ADDICTIONS

A COMPREHENSIVE GUIDEBOOK

ADDICTIONS

A COMPREHENSIVE GUIDEBOOK

EDITED BY

Barbara S. McCrady

Elizabeth E. Epstein

New York   Oxford
Oxford University Press
1999

Oxford University Press

Oxford   New York

Athens   Auckland   Bangkok   Bogotá   Buenos Aires   Calcutta
Cape Town   Chennai   Dar es Salaam   Delhi   Florence   Hong Kong   Istanbul
Karachi   Kuala Lumpur   Madrid   Melbourne   Mexico City   Mumbai
Nairobi   Paris   São Paulo   Singapore   Taipei   Tokyo   Toronto   Warsaw

and associated companies in
Berlin   Ibadan

Copyright © 1999 by Oxford University Press, Inc.

Published by Oxford University Press, Inc.
198 Madison Avenue, New York, New York 10016

Oxford is a registered trademark of Oxford University Press

Library of Congress Cataloging-in-Publication Data
McCrady, Barbara S.
Addictions : a comprehensive guidebook / Barbara S. McCrady,
Elizabeth E. Epstein.
p.   cm.
Includes index.
ISBN 0-19-511489-2
1. Substance abuse.   2. Alcoholism.   3. Drug abuse.   I. Epstein,
Elizabeth E.   II. Title.
RC564.M327   1999
616.86—dc21   98-51552

1 3 5 7 9 8 6 4 2

Printed in the United States of America
on acid-free paper

To Margaret Miller Sachs (1921–1994), my mother, my role model, my inspiration. —BSM

To my family—Joe, Jeremy, Eve, and Sam. —EEE

Foreword

Some years ago, before coming to the National Institute on Alcohol Abuse and Alcoholism, I directed a large alcoholism treatment program in New York City. At that time, our major goal was a relatively simple one: to get our patients sober and to help them remain so. The tools that we had available to help accomplish this goal also were relatively simple: the experience of those who had recovered primarily through Alcoholics Anonymous (AA) and our basic clinical "common sense" (i.e., approaches that seemed plausible and made intuitive sense but had not been validated with contemporary techniques of treatment outcome evaluation). The type of science-based information available to other health care practitioners through textbooks, health professions training, and other sources of information sharing that we take for granted today was, with a few notable exceptions, nonexistent just 15 years ago.

Today, the simple goal of treatment that we share as alcohol and other drug abuse scientists and practitioners has not changed. However, today's practitioners, unlike their predecessors, have access to an impressive array of clinical resources to help them to understand, diagnose, and treat the problems of alcohol and drug misuse. This textbook, *Addictions: A Comprehensive Guidebook*, is a fine example of such a resource. It presents a wide range of subjects written by experts from the many varied fields that impact in one way or another on the treatment of alcohol and other drug abuse. Its breadth and scope, in fact, are a testament to how far we have come in defining what we do and how we can do it effectively based not just on common sense, but on a growing body of quality basic and behavioral research.

This change from reliance solely on common sense to common sense and science, above all others, has led our fields to acceptance and respect by the professional health care field at large. It has also led to greater understanding by the public of alcohol and substance use disorders as bona fide medical conditions that can respond to treatment. This change is reflected in many different ways. For example, it is reflected in the growing recognition of the need for science-based information by policymakers and practitioners, a need deriving in part from demands by managed-care organizations, other third-party insurers, and state and federal policymakers for the same type of safety and efficacy evidence that is required for all other illnesses. It is also reflected in the increasing number of physicians' and other primary health care organizations that provide research-based findings about alcohol and other drug problems to their memberships. This change is also reflected in the extensive research effort underpinning new diagnostic classification systems, both nationally and internationally, and in the increasing attention to licensure and certification by professional organizations and by the states.

Because of these and other changes in how we do business, and the growing amount and complexity of information about alcohol and other drugs, having access to resources such as this book is a must. Here, in one source, is the information needed by alcohol and drug abuse specialists, primary-care providers, policymakers, and others who are involved in programs which are geared to helping those who abuse or are dependent on alcohol and other drugs to become informed about these problems, including the far-reaching effects of these substances on individuals and on society. I commend both Dr. McCrady and Dr. Epstein for their efforts in presenting such a wealth of material in a clear and concise manner appropriate for a variety of audiences, and for having pulled together the talented group of subject-matter experts represented in this book.

Enoch Gordis, M.D.
Director
National Institute on
Alcohol Abuse and Alcoholism

Acknowledgments

Several individuals were key to the completion of this book. First, we thank Larry Beutler, who recommended both the topic and the editors to Oxford University Press. Second, we express our tremendous appreciation to Joan Bossert at Oxford University Press, who was patient and encouraging in our work to conceptualize the book and bring it to fruition. The third key individual is Karen Rhines, both a promising clinical psychology graduate student at Rutgers and an utterly organized human being who has served as our editorial assistant. Fourth, the work could not have been completed in a more congenial and supportive setting than the Center of Alcohol Studies at Rutgers University. The enthusiasm for scholarship, being surrounded by colleagues conducting research and clinical work related to substance use and abuse, and the ready availability of the outstanding alcohol studies library—all provided the environment and resources necessary to complete this venture. Finally, our greatest appreciation goes to the authors and coauthors, a superb and renowned group of clinicians and researchers who produced wonderful chapters, and suffered patiently through our thorough and sometimes obsessive editing, to create this valuable resource for the field.

April 1998   B.S.M.
Piscataway, NJ   E.E.E.

Contents

Contributors

Lynn Abeita, B.A., Graduate Research Assistant, Department of Psychology, Arizona State University, Tempe, AZ

John P. Allen, Ph.D., Chief, Treatment Research Branch, National Institute on Alcohol Abuse and Alcoholism, Bethesda, MD

Raymond F. Anton, M.D., Professor of Psychiatry, Medical University of South Carolina, Institute of Psychiatry, Charleston, SC

Wayne S. Barber, M.D., Director of Behavioral Health Services, Rehoboth McKinley Christian Health Care Services and Chairman of Psychiatry, Rehoboth McKinley Christian Hospital, Gallup, NM

Rodger L. Beatty, Ph.D., Project Coordinator, Community AIDS Risk Reduction Project, Western Psychiatric Institute and Clinic, Pittsburgh, PA

Kathleen T. Brady, M.D., Ph.D., Associate Professor of Psychiatry, Department of Psychiatry and Behavioral Sciences, Medical University of South Carolina, Institute of Psychiatry, Charleston, SC

Kathleen M. Carroll, Ph.D., Associate Professor, Department of Psychiatry School of Medicine, Yale University School of Medicine, New Haven, CT

Felipe G. Castro, M.S.W., Ph.D., Professor, Department of Psychology, Arizona State University, Tempe, AZ

Deborah A. Dawson, Ph.D., Mathematical Statistician, Biometry Branch, Division of Biometry and Epidemiology—National Institute on Alcohol Abuse and Alcoholism, Bethesda, MD

George De Leon, Ph.D., Director, Center for Therapeutic Community Research at National Development and Research Institutes, Inc., Research Professor of Psychiatry, New York University School of Medicine, New York, NY

Dennis M. Donovan, Ph.D., Director, Alcohol and Drug Abuse Institute, Professor, Department of Psychiatry and Behavioral Sciences, University of Washington, Seattle, WA

Elizabeth E. Epstein, Ph.D., Assistant Research Professor, Center of Alcohol Studies, Rutgers, The State University of New Jersey, Piscataway, NJ

William Fals-Stewart, Ph.D., Assistant Professor of Psychology, Department of Psychology, Old Dominion University, Norfolk, VA

John W. Finney, Ph.D., Health Science Specialist, VA Palo Alto Health Care System, Center for Health Care Evaluation, Palo Alto, CA

Michelle O. Geckle, M.Ed., C.R.C., Senior Research Associate, Western Psychiatric Institute and Clinic, Pittsburgh, PA

Frederick B. Glaser, M.D., F.R.C.P. (C), Professor and Director, Division of Substance Abuse, Department of Psychiatric Medicine, East Carolina University School of Medicine, Greenville, NC

Edith S. Lisansky Gomberg, Ph.D., Professor of Psychology, Department of Psychiatry, University of Michigan Alcohol Research Center, Ann Arbor, MI

Bridget F. Grant, Ph.D., Chief, Biometry Branch, Division of Biometry and Epidemiology—National Institute on Alcohol Abuse and Alcoholism, Bethesda, MD

Robert Hendren, D.O., Director, Division of Child and Adolescent Psychiatry, University of Medicine and Dentistry of New Jersey, Robert Wood Johnson Medical School, Piscataway, NJ

Michie N. Hesselbrock, Ph.D., Professor, School of Social Work, University of Connecticut, West Hartford, CT

Victor M. Hesselbrock, Ph.D., Professor of Psychiatry, School of Medicine, University of Connecticut Health Center, Farmington, CT

Reid K. Hester, Ph.D., Director, Research Division, Behavior Therapy Associates, Albuquerque, NM

Harold D. Holder, Ph.D., Director and Senior Scientist, Prevention Research Center, Berkeley, CA

James Huggins, Ph.D., B.C.D., Associate Director, Persad, Pittsburgh, PA

Ronald M. Kadden, Ph.D., Professor, Department of Psychiatry, University of Connecticut Health Center, Farmington, CT

Carolyn Kapner, M.S.W., L.S.W., Therapist, Persad, Pittsburgh, PA

Thomas R. Kosten, M.D., Professor of Psychiatry, Yale University School of Medicine, VA Connecticut Healthcare System (Chief of Psychiatry Service), West Haven, CT

James W. Langenbucher, Ph.D., Associate Professor, Research Diagnostic Project, Center of Alcohol Studies, Rutgers, The State University of New Jersey, Piscataway, NJ

Karen Lewis, M.A., M.H.A., C.A.C., N.C.A.C., Psychologist, Private Practice, Pittsburgh, PA

Raye Z. Litten, Ph.D., Program Officer, Treatment Research Branch, National Institute on Alcohol Abuse and Alcoholism, Bethesda, MD

Robert Malcolm, M.D., Professor of Psychiatry, Department of Psychiatry and Behavioral Science, Medical University of South Carolina, Charleston, SC

G. Alan Marlatt, Ph.D., Professor of Psychology, Director, Addictive Behaviors Research Center, Addictive Behaviors Research Center, University of Washington, Seattle, WA

Barbara S. McCrady, Ph.D., Professor, Graduate School of Applied and Professional Psychology and Department of Psychology; Clinical Director, Center of Alcohol Studies, Rutgers University, Piscataway, NJ

Jeffrey Merrill, Ph.D., Director for Economic Policy and Research, Treatment Research Institute, University of Pennsylvania School of Medicine, Philadelphia, PA

William R. Miller, Ph.D., Regents Professor of Psychology and Psychiatry, Department of Psychology, University of New Mexico, Albuquerque, NM

Darlene H. Moak, M.D., Assistant Professor of Psychiatry, Medical University of South Carolina, Institute of Psychiatry, Charleston, SC

Rudolf H. Moos, Ph.D., Research Career Scientist, VA Palo Alto Health Care System, Center for Health Care Evaluation, Palo Alto, CA

Theresa B. Moyers, Ph.D., Clinical Director, Substance Abuse Treatment Program, VAMC Albuquerque, Albuquerque, NM

Hugh Myrick, M.D., Assistant Professor of Psychiatry, Department of Psychiatry and Behavioral Science, Medical University of South Carolina, Charleston, SC

Joseph Nowinski, Ph.D., Associate Adjunct Professor of Psychology, University of Connecticut, Storrs, CT

Charles P. O'Brien, M.D., Ph.D., Professor and Vice Chair, Department of Psychiatry, University of Pennsylvania, Chief of Psychiatry, VA Medical Center, University of Pennsylvania, Treatment Research Center, Philadelphia, PA

Timothy J. O'Farrell, Ph.D., Associate Professor of Psychology, Harvard Families and Addiction Program, Harvard Medical School Department of Psychiatry, Veterans Affairs Medical Center, Brockton and West Roxbury, MA

Patricia Owen, Ph.D., Director, Butler Center for Research and Learning, Hazelden Foundation, Center City, MN

Robert Pandina, Ph.D., Professor of Psychology, Director, Center of Alcohol Studies, Rutgers, The State University of New Jersey, Piscataway, NJ

Mary Ann Pentz, Ph.D., Associate Professor, Department of Preventive Medicine, Director, Center for Prevention Policy Research, University of Southern California, Los Angeles, CA

Rae Jean Proescholdbell, B.A., Graduate Research Assistant, Department of Psychology, Arizona State University, Tempe, AZ

Lori A. Quigley, Ph.D., Research Manager, UCSF Treatment Outcome Research Group, University of California—San Francisco, San Francisco, CA

Domingo Rodriguez, Vice President for Community Health and Human Services, Chicanos por la Causa, Phoenix, AZ

Susan J. Rose, Ph.D., Assistant Professor, University of Wisconsin–Milwaukee, School of Social Welfare, Milwaukee, WI

Richard N. Rosenthal, M.D., Associate Professor of Psychiatry, Director, Division of Substance Abuse, Albert Einstein College of Medicine; Associate Chairman, Department of Psychiatry, Beth Israel Medical Center, New York, NY

Dorothy J. Sandstrom, M.S., Project Coordinator, Western Psychiatric Institute and Clinic, Pittsburgh, PA

Pilar M. Sanjuan, B.A., Graduate Fellow, Center of Alcohol Studies, Rutgers, The State University of New Jersey, Piscataway, NJ

Sidney H. Schnoll, M.D., Ph.D., Professor, Departments of Internal Medicine and Psychiatry, Chairman, Division of Substance Abuse Medicine, Medical College of Virginia, Virginia Commonwealth University, Richmond, VA

Timothy Sheehan, Ph.D., Executive Director, Recovery Services, Hazelden Foundation, Center City, MN

Pamela M. Skerker, R.N., M.S., Psychiatric Nurse Practitioner, Department of Psychiatry, University of Connecticut Health Center, Farmington, CT

John Slade, M.D., Professor of Clinical Medicine, University of Medicine and Dentistry of New Jersey, New Brunswick, NJ

Robert S. Stephens, Ph.D., Associate Professor, Department of Psychology, Virginia Polytechnic Institute and State University, Blacksburg, VA

Susan M. Stine, M.D., Ph.D., Associate Professor, Department of Psychiatry and Behavioral Neurosciences, Wayne State University School of Medicine, Detroit, MI

Virginia Stoffel, M.S., Associate Professor, University of Wisconsin—Milwaukee, School of Social Welfare, Milwaukee, WI

Christine Timko, Ph.D., Health Science Specialist, VA Palo Alto Health Care System, Center for Health Care Evaluation, Palo Alto, CA

David G. Warren, J.D., Executive Director, North Carolina Governor's Institute on Alcohol and Substance Abuse, Professor, Department of Community and Family Medicine, Duke University Medical Center, Durham, NC

Michael F. Weaver, M.D., Assistant Professor of Internal Medicine, Division of Substance Abuse Medicine, Virginia Commonwealth University/Medical College of Virginia, Richmond, VA

Laurence Westreich, M.D., Assistant Clinical Professor of Psychiatry, New York University School of Medicine; Chief of Dual Diagnosis Program, Bellevue Hospital, New York, NY

Carolina E. Yahne, Ph.D., Psychologist, Center on Alcoholism, Substance Abuse, and Addictions, University of New Mexico, Albuquerque, NM

Allen Zweben, D.S.W., Associate Professor, University of Wisconsin–Milwaukee, School of Social Welfare, Milwaukee, WI

ADDICTIONS

A COMPREHENSIVE GUIDEBOOK

Introduction

Barbara S. McCrady
Elizabeth E. Epstein

If we could sniff or swallow something that would, for five or six hours each day, abolish our solitude as individuals, atone us with our fellows in a glowing exaltation of affection and make life in all its aspects seem not only worth living, but divinely beautiful and significant, and if this heavenly, world-transfiguring drug were of such a kind that we could wake up next morning with a clear head and an undamaged constitution—then, it seems to me, all our problems (and not merely the one small problem of discovering a novel pleasure) would be wholly solved and earth would become paradise.

Aldous Huxley, 1949

Aldous Huxley's romantic vision of substance use stands in stark contrast to the serious problems caused by substance use in the late 20th century. Substance use in the United States claims close to 600,000 lives per year, including approximately 440,000 attributable to nicotine use, 125,000 from alcohol use, and 10,000 from heroin and cocaine use (exclusive of deaths from HIV). Alcohol, tobacco, and other drug use and abuse are interwoven into many of the most pressing of our societal ills, including chronic illness, crime, violence, and homelessness. Concerns about the adverse effects of alcohol, tobacco, and other drugs date back to biblical times: "He shall separate himself from wine and strong drink, and shall drink no vinegar of wine, or vinegar of strong drink, neither shall he drink any liquor of grapes, nor eat moist grapes, or dried" (Bible Numbers 6:3).

Models of addiction have varied throughout history, and different treatment approaches have predominated, corresponding to the prevailing theoretical model of the time. Many models of addiction have held the view that abstinence is necessary to successful control of the addiction:

If an addict who has been completely cured starts smoking again he no longer experiences the discomfort of his first addiction. There exists, therefore, outside alkaloids and habit, a sense for opium, an intangible habit which lives on, despite the recasting of the organism. . . . The dead drug leaves a ghost behind. At certain hours it haunts the house. (Cocteau, 1929)

Contemporary thought, however, has introduced the possibility that moderation is an appropriate goal for the substance abuser, either as an interim goal to engage an individual in treatment, or as a long-term goal. Data on long-term use patterns of alcohol- and drug-abusing and -dependent individuals suggest that lifelong abstinence is an uncommon outcome: Most individuals experience fluctuating periods of moderation, abstinence, and heavy or problem use. Consequently, many professionals in the public health and clinical realm now embrace a harm reduction approach to minimize or decrease the adverse consequences of use.

Despite a rich and varied history of and literature on alcohol, tobacco, and other drugs, science has come lately to the field. The National Institute on Alcohol Abuse and Alcoholism (NIAAA) was established in 1971; the National Institute on Drug Abuse (NIDA), in 1973. Since the establishment of these two federal agencies, alcohol, tobacco, and other drugs have become increasingly legitimate topics of inquiry for scientists and targets for clinical care by health care professionals. Today, we have an impressive body of knowledge of the epidemiology, etiology, neuropharmacology, assessment, treatment, and prevention of substance use disorders. In all areas of health care delivery, professionals are being required to acquire and demonstrate mastery of the core knowledge in this field. Many professions now offer specialty credentialing in the substance use field, and alcohol and drug counseling is becoming an increasingly regulated field.

Our goal in developing this volume was to create a resource for several audiences. First, health care professionals and professionals in training in psychology, medicine, social work, nursing, and counseling will find the volume invaluable. As a training guide, for instance, the book covers material useful for credentialing exams, such as that required by the American Psychological Association College of Professional Psychology Certificate of Proficiency in the Treatment of Alcohol and Other Psychoactive Substance Use Disorders. The book is also suitable for scientists who would want easy access to a breadth of knowledge in the field that would complement the specialized knowledge they have in their own area of inquiry.

The volume is intended to be comprehensive yet manageable, accessible yet scholarly. In outlining the sections of the book, we attempted to include chapters on all aspects of substance abuse/dependence that a typical practitioner might need to be familiar with to understand and treat addictive disorders. In outlining each chapter, we envisioned neither a case-study–based "how-to" approach nor an arcane review of scientific knowledge. Rather, each author strove to strike a balance, to write a chapter that provides the best scientific knowledge, but in a format that is accessible and useful. We believe that

the authors have been successful in achieving this difficult balance.

The chapters are organized according to consistent themes within each section to facilitate comparability of topics across chapters. Part I (chapters 1–3) provides a broad background about substance use: epidemiology, current models of and knowledge about etiology, and information about the course in both treated and community samples. Part II (chapters 4–10) covers pharmacological and clinical information about major drug classes, including basic knowledge about each drug class, its metabolism, and its neuropharmacology as well as clinical information such as preparations, street names, symptoms of intoxication, dependence, and withdrawal.

Parts III, IV, and V provide core material for the practitioner. In part III (chapters 11–12), chapter 11 provides a comprehensive overview of approaches to assessment and measures, while chapter 12 focuses on treatment planning and decision making. Part IV (chapters 13–21) provides descriptions of a range of models of treatment that have empirical support for their efficacy and includes detailed information on historical origins, theory, therapeutic change, and empirical support for each approach. Part IV concludes with a summary chapter that highlights major psychological and pharmacological approaches to treatment. Part V (chapters 22–24) focuses on additional issues of direct concern to the practitioner: legal and ethical matters, credentialing, and the complex interface between the treatment of substance use and other social and health care systems.

Part VI (chapters 25–29) shifts attention from models of care to target populations. Authors in this section contributed chapters that review the best current knowledge about alcohol, tobacco, and other drug abuse in a range of populations: those with concomitant psychiatric disorders, age-limited populations (youth and the elderly), racial and ethnic minority groups, women, and gay men and lesbians.

Part VII (chapters 30–32) turns to the prevention and economics of substance use. The prevention chapters (30 and 31) describe strategies that target both the individual and the environment; the economics chapter (chapter 32) considers the larger context of the health economics of substance abuse treatment.

The reader may use the volume in three distinct ways: (1) As a textbook, the volume provides an orderly and comprehensive survey, suitable for a graduate course on the assessment and treatment of the abuse of alcohol, tobacco, and other drugs. The textbook reader should begin at the beginning and read through the entire volume. (2) When the book is used as a resource for treatment planning, the reader should first look to specific chapters relevant to the presenting drug(s) of abuse and the treatment population and should then use the index to identify assessment devices and treatment models related to the specific drug(s) of interest. (3) To use the book as a reference volume, the reader can find answers to specific questions in both the specific chapters and the index.

Knowledge evolves, both from the laboratory and from experience. We hope that this volume will provide you, the reader, with a firm grounding in current knowledge and clinical methods that will stimulate you to contribute to this exciting and evolving field.

References

Cocteau, Jean. *Opium*. (1929). Cited in *Columbia Dictionary of Quotations*. New York: Columbia University Press.

Huxley, Aldous. (1949). Wanted, a new pleasure. In *Music at Night and Other Essays*. Cited in *Columbia Dictionary of Quotations*. New York: Columbia University Press.

I

Epidemiology, Etiology, and Course of Substance Use Disorders

1

Alcohol and Drug Use, Abuse, and Dependence: Classification, Prevalence, and Comorbidity

Bridget F. Grant

Deborah A. Dawson

This chapter provides an epidemiological context for the remainder of this volume by describing the magnitude of the alcohol and drug problem in the United States. It also presents the most recent national statistics on alcohol and drug use, abuse and dependence, and comorbidity between alcohol, drug, and psychiatric disorders. Emphasis is placed on the summary of data from general population surveys, because prevalence statistics derived from treated samples are not representative and are subject to unique selection biases. Moreover, individuals in treatment are more likely to have multiple disorders than are individuals in the general population, thus spuriously inflating estimates of the prevalence of comorbidity and distorting the relationships existing between alcohol, drug, and other psychiatric disorders.

Preceding the prevalence and comorbidity statistics is a historical overview of classification systems in the alcohol and drug fields that includes a discussion of various approaches to subtyping alcohol and drug use disorders. Attempts to classify alcohol and drug use disorders have been problematic both contemporarily and historically. Although the lack of consensus is not unique to the alcohol and drug fields, there currently exists no consensus on how to classify alcohol and drug use disorders, and no such consensus is expected in the near future. Historical changes in these classification systems also adversely affect the collection and communication of accurate public health statistics over time. This chapter's discussion of changes in classification systems over time and the differences and similarities among alternative systems is intended to help researchers and clinicians gauge the degree to which current and future research findings can be integrated with one another and with results from earlier studies using historical classification systems. Only in this way can scientific knowledge in the alcohol and drug fields be advanced.

CLASSIFICATION OF ALCOHOL
AND DRUG USE DISORDERS:
HISTORICAL OVERVIEW

Up until the early 1800s, the classification of alcohol and drug use disorders received very little attention. At the institutional level, early official efforts at classification can be seen in 19th-century asylum records in which terms such as *delirium tremens, insanity caused by intemperance*, and *dipsomania* (drink seeking) were used to describe conditions resulting from alcohol use. In France, the statistical classification used throughout the 19th century to record morbidity and mortality included alcohol-related rubrics such as habitual drinking and socially induced heavy drinking (Babor, 1992).

Beginning in the early 19th century, a series of medical writers began to lay the groundwork for what would eventually become the disease concept of alcoholism. Among these early contributors was Bruhl-Cramer, who in 1819 introduced the concept of drink seeking, or dipsomania. Esquirol (1845) was the first to give drunkenness or monomania a place in psychiatric nomenclatures, and Huss (1849) was first to use the term *alcoholism*. By the latter part of the 19th century, Carpenter (1850), Crothers (1893), Kerr (1888), and McBride (1910) had promulgated the disease concept of inebriety as a concept very similar to what is referred to today as *dependence*. In this formulation, inebriety and dipsomania were diseases, and their presumed origin was biological or possibly genetic.

Although the early nosological history of drug use disorders is more vague than that of alcohol use disorders, it is likely that the first attempts at their classification occurred during the early drug epidemics of the late 19th century. At that time, addiction to opiates and cocaine gave rise to terms such as *morphism* and *narcomania*. These terms were used in much the same way as *inebriety* and *dipsomania* had been used to describe dependence on alcohol.

With the disease concept firmly entrenched by the end of the 19th century, diagnostic classifications for the next 50 years would continue to emphasize the concepts of addiction or dependence, giving very little attention to the social, psychological, and medical consequences of substance intoxication and chronic use. This trend began with Kraeplin (1909–1915), whose *Textbook of Psychiatry* included a ma-

jor category for intoxication psychosis but placed primary emphasis on organic disorders associated with chronic alcoholism.

It was not until the early 1960s that classification systems began to give some consideration to alcohol and drug use problems that did not involve addiction or dependence. The most well known of these classificatory systems was outlined by Jellinek (1960) in his classical work, "The Disease Concept of Alcoholism." In his classification, Jellinek clearly differentiated varieties of alcohol use disorders that involved a clear dependence process (gamma and delta types) from those that did not (alpha, beta, and epsilon types). It was not until the third edition of the *Diagnostic and Statistical Manual of Mental Disorders* (*DSM-III*; American Psychiatric Association [APA], 1980) and the eighth revision of the *International Classification of Diseases* (*ICD-8*; World Health Organization [WHO], 1968) that nondependent substance use disorders were introduced.

In the *ICD-8*, alcohol addiction was characterized by a state of physical and emotional dependence on regular or periodic heavy and uncontrolled alcohol consumption during which a person experiences a compulsion to drink and withdrawal symptoms upon cessation of drinking. The categories of episodic and habitual excessive drinking, which were not extended to other drugs, focused on pathological drinking patterns and were differentiated from alcohol addiction by the absence of compulsion and withdrawal. The alcohol and drug abuse and dependence categories of the *DSM-III* were characterized by patterns of pathological use, and by impairment in social or occupational functioning due to use, with dependence additionally requiring the presence of either tolerance or withdrawal.

In 1976, Edwards and Gross developed the concept of the alcohol dependence syndrome (ADS). The concept of the ADS was to become extremely influential in the formation of all further revisions of the *ICD* and *DSM* definitions of both alcohol and drug use disorders. The syndrome was provisionally endowed with the following seven elements: (1) narrowing of the drinking repertoire; (2) salience of drink-seeking behavior; (3) increased tolerance to alcohol; (4) repeated withdrawal symptoms; (5) relief or avoidance of withdrawal by further drinking; (6) subjective awareness of compulsion to drink; and (7) rapid reinstatement of symptoms after a period of abstinence.

The ADS was described not as an all-or-none disease state, but as a condition which existed in degrees of severity with the emphasis squarely placed on dimensionality of a learned phenomenon. Not all components of the syndrome needed always to be present in the same intensity. More important, the unidimensional ADS was kept theoretically distinct from other alcohol-related disabilities in what Edwards and his colleagues (Edwards, Gross, Keller, Moser, & Room, 1977) termed the biaxial concept. Alcohol- and drug-related physical, mental, and social problems were recognized as public health concerns that were significant in their own right, quite apart from dependence.

The ADS concept's impact on the current *ICD-10* and *DSM-IV* is evident (table 1.1). In both these definitions, the syndromal and dimensional components of the ADS are present in addition to the differentiation of the dependence category from nondependent categories of abuse and harmful use (table 1.2). Both classifications also share much of the content of their diagnostic criteria with those of the ADS. Changes that occurred with the ninth revision of the *ICD* (*ICD-9*; WHO, 1978) and the third edition, revised, of the *DSM* (*DSM-III-R*; APA, 1987) and that were retained in the tenth revision of the *ICD* (*ICD-10*; WHO, 1992) and fourth edition of the *DSM* (*DSM-IV*; APA, 1994) also included the adoption of the same criteria for abuse, harmful use, and dependence across all psychoactive substances. More important, the earlier defining criteria of compulsion, tolerance, and withdrawal were retained—but were no longer required—for a dependence diagnosis in either the *ICD-10*, the *DSM-IV*, or their immediate predecessors.

Although many subtle differences exist between the current *ICD* and *DSM* formulations of alcohol and drug use disorders, one important difference is worth noting. In the *ICD-10*, the harmful use category is characterized by actual physical or psychological harm to the user, whereas the *DSM-IV* abuse category additionally includes social, legal, and occupational consequences of use. Because cultural context is an important determinant of substance use patterns and consequences, it can be expected that the inclusion of social and legal problems in the *DSM-IV* will reduce the cross-cultural applicability of the abuse category. For example, changes in legal definitions or controls and differences between cultural mores of various countries will markedly influence how substance use relates to legal or social consequences, respectively.

Although the *ICD-10* and *DSM-IV* classifications of alcohol and drug use disorders do mirror many of the structural aspects of the ADS, they do not accept the learning theory underlying it. The *DSM-III*, *DSM-II-R*, and *DSM-IV* classifications were claimed to be largely atheoretical, as were the corresponding *ICD* classifications. (However, the *DSMs* have been criticized by social and behavioral scientists for failing to explicate the underpinnings of their nomenclature, even though it is clear that their classifications entail both ontological and epistemological assumptions arising from a medical model.) Rather, the *DSM* authors' claims of an atheoretical classification would seem to have been adopted to minimize opposition from other health professions concerned about the medicalization of the mental health field.

Over the past 30 years, behavioral scientists have proposed an alternative approach to the disease concept of alcohol and drug dependence that underlies the *DSM* classifications (Adesso, 1995; Nathan, 1981; Pattison, Sobell, & Sobell, 1977). In this approach, alcohol and drug use disorders are viewed not as unitary disorders defined in terms of a single disease label, but as acquired habits that emerge from biological, pharmacological and conditioning factors. Drinking behavior occurs on a continuum of severity, and excessive drinking occurs on a continuum with normal drinking. Emphasis is placed on environmental, affective, and cognitive antecedent conditions and on reinforcing consequences of drinking. The goal of this functional approach is a classification of pathological drinking that is governed by universal principles of human motivation and learning that guide us all (Wulfert, Greenway, & Dougher, 1996).

SUBTYPES OF ALCOHOL AND DRUG USE DISORDERS

From as early as the mid-19th century, clinicians and researchers recognized that individuals classified as alcoholics or as alcohol-dependent were far from homogeneous. Babor and Lauerman (1986) cited the development of 39 different classifications of alcoholic subtypes between 1850 and 1941. Although these early typologies were unsystematic and lacking in empirical foundation, they helped to identify de-

TABLE 1.1 *DSM-IV* and *ICD-10* Diagnostic Criteria for Alcohol and Drug Dependence

	DSM-IV	ICD-10
Clustering criterion	A. A maladaptive pattern of substance use, leading to clinically significant impairment or distress as manifested by three or more of the following occurring at any time in the same 12-month period:	A. Three or more of the following have been experienced or exhibited at some time during the previous year:
Tolerance	(1) Need for markedly increased amounts of a substance to achieve intoxication or desired effect; or markedly diminished effect with continued use of the same amount of the substance	(1) Evidence of tolerance, such that increased doses are required in order to achieve effects originally produced by lower doses
Withdrawal	(2) The characteristic withdrawal syndrome for a substance or use of a substance (or a closely related substance) to relieve or avoid withdrawal symptoms	(2) A physiological withdrawal state when substance use has ceased or been reduced as evidenced by: the characteristic substance withdrawal syndrome, or use of substance (or a closely related substance) to relieve or avoid withdrawal symptoms
Impaired control	(3) Persistent desire or one or more unsuccessful efforts to cut down or control substance use (4) Substance use in larger amounts or over a longer period than the person intended	(3) Difficulties in controlling substance use in terms of onset, termination, or levels of use
Neglect of activities	(5) Important social, occupational, or recreational activities given up or reduced because of substance use	(4) Progressive neglect of alternative pleasures or interests in favor of substance use; or
Time spent	(6) A great deal of time spent in activities necessary to obtain, to use, or to recover from the effects of substance used	A great deal of time spent in activities necessary to obtain, to use, or to recover from the effects of substance use
Inability to fulfill roles	None	None
Hazardous use	None	None
Continued use despite problems	(7) Continued substance use despite knowledge of having a persistent or recurrent physical or psychological problem that is likely to be caused or exacerbated by use	(5) Continued substance use despite clear evidence of overtly harmful physical or psychological consequences
Compulsive use	None	(6) A strong desire or sense of compulsion to use substance
Duration criterion	B. No duration criterion separately specified. However, several dependence criteria must occur repeatedly as specified by duration qualifiers associated with criteria (e.g., "often," "persistent," "continued")	B. No duration criterion separately specified
Criterion for subtyping dependence	With physiological dependence: Evidence of tolerance or withdrawal (i.e., any of items A(1) or A(2) above are present) Without physiological dependence: No evidence of tolerance or withdrawal (i.e., none of items A(1) or A(2) above are present)	None

TABLE 1.2 *DSM-IV* and *ICD-10* Diagnostic Criteria for Alcohol and Drug Abuse/Harmful Use

DSM-IV Alcohol and Drug Abuse

A. A maladaptive pattern of substance use leading to clinically significant impairment or distress, as manifested by one (or more) of the following occurring within a 12-month period:

   (1) recurrent substance use resulting in a failure to fulfill major role obligations at work, school, or home

   (2) recurrent substance use in situations in which use is physically hazardous

   (3) recurrent substance-related legal problems

   (4) continued substance use despite having persistent or recurrent social or interpersonal problems caused or exacerbated by the effects of alcohol

B. The symptoms have never met the criteria for substance dependence for the same class of substance.

ICD-10 Harmful Use of Alcohol and Drugs

A. A pattern of substance use that is causing damage to health. The damage may be physical or mental. The diagnosis requires that actual damage should have been caused to the mental or physical health of the user.

B. No concurrent diagnosis of the substance dependence syndrome for same class of substance.

---

fining characteristics, such as drinking patterns, family history of alcoholism, personality characteristics, and psychopathologies, that have served as the basis for subsequent alcoholism typologies (Babor, 1996). In 1941, Bowman and Jellinek synthesized a number of earlier typologies into a classification scheme that defined four types of alcoholics on the basis of their drinking patterns (continuous, periodic, or irregular) and etiology (endogenous or exogenous). These categories were later superseded by Jellinek's (1960) far more widely recognized categories of alpha, beta, gamma, delta, and epsilon alcoholism. Of these, Jellinek regarded only the gamma and delta varieties as conforming to the disease concept of alcoholism and distinguished these by more endogenous influences, more rapid progression, and greater loss of control among gamma alcoholics, and more exogenous influences, slower progression, and greater inability to abstain among delta alcoholics.

More recent alcohol typologies have refined these categories and added new defining characteristics, but the most well known of the current subtypes have maintained the distinction between two broad categories of alcoholics. For example, Cloninger, Bohman, and Sigvardsson (1981) proposed a Type 1 versus Type 2 distinction. Type 1 (milieu-limited) alcoholism is hypothesized to affect both men and women, to have a relatively late onset, to be influenced by both endogenous and exogenous factors, to involve relatively mild alcohol problems with little antisocial activity, and to be associated with low levels of novelty seeking and high levels of harm avoidance. In contrast, Type 2 (male-limited) alcoholism is characterized as occurring primarily among men and is associated with an early onset of alcoholism, a high level of familial alcoholism among male relatives (i.e., a primarily endogenous etiology), high levels of antisocial activity and novelty seeking, and low levels of harm avoidance (Cloninger, 1987; Cloninger et al., 1981).

Babor and associates (1992) used the technique of cluster analysis to identify 17 defining characteristics that distinguished their proposed categories of Type A and Type B alcoholism. They found that of the two groups, Type B alcoholics had a greater genetic predisposition toward alcoholism, more childhood risk factors such as conduct disorder, an earlier onset of alcoholism, more severe symptoms of dependence, more polydrug use, more psychopathology and life stress, and a more chronic treatment history. Subsequent attempts to replicate this dichotomy and extend it to substances other than alcohol have yielded different results in terms of which of the defining characteristics contribute most strongly to the Type A–Type B distinction, but medical conditions, dependence severity, and lifetime severity have been repeatedly identified as among the most important dimensions (Ball, 1996; Schuckit et al., 1995).

Although each new classification scheme has been based on modifications of existing subtypes, the similarities among the typologies are more striking than their differences. Babor (1996) argued that the dichotomy between what he terms the Apollonian and Dionysian types of alcoholism captures not only the delta-gamma, Type 1–Type 2, and Type A–Type B distinctions but also many of the other typologies that have been proposed during the last century, including the reactive versus essential and symptomatic subtypes (Knight, 1938), the family history negative versus positive dichotomy (Frances, Timm, & Buckey, 1980), affiliative versus schizoid drinkers (Morey & Skinner, 1986), developmentally cumulative versus antisocial and negative affect drinkers (Zucker, 1987), and the late- versus early-onset dichotomy (Buydens-Branchey, Branchey, & Noumair, 1989). Future research will undoubtedly continue to clarify the distinctions that characterize these two broad categories of alcoholism, to test the applicability of these categories to different drugs and within different subpopulations, and to extend their usefulness as predictors of response to different types of treatment.

Some of the typologies of alcohol dependence described above have been tested for their applicability to other substances. Wills, Vaccaro, and McNamara (1994) examined substance use and personality characteristics in a sample of 457 adolescents 12 to 15 years of age. Cluster analysis resulted in five distinct groups. The two groups with the highest levels of novelty seeking and lowest levels of harm avoidance and reward dependence were also those with the highest levels of cannabis use. Wills et al. interpreted these results as consistent with the Type1–Type 2 distinction, the adolescents in these two groups corresponding to the Type 2 subtype. The construct, concurrent, and predictive validity of the Type A–Type B distinction has been supported in a cluster analysis of 399 cocaine users that included both those seeking and those not seeking treatment (Ball, Carroll, Babor, & Rounsaville, 1995), and some but not all of the characteristics distinguishing these two subtypes were replicated in samples of cannabis and opiate users (Feingold, Ball, Kranzler, & Rounsaville, 1996). Other typologies that have been proposed for drug abuse and dependence include Cancrini's (1994) fourfold classification based on underlying psychopathology (adjustment disorders, neurotic disorders, psychosis/borderline disorders, and sociopathic personality disorders) and the distinction between recreational users and self-medicators that is based on underlying motivation (Carlin & Strauss, 1978).

PREVALENCE OF ALCOHOL AND DRUG USE

Prevalence figures on alcohol and drug use presented in this chapter are based on the 1992 National Longitudinal Alcohol Epidemiologic Survey (NLAES), a nationwide household survey sponsored by the National Institute on Alcohol Abuse and Alcoholism (Grant et al., 1994). The NLAES consisted of a representative sample of the U.S. population involving direct face-to-face interviews with 42,862 respondents, 18 years of age and older. The sampling design included clustering and stratification with the provisions for oversampling blacks and young adults (aged 18–29).

Data from the NLAES indicated that two thirds (66.0%) of adults 18 years of age and over were lifetime drinkers who had consumed at least 12 alcoholic drinks during any 1 year of their lives, and nearly half (44.4%) were past year drinkers who had consumed 12 or more drinks in the year preceding the interview (table 1.3). Drinking was more common among men than women with the gender differential strongest among blacks and was more common among nonblacks (including whites and all other races) than blacks with the racial differential strongest among women. The prevalence of lifetime drinking was highest (73.3%) for individuals in the age range of 30–44 years and lowest (47.8%) for those aged 65 years and older. The prevalence of past-year drinking was marginally higher for persons aged 18–29 than for those aged 30–44 (53.4% versus 50.2%) and declined sharply in the older age groups to 40.5% for persons aged 45–64 and 24.5% for those aged 65 years and older.

Heavy drinking may be defined in terms of drinking patterns (e.g., the frequency of drinking five or more, or some other number of, drinks) or in terms of volume of ethanol intake. Among volume-based measures, an average daily intake of more than 1 ounce of ethanol (the equivalent of more than two standard drinks) frequently has been used as a threshold for heavy drinking (Williams & Debakey, 1992). By this measure, nearly one quarter (23.4%) of U.S. adults were lifetime heavy drinkers, that is, they drank an average of more than 1 ounce of ethanol per day during their period of heaviest drinking (but not necessarily throughout their entire lives). Thus, slightly more than one third of all lifetime drinkers could be defined as heavy drinkers at some point during their drinking histories. In contrast, the prevalence of past-year heavy drinking was only 8.7%, less than one fifth of past-year drinkers.

The prevalence of heavy drinking was higher among men than women and higher among nonblacks than blacks. With respect to age, the preva-

TABLE 1.3 Prevalence (%) of Lifetime and Past-Year Alcohol Use[a] and Heavy Use,[b] by Gender, Ethnicity, and Age

Sociodemographic characteristic	Alcohol use[a]		Heavy use[b]	
	Lifetime	Past year	Lifetime	Past year
Total	66.0	44.4	23.4	8.7
18–29	68.0	53.4	25.3	11.2
30–44	73.3	50.2	27.2	8.4
45–64	66.1	40.5	23.0	8.9
65+	47.8	24.5	13.0	5.2
Total men	78.3	55.8	35.6	13.7
18–29	75.7	64.2	34.8	17.1
30–44	82.8	60.8	39.7	13.1
45–64	80.3	51.0	36.8	13.5
65+	68.2	36.4	25.0	9.1
Total women	54.7	33.9	12.1	4.1
18–29	60.4	42.6	15.7	5.3
30–44	63.9	39.8	15.0	3.8
45–64	52.8	30.7	10.3	4.5
65+	33.4	16.1	4.8	2.4
Total nonblack	67.9	45.9	24.1	8.8
18–29	71.7	56.4	27.2	11.5
30–44	75.3	51.7	28.1	8.4
45–64	67.3	41.7	23.3	9.1
65+	48.7	25.7	13.2	5.4
Nonblack men	79.6	56.9	36.5	13.7
18–29	77.9	66.1	36.4	17.2
30–44	84.2	62.0	40.8	13.0
45–64	80.9	51.8	37.0	13.7
65+	68.9	37.6	25.0	9.4
Nonblack women	56.9	35.6	12.6	4.2
18–29	65.3	46.5	17.6	5.7
30–44	66.4	41.4	15.3	3.7
45–64	54.3	32.1	10.3	4.7
65+	34.2	17.2	5.0	2.6
Total black	51.4	32.5	17.5	7.7
18–29	45.1	34.5	13.5	9.0
30–44	58.7	39.1	21.1	8.8
45–64	55.0	30.1	20.8	7.1
65+	37.9	11.7	11.0	2.4
Black men	67.6	46.6	28.6	13.3
18–29	60.5	50.9	23.4	16.2
30–44	71.8	51.3	30.9	14.3
45–64	74.0	43.5	34.1	11.8
65+	59.6	22.7	23.9	4.6
Black women	38.3	21.2	8.7	3.3
18–29	32.2	20.8	5.3	3.1
30–44	47.7	28.8	12.9	4.3
45–64	39.8	19.4	10.0	3.4
65+	24.0	4.8	3.2	1.0

Note. Data compiled from Source and accuracy statement for the National Longitudinal Alcohol Epidemiologic Survey. Rockville, MD: National Institute on Alcohol Abuse and Alcoholism.

[a]Consumption of 12 or more drinks within a 12-month period.
[b]Average daily consumption of more than 1.0 ounce of ethanol.

lence of lifetime heavy drinking generally was of about the same magnitude for all ages under 65 years, with lower rates among persons 65 years and older. Among nonblack women, though, the rates of lifetime heavy drinking were lower for those aged 45–64 than for those aged 18–29, and the opposite was true among black men and women. Past-year heavy drinking was equally common among persons aged 45–64 and those aged 30–44, the highest prevalence being found among those aged 18–29.

Table 1.4 shows the lifetime prevalence of illicit drug use, that is, the use of drugs at least 12 times without or beyond the limits of a doctor's prescription. Overall, 15.6% of U.S. adults reported a positive lifetime history of drug use. Cannabis was the most

commonly used drug (13.9%), followed by illicit use of prescription drugs (6.2% for all types combined, including 2.2% for sedatives, 2.4% each for opioids and tranquilizers, and 4.1% for amphetamines) and cocaine or crack (3.7%). Lifetime use of hallucinogens was reported by 2.0% of all adults. Considering all types of drugs combined, the lifetime prevalence of use was higher for men than women (23.0% vs. 13.2%), higher for individuals aged 18–29 than for those aged 30 and older (26.3% vs. 17.1%, with a smaller age differential for blacks than for nonblacks), and slightly higher for nonblacks than blacks (16.0% vs. 12.4%, with most of the difference occurring among individuals aged 18–29). These patterns held true for most of the individual types of drugs

TABLE 1.4 Prevalence (%) of Lifetime Illicit Use of Selected Types of Drugs, by Gender, Ethnicity, and Age

| Sociodemographic characteristic | Any drug | Prescription drugs | | | | | Cannabis | Hallu-cinogens | Cocaine |
		Total	Sedatives	Opioids	Tranquil-izers	Amphet-amines			
Total	15.6	6.2	2.2	2.4	2.4	4.1	13.9	2.0	3.7
18–29	23.0	8.4	2.6	3.6	3.2	5.8	21.1	3.4	5.6
30+	13.2	5.4	2.1	2.0	2.2	3.6	11.5	1.5	3.1
Total men	19.5	7.5	3.0	3.2	3.2	5.4	18.0	3.0	5.0
18–29	26.3	8.7	3.1	4.2	3.6	6.4	25.0	4.7	6.5
30+	17.1	7.1	2.9	2.8	3.0	5.0	15.5	2.5	4.5
Total women	12.0	4.9	1.6	1.7	1.8	3.0	10.1	1.0	2.6
18–29	19.8	8.1	2.1	2.9	2.7	5.3	17.2	2.1	4.7
30+	9.6	4.0	1.4	1.3	1.4	2.3	7.9	0.7	1.9
Total nonblack	16.0	6.5	2.4	2.5	2.6	4.5	14.3	2.2	3.8
18–29	24.4	9.3	2.8	3.9	3.6	6.6	22.4	3.8	6.0
30+	13.4	5.7	2.2	2.1	2.3	3.8	11.7	1.7	3.1
Nonblack men	19.8	7.9	3.1	3.3	3.4	5.7	18.2	3.3	5.1
18–29	27.2	9.5	3.3	4.5	4.0	7.1	25.8	5.2	6.9
30+	17.2	7.4	3.0	2.9	3.2	5.3	15.6	2.6	4.5
Nonblack women	12.5	5.3	1.7	1.7	1.8	3.3	10.6	1.2	2.7
18–29	21.5	9.0	2.3	3.2	3.1	6.1	18.8	2.3	5.2
30+	9.8	4.1	1.5	1.3	1.5	2.5	8.2	0.8	1.9
Total black	12.4	3.3	1.1	1.6	1.4	1.4	10.9	0.6	3.0
18–29	14.6	2.8	1.0	1.7	0.8	0.9	13.0	0.9	2.9
30+	11.4	3.6	1.2	1.6	1.7	1.6	9.9	0.5	3.0
Black men	17.4	4.1	1.7	1.8	1.7	2.2	16.3	1.1	4.2
18–29	20.1	3.2	1.4	2.0	1.1	1.3	18.9	1.4	4.2
30+	16.2	4.5	1.8	1.7	2.0	2.6	15.2	1.0	4.2
Black women	8.3	2.7	0.7	1.4	1.2	0.8	6.4	0.2	2.0
18–29	10.0	2.5	0.6	1.5	0.5	0.7	8.1	0.5	1.9
30+	7.6	2.9	0.7	1.4	1.4	0.8	5.8	0.1	2.0

Note. Data compiled from Source and accuracy statement for the National Longitudinal Alcohol Epidemiologic Survey. Rockville, MD: National Institute on Alcohol Abuse and Alcoholism.

TABLE 1.5 Prevalence (%) of Past-Year Illicit Use of Selected Types of Drugs, by Gender, Ethnicity, and Age

Sociodemographic characteristic	Any drug	Total	Prescription drugs				Cannabis	Hallu-cinogens	Cocaine
			Sedatives	Opioids	Tranquil-izers	Amphet-amines			
Total	4.9	1.5	0.2	0.6	0.5	0.4	3.9	0.3	0.6
18–29	10.7	3.0	0.4	1.2	0.9	1.3	9.3	1.0	1.3
30+	3.0	1.0	0.2	0.4	0.4	0.2	2.2	<0.1	0.4
Total men	6.4	1.5	0.2	0.6	0.6	0.5	5.5	0.4	0.9
18–29	13.2	2.9	0.4	1.2	0.9	1.5	12.1	1.4	1.7
30+	4.0	1.0	0.1	0.5	0.5	0.2	3.1	0.1	0.5
Total women	3.6	1.4	0.3	0.6	0.5	0.4	2.5	0.1	0.4
18–29	8.2	3.0	0.4	1.3	0.9	1.2	6.4	0.6	0.8
30+	2.1	0.9	0.2	0.4	0.5	0.1	1.3	<0.1	0.2
Total nonblack	4.9	1.5	0.2	0.6	0.5	0.5	4.0	0.3	0.5
18–29	11.2	3.2	0.5	1.3	1.0	1.5	9.7	1.1	1.3
30+	2.9	1.0	0.2	0.4	0.4	0.2	2.1	0.1	0.3
Nonblack men	6.3	1.6	0.2	0.7	0.6	0.6	5.4	0.5	0.8
18–29	13.5	3.2	0.4	1.3	0.9	1.7	12.4	1.6	1.8
30+	3.8	1.1	0.1	0.5	0.5	0.2	3.0	0.1	0.5
Nonblack women	3.6	1.5	0.3	0.6	0.5	0.4	2.6	0.2	0.3
18–29	8.8	3.3	0.5	1.4	1.0	1.4	7.0	0.7	0.8
30+	2.0	0.9	0.2	0.4	0.4	0.2	1.3	<0.1	0.2
Total black	4.7	1.0	0.1	0.5	0.4	<0.1	3.8	0.1	1.0
18–29	7.3	1.3	0.1	0.6	0.5	<0.1	6.5	0.2	1.0
30+	3.6	0.9	0.1	0.4	0.4	<0.1	2.7	0.0	1.0
Black men	6.9	0.9	0.1	0.4	0.4	<0.1	6.0	0.2	1.4
18–29	10.8	1.4	0.1	0.4	0.9	<0.1	10.4	0.5	1.4
30+	5.1	0.7	0.1	0.4	0.3	<0.1	4.1	0.0	1.4
Black women	3.0	1.1	0.1	0.6	0.4	<0.1	2.1	0.0	0.7
18–29	4.4	1.2	0.1	0.9	0.2	<0.1	3.3	0.0	0.7
30+	2.4	1.0	0.1	0.4	0.5	<0.1	1.6	0.0	0.7

Note. Data compiled from *Source and accuracy statement for the National Longitudinal Alcohol Epidemiologic Survey.* Rockville, MD: National Institute on Alcohol Abuse and Alcoholism.

except for illicitly used prescription drugs, especially tranquilizers and amphetamines, whose lifetime use was more common among older than younger blacks.

The prevalence of past-year use of any type of drug was 4.9%: 3.9% for cannabis; 1.5% for illicit use of prescription drugs, with opioids the most commonly used (0.6%) of these; 0.6% for cocaine or crack; and 0.3% for hallucinogens (table 1.5). As with lifetime use, past-year drug use for all types of drugs combined was more common among men than women (6.4% vs. 3.6%) and far more prevalent among individuals aged 18–29 (10.7%) than among those aged 30 and older (3.0%). For all ages combined, there was no significant difference by race,

but among persons aged 18–29, the prevalence of use was higher for nonblacks than blacks (11.2% vs. 7.3%). These patterns varied somewhat for individual drugs. For example, the age differential was particularly strong for hallucinogens, there was no gender differential in the illicit use of prescription drugs, and blacks aged 30 and older were more likely than nonblacks in that age range to have used cocaine or crack in the past year.

The gender, ethnic, and age differentials that were obtained from the NLAES data presented in tables 1.3–1.5 correspond closely to those based on the National Household Survey on Drug Abuse (NHSDA), despite differences in the age groups surveyed and the definitions of substance use. The

NHSDA sample included individuals age 12 and over and classified respondents as drug users on the basis of a single incident of use. Prevalence estimates based on the NHSDA are accordingly higher (e.g., 37.2% lifetime use and 11.8% past-year use in individuals aged 12 and over in 1993) (Substance Abuse and Mental Health Services Administration [SAMHSA], 1995a).

Data on adolescent substance use are also collected annually in the Monitoring the Future Study, whose findings indicated that in 1995 the lifetime prevalence of any drug use was 28.5% for 8th-graders, 40.9% for 10th-graders, and 48.4% for 12th-graders. The corresponding rates of past-year use were 21.4%, 33.3%, and 39.0%, respectively. Among 12th-graders, rates of lifetime drug use were highest for cannabis (41.7%), followed by inhalants (17.8%), stimulants (15.3%), hallucinogens (12.7%), barbiturates (7.4%), tranquilizers (7.1%), and cocaine (6.0%). The prevalence of lifetime alcohol use among 12th-graders was 80.7% (Johnston, O'Malley, & Bachman, 1996).

Data from the NHSDA (SAMHSA, 1995a) indicated that among individuals 12–17 and 18–25 years of age, the lifetime prevalence of alcohol use rose throughout the late 1970s and declined between 1979 and 1992, with a very slight upturn between 1992 and 1993. The same trend was observed for cannabis use, whereas the lifetime prevalence of cocaine use peaked in 1982 and declined between 1982 and 1993. The patterns for past-year use of alcohol and drugs followed the same pattern. Among individuals 26 years of age and older, the lifetime prevalence of alcohol consumption rose during the late 1970s, decreased between 1979 and 1982, and remained fairly stable between 1982 and 1993. Lifetime use of cannabis and cocaine increased steadily between 1986 and 1993 within this age group, although the increases in cannabis use after 1988 were slight. Data from the Monitoring the Future Study indicated that the prevalence of past-year cannabis use among 8th-, 10th-, and 12th-graders increased sharply between 1991 and 1995, reversing a long-term trend toward decreasing use that began in the early 1980s. These data also showed an increase during the 1990s in the prevalence of past-year use of other drugs (e.g., inhalants and hallucinogens), but the statistical significance of these increases cannot be assessed from the published data (Johnston et al., 1996).

Although both the NHSDA and the Monitoring the Future Survey collect information on the use of alcohol and various types of drugs, the descriptive publications based on these surveys do not indicate the prevalence of multiple drug use, that is, the use of more than one type of psychoactive substance within a given time frame. Data from the 1992 NLAES revealed that one third (33.1%) of all U.S. adults had never used either alcohol or drugs at any point during their lives. More than half (51.3%) reported lifetime use of alcohol but not drugs. The proportions using alcohol and either a single type of drug or multiple drugs were 8.3% and 6.3%, respectively. Lifetime use of a single drug or multiple drugs without alcohol use was rare, reported by 0.7% and 0.2% of adults, respectively. Patterns of past-year use were similar, except that the proportion using neither alcohol nor drugs was higher (54.8%) and the proportion using alcohol only was lower (40.3%) than for the corresponding lifetime estimates.

In addition to these national population estimates, studies of emergency room and clinical samples have revealed widespread multiple drug use. Of more than half a million drug-related emergency room episodes reported to the Drug Abuse Warning Network (DAWN) in 1994, nearly one third involved the use of alcohol in combination with drugs (SAMHSA, 1996). The annual National Drug and Alcoholism Treatment Unit Survey (NDATUS), which collects data from all providers of alcohol and/or drug treatment services, revealed that 40% of all clients in treatment in 1993 abused both alcohol and drugs, 35% abusing alcohol only and 25% abusing drugs only (SAMHSA, 1995b). In a sample of 212 subjects who provided full screening information for admission into an alcohol treatment program, the proportions of men and women who reported concurrent use of other drugs were 44% and 41%, respectively, for cannabis, 32% and 33% for amphetamines, 22% each for sedatives, 17% and 10% for opiates, and 17% and 13% for hallucinogens (Schmitz et al., 1993). In another study of an inpatient treatment sample, 63% of the subjects reported concurrent use of alcohol and any other type of drug, and almost all of these concurrent users reported at least one episode of simultaneous use (i.e., use on the same day) of alcohol and other drugs (Martin et al., 1996a). In a mixed treatment/community sample of adolescents, the mean number of illicit drugs ever used was highest (3.8) for adolescents meeting the *DSM-IV* criteria for alcohol dependence, next highest (3.1) for those meeting the criteria for alcohol abuse, and lowest (1.9) for those without either diagnosis (Martin, Kaczynski, Maisto, & Tarter, 1996b).

Data on multiple drug use have provided the foundation for research on the developmental staging of substance use, which indicates a fairly consistent sequencing in the initiation of alcohol and other drug use, and for the gateway theory of substance use, which proposes that adolescent alcohol and/or cigarette use leads to (or increases the risk of) cannabis use and ultimately the use of hard drugs such as cocaine (see, for example, Kandel &Logan, 1984; Kandel & Yamaguchi, 1993; Welte & Barnes, 1985). Multiple drug use also has important implications for treatment. Studies of treatment samples generally have indicated that multiple drug users are younger, more likely to be male, more likely to be single, and more likely to live alone than individuals with alcohol problems only (Brown, Seraganian, & Tremblay, 1993, 1994; Schuckit & Bogard, 1986). Other studies have shown that multiple drug users have more antisocial problems, a greater history of depression and suicide attempt, higher levels of impulsivity, lower levels of self-control, more severe interpersonal and intrapsychic conflicts, and fewer personal coping resources than persons with alcohol use problems only (Brown & Fayek, 1993; Schuckit & Bogard, 1986). Not surprisingly, multiple drug users often have a poorer treatment outcome than do individuals treated for alcohol problems alone (Brown et al., 1993; Schuckit & Bogard, 1986). Thus, multiple drug users may require forms of treatment that do not rely on strong personal resources or a social network of support, that do attend to comorbid psychiatric problems, and that additionally deal with the complex issues surrounding the reinforcement of craving and the inappropriateness of using certain types of drugs in treatment under the circumstances of multiple drug use.

PREVALENCE OF ALCOHOL AND DRUG USE DISORDERS

The Epidemiologic Catchment Area (ECA) survey was the first of three national studies to assess alcohol and drug use disorders according to psychiatric diagnostic criteria (Robins, Locke, & Regier, 1990). In this survey, 18,571 respondents, aged 18 and older, were interviewed in a series of five community-based

epidemiological studies in the early 1980s. The second was the National Comorbidity Survey (NCS), a national probability sample of 8,098 respondents aged 15–54, conducted in 1991 (Kessler, McGonagle, & Shanyang, 1994). The most recent national survey on the prevalence of alcohol and drug use disorders is the National Longitudinal Alcohol Epidemiologic Survey (NLAES), in which direct face-to-face interviews were administered to 42,862 respondents, aged 18 and older, residing in the noninstitutionalized population of the contiguous United States (Grant, Peterson, Dawson, & Chou, 1994).

Although these three major national surveys all measured alcohol and drug use disorders, they are not comparable. Considerable differences between the surveys existed in terms of the diagnostic criteria represented, the survey instruments used, the amount and type of psychometric testing of the instruments, and definitions of lifetime diagnoses. The NLAES was the first national survey to measure alcohol and drug use disorders according to the most recent psychiatric classification, the *DSM-IV*. Most notably, the NLAES survey instrument required alcohol and drug symptoms to cluster together chronologically in order for a diagnosis of dependence to be made. In the ECA and NCS surveys, dependence on alcohol or any drug was defined as the lifetime accumulation of the required number of dependence symptoms to achieve a diagnosis, even though their occurrence may have been spread out over many years. Unlike the survey instruments used in the ECA and NCS, the NLAES diagnostic instrument was also subjected to a test-retest study that assessed its reliability in a general population sample similar to the samples for which it was intended to be used (Grant, Harford, Dawson, Chou, & Pickering, 1995).

The most recent prevalence estimates of lifetime and past-year alcohol use disorders derived from the NLAES appear in table 1.6, disaggregated by gender, ethnicity, and age. The past-year prevalence of combined alcohol abuse and dependence was 7.4%, representing 13,760,000 Americans, while the lifetime rate was much higher (18.2%). More respondents were diagnosed with dependence during the past year (4.4%) and on a lifetime basis (13.3%) than were diagnosed with alcohol abuse for those two time periods (3.0% and 4.9%, respectively).

Regardless of time frame, prevalence rates for alcohol abuse and alcohol dependence were greater among men than women and greater among non-

TABLE 1.6 Prevalence (%) of Lifetime and Past-Year *DSM-IV* Alcohol Abuse and Dependence by Gender, Ethnicity, and Age

Sociodemographic characteristics	Alcohol abuse only		Alcohol dependence		Total alcohol abuse/dependence	
	Lifetime	Past year	Lifetime	Past year	Lifetime	Past year
Total	4.9	3.0	13.3	4.4	18.2	7.4
18–24	6.7	6.5	19.9	9.4	26.6	15.9
25–44	6.2	3.0	15.7	4.3	21.9	7.3
45–64	3.7	1.4	9.9	2.1	13.7	3.5
65+	1.3	0.3	3.4	0.4	4.7	0.7
Total men	7.0	4.7	18.6	6.3	25.5	11.0
18–24	8.6	9.3	25.0	12.8	33.7	22.1
25–44	8.2	4.6	21.2	6.1	29.4	10.7
45–64	6.1	2.4	15.1	3.2	21.2	5.6
65+	2.5	0.6	6.4	0.6	8.9	1.2
Total women	2.9	1.5	8.4	2.6	11.4	4.1
18–24	4.8	3.8	14.8	6.0	19.5	9.8
25–44	4.2	1.5	10.3	2.5	14.5	3.9
45–64	1.4	0.4	5.2	1.1	6.6	1.5
65+	0.4	<0.1	1.3	0.2	1.7	0.3
Total nonblack	5.2	3.2	13.9	4.5	19.1	7.7
18–24	7.3	7.2	21.7	10.1	29.0	17.3
25–44	6.7	3.2	16.5	4.2	23.2	7.4
45–64	3.9	1.4	9.9	2.0	13.8	3.5
65+	1.3	0.3	3.5	0.4	4.8	0.7
Nonblack men	7.4	4.9	19.2	6.4	26.6	11.3
18–24	9.3	10.0	26.7	13.5	36.0	23.5
25–44	8.8	4.8	22.2	6.1	30.9	10.9
45–64	6.4	2.5	14.9	3.1	21.3	5.6
65+	2.6	0.6	6.5	0.6	9.1	1.2
Nonblack women	3.2	1.6	8.9	2.6	12.1	4.3
18–24	5.3	4.3	16.6	6.7	21.9	10.9
25–44	4.6	1.6	10.9	2.4	15.5	3.9
45–64	1.5	0.4	5.2	1.0	6.7	1.5
65+	0.4	<0.1	1.3	0.3	1.7	0.3
Total black	2.2	1.5	8.6	3.8	10.8	5.3
18–24	2.6	2.5	8.7	5.0	11.3	7.4
25–44	2.5	1.8	9.5	4.5	12.0	6.3
45–64	2.2	0.5	9.9	2.9	12.0	3.4
65+	0.4	0.0	2.8	0.3	3.2	0.3
Black men	3.5	2.5	13.3	5.8	16.8	8.3
18–24	3.9	4.0	13.6	8.4	17.5	12.3
25–44	3.7	2.8	13.4	6.0	17.1	8.8
45–64	4.0	1.2	16.0	4.0	20.1	5.2
65+	0.8	0.0	5.8	0.8	6.6	0.8
Black women	1.1	0.7	4.8	2.2	5.9	2.9
18–24	1.5	1.2	4.5	2.1	6.1	3.3
25–44	1.4	1.0	6.3	3.2	7.7	4.2
45–64	0.6	<0.1	4.9	1.9	5.5	1.9
65+	0.1	0.0	0.8	0.0	1.0	0.0

Note. Data compiled from *Source and accuracy statement for the National Longitudinal Alcohol Epidemiologic Survey.* Rockville, MD: National Institute on Alcohol Abuse and Alcoholism.

blacks than blacks. Rates for nonblack men and women often exceeded the rates of their black counterparts by over 30%. Prevalence rates of alcohol abuse and dependence, measured separately or combined, also decreased as a function of age, with the highest rates among respondents 18–45 years old relative to those 45 years and older, regardless of gender or ethnicity. Possible explanations for the decline in both past-year and lifetime alcohol abuse and dependence rates with age may include faulty recall accompanying increasing age, lower survival rates among alcoholics, and various time-dependent response styles. Alternatively, the age gradient may reflect a true cohort effect, that is, that alcohol abuse and dependence are more prevalent among the younger generation of Americans.

Although alcohol abuse and dependence were more common among men than among women, there was evidence of convergence of the rates between the sexes in the youngest age groups. The men-to-women ratios (i.e., the men's rate divided by the women's rate) were lowest in the 18- to 29-year-old age group. However, when the men-to-women ratio was examined separately for each ethnic group, it was clear that the rate converged among the youngest age groups only among nonblacks, a finding suggesting that nonblack women may be catching up. This phenomenon does not generalize to black women because the men-to-women ratios in blacks were shown to decrease as a function of age.

Prevalences of DSM-IV drug use disorders were much lower than the corresponding rates of alcohol use disorders (table 1.7). Rates for past-year abuse and dependence for most drugs were less than 1% in this general population sample, with the exception of cannabis abuse and dependence combined (1.2%). The prevalence of past-year abuse and/or dependence on any drug was 1.5%, with the rate of dependence (1.1%) exceeding the rate of abuse (0.5%) (data not shown). Overall, the lifetime rate of any drug abuse and/or dependence was 6.1%. The rate for lifetime cannabis abuse and dependence (4.6%) was greater than the rates for all the other drugs, followed in order of magnitude by abuse and/or dependence on any prescription drug (2.0%; including sedatives, tranquilizers, amphetamines, and opioids), cocaine (1.7%), amphetamines (1.5%), sedatives (0.6%), tranquilizers (0.6%), and hallucinogens (0.6%) (data not shown).

The prevalences of lifetime and past-year DSM-IV drug use disorders by gender, ethnicity, and age are shown in table 1.6. With the exception of cannabis abuse and dependence, rates for past-year abuse and dependence for most drugs also were generally less than 1% for each gender, age, and ethnic subgroup of the population. Similar to trends observed for alcohol use disorders, the rates of abuse and/or dependence on all drugs taken singly were greater for men than women, greater for nonblacks than blacks, and greater among the younger age group (<30 years) than to the older age group (30 years and older).

COMORBIDITY BETWEEN ALCOHOL USE DISORDERS, DRUG USE DISORDERS, AND PSYCHIATRIC DISORDERS

Over the last two decades, there has been increasing interest in the relationship between alcohol and drug use disorders and various forms of other psychopathology. During this time, considerable controversy has arisen surrounding several issues in comorbidity research. Opinions have varied widely on the reasons for comorbidity. There are several possible explanations for comorbidity, including the toxicity hypothesis, in which alcohol or drug use disorders are viewed as causing the comorbid disorder, and the self-medication hypothesis, in which an individual drinks or uses drugs to self-medicate the comorbid disorder (i.e., the comorbid disorder causes the alcohol or drug use disorder). It is also possible that both disorders are caused by some common factor, or that the disorders are etiologically distinct but that each modifies the risk and/or course of the other. In view of the number of comorbid relationships recognized in the literature, it is very likely that each of these hypotheses pertains to various subsets of comorbidity.

Another controversy in the comorbidity field is whether rules can be developed to reliably differentiate organic or substance-induced disorders or syndromes that mimic psychiatric disorders but are actually the toxic effects of alcohol or drug intoxication or withdrawal from independent forms of the psychiatric disorder. A similar issue arises in the differential diagnosis between pure forms of a psychiatric disorder and those that are induced by a preexisting medical condition.

TABLE 1.7 Prevalence (%) of Lifetime and Past-Year DSM-IV Drug Use Disorders by Gender, Ethnicity, and Age

Drug Use Disorder	Lifetime						Past Year					
	Men	Women	Black	Nonblack	18–29 years	30+ years	Men	Women	Black	Nonblack	18–29 years	30+ years
Any drug abuse or dependence	8.1	4.2	4.0	6.3	10.2	4.7	2.2	0.9	1.2	1.6	4.0	0.7
Any drug abuse only	4.4	2.0	1.7	3.3	5.2	2.5	1.6	0.5	0.7	1.1	3.0	0.5
Any drug dependence	3.7	2.2	2.2	3.0	5.1	2.2	0.6	0.4	0.6	0.5	1.2	0.2
Prescription drug abuse or dependence	2.5	1.6	0.6	2.2	2.8	1.8	0.3	0.3	0.3	0.3	0.7	0.2
Prescription drug abuse only	1.3	0.7	0.2	1.1	1.3	0.9	0.3	0.2	<0.1	0.2	0.5	0.1
Prescription drug dependence	1.2	0.9	0.4	1.1	1.5	0.9	0.1	0.1	<0.1	0.1	0.2	0.1
Sedative abuse or dependence	0.8	0.4	0.3	0.7	0.7	0.6	0.0	<0.1	0.0	<0.1	<0.1	<0.1
Sedative abuse only	0.4	0.2	0.2	0.3	0.3	0.3	0.0	0.0	0.0	0.0	0.0	0.0
Sedative dependence	0.4	0.2	0.1	0.4	0.4	0.3	<0.1	<0.1	0.0	<0.1	<0.1	<0.1
Tranquilizer abuse or dependence	0.8	0.4	0.4	0.6	0.9	0.6	<0.1	0.1	<0.1	0.1	0.1	<0.1
Tranquilizer abuse only	0.4	0.2	0.2	0.3	0.5	0.3	<0.1	<0.1	0.0	0.1	0.1	<0.1
Tranquilizer dependence	0.4	0.2	0.2	0.3	0.4	0.3	<0.1	<0.1	<0.1	<0.1	<0.1	<0.1
Amphetamine abuse or dependence	2.0	1.0	0.4	1.6	2.1	1.3	0.2	0.1	0.0	0.1	0.4	<0.1
Amphetamine abuse only	1.0	0.3	0.2	0.8	1.0	0.7	0.1	0.1	0.0	0.1	0.3	<0.1
Amphetamine dependence	1.0	0.6	0.2	0.8	1.1	0.6	0.1	<0.1	0.0	0.1	0.1	<0.1
Cannabis abuse or dependence	6.6	2.9	2.9	4.9	8.2	3.5	1.9	0.5	0.8	1.3	3.4	0.5
Cannabis abuse only	4.1	1.7	1.6	3.0	4.9	2.2	1.5	0.4	0.6	1.0	2.6	0.4
Cannabis dependence	2.5	1.2	1.3	1.9	3.3	1.3	0.4	0.1	0.2	0.3	0.8	<0.1
Cocaine abuse or dependence	2.2	1.1	1.6	1.7	2.7	1.3	0.3	0.1	0.5	0.2	0.4	0.1
Cocaine abuse only	0.9	0.4	0.4	0.7	1.0	0.5	0.2	<0.1	0.1	0.1	0.2	<0.1
Cocaine dependence	1.3	0.7	1.2	1.0	1.7	0.8	0.1	0.1	0.4	0.1	0.2	0.1
Hallucinogen abuse or dependence	1.0	0.3	0.1	0.6	1.1	0.4	0.1	<0.1	<0.1	0.1	0.3	0.0
Hallucinogen abuse only	0.5	0.2	<0.1	0.3	0.6	0.2	0.1	0.0	0.0	<0.1	0.2	0.0
Hallucinogen dependence	0.5	0.1	<0.1	0.3	0.5	0.1	<0.1	<0.1	<0.1	<0.1	0.1	0.0

Note. Data compiled from *Source and accuracy statement for the National Longitudinal Alcohol Epidemiologic Survey.* Rockville, MD: National Institute on Alcohol Abuse and Alcoholism.

Disentangling independent from substance-induced disorders can be difficult, because this determination rests largely on a self-report clinical history that may be unreliable, particularly when chronic, long-standing disorders may be involved. In view of this issue, it is not surprising that much of the thinking about comorbidity has been focused on the primary-secondary distinction, or on which disorder appeared first chronologically. The assumption has been that a psychiatric disorder that is primary to an alcohol or drug use disorder is more likely to be an independent disease entity which will persist in abstinence and require appropriate treatment. Conversely, a chronologically secondary psychiatric disorder is thought to be more likely to result from the toxic effects of alcohol and drugs and to remit with abstinence.

Most of the research on comorbidity has been conducted in treated samples. Data from these clinical studies show wide variation in comorbidity rates between alcohol and drug use disorders and other psychiatric disorders. The observed variation in the rates is very likely due to differences in the diagnostic interviews and criteria used to arrive at diagnoses and differences in the demographic composition of the samples. Regardless of the reported variability, studies of medical, psychiatric, and substance-abusing patients are not well suited to the study of comorbidity. Individuals in treatment are more likely to have multiple disorders than cases in the general population, thereby spuriously inflating comorbidity rates and creating an environment ripe for what is referred to as *Berkson's bias* (Berkson, 1946).

Because of these problems, it is necessary to turn to general population samples for more accurate and precise estimates of comorbidity. However, general population surveys designed to reliably study comorbidity are rare. As previously mentioned, only three major studies in the United States have considered psychiatric comorbidity, including alcohol and drug use disorders and other psychopathology. These studies were the ECA conducted in the early 1980s, the NCS conducted in 1991, and the NLAES conducted in 1992.

The relationships between current and lifetime alcohol and drug use disorders and other psychiatric disorders from these three surveys are summarized in table 1.8. In this table, we present odds ratios as measures of the strength of an association between disorders. An odds ratio significantly greater than 1.0 reflects a positive association between two comorbid disorders. An odds ratio of 1.0 or indistinguishable from 1.0 is considered nonsignificant.

Despite major differences in interview schedules, diagnostic criteria, and algorithms, the relative magnitudes of the rates are quite consistent across the ECA, NCS, and NLAES and between past-year and lifetime odds ratios, with the majority of associations being smaller for lifetime than past-year time frames. These results suggest that while self-medication of depression with alcohol may be effective in the short term, it may lead to increased dysphoria and exacerbation of depressive symptoms in the long term. If self-medication were successful in the long term, we would have expected the associations to be lower for past-year diagnoses relative to lifetime diagnoses.

The level of association among alcohol and drug use disorders was greatest in the two most recent surveys, the NCS and NLAES (OR > 20), but much lower in the older (ECA) survey. The magnitude of this association and its consistency in the latest two surveys, despite their methodological differences, strongly suggest that alcohol and drug use disorders are more likely to co-occur today than they were a decade ago on both a lifetime and a concurrent basis. Alcohol and drug use disorders were also more highly related to major depression and antisocial personality disorder than to manic disorder or any of the anxiety disorders. This result is consistent with evidence from the clinical literature, in which alcohol and drug use disorders, major depression, and antisocial personality disorders sometimes aggregate in the same family and in the same individuals, indicating that the three disorders may simply be alternative manifestations of the same disorder (Winokur & Coryell, 1991; Winokur, Rimmer, & Reich, 1971). However, from the limited number of data available from adoption and genetic marker studies, there is no consistent evidence of genetic overlap among the disorders in this putative spectrum (Cloninger, Reich, & Wetzel, 1979; Goodwin et al., 1974; Goodwin, Schulsinger, Hermansen, Guze, & Winokur, 1973). Further research will be required to determine if these three disorders are heterogeneous clinically and etiologically or, alternatively, represent different expressions of the same underlying pathogenic mechanism.

Despite the findings from clinical studies that comorbidity rates vary by gender and age, these specifications have been largely ignored in previous general

TABLE 1.8 Comorbidity Between Current and Lifetime Alcohol and Drug Use Disorders and Other Major Psychiatric Disorders in the NLAES, NCS, and ECA: Odds Ratios

Disorder	Survey	Current[a]		Lifetime	
		Alcohol use disorder	Drug use disorder	Alcohol use disorder	Drug use disorder
Drug use disorder	NLAES	25.1	—	13.0	—
	NCS	20.6	—	13.7	—
	ECA	7.8	—	5.8	—
Major depression	NLAES	3.7	7.2	3.6	5.2
	NCS	2.6	3.0	1.9	2.4
	ECA	2.7	3.4	1.9	3.5
Mania	NCS	5.6	5.7	4.9	7.4
	ECA	3.8	3.2	4.6	
Obsessive-compulsive disorder	ECA	3.4	3.4	2.1	3.3
Phobia	NCS	2.3	3.9	1.7	2.2
	ECA	1.7	1.7	1.4	1.8
Panic disorder	NCS	1.4	3.9	1.6	3.0
	ECA	4.6	1.0	2.6	3.1
Generalized anxiety disorder	NCS	2.7	5.0	2.0	2.9
Posttraumatic stress disorder	NCS	2.2	2.9	1.7	3.2
Antisocial personality disorder	NCS	—	—	11.3	11.5
	ECA	—	—	14.6	8.9

[a]Current: ECA and NCS, 6 months; NLAES, 12 months.

population studies. In the NLAES, associations between lifetime alcohol and drug use disorders and major depression were presented for abuse and dependence separately by gender and age (Grant, 1995; Grant & Harford 1995) (see table 1.9). For alcohol and each drug, the dependence-depression association was greater than the corresponding abuse-depression association, and the odds ratios were greater for drug than for alcohol use disorders.

Associations between alcohol and drug use disorders for all drugs combined and between dependence and major depression did not differ by gender. With the exception of cocaine and hallucinogens, the risk for alcohol and other drug abuse and major depression was consistently greater for women than men. One reason for this observed risk differential relates directly to the definition of abuse underlying the comorbidity rates. The DSM-IV defines alcohol and drug abuse, separately from dependence, as social, occupational, legal, and interpersonal consequences arising from substance use. Indicators of patterns of compulsive use (e.g., impaired control over

the use, giving up important activities to use) and tolerance and withdrawal symptomatology were relegated to the dependence category. Unlike the indicators of DSM-IV dependence, the DSM-IV abuse criteria may reflect societal reactions to substance use behavior. Women's drinking and drug-taking behavior may be more heavily sanctioned than that of men (Makela, 1987; Park, 1983), thereby increasing their vulnerability to societal reaction as reflected in the DSM-IV formulation of abuse. The increased risk of major depression among women diagnosed as abusers therefore may reflect the development of major depression as the result of a more adverse societal reaction to their drinking and drug use than that experienced by men. The finding that women also do not demonstrate greater abuse-depression associations than men for cocaine and hallucinogens implicates the importance of the context in which drug taking occurs. Cocaine and hallucinogen use frequently takes place among subcultures of society within which women may be protected from societal reactions through peer support and approval.

TABLE 1.9 Lifetime Comorbidity Between *DSM-IV* Alcohol and Drug Use Disorders and *DSM-IV* Major Depression by Gender and Age: Odds Ratios

Alcohol/drug use disorder	Men	Women	18–29 years	30+ years	Total
Alcohol abuse or dependence	4.2	4.0	2.8	3.8	3.6
Alcohol abuse only	1.5	2.1	1.4	1.7	1.7
Alcohol dependence	4.3	4.3	2.9	4.1	3.8
Any drug abuse or dependence	5.5	5.9	4.3	5.3	5.2
Any drug abuse only	3.2	4.0	2.6	3.4	3.3
Any drug dependence	7.2	7.3	5.5	7.1	6.9
Prescription drug abuse or dependence	6.5	6.7	5.3	6.6	6.3
Prescription drug abuse only	3.9	5.1	3.6	4.3	4.1
Prescription drug dependence	9.7	8.0	7.1	9.1	8.6
Sedative abuse or dependence	6.7	6.1	5.2	6.5	6.1
Sedative abuse only	3.8	4.9	3.4	4.2	3.9
Sedative dependence	10.1	7.3	7.3	9.1	8.5
Tranquilizer abuse or dependence	6.6	7.1	5.3	6.9	6.5
Tranquilizer abuse only	4.2	6.6	4.1	4.9	4.8
Tranquilizer dependence	9.6	7.4	7.5	8.8	8.3
Amphetamine abuse or dependence	6.4	6.6	4.4	7.1	6.2
Amphetamine abuse only	3.7	5.2	2.9	4.6	4.0
Amphetamine dependence	10.3	8.0	6.0	10.5	8.9
Cannabis abuse or dependence	4.8	5.8	3.8	4.7	4.7
Cannabis abuse only	3.0	4.2	2.5	3.2	3.1
Cannabis dependence	7.3	8.0	5.4	7.4	7.0
Cocaine abuse or dependence	5.3	5.2	3.6	5.5	5.0
Cocaine abuse only	5.1	4.3	2.6	5.9	4.5
Cocaine dependence	5.1	5.7	4.2	5.1	5.1
Hallucinogen abuse or dependence	7.4	5.4	4.4	7.1	6.3
Hallucinogen abuse only	6.9	4.5	4.6	5.7	5.7
Hallucinogen dependence	7.6	7.2	4.1	8.6	6.8

Note. Data compiled from *Source and accuracy statement for the National Longitudinal Alcohol Epidemiologic Survey.* Rockville, MD: National Institute on Alcohol Abuse and Alcoholism.

The association between alcohol and drug use disorders and major depression was consistently greater in the older age group than in the younger age group. This result is consistent with evidence from clinical studies that suggest that a variety of drugs are often used to self-medicate depression. Specifically, the mood effects of central nervous system depressants, such as alcohol, tranquilizers, and sedatives, have been shown to be variable, initially causing euphoria, but then producing dysphoria, particularly with prolonged use among chronic users. The finding that risk of comorbidity increases with age appears to confirm that self-medication for depression with alcohol, tranquilizers, and sedatives may be effective in the short term but that chronic high-dose use is frequently accompanied by dysphoria (Ellinwood, 1979; Post, Kotlin, & Goodwin, 1974). Alternatively, these findings may merely reflect age differences in the lifetime risk of both drug use disorders and major depression. Although major depression was strongly related to both cannabis and hallucinogen abuse and dependence, these two drug classes are not usually associated with the self-medication paradigm as it relates to major depression. However, chronic high-dose use of cannabis and hallucinogens may be accompanied by the development of amotivational syndrome, characterized by anhedonia, chronic apathy, difficulty concentrating, and social withdrawal (Cohen, 1981), symptoms strikingly similar to those of major depression. Alternatively, failure to extract clear relations between specific drugs of choice predicted by the self-medication hypothesis as ameliorating major depression may be the result of the common phenomena of polydrug abuse and dependence.

FUTURE DIRECTIONS AND TRENDS: CLASSIFICATION, PREVALENCE, AND COMORBIDITY

The future evolution of the classification of alcohol and drug use disorders is likely to entail a continuation of the trend toward differentiating dependence disorders from other substance-related disabilities as well as the proliferation of subtypes defined in terms of comorbidity, family history, and other differentiating factors. It is also expected that future changes in classification systems will depend more and more on empirical data for their justification, a trend begun during the *ICD-10* and *DSM-IV* revision processes. Recent efforts by behaviorally oriented scientists should also yield more refined alternative approaches to classifications based on the disease concept of alcohol and drug dependence. Existing classifications based on current observable alcohol and drug symptoms will be refined through the incorporation of biological, social, genetic, and cultural antecedents and through validation studies based on outcome, course, and rehabilitation as knowledge is advanced in each of these fields.

Future advances in the epidemiology of alcohol and drug use disorders and their comorbidity with psychiatric disorders will depend critically on the continued development of reliable and valid assessment instruments. Assessment instruments are needed particularly to more accurately measure the timing of the onset of disorder and to differentiate substance-induced disorders from those that occur independently of substance use. Equally important will be the development of reliable and valid adjunct assessment instruments to measure personality disorders. The impact of long-standing personality disorders on the development of alcohol and drug use disorders and their comorbidity with major mood, anxiety, and psychotic disorders has been largely neglected in the research literature.

Longitudinal studies are also sorely needed to advance knowledge in the alcohol and drug epidemiology and psychiatric comorbidity research fields. Longitudinal data would help elucidate the causes and the natural history of alcohol and drug use disorders and would provide the basis for understanding the pathophysiological processes underlying them. Since adolescence is a high-risk period for the development of alcohol and drug use disorders, the longitudinal study of the chronology of alcohol and drug use disorders and other forms of psychopathology should prove to be most informative. Longitudinal research also has the potential to define important subtypes of alcohol and drug use disorders defined by comorbidity and to identify accompanying risk factors helpful in prevention, treatment, and rehabilitation.

Key References

Grant, B. F. (1995). Comorbidity between DSM-IV drug use disorders and major depression: Results of a national survey of adults. *Journal of Substance Abuse, 7*, 481–497.

Grant, B. F., Harford, T. C., Dawson, D. A., Chou, S. P., Dufour, M., & Pickering, R. (1994). Prevalence of DSM-IV alcohol abuse and dependence: United States, 1992. *Alcohol, Health and Research World, 18*, 243–247.

Robins, L. N., Locke, B. Z., & Regier, D. A. (1990). An overview of psychiatric disorders in America. In L. N. Robins & D. A. Regier (Eds.), *Psychiatric disorders in America: The Epidemiologic Catchment Area Study* (pp. 328–366). New York: Free Press.

References

Adesso, U. J. (1995). Cognitive factors in alcohol and drug use. In M. Galizio & S. A. Maisto (Eds.), *Determinants of substance abuse: Biological, psychological, and environmental factors* (pp. 179–208). New York: Plenum Press.

American Psychiatric Association. (1980). *Diagnostic and statistical manual of mental disorders* (3rd ed.). Washington, DC: Author.

American Psychiatric Association. (1987). *Diagnostic and statistical manual of mental disorders* (3rd ed., Rev.). Washington, DC: Author.

American Psychiatric Association. (1994). *Diagnostic and statistical manual of mental disorders* (4th ed.). Washington, DC: Author.

Babor, T. F. (1992). Substance-related problems in the context of international classification systems. In M. Lader, G. Edwards, & D. C. Drummond (Eds.), *The nature of alcohol and drug related problems* (pp. 83–97). New York: Oxford University Press.

Babor, T. F. (1996). The classification of alcoholics: Typology theories from the 19th century to the present. *Alcohol Health and Research World, 20,* 6–17.

Babor, T. F., Hofmann, M., DelBoca, F. K., Hesselbrock, V., Meyer, R. E., Dolinsky, Z. S., & Rounsaville, B. (1992). Types of alcoholics: 1. Evidence for an empirically derived typology based on indicators of vulnerability and severity. *Archives of General Psychiatry, 49,* 599–608.

Babor, T. F., & Lauerman, R. (1986). Classification and forms of inebriety: Historical antecedents of alcoholic typologies. In M. Galanter (Ed.), *Recent developments in alcoholism* (Vol. 5, pp. 113–144). New York: Plenum Press.

Ball, S. A. (1996). Type A and Type B alcoholism: Applicability across subpopulations and treatment settings. *Alcohol, Health and Research World, 20,* 30–35.

Ball, S. A., Carroll, K. M., Babor, T. F., & Rounsaville, B. J. (1995). Subtypes of cocaine abusers: Support for the Type A-Type B distinction. *Journal of Consulting and Clinical Psychology, 63,* 115–124.

Berkson, J. (1946). Limitations of the application of the 4-fold table analyses to hospital data. *Biometrics, 2,* 47–53.

Bowman, K. M., & Jellinek, E. M. (1941). Alcohol addiction and its treatment. *Quarterly Journal of Studies on Alcohol, 2,* 98–176.

Brown, T. G., & Fayek, A. (1993). Comparison of demographic characteristics and MMPI scores from alcohol and poly-drug alcohol and cocaine abusers. *Alcoholism Treatment Quarterly, 10,* 123–135.

Brown, T. G., Seraganian, P., & Tremblay, J. (1993). Alcohol and cocaine abusers 6 months after traditional treatment: Do they fare as well as problem drinkers? *Journal of Substance Abuse Treatment, 10,* 545–552.

Brown, T. G., Seraganian, P., & Tremblay, J. (1994). Alcoholics also dependent on cocaine in treatment: Do they differ from "pure" alcoholics? *Addictive Behaviors, 19,* 105–112.

Bruhl-Cramer, C. Von. (1819). *Urber die trunksucht and eine rationelle.* Berlin: Heilmethode Deserlben.

Buydens-Branchey, L., Branchey, M. H., & Noumair, D. (1989). Age of alcoholism onset: 1. Relationship to psychopathology. *Archives of General Psychiatry, 46,* 231–236.

Cancrini, L. (1994). The psychopathology of drug addiction: A review. *The Journal of Drug Issues, 24,* 597–622.

Carlin, A. S., & Strauss, F. F. (1978). Two typologies of polydrug abusers. In D. R. Wesson, A. S. Carlin, K. M. Adams et al. (Eds.), *Polydrug abuse: The re-sults of a national collaborative study* (pp. 97–127). New York: Academic Press.

Carpenter, W. B. (1850). *On the use and abuse of alcoholic liquors in health and disease.* Philadelphia: Blanchard & Lee.

Cloninger, C. R. (1987). Neurogenetic adaptive mechanisms in alcoholism. *Science, 236,* 410–416.

Cloninger, C. R., Bohman, M., & Sigvardsson, S. (1981). Inheritance of alcohol abuse: Cross-fostering analysis in adopted men. *Archives of General Psychiatry, 38,* 861–868.

Cloninger, C. R., Reich, T., & Wetzel, R. (1979). Alcoholism and affective disorders: Familial associations and genetic models. In D. Goodwin & C. K. Erickson (Eds.), *Alcoholism and affective disorders: Clinical, genetic and biochemical studies* (pp. 57–86). New York: S. P. Medical and Scientific Books.

Cohen, S. (1981). Cannabis: Impact on motivation, Part 2. *Drug Abuse and Alcohol Newsletter, 10,* 1–3.

Crothers, T. D. (1893). *The disease of inebriety.* New York: Treat.

Edwards, G., & Gross, M. M. (1976). Alcohol dependence: Provisional description of a clinical syndrome. *British Medical Journal, 1,* 1058–1061.

Edwards, G., Gross, M. M., Keller, M., Moser, J., & Room, R. (1977). *Alcohol-related disabilities.* Geneva: World Health Organization.

Ellinwood, E. H. (1979). Amphetamines/anorectics. In R. L. Dupont, A. Goldstein, & J. O'Donnell (Eds.), *Handbook on drug abuse* (pp. 46–54). Washington, DC: National Institute of Mental Health.

Esquirol, E. (1845). *Mental maladies treatise on insanity.* Philadelphia: Lea & Blanchard.

Feingold, A., Ball, S. A., Kranzler, H. R., & Rounsaville, B. J. (1996). Generalizability of the Type A/Type B distinction across different psychoactive substances. *American Journal of Drug and Alcohol Abuse, 22,* 449–462.

Frances, R. J., Timm, S., & Bucky, S. (1980). Studies of familial and nonfamilial alcoholism. *Archives of General Psychiatry, 37,* 564–566.

Goodwin, D. W., Schulsinger, F., Hermansen, L., Guze, S. B., & Winokur, G. (1973). Alcohol problems in adoptees raised apart from alcoholic biological parents. *Archives of General Psychiatry, 28,* 238–243.

Goodwin, D. W., Schulsinger, F., Miller, N., Hermansen, L., Winokur, G., & Guze, S. B. (1974). Drinking problems in adopted and nonadopted sons of alcoholics. *Archives of General Psychiatry, 31,* 164–169.

Grant, B. F. (1995). Comorbidity between DSM-IV drug use disorders and major depression: Results of a national survey of adults. *Journal of Substance Abuse, 7,* 481–497.

Grant, B. F., & Harford, T. C. (1995). Comorbidity between DSM-IV alcohol use disorders and major depression: Results of a national survey. *Drug and Alcohol Dependence, 39,* 197–206.

Grant, B. F., Harford, T. C., Dawson, D. A., Chou, S. P., Dufour, M., & Pickering, R. (1994). Prevalence of DSM-IV alcohol abuse and dependence: United States, 1992. *Alcohol, Health and Research World, 18,* 243–247.

Grant, B. F., Harford, T. C., Dawson, D. A, Chou, P. S., & Pickering, R. P. (1995). The Alcohol Use Disorder and Associated Disabilities Interview Schedule: Reliability of alcohol and drug modules in a general population sample. *Drug and Alcohol Dependence, 39,* 37–44.

Grant, B. F., Peterson, L. A., Dawson, D. S., & Chou, S. P. (1994). *Source and accuracy statement for the National Longitudinal Alcohol Epidemiologic Survey.* Rockville, MD: National Institute on Alcohol Abuse and Alcoholism.

Huss, M. (1849). *Alcoholismus chronicus eller.* Stockholm: Chronisk Alkolssjuk dom.

Jellinek, E. M. (1960). *The disease concept of alcoholism.* New Haven, CT: College and University Press.

Johnston, L. D., O'Malley, P. M., & Bachman, J. G. (1996). *National survey results on drug use from the Monitoring the Future Study, 1975–1995* (Vol. 1). Rockville, MD: National Institute on Drug Abuse.

Kandel, D., & Logan, J. (1984). Periods of drug use from adolescence to young adulthood: 1. Periods of risk for initiation, continued use, and discontinuation. *American Journal of Public Health, 74,* 660–666.

Kandel, D., & Yamaguchi, K. (1993). From beer to crack: Developmental patterns of drug involvement. *American Journal of Public Health, 83,* 851–854.

Kerr, N. (1888). *Inebriety or narcomania: Its etiology, pathology, treatment and jurisprudence.* London: H. K. Lewis.

Kessler, R. C., McGonagle, K. A., & Shanyang, Z. (1994). Lifetime and 12-month prevalence of DSM-III-R psychiatric disorders in the United States: Results from the National Comorbidity Survey. *Archives of General Psychiatry, 51,* 8–19.

Knight, P. R. (1938). Psychoanalytic treatment in a sanitorium of chronic addiction to alcohol. *Journal of the American Medical Association, 111,* 1443–1448.

Kraeplin, E. (1909–1915). *Psychiatric ein lehrbuch* (8th ed., Vols. 1–4). Leipzig, Germany: J. A. Barth.

Makela, K. (1987). Level of consumption and social consequences of drinking. In Y. Israel, F. Glaser, & R. Popham (Eds.), *Recent advances in alcohol and drug Problems* (pp. 87–116). New York: Plenum Press.

Martin, C. S., Clifford, P. R., Maisto, S. A., Earleywine, M., Kirisci, L., & Longabaugh, R. (1996a). Polydrug use in an inpatient treatment sample of problem drinkers. *Alcoholism: Clinical and Experimental Research, 20,* 413–417.

Martin, S., Kaczynski, N. A., Maisto, S. A., & Tarter, R. E. (1996b). Polydrug use in adolescent drinkers with and without DSM-IV alcohol abuse and dependence. *Alcoholism: Clinical and Experimental Research, 20,* 1099–1108.

McBride, C. A. (1910). *The modern treatment of alcoholism and drug narcotism.* London: Rebman.

Morey, L. C., & Skinner, J. A. (1986). Empirically derived classifications of alcohol-related problems. In M. Galanter (Ed.), *Recent developments in alcoholism,* (Vol. 5, pp. 145–168). New York: Plenum Press.

Nathan, P. E. (1981). Prospects for a behavioral approach to the diagnosis of alcoholism. In R. E. Meyer, T. F. Babor, B. C. Glueck, J. H. Jaffe, J. E. O'Brian, & J. R. Stabenau (Eds.), *Evaluation of the alcoholic; Implications for research, theory and treatment* (DHHS Publication No. ADM 81–1033, pp. 85–102). Washington, DC: National Institute on Alcohol Abuse and Alcoholism.

Park, P. (1983). Social class factors in alcoholism. In B. Kissin & H. Begleiter (Eds.), *The pathogenesis of alcoholism: Psychosocial factors* (pp. 272–302). New York: Plenum Press.

Pattison, E. M., Sobell, M. B., & Sobell, L. C. (1977). *Emerging concepts of alcohol dependence.* New York: Springer.

Post, R. M., Kotlin, J., & Goodwin, F. K. (1974). The effects of cocaine on depressed patients. *American Journal of Psychiatry, 131,* 511–515.

Robins, L. N., Locke, B. Z., & Regier, D. A. (1990). An overview of psychiatric disorders in America. In L. N. Robins & D. A. Regier (Eds.), *Psychiatric disorders in America: The Epidemiologic Catchment Area Study* (pp. 328–366). New York: Free Press.

Schmitz, J., DeJong, J., Roy, A., Garnett, D., Moore, V., Lamparski, D., Waxman, R., & Linnoila, M. (1993). Substance abuse among subjects screened out from an alcoholism research program. *American Journal of Drug and Alcohol Abuse, 19,* 359–368.

Schuckit, M. A., & Bogard, B. (1986). Intravenous drug use in alcoholics. *Journal of Clinical Psychiatry, 47,* 551–554.

Schuckit, M. A., Tipp, J. E., Smith, T. L., Shapiro, E., Hesselbrock, V. M., Bucholz, K. K., Reich, T., & Nurnberger, J. I., Jr. (1995). An evaluation of Type A and B alcoholics. *Addiction, 90,* 1189–1203.

Substance Abuse and Mental Health Services Administration. (1995a). *National Household Survey on Drug*

Abuse Main Findings 1993 (DHHS Pub. No. SMA 95–3020). Rockville, MD: Author.

Substance Abuse and Mental Health Services Administration. (1995b). *Overview of the FY94 National Drug and Alcoholism Treatment Unit Survey (NDATUS): Data from 1993 and 1980–1993.* Rockville, MD: Author.

Substance Abuse and Mental Health Services Administration. (1996). *Preliminary estimates from the Drug Abuse Warning Network.* Rockville, MD: Author.

Welte, H., & Barnes, G. (1985). Alcohol: The gateway to other drug use among secondary-school students. *Journal of Youth and Adolescence, 14,* 487–498.

Williams, G. D., & Debakey, S. F. (1992). Changes in levels of alcohol consumption: United States, 1983–1988. *Addiction, 87,* 643–648.

Wills, T. A., Vaccaro, D., & McNamara, G. (1994). Novelty seeking, risk taking, and related constructs as predictors of adolescent substance use: An application of Cloninger's theory. *Journal of Substance Abuse, 6,* 1–20.

Winokur, G., & Coryell, W. (1991). Familial alcoholism in primary unipolar major depressive disorder. *American Journal of Psychiatry, 148,* 184–188.

Winokur, G., Rimmer, J., & Reich, T. (1971). Alcoholism: 4. Is there more than one type of alcoholism? *British Journal of Psychiatry, 118,* 525–531.

World Health Organization. (1968). *International Classification of diseases* (8th Rev.). Geneva: Author.

World Health Organization. (1978). *International classification of diseases* (9th Rev.). Geneva: Author.

World Health Organization. (1992). *International classification of diseases and related health problems* (10th Rev.). Geneva: Author.

Wulfert, E., Greenway, D. E., & Dougher, M. J. (1996). A logical functional analysis of reinforcement-based disorders: Alcoholism and pedophilia. *Journal of Consulting and Clinical Psychology, 64,* 1140–1115.

Zucker, R. A. (1987). The four alcoholisms: A developmental account of the etiologic process. In P. C. Rivers (Ed.), *Alcohol and addictive behavior* (pp. 27–83). Lincoln: University of Nebraska Press.

2

The Course of Treated and Untreated Substance Use Disorders: Remission and Resolution, Relapse and Mortality

John W. Finney

Rudolf H. Moos

Christine Timko

Each person's life has its unique course, and that course can be understood in terms of multiple dimensions and behaviors. In this chapter, we focus on the course of substance abuse/dependence (disorders involving alcohol, nicotine, and other drugs—particularly, heroin) and describe the more common life trajectories and influences that alter the course of these disorders.

Practitioners offering substance abuse services often see patients return for treatment repeatedly over a period of years. As a result, they are likely to conclude that substance use disorders are chronic, progressive conditions. However, those beliefs are based on observations of a restricted subset of individuals: those with the most severe, chronic forms of substance use disorders. In this regard, substantial empirical evidence indicates that persons who seek treatment for substance abuse are more impaired than persons not seeking treatment (Finney & Moos, 1995; Fiore et al., 1990; Graeven & Graeven, 1983;

Rounsaville & Kleber, 1985; Sobell, Cunningham, & Sobell, 1996; Tucker & Gladsjo, 1993). Cohen and Cohen (1984) coined the term *clinician's illusion* to refer to the selective, pessimistic perceptions of practitioners regarding the course of the disorders they treat.

In contrast, some analysts have provided very optimistic views on the long-term outcome of psychoactive substance addiction. For example, based on a records search, Winick (1962) argued that, over time, about two thirds of persons treated for heroin addiction "mature out" of their dependence, typically in their 30s. Similarly, Drew (1968) suggested that alcoholism is a "self-limiting" disease.

The research reviewed in this chapter, though not without limitations, provides a more comprehensive and balanced perspective on the course of substance use disorders. We address the following questions: What is the course and long-term outcome of treated and untreated substance use disorders? To what extent do persons with substance abuse/dependence exhibit progression in the severity of their symptoms? Can persons who are stably remitted function as well as individuals who never have had substance use disorders?

After reviewing research on the course and long-term outcomes of substance use disorders, we focus on one end point for some addicted persons: premature death. We examine the link between active addiction and heightened mortality risk. Then, we focus on course changes and the role of personal and environmental factors in remission, resolution, lapse, and relapse. Because of the intended practitioner audience, we focus more attention on findings for treated samples, and in the concluding section, we consider implications for treatment. As will become apparent, there is a larger body of research on these issues with respect to alcohol use disorders than for smoking and other drug abuse.

THE COURSE OF SUBSTANCE USE DISORDERS

It is inaccurate to speak of *the* course of any addiction, as the course for any individual is affected by numerous personal and environmental factors, including any other addictions. Thus, in referring to the course of a substance use disorder, one is referring less to its "natural history" as it unfolds in some inexorable way (Edwards, 1984), than to the "careers" of the disorder (Edwards, 1984) as they are shaped by varying personal and environmental factors for different individuals. In this section, we focus on long-term outcomes and the typical course for alcohol, other drug (primarily heroin), and nicotine addiction.

Course of Alcohol Use Disorders

Two types of findings from longitudinal studies provide evidence on the course of alcohol use disorders: data on individuals' functioning at a long-term follow-up point and a smaller body of results on the course of alcohol use disorders for groups of individuals who have been studied repeatedly over time. We examine separately the data for community (essentially untreated) and clinical samples that have been tracked for 8 years or more.

Long-Term Functioning in Community Samples

We located only two long-term follow-up studies that focused on alcohol use disorders in community samples. In one, Ojesjo (1981) reported outcomes for 96 alcoholic men who had been interviewed initially 15 years earlier. The men, whose age at baseline averaged 47 years, were categorized at that point as "abusers" (heavy drinkers with "medical and social disabilities"); "addicts," with generalized dependence symptoms; or "chronics," who had dependence symptoms and medical comorbidities. None received intensive treatment during the course of the study. At the 15-year follow-up, 26% had died. Among the survivors, 41% (2.7% per follow-up year) were in remission. The surviving "abusers" had the best outcomes, with 64% in remission, followed by "addicts" (18% in remission), and "chronics" (none in remission).

Vaillant (1995, 1996) presented long-term follow-up data on two quite different community samples, whose members had met *DSM-III* criteria for alcohol abuse (some also met criteria for dependence) at some point in their lives. One group was made up of 150 inner-city men (the "Core City" sample) who had initially been control group members in a study of juvenile delinquency. The "College" sample consisted of 55 men originally assessed as sophomores at Harvard University for a study of "normal development."

Long-term follow-up data were secured on 112 men in the Core City sample and 44 men in the College sample. By age 60, 28% of the men in the Core City sample had died. Among the survivors, 59% were in remission, with about three abstainers for each controlled drinker (Vaillant, 1996). The men in Vaillant's College sample exhibited a different pattern of outcome when they were 60 years old. A smaller percentage had died (18%), and among the survivors, only 27% were in remission and about equally divided between abstainers and controlled drinkers. By age 70, 40% of the College sample men had died. Remission was slightly less prevalent (47%) among the survivors than continuing alcohol abuse (53%) (the Core City sample has been followed only to age 60 at this point).

Overall, these two studies of community samples suggest that around 3% of individuals with alcohol use disorders experience remission each year. However, annual remission rates are difficult to calculate for Vaillant's (1995, 1996) samples, where, unlike in Ojesjo's (1981) study, the follow-ups for some men began before their alcohol use disorders had developed.

Course of Alcohol Use Disorders in Community Samples

A more complete picture of the typical course of alcohol use disorders requires data on individuals' functioning at intervening points, in addition to functioning at a long-term follow-up. Using retrospective accounts from 286 essentially untreated persons (170 men and 116 women), Schuckit, Anthenelli, Bucholz, Hesselbrock, and Tipp (1995) outlined the course of alcoholism in terms of the typical age at which 44 life events occurred. Study participants reported drinking more than intended at an average age of 21 and developing tolerance at 23 years of age. Objections from family, friends, or physicians ensued at age 24, on average, and respondents first considered themselves excessive drinkers at age 26. A first period of abstinence of 3 months or more was experienced by 181 of these individuals at age 28, followed by a second period of 3 months or more at 30 ($N = 98$) and a third period of abstinence at 34 ($N = 50$).

Although retrospective data, such as those of Schuckit et al. (1995), are valuable, prospective studies provide a more accurate perspective of the variable courses that alcohol abuse/dependence takes in individuals' lives. Vaillant's (1995, 1996) is the most lengthy and in-depth prospective study of the course of alcoholism. Participants in both of Vaillant's samples completed multiple interviews, so it was possible to determine their status at various stages in their lives. Vaillant's (1995, 1996) analyses reveal a different pattern of functioning over time for his two samples. The relevant data for the Core City sample are presented in figure 2.1 and those for the College sample in figure 2.2.

For many of the Core City men, alcohol abuse began relatively early in their lives (over 25% met criteria for alcohol abuse by age 20). Although all of the men met criteria for alcohol abuse at some point, 51% also met criteria for alcohol dependence. The prevalence of alcohol abuse/dependence in the Core City sample was the highest at age 40 and decreased

thereafter. Age 40 also marks the point at which some men in the sample began dying; among those who died, more were active alcohol abusers than abstainers before their deaths. On a more optimistic note, many of the surviving men resolved their alcohol abuse, as noted earlier, by either becoming abstainers (the more prevalent form of resolution) or controlled drinkers.

The onset of alcohol abuse occurred at a later age for many College sample men than for the members of the Core City sample, and a smaller percentage (38%) of the College men ever met criteria for alcohol dependence (all met criteria for abuse at some point). The prevalence of alcohol abuse/dependence peaked at a later age (50) as well and continued later in the lives of many of the College sample men. Overall, Vaillant (1995) observed that "the reason that alcoholism is relatively uncommon after the age of 60 is that roughly 2 percent of alcohol-dependent individuals become stably abstinent every year and after age 40 roughly 2 percent die every year" (p. 152).

Clearly, various alcohol addiction careers are subsumed in the data for Vaillant's two samples. Some persons reached criteria for alcohol abuse at an early age and either became abstinent or engaged in controlled drinking before other persons in the sample first met criteria for alcohol abuse. We discuss later factors that may account for various courses and course changes when we focus on factors associated with remission, resolution, lapse, and relapse.

Progression of Alcohol Use Disorders

One of the questions that longitudinal studies of persons with alcohol use disorders can address is whether such conditions are progressive. Retrospective studies of alcohol-dependent persons have suggested progression. In one of the earliest, Jellinek (1952) interviewed members of Alcoholics Anonymous (AA), who reported a sequence of the symptoms characterizing the "disease of gamma alcoholism" that was similar to that described above in the study by Schuckit et al. (1995).

Thus, if one begins with a sample of persons who meet criteria for abuse/dependence and asks them to reconstruct the sequence of events, the results are likely to reveal progression. However, persons who do not exhibit progression would not be included in

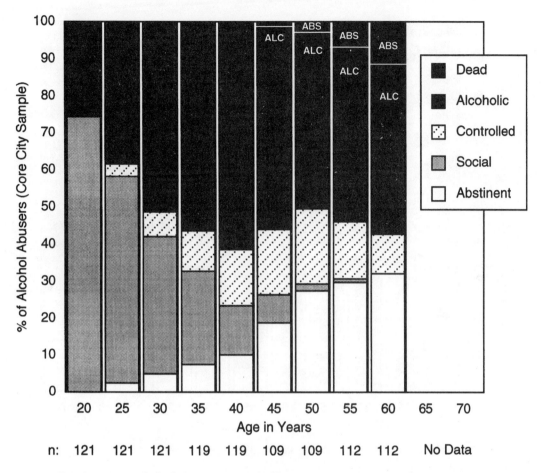

FIGURE 2.1 Quinquennial alcohol use status of the Core City men who met criteria for *DSM-III* alcohol abuse. ALC indicates the proportion of deaths that occurred among alcohol abusers; ABS, the proportion among stably abstinent men. Reprinted by permission from Vaillant (1996), *Archives of General Psychiatry*, 53, 243–249. Copyright 1996, American Medical Association.

such studies. Thus, retrospective and prospective studies of more representative samples that include persons who do and do not meet criteria for a diagnosis of alcohol dependence provide more accurate data on the issue of progression.

In a retrospective study with a general population sample, Nelson, Little, Heath, and Kessler (1996) investigated the lifetime prevalence and age of onset of each of nine symptom criteria for *DSM-III-R* alcohol dependence (roughly speaking, three criteria must have been present for a diagnosis of alcohol dependence). Symptoms were broken down into three clusters: symptoms of abuse; symptoms of tolerance, increasing time spent with alcohol use, and difficulty

in cutting down; and symptoms of withdrawal and restriction of activities. Among the individuals who indicated one or more symptoms, 44% of men and 50% of women exhibited symptoms in the first cluster; 31% of men and 28% of women, exhibited symptoms in the first and second clusters; and 17% of men and 13% of women exhibited symptoms in all three clusters. For 83% of the sample with symptoms in more than one cluster, transitions from one cluster to another, based on recalled age of onset of symptoms, reflected the expected progression from abuse to tolerance to withdrawal symptoms. Thus, not all persons with symptoms of alcohol dependence exhibited progression, but if they did, their symptoms

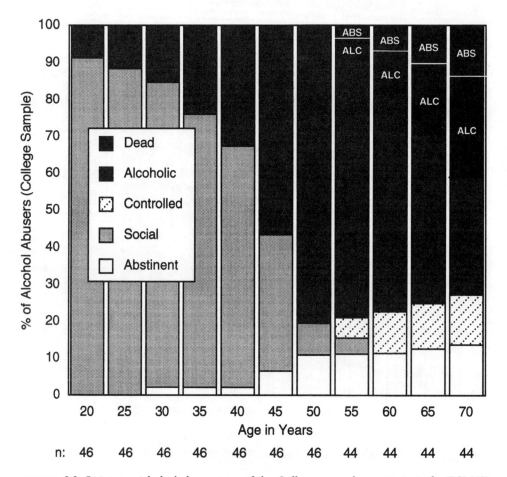

FIGURE 2.2 Quinquennial alcohol use status of the College men who met criteria for *DSM-III* alcohol abuse. ALC indicates the proportion of deaths that occurred among alcohol abusers; ABS, the proportion among stably abstinent men. Reprinted by permission from Vaillant (1996), *Archives of General Psychiatry, 53,* 243–249. Copyright 1996, American Medical Association.

followed a course similar to that identified in retrospective studies of treated alcohol-dependent persons.

In his prospective study, Vaillant (1995) observed that between the ages of 45 and 70, the majority of the men in the College sample did not change in terms of the severity of their alcohol abuse. Specifically, 20 of 22 men who met criteria for abuse did not progress to dependence and continued to exhibit abuse until their deaths or the final follow-up. Likewise, Hasin, Grant, and Endicott (1990) reported that only 30% of 71 men in a general population sample who initially reported only indicators of alcohol abuse exhibited symptoms of alcohol dependence 4 years later. In contrast, 46% were in remis-

sion. Overall, studies of (predominantly) untreated populations provide little support for the notion of an *inevitable* progression of symptoms for persons with earlier stage alcohol-use disorders. Both a "clinician's" and a "clinical researcher's illusion" may have been at work in promulgating the notion of inevitable progression.

Long-Term Outcome of Treated Alcoholism

Of particular interest to providers of specialized alcohol treatment services is what happens to patients in the long run after a treatment episode, the first of which occurs for many persons with alcohol use disorders in their early 40s (Schuckit, Smith, Anthenelli, & Irwin, 1993). Table 2.1 summarizes findings from 12 studies with long-term follow-ups that varied from 8 to 20 years. *Remission* is defined as abstinence, nonproblem drinking, or substantially improved drinking. Remission rates among successfully followed survivors ranged from 21% (Westermeyer & Peake, 1983) to 83% (O'Connor & Daly, 1985). Remission rates for survivors in samples followed over longer periods were generally higher, in part because of the winnowing out of chronic relapsers through premature death.

Remission rates divided by duration of follow-up yield annual rates that range from 2.1% to 7.6% and average 4.8%. This average remission rate is higher than the estimated 3% in studies of community samples, although caution should be exercised in attributing this difference to the effect of treatment. Broad comparisons between community and treated samples do not comprehensively control for population differences in risk factors associated with outcome, and the patient samples generally had higher mortal-

ity rates than did Ojesjo's (1981) and Vaillant's (1995, 1996) community samples. Thus, they may not have included as many persons who were more prone to relapse. On the other hand, the patients in the treated samples likely were more impaired initially, as we noted earlier.

Comparing Alcoholic Patients and Community Controls

Do patients experiencing remission at long-term follow-ups "fully recover"? Do they function in other life areas as well as similar persons who have not experienced alcohol use disorders? What are the costs of continuing alcohol abuse? Three long-term follow-up studies (Finney & Moos, 1991; Kurtines, Ball, & Wood, 1978; Vaillant & Milofsky, 1982) indicate that persons who exhibit long-term remission or resolution function as well as non-problem-drinking controls, but that continued alcohol abuse is associated with poorer functioning. However, full recovery

TABLE 2.1 Remission Rates in Long-term Follow-Ups of Treated Alcoholics

Study	Mean age at first contact (years)	Percentage married Time 1	Length of follow-up (years)	Percentage followed including deceased	Percentage deceased of those followed	Percentage remission for survivors	Annual remission rate (%)
Cross et al. (1990)	48	—	10.0	84	32	76	7.6
Edwards et al. (1983) Taylor et al. (1985)	41	100	11.3	87	20	40	3.5
Finney & Moos (1991)	—[a]	100	10.0	82[b]	19	57	5.7
Langle et al. (1993)	38	72	10.0	94	22	65	6.5
Mackenzie et al. (1986)	41	29	8.0	94	31	44	5.6
McCabe (1986)	45	100	16.6	88	44	65	3.9
Miller et al. (1992) Miller & Taylor (1980)	45	76	8.0	71	7	28	3.5
O'Connor & Daly (1985)	48	83[c]	20.0	70	56	83	4.1
Pendery et al. (1982) Sobell & Sobell (1973)	40	30	10.0	95	21	47	4.7
Vaillant et al. (1983)	30–50	35[d]	8.0	94	28	48	6.0
Walker (1987)	41	36	8.0–12.5	80	8[e]	43	4.2
Westermeyer & Peake (1983)	39	7[c]	10.0	93	22	21	2.1

[a]74% were age 40 or older.

[b]Of persons agreeing to a study extension at a six-month follow-up.

[c]Of those persons later followed.

[d]Living with spouse.

[e]Some known-to-be-deceased patients were excluded from the sample prior to a follow-up attempt.

takes time. De Soto, O'Donnell, and De Soto (1989) found a strong relationship in AA members between length of abstinence and improvement in psychiatric symptoms as assessed by the Brief Symptom Inventory. Symptoms dropped substantially within a year or two but continued to decline gradually for 10 years or more, at which point symptom levels were comparable to those in a general population sample.

Course of Drug Abuse

With the exception of a few studies of small, nonrepresentative samples of drug abusers in the community (e.g., Murphy, Reinarman, & Waldorf, 1989), long-term prospective studies of the course of drug abuse have focused on treated samples, primarily of opiate/opioid dependent patients.

Long-Term Outcome of Treated Opiate Dependence

We found 10 prospective studies (see table 2.2) of patients treated for drug abuse (usually opiate dependence) that included follow-ups of at least 8 years. Criteria for "remission" varied across studies. For example, some studies focused on complete abstinence, whereas others described only abstinence from opioids. The percentage of patients "in remission" in table 2.2 refers to "remission" among survivors as defined by the most stringent criterion available in the study (e.g., abstinence from all illicit drugs).

As was the case in the long-term studies of treated alcohol abuse, early death was the unfortunate outcome experienced by substantial percentages of patients, with long-term mortality rates varying from 10% to 54% across studies. For surviving patients, the percentage "in remission" ranged from 30% to 65% across the 10 studies. When remission rates are divided by the number of years of follow-up, the resulting annual remission rates varied from 1.7% (Hser, Anglin, & Powers, 1993) to 5.1% (Cottrell, Childs-Clarke, & Ghodse, 1985) and averaged 3.7%.

The remission rates in several of the studies are likely to have been inflated either because of reliance on record data rather than personal interviews or, in the case of Simpson, Joe, Lehman, and Sells (1986), because the 12-year follow-up sample was based on persons successfully followed at 6 years (and more likely to be doing well than those not followed), in-

stead of all patients entering treatment. Thus, we conclude that among survivors, about 3% experience remission each year, on average. This remission rate is somewhat lower than the rate of almost 5% found in long-term studies of persons treated for alcohol use disorders.

The Course of Treated Opiate Dependence

Several of the long-term follow-up studies listed in table 2.2 employed multiple follow-ups and thus provide some insight into addiction careers, particularly during the posttreatment period. In a follow-up of male heroin-addicted patients who had been treated at a Public Health Service (PHS) hospital, Vaillant (1966) observed that about 90% relapsed in the first 2 years. On the other hand, the percentage of men who exhibited active narcotic addiction declined from 53% at a 5-year follow-up to 25% at an 18-year follow-up (Vaillant, 1973).

Over the 12 years following an index treatment episode, around 75% of the patients tracked by Simpson et al. (1986; Simpson & Sells, 1990) used opioids daily for one or more periods. However, only 27% of these patients were actively addicted for more than 3 years at a time. The percentage of daily users in the entire sample declined from 47% in Year 1 to 24% in Year 12. Cessation of daily use was not invariably associated with cessation of criminal behavior, however. About half the patients who were no longer using opioids daily continued to engage in criminal activity.

The entire addiction careers (before and after the index treatment episode) for the opioid-addicted patients studied by Simpson and his colleagues (1986; Simpson & Sells, 1990) averaged about 10 years, with a range from 1 to 35 years. During their careers, these individuals had an average of six treatment episodes and, over time, tended to gravitate toward methadone therapy.

How stable are remissions among persons treated for narcotics dependence? For 78 patients who were both stably abstinent and employed at a 7-year follow-up by Haastrup and Jepsen (1988), 68% were similarly classified 4 years later and another 17% were in the next best outcome category. Not surprisingly, less stability in positive outcomes was found over a longer interval by Hser et al. (1993). Of the men testing negative for narcotics at a 10- to 12-year follow-up, 45% were in the same category at a 24-

TABLE 2.2 Remission Rates in Long-term Follow-Ups of Treated Drug Abuse/Dependence Patients

Study	Mean age at first contact (years)	Country	Type of treatment	Primary drug of abuse	Length of follow-up	Percentage deceased of those followed	Percentage remission for survivors	Annual remission rate (%)
Cottrell et al. (1985)	25	G.B.	DDC	Opiates	11.0	20	56	5.1
Edwards & Goldie (1987)	21	G.B.	DDC	Opiates	10.0	15	50	5.0
Gordon (1983)	22	G.B.	Drug clinic	Mixed	10.0	18	41	4.1
Haastrup & Jepsen (1988)	21	Den.	City treatment service or hosp.	IV opioid	11.0	29	37	3.4
Hser et al. (1993)	25	USA	CCAP	Opiate	23.0	31	39	1.7
Maddux & Desmond (1980)	26	USA	PHS hosp.	Opiate	9.5	13	30	3.2
O'Donnell (1969)	42	USA	PHS hosp.	Opiate	11.6	54	43	3.7
Simpson et al. (1986) Simpson et al. (1982)	22	USA	Varied	Opioid	12.0	10[a]	60	5.0
Tobutt et al. (1996) Stimson et al. (1978) Wille (1981)	25	G.B.	DDC	Opiate	22.0	36	65	3.0
Vaillant (1973)	25	USA	PHS hosp.	Opiate	18.0	23	45	2.5

Note. G.B. = Great Britain; Den. = Denmark; DDC = drug dependency clinics; PHS hosp. = Public Health Service hospital; MM = methadone maintenance; CCAP = California Civil Addict Program.

[a]Percentage who died between a 6-year and the 12-year follow-up; not from treatment entry.

year follow-up. Another 17% had died and 8% were incarcerated; the remaining individuals who were tracked were active narcotics users.

Course of Smoking

We could find no longitudinal study of the course of smoking comparable to those by Vaillant on the course of alcohol and drug abuse. However, a picture of a typical course, at least into middle adulthood, can be pieced together with information from various sources.

Although drinking and drug use are frequently initiated in the teenage years, addiction typically does not develop until at least early adulthood. Smoking typically begins in adolescence (Chen & Kandel, 1995) and is persistent. For example, Chassin, Presson, Rose, and Sherman (1996) found that the percentage of regular (at least weekly) smokers increased from 20% among 11th- and 12th-graders to 27% in young adulthood (age 23, on average) and remained stable (26%) into later adulthood (average age of 29). For adolescent smokers, 59% were smokers as adults versus only 10% for adolescent nonsmokers. For young adult smokers, 72% were adult smokers versus only 7% for young adult nonsmokers. Using data from various birth cohorts, Pierce and Gilpin (1996) projected that an adolescent smoker, born 1975–

1979, would continue to smoke for 15 years, on average, if a male and 20 years if a female.

Once initiated, nicotine addiction appears to have a higher remission rate than that found in the community samples of persons with alcohol use disorders. Among offspring of participants in the Framingham Heart study, a high 52% of 397 men and 49% of 497 women smoked when they were interviewed initially in 1971–1975 at age 20–29. When they were recontacted 8 years later, 32% of the men smokers and 23% of the women smokers had quit, 4% and 3% annual remission rates, respectively (Hubert et al., 1987). Presumably, most had quit on their own. We were unable to locate long-term follow-up studies of treated smokers.

The course of smoking is likely to exhibit stronger cohort effects than is the case for alcohol and other drug abuse. Whereas the broad social context (awareness of consequences, sanctions and controls, etc.) in which alcohol and drug abuse occur has been relatively constant over the past 30 years, there has been an increasing awareness of smoking's adverse health consequences, a declining number of locations in which it is acceptable or legal to smoke, and increasing social pressure against smoking. Thus, prior studies may be less accurate indicators of future trends than is the case for long-term studies of alcohol and drug abuse.

Summary

Vaillant (1995) observed that "if alcoholics can but survive, they will often recover" (p. 148). The data reviewed here suggest that this somewhat optimistic conclusion can be extended to persons with other substance use disorders. Among survivors, about 3% of alcohol abusers in community samples, 5% of treated persons with alcohol disorders, 3% of treated opiate-dependent persons, and 3–4% of smokers experience remission each year.

On the surface, the findings indicate that the annual remission rate for persons treated for alcohol use disorders is about two thirds greater than that for opiate-dependent patients (the single long-term follow-up of smokers is not a sufficient base on which to rest conclusions). However, that interpretation does not take into account the fact that the persons treated for alcohol use disorders in these studies (see table 2.1) tended to be older than persons treated for heroin dependence and other forms of drug abuse

(see table 2.2). To the extent that (a) individuals "mature out" of addictions and (b) death claims many who do not (see the next section), the rates of remission can be expected to be higher among older than among younger persons.

The studies we reviewed provide more good news for persons with alcohol use disorders. First, such disorders are not inevitably progressive, and if persons do recover, their psychosocial functioning is eventually comparable to sociodemographically similar persons who never had alcohol use disorders. In addition, as we describe in the next section, the mortality risk for persons who successfully resolve substance use disorders is lowered.

MORTALITY

Because the course of addictive disorders ends in premature death for many individuals, it is worth considering this end point in greater depth. We focus on two issues: first, the extent to which persons with addictive disorders die prematurely, and second, the extent to which persons whose substance use disorders are in remission, and whether patients who receive more treatment have a reduced mortality risk relative to those who continue as active substance abusers or receive less treatment.

Alcohol Use Disorders and Mortality

We first examine mortality in extended follow-ups of community and treated samples of persons with alcohol use disorders; we then determine the relationship of posttreatment drinking status to mortality risk.

Mortality in Community Samples

The paucity of long-term follow-ups of community samples means that few data are available on predominantly untreated samples of persons with alcohol use disorders. However, in Ojesjo's (1981) sample of untreated alcoholics, 26% died over the 15-year follow-up interval for an annual mortality rate of 1.7%. Among those individuals classified at baseline as "chronics," 44% had died, 24% of "addicts" had died, and 20% of "abusers" had died. Thus, presumably because it is associated with a higher likelihood of continued severity, severity of alcohol use disorder at baseline was a mortality risk factor. How these mortality rates compared with general population figures was not reported.

As noted earlier, 28% of the men in Vaillant's (1995, 1996) Core City sample died by age 60, as did 18% of the men in the University sample, rates two and three times as high, respectively, as estimates for demographically similar general population groups. Men who met criteria for alcohol dependence were more likely to die by age 60 in the College and Core City samples (62% and 32%, respectively) than men who met criteria for only alcohol abuse (17% and 18% in the two samples, respectively). Accidents and other violent deaths accounted for more deaths in the earlier years of follow-up; in later years, heart disease and cancer accounted for more deaths (see also Vaillant, Schnurr, Baron, & Gerber, 1991).

Mortality in Treated Samples

We have more extensive data on mortality for persons with treated alcohol use disorders. For 11 of the 12 long-term follow-up studies in table 2.1 (we excluded Walker, 1987, in which some known-to-be-deceased persons were excluded from the sample prior to initiating the follow-up), annual mortality rates ranged from .9% to 3.9% and averaged 2.8%. In an earlier review (Finney & Moos, 1991), we found that across seven long-term follow-ups, comparisons with general population data (usually adjusted for age, gender, and, less often, race) indicated that mortality rates among alcohol patients were 1.6 to 4.7 times greater than expected, and that they averaged 3.1 times the mortality rate in the general population.

More recent studies (Hurt et al., 1996; Lewis et al. 1995a, 1995b; Marshall, Edwards, & Taylor, 1994) have provided additional data on mortality rates and rates for different patient subgroups. Their results generally have been consistent with those we reviewed previously: 2.2–2.8% of patients died per year, rates that were 2.6–3.6 times higher than expected. Functioning prior to treatment was related to mortality risk. Patients classified as "moderately dependent" at baseline were 2.9 times as likely to die as community controls, whereas those who were "severely dependent" were 4.4 times as likely to die (this difference was not statistically significant, however; Marshall et al., 1994). Estimated years of life lost were related to more alcohol consumption at intake and younger age at which drinking was first seen as

a problem (Marshall et al., 1994). Time to death was significantly shorter for men than for women patients in a study by Lewis et al. (1995a).

Posttreatment Drinking Status and Mortality

The relationship of posttreatment drinking status to mortality risk may be of greater relevance to treatment providers than is patients' pretreatment functioning. Because of the infrequency of data from intervening follow-ups, such information is relatively scarce. However, Smith, Cloninger, and Bradford (1983) found that treated women who were abstainers at a 3-year follow-up had the lowest mortality rate (8%) 8–9 years later, followed by sporadic/variable drinkers (17%), social drinkers (20%), and problem drinkers (54%). At a 21-year follow-up, these percentages were 31%, 40%, 31%, and 66%, respectively (Smith, Lewis, Kercher, & Spitznagel, 1994). Likewise, in a study by Barr, Antes, Ottenbertg, and Rosen (1984) of 410 alcohol patients still alive at a 2-year follow-up, 6% of those classified as "not misusing" at that point died in the next 6 years, versus the significantly greater 15% of those classified as "misusing." In studies by Feuerlein, Kufner, and Flohrschutz (1994) and Bullock, Reed, and Grant (1992), the mortality risk for patients who had relapsed was three to five times as high as for those who were abstainers (cf. Finney & Moos, 1991; Pell & D'Alonzo, 1973). Overall, the bulk of the evidence suggests a substantial reduction in mortality risk for persons with alcohol use disorders who are able to abstain or to reduce their alcohol intake following treatment.

Mortality and Treated Drug Abuse/Dependence

Some variation exists in reported mortality rates for treated drug abuse patients, as might be expected, given the different countries in which the studies were conducted, the different treatment systems which were in place, and the variation in duration of follow-up. For nine studies in table 2.2 (excluding Simpson et al., 1986, in which only persons who were alive at a 6-year follow-up were "eligible" to die by a 12-year follow-up), annual mortality rates ranged from 1.3% (Hser et al., 1993; Vaillant, 1973) to 4.7% (O'Donnell, 1969), where the patients were older; the average annual mortality rate was 2.0%.

Although the 2.0% annual mortality rate among treated drug (primarily opiate) abusers is lower than the 2.8% rate for treated persons with alcohol use disorders, the mortality risk of drug abuse (primarily opiate-dependent) patients relative to members of the general population is much higher than that for alcohol patients. Specifically, across three studies (Goldstein & Herrera, 1995; Oppenheimer, Tobutt, Taylor, & Andrew, 1994; Tunving, 1988), patients being treated for narcotics addiction were from 4 times (Goldstein & Herrera, 1995—male patients only) to almost 12 times (Oppenheimer et al., 1994) as likely to die as their general population counterparts. The apparent inconsistency between the annual mortality rates and relative mortality risk for alcohol- and opiate-dependent patients is explained, at least partially, by the substantially greater age of the alcohol patients relative to the drug abuse patients (see tables 2.1 and 2.2). In this regard, the relative mortality risk was found to be higher in younger heroin-addicted patients (under 30) than in older patients (Oppenheimer et al., 1994; see also the study by O'Donnell, 1969).

Opiate addiction appears to be a particularly lethal form of drug abuse. Tunving (1988) attempted to track 524 patients receiving care at an inpatient treatment and detoxification unit in Lund, Sweden, between 1970 and 1978. The "dominating type of abuse" was determined for each patient: opiates, amphetamines, or mixed. Patients were traced via registers to 1984, at which point 62 had died at an average age of 27.6 years. Overall, patients were 3.5 times as likely to die as members of the general population. However, opiate addicts had a greater relative mortality risk (5.4 for men and 8.0 for women) than did amphetamine users (2.5 for men; no women died) or mixed drug users (3.0 for men and 2.0 for women) (see also Engstrom, Adamsson, Allebeck, & Rydberg, 1991).

Finally, although few long-term follow-up studies have examined the relationships between posttreatment substance use and mortality, the available evidence suggests that posttreatment drug abstinence is associated with a reduced mortality risk. Among active drug users at a 10- to 12-year follow-up by Hser et al. (1993), 23% had died by a 24-year follow-up, whereas 17% of persons not testing positive at the earlier point had died by the later follow-up. Another study (Gordon, 1983) found that active addiction

coupled with criminal conviction was associated with a heightened mortality risk for drug abuse patients over a 10-year follow-up.

Mortality and Smoking

Although smoking does not cause the social and psychological disruption in its active phase that alcohol and drug abuse do, because of its prevalence it ends more lives prematurely than alcohol and other drugs combined. Estimates are that over 400,000 persons in the United States (McGinnis & Foege, 1993) and 3 million people worldwide (Peto et al., 1996) die each year as a result of smoking. Heavy smoking shortens an individual's life by 8 years, on average, and by 16 years for those who die of causes related to smoking (Peto et al., 1996). Persons who are heavy smokers at age 25 can expect a 25% life reduction compared to nonsmokers (Rogers & Powell, 1991). Phillips, Wannamethee, Walker, Thomson, and Smith (1996) estimated that only 42% of smokers alive at age 20 would live to age 73 versus 78% of nonsmokers.

In their 15-year follow-up of British men aged 40–59 at baseline, Phillips et al. (1996) found that 8% of the nonsmokers had died versus 23% of the continuing smokers. Thus, middle-aged smokers appear to have almost three times the mortality risk of nonsmokers over a 15-year period.

Quitting smoking reduces an individual's mortality risk. Among former smokers included in a Coronary Artery Surgery Study Registry, there was an immediate decrease in mortality risk within 1 year of quitting, but for at least 20 years after quitting, former smokers still had a somewhat higher risk of mortality than nonsmokers (Omenn, Anderson, Kronmal, & Vlietstra, 1990). Similar results emerged in a study (Kawachi et al., 1993) of 117,000 registered nurses in the United States whose age range at baseline was 20–55. The relative risk of mortality for current smokers was 1.9 times greater than that for nonsmokers, whereas the relative risk for former smokers was 1.3. Nurses who started smoking before they were 15 years old had the highest relative mortality risk (3.2). Within 2 years of quitting, former smokers had a 24% reduction in their risk of mortality due to cardiovascular causes. However, it took 10–14 years of abstinence for the mortality risk of former smokers to approximate that of nonsmokers.

Summary

Clearly, substance use disorders place individuals at heightened risk of premature death. The relative lethality of alcohol, drug, and nicotine addiction is somewhat difficult to determine, as mentioned earlier, because of age and other differences in the samples studied. The data we have presented, as well as a study by Barr et al. (1984), indicate that alcohol patients are more likely to die over a given year than are drug abuse patients. However, alcohol patients tend to seek treatment at a substantially older age than drug abuse patients (see tables 2.1 and 2.2). The risk of death relative to that of general population members is similar for alcoholic patients and younger drug abuse patients.

Do drug and alcohol patients of the same age have similar mortality risks? We found only one study that addressed this issue. Among middle-aged and older patients in VA substance abuse treatment programs, the relative risk of mortality over a 4-year period was 2.42 for patients with only alcohol dependence diagnoses; patients with a drug dependence or drug psychosis diagnosis were 2.93 times as likely to die as demographically similar (age, gender, race) members of the general population (Moos, Brennan, & Mertens, 1994). Overall, we conclude that drug abuse (particularly opiate dependence; see Tunving, 1988) is a somewhat more lethal disorder than alcohol abuse or dependence.

In many cases, multiple addictions are interwoven as causes of early deaths. For example, Hurt et al. (1996) reported that among deceased persons who had received treatment primarily for alcoholism, 51% had a tobacco-related and 34% an alcohol-related cause of death. Concool, Smith, and Stimmel (1979) concluded that comorbid alcoholism was present in 60% of the deceased methadone patients they studied.

On a hopeful note, our review indicates that remission is linked to reduced mortality risk. Also of relevance to treatment providers is evidence that treatment involvement is associated with lower mortality rates. Patients who receive more methadone treatment are less likely to die than those receiving less treatment (Gearing & Schweitzer, 1974; Gronbladh, Ohlund, & Gunne, 1990; Segest, Mygind, & Bay, 1990). For example, Caplehorn, Dalton, Cluff, and Petrenas (1994) reported that patients who dropped out of methadone maintenance were almost three times more likely to die than were patients actively involved in treatment. For alcohol patients, longer periods of inpatient treatment have also been linked to a lower risk of premature death (Bunn, Booth, Loveland Cook, Blow, & Fortney, 1994). Although it is impossible in such studies to completely disentangle the effects of patient characteristics and of treatment, these findings should bolster the resolve of treatment providers and the motivation of patients to remain in treatment.

CESSATION, REMISSION, RESOLUTION, AND RELAPSE

The studies we have reviewed here indicate that substantial numbers of persons with alcohol, opiate, and nicotine abuse/dependence successfully resolve their disorders. How are such positive outcomes achieved? Stall and Biernacki (1986) concluded that the process of behavior change is influenced by multiple physiological, psychological, and social factors and is similar in many respects across different substance use disorders. The essence of current views on how most addictive behaviors are resolved was captured by Tuchfeld and Marcus (1984) in their two-stage model of (1) cessation and (2) maintenance.

Cessation of Substance Use

The primary impetus in the cessation process is the accumulation of substantial costs of substance use and the realization by the affected person that those negative experiences flow from his or her substance use. An individual may become aware of the costs of substance use gradually, or through the occurrence of some significant event or crisis (Tuchfeld, 1981), such as a life-threatening medical condition or a spouse's threatening divorce.

An individual's perception of the rising toll of substance use is influenced heavily by objective events that he or she has experienced with respect to health, psychological functioning, social relationships, employment, and legal status. In addition, perception of the costs of substance use may be influenced by anticipated future consequences. For example, the potential health consequences of smoking are a prominent impetus for many persons trying to quit, particularly if those risks are weighed in personal, rather than general, terms (Rose, Chassin, Presson, & Sherman, 1996).

In addition to the mounting costs of substance use, the addicted person may experience diminishing psychophysiological benefits (the "rush" or tranquillity) from substance use, due to the development of tolerance. At some point, perhaps after an extended period of ambivalence, the decisional balance of costs and benefits of substance use shifts to the negative side and the individual decides to quit (Sobell, Sobell, Toneatto, & Leo, 1993). In a sense, then, substance use disorders contain the seeds of their own resolution (Mulford, 1977; Orford, 1985).

The influential role of perceived negative consequences in prompting behavior change among unaided substance abusers is mirrored by its role in triggering treatment entry. In this regard, Finney and Moos (1995) found that the "effects" of hardship factors, which have been the most consistently identified precipitants of alcohol treatment entry in a number of studies, were mediated by individuals' perceived severity of their drinking problem. Similar findings emerged in a study of drug abuse patients by Power, Hartnoll, and Chalmers (1992).

What is perceived as a significant substance use problem by one person may not be by another. Among problem drinkers, persons of higher socioeconomic status (SES) tend to recognize a drinking problem sooner than lower SES persons: They hit a higher "bottom" (Humphreys, Moos, & Finney, 1995). Recognizing a substance use problem earlier, before a high level of dependence symptoms has developed, is associated with a greater likelihood of successful resolution (Cohen et al., 1989; Dawson, 1996; Rose et al., 1996). Also, the early realization of a drinking problem may provide persons with more options regarding attainable outcomes (e.g., nonproblem drinking).

Some persons may fall into an intermediate level of addiction, being sufficiently dependent so that substance use is not somewhat readily discontinued (especially at an earlier age; e.g., Cohen et al., 1989; Dawson, 1996; Rose et al., 1996), but not so dependent that the costs of substance use become exceedingly high. Recall that in Vaillant's (1995, 1996) study of the course of alcohol use disorders, fewer men in the College sample ever met criteria for dependence, but also fewer resolved their alcohol use disorders in comparison to the Core City sample

men. Instead, 20 of 22 men in the College sample drifted along in a state of alcohol abuse that while not optimal, apparently was tolerable.

Maintenance of Change: Remission and Resolution

Although important, the decision to change one's substance use behavior or to quit entirely may be fleeting ("It's easy to quit; I've done it many times"). In a widely cited analysis, Hunt, Barnett, and Branch (1971) charted time to relapse following treatment from 84 studies of smokers. The percentage of abstainers was about 35% at 3 months, 25% at 6 months, and 20% at 12 months. A study they reviewed of patients treated for alcohol abuse/dependence and one of heroin addiction patients showed similar relapse curves. Among unaided smokers making a quit attempt, rates of failure to maintain behavior change have been even higher. One study found that 62% of the individuals had returned to smoking within 15 days (Ward, Klesges, Zbikowski, Bliss, & Garvey, 1997); another reported that only 22% of unaided smokers who quit maintained abstinence for 14 days and only 8% were abstinent for 6 months (Hughes et al., 1992).

Short-term (e.g., 3–6 months) maintenance of change may be referred to as *remission*. Longer term change can be labeled *recovery* or *resolution*. In Tuchfeld and Marcus's (1984) two-stage model, a variety of factors contribute to remission and resolution. These "maintenance factors" include both intrapersonal and interpersonal determinants.

With respect to cognitive intrapersonal factors, a greater commitment to abstinence (Hall, Havassy, & Wasserman, 1990, 1991) and a stronger sense of self-efficacy (Garvey, Bliss, Hitchcock, Heinold, & Rosner, 1992; McKay, Maisto, & O'Farrell, 1993; Rose et al., 1996; Stephens, Wertz, & Roffman, 1993) are associated with a greater likelihood of maintaining remission/resolution. Behaviorally, individuals who possess skills to cope with relapse-inducing situations (Shiffman et al., 1996) and stressful situations in general (Moos et al., 1990) are more likely to have successful resolutions of their substance use disorders. Donovan (1996) suggests that individuals tend to cope initially by avoiding high-risk situations or, if they encounter such situations, by seeking social support. In later stages of resolution, individuals tend to rely less on behavioral coping approaches and more on cognitive coping responses, such as focusing on the negative consequences of prior substance use and the benefits that have accrued as a result of behavior change.

Abundant research indicates that factors outside the individual—the controls and support provided by others in his or her social environment—are also important in maintaining behavior change (Garvey et al., 1992; Havassy, Hall, & Wasserman, 1991; Rose et al., 1996; Sobell et al., 1993). In this regard, Vaillant (1988) identified three social conditions that, along with such substitute dependencies as meditation or exercise, were associated with long-term abstinence among both heroin addicts and persons who had met criteria for alcohol abuse. The social environment conditions included (a) some form of compulsory supervision (e.g., parole); (b) new social supports (e.g., new marriage); and/or (c) membership in an inspirational group, such as a self-help or religious group that provided hope, inspiration, and self-esteem. Vaillant (1988) viewed these factors as imposing structure on addicted persons' lives that counteracts the conditioned, unconscious aspects of substance use behavior.

During the maintenance process, the former substance abuser gradually assumes the identity and lifestyle of a nonaddicted person. For a former smoker, this lifestyle change may be nothing more profound than finding something else to do after eating or drinking, or drinking a glass of juice after waking up in the morning instead of having a cigarette. For a person with chronic alcohol or drug dependence, however, where sustained use has entailed involvement in a "deviant" subculture and perhaps criminal activity, this latter stage of the maintenance process entails developing an entirely new self-concept and way of life (Frykholm, 1985; Waldorf, 1983).

Relapse: The Failure to Maintain Remission or Resolution

Unfortunately, remitted substance abusers are often unable to maintain their behavior change. The relapse process, like the resolution process, has been conceptualized as occurring in two stages. First, there are factors that either make an individual vulnerable to or precipitate a slip or lapse. Second, there are "maintenance" factors that determine whether or not a lapse will lead to a full-blown relapse.

Marlatt and Gordon's (1985) conceptualization of the relapse process has been predominant and is described in more detail by Quigley and Marlatt (chapter 20, this volume). In brief, however, a lapse is seen as a result of a vulnerable person's confronting a high-risk situation. Eight types of high-risk intrapersonal or interpersonal situations have been reported by persons with alcohol, opiate, and nicotine dependence (Marlatt & Gordon, 1985). The most common two are negative affect and social pressure to use substances. Not all persons succumb to relapse-inducing situations, however. Vulnerability is caused by a breakdown in the maintenance factors described earlier. For example, a person may have a reduced sense of confidence that he or she can maintain abstinence (lowered sense of self-efficacy) or may fail to apply appropriate coping responses.

A lapse often leads to a full-blown relapse (Hughes et al., 1992; Ward et al., 1997), but not always (Gossop, Green, Phillips, & Bradley, 1989). In Marlatt's model, a lapse is more likely to lead to relapse if the person experiences the abstinence violation effect (AVE). The AVE consists of cognitive dissonance, caused by the discrepancy between the lapse and a person's self-concept as a former substance user, and by the person's attributing the lapse to stable, internal causal factors. The magnitude of the AVE is determined by the person's commitment to abstinence, the effort she or he has expended in maintaining abstinence prior to the lapse, and the perceived benefits of renewed substance use. Overall, there is less research support for the critical factors in Marlatt's second stage of the relapse process than there is for the first (Bradley, Phillips, Green, & Gossop, 1992; Brandon, Tiffany, Obremski, & Baker, 1990).

Summary

Persons with substance use disorders are both capable of cessation and resolution and vulnerable to lapse and relapse. Fortunately, substance use disorders provide the impetus for their own resolution in the form of accumulating negative consequences. In addition, the risk of lapse/relapse decreases as the duration of remission/resolution increases (De Soto et al., 1989; Loosen, Dew, & Prange, 1990; Vaillant, 1995). Both cessation/resolution and lapse/relapse are complicated processes in which a number of personal and environmental factors may play a role. Multiple change attempts, unaided or aided by other helping resources, are often involved in successful resolutions (Simpson & Sells, 1990; Timko, Finney, Moos, & Moos, 1995). As we discuss below, treatment providers can capitalize on "natural healing processes" to enhance the likelihood of successful resolutions of substance use disorders.

TREATMENT IMPLICATIONS

Researchers investigating the course of substance use disorders have typically been unimpressed with the role of treatment in the remission/resolution process (but see Simpson et al., 1986). Their research indicates that many persons resolve their substance use disorders without treatment, and for those receiving treatment, treatment episodes frequently are followed by relapses, resolutions often occur at points considerably after treatment has ended, and many treated persons who are functioning well point to other factors (e.g., family support) as being critical in the resolution process (Dawson, 1996; Saunders & Kershaw, 1979; Schachter, 1982; Vaillant, 1996; cf. Simpson et al., 1986). Orford (1985) spoke for many researchers when he argued that the personal and life context factors that impinge on the addicted person, although "'extraneous' when viewed from the treatment perspective, operate more intensively, for far longer, and hence seem likely to be by far the more influential" (p. 268).

Certainly, there are multiple pathways out of addiction, and not all involve treatment. Although an episode of treatment may have a modest impact in many cases, it may be a critical factor in particular instances. Stall and Biernacki (1986) noted that in the process of resolution of alcohol, heroin, and nicotine addiction, "significant accidents," which might have been "rather commonplace during the remitter's problem use career, served at that moment as a powerful catalyst to irrevocably change and reorient the remitter's self-concept and corresponding perspective" (p. 16). At times, treatment can play a similar role. Especially for persons receiving treatment for the first time, having sought treatment is a public declaration of an intent to change and may be an important "commitment mechanism" (Tuchfeld & Marcus, 1984). In addition, entering treatment may remoralize persons who have failed in multiple attempts to change on their own.

Because individuals usually seek treatment at times of crisis, it is a point that has significant potential for change. However, because crises are transitory, it is important that treatment seekers be engaged quickly in the treatment process. Initial therapeutic efforts should focus on strengthening the individual's decision and commitment to change. The findings reviewed in this chapter provide empirical data that can be brought to bear in helping patients to "take stock" (Sobell et al., 1993), that is, to weigh the costs and benefits of continued substance abuse versus abstinence or behavior change. For example, the findings on the heightened mortality risk of continued abuse, along with the reduced mortality risk that flows from abstinence, are concrete evidence of the severe consequences of continued abuse and the benefits of abstinence. More important, empirical data indicating that persons can resolve serious substance use disorders, and that those who do recover function as well as persons who were never addicted, can enhance patients' sense of self-efficacy that recovery is possible and can reinforce their perhaps tenuous beliefs that the effort will be worthwhile.

Findings on the course of substance use disorders also have implications for the role of treatment in the maintenance process. Edwards (1989) observed that a long-term perspective on substance abuse/dependence forces one "to place the treatment experience within the enormously important totality of the ebb and flow of what happens to that person's life—the job promotions and the redundancies, the broken marriages and the new lovers, children grown up, the death of parents, brain damage or growth in personal maturity, accidents and inheritances, boom and slump" (pp. 19–20). From this perspective, it makes sense that treatment should be directed toward helping patients improve their life circumstances and enhancing their ability to cope with the situations they confront in their everyday lives.

The protracted, fluctuating courses of many persons' substance use disorders, with periods of remission and relapse, suggest a temporal extension of treatment—that treatment should be available, as needed, over a long period, much as treatment is available for diseases, such as diabetes, that are chronic (O'Brien & McLellan, 1996). In that regard, mutual help groups, such as Alcoholics Anonymous, Cocaine Anonymous, Narcotics Anonymous, and

Nicotine Anonymous, can be a stable and consistent source of support (Humphreys et al., 1995).

Although progression in the severity of substance use disorders is not inevitable, it does occur. In addition, evidence reviewed here indicates that persons who have less serious substance use disorders (e.g., fewer symptoms of dependence) are more likely to experience successful resolutions than are more impaired individuals. These findings imply that interventions should be available for persons with less severe disorders (Sobell & Sobell, 1993). With respect to alcohol use disorders, one way to encourage problem drinkers to seek help earlier is to have nonabstinent treatment goals.

CONCLUSION

We still have much to learn about the course of treated and untreated substance use disorders. Although existing research has yielded important findings, it has limitations in the form of nonrepresentative samples; cohort effects; varying definitions of relapse, remission, and resolution; a heavy reliance on retrospective reports of the precipitants of relapse; and so forth. Overall, much of our current knowledge is based on what Taylor (1994) referred to as "a patchwork of cross-sectional and longitudinal studies, spread over different clinical and general populations, made in different countries and decades" (p. 50).

Despite these limitations, research on the course of substance use disorders has much to offer treatment providers. Recognition that persons who seek specialized treatment tend to be those with the most serious and chronic disorders, that treatment should capitalize on "natural healing processes" and be focused on improving patients' life circumstances and coping skills, and that, even with treatment, the process of resolution can be protracted can help treatment providers shape the interventions they offer, avoid burnout, and sustain their long-term commitment to helping persons with substance use disorders.

ACKNOWLEDGMENTS Preparation of this chapter was supported by NIAAA Grants AA08689 and AA06699, and in part by the Department of Veterans Affairs Mental Health Strategic Health Group and Health Services Research and Development Service.

Key References

Cohen, P., & Cohen, J. (1984). The clinician's illusion. *Archives of General Psychiatry, 41,* 1178–1182.

Stall, R., & Biernacki, P. (1986). Spontaneous remission from the problematic use of substances: An inductive model derived from a comparative analysis of the alcohol, opiate, tobacco, and food/obesity literatures. *International Journal of the Addictions, 21,* 1–23.

Vaillant, G. E. (1995). *The natural history of alcoholism revisited.* Cambridge: Harvard University Press.

References

Barr, H. L., Antes, D., Ottenbertg, D. J., & Rosen, A. (1984). Mortality of treated alcoholics and drug addicts: The benefits of abstinence. *Journal of Studies on Alcohol, 45,* 440–452.

Bradley, B. P., Phillips, G., Green, L., & Gossop, M. (1989). Circumstances surrounding the initial lapse to opiate use following detoxification. *British Journal of Psychiatry, 154,* 354–359.

Brandon, T. H., Tiffany, S. T., Obremski, K. M., & Baker, T. B. (1990). Postcessation cigarette use: The process of relapse. *Addictive Behaviors, 15,* 105–114.

Bullock, K. D., Reed, R. J., & Grant, I. (1992). Reduced mortality risk in alcoholics who achieve long-term abstinence. *Journal of the American Medical Association, 267,* 668–672.

Bunn, J. Y., Booth, B. M., Loveland Cook, C. A., Blow, F. C., & Fortney, J. C. (1994). The relationship between mortality and intensity of inpatient alcoholism treatment. *American Journal of Public Health, 84,* 211–214.

Caplehorn, J. R., Dalton, M. S., Cluff, M. C., & Petrenas, A. M. (1994). Retention in methadone maintenance and heroin addicts' risk of death. *Addiction, 89,* 203–209.

Chassin, L., Presson, C. C., Rose, J. S., & Sherman, S. J. (1996). The natural history of cigarette smoking from adolescence to adulthood: Demographic predictors of continuity and change. *Health Psychology, 15,* 478–484.

Chen, K., & Kandel, D. B. (1995). The natural history of drug use from adolescence to the mid-thirties in a general population sample. *American Journal of Public Health, 85,* 41–47.

Cohen, P., & Cohen, J. (1984). The clinician's illusion. *Archives of General Psychiatry, 41,* 1178–1182.

Cohen, S., Lichtenstein, E., Prochaska, J. O., Rossi, J. S., Gritz, E. R., Carr, C. R., Orleans, C. T., Schoenbach, V. J., Biener, L., Abrams, D., DeClemente, C., Curry, S., Marlatt, G. A., Cumming, K. M., Emount, S. L., Giovino, G., & Ossip-Klein, D. (1989). Debunking myths about self-quitting. *American Psychologist, 44*, 1355–1365.

Concool, B., Smith, H., & Stimmel, B. (1979). Mortality rates of persons entering methadone maintenance: A seven-year study. *American Journal of Drug and Alcohol Abuse, 6*, 345–353.

Cottrell, D., Childs-Clarke, A., & Ghodse, A. H. (1985). British opiate addicts: An 11-year follow-up. *British Journal of Psychiatry, 146*, 448–450.

Cross, G. M., Morgan, C. W., Mooney, A. J. I., Martin, C. A., & Rafter, J. A. (1990). Alcoholism treatment: A ten-year follow-up study. *Alcoholism: Clinical and Experimental Research, 14*, 169–173.

Dawson, D. A. (1996). Correlates of past-year status among treated and untreated persons with former alcohol dependence: United States, 1992. *Alcoholism: Clinical and Experimental Research, 20*, 763–779.

De Soto, C. B., O'Donnell, W. E., & De Soto, J. L. (1989). Long-term recovery in alcoholics. *Alcoholism: Clinical and Experimental Research, 13*, 693–697.

Donovan, D. M. (1996). Assessment issues and domains in the prediction of relapse. *Addiction, 91*(Supplement), S29–S36.

Drew, L. R. H. (1968). Alcoholism as a self-limiting disease. *Quarterly Journal of Studies on Alcohol, 29*, 956–967.

Edwards, G. (1984). Drinking in longitudinal perspective: Career and natural history. *British Journal of Addiction, 79*, 175–183.

Edwards, G. (1989). As the years go rolling by: Drinking problems in the time dimension. *British Journal of Psychiatry, 154*, 18–26.

Edwards, G., Oppenheimer, E., Duckitt, A., Sheehan, M., & Taylor, C. (1983, July 30). What happens to alcoholics? *Lancet*, pp. 269–271.

Edwards, J. G., & Goldie, A. (1987). A ten-year follow-up of Southampton opiate addicts. *British Journal of Psychiatry, 151*, 679–683.

Engstrom, A., Adamsson, C., Allebeck, P., & Rydberg, U. (1991). Mortality in patients with substance abuse: A follow-up in Stockholm County, 1973–1984. *International Journal of the Addictions, 26*, 91–106.

Feuerlein, W., Kufner, H., & Flohrschutz, T. (1994). Mortality in alcoholic patients given inpatient treatment. *Addiction, 89*, 841–849.

Finney, J. W., & Moos, R. H. (1991). The long-term course of treated alcoholism: 1. Mortality, relapse and remission rates and comparisons with commu-

nity controls. *Journal of Studies on Alcohol, 52*, 44–54.

Finney, J. W., & Moos, R. H. (1995). Entering treatment for alcohol abuse: A stress and coping model. *Addiction, 90*, 1223–1240.

Fiore, M. C., Novotny, T. E., Pierce, J. P., Giovino, G. A., Hatziandreu, E. J., Newcomb, P. A., Surawicz, T. S., & Davis, R. M. (1990). Methods used to quit smoking in the United States: Do cessation programs help? *Journal of the American Medical Association, 263*, 2760–2765.

Frykholm, B. (1985). The drug career. *Journal of Drug Issues, 15*, 333–346.

Garvey, A. L., Bliss, R. E., Hitchcock, J. L., Heinold, J. W., & Rosner, B. (1992). Predictors of smoking relapse among self-quitters: A report from the National Aging Study. *Additive Behaviors, 17*, 367–377.

Gearing, F. R., & Schweitzer, M. D. (1974). An epidemiologic evaluation of long-term methadone maintenance treatment for heroin addiction. *American Journal of Epidemiology, 100*, 101–112.

Goldstein, A., & Herrera, J. (1995). Heroin addicts and methadone treatment in Albuquerque: A 22-year follow-up. *Drug and Alcohol Dependence, 40*, 139–150.

Gordon, A. M. (1983). Drugs and delinquency: A ten-year follow-up of drug clinic patients. *British Journal of Psychiatry, 142*, 169–173.

Gossop, M., Green, L., Phillips, G., & Bradley, B. (1989). Lapse, relapse and survival among opiate addicts after treatment: A prospective follow-up study. *British Journal of Psychiatry, 154*, 348–353.

Graeven, D. B., & Graeven, K. A. (1983). Treated and untreated addicts: Factors associated with participation in treatment and cessation of heroin use. *Journal of Drug Issues, 13*, 207–236.

Gronbladh, L., Ohlund, L. S., & Gunne, L. M. (1990). Mortality in heroin addiction: Impact of methadone treatment. *Acta Psychiatrica Scandinavica, 82*, 223–227.

Haastrup, S., & Jepson, P. W. (1988). Eleven year follow-up of 300 young opioid addicts. *Acta Psychiatrica Scandinavica, 77*, 22–26.

Hall, S. M., Havassy, B. E., & Wasserman, D. A. (1990). Commitment to abstinence and acute stress in relapse to alcohol, opiates, and nicotine. *Journal of Consulting and Clinical Psychology, 58*, 175–181.

Hall, S. M., Havassy, B. E., & Wasserman, D. A. (1991). Effects of commitment to abstinence, positive moods, stress, and coping on relapse to cocaine use. *Journal of Consulting and Clinical Psychology, 59*, 526–532.

Hasin, D. S., Grant, B. F., & Endicott, J. (1990). The natural history of alcohol abuse: Implications for definitions of alcohol use disorders. *American Journal of Psychiatry, 147,* 1537–1541.

Havassy, B. E., Hall, S. M., & Wasserman, D. A. (1991). Social support and relapse: Commonalities among alcoholics, opiate users, and cigarette smokers. *Addictive Behaviors, 16,* 235–246.

Hser, Y. I., Anglin, D., & Powers, K. (1993). A 24-year follow-up of California narcotics addicts. *Archives of General Psychiatry, 50,* 577–584.

Hubert, H. B., Eaker, E. D., Garrison, R. J., & Castelli, W. P. (1987). Life-style correlates of risk factor change in young adults: An eight-year study of coronary heart disease risk factors in the Framingham offspring. *American Journal of Epidemiology, 125,* 812–831.

Hughes, J. R., Gulliver, S. B., Fenwick, J. W., Valliere, W. A., Cruser, K., Pepper, S., Shea, P., Solomon, L. J., & Flynn, B. S. (1992). Smoking cessation among self-quitters. *Health Psychology, 11,* 331–334.

Humphreys, K., Moos, R. H., & Finney, J. W. (1995). Two pathways out of drinking problems without professional treatment. *Addictive Behaviors, 20,* 427–441.

Hunt, W. A., Barnett, L. W., & Branch, L. G. (1971). Relapse rates in addiction programs. *Journal of Clinical Psychology, 27,* 455–456.

Hurt, R. D., Offord, K. P., Croghan, I. T., Gomaz-Dahl, L., Kottke, T. E., Morse, R. M., & Melton, J., III. (1996). Mortality following inpatient addictions treatment: Role of tobacco use in a community-based cohort. *Journal of the American Medical Association, 275,* 1097–1103.

Jellinek, E. M. (1952). Phases of alcohol addiction. *Quarterly Journal of Studies on Alcohol, 13,* 673–684.

Kawachi, I., Colditz, G. A., Stampfer, M. J., Willett, W. C., Manson, J. E., Rosner, B., Hunter, D. J., Hennekens, C. H., & Speizer, F. E. (1993). Smoking cessation in relation to total mortality rates in women. A prospective cohort study. *Annals of Internal Medicine, 119,* 992–1000.

Kurtines, W. M., Ball, L. R., & Wood, G. H. (1978). Personality characteristics of long-term recovered alcoholics: A comparative analysis. *Journal of Consulting and Clinical Psychology, 46,* 971–977.

Langle, G., Mann, K., Mundle, G., & Schied, H. W. (1993). Ten years after: The post-treatment course of alcoholism. *European Psychiatry, 8,* 95–100.

Lewis, C. E., Smith, E., Kercher, C., & Spitznagel, E. (1995a). Assessing gender interactions in the prediction of mortality in alcoholic men and women: A 20-year follow-up study. *Alcoholism: Clinical and Experimental Research, 19,* 1162–1172.

Lewis, C. E., Smith, E., Kercher, C., & Spitznagel, E. (1995b). Predictors of mortality in alcoholic men: A 20-year follow-up study. *Alcoholism: Clinical and Experimental Research, 19,* 984–991.

Loosen, P. T., Dew, B. W., & Prange, A. J. (1990). Long-term predictors of outcome in abstinent alcoholic men. *American Journal of Psychiatry, 147,* 1662–1666.

Mackenzie, A., Allen, R. P., & Funderburk, F. R. (1986). Mortality and illness in male alcoholics: An 8-year follow-up. *International Journal of the Addictions, 21,* 865–882.

Maddux, J. F., & Desmond, D. P. (1980). New light on the maturing out hypothesis in opioid dependence. *Bulletin on Narcotics, 31,* 15–25.

Marlatt, G.A., & Gordon, J. R. (1985). *Relapse prevention: Maintenance strategies in the treatment of addictive behaviors.* New York: Guilford Press.

Marshall, E. J., Edwards, G., & Taylor, C. (1994). Mortality in men with drinking problems: A 20-year follow-up. *Addiction, 89,* 1293–1298.

McCabe, R. J. R. (1986). Alcohol-dependent individuals sixteen years on. *Alcohol and Alcoholism, 21,* 85–91.

McGinnis, J. M., & Foege, W. H. (1993). Actual causes of death in the United States. *Journal of the American Medical Association, 270,* 2207–2212.

McKay, J. R., Maisto, S. A., & O'Farrell, T. J. (1993). End-of-treatment self-efficacy, aftercare, and drinking outcomes of alcoholic men. *Alcoholism: Clinical and Experimental Research, 17,* 1078–1083.

Miller, W. R., Leckman, A. L., Delaney, H. D., & Tinkcom, M. (1992). Long-term follow-up of behavioral self-control training. *Journal of Studies on Alcohol, 53,* 249–261.

Miller, W. R., & Taylor, C. A. (1980). Relative effectiveness of bibliotherapy, individual and group self-control training in the treatment of problem drinkers. *Addictive Behaviors, 5,* 13–24.

Moos, R. H., Brennan, P. L., & Mertens, J. R. (1994). Mortality rates and predictors of mortality among late-middle-aged and older substance abuse patients. *Alcoholism: Clinical and Experimental Research, 18,* 187–195.

Moos, R. H., Finney, J. W., & Cronkite, R. C. (1990). *Alcoholism treatment: Context, process, and outcome.* New York: Oxford University Press.

Mulford, H. A. (1977). Stages in the alcoholic process: Toward a cumulative, nonsequential index. *Journal of Studies on Alcohol, 38,* 563–583.

Murphy, S. B., Reinarman, C., & Waldorf, D. (1989). An 11-year follow-up of a network of cocaine users. *British Journal of Addiction, 84,* 427–436.

Nelson, C. B., Little, R. J. A., Heath, A. C., & Kessler, R. C. (1996). Patterns of DSM-III-R alcohol dependence symptom progression in a general population survey. *Psychological Medicine, 26,* 449–460.

O'Brien, C. P., & McLellan, A. T. (1996). Myths about the treatment of addiction. *Lancet, 347,* 237–240.

O'Connor, A., & Daly, J. (1985). Alcoholics: A twenty year follow-up study. *British Journal of Psychiatry, 146,* 645–647.

O'Donnell, J. A. (1969). *Narcotics addicts in Kentucky.* (U.S. Public Health Service Publication No. 1881). Washington, DC: U.S. Government Printing Office.

Ojesjo, L. (1981). Long-term outcome in alcohol abuse and alcoholism among males in the Lundby general population. *British Journal of Addiction, 76,* 391–400.

Omenn, G. S., Anderson, K. W., Kronmal, R. A., & Vlietstra, R. E. (1990). The temporal pattern of reduction of mortality risk after smoking cessation. *American Journal of Preventive Medicine, 6,* 251–257.

Oppenheimer, E., Tobutt, C., Taylor, C., & Andrew, T. (1994). Death and survival in a cohort of heroin addicts from London clinics: A 22-year follow-up study. *Addiction, 89,* 1299–1308.

Orford, J. (1985). *Excessive appetites: A psychological view of addictions.* New York: Wiley.

Pell, S., & D'Alonzo, C. A. (1973). A five year mortality study of alcoholics. *Journal of Occupational Medicine, 15,* 120–125.

Pendery, M. L., Maltzman, I. M., & West, L. J. (1982). Controlled drinking by alcoholics? New findings and a reevaluation of a major affirmative study. *Science, 217,* 169–174.

Peto, R., Lopez, A. D., Boreham, J., Thun, M., Heath, C. J., & Doll, R. (1996). Mortality from smoking worldwide. *British Medical Bulletin, 52,* 12–21.

Phillips, A. N., Wannamethee, S. G., Walker, M., Thomson, A., & Smith, G. D. (1996). Life expectancy in men who have never smoked and those who have smoked continuously: 15 year follow up of large cohort of middle aged British men. *British Medical Journal, 313*(7062), 907–908.

Pierce, J. P., & Gilpin, E. (1996). How long will today's new adolescent smoker be addicted to cigarettes? *American Journal of Public Health, 86,* 253–256.

Power, R., Hartnoll, R., & Chalmers, C. (1992). A study of help seeking patterns amongst illicit drug users: Concern and need for help. *International Journal of the Addictions, 27,* 887–904.

Rogers, R. G., & Powell, G. E. (1991). Life expectancies of cigarette smokers and nonsmokers in the United States. *Social Science and Medicine, 32,* 1151–1159.

Rose, J., Chassin, L., Presson, C. C., & Sherman, S. J. (1996). Demographic factors in adult smoking status: Mediating and moderating influences. *Psychology of Addictive Behaviors, 10,* 28–37.

Rounsaville, B. J., & Kleber, H. D. (1985). Untreated opiate addicts: How do they differ from those seeking treatment? *Archives of General Psychiatry, 42,* 1072–1077.

Saunders, W. M., & Kershaw, P. W. (1979). Spontaneous remission from alcoholism—A community study. *British Journal of Addiction, 74,* 251–265.

Schacter, S. (1982). Recidivism and self-cure of smoking and obesity. *American Psychologist, 37,* 436–444.

Schuckit, M. A., Anthenelli, R. M., Bucholz, K. K., Hesselbrock, V. M., & Tipp, J. (1995). The time course of development of alcohol-related problems in men and women. *Journal of Studies on Alcohol, 56,* 218–225.

Schuckit, M. A., Smith, T. L., Anthenelli, R., & Irwin, M. (1993). Clinical course of alcoholism in 636 male inpatients. *American Journal of Psychiatry, 150,* 786–792.

Segest, E., Mygind, O., & Bay, H. (1990). The influence of prolonged stable methadone maintenance treatment on mortality and employment: An 8 year follow-up. *International Journal of the Addictions, 25,* 53–63.

Shiffman, S., Hickcox, M., Paty, J. A., Gnys, M., Kassel, J. D., & Richards, T. J. (1996). Progression from a smoking lapse to relapse: Prediction from abstinence violation effects, nicotine dependence, and lapse characteristics. *Journal of Consulting and Clinical Psychology, 64,* 993–1002.

Simpson, D. D., Joe, G. W., & Bracy, S. A. (1982). Six-year follow-up of opioid addicts after admission to treatment. *Archives of General Psychiatry, 39,* 1318–1323.

Simpson, D. D., Joe, G. W., Lehman, W. E. K., & Sells, S. B. (1986). Addiction careers: Etiology, treatment, and 12-year follow-up outcomes. *Journal of Drug Issues, 16,* 107–121.

Simpson, D. D., & Sells, S. B. (Eds.). (1990). *Opioid addiction and treatment: A 12-year follow-up.* Malabar, FL: Krieger.

Smith, E. M., Cloninger, C. R., & Bradford, S. (1983). Predictors of mortality in alcoholic women: A prospective follow-up study. *Alcoholism: Clinical and Experimental Research, 7,* 237–243.

Smith, E. M., Lewis, C. E., Kercher, C., & Spitznagel, E. (1994). Predictors of mortality in alcoholic women: A 20-year follow-up study. *Alcoholism: Clinical and Experimental Research, 18,* 1177–1186.

Sobell, L. C., Cunningham, J. A., & Sobell, M. B. (1996). Recovery from alcohol problems with and without treatment: Prevalence in two population surveys. *American Journal of Public Health, 86,* 966–972.

Sobell, L. C., Sobell, M. B., Toneatto, T., & Leo, G. I. (1993). What triggers the resolution of alcohol problems without treatment? *Alcoholism: Clinical and Experimental Research, 17,* 217–224.

Sobell, M. B., & Sobell, L. C. (1973). Alcoholics treated by individualized behavior therapy: One year treatment outcome. *Behaviour Research and Therapy, 11,* 599–618.

Sobell, M. B., & Sobell, L. C. (1993). *Problem drinkers: Guided self-change treatment.* New York: Guilford Press.

Stall, R., & Biernacki, P. (1986). Spontaneous remission from the problematic use of substances: An inductive model derived from a comparative analysis of the alcohol, opiate, tobacco, and food/obesity literatures. *International Journal of the Addictions, 21,* 1–23.

Stephens, R. S., Wertz, J. S., & Roffman, R. A. (1993). Predictors of marijuana treatment outcomes: The role of self-efficacy. *Journal of Substance Abuse, 5,* 341–354

Stimson, G. V., Oppenheimer, E., & Thorley, A. (1978). Seven year follow-up of heroin addicts: Drug use and outcome. *British Medical Journal, 1,* 1190–1192.

Taylor, C. (1994). What happens over the long-term? *British Medical Bulletin, 50,* 50–66.

Taylor, C., Brown, D., Duckitt, A., Edwards, G., Oppenheimer, E., & Sheehan, M. (1985). Patterns of outcome: Drinking histories over ten years among a group of alcoholics. *British Journal of Addiction, 80,* 45–50.

Timko, C., Finney, J. W., Moos, R. H., & Moos, B. S. (1995). Short-term careers and outcomes of previously untreated alcoholics. *Journal of Studies on Alcohol, 56,* 597–610.

Tobutt, C., Oppenheimer, E., & Laranjeira, R. (1996). Health of a cohort of heroin addicts from London clinics: 22-year follow-up. *British Medical Journal, 312*(7044), 1458.

Tuchfeld, B. S. (1981). Spontaneous recovery in alcoholic persons: Empirical observations and theoretical implications. *Journal of Studies on Alcohol, 42,* 626–641.

Tuchfeld, B. S., & Marcus, S. H. (1984). The resolution of alcohol-related problems: In search of a model. *Journal of Drug Issues, 14,* 151–159.

Tucker, J. A., & Gladsjo, J. A. (1993). Help-seeking and recovery by problem drinkers: Characteristics of drinkers who attended Alcoholics Anonymous or formal treatment or who recovered without assistance. *Addictive Behaviors, 18,* 529–542.

Tunving, K. (1988). Fatal outcome in drug addiction. *Acta Psychiatrica Scandinavica, 77,* 551–566.

Vaillant, G. (1966). A twelve-year follow-up of New York narcotic addicts: Some characteristics and determinants of abstinence. *American Journal of Psychiatry, 123,* 573–585.

Vaillant, G. E. (1973). A 20-year follow-up of New York narcotic addicts. *Archives of General Psychiatry, 29,* 237–241.

Vaillant, G. E. (1988). What can long-term follow-up teach us about relapse and prevention of relapse in addiction. *British Journal of Addiction, 83,* 1147–1157.

Vaillant, G. E. (1995). *The natural history of alcoholism revisited.* Cambridge: Harvard University Press.

Vaillant, G. E. (1996). A long-term follow-up of male alcohol abuse. *Archives of General Psychiatry, 53,* 243–249.

Vaillant, G. E., Clark, W., Cyrus, C., Milofsky, E. S., Kopp, J., Wulsin, V. W., & Mogielnicki, N. P. (1983). Prospective study of alcoholism treatment: Eight-year follow-up. *American Journal of Medicine, 75,* 455–463.

Vaillant, G. E., & Milofsky, E. S. (1982). Natural history of male alcoholism: 4. Paths to recovery. *Archives of General Psychiatry, 39,* 127–133.

Vaillant, G. E., Schnurr, P. P., Baron, J. A., & Gerber, P. D. (1991). A prospective study of the effects of cigarette smoking and alcohol abuse on mortality. *Journal of General Internal Medicine, 6,* 299–304.

Waldorf, D. (1983). Natural recovery from opiate addiction: Some social-psychological processes of untreated recovery. *Journal of Drug Issues, 13,* 237–280.

Walker, N. D. (1987). Long term outcome for alcoholic patients treated in a hospital based unit. *New Zealand Medical Journal, 100,* 554–557.

Ward, K. D., Klesges, R. C., Zbikowski, S. M., Bliss, R. E., & Garvey, A. J. (1997). Gender differences in the outcome of an unaided smoking cessation attempt. *Addictive Behaviors, 22,* 521–533.

Westermeyer, J., & Peake, E. (1983). A ten-year follow-up of alcoholic Native Americans in Minnesota. *American Journal of Psychiatry, 140,* 189–193.

Wille, R. (1981). Ten-year follow-up of a representative sample of London heroin addicts: Clinic attendance, abstinence and mortality. *British Journal of Addiction, 76,* 259–266.

Winick, C. (1962). Maturing out of narcotic addiction. *Bulletin on Narcotics, 14,* 1–7.

3

Theories of Etiology of Alcohol and Other Drug Use Disorders

Michie N. Hesselbrock

Victor M. Hesselbrock

Elizabeth E. Epstein

Research on the etiology of alcohol and drug use disorders is a complex, multidiscipline endeavor, and the set of results reported in the literature is enormous. Etiology can be conceptualized on many levels, by means of several different theoretical approaches. For instance, individuals who take a disease model approach to addictions would be most interested in learning about genetic and biological contributions to the disorders. Researchers who adopt a behavioral approach might look for lawful systems of antecedent and consequent events that initiate and maintain drinking. Personality or developmental theorists, or those interested in comorbid psychopathology, might search for mediating pathways, such as certain psychiatric disorders or personality characteristics, to addictive disorders which are seen as end points of these other syndromes. Sociologists might examine factors on a more macro level, such as peer or societal influences that contribute to development and maintenance of addiction.

In this chapter, we summarize several major con-temporary bodies of literature in an attempt to elucidate the current state of research and knowledge on the etiology and maintenance of alcohol and drug use disorders. Of course, this task would better be accomplished in a multivolume book devoted solely to the topic of etiology, so by design, we hope to provide a framework here for readers to understand the basic issues in the study of etiology from several different theoretical viewpoints. First, evidence is presented for genetic contributions to alcohol and drug abuse/dependence. Mechanisms of heritability are illustrated through a brief discussion of research on antisocial personality as an etiological pathway to substance abuse/dependence. Then, biological models of the risk for developing alcohol abuse/dependence are reviewed. Clinical heterogeneity among substance abusers is then covered in some detail, since a complication in the study of etiology of addictive disorders is the phenotypic and possibly genotypic complexity of these disorders.

Mediating variables, or risk factors, are then dis-

cussed in a section reviewing the literature on psychopathology (conduct disorder and antisocial personality disorder), personality, and temperament as
related to development of alcohol and drug misuse.
Then, various other models of etiology are presented,
such as behavioral models, family models, peer influences, and sociocultural approaches.

Note that in this chapter, the term *alcoholism*
may be used interchangeably with and refers to *alcohol abuse/dependence*, and *alcoholic* is used in this
chapter to mean "an individual with alcohol abuse
or dependence."

GENETIC AND BIOLOGICAL MODELS

Genetic Factors and the Vulnerability to Developing Alcohol and Other Drug Abuse/Dependence

Many psychiatric disorders are familial in nature;
that is, the disorder is also often found among other
family members. While this increased prevalence
among family members is suggestive of a possible genetic contribution to the development of a disorder,
it is not conclusive. Other types of evidence are also
needed that examine the role of both environmental
and genetic factors. There is a substantial literature,
based upon studies of monozygotic and dizygotic
twins, half-siblings, adoptees, and extended-family
pedigrees, suggesting that the mode of transmission
of addiction problems and disorders from parent to
child has both a genetic and an environmental component.

Alcohol Abuse/Dependence

The familial nature of alcoholism has long been recognized and is well documented. A review of this
literature by Goodwin (1979) found that as many as
25% of fathers and brothers of alcoholic patients are
themselves affected with alcoholism, while studies of
hospitalized alcoholics indicate that as many as 80%
may have a close biological relative with a lifetime
history of alcohol-related problems (Hesselbrock &
Hesselbrock, 1992). Cotton's (1979) review of 39
family history studies estimated a four- to fivefold increase in the risk of developing alcoholism among
the first-degree relatives of alcoholics as compared to
the general population. More recently, Merikangas

(1990) reported a sevenfold increase in the risk for
developing alcoholism among the first-degree relatives of alcoholics as compared to controls.

The dramatic rate of risk for alcoholism reported
by these studies could be due to sampling bias (i.e.,
most studies reporting an increased risk of familial
alcoholism have been conducted on men). However,
pedigree studies of the biological relatives of female
alcoholic patients have found similar high rates of
alcoholism among both male and female relatives
(Cloninger, Christiansen, Reich, & Gottesman, 1978;
Hesselbrock et al., 1984). Further, a recent study of
female twins has found that both mothers and fathers
were equally likely to transmit the liability for developing alcoholism to their daughters, particularly in
its more severe forms (Kendler, Heath, Neale, Kessler, & Eaves, 1992).

While the reported prevalence of alcoholism
among biological family members varies from one
study to the other, higher rates of alcoholism are consistently found among the family members of alcoholic persons than among those of nonalcoholic persons. Further, there seems to be a positive association
between the rates of alcoholism and pedigree position (i.e., the rate drops as the biological distance
increases). However, it is difficult to separate biological (genetic) factors from possible environmental influences in family history studies, since members of
nuclear families typically share both genetic and environmental factors. Adoption studies enable the separation of genetic and environmental factors. A series
of adoption studies have found a strong link between
paternal alcoholism and the son's development of alcoholism. Using the Danish adoption registers, these
studies indicate that sons of an alcoholic parent have
a similar risk for alcoholism whether raised by the
alcoholic parent or not. Further, the sons were four
times more likely to develop alcoholism than sons
of nonalcoholics, even when adopted away at birth
(Goodwin et al., 1974). These findings have been
replicated by adoption studies conducted in Sweden
(Bohman, Sigvardsson, & Cloninger, 1981; Cloninger, Bohman, & Sigvardsson, 1981), as well as in
Iowa (Cadoret, Cain, & Grove, 1980).

Studies of twins also support the role of genetic
factors in the development of alcoholism (see review
by Hesselbrock, 1995). The majority of twin studies
report increased concordance rates of alcoholism
among monozygotic twins compared to dizygotic
twins (Kendler et al., 1992; McGue, Pickens, &

Svikis, 1992; Pickens et al., 1991). Further, a similarity in alcohol consumption among twins raised separately has also been reported (Hayakawa, 1987; Kaprio et al., 1987; Pedersen, Friberg, Floderus-Myrhed, McClearn, & Plomin, 1984). These studies provide additional support for the role of genetic factors (although unspecified) in the vulnerability to alcoholism.

Pickens et al. (1991) studied same-sex twin pairs of subjects who were treated for alcohol or other drug abuse and found a heterogeneous pattern of inheritance. Approximately half of the twins' biological parent or parents were themselves alcoholic. Heritability was much stronger for alcohol dependence than for alcohol abuse; heritability was also typically much stronger for men than for women (NIAAA, 1993). Further analysis by McGue et al. (1992) found that the rates of alcohol and drug dependence and conduct disorder were much higher among monozygotic male twin pairs than among dizygotic twins of males who were alcohol-dependent or abusing alcohol. Gender differences were apparent in that among female twins, similar rates of problem behaviors were reported by both female pairs. Further gender differences were found in terms of age of onset of alcohol problems and heritability of the problems. An association between early onset and heritability was found among male subjects, but not females. A study of twins in Australia has also suggested a genetic influence in their drinking patterns, with a higher heritability among men than among women (.66 h^2 vs. .42, h^2 respectively) (Heath, Meyer, Jardine, & Martin, 1991).

Drug Abuse and Dependence

Family pedigree studies have the potential to help to identify risk factors for other drug dependence as well as alcohol dependence, since they attempt to identify patterns of other substance abuse among biological relatives. However, only a few studies have sought to determine a familial influence in the development of substance use disorders other than ethanol. Among this small group of studies some patterns seem to be emerging. Croughan (1985) reviewed several family history studies and found that antisocial personality and criminality cluster in drug dependence families, just as in families with alcohol dependence. Meuller, Rinehart, Cadoret, and Troughton (1988) found a significant increase in the prevalence of drug dependence among the biological relatives of inpatients with nonalcohol chemical dependence.

The preference for similar types of drugs may occur among family members of drug abusers. For example, monozygotic twins appear to display greater similarity than dizygotic twin pairs in their preference for, and response to, certain types of drugs (Schuckit, 1987). However, not all researchers agree on these findings. Mirin, Weiss, Sollogub, and Michael (1984) and Mirin, Weiss, and Michael (1986), in a study of first-degree relatives of substance abusers in a treatment program, found differences in the prevalence of substance abuse in relation to the gender of the relative and the choice of substance. Their findings indicate that substance abuse disorders (excluding alcohol) were less frequent among both the male and female relatives of depressant abusers than among the relatives of opiate or stimulant abusers. Further, the prevalence of substance abuse disorders among the female relatives of stimulant and depressant abusers was higher than that among male relatives. The opposite was true of the relatives of opiate abusers, where more male relatives than female relatives were found to be affected with substance abuse.

More recently, Bierut et al. (1998) have examined the familial nature of substance abuse in the Collaborative Study on the Genetics of Alcoholism (COGA) sample. While COGA was designed to determine the genetic basis of alcoholism by using an extended-family study method, many of the persons in the sample with alcohol dependence were also affected with another comorbid substance use disorder. Data from this six-site study indicate some specificity of the familial nature of substance dependence, including alcohol dependence. In this study, the lifetime prevalence of alcohol, marijuana, and cocaine dependence was found to be higher in the biological siblings of alcohol-dependent persons than in those of control subjects, but an increased risk for marijuana or cocaine dependence in siblings was found only when marijuana or cocaine dependence was present in the probands. The risk of developing alcohol dependence in the siblings was not increased by comorbid substance dependence in probands.

Several investigators have examined the role of parents' influence on the drug of choice of their offspring. A high concordance rate of tranquilizer use (56%) between parent and child was found by Smart and Fejer (1972), while Annis (1974) found a positive relationship between adolescents' and parents' use of alcohol and painkillers. Although several studies of intergenerational drug use agree on the overall impact of parental substance abuse, no consistency of findings for parents' influence on the drug of choice by their offspring has been reported.

While investigators seem to agree on the role of genetic influences on the development of both alcoholism and other drug abuse/dependence, separate genetic risk factors may affect the transmission of alcohol dependence versus other drug dependencies. Hill, Cloninger, and Ayre (1977) found that the transmission of opioid dependence was independent of the transmission of alcoholism among the first-degree relatives of subjects who were dependent on opiates only, on alcohol only, and on both. Rounsaville, Weissman, Kleber, and Wilber (1982) compared the rates of drug abuse among the siblings of opiate addicts with or without a concurrent diagnosis of alcoholism. Although the differences in the rates were small, higher rates of drug abuse were reported by the siblings of opiate addicts without alcoholism. Similarly, Stabenau (1992) found evidence suggesting that the risk for alcohol dependence was independent of the risk for drug dependence in a sample of 219 nonhospitalized nontreated young male and female subjects. Further, it was found that antisocial personality disorder predicted alcohol abuse and dependence, family history of drug abuse predicted drug abuse/dependence, and additively, they predicted lifetime rates of alcohol and drug abuse/dependence.

Mechanisms of Heritability

The importance of the interaction between an inherited vulnerability and environmental risk factors has been stressed by Kendler (1995). He places an emphasis on gene-environment interaction $(G \times E)$ rather than an "additive model," which assumes that the impact of a pathogenic environment is independent of genotype. There is evidence from epidemiological studies that indicates a genetic influence on the self-selection of individuals into high-risk environments as well as supporting the role of environmental factors affecting the development of psychiatric disorders (Kendler, 1995).

In their attempt to clarify genetic and environmental contributions to the development of alcohol and other drug dependence, Cadoret, Yates, Trough-ton, Woodworth, and Stewart (1995) examined multipathways of transmission of these disorders from parent to offspring. Etiological pathways related to alcoholism, antisocial personality disorder, and drug dependence were examined in a sample 95 male adoptees in Iowa. In terms of the association between alcohol abuse and antisocial personality disorder, three independent pathways representing genetic and environmental factors were found. The first pathway demonstrated a direct genetic effect of one or both biological parents with alcoholism on the increased risk for alcoholism among the biological offspring. The second pathway, indicating environmental factors, showed a direct effect of alcohol problems in adoptive relatives contributing to the increased risk for alcoholism in adoptees. The third pathway, representing antisocial personality disorder in the biological parent, showed an increased risk of an intervening variable, antisocial personality disorder in adoptees. The presence of antisocial personality disorder, in turn, increased the risk for alcohol abuse/dependency in adoptees.

Similarly, alcohol abuse/dependence in the biological parent increased the risk for drug abuse/dependence in adoptees, while antisocial personality disorder in the biological parent increased the likelihood of aggressivity associated with antisocial personality disorder in the adoptees. Aggressivity functioned as an intervening variable for the development of drug abuse and/or dependency in adoptees. Environmental factors, characterized by parental divorce or separation as well as the presence of behavior problems in the adoptive parent, were also associated with an increased risk for drug abuse/dependence in adoptees (Cadoret et al., 1995).

The separate and independent role of antisocial personality disorder in the development of alcohol and other drug abuse/dependence found in the Cadoret et al. (1995) study is consistent with other published studies. Other investigators have demonstrated that alcohol abuse/dependence and antisocial personality disorders in biological parents appear to be transmitted to their offspring as separate traits, while both traits contribute to the risk of developing alcoholism and drug dependence in the offspring (Cloninger et al., 1978; Reich, Cloninger, Lewis, & Rice, 1981). Further, the heritability of aggressive behaviors has also been documented. (Eron & Huessman, 1990; Mattes & Fink, 1987; Plomin, Nitz, & Rowe, 1990). Similarly, conduct problems also distinguished children whose parents had antisocial personality disorder from those children whose parents did not (August & Stewart, 1983; Stewart, deBlois, & Cummings, 1980). Thus, conduct disorder, aggressivity, and antisocial personality contribute to the risk of alcohol/drug abuse independent of each other and independent of the risk due to parental alcohol/drug abuse (Cadoret & Wesner, 1990; Hesselbrock et al., 1984, 1992; Loney, 1980).

A twin study by Lyons et al. (1995) also investigated different mechanisms responsible for the familial transmission of alcoholism by separating possible genetic factors from environmental factors. Symptoms of antisocial personality disorder were examined in 3,226 male twin pairs. It was found that shared family environment was more important in predicting the concordance of individual juvenile symptoms, whereas genetic influences were more important for predicting adult symptoms.

Biological Factors in the Etiology of Substance Use Disorders

Central Nervous System: Neuropsychological Functioning and the Risk for Developing Alcoholism

A variety of studies implicate heritable physiological factors associated with central nervous system functioning in relation to an increased vulnerability to developing drug and alcohol abuse. Although the relative contribution of these specific inherited factors to an increased risk has not yet been identified, potential neurophysiological indicators of this vulnerability suggested in the literature include differences in body sway (static ataxia; Lipscomb, Carpenter, & Nathan, 1979), subjective feelings of intoxication, and an increased physiological response to ethanol (Schuckit, 1980, 1985; Schuckit, Gold, & Risch, 1987).

Neuropsychological functioning has also been examined as a risk factor. Aspects of neuropsychological functioning are heritable, and it has been postulated that certain cognitive deficits among children of alcoholics may contribute to the risk for developing alcoholism and other substance abuse disorders (see review by Hesselbrock, Bauer, Hesselbrock, & Gillen, 1991).

Several investigators have found central nervous system disturbances, including impaired cognitive functioning and electrophysiological disturbances, among persons affected with a substance abuse disorder. Impairment of brain functioning as well as structural abnormalities have been reported among chronic alcoholics (Deckel, Bauer, & Hesselbrock, 1995; Hesselbrock et al., 1991). The areas of impaired cognitive functioning include memory, attention span, visuospatial skills, abstract thinking, and verbal reasoning. DeObaldia, Parsons, and Yohman (1983), among others, reported an association between severe symptoms of alcohol dependence and poor cognitive test performance among alcoholics. Electroencephalographic (EEG) and event-related potential (ERP) disturbances among alcoholics have also been reported. Using event-related potential methods, Porjesz and Begleiter (1985) found reduced P3 ERP waveform amplitudes among alcoholics as compared to nonalcoholics. However, originally it was not clear whether these differences represented an indicator of risk for the development of alcoholism or were the result of chronic heavy drinking. Several studies of alcoholics have observed at least some level of recovery in cognitive functioning following abstinence.

Recent studies have provided evidence that electrophysiological factors as measured by the EEG and ERP may contribute to the vulnerability to alcohol dependence, independent of chronic alcohol consumption. Begleiter et al. (1984) reported reduced P3 ERP component amplitudes, particularly over the parietal area, among prepubescent, alcohol-naive sons of alcoholic fathers compared to sons of nonalcoholic fathers. These findings have been replicated by other investigators (cf. O'Connor, Hesselbrock, & Tasman, 1986; V. Hesselbrock, O'Connor, Tasman, & Weidenman, 1988). Further, the amplitude of the P3 waveform has been shown to be related to aspects of both figural memory and cognitive flexibility among young men at high risk for alcoholism (V. Hesselbrock, Bauer, O'Connor, & Gillen, 1993). Despite these findings indicating the possible contribution of both electrophysiological and neuropsychological factors to the development of alcohol dependence, the relationship between electrophysiological measures and behavioral (neuropsychological) measures of cognitive functioning are not well understood.

Deckel et al. (1995) examined neuropsychological and electrophysiological measures in relation to alcohol-related variables in young men at risk for alcoholism because of a positive family history of paternal alcoholism. Neuropsychological tests measuring frontal and/or temporal neocortical functioning were found to be predictive of the age of taking their first drink and the frequency of drinking to get intoxicated. Left-frontal slow-alpha EEG activity was also associated with these alcohol-related variables. These findings suggest that disturbances in the integrity of the anterior neocortex may be a risk factor in the development of alcohol-related behaviors.

Branchey, Buydens-Branchey, and Lieber (1993) suggest that a low P3 amplitude could antedate substance abuse and may be a risk factor for the development of substance misuse. They found that a subtype of alcoholics with lifelong aggressive behavior exhibited lower P3 voltages in the event-related potential. These patients were also characterized by a high genetic loading for alcoholism (Branchey et al., 1988, 1993). While the number of subjects examined was small ($n = 10$), low P3 amplitude was also observed among former cocaine and/or heroin addicts who had been abstinent for at least 6 months.

CLINICAL HETEROGENEITY AMONG ALCOHOL AND SUBSTANCE ABUSERS: IMPLICATIONS FOR ETIOLOGY

Type 1/Type 2

The independent contributions of genetic factors and environmental factors to the development of alcohol and drug addiction are difficult to separate. A primary reason for this difficulty is that neither alcohol nor other drug dependence is a unitary clinical disorder (Hesselbrock, 1986a, 1995). Both patient and general populations of persons so affected are heterogeneous in relation to their clinical presentation. An early, influential attempt to subclassify alcoholism was conducted in Sweden by the use of retrospective data obtained from adoption records. Cloninger et al. (1981) proposed two forms of alcoholism found among male adoptees based upon their own alcohol use and their parents' characteristics. The first form, Type 1, influenced by both genetic and environmental factors, is characterized by mild

or severe alcohol abuse in the probands and no history of criminality or alcohol abuse in their biological fathers. Type 2 alcoholism is thought to be highly heritable, male-limited (father-to-son transmission), and developed independent of environmental factors. It is characterized by moderate alcohol abuse in the probands and severe alcohol use and criminality in the fathers.

Bohman et al. (1981) examined female adoptees in the Swedish sample and found only Type 1 alcohol abuse. However, only 31 female adoptees were identified who met criteria for alcohol abuse. A replication study derived from a sample in Gothenburg, Sweden, was reported recently by this study team (Sigvardsson, Bohman, & Cloninger, 1996). The replication study essentially confirms the original findings for both male and female adoptees.

The phenotypic characteristics of persons with a family history of alcohol abuse in the Cloninger et al. study are different from those reported by Goodwin (1979, 1984), who found a severe form of alcoholism among adoptee probands with a paternal history of alcoholism. The differences in findings between the two studies could be due to sample differences, where the studies were conducted, and the source of the information upon which parental classifications were made. In the Swedish study, a subject was defined as having alcoholism based upon two or more contacts with local temperance boards or having been treated for alcoholism, while the Danish study defined a subject as having alcoholism based upon national hospitalization records.

Both Swedish adoption studies are limited by the rather small number of female alcohol abusers included in the study, the restricted sample selection methods, and the use of indirect measures of alcohol abuse for both the subjects and their fathers (Vanclay & Raphael, 1990). Efforts to replicate the Swedish adoption study in the United States have resulted in equivocal support.

Investigations of Type 1 and Type 2 alcoholism in U.S. samples have found that the principal distinguishing etiological factor is the age of onset of alcoholism. Type 2 alcoholism is characterized by an early age of onset, while Type 1 is more prevalent among later onset alcoholics. While many alcohol-related symptoms did not distinguish the two types of alcoholism among men treated at a VA hospital, the age of onset of alcoholism was an important factor in characterizing the two types of alcoholism (Penick et al., 1990). Similar findings were reported by Irwin, Schuckit, and Smith (1990) and von Knorring et al. (1987).

Buydens-Branchey, Branchey, and Noumair (1989a) also divided a sample of recently detoxified male alcoholic patients admitted to a rehabilitation program according to their age at the onset of alcoholism. Early-onset alcoholism included those patients who began alcohol abuse before 20 years of age, while the late-onset group had an onset of alcohol abuse sometime after 20 years of age. The early-onset group reported a higher prevalence rate of paternal alcoholism and were twice as likely as the late-onset alcoholics to have been incarcerated for crimes involving physical violence. Further, the early-onset subjects were found to be suffering from depression and were more likely to have attempted suicide than the late-onset alcoholics. Buydens-Branchey et al. (1989b) also suggested that early-onset alcoholics may have a preexisting serotonin deficit, manifesting itself by increased alcohol intake at an early age.

Type A/Type B

A more recent methodology of classifying alcoholics and drug abusers was proposed by Babor et al. (1992). Using a cluster analysis of variables derived from 17 different areas of clinical data, Babor et al. (1992) derived two types of alcoholism from 321 male and female hospitalized alcoholics. Two "types" of alcoholism were identified (Type A and Type B), which closely resembled Cloninger's Type 1 and Type 2. Type A was also characterized by a late onset of alcoholism, while a principal characteristic of Type B alcoholism was an early onset of alcohol problems and alcoholism. Further, the Type 2–like cluster (Type B) alcoholics displayed severe and chronic consequences of alcoholism and had a higher frequency of childhood risk factors, familial alcoholism, and a more chronic treatment history.

Ball and colleagues (Ball, Carroll, & Babor, 1995; Feingold, Ball, Kranzler, & Rounsaville, 1996), using cluster-analytic methods to subclassify a nonclinical sample of cocaine abusers, found support for the Type A and B classification of alcoholism among cocaine abusers. Their findings suggest that a multidimensional subclassification system may also have an impact on our understanding of etiology and course of both alcohol and other substance abuse. Relative

to Type A subjects, Type B cocaine abusers reported higher rates of premorbid risk factors, including a family history of drug abuse, childhood behavior problems, and an early age of onset of cocaine abuse. The course and consequences of the disorder among Type B cocaine abusers were also more severe (i.e., more severe drug and alcohol abuse, more addiction-related psychosocial impairment, more antisocial behavior, and more comorbid psychiatric problems) than among Type A cocaine abusers.

Gender Differences in Clinical Heterogeneity

While typologies developed on the Swedish sample and an empirically derived typology in the United States seem to have etiological significance for the development of alcoholism for men, they do not necessarily apply to the women in the United States with alcohol or other substance abuse problems. Unlike the female subjects in the Swedish adoptee study, who were found to be of only one type (Type 1), a female sample in the United States was found to include both Type 1 and Type 2 alcoholism. The Type 2 female alcoholics were characterized by early age of onset, high familial density, and paternal alcoholism (Glenn & Nixon, 1991).

In another study with a small sample, Hesselbrock (1991) found that antisocial personality (ASP) alcoholic women had characteristics similar to those of male Type 2 alcoholism. In order to further consider possible gender differences, DelBoca and Hesselbrock (1996) conducted a reanalysis of the original Type A and B (Babor et al., 1992) data set by deriving a four-cluster solution (vs. the original two-group solution). As in the original analysis, the clusters appeared to separate, in part, along "risk" and "severity" dimensions. The risk dimension included vulnerability factors such as a family history for alcoholism, early onset of alcohol problems, and a history of childhood conduct problems. The severity dimension included indicators of physiological dependence (tolerance and withdrawal), alcohol-related problems, and comorbid or alcohol-induced psychiatric symptoms (e.g., anxiety, affective disturbance). The proportions of men and women found in the low risk–low severity group (39% women and 28% men) and the high risk–high severity group (22% women and 22% men) were similar. The two intermediate subgroups were more gender-specific. The "internalizing" subtype, characterized by moderate risk and high alcohol involvement, included more women than men. This group displayed a high level of depression and anxiety symptoms, but a low prevalence of ASP. The gender composition of the "externalizers," with moderate risk and high severity, included more men than women. The rate of ASP among subjects in this subtype was high, while the prevalence of depression and anxiety was lower than in the other groups. These findings indicate the importance of gender considerations in the examination of the etiology and the clinical presentation of alcohol dependence.

PSYCHOPATHOLOGY, PERSONALITY, AND TEMPERAMENT AS RISK FACTORS FOR ALCOHOL AND DRUG USE DISORDERS

Association of Conduct Disorder and Antisocial Personality Disorder as Risk Factors for Alcoholism

The association of childhood behavioral problems and the development of alcoholism has been documented repeatedly in longitudinal studies of both clinical and nonclinical samples over the past 30 years. The classic study conducted by Robins (1966) found that childhood conduct problems predicted the later development of alcoholism in men treated initially at a child guidance clinic as children. In an earlier study, McCord and McCord (1960) found that aggression and sadistic behaviors in delinquent boys were predictive of the development of alcoholism in adulthood. These findings have been replicated in longitudinal studies of community samples as well as in retrospective studies of adults with drinking problems (Cahalan & Room, 1974; Jones, 1968).

Childhood hyperactivity, when combined with childhood conduct disorder, has been linked to adult alcoholism through studies of hospitalized alcoholics. Using a retrospective assessment, Tarter, McBride, Buopane, and Schneider (1977) reported a higher frequency of childhood hyperactivity and minimal brain dysfunction (MBD) behaviors among primary or "essential" alcoholics than among "reactive" alcoholics. DeObaldia et al. (1983) also found an association between hyperactivity/MBD in childhood and severe symptoms of alcohol dependence in adulthood. More recently, Boyle et al. (1992) examined prospectively the association between conduct disorder in early adolescence and substance use. The children were first assessed at 12–16 years of age regarding their substance use (e.g., tobacco, alcohol, marijuana, and hard drugs) and the presence of psychiatric disorders (conduct disorder, attention deficit disorder) and emotional problems (feelings of anxiety and depression). A follow-up assessment was conducted 4 years later. Even after controlling for potential confounding factors measured at the first assessment (including drug use, attention deficit, and emotional disorder), Boyle et al. found that the association between conduct disorder in early adolescence and marijuana and hard drug use in late adolescence remained statistically significant.

It is difficult to delineate clearly a specific etiological mechanism that ties childhood problem behaviors to the development of alcoholism or substance abuse in adulthood. First, the concept of "childhood problem behavior" includes a broad range of behavior problems in children, including hyperactivity, MBD, emotional problems, and deviant behavior (including vandalism, aggression, and hostility). This constellation of behaviors has often been found to predict substance use in adolescents, substance use problems in young adults, and onset and severity of a substance use disorder in adult patients. Most investigators typically have not examined a broad, comprehensive range of behavior problems. Instead, only some of the selected behaviors mentioned above have been examined, and none have studied a comprehensive list of behaviors/problems. Consequently, it is difficult to identify a specific behavior(s) that influences the development of substance abuse. Several attempts have been made to identify clusters or groups of risk behaviors that are related to the development of substance abuse. Windle (1996) found a high intercorrelation among measures of different externalizing behaviors, including conduct disorder, attention deficit/hyperactivity disorder, and oppositional disorder, among teenagers. Further, teenaged moderate drinkers reported a higher frequency of these behaviors than light drinkers, and problem drinkers reported more problem behaviors than moderate drinkers, demonstrating a direct positive relationship between childhood problem behaviors and both the level of consumption and the severity of drinking problems in adolescents. M. N. Hesselbrock (1986b) divided Tarter et al.'s (1977) list of problem behaviors into hyperactivity, attention deficit, impulsivity, and conduct problems to examine their independent contribution to the prediction of alcoholism. Only childhood conduct problems were related to a certain type of alcoholism in adulthood, namely, alcoholism with antisocial personality disorder. Similarly, other investigators have found that conduct problems also distinguished children whose parents were diagnosed with antisocial personality disorders from those whose parents were not (August & Stewart, 1983; Stewart et al., 1980).

It may be of importance to differentiate conduct disorder from attention deficit disorder, although they frequently co-occur (Murphy & Barkley, 1996). Boyle et al. (1992) found a significant independent contribution of conduct disorder in predicting marijuana and hard drug use among adolescents, but little evidence of an independent contribution of attention deficit disorder apart from conduct disorder. A similar finding was reported by August and Stewart (1983).

A review of longitudinal developmental studies of alcoholism indicates that antisocial behavior and difficulty in achievement-related activities in childhood and adolescence are consistently related to the development of alcoholism in adulthood (Zucker & Gomberg, 1986). The _____ ̄ in
                                                                  rs,

_____ ulat only about one third become antisocial adults (Robins, 1966; Robins & Price, 1991). Violent and aggressive behavior typically does not appear in adulthood if it has been absent in childhood. The distinguishing features of those who do not improve is the presence of under-

socialization and aggressiveness (see review by Loeber & Dishion, 1983). Children who continue to be inattentive and impulsive are often characterized as aggressive, noncompliant, and antisocial and use alcohol in their teens.

Importantly, persons who continue to use alcohol and drugs in their teens continue to use substances as young adults. These results are supported by Kandel, Simcha-Fagan, and Davies (1986), who found that illicit drug use by boys during adolescence (ages 15–16) was a strong predictor of continued drug use as long as 9 years later. Early drug use also predicted later delinquent behavior among women. The findings of Kandel et al. suggest that gender differences influence the role played by delinquency, early drug use, and other problems as risk factors for adult substance use and misuse. Adult role deviations (e.g., unstable employment, not being married) were also identified as risk factors for illicit drug use in young adulthood.

Temperament as a Risk Factor for Alcohol and Other Drug Abuse

A search of the developmental process of childhood problem behavior suggests that aspects of temperament may predict both behavior problems and later substance abuse, particularly in adolescence. Temperament traits are expressed at an early stage of child development and seem to differentially predict boys' and girls' later behaviors. For example, a longitudinal study of very young children found that girls who were low in ego resiliency and ego control in nursery school were using marijuana at age 14, while marijuana use in boys was predicted by low ego control, but not by early ego resilience (Block, Block, & Keyes, 1988).

Temperament has been identified as an important factor in several theoretical formulations related to the development of pathological alcohol involvement (Cloninger, 1987; Lerner & Vicary, 1984; 1991; Tarter, 1988). While prior research has shown that a predisposition to the development of alcoholism is due partially to the individual's genetic makeup, several studies suggest that this genetic predisposition may be expressed, in part, through the individual's temperament. Temperament characteristics and extreme deviations in temperament characteristics have been found to be highly heritable (cf. Cloninger, 1987) and to manifest early in a child's development. Studies of adolescent problem drinkers have identified tolerance of deviance and related personality traits (e.g., distrust, aggressive sociality, cynicism) as being associated with acute alcohol problems in adolescence.

Currently, two of the more prominent theoretical models of the development of alcoholism include temperament as a key feature (Cloninger, 1987; Cloninger & Gottesman, 1987; Tarter, 1988). In both models, temperament and personality characteristics are linked to alcoholism through clusters of temperament and personality attributes that may be transmitted from parents to their offspring. Cloninger (1987) has hypothesized that biologically based personality differences distinguish between Type 1 and Type 2 alcoholism. Type 1 alcoholism was theorized to be associated with three heritable dimensions of personality: low novelty seeking, high harm avoidance, and high reward dependence. Type 2 alcoholism was thought to be associated with the opposite spectrum of these personality characteristics. Masse and Tremblay (1997) found that two of the personality traits of the Type 1/Type 2 typology are predictors of early onset of substance use. In a study of kindergarten boys, they found that high novelty seeking and low harm avoidance measured at age 6 predicted early onset of cigarette smoking, getting drunk, and other drug use in adolescence. Further, there was some stability of the three traits from age 6 to age 10, with novelty seeking $r = .38$; harm avoidance $r = .24$; and reward dependence $r = .18$ in a sample of about 900 boys.

Irwin et al. (1990) examined the usefulness of novelty seeking, harm avoidance and reward dependence for predicting alcohol-related problems among young men whose fathers had alcohol problems, but they found no significant relationship between the personality traits proposed by Cloninger and Gottesman (1987) and either a family history of alcoholism or the young men's drinking pattern (Irwin et al., 1990; Schuckit, Irwin, & Mahler, 1990). Hesselbrock and Hesselbrock (1990) examined a sample of nonalcoholic young adult men at high risk for developing alcoholism. In addition, antisocial personality disorder, regardless of a family history of alcoholism, was found to be an important factor in the prediction of the development of alcohol use. Antisocial personality disorder was also associated with the three personality characteristics among young men at high risk for developing alcohol abuse.

As described above, harm avoidance, novelty seeking, and reward dependence they are thought to be genetically based and to be transmitted independently from parent to offspring, and they are thought to represent variations in the individual's neurological makeup and influence susceptibility to the development of alcoholism. Although Cloninger has replicated his own findings in a separate Swedish sample (Sigvardsson et al., 1996), few investigators have been able to identify these three specific personality traits as distinguishing features of either alcohol-dependent persons or high-risk subjects among U.S. samples (Hesselbrock & Hesselbrock, 1992; Masse & Tremblay, 1997).

Tarter and colleagues have proposed a broader temperament model of alcoholism. This model includes six dimensions of temperament that may be inherited: activity level, attention span persistence, soothability, emotionality, reaction to food, and sociability. Indeed, low attentional capacity, high emotionality, and low sociability have been found to be associated with an increased risk for developing alcohol-related problems (Tarter, 1988; Tarter, Kabene, Escallier, Laird, & Jacob, 1990). In addition, Lerner and Vicary (1984), as well as Ohannessian and Hesselbrock (1995), found that certain clusters of temperament traits, which constitute a "difficult temperament" (high activity level, low flexibility and task orientation, mood instability, and social withdrawal), are related to substance use/abuse.

Mezzich et al. (1993) identified adolescents with alcohol abuse/dependence that could be clustered into two groups according to an internalizing/externalizing behavior dimension. The first group was characterized by negative affect, while the second group was better characterized by behavioral disturbances, reduced depression, and anxiety symptoms (i.e., behavioral dyscontrol and hypophoria). The second group also had increased substance use, increased problems at school and with peers, and increased behavioral problems. These findings provide some confirmatory evidence for an adolescent typology of alcohol dependence based upon personality factors that is similar to the Type A/Type B dichotomy developed by Babor et al. (1992).

More recently, personality research has focused upon what has been termed the five-factor model of personality. This work traces its origins to Gordon Allport (1937) and Cattell (1947) and over the years has led to the identification of five robust factors:

(a) neuroticism—a tendency to experience negative affect; (b) extroversion—gregariousness, activity; (c) openness to experience—intellectual curiosity, awareness of inner feelings, need for variety in actions; (d) agreeableness—altruism, emotional support, helpfulness; and (e) conscientiousness—will to achieve, dependability, responsibility. These factors, which combine aspects of the temperament traits proposed by Cloninger and by Tarter as having etiological significance, consider the effects of more "normal" traits rather than deviations. A study of the risk for alcoholism in relation to the five-factor model of personality found that a family history of alcoholism was positively associated with openness and negatively associated with agreeableness and conscientiousness (Martin & Sher, 1994). Alcohol use was positively correlated with neuroticism and negatively correlated with agreeableness and conscientiousness. No interaction was found between a family history of alcoholism and gender in relation to the five dimensions of personality, nor was antisocial personality disorder related to any of the five dimensions in subjects with alcohol use disorders.

Association of Temperament and Conduct Problems as Precursors to Substance Abuse

The association between other aspects of children's temperament and conduct problems as precursors to substance abuse has been studied. "Difficult temperament disposition" or "temperament deviation" was found to be associated with conduct disorder in childhood/adolescence, progressing to antisocial personality disorder in adulthood, while "normative temperament" was associated with time-limited delinquent behavior (Moffit, 1993; Windle, 1996). In another study, 10- to 12-year-old sons of fathers with and without substance abuse were separated by means of a cluster analysis. The resulting two-cluster solution classified boys along the dimensions of difficult and normative temperament. The sons' temperament cluster membership was a more salient predictor of deviancy than a family history of substance abuse. The boys classified as having difficult temperament were high on aggressivity, maladaptive discipline, family dysfunction, attributional errors in perception of self, and high peer affiliations associated with unconventionality and delinquent behavior. Furthermore, these characteristics were predictive of the boys' alcohol and drug use 2 years later, when

they were 12–14 years old (Blackson & Tarter, 1994). Martin, Kaczynski, Maisto, and Tarter (1996) found that dispositional traits characterized by heightened negative affect (depressed mood and anxiety) and behavioral undercontrol reflecting impulsivity, aggressivity, acting out, and sensation seeking were significant predictors of the number of drugs used by adolescents. Assuming that "difficult temperament" is predictive of adult antisocial personality disorder, the findings of Martin et al. are supported by a study of unaffected young men in their early 20s which found that a diagnosis of antisocial personality disorder was a more powerful predictor of heavy drinking (Hesselbrock & Hesselbrock, 1992).

Individual differences in temperament can be conceptualized in terms of the developmental process, along with the personality development of children and adolescents. Rothbart and Ahadi (1994) proposed temperament as being constitutionally based and including an individual's reactivity (responsiveness of emotional activation and arousal systems) and development of ability for self-regulation, interacting over time with heredity, maturation, and experience. Conversely, temperament may influence the way children interact with their environment. Barron and Earls (1984) found that temperamental inflexibility, negative parent-child interaction and high family stress showed a strong association with problem behavior in 3-year-old children. Others suggest that temperament deviation in children may promote maladaptive behavior and a tendency to associate with deviant peers. Deviation in temperament is also associated with aggression and poor responsiveness to parental discipline, both of which are predictive of conduct disorders (Blackson, 1994).

PSYCHOLOGICAL MODELS OF ETIOLOGY AND MAINTENANCE OF ALCOHOL AND DRUG USE DISORDERS

Psychoanalytic Models

Leeds and Morgenstern (1995) reviewed several theories of substance use that relate to various aspects of psychoanalytic theory. Wurmser (1984) viewed substance abusers as having severe intrapsychic conflict in the form of overly harsh superegos, so that these individuals use alcohol or drugs to escape intense feelings of rage and fear. Khantzian, Halliday, and

McAuliffe (1990) took a self-deficit approach, positing that inadequacies of the ego underlie substance abuse. This theory takes into account the notion that an individual's drug of choice has particular "self-medicating" properties for his or her particular type of ego deficit. Krystal's (1984) theory focuses on disturbed object relations as the basis of substance abuse/dependence and disturbed affective regulation. McDougall (1989) proposed that all addictive disorders are psychosomatic defenses against psychic conflict.

In general, psychoanalytic models have been less widely accepted as underlying substance abuse/dependence, though they are thought-provoking and interesting. The reader is referred to Morgenstern and Leeds (1993) and Leeds and Morgenstern (1995) for more detailed discussion of psychoanalytic theories of etiology of substance use disorders.

Behavioral, Cognitive Behavioral, and Social Learning Theory Models

Historically, behavioral models of substance use disorders postulated that substance use behavior is learned and maintained through either classical or operant conditioning (chapter 14, this volume). The contemporary cognitive behavioral (CB) models such as social learning theory (SLT) incorporate thoughts and feelings as important determinants of behavior and responses to the environment. Behavioral and cognitive behavioral models are described in detail in chapter 14 of this book and elsewhere (Rotgers, 1996). Here, we will briefly review the basic tenets of each approach to the etiology of substance abuse/dependence disorder.

Classical Conditioning

Classical conditioning is thought to facilitate development of a drinking or drug problem or craving through pairing of conditioned stimuli (CS) such as particular sites of use or people and the unconditioned stimulus (US; alcohol or drugs), the result being a conditioned response (CR), or conditioned craving.

Conditioned tolerance has been proposed as a classical conditioning paradigm, in which the substance is the US and the physiological effects are the unconditioned response (UR); substance-related cues become the US, eliciting a CR which Wikler (1973)

and Siegel (1979) noticed are often the opposite of the initial drug effects. Siegel called these unexpected CRs "conditioned compensatory responses" (CCRs). The CCRs were noted to increase in strength with repeated trials, thus decreasing the observed drug effect (see Sherman, Jorenby, & Baker, 1988).

Wikler (1973) also noticed that heroin addicts exhibited withdrawal symptoms simply by looking at paraphernalia associated with heroin use. He called this "conditioned withdrawal" and carried out a series of studies using heroin as the US, resulting in withdrawal symptoms as the UR. The CS was the heroin-related paraphernalia, and the CR was an experience of withdrawal after the injection of an inert substance (see also Rotgers, 1996).

Operant Conditioning

Operant conditioning principles apply to the positive reinforcing effects of alcohol and drugs as social reinforcers, and to the avoidance or cessation of withdrawal symptoms. That is, an individual drinks in response to an antecedent stimulus, such as a glass of beer or an angry mood, and then associates the reinforcing effects of alcohol (i.e., euphoria or elevated mood) with the antecedent stimulus. Substance-using behavior increases as a result of the positive or negative reinforcing effects of the alcohol or drug.

For instance, the putative effects of alcohol on tension reduction have been well documented. The literature documents variable effects of alcohol and drugs across different settings, individual characteristics of drinkers, and different sources of stress. Recent studies have conceptualized a self-medicating theory in terms of conditioned behavioral responses resulting from positive reinforcement received through the consumption of alcohol and other drugs. Kushner, Sher, Wood, and Wood (1994) examined the moderating effects of alcohol expectancies on tension reduction, level of anxiety symptoms, and drinking behavior among college students. A strong association between anxiety symptoms and alcohol consumption was found among men with high tension-reduction outcome expectancies, but not among women. However, recent investigations of both clinical and nonclinical samples have found anxiety disorders, while highly comorbid with alcohol and substance use disorders, typically follow the development of alcohol and other drug abuse rather than precede their development (Hesselbrock, Hesselbrock, & Stabenau,

1985; Schuckit & Hesselbrock, 1995; Schuckit et al., 1995).

Cognitive Behavioral/SLT Models

Cognitive behavioral (CB) models highlight the importance of cognitions and feelings as preceding and directing behavior. Social learning theory (SLT) focuses on constructs such as expectancies, self-efficacy, and attributions, all types of cognitions that are thought to mediate the pathway from stimuli to use of substances as response. Expectancies of the positive effects of substance use develop from repeated classical and/or operant pairings of the alcohol or drug with its reinforcing effects. Expectancies can be thought of as conditioned cognitions, which can themselves be associated with positive experiences, or positive subjective responses, to alcohol or drug-related cues. Positive expectancies, such as expectancies of relief from withdrawal symptoms or of relaxation following a drink, can facilitate more frequent alcohol or drug use and thus contribute to the development of dependence (see Rotgers, 1996).

Self-efficacy, according to SLT, is an individual's expectation or confidence in his or her ability to perform particular coping behaviors in certain situations and the expectation that the coping behavior will be reinforced (see Rotgers, 1996, for a more detailed discussion). Since SLT views substance use disorders as a failure of coping, it is assumed that self-efficacy for coping without alcohol or drugs is low among active users, and this type of cognition contributes to increased use and development of dependence on the substance.

CB theory postulates that initial heavy use of substances is the result of several interacting factors, such as an individual's biological makeup (genetic risk, temperament), which determines if the substance use will be reinforcing or punishing; the social environment, which may facilitate or condone use; and the basic principles of operant conditioning, which reward and maintain use. As an individual uses more, he or she uses other coping skills less and develops reduced self-efficacy and increased positive expectancies of the effects of the substance, the result being more use. In later stages, classical conditioning principles such as conditioned craving, tolerance, and withdrawal play an important role in the development and maintenance of heavy problem use of alcohol or drugs (see Rotgers, 1996, for an excellent

description of the CB model of the etiology of substance use disorders).

An example of a specific SLT is that of Petraitis, Flay, and Miller (1995), who proposed the cognitive affective approach to explain adolescents' experimentation with alcohol and other drugs. Their conceptualization is based on a social learning theory which asserts that the decision to experiment with substances is influenced, in part, by the adolescent's belief regarding the cost-benefit ratio of substance use. The process of forming the belief to using substances progresses through several stages. The first cognitive process is the evaluation that the costs are smaller than the benefits of substance use; this is followed by the formation of positive attitudes toward substance use and the perception that substance use is endorsed by the people around the adolescent. The authors also cited the lack of self-efficacy in being able to refuse alcohol/drug use as an important reason for forming the decision to use substances.

SOCIOCULTURAL MODELS OF ETIOLOGY AND MAINTENANCE

Familial Factors

As noted, alcohol and drug use disorders are multiply determined by a complex association of genetic, environmental, personality, and other factors. Because of these factors, often more than one family member is substance-dependent, which further complicates the task of teasing apart the specific influences that family environment, rearing, and interspousal relationships have on the development of alcoholism. Three contemporary models of family influence on the development and maintenance of substance dependence each take a different approach (see chapter 16, this volume; McCrady & Epstein, 1996; McCrady, Kahler, & Epstein, 1998). The family disease model posits that all family members suffer from a "family disease" of either alcoholism or codependency, and that alcoholism and codependency are interrelated in such a way as to "enable" (perpetuate) the alcohol problem. Thus, according to this model, the specific etiology of the alcoholism is biological, but the alcoholism is then maintained by a family disease.

Research by means of the family systems model on the role of the family of origin of the drinker and the spouse in the etiology of the substance abuse has focused on family behavior around drinking. Originally developed by Steinglass and associates (Davis, Berenson, Steinglass, & Davis, 1974; Steinglass, Weiner, & Mendelson, 1971), the family systems model assumes that alcohol serves to stabilize family equilibrium, and that families organize their interactions and structure around the alcohol to continue the "homeostasis" (i.e., to maintain the alcohol problem despite the problems associated with such a system). The degree to which alcoholic families uphold "family rituals" (e.g., dinnertime, celebration of holidays) may protect against development of alcoholism in offspring or at least may serve as a marker of transmission (Bennett, Wolin, Reiss, & Teitelbaum, 1987; Steinglass, Bennett, Wolin, & Reiss, 1987; Wolin, Bennett, Noonan, & Teitelbaum, 1980). More recently, Bennett and Wolin (1990) reported that continuing interaction between alcoholic parents and their adult offspring is associated with increased rates of alcoholism among the male offspring.

The third contemporary model is the behavioral family approach, which examines the family's (especially the spouse's) behaviors as antecedents to and reinforcing consequences of substance use. These behaviors serve to help develop and maintain the drinking problem. This model is outlined in detail in chapter 16 of this book.

Peer Influences

Peer group influences have been cited consistently as risk factors for the initiation of alcohol and other drugs among adolescents (Kandel, Kessler, & Margulies, 1978; Wills, Vaccaro, & McNamara, 1992). Peers influence adolescents' behavior, values, and attitudes. The association with deviant friends has been found to promote the acceptance of deviant behaviors (Loeber, Stouthamer, Van Kammen, & Farrington, 1991) and to increase the risk for alcohol and drug use among adolescents (Robins & McEvoy, 1990). Further, peer relationships can either promote or reduce the student's motivation for school performance and can affect self-esteem and social relationships in adolescents (O'Connell, 1989). Segal and Stewart (1996) found adolescents citing their perception of the positive aspects of substance use involving peers, along with the tension reduction effects of alcohol, as reasons for alcohol/substance use. In this study, the most important reasons cited by

adolescents for using alcohol were to socialize with friends; to alleviate tension and anxiety, especially in mixed-gender situations; to get high; to "cheer up"; and to reduce boredom.

It is not clear whether association with a deviant peer group is a risk factor for, or a result of, maladaptive behavior. It has been suggested that adolescents who abuse alcohol and drugs tend to associate with peers who are positive toward the abuse of alcohol and other drugs, providing support and reinforcement for these risky behaviors (Freeman & Dyer, 1993; Harford & Grant, 1987). Furthermore, adolescents' deviant peer-group involvement interacts with other risk factors, including family problems, stress and other mental health problems, and low self-esteem. Thus, it can be difficult to separate etiological factors from the consequences of substance abuse and other behavior problems (Freeman & Dyer, 1993). Gender differences are evident, as males report a higher rate of deviant peer involvement, providing explanatory support for a higher rate of alcohol and drug use in adolescent boys (Wills et al., 1992). Further, cultural differences seem to affect the differential influence of parental support for alcohol and drug abuse in young adults. Gillmore (1990) found that the initiation of alcohol, tobacco, and marijuana use, as well as the intention to use substances as an adult, was also related to substance availability and perceived parental approval, which varied among Caucasians, Asian-Americans, and African-Americans.

Social Environments That Support Substance Use

The social learning theories have relevance only within the context of both the micro- and the macrocommunity. Petraitis et al. (1995) proposed a social control theory which asserts that acceptance by or attachment to family, school, or community is a social bond to the conventional society. These social bonds prevent adolescents from expressing deviant behavior. According to this theory, the use of alcohol and other drugs is caused by a lack of social bonds. Petraitis et al.'s conceptualization of social control theory regarding adolescents' experimentation with drugs and alcohol is supported by the work of Segal and Stewart.

Segal and Stewart (1996) found that recent changes in cultural factors interact with individual factors in the development of substance abuse. They noted that a cultural vacuum, produced by the declining role of family values, leads to the glorification of fun and violence, as well as the use of alcohol and drugs associated with promiscuous sexual practice, as a means of escape from identity problems, frustration, disappointments, boredom, and so on. They also regard the imitation of adult behavior, curiosity, and a rebellion against age-related restrictions and taboos as reasons for adolescent drug use. These factors seem to apply both to the first experimental use of a substance and to the development of the abuse of alcohol and drugs. Segal and Stewart view the abuse of alcohol and other drugs as being associated with more serious psychological factors but do not provide specific empirical support for their thoughts.

Certain characteristics of neighborhoods also seem to contribute to the development of problems related to drug and alcohol use among their inhabitants. Hawkins, Catalano, and Miller (1992) reviewed several studies supporting the notion of "neighborhood disorganization" as a risk factor for adolescent drug abuse. This general term encompasses a variety of factors, including high population density, physical deterioration, high levels of adult crime, and illegal drug trafficking.

Hawkins and Weis (1985) proposed a developmental approach that integrates social control theory and social learning theory as an etiological explanation of delinquency. According to this approach, the person interacts sequentially with the smallest to the largest social system. Thus, "social development" is a process in which the most important units of socialization—families, schools, and peers—influence behavior sequentially, both directly and indirectly. Social bonding and attachments to family, school, and the community increase the level of commitment to conventionality among youths. However, youths develop attachment and commitment to conventionality only when they have opportunity to interact with conventional activities that provide positive experiences for them. The bonding of youths to the social norms occurs only when the youths' association with conventional units is more rewarding than their association with delinquent peers. Thus, the value and activities of conventionality must be viewed as rewarding. Poor parenting skills and high levels of family stress (often associated with parental substance abuse) fail to provide children with conventional values and attitudes (Azzi-Lessing & Olsen, 1996). Furthermore, the role of a particular culture as well as the value system of a neighborhood, has been changing in recent years and plays a significant role in the development of complex postindustrial society. These apparent changes are characterized as a decline in the support and interaction among neighbors, a weakening of the neighborhood's ability to exert social control, social disorganization, and the loss of a sense of continuity and belonging among neighborhood members. These social factors may result in an individual's increase in feelings of alienation, narcissistic escapism, and deviant behavior (Segal & Stewart, 1996). Hawkins et al. identified a deterioration in parental socialization and supervision, consistent with this explanation of neighborhood disorganization, as a risk factor in adolescent drug abuse.

Socioeconomic Status as a Risk Factor

Studies of the relationship between socioeconomic status and alcohol and other drug abuse have found a bimodal distribution of risk factors. Hawkins et al.'s (1992) review confirmed a positive correlation between parental education level and marijuana use and drinking among teens. However, the poverty associated with childhood behavior problems has been found to increase the risk for later alcoholism and drug problems (Robins & Ratcliff, 1979). The relationship of poverty to the development of drug abuse could be explained by the environmental conditions that define poverty, including unemployment, welfare dependency, single parenthood, and an abundance of illicit drugs in the neighborhood (Gitlin, 1990). In a study of alcohol abuse/dependence and associated patterns of psychiatric comorbidity in an Ontario, Canada, household sample, Ross (1995) found that high income was associated with pure alcohol abuse, but not with alcohol dependence. Low income was associated with alcohol dependence complicated by comorbid psychiatric disorders. Together, these findings suggest a complex role of socioeconomic status for both the etiology and the consequences of alcohol/substance use and abuse. Further research is needed to clarify the role of socioeconomic status in relation to the level of severity of use and abuse of substances, the specific types of substances abused, and other possible etiological factors, including comorbid psychopathology.

Social Policy Considerations

Social policy considerations, discussed in more detail in chapter 31 of this volume, can be considered more distal factors related to the etiology of substance abuse/dependence. Social policy influences the availability of substances to the population and the punitive effects of consuming particular substances. To some extent, lack of exposure and access to alcohol and drugs would serve as a protecting factor against use, abuse, and development of dependence on substances.

Over the years, society (through governmental action) has employed a variety of measures to restrict the availability of alcoholic beverages. Prohibition enacted through an amendment to the U.S. Constitution at the national level, local and federal taxation policies, and the legislation of minimum legal drinking ages have had both short- and long-term effects on the availability of beverage alcohol. Legal restrictions (e.g., based upon a minimum age) on the purchase of alcohol have had recent favor as a means of controlling adolescent morbidity and mortality resulting from alcohol use, apparently with some success. Between 1970 and 1975, when 29 states lowered their minimum legal drinking ages, increases in teen alcohol consumption, auto fatalities, and injuries were recorded. As the legal drinking age was raised over the following years, reductions in adolescent alcohol consumption (particularly beer), injuries, and auto fatalities were generally noted (Wagenaar, 1993).The effect of raising the minimum drinking age on the prevalence of other alcohol-related behaviors among adolescents, such as assaults, teen pregnancy, drownings, and sexually transmitted diseases, is less clear as is the effect on the incidence of alcohol abuse and dependence in subsequent years. Such changes are difficult to determine directly because minimum drinking laws vary across states, and because of the rather ready availability of alcohol from other sources.

Taxation has also been viewed as a means of controlling the availability of alcohol. The typical view is that higher taxes on alcohol (resulting in an increase in unit price) lead to reduced consumption. In general, increased taxes on (i.e., increased cost of)

alcoholic beverages are associated with decreased drinking. Manning et al. (1991) reported that both light and heavier drinkers appear to be less responsive to price than moderate drinkers. However, Kenkel (1996) noted that this effect may be due to a lack of information about the health consequences of heavy drinking among both the light and heavy drinkers rather than to concern over cost. In Kenkel's study, better informed consumers showed greater reductions in drinking due to price increases than less informed consumers, including heavy drinkers. The use of taxation to increase the cost of obtaining alcohol is not straightforward. Federal taxes on alcohol, for example, are applied uniformly on each unit of alcoholic beverage produced. However, different manufacturers and different retailers operating in a competitive market may choose to differentially pass this cost along to the consumer. Thus, the cost of alcohol may rise in some locales, but not in others.

Further, the cost of any particular brand of an alcoholic beverage may vary considerably within a specified geographic region, depending upon the type of establishment where the beverage is purchased. The package outlet price of a can of beer is typically lower than its cost at a restaurant, even though the unit tax is the same for both. This effect may be manifested through an "ability to pay" in relation to younger drinkers. Sloan, Reilly, and Schenzler (1994) estimated that the price of alcohol had a significant effect on motor vehicle fatalities among 18- to 20-year olds, but not older age groups.

SUMMARY

This chapter reviewed a variety of etiological factors that are related to development of alcohol and other drug abuse. While the biological factors, including genetics, and the neuropsychological factors have become increasingly important as etiological factors in the development of alcohol and other drug abuse problems, specific mechanisms of heredity are not known.

Further, each biological factor interacts with personality, behavior, and development within the context of environment in which a person grows up and resides. Several environmental factors appear to affect the expression of genetic factors. For example, a variety of studies indicate that peer influences, stressful and negative life events, and family environment (including poor parenting styles) seem to enhance the likelihood of developing alcohol or addictive drug use behavior among adolescents and young adults at high risk for developing problems with alcohol and other addictive substances. On the other hand, certain social and environmental factors appear to attenuate the risk for developing alcohol and drug use problems conferred by a family history of alcoholism or drug abuse. Good relations with non-drug-using peers, family rituals that actively seek to prevent alcohol/drug use, and consistency of parental discipline appear to reduce exposure to alcohol and drugs among youth. Reduced exposure reduces the likelihood that genes responsible for developing alcoholism or other drug use disorders will become activated (Hesselbrock & Hesselbrock, 1990).

The interaction between biological and environmental factors is constantly changing, and new models of etiology are being introduced. Prevention and treatment efforts should consider these new developments and evaluate their validity and applicability to work with those who are affected.

ACKNOWLEDGMENT   This work was supported by NIAAA grants P50-AA35010 and U10-AA08403.

Key References

Cadoret, J. J., & Wesner, R. B. (1990). Use of the adoption paradigm to elucidate the role of genes and environment and their interaction in the genesis of alcoholism. In C. R. Cloninger & H. Begleiter (Eds.), *Genetics and biology of alcoholism* (pp. 31–42). Cold Spring Harbor, NY: Cold Spring Harbor Laboratory Press.

Hesselbrock, V. (1995). The genetic epidemiology of alcoholism. In H. Begleiter & B. Kissin (Eds.), *The genetics of alcoholism* (pp. 17–39). New York: Oxford University Press.

National Institute on Alcohol Abuse and Alcoholism. (1993). Genetic and other risk factors for alcoholism. In *Alcohol and Health: Eighth Special Report to the U.S. Congress* (NIH Publication No. 94-3699, pp. 61–83). Washington, DC: National Institutes of Health.

References

Allport, G. W. (1937). *Personality: A psychological interpretation.* New York: Holt.

Annis, H. (1974). Patterns of inter-familial drug use. *British Journal of Addiction, 69,* 361–369.

August, G. J., & Stewart, M. A. (1983). Familial subtypes of childhood hyperactivity. *Journal of Nervous and Mental Disease, 170,* 147–154.

Azzi-Lessing, L., & Olsen, L. J. (1996). Substance abuse-affected families in the child welfare system: New challenges, new alliances. *Social Work, 41*(1), 15–23.

Babor, T. F., Dolinsky, Z. S., Meyer, R. E., Hesselbrock, M. N., Hofmann, M., & Tennen, H. (1992). Types of alcoholics: Concurrent and predictive validity of some common classification schemes. *British Journal of Addiction, 87,* 1415–1431.

Ball, S. A., Carroll, K. M., & Babor, T. F. (1995). Subtypes of cocaine abusers: Support for a type A-type B distinction. *Journal of Consulting and Clinical Psychology, 63*(1), 115–124.

Barron, A. P., & Earls, F. (1984). The relation of temperament and social factors to behavior problems in three-year-old children. *Jounal of Child Psychology and Psychiatry, 25*(1), 23–33.

Begleiter, H., Porjesz, B., Bihari, B., et al. (1984). Event related brain potentials in boys at risk for alcoholism. *Science, 225,* 1493–1495.

Bennett, L. A., & Wolin, S. J. (1990). Family culture and alcoholism transmission. In R. L. Collins, K. E. Leonard, & J. S. Searles (Eds.), *Alcohol and the Family: Research and Clinical Perspectives.* New York: Guilford Press.

Bennett, L. A., Wolin, S. J., Reiss, D., & Teitelbaum, M. A. (1987). Marital conflict resolution of alcoholic and nonalcoholic couples during drinking and non drinking sessions. *Journal of Studies on Alcohol, 40,* 183–195.

Bierut, L. J., Dinwiddie, S., Begleiter, H., Crowe, R. R., Heselbrock, V. M., Nurnberger, J. I., Jr., Schuckit, M. A., & Reich, T. R. (1998). Familial transmission of substance dependence: Alcohol, marijuana, and cocaine. *Archives of General Psychiatry, 55,* 982–988.

Blackson, T. C. (1994). Temperament: a salient correlate of risk factors for alcohol and drug abuse. *Drug and Alcohol Dependence, 36,* 205–214.

Blackson, T. C., & Tarter, R. E. (1994). Individual, family, and peer affiliation factors predisposing to early-age onset of alcohol and drug use. *Alcoholism: Clinical and Experimental Research, 18*(4), 813–821.

Block, J., Block, J. H., & Keyes, S. (1988). Longitudinally foretelling drug usage in adolescence: Early childhood personality and environmental precursors. *Child Development, 59,* 336–355.

Bohman, M., Sigvardsson, S., & Cloninger, C. (1981). Maternal inheritance of alcohol abuse: Cross-fostering analysis of adopted women. *Archives of General Psychiatry, 38,* 965–969.

Boyle, M. H., Offord, D. R., Racine, Y. A., Szatmary, P., Fleming, J. E., & Links, P. S. (1992). Predicting substance use in alte adolescence: Results from the Ontario child health study follow-up. *American Journal of Psychiatry, 149,* 761–767.

Branchey, M. H., Buydens-Branchey, L., & Horvath, T. B. (1993). Event-related potentials in substance-abusing individuals after long-term abstinence. *American Journal on Addictions, 2*(2), 141–148.

Branchey, M. H., Buydens-Branchey, L., & Lieber, C. S. (1988). P3 in alcoholics with disordered regulation of aggression. *Psychiatry Research, 25,* 49–58.

Buydens-Branchey, L., Branchey, M. H., & Noumair, D. (1989a). Age of alcoholism onset: Relationship to psychopathology. *Archives of General Psychiatry, 46,* 225–230.

Buydens-Branchey, L., Branchey, M. H., & Noumair, D. (1989b). Age of alcoholism onset: Relationship to susceptibility to serotonin precursor availability. *Archives of General Psychiatry, 46,* 231–236.

Cadoret, R. J., Cain, C. A., & Grove, W. M. (1980). Development of alcoholism in adoptees raised apart from alcoholic biologic relatives. *Archives of General Psychiatry, 37,* 561–563.

Cadoret, J. J., & Wesner, R. B. (1990). Use of the adoption paradigm to elucidate the role of genes and environment and their interaction in the genesis of alcoholism. In C. R. Cloninger & H. Begleiter (Eds.), *Genetics and biology of alcoholism* (pp. 31–42). Cold Spring Harbor, NY: Cold Spring Harbor Laboratory Press.

Cadoret, R. J., Yates, W. R., Troughton, E., Woodworth, G., & Stewart, M. A. (1995). Adoption study demonstrating two genetic pathways to drug abuse. *Archives of General Psychiatry, 52,* 42–52.

Cahalan, D., & Room, R. (1974). *Problem drinking among American men.* New Brunswick, NJ: Rutgers Center of Alcohol Studies.

Cattell, R. B. (1947). Confirmation and clarification of primary personality factors. *Psychometrica 12,* 197–220.

Cloninger, C. R. (1987). Neurogenetic adaptive mechanisms in alcoholism. *Science, 236,* 410–416.

Cloninger, C. R., Bohman, M., & Sigvardsson, S. (1981). Inheritance of alcohol abuse: Cross-fostering analysis of adopted men. *Archives of General Psychiatry, 38,* 861–868.

Cloninger, C. R., Christiansen, K. O., Reich, T., & Gottesman, I. (1978). Implications of sex differences in the prevalence of antisocial personality, alcoholism, and criminality for models of familial transmission. *Archives of General Psychiatry, 35,* 941–951.

Cloninger, C. R., & Gottesman, I. I. (1987). Genetic and environmental factors in antisocial behavior disorders. In S. Mednick, T. Moffitt, & S. Stack (Eds.), *The cause of crime: New biological approaches.* New York: Cambridge University Press.

Cotton, N. (1979). The familial incidence of alcoholism. *Journal of Studies on Alcohol, 40,* 89–116.

Croughan, J. L. (1985). Contribution of family studies to understanding drug abuse. In L. N. Robins (Ed.), *Studying drug abuse* (series in psychosomatic epidemiology, Vol. 6, pp. 93–116). New Brunswick, NJ: Rutgers University Press.

Davis, D. I., Berenson, D., Steinglass, P., & Davis, S. (1974). The adaptive consequences of drinking. *Psychiatry, 37,* 209–215.

Deckel, A. W., Bauer, L., & Hesselbrock, V. (1995). Anterior brain dysfunctioning as a risk factor in alcoholic behaviors. *Addiction, 90,* 1323–1334.

DelBoca, F., & Hesselbrock, M. N. (1996). Gender and alcoholic subtypes. *Alcohol, Health and Research World, 20,* 56–62.

DeObaldia, R., Parsons, O., & Yohman, J. (1983). Minimal brain dysfunction symptoms claimed by primary and secondary alcoholics: Relation to cognitive functioning. *International Journal of Neuroscience, 20,* 173–182.

Eron, L., & Huessman, L. (1990). The stability of aggressive behavior—even unto the third generation. In M. Lewis & S. Miller (Eds.), *Handbook of developmental psychopathology* (pp. 147–156). New York: Plenum Press.

Feingold, A., Ball, S. A., Kranzler, H. R., & Rounsaville, B. J. (1996) Generalizability of the Type A/Type B distinction across different psychoactive substances. *American Journal of Drug and Alcohol Abuse, 22*(3), 449–462.

Freeman, E. M., & Dyer, L. (1993, September). High-risk children and adolescents: Family and community environments. *Families in Society: The Journal of Contemporary Human Services,* pp. 422–431.

Gillmore, M. R. (1990). Racial differences in acceptability and availability of drugs and early initiation of substance use. *American Journal of Drug and Alcohol Abuse, 16,* 185–206.

Gitlin, T. (1990). On drugs and mass media in America's consumer society. In Resnik (Ed.), *Youth and drugs: Society's mixed messages* (pp. 31–52). OSAP Prevention Monograph 6. Rockville, MD: U.S. Department of Health and Human Services.

Glenn, S. W., & Nixon, S. J. (1991). Application of Cloninger's subtypes in a female alcoholic sample. *Alcoholism: Clinical and Experimental Research 15,* 851–857.

Goodwin, D. W. (1979). Alcoholism and heredity: A review and hypothesis. *Archives of General Psychiatry. 36*, 57–61.

Goodwin, D. W. (1984). Studies of familial alcoholism: A review. *Journal of Clinical Psychiatry, 45*, 14–17.

Goodwin, D. W., Schulsinger, F., Moller, N., Hermansen, L., Winokur, G., & Guze, S. (1974). Drinking problems in adopted and nonadopted sons of alcoholics. *Archives of General Psychiatry, 31*, 164–169.

Harford, T., & Grant, B. (1987). Psychosocial factors in adolescent drinking contexts. *Journal of Studies on Alcohol, 48*, 551–557.

Hawkins, J. D., Catalano, R. F., & Miller, J. Y. (1992). Risk and protective factors for alcohol and other drug problems in adolescence and early adulthood: Implications for substance abuse prevention. *Psychological Bulletin, 112*(1), 64–105.

Hawkins, J. D., & Weis, J. G. (1985). The social development model: An integrated approach to delinquency prevention. *Journal of Primary Prevention, 6*(2), 73–97.

Hayakawa, K. (1987). Smoking and drinking discordance and health condition: Japanese identical twins reared apart and together. *Acta Geneticae Medicae et Gemellologiae, 36*, 493–502.

Heath, A. C., Meyer, J., Jardine, R., & Martin, N. G. (1991) The inheritance of alcohol consumption patterns in a general population twin sample: 2. Determinants of consumption frequency and quantity consumed. *Journal of Studies on Alcohol, 52*, 425–433.

Hesselbrock, M. N. (1986a). Alcoholic typologies: A review of empirical evaluations of common classification schemes. In M. Galanter (Ed.), *Recent development in alcoholism* (Vol. 4, pp. 191–206). New York: Plenum.

Hesselbrock, M. N. (1986b). Childhood behavior problems and adult antisocial personality disorder in alcoholism. In R. E. Meyer (Ed.), *Psychopathology and addictive disorders* (pp. 78–94). New York: Guilford Press.

Hesselbrock, M. N. (1991). Gender comparison of antisocial personality disorder and depression in alcoholism. *Journal of Substance Abuse, 3*, 205–209

Hesselbrock, M. N. (1995). Genetic determinants of alcoholic subtypes. In H. Begleiter & B. Kissin (Eds.), *The genetics of alcoholism* (pp. 40–69). New York: Oxford University Press.

Hesselbrock, M. N., & Hesselbrock, V. (1992). Relationship of family history, antisocial personality disorder and personality traits in young men at risk for alcoholism. *Journal of Studies on Alcohol, 53*, 619–625.

Hesselbrock, M. N., Hesselbrock, V., Babor, T. F., Stabenau, J. R., Meyer, R. E., & Weidenman, M. (1984). Antisocial behavior, psychopathology and problem drinking in the natural history of alcoholism. In D. W. Goodwin, K. T. Van Dusen, & S. A. Mednick (Eds.), *Longitudinal research in alcoholism* (pp. 197–214). Boston: Kluwer-Nijhoff.

Hesselbrock, V. (1995). The genetic epidemiology of alcoholism. In H. Begleiter & B. Kissin (Eds.), *The genetics of alcoholism* (pp. 17–39). New York: Oxford University Press.

Hesselbrock, V., Bauer, L. O., Hesselbrock, M. N., & Gillen, R. (1991). Neuropsychological factors in individuals at high risk for alcoholism. In M. Galanter (Ed.), *Recent developments in alcoholism* (Vol. 9, pp. 21–29). New York: Plenum Press.

Hesselbrock, V., Hesselbrock, M. N., & Stabenau, J. R. (1985). Alcoholism in men patients subtyped by family history and antisocial personality. *Journal of Studies on Alcohol, 46*(1), 59–64.

Hesselbrock, V., O'Connor, S., Tasman, A., & Weidenman, M. (1988). Cognitive and evoked potential indications of risk for alcoholism in young men. In K. Kuriyama, A. Takada, & H. Ishii (Eds.), *Biomedical and social aspects of alcohol and alcoholism: Proceedings of the Fourth Congress of the International Society for Biomedical Research on Alcoholism* (ISBRA). Kyoto, Japan, June 26–July 2. (pp. 583–585). Amsterdam: Excerpta Medica.

Hesselbrock, V., Bauer, L., O'Connor, S., & Gillen, R. (1993). Reduced P300 amplitude in relation to family history of alcoholism and antisocial personality disorder among young men at risk for alcoholism. *Alcohol and Alcoholism* (Suppl. 2), 95–100.

Hesselbrock, V. M., & Hesselbrock, M. N. (1990). Behavioral/social factors that may enhance or attenuate genetic effects. In C. R. Cloninger and H. Begleiter (Eds.), *Banbury Report 33: Genetics and biology of alcoholism* (pp. 75–85). New York: Cold Spring Harbor.

Hill, S. Y., Cloninger, R. C., & Ayre, F. R. (1977). Independent familial transmission of alcoholism and opiate abuse. *Alcoholism: Clinical and Experimental Research, 1*, 1335–1342.

Irwin, M., Schuckit, M., & Smith, T. (1990). Clinical importance of age at onset in Type 1 and Type 2 primary alcoholics. *Archives of General Psychiatry, 47*, 320–324.

Jones, M. C. (1968) Personality correlates and antecedents of drinking patterns in adult males. *Journal of Consulting and Clinical Psychology, 32*, 2–12.

Kandel, D. B., Kessler, R. C., & Margulies, R. Z. (1978). Antecedents of adolescent initiation into stages of drug use: A developmental analysis. *Journal of Youth and Adolescence, 7,* 13–40.

Kandel, D., Simcha-Fagan, O., & Davies, M. (1986). Risk factors for deliquency and illicit drug use from adolescence to young adulthood. *Journal of Drug Issues, 16*(1), 67–90.

Kaprio, J., Koskenvuo, M., Langinvainio, H., Romanov, K., Sarna, S., & Rose, R. J. (1987). Genetic influence on use and abuse of alcohol: A study of 5,638 adult Finnish twin brothers. *Alcoholism: Clinical and Experimental Research, 11,* 349–356.

Kendler, K. S. (1995). Genetic epidemiology in psychiatry; Taking both genes and environment seriously: Commentary. *Archives of General Psychiatry, 52,* 895–899.

Kendler, K., Heath, A. C., Neale, M. C., Kessler, R. C., & Eaves, L. J. (1992). A population-based twin study of alcoholism in women. *Journal of the American Medical Association, 268,* 1877–1882.

Kenkel, D. S. (1996) New estimates of the optimal tax on alcohol. *Economic Inquiry, 34,* 296–319.

Khantzian, E. J., Halliday, K. S., & McAuliffe, W. E. (1990). *Addiction and the vulnerable self: Modified dynamic group therapy for substance abusers.* New York: Guilford Press.

Krystal, H. (1984). Character disorders: Characterological specificity and the alcoholic. In E. M. Pattison & E. Kaufman (Eds.), *Encyclopedic handbook of alcoholism.* New York: Gardner Press.

Kushner, M. G., Sher, K. J., Wood, M. D., & Wood, P. K. (1994). Anxiety and drinking behavior: Moderating effects of tension-reduction alcohol outcome expectancies. *Alcoholism: Clinical and Experimental Research, 18*(4), 852–860.

Leeds, J., & Morgenstern, J. (1995). Psychoanalytic theories of substance abuse. In F. Rotgers, D. S. Keller, & J. Morgenstern (Eds.), *Treating substance abuse: Theory and technique* (pp. 68–83). New York: Guilford Press.

Lerner, J. V., & Vicary J. R. (1984). Difficult temperament and drug use: Analyses from the New York Longitudinal Study. *Journal of Drug Education, 14,* 1–8.

Lipscomb, T. R., Carpenter, J. A., & Nathan, P. E. (1979). Static ataxia: A predictor of alcoholism? *British Journal of the Addictions, 74,* 289–294.

Loeber, R., & Dishion, T. (1983). Early predictors of male deliquency: A review. *Psychological Bulletin, 94*(1), 68–99.

Loeber, R., Stouthamer, M., Van Kammen, W., & Farrington, D. (1991). Initiation, escalation, and desistence in juvenile offending and their correlates. *Journal of Criminal Law and Criminology, 82,* 36–82.

Loney, J. (1980). The Iowa theory of substance abuse among hyperactive adolescents. In J. J. Lettieri, M. Sayers, & H. W. Pearson (Eds.), *Theories on drug abusers: Selected contemporary perspectives.* NIDA Research Monograph #30. Rockville, MD: National Institute on Drug Abuse.

Lyons, M. J., True, W. R., Eisen, S. A., Goldberg, J., Meyer, J. M., Faraone, S. V., Eaves, L. J., & Tsuang, M. T. (1995). Differential heritability of adult and juvenile antisocial traits. *Archives of General Psychiatry, 52,* 906–915.

Manning, W. G., Keeler, E. B., Newhouse, J. P., Sloss, E. M, & Wasserman, J. (1991). *The costs of poor health habits: A RAND study.* London: Harvard University Press.

Martin, C. S., Kaczynski, N. A., Maisto, S. A., & Tarter, R. E. (1996). Polydrug use in adolescent drinkers with and without DSM-IV alcohol abuse and dependence. *Alcoholism: Clinical and Experimental Research, 20,* 1099–1108.

Martin, E. D., & Sher, K. J. (1994). Family history of alcoholism, alcohol use disorders, and the five factor model of personality. *Journal of Studies on Alcohol, 55,* 81–90.

Masse, L. C., & Tremblay, R. E. (1997). Behavior of boys in kindergarten and the onset of substance use during adolescence. *Archives of General Psychiatry, 54,* 62–68.

Mattes, J., & Fink, M. (1987). A family study of patients with temper outbursts. *Journal of Psychiatric Research, 21,* 249–255.

McCord, W., & McCord, J. (1960). *Origins of alcoholism.* Stanford, CA: Stanford University Press.

McCrady, B. S., & Epstein, E. E. (1996). Theoretical bases of family approaches. In F. Rotgers, D. S. Keller, & J. Morgenstern (Eds.), *Treating substance abuse: Theory and Technique.* New York: Guilford Press.

McCrady, B. S., Kahler, C., & Epstein, E. E. (1998). Families of alcoholics. In N. N. Singh (Ed.), *Comprehensive clinical psychology: Vol. 9. Applications in diverse populations* (pp. 199–218). Oxford, England: Elsevier Science.

McDougall, J. (1989). *Theaters of the body.* New York: Norton.

McGue, M., Pickens, R. W., & Svikis, D. S. (1992). Sex and age effects on the inheritance of alcohol problems: A twin study. *Journal of Abnormal Psychology, 101,* 3–17.

Merikangas, K. R. (1990). The genetic epidemiology of alcoholism. *Psychological Medicine, 20,* 11–22.

Meuller, W. H., Rinehart, R., Cadoret, R., & Troughton, E. (1988). Specific familial transmission in substance abuse. *International Journal of the Addictions*, 23, 1029–1039.

Mezzich, A., Tarter, R., Kinsci, L., Clark, D., Bukstein, O., & Martin, C. (1993). Subtypes of early onset alcoholism. *Alcoholism: Clinical and Experimental Research*, 17, 767–770.

Mirin, S., Weiss, R., & Michael, J. (1986). Family pedigree and psychopathology in substance abusers. In R. E. Meyer (Ed.), *Psychopathology and addictive disorders* (pp. 57–77). New York: Guilford Press.

Mirin, S. M., Weiss, R. D., Sollogub, A., & Michael, J. (1984). Psychopathology in families of drug abusers. In S. M. Mirin (Ed), *Substance abuse and psychopathology* (pp. 79–106). Washington, DC: American Psychiatric Association Press.

Moffit, T. (1993). Adolescence—Limited and life-course-persistent antisocial behavior. *Psychology Review*, 100, 674–701.

Morgenstern, J., & Leeds, J. (1993). Contemporary psychoanalytic theories of substance abuse: A disorder in search of a paradigm. *Psychotherapy*, 30, 194–206.

Murphy, K., & Barkley, R. A. (1996). Attention deficit hyperactivity disorder adults: comorbidities and adaptive impairments. *Comprehensive Psychiatry*, 37, 393–401.

National Institute on Alcohol Abuse and Alcoholism. (1993). Genetic and other risk factors for alcoholism. In *Alcohol and Health: Eighth Special Report to the U.S. Congress* (NIH Publication No. 94-3699, pp. 61–83). Washington, DC: National Institutes of Health.

O'Connell, D. F. (1989). Treating the high risk adolescent: A survey of effective programs and interventions. In P. B. Henry (Ed.), *Practical approaches in treating adolescent chemical dependency: A guide to clinical assessment and intervention* (pp. 49–69). New York: Haworth Press.

O'Connor, S., Hesselbrock, V., & Tasman, A. (1986). Correlates of increased risk for alcoholism in young men. *Progress in Neuropsychopharmacology and Biological Psychiatry*, 10, 211–218.

Ohannessian, C. M., & Hesselbrock, V. (1995). Temperament and personality typologies in adult offspring of alcoholics. *Journal of Studies on Alcohol*, 56, 318–327.

Pedersen, N., Friberg, L., Floderus-Myrhed, B., McClearn, G. E., & Plomin, R. (1984). Swedish early separated twins: Identification and characterization. *Acta Geneticae Medicae et Gemellologiae*, 33, 243–250.

Penick, E. C., Powell, B. J., Nickel, E. J., Read, M. R., Gabrieli, W. F., & Liskow, B. I. (1990). Examination of Cloninger's Type I and Type II alcoholism with a sample of men alcoholics in treatment. *Alcoholism: Clinical and Experimental Research*, 14, 623–629.

Petraitis, J., Flay, B. R., & Miller, T. Q. (1995). Reviewing theories of adolescent substance use: Organizing pieces in the puzzle. *Psychological Bulletin*, 117(1), 67–86.

Pickens, R. W., Sivikis, D. S., McGue, M., Lykken, D. T., Heston, L. L., & Clayton, P. J. (1991). Heterogeneity in the inheritance of alcoholism: A study of male and female twins. *Archives of General Psychiatry*, 48, 10–28.

Plomin, R., Nitz, K., & Rowe, D. (1990). Behavioral genetics and aggressive behavior in childhood. In M. Lewis & S. Miller (Eds.), *Handbook of developmental psychopathology* (pp. 119–133). New York: Plenum Press.

Porjesz, B., & Begleiter, H. (1985). Human brain electrophysiology and alcoholism. In R. E. Tarter & D. Van Thiel (Eds.), *Alcohol and the brain*. New York: Plenum Press.

Reich, T. R., Cloninger, C. R., Lewis, C., & Rice, J. P. (1981) Some recent findings in the study of genotype-environment interaction in alcoholism. In R. E. Meyer (Ed.), *Evaluation of the alcoholic: Implications for research, theory, and treatment*. Washington, DC: Government Printing Office.

Robins, L. N. (1966). *Deviant children grown-up*. Baltimore: Williams & Wilkins.

Robins, L. N., & McEvoy, L. T. (1990). Conduct problems as predictors of substance abuse. In L. N. Robins & M. R. Rutter (Eds.), *Straight and devious pathways to adulthood*. Cambridge, England: Cambridge University Press.

Robins, L. N., & Price, R. K. (1991). Adult disorders predicted by childhood conduct problems: Results form the NIMH Epidemiologic Catchment Area Project. *Psychiatry*, 54, 116–132.

Robins, L. N., & Ratcliff, K. S. (1979). Risk factors in the continuation of childhood antisocial behavior into adulthood. *International Journal of Mental Health*, 7, 526–530.

Ross, H. E. (1995). DSM-III-R alcohol abuse and dependence and psychiatric comorbidity in Ontario: Results from the mental health supplement to the Ontario health survey. *Drug and Alcohol Dependence*, 39, 111–128.

Rotgers, F. (1996). Behavioral theory of substance abuse treatment: Bringing science to bear on practice. In F. Rotgers, D. S. Keller, & J. Morgenstern (Eds.), *Treating substance abuse: Theory and technique*. New York: Guilford Press.

Rothbart, M. K., & Ahadi, S. A. (1994). Temperament and the development. *Journal of Abnormal Psychology*, 103(1), 55–66.

Rounsaville, B., Weissman, M. M., Kleber, H., & Wilber, C. (1982). Heterogeneity of psychiatric diagnosis in treated opiate addicts. *Archives of General Psychiatry, 39,* 161–166.

Schuckit, M. (1980). Self-rating alcohol intoxication by young men with and without family histories of alcoholism. *Journal of Studies on Alcohol, 41,* 242–249.

Schuckit, M.A. (1985). Ethanol-induced changes in body sway seen at high alcoholism risk. *Archives of General Psychiatry, 42,* 375–379.

Schuckit, M. A. (1987). Biological vulnerability to alcoholism. *Journal of Consulting and Clinical Psychology, 55,* 301–310.

Schuckit, M. A., Gold, E. O., & Risch, C. (1987). Serum prolactin levels in sons of alcoholic and control subjects. *American Journal of Psychiatry, 144,* 854–859.

Schuckit, M. A., & Hesselbrock, V. (1995). Alcohol dependence and anxiety disorders: What is the relationship? *American Journal of Psychiatry, 151,* 1723–1734.

Schuckit, M. A., Hesselbrock, V., Tipp, J., Nurnberger, J. I., Anthenelli, R. M., & Crowe, R. R. (1995). The prevalence of major anxiety disorders in relatives of alcohol dependent men and women. *Journal of Studies on Alcohol, 56,* 309–317.

Schuckit, M. A., Irwin, M., & Mahler, H. (1990). Tridimensional Personality Questionnaire scores of sons of alcoholic and nonalcoholic fathers. *American Journal of Psychiatry, 147,* 481–487.

Segal, B. M., & Stewart, J. C. (1996). Substance use and abuse in adolescence: An overview. *Child Psychiatry and Human Development, 26,* 193–210.

Sher, K. J. (1991). *Children of alcoholics: A critical appraisal of theory and research.* Chicago: University of Chicago Press.

Sherman, J. E., Jorenby, D. E., & Baker, T. B. (1988). Classical conditioning with alcohol: Acquired preferences and aversions, tolerance, and urges/cravings. In C. D. Chaudron & D. A. Wilkinson (Eds.), *Theories on alcoholism* (pp. 173–237). Toronto: Addiction Research Foundation.

Siegel, S. (1979). The role of conditioning in drug tolerance and addiction. In J. D. Keehn (Ed.), *Psychopathology in animals: Research and treatment implications.* New York: Academic Press.

Sigvardsson, S., Bohman, M., & Cloninger, C. R. (1996). Replication of the Stockholm adoption study of alcoholism. *Archives of General Psychiatry, 53,* 681–687.

Sloan, F. A., Reilly, B. A., & Schenzler, C. M. (1994). Effects of price, civil, and criminal sanctions, and law enforcement on alcohol-related mortality. *Journal of Studies on Alcohol, 55,* 454–465.

Smart, R., & Fejer, D. (1972). Drug use among adolescents and their parents. *Journal of Abnormal Psychology, 79,* 153–160.

Stabenau, J. R. (1992). Is risk for substance abuse unitary? *Journal of Nervous and Mental Disease, 180(9),* 583–588.

Steinglass, P., Bennett, L. A., Wolin, S. J., & Reiss, D. (1987). *The alcoholic family.* New York: Basic Books.

Steinglass, P., Weiner, S., & Mendelson, J. H. (1971). Interactional issues as determinants of alcoholism. *American Journal of Psychiatry, 128,* 275–280.

Stewart, M. A., deBlois, G. S., & Cummings, C. (1980). Psychiatric disorder in the parents of hyperactive boys and those with conduct disorder. *Journal of Child Psychology and Psychiatry, 21,* 283–292.

Tarter, R E. (1988). Are there inherited behavioral traits that predispose to substance abuse? *Journal of Consulting and Clinical Psychology, 56,* 189–196.

Tarter, R. E., Kabene, M., Escallier, E. A., Laird, S. B., & Jacob, T. (1990). Temperament deviation and risk for alcoholism. *Alcoholism: Clinical & Experimental Research, 14,* 380–382.

Tarter, R. E., McBride, H., Buopane, N., & Schneider, D. (1977). Differentiation of alcoholics according to childhood history of minimal brain dysfunction, family history, and drinking patterns. *Archives of General Psychiatry, 43,* 761–768.

Vanclay, F. M., & Raphael, B. (1990). Type 1 and Type 2 alcoholics: Schuckit and Irwin's negative findings. *British Journal of the Addictions. 78,* 317–326.

von Knorring, L., von Knorring, A.-L., Smigan, L., Lindberg, U., & Edholm, M. (1987). Personality traits in subtypes of alcoholics. *Journal of Studies on Alcohol, 48,* 523–527.

Wagenaar, A. C. (1993). Minimum drinking age and alcohol availability to youth: Issues and research needs. In M. E. Hilton & G. Bloss (Eds.), *Economics and the prevention of alcohol-related problems.* (pp. 175–200). National Institute on Alcohol Abuse and Alcoholism Research Monograph No. 25. Washington, DC: Government Printing Office.

Wikler, A. (1973). Dynamics of drug dependence: Implications of a conditioning theory for research and treatment. *Archives of General Psychiatry, 28,* 611–616.

Wills, T. A., Vaccaro, D., & McNamara, G. (1992). The role of life events, family support, and competence in adolescent substance use: A test of vulnerability and protective factors. *American Journal of Community Psychology, 20(3),* 349–374.

Windle, M. (1996). An alcohol involvement typology for adolescents: Convergent validity and longitudinal stability. *Journal of Studies on Alcohol, 57,* 627–637.

Wolin, S. J., Bennett, L. A., Noonan, D. L., & Teitelbaum, M. A. (1980). Disrupted family rituals: A factor in the intergenerational transmission of alcoholism. *Journal of Studies on Alcohol, 41,* 199–214.

Wurmser, L. (1984). The role of superego conflicts in substance abuse and their treatment. *International Journal of Psychoanalytic Psychotherapy, 10,* 227–258.

Zucker, R. A., & Gomberg, E. (1986). Etiology of alcoholism reconsidered: The case for a biopsychosocial process. *American Psychologist, 41,* 783–793.

II

Specific Drugs of Abuse: Pharmacological and Clinical Aspects

4

Alcohol

Darlene H. Moak
Raymond F. Anton

Among substances commonly abused by humans, alcohol has by far the simplest structure, consisting of only two carbon atoms, six hydrogen atoms, and a single oxygen atom. It is also a relatively "weak" drug, since *grams* of alcohol must be consumed in order to achieve any measurable effect in contrast to the milligram (1/1000 gram) dosages of other abused substances. Alcohol, in contrast to other abused substances, is a legal or licit substance (at least for persons over a certain age). Yet the misuse and abuse of alcohol result in a complex biological, psychological, and social disorder of enormous impact on society. In 1993, the last year for which complete statistics are available, alcohol was believed to be responsible for 19,557 deaths, with an age-adjusted death rate of 6.7 per 100,000 (Gardner & Hudson, 1996), and to cost American society close to $100 billion annually in loss of life, property, and productivity.

This chapter will address the basic biological properties of this drug and its impact on human function, including the metabolic pathways for alco-

hol; its actions in the central nervous system; the physical symptoms of use, abuse, and dependence; the symptoms and course of alcohol withdrawal; and the pathological effects of its use. The diagnosis and treatment of the alcohol use disorders will be addressed in a subsequent chapters.

MAJOR PHARMACOLOGICAL ACTIONS

Metabolic Pathways

Metabolism is the process by which the human body converts an ingested substance to other compounds which are either more or less toxic than the parent compound. The primary metabolic pathway by which alcohol is detoxified, shown in figure 4.1, is "oxidation," most of which takes place in the liver. A small amount, about 5–10% of alcohol consumed under normal conditions, bypasses this pathway and is excreted unchanged from the lungs or in the

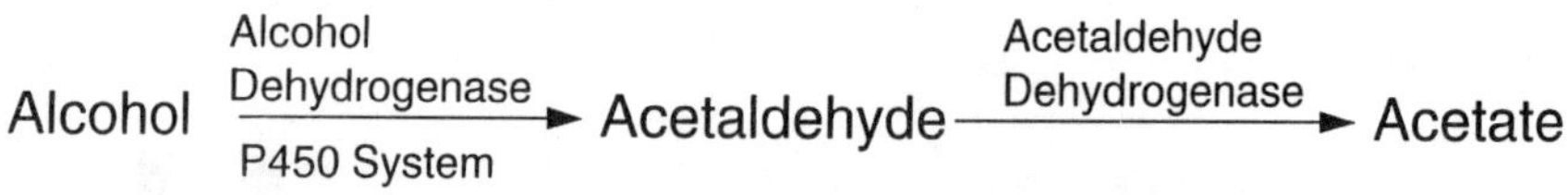

Alcohol $\xrightarrow[\text{P450 System}]{\text{Alcohol Dehydrogenase}}$ Acetaldehyde $\xrightarrow{\text{Acetaldehyde Dehydrogenase}}$ Acetate

FIGURE 4.1 Metabolism of alcohol via the major pathway, oxidation.

urine. Oxidation of alcohol in the liver is accomplished through the action of the enzyme alcohol dehydrogenase, which converts alcohol to acetaldehyde. Acetaldehyde, in turn, is converted to acetate by aldehyde dehydrogenase. This metabolic pathway has been known since the 1940s.

Although alcohol dehydrogenase is contained largely in the human liver, it is also found in the lining of the stomach. Alcohol dehydrogenase in the stomach may play a major role in alcohol metabolism (Haber et al., 1996), although the exact contribution of this gastric component remains somewhat controversial. Women appear to have less alcohol dehydrogenase in the stomach lining than men and, consequently, less activity of this enzyme (Frezza et al., 1990). Thus, women may develop liver damage after less extensive drinking careers than men because of exposure of the liver to higher alcohol concentrations. It is now known that there are at least eight subtypes, or isozymes, of human alcohol dehydrogenase in the liver alone (Ehrig, Bosron, & Li, 1990), and many of the genes responsible for their expression have been identified.

The enzyme aldehyde dehydrogenase has also been studied extensively. The widely used medication disulfiram (Antabuse) exerts its effect on alcohol metabolism by inhibiting the activity of aldehyde dehydrogenase. This inhibitor causes a buildup of the toxic metabolite acetaldehyde, which is normally present in only very small amounts in individuals consuming alcohol. This buildup, in turn causes a distressing clinical syndrome characterized by extreme flushing, nausea, and decreased blood pressure (the "disulfiram reaction"). Only two genetic variants of this enzyme have been identified. Most individuals of Asian background have a variant with low activity, which results in poor tolerance of alcohol consumption and relatively low rates of alcohol dependence (Mizoi et al., 1983).

Alcohol is also metabolized via an alternative pathway involving the liver enzyme cytochrome P450IIE1 (CYP2E1). This pathway exhibits increased activity in individuals who have ingested alcohol chronically (Lieber, 1994). Acetaminophen

(Tylenol) is also metabolized by CYP2E1, and in chronic heavy drinkers, there is evidence that acetaminophen use results in liver damage due to the accumulation of toxic metabolites (Seeff, Cuccherini, Zimmerman, Adler, & Benjamin, 1986). The CYP2E1 system is also responsible for the metabolism of many other medications, and the increased activity of this system in chronic heavy drinkers typically results in lower blood levels for many important medications (Kalant, Khanna, Lin, & Chung, 1976).

Actions in the Central Nervous System

Impact on Neurotransmitter Systems

Unlike other substances of abuse, which typically affect a particular transmitter system more strongly than others (e.g., dopamine in the case of cocaine and the opioid system in the case of heroin), alcohol is believed to affect many different neurotransmitter systems, with no single system predominating. The findings of animal research have been reviewed recently by De Witte (1996). Acute alcohol consumption in animals enhances release of serotonin, gamma aminobutyric acid (GABA), and taurine. However, chronic alcohol consumption decreases serotonin release and increases concentrations of endogenous opioid peptides and glutamate binding sites. Most likely the reward pathways mediated by dopamine are also involved (Koob, 1992). Subtypes of receptors in each transmitter system probably play an important role in the initiation and maintenance of drinking behaviors.

The possible interactions of neurotransmitter systems and alcohol in the human brain have been explored by Kranzler and Anton (1994) and are outlined in table 4.1. A key tenet of these relationships is that the dysfunctions in transmitter systems probably vary among subtypes of individuals affected by alcohol use disorders. Naltrexone, an opioid receptor blocker, has been found to be efficacious in the treatment of alcohol-dependent subjects, a finding that suggests the direct or indirect involvement of the opi-

TABLE 4.1 Relationships of Alcohol and Neurotransmitter Systems

Neurotransmitter system	Relationship to alcohol	Possible clinical manifestations
GABA-A	Enhanced activity with acute exposure Desensitization with chronic exposure	Sedation Withdrawal symptoms, seizures
Dopamine	Increased release of dopamine (may be mediated by opioidergic mechanism) during acute exposure	Stimulation of motor system, reinforcing properties of alcohol
Opioid	Decreased basal levels of beta-endorphins in abstinent alcoholics and in children of alcoholics	Increased craving
	Inhibition of opioid receptor binding by opioid antagonists	Decreased alcohol consumption, decreased tendency to relapse
Serotonin	Alcohol causes increased serotonergic activity in brain (may "normalize" low baseline levels)	Low serotonin levels in central nervous system may be associated with impulsivity and tendency toward violence
	Serotonin agonists decrease alcohol intake in animals; inconsistent results on alcohol intake in human studies	
N-methyl-D-aspartate (NMDA) and glutamate	Inhibition of transmission with acute exposure to alcohol	None identified at this time
	Possible upregulation of NMDA receptors with chronic exposure to alcohol	Behavioral tolerance Seizures Alcoholic dementia due to loss of long-term potentiation (needed for memory)

Note. From Kranzler and Anton (1994).

oid system (O'Malley et al., 1992; Volpicelli, Alterman, Hayashida, & O'Brien, 1992). An important role for the serotonergic system is supported by findings of decreased metabolites of serotonin in the cerebrospinal fluid of alcohol-dependent individuals (Ballenger, Goodwin, Major, & Brown, 1979). Treatment studies utilizing medications that alter serotonergic function have shown varying results, depending on the population studied (Kranzler et al., 1995; Sellers, Higgins, Tompkins, & Romach, 1992). A new medication, acamprosate, which is believed to modulate the action of the excitatory amino acid glutamate, has been shown to be helpful in improving outcomes (Sass, Soyka, Mann, & Zieglgansberger, 1996). Ultimately, combinations of pharmacotherapy that impact on several different neurotransmitter systems may be of help in treating individuals with alcohol use disorders. This approach will be explored in greater detail in chapter 19.

Mechanisms of Tolerance and Dependence

Tolerance is defined as a reduction over time in the behavioral effects after ingestion of the same dose of alcohol. Tolerance has been shown to develop rapidly in both animals and humans. Mechanisms underlying the development of tolerance in humans include increasing the activity (induction) of the enzymes responsible for the metabolism of alcohol as outlined above (metabolic tolerance), the ability of an organism to function in spite of the presence of alcohol (behavioral tolerance), and adaptation of central nervous system cells to the effects of alcohol (neuronal tolerance) (Harris & Buck, 1990).

Behavioral tolerance has been shown to be environmentally dependent in animals (Tabakoff & Melchior, 1981), since mice who developed tolerance in one environment showed less tolerance in a novel environment. The N-methyl-D-aspartate (NMDA) receptor may be particularly important in this process (Szabo, Tabakoff, & Hoffman, 1994).

As a finding of great theoretical and practical interest, sons of alcoholics who show less intoxication (i.e., demonstrate greater tolerance) when given a single dose of alcohol are at higher risk of subsequent development of alcohol use disorders. This finding suggests that more rapid development of tolerance in individuals with a family history of alcoholism may be genetically mediated (Schuckit & Smith, 1997).

While tolerance and physical dependence may share some mechanisms, there appear to be significant differences between these two processes as well. Not all individuals who exhibit tolerance to alcohol are physically dependent, and conversely, some individuals who are physically dependent on alcohol may not display tolerance. Physical dependence on alcohol occurs when central nervous system cells require the presence of alcohol to function normally. When alcohol intake is discontinued, there are clear signs of withdrawal. Although withdrawal can be demonstrated after smaller doses of alcohol in both animals and humans (the typical "hangover"), a more severe syndrome is seen after prolonged, chronic use of alcohol. This syndrome will be more fully described later in this chapter.

The propensity to develop physical dependence may also be genetically mediated. Different strains of mice have been bred which are differentially sensitive to withdrawal seizures (Phillips, Feller, & Crabbe, 1989). Although the exact mechanism by which physical dependence develops is not known, there is evidence to support a role for several different central nervous system pathways. These include changes in neuronal membranes (Hunt, 1985); changes in excitability and function of nerve cells mediated through the transport of charged atoms (ions) especially calcium (Daniell & Leslie, 1986) and the GABA receptor/chloride channel (Allan & Harris, 1987); changes in the activity of excitatory neurotransmitter systems such as the glutamate system (Tsai, Gastfriend, & Coyle, 1995); and changes in "second messenger" systems (Gordon, Collier, & Diamond, 1992).

CLINICAL ASPECTS

Blood alcohol concentration is most commonly expressed as milligrams of alcohol per 100 milliliters of volume, or milligrams percent. The level at which a social drinker might display symptoms of intoxication is 100 milligrams percent, or .100. Alternatively, blood alcohol concentration can be expressed as millimoles per liter, in which case the level of intoxication becomes 10 millimoles per liter.

The absorption of alcohol from the gastrointestinal tract largely determines the rate of increase of the blood alcohol concentration (BAC), the peak BAC that occurs, and the time at which the peak occurs.

When alcohol is consumed, it is first absorbed through the stomach wall. The rate at which it is absorbed, and at which it subsequently enters the general circulation, depends upon the concentration. Therefore, the alcohol in a strong drink is absorbed more quickly than that in a weaker drink (Goldstein, 1992). Because absorption of alcohol in the stomach is slower than in the small intestine, absorption can also be slowed by the presence of food in the stomach, which delays the emptying of the stomach contents into the small intestine. Whatever alcohol is not metabolized through "first-pass" metabolism (either by alcohol dehydrogenase in the stomach lining or by the liver) enters the general circulation and reaches the brain, where it results in characteristic behavioral effects (see below).

In general, the same dose of alcohol will result in a higher BAC in females than in males (Frezza et al., 1990; Sutker, Tabakoff, Goist, & Randall, 1983). This effect is felt to be due largely to the smaller proportion of body water in women than in men, which leads to a smaller volume of distribution (Arthur, Lee, & Wright, 1984) and to the decreased activity of alcohol dehydrogenase in the stomachs of women. There is no predictable effect of menstrual phase on blood alcohol concentration (Lammers, Mainzer, & Breteler, 1995).

Although the concentration of alcohol in a drink may affect the rate at which it is absorbed, it does not affect the total amount of alcohol delivered. A standard drink contains approximately 13.6 g of absolute alcohol. A standard drink may therefore be 12 oz of beer containing 5% alcohol by volume, 5 oz of wine at 12% alcohol by volume, or 1.5 oz of hard liquor containing 40% alcohol by volume. Since "one drink" can mean quite different amounts to different people, it is important to use standardized methodology when determining how much alcohol an individual is consuming. A widely used method is the time-line follow back (Sobell, Sobell, Klanjner, Pavan, & Basian, 1986). The utilization of surrogate fluids (i.e., water) and standard glasses, allowing direct estimation of consumed volume, results in increased accuracy for this method (Miller & Del Boca, 1994).

The rate at which alcohol is eliminated from the human body has been of interest because of its medicolegal implications, particularly in regard to operation of motor vehicles while under the influence of alcohol. Jones and Andersson (1996) studied blood samples from a large sample of individuals who had been charged with driving under the influence and found significantly higher rates of elimination for women $(0.214 \pm 0.053$ mg/ml/hr) than for men $(0.189 \pm 0.048$ mg/ml/hr). Of individuals in this study, 95% had an elimination rate between 0.09 and 0.29 mg/ml/hr. This rate suggests that, since ingestion of one standard drink typically results in a blood alcohol concentration of approximately 20 mg%, one standard drink is eliminated in approximately 1 hr. The approximate blood alcohol concentrations for men and women resulting from ingestion of various amounts of alcohol and the decrease over varying amounts of time are shown in table 4.2.

Drug Interactions

Acute alcohol exposure tends to inhibit the CYP2E1 enzyme system in the liver and thus to increase blood levels of many common medications, such as warfarin, barbiturates, benzodiazepines, phenothiazines, and opiates. Conversely, chronic exposure to alcohol results in increased activity, or induction, of this enzyme system, resulting in decreased levels of these medications. A few medications, such as cimetidine and ranitidine (histamine H_2-receptor antagonists), appear to be able to increase alcohol concentrations through inhibition of gastric alcohol dehydrogenase (DiPadova et al., 1992). Table 4.3 shows interactions of both acute and chronic alcohol use with commonly used medications.

Many individuals who abuse alcohol also abuse other substances. A common abuse pattern is the combination of cocaine and alcohol. Cocaethylene, an active metabolite of cocaine, is formed by concurrent use of alcohol and cocaine and has been found to be pharmacologically similar to cocaine but is eliminated more slowly than cocaine (McCance, Price, Kosten, & Jatlow, 1995). In animals, cocaethylene has been reported to cause increased lethality

TABLE 4.2 Blood Alcohol Concentrations (Milligrams Percent) by Gender, Weight, and Number of Drinks Over Time

	Males			Females		
	Weight (lb)			Weight (lb)		
	150	200	250	100	120	150
1 SD[*a]						
After 1 hour	12	5	1	34	26	18
2 SD						
After 1 hour	40	32	18	84	67	51
After 2 hours	25	17	3	69	52	36
3 SD						
After 1 hour	67	47	34	133	108	84
After 2 hours	52	32	19	118	93	69
After 3 hours	37	17	4	103	78	54
4 SD						
After 1 hour	95	67	51	183	149	117
After 2 hours	80	52	36	168	134	102
After 3 hours	65	37	21	153	119	87
After 4 hours	50	22	6	137	104	72
5 SD						
After 1 hour	122	88	67	232	191	150
After 2 hours	107	73	52	217	176	135
After 3 hours	92	58	37	202	161	120
After 4 hours	77	43	22	187	146	105
After 5 hours	62	28	7	172	131	90

Note. Adapted from Fisher, Simpson, and Kapur (1987).

[a]SD = standard drink as defined.

TABLE 4.3 Interactions of Alcohol With Commonly Used Medications

Medication	Acute alcohol use	Chronic alcohol use
Acetaminophen (Tylenol)	Unclear	Liver damage (can be fatal)
Nonsteroidal antiinflammatories (aspirin, Advil, etc.)	Aspirin may increase effect of alcohol	Damage to gastrointestinal tract (bleeding, ulceration)
Benzodiazepines (Valium, etc.)	Increased sedation Decreased motor coordination	Same
Anticonvulsants (Dilantin, etc.)	Increased blood level and increased side effects	Increased risk of seizures
Antidepressants Tricyclics Serotonin uptake inhibitors Monoamine oxidase inhibitors	Increased blood level (increased side effects) Hypertensive reaction	Decreased effectiveness due to decreased blood levels
Antipsychotics (Thorazine, etc.)	Increased sedation	Increased risk of liver damage
Anticoagulants (warfarin)	Increased risk of bleeding	Increased risk of blood clotting

Note. From National Institute on Alcohol Abuse and Alcoholism: Alcohol Alert (1995).

over cocaine (Hearn, Rose, Wagner, Ciarleglio, & Mash, 1991), but in humans, concurrent cocaine use was associated with decreased alcohol withdrawal symptoms (Castaneda, Lifshutz, Westreich, & Galanter, 1995) and a decreased risk of seizures (Moak & Anton, 1996). However, inpatients who abused both cocaine and alcohol were found to be more depressed and to have higher global severity scores than inpatients who abused only cocaine (Brady, Sonne, Randall, Adinoff, & Malcolm, 1995).

Nicotine abuse also commonly occurs with alcohol use and abuse. While approximately one quarter of the population of the United States has a history of tobacco dependence and one seventh has a history of alcohol dependence (Anthony, Warner, & Kessler, 1994), prevalence rates of smoking among alcohol-dependent individuals range from 71% to 97%, and in contrast to trends in the general population, there has been no decrease in smoking rates in alcoholics in the last two decades (Monti, Rohsenow, Colby, & Abrams, 1995). Furthermore, alcohol-dependent individuals tend to smoke more heavily than nonalcoholic smokers (Kozlowski, Skinner, Kent, & Pope, 1989). Nicotine has been shown to cause tolerance to several effects of alcohol in mice, including hypothermia, open-field activity, and sleep time (Collins, Wilkins, Slobe, Cao, & Bullock, 1996). These findings suggest that concurrent use of nicotine may allow increased amounts of alcohol to be consumed with less immediate adverse effects but without protection against long-term negative sequelae. In fact,

individuals who abuse alcohol are more likely to die from nicotine-related diseases than from the direct effects of alcohol (Hurt et al., 1996). Since humans may also develop cross-tolerance to alcohol and nicotine, exposure to nicotine-related stimuli may affect craving of and relapse to alcohol (Monti et al., 1995).

Marijuana is also commonly used with alcohol, and the combined effects of these two substances have not been studied extensively. When normal subjects were administered the two substances either alone or together (Chait & Perry, 1994), additive effects on performance impairment and subjective mood ratings were noted.

Physical Symptoms of Use, Abuse, and Dependence

In normal drinkers, acute alcohol use results in characteristic effects at different BAC levels. Typically, mild euphoria is detected at levels of 30 mg/dl (mg%); mild incoordination at 50 mg/dl; ataxia, or difficulty walking, at 100 mg/dl; and at 200 mg/dl, confusion and a reduced level of mental activity. At 300 mg/dl, most individuals have become stuporous, and above 400 mg/dl, there is deep anesthesia (Victor, 1992).

Frequently, intoxicated individuals exhibit an inability to recall events that occurred during their drinking, a phenomenon known as a *blackout*. The precise mechanism by which blackouts occur is not known, although inhibition of N-methyl-D-aspartate

(NMDA) receptor-stimulated calcium flux has been implicated (Diamond & Messing, 1994). Blackouts are felt to be associated with more severe degrees of alcohol misuse and may be an early warning sign of developing abuse and dependence.

As mentioned previously, alcohol-abusing and -dependent individuals frequently show less effect at each BAC mentioned above, as they have developed tolerance to the acute effects of alcohol.

Symptoms and Course of Withdrawal

There appears to be considerable interindividual variability in the presentation of alcohol withdrawal (AW) symptoms. Individuals with quite similar drinking careers may exhibit quite different degrees of withdrawal symptoms, a finding that again suggests the strong influence of individual genetic vulnerability to the withdrawal syndrome. The typical hangover is a mild form of AW. Severe, life-threatening withdrawal accompanied by loss of orientation and hallucinations is known as *delerium tremens* (DTs). DTs occur in less than 5% of individuals with AW, and mortality resulting from this syndrome when untreated is estimated to be 15% (Victor, 1992) but is less than 2% when the syndrome is recognized and treated properly (Ozdemir, Bremner, & Naranjo, 1993).

Delerium tremens is more likely to occur in medical settings, a finding that suggests that other organ pathology, such as pancreatitis, pneumonia, and hepatitis, may predispose toward the development of DTs (Thompson, 1975). Seizures may occur during withdrawal from alcohol, most likely occurring in 5–15% of alcohol-dependent individuals (Victor & Brausch, 1967). Seizure risk increases as daily intake of alcohol increases, with an approximately 3-fold increase in risk at 51–100 g alcohol/day (4–8 standard drinks/day), an 8-fold increase in risk at 101–200 g/day (9–14 standard drinks/day), and an almost 20-fold increased in risk at more than 200 g/day (more than 14 standard drinks/day) (Ng, Hauser, Brust, & Susser, 1988). When seizures are due solely to alcohol withdrawal, ongoing treatment with standard anticonvulsant medication is usually not required, in contrast to requirements for seizures associated with idiopathic or posttraumatic epilepsy (Rathlev et al., 1994).

AW symptoms usually begin within 24–48 hr of decreasing or discontinuing drinking, most commonly within 6–8 hr, and typically last 48–72 hr in uncomplicated cases. DTs usually manifest between 48 and 96 hr after cessation of drinking and, with adequate treatment, usually last for 48–72 hr. Although seizures typically occur within the first 24 hr after drinking ceases, they can occur up to 5 days afterward. At least two of the following symptoms are required to meet the definition of AW found in the fourth edition of the *Diagnostic and Statistical Manual of Mental Disorders (DSM-IV)*: nausea and vomiting, tremor, sweating, anxiety and irritability, motor arousal (agitation), skin sensations, heightened sensitivity to light and sound, headache, and problems with concentration and orientation (Sellers, Sullivan, Somer, & Sykora, 1991). Increased blood pressure and increased heart rate (pulse) are often found. Most individuals with AW also exhibit decreased appetite and abnormal sleep architecture. A commonly used rating instrument that measures the intensity of AW symptoms reliably is the Clinical Institute Withdrawal Assessment for Alcohol (revised) (CIWA-Ar; Sullivan, Sykora, Schneiderman, Naranjo, & Sellers, 1989). Scores over 10 on this scale generally indicate withdrawal that should be managed with medication and supportive care.

Although many clinicians and researchers believe that there is a "protracted" AW syndrome, defined as AW symptoms that persist after the first several days of cessation of drinking, the nature of this syndrome remains ill defined. Abnormalities in brain function, as demonstrated in electroencephalographic (EEG) sleep recordings and positron emission tomography (PET) scans, lasting at least several weeks after drinking has been discontinued, have been documented (Gillin, Smith, Irwin, Kripke, & Schuckit, 1990; Volkow et al., 1994) and support the notion that more subtle AW symptoms may continue to affect alcoholics. Distinguishing possible protracted AW symptoms from the symptoms and signs of other psychiatric disorders, such as affective and anxiety disorders, remains challenging.

There are many effective pharmacological treatments for AW that are discussed in chapter 19. There is increasing evidence that repeated episodes of AW lead to more serious AW symptoms in subsequent episodes (Booth & Blow, 1993; Brown, Anton, Malcolm, & Ballenger, 1988; Moak & Anton, 1996) which may be due to a "kindling" or sensitization phenomenon as originally hypothesized by Ballenger and Post (1978). If the severity of AW episodes is mediated by a kindling process, anticonvulsants such as carbamazepine and valproate might reduce the progressive worsening of AW symptoms over repeated AW episodes better than benzodiazepines, which are the current standard treatment. Research to define the role of these medications in the treatment of AW is ongoing.

Not all episodes of AW may require pharmacological treatment. Concern has been expressed regarding the use of medications which themselves possess addictive potential, such as the benzodiazepines, in the treatment of a substance use disorder. A small but well-designed study by Naranjo and colleagues (1983) of alcoholics with mild to moderate AW symptoms showed similar outcomes for both pharmacological and nonpharmacological treatment. More research is needed to better define the optimal use of medications in the treatment of AW episodes.

PATHOLOGICAL EFFECTS

Physiological Effects

Organ systems that are particularly vulnerable to the adverse effects of excessive alcohol use are the central nervous system; the gastrointestinal system, in particular the liver, and the cardiovascular system. Table 4.4 summarizes the clinical syndromes that are a result of the toxic effects of alcohol.

Central Nervous System

The alcohol withdrawal syndromes, which are manifestations of alcohol's toxicity on the central nervous system, have already been discussed. Additionally, chronic exposure to alcohol can give rise to a number of more pervasive neurological syndromes. Some may be due to an interaction with nutrition, such as Wernicke's encephalopathy, caused by thiamine deficiency. Other disorders are most likely due to the direct neurotoxicity of alcohol, such as alcoholic dementia and disorders of the nerves (neuropathy) and muscles (myopathy) (Diamond & Messing, 1994).

Wernicke's encephalopathy is characterized by a triad of ataxia (difficulty with walking), oculomotor abnormalities (difficulty with eye movement), and global confusion (Reuler, Giard, & Cooney, 1985). It usually occurs in combination with Korsakoff's psychosis, which consists of a complete inability to learn new information. Confabulation, which is characterized by verbal responses that are grossly inaccurate and often bizarre and fantastic, is common as an attempt to partially compensate for the defect. Korsakoff's psychosis is permanent in 25% of individuals in which it develops. Both of these severe syndromes can largely be prevented by the prompt administration of thiamine, either orally or by intramuscular injection, in individuals entering alcohol withdrawal.

Many alcoholics develop a cerebellar syndrome with profound ataxia, more pronounced in the legs than in the arms. Chronic use of alcohol also appears to lead to a typical dementia, with clinical manifestations of cognitive deficits including memory impairment and pathological findings of cortical atrophy, enlargement of the lateral ventricles, and a loss of cortical neurons. Modern brain-imaging techniques bear promise in better defining the changes that occur and their possible resolution with abstinence from alcohol (Mann, Mundle, Strayle, & Wakat, 1995).

Polyneuropathy is the most common neurological complication in alcoholism. Affected individuals complain of numbness (paresthesias), pain, and weakness, especially in the feet. This can be severe enough to interfere with walking. Finally, an acute and even life-threatening myopathy can occur after binge drinking, with muscle swelling, weakness, and pain; elevated blood levels of creatine kinase; and myoglobinuria, which can result in kidney damage. A more chronic, usually painless, and commonly undiagnosed myopathy can also develop.

Gastrointestinal System and Liver

Alcohol is detoxified primarily in the liver and affects this organ in a number of ways (French, 1996). Alcohol appears to induce a hypermetabolic state in liver cells (hepatocytes), which results in a relative oxygen deficiency. This may in turn promote the formation of "free radicals" which lead to fibrosis (Ishii et al., 1996). Liver damage is first manifested by fatty change (steatosis) which is reversible and clinically silent. This is followed by the development of alcoholic hepatitis, which can present with jaundice, fever, anorexia, and right upper quadrant abdominal pain.

Cirrhosis, or irreversible liver damage, is the most severe form of alcoholic liver disease. It was the 11th leading cause of death in the United States in 1993,

TABLE 4.4 Medical Disorders Caused by Alcoholism

Organ system	Disorder
Central nervous system	Wernicke's encephalopathy
	Korsakoff's psychosis
	Cerebellar ataxia
	Alcoholic dementia
	Polyneuropathy
	Myopathy
Gastrointestinal system and liver	Steatosis (fatty change)
	Alcoholic hepatitis
	Cirrhosis
	Pancreatitis
	Gastritis
Cardiovascular system	Cardiomyopathy
	Arrhythmias
	Hypertension
	Increased cholesterol and blood lipids
	Decreased platelet aggregation
Endocrine system	Hypoglycemia with acute exposure
	Hyperglycemia with chronic exposure
	Osteoporosis
	Menstrual cycle irregularity in women
	Decreased testosterone levels in men

although it ranked as high as 7th among women between the ages of 45 and 64 (Gardner & Hudson, 1996). Cirrhosis appears to develop more quickly in women (Morgan, 1994), perhaps partly because of early exposure to higher levels of alcohol due to the lower activity of gastric alcohol dehydrogenase. Concomitant physical findings can include an enlarged spleen, abdominal fluid (ascites), testicular atrophy, enlarged breasts in males (gynecomastia), enlarged superficial blood vessels (spider angiomata), and palmar erythema. Frequently, the liver enzyme abnormalities characteristic of earlier stages of damage may actually normalize in cirrhosis, although a decrease in serum albumin and increase in serum globulin may persist.

Because cirrhosis causes obstruction of blood flow through the liver and increased pressure in the circulation proximal to the liver (portal hypertension), veins in the esophagus frequently become enlarged and are termed *varices*. These varices can bleed spontaneously and lead to fatal gastrointestinal hemorrhage. Late complications of cirrhosis include hepatic encephalopathy and the hepatorenal syndrome. Hepatic encephalopathy is a complex neuropsychiatric syndrome consisting of disturbances in conciousness and behavior, personality changes, asterixis (a characteristic "flapping" tremor), fluctuating neurological signs, and distinctive changes on electroencephalogram and is associated with elevated blood levels of ammonia. The hepatorenal syndrome, in which blood flow to the kidneys is critically decreased, manifests clinically as a decreased urine production and a retention of sodium and fluid.

The interaction of alcohol and viruses causing acute and chronic hepatitis is of great interest. Evidence of hepatitis C virus infection, in particular, has been found to be more common among individuals with alcoholic liver disease than in either patients without alcoholism or patients with alcoholism but without alcoholic liver disease (Mendenhall et al., 1991) and appears to be associated with more severe liver disease (Pares et al., 1990). An increased prevalence of hepatitis B virus antibodies has been found in some studies as well (Brechot, Nalpas, & Feitelson, 1996). In addition to contributing to an accelerated course of progression to cirrhosis, infection with hepatitis viruses appears also to play a role in the development of cancer of the liver (Brechot et al., 1996).

Other gastrointestinal complications of excessive alcohol use are inflammation of the pancreas, or pancreatitis, and injury to the stomach lining, or gastritis. The symptoms of pancreatitis are abdominal pain, usually of a boring and steady quality and originating in the upper abdomen with radiation through to the back, and vomiting. Although most attacks are limited and last 2–3 days, severe attacks may result in hospitalization, and there is a mortality of up to 30%. Gastritis typically presents as pain in the upper abdomen and vomiting of blood. While bleeding from gastritis is usually self-limited, it is important to distinguish it from bleeding from esophageal varices, as described above.

Cardiovascular System

Alcohol has been known for over a century to have a direct toxic effect upon the heart, having been first described in 1884 as occurring in persons who consumed large amounts of beer in Germany (the Munich "beer heart") (Rubin & Thomas, 1992). Although initially felt to be a manifestation of concomitant thiamine deficiency, it is now known that chronic use of alcohol results in a condition of heart muscle weakening known as *cardiomyopathy*. This condition may lead to irregular rhythms that sometimes result in sudden death (Ettinger et al., 1978). Acute alcohol abuse can also result in deleterious effects on the heart. Kelly and colleagues (1996) found decreases in heart muscle contractile force in healthy adult subjects at alcohol concentrations common among social drinkers.

Hypertension, or elevated blood pressure, is more common among alcohol-abusing and -dependent individuals than in nonalcoholic members of the general population (Klatsky, 1996). This has been found to be true for both sexes, across various age groups, among different racial groups, and for drinkers of liquor, wine, or beer. Even though this relationship was first identified early in this century, the exact mechanism by which alcohol causes hypertension is not known. Some researchers have felt that hypertension is a manifestation of mild alcohol withdrawal, while others have focused on the use of salt in the diets of alcoholics.

Of importance in relation to these direct effects on the cardiovascular system is the effect of alcohol on lipids (Frohlich, 1996). This has been an area of some interest and also of controversy in recent years, with several studies supporting a beneficial effect of moderate alcohol use on lipid profiles through increase in high-density lipoprotein (HDL), which is believed to result in a protective cardiovascular effect (Gaziano et al., 1993). It is important to note that any positive effects of alcohol that have been documented have occurred in individuals who are moderate drinkers (less than three drinks per day) and that these benefits are quickly offset when drinking exceeds truly moderate levels, currently defined as two standard drinks per day for men and one standard drink per day for women.

Alcohol use also impacts the cardiovascular system through its effect on platelet function (Renaud & Ruf, 1996). Platelets play a critical role in blood clotting through their ability to clump at sites of injury. Alcohol has been shown to inhibit platelet aggregation in both humans and animals. This may be an underlying cause of the increased incidence of cerebral hemorrhages observed in alcoholics. It has also been shown that, after heavy alcohol use, platelets will "rebound" and exhibit enhanced aggregation. This rebound aggregation may lead to an increased occurrence of cardiovascular events, including myocardial infarction, or heart attack, and stroke. Interestingly, this rebound aggregation is not observed in animals given red wine (Ruf, Berger, & Renaud, 1995), in humans drinking red wine (Renaud, Dumont, Godsey, Suplisson, & Thevenon, 1979), or when grape tannins are added to alcohol (Ruf et al., 1995).

Endocrine System

Alcohol influences the function of several important hormonal and metabolic systems. In particular, it can affect the metabolism of glucose and calcium and the function of the reproductive system. Acute alcohol use can result in low blood sugar (hypoglycemia) through exhaustion of glycogen stores and inhibition of glucose metabolism (Gordon & Lieber, 1992). Chronic heavy drinking is more likely to result in elevated blood glucose (hyperglycemia) and can be especially harmful in those individuals who are predisposed to the development of diabetes mellitus (Crane & Sereny, 1988).

Alcohol interferes with calcium metabolism at several levels. Acute alcohol use may lead to a transient insufficiency of the important calcium regulatory glands, the parathyroids (Laitinen et al., 1991). This results in increased loss of calcium from the body. Chronic alcohol use frequently leads to dietary insufficiency of calcium and vitamin D, which can lead to softening of the bones (i.e., osteoporosis). Liver disease, through alteration of reproductive hormone levels, can also affect bone and calcium metabolism (Laitinen & Valimaki, 1993). In individuals with osteoporosis, the increased risk of falls associated with alcohol use can result in an increased incidence of fractures (Hingson & Howland, 1987).

Many studies have found evidence of dysfunction of the reproductive system in heavy drinkers and alcoholics (Mendelson & Mello, 1988). Amenorrhea, or absence of menstrual cycles, has been observed in women who drink heavily. Low levels of alcohol use (three to six drinks per week) in postmenopausal women have been shown to be associated with increased levels of estradiol, which may result in a decreased risk of cardiovascular disease (Stampfer, Colditz, Willett, Speizer, & Hennekens, 1988) but may also increase risk of breast cancer (Singletary, Dorgan, Gapstur, & Anderson, 1996). Testicular function is also profoundly affected by heavy alcohol use, with findings of decreased testosterone levels (Gordon, Altman, Southren, Rubin, & Lieber, 1976) and the appearance of female sexual characteristics, such as enlarged breasts (Bannister & Lowosky, 1987).

Fetal Alcohol Syndrome

Fetal alcohol syndrome (FAS) is very likely the most common known cause of mental retardation and affects from 1 to 3 of every 1,000 infants born in the United States. The risk to fetal health from alcohol has been recognized since the writing of the Bible, and in 1899, a publication by Sullivan documented an increased rate of stillbirth and infant death in the children of alcoholic women.

The full manifestation of FAS is characterized by the triad of characteristic facial malformations, prenatal and postnatal growth deficiency, and central nervous system dysfunction. Facial malformations include short palpebral fissures (eye openings), elongated midface, long and flat philtrum (area between the mouth and nose), thin upper vermilion (lip), flattened maxilla (cheeks), and flattening of the nasal bridge (Sokol & Clarren, 1989). Central nervous system involvement is demonstrated by findings of IQs between 60 and 65, although a wide range is frequently seen (Streissguth, Herman, & Smith, 1978). Infants who display some features of FAS but do not meet the full diagnosis were once described as having fetal alcohol effects (FAE). More recently, it has

been suggested that such infant characteristics be called alcohol-related birth defects (ARBD; Hannigan, Welch, & Sokol, 1992).

The mechanisms by which alcohol use results in fetal effects are most likely complex. Four pathways have been suggested by Pratt (1984). Early in pregnancy, alcohol acts as a direct teratogen, causing either cell death or chromosomal aberrations. Later in development, between 4 and 10 weeks after conception, alcohol may act as a toxin to cells. Subsequently, from 8 to 10 weeks onward, alcohol causes disorganization and delay of cell migration and development. Finally, alcohol interferes with the production of important brain transmitters and thus probably leads to behavioral problems. Growth deficiency may be mediated in part by alcohol effects on growth hormone in these infants. Additionally, it has been suggested that alcohol use causes perinatal hypoxia and acidosis in the fetus due to impairment of umbilical circulation (Randall, Ekblud, & Anton, 1990). It is not clear whether alcohol itself or its metabolite acetaldehyde causes this effect.

Longitudinal follow-up of infants and children with FAS into adulthood is still in its early stages. It has been shown that many children with FAS are able to "catch up" in adolescence in regard to growth and that some of the facial anomalies resolve, but that maladaptive behaviors, including poor judgment, distractibility, and difficulty perceiving social cues, persist (Streissguth et al., 1991).

It has been shown that increased maternal age is associated with greater fetal risk from alcohol use (Jacobson, Jacobson, & Sokol, 1996). Currently, the safest approach to alcohol use during pregnancy is believed to be the recommendation of complete abstinence. The possibility that such a stringent recommendation might unnecessarily alarm women who may have drunk at very low levels during early pregnancy is of some concern (Abel, 1996).

Psychological Effects

Alcohol profoundly affects both affective states and cognitive functioning. These effects can be seen in social drinkers, in chronic heavy drinkers, in alcoholics, and in dually diagnosed individuals (those individuals with both an alcohol use disorder and another psychiatric disorder). Relationships between psychiatric symptomatology and alcohol use are very likely complex and bidirectional; that is, alcohol use results in characteristic affective changes, but preexisting affective disorders and expectancy sets may strongly influence the effect and pattern of drinking. Alcohol use disorders are more common among individuals who meet criteria for affective and anxiety disorders (Kessler et al., 1997) than in individuals without these disorders, but it is often not clear if the alcohol use disorder preceded or followed the onset of the affective or anxiety disorder. Structured interviews that attempt to distinguish between so-called primary disorders (disorders that predate the onset of alcohol and other substance use disorders) and those disorders that occur secondary to substance use are useful (Hasin et al., 1996).

It is also crucial, when reviewing experimental data, to be aware of the population being studied, as it is likely that social drinkers and alcohol-abusing and -dependent individuals differ in important ways in their reasons for drinking and their response to alcohol.

Cognitive Effects

The effect of alcohol on cognitive functioning in abusing and dependent populations is clearly a negative one. In social drinkers, however, the situation is not as clear. Individuals under the influence of alcohol perform poorly on cognitive tests (Lex, Greenwald, Lukas, Slater, & Mendelson, 1988) but probably of greater interest is the long-term effect of alcohol on cognitive performance of social drinkers. Important early studies (Hannon, Day, Butler, Larson, & Casey, 1983; Jones & Jones, 1980; Parker & Noble, 1977) showed an association between decreased performance on cognitive tasks and higher levels of alcohol consumption among social drinkers. Other studies have been less supportive of a significant role of chronic alcohol use in decreased cognitive functioning, although recent heavy alcohol intake was associated with mild cognitive defects (Bergman, 1985).

Longitudinal studies have substantiated persistently poorer performance on cognitive testing among heavy drinkers than among social drinkers and nondrinkers (Arbuckle, Chaikelson, & Gold, 1994). In abusing and dependent populations, deficits are observed in perceptual-motor skills, visual-spatial performance, abstraction and problem solving, and learning and memory processes (Parsons & Nixon, 1993). Abstinence does lead to recovery of some cognitive functions, with verbal skills returning most quickly, usually within a month of attaining abstinence. Difficulties with abstraction and problem solving appear to be more long-lasting. Younger age and length of abstinence are predictive of better recovery of cognitive functioning, while pattern and duration of alcohol use appear to be relatively weak determinants of cognitive impairment (Fein, Bachman, Fisher, & Davenport, 1990). With continued abstinence, scores on tests tend to improve but appear to remain inferior to those in age-matched controls.

Effects of Affective and Anxiety States

Many individuals, particularly heavier social drinkers, use alcohol as a means to ameliorate uncomfortable affective and anxiety states (Lex, Mello, Mendelson, & Babor, 1989). Because of alcohol's propensity to cause anxiety and depression, both through its direct action on the central nervous system and through subsequent withdrawal states, this "self-medication" with alcohol is likely to worsen existing psychological symptoms. Kushner, Sher, and Beitman (1990) found that while agoraphobia and social phobia were more likely to precede the onset of an alcohol use disorder, panic disorder and generalized anxiety disorder were more likely to follow onset of alcohol abuse and dependence.

Although depressive symptoms are common in individuals with alcohol use disorders, these symptoms frequently remit with even short periods of abstinence (Brown & Schuckit, 1988). In some individuals, particularly in women and in those experiencing a disruption of social support, depressive disorders can occur independent of alcohol use and persist after sobriety is achieved (Beck, Steer, & McElroy, 1982; Overall, Reilly, Kelley, & Hollister, 1985). Suicide is a serious consequence of both alcohol use disorders and depression (Winokur & Black, 1987), and suicide attempts by depressed alcoholics are typically impulsive in nature, involving little if any premeditation (Cornelius, Salloum, Day, Thase, & Mann, 1996). Suicide attempts are common among alcoholics, with 21% of men and 41% of women reporting at least one lifetime attempt in one study (Hesselbrock, Hesselbrock, Syzmanski, & Weidenman, 1988). This report underscores the importance of assessing suicidality in individuals with alcohol use disorders.

It would also appear that personality attributes that are considered persistent and enduring may in fact change after the cessation of drinking, since the Minnesota Multiphasic Personality Inventory, as well as the diagnostic criteria for personality disorders (SCID-P), shows change when repeated after a period of abstinence (Pettinati, 1990; Pettinati, Sugerman, & Maurer, 1982).

Expectancies of Alcohol Use

In a study of a social drinking population interviewed by telephone, the typical reasons for alcohol use were drinking to cope, drinking to be sociable, drinking to enhance social confidence, and drinking for enjoyment (Smith, Abbey, & Scott, 1993). More positive expectancies of alcohol use were found to predict current drinking patterns and symptoms of alcohol dependence in young adults (Williams & Ricciardelli, 1996). However, among "highly sexually insecure" male and female college students, the expectation that alcohol would enhance sexuality did not predict drinking patterns (Mooney, 1995).

Social and Interpersonal Effects

This section will discuss the relationship of alcohol use and the following aspects of social functioning: impulsivity and lack of social restraint, family function and domestic violence, other forms of violence, motor vehicle trauma and other trauma, work performance, and legal consequences. The important effects of gender and age on the impact of alcohol use on social functioning are considered in other sections of this book.

Impulsivity and Lack of Social Restraint

Similar to the relationship of cognition and affect to alcohol use as discussed above, the relationship of social functioning to alcohol use appears to be bidirectional. It is important, but sometimes difficult, to distinguish the pathological effects of alcohol use on social functioning from those deficiencies in social functioning that can lead to problem drinking. In a sample of young adult drinkers, low self-restraint, a measure of social functioning, was a strong predictor of alcohol-related problems, especially when combined with a high level of distress (Weinberger & Bartholomew, 1996). Both male and female alcohol-

ics have been found to have interpersonal problem-solving deficits (Nixon, Tivis, & Parsons, 1992), and more improvement on a social skills task battery has been found to be associated with better adjustment in alcoholics who were followed up 1 year after treatment (Jones & Lanyon, 1981). Since alcoholics have been shown to have decreased functioning of the prefrontal lobes of the brain (Volkow et al., 1992), where social judgment and behavior or restraint are mediated, it is possible that the impaired social functioning, judgment, impulsivity, and lack of insight manifested by actively drinking alcoholics are attributable to a direct toxic effect on the brain.

Family Function and Domestic Violence

Alcohol use and misuse are frequently associated with family dysfunction and domestic violence. Alcohol and other drug use by parents has been found to contribute to sexual and physical abuse of children, although it is difficult at this time to estimate the extent of increased risk given the methodological limitations of the studies that have been done, and there is also evidence to support a link between the experience of childhood violence and later alcohol and other drug abuse (Miller, Maguin, & Downs, 1997). Although homicides caused by domestic violence were less likely to involve alcohol and drugs than homicides resulting from causes other than domestic violence, the proportion of domestic violence homicides in which substance use was involved (54%) was still high (Arbuckle et al., 1996). It is important to assess substance use in the victim as well as in the perpetrator of domestic violence, since exposure to trauma has been shown to be both a predictor and a consequence of alcohol use disorders (Stewart, 1996).

Motor Vehicle and Other Trauma

Alcohol use also frequently plays a role in motor vehicle accidents, burn injuries, and other trauma. Alcohol intoxication, defined as a blood alcohol concentration of 100 mg%, is associated with 40–50% of traffic fatalities, 25–35% of nonfatal motor vehicle injuries, and up to 64% of fires and burns (National Institute on Alcohol Abuse and Alcoholism [NIAAA], 1989). Burn victims who tested positively for alcohol and other substances had significantly greater total body surface area involvement (McGill, Kowal-Vern,

Fisher, Kahn, & Gamelli, 1995) and overall mortality (Haum et al., 1995; McGill et al. 1995). Interestingly, a stronger association was found between drinking variables and injuries that resulted from violence in a study of individuals requiring an emergency room visit than for other frequent sequelae of alcohol use, including motor vehicle accidents, penetrating traumas not caused by violence, and fires (Cherpitel, 1996).

Occupational Performance

Alcohol use has long been believed to cause decreased work performance (Berry & Boland, 1977; U.S. General Accounting Office, 1970). However, many studies in this area have methdological flaws that have resulted in contradictory findings, suggesting a more complicated relationship between levels of alcohol use and occupational performance (Webb et al., 1994). Problem drinkers were found to be more likely to sustain occupational injuries and to have more absences due to these injuries (Hingson & Howland, 1987). Hangovers and drinking while at work were better predictors of work-related problems than overall levels of drinking in a study of workers at a manufacturing facility (Ames, Grube, & Moore, 1997). Additionally, level of job satisfaction and belief in drinking as a coping mechanism were found to be important mediators of the effect of drinking on work performance (Greenberg & Grunberg, 1995; Webb et al., 1994). A study of the interaction of ethnicity and socioeconomic status on social consequences of drinking found that less affluent black men had more drinking-related problems than less affluent white men, while affluent black men reported fewer problems related to drinking than affluent white men (Jones-Webb, Hsiao, & Hannan, 1995).

Legal Consequences

Substance use, in particular alcohol use, is an important correlate of criminal violent behavior, but the relationship of alcohol use to this type of behavior is not a simple one (Bradford, Greenberg, & Motayne, 1992). Current estimates are that approximately 50% of violent crime in the United States involves the concurrent use of alcohol. Moreover, violent offenders have been found to be more likely to be drunk than nonviolent offenders at the time of committing

a crime (66% of the former group vs. 38% of the latter group) (Roslund & Larson, 1979). Based on these statistics, rehabilitation of imprisoned individuals that includes attention to treatment of substance use disorders would seem to be appropriate, but studies of the effectiveness of such treatment programs are lacking at the present time (Roesch, Ogloff, & Eaves, 1995).

SUMMARY

The consumption of alcoholic beverages can be a pleasant aspect of many family and social activities, and there is evidence that truly moderate alcohol use may offer some health benefits. However, the misuse of alcohol, leading to the development of alcohol use disorders, has a negative impact on society at many different levels. The medical disorders that result from excessive alcohol use are significant causes of morbidity and mortality. Psychological disturbances and social and interpersonal dysfunction caused by or worsened by alcohol use result in immense economic loss for society as well as human suffering that cannot be measured in dollars. Exposure of a fetus to alcohol extends the impact of alcohol use disorders to future generations.

Research, both animal and human, which seeks to improve our understanding of the action of alcohol at the molecular and biochemical level of the central nervous system, as well as the development of new psychotherapies and pharmacotherapies, offers hope to the millions of human beings affected by these disorders.

Key References

Koob, G. F. (1992). Drugs of abuse: anatomy, pharmacology and function of reward pathways. *Trends in Pharmacological Sciences, 13,* 177–184.

Lieber, C. S. (1995). Medical disorders of alcoholism. *New England Journal of Medicine, 333,* 1058–1065.

Niccols, G. A. (1994). Fetal alcohol syndrome: implications for psychologists. *Clinical Psychology Review, 14,* 91–111.

References

Abel, E. L. (1996). "Moderate" drinking during pregnancy: Cause for concern? *Clinica Chimica Acta, 246,* 149–154.

Allan, A. M., & Harris, R. A. (1987). Acute and chronic ethanol treatments alter GABA receptor-operated chloride channels. *Pharmacology, Biochemistry and Behavior, 27*, 665–670.

Ames, G. M., Grube, J. W., & Moore, R. S. (1997). The relationship of drinking and hangovers to workplace problems: an empirical study. *Journal of Studies on Alcohol, 58*, 37–47.

Anthony, J. C., Warner, L. A., & Kessler, R. C. (1994). Comparative epidemiology of dependence on tobacco, alcohol, controlled substances, and inhalants: Basic findings from the national comorbidity survey. *Experimental and Clinical Psychopharmacology, 2*, 244–268.

Arbuckle, J., Olson, L., Howard, M., Brilman, J., Anctil, C., & Sklar, D. (1996). Safe at home? Domestic violence and other homicides among women in New Mexico. *Annals of Emergency Medicine, 27*, 210–215.

Arbuckle, T. Y., Chaikelson, J. S., & Gold, D. P. (1994). Social drinking and cognitive functioning revisited: The role of intellectual endowment and psychological distress. *Journal of Studies on Alcohol, 55*, 352–361.

Arthur, M. J. P., Lee, A., & Wright, R. (1984). Sex differences in the metabolism of ethanol and acetaldehyde in normal subjects. *Clinical Science, 67*, 397–401.

Ballenger, J. C., Goodwin, F. K., Major, L. F., & Brown, G. L. (1979). Alcohol and central serotonin metabolism in man. *Archives of General Psychiatry 1979, 36*, 224–227.

Ballenger, J. C., & Post, R. M. (1978). Kindling as a model for alcohol withdrawal syndromes. *British Journal of Psychiatry, 133*, 1–14.

Bannister, P., & Lowosky, M. S. (1987). Ethanol and hypogonadism. *Alcohol and Alcoholism, 22*, 213–217.

Beck, A. T., Steer, R. A., & McElroy, M. G. (1982). Self-reported precedence of depression in alcoholism. *Drug and Alcohol Dependence, 10*, 185–190.

Bergman, H. (1985). Cognitive deficits and morphological cerebral changes in a random sample of social drinkers. *Recent Developments in Alcoholism, 3*, 265–275.

Berry, R. E., & Boland, J. P. (1977). *The economic cost of alcohol abuse*. New York: Macmillan.

Black, M. (1984). Acetaminophen hepatotoxicity. *Annual Review of Medicine, 35*, 577–593.

Booth, B. M., & Blow, F. C. (1993). The kindling hypothesis: Further evidence from a U.S. national study of alcoholic men. *Alcohol and Alcoholism, 28*, 593–598.

Bradford, J. M. W., Greenberg, D. M., & Motayne, G. G., (1992). Substance abuse and criminal behavior. *Psychiatric Clinics of North America, 15*, 605–622.

Brady, K. T., Sonne, S., Randall, C. L., Adinoff, B., & Malcolm, R. (1995). Features of cocaine dependence with concurrent alcohol abuse. *Drug and Alcohol Dependence, 39*, 69–71.

Brechot, C., Nalpas, B., & Feitelson, M. A. (1996). Interactions between alcohol and hepatitis viruses in the liver. *Clinics in Laboratory Medicine, 16*, 273–287.

Brown, M. E., Anton, R. F., Malcolm, R., & Ballenger, J. C. (1988). Alcohol detoxification and withdrawal seizure: Clinical support for a kindling hypothesis. *Biological Psychiatry, 23*, 507–514.

Brown, S. A., & Schuckit, M. A. (1988). Changes in depression among abstinent alcoholics. *Journal of Studies on Alcohol, 49*, 412–417.

Castaneda, R., Lifshutz, H., Westreich, L., & Galanter, M. (1995). Concurrent cocaine withdrawal is associated with reduced severity of alcohol withdrawal. *Comprehensive Psychiatry, 36*, 441–447.

Chait, L. D., & Perry, J. J. (1994). Acute and residual effects of alcohol and marijuana, alone and in combination, on mood and performance. *Psychopharmacology, 115*, 340–349.

Cherpitel, C. J. (1996). Drinking patterns and problems and drinking in the event: An analysis of injury by cause among casualty patients. *Alcoholism: Clinical and Experimental Research, 20*, 1130–1137.

Collins, A. C., Wilkins, L. H., Slobe, B. S., Cao, J-Z., & Bullock, A. E. (1996). Long-term ethanol and nicotine treatment elicit tolerance to ethanol. *Alcoholism: Clinical and Experimental Research, 20*, 990–999.

Cornelius, J. R., Salloum, I. J., Day, N. L., Thase, M. E., & Mann, J. J. (1996). Patterns of suicidality and alcohol use in alcoholics with major depression. *Alcoholism: Clinical and Experimental Research, 20*, 1451–1455.

Crane, M., & Sereny, G. (1988). Alcohol and diabetes. *British Journal of Addiction, 83*, 1357–1358.

Daniell, L. C., & Leslie, S. W. (1986). Inhibition of fast-phase calcium uptake and endogenous norepinephrine release in rat brain region synaptosomes. *Brain Research, 377*, 18–28.

DeWitte, P. (1996). The role of neurotransmitters in alcohol dependence: Animal research. *Alcohol and Alcoholism, 31*, 13–16.

Diamond, I., & Messing, R. O. (1994). Neurologic effects of alcoholism. *Western Journal of Medicine, 161*, 279–287.

DiPadova, C., Roine, R., Frezza, M., Gentry, T., Baraona, E., & Lieber, C. (1992). Effects of ranitidine on blood alcohol levels after ethanol ingestion. *Journal of the American Medical Association, 267,* 83–86.

Ehrig, T., Bosron, W. F., & Li,T-K. (1990). Alcohol and acetaldehyde dehydrogenase. *Alcohol, 25,* 105–116.

Ettinger, P. O., Wu, C. F., De La Cruz, C., Weisse, A. B., Ahmed, S. S., & Regan, T. J. (1978). Arrhythmias and the "holiday heart": Alcohol-associated cardiac rhythm disorders. *American Heart Journal, 95,* 555–562.

Fein, G., Bachman, L., Fisher, S., & Davenport, L. (1990). Cognitive impairments in abstinent alcoholics. *Western Journal of Medicine, 152,* 531–537.

Fisher, H. R., Simpson, R. I., & Kapur, B. M. (1987). Calculation of blood alcohol concentration (BAC) by sex, weight, number of drinks and time. *Canadian Journal of Public Health, 78,* 300–304.

French, S. W. (1996). Ethanol and hepatocellular injury. *Clinics in Laboratory Medicine, 16,* 289–306.

Frezza, M., Di Padova, C., Pozzato, G., Terpin, M., Baraona, E., & Lieber, C. S. (1990). High blood alcohol levels in women: the role of decreased gastric alcohol dehydrogenase activity and first-pass metabolism. *New England Journal of Medicine, 322,* 95–9.

Frohlich, J. J. (1996). Effects of alcohol on plasma lipoprotein metabolism. *Clinica Chimica Acta, 246,* 39–49.

Gardner, P., & Hudson, B. L. (1996). Advance report of final mortality statistics, 1993. *Monthly Vital Statistics Report, 44 (Supplement).*

Gaziano, J. M., Buring, J. E., Breslow, J. L., Goldhaber, S. Z., Rosner, B., VanDenburgh, M., Willett, W., & Hennekens, C. H. (1993). Moderate alcohol intake, increased levels of HDL and its subfractions, and decreased risk of myocardial infarction. *New England Journal of Medicine, 329,* 1829–1834.

Gillin, J. C., Smith, T. L., Irwin, M., Kripke, D. F., & Schuckit, M. (1990). EEG sleep studies in "pure" primary alcoholism during subacute withdrawal: Relationships to normal controls, age and other clinical variables. *Biological Psychiatry, 27,* 477–488.

Goldstein, D. B. (1992). Pharmacokinetics of alcohol. In J. H. Mendelson & N. K. Mello (Eds.), *The medical diagnosis and treatment of alcoholism.* New York: McGraw-Hill.

Gordon, A. S., Collier, K., & Diamond, I. (1992). Ethanol regulation of adenosine receptor stimulated cAMP levels in a clonal neural cells line: An in vitro model of cellular tolerance to alcohol. *Proceedings of the National Academy of Sciences USA, 83,* 2105–2108.

Gordon, G. C., Altman, K., Southren, A. L., Rubin, E., & Lieber, C. S. (1976). The effects of alcohol (ethanol) administration on sex hormone metabolism in normal men. *New England Journal of Medicine, 295,* 793–797.

Gordon, G. G., & Lieber, C. S. (1992). Alcohol, hormones and metabolism. In C. S. Lieber (Ed.), *Medical and nutritional complications of alcoholism.* New York: Plenum.

Greenberg, E. S., & Grunberg, L. (1995).Work alienation and problem alcohol behavior. *Journal of Health and Social Behavior, 36,* 83–102.

Haber, P. S., Gentry, R. T., Mak, K. M., Mirmiran-Yazdy, S. A. A., Greenstein, R. J., & Lieber, C. S. (1996). Metabolism of alcohol by human gastric cells: relation to first-pass metabolism. *Gastroenterology, 111,* 863–870.

Hannigan, J. H., Welch, R. A., & Sokol, R. J. (1992). Recognition of fetal alcohol syndrome and alcohol-related birth defects. In J. H. Mendelson & J. H. Mello (Eds.), *The medical diagnosis of alcoholism* (pp. 639–667). New York: McGraw-Hill.

Hannon, R., Day, C. L., Butler, A. M., Larson, A. J., & Casey, M. (1983). Alcohol consumption and cognitive functioning in college students. *Journal of Studies on Alcohol, 44,* 283–298.

Harris, R. A., & Buck, K. J. (1990). The processes of alcohol tolerance & dependence. *Alcohol Health and Research World, 14,* 105–110.

Hasin, D. S., Trautman, K. D., Miele, G. M., Samet, S., Smith, M., & Endicott, J. (1996). Psychiatric Research Interview for Substance and Mental Disorders (PRISM): Reliability for substance abusers. *American Journal of Psychiatry, 153,* 1195–1201.

Haum, A., Perbix, W., Hack, H. J., Stark, G. B., Spilker, G., & Doehn, M. (1995). Alcohol and drug abuse in burn injuries. *Burns, 21,* 194–199.

Hearn, W. L., Rose, S., Wagner, J., Ciarleglio, A., & Mash, D. C. (1991). Cocaethylene is more potent than cocaine in mediating lethality. *Pharmacology, Biochemistry and Behavior, 39,* 531–533.

Hesselbrock, M., Hesselbrock, V., Syzmanski, K., & Weidenman, M. (1988). Suicide attempts and alcoholism. *Journal of Studies on Alcohol, 49,* 436–442.

Hingson, R., & Howland, J. (1987). Alcohol as a risk factor for injury or death resulting from accidental falls: A review of the literature. *Journal of Studies on Alcohol, 48,* 212–219.

Hunt, W. A. (1985). *Alcohol and biological membranes.* New York: Guilford Press.

Hurt, R. D., Offord, K. P., Croghan, I. T., Gomez-Dahl, L., Kottke, T. E., Morse, R. M., & Melton, L. J. (1996). Mortality following inpatient addictions treatment: Role of tobacco use in a community-based cohort. *Journal of the American Medical Association, 275,* 1097–1103.

Ishii, H., Thurman, R. G., Ingelman-Sundberg, M., Cederbaum, A. I., Fernandez-Checa, J. C., Kato, S., Yokoyama, H., & Tsukamoto, H. (1996). Oxidative stress in alcoholic liver injury (symposium). *Alcoholism: Clinical and Experimental Research, 20,* 162A–167A.

Jacobson, J. L., Jacobson, S. W., & Sokol, R. J. (1996). Increased vulnerability to alcohol related birth defects in the offspring of mothers over 30. *Alcoholism: Clinical and Experimental Research, 20,* 359–363.

Jones, A. W. & Andersson, L. (1996). Influence of age, gender, and blood-alcohol concentration on the disappearance rate of alcohol from blood in drinking drivers. *Journal of Forensic Science, 41,* 922–926.

Jones, M. K., & Jones, B. M. (1980). The relationship of age and drinking habits to the effects of alcohol on memory in women. *Journal of Studies on Alcohol, 41,* 179–186.

Jones, S. L., & Lanyon, R. I. (1981). Relationship between adaptive skills and outcome of alcoholism treatment. *Journal of Studies on Alcohol, 42,* 521–525.

Jones-Webb, R. J., Hsiao, C-Y., & Hannan, P. (1995). Relationships between socioeconomic status and drinking problems among black and white men. *Alcoholism: Clinical and Experimental Research, 19,* 623–627.

Kalant, H., Khanna, J. M., Lin, G. Y., & Chung, S. (1976). Ethanol—A direct inducer of drug metabolism. *Biochemical Pharmacology, 25,* 337–42.

Kelly, L. F., Goldberg, S. J., Donnerstein, R. L., Cardy, M. A., & Palombo, G. M. (1996). Hemodynamic effects of acute ethanol in young adults. *American Journal of Cardiology, 78,* 851–854.

Kessler, R. C., Crum, R. M., Warner, L. A., Nelson, C. B., Schulenberg, J., & Anthony, J. C. (1997). Lifetime co-occurrence of DSM-III-R alcohol abuse and dependence with other psychiatric disorders in the National Comorbidity Survey. *Archives of General Psychiatry, 54,* 313–321.

Klatsky, A. L. (1996). Alcohol and hypertension. *Clinica Chimica Acta, 246,* 91–105.

Koob, G. F. (1992). Drugs of abuse: Anatomy, pharmacology and function of reward pathways. *Trends in Pharmacological Sciences, 13,* 177–193.

Kozlowski, L. T., Skinner, W., Kent, C., & Pope, M. A. (1989). Prospects for smoking treatment in individuals seeking treatment for alcohol and other drug problems. *Addictive Behavior, 14,* 273–278.

Kranzler, H. R., & Anton, R. F. (1994). Implications of recent neuropsychopharmacologic research for understanding the etiology and development of alcoholism. *Journal of Consulting and Clinical Psychology, 62,* 1116–1126.

Kranzler, H. R., Burleson, J. A., Korner, P., Del Boca, F. K., Bohn, M. J., Brown, J., & Liebowitz, N. (1995). Placebo-controlled trial of fluoxetine as an adjunct to relapse prevention in alcoholics. *American Journal of Psychiatry, 152,* 391–397.

Kushner, M. G., Sher, K. J., & Beitman, B. D. (1990). The relation between alcohol problems and the anxiety disorders. *American Journal of Psychiatry, 147,* 685–695.

Laitinen, K., Lamberg-Allardt, C., Tunninen, R., Karonen, S. L., Tahetia, R., Yikahri, R., & Valimaki, M. (1991). Transient hypoparathyroidism during acute alcohol intoxication. *New England Journal of Medicine, 324,* 721–727.

Laitinen, K., & Valimaki, M. (1993). Bone and the "comforts of life." *Annals of Medicine, 25,* 413–425.

Lammers, S. M. M., Mainzer, D. E. H., & Breteler, M. H. M. (1995). Do alcohol pharmacokinetics in women vary due to menstrual cycle? *Addiction, 90,* 23–30.

Lex, B. W., Greenwald, N. E., Lukas, S. E., Slater, J. P., & Mendelson, J. H. (1988). Blood ethanol levels, self-rated ethanol effects, and cognitive-perceptual tasks. *Pharmacology, Biochemistry and Behavior, 29,* 509–515.

Lex, B. W., Mello, N. K., Mendelson, J. H., & Babor, T. F. (1989). Reasons for alcohol use by female heavy, moderate and occasional social drinkers. *Alcohol, 6,* 281–287.

Lieber, C. S. (1994). Hepatic and metabolic effects of ethanol: Pathogenesis and prevention. *Annals of Medicine, 26,* 325–30.

Lieber, C. S. (1995). Medical disorders of alcoholism. *New England Journal of Medicine, 333,* 1058–1065.

Mann, K., Mundle, G., Strayle, M., & Wakat, P. (1995). Neuroimaging in alcoholism: CT and MRI results and clinical correlates. *Journal of Neural Transmission, 99,* 145–155.

Manzo, L., Locatelli, C., Candura, S. M., & Costa, L. G. (1994). Nutrition and alcohol neurotoxicity. *Neurotoxicology, 15,* 555–566.

McCance, E. F., Price, L. H., Kosten, T. R., & Jatlow, P. I. (1995). Cocaethylene: Pharmacology, physiology and behavioral effects in humans. *Journal of Pharmacology and Experimental Therapeutics, 274,* 215–223.

McGill, V., Kowal-Vern, A., Fisher, S. G., Kahn, S., & Gamelli, R. L. (1995). The impact of substance use on mortality and morbidity from thermal injury. *Journal of Trauma, Injury, Infection and Critical Care, 38,* 931–934.

Mendelson, J. H., & Mello, N. K. (1988). Chronic alcohol effects on anterior pituitary and ovarian hormones in heathy women. *Journal of Pharmacology and Experimental Therapeutics, 245,* 407–412.

Mendenhall, C. L., Seeff, L., Diehl, A. M., Ghosn, S. J., French, S. W., Gartside, P. S., Rouster, S. D., Buskell-Bales, Z., Grossman, C. J., Roselle, G. A., Weesner, R. E., Garcia-Pont, P., Goldberg, S. J., Kiernan, T. W., Tamburro, C. H., Zetterman, R., Chedid, A., Chen, T., Rabin, L., & VA Cooperative Study Group (No. 119). (1991). Antibodies to hepatitis b virus and hepatitis c virus in alcoholic hepatitis and cirrhosis; their prevalence and clinical relevance. *Hepatology, 14,* 581–589.

Miller, B. A., Maguin, E., & Downs, W. R. (1997). Alcohol, drugs and violence in children's lives. *Recent Developments in Alcoholism, 13,* 357–385.

Miller, W. R., & Del Boca, F. K. (1994). Measurement of drinking using the Form 90 family of instruments. *Journal of Studies on Alcohol, 12,* 112–118.

Mizoi, T., Tatsuno, Y., Adachi, J., Kogame, M., Fukunaga, T., Fujiwara, S., Hishida, S., & Ijiri, I. (1983). Alcohol sensitivity related to polymorphism of alcohol-metabolizing enzymes in Japanese. *Pharmacology, Biochemistry and Behavior, 18,* 127–133.

Moak, D. H., & Anton, R. F. (1996). Alcohol-related seizures and the kindling effect of repeated detoxifications: The influence of cocaine. *Alcohol and Alcoholism, 31,* 135–143.

Monti, P. M., Rohsenow, D. J., Colby, S. M., & Abrams, D. B. (1995). Smoking among alcoholics during and after treatment: Implications for models, treatment strategies, and policy. *National Institute on Alcohol Abuse and Alcoholism Research Monograph, 30,* 187–206.

Mooney, D. (1995). The relationship between sexual insecurity, the alcohol expectation for enhanced sexual experience, and consumption patterns. *Addictive Behaviors, 20,* 243–250.

Morgan, M. Y. (1994). The prognosis and outcome of alcoholic liver disease. *Alcohol and Alcoholism, 2,* 335–343.

Naranjo, C. A., Sellers, E. M., Chater, K., Iversen, P., Roach, C., & Sykora, K. (1983). Nonpharmacologic intervention in acute alcohol withdrawal. *Clinical Pharmacology and Therapeutics, 34,* 214–219.

National Institute on Alcohol Abuse and Alcoholism, (1989). Alcohol and trauma. *Alcohol Alert, 3.*

National Institute on Alcohol Abuse and Alcoholism, (1995). Alcohol-medication interactions. *Alcohol Alert, 27.*

Ng, S. K. C., Hauser, W. A., Brust, J. C. M., & Susser, M. (1988). Alcohol consumption and withdrawal in new-onset seizures. *New England Journal of Medicine, 319,* 666–673.

Niccols, G. A. (1994). Fetal alcohol syndrome: Implications for psychologists. *Clinical Psychology Review, 14,* 91–111.

Nixon, S. J., Tivis, R., & Parsons, O. A. (1992). Interpersonal problem-solving in male and female alcoholics. *Alcoholism: Clinical and Experimental Research, 16,* 684–687.

O'Malley, S. S., Jaffe, A. J., Chang, G., Schottenfeld, R. S., Meyer, R. E., & Rounsaville, B. (1992). Naltrexone and coping skills therapy for alcohol dependence: A controlled study. *Archives of General Psychiatry, 49,* 881–887.

Overall, J. E., Reilly, E. L., Kelley, J. T., & Hollister, L. E. (1985). Persistence of depression in detoxified alcoholics. *Alcoholism: Clinical and Experimental Research, 9,* 331–333.

Ozdemir, V., Bremner, K. E., & Naranjo, C. A. (1993). Treatment of alcohol withdrawal syndrome. *Annals of Medicine, 26,* 101–105.

Pares, A., Barrera, J. M., Caballeria, J., Ercilla, G., Bruguera, M., Caballeria, L., Castillo, R., & Rodes, J. (1990). Hepatitis c virus antibodies in chronic alcoholic patients: Association with severity of liver injury. *Hepatology, 12,* 1295–1299.

Parker, E. S., & Noble, E. P. (1977). Alcohol consumption and cognitive functioning in social drinkers. *Journal of Studies on Alcohol, 38,* 1224–1232.

Parsons, O. A., & Nixon, S. J. (1993). Neurobehavioral sequelae of alcoholism. *Behavioral Neurology 11,* 205–218.

Pettinati, H. M. (1990). Diagnosing personality disorders in substance abusers. *National Institute of Drug Abuse Research Monograph, 105,* 236–242.

Pettinati, H. M., Sugerman, A. A., & Maurer, H. S. (1982). Four year MMPI changes in abstinent and drinking alcoholics. *Alcoholism: Clinical and Experimental Research, 6,* 487–494.

Phillips, T. J., Feller, D. J., & Crabbe, J. C. (1989). Selected mouse lines, alcohol and behavior. *Experientia, 45,* 805–827.

Pratt, O. E. (1984). Introduction: What do we know of the mechanisms of alcohol damage in utero? In *Ciba Foundation Symposium 105: Mechanisms of alcohol damage in utero.* London: Pitman.

Randall, C. L., Ekblud, U., & Anton, R. F. (1990). Perspectives on the pathophysiology of fetal alcohol syndrome. *Alcoholism: Clinical and Experimental Research, 14,* 807–812.

Rathlev, N. K., D'Onofrio, G., Fish, S. S., Harrison, P. M., Bernstein, E., Hossack, R. W., & Pickens, L. (1994). The lack of efficacy of phenytoin in the prevention of recurrent alcoholrelated seizures. *Annals of Emergency Medicine, 23,* 513–518.

Renaud, S., Dumont, E., Godsey, F., Suplisson, A., & Thevenon, C. (1979). Platelet functions in relation to dietary fats in farmers from two regions of France. *Thrombosis and Haemostasis, 40*, 518–531.

Renaud, S. C., & Ruf, J-C. (1996). Effects of alcohol on platelet functions. *Clinica Chimica Acta, 246*, 77–89.

Reuler, J. B., Giard, D. E., & Cooney, T. G. (1985). Wernicke's encephalopathy. *New England Journal of Medicine, 312*, 1035–1038.

Roesch, R., Ogloff, J. R., & Eaves, D. (1995). Mental health research in the criminal justice system: The need for common approaches and international perspective. *International Journal of Law and Psychiatry, 18*, 1–14.

Roslund, B., & Larson, C. A. (1979). Crimes of violence and alcohol abuse in Sweden. *International Journal of the Addictions, 14*, 1103–1115.

Rubin, E., & Thomas, A. P. (1992). Effects of alcohol on the heart and cardiovascular system. In J. H. Mendelson & N. K. Mello (Eds.), *Medical diagnosis and treatment of alcoholism* (pp. 263–287). New York: McGraw-Hill.

Ruf, J. C., Berger, J. L., & Renaud, S. (1995). Platelet rebound effect of alcohol withdrawal and wine drinking in rats. Relation to tannins and lipid peroxidation. *Arteriosclerosis, Thrombosis and Vascular Biology, 15*, 140–144.

Sass, H., Soyka, M., Mann, K., & Zieglgansberger, W. (1996). Relapse prevention by acamprosate: Results from a placebo-controlled study on alcohol dependence. *Archives of General Psychiatry, 53*, 673–680.

Savolainen, M. J., & Kesaniemi, A. Y. (1995). Effects of alcohol on lipoproteins in relation to coronary artery disease. *Current Opinion in Lipidology, 6*, 191–195.

Schuckit, M. A., & Smith, T. L. (1997). Assessing the risk for alcoholism among sons of alcoholics. *Journal of Studies on Alcohol, 58*, 141–145.

Seeff, L. B., Cuccherini, B. A., Zimmerman, H. J., Adler, E., & Benjamin, S. B. (1986). Acetaminophen hepatoxocity in alcoholics: A therapeutic misadventure. *Annals of Internal Medicine, 104*, 399–404.

Sellers, E. M., Higgins, G. A., Tompkins, D. M., & Romach, M. K. (1992). Serotonin and alcohol drinking. *National Institute of Drug Abuse Research Monograph, 119*, 141–145.

Sellers, E. M., Sullivan, J. T., Somer, G., & Sykora, K. (1991). Characterization of DSM-III-R criteria for uncomplicated alcohol withdrawal provides an empircal basis for DSM-IV. *Archives of General Psychiatry, 48*, 442–447.

Singletary, K. W., Dorgan, J., Gapstur, S. M., & Anderson, L. M. (1996). Alcohol and breast cancer: Interactions between alcohol and other risk factors. *Alcoholism: Clinical and Experimental Research, 20*, 57A–61A.

Smith, M. J., Abbey, A., & Scott, R. O. (1993). Reasons for drinking alcohol: Their relationship to psychosocial variables and alcohol consumption. *International Journal of the Addictions, 28*, 881–908.

Sobell, M. K., Sobell, L. C., Klanjner, F., Pavan, D., & Basian, E. (1986). The reliability of a timeline method for assessing normal drinker college students' recent drinking history: Utility for alcohol research. *Addictive Behaviors, 11*, 149–161.

Sokol, R. J., & Clarren, S. K. (1989). Guidelines for the use of terminology describing the impact of prenatal alcohol on the offspring. *Alcoholism: Clinical and Experimental Research, 13*, 597–598.

Stampfer, M. J., Colditz, G. A., Willett, W. C., Speizer, F. E., & Hennekens, C. H. (1988). A prospective study of moderate alcohol consumption and the risk of coronary disease and stroke in women. *New England Journal of Medicine, 319*, 267–273.

Stewart, S. H. (1996). Alcohol abuse in individuals exposed to trauma: A critical review. *Psychological Bulletin, 120*, 83–112.

Streissguth, A. P., Aase, J. M., Clarren, S. K., Randels, S. P., LaDue, R. A., & Smith, D. F. (1991). Fetal alcohol syndrome in adolescents and adults. *Journal of the American Medical Association, 265*, 1961–1967.

Streissguth, A. P., Herman, C. S., & Smith, D. W. (1978). Intelligence, behavior and dysmorphogenesis in the fetal alcohol syndrome: a report on 20 patients. *Journal of Pediatrics, 92*, 363–367.

Sullivan, J. T., Sykora, K., Schneiderman, J., Naranjo, C. A., & Sellers, E. M. (1989). Assessment of alcohol withdrawal: The revised clinical institute withdrawal assessment for alcohol scale (CIWA-Ar). *British Journal of Addiction, 84*, 1353–1357.

Sullivan, W. C. (1899). A note on the influence of maternal inebriety on the offspring. *Journal of Mental Science, 45*, 489–503.

Sutker, P. B., Tabakoff, B., Goist, K. C., & Randall, C. L. (1983). Acute alcohol intoxication, mood states and alcohol metabolism in women and men. *Pharmacology, Biochemistry and Behavior, 18*, 349–354.

Szabo, G., Tabakoff, B., & Hoffman, P. L. (1994). The NMDA receptor antagonist dizocilpine differentially affects environment-dependent and environment-independent ethanol tolerance. *Psychopharmacology, 113*, 511–517.

Tabakoff, B., & Melchior, C. L. (1981). Modification of environmentally cued tolerance to ethanol in mice. *Journal of Pharmacology and Experimental Therapy, 291*, 175–180.

Thompson, W. L. (1975). Management of alcohol withdrawal syndromes. *Archives of Internal Medicine, 138,* 278–283.

Tsai, G., Gastfriend, D. R., & Coyle, J. T. (1995). The glutamatergic basis of human alcoholism. *American Journal of Psychiatry, 152,* 332–340.

U.S. General Accounting Office. (1970). *Comptroller General's report to subcommittee on alcoholism and narcotics.* Washington, DC: Government Printing Office.

Victor, M. (1992). The effects of alcohol on the nervous system. In J. H. Mendelson & N. K. Mello (Ed.), *The medical diagnosis and treatment of alcoholism* (pp. 201–262). New York: McGraw-Hill.

Victor, M., & Brausch, C. (1967). The role of abstinence in the genesis of alcoholic epilepsy. *Epilepsia, 8,* 1–20.

Volkow, N. D., Hitzemann, R., Wang, G-J., Fowler, J. S., Burr, G., Pascani, K., Dewey, S. L., & Wolf, A. P. (1992). Decreased brain metabolism in neurologically intact healthy alcoholics. *American Journal of Psychiatry, 149,* 1016–1022.

Volkow, N. D., Wang, G-J., Hitzemann, R., Fowler, J. S., Overall, J. E., Burr, G., & Wolf, A. P. (1994). Recovery of brain glucose metabolism in detoxified alcoholics. *American Journal of Psychiatry, 151,* 178–183.

Volpicelli, J. R., Alterman, A. I., Hayashida, M., & O'Brien, C. P. (1992). Naltrexone in the treatment of alcohol dependence. *Archives of General Psychiatry, 49,* 876–880.

Webb, G. R., Redman, S., Hennrikus, D. J., Kelman, G. R., Gibberd, R. W., & Sanson-Fisher, R. W. (1994). The relationships between high-risk and problem drinking and the occurrence of work injuries and related absences. *Journal of Studies on Alcohol, 55,* 434–446.

Weinberger, D. A., & Bartholomew, K. (1996). Social-emotional adjustment and patterns of alcohol use among young adults. *Journal of Personality, 64,* 495–527.

Williams, R. J., & Ricciardelli, L. A. (1996). Expectancies related to symptoms of alcohol dependence in young adults. *Addiction, 91,* 1031–1039.

Winokur, G., & Black, D. W. (1987). Psychiatric and medical diagnoses as risk factors for mortality in psychiatric patients: A case-control study. *American Journal of Psychiatry, 144,* 208–211.

5

Sedative-Hypnotic and Anxiolytic Agents

Kathleen T. Brady

Hugh Myrick

Robert Malcolm

Sedative and anxiolytic agents have long been used for the reduction of anxiety and the induction of sleep. Most of these drugs have a similar spectrum of activity along a continuum of central nervous system (CNS) depression, producing a calming, anxiolytic effect at low doses (sedation) and drowsiness and sleep at higher doses (hypnosis). Barbiturates were introduced into clinical practice in the early 1900s and were the most commonly used drugs in the treatment of anxiety, insomnia, and seizure disorders until the introduction of the benzodiazepines in the early 1960s. The benzodiazepines offered substantial advantages over the barbiturates in terms of safety and selectivity of activity.

After the benzodiazepines became available in the 1960s, prescriptions for sedative-hypnotics steadily increased to a peak level of approximately 100 million prescriptions per year in 1975. Prescriptions then decreased to 65 million in 1981 and have leveled off since then (Griffiths & Sannerud, 1987). The tendency toward more conservative anxiolytic

use is probably, in part, attributable to an increase in negative attitudes toward the use of these compounds. Of medical specialists, family physicians and internists are the major prescribers of benzodiazepines, followed by psychiatrists. With the increased use of benzodiazepines, the use of nonbenzodiazepine sedative-hypnotics has decreased to the point where trends in the prescription of benzodiazepines accurately reflect the prescription of sedative-hypnotics generally.

Despite a trend toward the decreasing use of sedative-hypnotics, they remain commonly prescribed agents. Data from the National Prescription Audit and the National Disease and Therapeutic Index indicated that retail pharmacies dispensed 20.8 million prescriptions in 1989 (Wysowski & Baum, 1991). Nevertheless, only 0.9% of the general adult population endorsed nonmedical use of sedatives in 1992 (U.S. Department of Health and Human Services, 1992). Furthermore, data seem to indicate that these are valuable therapeutic agents and, for the most part, are being prescribed appropriately within the context of health care provision (Griffiths & Sannerud, 1987).

It is important to note that many antidepressant agents (tricyclic antidepressants, selective serotonin reuptake inhibitors) are effective in the treatment of anxiety disorders. These agents, however, are not marketed primarily as anxiolytic agents, and discussion of their use is beyond the scope of this chapter. These agents do have a clear role in the treatment of anxiety disorders and little abuse potential. Thus, they are clearly agents that warrant serious consideration in the treatment of anxiety disorders in the substance-abusing population.

Two newer agents have been introduced that have unique spectrums of clinical activity. Buspirone (Buspar) is an anxiolytic drug, shown to be effective in the treatment of generalized anxiety disorder, but not in the treatment of other anxiety disorders. Buspirone is of particular interest because, unlike the benzodiazepines, it has no abuse potential. A recent study of the use of buspirone in anxious alcoholics indicated that this drug could be useful both in decreasing anxiety in an alcoholic population and in improving some alcohol-related outcomes (Kranzler et al., 1994). Thus, this agent may be of particular interest as an anxiolytic in substance abusers but appears to have a limited spectrum of clinical efficacy.

Zolpidem (Ambien) was introduced in 1993 in the United States as a short-acting nonbenzodiazepine hypnotic agent. This agent does, however, work through the GABA-ergic neurotransmitter system, has metabolites which are active at benzodiazepine receptor sites, and shares many properties with the benzodiazepines. In addition, there has been at least one case of dose escalation and withdrawal in individuals with a history of a substance use disorder (Bruun, 1993). Other newer agents, such as abecarnil, gepirone, and alpidem, are not currently available in the United States and there are few data concerning their usefulness as hypnotic agents or their abuse potential.

MAJOR PHARMACOLOGICAL ACTIONS

All of the sedative-hypnotic and anxiolytic agents have the ability to produce widespread CNS depression. In lower doses, most decrease activity, moderate excitement, and have a calming, anxiolytic effect. In higher doses, they produce drowsiness and facilitate the onset and maintenance of sleep. Some sedative-hypnotics (i.e., barbiturates) have the capacity to induce general anesthesia. However, it is important to note that the benzodiazepines do not induce general anesthesia. While there are variations in the specificity and spectrum of clinical activity among sedative-hypnotic agents, many of these drugs have anticonvulsant, anxiolytic, and muscle-relaxant properties. In clinical practice today, the most common uses of the sedative-hypnotics include sleep induction, anxiety reduction, anticonvulsant activity, and muscle relaxation. Buspirone, an anxiolytic agent which is not a sedative-hypnotic agent, does not produce widespread CNS depression or sleep induction.

Sedative-hypnotic and anxiolytic agents have other important pharmacological differences. These include variation in onset of clinical activity, variation in half-life, the presence or absence of active metabolites, and differences in the specificity of the various sedative-hypnotics in producing various clinical effects. For instance, it appears that the benzodiazepines are more specific in their anxiolytic properties than the barbiturates. Thus, the benzodiazepines have an anxiolytic effect at nonsedating doses, whereas barbiturates do not. Benzodiazepines are also far safer to use than barbiturates. Barbiturates suppress the respiratory drive at doses only three times greater than those used to induce sleep and hence are very dangerous in overdose.

Metabolic Pathways

The chemical and pharmacokinetic properties of the sedative-hypnotics affect their clinical utility. They are all lipophilic and essentially completely absorbed. As can be seen in tables 5.1 and 5.2, they have very different elimination half-lives, however, and may thus be divided into four categories: (a) ultra-short-acting (midazolam); (b) short-acting (T½ < 6 hr; triazolam, zolpedim); (c) intermediate-acting (T½ = 6–24 hr. temazepam, lorazepam, oxazepam); and (d) long-acting (T½ > 24 hr.; flurazepam, diazepam). The benzodiazepines and their active metabolites bind to plasma proteins. The concentration in the cerebrospinal fluid (CSF) is approximately equal to that of free drug in plasma. The benzodiazepines are extensively metabolized in the liver (Hobbs, Rall, & Verdoorn, 1996). Many have active metabolites that are biotransformed more slowly than the

TABLE 5.1 Names, Routes of Administration, Dosage, and Half-Life of Commonly Used Benzodiazepines

Generic/trade name (street name)	Routes of administration	Half-life (hours)	Usual therapeutic use	Usual dosage (mg)
Alprazolam/Xanax (blue haze)	Oral	6–16	Anxiety disorder	0.125–3.0 bid–qid
Chlordiazepoxide/Librium (libs, tranqs)	Oral, IM, IV	5–15	Anxiety/alcohol withdrawal	50–100 qd–qid
Clonazepam/Klonopin	Oral	30–60	Seizure disorders/agitation/ anxiety	1–5 qd–bid
Diazepam/Valium (CVs, vals, yellow-and-blues)	Oral	20–70	Anxiety/withdrawal/seizures	5–10 tid–qid
Flurazepam/Dalmane	Oral	47–100	Insomnia	15–30 qhs
Lorazepam/Ativan	Oral	12–18	Anxiety/agitation/withdrawal	1–5 bid–qid
Midazolam/Versed	IV or IM	1.2–12.3	Preanesthetic	5.0 mg
Oxazepam/Serax	Oral	5.7–10.9	Anxiety/withdrawal	15–30, tid–qid
Temazepam/Restoril	Oral	3.5–18.4	Insomnia	7.5–30.0 qhs
Triazolam/Halcion	Oral	1.5–5.5	Insomnia	0.125–0.25 qhs

TABLE 5.2 Other Sedative-Hypnotics/Anxiolytics

Generic/trade name (street name)	Routes of administration	Half-life (hours)	Usual therapeutic use	Usual sedative/ anxiolytic dosage
Barbiturates				
Amobarbital/Amytal (blue devil/blue doll)	Oral, IM, IV	10–40	Insomnia/preoperative/ seizures	40–50 bid–tid
Butabarbital/Butisol	Oral	35–88	Insomnia in combination with analgesics for headache	15–30, tid–qid
Methohexital/Brevital	IV	3–5	Preoperative	—
Pentobarbital/Nembutal (yellow jackets/yellows)	Oral, IM, IV, rectal	15–50	Insomnia/seizures/ preoperative	100 qhs
Phenobarbital/Luminal (phennies)	Oral, IM, IV	80–120	Seizures	30–120 bid–tid
Secobarbital/Seconal (red devils/reds)	Oral, IM, IV, rectal	15–40	Insomnia/seizures	100 qhs
Others				
Buspirone/Buspar	Oral	10–16	Anxiety	10–60 bid–tid
Chloral Hydrate/Noctec (miki's/mickey finn)	Oral, rectal	5–10	Insomnia	500 @ hs
Ethchlorvynol/Placidyl	Oral	10–20	Insomnia	500 @ hs
Glutethemide/Doriden	Oral	7–15	Insomnia	250–500 @ hs
Meprobamate/Miltown (goof balls)	Oral	6–7	Anxiety	1200–1600 bid–tid
Zolpidem/Ambien	Oral	2–4	Insomnia	5–20 qhs

parent compounds, explaining the long duration of effects. Metabolism occurs in three major stages. For those compounds that have a substituent on the diazepine ring, the initial phase of metabolism is the removal of the substituent producing an N-desalkylated compound which is biologically active. One such compound, nordiazepam, is an active metabolite common to the metabolic pathway of diazepam, clorazepate, prazepam, and halazepam. The second phase of metabolism involves hydroxylation and also usually yields an active metabolite. The third major stage of metabolism is conjugation, principally with glucuronic acid to an inactive metabolite.

Actions in the Central Nervous System

Impact on Neurotransmitter Systems

Since the 1970s, much attention has been focused on the neurobiology of sedative-hypnotic and anxiolytic agents. While most of the work has focused on the benzodiazepines, it is likely that most sedative-hypnotics have important similarities in the mechanism of action. Most of the actions of sedative-hypnotic agents are a result of potentiation of neural inhibition mediated through the gamma-aminobutyric acid (GABA) neurotransmitter system. Ninety percent of all inhibitory neurons are believed to be GABA-mediated. Animal and clinical studies have demonstrated that drugs with an intrinsic positive effect at the GABA-benzodiazepine-chloride channel complex (e.g., GABA agonists, benzodiazepine agonists, barbiturates, and alcohol) facilitate GABA-mediated chloride conductance and possess anxiolytic and anticonvulsant activity (Aaronson, Hinman, & Okamoto, 1984; Frye, McGown, & Breese, 1983). The mechanism of inhibitory activity appears to be activation of the central benzodiazepine receptor or the GABA-A receptor, which increases chloride conductance through the ionophore, thereby hyperpolarizing the cell membrane and stabilizing the cell (Potter, Rudorfer, & Manji, 1990). Specific benzodiazepine receptors associated with the GABA receptor/chloride ion channel have been identified, and benzodiazepine antagonists have been developed. GABA receptors are present at all levels within the central nervous system. The many different pharmacological activities of the benzodiazepines are due to activities in varying, specific brain regions.

Mechanisms of Tolerance and Dependence

Tolerance is defined as a reduction in response to a drug after repeated administrations (Hobbs et al., 1996). Pharmacokinetic tolerance occurs with the barbiturates, but not the benzodiazepines, and refers to changes in the distribution or metabolism of a drug after repeated administration so that reduced concentrations are present in the blood. Barbiturates stimulate the activity of the hepatic microsomal enzymes and therefore cause more rapid metabolism of the barbiturates themselves as well as of many other drugs. Hence, barbiturate administration can cause a decreased plasma level and therefore therapeutic effects of a number of other agents. Benzodiazepines do not stimulate activity of the hepatic microsomal system.

Pharmacodynamic tolerance occurs with chronic benzodiazepine administration and is most likely caused by drug-induced changes in receptor density or function. Tolerance to the various effects of drugs develops at differing rates. For the benzodiazepines, although tolerance develops fairly rapidly to the sleep-inducing properties, tolerance to anxiolytic activity and memory impairment is generally not seen.

Physical dependence is the state that develops as a result of the resetting of physiological responses as a consequence of repeated drug use. The GABA-ergic system adjusts to the chronic presence of benzodiazepines, so that when the agents are stopped abruptly, physical signs and symptoms occur (table 5.3) that are manifestations of central nervous system hyperarousal due to readaptation to the absence of the drug. As will be discussed in a later section, withdrawal from sedative-hypnotic agents can be life-threatening.

CLINICAL ASPECTS

Abuse Potential and Toxicity

In tables 5.1 and 5.2, the names, route of administration, usual dosages, and half-lives of benzodiazepines (table 5.1) and other sedative-hypnotics and anxiolytics (table 5.2) are displayed. Generally, these drugs are taken orally. The benzodiazepines have low toxicity and few drug interactions but can produce additive sedation in combination with alcohol. The barbiturates have complex drug interactions. These drugs inhibit the metabolism of many other drugs

TABLE 5.3 Sedative-Hypnotic Withdrawal Symptoms

Mild	Moderate	Severe
Anxiety	Panic	Hypothermia
Insomnia	Decreased concentration	Vital sign instability
Dizziness	Tremor	Muscle fasciculations
Headache	Sweating	Seizures
Anorexia	Palpitations	Delirium
Perceptual hyperacusis	Perceptual distortions	Psychosis
Irritability	Muscle aches	
Agitation	GI upset	
	Insomnia	
	Elevated vital signs	
	Depression	

and can cause life-threatening CNS depression in combination with alcohol and other CNS depressants.

The potential for sedative-hypnotic and anxiolytic abuse and dependence is apparent from laboratory as well as clinical settings. Drug self-administration procedures in laboratory animals provide valuable information concerning the potential for the abuse of pharmacological agents in humans. Multiple experimental studies with rats and nonhuman primates have indicated that a variety of sedative-hypnotic and anxiolytic agents are self-administered. These studies indicated that benzodiazepines are less efficacious reinforcers than barbiturates and psychomotor stimulants (Griffiths & Sannerud, 1987). Of interest, in self-administration paradigms, buspirone has not been shown to be self-administered by animals or humans or to produce physical dependence. In this regard, buspirone clearly has a different pharmacological profile from the sedative-hypnotic agents. However, self-administration in animal laboratory paradigms, as well as dependence and tolerance, has been established with zolpidem (Griffiths, Sannerud, Ator, & Brady, 1992).

Studies comparing the abuse liability of various benzodiazepines have found that there are meaningful differences among these compounds. Oxazepam, halazepam, and chlordiazepoxide all appear to have less abuse potential than lorazepam, diazepam, and alprazolam (Griffiths & Sannerud, 1987). It may be that a rapid onset of effect is an important determinant of differential abuse liability among drugs in the same class. This finding is paralleled in the studies of barbiturates in which phenobarbital has been shown to produce less preference and euphoria than pentobarbital and secobarbital, both of which have a rapid onset of action.

Physical Symptoms of Abuse and Dependence

An area of major concern if a decision is made to discontinue a sedative-hypnotic agent is the physical dependence and withdrawal that can occur with nearly all of these agents. It is important to note that withdrawal has not been reported for buspirone, which is an anxiolytic but not a sedative-hypnotic agent. Studies have confirmed that withdrawal symptoms can occur both with high-dose use and after prolonged treatment at therapeutic doses (Griffiths & Sannerud, 1987). Withdrawal manifestations are quite variable (table 5.3) and are related to the sedative-hypnotic used, the half-life and dosage of the agent, and patient characteristics such as personality factors, age, and general health. Rickels, Schweizer, Case, and Garcia-Espana (1988) found that personality factors, such as neuroticism and dependence, made significant contributions to the severity of withdrawal from sedative-hypnotics and were good predictors of difficulty with sedative-hypnotic discontinuation. Older age and male sex were favorable demographic features for sedative-hypnotic-dependent patients wishing to discontinue intake.

Withdrawal following cessation of short-half-life drugs (e.g., alprazolam and oxazepam) generally begins within 1–3 days, while withdrawal from longer-half-life drugs (e.g., diazepam, chlordiazepoxide) usually begins after 4–7 days. The time course for such symptoms may be only a few days or, less commonly, 1–4 weeks. For short-half-life agents, withdrawal is likely to begin and peak within a few days and be over within a week. For agents with a longer half-life, the symptoms may last for several days to weeks.

Minor withdrawal is often described by patients as involving increased acuity to sound or smell and sometimes vision, with colors often being "too vivid"; anxiety that may exceed the pretreatment level, at least temporarily; and irritability, insomnia, agitation, dizziness, and anorexia. Moderate withdrawal may be characterized by some vital sign elevations, panic-like symptoms, decreased concentration, tremor, sweating, headache, palpitations, insomnia, perceptual distortions, muscle aches, GI symptoms, and depression. Severe withdrawal is generally not seen in individuals with therapeutic dose dependence. Severe withdrawal has been characterized as similar to that of delirium tremens following alcohol cessation and can include hypothermia, vital sign fluctuations, muscle fasciculations, delirium, seizures, and psychotic symptoms including depersonalization, derealization, and paranoid ideation. Debate continues over the existence of a protracted abstinence syndrome lasting months to years. Smith and Wesson (1995) postulate that low-dose sedative-hypnotic withdrawal is receptor-mediated. This theory posits that because of this receptor mediation, symptoms worsen when patients are tapered from the last few milligrams of drug and may last for 6 months to 1 year.

Despite the total number of doses of benzodiazepines prescribed per year, the number of withdrawal reactions reported is relatively small. However, estimates are that 40% of benzodiazepine users will experience clinically distressing signs of withdrawal with abrupt cessation and constitute a significant population of patients (Tyrer & Seivewright, 1984). The duration of sedative-hypnotic treatment that can produce physical dependence is not well characterized. Some estimate it to be as short as 4–6 weeks (Fontaine, Chouinard, & Annable, 1984). If rebound insomnia is considered a measure of withdrawal, this has been demonstrated after only 2 weeks of daily drug administration (Bixler, Kales, Kales, Jacoby, & Soldatos, 1985).

There is suggestion from recent reports that the triazolobenzodiazepines, alprazolam and triazolam,

may present special problems during withdrawal. Brown and Hauge (1986) noted that the triazolo group may lead to greater binding affinity for a subpopulation of benzodiazepine receptors that are not influenced by other benzodiazepines. They believe that other benzodiazepines are therefore not totally effective in producing cross-tolerance for triazolobenzodiazepines and therefore are less effective in treating their withdrawal symptoms. Other case reports substituting clonazepam for triazolobenzodiazepines would seem to contradict this belief (Herman, Rosenbaum, & Brotman, 1987).

It is important to distinguish withdrawal symptoms from the reemergence of symptoms, as well as symptom rebound, in individuals with anxiety disorder. For the most part, this can be done by careful assessment of the profile and time course of symptoms that emerge upon drug termination. Symptom reemergence involves a gradual return of the original symptoms. Rebound anxiety is anxiety symptoms more severe than the original symptoms, which subsequently return to original levels. Withdrawal symptoms appear during drug taper and disappear in a matter of days to weeks. It is necessary for patients to remain medication-free for at least 2–3 weeks to distinguish fully among these three phenomena, but certain symptoms experienced for the first time after a benzodiazepine has been discontinued should probably be considered withdrawal symptoms.

Treatment of Sedative-Hypnotic Withdrawal

Patient education is one of the most important aspects of managing sedative-hypnotic withdrawal, particularly with therapeutic dose dependence. Patients should be informed of the need for withdrawal and educated about potential signs and symptoms, and the approach to discontinuation should be discussed with the patient. Several strategies may be used in the management of sedative-hypnotic withdrawal. The first two approaches, which involve drug tapering, are the most commonly used in situations of therapeutic drug dependence in which a slow discontinuation of drug can be tolerated and the withdrawal can be managed on an outpatient basis. The third approach, phenobarbital substitution, is more appropriate in situations where sedative-hypnotic abuse is clearly established and detoxification needs to be done rapidly. This strategy is designed to be used where close observation is possible, such as in an inpatient setting. It is important to note that withdrawal from high-dose sedative-hypnotic use can be life-threatening and often requires an inpatient setting.

In the approach of drug tapering, perhaps the most common approach is to taper the therapeutic agent over a 6- to 12-week period, using small reduction increments. It is appropriate to reduce by one fourth the prescribed dosage per week for the first several weeks, but as lower doses of medication are approached, even smaller decrements should be used. This is particularly true if the half-life of the drug is short. With shorter half-life drugs, this may mean dosing three to four times per day or more toward the end of the taper. For individuals who experience withdrawal symptoms using this regimen, a switch to a longer acting agent, such as clonazepam (Herman et al., 1987), which can then be tapered over several weeks, may be indicated. Clonazepam is a particularly good agent to use when a decision has been made to switch to a long-half-life agent. It has a slower onset of activity and relatively less abuse potential than other agents with long half-lives (e.g., diazepam).

A protocol for switching patients to phenobarbital has been described by Smith and Wesson (1995). Their article provides conversion dosages between phenobarbital and most sedative-hypnotics. For individuals for whom the daily administered dose of sedative-hypnotic is unclear, a protocol for using a pentobarbital challenge to determine the phenobarbital dosing strategy for detoxification has been described by Jackson and Shader (1973).

A carbamazepine substitution protocol has been shown preliminarily to be an effective treatment for benzodiazepine withdrawal. Carbamazepine has been shown to be as effective in the treatment of alcohol withdrawal as oxazepam (Malcolm, Ballenger, Sturgis, & Anton, 1989). In two preliminary open-label studies, carbamazepine in dosages of 200 mg tid for 7–10 days was effective in managing patients with difficult benzodiazepine withdrawal (Klein, Uhde, & Post, 1986; Ries, Roy-Byrne, Ward, Nepper, & Cullison, 1989). In a multisite, placebo-controlled study of the use of carbamazepine in alprazolam withdrawal (Ballenger, Lydiard, Laraia, Fossey, & Zealberg, 1991), carbamazepine showed some promise in the management of withdrawal, but the high dropout rates made definite conclusions im-

possible. Because of the preliminary nature of the controlled evidence supporting the use of carbamazepine and the potential for serious adverse consequences with inadequately managed sedative-hypnotic withdrawal, a benzodiazepine backup for elevated vital signs or other signs of withdrawal in individuals being detoxified with carbamazepine should always be used.

Pathological Effects

Sedative-hypnotic abuse appears to be predominant in certain populations clinically. In the majority of cases, sedative-hypnotic abuse occurs in the context of polysubstance abuse. In these cases, the sedative-hypnotics are often taken to ameliorate adverse effects of psychostimulants, to self-medicate heroin or alcohol withdrawal, or to produce intoxication when other drugs are not available. Sedative-hypnotics are rarely the drug of choice in these individuals. In one study of individuals in an inpatient substance-abuse treatment setting, 96% of individuals presenting with sedative-hypnotic abuse or dependence also had another substance-use disorder (Malcolm, Brady, Johnston, & Cunningham, 1993).

Another population at risk for the development of sedative-hypnotic abuse or dependence is individuals seeking treatment for anxiety or depression who also have a history of, or current, substance use disorder. A history of a substance use disorder or a strong family history of a substance use disorder should alert the physician that the risk-benefit ratio for sedative-hypnotic use must be assessed carefully. Covert alcoholism presents a great challenge to the clinician in prescribing sedative-hypnotics because it often presents as an anxiety disorder. However, Ciraulo, Sands, and Shader (1988) challenged the assertion that alcoholics have a greater liability for sedative-hypnotic abuse. In their review, they asserted that the liability for abuse may be greater for alcoholics, but there are such methodological deficiencies in the present studies that such a conclusion cannot automatically be reached. In light of the potential for serious interactions and the clinical experience that alcoholics abuse both alcohol and sedative-hypnotics, it seems that the use of sedative-hypnotics by alcoholics, whether drinking or in recovery, should be undertaken with great caution even on a short-term basis and probably should not be prescribed long term.

Physiological Effects

Benzodiazepines and other sedative hypnotics can cause varying degrees of light-headedness, lassitude, increased reaction time and motor incoordination, impairment of mental and motor function, confusion, and anterograde amnesia. All of these effects can impair driving and other psychomotor skills. As previously mentioned, interaction with ethanol may be particularly dangerous. These agents may also cause paradoxical effects. There have been reports of increased nightmares, anxiety, and irritability and the release of bizarre, uninhibited behavior with the use of benzodiazepines, referred to as disinhibition or dyscontrol reactions (Rashi, Patrissi, & Cook, 1988). The most serious physiological consequence of chronic use of these agents is the risk of physical dependence and life-threatening physical withdrawal with discontinuation of use.

Psychological Effects

As mentioned above, benzodiazepines have profound effects on cognition and memory. Paranoia, depression, and suicidal ideation have also been reported in several small case series associated with chronic use of benzodiazepines. These effects have not been investigated in any well-controlled studies.

Social/Interpersonal Effects

Like all addictive disorders, sedative hypnotic abuse and dependence generally have profound effects on social and interpersonal functioning. Because of effects on cognition, memory, and psychomotor performance, work and/or school performance is impaired. Like any addiction, sedative-hypnotic abuse and dependence impair consistent performance in social roles (wife/husband/parent) and interfere with the development of healthy interpersonal relationships.

SUMMARY

Sedative-hypnotics and anxiolytics remain one of the most useful classes of medication for the management of numerous disorders, particularly the anxiety disorders. As with all medications, treatment requires accurate diagnosis, knowledge of indications and side effects, and the willingness to monitor outcome repeatedly and frequently. The vast majority of sedative-hypnotic and anxiolytic users use them appropriately and as prescribed by their physicians.

Guidelines regarding benzodiazepine prescribing have been published by the American Psychiatric Association in a task force report (1990). In the report, therapeutic dose dependence is clearly acknowledged and discussed. The importance of informing patients concerning this potential before initiating long-term treatment is made clear, and strategies for managing withdrawal are discussed. This task force report recommends that benzodiazepines be used for the short-term treatment of anxiety or insomnia that interferes with daily functioning. Long-term use is recommended for only two groups of patients: the medically ill with persistent anxiety as a component of the medical illness that cannot be treated in other ways and individuals with chronic panic or agoraphobia for which benzodiazepines are decided to be the agent of choice by the treating physician. The task force report discourages the long-term use of benzodiazepines by patients with chronic sleep disorders. It is recommended that the lowest dose possible be used and that patients be treated for the briefest period of time indicated for their clinical condition. The task force urges particular caution in prescribing benzodiazepines to the elderly and to individuals with substance use disorders. Clear and more limited guidelines for sedative-hypnotic prescribing practices will probably greatly reduce the risk of sedative-hypnotic abuse.

While withdrawal reactions are likely with long-term sedative-hypnotic use, these can be clinically managed and should not militate against appropriate use. Withdrawal symptoms are generally mild in routine clinical use of sedative-hypnotics and controlled by sensible drug tapering. The potential for withdrawal phenomena should be discussed with all patients at the initiation of therapy. Current or past substance abuse appears to be the most prominent risk factor for sedative-hypnotic abuse and should be carefully assessed in all patients. Clinicians must be mindful of the risks of prescribing sedative-hypnotics. With both physicians and patients fully informed concerning the risks and benefits of these drugs, their use can be safe, appropriate, and important in the care of many patients.

Key References

American Psychiatric Association. (1990). *Benzodiazepine dependence, toxicity and abuse*. Washington, DC: American Psychiatric Press.

Griffiths, R. R., & Sannerud, C. A. (1987). Abuse and dependence on benzodiazepines and other anxiolytic/sedative drugs. In Y. Herbert, Meltzer, & J. T. Coyle (Eds.), *Psychopharmacology: The third generation of progress* (2nd ed., pp. 1535–1541). New York: Raven Press.

Hobbs, W. R., Rall, T. W., & Verdoorn, T. A. (1996). Hypnotics and sedatives: Ethanol. In J. G. G. Hardman, A. Gilman, & L. L. Limbird (Eds.), *Goodman & Gilman's the Pharmacological Basis of Therapeutics* (9th ed., pp. 361–396). New York: McGraw-Hill.

References

Aaronson, L. M., Hinman D. J., & Okamoto, M. (1984). Effects of diazepam on ethanol withdrawal. *Journal of Pharmacology and Experimental Therapeutics, 221*, 319–325.

American Psychiatric Association. (1990). *Benzodiazepine dependence, toxicity and abuse*. Washington, DC: American Psychiatric Press.

Ballenger, J. C., Lydiard, R. B., Laraia, M. D., Fossey, M. D., & Zealberg, J. J. (1991, May). *Use of carbamazepine in alprazolam discontinuation*. New research abstract. New Orleans: American Psychiatric Association.

Bixler, E. O., Kales, J. D., Kales, A., Jacoby, J. A., & Soldatos, C. R. (1985). Rebound insomnia and elimination half-life: assessment of individual subject response. *Journal of Clinical Pharmacology, 25*(2), 115–124.

Brown, J. L., & Hauge, K. J. (1986). A review of alprazolam withdrawal. *Drug Intelligence and Clinical Pharmacy, 20*, 837–884.

Bruun, T. G. (1993). Abuse potential during use and withdrawal psychosis after treatment with the hypnotic zolpidem. *Ugeskr Laeg, 155*, 2711–2713.

Ciraulo, D. A., Sands, B. F., & Shader, R. I. (1988). Critical review of liability for benzodiazepine abuse among alcoholics. *American Journal of Psychiatry, 145*(12), 1501–1506.

Fontaine, R., Chouinard, G., & Annable, L. (1984). Rebound anxiety in anxious patients after abrupt withdrawal of benzodiazepine treatment. *American Journal of Psychiatry, 141*(7), 848–852.

Frye, G. D., McCown, T. J., & Breese, G. R. (1983). Differential sensitivity of ethanol withdrawal signs in the rat to gamma-aminobutyric acid (GABA)mimet-
ics: Blockade of audiogenic seizures but not forelimb tremors. *Journal of Pharmacology and Experimental Therapeutics, 226*(3), 720–725.

Griffiths, R. R., & Sannerud, C. A. (1987). Abuse and dependence on benzodiazepines and other anxiolytic/sedative drugs. In Y. Herbert, Meltzer, & J. T. Coyle (Eds.), *Psychopharmacology: The third generation of progress* (2nd ed., pp. 1535–1541). New York: Raven Press.

Griffiths, R. R., Sannerud, C. A., Ator, N. A., & Brady, J. V. (1992). Zolpidem behavioral pharmacology in baboons: Self-injection, discrimination, tolerance and withdrawal. *Journal of Pharmacology and Experimental Therapeutics, 260*(3), 1199–1208.

Herman, J. B., Rosenbaum, J. F., & Brotman, A. W. (1987). The alprazolam to clonazepam switch for the treatment of panic disorder. *Journal of Clinical Psychopharmacology, 7*(3), 175–178.

Hobbs, W. R., Rall, T. W., & Verdoorn, T. A. (1996). Hypnotics and sedatives: Ethanol. In J. G. G. Hardman, A. Gilman, & L. L. Limbird (Eds.), *Goodman & Gilman's the Pharmacological Basis of Therapeutics* (9th ed., pp. 361–396). New York: McGraw-Hill.

Jackson, A. H., & Shader, R. I. (1973). Guidelines for the withdrawal of narcotic and general depressant drugs. *Diseases of the Nervous System, 34*(3), 162–166.

Klein, E., Uhde, T. W., & Post, R. M. (1986). Preliminary evidence for the utility of carbamazepine in alprazolam withdrawal. *American Journal of Psychiatry, 143*(2), 235–236.

Kranzler, H. R., Burleson, J. A., Del Boca, F. K., Babor, T. F., Korner, P., Brown, J., & Bohn, M. J. (1994). Buspirone treatment of anxious alcoholics: A placebo-controlled trial. *Archives of General Psychiatry, 51*(9), 720–731.

Malcolm, R., Ballenger, J. C., Sturgis, E. T., & Anton, R. (1989). Double-blind controlled trial comparing carbamazepine to oxazepam treatment of alcohol withdrawal [see comments]. *American Journal of Psychiatry, 146*(5), 617–621.

Malcolm, R., Brady, K. T., Johnston, A. L., & Cunningham, M. (1993). Types of benzodiazepines abused by chemically dependent inpatients. *Journal of Psychoactive Drugs, 25*(4), 315–319.

Potter, W. Z. (1984). Psychotherapeutic drugs and biogenic amines: Current concepts and therapeutic implications. *Drugs, 28*, 127–143.

Rashi, K., Patrissi, G., & Cook, B. (1988, July 15). Alprazolam found to have serious side effects. *Psychiatric News*, pp. 14–16.

Rickels, K., Schweizer E., Case, G. W., & Garcia-Espana, F. (1988). Benzodiazepine dependence, withdrawal severity, and clinical outcome: Effects of personality. *Psychopharmacology Bulletin, 24,* 415–420.

Ries, R. K., Roy-Byrne, P. P., Ward, N. G., Neppe, V., & Cullison, S. (1989). Carbamazepine treatment for benzodiazepine withdrawal. *American Journal of Psychiatry, 146*(4), 536–537.

Schweizer, E., Case, W. G., & Rickels, K. (1989). Benzodiazepine dependence and withdrawal in elderly patients. *American Journal of Psychiatry, 146*(4), 529–531.

Smith, D. E., & Wesson, D. R. (1995). Benzodiazepines and other sedative-hypnotics. In M. Galanter & H. Kleber (Eds.), *American psychiatric press textbook of substance abuse treatment* (1st ed.). Washington, DC: American Psychiatric Press.

Tyrer, P., & Seivewright, N. (1984). Identification and management of benzodiazepine dependence. *Post Graduate Medical Journal, 605,* 41–46.

U.S. Department of Health and Human Services (1992). *National household survey on drug abuse: population estimates.* Publication No. SMA-93-2053. Washington, DC: Government Printing Office.

Wysowski, D. K., & Baum, C. (1991). Outpatient use of prescription sedative-hypnotic drugs in the United States, 1970 through 1989. *Archives of Internal Medicine, 151*(9), 1779–1783.

6

Stimulants:
Amphetamines and Cocaine

Michael F. Weaver
Sidney H. Schnoll

Stimulants are drugs that stimulate the central nervous system (CNS) to produce increased psychomotor activity. Stimulants are widely used throughout the world, and nearly every society has some form of stimulant, whether it is caffeine in the West, khat in the Middle East, or methamphetamine throughout the world. Amphetamines and cocaine are the most prevalent stimulants of abuse. Smokable methamphetamine has been growing in popularity since the early 1980s, and over 4 million people in the United States have tried it (Substance Abuse and Mental Health Services Administration, 1995).

Stimulant abuse is cyclic in nature. A new drug will become popular on the illicit market and reach a peak of abuse among addicts, often generating panic in the general population. However, rates of abuse will gradually decline over time through death or disinterest until another new drug comes along to start the cycle again. Stimulant epidemics, like stimulant problem users, have a natural tendency to burn themselves out (Kaplan, Husch, & Bieleman, 1994).

This has been the case with amphetamine in the 1960s and methylenedioxymethamphetamine (MDMA) in the 1980s. The United States is currently experiencing a cocaine epidemic and the rise of a new cycle of smokable methamphetamine abuse. Understanding the effects of stimulants on the individual as well as on society is essential to the effective treatment of stimulant addiction.

MAJOR PHARMACOLOGICAL ACTIONS

Metabolic Pathways

Amphetamine is metabolized extensively in the liver into several biologically active metabolites (see figure 6.1), and nearly half is excreted unchanged in the urine while the rest is eliminated by biotransformation. The biological half-life of most amphetamines is 6–12 hr (Lader, 1983).

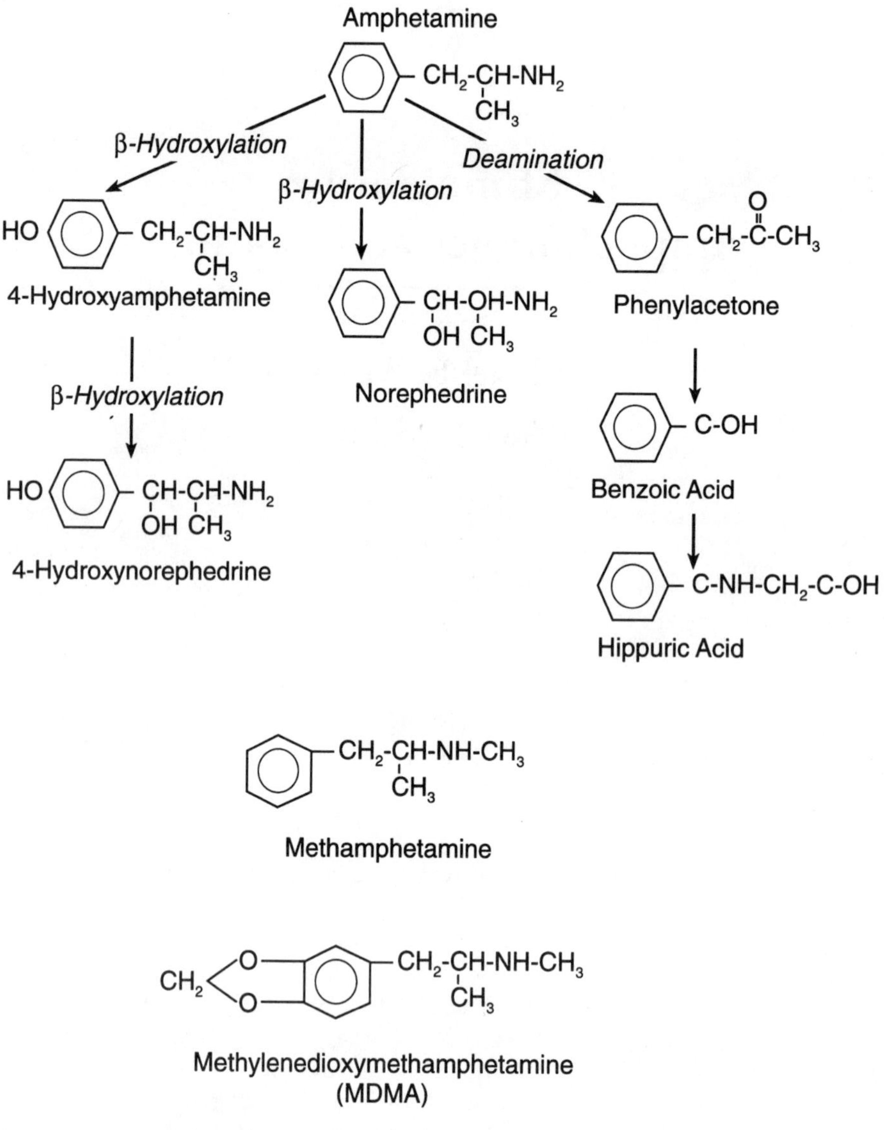

FIGURE 6.1 Structures and metabolism of some amphetamines.

Cocaine is also rapidly and extensively metabolized (see figure 6.2), then excreted in the urine. Its chemical name is benzoylmethylecgonine and it is broken down into both active and inactive metabolites by cholinesterases found in serum and the liver. The vast majority is hydrolyzed to two inactive metabolites (benzoylecgonine and ecgonine methyl-ester) with half-lives of 4–6 hr. Both are detectable on a urine drug screen within 4 hours of inhalation and up to 48 hours after cocaine use or even longer in chronic users (Quandt, Sommi, Pipkin, & McCal-lum, 1988; Weiss & Gawin, 1988). Cocaine undergoes oxidative metabolism by cytochrome P-450 monooxygenases in the liver to a potentially toxic active metabolite, norcocaine, but less than 10% is metabolized by this pathway (Roberts, Harbison, & James, 1991). Another active metabolite is ethylcocaine (cocaethylene), which is formed by the liver only in the presence of alcohol. Ethylcocaine has a potency equal to cocaine, which heightens the risk of toxicity from cocaine when it is taken with alcohol (Benowitz, 1993).

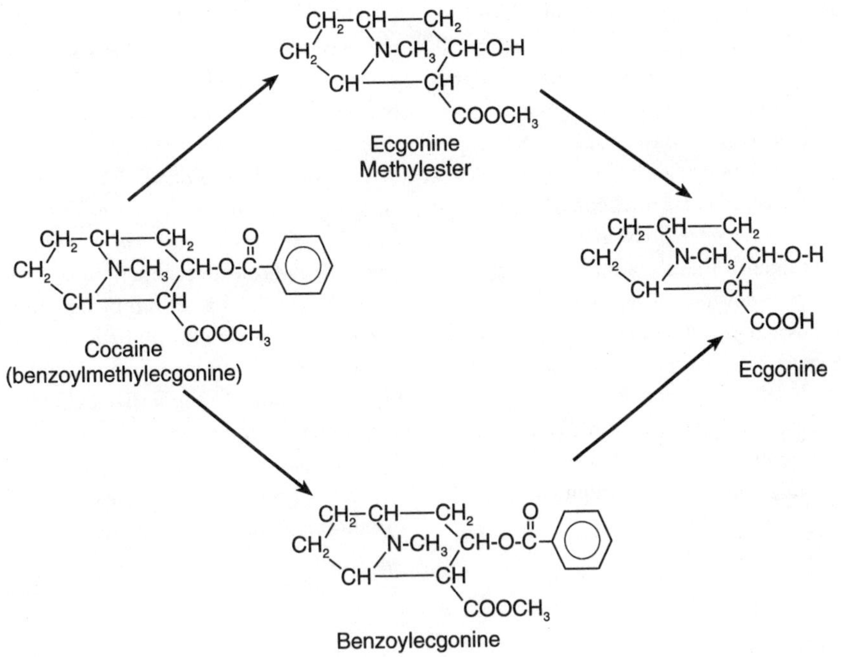

FIGURE 6.2 Metabolism of cocaine.

Certain types of patients are at higher risk for developing cocaine toxicity. Those who have deficient plasma cholinesterase, about 3% of the U.S. population (Becker, 1972), will metabolize it more slowly, so that they are at higher risk for adverse effects (Hoffman et al., 1992). Cholinesterase activity is lower in the elderly, patients with liver disease, pregnant women, and infants. Agents that induce cytochrome P-450 enzymes, such as alcohol or phenobarbital, can increase the percentage of cocaine that is converted to norcocaine and other active metabolites which are toxic. Care should be taken to prevent cocaine use in those populations that are more vulnerable to its toxic effects.

Actions in the Central Nervous System

Impacts on Neurotransmitter Systems

Despite structural and neuropharmacological differences, all stimulants are indirect sympathomimetic drugs. By blocking neurotransmitter (NT) reuptake at the synaptic junction, which raises the concentration of NT in the synapse, they produce activation of dopamine (DA), norepinephrine (NE), and serotonin (5-HT) systems. These pathways are closely asso-

ciated with expression of behavior and emotions, a heightened state of arousal, and pleasure. The simultaneous interaction between these different NT pathways is fundamental to stimulant euphoria and reward behavior (Gawin, 1991).

Amphetamine binds to the DA transporter (reuptake pump) on the presynaptic neuron in the synaptic cleft, then causes reversal of the pump mechanism, which allows DA to be released back into the synaptic cleft to stimulate postsynaptic receptors (Raiteri, Bertollini, Angelini, & Levi, 1975). Amphetamine also enhances release of excitatory NT from intracellular vesicles (Knepper, Grunewald, & Rutledge, 1988) and inhibits monoamine oxidase from breaking down NT in the synaptic cleft (Miller, Shore, & Clarke, 1980), an action that accounts for its long duration of effect. The primary mechanism of cocaine's effects is blockade of the DA transporter (Ritz, Lamb, Goldberg, & Kuhar, 1987), but without reversal of DA reuptake or inhibition of monoamine oxidase. Therefore, the acute effects of cocaine are transient and soon result in rapid depletion of NT. Cocaine acts very rapidly and can increase NE levels in the brain within 10 min of administration, but there is a subsequent decrease to subnormal levels within 20 min (Pradhan, Roy, & Pradhan, 1978).

Thus, there is a rapid onset of euphoria, but once the available NT is depleted, the euphoric effects diminish rapidly, to be replaced by feelings of depression and craving for a repeat of the euphoria.

Chronic use of stimulants results in NT depletion. Synapses operate using a negative feedback system, so compensatory changes occur that allow the neurons to adapt to alterations in the NT milieu caused by stimulants. Brain reward regions affected by stimulants are down-regulated and become subsensitive, the reaction responsible for the protracted anhedonia experienced when chronic stimulant users become abstinent (Gawin, 1991). High-dose use of stimulants over long periods of time causes neurophysiological changes in brain systems, which can take months to resolve after cessation of stimulant use.

Mechanisms of Tolerance and Dependence

Tolerance is the need to take larger doses of a drug to get the same initial effect. Tolerance to stimulant effects develops rapidly, especially to some properties such as anorexic effects, some cardiovascular effects, euphoria, and many CNS actions. Acute tolerance may be due to enhanced synaptic clearance and/or decreased release of DA, which may explain the dose escalation that occurs when people use increasingly larger doses at frequent intervals during a binge. Only partial tolerance develops to arrhythmias or seizures (Ambre et al., 1988), which raises the risk for development of toxicity during a binge. Development of tolerance indicates that a user is at risk for developing dependence on stimulants.

Psychological dependence is the feeling that a drug is essential to normal functioning. Stimulants were previously believed not to have a withdrawal syndrome or to produce dependence, but this misconception may have arisen because most early studies were done on subjects who used relatively low doses for short periods of time. Cocaine and amphetamines are the most potent reinforcing agents known, and they produce intense classical and operant conditioning. Animals trained to acquire cocaine will continue to take the drug, disregarding food and sex. In similar fashion, addicts report that during binges, virtually all thoughts are focused on stimulants: sleep, nourishment, money, loved ones, responsibility, and survival lose all significance (Gawin & Kleber, 1986). A stimulant addict focuses

on pharmacologically based euphoria despite a progressive inability to attain this state (tolerance) and adverse consequences. Controlled use shifts to compulsive use when users attain increased access to these drugs and escalate dosage or when they switch to a more rapid route of administration, such as from chewing leaves to insufflation to smoking or intravenous injection. The absence of a daily use pattern does not indicate less impairment, since stimulant dependence is characterized by binges, or "runs," of intense use alternating with periods of decreased use or short periods of abstinence without an intention to quit permanently. Subjective experiences or symptoms other than physiological discomfort are crucial in addiction to stimulants. Numerous periods of extreme euphoria are experienced during a binge, forming vivid memories that are later contrasted with the depression resulting after the stimulant effects have worn off, so and craving results (Gawin & Kleber, 1986). Addicts continue to use stimulants to avoid the depressed mood when the effects wear off; the result is binging, with acute tolerance causing rapid dose escalation until drug supplies are exhausted. Neurochemical changes cause long-term mood alteration and create psychological dependence that leads to recurrent binges. Stimulants cause physiological dependence at the NT level, which is clinically expressed as psychological dependence. According to estimates by the National Institute on Drug Abuse (NIDA), only 10–15% of those who initially try stimulants (specifically cocaine) intranasally become abusers. No set of characteristics has been identified predicting whether a recreational user will become chemically dependent.

CLINICAL ASPECTS

Clinical Pharmacological Aspects

Preparations

Amphetamines come in a variety of commercial and illicit preparations and can be used orally or intranasally, smoked, or injected intravenously (IV) (see table 6.1). They are most commonly taken as tablets when used for therapeutic purposes such as treatment of attention deficit disorder (ADD), narcolepsy, or exogenous obesity. One of the earliest amphetamines available for commercial use was benzathine nasal spray used to treat asthma and rhinitis. Meth-

TABLE 6.1 Names of Common Stimulant Preparations

Generic name	Trade name	Street names
Amphetamines		
Amphetamine sulfate	Benzedrine	Bennies, peaches
Dextroamphetamine	Dexedrine	Dexies, footballs
Amphetamine + dextroamphetamine	Adderall Biphetamine	
Phenmetrazine	Preludin	
Methylphenidate	Ritalin	Rits
Methamphetamine	Methedrine Desoxyn	Uppers, white crosses, black beauties, pep pills, speed, meth, crystal, crank
Freebase methamphetamine		Ice, crystal
Designer drugs		
DOM (dimethoxymethylamphetamine)		STP (serenity, tranquility, and peace), sweet tart, wedge
MDA (methylenedioxyamphetamine)		The love drug
MDMA (methylenedioxymethamphetamine)		Ecstacy, XTC, Adam, M & M
MDEA (methylenedioxyethamphetamine)		Eve
Cocaine		
Coca paste		Pasta, bazooka
Cocaine HCl		Blow, snow, nose candy, white lady, flake, paradise, girl, coke
Alkaloid (freebase)		Freebase crack, rock, supercoke, gravel, Roxanne

amphetamine is a more potent form of amphetamine used for therapeutic and illicit purposes. The free-based form of methamphetamine hydrochloride (HCl) is highly pure and smokable and is known on the street as *ice*.

"Designer drugs" are synthetic derivatives of federally controlled substances, created by a slight alteration in the molecular structure of existing drugs and produced illegally in clandestine laboratories for illicit use. The most popular of these is methylenedioxymethamphetamine (MDMA), known on the street as *ecstasy*. Initially, it was used legally as an adjunct to psychotherapy, but it became popular on the illicit market for its intoxicating effects. There are at least half a dozen amphetamine designer drugs available on the illicit market today (see table 6.1). Most have some psychoactive properties and cause visual disturbances but are not true hallucinogens like lysergic acid diethylamide (LSD) (Beebe & Walley, 1991).

Cocaine comes in a variety of commercial and illicit preparations and, like amphetamines, can be used by multiple routes (see table 6.1). It is found naturally in the leaves of the *Erythroxylon coca* plant indigenous to South America, which contain about 1% cocaine by weight. South American natives chew coca leaves to reduce hunger and fatigue as well as to increase their sense of well-being. The leaves can be steeped in tea or incorporated into beverages such as wine or the original formulation of Coca-Cola. Coca paste is a crude extract of coca leaves containing 40–85% cocaine sulfate, which is smoked (Karan, Haller, & Schnoll, 1991). This is used primarily in South America, while more potent preparations are used throughout the rest of the world.

Cocaine HCl is the most common form of cocaine used for illicit or therapeutic purposes. It is processed from the leaves of the coca plant. Since it is easily absorbed through any mucous membrane, it can be ingested orally or used topically as a local anesthetic. Commercial generic cocaine HCl is available for therapeutic use in the form of crystals, flakes, or tablets that can be dissolved, or in a prepackaged solution. It is also available for pediatric local anesthesia in fixed combination with tetracaine and adrenaline as TAC solution (Pryor, Kilpatrick, & Opp, 1980). Alkaloid forms of cocaine can be made by different techniques to produce either "freebase" or "crack." Unlike cocaine HCl, which decomposes at high temperatures, alkaloid cocaine vaporizes at a much lower temperature, so that it is suitable for smoking.

Routes and Dosages

Routes of Administration (See Table 6.2)   As with other classes of abused drugs, certain routes of administration of stimulants carry higher risk for acute toxicity as well as potential for the development of addiction. Stimulants can be taken by several different methods, and some formulations are more suitable for certain routes. In general, the faster a drug has its euphoric effect on the brain, the higher the potential for addiction and toxicity. Rapid onset of

euphoria, or the "rush," leads to immediate gratification and provides a powerful stimulus for readministration of the drug to maintain the euphoria, or "high." Most often, the more rapid the onset of action, the shorter the duration, so that more frequent administration is required. The routes of administration having the most rapid onset of action are IV and smoking. When injected IV, stimulants reach cerebral circulation in 10–15 sec. When smoked, they reach the brain in 6–8 sec, but this route is less potent than IV since smoked stimulants have only 50–60% of the bioavailability of IV stimulants. Smoking can achieve blood levels comparable to those reached through IV injection (Cook & Jeffcoat, 1990) despite lower bioavailability because the lungs provide a very large surface for rapid absorption of drug and the smoker can rapidly titrate the amount administered to provide the desired blood level based on effect. These routes also have the most potential for toxicity due to rapid dose escalation. They are more dangerous than other routes because of the

TABLE 6.2 Common Stimulant Dosages

	Administration		Common Dosage	
Drug	Route	Street terminology	Usual dose	Street terminology
Amphetamine	Oral		5–20 mg/day	(Therapeutic)
Amphetamine + dextroamphetamine	Oral		10-mg tablets 20-mg tablets	
Methamphetamine	Intravenous	Run	average 1/10 g	Hit
Coca leaves	Oral (chew)		1% cocaine by weight	Cocada
Coca paste	Smoke	Bazooka	40–85% cocaine sulfate	
Cocaine HCl	Oral		135-mg soluble tablets	
	Topical		40–100 mg/ml solution 5–25-g powder (200–400 mg in adults)	(Therapeutic)
	Intranasal insufflation	Snort, sniff, toot	10–30 mg powder per line, 30 lines from 1 g	Line, rail
	Intravenous	Shoot, mainline	3 g 6–8 g or 1/4 oz/week	Eight-ball binge, run, spree
Alkaloid cocaine (crack)	Smoke (pipe)	Bong	2–3 inhalations/rock, 2–3 rocks/vial	Rock, vial
TAC (tetracaine, adrenaline, cocaine) solution	Topical		11.8% cocaine HCl	(Therapeutic)

need for specialized equipment ("works") such as syringes or pipes, which pose additional risks, such as spread of infection or injury by fire. Intranasal insufflation ("snorting") is the most common route of administration for stimulants (Cregler & Mark, 1986) since it requires no specialized equipment. Euphoria is achieved in 3–5 min, but bioavailability is only 20–60% (Jatlow, 1987). The amount absorbed is limited by vasoconstriction of the nasal mucosa, especially for cocaine. About 90% of cocaine users have snorted, around 33% have smoked, and less than 10% have injected (National Institute on Drug Abuse [NIDA], 1991). Smoked and IV stimulants appear to be more behaviorally reinforcing than snorted stimulants, due to binging.

A stimulant is absorbed orally with a bioavailability of 30–40%; the remainder is eliminated by first-pass hepatic metabolism. Absorption occurs more slowly from the intestines, with peak plasma levels being reached 30–120 min after dosing. In South America, the chewing of coca leaves is very common, but because the amount of cocaine in the leaves is so low, there is no evidence that this practice causes chronic toxicity or dependence.

Dosages (See Table 6.2) Amphetamines are available by prescription for treatment of exogenous obesity, narcolepsy, and ADD; the dosage is titrated by the treating physician. Prior to the introduction of tricyclic antidepressants, amphetamines were used as symptomatic treatment of depression in doses of 5–20 mg/day (Lader, 1983). Dosage varies between amphetamines and methamphetamines, since the effect of methamphetamines on the CNS is twice that of amphetamines because of higher penetration across the blood-brain barrier. Illicit amphetamines do not come in standardized doses. Most illegally produced amphetamine is adulterated, or "cut," with virtually any amount of another compound—which varies widely among dealers and batches of drug—so the actual dose of amphetamine taken is difficult to determine and varies with each use.

Generic cocaine is available commercially for use as a topical anesthetic. In children it is used in TAC solution for anesthesia during repair of minor lacerations, but there is a risk of toxicity if the solution is accidentally swallowed (Dailey, 1988). In South America, chewing coca leaves to relieve fatigue is widely prevalent among natives in the higher eleva-

tions of the Andes Mountains, and the distance a person can travel in the time it takes to chew a wad of coca leaves is known as a *cocada* (Karan et al., 1991).

Because it is illegal in the United States to use cocaine except as a topical anesthetic, any other use may be considered misuse. Out of the millions of people in the United States who have tried cocaine, 80% have not become regular users and 95% have not developed compulsive use or addiction (Gawin & Ellinwood, 1988). In one study, the average user seeking treatment for cocaine abuse reported using 6–8 g or one-quarter ounce per week (Schnoll, Daghestani, & Hansen, 1985). Those who smoked or injected cocaine consumed larger quantities than those who snorted it. Like amphetamines, cocaine is cut with varying amounts of other drugs, so the actual dose is difficult to determine. Crack has grown in popularity in recent years and may have more abuse potential because of its rapid onset of action, short duration, and widespread availability. Individuals who use stimulants in escalating doses over a period as short as several days are vulnerable to developing problems of dependence. Users may average 1 to 7 binges per week, each binge lasting 4–24 hr. Addicts may readminister the drug as often as every 10–30 min. The duration of action of methamphetamine is much longer than that of cocaine, and the effects of methamphetamine may last 10 times as long as the effects of cocaine (Derlet & Heischober, 1990), so readministration of the drug is not as frequent.

Drug Interactions

Adulterants In order to increase profits, street dealers adulterate the drugs with other compounds, including inert and active substances. Most stimulants are in the form of white powder, so dealers cut them with other white powders. These may be inert substances that provide bulk, such as talc, flour, cornstarch, or sugars. These can lead to problems by traveling through the circulation as emboli to the lungs or by causing infection since they are usually not sterile. Other adulterants may be active drugs that potentiate some aspect of cocaine or amphetamines, such as local anesthetics or cheaper stimulants. These additives may raise the risk of toxicity by increasing the sympathetic effects or chances of car-

TABLE 6.3 Primary Drug Interactions with Stimulants

Effect	Drugs causing effect when taken with a stimulant (amphetamines or cocaine)
Increase in blood pressure and/or heart rate	MAOIs,[a] alcohol, marijuana, carbamazepine, caffeine, beta-blockers, NSAIDs[b]
Decrease in blood pressure	Haloperidol, calcium channel blockers
Increase in coronary vasoconstriction	Beta-adrenergic blockers (propranolol)
Reduction in vasoconstriction	Tricyclic antidepressants (TCAs)
Arrhythmias	Anticholinergics, bromocriptine, digoxin, anesthetics (enflurane, halothane)
Enhancement of euphoria	Heroin, buprenorphine, naloxone
Lessening of craving	Flupenthixol, amantadine, TCAs
Addictive toxic metabolite	Alcohol (only with cocaine)

[a]MAOIs: monoamine oxidase inhibitor medications.

[b]NSAIDs: nonsteroidal anti-inflammatory drugs.

diac arrhythmias. Stimulants may be cut with nearly any compound, so if a patient presents with acute intoxication or overdose, a general laboratory screen of urine or serum for unknown drugs is indicated in addition to a screening test for common drugs of abuse.

Common Illicit Drug Combinations (See Tables 6.3 and 6.4) Polysubstance abuse is common, and any drug combination is possible. Users coadminister other drugs to reduce unpleasant components of the stimulant experience, such as anxiety. However, the consequences of combining stimulants with other drugs are poorly understood. The regular use of other addictive drugs is prevalent: In one survey, 53% of stimulant users also used marijuana, 35% also used

alcohol, 20% used another depressant such as methaqualone or benzodiazepines, and 11% also used heroin (Chitwood, 1985).

Stimulants can be mixed with marijuana or tobacco and smoked in a cigarette. Marijuana potentiates some sympathetic effects of stimulants, and the combination can elevate heart rate by up to 50 beats per minute, an effect that is maintained longer than with either drug alone (Foltin, Fischman, Pedroso, & Pearlson, 1987). Heroin is used with stimulants to enhance euphoria and offset overstimulation. Phencyclidine and hallucinogens have also been used with stimulants but less commonly. Methamphetamine and crack have been used together in a combination sometimes known on the street as *ice*, which has the potential to cause dangerous sympa-

TABLE 6.4 Street Names for Common Illicit Drug Combinations

Drug combination	Street name
Methamphetamine + alkaloid cocaine (crack)	Ice
Methamphetamine + heroin	Poor man's speedball
Methylphenidate + heroin	Pineapple
Cocaine + heroin	Speedball, girls and boys, whiz bang
Cocaine + alcohol	Liquid lady
Cocaine + marijuana	C & M
Cocaine + strychnine (adulterant)	Death hit
Cocaine + phencyclidine	Ghostbuster, space blaster

thetic overstimulation. Alcohol is used to lessen anxiety during the high, to induce sleep during the crash, or to help the addict cope with mood disturbances. The combination of alcohol and cocaine produces ethylcocaine, previously described. Alcohol also potentiates stimulant-induced increases in resting heart rate (Foltin & Fischman, 1989).

Potential Therapeutic Agents (See Table 6.5) Many different medications have been tried in attempts to lessen craving for stimulants or to attenuate their euphoric effects. Stimulant abusers are a heterogeneous population, so that controlled trials are difficult to carry out and much of the evidence for efficacy is anecdotal or based on limited open trials. The literature reveals no pharmacological agent that has been demonstrated in large double-blind controlled clinical trials to be significantly better than placebo for stimulant-dependent men and women (Schuckit, 1994).

Physical Symptoms of Use, Abuse, and Dependence

Small initial doses of stimulants cause acute dopaminergic stimulation of the brain's endogenous pleasure center. Users experience euphoria, heightened energy and libido, decreased appetite, hyperalertness, and increased self-confidence. Objective signs of small doses are acute NE effects such as mild elevation of pulse and blood pressure or reduction in skin temperature, which reflects cutaneous vasoconstriction.

Higher doses cause intensification of euphoria, accompanied by heightened CNS stimulation shown as increased alertness, talkativeness, repetitive be-

TABLE 6.5 Potential Therapeutic Agents

Agent	Action
Tricyclic antidepressants Desipramine Imipramine	Block catecholamine uptake to stabilize DA and NE receptors
Monoamine oxidase inhibitors	Block NT metabolism at synaptic cleft and counteract intraneuronal NT depletion of stimulant withdrawal
Other antidepressants Fluoxetine Trazodone	Selective serotonin reuptake inhibition to prevent 5-HT depletion by stimulants
Neuroleptics Haloperidol Flupenthixol	Block DA receptor Selective blockade of D2 autoreceptors
Antiparkinsonian medications Levodopa Bromocriptine Amantidine	 DA precursor DA receptor agonist Raises brain DA levels
Antiepileptics Carbamazepine Valproate	Prevent subclinical seizures, which may be related to craving
Opioid agonists and antagonists Methadone Buprenorphine Naloxone	 Opioid agonist Partial agonist Opioid antagonist
Stimulants Methylphenidate Mazindol	Replacement therapy
Lithium	Mood stabilizer

havior, and altered sexual behavior. Users have increased sympathomimetic effects such as dizziness, tremor, hyperreflexia (rapid reflexes), hyperpyrexia (fever), mydriasis (dilated pupils), diaphoresis (sweating), tachypnea (rapid breathing), tachycardia (rapid heartbeat), and hypertension (high blood pressure). If at least two of these signs are present within 1 hr of use, criteria are met for stimulant intoxication (American Psychiatric Association, 1994). Behavioral changes are also part of the criteria for stimulant intoxication; these include fighting, grandiosity, hypervigilance, psychomotor agitation, impaired judgment, and impaired social or occupational functioning. Intravenous users are unable to tell apart the effects of different stimulants and cannot distinguish cocaine from amphetamines (Fischman & Schuster, 1982). Acute intoxication usually resolves within 6–24 hr, especially for short-acting stimulants like cocaine.

Repeated phasic use of low-dose stimulants leads to enhanced sensitivity and potentiation of motor activity, such as exaggerated "startle" reactions, dyskinesia (disturbances of movement), and postural abnormalities. The clinical features of chronic use are depression, fatigue, poor concentration, and mild Parkinsonian features such as myoclonus (inappropriate, spontaneous muscle contractions), tremor, or bradykinesia (slowing of movements). Patients presenting with these signs should be suspected of stimulant abuse and screened carefully.

Symptoms and Course of Withdrawal

Abrupt cessation of stimulants has no gross physiological changes, so for many years it was assumed that there was no discrete withdrawal syndrome. However, more recent research has revealed an abstinence syndrome with symptoms more subtle and complex than those previously associated with drug withdrawal. Biological measures suggest derangement of neurochemical activity, which appears to be linked to a reduction in dopaminergic tone following abrupt cessation of stimulant use (Lago & Kosten, 1994). The stimulant withdrawal syndrome has a triphasic pattern of symptoms which begins immediately after the last use and may last for many months (Gawin & Kleber, 1986).

Phase 1 begins with the "crash," or drastic reduction in mood and energy, starting 15–30 min after cessation of a stimulant binge. This is caused by the rapid depletion of NT at the synaptic level. Addicts experience craving, depression, anxiety, and paranoia. The craving for stimulants decreases over 1–4 hr, to be replaced by craving for sleep and rejection of further stimulant use. The late part of Phase 1 consists of hypersomnolence lasting 8 hr to 4 days and is accompanied by electroencephalographic changes (Kowatch, Schnoll, Knisely, Green, & Elswick, 1992). Sleep is punctuated by brief awakenings during which the addict experiences hyperphagia ("the munchies"). Phase 1 parallels the hangover after an alcohol binge.

Phase 2 begins 12–96 hr after the crash and lasts 2–12 weeks. The first 1–4 days consist of euthymia, sleep, and little craving. Then starts a protracted dysphoric syndrome in which the addict experiences anhedonia, boredom, anxiety, generalized malaise, problems with memory and concentration, and occasional suicidal ideation. This syndrome induces severe craving, which may lead to resumption of stimulant use and a vicious circle of recurrent binges. The delayed effects of withdrawal are due to neuroadaptations caused by stimulants, such as higher density of receptors and supersensitivity to NT, which may normalize over about a month after cessation of use. Phase 2 parallels the syndrome of withdrawal from other abused drugs, except for the absence of gross physiological changes.

Phase 3 is the extinction phase. There is no anhedonia, but there is intermittent conditioned craving lasting months to years after the last stimulant use; this craving is gradually extinguished over time. Craving is the most prominent and disturbing symptom of stimulant withdrawal. There are two types of craving: anhedonic and conditioned. Anhedonic craving arises from boredom and a general desire to get high. Conditioned craving, also known as *evoked* or *cue craving*, arises from stimuli in the environment that remind the addict of the pleasures associated with using stimulants. Conditioned craving is more intense for stimulants than in other addictive disorders because stimulants are such powerful reinforcers.

The severity and duration of withdrawal depends on the intensity of the preceding months of chronic abuse and the presence of predisposing psychiatric disorders, which amplify withdrawal symptoms. Neuroadaptation from high-intensity binge use may be required before withdrawal occurs, and infrequent users without psychiatric comorbidity may not experience withdrawal (Gawin, 1991). Since abrupt discontinuation of stimulants does not cause gross physiological sequelae, they are not tapered off or replaced with a cross-tolerant drug during medically supervised withdrawal.

Pathological Effects

Physiological

Stimulants are widely distributed throughout the body, the highest concentrations appearing in the brain, spleen, kidney, and lungs (Prakash & Das, 1993). They activate the sympathetic nervous system (SNS), which causes a fight-or-flight response, affecting the heart, lungs, vasculature (including the brain and intestinal arteries), and even sexual performance. The acute effects of large doses of stimulants or cumulative effects of long-term use can result in serious medical sequelae (see table 6.6).

Tachycardia and hypertension are classic sympathetic responses even at low doses. Activation of NE-mediated systems in the heart causes coronary artery vasoconstriction so that coronary blood flow is decreased during a period of high oxygen demand. There is a high incidence of silent ischemia (lack of blood flow to cardiac tissue) during withdrawal (Nademanee et al., 1989), or a susceptible individual may have a myocardial infarction during a binge. Stimulants potentiate the effects of NE in cardiac cells, an effect that leads to arrhythmias (Wilkerson, 1988). Long-term use can lead to myocarditis or catecholamine-related cardiomyopathy (Virmani, Robinowitz, Smialek, & Smyth, 1988).

The CNS has many affected areas in addition to the pleasure centers: Direct effects on the thermoregulatory center may result in hyperpyrexia or even malignant hyperthermia (Roberts, Quattrocchi, & Howland, 1984); depression of medullary centers can cause respiratory paralysis (Gay, 1982); stimulants also lower the seizure threshold. Cerebral vasculature is particularly affected: Vasoconstriction with ischemia may lead to a transient ischemic attack or a cerebral infarct (stroke), which is more common with crack; cocaine HCl is associated with hemorrhagic strokes (Levine et al., 1991); migrainelike vascular headaches during withdrawal have been linked to serotonin dysregulation (Satel & Gawin, 1989). Long-term users develop cerebral atrophy, especially

in the frontal and temporal lobes (Pascual-Leone, Dhuna, & Anderson, 1991).

Pulmonary complications occur mainly when stimulants are smoked. The most common complaint is a chronic cough with black sputum (Warner, 1995). Pulmonary edema (accumulation of fluid in lung tissue) develops rapidly and may be due to capillary membrane disruption with altered permeability; fortunately, it usually resolves with supportive therapy without specific treatment (Cucco, Yoo, Cregler, & Chang, 1987). Granulomatous pneumonitis with pulmonary hypertension may develop as a result of talc in the lungs from IV injection (Estroff & Gold, 1986). "Crack lung" is a syndrome of chest pain, hemoptysis (coughing up blood), and diffuse alveolar infiltrates that may be due to lung hypersensitivity to cocaine (Forrester, Steele, Waldron, & Parsons, 1990). Long-term use results in an abnormal reduction in alveolar membrane diffusing capacity (Itkonen, Schnoll, & Glassroth, 1984).

Repeated intranasal insufflation results in inflammation and atrophy of nasal mucosa, chronic sinusitis, or even necrosis with perforation of the nasal septum. Smoking stimulants in a pipe may result in singed eyebrows, facial burns, or laryngeal edema due to hot smoke. Gingival ulceration may occur at the site of application of oral cocaine (Quart, Small, & Klein, 1991). Stimulants may cause intestinal ischemia as a result of vasoconstriction (Texter, Chou, Merrill, Laureton, & Frohlich, 1964). Acute renal failure may occur as a result of rhabdomyolysis (muscle tissue breakdown) from stimulant use, but the mechanism for rhabdomyolysis is unclear.

Stimulants have variable effects on sexual function: It may be enhanced or inhibited. Sexual arousal may be heightened along with a delay in orgasm. Priapism (continuous painful penile erection) may also result. High doses for prolonged periods can result in aberrant sexual behavior (Smith, Wesson, & Apter-Marsh, 1984).

Use of stimulants during pregnancy can cause obstetric complications including preterm labor, spontaneous abortion, or fetal distress (Oro & Dixon, 1987). From 10% to 20% of inner-city pregnant women in the United States use cocaine (Zuckerman et al., 1989), so effects on the fetus have been well studied. The consequences of prenatal exposure to methamphetamine are believed to be similar to those of cocaine. Higher rates of congenital malformations and intrauterine growth retardation may be

TABLE 6.6 Consequences of Stimulant Abuse

Physical

Cardiovascular
  Hypertension
  Arrhythmias
  Myocarditis
  Cardiomyopathy
  Myocardial ischemia
  Myocardial infarction

Central nervous system
  Headache
  Seizures
  Transient focal neurological
    deficits
  Cerebral hemorrhage
  Cerebral infarction
  Cerebral edema
  Cerebral atrophy
  Cerebral vasculitis
  Toxic encephalopathy/coma

Gastrointestinal
  Nausea/vomiting/diarrhea
  Anorexia
  Malnutrition
  Intestinal ischemia
  Gastroduodenal perforation

Head and neck
  Erosion of dental enamel
  Gingival ulceration
  Keratitis
  Mydriasis
  Altered olfaction
  Chronic rhinitis
  Nasal septal perforation

Renal
  Acute renal failure

Endocrine
  Hyperprolactinemia
  Elevated thyroxin level

Pulmonary
  Chronic productive cough
  Pneumothorax
  Pneumomediastinum
  Pneumopericardium
  Asthma exacerbation
  Pulmonary edema
  Pulmonary hemorrhage
  Bronchiolitis obliterans
  "Crack lung"

Other
  Hyperthermia
  Rhabdomyolysis
  Sudden death
  Sexual dysfunction

Reproductive
  Obstetric
    Spontaneous abortion
    Placental abruption
    Placenta previa
    Premature rupture of membranes
  Fetal
    Intrauterine growth retardation
    Congenital malformations
  Neonatal
    Cerebral infarction
    Delayed neurobehavioral development
    Sudden infant death syndrome

Infectious (from sharing needles)
  Human immunodeficiency virus (HIV)
  Infectious endocarditis
  Hepatitis B and/or C
  Tetanus

Psychological

Emotional lability
Insomnia
Altered self-esteem
Aberrant sexual behavior
Irritability

Anxiety
Depression
Aggressive behavior
Paranoia
Hallucinations

Delerium
Toxic psychosis
Suicide

Social

Less social participation
Loss of judgment
Loss of family structure
Child neglect or abuse

Lost job productivity
Criminal activity
Prostitution
Spread of infection

Violent behavior
Higher incidence of trauma
Homicide
Accidental death

---

due to fetal hypoxia from placental vasoconstriction and altered circulating levels of DA and NE. Stimulants cross the placenta freely and accumulate in fetal tissue (Ellis, Byrd, Sexson, & Patterson-Barnett, 1993). Babies born to stimulant-using mothers often have alterations in birth weight or length, and congenital abnormalities include malformations of the skull, limbs, CNS, intestines, and genitourinary system. However, many of the abnormalities attributed to cocaine are occasionally observed in premature infants independent of any drug involvement (Rosenkrantz, 1987). In most studies, the experimental con-

trol needed to disentangle the effects of complex interactions of drug use, lifestyle, and subject history is difficult to achieve (Ellis et al., 1993). Neurobehavioral abnormalities include irritability, abnormal sleep-wake cycles, tremulousness, poor feeding, and hypo- or hypertonia (Oro & Dixon, 1987). In neonates, cerebral infarction can result from maternal stimulant use near term. These children are also at high risk for sudden infant death syndrome (Riley, Brodsky, & Porat, 1988). Longitudinal studies of these children have not been completed, so little is known about potential long-term adverse effects, but abnormalities suggesting frontal lobe dysfunction may manifest at school age (Dixon, 1989). Even after birth, children are at risk from maternal stimulant use because it passes into breast milk (Chasnoff, Lewis, & Squires, 1987).

Psychological

Small doses of stimulants cause euphoria with a sense of heightened alertness and energy. Moderate doses cause the classical high in which the user feels intensely euphoric but becomes hyperexcitable and exhibits grandiose behavior. Larger doses cause severe alterations of behavior with impairment of judgment, memory, and control on thought processes, so the user appears confused. Users may experience extreme fear or paranoia and frequently resort to violence. There may also be psychotic manifestations such as hallucinations or paranoid delusions, which may lead to suicide. Anxiety, delusions, and depression become more pronounced with increasing use. Between episodes of drug use, abusers are irritable, suspicious, and dysphoric. Visual hallucinations are not uncommon with cocaine use and are known as *snow lights*. Formication is the sensation of insects crawling on or under the skin, compelling the addict to pick at the skin, causing excoriations. This phenomenon is known as having *crank bugs* or *coke bugs*.

Known psychiatric disorders may be exacerbated by stimulant use. Schizophrenia is more susceptible to relapse, and panic disorder may have an increase in the intensity and frequency of attacks. Drug use frequently represents an attempt to manage preexisting psychiatric symptoms; this is known as the *self-medication hypothesis*. Crack smokers have a higher incidence of psychiatric problems, psychosis, and associated violence than users of other forms of cocaine (Honer, Gewirtz, & Turey, 1987).

Stimulant use can cause a full-blown toxic psychosis (Karan et al., 1991) with extreme paranoia, panic, and hypervigilance as well as insomnia and visual hallucinations. Patients may exhibit unusual aggressiveness, which can lead to property damage and suicidal or homicidal behavior. Unlike cocaine-induced toxic psychosis, methamphetamine psychosis lasts much longer than a few hours. It usually resolves within 10 days of cessation of drug use, but in about 10% of patients, it persists for up to 6 months (Beebe & Walley, 1995). After resolution of toxic psy-

chosis, further stimulant use may induce another psychotic episode within a shorter time than initially.

Chronic stimulant users may develop anxiety or paranoia, and chronic use is associated with weight loss, insomnia, and depression. Chronic use of MDMA in particular can lead to a paranoid psychosis that is clinically indistinguishable from schizophrenia; fortunately, it is usually reversible after a prolonged drug-free state (Buchanan & Brown, 1988).

Social/Interpersonal

In the 1960s and 1970s, stimulants were thought to promote conviviality and good spirits and were used as "party drugs." People initially use stimulants to reduce social inhibitions and promote interpersonal communication, but as usage goes up, social participation drops precipitously. Continued use causes paranoia, so addicts withdraw from their friends to avoid other people who might disrupt the high.

Active stimulant use causes progressive loss of judgment concerning "safe" drug use habits. The risk of accidents is increased in users owing to poor judgment and psychomotor hyperactivity when high. Substantial personal and societal injury may result from infection due to IV drug use, trauma, criminal activities, child neglect, and lost job productivity.

Violent behavior is the leading cause of death among stimulant users. The most common forms of death are accidents, suicide, and homicide (Warner, 1993). In fact, cocaine has been associated with more deaths than any other illicit drug (NIDA, 1990).

Use of stimulants increases the risk and spread of sexually transmitted diseases (STDs), including human immunodeficiency virus (HIV). Some women use prostitution as a means of securing stimulants to maintain an addiction, men may exchange drugs for sex with a prostitute, or multiple users may have sex in a "crack house," all of which are high-risk behaviors.

Stimulant abuse can have adverse health consequences for children, such as child neglect and abuse or loss of family structure. Society also faces the economic burden of prolonged hospitalization of newborns or foster care for children of addicts. The often chaotic environment of an addicted mother, combined with lack of appropriate stimulation and an inappropriate role model, may cause substantial impairment of intellectual capability as well as of social and ethical behavior among children growing up in that environment (Chasnoff, 1988). This situation sets the stage for another generation of drug users.

SUMMARY

Stimulants are metabolized extensively in the serum and liver. Certain patient populations are at higher risk for developing toxicity from concomitant alcohol use or if they have lower cholinesterase activity, resulting in abnormal drug metabolism. All stimulants activate the SNS and the brain's pleasure centers. Chronic use causes long-term changes in these systems, especially DA. Acute tolerance is due to release and/or secretion of DA and is responsible for dose escalation during a binge. Dependence is due to long-term neurochemical changes and the powerful reinforcing effects of stimulant euphoria, as well as avoidance of depression caused by cessation of use.

Stimulants have therapeutic and illicit uses. They come in a variety of preparations and can be administered by almost any route. Smoking and IV are the routes with the most potential for addiction and toxicity but insufflation is the most common route of abuse. Illicit stimulants are adulterated with many compounds at the whim of the dealer, so actual dosages are unpredictable. During binges, addicts administer as much drug as possible until supplies are exhausted. Dangerous consequences can result from interactions with adulterants, other drugs of abuse, or potential therapeutic agents if the addict relapses.

Small doses cause mild sympathetic signs, while larger doses or chronic use causes exaggerated signs and behavioral changes. Abrupt cessation results in a triphasic withdrawal syndrome without gross physiological changes which begins immediately, and craving may last many months.

Stimulants can have many pathological effects due to overstimulation of the SNS. Physiological effects include arrhythmias, pulmonary edema, and possibly birth defects. Psychological effects include toxic psychosis and paranoia. Social effects include violent behavior, spread of STDs, and child neglect.

Stimulant abuse has broad consequences, not only for individual relationships, but for society as a whole. Understanding the full impact of stimulant use can help health care providers to educate people about stimulants in order to decrease stimulant abuse and prevent its spread.

Key References

Beebe, D. K., & Walley, E. (1995). Smokable methamphetamine ("ice"): An old drug in a different form. *American Family Physician, 51*(2), 449–453.

Gawin, F. H. (1991). Cocaine addiction: Psychology and neurophysiology. *Science, 251,* 1580–1586.

Karan, L. D., Haller, D. L., & Schnoll, S. H. (1991). Cocaine. In R. J. Frances & S. I. Miller (Eds.), *Clinical textbook of addictive disorders* (pp. 121–145). New York: Guilford Press.

References

Ambre, J. J., Belknap, S. M., Nelson, J., Ruo, T. I., Shin, S., & Atkinson, A. J., Jr. (1988). Acute tolerance to cocaine in humans. *Clinical Pharmacology and Therapeutics, 44,* 1–8.

American Psychiatric Association. (1994). *Diagnostic and statistical manual of mental disorders* (4th ed.). Washington, DC: Author.

Becker, C. E. (1972). Screening of 563 students for cholinesterase variants. *Clinical Chemistry, 18,* 75–76.

Beebe, D. K., & Walley, E. (1991). Substance abuse: the designer drugs. *American Family Physician, 43*(5), 1689–1698.

Beebe, D. K., & Walley, E. (1995). Smokable methamphetamine ("ice"): An old drug in a different form. *American Family Physician, 51*(2), 449–453.

Benowitz, N. L. (1993). Clinical pharmacology and toxicology of cocaine. *Pharmacology and Toxicology, 72,* 3–12.

Buchanan, J. F., & Brown, C. R. (1988). "Designer drugs": A problem in clinical toxicology. *Medical Toxicology and Adverse Drug Exposure, 3,* 1–17.

Chasnoff, I. J. (1988). Drug use in pregnancy: Parameters of risk. *Pediatric Clinics of North America, 35,* 1403–1412.

Chasnoff, I. J., Lewis, D. E., & Squires, L. (1987). Cocaine intoxication in a breast-fed infant. *Pediatrics, 80,* 836–838.

Chitwood, D. D. (1985). Patterns and consequences of cocaine use. *NIDA Research Monograph, 61,* 111–129.

Cook, C. E., & Jeffcoat, A. R. (1990). Pyrolytic degradation of heroin, phencyclidine, and cocaine: Identification of products and some observations on their metabolism. *NIDA Research Monograph, 99,* 97–120.

Cregler, L. L., & Mark, H. (1986). Medical complications of cocaine abuse. *New England Journal of Medicine, 315*(23), 1495–1500.

Cucco, R. A., Yoo, O. H., Cregler, L., & Chang, J. C. (1987). Nonfatal pulmonary edema after "freebase" cocaine smoking. *American Review of Respiratory Disease, 136,* 179–181.

Dailey, R. H. (1988). Fatality secondary to misuse of TAC solution. *Annals of Emergency Medicine, 17,* 646–648.

Derlet, R. W., & Heischober, B. (1990). Methamphetamine: Stimulant of the 1990's? *Western Journal of Medicine, 153,* 625–628.

Dixon, S. D. (1989). Effects of transplacental exposure to cocaine and methamphetamine on the neonate. *Western Journal of Medicine, 150,* 436–442.

Ellis, J. E., Byrd, L. D., Sexson, W. R., & Patterson-Barnett, C. A. (1993). In utero exposure to cocaine: A review. *Southern Medical Journal, 86*(7), 725–731.

Estroff, T. W., & Gold, M. S. (1986). Medical and psychiatric complications of cocaine abuse with possible points of pharmacological treatment. In B. Stimmel (Ed.), *Controversies in alcoholism and substance abuse* (pp. 61–75). New York: Haworth Press.

Fischman, M. W., & Schuster, C. R. (1982). Cocaine self-administration in humans, *Federal Proceedings, 41*(2), 241–246.

Foltin, R. W., & Fischman, M. W. (1989). Effects of the combination of cocaine and marijuana on the task-elicited physiological response. *NIDA Research Monograph, 95,* 359–360.

Foltin, R. W., Fischman, M. W., Pedroso, J. J., & Pearlson, G. D. (1987). Marijuana and cocaine interactions in humans: Cardiovascular consequences. *Pharmacology Biochemistry and Behavior 28,* 459–464.

Forrester, J. M., Steele, A. W., Waldron, J. A., & Parsons, P. E. (1990). Crack lung: An acute pulmonary syndrome with a spectrum of clinical and histopathologic findings. *American Review of Respiratory Disease, 142,* 462–467.

Gawin, F. H. (1991). Cocaine addiction: Psychology and neurophysiology. *Science, 251,* 1580–1586.

Gawin, F. H., & Ellinwood, E. H., Jr. (1988). Cocaine and other stimulants: Actions, abuse, and treatment. *New England Journal of Medicine, 318,* 1173–1182.

Gawin, F. H., & Kleber, H. D. (1986). Abstinence symptomatology and psychiatric diagnosis in cocaine abusers: Clinical observations. *Archives of General Psychiatry, 43,* 107–113.

Gay, G. R. (1982). Clinical management of acute and chronic cocaine poisoning. *Annals of Emergency Medicine, 11,* 562–572.

Hoffman, R. S., Henry, G. C., Howland, M. A., Weisman, R. S., Weil, L., & Goldfrank, L. R. (1992). Association between life-threatening cocaine toxicity and plasma cholinesterase activity. *Annals of Emergency Medicine, 21,* 247–253.

Honer, W. G., Gewirtz, G., & Turey, M. (1987). Psychosis and violence in cocaine smokers [letter]. *Lancet, 2*(8556), 451.

Itkonen, J., Schnoll, S. H., & Glassroth, J. (1984). Pulmonary function in freebase cocaine users. *Archives of Internal Medicine, 144,* 2195–2197.

Jatlow, P. I. (1987). Drug of abuse profile: Cocaine. *Clinical Chemistry, 33*(11 Suppl), 66B–71B.

Kaplan, C. D., Husch, J. A., & Bieleman, B. (1994). The prevention of stimulant misuse. *Addiction, 89,* 1517–1521.

Karan, L. D., Haller, D. L., & Schnoll, S. H. (1991). Cocaine. In R. J. Frances & S. I. Miller (Eds.), *Clinical textbook of addictive disorders* (pp. 121–145). New York: Guilford Press.

Knepper, S. M., Grunewald, G. L., & Rutledge, C. O. (1988). Inhibition of norepinephrine transport into synaptic vesicles by amphetamine analogs. *Journal of Pharmacology and Experimental therapeutics, 247,* 487–494.

Kowatch, R. A., Schnoll, S. H., Knisely, J. S., Green, D., & Elswick, R. K. (1992). Electroencephalographics, sleep, and mood during cocaine withdrawal. *Journal of Addictive Diseases, 11*(4), 21–45.

Lader, M. (1983). *Introduction to psychopharmacology.* Kalamazoo, MI: Upjohn Company.

Lago, J. A., & Kosten, T. R. (1994). Stimulant withdrawal. *Addiction, 89,* 1477–1481.

Levine, S. R., Brust, J. C., Futrell, N., Brass, L. M., Blake, D., Fayad, P., Schultz, L. R., Millikan, C. H., Ho, K. L., & Welch, K. M. (1991). A comparative study of the cerebrovascular complications of cocaine: Alkaloidal versus hydrochloride—a review. *Neurology, 41,* 1173–1177.

Miller, H. H., Shore, P. A., & Clarke, D. E. (1980). In vivo monoamine oxidase inhibition by d-amphetamine. *Biochemistry and Pharmacology, 29,* 1347–1354.

Nademanee, K., Gorelick, D. A., Josephson, M. A., Ryan, M. A., Wilkins, N. J., Robertson, H. A., Mody, F. V., & Intarachot, V. (1989). Myocardial ischemia during cocaine withdrawal. *Annals of Internal Medicine, 111,* 876–880.

National Institute on Drug Abuse. (1990). *Data from the drug abuse warning network, Series 1, No. 9* (No. 90-1717). Washington, DC: Alcohol, Drug Abuse, and Mental Administration.

National Institute on Drug Abuse. (1991). *National household survey on drug abuse: Main findings 1990* (No. 91-1788). Washington, DC: U.S. Department of Health and Human Services.

Oro, S., & Dixon, S. D. (1987). Perinatal cocaine and methamphetamine exposure: Maternal and neonatal correlates. *Journal of Pediatrics, 111,* 571–578.

Pascual-Leone, A., Dhuna, A., & Anderson, D. C. (1991). Cerebral atrophy in habitual cocaine abusers: A planimetric CT study. *Neurology, 41,* 34–38.

Pradhan, S., Roy, S. N., & Pradhan, S. N. (1978). Correlation of behavioral and neurochemical effects of acute administration of cocaine in rats. *Life Science, 22,* 1737–1743.

Prakash, A., & Das, G. (1993). Cocaine and the nervous system. *International Journal of Clinical Pharmacology and Therapeutic Toxicology, 31*(12), 575–581.

Pryor, G. J., Kilpatrick, W. R., & Opp, D. R. (1980). Local anesthesia in minor lacerations: Topical TAC vs. Lidocaine infiltration. *Annals of Emergency Medicine, 9,* 568–571.

Quandt, C. M., Sommi, R. W., Jr., Pipkin, T., & McCallum, M. H. (1988). Differentiation of cocaine toxicity: Role of the toxicology drug screen. *Drug Intelligence and Clinical Pharmacy, 22,* 582–587.

Quart, A. M., Small, C. B., & Klein, R. S. (1991). The cocaine connection: Users imperil their gingiva. *Journal of the American Dental Association, 122,* 85–87.

Raiteri, M., Bertollini, A., Angelini, F., & Levi, G. (1975). D-Amphetamine as a releaser or reuptake inhibitor of biogenic amines in synaptosomes. *European Journal of Pharmacology, 34,* 189–195.

Riley, J. G., Brodsky, N. L., & Porat, R. (1988). Risk for SIDS in infants with in utero cocaine exposure: A prospective study. *Pediatric Research, 23,* 454A.

Ritz, M. C., Lamb, R. J., Goldberg, S. R., & Kuhar, M. J. (1987). Cocaine receptors on dopamine transporters are related to self-administration of cocaine. *Science, 237,* 1219–1223.

Roberts, J. R., Quattrocchi, E., & Howland, M. A. (1984). Severe hyperthermia secondary to intravenous drug abuse. *American Journal of Emergency Medicine, 2,* 373.

Roberts, S. M., Harbison, R. D., & James, R. C. (1991). Human microsomal N-oxidative metabolism of cocaine. *Drug Metabolism and Disposition, 19,* 1046–1051.

Rosenkrantz, T. S. (1987). Neonatology. In P. H. Dworkin (Ed.), *Pediatrics* (pp. 99–135). New York: Wiley.

Satel, S. L., & Gawin, F. H. (1989). Migrainelike headache and cocaine use. *Journal of the American Medical Association, 261,* 2995–2996.

Schnoll, S. H., Daghestani, A. N., & Hansen, T. R. (1985). Cocaine dependence. *Medical Times, 113*(4), 46–62.

Schuckit, M. A. (1994). The treatment of stimulant dependence. *Addiction, 89,* 1559–1563.

Smith, D. E., Wesson, D. R., & Apter-Marsh, M. (1984). Cocaine and alcohol induced sexual dysfunction in patients with addictive diseases. *Journal of Psychoactive Drugs, 16,* 359–361.

Substance Abuse and Mental Health Services Administration. (1995). *National household survey on drug abuse: Main findings, 1993.* Rockville, MD: U.S. Department of Health and Human Services, Public Health Service, Substance Abuse and Mental Health Services Administration.

Texter, E. C., Chou, C. C., Merrill, S. L., Laureton, H. C., & Frohlich, E. D. (1964). Direct effects of vasoactive agents on segmental resistance of the mesenteric and portal circulation: Studies with l-epinephrine, levarterenal, angiotensin, vasopressin, acetylcholine, methacholine, histamine, and serotonin. *Journal of Laboratory and Clinical Medicine, 64,* 624–633.

Virmani, R., Robinowitz, M., Smialek, J. E., & Smyth, D. F. (1988). Cardiovascular effects of cocaine: an autopsy study of 40 patients. *American Heart Journal, 115,* 1068–1076.

Warner, E. A. (1993). Cocaine abuse. *Annals of Internal Medicine, 119,* 226–235.

Warner, E. A. (1995). Is your patient using cocaine? *Postgraduate Medicine, 98*(2), 173–180.

Weiss, R. D., & Gawin, F. H. (1988). Protracted elimination of cocaine metabolites in long-term high-dose cocaine abusers. *American Journal of Medicine, 85,* 879–880.

Wilkerson, R. D. (1988). Cardiovascular toxicity of cocaine. *NIDA Research Monograph, 88,* 304–324.

Zuckerman, B., Frank, D. A., Hingson, R., Amaro, H., Levenson, S. M., Kayne, H., Parker, S., Vinci, R., Aboagye, K., Fried, L. E., Cabral, H., Timperi, R., & Bauchner, H. (1989). Effects of maternal marijuana and cocaine use on fetal growth. *New England Journal of Medicine, 320,* 762–768.

7

Cannabis and Hallucinogens

Robert S. Stephens

Cannabis, hallucinogens, and phencyclidine (PCP) are molecularly distinct drugs that share an ability to alter perception and produce euphoria. As a group, they represent some of the least toxic psychoactive substances, but there are important exceptions. They are also linked by strong associations with the alternative culture that emerged during the 1960s in the United States that had as its motto, "Turn on, tune in, and drop out." They continue to be used recreationally today, and much information has accumulated on the patterns of use, pharmacology, and biobehavioral consequences of use and abuse.

Cannabis is the illicit substance most frequently used in the United States. According to the National Household Survey on Drug Abuse in 1994 (NHSDA; Substance Abuse and Mental Health Administration, 1995), 8.5% of the population (approximately 17.8 million people) used cannabis, and over one quarter of users (approximately 5.1 million people) reported using it one or more times each week. A press release from the 1994 annual national survey of high school

students indicates that cannabis use is increasing again (Johnston, Bachman, & O'Malley, 1994). Almost one third of high school seniors used cannabis in 1994, and daily use of cannabis climbed to 3.6% among high school seniors—up by 50% from 1993 levels. The increases in cannabis use occurred concurrently with a steady and accelerating decline in perceived risk of use and an increase in peer approval.

On the other hand, hallucinogens are among the illicit substances least frequently used in the Western world. In a representative survey of the U.S. adult population conducted between 1990 and 1992, only 11% had ever used hallucinogens, ranking them lower than all other drugs except heroin, extramedical use of analgesics, and inhalants (Anthony, Warner, & Kessler, 1994). Use of hallucinogens peaked in the 1970s, declined through much of the 1980s, and remained stable at a low rate throughout the late 1980s (e.g., Johnston, O'Malley, & Bachman, 1989). However, there are indications that use of hallucinogens is increasing again (e.g., Cuomo, Dyment, & Gammino, 1994; Johnston, O'Malley, & Bachman, 1994; Millman & Beeder, 1994).

CANNABIS

Cannabis is derived from the plant of the same name. Actually, there is still debate on whether there is only one species of *Cannabis* with two subtypes or several species of *Cannabis* with differing psychoactive potencies (McKim, 1997; Stafford, 1992). Large variations in the size and shape of different varieties of the plant fuel this debate. One variety matures rapidly and grows as a lanky plant up to 20 feet in height and is cultivated for the fiber known as hemp *(Cannabis sativa)*. It is used to make rope and has a relatively low psychoactive potency in comparison with other varieties that are more compact, grow more slowly, and are cultivated for their psychoactive properties *(Cannabis indica)*.

Regardless of the correct botanical classification, the potency of the plant varies primarily as a function of the concentration of delta-9-tetrahydrocannabinol (THC), the main psychoactive ingredient in cannabis. However, there are more than 60 molecular compounds unique to cannabis. While most of these other cannabinoids appear to be relatively inactive in regard to psychological and behavioral effects, it is possible that some are weakly psychoactive or that they alter the potency of the preparation by interacting with THC (Abood & Martin, 1992). Still other cannabinoids may affect other cells or organs but may not have effects on the mental state (Mechoulam, Hanus, & Martin, 1994). It is known that new cannabinoids may be created in the process of burning (smoking) or through the digestion process when cannabis is taken orally. Thus, the combination of cannabinoids responsible for the psychoactive effects is complex and not completely understood. THC isolated from the plant may not produce exactly the same effects as cannabis consumed intact.

Absorption and Metabolism

THC is absorbed rapidly from the lungs into the bloodstream with peak blood levels occurring within 10 min of smoking. However, the decline of THC in the blood is equally rapid, so that after 1 hr only 5–

10% of the initial blood level may remain. Absorption is much slower if THC is taken orally, and the onset of effects may be delayed for 1 hr or more and may last as long as 5 hr. Rapid metabolism and redistribution to the brain and other fatty tissues accounts for the rapidly falling blood levels of THC (Hall, Solowij, & Lemon, 1994; McKim, 1997).

Metabolism of THC begins immediately in the lungs (if smoked) or the intestine (if ingested orally), but the majority is absorbed into the bloodstream and carried to the liver, where it is converted primarily into 9-carboxy-THC and 11-hydroxy-delta-9-THC (Hall et al., 1994; McKim, 1997). Although 9-carboxy-THC is not psychoactive, 11-hydroxy-delta-9-THC may actually be more potent than THC and may account for much of the psychoactive effect of cannabis, particularly when it is consumed orally (Hawks, 1982). THC is highly lipid-soluble and is readily stored in fatty tissue. The gradual release of THC from storage in fat cells explains the relatively long time it takes to eliminate a single dose from the body. The half-life of THC in the body may be from 3 to 5 days (Johansson, Agurell, Hollister, & Halldin, 1988; Seth & Sinha, 1991), and traces may be detectable for weeks or even months after chronic use (Ellis, Mann, Judson, Schramm, & Taschian, 1985).

Blood levels of THC do not show strong correspondence to the subjective intoxication or "high" reported by users. A peak high typically occurs sometime after blood levels of THC start falling, a phenomenon suggesting either that other metabolites contribute to the subjective high or that levels of THC in the brain increase even after blood levels begin to fall (e.g., Bronson, Latour, & Nahas, 1984). Large interindividual differences, the development of tolerance, and the gradual release of THC stored in fat cells also hamper efforts to estimate impairment from blood or urine specimens (Hall et al., 1994).

Neuropharmacology

The neuropharmacological processes through which THC exerts its psychoactive effects were poorly understood until recently. In 1990, several investigators converged on the finding of a specific neuronal receptor for cannabinoids (Bidaut-Russell, Devane, & Howlett, 1990; Herkenham et al., 1990; Matsuda, Lolait, Brownstein, Young, & Bonner 1990). High densities of the receptor have been identified in the cerebral cortex, hippocampus, cerebellum, and basal ganglia. It is noteworthy that the functions served by those portions of the brain with the highest concentration of cannabinoid receptors correspond to long-established effects of marijuana on fragmented thought (cortex), memory (hippocampus), and motor coordination (cerebellum). Further, the euphoria produced by marijuana appears to be related to the cannabinoid receptor's modulation of the mesolimbic dopaminergic pathways in the brain (Gardner, 1992). This dopaminergic pathway mediates the experience of reward or reinforcement produced by nearly all drugs that are typically abused. At least some of THC's effect occurs through modulation of the endogenous opioid system, which then interacts with the dopaminergic system (Gardner, 1992; Tanda, Pontieri, & DiChiara, 1997). Recent research in animals indicates that chronic cannabis exposure produces neuroadaptive changes in the limbic system similar to the changes produced by other drugs of abuse, an effect that may explain the withdrawal and craving phenomena associated with abstinence (De-Fonseca, Carrera, Navarro, Koob, & Weiss, 1997).

Devane and colleagues (1992) identified a naturally occurring brain molecule that binds to the receptor. Named *anandamide*, a term derived from the Sanskrit word *ananda* and meaning "internal bliss," it appears to mimic the action of cannabinoids. Although the role of anandamide in human physiology is not yet understood, these findings have led to an explosion of research that promises to better explicate the mechanisms of action of cannabis. A likely outcome will be the development of new medicines that make use of the cannabinoid receptor family (McKim, 1997).

Preparations, Dosage, and Routes of Administration

Common street names, preparations, dosages, and routes of administration of marijuana are summarized in table 7.1. Marijuana is the most common form of cannabis used in the United States. Marijuana consists of a mixture of the flowering tops, leaves, and stems of the dried cannabis plant. THC is concentrated most highly in the flowering tops, then the upper leaves, then the lower leaves, and finally the stems and seeds. The concentration of

THC in marijuana may vary from 0.5% to 14%, or even higher, depending upon the parts of the plant used, the growing conditions, and the genetic characteristics of the plant (Hall et al., 1994; McKim, 1997; Ray & Ksir, 1996). Sinsemilla is a particularly potent variety of marijuana that consists largely of the flowering tops of female plants. Sinsemilla (Spanish for "without seeds") is produced by removal of the male plants from the growing area, which prevents fertilization of the female plant. The female plant's energy, then, is not wasted producing seeds, and the result is THC concentrations in the range of 7–14% or higher.

Hashish is a potent cannabis preparation created by squeezing or otherwise extracting the yellowish resin from the flowering tops of the plant. It turns dark brown or black as it dries and is shaped into small rocks that may be smoked in a pipe or baked in cookies or other confections for oral consumption (e.g., "hash brownies"). The concentration of THC in hashish varies widely and is typically in the range of 2–8% but may be as high as 10–20% (Hall et al., 1994; McKim, 1997; Ray & Ksir, 1996). Hash oil is a purified variation of hashish in which THC and other cannabinoids have been extracted and concentrated through the use of an organic solvent. The oily substance is typically black or red and may be added to tobacco and smoked or heated on a piece of foil or in a pipe and inhaled. The concentration of THC in hash oil may be as high as 60% but is generally between 15% and 50%.

The large variability in the concentration of THC in marijuana and related preparations makes it difficult to establish the dose typically consumed by the average user. Only 2 mg to 3 mg of intravenous THC is needed to produce the desired effects (Perez-Reyes, Timmons, & Wall, 1974). A single marijuana cigarette or "joint," may have between 5 mg and 150 mg of THC, but anywhere between 30% and 80% of the THC may be lost in the combustion process or through sidestream smoke that is never inhaled. Further, the fraction of inhaled THC that actually reaches the bloodstream may be as low as 5–24% (Hall et al., 1994). It is estimated that the average daily user in the United States may consume 50 mg of THC per day in comparison to heavy users in Jamaica or Asia, who may consume 200–400 mg per day (Hall et al., 1994; McKim, 1997). There is some evidence that marijuana users titrate or adjust the

TABLE 7.1 Cannabis and Hallucinogens: Common Names, Dosages, Routes of Administration, and Preparations

Drug	Common names	Dosage	Routes of administration	Preparations
Cannabis	Aunt Mary, boom, bud, chronic, dope, gangster, ganja, grass, herb, kif, Mary Jane, pot, reefer, scooby snack, skunk, smoke, weed	5–150 mg of THC	Smoked Oral	Marijuana—Mixture of dried flowering tops, leaves, and stems Hashish—Brown or black resin from flowering tops shaped into small rocks Hash oil—Black or red oily substance derived from resin
Lysergic acid diethylamide (LSD)	Acid, Bart Simpson, Bartman, blue heaven, blotter, doses, hits, gelatin chips, microdots, sugar cubes, tabs, trips, windowpane	30–300 mcg	Oral	Absorbed on paper ("blotter") or in sugar cubes; capsules
Psilocybin	Caps, liberty caps, magic or Mexican mushrooms, 'shrooms	4–60 mg; 4–60 mushrooms	Oral	Dried mushrooms eaten whole, boiled to make tea, or mixed with other foods
Dimethyltryptamine (DMT)	Businessman's lunch, businessman's LSD	15–40 mg	Smoked Intranasal Injected	Crystals or oil mixed with marijuana, tobacco, or other herbs and smoked or inhaled; dissolved and injected
Mescaline	Mesc, mescal buttons, peyote	200–500 mg	Oral	Fresh or dried peyote buttons chewed, boiled into tea, or mixed with other foods; crystals in capsules
Dimethoxymethyl amphetamine (DOM)	STP	1–5 mg	Oral	Powder, crystals, tablets, or capsules
Methylenedioxyphenylisopropylamine (MDA) and methylenedioxymethamphetamine (MDMA)	Love drug	75–100 mg	Oral	Powder, crystals, tablets, or capsules
Phencyclidine (PCP)	Angel dust, dust, elephant or horse tranquilizer, hog, ozone, peace pill, rocket fuel, tranq, wack	5 mg–15 mg	Smoked Intranasal Injected Oral	Crystals mixed with tobacco, marijuana ("sherms"), or other herbs and smoked; crystals snuffed or dissolved in water and injected; tablets and capsules
Ketamine	K, ket, psychedelic heroin, special K, vitamin K	50–375 mg	Oral Intranasal Injected	Tablets or capsules; crystals snuffed
Amanita muscaria	Fly agaric	1–10 mushrooms	Oral	Dried mushrooms eaten whole or chopped and mixed with other foods

amount they smoke to compensate for the varying concentrations of THC (Perez-Reyes, DiGuiseppi, Davis, Shindler, & Cook, 1982), but the data are mixed and learned smoking habits may play a larger role (Wu, Tashkin, Rose, & Djahed, 1988).

Smoking is by far the most common route of administration of cannabis in the United States. Marijuana is typically rolled in cigarette papers to make "joints" or "nails." It may also be smoked in pipes, as are hashish and hash oil. Recently, it has become popular to roll marijuana in cigar wrappers, which are called *blunts.* Water pipes ("bongs") force the smoke through a chamber of water prior to inhalation and are used by some individuals to cool the smoke and filter unwanted constituents. Oral consumption of marijuana and hashish is less common and is accomplished by baking the substance in cookies, brownies, or cakes. When consumed orally, the effects are delayed by about 1 hr and are typically not as intense (Agurell, Lindgren, Ohlsson, Gillespie, & Hollister, 1984). On the other hand, oral consumption prolongs the effects, which are experienced for several hours or more depending upon the amount consumed. The inability to titrate the dose when consumed orally and the prolonged duration of effects may increase the likelihood of anxiety and panic reactions.

Marijuana is used in combination with many other drugs, and particular combinations vary in popularity by geographic region or as trends over time. Alcohol is the drug most commonly used in conjunction with marijuana and appears to augment the degree of intoxication and behavioral impairment in an approximately additive fashion (Chait & Perry; 1994; Hall et al., 1994). Smoking cannabis has also been shown to increase the subjective high from intranasal cocaine use, perhaps by increasing the availability of cocaine in the plasma (Lukas, Sholar, Kouri, Fukuzako, & Mendelson, 1994). Marijuana and amphetamines increase autonomic nervous system activity through different means, so that their combined effects on arousal may be perceived as aversive. On the other hand, stimulants may antagonize the sedative effects of cannabis and offset the decreases in behavior that are typically observed (Hall et al., 1994). Marijuana may also be laced with PCP or other hallucinogens whose effects tend to overpower the effects of THC. Substantial increases in toxicity are not seen when cannabis is used in combination with other drugs.

Acute Effects

Cannabis is known to produce a wide variety of cognitive, emotional, physiological, and behavioral effects that vary as a function of the dose, the setting, the current state of the user, the user's prior experience with the drug, and the user's expectations and attitudes. For most users, cannabis produces a mild state of euphoria or relaxation referred to as being *high* or *stoned.* It is often perceived to enhance other experiences such as listening to music, the taste of food, or the enjoyment of sexual interactions. Distortions in the sense of time may make experiences seem to last longer. Increased talkativeness and laughter are common in social situations, but there may be swings in mood, with increased sociability replaced by an introspective dreaminess. Lethargy and sleepiness are common as the effects of a dose wear off.

Cannabis intoxication can cause increased anxiety, paranoia, and even panic, particularly in naive users (Thomas, 1993). Even experienced users may experience these feelings occasionally after consuming larger doses than usual or after oral doses with slower onset but longer duration. Increased heart rate may augment the experience of panic in naive users who misinterpret the sensation as indicative of a dangerous reaction. Blood pressure fluctuates unpredictably, and light-headedness or fainting upon rising to a standing position sometimes occurs. Although these symptoms may be experienced as uncomfortable, tolerance to most of these effects develops in regular users, and the actual health risk from an acute dose is minimal. Individuals with known cardiovascular disease or defects should be cautioned, but from information based on animal studies, the dose that would cause death in otherwise healthy humans is 1,000 times the dose that produces the desired feelings of being high (Hall et al., 1994). There are no reports of death from acute administration of cannabis.

Cannabis intoxication impairs short-term memory and attention and thus frequently results in disjointed thought patterns and speech, so that individuals lose track of what they were thinking or saying in midstream. For occasional users, this disruption in thought may be little more than an amusing side effect or even a desired outcome that allows the user's mind to wander easily from thought to thought. Cannabis has been shown repeatedly to affect performance on a variety of laboratory tasks requiring attention, concentration, eye-hand motor coordination, and memory, although mixed findings and large interindividual differences suggest that the effects may not be very robust (Chait & Pierri, 1992; Hall et al., 1994). The debilitating effects are seen more reliably when complex tasks are used that require attention to multiple stimuli simultaneously or when attentional demands have been prolonged (e.g., to more than an hour). There do not seem to be substantial effects on mood or performance the day after marijuana use (e.g., Chait & Perry, 1994).

Tolerance, Withdrawal, and Dependence

Despite the prevalence of use there is a surprisingly small literature on problematic use of cannabis. The lack of research on clinical issues probably stemmed from controversy over the addictive potential of cannabis and the perception that it was clinically relevant only as a secondary drug of abuse among more seriously impaired polydrug abusers (see Roffman, Stephens, Simpson, & Whitaker, 1988). However, recent data show that a subgroup of marijuana users develops a dependence syndrome and may experience increased risks of negative health, safety, and social consequences.

The relative absence of tolerance and withdrawal effects in humans fueled debate on the addictive potential of cannabis throughout much of the 1960s and 1970s. In fact, many users report the phenomenon of reverse tolerance or sensitization to the effects of cannabis upon early repeated use. Reverse tolerance has never been demonstrated in the laboratory and is probably related more to experienced users' learning to smoke more efficiently and learning to better identify and label the effects of cannabis rather than to its neuropharmacology.

On the other hand, tolerance to many of the effects of cannabis has been demonstrated in both animal (Abel, McMillan, & Harris, 1974; Kosersky, McMillan, & Harris, 1974) and human studies (Babor, Mendelson, Greenberg, & Kuehnle, 1975); Georgotas & Zeidenberg, 1979; Jones & Benowitz, 1976; Jones, Benowitz, & Herning, 1981). Jones and Benowitz (1976) administered high doses of THC orally every 4 hr to healthy male marijuana users over a period of 30 days. Their results showed that subjects' ratings of subjective "highs" decreased as the duration of the daily dosing increased. The increase in

heart rate associated with cannabis use declined with repeated dosing, and observations of initial negative effects on subjects' social interactions were almost entirely gone by the end of the daily dosing period. Similar recovery of cognitive and psychomotor performance with repeated dosing was witnessed as well. Evidence of tolerance to the subjective high also emerged in a study in which subjects smoked an average of 10 marijuana cigarettes per day (Georgotas & Zeidenberg, 1979), but another study that required subjects to smoke only a single marijuana cigarette per day for 28 days did not find any evidence of tolerance (Frank, Lessin, Tyrrell, Hahn, & Szara, 1976). These findings suggest that casual use of cannabis is unlikely to produce significant tolerance, but that large daily doses result in tolerance for many of the physiological, cognitive, and social effects of THC.

These same studies have generally found evidence of withdrawal upon sudden cessation of large daily doses (Georgotas & Zeidenberg, 1979; Jones & Benowitz, 1976). Subjects reported "inner unrest" within hours of the last dose of THC. Irritability, hot flashes, insomnia, sweating, restlessness, runny nose, loose stools, hiccups, and loss of appetite were commonly reported 12 hr after the last dose (Jones & Benowitz, 1976). Uncooperative and even resistant behavior was noted in some cases (Georgotas & Zeidenberg, 1979). Although the doses used to produce these effects were large (e.g., 210 mg/day), there is some evidence that under conditions of chronic administration, doses as low as 10 mg/day for 10 days can produce tolerance and withdrawal symptoms (Jones et al., 1981). Yet, withdrawal symptoms are not always apparent even with moderately high daily doses (e.g., Mendelson, Kuehnle, Greenberg, & Mello, 1976).

Although laboratory studies have demonstrated that tolerance and withdrawal develop under specific conditions, there are fewer data on the occurrence of tolerance and withdrawal among users in the natural environment. Case studies and the uncontrolled observations of treatment professionals have reported withdrawal phenomena but have not ruled out the possibility that the symptoms reflected preexisting psychopathology or withdrawal from other substances. In one study, about 15% of moderate to heavy users reported a withdrawal syndrome that primarily included nervousness, sleep disturbance, and appetite change (Wiesbeck et al., 1996). Symptoms appeared to be related to the duration of daily use and were not totally accounted for by a history of other drug dependence or personality characteristics. It is important to remember, however, that the withdrawal symptoms reported by cannabis users are mild and generally cease within 1–3 days. Further, nearly half of the daily users seeking treatment do not report withdrawal symptoms (Stephens, Roffman, & Simpson, 1993). Thus, the role of physical dependence in determining chronic, problem use is far from certain.

The diagnosis of drug dependence today relies less on the occurrence of signs of physical dependence and more on a drug-dependence syndrome defined behaviorally by the high salience of drug use in the user's life, difficulty quitting or controlling use, a narrowing of the drug-using repertoire, and rapid reinstatement of dependence after abstinence (Edwards, Arif, & Hodgson, 1981; Edwards & Gross, 1976). Withdrawal and tolerance are seen as co-occurring aspects of the dependence syndrome but are neither necessary nor sufficient. Several psychometric studies of these dependence criteria indicate that they provide an accurate description of dependence on cannabis, as well as on most other drugs of abuse (Kosten, Rounsaville, Babor, Spitzer, & Williams, 1987; Newcombe, 1992; Rounsaville, Bryant, Babor, Kranzler, & Kadden, 1993). Daily marijuana users who sought treatment showed evidence of this syndrome (Stephens & Roffman, 1993). They averaged over 10 years of near-daily use and over six serious attempts at quitting. Their use had persisted in the face of multiple forms of impairment (i.e., social, psychological, physical), and most perceived themselves as unable to stop (Stephens et al., 1993; Stephens, Roffman, & Simpson, 1994).

Epidemiological studies using *DSM* diagnostic criteria converge on the relative risk for a lifetime diagnosis of cannabis dependence. Both the Epidemiological Catchment Area (ECA; Anthony & Helzer, 1991) and the National Comorbidity Study (NCS; Anthony et al., 1994) estimate that slightly more than 4% of the population develops a dependency on marijuana—the highest prevalence rate of any illicit drug. Approximately 9% of those who had ever used marijuana qualified for this diagnosis, a rate comparable to that for sedatives, antianxiety medications, and stimulants but somewhat less than that for alcohol (15%) and substantially less than that for tobacco (32%) and heroin (23%) (Anthony et al.,

1994). As with other drugs of abuse, the risk of dependence appears to be higher in men than in women. Given the difficulty of quantifying the dose of cannabis that reaches the bloodstream, there are no clear guidelines on the amount of THC that must be consumed to produce dependence. It is clear that the risk of dependence increases as the frequency of use increases. Yet, even daily use is not synonymous with dependence, and many daily users do not report significant negative consequences or a desire to quit (Haas & Hendin, 1987; Rainone, Deren, Kleinman, & Wish, 1987). Thus, the vast majority of marijuana users do not become dependent, while a small minority develop a syndrome of compulsive use that is similar to the dependence syndromes described for most other drugs.

Adverse Effects on Health, Safety, and Adjustment

A primary area of concern for cannabis users is related more to the mode of use than to the psychoactive ingredient, THC. Cannabis smoke is similar to tobacco smoke in many of its constituents and may pose similar health risks. Currently, there are no studies clearly linking marijuana use with cancers of the aerodigestive tract or lungs in humans, but marijuana smoking, independent of tobacco smoking, has been shown to increase chronic and acute bronchitis, to cause functional alterations in the respiratory tract, and to produce morphological changes in the airways that may precede malignant change (see for reviews Hall et al., 1994; Tashkin et al., 1990). The adverse effects appear to occur with fewer marijuana cigarettes per day and at earlier ages than for tobacco smokers. In addition, concurrent tobacco smoking augments many of the effects of marijuana smoking in an additive fashion. Notably, 50% of the chronic, heavy marijuana users seeking treatment also smoke tobacco (Stephens et al., 1993). A study of the medical records of daily "cannabis-only" smokers receiving care in a large health maintenance organization found a slight increase in outpatient visits related to respiratory complaints over the visit frequency of nonsmokers (Polen, Sidney, Tekawa, Sadler, & Friedman, 1993). The full effects of chronic marijuana use on the respiratory system may not yet be known given the relatively short period of widespread use in the Western world.

The majority of studies and reviews have concluded that there is little evidence of any substantial permanent damage to the brain even from chronic cannabis use (Hollister, 1986; Wert & Raulin, 1986a, 1986b). Methodological problems in many studies and the failure to replicate occasional adverse findings make definitive statements impossible, but it seems clear that major impairments are unlikely. However, some studies using recordings of event-related potentials that are indicative of the ability to focus attention and to filter irrelevant distracting stimuli have found evidence of impairment related to duration and frequency of marijuana use (Solowij, Michie, & Fox, 1991, 1995). The relationship of the findings to daily intellectual functioning is not known, and there are null findings with the use of similar tasks (Patrick et al, 1995). More sensitive neuropsychological tests have also revealed small but significant impairments in the attentional and executive functioning of heavy-marijuana-using college students that does not show up in more global estimates of intelligence (Pope & Yurgelun-Todd, 1996). They may be due to a drug residue effect that will diminish with longer abstinence, rather than a more permanent alteration of the central nervous system (Pope, Gruber, & Yurgelun-Todd, 1995). However, several investigators have warned that the significance of marijuana's effect on cognitive functioning may be underestimated by these studies of more highly functioning individuals and that the effects could be much greater on those whose intellectual abilities are compromised (e.g., by learning disabilities or lower intelligence).

Animal research suggests that cannabis may reduce the immune response and leave the organism susceptible to infection by bacteria and viruses, but the clinical relevance of these findings is questionable in humans (Hall et al., 1994; Hollister, 1986). When small adverse effects on the human immune system have been found, they have typically not been replicated (Hall et al., 1994; Hollister, 1986).

Smoking marijuana during pregnancy may be associated with a shorter period of gestation and lower birth weight (Hatch & Bracken, 1986; Zuckerman et al., 1989), but a large multicenter study failed to find these effects (Shiono et al., 1995). Prenatal marijuana use does not seem to cause major birth defects (Zuckerman et al., 1989) and does not impair gross motor development (Chandler, Richardson, Gallagher, & Day, 1996). One study implicates maternal marijuana use during pregnancy with an increased risk of a rare form of childhood cancer (Robinson et al., 1989), but the unexpected nature of the finding suggests the need for replication. The Ottawa Prenatal Prospective Study followed a group of children born to mothers who used marijuana during pregnancy and matched controls through 9 years of age (Fried, 1995; Fried, O'Connell, & Watkinson, 1992; Fried & Watkinson, 1990). Early findings of differences between groups were largely negative on measures of global scores of intelligence. Specific deficits related to prenatal marijuana use were found at ages 4–9 on several neurobehavioral tasks. Fried (1995) speculated that the late emergence of differences in sustained attention, language comprehension, and visual perceptual tasks indicated more general impairment in the executive functions of the prefrontal lobe, which becomes fully active only at later stages of development. There are other findings consistent with this interpretation, but the absolute differences in intellectual functioning appear to be very small (Day et al., 1994; Richardson, Day, & Goldschmidt, 1995). The clinical significance of these findings await further follow-ups of this cohort and replication in other prospective studies.

Research on experimental driving simulators and on-road research found mixed evidence of impairment after cannabis use, lane control errors being the most frequent type of error found (Smiley, 1986). The most reliable finding has been a reduction in risk taking (e.g., by driving slower or maintaining a greater distance from other cars) after smoking marijuana that may partially explain the relative lack of impairment on driving tasks. More driving errors were seen under unexpected emergency conditions when drivers were not able to compensate for the effects of intoxication (Smiley, 1986). Reviews of studies examining the presence of cannabinoids in relation to automobile accident mortality are inconclusive (McBay, 1986; Simpson, 1986). Although cannabis has been found to be present in the bodies of accident victims at rates of 4–37%, it is not known whether this prevalence exceeded the base rate of cannabis use in the population under consideration (e.g., young male drivers; Terhune, 1986). In addition, most victims who are positive for cannabinoids are also positive for alcohol, which has a known association with increases driving accidents (McBay, 1986).

A major question about the use of marijuana is

its role in promoting the use of harder drugs. The "gateway" hypothesis holds that marijuana is a "stepping-stone" to the use of harder drugs. Although numerous studies confirm a progression of drug use in the United States, starting with alcohol and tobacco use and proceeding to marijuana and then harder drugs (e.g., Ellickson, Hays, & Bell, 1992; Huba, Wingard, & Bentler, 1981; Kandel & Faust, 1975), the causal role of marijuana in this progression is doubtful (e.g., Kandel 1988). More likely, it reflects a societal phenomenon of the use of legal drugs followed by marijuana, the mildest and most available of the illicit drugs (Miller, 1994). A subset of marijuana users go on to experiment with harder drugs, perhaps because of the association with drug users (e.g., Kandel, 1984), other risk factors (see Newcombe, 1992), or preexisting differences in personality characteristics (Baumrind, 1983; Perry & Mandell, 1995), but the progression is far from inevitable and is not likely to be directly linked to the pharmacology of cannabis.

Regardless of whether it leads to harder drug use, regular cannabis use by adolescents raises concerns about negative educational, occupational, social, and psychological consequences. Longitudinal studies have generally confirmed that heavier marijuana and other drug involvement in adolescence is predictive of less stability in a variety of adult roles, including college involvement, occupational stability, and marriage (Kandel, Davies, Karus, & Yamaguchi, 1986; Newcombe & Bentler, 1988). These outcomes may be explained by preexisting differences in the adjustment of those who choose to use cannabis (e.g., Brook, Cohen, Whiteman, & Gordon, 1992; Kandel & Davies, 1992; Newcombe & Bentler, 1988; Shedler & Block, 1990) or by the combined use of cannabis, alcohol, and other drugs (see Newcombe & Bentler, 1988). Nevertheless, the acute effects of cannabis on cognition and behavior recommend against its use when attending school, performing complex tasks, or mastering new social skills.

Related to concerns about impaired educational and occupational performance is the notion that marijuana produces an "amotivational syndrome" characterized by low motivation, apathy, lethargy, mental dulling, and social withdrawal. While there are many clinical observations and case reports of chronic marijuana users who fit this picture, it is also clear that many other equally heavy users perform well in school and in complex and demanding occu-

pations. Field studies of heavy users in comparison with nonusers in other cultures (Carter, Coggins, & Doughty, 1980; Rubin & Comitas, 1975) have generally not yielded findings of decreased productivity. Laboratory studies provide mixed evidence that marijuana decreases motivation, but these studies rely on relatively short periods of use under artificial circumstances (Hall et al., 1994). It seems unlikely that marijuana directly causes motivational problems; rather, it may interact with predisposing personality characteristics in some individuals to produce this clinical phenomenon. Surveys of self-identified marijuana users in three separate communities in the United States indicate that a majority of regular, heavy users report impairment of memory, concentration, motivation, self-esteem, interpersonal relationships, health, employment, or finances related to their marijuana use (Haas & Hendin, 1987; Rainone et al., 1987; Roffman & Barnhart, 1987), indicating that at least a subset of users may be adversely affected. Some of these users seek treatment and appear to profit from it (Stephens et al., 1993, 1994).

Although there is some evidence that cannabis use rarely produces an acute psychosis consisting of confusion, agitation, anxiety, delusions, and hallucinations, it does not appear to persist beyond the period of intoxication (Gruber & Pope, 1994; Thomas, 1993). Verbal support, a quiet place, and, perhaps, small doses of tranquilizers are typically sufficient to reassure the individual until the acute effects wear off. One of the difficulties of research in this area is distinguishing between psychotic symptoms caused by cannabis use and the emergence of preexisting psychotic conditions such as schizophrenia and manic-depressive psychoses following cannabis use. Cannabis may precipitate the expression of latent schizophrenia or exacerbate the course of the disorder (e.g., Linszen, Dingemans, & Lenior, 1994), but there is little systematic evidence that it causes any form of chronic mental disorder in psychiatrically normal individuals (Taylor & Warner, 1994; Thomas, 1993).

There is ongoing debate on whether the potency of marijuana available in the United States today is significantly greater than that available during the early 1970s, when much of the research on the addictive potential and harmful effects of cannabis was conducted (Cohen, 1986; Mikuriya & Aldrich, 1988). If so, it is possible that the older research underestimates the adverse effects of cannabis. Analyses of marijuana seized by the Drug Enforcement Agency

(DEA) in the 1970s showed lower concentrations of THC than those found in samples seized in the 1980s, but there was no systematic increase in the potency of confiscated samples throughout the 1980s and early 1990s. It is probable that samples from the 1970s showed lower amounts of THC because they were stored improperly and degraded (Mikuriya & Aldrich, 1988). It is also not clear that these confiscated samples were representative of what was generally available to users. Further, if users titrate their dose, or if the effects of THC on long-term functioning are not dose-dependent, any change in average potency would not necessarily translate into greater adverse consequences. These issues remain to be resolved.

Cannabis Summary

Cannabis is a complex psychoactive substance with a variety of acute effects on mood, cognition, and physiology that appear to be mediated largely through specific cannabinoid receptors in the brain. Most users find these effects reinforcing, and acute toxicity is minimal, anxiety and panic reactions being the most commonly reported adverse effects. Death from cannabis intoxication does not occur in humans. Tolerance and withdrawal have been demonstrated in the laboratory after large chronic doses and have been reported by heavy users, but the withdrawal syndrome appears to be mild and is not likely to account for the behavioral dependence documented in a subset of frequent users. The largest concern related to chronic use is the deleterious effects of smoking on the lungs. There are also recent data suggesting subtle residual cognitive impairment in chronic heavy users and delayed effects on the cognitive development of children born to mothers who used marijuana. These findings require replication before great weight is placed on them because of mixed results and the more frequently reported failure to find significant adverse effects on intellectual abilities. On the whole, cannabis use does not seem to cause mental disorders or to grossly affect psychosocial functioning, although it may exacerbate preexisting psychotic conditions or subclinical personality dysfunction. A subset of heavy users develop dependence and report adverse effects on their social, occupational, and personal lives. Such users who present for treatment appear to respond to psychosocial interventions similarly to other drug-dependent individuals.

HALLUCINOGENS

Hallucinogens constitute a broad group of substances that share an ability to produce sensory distortions and hallucinations at doses that are not otherwise toxic to the body. In contrast to cannabis, these drugs produce more intense perceptual-emotional experiences and stronger physiological effects. Hallucinogens have been used throughout history as part of a variety of religious and spiritual rituals and are still used in this manner by some. Other names given to these drugs include *psychedelics*, *phantasticants*, and *psychotomimetics*. The former two terms derive from the use of these drugs to achieve enlightening visual and emotional experiences or to create fantasylike experiences, respectively. *Psychotomimetics* refers to the similarity between the drug effects and the symptoms of psychosis.

There are over 100 different hallucinogens with substantially different molecular structures. They are commonly grouped by their similarity to particular neurotransmitters (e.g., McKim, 1997; Ray & Ksir, 1996). For instance, d-lysergic acid diethylamide (LSD), psilocybin, and dimethyltryptamine (DMT) share the indole nucleus that provides the basic structure of the neurotransmitter serotonin. Mescaline and numerous amphetamine derivatives (e.g., dimethoxymethylamphetamine [DOM], methylenedioxyphenylisopropylamine [MDA], methylenedioxymethamphetamine [MDMA]) are based on the catechol nucleus and are more similar to the catecholamine neurotransmitters, norepinephrine and dopamine. A group of hallucinogens less frequently used in the United States block the receptors for the neurotransmitter acetylcholine but do not activate it. These anticholinergic hallucinogens include belladonna, mandrake, henbane, datura, and several synthetic drugs used to treat parkinsonian symptoms (e.g., benzotropine and trihexyphenidyl). Phencyclidine, ketamine, and *Amanita muscaria* (fly agaric) constitute a miscellaneous group that share some effects with the hallucinogens but also produce distinct effects.

Acute Effects

Despite their chemical diversity, the subjective experiences or "trips" these substances produce have many common features (Abraham, Aldridge, & Gogia, 1996; Grinspoon & Bakalar, 1983; Stafford, 1992; Strassman, Qualls, Uhlenhuth, & Kellner, 1994; Weiss &

Millman, 1991). Hallucinogens typically have their most immediate effects on the autonomic nervous system and produce an increase in heart rate and body temperature and slightly elevate blood pressure. The individual may experience a dry mouth, dizziness, and subjective feelings of being hot or cold. Gradually, the focus on physiological changes fades into the background and perceptual distortions and hallucinations become prominent.

Although hallucinations occur in all sensory systems, visual effects are the most common and auditory effects the least common (Abraham & Aldridge, 1993; Grinspoon & Bakalar, 1983). Aesthetic experience is altered so that colors seem more intense, objects and events look sharper and take on new significance, and music may seem richer and more meaningful. Synesthesia, the crossing of senses so that sounds are seen or objects heard, has been reported. The sense of time slows or even comes to a complete stop. Geometric patterns often appear with or without the eyes open early in the experience and give way later to visions of landscapes, people, or symbolic objects. Anxiety and increased energy coexist with euphoria and even relaxation, and there is often rapid alteration between emotional states. Set (the user's expectations and cognitive/emotional state prior to use) and setting (the physical surroundings and circumstances) profoundly affect the experience. There may be intense feelings of closeness to others whereas, later in the experience or on a different occasion, the user may feel distant and isolated. Short-term memory is impaired, but memories from the past may emerge and feel more vivid and real. The number and intensity of effects are dose-dependent, and some of the more extreme perceptual distortions are probably not experienced by many recreational users who consume low to moderate doses. At very low doses, the effects of hallucinogens may be more somatic and less perceptual/cognitive, the result being uncomfortable feelings of physical tension (Strassman et al., 1994).

LSD impairs functioning on a variety of cognitive tasks (Hollister, 1978), and animal research suggests that PCP disrupts short-term memory. However, controlled research on the effects of hallucinogens on performance is difficult to interpret because of the difficulty in maintaining the subject's motivation for the tasks in the midst of the hallucinogenic experience (McKim, 1997). There is no systematic evidence to support the claims that hallucinogens in-crease creativity, and in fact, studies suggest that they impair performance on laboratory creativity tasks (McKim, 1997; Ray & Ksir, 1996).

"Bad trips" are one of the undesirable acute effects of hallucinogen use. These are characteristically panic reactions that develop when individuals feel that the hallucinogenic experience will never end or when have difficulty distinguishing drug effects from reality. In most cases, users can be "talked down" by being reassured that their experiences are drug-induced and will end soon. Most of these bad trips are thought to be related to an interaction of a negative mood state or adverse environmental circumstances with the drug effects. Adverse reactions are extremely rare in controlled studies of LSD use, where individuals are carefully screened for psychological adjustment and consume the drug in safe and secure situations (Levine & Ludwig, 1964), but they may be somewhat more common under street conditions in less psychologically stable users. It is also important to note that the true content of hallucinogenic drugs purchased on the street is always in doubt and has often been misidentified or adulterated with other drugs.

Neuropharmacology, Dosage, Preparations, Absorption, and Metabolism

There is little systematic research on many of the hallucinogens, and detailed information on neuropharmacology, typical dosages, and metabolic pathways is lacking (Abraham et al., 1996). It is clear that LSD and other hallucinogens block serotonin receptors or otherwise alter serotonergic activity, but so do other drugs that do not produce hallucinations. Some evidence exists that LSD and other hallucinogens (e.g., psilocybin and mescaline) produce effects by stimulating a specific subtype of serotonin receptor known as 5-HT_2 (see Abraham & Aldridge, 1993; McKim, 1997).

Table 7.1 presents the common street names, typical dosages, routes of administration, and common preparations of the hallucinogens most frequently used in the United States. It is important to note that many of the hallucinogens are derived from plants and are often consumed in this organic form. As in cannabis, the active ingredients in these plants vary widely. Typical users are often not aware of the dose they are taking. The ranges of dosages given in table 7.1 are derived both from scientific studies that isolate the active ingredients and from anecdotal or case reports (see Gable, 1993; Stafford, 1992). The wide range in dosages reflects, in part, the fact that users have different preferences for the intensity of the hallucinogenic experience. Values at the lower end of the ranges typically reflect the minimal effective dose and are associated with autonomic effects and mild feelings of euphoria, while values at the higher end constitute dosages that produce more intense hallucinogenic experiences. These ranges also represent differences in dosages related to routes of administration. Smaller doses are typically used in injecting or smoking the drug than in oral consumption.

LSD

LSD is the classic hallucinogen and its discovery by Albert Hoffman in 1943 is credited with introducing hallucinogen use to the Western world. It is produced synthetically and is the most potent of the hallucinogens. After its accidental discovery, LSD was produced legally for research and used briefly as an adjunct to psychotherapy before becoming illegal. The lack of carefully controlled studies and its unpredictable effects made LSD's utility as an aid to exploring the mind highly debatable (see Abraham et al., 1996). It was adopted as a drug of choice by the hippie movement of the 1960s and was actively promoted by psychologist Timothy Leary as a mind-expanding drug (see Grinspoon & Bakalar, 1979; Stafford, 1992). Use peaked in the late 1960s and early 1970s. It has been suggested that today's users are more interested in it for pleasure than for the self-enlightenment sought by the flower children of that era (Baumeister & Placidi, 1983). Consequently, it is probably taken in smaller doses today and thus produces more of a euphoric effect than the intensely hallucinogenic trips of the 1960s (McKim, 1997).

LSD is metabolized in the liver, and the half-life of the drug in the body is approximately 2 hr. The metabolites do not appear to be psychoactive. Effects begin within 30–90 min and last from 6–12 hr (Abraham & Aldridge, 1993; McKim, 1997). The lethal toxicity of LSD is very low, as the dose that is likely to be lethal to humans is probably 200–300 times the effective dose of 30–100 mcg (Gable, 1993). Reports of death by overdose are very rare, and there are numerous cases of individuals who have taken massive doses (e.g., 40,000 mcg; see Stafford, 1992) and survived.

Psilocybin

Psilocybin is found in mushrooms native to North America and has been used in religious rituals by Mexican and Central American Indians for thousands of years (McKim, 1997; Stafford, 1992). Psilocybin is much less potent than LSD but produces similar effects if the dose is adjusted. Lethality is effectively nil; a dose likely to produce death is about 3,500 times the effective dose (Gable, 1993). Psilocybin is converted in the body to psilocin, which apparently is more psychoactive and accounts for most of the effects (McKim 1997; Ray & Ksir, 1996).

DMT

Dimethyltriptamine is the active ingredient found in a variety of plants around the world. It is extracted and snuffed by South American Indians (McKim, 1997; Stafford, 1992). It is typically produced synthetically when available in the United States. Although never widely used in the United States, DMT was named the *businessman's lunch* or *businessman's LSD* because of the rapid onset of its effects and its relatively short duration of action. Onset is very rapid, and effects are completely resolved within 30 min to 1 hr (Ray & Ksir, 1996; Stafford, 1992; Strassman et al., 1994).

Mescaline

Mescaline is derived from the small, carrot-shaped peyote cactus which is indigenous to the deserts of Mexico and the Southwestern United States. It is used legally in some states as part of religious ceremonies by members of the Native American Church (McKim, 1997). Typically, the cactus is cut into thick slices and dried, producing "mescal buttons" that are chewed and eventually swallowed. Nausea is common after eating the buttons. Mescaline appears to be the ingredient responsible for visual hallucinations, but other psychoactive alkaloids have been identified in peyote. Mescaline is also produced synthetically as a saltlike crystal but may not produce effects identical to peyote in this form (Ray & Ksir, 1996; Stafford, 1992).

Mescaline is absorbed into the bloodstream from the digestive tract and reaches maximum concentrations in the brain within 30 to 120 min. Most of the drug is excreted unchanged. It has a half-life of approximately 2 hr and effects may last up to 8 or 9 hr. The lethal dose of mescaline is estimated to be only 10–30 times the effective dose, so the risk of toxicity relative to LSD and other indole hallucinogens is increased (Gable, 1993; Ray & Ksir, 1996).

MDA, DOM, and Other Designer Drugs

MDA (3,4-methylenedioxyphenylisopropylamine) and DOM (2,5-dimethoxy-4-methyl-amphetamine) were two of the earliest hallucinogens created synthetically by alteration of the amphetamine molecule. However, they have psychoactive properties more similar to mescaline (McKim, 1997; Stafford, 1992). The oils from a variety of plants, including nutmeg, contain precursors of the MDA molecule and are sometimes ingested to produce psychoactive effect (Stafford, 1992). In the 1970s, MDA was known as the love drug because of its ability to produce a profound sense of closeness to others along with some milder stimulant effects. DOM was introduced to the streets as STP (serenity, tranquility, peace) during this same period. It produces effects very similar to those of mescaline and LSD that last 6–8 hr. Although not widely available today, these drugs were the forerunners of numerous designer drugs, the best known of which is ecstasy, or 3,4-methylenedioxymethamphetamine (MDMA; Steele, McCann, & Ricaurte, 1994). These drugs are discussed in more detail in chapter 10 and are not considered further here.

PCP

PCP was developed as an analgesic and anesthetic and has the desirable effect of reducing the perception of pain by inducing a dissociative or trancelike state without the irregularities of heart rate, blood pressure, or respiration associated with many general anesthetics (McKim, 1997; Ray & Ksir, 1996). However, it had other unpredictable psychoactive effects on some individuals that made it unsuitable for use as a human anesthetic, although it is still used with animals. PCP is easily synthesized and began appearing on the streets in the 1960s and 1970s. It was often misrepresented as THC, LSD, or other hallucinogens. It can be produced as tablets or capsules that are taken orally, but most often, it is found in a salt-like crystal form that is sprinkled on plant material (e.g., tobacco, marijuana, various herbs) and smoked. It can also be snuffed or absorbed through any moist membrane (eyes, rectum, vagina) or dissolved in water and injected (McKim, 1997). There is evidence that PCP's reinforcing properties result from stimulation of the mesolimbic dopaminergic system. There is also evidence that PCP may have its own receptor, and it is known to affect receptors for excitatory amino acids in the cortex and other parts of the brain (Johnson, 1987).

At lower doses (5–10 mg), PCP produces a sense of relaxation, tingling sensations, and numbness. It does not produce true hallucinations like LSD, but there are distortions of body image, floating sensations, and euphoria that last 4–6 hr (McKim, 1997). Depression sometimes follows the acute dose and may last 24 hr. At higher doses, some individuals develop a psychoticlike state including confusion, depersonalization, persecution, depression, and intense anxiety that may last several days (Brecher, Wang, Wong, & Morgan, 1988; Ray & Ksir, 1996). Individuals in this acute psychotic state are known to be difficult to manage, and there is popular lore that PCP induces violence. However, careful examination of the literature suggests that PCP does not directly induce violence in individuals who are otherwise not prone to violence (Brecher et al., 1988). Rather, it appears that injuries occur in the context of trying to subdue the agitated and irrational user who, by virtue of being relatively anesthetized to pain, will not respond to typical means of subjugation and may seem to have "superhuman" strength. The lethal dose in humans is estimated to be 40 times the effective dose (Gable, 1993) although some reviewers have estimated the toxic dose to be substantially lower (McKim, 1997).

Ketamine

Ketamine has recently gained notoriety as a "club drug" because of its frequent use at dance clubs and all night "raves." It is closely related to PCP and produces similar dissociative effects. It was developed as an anesthetic for children and is also used in veterinary medicine (McKim, 1997). Some users report spiritual experiences and entry into alternate realities, while others note unpleasant excitability, confusion, and irrational behavior. More negative effects appear to occur at the upper end of the range of dosages (see table 7.1). The effects typically last from 1 to 4 hr, depending upon dose and route of administration.

Amanita muscaria

The *Amanita muscaria* mushroom typically grows in forests and can be found on most of the world's continents, including North America. It is commonly referred to as *fly agaric* because of its ability to sedate flies for several hours without causing death. The mushroom has a toadstool shape and ranges in color from creamy white to pinkish orange to scarlet. The active ingredient is thought to be ibotinic acid or its metabolite, muscamole (McKim, 1997; Stafford, 1992). It is suggested that from 1 to 10 of the dried mushrooms consumed orally produce the desired effects (Ray & Ksir, 1996; Stafford, 1992). At lower doses, there is twitching and trembling of the limbs and a euphoric feeling, followed by colorful hallucinations. At higher doses, it has been noted to produce hyperactivity and violence on occasion (McKim, 1997). The user eventually falls into a prolonged deep sleep with partial paralysis. The high toxicity and potential for death of these mushrooms are well known.

Anticholinergic Hallucinogens

The anticholinergic hallucinogens are rarely used recreationally in the United States. Atropine, scopolamine, and hyoscyamine are the naturally occurring active ingredients in a variety of plants that grow around the world (e.g., belladonna, mandrake, henbane, datura). They block the acetylcholine receptor in both the central and the peripheral nervous systems, but they do not activate it. Their acute effects are different from those of other hallucinogens and resemble a toxic psychosis with delirium, confusion, and loss of memory for recent events (Ray & Ksir, 1996). There are no visual hallucinations. In addition to this clouding of consciousness, these drugs produce a number of undesirable peripheral effects, including dry mouth, blurred vision, and increased body temperature. Toxicity is generally high, and accidental death from overdose is not uncommon (McKim, 1997). Although there are some recent reports of abuse of synthetic varieties that were created for medical reasons (Dilsaver, 1988), little informa-

tion is available on street names and typical dosages. Hence, these drugs are not included in table 7.1.

Tolerance, Withdrawal, and Dependence

Tolerance builds rapidly to LSD, psilocybin, and mescaline, and it becomes impossible to achieve the desired effects with any dose after several successive days of use. Tolerance is lost equally rapidly, however, and the same dose may again be used after a few days. There is cross-tolerance between LSD, psilocybin, and mescaline (McKim, 1997). The rapidly developing tolerance dictates that hallucinogens be used only occasionally, and even the heaviest users may trip only a few times per month. True withdrawal syndromes do not occur for these hallucinogens (Abraham & Aldridge, 1993; McKim, 1997). Hallucinogens also have one of the lowest potentials for the development of dependence (Gable, 1993). Only about 5% of users ever meet diagnostic criteria for dependence (Anthony et al., 1994), and very few users report not being able to stop or cut down their use (Morgenstern, Langenbucher, & Labouvie, 1994).

An exception to the lack of tolerance and withdrawal among hallucinogens is PCP, which has been shown to produce tolerance in both animals and humans (Balster, 1987). Withdrawal symptoms have also been demonstrated in animals and may be related to depletion of norepinephrine, dopamine, and serotonin neurotransmitters with chronic use (Giannini, Loiselle, Graham, & Folts, 1993). No systematic human studies of withdrawal and dependence have been conducted, but based on animal research, PCP is considered to have moderate to high potential to produce dependence (Gable, 1993). Similarly, there are anecdotal reports of compulsive use patterns with ketamine, but it is not clear to what extent this is related to tolerance and withdrawal (Stafford, 1992). The finding that animals will self-administer PCP, but not other hallucinogens, suggests that it possesses rewarding properties not shared by other hallucinogens (Balster, 1987).

Adverse Effects on Health, Safety, and Adjustment

There is little evidence that LSD and other hallucinogens produce genetic damage or cause birth defects in the children of users (Abraham & Aldridge, 1993; Grinspoon & Bakalar, 1979). No chronic diseases or medical conditions are known to be associated with hallucinogen use. However, it is important to remember that hallucinogen use is rare in the population. Thus, it is difficult to obtain adequate samples to study these potential outcomes, particularly if they result only from years of cumulative use. Further, hallucinogen users frequently use multiple drugs, so it is difficult to identify their independent effects.

The primary area of concern for hallucinogen use is the production of enduring psychoses. Cases of prolonged psychoses following hallucinogen use are well documented, but the extent to which these disorders were caused by the drug is not known (Abraham & Aldridge, 1993; Abraham et al., 1996; Steele et al., 1994). Many cases clearly occur in individuals with schizophrenia or in those who showed poor premorbid adjustment indicative of a latent psychosis. However, other cases appear to have developed in psychologically stable individuals. The low incidence of these reactions in controlled administration studies suggests that unidentified predisposing characteristics interact with the hallucinogenic experience to produce chronic psychoses.

Other concerns center on the accidental injuries or deaths that occur during the acute hallucinogenic state. The frequency of these events is probably exaggerated by sensationalized media reports, but it is clear that judgment is sometimes impaired during hallucinogen use and can lead to injury. This is particularly likely in the case of high doses of PCP, where the hallucinogenic state is associated more with confusion, disorientation, paranoia, and resistance to intervention.

Flashbacks, or the recurrence of acute effects of the drug, weeks or months after use are sometimes reported even after a single use of LSD. They are unpredictable in timing and frequency, and some may be nothing more than intense memories of the previous trip (Ray & Ksir, 1996). They vary widely in content (e.g., perceptual, somatic, emotional) and in duration (from fractions of a second to 5 years; Abraham & Aldridge, 1993). They typically diminish with time if the person stops using psychoactive drugs. Flashbacks involving the reexperiencing of visual hallucinations and distortions have been termed *posthallucinogen perception disorder* and *hallucinogen persisting perception disorder* in the two most recent editions of the *DSM*, respectively (American Psychiatric Association, 1987, 1994). Most common-

ly, they consist of trails of moving objects, flashes of color, lights in the peripheral fields, afterimages, and stroboscopic-like effects. These visual phenomena often occur when the person enters a dark room or when other psychoactive drugs are used. They may also be self-induced by an intentional remembering of the experience. There is some evidence that the phenomena may be related to relatively permanent changes in the central nervous system's processing of visual stimuli (Abraham & Aldridge, 1993).

Hallucinogen Summary

Hallucinogens are a molecularly diverse set of drugs with surprisingly similar psychoactive effects. Autonomic effects predominate shortly after use and are later overshadowed by powerful hallucinogenic effects on perception and emotion. The most common adverse reaction is panic, although more psychotic-like confusion and disorientation occur occasionally, particularly with PCP, which is generally more disruptive to behavior when taken in high doses. The rapid acquisition of tolerance prevents daily or near-daily use of many hallucinogens, and there is no withdrawal syndrome. Dependence on these drugs is rare. PCP is an exception and does produce tolerance, withdrawal, and behavioral indications of dependence in some users. There are few indications of longer term adverse consequences, but infrequent use in the population makes it difficult to detect such outcomes if they do exist. Chronic psychoses may be precipitated by hallucinogen use, but they are rare and appear to be more likely in psychiatrically predisposed individuals. Impaired judgment and rare acute psychoticlike states may increase injuries and accidental deaths.

Key References

Hall, W., Solowij, N., & Lemon, J. (1994). *The health and psychological consequences of cannabis use.* National Drug Strategy Monograph Series No. 25. Canberra: Australian Government Publishing Service.

McKim, W. A. (1997). *Drugs and behavior: An introduction to behavioral pharmacology* (3rd ed.). Upper Saddle River, NJ: Prentice Hall.

Stafford, P. (1992). *Psychedelics encyclopedia* (3rd ed.). Berkeley, CA: Ronin.

References

Abel, E. L., McMillan, D. E., & Harris, L. S. (1974). Delta-9-tetrahydrocannabinol: Effects of route of administration on onset and duration of activity and tolerance development. *Psychopharmacologia, 35,* 29–38.

Abood, M. E., & Martin, B. R. (1992). Neurobiology of marijuana abuse. *Trends in Pharmacological Science, 13,* 201–206.

Abraham, H. D., & Aldridge, A. M. (1993). Adverse consequences of lysergic acid diethylamide. *Addiction, 88,* 1327–1334.

Abraham, H. D., Aldridge, A. M., & Gogia, P. (1996). The psychopharmacology of hallucinogens. *Neuropsychopharmacology,14,* 285–298.

Agurell, S., Lindgren, J., Ohlsson, A., Gillespie, H. K., & Hollister, L. (1984). Recent studies on the pharmacokinetics of delta-1-tetrahydrocannabinol in man. In S. Agurell, W. L. Dewey, & R. E. Willett (Eds.), *The cannabinoids; Chemical, pharmacologial, and therapeutic aspects* (pp. 165–184). Orlando, FL: Academic Press.

American Psychiatric Association. (1987). *Diagnostic and statistical manual of mental disorders (DSM-III-R;* 3rd ed. Rev.). Washington, DC: Author.

American Psychiatric Association. (1994). *Diagnostic and statistical manual of mental disorders (DSM-IV;* 4th ed.). Washington, DC: Author.

Anthony, J. C., & Helzer, J. E. (1991). Syndromes of drug abuse and dependence. In L. N. Robins & D. A. Regier (Eds.), *Psychiatric disorders in America* (pp. 116–154). New York: Free Press.

Anthony, J. C., Warner, L. A., & Kessler, R. C. (1994). Comparative epidemiology of dependence on tobacco, alcohol, controlled substances, and inhalants: Basic findings from the national comorbidity survey. *Experimental and Clinical Psychopharmacology, 2,* 244–268.

Babor, T. F., Mendelson, J. H., Greenberg, I., & Kuehnle, J. C. (1975). Marijuana consumption and tolerance to physiological and subjective effects. *Archives of General Psychiatry, 32,* 1548–1552.

Balster, R. L. (1987). The behavioral pharmacology of phencyclidine. In H. Y. Meltzer (Ed.), *Psychopharmacology: The third generation of progress* (pp. 1573–1579). New York: Raven Press.

Baumeister, R. F., & Placidi, K. S. (1983). A social history and analysis of the LSD controversy. *Journal of Humanistic Psychology, 23,* 25–58.

Baumrind, D. (1983). Specious causal attribution in the social sciences: The reformulated stepping stone hypothesis as exemplar. *Journal of Personality and Social Psychology, 45,* 1289–1298.

Bidaut-Russell, M., Devane, W. A., & Howlett, A. C. (1990). Cannabinoid receptors and modulation of cyclic AMP accumulation in the rat brain. *Journal of Neurochemistry, 55,* 21–55.

Brecher, M., Wang, B-W., Wong, H., & Morgan, J. P. (1988). Phencyclidine and violence: Clinical and legal issues. *Journal of Clinical Psychopharmacology, 8,* 397–401.

Bronson, M., Latour, C., & Nahas, G. G. (1984). Distribution and disposition of delta-9-tetrahydrocannabinol (THC) in different tissues in the rat. In S. Agurell, W. L. Dewey, & R. E. Willette (Eds.), *The cannabinoids: Chemical, pharmacologic, and therapeutic aspects* (pp. 309–317). Orlando, FL: Academic Press.

Brook, J. S., Cohen, P., Whiteman, M., & Gordon, A. S. (1992). Psychosocial risk factors in the transition from moderate to heavy use or abuse of drugs. In M. Glantz & R. Pickens (Eds.), *Vulnerability to drug abuse.* Washington: American Psychological Association.

Carter, W. E., Coggins, W., & Doughty, P. L. (1980). *Cannabis in Costa Rica: A study of chronic marihuana use.* Philadelphia: Institute for the Study of Human Issues.

Chait, L. D., & Perry, J. L. (1994). Acute and residual effects of alcohol and marijuana, alone and in combination, on mood and performance. *Psychopharmacology, 115,* 340–349.

Chait, L. D., & Pierri, J. (1992). Effects of smoked marijuana on human performance: A critical review. In L. Murphy and A. Bartke (Eds.), *Marijuana/cannabinoids: Neurobiology and neurophysiology* (pp. 387–424). Boca Raton, FL: CRC Press.

Chandler, L. S., Richardson, G. A., Gallagher, J. D., & Day, N. L. (1996). Prenatal exposure to alcohol and marijuana: Effects on motor development of preschool children. *Alcoholism: Clinical and Experimental Research, 20,* 455–461.

Cohen, S. (1986). Marijuana research: Selected recent findings. *Drug Abuse and Alcoholism Newsletter, 15,* 1–3.

Cuomo, M. J., Dyment, P. G., & Gammino, V. M. (1994). Increasing use of "ecstasy" (MDMA) and other hallucinogens on a college campus. *Journal of American College Health, 42,* 271–274.

Day, N. L., Richardson, G. A., Goldschmidt, L., Robles, N., Taylor, P. M., Stoffer, D. S., Cornelius, M. D., & Geva, D. (1994). *Neurotoxicology and Teratology, 16,* 169–175.

DeFonseca, F. R., Carrera, M. R. A., Navarro, M., Koob, G. F., & Weiss, F. (1997). Activation of corticotropin-releasing factor in the limbic system during cannabinoid withdrawal. *Science, 276,* 2050–2053.

Devane, W. A., Hanus, L., Breuer, A., Pertwee, R. G., Stevenson, L. A., Griffin, G., Gibson, D., Mandelbaum, A., Etinger, A., & Mechoulam, R. (1992). Isolation and structure of a brain constituent that binds to the cannabinoid receptor. *Science, 258,* 1946–1949.

Dilsaver, S. C. (1988). Antimuscarinic agents as substances of abuse: A review. *Journal of Clinical Psychopharmacology, 8,* 14–22.

Edwards, G., Arif, A., & Hodgson, R. (1981). Nomenclature and classification of drug- and alcohol-related problems: A WHO memorandum. *Bulletin of the World Health Organization, 59,* 225–242.

Edwards, G., & Gross, M. M. (1976). Alcohol dependence: Provisional description of a clinical syndrome. *British Medical Journal, 1,* 1058–1061.

Ellickson, P. L., Hays, R. D., & Bell, R. M. (1992). Stepping through the drug use sequence: Longitudinal scalogram analysis of initiation and regular use. *Journal of Abnormal Psychology, 101,* 441–451.

Ellis, G. M., Mann, M. A., Judson, B. A., Schramm, N. T., & Tashchian, A. (1985). Excretion patterns of cannabinoid metabolites after last use in a group of chronic users. *Clinical Pharmacology and Therapeutics, 38,* 572–578.

Frank, I. M., Lessin, P. J., Tyrrell, E. D., Hahn, P. M., & Szara, S. (1976). Acute and cumulative effects of marijuana smoking on hospitalized subjects: A 36-day study. In M. C. Braude & S. Szara (Eds.), *Pharmacology of marijuana* (Vol. 2, pp. 673–680). Orlando, FL: Academic Press.

Fried, P. A. (1995). The Ottawa prenatal prospective study (OPPS): Methodological issues and findings—It's easy to throw the baby out with the bath water. *Life Sciences, 56,* 2159–2168.

Fried, P. A., O'Connell, C. M., & Watkinson, B. (1992). 60- and 72-month follow-up of children prenatally exposed to marijuana, cigarettes, and alcohol: Cognitive and language assessment. *Developmental and Behavioral Pediatrics, 13,* 383–391.

Fried, P. A., & Watkinson, B. (1990). 36- and 48-month neurobehavioral follow-up of children prenatally exposed to marijuana, cigarettes and alcohol. *Developmental and Behavioral Pediatrics, 11,* 48–58.

Gable, R. S. (1993). Toward a comparative overview of dependence potential and acute toxicity of psychoactive substances used nonmedically. *American Journal of Drug and Alcohol Abuse, 19,* 263–281.

Gardner, E. L. (1992). Cannabinoid interactions with brain reward systems—The neurobiological basis of cannabinoid abuse. In L. Murphy & A. Bartke (Eds.), *Marijuana/cannabinoids neurology and neurophysiology* (pp. 275–336). Boca Raton, FL: CRC Press.

Georgotas, A., & Zeidenberg, P. (1979). Observations on the effects of four weeks of heavy marijuana smoking on group interaction and individual behavior. *Comprehensive Psychiatry, 20,* 427–432.

Giannini, A. J., Loiselle, R. H., Graham, B. H., & Folts, D. J. (1993). Behavioral response to buspirone in cocaine and phencyclidine withdrawal. *Journal of Substance Abuse Treatment, 10,* 523–527.

Grinspoon, L., & Bakalar, J. B. (1979). *Psychedelic drugs reconsidered.* New York: Basic Books.

Grinspoon, L., & Bakalar, J. B. (Eds.) (1983). *Psychedelic reflections.* New York: Human Sciences Press.

Gruber, A. J., & Pope, H. G. (1994). Cannabis psychotic disorder: Does it exist? *American Journal on Addictions, 3,* 72–83.

Haas, A. P., & Hendin, H. (1987). The meaning of chronic marijuana use among adults: A psychosocial perspective. *Journal of Drug Issues, 17,* 333–348.

Hall, W., Solowij, N., & Lemon, J. (1994). *The health and psychological consequences of cannabis use.* National drug strategy monograph series No. 25. Canberra: Australian Government Publishing Service.

Hatch, E. E., & Bracken, M. B. (1986). Effect of marijuana use in pregnancy on fetal growth. *American Journal of Epidemiology, 124,* 986–993.

Hawks, R. L. (1982). The constituents of cannabis and the disposition and metabolism of cannabinoids. In R. L. Hawks (Ed.), *The analysis of cannabinoids in biological fluids* (pp. 125–137). (National Institute on Drug Abuse Research Monograph No. 42). Rockville, MD: U. S. Department of Health and Human Services.

Herkenham, M., Lynn, A. B., Little, M. D., Johnson, M. R., Melvin, L. S., De Costa, B. R., & Rice, K. C. (1990). Cannabinoid receptor localization in brain. *Proceedings of the National Academy of Sciences, USA, 87,* 1932–1936.

Hollister, L. E. (1978). Psychotomimetic drugs in man. In L. L. Iverson, S. D. Iverson, & S. H. Snyder (Eds.), *Handbook of psychopharmacology* (Vol. 11, pp. 389–425). New York: Plenum.

Hollister, L. E. (1986). Health aspects of cannabis. *Pharmacological Reviews, 38,* 1–20.

Huba, G. J., Wingard, J. A., & Bentler, P. M. (1981). A comparison of two latent variables causal models of adolescent drug use. *Journal of Personality and Social Psychology, 40,* 180–193.

Johansson, E., Agurell, S., Hollister, L. E., & Halldin, M. M. (1988). Prolonged apparent half-life of 1-tetrahydrocannabinol in plasma of chronic marijuana users. *Journal of Pharmacy and Pharmacology, 40,* 374–375.

Johnson, K. M., Jr. (1987). Neurochemistry and neurophysiology of phencyclidine. In H. Y. Meltzer (Ed.),

Psychopharmacology: The third generation of progress (pp. 1581–1588). New York: Raven Press.

Johnston, L. D., Bachman, J. G., & O'Malley, P. M. (1994). Press release—News and information services, University of Michigan, January 31.

Johnston, L. D., O'Malley, P. M., & Bachman, J. G. (1989). *National trends in drug use and related factors among American high school students and young adults, 1975–1988* (DHHS Publication No. ADM 87-1535). Washington, DC: Government Printing Office.

Johnston, L. D., O'Malley, P. M., & Bachman, J. G. (1994). *National survey results on drug use from monitoring the future study, 1975–1993* (NIH Publication No. 94-3809). Bethesda, MD: National Institute on Drug Abuse.

Jones, R. T., & Benowitz, N. (1976). The 30-day trip: Clinical studies of cannabis tolerance and dependence. In M. C. Braude & S. Szara (Eds.), *Pharmacology of marijuana* (Vol. 2, pp. 627–642). Orlando, FL: Academic Press.

Jones, R. T., Benowitz, N., & Herning, R. I. (1981). The clinical relevance of cannabis tolerance and dependence. *Journal of Clinical Pharmacology, 21,* 143S–152S.

Kandel, D. B. (1984). Marijuana users in young adulthood. *Archives of General Psychiatry, 41,* 200–209.

Kandel, D. B. (1988). Issues of sequencing of adolescent drug use and other problem behaviors. *Drugs and Society, 3,* 55–76.

Kandel, D., & Davies, M. (1992). Progression to regular marijuana involvement: Phenomenology and risk factors for near daily use. In M. Glantz & R. Pickens (Eds.), *Vulnerability to drug abuse.* Washington: American Psychological Association.

Kandel, D. B., Davies, M., Karus, D., & Yamaguchi, K. (1986). The consequences in young adulthood of adolescent drug involvement. *Archives of General Psychiatry, 43,* 746–754.

Kandel, D., & Faust, R. (1975). Sequence and stages in patterns of adolescent drug use. *Archives of General Psychiatry, 32,* 923–932.

Kosersky, D. S., McMillan, D. E., & Harris, L. S. (1974). Delta-9-tetrahydrocannabinol and 11-hydroxy-delta-9-tetrahydrocannabinol: Behavioral effects and tolerance development. *Journal of Pharmacology and Experimental Therapeutics, 189,* 61–65.

Kosten, T. R., Rounsaville, B. J., Babor, T. F., Spitzer, R. L., & Williams, J. B. W. (1987). Substance-use disorders in DSM-III-R. *British Journal of Psychiatry, 151,* 834–843.

Levine, J., & Ludwig, A. M. (1964). The LSD controversy. *Comprehensive Psychiatry, 5,* 314–321.

Linszen, D. H., Dingemans, P. M., & Lenior, M. E. (1994). Cannabis abuse and the course of recent-onset schizophrenic disorders. *Archives of General Psychiatry, 51,* 273–279.

Lukas, S. E., Sholar, M., Kouri, E., Fukuzako, H., & Mendelson, J. H. (1994). Marihuana smoking increases plasma cocaine levels and subjective reports of euphoria in male volunteers. *Pharmacology Biochemistry and Behavior, 48,* 715–721.

Matsuda, L. A., Lolait, S. J., Brownstein, M., Young, A., & Bonner, T. I. (1990). Structure of a cannabinoid receptor and functional expression of the cloned cDNA. *Nature, 346,* 561–564.

McBay, A. J. (1986). Drug concentrations and traffic safety. *Alcohol, Drugs, and Driving, 2,* 51–59.

McKim, W. A. (1997). *Drugs and behavior: An introduction to behavioral pharmacology* (3rd ed.). Upper Saddle River, NJ: Prentice Hall.

Mechoulam, R., Hanus, L., & Martin, B. (1994). The search for endogenous ligands of the cannabinoid receptor. *Biochemical Pharmacology, 48,* 1537–1544.

Mendelson, J. H., Kuehnle, J. C., Greenberg, I., & Mello, N. K. (1976). The effects of marijuana use on human operant behavior: Individual data. In M. C. Braude & S. Szara (Eds.), *Pharmacology of marijuana* (Vol. 2, pp. 643–653). Orlando, FL: Academic Press.

Mikuriya, T. H., & Aldrich, M. R. (1988). Cannabis 1988: Old drug, new dangers, the potency question. *Journal of Psychoactive Drugs, 20,* 47–55.

Miller, T. Q. (1994). A test of alternative explanations for the stage-like progression of adolescent substance use in four national samples. *Addictive Behaviors, 19,* 287–293.

Millman, R. B., & Beeder, A. B. (1994). The new psychedelic culture: LSD, ecstasy, "rave" parties and the Grateful Dead. *Psychiatric Annals, 24,* 148–150.

Morgenstern, J., Langenbucher, J., & Labouvie, E. W. (1994). The generalizability of the dependence syndrome across substances: An examination of some properties of the proposed DSM-IV dependence criteria. *Addiction, 89,* 1105–1113.

Newcombe, M. D. (1992). Understanding the multidimensional nature of drug use and abuse: The role of consumption, risk factors and protective factors. In M. Glantz & R. Pickens (Eds.), *Vulnerability to drug abuse.* Washington, DC: American Psychological Association.

Newcombe, M. D., & Bentler, P. (1988). *Consequences of adolescent drug use: Impact on the lives of young adults.* Newbury Park, CA: Sage.

Office of Applied Studies, Substance Abuse and Mental Health Administration. (1995). Preliminary estimates from the 1994 national household survey on drug abuse. *Advance Report No. 10*. Rockville, MD: Author.

Patrick, G., Straumanis, J. J., Struve, F. A., Nixon, F., Fitz-Gerald, M. J., Manno, J. E., & Soucair, M. (1995). Auditory and visual P300 event-related potentials are not altered in medically and psychiatrically normal chronic marihuana users. *Life Sciences, 56*, 2135–2140.

Perez-Reyes, M., DiGuiseppi, S., Davis, K. H., Schindler, V. H., & Cook, C. E. (1982). Comparison of effects of marihuana cigarettes of three different potencies. *Clinical Pharmacology and Therapeutics, 31*, 617–624.

Perez-Reyes, M., Timmons, M. C., & Wall, M. E. (1974). Long-term use of marijuana and the development of tolerance or sensitivity to 9-tetrahydrocannabinol. *Archives of General Psychiatry, 31*, 89–91.

Perry, M. J., & Mandell, W. (1995). Psychosocial factors associated with the initiation of cocaine use amongh marijuana users. *Psychology of Addictive Behaviors, 9*, 91–100.

Polen, M. R., Sidney, S., Tekawa, I. S., Sadler, M., & Friedman, G. D. (1993). Health care use by frequent marijuana smokers who do not smoke tobacco. *Western Journal of Medicine, 158*, 596–601.

Pope, H. G., Gruber, A. J., & Yurgelun-Todd, D. (1995). The residual neuropsychological effects of cannabis: The current status of research. *Drug and Alcohol Dependence, 38*, 25–34.

Pope, H. G., & Yurgelun-Todd, D. (1996). The residual cognitive effects of heavy marijuana use in college students. *Journal of the American Medical Association, 275*, 521–527.

Rainone, G. A., Deren, S., Kleinman, P. H., & Wish, E. D. (1987). Heavy marijuana users not in treatment: The continuing search for the "pure" marijuana user. *Journal of Psychoactive Drugs, 19*, 353–359.

Ray, O., & Ksir, C. (1996). *Drugs, society, and human behavior* (7th ed.). St. Louis: Mosby.

Richardson, G. A., Day, N. L., & Goldschmidt, L. (1995). Prenatal alcohol, marijuana, and tobacco use: Infant mental and motor development. *Neurotoxicology and Teratology, 17*, 479–487.

Robinson, L. I., Buckley, J. D., Daigle, A. E., Wells, R., Benjamin, D., Arthur, D. C., & Hammond, G. D. (1989). Maternal drug use and the risk of childhood nonlymphoblastic leukemia among offspring: An epidemiologic investigation implicating marijuana. *Cancer, 63*, 1904–1911.

Roffman, R. A., & Barnhart, R. (1987). Assessing need for marijuana dependence treatment through an anonymous telephone interview. *International Journal of the Addictions, 22*, 639–651.

Roffman, R. A., Stephens, R. S., Simpson, E. E., & Whitaker, D. L. (1988). Treatment of marijuana dependence: Preliminary results. *Journal of Psychoactive Drugs, 20*, 129–137.

Rounsaville, B. J., Bryant, K., Babor, T., Kranzler, H., & Kadden, R. (1993). Cross-system agreement for substance use disorders. *Addiction, 88*, 337–348.

Rubin, V., & Comitas, L. (1975). *Ganja in Jamaica: A medical anthropological study of chronic marihuana use*. Hague: Mouton Publishers.

Seth, R., & Sinha, S. (1991). Chemistry and pharmacology of cannabis. *Progress in Drug Research, 36*, 71–115.

Shedler, J., & Block, J. (1990). Adolescent drug use and psychological health. *American Psychologist, 45*, 612–630.

Shiono, P. H., Klebanoff, M. A., Nugent, R. P., Cotch, M. F., Wilkins, D. G., Rollins, D. E., Carey, J. C., & Behrman, R. E. (1995). The impact of cocaine and marijuana use on low birth weight and preterm birth: A multicenter study. *American Journal of Obstetrics and Gynecology, 172*, 19–27.

Simpson, H. M. (1986). Epidemiology of road accidents involving marijuana. *Alcohol, Drugs, and Driving, 2*, 15–30.

Smiley, A. (1986). Marijuana: On-road and driving simulator studies. *Alcohol, Drugs, and Driving, 2*, 121–134.

Solowij, N., Michie, P. T., & Fox, A. M. (1991). Effects of long-term cannabis use on selective attention: An event-related potential study. *Pharmacology Biochemistry and Behavior, 40*, 683–688.

Solowij, N., Michie, P. T., & Fox, A. M. (1995). Differential impairments of selective attention due to frequency and duration of cannabis use. *Society of Biological Psychiatry, 37*, 731–739.

Stafford, P. (1992). *Psychedelics encyclopedia* (3rd ed.). Berkeley, CA: Ronin.

Steele, T. D., McCann, U. D., & Ricaurte, G. A. (1994). 3,4-Methylenedioxymethamphetamine (MDMA, "ecstasy"): Pharmacology and toxicology in animals and humans. *Addiction, 89*, 539–551.

Stephens, R. S., & Roffman, R. A. (1993). Adult marijuana dependence. In J. S. Baer, G. A. Marlatt, & R. J. McMahon (Eds.), *Addictive behaviors across the lifespan: Prevention, treatment, and policy issues*. Newbury Park, CA: Sage.

Stephens, R. S., Roffman, R. A., & Simpson, E. E. (1993). Adult marijuana users seeking treatment. *Journal of Consulting and Clinical Psychology, 61*, 1100–1104.

Stephens, R. S., Roffman, R. A., & Simpson, E. E. (1994). Treating adult marijuana dependence: A test of the relapse prevention model. *Journal of Consulting and Clinical Psychology, 62,* 92–99.

Strassman, R. J., Qualls, C. R., Uhlenhuth, E. H., & Kellner, R. (1994). Dose-response study of N,N-Dimethyltryptamine in humans: 2. Subjective effects and preliminary results of a new rating scale. *Archives of General Psychiatry, 51,* 98–108.

Tanda, G., Pontieri, F. E., & DiChiara, G. (1997). Cannabinoid and heroin activation of mesolimbic dopamine transmission by a common μ_1 opioid receptor mechanism. *Science, 276,* 2048–250.

Tashkin, D. P., Fligiel, S., Wu, T., Gong, H., Jr., Barbers, R. G., Coulson, A. H., Simmons, M. S., & Beals, T. F. (1990). Effects of habitual use of marijuana and/or cocaine on the lung. In C. N. Chiang & R. L. Hawks (Eds.), *Research findings on smoking of abused substances.* (National Institute on Drug Abuse Research Monograph No. 99). Washington, DC: Government Printing Office. DHHS Publication No. 90-1690.

Taylor, D., & Warner, R. (1994). Does substance use precipitate the onset of functional psychosis? *Social Work and Social Sciences Review, 5,* 64–75.

Terhune, K. W. (1986). Problems and methods in studying drug crash effects. *Alcohol, Drugs, and Driving, 2,* 1–13.

Thomas, H. (1993). Psychiatric symptoms in cannabis users. *British Journal of Psychiatry, 163,* 141–149.

Weiss, C. J., & Millman, R. B. (1991). Hallucinogens, phencyclidine, marijuana, inhalants. In R. J. Frances & S. I. Miller (Eds.), *Clinical textbook of addictive disorders* (pp. 146–170). New York: Guilford Press.

Wert, R. C., & Raulin, M. L. (1986a). The chronic cerebral effects of cannabis use: 1. Methodological issues and neurological findings. *International Journal of the Addictions, 21,* 605–628.

Wert, R. C., & Raulin, M. L. (1986b). The chronic cerebral effects of cannabis use: 2. Psychological findings and conclusions. *International Journal of the Addictions, 21,* 629–642.

Wiesbeck, G. A., Schuckit, M. A., Kalmijn, J. A., Tipp, J. E., Bucholz, K. K., & Smith, T. L. (1996). An evaluation of the history of a marijuana withdrawal syndrome in a large population. *Addiction, 91,* 1469–1478.

Wu, T. C., Tashkin, D. P., Rose, J. E., & Djahed, B. (1988). Influence of marijuana potency and amount of cigarette consumed on marijuana smoking pattern. *Journal of Psychoactive Drugs, 20,* 43–46.

Zuckerman, B., Frank, D., Hingson, R., Amaro, H., Levenson, S., Kayne, H., Parker, S., Vinci, R., Aboagye, K., Fried, L., Cabral, H., Timperi, R., & Bauchner, H. (1989). Effects of maternal marijuana and cocaine use on fetal growth. *New England Journal of Medicine, 320,* 762–768.

8

Opioids

Susan M. Stine
Thomas R. Kosten

The term *opioids* includes all known agents with morphinelike and morphine-blocking activity as well as naturally occurring and synthetic opioid peptides. *Opiates* constitute that subclass of opioids that are alkaloids extracted from opium, including morphine and codeine, and a wide variety of semisynthetic derivative compounds from them and from thebaine, another component of opium. Opium contains more than 20 distinct alkaloids, the first of which (morphine) was isolated in 1806. Many semisynthetic derivatives are made by relatively simple modifications of the major opium alkaloids, morphine or thebaine. Thebaine has little analgesic action but is a precursor of several important compounds, such as oxycodone and naloxone. In addition to morphine, codeine, and the semisynthetic derivatives of the natural opium alkaloids, a number of other structurally distinct chemical classes of drugs have pharmacological actions similar to those of morphine. (See table 8.1.)

Endorphin is a term referring to the opioid subclass of endogenous opioid peptides that consists of three families: the enkephalins, the dynorphins, and the beta-endorphins. Each family is derived from a distinct precursor polypeptide and has a characteristic anatomical distribution. These precursors are designated as proopiomelanocortin (POMC), proenkephalin, and prodynorphin. A detailed description of the processing of these peptides is provided by Hollt (1986). The distribution of peptides from POMC is relatively limited (compared to the distribution of other families). In the human brain, the distribution of POMC corresponds to areas where electrical stimulation can produce pain relief (Pilcher, Joseph, & MacDonald, 1988), such as the arcuate nucleus, which projects its fibers widely to limbic and brain stem areas. Some POMC-containing fibers descend to the spinal cord (Lewis, Mansour, Khachaturian, Watson, & Akil, 1987). POMC peptides are also found in endocrine organs such as the pituitary and pancreas. The peptides from prodynorphin and proenkephalin are distributed more widely throughout the CNS, and the pattern is more complex. Pro-

TABLE 8.1 Commonly Abused and Prescribed Opiates

Generic name	Trade name	Street name[a]	Dose and route of administration[b,c]	Duration (hr)[b]	Comments
Illegal					
Heroin (diacetyl-morphine)	None	Smack, horse; many and varied brand markings (e.g., DOA, Silence of the Lamb, Predator, Brain Damage)[d]	IM, IV, SC (5 mg); IN, O (60 mg) (street supply, bags, 0.1–0.2 g for $5, $10, $15; variable purity 15–90%)[d]	4–5	Illegal in US. Not available by prescription.
Legally available by prescription					
Morphine	Astramorph/PF Duramorph, Infumorph MS Contin, Oramorph, Roxanol	Morpho, morph, stuff, monkey, M, tab.	IM, SC (10 mg) O (60 mg)	4–5 4–7	Oral dose only 1/6 as effective as parenteral, wide variability in first-pass metabolism.
Codeine	(Many brands of combination meds for cough)	School boy	IM (130 mg); O (200 mg) (10–20 for antitussive effect).	4–6	
Hydromorphone	Dilaudid	Dillies[e]	IM, SC (1–2 mg); O (2 mg)	4–5	
Hydrocodone	Hycodan, others	Little D, lords	O (5–10 mg)	4–5	
Oxycodone	Percodan; Percocet	Percs	O (5–10 mg)	4–5	Used with other ingredients (aspirin, acetaminophen).
Propoxyphene	Darvon	Unknown	O (65 mg)	4–6	Related structurally to methadone, can cause positive urine toxicology for methadone. Very irritating, damages veins and tissues if used IV or SC.
Pentazocine	Talwin	Unknown	IM, SC (30–60 mg) O(180 mg)	4–6 4–7	Can cause withdrawal in physically dependent persons (due to partial agonist properties at μ receptors). Irritating if given IV.

Drug	Brand name	Street name	Route (dose)[b]		Comments
Meperidine	Demerol	Cubes[e]	IM, SC (75 mg) O (300 mg)	3–5 4–6	Complicated metabolism, notably normeperidine (long-lasting active compound with stimulant properties, risk of seizure with accumulation).
Fentanyl	Sublimaze	P dope	IM, IV (0.1 mg)	1–2	When abused often not measured in urine toxicology due to potency, short action. Often abused by professionals with access. Reported to be active compound in "P dope."[f]
Maintenance agents Methadone	Dolophine	Dollies, Dolls, amidone	IM (10 mg) O (20 mg)	4–5	Other nonanalgesic effects have longer duration. Oral dose longer acting. Maintenance dose usually 40–100 mg effective 24 hr.
LAAM (Levo-alpha-acetymethadol)	ORLAAM	Unknown		4–6	Duration of parent drug and long-lasting active metabolites 48–72 hr. Street availability unlikely due to federal regulations prohibiting take-home doses.
Buprenorphine	Buprenex	Unknown	IM (0.4 mg) SL (0.8 mg)	4–5 5–6	Current investigational use as maintenance agent for opiate dependence, usual dose 8–20 mg SL, duration 24–72 hr (dose-dependent).

[a]Witters (1992).

[b]Dose producing equivalent analgesic effect to 10 mg morphine: IH—inhalation; IM—intramuscular; IN—intranasal; IV—intravenous; O—oral; SC—subcutaneous; SL—sublingual.

[c]Reisine and Pasternak (1996).

[d]Office of National Drug Control Policy (1994).

[e]Johnson (1990).

[f]"P dope" often contains heroin as active agent.

enkephalin peptides are present in areas of the CNS that are presumed to be related to the perception of pain (e.g., laminae I and II of the spinal cord, the spinal trigeminal nucleus, and the periaqueductal gray); to the modulation of affective behavior (e.g., amygdala, hippocampus, locus ceruleus, and cerebral cortex) and motor control (caudate nucleus and globus pallidus); and to the regulation of the autonomic nervous system (medulla oblongata) and neuroendocrinological functions (median eminence). Similar to the POMC-derived peptides, the peptides derived from proenkephalin and prodynorphins are also not confined to the CNS.

MAJOR PHARMACOLOGICAL ACTIONS

Metabolic Pathways

Morphine and most opioids act most rapidly when they are given intravenously. Most opioids are also absorbed from the gastrointestinal tract and through the rectal mucosa (e.g., morphine and hydromorphone are available in suppositories). The more lipophilic opioids are also readily absorbed through the nasal or buccal mucosa, and the latter route of administration is under investigation (Weinberg 1988), notably with the new maintenance medication buprenorphine. Opioids are also absorbed after subcutaneous or intramuscular injection and also penetrate the spinal cord following epidural or intrathecal administration. Transdermal absorption is related to lipid solubility. More lipid-soluble opioids also act even more rapidly than morphine after subcutaneous administration. Opioids have many pharmacological actions, and the specific effects differ in time course and in relation to drug absorption and metabolic rates. For example, when opioids such as morphine are given initially, their durations of euphoria or analgesic action show relatively little variation regardless of rate of metabolism, while other effects may persist longer and some metabolites may accumulate with repeated administration, increasing this complexity.

Opiates are metabolized by the liver, and in patients with hepatic disease, increased bioavailability after oral administration or cumulative effects may occur (Sawe, Dahlstrom, Paalzow, & Rane, 1981). Renal disease can also significantly alter the pharmacokinetics of some opioids. Although there is overall

similarity in the way most opioid drugs are metabolized, there are also some specific unique issues with individual compounds and the action of their metabolites. Only a few important examples can be mentioned here. Heroin (diacetylmorphine) has a plasma half-life of only 0.5 hr but has a 4- to 5-hr duration of action due to its active metabolites (Reisine & Pasternak, 1996). Heroin is mainly excreted in the urine, largely as free and conjugated morphine. The major pathway for the metabolism of morphine in turn is conjugation with glucuronic acid to form both active and inactive products. One product, morphine-6-glucuronide, is excreted by the kidney, and in renal failure, the levels of morphine-6-glucuronide can accumulate. The absorption, fate, and distribution of morphinelike drugs have been reviewed by Misra (1978) and by Chan and Matzke (1987), and opioid pharmacology is also comprehensively summarized in Reisine and Pasternak (1996).

One specific example of opiate metabolism deserves mention because of its clinical significance. Meperidine (Demerol), a commonly used opioid medication, is hydrolyzed to normeperidinic acid, which, in turn, is partially conjugated. Meperidine is also N-demethylated to normeperidine, which may lead to tremors, muscle twitches, dilated pupils, hyperactive reflexes, and convulsions due to the accumulation of this metabolite, which has a half-life of 15–20 hr compared with 3 hr for meperidine. Since normeperidine is eliminated by both the kidney and the liver, decreased renal or hepatic function increases the likelihood of such toxicity (Kaiko et al., 1983). Only a small amount of meperidine is excreted unchanged.

Actions in the Central Nervous System

Effects on Neurotransmitter Systems

Although the endogenous opioid peptides appear to function as neurotransmitters, modulators of neurotransmission, or neurohormones, their role in physiological processes is not completely understood and is made more difficult by their frequent coexistence with other peptides or biogenic amines within a given neuron.

In vivo studies in animal models initially demonstrated the importance of many neurotransmitters in the action of opioid drugs. Since the discovery of the endorphins, the interactions of other neurotransmitters with opioid pathways have continued to be important in the understanding of the function of these systems. For example, the involvement of glutamatergic and the noradrenergic systems in opioid withdrawal is discussed below in the next section and has led to important pharmacotherapeutic approaches.

Dopamine effects, especially in the mesolimbic dopamine system, have been similarly implicated in opiate reinforcement. Virtually any drug abused by humans, including opiates and cocaine, causes increased dopamine release after acute administration (Chen, Mestek, Liu, Hurley, & Yu, 1993). Acute systemic administration of opiates to rats excites dopaminergic neurons of the ventral tegmental area (VTA). However, studies in brain slices in vitro have shown that such activation also represents an indirect effect of the opiates: Opiates, apparently via activation of mu receptors, directly inhibit GABA-ergic neurons within the VTA and thereby reduce the inhibitory influence of these cells on the dopaminergic neurons (Johnson & North, 1992) and increase dopaminergic transmission to the nucleus accumbens (NAc). This dopaminergic input is inhibitory to most cells in that brain region. There are also numerous reports that chronic opiate exposure can alter extracellular levels of dopamine in the VTA-NAc pathway as determined by in vivo microdialysis (e.g., Acquas, Carboni, & DiChiara, 1990). Such changes in dopamine levels are proposed to be involved in chronic opiate-induced alterations in drug reward mechanisms. There are also nondopaminergic mechanisms of opiate reward (Koob, 1992).

Mechanisms of Tolerance and Dependence

The mechanisms by which opiates induce addiction have long been a subject of great interest. Model systems to explain tolerance and dependence exist on three levels: the neuroanatomical level, the cellular (neurotransmitter release and receptor-binding) level, and the subcellular ("second-message") level.

Neuroanatomical Systems   Neuroanatomically, many regions of the central nervous system are opiate-responsive, but certain well-characterized regions have provided particularly useful model systems in which to study the mechanisms underlying the acute and chronic actions of opiates on the nervous system.

Three neuroanatomical systems are most important: pathways originating from and impinging upon the locus coeruleus (LC), the mesolimbic dopamine system, and the dorsal root ganglion-spinal cord. The first two systems are the most relevant to addictive actions. The LC is located on the floor of the fourth ventricle in the anterior pons and is the major noradrenergic nucleus in the brain, with widespread projections to both the brain and spinal cord. An important role for the LC in opiate physical dependence and withdrawal has been established at both the behavioral and the electrophysiological levels: Overactivation of LC neurons and decreased release of norepinephrine (NE) are both necessary and sufficient for producing many of the behavioral signs of withdrawal (Aghajanian, 1978; Maldonado & Koob, 1988; Nestler, 1992; Nestler, Hope, & Widnell, 1993; Rasmussen & Aghajanian, 1989). Chronically, LC neurons develop tolerance to acute inhibitory actions of opiates, as neuronal activity recovers toward preexposure levels (Aghajanian, 1978; Christie, Williams, & North, 1987). Abrupt cessation of opiate treatment—for example, via administration of an opioid receptor antagonist—causes a marked increase in neuronal firing rates above preexposure levels (Aghajanian, 1978; Kogan, Nestler, & Aghajanian, 1992; Rasmussen, Beitner-Johnson, Krystal, Aghajanian, & Nestler, 1990). Overactivation of LC neurons during withdrawal arises from both extrinsic and intrinsic sources. The extrinsic source involves a hyperactive excitatory glutamatergic input to the LC (Akaoka & Aston-Jones, 1991; Rasmussen & Aghajanian, 1989). The intrinsic source involves intracellular adaptations in signal transduction pathways coupled to opioid receptors in the LC neurons (see below for subcellular mechanism).

Increasing evidence indicates that the mesolimbic dopamine system—consisting of dopaminergic neurons in the VTA and their projection regions, most notably the nucleus accumbens—plays an important role in mediating the reinforcing actions of opiates on brain function. Animals will self-administer opiates directly into the VTA and NAc and will develop conditioned place preference after such local drug administration (Koob, 1992; Self & Nestler, 1995; Wise, 1990).

Cellular (Synaptic) Mechanisms   The discovery of opioid receptors raised the possibility that aspects of opiate addiction might involve these endogenous receptors. However, over 15 years of research have failed to identify consistent changes in the number of opiate receptors, or changes in their affinity for opiate ligands, under conditions of opiate addiction, which has led to a focus on subcellular mechanisms (see below). Nevertheless, the receptor and cellular mechanisms of addiction remain important, and the identification of opioid receptors in the 1970s represented a major advance in our understanding of the mechanisms of addiction. There are three major classes of opioid receptors in the CNS, designated mu, delta, and kappa, as well as subtypes within each class. Members of each class of opioid receptor have been cloned from human cDNA and their predicted amino acid sequences obtained. Their amino acid sequences are approximately 65% identical, and they have little sequence similarity to other G-protein-coupled receptors, except receptors for somatostatin (Reisine & Bell, 1993).

There have been numerous claims over the years that multiple subtypes of the mu, delta, and kappa receptors exist in the brain (e.g., Pasternak, 1993). However, the molecular basis of some of these variants remains uncertain, since molecular cloning studies have, so far, failed to confirm them, notably, mu_1 and mu_2 (Reisine & Pasternak, 1996). The primary approach used to define the unique pharmacological profiles of the receptor classes has been the design of functional studies (as opposed to receptor chemistry and binding studies). Although biochemical and pharmacological evidence indicates that mu, delta, and kappa receptors are distinct molecular entities, they share a number of pharmacological characteristics. First, they all appear to function primarily by exerting inhibitory modulation of synaptic transmission in both the CNS and the myenteric plexus. Although their location varies, they are often found on presynaptic nerve terminals, where their action results in decreased release of excitatory neurotransmitters. Second, they all appear to be coupled to the guanidine nucleotide, which is involved in the subcellular mechanisms of addiction.

Of the endogenous opioid peptides, beta-endorphin has the greatest affinity for mu receptors, enkephalins for delta receptors, and dynorphin for kappa receptors. Morphinelike opiates, such as heroin, preferentially bind to the mu opiate receptor, whereas the benzomorphan opiates, such as pentazocine, preferentially bind to the kappa receptor. With respect to psychological addiction to opiates, mu and delta receptors are primarily implicated in mediating the reinforcing actions of opiates and kappa receptors

in mediating their aversive actions (Koob, 1992; Self & Nestler, 1995). However, opioids that are relatively selective at standard doses will interact with additional receptor classes when given at sufficiently high doses. This is especially true as doses are escalated to overcome tolerance. Some drugs, particularly mixed agonist/antagonist agents, interact with more than one receptor class at usual clinical doses, and they may act as an agonist at one receptor and an antagonist at another.

Numerous receptor-binding studies have been carried out to investigate changes induced by chronic opiate exposure. Long-term incubation of cultured cell lines with receptor ligands results in downregulation of opioid receptors as evidenced by a decrease in maximal specific binding, but many other studies have failed to detect changes in opiate binding after chronic opiate exposure (Harris & Nestler, 1993). The involvement of other transmitter systems, as described above at the beginning of this section, has perhaps been more useful in the elucidation of tolerance and dependence than of the opiate mechanisms themselves. For example, blockade of glutamate actions by noncompetitive and competitive NMDA (N-methyl-D-aspartate) antagonists blocks morphine tolerance (Elliott et al., 1994; Trujillo & Akil, 1991). Since these NMDA antagonists have no effect on the potency of morphine in naive animals, their effect cannot be attributed to a simple potentiation of opioid actions. Blockade of the glycine regulatory site on NMDA receptors also has the ability to block tolerance (Kolesnikov, Maccehini, & Pasternak, 1994). Inhibition of nitric oxide synthase also blocks morphine tolerance (Kolesnikov, Pick, Ciszewska, & Pasternak, 1993) and reverses tolerance in morphine-tolerant animals, despite continued opioid administration. Although the NMDA antagonists and nitric oxide synthase inhibitors are effective against tolerance to morphine and other mu agonists, they have little effect against tolerance to the kappa agonists.

Pharmacological dependence (abstinence symptoms or naloxone-precipitated symptoms) seems to be closely related to tolerance (decreased effect with long-term exposure), since the same treatments that block tolerance to morphine also often block dependence. Coadministration of the alpha$_2$-adrenergic antagonist yohimbine, however, has been reported to prevent naloxone-precipitated withdrawal (dependence) in animals without diminishing the analgesic effect (tolerance) (Taylor et al., 1991), so it may be possible to differentially affect these phenomena.

Subcellular Mechanisms   In contrast to the difficulty in establishing consistent effects of chronic opiate exposure on opioid receptors, studies of the chronic effects of opiates on postreceptor signal transduction pathways have been more fruitful (Nestler et al., 1993). Opiates regulate adenyl cyclase, Ca^{2+} channels, and phosphatidylinositol turnover, suggesting that opiates may also produce changes in cyclic AMP-dependent and calcium-dependent protein phosphorylation in specific target neurons. However, a definitive demonstration of opioid receptor phosphorylation has yet to appear. These studies are reviewed elsewhere (Harris & Nestler, 1993; Johnson & Fleming, 1989; Loh & Smith, 1990).

Acutely, opiates were found to decrease cellular levels of cyclic AMP in neuroblastoma x glioma cells (Sharma, Klee, & Nirenberg, 1975), and chronic exposure was found to result in substantial increases in adenyl cyclase activity in this system. More recently, similar types of mechanisms have been identified in specific regions of the central nervous system. Chronic exposure to opiates produces long-term changes in levels of specific G protein subunits and in the individual proteins that comprise the cyclic AMP system. While there are very likely other mechanisms of opiate dependence in the locus coeruleus and elsewhere, upregulation of the cyclic AMP pathway after chronic opiate exposure represents one example of a specific behavioral manifestation of opiate dependence that can be attributed directly to molecular and cellular adaptations in specific neurons. The subject of subcellular mechanisms of addiction has been extensively reviewed by Nestler (1997).

Summary of Opioid Pharmacology

In summary the understanding of opiate pharmacology has increased exponentially in recent years and has occurred on multiple levels. The effects of natural, synthetic, and endogenous opioids are determined initially by the unique and varied aspects of their metabolism. The examples in this chapter are far from a comprehensive description but serve as illustrations of the fundamental importance of this process. In addition to metabolic properties, the activity of opioids is determined by effects on central nervous system neurotransmitters and receptors, including endogenous opioid systems, as well as other neurotransmitters such as dopamine, GABA, and glutamate. Opioid acute effects as well as mechanisms of tolerance and dependence also occur on multiple levels: the neuroanatomical level (locus coeruleus, mesolimbic dopamine system, dorsal root ganglia, spinal cord), the cellular or synaptic level, and the subcellular level. Opiate pharmacology continues to be an area of extremely active research with increasing numbers of pharmacological agents available exhibiting complex and diverse mechanisms of action. Nevertheless, despite the excitement and therapeutic potential of these developments, many questions remain to be answered before the neuroscience of opiate dependence and tolerance is completely understood.

MAJOR CLINICAL ASPECTS

Clinical aspects of opioid use include physiological and psychological phenomena, therapeutic and toxic effects, and the specific direct and indirect consequences of abuse and dependence.

General Physical Symptoms of Opioid Action

In addition to other subdivisions among opioids (e.g., families of opium alkaloids and derivatives, endogenous vs. pharmacological agents discussed previously), opioids have also been divided into three functional groups with respect to pharmacological action on receptors: opioid agonists (or agents which act similarly to morphine); opioids with mixed actions, such as nalorphine and pentazocine, which are agonists on some receptors and antagonists or very weak partial agonists at others; and opioid antagonists (or agents which block morphinelike actions of other drugs), such as naloxone. This classification, as well as which receptors are affected, determines the physical symptoms produced by the opioid drug.

Although analgesia occurs without loss of consciousness, there may be feelings of drowsiness, difficulty in mentation, apathy, and lessened physical activity. The effect of opioids on pain is complex. All types of painful experiences include both the original sensation and the reaction to that sensation and can be affected by both mu and kappa agonist mechanisms in the brain and spinal cord. Analgesic responses of an individual patient may also vary dramatically with different morphinelike drugs. For example, some patients unable to tolerate morphine may have no problems with an equianalgesic dose of methadone, whereas others can take morphine and not methadone. The complexity of these effects is reviewed by Pasternak (1993).

Respiratory depression is of paramount clinical importance and is produced at least in part by virtue of a direct effect of morphinelike opioids on the brain stem respiratory centers. The depression of respiratory rate is discernible even with doses too small to disturb consciousness, and it increases progressively as the dose is increased. The combination of opiates with other medications may present a greater risk of respiratory depression. The primary mechanism of respiratory depression by opioids involves a reduction in the responsiveness of brain stem respiratory centers to carbon dioxide, but opioids also depress the pontine and medullary centers regulating respiratory rhythmicity and the responsiveness of medullary respiratory centers to electrical stimulation (Martin, 1983). Partial agonist opiods (e.g., buprenorphine and pentazocine) are less likely to cause severe respiratory depression and are far less commonly associated with death caused by overdose.

The cardiovascular system is not affected as significantly by direct action of morphinelike opioids. In the supine patient, therapeutic doses of these drugs have no major effect on blood pressure or cardiac rate and rhythm, although such doses do produce peripheral vasodilatation. Morphine and some other opioids also provoke release of histamine, which can play a large role in hypotension. Although effects on the myocardium are not significant in normal humans, morphine and other opiates should be used with great care in patients with cor pulmonale and chronic pulmonary disease, since deaths following ordinary therapeutic doses have been reported (Reisine & Pasternak, 1996).

Effects of opioids on the gastrointestinal system are also of great clinical significance. Nausea and vomiting are commonly produced and are caused by direct stimulation of the chemoreceptor trigger zone for emesis, in the area postrema of the medulla. Morphine and other mu agonists usually decrease the secretion of hydrochloric acid, although stimulation is sometimes evident. Relatively low doses of morphine decrease gastric motility, thereby prolonging gastric emptying time; this can increase the likelihood of esophageal reflux (Duthie & Nimmo, 1987). Morphine also diminishes biliary, pancreatic, and intestinal secretions (Dooley, Saad, & Valenzuela, 1988) and delays digestion of food in the small intestine. Propulsive peristaltic waves in the colon are diminished or abolished after morphine administration, and tone is increased to the point of spasm. The resulting delay in the passage of the contents causes considerable desiccation of the feces. Constipation is an exceedingly common problem when opioids are used and can lead to life-threatening complications, and the use of stool softeners and laxatives should be initiated early.

Although some opioid peptides can affect the immune system by producing a number of naloxone-sensitive effects on the function of macrophages and leukocytes, morphine itself is rarely active. The most firmly established effect of morphine on the immune system is its ability to inhibit the formation of rosettes by human lymphocytes. The administration of morphine to animals causes suppression of the cytotoxic activity of natural killer cells and enhances the growth of implanted tumors. Of interest, these effects are mediated by actions within the CNS. By contrast, beta-endorphin enhances the cytotoxic activity of human monocytes in vitro and increases the recruitment of precursor cells into the killer cell population: This peptide can also exert a potent chemotactic effect on these cells. The immune system effects of these drugs has become an intensified focus of interest due to the comorbidity of HIV infection in the opioid-dependent population.

Other miscellaneous effects of opioids merit brief mention. Opioids have action on various aspects of neuroendocrine function which have been reviewed by Howlett and Rees (1986) and by Grossman (1988). Opioids also affect the uterus, and therapeutic doses of morphine may prolong labor. Neonatal mortality may thus be increased by the injudicious use of morphinelike opioids. Skin effects also occur, and therapeutic doses of morphine commonly cause urticaria, probably by dilatation of cutaneous blood vessels due to the release of histamine.

Acute Opioid Effects:
Intoxication and Overdose

While mild opioid intoxication and opioid withdrawal are not usually life-threatening, severe intoxication or overdose is a medical emergency that requires immediate attention. Of primary concern in the management of overdose are interactions with mu receptors in the central nervous system, which can lead to signs of intoxication such as sedation and respiratory depression. These signs are perhaps less specific than miosis ("pinpoint pupils"), which is an important pharmacological effect that can be used to identify possible opioid intoxication. Symptoms of opioid intoxication are distinct. Euphoria occurs immediately after initial ingestion, and the individual experiences a dramatic decrease in anxiety or tension; the individual also often experiences an initial burst of energy within a few minutes after ingestion. Apathy follows the initial euphoria, and "nodding," a state between alertness and sleep, occurs. Physically, the individual exhibits miosis (constricted pupils), slow and regular respirations, slurred speech, and hypoactive bowel sounds. Judgment, attention, concentration, and memory are impaired (Thomason & Dilts, 1991).

The triad of coma, pinpoint pupils, and depressed respiration strongly suggests opioid poisoning. Because this often occurs in combination with other drugs, pharmacological therapy for opioid dependence should be instituted immediately as well as screening for the presence of other drugs and metabolites. The finding of needle marks suggestive of addiction further supports the diagnosis. Examination of the urine and gastric contents for drugs may aid in diagnosis, but the results usually become available too late to influence treatment. Naloxone hydrochloride, a pure opioid antagonist, can effectively reverse the central nervous system effects of opioid intoxication and overdose. An initial intravenous dose of 0.4–0.8 mg will dramatically reverse neurological and cardiorespiratory depression, in approximately 2 min, but care should be taken to avoid precipitating withdrawal in dependent patients who may be extremely sensitive to antagonists. The safest approach is to dilute the standard naloxone dose (0.4 mg) and slowly administer it intravenously, monitoring arousal and respiratory function. With care, it is usually possible to reverse the respiratory depression without precipitating a major withdrawal syndrome. If no response is seen with the first dose, additional doses can be given. Patients should be observed for rebound increases in sympathetic nervous system activity, which may result in cardiac arrhythmia and pulmonary edema (Duthie & Nimmo, 1987). Pulmonary edema sometimes associated with opioid overdosage may be countered by positive-pressure respiration. Tonic-clonic seizures, occasionally seen as part of the toxic syndrome with meperidine and propoxyphene, are ameliorated by treatment with naloxone. Overdose with more potent (e.g., fentanyl) or longer acting (methadone) opioids may require higher doses of naloxone given over longer periods of time, thus necessitating the use of ongoing naloxone infusion.

Chronic Opioid Effects: Symptoms of Dependence and Withdrawal

Two prominent pharmacological features of chronic opiate administration have been described: tolerance, characterized by a diminishing drug effect after repeated administration, and dependence, revealed by a withdrawal syndrome after abrupt discontinuation of opiate exposure. It should be noted that this use of the word *dependence* has a pharmacological meaning, as contrasted with *behavioral* and *psychological dependence* as defined in *DSM-IV* (discussed elsewhere in this volume).

Withdrawal from opioids results in a specific constellation of symptoms as well as some relatively nonspecific symptoms. Although some opioid withdrawal symptoms overlap with withdrawal from sedative-hypnotics, opioid withdrawal is generally considered less likely to produce severe morbidity or mortality. Clinical phenomena associated with opioid withdrawal generally consist of symptoms related to neurophysiological rebound in the organ systems on which opioids have their primary actions (Jaffe & Martin, 1990), and the severity of opioid withdrawal varies with the dose and duration of drug use. The time to onset of opioid withdrawal symptoms depends on the half-life of the drug being used. For example, withdrawal may begin 4–6 hr after last use of heroin, but up to 36 hr after last use of methadone (Gold, Pottash, Sweeney, & Kleber, 1980; Gunne, 1959).

Early withdrawal symptoms may include abnormalities in vital signs, including tachycardia and hypertension. Pupillary dilation can be marked. CNS symptoms include restlessness, irritability, and insomnia. Opioid craving also occurs in proportion to the severity of physiological withdrawal symptoms. Patients frequently note yawning and sneezing, gastrointestinal symptoms (which may initially be simply anorexia but can progress to include nausea, vomiting, and diarrhea), and a variety of cutaneous and mucocutaneous symptoms (including lacrimation, or eye watering; rhinorrhea, or runny nose; and piloerection, also known as *gooseflesh*). This combination of symptomatology and intense craving frequently leads to relapse to drug use.

As with the onset of withdrawal, the duration also varies with the drug used. In patients hospitalized for medical illnesses, the severity of the underlying clinical conditions can alter the selection of withdrawal therapy (O'Connor, Samet, & Stein, 1994). The decision as to whether to perform opioid detoxification on an outpatient or inpatient basis depends on the presence of comorbid medical and psychiatric problems, the availability of social support (e.g., family members to provide monitoring and transportation), and the presence of polydrug abuse. The available methods of detoxification also may affect this decision; for example, methadone detoxification is legally restricted by federal legislation to inpatient settings or specialized, licensed outpatient drug treatment programs (*Federal Register*, 1989).

A variety of pharmacological therapies have been developed to assist patients through a safer, more comfortable opioid withdrawal. These therapies involve the use of opioid agonists (e.g., methadone) and alpha-2 adrenergic agonists such as clonidine; an opioid antagonist, naltrexone, in combination with clonidine; and a mixed opioid agonist/antagonist, buprenorphine.

The simplest approach to detoxification is to substitute a prescribed opioid for the heroin the addict is dependent on, and then to gradually lower the dose of the prescribed opioid. The prescribed opioid commonly is methadone (Senay, Dorus, & Showalter, 1981; Silsby & Tennant, 1974; Wilson, Elms, & Thomson, 1974), but levo-alpha acetyl methadol (LAAM) can also be used, and the withdrawal from LAAM has a delayed onset, relative to methadone discontinuation, but a similar time course (Fraser & Isbell, 1952; Sorensen, Hargreaves, & Weinberg, 1982). Buprenorphine is a partial mu agonist with an extremely high receptor affinity (Gal, 1989; Lewis, 1985; Neil, 1984) and can also be used.

The noradrenergic approach to detoxification avoids the difficulties of prescribing an opioid to an addict. This approach is based on the established role of increased central nervous system noradrenergic hyperactivity in opiate withdrawal symptoms described earlier in this chapter (see Redmond & Huang, 1982, for review). Clonidine, which acts on presynaptic receptors to reduce noradrenergic release, is generally used, but this method is less effective against many of the more subjective complaints during withdrawal, such as lethargy, restlessness, and dysphoria (Jasinski, Johnson, & Kocher, 1985). However, the method is safe and effective against most symptoms and is also faster than methadone detoxification (Stine & Kosten, 1992). In outpatients, clonidine's efficacy in the treatment of opiate withdrawal is controversial (Gold et al., 1980; Jasinski et al., 1985).

One very interesting pharmacological discovery is the ability of opiate antagonists to reverse opiate dependence and accelerate detoxification. Administration of naloxone in dependent monkeys causes a desensitization to subsequent naloxone doses (Krystal, Walker, & Heninger, 1989). The use of an antagonist along with another medication like clonidine to relieve the discomfort also seems to accelerate treatment in humans. Administering an antagonist such as naltrexone precipitates withdrawal within minutes for both methadone-maintained and ordinary heroin addicts, and this process of precipitation appears to decrease the duration of subsequent withdrawal symptoms. The amount of clonidine needed to ameliorate these symptoms when naltrexone and clonidine are used together is also lessened by using larger initial doses of naltrexone (Brewer, Rezae, & Bailey, 1988; Charney et al., 1982; Vining, Kosten, & Kleber, 1988). Recently, very rapid inpatient detoxification from opiates using sedatives and anesthetics in combination with opiate antagonists has been reported (Loimer, Lenz, Schmid, & Presslich, 1991; Loimer, Schmid, Lenz, Presslich, & Grunberger, 1990) but these procedures require intensive medical treatment (intubation, artificial ventilation) as well as the risk of anesthesia and are therefore controversial.

In addition to acute withdrawal and detoxification, another issue is that of "protracted withdrawal," which has been implicated in such clinically crucial phenomena as the difficulty of maintaining abstinence after detoxification from methadone maintenance (Senay, Dorus, Goldberg, & Thorton, 1977), high rates of relapse after abstinence (Dole, 1972), and drug craving (Mirin, Meyer, & McNamee, 1976). Chronic use of opioids is followed by neurobiological alterations that persist for months after discontinuation of the opiates. Up to 9 months after detoxification, opiate addicts manifest abstinence symptoms of weight gain, increased basal metabolic rate, decreased temperature, increased respiration, increased blood pressure, and decreased erythrocyte sedimentation rate (Himmelsbach, 1942). However, because these symptoms are nonspecific and are not clearly opposite in nature to opiate agonist effects, as acute withdrawal symptoms are, the protracted withdrawal phenomenon is controversial (Satel, Kosten, Schuckit, & Fischman, 1993).

Patterns of Abuse and Psychological Dependence

Heroin use existed among whites and other ethnic groups prior to the 1950s but began to spread among black males in Harlem during the 1950s. Among young men in Manhattan, heroin use increased from 3% in 1963 to a peak of 20% in 1972 (13% used heroin in 1974) (Hunt, 1965; Malcolm X & Haley, 1965). The proportion using heroin then declined some and remained relatively low in the late 1970s. In the late 1970s and the 1980s in New York's hard drug scene, low proportions of youths reaching adulthood in Harlem and the inner city initiated use of heroin or became regular users, but sizable proportions of those who did initiate heroin injection became addicted within 2 years, and half of these persisted in their addiction. Thus, the heroin era cohort constitutes a large proportion of the heroin addicts who continue to need treatment today (Frank, 1986).

In addition to the traditional association of heroin addiction with a lower socioeconomic group, use itself leads to further social and interpersonal deterioration. Since opioids are severely regulated, especially in the United States, demand by addicts results in the existence of a black market characterized by crime, disease, poverty, and loss of personal and social productivity. Prostitution is closely linked with drug abuse in general and opioid use in particular and contributes to the spread of HIV, as well as other venereal and infectious diseases. High overall death rates are associated with opioid abuse: approximately 10–15 per 1,000 users in the United States (Jaffe, 1989). Statistics indicate a dramatic increase in heroin-related deaths between 1993 and 1994 (National Drug Control Strategy, 1997). This same source reports that the annual number of heroin-related emergency room mentions increased from 34,000 in 1990 to 76,023 in 1995. Opioids have the capacity to absorb all of an individual's attention, resources, and energy, which become devoted exclusively to obtaining the next dose at any cost. This vicious circle of-

ten persists for decades. The consequent pervasive and devastating deterioration leads to the need for long-term treatments and intense psychosocial interventions.

During the last 5 years, a substantial new epidemic of heroin abuse has been developing in the United States and spreading to middle-class users, who were formerly more likely to abuse only cocaine. *Pulse Check*, a publication by the Office of National Drug Control Policy (ONDCP), reported in December 1991 four key trends in heroin use: More teenagers and young adults, more middle- and upper-middle-class people were using purer heroin, and the proportion of people inhaling or smoking heroin, as well as the number of people seeking treatment, continued to increase. At a September 1997 NIDA conference, Donna Shalala, Health and Human Services Secretary, stated that in 1995, more than 140,000 people tried heroin for the first time, most of them under the age of 26 ("Shalala Joins," 1997). The National Drug Control Strategy (1995) reported that the strongest sign of an epidemic is the entry of a large number of new users (new initiates), and this new influx of heroin users defines such an epidemic. New users, because they have had less exposure and fewer chronic health (at least with respect to infectious disease) and legal adverse consequences, are more likely to recruit other new users. Many drug abusers mistakenly believe that inhaling heroin, rather than injecting it, reduces the risks of addiction or overdose. In some areas, "shabanging"—picking up cooked heroin with a syringe and squirting it up the nose—has increased in popularity (Addiction Treatment Forum, 1997). Commonly known as *smack* or *horse* for years, the new pure heroin is more life-threatening, which is reflected in the new street terminology (*DOA, body bag, instant death*, and *silence of the lamb*), and the implied danger seems to actually increase the drug's allure (Addiction Treatment Forum, 1997). In general, inhaling predominates in cities where there is high heroin purity, and IV use predominates where purity is lower (e.g., California and Colorado), but *Pulse Check* (1994) also reports that many young users in "high-purity" cities such as Chicago and New York City have switched to injection.

This expanding market for heroin fortunately coincides with a variety of new treatments that have become available, for example, developments in the treatment of acute withdrawal and the treatment of chronic dependence by antagonist and agonist pharmacotherapy, including ways to optimize the delivery of methadone maintenance and newly available breakthrough pharmocotherapies. These treatments as discussed in detail elsewhere in this volume.

In addition to heroin, many other opioid drugs, including oral prescription analgesics, can also be abused and lead to opiate dependence. When given for clinical need—for example, in the treatment of pain associated with acute surgical procedures—these medications can generally be used without resulting in opioid abuse or dependence. Even when longer term use of an opioid analgesic is necessary and some physiological tolerance results, this does not usually constitute opioid dependence as defined by *DSM-IV*. Chronic pain, however, can present a problem. Of all patients with chronic pain, 50% take between one and five medications per day, and 25% of these become addicted (Maruta, Swanson, & Finlayson, 1979). These patients also frequently use alcohol, and this combination can result in accidental overdose and death. One study at the Seattle VA (Chabal, Erjavec, Jacobson, Mariano, & Chaney, 1997) reported that a total of 19% (76 out of 403) of all pain patients seen were using chronic opiates and that 34% of these met one and 27.6% met three or more *DSM-III-R* abuse criteria. It was further noted in that study that prior opiate and alcohol abuse did not predict who would become an opiate abuser. The use of increased amounts by these patients may, in turn, enhance the risk of toxic effects and may lead to other problems, such as seeking multiple physicians and pharmacies and obtaining the opioid illicitly (Jaffe & Martin, 1990). These medications are also available illegally on the street and are also abused by individuals who have opiate dependence without a history of treatment for chronic pain. Most are essentially similar to heroin and morphine but some have some differences and associated special problems (see table 8.1). Of the orally prescribed medications, propoxyphene (Darvon) is commonly quoted as being related to frequent emergency-room overdose visits and medical examiner statistics (Soumerai, Avorn, Gortmaker, & Hawley, 1987). Hydrocodone is also gaining recognition. The available maintenance pharmacotherapy drugs may also be abused if access is available on the street. The commonly abused illegal and prescription opioids are listed in table 8.1, along with some of their special properties.

Summary of Clinical Aspects

Clinical effects of opioids as described above include general beneficial effects of the medications such as analgesia as well as life-threatening effects such as respiratory depression. Opiates act on multiple systems to produce effects on almost all aspects of human physiological functioning, such as the gastrointestinal, cardiovascular, immune, and endocrine functions. Acute clinical phenomena such as intoxication and overdose have been described and are contrasted with chronic effects such as symptoms of dependence and withdrawal. Both tolerance and dependence and intensity of withdrawal symptoms are functions of the potency of and length of exposure to an opiate, while the time course of such symptoms is related to the duration of action of the opiate. Detoxification is an area of active clinical research, and new, efficient treatments are continually being developed. Currently, opioid agents such as antagonists (naloxone and naltrexone) and partial agonists (buprenorphine), as well as adrenergic agents, have been studied for use in detoxification and have shortened the time needed for this treatment.

Opiate dependence (in a behavioral or *DSM-IV*-defined as opposed to pharmacological sense) has been an important public health concern throughout the 20th century and is now a growing epidemic on the eve of the 21st century. The many and varied available opioid medications all have some degree of abuse potential and can present special problems. Some of the most common of these are summarized in table 8.1. Of the available opiates, heroin, and the current epidemic of its increased abuse and dependence, is the most significant threat to individual and public health well-being. Health problems associated with opioid and especially heroin abuse are discussed below.

ASSOCIATED PATHOLOGY AND PROBLEMS

Opioid Dependence and the HIV Infection

Public Health Issues

As of June 30, 1991, 58,879 or 32.2% of all AIDS cases reported to the Centers for Disease Control (CDC) were associated with illicit drug use (Nwanyanwu, Chu, Green, Buehler, & Berkelman, 1993). From 1989 to 1991, the geographic regions with highest increase in AIDS were the South and the North-central compared with the Northeast, which was the lowest. Although there is some stabilization of reported infection rates, the HIV seroprevalence in New York City IV drug users remains close to 50%, a prevalence which is maintained by new cases, since some individuals have died. As is apparent from the above statistics, HIV infection rates among intravenous drug abusers in New York remain significant and are on the increase nationally. The infection rate in the group of IV drug users in methadone treatment, however, is low (Ball & Ross, 1991; Hartel et al., 1995), making treatment of opioid dependence a clear public health need (O'Connor et al., 1994).

In addition to treating and preventing opioid dependence, harm reduction among actively using opiate addicts has also become an important goal. One highly publicized new intervention which has recently been developed to reduce risks of transmission of HIV and other blood-borne disease is the syringe exchange program (SEP). These programs have been controversial since their introduction due to concern that providing easy access to needles would lead to increased intravenous drug use. There is, however, no evidence for this according to Ellie Schoenbaum, M.D., Director of the AIDS Research Program, Department of Epidemiology and Social Medicine at Montefiore Medical Center in the Bronx, New York, speaking at a September 1997 NIDA conference ("Shalala Joins," 1997). Needle exchange programs now exist in many locations in North America, Europe, and Australia (Lurie et al., 1993; Stimson, 1989; Stryker & Smith, 1993). In an April 1995 survey by the North American Syringe Exchange Network, 60 SEPs reported operating in 46 cities in 21 states. The legality and acceptance of these programs vary from state to state and range from "legal" (states with no law requiring prescriptions for needles), to "illegal but tolerated" (by local authorities) in spite of laws requiring needle prescription, to "illegal/underground" (Titus, 1996). In addition to exchanging needles and providing condoms and related education, most SEPs also counsel injection drug users to follow medical hygiene standards (e.g., use a new sterile needle and syringe for each injection, use clean water to prepare drugs; "Syringe Exchange," 1995). These programs have also often served as an important link between active drug injectors and medical and social services. Studies have consistently shown that needle exchange, in addition to improving access to and engagement with needed services, is also independently associated with decreased needle sharing and related high-risk behavior (Stimson, 1989; Stryker & Smith, 1993; Watters, Estilo, Clark, & Lorvick, 1994). Thus, the available research suggests that a stabilization in HIV infection rates is associated with needle and syringe exchange programs (DesJarlais et al., 1994; Stryker & Smith, 1993). Although this has not been directly demonstrated, additional interesting data supporting that conclusion have been reported by an innovative needle exchange and research program in New Haven, Connecticut. The prevalence of HIV infection and used syringes in that city has steadily declined since the program was introduced. Using these data, researchers have determined that the likelihood of HIV transmission via contaminated needles may have been reduced by as much as one third in this environment as a result of the increased availability of sterile needles through the needle exchange program (Kaplan, Khoshnood, & Heimer, 1994). Even though early data support the effectiveness of SEPs, they remain controversial, and continued research is necessary to establish their efficacy.

Treatment Needs of Comorbid Opiate Dependent and HIV Infected Patients

In addition to risk reduction or prevention of infection, there is also need for treatment of an increasing number of existing HIV-positive opiate-dependent patients both in and out of opiate treatment. Inner-city HIV-positive drug abusers have need of extensive medical and social services (London et al., 1995), which are most effectively delivered at a central site (Selwyn, Budner, Wasserman, & Arno, 1993). Where this is feasible, the psychosocial intervention should include mechanisms for ensuring that on-site services are used appropriately. Where on-site delivery of medical and social services is not possible, interventions for improving patients' compliance with medical regimens (e.g., keeping appointments, taking antiretroviral medications and prophylaxes against *Pneumocystis carinii* pneumonia and tuberculosis) and for connecting patients to community social service resources is essential. Compliance with medical regimens has the potential to improve the quality and quantity of life and thus impacts on motivation for changing high-risk behaviors regardless of whether opiate dependence treatment is accepted.

For those individuals who are in treatment for opiate dependence, special issues in the concurrent management of methadone and medications for HIV necessitate integration of medical services and opiate treatment. Risk reduction education by staff and special training in HIV spectrum disease, distribution of condoms, and assistance with referrals to infectious disease clinics are further examples of such integrated services. Primary medical care, including T cell monitoring and prescriptions for zidovudine (azidothymidine, or AZT) and other HIV medications, is provided along with prophylaxis for *Pneumocystis carinii* (PCP) pneumonia and other opportunistic infections. TB case management projects and the provision of medications for prevention and treatment have developed in response to an increase in tuberculosis, especially treatment-resistant tuberculosis, within this group (Albert Einstein College of Medicine, 1989; Joseph & Springer, 1990).

Medication Interaction Concerns

The assessment of antiretroviral drug efficacy, as well as the determination of patients' prognosis and rate of disease progression, was revolutionized in 1996 with the introduction of commercial assays that quantitate the amount of HIV RNA in plasma. These blood tests, also called *viral load tests*, are performed by commercial laboratories and are now routinely available. HIV viral load measures have been shown in several studies to provide powerful new tools to estimate the risk of disease and long-term morbidity and mortality (Carpenter et al., 1996; Mellors et al., 1995; Mellors et al., 1996; O'Brien et al., 1996). Viral load assays should be performed as part of all HIV-infected patients' baseline evaluations and, in addition, should be used to assess prognosis, to determine the appropriateness of initiating antiretroviral therapy, and to evaluate responses to therapy.

The introduction of new antiretroviral agents has raised justifiable hope of a new therapeutic era for HIV-infected patients. However, these agents have also introduced new complexities in patient management, particularly for injection drug users, due in large part to potential drug toxicities and drug interactions. The principal toxicities of the nucleoside analogues consist mostly of bone marrow suppression (zidovudine), peripheral neuropathy and pancreatitis (didanosine, zalcitabine, and stavudine, to varying degrees), and less commonly, hepatitis (zidovudine, didanosine, zalcitabine), and diarrhea (lamivudine). Some of these toxicities may be particularly important in populations of HIV-infected drug users, in whom underlying rates of peripheral nerve disease, pancreatitis (due to coexisting alcohol abuse), and hepatitis due to underlying alcoholic, drug-induced, or viral hepatitis may be very high compared to the rates in other HIV-infected populations (Cherubin & Sapira, 1993; Kreek, 1973).

The principal toxicity of the nonnucleoside reverse transcriptase inhibitors (nevirapine, delavirdine) is rash. The protease inhibitors, in contrast, while very potent antiretroviral agents, can have significant side effects: gastrointestinal distress (saquinavir, indivanir, ritonavir) and liver function and lipid abnormalities (ritonavir). Of the three available by prescription in mid-1995 (saquinavir, ritonavir, indinavir), saquinavir and indinavir are generally better tolerated than ritonavir, but ritonavir may be one of the most potent of the three.

With the increasing number of HIV-infected patients in treatment programs for opiate dependence, potential interactions between methadone and other opiate pharmacotherapies and antiviral agents used in the treatment of HIV are particularly important to define. The ability of opioid-maintained patients to tolerate most of these medications has not been specifically studied. Therefore, clinicians are hesitant to use these powerful new agents in the opioid-dependent and agonist-maintained patient for fear of enhanced drug toxicity. A study of possible interactions between methadone and zidovudine (azidothymidine, or AZT) has shown that serum levels of methadone are not affected by this drug, but that some patients who receive methadone maintenance treatment may show a potentially toxic increase in serum levels of AZT (Friedland et al., 1992; McCance-Katz, Jatlow, Rainey, & Friedland, in press; Schwartz et al., 1992;). However, these authors caution against making changes in the dosage of AZT and suggest instead careful clinical monitoring for signs of dose-related AZT toxicity in such patients. In the case of protease inhibitors, there is even less information concerning interaction with methadone. All the protease inhibitors are metabolized by the hepatic cytochrome P450 microsomal enzyme system and, to varying degrees, may inhibit the metabolism of other drugs that are handled by this system. These drugs include methadone, other opioids, barbiturates, benzodiazepines, anticonvulsants, and a variety of other medications. Thus, dosing adjustments may be required, and in some cases, certain medications may be contraindicated. Clinical and pharmaceutical studies are urgently needed to evaluate the possibly wide range of drug interactions for which HIV-infected drug users may be at risk through the use of this important new group of antiretroviral medications.

Other Medical Problems

Liver Disease

In addition to the direct physiological effects described above with opioid use and abstinence, there are multiple indirectly associated medical problems. Chronic liver disease is the most common medical problem. Fifty to sixty percent of all heroin addicts entering methadone maintenance have biochemical evidence of chronic liver disease primarily of two etiological types: (a) sequelae of earlier acute infection with hepatitis B or hepatitis C virus; (b) alcohol-induced liver disease, including fatty liver, alcoholic hepatitis, and alcohol cirrhosis. Each of the major forms of viral hepatitis has been associated with injection-drug use, with hepatitis B and C being the most important.

A variety of studies have shown that over half of injection-drug users are likely to show serological evidence of past hepatitis B infection (positive serological test for hepatitis B surface antibody and/or hepatitis B core antibody), and a substantial proportion of this population also show evidence of active hepatitis B (hepatitis surface antigen positive) infection (Chu & Wortley, 1995). These chronic carriers are at risk for transmitting hepatitis B infection and are more likely to experience chronic liver disease.

Hepatitis C is an important cause of posttransfusion hepatitis, as well as hepatitis infection among injection-drug users (Cherubin & Sapira, 1993; O'Connor, Selwyn, & Schottenfeld, 1994). A variety of serological studies of hepatitis C virus infection has found that the majority (over two thirds) of injection-drug users examined have shown evidence of hepatitis C like hepatitis B, infection (Esteban et al., 1989; Simmonds et al., 1990). Hepatitis C is also associated with chronic liver disease, and there are similar implications concerning the use of potentially

hepatotoxic drugs in such patients (Cherubin & Sapira, 1993; O'Connor et al., 1994).

Chronic liver disease in all its forms has major implications concerning medication use. For example, opioid medications for treatment of dependence on drugs such as methadone, LAAM, and buprenorphine, medications commonly prescribed to treat diseases that are prevalent in drug users such as tuberculosis (e.g., isoniazid, rifampin), and drugs used to treat or prevent opportunistic infections (e.g., trimethoprim-sulfamethoxazole) and some antiretroviral agents (e.g., didanosine) may have hepatotoxic influence (Kreek, Garfield, Gutjahr, & Giusti, 1976; O'Connor et al., 1994; Sawyer, Brown, Narong, & Li, 1993; Schwartz et al., 1990).

The bulk of severe chronic opioid addicts in treatment receive methadone, and the liver may play a central role in several aspects of methadone disposition, including not only methadone metabolism and clearance but also storage and subsequent release of unchanged methadone. However, clinically methadone use has been well described in milder liver disease and used successfully in these patients. Very severe liver disease or abrupt changes in hepatic status may cause significant alterations in methadone disposition with concomitant clinical symptoms (Kreek, Oratz, & Rothchild, 1978).

Other Infectious Diseases

A variety of bacterial infections have been well documented to be associated with drug use in general, and with injection-drug use in particular. For example, individuals with IV drug use (especially if they also have HIV disease) are at further risk for important bacterial infections, including skin and soft tissue infection, pneumonia, and endocarditis and sepsis. Tuberculosis is an especially significant problem in this population. As with bacterial infections, tuberculosis has long been known to be prevalent in drug users (Cherubin, 1967), but the AIDS epidemic has resulted in a major increase in the number of cases of tuberculosis, particularly among drug users (Selwyn et al., 1992). Generally tuberculosis in HIV-infected individuals may represent reactivation of latent disease in the setting of immunosuppression, but it is also brought on in other addicts by environmental and "social" factors related to drug use (O'Connor, Selwyn, & Schottenfeld, 1994). HIV-infected individuals within the opiate-dependent population are at particularly high risk for "extrapulmonary" manifestations of tuberculosis (Barnes, Bloch, Davidson, & Snider, 1991; Braun et al., 1990), including infection of the gastrointestinal system or central nervous system.

Complications of Pregnancy

The potential medical and social costs of opiate dependence during pregnancy are great. Pregnant opiate-dependent women experience a sixfold increase in maternal obstetric complications and significant increases in neonatal complications (Dattel, 1990). Pregnancy complications associated with opiate dependence include low birth weight, toxemia, third-trimester bleeding, malpresentation, postchildbirth morbidity, fetal distress, and meconium in the amniotic fluid. Neonatal complications include narcotic withdrawal, postnatal growth deficiency, microcephaly, neurobehavioral problems, and a 74-fold increase in sudden infant death syndrome (SIDS) (Dattel, 1990).

Psychiatric Problems

There is a large subgroup of opioid-dependent patients with psychiatric comorbidity, and inability to treat the psychiatric disorders of the opiate-dependent patient contributes to poor treatment response and increased severity of all medical, addictive, and psychiatric problems. Studies have found that addicts can have almost every psychiatric illness that occurs in nonaddicts. A comprehensive evaluation of psychiatric disorders in addicts was completed by Rounsaville, Weissman, Kleber, and Wilber (1982) in a sample of 533 opiate addicts. In that study, depression was the most frequently diagnosed illness, with about 53.9% of the sample having had some form of depression at least once. Alcoholism was the next most common problem (34.5%), followed by antisocial personality (26.5%) and anxiety disorders (9.6% for phobic disorder and 5.4% for generalized anxiety). Schizophrenia, other types of personality disorders, mania, and hypomania occurred with a much lower frequency. Eighty-five percent of the patient sample were found to have had a psychiatric disorder in addition to opiate dependence at some time in their lives. Many symptoms not systematically studied in the above report, but also seen regularly, are acute situational reactions that involve intense but transient feelings of anger, anxiety, or depression; psychiatric disorders complicated by medical conditions such as hepatitis; and illnesses or injuries that produce chronic pain such as pancreatitis, sickle cell anemia, or trauma resulting in nerve root irritation. Rounsaville, Weissman, Crits-Christoph, Wilber, and Kleber (1982) also found that untreated addicts had similar types of psychiatric illnesses in relatively similar proportions to patients who were in treatment. However, treated addicts were less likely to have a current psychiatric illness.

Summary of Associated Pathology and Problems

In summary, opiate dependence presents a diverse array of associated medical, psychosocial, and psychiatric problems with a large public health impact. Treatment and prevention of HIV infection in particular requires an active approach using active psychosocial services such as education and support of medication compliance. Controversial approaches such as syringe exchange programs require ongoing investigation. Pharmacokinetic interaction of important medications for the opiate-dependent/HIV-comorbid population is also an area of urgently needed research.

Key References

Stine, S. M. (1997). New developments in methadone treatment and matching treatments to patient. In S. M. Stine & T. R. Kosten (Eds.), *New treatments for opiate dependence* (Vol. 3, pp. 121–172). New York: Guilford Press.

Reisine, T., & Pasternak, G. (1996). Opioid analgesics and antagonists. In J. G. Hardman & L. E. Limbird (Eds.), *Pharmacological basis of therapeutics* (9th ed., pp. 521–557).

Kreek, M. J. (1994). Pharmacology and medical aspects of methadone treatment. In R. A. Rettig & A. Yarnolinsky (Eds.), *Federal regulation of methadone treatment* (pp. 37–60). Washington, DC: National Academy of Science, National Academy Press.

References

Acquas, E., Carboni, E., & DiChiara, G. (1990). Profound depression of mesolimbic dopamine release after morphine withdrawal in dependent rats. *European Journal of Pharmacology, 193,* 133–134.

Addiction Treatment Forum. (1997). Smack is back—big time! *Addiction Treatment Forum, 6,* 1.

Aghajanian, G. K. (1978). Tolerance of locus coeruleus neurons to morphine and suppression of withdrawal response by clonidine. *Nature, 267,* 186–188.

Akaoka, A., & Aston-Jones, G. (1991). Opiate withdrawal-induced hyperactivity of locus coeruleus neurons is substantially mediated by augmented excitatory amino acid input. *Journal of Neuroscience, 11,* 3830–3839.

Ball, J. C., & Ross, A. (1991). *The effectiveness of methadone maintenance treatment.* New York: Springer-Verlag.

Barnes, P. F., Bloch, A. B., Davidson, P. T., & Snider, D. E., Jr. (1991). Tuberculosis in patients with human immunodeficiency virus infection. *New England Journal of Medicine, 324(23),* 1644–1650.

Braun, M. M., Byers, R. H., Heyward, W. L., Ciesielski, C. A., Bloch, A. B., Berkelman, R. L., & Snider, D. E. (1990). Acquired immunodeficiency syndrome and extrapulmonary tuberculosis in the United States. *Archives of Internal Medicine, 150,* 1913–1916.

Brewer, C., Rezae, H., & Bailey, C. (1988). Opioid withdrawal and naltrexone induction in 48–72 hours with minimal drop out, using a modification of the naltrexone-clonidine technique. *British Journal of Psychiatry, 153,* 340–343.

Brown, C. (1965). *Manchild in the promised land.* New York: Macmillan.

Carpenter, C. C., Fischl, M., Hammer, S. M., Hirsch, M. S., Jacobsen, D. M., Katzenstein, D. A., Montaner, J. S., Richman, D. D., Saag, M. S., Schooley, R. T., Thompson, M. A., Vella, S., Yeni, P. G., & Volberding, P. A. (1996). Antiretroviral therapy for HIV infection in 1996. *Journal of the American Medical Association, 276,* 146–154.

Chabal, C., Erjavec, M. K., Jacobson, L., Mariano, A., & Chaney, E. (1997). Prescription opiate abuse in chronic pain patients: Clinical criteria, incidence, and predictors. *Clinical Journal on Pain, 13,* 150–155.

Chan, G. L. C., & Matzke, G. R. (1987). Effects of renal insufficiency on the pharmacokinetics and pharmacodynamics of opioid nalgesics. *Drug Intelligence and Clinical Pharmacy, 21,* 773–783.

Charney, D. S., Riordan, C. E., Kleber, H. D., Murburg, M., Braverman, P., Sternberg, D. E., Heninger, G. R., & Redmond, D. E. (1982). Clonidine and naltrexone: A safe, effective and rapid treatment of abrupt withdrawal from methadone therapy. *Archives of General Psychiatry, 39,* 1327–1332.

Chen, Y., Mestek, A., Liu, J., Hurley, J.A., & Yu, L. (1993). Molecular cloning and functional expression of a mu-opioid receptor from rat brain. *Molecular Pharmocology, 44,* 8–12.

Cherubin, C. E. (1967). The medical sequelae of narcotic addiction. *Annals of Internal Medicine, 67,* 23–33.

Cherubin, C. E., & Sapira, J. D. (1993). The medical complications of drug addiction and the medical assessment of the intravenous drug user: 25 years later. *Annals of Internal Medicine, 119,* 1017–1028.

Christie, M. J., Williams, J. T., & North, R. A. (1987). Cellular mechanisms of opioid tolerance: Studies in single brain neurons. *Molecular Pharmacology, 32,* 633–638.

Chu, S. Y., & Wortley, P. M. (1995). Epidemiology of HIV/AIDS in women. In H. J. Minkoff & J. A. DeHovitz (Eds.), *HIV infection in women.* New York: Raven Press.

Dattel, B. J. (1990). Substance abuse in pregnancy. *Seminars in Perinatology, 14(2),* 179–187.

DesJarlais, D. C., Friedman, S. R., Sotheran, J. L., Wenston, J., Maror, M., Yancovitz, S. R., Frank, B., Beatrice, S., & Mildvan, D. (1994). Continuity and change within an HIV epidemic: Injecting drug users in New York City, 1984 through 1992. *Journal of the American Medical Association, 271,* 121–127.

Dole, V. P. (1972). Narcotic addition, physical dependence, and relapse. *New England Journal of Medicine, 286(18),* 988–992.

Dooley, C. P., Saad, C., & Valenzuela, J. E. (1988). Studies of the role of opioids in control of human pancreatic secreation. *Digestive Diseases and Sciences, 33,* 598–604.

Duthie, D. J. R., & Nimmo, W. S. (1987). Adverse effects of opioid analgesic drugs. *British Journal of Anaesthesia, 59,* 61–77.

Elliott, K., Minami, M., Kolesnikov, Y. A., Pasternak, G. W., & Inturrisi, C. E. (1994). The NMDA receptor antagonists, LY274614 and MK-801, and the nitric oxide synthase inhibitor, NG-nitro-L-arginine, attenuate analgesic tolerance to the mu-opioid morphine but not to kappa opioids. *Pain, 56(1),* 69–75.

Esteban, J. I. et al. (1989). Hepatitis C virus antibodies among risk groups in Spain. *Lancet, 2,* 294–297.

Federal Register. (1989, March 2). *Methadone: Rule, proposed rule, and notice.* (Vol. 54, No. 40, p. 8965). Washington, DC: Department of Health and Human Services, Food and Drug Administration, 21 CFR Part 291.

Frank, B. (1986). *What is the future of the heroin problem in New York City?* Paper presented at the 3rd annual Northeast regional methadone conference, Baltimore.

Fraser, H. F., & Isbell, H. (1952). Actions and addiction liabilities of alpha-acetylmethadols in man. *Journal of Pharmacology and Experimental Therapeutics, 105*, 458–465.

Friedland, A., Schwartz, E., Brechbuhl, A. B., Kahl, P., Miller, M., & Selwyn, P. (1992). Pharmacokentic interactions of zidovudine and methadone in intravenous drug using patients with HIV infection. *Journal of Acquired Immune Deficiency Syndromes, 5*, 619–626.

Gal, T. J. (1989). Naloxone reversal of buprenorphine-induced respiratory depression. *Clinical Pharmacology and Therapeutics, 45*, 66–71.

Gold, M. S., Pottash, A. C., Sweeney, D. R., & Kleber, H. D. (1980). Opiate withdrawal using clonidine. *Journal of the American Medical Association, 243*(4), 343–346.

Grossman, A. (1988). Opioids and stress in man. *Journal of Endocrinology, 119*, 377–381.

Gunne, L. N. (1959). Noradrenaline and adrenaline in the rat brain during acute and chronic morphine administration and during withdrawal. *Nature, 184*, 150–151.

Harris, H. W., & Nestler, E. J. (1993). Opiate regulation of signal transduction pathways. In R. P. Hammer, Jr. (Ed.), *The neurobiology of opiates.* (pp. 301–332). Boca Raton, FL: CRC Press.

Hartel, D. M, Schoenbaum, E. E., Selwyn, P. A., Kline, J., Davenny, K., Klein, R. S., & Friedland, G. H. (1995). Heroin use during methadone maintenance treatment: The importance of methadone dose and cocaine use. *American Journal of Public Health, 85*, 83–88.

Himmelsbach, C. K. (1942). Clinical studies of drug addiction: Physical dependence, withdrawal and recovery. *Archives of Internal Medicine, 69*, 766–772.

Hollt, V. (1986). Opioid peptide processing and receptor selectivity. *Annual Review of Pharmacology Toxicology, 26*, 59–77.

Howlett, T. A., & Rees, L. H. (1986). Endogenous opioid peptides and hypo-thalamo-pituitary function. *Annual Review of Physiology, 48*, 527–537.

Jaffe, J. H. (1989). Psychoactive substance use disorders. In H. I. Kaplan & B. J. Sadock (Eds.), *Comprehensive textbook of psychiatry* (5th ed., pp. 642–698). Baltimore: Williams & Wilkins.

Jaffe, J. H., & Martin, W. R. (1990). Opioid analgesics and antagonists. In A. G. Gilman, T. W. Rall, A. S. Nies, & P. Taylor (Eds.), *Goodman and Gilman's: The pharmacological basis of therapeutics* (8th ed., pp. 485–521). New York: Pergamon Press.

Jasinski, D. R., Johnson, R. E., & Kocher, T. R. (1985). Clonidine in morphine withdrawal: Differential effects on signs and symptoms. *Archives of General Psychiatry, 42*(11), 1063–1066.

Johnson, N. P. (1990). What'd he say? Street drug terminology. *Journal of the South Carolina Medical Association*, 51–56.

Johnson, S. M., & Fleming, W. W. (1989). Mechanisms of cellular adaptive sensitivity changes: Applications to opioid tolerance and dependence. *Pharmacology Review, 41*, 435–488.

Johnson, S. W., & North, R. A. (1992). Opioids excite dopamine neurons by hyperpolarization of local interneurons. *Journal of Neuroscience, 12*, 483–488.

Joseph, H., & Springer, E. (1990). Methadone maintenance treatment and the AIDS epidemic. In J. J. Platt, C. D. Kaplan, & P. J. Kim (Eds.), *The effectiveness of drug abuse treatment: Dutch and American perspectives* (pp. 261–274). Malabar, FL: Robert E. Krieger.

Kaiko, R. F., Foley, K. M., Grabinski, P. Y., Heidrich, G., Rogers, A. G., Inturrisi, C. E., & Reidenberg, M. M. (1983). Central nervous system excitatory effects of meperidine in cancer patients. *Annals of Neurology, 13*, 180–185.

Kaplan, E. H., Khoshnood, K., & Heimer, R. (1994). A decline in HIV-infected needles returned to New Haven's needle exchange program: Client shift or needle exchange? *American Journal of Public Health, 84*, 1991–1994.

Kogan, J. H., Nestler, E. J., & Aghajanian, G. K. (1992). Elevated basal firing rates and enhanced responses to 8-Br-cAMP in locus coeruleus neurons in brain slices from opiate-dependent rats. *European Journal of Pharmacology, 211*, 47–53.

Kolesnikov, Y. A., Maccehini, M. L., & Pasternak, G. W. (1994). 1-Aminocyclopropane carboxylic acid (ACPC) prevents mu and delta opioid tolerance. *Life Science, 55*, 1393–1398.

Kolesnikov, Y. A., Pick, C. G., Ciszewska, G., & Pasternak, G. W. (1993). Blockade of tolerance to morphine but not kappa opioids by a nitric oxide synthase inhibitor. *Proceeding of the National Academy of Science USA, 90*, 5162–5166.

Koob, G. F. (1992). Drugs of abuse: Anatomy, pharmacology, and function of reward pathways. *Trends in Pharmacological Sciences, 13*, 177–184.

Kreek, M. J. (1973). Medical safety and side effects of methadone in tolerant individuals. *Journal of the American Medical Association, 223*, 665–668.

Kreek, M. J., Garfield, J. W., Gutjahr, C. L., & Giusti, L. M. (1976). Rifampin-induced methadone withdrawal. *New England Journal of Medicine, 294*, 1104–1106.

Kreek, M. J., Oratz, M., & Rothschild, M. A. (1978). Hepatic extraction of long- and short-acting narcotics in the isolated perfused rabbit liver. *Gastroenterology, 75*, 88–94.

Krystal, J. H., Walker, M. W., & Heninger, G. R. (1989). Intermittent naloxone attenuates the development of physical dependence on methadone in rhesus monkeys. *European Journal of Pharmacology, 160,* 331–338.

Lewis, J., Mansour, A., Khachaturian, H., Watson, S. J., & Akil, H. (1987). Opioids and pain regulation. In H. Akil & J. W. Lewis (Eds.), *Neurotransmitters and pain control, pain and headache* (Vol. 9, pp 129–159). Basel: S. Karger.

Lewis, J. W. (1985). Buprenorphine. *Drug and Alcohol Dependence, 14,* 363–372.

Loh, H. H., & Smith, A. P. (1990). Molecular characterization of opioid receptors. *Annual Review of Pharmacology Toxicology, 30,* 123–147.

Loimer, N., Lenz, K., Schmid, R., & Presslich, O. (1991). Technique for greatly shortening the transition from methadone to naltrexone maintenance of patients addicted to opiates. *American Journal Psychiatry, 148,* 933–935.

Loimer, N., Schmid, R., Lenz, K., Presslich, O., & Grunberger, J. (1990). Acute blocking of naloxone-precipitated opiate withdrawal symptoms by methohexitone. *British Journal of Psychiatry, 157,* 748–752.

London, J., Miller, M., Sorensen, J. L., Delucchi, K., Dilley, J., Dotson, J., Schwartz, B., & Okin, R. (1995). *Problems of HIV-infected substance abusers entering case management.* Paper presented at the 57th annual scientific meeting of the College on Problems of Drug Dependenc, Scottsdale, AZ.

Lurie, P., Reingold, A. L., Bowser, B., et al. (1993). *The public health impact of needle exchange programs in the United States and abroad.* San Francisco: University of California Press.

Malcolm X, & Haley, A. (1965). *Autobiography of Malcolm X.* New York: Signet.

Maldonado, R., & Koob, G. F. (1988). Destruction of the locus coeruleus decreases physical signs of opiate withdrawal. *Brain Research, 605,* 128–138.

Martin, W. R. (1983). Pharmacology of opioids. *Pharmacology Reviews, 35,* 283–323.

Maruta, T., Swanson, P. W., & Finlayson, R. E. (1979). Drug abuse and dependency in patients with chronic pain. *Mayo Clinical Proceedings, 54*(4), 241–244.

McCance-Katz, E. F., Jatlow, P., Rainey, P. M., & Friedland, G. (in press). Methadone effects on zidovudine disposition (ACTG 262). *Journal of Acquired Immune Deficiency Syndromes and Human Retrovirology.*

Mellors, J. W., Kingsley, L. A., Rinaldo, C. R., Jr., Todd, J. A., Hoo, B. S., Kokka, R. P., & Gupta, P. (1995). Quantitation of HIV-1 RNA in plasma predicts out-

come after seroconversion. *Annals of Internal Medicine, 122,* 573–579.

Mellors, J. W., Rinaldo, C. R., Gupta, P., White, R. M., Todd, J. A., & Kingsley, L. A. (1996). Prognosis in HIV-1 infection predicted by the quantity of virus in plasma. *Science, 272,* 1167–1170.

Mirin, S. M., Meyer, R. E., & McNamee, B. H. (1976). Psychopathology and mood during heroin use: Acute vs. chronic effects. *Archives of General Psychiatry, 33,* 1503–1508.

Misra, A. L. (1978). Metabolism of opiates. In M. L. Adler, L. Manara, & R. Samanin (Eds.), *Factors affecting the action of narcotics* (pp. 297–343). New York: Raven Press.

National Drug Control Strategy. (1995). *Strengthening communities' response to drugs and crime.* Washington, DC: Government Printing Office.

National Drug Control Strategy. (1997). Washington, DC: Government Printing Office.

Neil, A. (1984). Affinities of some common opioid analgesics towards four binding sites in mouse brain. *Naunyn-Schmeideberg's Archives of Pharmacology, 328,* 24–29

Nestler, E. J. (1992). Molecular mechanisms of drug addiction. *Journal of Neuroscience, 12,* 2439–2450.

Nestler, E. J. (1997). Basic neurobiology of opiate addiction. In S. M. Stine & T. R. Kosten (Eds.), *New treatments for opiate dependence.* New York: Guilford Press.

Nestler, E. J., Hope, B. T., & Widnell, K. L. (1993). Drug addiction: A model for the molecular basis of neural plasticity. *Neuron, 11,* 995–1006.

Nwanyanwu, O. C., Chu, S. Y., Green, T. A., Buehler, J. W., & Berkelman, R. L. (1993). Acquired immunodeficiency syndrome in the United States associated with injecting drug use, 1981–1991. *American Journal on Drug and Alcohol Abuse, 19*(4), 399–408.

O'Brien, W. A., Hartigan, P. M., Martin, D., Esinhart, J., Hill, A., Benoit, S., Rubin, M., Simberkoff, M. S., & Hamilton, J. D. (1996). Changes in plasma HIV-1 RNA and CD4++ lymphocyte counts and the risk of progression to AIDS. *New England Journal of Medicine, 334,* 426–431.

O'Connor, P. G., Samet, J. H., & Stein, M. D. (1994). Management of hospitalized intravenous drug users: Role of the internist. *American Journal of Medicine, 96,* 551–558.

O'Connor, P. G., Selwyn, P. A., & Schottenfeld, R. S. (1994). Medical care for injection-drug users with human immunodeficiency virus infection. *New England Journal of Medicine, 331*(7), 450–459.

Office of National Drug Control Policy (1991). *Pulse check: National trends in drug abuse.* Washington, DC: Executive Office of the President.

Pasternak, G. W. (1993). Pharmacological mechanisms of opioid analgesics. *Clinical Neuropharmacology, 16,* 1–18.

Pilcher, W. H., Joseph, S. A., & McDonald, J. V. (1988). Immunocyto chemical localization of pro-opiomelanocortin neurons in human brain areas subserving stimulation analgesia. *Journal of Neurosurgery, 68,* 621–629.

Rasmussen, K., & Aghajanian, G.K. (1989). Withdrawal-induced activation of locus coeruleus neurons in opiate-dependent rats: Attenuation by lesions of the nucleus paragigan to cellularis. *Brain Research, 505,* 346–350.

Rasmussen, K., Beitner-Johnson, D., Krystal, J. H., Aghajanian, G. K., & Nestler, E. J. (1990). Opiate withdrawal and the rat locus coeruleus: Behavioral, electrophysiological, and biochemical correlates. *Journal of Neuroscience, 10,* 2308–2317.

Redmond, D. E., Jr., & Huang, Y. H. (1982). The primate locus coeruleus and effects of clonidine on opiate withdrawal. *Journal of Clinical Psychiatry, 43*(6 Pt 2), 25–29.

Reisine, T., & Bell, G. I. (1993). Molecular biology of opioid receptors. *Trends in Neurosciences, 16,* 506–510.

Reisine, T., & Pasternak, G. (1996). Opioid analgesics and antagonists. In J. G. Hardman, A. Gilman, & L. E. Limbird (Eds.), *Pharmacological basis of therapeutics* (9th ed., pp. 521–557). New York: McGraw-Hill.

Rounsaville, B. J., Weissman, M. M., Chrits-Christoph, K., Wilber, C., & Kleber, H. D. (1982). Diagnosis and symptoms of depressions in opiate addicts. *Archives of General Psychiatry, 39,* 151–156.

Rounsaville, B. J., Weissman, M. M., Kleber, H. D., & Wilber, C. H. (1982). The heterogeneity of psychiatric diagnosis in treated opiate addicts. *Archives of General Psychiatry, 39,* 161–166.

Satel, S. L., Kosten, T. R., Schuckit, M. A., & Fischman, M. W. (1993). Should protracted withdrawal from drugs be included in DSM-IV. *American Journal of Psychiatry, 150,* 695–704.

Sawe, J., Dahlstrom, B., Paalzow, L., & Rane, A. (1981). Morphine kinetics in cancer patients. *Clinical Pharmacology and Therapeutics, 30,* 629–635.

Sawyer, R. C., Brown, L. S., Narong, P. G., & Li, R. (1993, June 6–11). Evaluation of a possible pharmacological interaction between rifampin and methadone in HIV seropositive injecting drug users. In *Abstracts of the Ninth International Conference on AIDS/Fourth STD World Congress,* (p. 501, abstract). Berlin, Germany. London: Wellcome Foundation.

Schwartz, E. L., Brechbuhl, A. B., Kahl, P., Miller, M.

H., Selwyn, P. A., & Friedland, G. H. (1990, June 20–24). Altered pharmacokinetics of zidovudine in former IV drug-using patients receiving methadone. In *Abstracts of the Sixth International Conference on AIDS,* San Francisco (Vol 3, p. 194, abstract). San Francisco: University of California.

Schwartz, E. L., Brechbuhl, A. B., Kahl, P., Miller, M. A., Selwyn, P. A., & Friedland, G. H.. (1992). Pharmocokinetics interactions of zidovudine and methadone in intravenous drug-using patient with HIV infection. *Journal of Acquired Immune Deficiency Syndromes, 5*(6), 619–626.

Self, D. W., & Nestler, E. J. (1995). Molecular mechanisms of drug reinforcement and addiction [Review]. *Annual Review Neuroscience, 18,* 463–495.

Selwyn, P. A., Budner, N. S., Wasserman, W. C., & Arno, P. S. (1993). Utilization of on-site primary care services by HIV-seropositive and seronegative drug users in a methadone maintenance program. *Public Health Report, 108,* 492–500.

Selwyn, P. A., Sckell, B. M., Alcabes, P., Friedland, G. H., Klein, R. S., & Schoenbaum, E. E. (1992). High risk of active tuberculosis in HIV-infected drug users with cutaneous anergy. *Journal of the American Medical Association, 268,* 504–509.

Senay, E. C., Dorus, W., Goldberg, F., & Thornton, W. (1977). Withdrawal from methadone maintenance: Rate of withdrawal and expectation. *Archives of General Psychiatry, 34,* 361–367.

Senay, E. C., Dorus, W., & Showalter, C. V. (1981). Short-term detoxification with methadone. *Annals of the New York Academy of Sciences, 362,* 203–216.

Shalala joins NIDA in concern over heroin use. (1997, December 5). *Psychiatric News,* p. 2.

Sharma. S. K., Klee, W. A., & Nirenberg, M. (1975). Dual regulation of adenylate cyclase accounts for narcotic dependence and tolerance. *Proceedings of the National Academy of Science USA, 72,* 3092–3096.

Silsby, H., & Tennant, F.S., Jr. (1974). Short-term, ambulatory detoxification of opiate addicts using methadone. *International Journal of the Addictions, 9*(1), 167–170.

Simmonds, P., Zhang, L. Q., Watson, H. G., Rebus, S., Ferguson, E. D., Balfe, P., Leadbetter, G. H., Yap, P. L., Peutherer, J. F., & Ludlam, C. A.. (1990). Hepatitis C quantification and sequencing in blood products, haemophiliacs, and drug users. *Lancet, 336,* 1469–1472.

Sorensen, J. L., Hargreaves, W. A., & Weinberg, J. A. (1982). Withdrawal from heroin in three or six weeks—comparison of methadylacetate and methadone. *Archives of General Psychiatry, 39,* 167–171.

Soumerai, S. B., Avorn, J., Gortmaker, S., & Hawley, S. (1987). Effect of government and commercial warnings on reducing prescription misuse: the case of propoxyphene. *American Journal of Public Health.* 77(12), 1518–1523.

Stimson, G. V. (1989). Syringe-exchange programmes for injecting drug users. *AIDS, 3,* 253–260.

Stine, S. M. (1997). New developments in methadone treatment and matching treatments to patient. In S. M. Stine & T. R. Kosten (Eds.), *New treatments for opiate dependence* (Vol. 3, pp. 121–172). New York: Guilford Press.

Stine, S. M., & Kosten, T. R. (1992). The use of drug combinations in treatment of opioid withdrawal. *Journal of Clinical Psychopharmacology, 12,* 203–209.

Stryker, J., & Smith, M. D. (1993). *Dimensions of HIV prevention: Needle exchange.* Menlo Park, CA: Henry J. Kaiser Family Foundation.

Syringe exchange programs—United States, 1994–1995. *Journal of the American Medical Association, 274*(16), 1260–1261.

Taylor, J. R., Lewis, V. O., Elsworth, J. D., Pivirotto, P., Roth, R. H., & Redmond Jr., D. E. (1991). Yohimbine co-treatment during chronic morphine administration attenuates naloxone-precipitated withdrawal without diminishing tail-flick analgesia in rats. *Psychopharmacology, 103,* 407–414.

Thomason, H. H., Jr., & Dilts, S. L. (1991). Opioids. In R. J. Frances & S. I. Miller (Eds.), *Clinical textbook of addictive disorders* (pp. 103–120). New York: Guilford Press.

Titus, K. (1996). Special consultation on syringe laws addresses epidemics, airs controversy. *Journal of the American Medical Association, 275*(21), 1621–1622.

Trujillo, K. A., & Akil, H. (1991). Inhibition of morphine tolerance and dependence by the NMDA receptor antagonist MD-801. *Science, 251,* 85–87.

Vining, E., Kosten, T. R., & Kleber, H. D. (1988). Clinical utility of rapid clonidine naltrexone detoxification for opioid abusers. *British Journal of Addictions,* 83, 567–575.

Watters, J. K., Estilo, M. J., Clark, G. L., & Lorvick, J. (1994). Syringe and needle exchange as HIV/AIDS prevention for injection drug users. *Journal of the American Medical Association, 271,* 115–120.

Weinberg, D. S., Inturrisi, C. E., Reidenberg, B., Moulin, D. W., Nip, T. J., Wallenstein, S., Houde, R. W., & Foley, K. M. (1988). Sublingual absorption of selected opioid analgesics. *Clinical Pharmacology and Therapeutics, 44,* 335–342.

Wilson, B. K., Elms, R. R., & Thomson, C. P. (1974). Low-dosage use of methadone in extended detoxification. *Archives of General Psychiatry, 31,* 233–236.

Wise, R. A. (1990). The role of reward pathways in the development of drug dependence. In D. J. K. Balfour (Ed.), *Psychotropic drugs of abuse* (pp. 23–57). Oxford: Pergamon Press.

Witters, W. L. (1992). Drug use: an introduction. In W. L. Witters, P. J. Venturelli, & G. R. Hanson (Eds.), *Drugs and society* (3rd ed.). Boston: Jones & Barlett.

9

Nicotine

John Slade

But for nicotine and addiction to it, tobacco products would very likely not be the public health menace they are. While other components of tobacco products and tobacco smoke are in the main responsible for the direct toxicity of tobacco, it is nicotine that keeps consumers interested in using. But for the enormous burden of illness and death that tobacco causes, nicotine dependence would very likely not be an important clinical entity.

As it is, though, the cigarette is the leading cause of preventable death, and nicotine is largely responsible for the high prevalence of its use. The high rate of tobacco use among people who use other dependence-producing drugs presents special concerns and challenges.

MAJOR PHARMACOLOGICAL ACTIONS

Metabolic Pathways

The nicotine molecule may exist as a salt or as a free base; the relative proportion of each species depends on the pH of the medium in which it is dissolved. The two are precisely equal in concentration at the somewhat alkaline pH of 8.0. Although dissolved salts of nicotine are not readily absorbed because they are ionized, the neutral free base freely crosses biological membranes. Available nicotine delivery devices present nicotine to the skin (patches), the nasal mucosa (nasal snuff and nasal spray), the oropharyngeal mucosa (cigars, pipe tobacco, spit tobacco, gum, inhaler), and the lower respiratory tract (cigarettes and cigars).

Nicotine is rapidly metabolized, mostly to cotinine and nicotine oxide (Henningfield, Cohen, & Pickworth, 1993). Most (85–90%) of the biotransformation occurs in the liver. (When nicotine is ingested orally, it is absorbed in the small intestine, but little reaches the systemic circulation because of first-pass metabolism in the liver.) Cotinine formation depends on the cytochrome P450 system (described in chapter 4). Most cotinine is further metabolized to other products.

Overall, only 5–10% of ingested nicotine is excreted unchanged. Total clearance of nicotine averages 1,300 ml/min of which only 200 ml/min is accomplished by the kidney. The balance (1,100 ml/min) is equal to about 70% of hepatic blood flow; since the liver is responsible for most of the disappearance of nicotine from the blood, this indicates that the liver takes up nicotine from the blood with about a 70% efficiency.

Nicotine has a half-life in the circulation of about 2 hr. This contributes to the peaks and valleys of nicotine levels seen in persons using tobacco products. For instance, with cigarettes, after an overnight abstinence, the venous level might be about 5 ng/ml. Over 6–8 hr of regular smoking, the level rises to between 20 and 40 ng/ml, a level punctuated by surges associated with the smoking of each cigarette (and, indeed, each puff). Overnight, the level falls again. While nicotine levels vary greatly over the course of a day, a regular smoker always has nicotine on board.

The half-life of cotinine is about 18–20 hr. This compound does not, then, show the acute cigarette-to-cigarette or puff-to-puff variation in level that nicotine does. However, the longer half-life of cotinine has made this compound useful as a marker for recent nicotine ingestion. Blood levels of cotinine in a smoker are on the order of 250 ng/ml. There is a useful relationship between the random level of cotinine in the blood and total daily nicotine dose (Benowitz, 1988). Multiplying the blood cotinine level by 0.12 provides an estimate of the amount of nicotine ingested over the previous 24 hr. Depending on how they are smoked, single cigarettes, across a wide range of FTC-rated, machine-measured nicotine deliveries, deliver between 1 and 3 mg of nicotine to the consumer (U.S. Department of Health and Human Services [USDHHS], 1988; NCI Expert Committee, 1996).

Actions in the Central Nervous System

Impacts on Neurotransmitter Systems

Two cholinergic agonists, nicotine from tobacco and muscarine from a species of *Amanita* mushroom, have long defined two basic types of biological receptor for acetylcholine. Receptors for nicotine are widely distributed in the body (Benowitz, 1996). They are found at the neuromuscular junction, in autonomic ganglia, and in the central nervous system. In the brain, nicotinic receptors are especially prominent in the cortex, thalamus, ventral tegmental area, interpeduncular nucleus, amygdala, septum, brain stem motor nuclei, and locus coeruleus. Neuronal nicotinic acetylcholine receptors have protein subunits designated α and β. Eight different varieties of α and three different varieties of β subunits are found in the brain, but the predominant combination in rat brain is $\alpha_4\beta_2$. Different receptors have varying affinities for nicotine and varying conductances for sodium and calcium. These differences may explain some of the diversity of action of nicotine.

Nicotinic receptors are present both on cell bodies and at nerve terminals and thus provide the potential for modulation of neural activity in a number of different ways. Stimulation of these receptors leads to release of a wide variety of neurotransmitters, including acetylcholine, norepinephrine, dopamine, serotonin, and β-endorphin. The hormones prolactin, growth hormone, and ACTH are also released by nicotine. Of note outside the CNS, nicotine stimulates the release of epinephrine and β-endorphin from the adrenal gland.

Mechanisms of Tolerance and Dependence

Nicotine both activates and desensitizes nicotinic cholinergic receptors (Benowitz, 1996). Desensitization may explain the rapid acquisition of tolerance (tachyphylaxis) seen with nicotine exposure and the upregulation of nicotinic cholinergic receptors characteristic of sustained exposure to nicotine.

Nicotine stimulates the release of dopamine from the mesolimbic system in the ventral tegmental area, projecting into the nucleus accumbens. This action is regarded as central to its reinforcing and dependence-producing effects and is similar to the action by which other addicting drugs such as cocaine and heroin affect this brain region.

CLINICAL ASPECTS

Preparations and Dosing

The nicotine market should be considered broadly (Warner, Slade, & Sweanor, 1997). While nicotine is usually consumed in the form of conventional tobacco products, other dosage forms are increasingly available, and novel tobacco products are under development and beginning to appear (table 9.1).[1] Nicotine delivery devices include conventional tobacco

TABLE 9.1 Nicotine Delivery Devices

Product	Route of nicotine absorption	Relative addictive potential	Relative toxicity
Traditional tobacco products			
Cigarette	Lung	4	4
Cigar	Mouth and lung	3	3
Pipe	Mouth and lung	3	3
Chewing tobacco and moist snuff	Mouth	3	3
Nicotine replacement products			
Gum	Mouth	1	1
Patch	Skin	0	1
Nasal spray	Nose	2	1
Inhaler	Mouth and throat	1	1
Novel tobacco products			
Eclipse	Lung	3	2
Tobacco gum	Mouth	1	1
Tobacco lozenge	Mouth	1	1

Note. The likely relative addictive potential and potential toxicity have been estimated for illustrative purposes by the author on a scale of 0 to 4. Eclipse is the brand name for a novel nicotine delivery device undergoing test marketing by the R. J. Reynolds Tobacco Company. The tobacco gum and tobacco lozenge referred to in the table are products under development by the Star Tobacco and Pharmaceutical Company.

products, medicinal forms of nicotine from pharmaceutical companies, and novel tobacco products. There are hundreds of different brands of nicotine delivery device on the market. Street names include *fag, cig, smoke, chew, dip, spit tobacco,* and *stogie.*

Tobacco products are, at root, devices for the delivery of nicotine (U.S. Food and Drug Administration [USFDA], 1996). There is now a wealth of evidence from previously secret files of tobacco product manufacturers that this has long been the view within the companies (Glantz, Slade, Bero, Hanauer, & Barnes, 1996).

Cigarette smoke is usually inhaled, and nicotine is absorbed in the lungs following inhalation. The acidity of cigarette smoke precludes absorption from the mouth, so inhalation is necessary for nicotine absorption (Slade, 1993). Inhalation has two important effects: With pulmonary absorption, the arterial level of nicotine rises very rapidly to levels of 80 ng/ml or more (Henningfield, London, & Benowitz, 1990), and inhalation exposes the lungs to all the other components of cigarette smoke, leading to more widespread distribution of these toxic materials than occurs with other forms of nicotine ingestion. The surges of nicotine reaching the brain following inhalation are thought to make the inhalation route more reinforcing than other routes of administration (Henningfield & Keenan, 1993).

Cigars are engineered to produce a more alkaline smoke than cigarettes, making oral absorption of cigar smoke possible. Testimony from cigar executives before Congress has indicated that the oral absorption of nicotine from cigar smoke is intended by the manufacturers (American Society of Addiction Medicine, 1995). However, many smokers of cigars also inhale the smoke; inhalation leads to rapid absorption of nicotine and widespread dissemination of numerous toxins and thus to adverse health effects which are similar to those from smoking cigarettes. Pipe tobaccos, while usually designed to produce alkaline smoke, may have a lower pH as well, which would require inhalation for nicotine delivery. Puffing, rather than inhaling, though, seems the more usual way of using pipes.

Oral tobaccos (such as chewing tobacco and moist snuff) are manufactured to facilitate nicotine absorption in the mouth. The manufacturers of moist snuff manipulate the pH of their products so that products that are widely used by novices have lower nicotine deliveries than products used by experienced dippers (Djordjevic, Hoffman, Glynn, & Connolly, 1995; Henningfield, Radzius, & Cone, 1995).

Nicotine replacement products are marketed as adjuncts for the management of nicotine dependence. However, it is not uncommon for people to use some of these products for prolonged periods of time (Warner et al., 1997). The use of those products that deliver nicotine in discrete doses (gum, nasal spray, inhaler) can become paired with internal or external cues. Thus, these nicotine delivery devices may be at least mildly reinforcing in and of themselves. There are no reports, however, of anything resembling a dependence syndrome associated with use of the nicotine patch, as would be expected, since there is no way for the consumer to modulate the slowly absorbed dose from the patch apart from applying or removing the product.

A variety of novel products is emerging that defy conventional categories. Eclipse is a device manufactured by R. J. Reynolds that resembles a cigarette but generates heat from a carbon fuel element and produces a nicotine-laden aerosol from papers made from tobacco and other materials. In use, the consumer inhales an aerosol that contains a substantial dose of nicotine but lower doses of the other materials than are found in most cigarettes (Slade, in press). Star Tobacco and Pharmaceuticals is developing a tobacco-containing gum and lozenge using leaf tobacco that has been treated to eliminate tobacco-specific nitrosamines. The company is testing its products and plans to submit them to the FDA for approval as therapeutic agents (Sears, 1997).

Both confusion and gaps in knowledge exist about the dose of nicotine that consumers of these various products actually ingest. The nicotine yield of cigarettes as measured on a machine has been the primary source of information available to consumers about nicotine dosing since the mid-1960s. These results, though, bear little relationship to the actual amounts of nicotine that consumers ingest (NCI Expert Committee, 1996) because, simply, people don't smoke like machines. They often take larger and more frequent puffs, and they often block the tiny ventilation holes that surround the filter of most cigarettes on the market, a behavior that results in more concentrated smoke being inhaled. The way smokers actually smoke increases the yields of their cigarettes from two- to fourfold (Djordjevic, Fan, Ferguson, & Hoffman, 1995). Moreover, there is little difference in the dose of nicotine people actually absorb across a broad range of brands having different FTC-rated nicotine yields (NCI Expert Committee, 1996). A relatively constant phenomenon, however, is the nicotine content of a cigarette. On average, each cigarette, regardless of brand or brand style, contains about 8–10 mg of nicotine (USDHHS, 1988).

The nicotine deliveries expected from cigars and moist snuff products vary considerably. Cigars exhibit a wide range of nicotine contents, in large part related to the great variety of sizes and weights of cigars (USDHHS, 1998). Moist snuff brands seem engineered to deliver nicotine at varying rates depending on the market niche for which particular brands are designed (Connolly, 1995; Slade, 1995; Tomar, Giovino, & Eriksen, 1995). While nicotine content is similar from brand to brand, the pH of the products varies enormously, which affects the rate at which nicotine can be absorbed in the mouth of a consumer. Starter products (e.g., Skoal Long Cut) deliver nicotine more slowly than products that are more often used by experienced, tolerant users (e.g., Copenhagen) (Djordjevic et al., 1995; Henningfield et al., 1995).

Unlike cigarettes, which are rated by supposed nicotine yield, nicotine gum is rated by nicotine content. The available dosage strengths, 2 mg and 4 mg, actually deliver less than half of these doses to the consumer. Unlike nicotine gum, nicotine patches are categorized by the delivered dose of nicotine over either 16 or 24 hr, depending on the brand (e.g., one brand offers patches in three sizes which deliver 7, 14, and 21 mg of nicotine over 24 hr, while another brand provides one size which delivers 15 mg over 16 hr). Nicotine nasal spray is labeled by the delivered dose of nicotine, 0.5 mg per activation of the spray device.

Physical Symptoms of Use, Abuse, and Dependence

Initial ingestion of nicotine is often an aversive experience. Nausea, headache, and a generalized feeling of being unwell are common initial impressions. Tolerance develops rapidly to these symptoms. With the regular use of tobacco products, nicotine ingestion is reinforced and often becomes compulsive. Nicotine ingestion becomes paired with an enormous range of internal and external cues, so that these cues become additional stimuli for more nicotine ingestion. Symptoms of dependence commonly occur prior to the onset of daily smoking (McNeill, West, Jarvis, Jackson, & Bryant, 1986).

Many find in the course of regular use that nicotine ingestion in the form of tobacco products facilitates relaxation and helps focus attention. Nicotine delivered in the form of the cigarette has effects on appetite and on metabolism. Regular use of cigarettes is associated with a modestly lower weight (6–8 lb) than that seen in an appropriate comparison group of never smokers. Adolescent females who smoke know this and often explain their smoking as part of their keeping on a diet. Nicotine gum has a tendency to suppress appetite as well. Tobacco use may suppress depressed mood. Cigarette smoking is more common among people who have a history of depression. Such people often have great difficulty quitting, and symptoms of depression may emerge during nicotine withdrawal. There are suggestions in the literature both that depression leads to smoking and that smoking leads to depression (Breslau, Peterson, Schultz, Chilcoat, & Andreski, 1998; Choi, Patten, Gillin, Kaplan, & Pierce, 1997).

In the doses usually ingested, nicotine does not cause intoxication. Thus, it can be used in many more settings than would be possible if it produced intoxication.

Symptoms and Course of Withdrawal

The symptoms of nicotine withdrawal that an individual manifests vary from person to person. The following phenomena are listed as having diagnostic importance in recognizing nicotine withdrawal in the *DSM-IV* (American Psychiatric Association, 1994): (a) dysphoric or depressed mood; (b) insomnia; (c) irritability; frustration, or anger; (d) anxiety; (e) difficulty concentrating; (f) restlessness; (g) decreased heart rate; and (h) increased appetite or weight gain. In addition to these, craving or urges to use tobacco are also symptoms of nicotine withdrawal.

Nicotine withdrawal begins with a few hours of the last dose of nicotine. It has a variable course, with clinical symptoms varying from days to weeks. One laboratory study found persistent abnormalities for the entire 10-day duration of the experiment (USDHHS, 1988). Patients often do not feel comfortable for weeks or even months after stopping. Like other withdrawal syndromes, nicotine withdrawal is a complex function of dose, set, and setting.

Pathological Effects

The adverse pathological effects of tobacco use are legion (London, Whelan, & Case, 1996). No other psychoactive substance causes as much illness and death. Overall, half of those who continue to smoke cigarettes will die prematurely as a direct result

(Doll, Peto, Wheatley, Gray, & Sutherland, 1994). About half of deaths from smoking occur in the middle years of life and half in the later years. Stopping smoking at any age reduces both morbidity and mortality from smoking.

In the United States, more than 400,000 persons die each year because of cigarettes; the risk of illness and death is strongly related to the amount and duration of use (USDHHS, 1989). Cigar use is a cause of cancers in the mouth and throat, and if cigar smoke is inhaled, the risks of lung cancer, emphysema, and fatal heart disease rise steeply (USDHHS, 1998). Smokeless tobacco causes a wide range of oral lesions, including cancer (USDHHS, 1986).

While most attention has been paid to lung cancer, heart disease, and chronic obstructive pulmonary disease (chronic bronchitis and emphysema), cigarettes cause many additional serious problems. Stroke and peripheral vascular disease, including aortic aneurysm, are caused by cigarettes. The occurrence of cancers of the mouth, throat, larynx, esophagus, pancreas, uterine cervix, and bladder are related to the cigarette. Poor wound healing, reduced fertility, impotence, earlier age at menopause, increased risk of osteoporosis, cataracts, and peptic ulcer disease are some of the other robust associations with cigarette use (London et al., 1996).

Adverse pregnancy outcomes have long been known to be caused by maternal cigarette use. Placenta previa and placental abruption are both related to maternal smoking. Low birth weight, with its attendant increased risk of illness and death, is more common in this group of infants. The risk of SIDS is high among infants exposed to tobacco smoke both in utero and postnatally (California Environmental Protection Agency, 1997).

The precise role that nicotine itself plays in producing these effects is not known. Nicotine is not a carcinogen, but it has cardiovascular effects, including effects on heart rate and blood pressure. However, nicotine does not appear to be responsible for many of the phenomena associated with atherogenesis from smoking (Benowitz & Gourlay, 1997), and the ingestion of nicotine in forms other than the cigarette and the cigar are, by and large, not associated with cardiac complications.

Nicotine itself is suspected of being causally related to adverse pregnancy outcomes (Oncken, in press) and to the occurrence of SIDS (Slotkin, Lappi, McCook, Lorber, & Seidler, 1995).

Psychological, Including Affective and Cognitive Effects

While nicotine is usually regarded as a drug with few or no negative psychological effects, a number of phenomena suggest that nicotine may not be free of negative effects. A large literature exists on performance effects related to tobacco use. Unfortunately, much of this literature compares deprived with undeprived smokers (Heishman, Taylor, & Henningfield, 1994). Moreover, the tasks employed have tended not to be as complex as tasks in daily life. Overall, the data are clear that smoking reverses decrements in performance associated with withdrawal. However, there is as yet no clear indication that smoking actually enhances performance. Using appropriate controls, Spilich, June, and Renner (1992) have shown that smoking is associated with impaired performance on several cognitive tests, including a reading comprehension test and a driving simulation. These results are congruent with epidemiological data indicating that people who smoke are at increased risk of experiencing automobile crashes compared to appropriate controls, a result which is not explained by distractions caused by manipulating cigarettes (DiFranza, Winters, Goldberg, Cirillo, & Biliouris, 1986).

Many who use tobacco explain their use as a way of coping with stress. Indeed, an increase in stressful feelings accompanies many attempts to withdraw from tobacco use. However, people who smoke are, at baseline, under a higher level of self-perceived stress than those who do not smoke. After quitting, people feel under less stress (Parrott, 1998). Thus, it may be that, as with alcohol, smoking induces some of the adverse affective symptoms which users believe their use of tobacco relieves.

People addicted to other drugs, including alcohol, are about three times more likely than those without other drug problems to smoke cigarettes: The prevalence of smoking in this population is in the range of 60–80% (Hurt, Eberman, Slade, & Karan, 1993). In animal studies, cross-tolerance has been demonstrated between alcohol and nicotine (Dar, Li, & Bowman, 1993). Stuyt has suggested a possible mechanism for the interaction (Stuyt, 1997). In a follow-up study of people treated for drug dependence, relapse rates were substantially lower among persons who did not use tobacco if the other drug problem was either alcohol or heroin. Among cocaine users, however, relapse rates were the same regardless of tobacco use. Since nicotine is, primarily, a stimulant, it may be that nicotine facilitates the abuse of depressant drugs such as alcohol and heroin while having no effect on the abuse of another stimulant, cocaine.

Social and Interpersonal Effects

Tobacco smoke is a cause of illness and death in nonsmokers (California Environmental Protection Agency, 1997; Hackshaw, Law, & Wald, 1997; Howard et al., 1998; Law, Morris, & Wald, 1997; U.S. Environmental Protection Agency, 1992). In adults, environmental tobacco smoke (ETS) is a cause of lung cancer and heart disease, leading to as many as 50,000 deaths in the United States each year (Glantz & Parmley, 1995). ETS makes asthma and other respiratory conditions worse. Among children, ETS is a cause of otitis media, bronchitis, and pneumonia.

The evidence that ETS is harmful to nonsmokers is compelling. Unlike pollution problems such as those of asbestos and radon, for which most of the evidence of serious environmental hazard involves extrapolations from high dose exposures, ETS is known to be harmful both from studies of high dose exposures (among smokers) and from a wealth of studies at the actual levels of exposure of nonsmokers. Moreover, the problem is enormous because of the widespread exposure nonsmokers have to ETS. Although only about 25% of adults smoke in the United States, nearly 40% of children live in a household in which at least one person smokes.

Smoking by others is a factor in taking up smoking (USDHHS, 1994), and smoking by others is a common precipitant of relapse for those who have recently stopped (USDHHS, 1990).

SUMMARY

Nicotine stimulates nicotinic cholinergic receptors in the body. Within the brain, responsive receptors are found in many locations, including in the ventral tegmental area. Tolerance and dependence result from repeated ingestion of nicotine from tobacco products. Tobacco product use regularly leads to serious health problems for both users and nonsmokers exposed to tobacco smoke. While nicotine itself is addicting and has a variety of other pharmacological properties, it is probably not directly responsible for most of the harm tobacco products cause. This fact makes it possible to use nicotine in medicinal forms in the treatment of nicotine dependence.

Note

1. The designations of relative addictive potential and relative toxicity presented in table 9.1 are estimates by the author.

Key References

Benowitz, N. L. (1996). Pharmacology of nicotine: Addiction and therapeutics. *Annual Review of Pharmacology and Toxicology, 36,* 597–613.

Slade, J. (1993). Nicotine delivery devices. In C. T. Orleans & J. Slade (Eds.), *Nicotine addiction: Principles and management* (pp. 3–23). New York: Oxford University Press.

Warner, K. E., Slade, J., & Sweanor, D. T. (1997). The emerging market for long-term nicotine maintenance. *JAMA, 278,* 1087–1092.

References

American Psychiatric Association. (1994). *Diagnostic and statistical manual of mental disorders* (4th ed.). Washington, DC: Author.

American Society of Addiction Medicine. (1995). *Submission to the Food and Drug Administration: Comments for Docket No. 95N-0253J and 95N-0253.* Chevy Chase, MD: American Society of Addiction Medicine.

Benowitz, N. L. (1988). Pharmacologic aspects of cigarette smoking and nicotine addiction. *New England Journal of Medicine, 319,* 1318–1330.

Benowitz, N. L. (1996). Pharmacology of nicotine: Addiction and therapeutics. *Annual Review of Pharmacology and Toxicology, 36,* 597–613.

Benowitz, N. L., & Gourlay, S. G. (1997). Cardiovascular toxicity of nicotine: Implications for nicotine replacement therapy. *Journal of the American College of Cardiology, 29,* 1422–1431.

Breslau, N., Peterson, E. L., Schultz, L. R., Chilcoat, H. D., & Andreski, P. (1998). Major depression and stages of smoking. *Archives of General Psychiatry, 55,* 161–166.

California Environmental Protection Agency. (1997). *Health effects of exposure to environmental tobacco smoke.* California Environmental Protection Agency, Office of Environmental Health Hazard Assessment.

Choi, W. S., Patten, C. A., Gillin, J. C., Kaplan, R. M., & Pierce, J. P. (1997). Cigarette smoking predicts development of depressive symptoms among U.S. adolescents. *Annals of Behavioral Medicine, 19,* 42–50.

Connolly, G. N. (1995). The marketing of nicotine addiction by one oral snuff manufacturer. *Tobacco Control, 4,* 73–79.

Dar, M. S., Li, C., & Bowman, E. R. (1993). Central behavioral interactions between ethanol, (-)-nicotine, and (-)-cotinine in mice. *Brain Research Bulletin, 32,* 23–28.

DiFranza, J. R., Winters, T. H., Goldberg, R. J., Cirillo, L., & Biliouris, T. (1986). The relationship of smoking to motor vehicle accidents and traffic violations. *New York State Journal of Medicine, 86,* 464–467.

Djordjevic, M. V., Fan, J., Ferguson, S., & Hoffman, D. (1995). Self-regulation of smoking intensity: Smoke yields of the low-nicotine, low-"tar" cigarettes. *Carcinogenesis, 16,* 2015–2021.

Djordjevic, M. V., Hoffman, D., Glynn, T., & Connolly, G. N. (1995). US commercial brands of moist snuff, 1994: 1. Assessment of nicotine, moisture, and pH. *Tobacco Control, 4,* 62–65.

Doll, R., Peto, R., Wheatley, K., Gray, R., & Sutherland, I. (1994). Mortality in relation to smoking: 40 years' observations on male British doctors. *British Medical Journal, 309,* 901–911.

Glantz, S. A., & Parmley, W. W. (1995). Passive smoking and heart disease mechanisms and risk. *JAMA, 273,* 1047–1053.

Glantz, S. A., Slade J., Bero, L. A., Hanauer, P., & Barnes, D. E. (1996). *The cigarette papers.* Berkeley: University of California Press.

Hackshaw, A. K., Law, M. R., & Wald, N. J. (1997). The accumulated evidence on lung cancer and environmental tobacco smoke. *British Medical Journal, 315,* 980–988.

Heishman, S. J., Taylor, R. C., & Henningfield, J. E. (1994). Nicotine and smoking: A review of the effects on human performance. *Experimental and Clinical Psychopharmacology, 2,* 345–395.

Henningfield, J. E., Cohen, C., & Pickworth, W. B. (1993). Psychopharmacology of nicotine. In C. T. Orleans & J. Slade (Eds.), *Nicotine addiction: Principles and management* (pp. 24–45). New York: Oxford University Press.

Henningfield, J. E., & Keenan, R. M. (1993). Nicotine delivery kinetics and abuse liability. *Journal of Consulting and Clinical Psychology, 61,* 743–750.

Henningfield, J. E., London, E. D., & Benowitz, N. L. (1990). Arterial-venous differences in plasma concentrations of nicotine after cigarette smoking. *JAMA, 263,* 2049–2050.

Henningfield, J. E., Radzius, A., & Cone, E. J. (1995). Estimation of available nicotine content of six smoke-less tobacco products. *Tobacco Control, 4*, 57–61.

Howard, G., Wagenknecht, L. E., Burke, G. L., Diez-Roux, A., Evans, G. W., et al. (1998). Cigarette smoking and progression of atherosclerosis: The atherosclerosis risk in communities (ARIC) study. *JAMA, 279*, 119–124.

Hurt, R. D., Eberman, K. M., Slade, J., & Karan, L. (1993). Treating nicotine addiction in patients with other addictive disorders. In C. T. Orleans & J. Slade (Eds.), *Nicotine addiction: Principles and management* (pp. 310–326). New York: Oxford University Press.

Law, M. D., Morris, J. K., & Wald, N. J. (1997). Environmental tobacco smoke exposure and ischaemic heart disease: An evaluation of the evidence. *British Medical Journal, 315*, 973–980.

London, W. M., Whelan, E. M., & Case, A. G. (Eds.). (1996). *Cigarettes: What the warning label doesn't tell you.* New York: American Council on Science and Health.

McNeill, A. D., West, R., Jarvis, M., Jackson, P., & Bryant, A. (1986). Cigarette withdrawal symptoms in adolescent smokers. *Psychopharmacology, 90*, 533–536.

NCI Expert Committee. (1996). *The FTC cigarette test method for determining tar, nicotine, and carbon monoxide yields of U.S. cigarettes.* (NIH Publication No. 96-4028). U.S. Department of Health and Human Services, Public Health Service, National Institutes of Health, National Cancer Institute.

Oncken, C. A. (in press). Toxicity and pharmacodynamic effects of nicotine during pregnancy. In R. Ferrence, M. Pope, R. Room, & J. Slade (Eds.), *Nicotine and public health.* Washington, DC: American Public Health Association.

Parrott, A. C. (1998). Nesbitt's paradox resolved? Stress and arousal modulation during cigarette smoking. *Addiction, 93*, 27–39.

Sears, S. P., Jr. (1997). Letter of 4 September to U.S. Senator Patrick Leahy. Petersburg, VA: Star Tobacco & Pharmaceuticals.

Slade, J. (1993). Nicotine delivery devices. In C. T. Orleans & J. Slade (Eds.), *Nicotine addiction: Principles and management* (pp. 3–23). New York: Oxford University Press.

Slade, J. (1995). Are tobacco products drugs? Evidence from US Tobacco. *Tobacco Control, 4*, 1–2.

Slade, J. (in press). Innovative nicotine delivery devices. In R. Ferrence, M. Pope, R. Room, & J. Slade (Eds.), *Nicotine and public health.* Washington, DC: American Public Health Association.

Slotkin, T. A., Lappi, S. E., McCook, E. C., Lorber, B. A., & Seidler, F. J. (1995). Loss of neonatal hypoxia tolerance after prenatal nicotine exposure: Implications for sudden infant death syndrome. *Brain Research Bulletin, 38*, 69–75.

Spilich, G. J, June, L., & Renner, J. (1992). Cigarette smoking and cognitive performance. *British Journal of Addiction, 87*, 113–126.

Stuyt, E. B. (1997). Recovery rates after treatment for alcohol/drug dependence. *American Journal on Addictions, 6*, 159–167.

Tomar, S. L., Giovino, G. A., & Eriksen, M. P. (1995). Smokeless tobacco brand preference and brand switching among US adolescents and young adults. *Tobacco Control, 4*, 67–72.

U.S. Department of Health and Human Services. (1986). *The health consequences of using smokeless tobacco: A report of the Advisory Committee to the Surgeon General.* (NIH Publication No. 86-2874). U.S. Department of Health and Human Services, Public Health Service, National Institutes of Health.

U.S. Department of Health and Human Services. (1988). *The health consequences of smoking: Nicotine addiction—A report of the Surgeon General.* (DHHS Publication No. (CDC) 88-8406). U.S. Department of Health and Human Services, Public Health Service, Centers for Disease Control, Center for Health Promotion and Education, Office on Smoking and Health.

U.S. Department of Health and Human Services. (1989). *Reducing the health consequences of smoking: 25 years of progress—A report of the Surgeon General.* (DHHS Publication No. (CDC) 89-8411). U.S. Department of Health and Human Services, Public Health Service, Centers for Disease Control, Center for Chronic Disease Prevention and Health Promotion, Office on Smoking and Health.

U.S. Department of Health and Human Services. (1990). *The health benefits of smoking cessation: A report of the Surgeon General.* (DHHS Publication No. (CDC) 90-8416). U.S. Department of Health and Human Services, Public Health Service, Centers for Disease Control, Center for Chronic Disease Prevention and Health Promotion, Office on Smoking and Health.

U.S. Department of Health and Human Services. (1994). *Preventing tobacco use among young people: A report of the Surgeon General.* U.S. Department of Health and Human Services, Public Health Service, Centers for Disease Control and Prevention, National Center for Chronic Disease Prevention and Health Promotion, Office on Smoking and Health.

U.S. Department of Health and Human Services. (1998). *Cigars: Health effects and trends—Smoking and Health Monograph 9.* D. Burns, K. M. Cumming, & D. Hoffman (Eds.). U.S. Department of

Health and Human Services, Public Health Service, National Institutes of Health. (NIH Publication No. 98-4302)

U.S. Environmental Protection Agency. (1992). *Respiratory health effects of passive smoking: Lung cancer and other disorders.* (EPA/600/6-90/006F). U.S. Environmental Protection Agency, Office of Research and Development, Office of Health and Environmental Assessment.

U.S. Food and Drug Administration. (1996). Nicotine in cigarettes and smokeless tobacco is a drug and these products are nicotine delivery devices under the federal Food, Drug and Cosmetic Act: Jurisdictional determination. *Federal Register 61:* 44619–45318.

Warner, K. E., Slade, J., & Sweanor, D. T. (1997). The emerging market for long-term nicotine maintenance. *JAMA, 278,* 1087–1092.

10

Other Drugs of Abuse:
Inhalants, Designer Drugs, and Steroids

Robert Pandina

Robert Hendren

Typically, substances included in a general drug class are comparable on many, if not all, basic parameters, including chemical structure, mechanisms of action, and metabolic pathways, as well as physiological, psychological, and behavioral effects. In fact, commonalities along such parametric dimensions are clearly evident among the classes of drug of abuse discussed in the preceding chapters of this volume (e.g., opiates, stimulants, hallucinogens, sedatives).

This chapter focuses upon three broad and somewhat anomalous drug "classes." Each of these "other" drug classes is anomalous for different reasons. Even the characterization and nomenclature of inhalants, designer drugs, and steroids are derived from different roots. For example, inhalant (IH) commonalities include their volatile nature and gaseous properties—hence, a common route of administration. The substances often subsumed under the rubric of inhalants are widely disparate on many other basic parameters, including chemical structure.

Of the classes to be discussed in this chapter, anabolic-androgenic steroids are the most traditional in terms of commonalities. This chapter limits discussion to the general characteristics of those dozen or so anabolic-androgenic steroids (AASs) that are taken illicitly for their equivocal anabolic utilitarian effects, that is, their purported ability to enhance muscle mass. Even so, discussion of this drug class is somewhat problematic. Significantly, several authorities (e.g., Cicero & O'Connor, 1990) have questioned the notion that AASs adequately meet the standard criteria (e.g., use intentions, evidence of psychological or physiological dependence) for classification as abused drugs. Others suggest such a role can be demonstrated (e.g., Brower, 1993a).

Designer drugs (DDs) have as a common property the fact that, typically, they are created purposefully in the laboratory for specific effects, capitalizing on the same general technology and strategy employed in crafting psychotropic medications. Often, such drugs are derivations of existing drugs. Designer drugs are often touted as "new and improved" versions of parent compounds, claiming elimination of unwanted "side effects" (e.g., bad "trips") or enhanced main effects (e.g., effect duration). They are often employed by the "recreational" user for purposes never intended by their creators. This chapter will present an overview of the prototype designer drug MDMA (3,4-methylenedioxymethamphetamine), known on the street as *ecstasy*, and will comment on others often referred to as designer drugs.

These three anomalous drug classes are often subsumed along with other low-use-frequency substances under the dreaded "other drug" use category or are aggregated within global classes in summary reports. Furthermore, a given aggregated class (e.g., inhalants, hallucinogens) often subsumes drugs widely disparate in terms of use profiles, consequences, and other important parameters. Use patterns for such drug classes may be reported as aggregated data and are treated as low-frequency events, receiving relatively sparse analytic treatment even when more detailed information is gathered. The result is that sometimes it is difficult to conduct finer grained analyses of use patterns, consequences, and risk factor profiles for these drugs. Other circumstances hamper our understanding of salient dimensions associated with other drugs of abuse. For example, use of these other drugs tends to fluctuate somewhat rapidly (e.g., ecstasy). Use prevalence is relatively low and often confined to certain difficult-to-access, "hidden" subpopulations (e.g., steroid use among athletes, inhalant use among Hispanic and Native American youth in rural areas or on reservations), and use, when it occurs, may be erratic.

In spite of the relatively low prevalence, idiosyncratic use patterns, and difficulties associated with studying these substances, the consequences of inhalant, designer drug, and anabolic steroid use for the individual user and for society at large represent serious public health problems that warrant the attention of the clinical and scientific communities. What does unite these three classes is the fact that they tend to be substances of choice among adolescents and young adults. Further, use of these drugs is accompanied by serious health consequences.

Given the limitations of space and the range of information available, coverage of each substance category is far from encyclopedic. This chapter attempts to summarize basic information regarding these substance categories. Where possible, we will identify references that provide more complete coverage of certain topics.

INHALANT ABUSE

Clinical Aspects and Epidemiology

Inhalants (also called *solvents* and *volatile substances*) are a chemically diverse group of abused psychoactive substances found in volatile solvents. Inhalant abuse involves a wide variety of substances, including gasoline, glue, solvents, spray paints, aerosols, and thinners, which contain a wide spectrum of chemicals (hydrocarbons, nitrites, ketones, toluene esters). (See table 10.1.) Vasodilators such as amyl or butyl nitrate and general anesthetics are also abused inhalants but are considered as separate substances of abuse (Dinwiddie, 1994; Johnston, O'Malley, & Bachman, 1996). Inhalation of commercial contact cement containing n-hexanes and spray paints containing toluene and gasoline is popular, particularly because of the euphoric effect, availability, and relatively low cost.

Availability and ease of procurement appear to be the primary reasons inhalants are abused and ac-

TABLE 10.1 Common Inhalants

Aerosols
   Spray paint
   Hair spray
   Deodorant, air freshener
   Analgesic spray, asthma spray

Solvents and Gases
   Paint thinner and remover
   Typing correction fluid "white-out"
   Gasoline
   Cigarette lighter fluid
   Nail polish remover
   Bottled fuel gas
   Felt-tipped markers

Adhesives
   Airplane glue
   Contact cement

Cleaning agents
   Dry-cleaning fluid
   Spot remover
   Degreaser "STP"

count for the greater prevalence among disadvantaged youth (Fornazzari, Wilkinson, Kapur, & Carlen, 1983). Particularly vulnerable are those who live in areas where other substances of abuse are not readily available (e.g., rural areas, reservations).

The annual High School Senior Drug Use Survey (Johnston et al., 1996) indicates that while the overall use of inhalants peaked in 1979, solvent abuse per se has actually been increasing. In 1995, inhalant use in the past year had been reported by about 13% of 8th-graders, 10% of 10th-graders, and 8% of 12th-graders. Estimates may be conservative due to underreporting and the probability that solvent-abusing youth have dropped out of school by the 12th grade. The lifetime prevalence rate was about 22%, 19%, and 17% respectively for 8th, 10th, and 12th graders. Inhalant use tends to occur at relatively young ages and decreases in late adolescence. However, amyl and butyl nitrates ("poppers" or "whippettes") are used as purported sexual enhancers by some adults (particularly those in the gay community). Nitrous oxide ("laughing gas") is difficult to obtain. Much of the reported use of this anesthetic agent can be attributed to the mislabeling of amyl or butyl nitrates. Inhalant users may sample a wide variety of these products (Rosenberg & Sharp, 1992) and use other drugs and alcohol (Beauvais, 1992; Oetting & Webb, 1992).

Studies of selected populations suggest that prevalence may be higher among Mexican-Americans and Native Americans, especially those living in impoverished environments (characterized by economic disadvantages, disorganized family structures, high levels of crime, social isolation, etc.). However, considerable variability among Hispanic and Native American ethnic groups has been noted (Beauvais, 1992; May, 1988; Oetting & Beauvais, 1990; Tapia-Conyer, Cravioto, De La Rosa, & Velez, 1995).

A relationship between inhalant abuse and delinquency has been suggested. The relationship may be strongest among Hispanics from large, poor, and disrupted families with siblings who are also inhalant abusers (Reed & May, 1984). Among delinquents, inhalant abusers tend to be more criminally involved as measured by the number and violent nature of their offenses.

The hidden and highly variable nature of inhalant-using groups makes definitive characterization most difficult. It is likely that low cost, universal availability, ease of access, and local custom are factors as important as ethnicity in determining user profiles.

Metabolic Pathways and Mechanisms of Action

Inhalants are "sniffed" from an open container or plastic bag or "huffed" from a rag soaked in the substance ("toques") and placed near or on the nose and mouth. Abusers may prefer one inhalant to another but commonly use a variety of agents depending on availability and potency. For instance, gold and silver spray paint are preferred over other colors because the greater weight of gold and silver molecules requires a larger amount of toluene propellant.

Inhalants are absorbed rapidly into the blood supply through the rich capillary surface of the lungs. Peak concentrations are reached within minutes, and effects last about 5–15 min. Hydrocarbons are the chief chemicals of inhalants. They are rapidly taken into fat stores, including lipids in the central nervous system, making accurate measurement of blood levels difficult. The mechanism of action may involve the fluidization of cell membranes. The GABA-A receptor complex appears to be the primary target of most inhalants. Effects are mediated through control of ion channels. Metabolism and excretion are variable for different compounds. Inhalant degradation and elimination are accomplished by the lungs, kidneys, and liver.

Inhalant intoxication resembles alcohol intoxication, with initial stimulation and euphoria followed by depression. Onset of effects is rapid and intense. Visual, auditory, and tactile distortions may develop into hallucinations with higher dosage. Giddiness, staggering gait, disinhibition, nausea, vomiting, headache, double vision, ringing in the ears, and palpitations may occur with flushing, coughing, and excessive salivation. Users may have an odor of paint or solvents, discolored hands and nose from paint, and a rash around the nose and mouth (Dinwiddie, 1994).

Tolerance appears to develop, as does withdrawal. The withdrawal period lasts from 2 to 5 days; it is unclear what is the intensity of exposure (either duration or dosage) that results in withdrawal. Symptoms include sleep disturbance, tremors, irritability, rapid respiration, nausea, and discomfort in the abdomen and chest.

Biological, Psychological, and Behavioral Consequences of Inhalant Use

The consequences of inhalant abuse are thought to be grim, but there are few studies of long-term sequelae or of the relationship of the duration and extent of abuse to the extent and duration of the damage. One important reason is the difficulty in designing a study that can control for the majority of significant and potentially confounding variables. While it is generally accepted that emotional problems and social deprivation precede inhalant abuse, the long-term effects of solvent abuse on the emotional and cognitive functioning of solvent-abusing youth are not known.

Inhalant abuse has been linked to sudden death, usually due to heart failure, referred to as *sudden sniffing death syndrome*. In addition, there is chronic damage to the heart, lungs, kidneys, liver, and peripheral nerves related to the specific chemicals found in the inhalant. There also are risks from handling volatile substances. Between 1981 and 1990, 605 children reportedly died from the misuse of volatile substances. The largest single cause of death was misuse of butane gas lighter refills (Esmail, Meyer, Pottier, & Wright, 1993). Suffocation can occur when a plastic bag is used for delivery of the inhalant.

Neurological abnormalities include pyramidal, cerebellar, and brain stem dysfunctions including functional and, to a lesser extent, structural changes (Fornazzari et al., 1983; Rosenberg, Sptiz, Filley, Davis, & Schaumburg, 1988). Cerebellar abnormalities are likely to be seen with severe and prolonged abuse and therefore are more likely to occur in young adults than in children (Ron, 1986).

Neuroimaging studies clearly suggest that solvent abuse may affect brain function. Methodological difficulties, discussed below, preclude firm conclusions. CT scans have demonstrated cerebral cortical or cerebellar atrophy, including widening of sulci and enlargement of the ventricular system (Shickler, Seitz, Rice, & Strader, 1982). Further, these structural anomalies were significantly related to neuropsychological deficits in concentration, attention, memory, and motor coordination (Fornazzari et al., 1983).

Chronic toluene abuse has been demonstrated to result in MRI-documented anomalies (atrophy and loss of differentiation) in cerebral, cerebellar, brain stem, periventricular, and thalamic sites (Escobar & Aruffo, 1980; Rosenberg et al., 1988; Xiong, Matthews, Li, & Jinkins, 1993). Severe and prolonged abuse may be related to frequency of anomalies in some sites (e.g., cerebellum) (Ron, 1986). Not all subjects studied exhibited MRI abnormalities. When anomalies are detected, some recovery occurs, although signs may persist for some time (e.g., up to 18 months) (King, Day, Oliver, Lush, & Watson, 1981).

Myelin is thought to be severely affected by solvents and inhalants in developing brains (Escobar & Aruffo, 1980; Wiggins, 1986). White matter hyperintensities in the cerebrum, brain stem, and cerebellum are reported in chronic toluene abusers (Yamanouchi et al., 1995). Myelin changes have also been found to persist for up to 18 months after abstinence (Rosenberg et al., 1988). The degree of white matter abnormality found in chronic toluene abusers is found to correlate with neuropsychological impairment (Filley, Heaton, & Rosenberg, 1990).

Poor performance on neuropsychological tests measuring concentration, attention, visual perceptual abilities, learning skills, and memory is found in chronic toluene abusers (Fornazzari, 1990; Zur & Yule, 1990a). The extent of cognitive decline appears to be related to the severity of cerebral white matter involvement (Filley et al., 1990; Katzelnick, Davar, & Scanlon, 1991). However, differences between inhalant abusers and well-matched controls are often not found to be significant (Jansen, Richter, & Griesel, 1992), especially when young abusers are tested after several weeks of abstinence, and when socioeconomic status is taken into account (Chadwick & Anderson, 1989).

Numerous limitations in the available studies make it difficult to judge whether consistent neuropsychological deficits are present in solvent abusers and whether the deficits are transient or permanent (Ron, 1986). In a thorough review, Chadwick and Anderson (1989) noted problems consequent to small sample sizes, absence of data on prior performance, lack of evidence for abstinence, and insufficient control for group differences that could be due to effects other than substance abuse (e.g., SES and delinquency). Other shortcomings include lack of differentiation between acute and chronic effects, questionable validity of measures of the dysfunction, and sociocultural confounds (Tenenbein, 1992). It is also uncertain whether the deficits are best explained as the direct effect of solvent abuse or by factors such as background, social disadvantages, or history of delinquency.

Evidence for preexisting personality traits that predispose to inhalant abuse is not clear from the literature to date. One study suggests that the initiation of inhalant use is associated with a sensation-seeking trait (Morita et al., 1994). This is consistent with the finding that inhalant abusers are over five times more likely than nonabusers to have injected drugs even after statistical adjustments for sex, age, socioeconomic status, and the use of marijuana (Schutz, Chilcoat, & Anthony, 1994).

Solvent abuse is found to occur more frequently in emotionally disturbed and depressed youth than in the general population (Skuse & Burrell, 1982). Other studies find depression to be more common in toluene abusers than in young delinquents used as controls (Zur & Yule, 1990b). In populations of drug and alcohol abusers, those who abuse solvents appear to have more severely disturbed personalities, but there is little evidence that specific or persistent psychiatric disability either causes or results directly from solvent abuse (Ron, 1986).

As mentioned previously, a strong relationship exists between inhalant abuse and juvenile delinquency, with more criminal and violent offenses among solvent-abusing delinquents (Reed & May, 1984). Solvent abuse in young adulthood is strongly associated with antisocial personality disorder and polysubstance abuse (Crites & Schuckit, 1979; Dinwiddie, 1994; Dinwiddie, Reich, & Cloninger, 1991). However, there are no conclusive findings regarding whether psychiatric symptoms precede or result from solvent abuse in youth. Identification of particular patterns of psychiatric disorders and whether they precede, are exacerbated by, or are the result of solvent abuse will be helpful in prevention and intervention planning.

ANABOLIC-ANDROGENIC STEROIDS

Clinical Aspects and Epidemiology

Anabolic-androgenic steroids (hereafter referenced as AASs, steroids, or "roids") are derivatives of, or synthetically modeled after, testosterone, a prototypical androgen that is produced naturally in the testes by males. This androgen has two primary effects. Androgenic effects account for the development of the male reproductive tract, other aspects of sexual differentiation (including central nervous system development), and associated characteristics (e.g., differentiation and growth of genitalia, stimulation of hair growth, enhancement of libido and sexual potency), that is, so-called virilizing or masculinizing actions. Anabolic effects contribute to linear body growth and the development of body mass.

A broader role for androgens in central nervous system (CNS) functioning and behavioral and psychological processes under CNS regulation has been claimed, including modulation of aggression and mood. AASs have several valid though limited medical uses, including limited treatment of asthma and specific anemias, control of metastatic breast cancer, and augmentation of sexual development in hypogonadal males (see also American Medical Association, 1990; Kochakian, 1993). However, it is the latter anabolic effects that have apparently resulted in the current patterns of illicit use, prompting continuing concern in clinical, scientific, and sporting communities. Particularly important is the view that lean body mass and strength can be significantly enhanced. There is additionally some credence to reports that increased intensity in training and increased aggressivity in competitive sports venues (e.g., football, track and field) are not unwanted side benefits of AAS use. In the user community, the most popular "roids" are touted for their anabolic activity, hence the emphasis on the terminology *anabolic steroids*. Nevertheless, all AASs appear to retain some androgenic actions, most of which are viewed negatively by illicit roid users. In fact, a substantial aspect of the marketplace attempts to capitalize on the purported "pure" anabolic actions of new derivatives as they become available.

There are estimated to be over 100 different compounds claimed to have anabolic actions (Nuwer, 1990). Table 10.2 (after Strauss & Yesalis, 1991) lists a sample of the more commonly used AASs; trade and generic names are listed. Steroid preparations come in two forms for administration: oral and parenteral (typically by intramuscular injection). Oral preparations are derived principally from 17-alpha-methyl, 17-alpha-ethyl, and 1-methyl testosterone derivatives; intramuscular preparations are typically esters of testosterone or esters of 19-nortestosterone (Haupt & Rovere, 1984; Kochakian, 1993).

Popular attention began to focus upon steroid use during the early 1960s, when the success of Soviet strength athletes was attributed, in part, to the use of AASs. Haupt and Rovere (1984) and Kochakian

TABLE 10.2 Trade Names and Dosages of Commonly Used Anabolic Steroids

Oral anabolic steroids	Dosages	Injectable anabolic steroids	Dosages
Anadrol (oxymetholone)	1–5 mg/kg daily	Anatrofin (stenobolone)	—
Anavar (oxandrolone)	5–10 mg daily	Bolfortan (testosterone nicotinate)	200–400 mg weekly
Dianabol (methandrostenolone)	15–45 mg daily	Deca-Durabolin (nandrolone decanoate)	50–100 mg 3–4x weekly
Maxibolin (ethylestrenol)	4–8 mg daily	Delatestryl (testosterone enanthate)	50–400 mg 2–3x weekly
Android (methyltestosterone)	10–40 mg daily	Depo-Testosterone (testosterone cypionate)	50–400 mg 2–4x weekly
Primobolan (methenolone)	1–5 mg/kg daily	Dianabol (methandrostenolone)	200 mg weekly
Proviron (mesterolone)	75–100 mg daily	Durabolin (nandrolone phenpropionate)	25–50 mg weekly
Winstrol (stanozolol)	6–8 mg daily	Enoltestovis (hexoxymestrolum)	—
		Equipoise (boldenone—veterinary)	—
		Finajet (trenbolone)	200–400 mg weekly
		Primobolan (methenolone enanthate)	—
		Sustanon 250 (a mixture of testosterone esters)	—
		Therobolin	200 mg weekly
		Trophobolene	—
		Winstrol V (stanozolol—veterinary)	—

Note. After Strauss and Yesalis (1991). Dosages are highly variable among users. Missing values indicate that "typical" doses in humans have not been established.

(1990, 1993) provide interesting historical perspectives on the use and development of testosterone and its offspring, the AASs. Attention in the United States was catalyzed by the acknowledgment of American athletes that AASs played an important role in their successes. Hence, by the 1960s, a substantial community of elite and professional athletes as well as serious amateurs, particularly those interested in strength conditioning and body building, had begun using AASs. By the 1970s, serious concerns about the impact of such substances on the "level playing field" had generated the present attempts to regulate the use of these substances among competitive athletes. By the 1980s, several authorities considered AAS use among elite athletes to be epidemic in proportion (Haupt & Rovere, 1984) in spite of evidence of negative consequences. The technological advances that permitted derivation of AASs with purportedly relatively high anabolic and low androgenic properties very likely contributed to their rise in popularity. These substrata, then, formed the platform for current concerns.

Not surprisingly, reliable prevalence data are sparse, particularly for the decades of the 1960s, 1970s, and 1980s, for both the general public and for high-risk segments such as professional and elite athletes. Ethnographic and anecdotal reports suggest that use among professionals such as football players, serious weight lifters, elite track-and-field contenders, and other serious competitive athletes (including body builders) was endemic during this period (Yesalis, Courson, & Wright, 1993). In fact, in some quarters, it was considered necessary in order to maintain a competitive equilibrium, let alone an advantage! Whether accurate or not, these perceptions probably contributed substantially to the view of the general public that in spite of the risks, AAS use could yield substantial rewards for those valuing strength, endurance, lean muscle mass, and a competitive advantage. From this perspective, it is easier to understand the attraction that AAS use has had to segments of the youth- and performance-oriented American culture of the 1980s and 1990s. A clear barrier to obtaining reliable data resulted from efforts of professional (e.g., National Football League) and elite amateur sports regulatory bodies (e.g., International Olympic Committee) to control steroid use among competitors. Though these bodies acted appropriately to prevent, or at least limit, such abuses, the net effect was to drive AAS use underground and to stimulate relatively creative means on the part of athletes to mask AAS use detection.

During the 1980s and 1990s, however, a number of serious attempts were made to obtain estimates of AAS use among a number of target populations, including high-school- and college-aged students in the general population. These efforts have yielded useful prevalence data. Johnston et al.'s (1996) annual survey of high school students, arguably the most representative sample (N = approximately 15,400) of students in school, added questions about steroid use in the mid-1990s. Their data indicate a lifetime prevalence rate of about 2%, the overwhelming proportion of users being males; monthly rates are about 0.6%.

Results from a more limited study focusing specifically on AAS use that surveyed a selected sample (N = 3,403) of male 12th-graders (Buckley et al., 1988) yielded higher prevalence rates of 6.6%. In Buckley, Yesalis, and Bennell's (1993) more focused study, students who participated in sports (particularly football and wrestling) were likely to use steroids; however, a substantial proportion of users (about a third) were not involved in school-sponsored programs. Pope, Katz, and Champoux (1988) reported results of an exploratory study of college men that yielded prevalence rates of about 2% consistent with the results of the Johnston et al. (1996) ongoing study of high school seniors. Again, the larger proportion of users were likely to be varsity athletes. Another, more comprehensive population-based study (Yesalis, Kennedy, Kopstein, & Bahrke, 1993) yielded results more in agreement with Johnston and colleagues. While much of the focus has been on males, particularly competitive athletes and bodybuilders, some attempts have been made to study females, especially athletes who should be at greater risk. What sparse data are available indicate an increasing trend toward AAS use among these athletes (e.g., Buckley et al., 1993). The paucity of data about women probably gives an unrealistically benign view of AAS use, particularly among competitive athletes. For example, Strauss and Yesalis (1993) (see also Tricker, O'Neill, & Cook, 1989) reported use rates of between 6% and 10% for female athletes in various sports.

Metabolic Pathways and Mechanisms of Action

AASs have the capacity to increase protein synthesis by acting at specific receptor sites that are distributed across a wide range of body tissues, including skeletal and cardiac muscle, a range of receptor systems and locations with the CNS, and a number of other body organs, including the skin, testes, and prostate gland. AASs probably act by increasing protein synthesis through inhibiting the catabolic effects of glucocorticoids (especially under conditions of extreme stress, including that resulting from physically induced fatigue) and interactions with receptors at neuromuscular junctions, and possibly by modulating complex CNS functions in a variety of neurotransmitter systems (Haupt & Rovere, 1984; Lombardo, 1993; Rubinow & Schmidt, 1996). Hence, precise identification of the mechanisms of action of AASs is complicated by the range of target tissues affected, the variety of AASs, and the general complexity of hormonally regulated processes (Kochakian, 1990). In a similar vein, specification of metabolic pathways is difficult, though metabolism is accomplished through pathways generally reserved for naturally occurring testosterone and related androgens. Testosterone is metabolized by the liver to 5-alpha-androsterone and 5-beta-etiocholanolone (both 17 ketosteroids) and excreted in urine. Small amounts are secreted unchanged in urine. Testosterone is converted to other active compounds in some target organs (e.g., the prostate) (Wadler & Hainline, 1989; Winters, 1990).

Given the wide range of potential targets, the variety of action mechanisms, and the number of CNS systems susceptible to AAS influences, it is not surprising that a role for AAS use in the abuse of other substances, particularly alcohol and morphine, has been proposed. Cicero and O'Connor (1990), for example, citing literature examining testosterone-mediated alcohol tolerance, suggest a possible indirect role in key dependence processes. This suggestion is intriguing, especially in light of limited case reports regarding behavioral anomalies of reported AAS users coincident with ingestion of alcohol and other substances (e.g., Conacher & Workman, 1989). Other anecdotal evidence involving professional athletes who have been AAS users and users of other substances, particularly alcohol and cocaine, is also suggestive of possible interactive effects. Documentation of such interactions remains speculative.

In spite of the controversy about the risk of dependence (Cicero & O'Connor, 1990), ample case material and recent survey data appear (e.g., Brower, 1993a) to document the dependence liability of AAS users. The mechanisms that lead to and sustain dependence are far from clear. Issues regarding the frequency, duration, and dosages required to produce dependence are not easy to ascertain for a variety of reasons, particularly because of the manner in which AASs are used. Typically, AAS users take them on an intermittent schedule, a practice termed *cycling*. The period of use may vary, but use often occurs over several weeks or months during training and is then interrupted for several weeks. Another practice, termed *stacking*, involves the use of several different AASs. The purposes for which they are employed also cause difficulties in assessing dependence liability. As indicated above, a primary motivation for AAS use is performance enhancement. Other effects, such as increased training intensity, aggressivity, and other mood alterations, may be considered secondary and, to some extent, unwanted. Hence, AASs are somewhat atypical compared to other psychotropics in terms of their primary expected and sought-after effects. Nonetheless, users do report subjective experiences of well-being and other affective changes, an inability and unwillingness to cut back on use, and other effects consistent with those reported for other drugs of abuse.

Tolerance and withdrawal have been reported by AAS users (Brower, 1993b). Withdrawal symptomatology, when reported, appears more similar to a depressive profile (than to agitation); however, anxiety and increased aggression have been noted in limited case reports.

Biological, Psychological, and Behavioral Consequences of AAS Use

As with other aspects of AAS use, a clear and concise picture of consequences is difficult to paint. By this point, readers have probably asked themselves, "Does AAS use meet its advertized claims?" that is, are AASs effective in providing enhanced performance, however measured? The answer to this question is far from resolved. The consensus appears to be that

under some circumstances (e.g., combined with appropriate training and dieting programs), in some individuals (e.g., mature competitive athletes with substantial pretreatment histories of training), and for limited periods of time, some physical gains may be appreciated. However, even relatively comprehensive assessments of the available literature (e.g., Haupt & Rovere, 1984; Lombardo, 1993) point out that the number of positive and negative reports in the literature are close to equal. Reports appear to be clear that for many individuals, the subjective value of AAS use is substantial even when physical gains or advantages are not clearly demonstrable. This observation suggests a strong role for psychologically mediated processes in use initiation and maintenance as well as other aspects of dependence. Hence, AAS-induced changes in affect modulation and affective experience may serve to sustain use.

The costs or negative effects of use are also difficult to ascertain. Part of the difficulty results from the hidden nature of use and the clustering of users among specific risk groups, as well as the use practices of cycling and stacking described above. Given the wide range of target organs potentially affected by AASs, it is not surprising that a broad range of negative consequences have been reported.

Pathological outcomes have been reported for almost all body tissues that are AAS targets (Friedl, 1990; Haupt & Rovere, 1984; Lombardo, 1993). Hence, cancers and other abnormalities of the liver (including peliosis hepatis and tumors), colon, kidneys, and prostate have been identified among users. Case reports of cerebrovascular disease include occurrences of myocardial infarction and thrombosis. Increases in blood pressure and cholesterol have been documented and may be, in part, mechanisms related to cerebrovascular outcomes. However, cardiovascular risks are viewed as equivocal by some authorities. Cosmetic consequences include induction of baldness and increase or alteration in growth patterns of other body hair (including facial hair in women) and occurrences of acne in many body regions. Changes in reproductive system organs and their functions have been observed. These include testicular atrophy, enlargement of the clitoris, gynecomastia (in males), sterility, impotence, and loss of menses.

In spite of attempts to document adverse medical outcomes of AAs use, the knowledge base remains somewhat sparse. Such issues as dose and use duration, linkage of effects to specific AASs, and differentiation of drug-related outcomes from other risk factors (e.g., training protocols, diet, lifestyle) remain to be addressed more fully. Perhaps, one of the most disconcerting conclusions reached regarding medical consequences is that AASs have the potential to alter functioning in such a variety of vital bodily tissues that it would be foolish to conclude that they could be safely used by athletes or, we would add, any other individual expecting to enhance performance markedly through their use (Friedl, 1993). Further, inasmuch as an important route of administration is needle injection, the risk of HIV infection is potentially significant.

A firm grasp of the undesirable psychological and behavioral consequences of AAS use is even more difficult to achieve than the rudimentary consensus view of medical sequelae summarized above. Aggression, anger, anxiety, depression, euphoria, hostility, irritability, and libidinal alterations (both increases and decreases) have been reported. Much of the evidence is based on anecdotal reports, case histories, and ethnographic studies (several of professional athletes). Few controlled studies or studies using standard psychological inventories or other assessment tools have been reported. One such study (Bahrke, Wright, Strauss, & Catlin, 1992) failed to find reliable differences among users, former users, and nonusers in scores on two standardized psychometric tools (Profile of Mood States and Buss-Durkee Hostility Inventory), even though steroid users reported subjective effects of aggression and hostility. Subjects were all weight lifters, and the sample size was small, although within the range for other such investigations. In contrast, investigations relying on standardized assessments of more severe symptomatology appear to obtain more positive results. For example, Pope and Katz (1994) reported increased occurrences of "major mood disturbances," such as major depression, dysthymia, generalized anxiety, and panic disorder (though not other psychiatric dysfunctions), among steroid-using athletes as determined by the Structured Clinical Interview for *DSM-III-R* (SCID). Interview information also suggested increased aggressive behavior among those experiencing mood disturbances. The study attempted to address several key methodological issues, including dose effects and use patterns. Analyses also suggested the importance of high doses in the emergence of symptomatology. Several case reports by the same team of investigators (Pope & Katz, 1990) have attempted to link steroid use to episodes of violence, including homicide. Note that few female AAS users have been systematically studied. These studies have provided no systematic information regarding alterations in perceived aggression and mood changes. Limited ethnographic observations suggest subjective effects similar to those for males.

Hence, a pattern is beginning to emerge from the limited studies available. Some, though not all, AAS users appear to experience a variety of changes in mood and affective states. Two dominant clusters of symptoms appear common. One cluster appears to comprise feelings of irritability, aggression, and hostility. A second appears to be characterized by feelings of anxiety and depression. The "irritable" cluster may be accompanied by episodes of acting out, while the other, more internally focused cluster may be accompanied by withdrawal and isolation. It also appears that the majority of central questions remain not only unresolved but also minimally addressed.

DESIGNER DRUGS

Clinical Aspects and Epidemiology

The designation of a substance as a *designer drug* is more a term of convention than one of accurate pharmacological classification. This terminology became popular during the 1960s and 1970s, when the legitimate pharmaceutical industry was actively engaged in developing a variety of new compounds to treat psychiatric disorders. Many of the newly developed drugs were variants of prototype substances (e.g., diazepam as a variant of chlordiazepoxide). Often, these new substances were viewed as possessing considerable advantages over the prototypes, such as greater potency, longer or shorter durations of action, fewer side effects, or more specific action. Given the technical advancements in pharmacology, hundreds of new compounds could be and were synthesized and tested (at least in animal models).

These concepts soon caught the attention of individuals interested in applying these technologically sophisticated methods in the development of drugs for the illicit marketplace. Indeed, the era of "better living through chemistry," a slogan of one of the legitimate pharmaceutical giants, had come to the world of drug abuse. Ironically, some of the drugs that set the pattern for the illicit use of designer drugs had been available for some time prior to their introduction into the illicit marketplace. For example, it was during this same time that LSD use began a sharp rise in popularity. In a sense, LSD was the precursor of what was to come in the line of designer drugs, a step in the evolution from experiences derived from plants to those derived from the laboratory.

The historic patterns of use of MDMA and related designer drugs (e.g., 3,4 methelenedioxyethamphetamine, MDEA, "Eve") have been somewhat erratic and hence difficult to trace. Even with the closer tracking of drug use patterns beginning in the 1970s, documentation is at best sparse. MDMA use appears to be most popular among 16- to 25-year-olds (both male and female). Surveys of adolescents indicate a lifetime prevalence of about 2% (Johnston et al., 1996). In the late 1970s and early 1980s, the drug was touted as the "love drug," reportedly enhancing the intensity of sexual encounters. It was also billed as the "businessman's LSD," given its hallucinogenic and stimulant properties and its shorter duration of action in comparison to LSD. In the 1990s, the drug is most often used by adolescents and young adults. Its use is particularly popular at "raves" (intensive all-night dance parties) and is generally considered safe by users. The majority of users seem to experience few immediate toxic effects beyond those viewed as part of the intoxication that occurs. However, based on the animal literature and the growing number of clinical case reports on humans, there is no question that MDMA and related designer drugs carry significant physical and psychological health risks even for otherwise symptom-free users or MDMA-experienced users. The risks appear to be related to acute episodes of intoxication; however, there are few long-term studies, including case studies that track users longitudinally. However, animal studies document the potential of long-term irreversible neurotoxicity (Fischer, Hatzidimitriou, Wlos, Katz, & Ricaurte, 1995). There is little evidence of dependence development among MDMA users. Here again, the literature is marked by the absence of suitable data that would allow a firm conclusion to be drawn. If on the one hand designer drugs follow the pattern set by hallucinogens (e.g., LSD), dependence liability would seem relatively small. On the other hand, were they to follow the pattern set by amphetamines, the liability could be much higher.

Metabolic Pathways and Mechanisms of Action

MDMA, commonly referred to as *ecstacy* (also *love boat*) is a methamphetamine derivative that was synthesized in 1914. MDMA is considered a prototype of designer drugs. It is likely that much of what is sold on the street under various names is, in fact, MDMA, inasmuch as it is relatively easy to synthesize. Further, other related compounds have severe neurotoxicity. MDMA was first introduced as an appetite suppressant and was thought to be relatively safe (Green, Cross, & Goodwin, 1995; Steele, McCann, & Ricaurte, 1994). It was viewed subsequently as a nontoxic drug that could induce feelings of "warm, loving relaxation." MDMA is believed to act on reward systems of the brain through stimulation of dopamine and serotonin pathways, probably by increasing extracellular concentrations of both neurotransmitters (White, Obradovic, Imel, & Wheaton, 1996). Recent studies in animals have documented significant neurotoxicity, particularly in serotonin neurons, that may be relatively permanent (Fischer et al., 1995). However, such neurotoxicity has not been demonstrated conclusively in humans even though clinical reports of toxic effects, including fatalities, document the serious harm potential of the substance (Dar & McBrien, 1996; Demirkiran, Jankovic, & Dean, 1996; Green et al., 1995).

MDMA effects are experienced as a combination of those induced by hallucinogens and amphetamines. The MDMA "trip" may last for several hours, although its duration is shorter and intensity less than that occurring with LSD; however, users frequently take additional doses as the effects dissipate. Users experience a dreamy state sometimes accompanied by hallucinations and delusions, along with an amphetamine-like increase in motor activation, stimulation, and general arousal. A variety of signs and symptoms may occur that indicate acute toxic reactions: dilated pupils, agitation, excitement, hallucinations, tachycardia, palpitations, CNS depression, incontinence (occasionally), and signs of cognitive disorganization and distortion (Watson, Ferguson, Hinds, Skinner, & Coakley, 1993). The drug also induces hyperthermia, which can seriously compromise a variety of bodily functions.

Biological, Psychological, and Behavioral Consequences

On those occasions when toxic reactions occur, a variety of functions of several organ systems appear adversely affected. Cardiovascular effects include increased heart rate and blood pressure that may be accompanied by tachycardia. Blood coagulation disorders (e.g., coagulopathy) have been noted in cases of fatalities. Also, liver toxicity and kidney failure have been observed in fatalities. Rhabdomyolysis (disease of the skeletal muscle characterized by tissue disintegration) and general muscle rigidity may also occur. At least one case of cerebral infarction in an otherwise healthy male has been attributed to MDMA intoxication. Hyperthermia is a common consequence; this condition may be exacerbated in cases where individuals are engaged in prolonged or intensive motor activity such as dancing, especially when dehydration occurs. Given the range of affective and cognitive changes that occur and in light of the animal literature regarding neurotoxicity, it is probable that significant alterations occur in dopaminergic and serotonergic neural networks. However, the duration and extent of neural toxicity in humans remain to be resolved (Fischer et al., 1995; Steele et al., 1994). The degree to which these consequences occur in cases that do not result in the full-blown toxic reaction is unknown.

Psychological and behavioral consequences that extend beyond the period of acute intoxication or are not concomitant with acute toxic reactions have not been well documented. The most commonly, though not frequently, reported outcomes are protracted changes in mood, manifesting as depression and anxiety. Cognitive disorganization resulting in decreased capacity has also been observed (Steele et al., 1994). Documentation has occurred primarily through clinical case reports; few ethnographic or observational studies have been reported. Hence, one might conclude that effects are limited to episodes of acute intoxication and toxic reactions or to the brief postintoxication periods possibly coincident with detoxification. However, such a conclusion would be premature, especially given the high potency and dramatic effects of designer drugs.

FINAL COMMENT

The use of inhalants, anabolic-androgenic steroids, and designer drugs represents a wide range of serious health risks even though prevalence rates are relatively low in comparison to the use of many other substances (e.g., alcohol, marijuana) and the magnitude of consequences may not seem as large. Furthermore, the fact that key information is somewhat sketchy provides both challenges for basic researchers seeking to fill the voids and problems for clinicians confronted with treating users of these substances. Hopefully, this chapter not only provides a useful summary of relevant facts but will also stimulate much-needed basic and clinical research.

Key References

Brower, K. J. (1993a). Anabolic steroids: Potential for physical and psychological dependence. In C. E. Yesalis (Ed.), *Anabolic steroids in sport and exercise* (pp. 193–213). Champaign, IL: Human Kinetics Publishers.

Steele, T. D., McCann, U. D., & Ricaurte, G. A. (1994). 3,4-Methylenedioxymethamphetamine (MDMA, "ecstasy"): Pharmacology and toxicology in animals and humans. [Review]. *Addiction*, 89(5), 539–551.

Tenenbein, M. (1992). Clinical/biophysiologic aspects of inhalant abuse. In C. W. Sharp, F. Beauvais, & R. Spence (Eds.), *Inhalant abuse: A volatile research agenda* (pp. 173–180). Rockville, MD: National Institute on Drug Abuse (Research Monograph 129).

References

American Medical Association, Council on Scientific Affairs. (1990). Medical and nonmedical use of anabolic-androgenic steroids. *Journal of the American Medical Association*, 264, 2923–2927.

Bahrke, M. S., Wright, J. E., Strauss, R. H., & Catlin, D. H. (1992). Psychological moods and subjectively perceived behavioral and somatic changes accompanying anabolic-androgenic steroid use. *American Journal of Sports Medicine*, 20(6), 717–723.

Beauvais, F. (1992). Volatile substance abuse: Trends and patterns. In C. W. Sharp, F. Beauvais, & R. Spence (Eds.), *Inhalant abuse: A volatile research agenda* (pp. 13–42). Rockville, MD: National Institute on Drug Abuse (Research Monograph 129).

Brower, K. J. (1993a). Anabolic steroids: Potential for physical and psychological dependence. In C. E. Yesalis (Ed.), *Anabolic steroids in sport and exercise* (pp.

193–213). Champaign, IL: Human Kinetics Publishers.

Brower, K. J. (1993b). Assessment and treatment of anabolic steroid withdrawal. In C. E. Yesalis (Ed.), *Anabolic steroids in sport and exercise* (pp. 231–250). Champaign, IL: Human Kinetics Publishers.

Buckley, W. E., Yesalis, C. E., & Bennell, D. L. (1993). A study of anabolic steroid use at the secondary school level: Recommendations for prevention. In C. E. Yesalis (Ed.), *Anabolic steroids in sport and exercise* (pp. 71–86). Champaign, IL: Human Kinetics Publishers.

Buckley, W. E., Yesalis, C. E., III., Friedl, K. E., Anderson, W. A., Streit, A. L., & Wright, J. E. (1988). Estimated prevalence of anabolic steroid use among male high school seniors. *Journal of the American Medical Association, 260*(23), 3441–3445.

Chadwick, O. F. D., & Anderson, H. R. (1989). Neuropsychological consequences of volatile substance abuse: A review. *Human Toxicology, 8,* 307–312.

Cicero, T. J., & O'Connor, L. H. (1990). Abuse liability of anabolic steroids and their possible role in the abuse of alcohol, morphine, and other substances. In G. C. Lin & L. Erinoff (Eds.), *Anabolic steroid abuse* (pp. 1–28). Rockville, MD: National Institute on Drug Abuse (Research Monograph 102).

Conacher, G. N., & Workman, D. G. (1989). Violent crime possibly associated with anabolic steroid use. [Letter to the editor]. *American Journal of Psychiatry, 146*(5), 679.

Crites, J., & Schuckit, M. (1979). Solvent misuse in adolescents at a community alcohol center. *Journal of Clinical Psychiatry, 40,* 39–43.

Dar, K. J., & McBrien, M. E. (1996). MDMA induced hyperthermia: Report of a fatality and review of current therapy. [Review]. *Intensive Care Medicine, 22*(9), 995–996.

Demirkiran, M., Jankovic, J., & Dean, J. M. (1996). Ecstasy intoxication: An overlap between serotonin syndrome and neuroleptic malignant syndrome. [Review]. *Clinical Neuropharmacology, 19*(2), 157–164.

Dinwiddie, S. H., Reich, T., & Cloninger, C. K. (1991). The relationship of solvent use to other substance use. *American Journal of Drug and Alcohol Abuse, 17,* 173–186.

Dinwiddie, S. W. (1994). Abuse of inhalants: A review. *Addiction, 89,* 925–929.

Escobar, A., & Aruffo, C. (1980). Chronic thinner intoxication: Clinico-pathologic report of a human case. *Journal of Neurology, Neurosurgery, and Psychiatry, 43,* 986–994.

Esmail, A., Meyer, L., Pottier, A., & Wright, S. (1993). Deaths from volatile substance abuse in those under 18 years: Results from a national epidemiological study. *Archives in Disease of Childhood, 69*(3), 356–360.

Filley, C., Heaton, R. K., & Rosenberg, N. L. (1990). White matter dementia in chronic toluene abuse. *Neurology, 40,* 532–534.

Fischer, C., Hatzidimitriou, G., Wlos, J., Katz, J., & Ricaurte, G. (1995). Reorganization of ascending 5-HT axon projections in animals previously exposed to recreational drug 3,4-methylenedioxymethamphetamine (MDMA, "ecstasy"). *Journal of Neuroscience, 15,* 5476–5485.

Fornazzari, L. (1990). The neurotoxicity of inhaled toulene. [Letter to the editor]. *Canadian Journal of Psychiatry, 35,* 723.

Fornazzari, L., Wilkinson, D. A., Kapur, B. M., & Carlen, P. L. (1983). Cerebellar, cortical and functional impairment in toulene abusers. *Acta Neurologica Scandinavica, 67,* 319–329.

Friedl, K. E. (1990). Reappraisal of the health risks associated with the use of high doses of oral and injectable androgenic steroids. In G. C. Lin & L. Erinoff (Eds.), *Anabolic steroid abuse* (pp. 143–177). Rockville, MD: National Institute on Drug Abuse (Research Monograph 102).

Friedl, K. E. (1993). Effects of anabolic steroids on physical health. In C. E. Yesalis (Ed.), *Anabolic steroids in sport and exercise* (pp. 107–150). Champaign, IL: Human Kinetics Publishers.

Green, A. R., Cross, A. J., & Goodwin, G. M. (1995). Review of the pharmacology and clinical pharmacology of 3,4-methylenedioxymethamphetamine (MDMA or "ecstasy"). [Review]. *Psychopharmacology, 119*(3), 247–260.

Haupt, H. A., & Rovere, G. D. (1984). Anabolic steroids: A review of the literature. *American Journal of Sports Medicine, 12*(6), 469–484.

Jansen, P., Richter, L. M., & Griesel, R. D. (1992). Glue sniffing: A comparison study of sniffers and non-sniffers. *Journal of Adolescence, 15*(1), 29–37.

Johnston, O. D., O'Malley, P. M., & Bachman, J. G. (1996). *National survey results on drug use from the monitoring the future survey 1975–1995: Vol. 1. Secondary schools students* (NIH Publication No. 96-4139). Washington, DC: U.S. Department of Health and Human Services.

Katzelnick, D. J., Davar, G., & Scanlon, J. P. (1991). Reversibility of psychiatric symptoms in a chronic solvent abuser: A case report. *Journal of Neuropsychiatry, 3,* 319–321.

King, M. D., Day, R. E., Oliver, J. S., Lush, M., & Watson, J. (1981). Solvent encephalopathy. *British Medical Journal, 283,* 663–665.

Kochakian, C. D. (1990). History of anabolic-androgenic steroids. In G. C. Lin & L. Erinoff (Eds.),

Anabolic steroid abuse (pp. 29–59). Rockville, MD: National Institute on Drug Abuse (Research Monograph 102).

Kochakian, C. D. (1993). Anabolic-androgenic steroids: A historical perspective and definition. In C. E. Yesalis (Ed.), Anabolic steroids in sport and exercise (pp. 3–33). Champaign, IL: Human Kinetics Publishers.

Lombardo, J. (1993). The efficacy and mechanisms of action of anabolic steroids. In C. E. Yesalis (Ed.), Anabolic steroids in sport and exercise (pp. 89–106). Champaign, IL: Human Kinetics Publishers.

May, P. A. (1988). Final report: Native American Adolescent Injury Prevention Project. Albuquerque: University of New Mexico.

Morita, N., Satoh, S., Oda, S., Tomita, H., Shoji, M., Seno, E., Abe, K., & Konishi, T. (1994). A study of relationships among solvent inhalation, personality and expectancy; especially an affinity to hallucination, sensation seeking and neurotic tendency. (Japanese) Arukoru Kenkyu-To Yakubutsu Ison Japanese Journal of Alcohol Studies & Drug Dependence, 29(5), 445–468.

Nuwer, H. (1990). Steroids. New York: Franklin Watts.

Oetting, E., & Beauvais, F. (1990). Adolescent drug abuse: Finding of national and local surveys. Journal of Consulting and Clinical Psychology, 58, 385–394.

Oetting, E. R., & Webb, J. (1992). Psychosocial characteristics and their links with inhalants: A research agenda. In C. W. Sharp, F. Beauvais, & R. Spence (Eds.), Inhalant abuse: A volatile research agenda (pp. 59–96). Rockville, MD: National Institute on Drug Abuse (Research Monograph 129).

Pope, H. G., Jr., & Katz, D. L. (1990). Homicide and near-homicide by anabolic steroid users. Journal of Clinical Psychiatry, 51, 28–31.

Pope, H. G., Jr., & Katz, D. L. (1994). Psychiatric and medical effects of anabolic-androgenic steroid use: A controlled study of 160 athletes. Archives of General Psychiatry, 51, 375–382.

Pope, H. G., Jr., Katz, D. L., & Champoux, R. (1988). Anabolic-androgenic steroid use among 1,010 college men. The Physician and Sports Medicine, 16(7), 75–81.

Reed, B. J., & May, P. A. (1984). Inhalant abuse and juvenile delinquency: A control study in Albuquerque, New Mexico. International Journal of Addiction, 19, 789–803.

Ron, M. A. (1986). Volatile substance abuse: A review of possible long-term neurological, intellectual, and psychiatric sequelae. British Journal of Psychiatry, 148, 235–246.

Rosenberg, N., & Sharp, C. W. (1992). Solvent toxicity: A neurological focus. In C. W. Sharp, F. Beauvais, & R. Spence (Eds.), Inhalant abuse: A volatile research agenda (pp. 117–171). Rockville, MD: National Institute on Drug Abuse (Research Monograph 129).

Rosenberg, N. L., Sptiz, M. C., Filley, C. M., Davis, K. A., & Schaumburg, H. H. (1988). Central nervous system effects of chronic toluene abuse—Clinical, brain stem evoked response and magnetic resonance imaging studies. Neurotoxicology and Teratology, 10, 489–495.

Rubinow, D. R., & Schmidt, P. J. (1996). Androgens, brain, and behavior. American Journal of Psychiatry, 153(8), 974–984.

Schutz, C. G., Chilcoat, H. D., & Anthony, J. C. (1994). The association between sniffing inhalants and injecting drugs. Comprehensive Psychiatry, 35(2), 99–105.

Shickler, K. N., Seitz, K., Rice, J. F., & Strader, T. (1982). Solvent abuse associated cortical atrophy. Journal of Adolescent Health Care, 3, 37–39.

Skuse, D., & Burrell, S. (1982). A review of solvent abusers and their management by a child psychiatric out-patient service. Human Toxicology, 1, 321–329.

Steele, T. D., McCann, U. D., & Ricaurte, G. A. (1994). 3,4-Methylenedioxymethamphetamine (MDMA, "ecstasy"): Pharmacology and toxicology in animals and humans. [Review]. Addiction, 89(5), 539–551.

Strauss, R. H., & Yesalis, C. E. (1991). Anabolic steroids in the athlete. Annual Review of Medicine, 42, 449–457.

Strauss, R. H., & Yesalis, C. E. (1993). Additional effects of anabolic steroids on women. In C. E. Yesalis (Ed.), Anabolic steroids in sport and exercise (pp. 151–160). Champaign, IL: Human Kinetics Publishers.

Tapia-Conyer, R., Cravioto, P., De La Rosa, B., & Velez, C. (1995). Risk factors for inhalant abuse in juvenile offenders: The case of Mexico. Addiction, 90(1), 43–49.

Tenenbein, M. (1992). Clinical/biophysiologic aspects of inhalant abuse. In C. W. Sharp, F. Beauvais, & R. Spence (Eds.), Inhalant abuse: A volatile research agenda (pp. 173–180). Rockville, MD: National Institute on Drug Abuse (Research Monograph 129).

Tricker, R., O'Neill, M. R., & Cook, D. (1989). The incidence of anabolic steroid use among competitive bodybuilders. Journal of Drug Education, 19(4), 313–325.

Wadler, G. I., & Hainline, B. (1989). Anabolic steroids. In A. J. Ryan (Ed.), Drugs and the athlete (pp. 55–69). Philadelphia: F. A. Davis.

Watson, J. D., Ferguson, C., Hinds, C. J., Skinner, R., & Coakley, J. H. (1993). Exertional heat stroke induced by amphetamine analogues: Does dantrolene have a place? [Review]. Anaesthesia, 48(12), 1057–1060.

White, S. R., Obradovic, T., Imel, K. M., & Wheaton, M. J. (1996). The effects of methylenedioxymethamphetamine (MDMA, "ecstasy") on monoaminergic neurotransmission in the central nervous system. [Review]. *Progress in Neurobiology, 49*(5), 455–479.

Wiggins, R. C. (1986). Myelination: A critical stage in development. *Neurotoxicology, 7,* 103–230.

Winters, S. J. (1990). Androgens: Endocrine physiology and pharmacology. In G. C. Lin & L. Erinoff (Eds.), *Anabolic steroid abuse* (pp. 113–130). Rockville, MD: National Institute on Drug Abuse (Research Monograph 102).

Xiong, L., Matthews, J. D., Li, J., & Jinkins, J. R. (1993). MR imaging of "spray heads": Toluene abuse via aerosol paint inhalation. *American Journal of Neuroradiology, 14*(5), 1195–1199.

Yamanouchi, N., Okada, S., Kodama, K., Hirai, S., Sekine, H., Murakami, A., Komatsu, N., Sakamoto, T., & Sato, T. (1995). White matter changes caused by chronic solvent abuse. *American Journal of Neuroradiology, 16*(8), 1643–1649.

Yesalis, C. E., Courson, S. P., & Wright, J. (1993). History of anabolic steroid use in sport and exercise. In C. E. Yesalis (Ed.), *Anabolic steroids in sport and exercise* (pp. 35–47). Champaign, IL: Human Kinetics Publishers.

Yesalis, C. E., Kennedy, N. J., Kopstein, A. N., & Bahrke, M. S. (1993). Anabolic-androgenic steroid use in the United States. *Journal of the American Medical Association, 270*(10), 1217–1221.

Zur, J., & Yule, W. (1990a). Chronic solvent abuse: Cognitive sequelae. *Child Care and Health Development, 16,* 1–20.

Zur, J., & Yule, W. (1990b). Chronic solvent abuse: 2. Relationship with depression. *Child Care and Health Development, 16,* 21–24.

III

Case Identification, Assessment, and Treatment Planning

11

Assessment Strategies and Measures in Addictive Behaviors

Dennis M. Donovan

Given the high prevalence of alcohol and drug use disorders in the general population and, even higher, among those with psychological problems (Regier et al., 1990; Ross, Glaser, & Germanson, 1988), it is quite likely that all mental health practitioners will be faced with the task of assessing and treating individuals with a substance use disorder, regardless of the clinical setting in which they work. However, while clinicians are likely to agree that assessment is a cornerstone of the therapeutic process with substance abusers and to endorse the ideal of providing a comprehensive assessment of those seeking treatment for addictive disorders, this agreement will not necessarily lead to the actual practice of such an assessment process in clinical settings (Institute of Medicine, 1990). A number of practical considerations contribute to this discrepancy between the ideal and the actual in clinical practice, some of which appear to be inherent in the complexity of substance abuse and others that are more attributable to mental health practitioners' attitudes and skill level (Allen,

1991; Sobell, Sobell, & Nirenberg, 1988). Clinicians are often ill prepared for such an undertaking due to a lack of formal training in the areas of alcohol and drug abuse (e.g., Sobell et al., 1988). For example, graduate training programs in both clinical and counseling psychology have been found to provide only minimal training in alcohol and drug problems (Lubin, Brady, Woodward, & Thomas, 1986); this deficiency is often not rectified during clinical internship (Bacorn & Connors, 1989).

The purpose of this chapter is to provide a brief overview of issues involved in the assessment process in addictive behaviors with the hope of both increasing clinicians' familiarity with this area and enhancing its clinical application. A number of more thorough reviews of these issues and of specific instruments for the assessment of alcohol and drug problems are available to the interested reader (e.g., Addiction Research Foundation, 1994; Allen & Columbus, 1995; Carey & Teitelbaum, 1996; Carroll, 1995; Donovan, 1988, 1992, 1995; Donovan & Marlatt, 1988; Litten & Allen, 1992; Nirenberg & Maisto, 1987; Rounsaville, Tims, Horton, & Sowder, 1993; Sobell, Toneatto, & Sobell, 1994).

WHY ASSESS: PURPOSES OF ASSESSMENT

Assessment serves multiple functions (e.g., Allen & Columbus, 1995; Allen & Mattson, 1993; Carey & Teitelbaum, 1996; Institute of Medicine, 1990; Jacobson, 1989a, 1989b; Shaffer & Kauffman, 1985): screening and case finding, motivating clients to enter treatment, problem description, diagnosis, treatment planning, and evaluation of treatment process and outcome. Some of these functions are related to information acquisition and integration, while others are more directly related to motivating the individual and inducing him or her into the role of a client in a help-seeking relationship. In this chapter, the outcome evaluation function will not be reviewed. Information about this function can be found elsewhere (e.g., Allen & Columbus, 1995; Longabaugh & Clifford, 1992).

Screening: Identifying Individuals with Potential Substance Use Disorders

An initial function of assessment is identifying individuals who may have a substance abuse problem or who are at increased risk of developing one. Such screening and case-finding approaches are typically relatively brief and inexpensive and are applied to relatively large groups of individuals. An attempt is made, through questionnaires or interviews, to accurately classify an individual either as having a problem (a true positive) or as not having a problem (a true negative). A concern that must be taken into account in this process is the probability of incorrectly identifying someone as having a problem when he or she does not (a false positive) or as not having a problem when in fact he or she does (a false negative). The accuracy of the identification process is somewhat relative, in that it will vary according to the base rate of the substance abuse problem in the population being screened. Also, the relative degree of inaccuracy that is tolerable depends on the purpose of the screening procedure. An attempt is made to use assessment instruments or procedures that maximize both sensitivity (the ability to accurately

identify those who have alcohol or drug abuse problems while minimizing false negatives) and specificity (the ability to accurately identify those who do not have a problem while minimizing false positives). However, in most screening applications, an attempt is made to identify as large a group of potential cases as possible, so that the sensitivity of the screening instrument may be more important than its specificity, with more thorough assessments being used subsequently to increase the accuracy of the initial screening (Carey & Teitelbaum, 1996; Connors, 1995).

The Institute of Medicine (1990) has suggested that the screening and case-finding function should be expanded beyond traditional substance abuse treatment settings to other areas and populations that have a relatively high probability of alcohol or drug use problems. Such populations, which include many individuals who may have problems but who are not actively seeking treatment, might include pregnant women (Russell, 1994), the mothers of small children (Kemper, Greteman, Bennett, & Babonis, 1993), and individuals brought to the attention of child welfare authorities (Dore, Doris, & Wright, 1995); patients seen in community health clinics (Kipke, Montgomery, & McKenzie, 1993), family practice settings (Nilssen & Cone, 1994), emergency rooms (Cherpitel, 1995), trauma centers (Gentilello, Donovan, Dunn, & Rivara, 1995), and psychiatric settings (Teitelbaum & Carey, 1996); individuals arrested for driving while intoxicated (Lapham et al., 1995) and other individuals involved in the criminal justice system (Peters & Schonfeld, 1993); high-risk youth (Dembo, Turner, Borden, Schmeidler, & Manning, 1994; Leccese & Waldron, 1994) and older adults (DeHart & Hoffman, 1995).

A number of instruments have been developed for use in screening for substance abuse problems, more of these focusing on alcohol use than on drug use. Connors (1995) has identified and provides detailed information on 25 different measures for use in screening for alcohol problems in both adolescents and adults. The comparative utility of a number of these alcohol screening tests has been evaluated (Maisto, Connors, & Allen, 1995). Screening tests range from as few as two questions (e.g., Brown, Leonard, Saunders, & Papasouliotis, 1997; Cyr & Wartman, 1988) to much longer and more structured procedures (e.g., Tarter & Hegedus, 1991).

The Drug Abuse Screening Test (DAST; Gavin, Ross & Skinner, 1989; Skinner, 1982) was developed specifically for and has been used frequently for screening for drug abuse. The usefulness of any of the available screening measures varies with the characteristics of the population being studied. Thus, there may be differences in the likelihood of a person's being identified as having a substance abuse problem at an individual level, as well as in the estimates of prevalence and incidence at the larger epidemiological level, based on the instrument when used with men versus women, different ethnic groups, and different age groups (e.g., Cherpitel & Clark, 1995; Connors, 1995; Lapham et al., 1995; Russell, 1994). Therefore, either specialized screening methods have been derived for some of these subgroups (e.g., Leccese & Waldron, 1994; Russell, 1994) or normative information has been developed for standard instruments when used with such subgroups. Table 11.1 presents a listing of a number of frequently employed screening measures as well as measures appropriate for each of the different stages and domains of the assessment process.

Motivating the Help Seeker

A set of interrelated goals of screening for substance abuse problems includes identifying an individual with a present or potential problem, increasing the individual's problem awareness, suggesting the need for a more thorough assessment, and increasing the individual's interest in and readiness for treatment if recommended from the assessment (Connors, 1995). Assessment is often one of the first steps in the process of treatment for those seeking help for an addictive disorder. Choosing to give up alcohol or drugs is not a decision arrived at easily, and there are many barriers to doing so (e.g., Marlatt, Tucker, Donovan, & Vuchinich, 1997). Thus, the decision to seek treatment is one that may have taken much time and determination to make. There is often a sense of uncertainty and ambivalence in the individual who may be aware that change is needed yet unsure that it will be possible to change or whether she or he wants to give up the positive features associated with the addictive behavior (Kanfer, 1986).

Prochaska and DiClemente (1986) suggested that individuals go through a series of stages in this decision-making process, ranging from precontemplation (e.g., not feeling as if one has a problem) to taking positive steps to initiate change. Many have gone for years without perceiving that they have a problem, seemingly oblivious of the negative consequences that others are able to observe. This behavior has often been described as being in denial. Other individuals have contemplated the need for changing their drinking or drug use for some time but have not been sufficiently committed to take any action. Others may have attempted action in the past but have since resumed use, raising questions in their minds about the efficacy of treatment and their ability to reach their goals. Others, acknowledging the need to change, may still be influenced more by their perceptions of the positive and more proximal benefits derived from using than by the anticipated but more distal benefits of stopping use and thus are unable to make a firm commitment to take action.

Given the somewhat tenuous nature of the individual's commitment in light of such ambivalence, the clinician may have a unique therapeutic opportunity to facilitate a transition between an individual's contemplating the need for change, making a commitment to change, and actually taking steps to modify behavior patterns (Prochaska & DiClemente, 1986). The task of the clinician in such circumstances is to help reinforce the individual's commitment to seek help and to change his or her behavior. This task may require "hooking" the positive side of the person's ambivalence by focusing on her or his commitment and motivation to change, by making the new behavior pattern and lifestyle associated with giving up alcohol or drugs appear as rewarding as continuing to use, and by helping reduce fears and concerns about change (Donovan, 1988; Kanfer, 1986; Miller, 1983).

The approach that the clinician takes in attempting to accomplish this task will differ depending on the client's readiness to change (Prochaska & DiClemente, 1986; Prochaska, DiClemente, & Norcross, 1992). A client who is in the early stages of the behavior change process, in which he or she is contemplating change and moving toward making a commitment and taking action, appears to benefit most by approaches that increase his or her information and awareness about himself or herself and the nature of the problem, that lead to an assessment of how he or she feels and thinks about himself or herself in light of a problem, that increase his or her belief in the ability to change, and that reaffirm his or her commitment to take active steps to change

TABLE 11.1 Examples of Instruments and Interviews Appropriate for Use in Multidimensional Assessments of Substance Use Disorders Across Different Stages of the Assessment Process

Stage of assessment	Assessment domain	Examples of instruments	Reference
Screening	Alcohol use	CAGE Questions	Mayfield et al., 1974
		Two Item Alcohol Screening Questions	Cyr & Wartman, 1988
		NET	Russell, 1994
		T-ACE	Sokol et al., 1989
		TWEAK	Russell et al., 1991
		Alcohol Use Disorders Identification Test (AUDIT)	Saunders et al., 1993
		Michigan Alcoholism Screening Test (MAST)	Selzer, 1971
		Brief Michigan Alcoholism Screening Test (bMAST)	Pokorny et al., 1972
		Short Michigan Alcoholism Screening Test (sMAST)	Zung, 1984
	Drug use	Two Item Alcohol and Drug Screening Questions	Brown et al., 1997
		Drug Abuse Screening Test (DAST)	Skinner, 1982
Problem assessment	Alcohol use patterns	Time-Line Follow Back	Sobell & Sobell, 1992
		Form-90	Miller, 1996
		Comprehensive Drinker Profile (CDP)	Miller & Marlatt, 1984
		Alcohol Use Inventory (AUI)	Wanberg et al., 1977
	Drug use patterns	Addiction Severity Index (ASI)	McLellan et al., 1992
		Drug History Questionnaire (DHQ)	Sobell et al., 1995
		Individual Assessment Profile (IAP)	Flynn et al., 1995
	Diagnoses	Psychiatric Research Interview for Substance and Mental Disorders (PRISM)[a]	Hasin et al., 1996
		Diagnostic Interview Schedule (DIS)	Robins et al., 1981
		Schedules for Clinical Assessment in Neuropsychiatry (SCAN)	Wing et al., 1990
		Composite International Diagnostic Interview (CIDI)	Robins et al., 1988
		Alcohol Use Disorders and Associated Disabilities Interview Schedule (AUDASIS)	Grant & Hasin, 1990
	Outcome expectancies— Alcohol	Negative Alcohol Expectancy Questionnaire (NAEQ)	Jones & McMahon, 1993
		Alcohol Expectancy Questionnaire (AEQ)	Brown et al., 1987
		Drinking Expectancy Questionnaire (DEQ)	Young & Knight, 1989
		Alcohol Beliefs Scale (ABS)	Connors & Maisto, 1988
		Effects of Drinking Alcohol (EDA)	Leigh, 1987
		Comprehensive Effects of Alcohol Scale (CEOA)	Fromme et al., 1993
	Outcome expectancies— Drugs	Cocaine Expectancy Questionnaire (CEQ)	Jaffe & Kilbey, 1994
		Cocaine Effect Expectancy Questionnaire— Likert (CEEF-L)	Schafer & Fals-Stewart, 1993
		Cocaine Effect Expectancy Questionnaire (CEEQ)	Schafer & Brown, 1991
		Marijuana Effects Expectancy Questionnaire (MEEQ)	Schafer & Brown, 1991

(continued)

TABLE 11.1 *(continued)*

Stage of assessment	Assessment domain	Examples of instruments	Reference
Problem assessment (continued)	Relapse risk	Substance Abuse Relapse Assessment (SARA)	Schonfeld et al., 1993
		Cocaine Relapse Interview (CRI)	McKay et al., 1996
		Cocaine High-Risk Situations Questionnaire (CHRSQ)	Michalec et al., 1992
		Situational Competency Test (SCT)	Chaney et al., 1978
		Reasons for Drinking Questionnaire (RFDQ)	Zywiak et al., 1996
		Reasons for Heroin Use Questionnaire (RFHUQ)	Heather et al., 1991
		Relapse Situation Appraisal Questionnaire (RSAQ)	Myers et al., 1996
	Coping: substance-related	Coping Behaviors Inventory (CBI)	Litman et al., 1983
		Problem Skills Inventory (PSI)	Hawkins et al., 1986
		Alcohol Specific Role Play Test (ASRPT)	Monti et al., 1993
	Coping: general	Ways of Coping Checklist (WOC)	Folkman & Lazarus, 1980
		COPE	Carver et al., 1989
		Coping Responses Inventory (CRI)	Moos, 1995
	Self-efficacy—Alcohol	Alcohol Abstinence Self-Efficacy Scale (AASE)	DiClemente et al., 1994
		Drinking Refusal Self-Efficacy Questionnaire (DRSEQ)	Young et al., 1991
		Individualized Self-Efficacy Survey (ISS)	Miller et al., 1994
		Inventory of Drinking Situations (IDS)	Annis et al., 1987
		Situational Confidence Questionnaire (SCQ)	Annis & Graham, 1988
	Self-efficacy—Drugs	Inventory of Drug-Taking Situations (IDTS)	Annis & Graham, 1991
		Drug Abuse Self-Efficacy Scale (DASES)	Martin et al., 1995
		Situational Confidence Questionnaire—Heroin (SCQ-Heroin)	Barber et al., 1991
Personal assessment	Personality	California Psychological Inventory (CPI)	Gough, 1975
		NEO Personality Inventory	Costa & McCrae, 1992
		Personality Research Form (PRF)	Jackson, 1994
	Psychopathology	Minnesota Multiphasic Personality Inventory (MMPI-2)	Hathaway et al., 1989
		Millon Clinical Multiaxial Inventory (MCMI-II)	Millon, 1992
		Psychological Screening Inventory (PSI)	Lanyon, 1970
	Emotional state	Symptom Checklist-90 (SCL-90)	Derogatis, 1977
	Anger	State-Trait Anger Inventory	Spielberger et al., 1983
		Multidimensional Anger Inventory	Siegel, 1986
	Anxiety	State-Trait Anxiety Inventory	Spielberger et al., 1970
		Beck Anxiety Inventory	Beck et al., 1988
	Depression	Beck Depression Inventory (BDI)	Beck et al., 1961
		Center for Epidemiologic Studies Depression Scale (CES-D)	Radloff, 1977
		Inventory to Diagnose Depression (IDD)	Zimmerman & Coryell, 1987
	General life/social function	Addiction Severity Index (ASI)	McLellan et al., 1992
		Psychosocial Functioning Inventory (PFI)	Feragne et al., 1983

(continued)

TABLE 11.1 (*continued*)

Stage of assessment	Assessment domain	Examples of instruments	Reference
Treatment-related factors	Readiness to change	Stages of Change Readiness and Treatment Eagerness Scale (SOCRATES)	Miller & Tonigan, 1996
		Readiness to Change Questionnaire (RTCQ)	Rollnick et al., 1992
		University of Rhode Island Readiness to Change Assessment (URICA)	McConnaughy et al., 1983
		Desire for Help Scale (DHS)	Simpson & Joe, 1993
		Intrinsic/Extrinsic Motivation to Quit Questionnaire (IEMQ)	Curry et al., 1990 McBride et al., 1994
	Barriers to treatment	Barriers to Treatment Instrument (BTI)	Allen, 1994
		Reasons for Delaying Seeking Treatment (RDST)	Cunningham et al., 1993
		Fears About Treatment Questionnaire (FTQ)	Oppenheimer et al., 1988
	Reasons for seeking treatment	Treatment Seeking Scale (TSS)	Cunningham et al., 1994
		Treatment Motivation Questionnaire (TMQ)	Ryan et al., 1995
		Readiness for Treatment Scale (RTS)	Simpson & Joe, 1993
		Reasons for Giving Up Drugs and Alcohol	Murphy & Bentall, 1992
		Reasons for Coming to Treatment Questionnaire (RCTQ)	Oppenheimer et al., 1988
		Circumstances, Motivation, Readiness, and Suitability Scales (CMRS)	DeLeon et al., 1994
	Treatment goals	Treatment Goals Inventory (TGI)	Glaser & Skinner, 1981
	Treatment services utilization	Treatment Services Review (TSR)	McLellan et al., 1992
Collateral information	Collateral reports	Form-90	Miller, 1996
		Comprehensive Drinker Profile (CDP)	Miller & Marlatt, 1984, 1987

[a]PRISM was formerly known as the SCID-A.

(Prochaska et al., 1992). In addition to being consistent with "practice wisdom" and theoretical approaches to change, the proposed focus on such awareness-raising factors for those in the precontemplation and contemplation phases is also consistent with recent evidence from individuals who resolved an alcohol problem on their own without the aid of formal treatment. Sobell, Sobell, Toneatto, and Leo (1993) found that over half of the recoveries of such individuals could be characterized by their cognitive evaluation of the pros and cons of continued drinking.

For a subset of individuals, the reasons that led to contemplating the need for change or seeking help may be sufficient to lead to long-term change in the absence of more formal treatment (Mariezcurrena, 1994; Marlatt et al., 1997; Sobell, Cunningham, & Sobell, 1996; Stall & Biernacki, 1986; Tucker & Gladsjo, 1993). For others, the assessment process, when combined with detailed feedback about the nature of the addictive behavior and advice about possible alternative coping strategies, may enhance motivation to change and may serve as an effective form of intervention which either may preclude the need for more extensive treatment or may increase the likelihood of accepting treatment referrals (e.g., Bien, Miller, & Tonigan, 1993; Heather, 1989; Miller, 1989).

Problem Assessment

The task of screening is to determine whether a problem exists; the task of problem assessment is to determine the extent of the identified problem. If an individual has been identified during the screening process as potentially having a problem, he or she should be referred for a more thorough evaluation. This action is consistent with the view that assessment is a sequential process (Donovan, 1988; Institute of Medicine, 1990; Sobell et al., 1994). This next level of assessment involves problem assessment, which involves a characterization of the nature, scope, and severity of the potential substance use disorder identified in the screening stage (Institute of Medicine, 1990). This stage of assessment requires more time and resources to conduct and thus is more costly than screening, but it is important in order to determine whether specialized treatment is needed and, if so, which available type or intensity of treatment is appropriate. Figure 11.1 depicts an assessment "funnel" that suggests that each step of the assessment process becomes more intensive and focused, with an attendant increase in expense and sensitivity. It also suggests that assessment is an ongoing and sequential process that interacts with the stage of treatment (Donovan, 1988).

Defining the Parameters of the Target Behavior

The most notable aspect of assessment is that it involves the collection, integration, and interpretation of information from and about the individual to allow a clear picture of the problem for which treatment is sought. While on the surface this appears to be a straightforward task, a biopsychosocial perspective of addictive behaviors suggests that multiple systems are involved in the development and maintenance of these behavior patterns (Donovan, 1988; Institute of Medicine, 1990; Skinner, 1988). Therefore, it is necessary for assessment to be multidimensional, focusing on the physiological, behavioral, psychological, and social factors that define or are related to the disorder. Consistent with this view, Harrell, Honaker, and Davis (1991) factor-analyzed assessment information collected from alcohol abusers and polydrug abusers. The assessment included measures of quantity/frequency of alcohol or drug use, physiological symptoms, situational stressors, antisocial behaviors, interpersonal problems, affective dysfunction, attitude toward treatment, degree of impact of problems on one's life, and expectancies about the substance's perceived ability to reduce tension, facilitate social interactions, and enhance mood. Three broad dimensions were found: behavioral/physiological, social, and cognitive. Alcohol and polydrug abusers, although demonstrating some differences, had relatively similar and parallel patterns of dysfunction across these three domains.

Within this context, the Institute of Medicine (1990) suggested that the assessment of alcohol problems should minimally include an evaluation of the parameters of alcohol use (e.g., quantity, frequency, pattern), the signs and symptoms of alcohol use, and

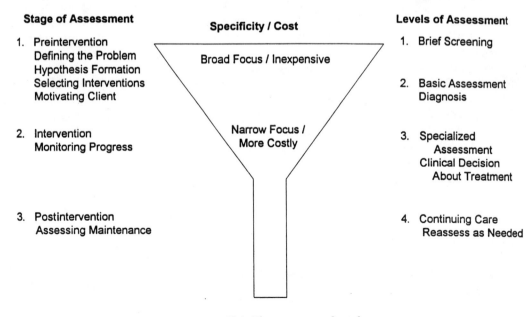

FIGURE 11.1 The assessment funnel.

the consequences of alcohol use. The same general dimensions should also be included in the assessment of the use of drugs other than (or in addition to) alcohol. However, it has been suggested that a greater focus be placed on the frequency of drug use rather than the quantity of substance consumed, due to difficulties in quantifying "doses" of a given drug, the amount of the active ingredients, and uncertainty about the actual drug(s) being used (Addiction Research Foundation, 1994). Additionally, other information about drug use should be collected, such as route of administration and pattern of use. The degree of consistency across these assessment domains is less than one might assume, with a wide degree of variability in the manifestations of substance use problems both within and across individuals. Sobell et al. (1988, 1994) provided detailed descriptions of the types of information that should be included in a comprehensive behavioral analysis and assessment of alcohol and drug problems that address multiple systems and dimensions of the target behavior. Similarly, Sobell and Sobell (1995) provide a detailed description, comparison, and recommendations of measures useful in assessing alcohol consumption. Maisto and McKay (1995) also provided information on measures appropriate for assessing the degree of alcohol dependence and the negative consequences associated with problem drinking.

Determining a Diagnosis

Beyond facilitating client motivation and treatment entry, assessment serves a number of other important functions in the management of substance abuse disorders (Allen & Mattson, 1993). One of these is the development of a diagnostic formulation, which is typically developed through the integration of information derived from the client's history of substance use, clinical interviews based on the specific criteria of the diagnostic system being employed, psychometric tests, and laboratory data. Kranzler, Tennen, Babor, Kadden, and Rounsaville (1997) suggested that, where possible, a longitudinal procedure in which an experienced, expert clinician uses all available data collected from multiple sources across time is a helpful method to arrive at valid diagnoses among substance abusers. The diagnostic system employed by the clinician is determined in part by one's theoretical perspective and provides a method of organizing the range of information gathered from a comprehensive assessment (Jacquot, 1992; Shaffer &

Kauffman, 1985). In addition to having practical reimbursement value for the clinician, the clinical diagnosis is meant to convey an understanding of the etiology, development, and manifestation of the substance use disorder; to aid in the development of appropriate treatment plans; and to provide some indication of the likely prognosis of the disorder (Jacobson, 1989a).

Substance-Related Diagnoses

The two diagnostic systems that are currently most commonly employed in substance abuse treatment settings include the *ICD-10* (World Health Organization, 1990) and the *DSM-IV* (American Psychiatric Association, 1994; Grant & Towle, 1991; Hasin, Li, McCloud, & Endicott, 1997). The set of core symptoms and related diagnostic criteria that define a substance use disorder in these systems, and the interrelationship among them, have been influenced greatly by the conceptualization of a substance dependence syndrome. This syndrome consists of a constellation of related features, the most prominent of which include a narrowing of the drinking or drug use repertoire, a salience of drink- or drug-seeking behavior, increased tolerance, repeated withdrawal symptoms, relief or avoidance of withdrawal symptoms, a subjective awareness of a compulsion to drink or use drugs, and a reinstatement of use patterns after an initial relapse following a period of abstinence. Not all of these features need to be present at all times or with the same degree of intensity across time for an individual or across individuals. The dependence construct, which had its origins in describing alcohol problems, appears to have been generalized successfully to other drugs of abuse (Babor, Cooney, & Lauerman, 1987; Blaine, Horton, & Towle, 1995; Edwards, 1986; Feingold & Rounsaville, 1995; Hasin, Grant, Harford, & Endicott, 1988; Morgenstern, Langenbucher, & Labouvie, 1994).

An important contribution made by the syndrome concept is that dependence can be rated along a continuum of the degree or severity of dependence rather than being viewed only as a dichotomous diagnostic classification (e.g., Hasin & Glick, 1992). Another important feature of the dependence syndrome is the distinction made between "dependence" and alcohol- or drug-related "disabilities," or the negative physical, mental, and psychosocial consequences in which alcohol or drug use is implicated. These disabilities are considered to be related to, but conceptually distinct from, the dependence syndrome. That is, it is possible to be dependent either with or without experiencing negative psychosocial consequences; similarly, it is possible to experience such negative consequences without necessarily meeting the criteria for dependence.

Many concerns exist about the adequacy of the currently available diagnostic systems and the general conceptual framework on which they rest (e.g., Beutler & Clarkin, 1990; Nathan, 1991; Sellman, 1994; Tarter, Moss, Arria, Mezzich, & Vanyukov, 1992; Widiger & Smith, 1994), as well as about difficulties in the practical translation of diagnostic concepts to clinical decision making and treatment planning (Babor, Orrok, Liebowitz, Salomon, & Brown, 1990). Also, despite the widespread adoption of the dependence syndrome in current diagnostic systems, concerns have been raised about a number of the elements of the syndrome, such as the need for tolerance and withdrawal (e.g., Carroll, Rounsaville, & Bryant, 1994) and the narrowing of the drinking or drug use repertoire (Cottler, Phelps, & Compton, 1995). A number of authors have also questioned the conceptual distinction between dependence and disabilities. Empirical evidence suggests that the constellation of core elements of the dependence syndrome are highly related to measures of health, social, and emotional problems attributable to alcohol or drug use and that they appear to represent a single factor, rather than two distinct dimensions (e.g., Hasin et al., 1988; Hasin, Muthuen, & Grant, 1994). However, from a practical clinical perspective, to be complete, a diagnostic assessment of substance use disorder should include an assessment of both the dependence syndrome, graded along a continuum of severity, and the types of negative consequences that have been experienced by the individual. Also, most diagnostic systems allow the determination of both "lifetime" occurrence of the diagnosis and whether the individual meets the diagnostic criteria based on symptom manifestation over a more recent time frame (e.g., the last 6 months).

Other Psychiatric Diagnoses

While the primary focus of the diagnostic interview is on the client's stated drug of choice, it must be more broadly based than this. Substance use or dependence does not usually exist in isolation. Dependence on a substance may represent a primary disorder, may occur in conjunction with other drug use

and/or dependence, may be secondary to other psychiatric conditions, or may coexist concurrently and independently with other psychiatric disorders (Craig, 1988; N. S. Miller, 1993). The presence of additional substance use and psychiatric problems increases both the complexity of the diagnostic and assessment processes (e.g., Dawes, Frank, & Rost, 1993; Teitelbaum & Carey, 1996; Woolf-Reeve, 1990) and the clinical determination of the most appropriate therapeutic approach (e.g., Rubenstein, Campbell, & Daley, 1990). This is true for major psychiatric disorders (e.g., Axis I) such as affective disorders and concurrent drug dependence. The presence of additional Axis I disorders, as well as the relative severity of more generalized psychiatric problems, is prognostic of poorer treatment outcome (McLellan, 1986; Rounsaville, Dolinsky, Babor, & Meyer, 1987) and most often requires the provision of more intensive treatment services (Alterman, McLellan, & Shifman, 1993). Axis II diagnoses are also relevant, given the strong relationship between certain addictive behaviors and personality disorders, particularly antisocial personality (e.g., Blume, 1989; Nace, Davis, & Gaspari, 1991). Again, the presence of a concurrent personality disorder may lead to poorer outcomes around substance use (Rounsaville, et al., 1987) or with respect to other areas of life function such as emotional health, social life, relationship with friends, or overall life satisfaction (Nace & Davis, 1993).

A number of structured, semistructured, and unstructured clinical interviews are available to assist the clinician with determining a diagnosis both of substance use disorders and other psychiatric disorders (see table 11.1). Hasin (1991), Grant and Towle (1990), and Maisto and McKay (1995) have provided extensive information on measures used in clinical and research settings to assess the alcohol dependence syndrome, provide a diagnostic classification of alcohol dependence or abuse, and measure aspects of problems and negative consequences related to alcohol use. Similarly, Rounsaville et al. (1993) provided a similar review of diagnostic measures used with drug abuse clients.

Other Substance-Related Domains

In order to gain a more thorough understanding of the individual's substance use disorder and to help develop appropriate plans for intervention, a number of additional features related to substance use need to be assessed. To a large extent, the domains to assess derive from cognitive behavioral models of substance abuse problems and factors that may be involved in relapse once the individual has reduced or stopped alcohol or drug use (e.g., Connors, Maisto, & Donovan, 1996; Donovan, 1996; Donovan & Chaney, 1985; Marlatt & Gordon, 1985; Rawson, Obert, McCann, & Marinelli, 1993). Such models suggest that individuals may develop substance abuse or dependence in part based upon the perception that substance use is functionally useful in dealing with interpersonal and intrapersonal situations that are stressful, are associated with prior use, or involve social pressures to use, for which the individual may not have adequate coping skills. In such situations the anticipated effects of the substance are seen as being able to bring about positive effects by its influence on moods and social behavior. Thus, assessment of these domains should include measures of the individual's beliefs about the anticipated effects of the substance on mood and behavior (outcome expectancies), the nature of those situations that may pose the greatest risk of relapse, the relative availability of or deficits in the individual's substance-specific and general coping abilities, and the person's belief about the relative availability of appropriate coping skills and the ability to use them successfully to deal effectively with potential risks of relapse (self-efficacy expectancies).

Outcome Expectancies

There has been an increased focus on the role played by the individual's expectancies concerning the anticipated effects of alcohol or drugs on mood and behavior in the development and maintenance of substance use problems, as well as their potential contribution to relapse following behavior change (e.g., Brown, 1993; Oei & Baldwin, 1994). In general, substance-related expectancies typically refer to the beliefs or cognitive representations held by the individual concerning the anticipated effects or outcomes expected to occur after consuming alcohol. These expectancies are shaped by an individual's past direct or indirect experiences with substances and the behaviors associated with their use (Connors & Maisto, 1988). To the extent that these representations are activated and accessible to the individual in situations associated with using, they are hypothesized to determine the anticipated outcomes

in drinking or drug use and to mediate subsequent drinking behavior (Rather & Goldman, 1994; Stacy, Leigh, & Weingardt, 1994). It is typically presumed that individuals drink or use drugs in order to achieve or enhance the emotional or behavioral outcomes that they expect; thus, expectancies are viewed as reflective of possible reasons for using.

There is considerably more information available about alcohol-related expectancies than about expectancies of the effects of other drugs (Brown, 1993). Donovan (1995) provides a review of a number of the measures assessing alcohol-related expectancies. There has been a recent increase in the development of assessment instruments focusing on expectancies related to use of other substances such as cocaine and marijuana (e.g., Jaffe & Kilbey, 1994; Schafer & Brown, 1991). Initial efforts at assessing alcohol-related expectancies focused primarily on anticipated positive outcomes (e.g., Goldman, Brown, & Christiansen, 1987). It was assumed that these positive expectancies created a "pull" toward alcohol by developing a positively valenced incentive to drink. More recently, increasing attention has been paid to the role of expectancies about the negative effects of alcohol or other drugs which may serve as a deterrent or disincentive to use (e.g., Jones & McMahon, 1994). It appears, then, that there are different motivational factors represented by positive and negative expectancies in relationship to drinking behavior (McMahon & Jones, 1993), and that each may contribute to the prediction of relapse and treatment outcome (Jones & McMahon, 1994). Therefore, it is important to assess both positive and negative expectancies.

Relapse Risk

Marlatt and Gordon (1985) suggested that a number of different types of situations may increase the likelihood of relapse. The three primary categories include negative emotional states such as anger and resentment associated with interpersonal encounters, negative emotions such as depression and boredom which are more intrapersonal, and either direct or indirect social pressure to use. Cognitive behavioral relapse models suggest that if individuals encounter such high-risk situations and do not have available adequate or appropriate coping skills to deal with the situational demands, they experience a decrease in self-efficacy, the salience of the anticipated positive outcomes of substance use increase, and relapse is more likely to occur.

A number of measures have been developed to assess each of these domains. Annis and colleagues, for example, have developed parallel measures to assess drinking and drug use situations (Annis, Graham, & Davis, 1987; Annis & Graham, 1991). The situations presented in these scales are based on those found in Marlatt and Gordon's (1980) taxonomy of high-risk relapse situations. Individuals are asked to indicate how frequently they have consumed alcohol or used drugs either in these situations or in response to them. The assumption underlying the assessment model is that the more frequently one has drunk or used drugs in these settings, the greater the associative strength between the situation and drinking or using, and the greater the likelihood of drinking and using in such settings in the future. From the client's responses, a "problem index" score is calculated for each of the categories of drinking situations, allowing the construction of a client profile showing the individual's areas of greatest risk for heavy drinking and helping to target and guide interventions. It should be noted that the presumed high-risk situations identified by such measures have been associated only with heavy drinking or drug use; therefore, it may be inappropriate to presume a causal link between the types of situations endorsed, drinking or drug use behavior, and the likelihood of relapse (Sobell et al., 1994). Sobell et al. (1994) suggested that other factors, such as coping skills deficits, may represent a common third factor that may moderate the relationship between a given situation and relapse risk. Similarly, the categories assessed by such inventories provide information only about general categories of situations or general problem areas and may be lacking in detail about more personalized risk situations. Sobell et al. (1994) indicated that it is important to explore in more depth the unique and personally relevant high-risk situations or areas where the client lacks self-confidence for resisting drinking or drug use. Other methods, primarily interviews, attempt to gain a more individualized assessment of the antecedents to and consequences of previous relapse episodes (e.g., Schonfeld, Peters, & Dolente, 1993).

Coping

Cognitive behavioral models of relapse assume that the strength of self-efficacy expectancies depends on the availability and accessibility of the emotional and behavioral skills necessary to cope with situations that are appraised as a challenge to one's perception of control and that therefore may precipitate a relapse. It is assumed that the greater the individual's available repertoire of coping skills, the greater the strength of self-efficacy, and the lower the probability of relapse or drinking in a given situation.

A number of measures have been developed that assess coping skills, specifically targeting alcohol or drug use. These include both self-report measures (e.g., Litman, Stapleton, Oppenheim, & Peleg, 1983) and behavioral analogue or role play methods (e.g., Chaney, Marlatt, & O'Leary, 1978; Hawkins, Catalano, & Wells, 1986; Monti et al., 1993). The self-report measures assess the behavioral and emotional coping strategies that the individual uses to avoid relapse and the perceived effectiveness of these strategies. Individuals more likely to maintain posttreatment abstinence tended, when assessed at treatment entry, to perceive themselves as having more effective coping strategies overall and as rating the positive thinking and avoidance approaches as more effective than those who would relapse during follow-up (Litman, Stapleton, Oppenheim, Peleg, & Jackson, 1984). The role play methods present individuals with hypothetical high-risk relapse situations and ask them to respond as they would if actually in those situations. Microelements of the responses (e.g., latency to respond, length of response), observer-rated skillfulness or adequacy of the response to resolve the situation without drinking or using drugs, and self-reported anxiety and craving in the situations have been assessed (e.g., Schmitz, Oswald, Damin, & Mattis, 1995). Latency to respond, observer-rated anxiety and observer-rated estimates of skill deficits, and self-reported urges to drink have been found to predict poorer drinking-related posttreatment outcomes among alcoholics (Chaney et al., 1978; Kadden, Litt, Cooney, & Busher, 1992). Also, Kadden et al. (1992) found that those individuals who had more difficulty in the role play benefited more from a coping-skills training program of aftercare than from a supportive interactional therapy.

While it appears that substance abusers' coping ability is dependent in part on situational parameters in high-risk situations (Schmitz et al., 1995), it is also important to assess their more general coping and problem-solving skills (Beutler & Clarkin, 1990). DeNelsky and Boat (1986) provided a model of psychological assessment and treatment that is based on the assessment of the individual's coping skills and deficits in dealing with interpersonal relationships, thoughts and feelings, approaches to herself or himself and life, and the ability to sustain goal-directed effort. The availability of such skills is seen as important in dealing with problems that can be anticipated during the course of the treatment and maintenance phases and therefore should have an effect on the probability of relapse. A number of measures of coping ability are available and are consistent with this general model (e.g., Folkman & Lazarus, 1980; Moos, 1995).

Self-Efficacy

A second major cognitive factor to be incorporated into the assessment of substance abusers is self-efficacy (DiClemente, 1986; Rollnick & Heather, 1982; Wilson, 1987). While this construct plays a prominent role in cognitive behavioral models of problem drinking, considerably less research attention has been focused on its assessment and its relationship to drinking behavior than has been given to alcohol-related outcome expectancies (Young, Oei, & Crook, 1991). Also, as is true of outcome expectancies, considerably more work appears to have been done to date in the assessment of self-efficacy associated with alcohol than with other drugs. This self-efficacy construct has been defined in terms of the beliefs that individuals hold or their level of confidence concerning their ability to resist engaging in drinking or drug use behavior (Oei & Baldwin, 1994; Young et al., 1991). In addition to attempting to infer an individual's relative degree of self-efficacy from an assessment of coping skills, a number of measures have been developed to assess this domain more directly. For example, Annis and colleagues have developed a set of measures, paralleling those that assess high-risk situations, that ask the individual's level of confidence that he or she would not drink or not drink heavily or use drugs in each of these situations (Annis & Graham, 1988; Martin, Wilkinson, & Poulos, 1995). Similarly, DiClemente, Carbonari, Montgomery, and Hughes (1994) assessed the degree of confidence and the degree of temptation the individual might experience in a number of high-risk situations. Each of these approaches allows the clinician to evaluate the strength of the "pull" to drink or use drugs relative to the degree of confidence that one will not

do so. Again, more individualized assessments of self-efficacy and prioritization of high-risk situations may provide the more specific information needed to tailor interventions than is possible with measures of confidence and temptation in more general categories of risk situations (Miller, McCrady, Abrams, & Labouvie, 1994).

Personal Assessment: Domains of Assessment

The role of assessment goes well beyond classifying the individual's problem diagnostically to providing a more extensive picture of other areas of life functioning. Individuals who seek treatment usually have multiple problems in a number of life areas, such as employment, legal status, emotional function, social role function, medical status, and family relations (e.g., Siegal et al., 1995; Wallace, 1986). The assessment of functioning in these life areas, following screening and problem assessment, has been described by the Institute of Medicine (1990) as personal assessment. It is in this stage that a comprehensive assessment of the individual and his or her life problems is conducted. The nature, scope, and severity of such problems contribute to the treatment-planning process as well as to subsequent treatment outcome. The severity of problems in these life areas at the point of initial assessment and entry into treatment has also been found to predict poorer outcomes among alcohol-, opiate-, and cocaine-dependent clients in both publicly and privately funded treatment programs (McLellan et al. 1994). However, the more treatment services individuals receive specifically targeting these problem areas, the better the outcome compared to the outcome of those with similar problem severity who do not receive as much specifically targeted clinical service (McLellan et al., 1994).

In addition to an assessment of problem areas in psychosocial and role functioning, a number of other domains need to be considered. One is personality and psychopathology. The role of personality variables has been investigated with respect to the development of substance use disorders, their correlates with substance use patterns, and their prognostic utility in predicting treatment outcome (Craig, 1995; Sutker & Allain, 1988). Also, personality factors appear to represent one of several categories of interacting variables that may contribute to the "reasons" or motivation for using alcohol and drugs (Cox & Klinger, 1987). A number of authors have made the distinction between personality factors that antedate the onset of substance abuse problems and may contribute to their development (e.g., the "preaddict personality") and "clinical personality" variables, representing the characteristics of substance abusers who have sought out and are involved in treatment (Barnes, 1983; Craig, 1995). Craig (1995) described the "clinical personality" of substance abusers as frequently including the following traits: passivity and dependence, an external locus of control, low self-esteem, cognitions that are self-derogatory, depression, anxiety, immaturity, impulsivity, anger, low self-esteem, and psychopathic traits. While not all substance abusers present such characteristics and different combinations of these traits may be seen in others, these are traits that the clinician has to work with regardless of their origin.

To some extent, this area is related to some approaches that might be used in determining diagnoses, in that one would be looking for other forms of psychological/psychiatric problems (Axis I) and personality disorders (Axis II) as part of the diagnostic process. Other measures can provide continuous measures of personality traits that may be useful. Measures such as the MMPI-2 (Hathaway et al., 1989) and MCMI-II (Millon, 1992) have been found useful in assessing and determining treatment approaches for alcohol- and drug-dependent populations (e.g., Craig & Olson, 1992; Craig & Weinberg, 1992a, 1992b). Similarly, there is a high prevalence of sociopathy and antisocial behavior among alcoholics and substance abusers. Cooney, Kadden, and Litt (1990) found that the Socialization scale on the California Psychological Inventory (CPI; Gough, 1975) is a particularly good index of this measure and that it might have merit in matching clients to appropriate treatments (Kadden, Cooney, Getter, & Litt, 1989).

Two issues should be noted in regard to the utility of measures of personality and psychopathology. First, it is often difficult to determine whether the features seen in substance abusers in treatment contributed etiologically to the development of their substance use disorders or whether these are features that have developed secondary to their abuse of the substances (Craig, 1995). Second, those substance abusers who enter treatment are not representative of the broader population of substance abusers; those entering treatment often have a broader range and

greater severity of psychological and psychosocial problems than those who do not seek treatment (Marlatt et al., 1997).

It is also relevant to consider a more thorough assessment of individuals' general emotional state. This can be done by use of measures that attempt to provide an overview of a number of dimensions of emotional function, such as the SCL-90 (Derogatis, 1977), or by use of scales that are specific to a particular emotion. If one chooses the latter approach, it would seem appropriate that the assessment minimally include assessment of depression, anger, and anxiety, each of which has been associated with alcohol and drug use as either possible contributors to or consequences of use.

Determining Readiness to Change and Readiness for Treatment

As noted previously, individuals may be in different stages of readiness to change their alcohol and drug use behaviors. The assessment process can assist in determining where they fall with respect to this dimension. Three measures are available to assist; each is based on Prochaska and DiClemente's model of stages of behavior change (Prochaska et al., 1992). Two of these scales, the University of Rhode Island Change Assessment Instrument (URICA; McConnaughy, Prochaska, & Velicer, 1983) and the Stages of Change Readiness and Treatment Eagerness Scale (SOCRATES; Miller & Tonigan, 1996) have been used primarily with substance abusers who have sought treatment. The other, the Readiness to Change Questionnaire (Rollnick, Heather, Gold, & Hall, 1992), was designed not for those seeking treatment but for use as part of a screening of medical patients who might have alcohol abuse problems. Each of these measures provides a determination of the stage of change (e.g., precontemplation, contemplation, preparation, action) that best categorizes the individual's readiness to change.

Even if a person evidences a willingness to change his or her addictive behavior, this does not mean that he or she is necessarily interested in treatment (Marlatt et al., 1997). There may be a number of reasons why individuals might choose not to seek or to delay seeking treatment, ranging from fear of stigmatization, to concerns about whether treatment will be effective or not, to wanting to try to quit without formal treatment, as well as a number of more practical logistical barriers, such as the lack of child care. Similarly, there are many reasons why an individual seeks treatment at a given time. The factors influencing this decision may be external pressure, such as from the legal system, family, or employer; internal sources of motivation, such as concerns about one's health or the result of weighing the costs of continued use against the benefits of stopping, might also be involved. Ryan, Plant, and O'Malley (1995) found that a group of cocaine-dependent clients who had high levels of both external and internal motivation for seeking treatment were more compliant with outpatient treatment and had better short-term outcomes than those having other combinations of these two sources of motivation. Thus, it is important to know what barriers individuals may have overcome in their pursuit of treatment, as well as to determine the nature, degree, and sources of motivation for seeking treatment at this particular time. Additionally, it is helpful to know the individual's perception of the type of treatment that he or she feels is most appropriate for the particular substance use disorder and problems in other life areas that has led to seeking help. A number of scales have been developed to assist the clinician to systematically assess potential barriers to and motivation for treatment entry as well as the individual's goals and the types of treatment being sought (e.g., Allen 1994; Cunningham, Sobell, Sobell, & Gaskin, 1994; Curry, Wagner, & Grothaus, 1990; DeLeon, Melnick, Kressel, & Jainchill, 1994; Glaser & Skinner, 1981; McBride et al., 1994; Murphy & Bentall, 1992; Oppenheimer, Sheehan, & Taylor, 1988; Ryan, et al., 1995; Simpson & Joe, 1993).

Treatment Planning: Matching Clients to Treatments

Within the clinical context, the primary goal of assessment is to determine those characteristics of the client and his or her current life situation that may influence decisions about treatment and that may contribute to the success of treatment (Allen, 1991). Assessment procedures are crucial to and provide information necessary for the treatment-planning process. Treatment planning involves the integration of assessment information concerning the person's drinking behavior, alcohol-related problems (problem assessment), and other areas of psychological and social functioning (personal assessment) to assist

the client and the clinician in developing and prioritizing short- and long-term goals for treatment, in selecting the most appropriate interventions to address the identified problems, in determining and addressing perceived barriers to treatment engagement and compliance, and in monitoring progress toward the specified goals, improved psychosocial functioning, and harm reduction (Bois & Graham, 1993; Miller & Mastria, 1977; Sobell et al., 1988). The assessment and treatment-planning processes should lead to the individualization of treatment, appropriate client-treatment matching, and the monitoring of goal attainment (Allen & Mattson, 1993), based on the assumption that more appropriate matches between client and therapy will lead to both a better outcome and a more cost-effective delivery of services. While assessment at intake is instrumental attempts to match clients to the most appropriate available treatment options, it should also be viewed as a continuous process that allows monitoring of treatment progress, refocusing and reprioritizing of treatment goals and interventions across time, and determination of outcome (Donovan, 1988; Institute of Medicine, 1990; Sobell et al., 1994).

HOW AND WHEN TO ASSESS: PRACTICAL ASPECTS OF THE ASSESSMENT PROCESS

How Much Is Enough? Balancing Scope of Assessment with Cost and Utility

There is a tendency for those working in the mental health field generally and in substance abuse more specifically to want to know as much about the client as we can. This information is important in our attempt to understand the individual, the issues that historically contributed to his or her personal development and the etiology of a substance use disorder, and the client's current life circumstances. However, there is the risk that we may be collecting more information than is necessary to adequately plan appropriate treatments for the individual. The assessment process should be comprehensive; however, from a practical perspective, it should also be relatively parsimonious, given the array of areas that can be assessed (Donovan, 1988; Institute of Medicine, 1990). As Geller (1991) pointed out, for assessment procedures and instruments to be useful in clinical settings, they must provide a sufficient breadth of coverage of those client symptoms (problem assessment) and other areas of concern (personal assessment) that are relevant to clinical decision making, their use must be economically feasible, and the information obtained must be specific to those treatment options that are realistically available to the client. Similarly, Sobell et al. (1994) suggested that there is no standard formula for determining the length, breadth, or depth of a clinical assessment. Rather, the ultimate parameters of an assessment should be individually determined by both clinical judgment and common sense. A number of different strategies can be used to provide a framework and direction for the assessment process in each of the systems and domains noted above. Skinner (1988) and the Institute of Medicine (1990) have distinguished between two types of content in the personal assessment stage. The first is noncontingent content, which involves information that should be routinely and always collected on the individual (e.g., demographics, family history of substance abuse, prior treatment history). The contingent problem assessment employs a sequential approach, in which a less intensive screening of a broad range of life areas is conducted; those areas noted as being potentially problematic can be pursued further with more intensive and specialized assessments. A second strategy is the use of clinical hypothesis testing, in which the clinician formulates hypotheses about the individual's behavior based on his or her theoretical perspective and collects information through the assessment process to test the apparent validity of the hypotheses (Shaffer & Kauffman, 1985; Shaffer & Neuhaus, 1985). Each of these approaches is meant to provide information about the most critical factors in determining the assignment of the client to treatment.

Timing and Sequence of Assessments

Few guidelines have been developed to assist clinicians in determining the appropriate timing and sequencing of assessments of substance abusers (Allen, Columbus, & Fertig, 1995; Rounsaville, 1993; Schottenfeld, 1994). While the assessment process may include the collection of information from collateral sources, such as significant others and laboratory findings, most will rely heavily on the client's self-report. A major consideration in trying to determine the timing of the assessment and the ordering of different types of measures within it is the amount of time that has passed since the last drink or use of drugs. To be maximally useful to the clinician, assessments need to be conducted as soon as possible after the client is admitted to treatment in order to allow the integration of the obtained information into a treatment plan; however, it must not be so soon after the last use of alcohol or drugs that the information is distorted by the residual effects of acute intoxication, withdrawal, or emotional distress. The issue of timing becomes more complex since the length of stay in inpatient treatment settings is being reduced markedly and more treatment functions are being moved to outpatient settings.

It appears that a determination of the timing should take into account both the nature of the measures being used and the type of substance the client has been using. Allen et al. (1995) suggested that those tests requiring a high level of cognitive function should be delayed longer and be sequenced later in the assessment process than measures that focus on traitlike personality characteristics. However, there is no standard recommended length of time before such tests should be administered. Sherer, Haygood, and Alfano (1984) examined different time frames for administering both personality and cognitive function measures to newly admitted alcoholics who were toxic upon admission. Test results were quite unstable at the earliest testing point (4 days after admission) but appeared to be relatively stable on most measures at 10 days or later. Goldman (1987) found that alcoholics evidence a very marked recovery of neuropsychological functioning in the first month after they stop drinking; evaluation of cognitive functions before at least 2–3 weeks following cessation thus are likely to be quite unstable and to underestimate the individual's level of abilities. Also, the rate of recovery in this early period of recovery was often slower for older alcoholics and those with a more chronic history of alcoholism. Brown and colleagues (Brown et al., 1995; Brown, Irwin, & Schuckit, 1991; Brown & Schuckit, 1988) have also examined the time course of changes in both anxiety and depression during the early phases of treatment and recovery. Alcoholics evidenced an initially high level of state anxiety immediately following admission to inpatient treatment, but their scores typically returned to the normal range by the second week of treatment. Similarly, the symptoms of depression appeared to abate fairly quickly after the initiation of treatment. At admission, nearly half the patients had clinically significant depression, but only 6% remained clinically depressed at the end of 4 weeks of treatment. The greatest reduction in depression appeared to occur during the second week. It further appears that at least 3 weeks of abstinence from alcohol are needed to differentiate consistently between primary alcoholics who are depressed from alcoholics with primary affective disorder on the basis of their depressive symptomatology.

Based on these results, it appears that minimally 10 days to 3 weeks should pass from last drink or use before the resultant variables being assessed can be considered somewhat more stable and no longer being distorted by acute alcohol or drug effects or withdrawal distress. This time frame may represent an "ideal," given that managed-care programs often mandate inpatient stays of less than 10 days. Given the need for information useful for treatment planning purposes within this "real" time frame, measures that are less likely to be affected by alcohol or drug effects or withdrawal (e.g., demographic characteristics, legal history, trait-based client attributes) should be given earlier in the assessment sequence; measures that are more likely to be affected by alcohol or drug effects (e.g., cognitive function, current mood states) should occur later in the sequence, when the individual is more likely to have had a more extended period of abstinence (Allen et al., 1995; Rounsaville, 1993). A number of client characteristics such as age, length of heavy use, time since last use, and the presence of other comorbid psychiatric or physical conditions may moderate the rate of recovery of a number of functions; thus, interpretations of the assessment results need to take these factors into account. Given that individuals often continue to evidence improvements in cognitive and psychological functioning beyond these time frames, the process of assessment should be viewed as an ongoing process rather than one taking place only at a single point (Donovan, 1988).

Variability Based on Substance of Use and Abuse

In addition to the influence of client characteristics on the reliability and validity of information derived from assessment, the types of substances and a number of their characteristics must also be taken into account (Rounsaville, 1993). Substance abusers in-

volved in an assessment may be in one of four general phases related to their substance use: (a) acute intoxication (usually less that 24 hours since ingestion); (b) steady state use of the drug (having taken sufficient quantities in a time frame to avoid withdrawal); (c) withdrawal—both acute and prolonged; and (d) extended abstinence. Rounsaville (1993) suggested that the rate of absorption and the half-life of the drugs being used do affect the assessment process. In general, the more rapid the absorption and the shorter the half-life, the more intense and briefer the duration of the "high" or intoxicated state, and the more intense and briefer the withdrawal syndrome. Given the four states that must be considered for each class of drugs, the variability in absorption and half-life of each class, and the likelihood that an individual may be using multiple drugs from the same or different classes of drugs, the determination of timing of assessments is extremely complex. Rounsaville (1993) provided a number of useful steps that could make this determination somewhat more manageable. Before the evaluation, the clinician should get detailed information about the types of substances used, the amount and frequency of use, and the amounts used in the past day, week, and 30 days and should perform a cursory evaluation of the individual's current subjective state vis-à-vis the drugs he or she is taking. Those who report themselves as being either acutely intoxicated or in acute withdrawal should be rescheduled for assessment. In those cases where more than one assessment session is necessary, it may be appropriate to group together those measures that are likely to be unaffected by the influence of substances and to administer them separately from those likely to be affected by drugs. Also, given that a number of drug-induced effects may mimic symptoms of psychiatric disorders, it is important to conduct psychiatric interviews only after a history of recent drug use has been completed and the individual is not currently intoxicated or in withdrawal.

Methods to Enhance Validity and Reliability of Assessments

A common clinical concern is that substance abusers may not provide an accurate picture of their alcohol or drug use or of other aspects of their life potentially relevant to treatment planning. Substance abusers are often described as having a predisposition to minimize their drug use and related problems (e.g., Fuller, 1988; Schottenfeld, 1994; Watson, Tilleskjor, Hoodecheck-Schow, Pucel, & Jacobs, 1984), thus potentially adding another source of variability to the accuracy of self reports. While many substance abusers tend to underreport their use, others, particularly in treatment-seeking settings, may exaggerate their use. Regardless of the direction, the fear among clinicians is that the resulting self-reports are of questionable reliability and/or validity.

Despite this clinical concern, research suggests that the possible distortion in the self-report process is less problematic than it is feared to be. Babor and colleagues (Babor, Brown, & DelBoca, 1990; Babor & DelBoca, 1992; Babor, Stephens, & Marlatt, 1987), as well as the Institute of Medicine (1990), have noted that self-reports provided by alcoholic subjects are by and large reliable and valid. There is, however, a fairly large degree of variability across individuals. This appears to be related to the sensitivity of the information being gathered, the nature and specificity of the information against which the self-reports are being validated, the level of sobriety at the time of the assessment, the time window to be covered by the information being collected, and the demand characteristics of the assessment setting and purpose.

While a large body of evidence suggests that self-reports of substance use, negative consequences, and life events of alcohol- and drug-dependent clients are valid and reliable (e.g., Cordingley, Wilkinson, & Martin, 1990; Gladsjo, Tucker, Hawkins, & Vuchinich, 1992; Miller, Crawford, & Taylor, 1979; Sobell & Sobell, 1986; Stasiewicz, Bradizza, & Connors, 1997; Wilson & Grube, 1994), Fuller (1988) and Watson et al. (1984) have suggested that self-reports alone are insufficient. The use of multiple sources (e.g., collateral informants), the assessment of multiple systems (e.g., biochemical markers as well as self-report), the use of "bogus pipeline techniques," and the establishment of an interpersonal context that enhances rapport and motivation all appear to be important in maximizing the honesty of reports (Rankin, 1990).

Collateral Informants

A collateral informant, typically a spouse, parent, child, significant other, and/or friend of the client, is often asked to provide information about the client's alcohol and drug use as a way of both broadening the scope of the assessment process and verifying the client's self-report (Maisto & Connors, 1990). Such verification is strongly recommended, since the validity of self-reports appears to be enhanced (Wilson & Grube, 1994), and involvement of a significant other in the assessment and treatment process appears to improve treatment outcome (Waltman, 1995). When differences are found between the reports of clients and those of collaterals, the percentage of collaterals who overestimate clients' substance use is about equal to the percentage of clients who underestimate self-reported substance use (Miller et al., 1979). Cordingley et al. (1990) found that poly-drug users reported more drug use than collateral informants but were less likely to report negative drug-related consequences. Investigators have found that the likelihood and degree of discrepancies between client and collateral vary as a function of the relative ability of the collateral to observe the drinking and drug use behaviors of the client, the degree of certainty concerning the accuracy of her or his reports, the degree to which the clients are concerned about issues of confidentiality, and the relative familiarity and frequency of contact the collateral has had with the client (e.g., Gladsjo et al., 1992; Wilson & Grube, 1994). It is also felt that the validity of self-reports increases when clients expect independent corroboration of their reports. This is the assumption underlying the "bogus pipeline procedure," in which individuals are led to believe that the clinical staff has an independent and objective measure of substance use and severity of consequences. A number of standardized measures, such as the Form-90 (Miller, 1996) and the Comprehensive Drinker Profile (Miller & Marlatt, 1984, 1987), include interview protocols for use in collecting information from collaterals.

Biological Measures

A second area of assessment that provides useful information about the client's alcohol and drug use is biological markers that can be derived from blood and urine samples. A number of markers have been used to identify those individuals who may be vulnerable to the development of alcohol problems (e.g., "trait measures"; Helander & Tabakoff, 1997) and both chronic and more recent (e.g., "state") alcohol consumption (Allen, Fertig, Litten, Sillanaukee, & Anton, 1997; Anton, Litten, & Allen, 1995; Conigrave, Saunders, & Whitfield, 1995). Anton et al. (1995) suggested that biological measures are best seen as markers of alcohol consumption rather than as markers of alcoholism. This view is also more consistent with the application of such measures in clinical settings. Measures that have been evaluated have included gamma-glutamyltransferase (GGT), aspartate aminotransferase (AST), carbohydrate-deficient transferrin (CDT), and mean corpuscular volume (MCV). Anton et al. (1995) provided a thorough review of biological measures appropriate to assessing recent alcohol intake, acute intake, subacute intake, and chronic intake, including information about sensitivity and specificity, detection limits, ease of use, availability of assays, and the relative costs of each measure. Given that each test has limitations around its specificity and sensitivity, it is typically recommended that multiple biological measures be used together and in conjunction with self-report.

Measures used to screen for drug use are derived from both urinalysis and hair analysis. These two approaches to assessment have different but complementary functions (Vereby, 1992): Urinalysis provides an index of more recent or concurrent drug use, while hair analysis provides a long-term drug use history. Different laboratory methods used in assaying urine samples for drugs are available (e.g., thin-layer chromatography [TLC], radioimmunoassay [RIA], and enzyme immunoassay [EIA], including enzyme multiplied immunoassay technique [EMIT]; Saxon, Calsyn, Haver, & DeLaney, 1988). There are typically two types of tests conducted (Saxon et al., 1988). Screening laboratory tests are typically simple, efficient, and inexpensive and are used as a first step in assaying large numbers of urine samples. The second test is confirmatory and is employed when the initial screening test is positive for drug use; these confirmatory tests are usually more time-intensive and expensive. The preponderance of research on the validity of self-report use by drug abusers has been found to be positively correlated with the results of urinalysis (e.g., Harrison, 1995; Maisto, McKay, & Connors, 1990; Zanis, McLellan, & Randall, 1994). The variability in the validity of self-report appears to be related to the recency of the drug use (e.g., a discrepancy may exist because the window of measurement for certain drugs in urinalysis is relatively short, whereas self-report may cover a longer period of time), the social desirability of the drug being used (e.g., marijuana vs. heroin), contin-

gencies involved in treatment for positive urine results, the frequency and nature of the urine collection protocol (e.g., random vs. fixed), and the method employed in collecting the urine samples (e.g., supervised vs. unsupervised) (Harrison, 1995; Maisto et al., 1990; Moran, Mayberry, Kinniburgh, & James, 1995; Sherman & Bigelow, 1992).

The radioimmunoassay of hair (RIAH) is a more recent development in the screening process for identifying drug use. As blood circulates, it supplies hair follicles; when drugs are present in the blood, elements of the drugs are incorporated into and remain in the hair as it grows. Thus, a strand of hair can provide a history of drug use and abstinence for up to approximately a year; it may be possible to detect drug use for months after 2 or 3 days' use (Vereby, 1992). To a large extent, the results of hair analyses have been found to be positively related to the results of both self-reports of drug use and urinalysis in detecting cocaine, marijuana, and heroin use among substance-dependent clients (Hindin et al., 1994; Magura, Freeman, Siddiqi, & Lipton, 1992). The apparent agreement among hair analysis, urinalysis, and self-report measures of drug use suggests a high degree of convergence among these three indicators. It appears that use of the combination of self-report, urinalysis, and hair analysis provides the most accurate account of the client's recent drug use patterns and history (Cook, Bernstein, Arrington, Andrews, & Marshall, 1995).

Within the context of clinical assessment, a particular biochemical marker or set of markers can be used to corroborate self-reports of alcohol and/or drug use or may provide valuable independent information when an individual is unable or unwilling to offer valid data about alcohol or drug use. Such markers can also serve as methods to screen for problem alcohol or drug use, to determine whether a health problem is likely to be substance-related, and to monitor alcoholics and drug addicts for continued use or relapse during and after treatment (Allen et al., 1997). It is often difficult to decide which of the measures should serve as the "gold standard." It is clear that self-report, collateral information, and biological measures have limitations. As noted above, it is recommended, where possible, to get measures from all three of these sources. A common practice is to assume a conservative stance and to use that source having the most negative outcome for the client as an index of alcohol or drug use. This approach is similar to using the "lead" standard, which suggests that clinicians use a "longitudinal, expert, all-data" procedure in determining the client's clinical status (Kranzler et al., 1997).

Babor et al. (1990) and the Institute of Medicine (1990) have provided a number of additional, more specific approaches to the clinical assessment process that are meant to enhance the validity of self-report. A number of these are presented in table 11.2.

Interviewing Techniques and Style

Traditional views within the substance abuse field have suggested that the alcoholic and the drug abuser are to a large extent unmotivated, may be in denial, and are resistant to looking at their behavior or to make changes. In order to deal with this constellation of traits, a confrontive stance has often been suggested to facilitate clients' acceptance of their problem and their maximum benefit from treatment. A concern about this more traditional approach to clients, especially as they are seeking treatment, is that a confrontive therapist style, the attribution of denial and resistance to the alcoholic or addict, and the ex-

TABLE 11.2 Factors Enhancing the Reliability and Validity of Self-Reports Among Substance Abusers

The client is alcohol- and drug-free when interviewed.

Sufficient time has passed since last drink/drug use to allow clear responses.

Confidentiality is assured.

The setting is nonthreatening and nonjudgmental and encourages honest reporting.

The client does not feel pressure to respond in a particular way.

The client has no reason to distort reports (e.g., abstinence being a condition of parole).

The client is aware that corroborating information is available and will be collected (e.g., breath test, report of spouse), and that this information from other sources will be used to confirm what he or she reports.

Care is taken to ensure that questions are clearly worded and valid measurement approaches are used.

The assessment worker or therapist has a good rapport with the client.

The person administering the measures should be able to communicate clearly with the client.

Note. Adapted from National Institute on Alcohol Abuse and Alcoholism (1990) and the Addiction Research Foundation (1994).

pectation that the person will assume the label of *alcoholic* or *addict* as a prerequisite to change will lead to a negative reaction in the client. The negative feelings that may be engendered by such a confrontive intervention, in conjunction with a variety of other potential barriers to treatment, may lead the ambivalent client to pull away from rather than to approach treatment.

The more traditional view has been challenged recently by Miller and colleagues (Miller, 1983, 1989; Miller, Benefield, & Tonigan, 1993; Miller & Rollnick, 1991). A view more consistent with the clinician's task and the goal of increasing commitment to change has begun to emerge. In addition to a number of more specific clinical approaches helpful in minimizing therapist-generated barriers and enhancing clients' commitment during the initial phases of the assessment process (e.g., viewing "denial" or "resistance" not as stable personality traits but as states that can be modified within the context of the working alliance developed between the client and the clinician; reducing the emphasis on the individual's accepting the label *addict* or *alcoholic*; eliciting client self-motivational statements which reflect an increased level of cognitive awareness of the problems associated with the addiction, express an affective concern about the problem, and evidence a need to make behavioral changes), the clinician's interpersonal and therapeutic style is quite important. A therapist style based on the principles of motivational interviewing and a nondirective, supportive approach has been found to generate less "resistance" from clients, to be more successful in engaging individuals with alcohol problems in the therapeutic process, and to predict better outcomes than a more directive, confrontive style (Miller et al., 1993). In this regard, it has been found that alcoholic clients' perception of the quality of the therapeutic relationship with the staff member conducting an initial assessment is highly related to subsequent engagement in treatment (Hyams, Cartwright, & Spratley, 1996). Clients were more willing to engage if they felt they liked the staff member, felt understood, felt at ease with the worker, and felt very satisfied with the way they were treated; if the worker was warm and friendly with the client and expressed a high degree of understanding; and if the client had both a sense of catharsis in the assessment session and an opportunity to ask questions. Clients were less likely to engage if they felt criticized by the worker, if they felt the worker treated them as "stupid," if they perceived the worker not as being warm and genuine, but as merely acting a professional role, and if they perceived the worker as withholding information.

SUMMARY

Assessment is the initial step in the longer term process of therapy and behavior change. Its functions extend well beyond information gathering. The hope is that the clinician, through the assessment process, will motivate the individual, helping him or her move from the point of contemplating the need to change, through the action phase of change, and into a productive maintenance of the desired new behavior pattern. It is also hoped that the clinician can use the results of the assessment to facilitate the selection of the most appropriate treatment and in so doing maximize the chances of success for the client.

Key References

Addiction Research Foundation. (1994). *Directory of client outcome measures for addiction treatment programs.* Toronto: Addiction Research Foundation.

Allen, J. P., & Columbus, M. (Eds.). (1995). *Assessing alcohol problems: A guide for clinicians and researchers.* Treatment Handbook Series, Number 4. Bethesda, MD: National Institute on Alcohol Abuse and Alcoholism.

Rounsaville, B. J., Tims, F. M., Horton, A. M., Jr., & Sowder, B. J. (Eds.). (1993). *Diagnostic source book on drug abuse research and treatment.* National Institute on Drug Abuse. NIH Pub. No. 93-3508. Washington, DC: Government Printing Office.

References

Addiction Research Foundation. (1994). *Directory of client outcome measures for addiction treatment programs.* Toronto: Addiction Research Foundation.

Allen, J. P. (1991). The interrelationship of alcoholism assessment and treatment. *Alcohol Health and Research World, 15,* 178–185.

Allen, J. P., & Columbus, M. (1995). *Assessing alcohol problems: A guide for clinicians and researchers.* Treatment Handbook Series, Number 4. Bethesda, MD: National Institute on Alcohol Abuse and Alcoholism.

Allen, J. P., Columbus, M., & Fertig, J. B. (1995). Assessment in alcoholism treatment: An overview. In J. P. Allen & M. Columbus (Eds.), *Assessing alcohol problems: A guide for clinicians and researchers* (pp. 1–9). Treatment Handbook Series, Number 4. Bethesda, MD: National Institute on Alcohol Abuse and Alcoholism.

Allen, J. P., Fertig, J. B., Litten, R. Z., Sillanaukee, P., & Anton, R. F. (1997). Proposed recommendations for research on biochemical markers for problematic drinking. *Alcoholism: Clinical and Experimental Research, 21,* 244–247.

Allen, J. P., & Mattson, M. E. (1993). Psychometric instruments to assist in alcoholism treatment planning. *Journal of Substance Abuse Treatment, 10,* 289–296.

Allen, K. (1994). Development of an instrument to identify barriers to treatment for addicted women, from their perspective. *International Journal of the Addictions, 29,* 429–444.

Alterman, A. I., McLellan, A. T., & Shifman, R. B. (1993). Do substance abuse patients with more psychopathology receive more treatment? *Journal of Nervous and Mental Disease, 181,* 576–582.

American Psychiatric Association. (1994). *Diagnostic and statistical manual of mental disorders* (4th ed.). Washington, DC: Author.

Annis, H. M., & Graham, J. M. (1988). *Situational Confidence Questionnaire (SCQ-39): User's Guide.* Toronto: Addiction Research Foundation.

Annis, H. M., & Graham, J. M. (1991). *Inventory of Drug-Taking Situations (IDTA): User's Guide.* Toronto: Alcoholism and Drug Addiction Research Foundation.

Annis, H. M., Graham, J. M., & Davis, C. S. (1987). *Inventory of Drinking Situations (IDS): User's Guide.* Toronto: Addictions Research Foundation of Ontario.

Anton, R. F., Litten, R. Z., & Allen, J. P. (1995). Biological assessment of alcohol consumption. In J. P. Allen & M. Columbus (Eds.), *Assessing alcohol problems: A guide for clinicians and researchers* (pp. 31–40). Treatment Handbook Series 4. Bethesda, MD: National Institute on Alcohol Abuse and Alcoholism..

Babor, T. F., Brown, J., & DelBoca, F. K. (1990). Validity of self-reports in applied research on addictive behaviors: Fact or fiction? *Behavioral Assessment, 12,* 5–31.

Babor, T. F., Cooney, N. L., & Lauerman, R. J. (1987). The dependence syndrome concept as a psychological theory of relapse behaviour: An empirical evaluation of alcoholic and opiate addicts. *British Journal of Addiction, 82,* 393–405.

Babor, T. F., & DelBoca, F. K. (1992). Just the facts: Enhancing measurement of alcohol consumption using self-report methods. In R. Z. Litten & J. P. Allen (Eds.), *Measuring alcohol consumption: Psy-*

chosocial and biochemical methods (pp. 3–19). Totowa, NJ: Humana Press.

Babor, T. F., Orrok, B., Liebowitz, N., Salomon, R., & Brown, J. (1990). From basic concepts to clinical reality: Unresolved issues in the diagnosis of dependence. In M. Galanter (Ed.), Recent advances in alcoholism: Vol. 8. Combined alcohol and other drug dependence (pp. 85–104). New York: Plenum Press.

Babor, T. F., Stephens, R. S., & Marlatt, G. A. (1987). Verbal report methods in clinical research on alcoholism: Response bias and its minimization. Journal of Studies on Alcohol, 48, 410–424.

Bacorn, C. N., & Connors, G. J. (1989). Alcohol treatment training in psychology internship programs. Professional Psychology: Research and Practice, 20, 51–53.

Barber, J. G., Cooper, B. K., & Heather, N. (1991). The Situational Confidence Questionnaire (Heroin). International Journal of the Addictions, 26, 565–575.

Barnes, G. E. (1983). Clinical and prealcoholic personality characteristics. In B. Kissin & H. Begleiter (Eds.), The biology of alcoholism (Vol. 6, pp. 113–195). New York: Plenum Press.

Beck, A. T., Epstein, N., Brown, G., & Steer, R. A. (1988). An inventory for measuring clinical anxiety: Psychometric properties. Journal of Consulting and Clinical Psychology, 56, 893–897.

Beck, A. T., Ward, C. H., Mendelson, M., Mock, J., & Erbaugh, J. (1961). An inventory for measuring depression. Archives of General Psychiatry, 4, 561–571.

Beutler, L. E., & Clarkin, J. F. (1990). Systematic treatment selection: Toward targeted therapeutic interventions. New York: Brunner/Mazel.

Bien, T. H., Miller, W. R., & Tonigan, J. S. (1993). Brief interventions for alcohol problems: A review. Addiction, 88, 315–335.

Blaine, J. D., Horton, A. M., Jr., & Towle, L. H. (Eds.). (1995). Diagnosis and severity of drug abuse and dependence. Rockville, MD: National Institute on Drug Abuse.

Blume, S. A. (1989). Dual diagnosis: Psychoactive substance dependence and the personality disorders. Journal of Psychoactive Drugs, 21, 139–144.

Bois, C., & Graham, K. (1993). Assessment, case management, and treatment planning. In B. A. M. Howard, S. Harrison, V. Carver, & L. Lightfoot (Eds.), Alcohol and drug problems: A practical guide for counselors (pp. 87–101). Toronto: Addiction Research Foundation.

Bottoms, S. F., Martier, S. S., & Sokol, R. J. (1989). Refinements in screening for risk-drinking in reproductive-aged women: The "net" results. Alcohol: Clinical and Experimental Research, 13, 339.

Brown, R. L., Leonard, T., Saunders, L. A., & Papasouliotis, O. (1997). Two-item screening test for alcohol and other drug problems. Journal of Family Practice, 44, 151–160.

Brown, S. A. (1993). Drug effect expectancies and addictive behaviors. Experimental and Clinical Psychopharmacology, 1, 55–67.

Brown, S. A., Christiansen, B. A., & Goldman, M. S. (1987). The Alcohol Expectancy Questionnaire: An instrument for the assessment of adolescent and adult alcohol expectancies. Journal of Studies on Alcohol, 48, 483–491.

Brown, S. A., Inaba, R. K., Gillin, J. C., Schuckit, M. A., Stewart, M. A., & Irwin, M. R. (1995). Alcoholism and affective disorder: Clinical course of depressive symptoms. American Journal of Psychiatry, 152, 45–52.

Brown, S. A., Irwin, M., & Schuckit, M. A. (1991). Changes in anxiety among abstinent male alcoholics. Journal of Studies on Alcohol, 52, 55–61.

Brown, S. A., & Schuckit, M. A. (1988). Changes in depression among abstinent alcoholics. Journal of Studies on Alcohol, 49, 412–417.

Carey, K. B., & Teitelbaum, L. M. (1996). Goals and methods of alcohol assessment. Professional Psychology: Research and Practice, 27, 460–466.

Carroll, K. M. (1995). Methodological issues and problems in the assessment of substance use. Psychological Assessment, 7, 349–358.

Carroll, K. M., Rounsaville, B. J., & Bryant, K. J. (1994). Should tolerance and withdrawal be required for substance dependence disorders? Drug & Alcohol Addiction, 36, 15–22.

Carver, C. S., Scheier, M. F., & Weintraub, J. K. (1989). Assessing coping strategies: A theoretically based approach. Journal of Personality and Social Psychology, 56, 267–283.

Chaney, E. F., Marlatt, G. A., & O'Leary, M. R. (1978). Skill training with alcoholics. Journal of Consulting and Clinical Psychology, 46, 1092–1104.

Cherpitel, C. J. (1995). Screening for alcohol problems in the emergency room: A rapid alcohol problem screen. Drug and Alcohol Dependence, 40, 133–137.

Cherpitel, C. J., & Clark, W. B. (1995). Ethnic differences in performance of screening instruments for identifying harmful drinking and alcohol dependence in the emergency room. Alcoholism: Clinical and Experimental Research, 19, 628–634.

Conigrave, K. M., Saunders, J. B., & Whitfield, J. B. (1995). Diagnostic tests for alcohol consumption. Alcohol and Alcoholism, 30, 13–26.

Connors, G. J. (1995). Screening for alcohol problems. In J. P. Allen & M. Columbus (Eds.), Assessing alcohol problems: A guide for clinicians and researchers (pp. 17–29). Treatment Handbook Series, Number 4. Bethesda, MD: National Institute on Alcohol Abuse and Alcoholism.

Connors, G. J., & Maisto, S. A. (1988). The Alcohol Beliefs Scale. In M. Hersen & A. S. Bellack (Eds.), *Dictionary of behavioral assessment techniques* (pp. 24–26). New York: Pergamon Press.

Connors, G. J., Maisto, S. A., & Donovan, D. M. (1996). Conceptualizations of relapse: A summary of psychological and psychobiological models. *Addiction, 91*(Supplement), S5–S13.

Cook, R. F., Bernstein, A. D., Arrington, T. L., Andrews, C. M., & Marshall, G. A. (1995). Methods for assessing drug use prevalence in the workplace: A comparison of self-report, urinalysis, and hair analysis. *International Journal of the Addictions, 30*, 403–426.

Cooney, N. L., Kadden, R. M., & Litt, M. D. (1990). A comparison of measures for assessing sociopathy in male and female alcoholics. *Journal of Studies on Alcohol, 51*, 42–48.

Cordingley, J. Wilkinson, D. A., & Martin, G. W. (1990). Corroborating multiple drug users' posttreatment self-reports by collaterals. *Behavioral Assessment, 12*, 253–264.

Costa, P. T., & McCrae, R. R. (1992). Normal personality assessment in clinical practice: The NEO Personality Inventory. Special Section: Assessing personality characteristics in clinical settings. *Psychological Assessment, 4*, 5–13.

Cottler, L. B., Phelps, D. L., & Compton, W. M. (1995). Narrowing the drinking repertoire criterion: Should it be dropped from ICD-10? *Journal of Studies on Alcohol, 56*, 173–176.

Cox, W. M., & Klinger, E. (1987). Research on the personality correlates of alcohol use: Its impact on personality and motivation. *Drugs and Society, 1*, 61–83.

Craig, R. J. (1988). Diagnostic interviewing with drug abusers. *Professional Psychology: Research and Practice, 19*, 14–20.

Craig, R. J. (1995). The role of personality in understanding substance abuse. *Alcoholism Treatment Quarterly, 13*, 17–27.

Craig, R. J., & Olson, R. (1992). MMPI subtypes for cocaine abusers. *American Journal of Drug and Alcohol Abuse, 18*, 197–205.

Craig, R. J., & Weinberg, D. (1992a). Assessing alcoholics with the Millon Clinical Multiaxial Inventory: A review. *Psychology of Addictive Behaviors, 6*, 200–208.

Craig, R. J., & Weinberg, D. (1992b). Assessing drug abusers with the Millon Clinical Multiaxial Inventory: A review. *Journal of Substance Abuse Treatment, 9*, 249–255.

Cunningham, J. A., Sobell, L. C., Sobell, M. B., Agrawal, S., & Toneatto, T. (1993). Barriers to treatment: Why alcohol and drug abusers delay or never seek treatment. *Addictive Behaviors, 18*, 347–353.

Cunningham, J. A., Sobell, L. C., Sobell, M. B., & Gaskin, J. (1994). Alcohol and drug abusers' reasons for seeking treatment. *Addictive Behaviors, 19*, 691–696.

Curry, S. J., Wagner, E. H., & Grothaus, L. C. (1990). Intrinsic and extrinsic motivation for smoking cessation. *Journal of Consulting and Clinical Psychology, 58*, 310–316.

Cyr, M. G., & Wartman, S. A. (1988). The effectiveness of routine screening questions in the detection of alcoholism. *Journal of the American Medical Association, 259*, 51–54.

Dawes, M. A., Frank, S., & Rost, K. (1993). Clinician assessment of psychiatric comorbidity and alcoholism severity in adult alcoholic inpatients. *American Journal of Drug and Alcohol Abuse, 19*, 377–386.

DeHart, S. S., & Hoffman, N. G. (1995). Screening and diagnosis of "alcohol abuse and dependence" in older adults. *International Journal of the Addictions, 30*, 1717–1747.

DeLeon, G., Melnick, G., Kressel, D., & Jainchill, N. (1994). Circumstances, motivation, readiness, and suitability (The CMRS Scales): Predicting retention in therapeutic community treatment. *American Journal of Drug and Alcohol Abuse, 20*, 495–514.

Dembo, R., Turner, G., Borden, P., Schmeidler, J., & Manning, D. (1994). Screening high risk youths for potential problems: Field application in the use of the Problem Oriented Screening Instrument for Teenagers (POSIT). *Journal of Child and Adolescent Substance Abuse, 3*, 69–93.

DeNelsky, G. Y., & Boat, B. W. (1986). A coping skills model of psychological diagnosis and treatment. *Professional Psychology: Research and Practice, 17*, 322–330.

Derogatis, L. R. (1977). *SCL-90: Administration, scoring and procedures manual for the revised version.* Baltimore: Clinical Psychometrics Research.

DiClemente, C. C. (1986). Self-efficacy and the addictive behaviors. *Journal of Social and Clinical Psychology, 4*, 302–315.

DiClemente, C. C., Carbonari, J. P., Montgomery, R. P. G., & Hughes, S. O. (1994). The Alcohol Abstinence Self-Efficacy Scale. *Journal of Studies on Alcohol, 55*, 141–148.

Donovan, D., & Chaney, E. (1985). Alcoholic relapse prevention and intervention: Models and methods. In G. A. Marlatt & J. R. Gordon (Eds.), *Relapse prevention: Maintenance strategies in the treatment of addictive behaviors* (pp. 351–416). New York: Guilford Press.

Donovan, D. M. (1988). Assessment of addictive behaviors: Implications of an emerging biopsychosocial model. In D. M. Donovan & G. A. Marlatt (Eds.), *Assessment of addictive behaviors* (pp. 3–48). New York: Guilford Press.

Donovan, D. M. (1992). The assessment process in addictive behaviors. *The Behavior Therapist, 15,* 18- 20.

Donovan, D. M. (1995). Assessments to aid in the treatment planning process. In J. P. Allen & M. Columbus (Eds.), *Assessing alcohol problems: A guide for clinicians and researchers* (pp. 75–122). Treatment Handbook Series, Number 4. Bethesda, MD: National Institute on Alcohol Abuse and Alcoholism.

Donovan, D. M. (1996). Assessment issues and domains in the prediction of relapse. *Addiction, 91*(Supplement), S29–S36.

Donovan, D. M., & Marlatt, G. A. (Eds.). (1988). *Assessment of addictive behaviors.* New York: Guilford Press.

Dore, M. M., Doris, J. M., & Wright, P. (1995). Identifying substance abuse in maltreating families: A child welfare challenge. *Child Abuse and Neglect, 19,* 531–543.

Edwards, G. (1986). The alcohol dependence syndrome: A concept as stimulus to inquiry. *British Journal of Addiction, 81,* 171–183.

Feingold, A., & Rounsaville, B. (1995). Construct validity of the dependence syndrome as measured by DSM-IV for different psychoactive substances. *Addiction, 90,* 1661–1669.

Feragne, M. A., Longabaugh, R., & Stevenson, J. F. (1983). The Psychosocial Functioning Inventory. *Evaluation and the Health Professions, 6,* 25–48.

Flynn, P. M., Hubbard, R. L., Luckey, J. W., Forsyth, B. H., et al. (1995). Individual Assessment Profile: Standardizing the assessment of substance abuse. *Journal of Substance Abuse Treatment, 12,* 213–221.

Folkman, S., & Lazarus, R. S. (1980). An analysis of coping in a middle-aged community sample. *Journal of Health and Social Behavior, 21,* 219–239.

Fromme, K., Stroot, E. A., & Kaplan, D. (1993). Comprehensive effects of alcohol: Development and psychometric assessment of a new expectancy questionnaire. *Psychological Assessment, 5,* 19–26.

Fuller, R. K. (1988). Can treatment outcome research rely on alcoholics' self-reports? *Alcohol Health and Research World, 12,* 180–186.

Gavin, D. R., Ross, H. E., & Skinner, H. (1989). Diagnostic validity of the Drug Abuse Screening Test in the assessment of DSM-III drug disorders. *British Journal of Addiction, 84,* 301–307.

Geller, A. (1991). Practical concerns for use of assessment instruments in a clinical setting. *Alcohol Health and Research World, 15,* 186–187.

Gentilello, L. M., Donovan, D. M., Dunn, C. W., & Rivara, F. P. (1995). Alcohol interventions in trauma centers: Current practice, future directions. *Journal of the American Medical Association, 274*(13), 1043–1048.

Gladsjo, J. A., Tucker, J. A., Hawkins, J. L., & Vuchinich, R. E. (1992). Adequacy of recall of drinking patterns and event occurrences associated with natural recovery from alcohol problems. *Addictive Behaviors, 17,* 347–358.

Glaser, F. B., & Skinner, H. A. (1981). Matching in the real world: A practical approach. In E. A. Gotthiel, A. T. McLellan, & K. A. Druley (Eds.), *Matching patient needs and treatment methods in alcoholism and drug abuse* (pp. 295–324). Springfield, IL: Charles C Thomas.

Goldman, M. S. (1987). The role of time and practice in recovery of function in alcoholics. In O. A. Parsons, N. Butters, & P. E. Nathan (Eds.), *Neuropsychology of alcoholism: Implications for diagnosis and treatment* (pp. 291–321). New York: Guilford Press.

Goldman, M. S., Brown, S. A., & Christiansen, B. A. (1987). Expectancy theory: Thinking about drinking. In H. T. Blane & K. E. Leonard (Eds.), *Psychological theories of drinking and alcoholism* (pp. 181–226). New York: Guilford Press.

Gough, H. G. (1975). *California Psychological Inventory manual.* Palo Alto, CA: Consulting Psychologists Press.

Grant, B. F., & Hasin, D. S. (1990). *The Alcohol Use Disorders and Associated Disabilities Interview Schedule (AUDADIS).* Rockville, MD: National Institute on Alcohol Abuse and Alcoholism.

Grant, B. F., & Towle, L. H. (1990). Standardized diagnostic interviews for alcohol research. *Alcohol Health and Research World, 14,* 340–348.

Grant, B. F., & Towle, L. H. (1991). A comparison of diagnostic criteria: DSM-III-R, proposed DSM-IV, and proposed ICD-10. *Alcohol Health and Research World, 15,* 284–292.

Harrell, T. H., Honaker, L. M., & Davis, E. (1991). Cognitive and behavioral dimensions of dysfunction in alcohol and polydrug abusers. *Journal of Substance Abuse, 3,* 415–426.

Harrison, L. D. (1995). The validity of self-reported data on drug use. *Journal of Drug Issues, 25,* 91–111.

Hasin, D. S. (1991). Diagnostic interviews for assessment: Background, reliability, validity. *Alcohol Health and Research World, 15,* 293–302.

Hasin, D. S., & Glick, H. (1992). Severity of DSM-III-R alcohol dependence: United States, 1988. *British Journal of Addiction, 87,* 1725–1730.

Hasin, D. S., Grant, B. F., Harford, T. C., & Endicott, J. (1988). The drug dependence syndrome and related disabilities. *British Journal of Addiction, 83,* 45–55.

Hasin, D. S., Li, Q., McCloud, S., & Endicott, J. (1997). Agreement between DSM-III, DSM-III-R, DSM-IV, and ICD-10 alcohol diagnoses in a U.S. community sample of heavy drinkers. *Addiction, 91,* 1517–1527.

Hasin, D. S., Muthuen, B., & Grant, B. F. (1994). Validity of the bi-axial dependence concept: A test in the US general population. *Addiction, 89,* 573–579.

Hasin, D. S., Trautman, K. D., Miele, G. M., Samet, S., et al. (1996). Psychiatric Research Interview for Substance and Mental Disorders (PRISM): Reliability for substance abusers. *American Journal of Psychiatry, 153,* 1195–1201.

Hathaway, S. R., McKinley, J. C., Butcher, J. N., Dahlstrom, W. G., Graham, J. R., Tellegen, A., & Kaemmer, B. (1989). *Minnesota Multiphasic Personality Inventory-2: Manual for administration and scoring.* Minneapolis: University of Minnesota Press.

Hawkins, J. D., Catalano, R. F., & Wells, E. A. (1986). Measuring the effects of a skills training intervention for drug abusers. *Journal of Consulting and Clinical Psychology, 54,* 661–664.

Heather, N. (1989). Brief interventions. In R. K. Hester & W. R. Miller (Eds.), *Handbook of alcoholism treatment approaches: Effective alternatives* (pp. 93–116). New York: Pergamon Press.

Heather, N., Stallard, A., & Tebbutt, J. (1991). Importance of substance cues in relapse among heroin users: Comparison of two methods of investigation. *Addictive Behaviors, 16,* 41–49.

Helander, A., & Tabakoff, B. (1997). Biochemical markers of alcohol use and abuse: Experiences from the pilot study of the WHO/ISBRA collaborative project on state and trait markers of alcohol. *Alcohol and Alcoholism, 32,* 133–144.

Hindin, R., McCusker, J., Vickers, L. M., Bigelow, C., Garfield, F., & Lewis, B. (1994). Radioimmunoassay of hair for determination of cocaine, heroin, and marijuana exposure: Comparison with self-report. *International Journal of the Addictions, 29,* 771–789.

Hyams, G., Cartwright, A., & Spratley, T. (1996). Engagement in alcohol treatment: The client's experience of, and satisfaction with, the assessment interview. *Addiction Research, 4,* 105–123.

Institute of Medicine. (1990). *Broadening the base of treatment for alcohol problems.* Washington, DC: National Academy Press.

Jackson, D. N. (1994). *Personality Research Form manual* (3rd ed.). Port Huron, MI: Research Psychologists Press.

Jacobson, G. R. (1989a). A comprehensive approach to pretreatment evaluation: 1. Detection, assessment, and diagnosis of alcoholism. In R. K. Hester & W. R. Miller (Eds.), *Handbook of alcoholism treatment approaches: Effective alternatives* (pp. 17–53). New York: Pergamon Press.

Jacobson, G. R. (1989b). A comprehensive approach to pretreatment evaluation: 2. Other clinical considerations. In R. K. Hester & W. R. Miller (Eds.), *Handbook of alcoholism treatment approaches: Effective alternatives* (pp. 54–66). New York: Pergamon Press.

Jacquot, M. M. (1992). Assessment of substance abuse: An integrated approach. In C. E. Stout, J. L. Levitt, & D. H. Ruben (Eds.), *Handbook for assessing and treating addictive disorders* (pp. 61–82). New York: Greenwood Press.

Jaffe, A. J., & Kilbey, M. M. (1994). The Cocaine Expectancy Questionnaire (CEQ): Construction and predictive utility. *Psychological Assessment, 6,* 18–26.

Jones, B. T., & McMahon, J. (1993). The reliability of the Negative Alcohol Expectancy Questionnaire and its use. *Journal of Association of Nurses in Substance Abuse, 12,* 15–16

Jones, B. T., & McMahon, J. (1994). Negative alcohol expectancy predicts post-treatment abstinence survivorship: The whether, when, and why of relapse to a first drink. *Addiction, 89,* 1653–1665.

Kadden, R., Cooney, N., Getter, H., & Litt, M. (1989). Matching alcoholics to coping skills or interactional therapies: Posttreatment results. *Journal of Consulting and Clinical Psychology, 57,* 698–704.

Kadden, R. M., Litt, M. D., Cooney, N. L., & Busher, D. A. (1992). Relationship between role-play measures of coping skills and alcoholism treatment outcome. *Addictive Behaviors, 17,* 425–437.

Kanfer, F. H. (1986). Implications of a self-regulation model of therapy for treatment of addictive behaviors. In W. R. Miller & N. Heather (Eds.), *Treating addictive behaviors: Processes of change* (pp. 29–47). New York: Plenum Press.

Kemper, K., Greteman, A., Bennett, E., & Babonis, T. R. (1993). Screening mothers of young children for substance abuse. *Journal of Developmental & Behavioral Pediatrics, 14,* 308–312.

Kipke, M. D., Montgomery, S., & McKenzie, R. G. (1993). Substance abuse among youth seen at a community-based health clinic. *Journal of Adolescent Health, 14,* 289–294.

Kranzler, H. R., Tennen, H., Babor, T. F., Kadden, R. M., & Rounsaville, B. J. (1997). Validity of the longitudinal, expert, all data procedure of psychiatric diagnosis in patients with psychoactive substance use disorders. *Drug and Alcohol Dependence, 45,* 93–104.

Lanyon, R. I. (1970). Development and validation of a psychological screening inventory. *Journal of Consulting and Clinical Psychology, 35* (1, Pt. 2), 24 p.

Lapham, S. C., Skipper, B. J., Owen, J. P., Kleyboecker, K., Teaf, D., Thompson, B., & Simpson, G. (1995).

Alcohol abuse screening instruments: Normative test data collected from a first DWI offender screening program. *Journal of Studies on Alcohol, 56,* 51–59.

Leccese, M., & Waldron, H. B. (1994). Assessing adolescent substance use: A critique of current measurement instruments. *Journal of Substance Abuse Treatment, 11,* 553–563.

Leigh, B. C. (1987). Beliefs about the effects of alcohol on self and others. *Journal of Studies on Alcohol, 48,* 467–475.

Litman, G. K., Stapleton, J., Oppenheim, A. N., & Peleg, M. (1983). An instrument for measuring coping behaviours in hospitalized alcoholics: Implications for relapse prevention and treatment. *British Journal of Addiction, 78,* 269–276.

Litman, G. K., Stapleton, J., Oppenheim, A. N., Peleg, M., & Jackson, P. (1984). The relationship between coping behaviours and their effectiveness and alcoholism relapse and survival. *British Journal of Addiction, 79,* 283–291.

Litten, R. Z., & Allen, J. P. (Eds.). (1992). *Measuring alcohol consumption: Psychosocial and biochemical methods.* Totowa, NJ: Humana Press.

Longabaugh, R., & Clifford, P. R. (1992). Program evaluation and treatment outcome. *Annual Review of Addictions Research and Treatment, 2,* 223–247.

Lubin, B., Brady, K., Woodward, L., & Thomas, E. A. (1986). Graduate professional training in alcoholism and substance abuse: 1984. *Professional Psychology: Research and Practice, 17,* 151–154.

Magura, S., Freeman, R. C., Siddiqi, Q., & Lipton, D. S. (1992). The validity of hair analysis for detecting cocaine and heroin use among addicts. *International Journal of the Addictions, 27,* 51–69.

Maisto, S. A., & Connors, G. J. (1992). Using subject and collateral reports to measure alcohol consumption. In R. Z. Litten & J. P. Allen (Eds.), *Measuring alcohol consumption: Psychosocial and biochemical methods* (pp. 73–96). Totowa, NJ: Humana Press.

Maisto, S. A., Connors, G. J., & Allen, J. P. (1995). Contrasting self-report screens for alcohol problems: A review. *Alcoholism: Clinical and Experimental Research, 19,* 1510–1516.

Maisto, S. A., & McKay, J. R. (1995). Diagnosis. In J. P. Allen & M. Columbus (Eds.), *Assessing alcohol problems: A guide for clinicians and researchers* (pp. 41–54). Treatment Handbook Series, Number 4. Bethesda, MD: National Institute on Alcohol Abuse and Alcoholism.

Maisto, S. A., McKay, J. R., & Connors, G. J. (1990). Self-report issues in substance abuse: State of the art and future directions. Special Issue: Self-reports across addictive behaviors: Issues and future directions in clinical and research settings. *Behavioral Assessment, 12,* 117–134.

Mariezcurrena, R. (1994). Recovery from addictions without treatment: Literature review. *Scandinavian Journal of Behaviour Therapy, 23,* 131–154

Marlatt, G. A., & Gordon, J. R. (1980). Determinants of relapse: Implications for the maintenance of behavior change. In P. O. Davidson & S. M. Davidson (Eds.), *Behavioral medicine: Changing health lifestyles* (pp. 410–452). New York: Brunner/Mazel.

Marlatt, G. A., & Gordon, J. R. (Eds.). (1985). *Relapse prevention: Maintenance strategies in the treatment of addictive behaviors.* New York: Guilford Press.

Marlatt, G. A., Tucker, J. A., Donovan, D. M., & Vuchinich, R. E. (1997). Help-seeking by substance abusers: The role of harm reduction and behavioral-economic approaches to facilitate treatment entry and retention by substance abusers. In L. S. Onken, J. D. Blaine, & J. J. Boren (Eds.), *Beyond the therapeutic alliance: Keeping the drug dependent individual in treatment* (pp. 44–84). Rockville, MD: National Institute on Drug Abuse Research Monograph, Number 165, U.S. Department of Health and Human Services, Public Health Service, National Institutes of Health.

Martin, G. W., Wilkinson, D. A., & Poulos, C. X. (1995). The Drug Avoidance Self-Efficacy Scale. *Journal of Substance Abuse, 7,* 151–163.

Mayfield, D., McLeod, G., & Hall, P. (1974). The CAGE questionnaire: Validation of a new alcoholism instrument. *American Journal of Psychiatry, 131,* 1121–1123.

McBride, C. M., Curry, S. J., Stephens, R. S., Wells, E. A., Roffman, R. A., & Hawkins, J. D. (1994). Intrinsic and extrinsic motivation for change in cigarette smokers, marijuana smokers, and cocaine users. *Psychology of Addictive Behaviors, 8,* 243–250.

McConnaughy, E. A., Prochaska, J. O., & Velicer, W. F. (1983). Stages of change in psychotherapy: Measurement and sample profiles. *Psychotherapy: Theory, Research, and Practice, 20,* 368–375

McKay, J. R., Rutherford, M. J., Alterman, A. I., & Cacciola, J. S. (1996). Development of the Cocaine Relapse Interview: An initial report. *Addiction, 91,* 535–548.

McLellan, A. T. (1986). "Psychiatric severity" as a predictor of outcome from substance abuse treatment. In R. E. Meyer (Ed.), *Psychopathology and addictive disorders* (pp. 97–139). New York: Guilford Press.

McLellan, A. T., Alterman, A. I., Metzger, D. S., Grisson, G. R., Woody, G. E., Luborsky, L., & O'Brien, C. P. (1994). Similarity of outcome predictors across opiate, cocaine, and alcohol treatments: Role of treatment services. *Journal of Consulting and Clinical Psychology, 62*, 1141–1158.

McLellan, A. T., Kushner, H., Metzger, D., Peters, R., Smith, I., Grissom, G., Pettinati, H., & Argeriou, M. (1992). The fifth edition of the Addiction Severity Index. *Journal of Substance Abuse Treatment, 9*, 199–213

McMahon, J., & Jones, B. T. (1993b). Negative expectancy in motivation. *Addiction Research, 1*, 145–155

Michalec, E., Zwick, W. R., Monti, P. M., Rohsenow, D. J., et al. (1992). A Cocaine High-Risk Situations Questionnaire: Development and psychometric properties. *Journal of Substance Abuse, 4*, 377–391.

Miller, K. J., McCrady, B. S., Abrams, D. B., & Labouvie, E. W. (1994). Taking an individualized approach to the assessment of self-efficacy and the prediction of alcoholic relapse. *Journal of Psychopathology and Behavioral Assessment, 16*, 111–120.

Miller, N. S. (1993). Comorbidity of psychiatric and alcoholic/drug disorders: Interactions and independent status. *Journal of Addictive Diseases, 12*, 5–16.

Miller, P. M., & Mastria, M. A. (1977). *Alternatives to alcohol abuse: A social learning model* (pp. 37–48). Champaign, IL: Research Press.

Miller, W. R. (1983). Motivational interviewing with problem drinkers. *Behavioral Psychotherapy, 11*, 147–172.

Miller, W. R. (1989). Increasing motivation for change. In R. K. Hester & W. R. Miller (Eds.), *Handbook of alcoholism treatment approaches: Effective alternatives* (pp. 67–80). New York: Pergamon Press.

Miller, W. R. (1996). *Manual for Form-90: A structured interview for drinking and related behaviors.* Project MATCH Monograph Series, Vol. 5. Rockville, MD: National Institute on Alcohol Abuse and Alcoholism.

Miller, W. R., Benefield, R. G., & Tonnigan, J. S. (1993). Enhancing motivation for change in problem drinking: A controlled comparison of two therapist styles. *Journal of Consulting and Clinical Psychology, 61*, 455–461.

Miller, W. R., Crawford, V. L., & Taylor, C. A. (1979). Significant others as corroborative sources for problem drinkers. *Addictive Behaviors, 4*, 67–70.

Miller, W. R., & Marlatt, G. A. (1984). *Manual for the Comprehensive Drinker Profile.* Odessa, FL: Psychological Assessment Resources.

Miller, W. R., & Marlatt, G. A. (1987). *Comprehensive Drinker Profile manual supplement for use with Brief Drinker Profile, Follow-up Drinker Profile, collateral interview form.* Odessa, FL: Psychological Assessment Resources

Miller, W. R., & Rollnick, S. (1991). *Motivational interviewing: Preparing people to change addictive behavior.* New York: Guilford Press.

Miller, W. R., & Tonigan, J. S. (1996). Assessing drinkers' motivation for change: The Stages of Change Readiness and Treatment Eagerness Scale (SOCRATES). *Psychology of Addictive Behaviors, 10*, 81–89.

Millon, T. (1992). Millon Clinical Multiaxial Inventory: 1 and 2. *Journal of Counseling and Development, 70*, 421–426.

Monti, P. M., Rohsenhow, D. J., Abrams, D. B., Zwick, W. R., Binkoff, J. A., Munroe, S. M., Fingeret, A. L., Nirenberg, T. D., Liepman, M. R., Pedraza, M., Kadden, R. M., & Cooney, N. L. (1993). Development of a behavior analytically derived alcohol-specific role-play assessment instrument. *Journal of Studies on Alcohol, 54*, 710–721.

Moos, R. H. (1995). Development and application of new measures of life stressors, social resources, and coping responses. *European Journal of Psychological Assessment, 11*, 1–13.

Moran, J., Mayberry, C., Kinniburgh, D., & James, D. (1995). Program monitoring for clinical practice: Specimen positivity across urine collection methods. *Journal of Substance Abuse Treatment, 12*, 223–226.

Morgenstern, J., Langenbucher, J., & Labouvie, E. W. (1994). The generalizability of the dependence syndrome across substances: An examination of some properties of the proposed DSM-IV dependence criteria. *Addiction, 89*, 1105–1113.

Murphy, P. N., & Bentall, R. P. (1992). Motivation to withdraw from heroin: A factor analytic study. *British Journal of Addiction, 87*, 245–250.

Myers, M. G., Martin, R. A., Rohsenow, D. J., & Monti, P. M. (1996). The relapse situation appraisal questionnaire: Initial psychometric characteristics and validation. *Psychology of Addictive Behaviors, 10*, 237–247.

Nace, E. P., & Davis, C. W. (1993). Treatment outcome in substance-abusing patients with a personality disorder. *American Journal on Addictions, 2*, 26–33.

Nace, E. P., Davis, C. W., & Gaspari, J. P. (1991). Axis II comorbidity in substance abusers. *American Journal of Psychiatry, 148*, 118–120.

Nathan, P. E. (1991). Substance use disorders in the DSM-IV. *Journal of Abnormal Psychology, 100*, 356–361.

National Institute of Alcohol Abuse and Alcoholism. (1990). *Alcohol and health: Seventh special report to the U.S. Congress.* Washington, DC: U.S. Department of Health and Human Services.

Nilssen, O., & Cone, H. (1994). Screening patients for alcohol problems in primary health care settings. *Alcohol Health and Research World, 18*, 136–139.

Nirenberg, T. D., & Maisto, S. A. (Eds.). (1987). *Developments in the assessment and treatment of addictive behaviors.* Norwood, NJ: Ablex.

Oei, T. P. S., & Baldwin, A. (1994). Expectancy theory: A two-process model of alcohol use and abuse. *Journal of Studies on Alcohol, 55,* 525–534.

Oppenheimer, E., Sheehan, M., & Taylor, C. (1988). Letting the client speak: Drug misusers and the process of help seeking. *British Journal of Addiction, 83,* 635–647.

Peters, R. H., & Schonfeld, L. (1993). Determinants of recent substance abuse among jail inmates referred for treatment. *Journal of Drug Issues, 23,* 101–117.

Pokorny, A. D., Miller, B-A., & Kaplan, H. B. (1972). The brief MAST: A shortened version of the Michigan Alcoholism Screening Test. *American Journal of Psychiatry, 129,* 342–345.

Prochaska, J. O., & DiClemente, C. D. (1986). Toward a comprehensive model of change. In W. R. Miller & N. Heather (Eds.), *Treating addictive behaviors: Processes of change* (pp. 3–27). New York: Plenum.

Prochaska, J. O., DiClemente, C. C., & Norcross, J. C. (1992). In search of how people change: Applications to addictive behaviors. *American Psychologist, 47,* 1102–1114.

Radloff, L. S. (1977). The CES-D: A self-report depression scale for research in the general population. *Applied Psychological Measurement, 1,* 385–401.

Rankin, H. (1990). Validity of self-reports in clinical settings. Special Issue: Self-reports across addictive behaviors: Issues and future directions in clinical and research settings. *Behavioral Assessment, 12,* 107–116.

Rather, B. C., & Goldman, M. S. (1994). Drinking-related differences in the memory organization of alcohol expectancies. *Experimental and Clinical Psychopharmocology, 2,* 167–183

Rawson, R. A., Obert, J. L., McCann, M. J., & Marinelli, C. P. (1993). Relapse prevention models for substance abuse treatment. *Psychotherapy, 30,* 284–298.

Regier, D. A., Farmer, M. E., Rae, D. S., Locke, B. Z., Keith, S. J., Judd, L. L., & Goodwin, F. K. (1990). Comorbidity of mental disorders with alcohol and other drug abuse: Results from the Epidemiological Catchment Area (ECA) study. *Journal of the American Medical Association, 264,* 2511–2518.

Robins, L. N., Helzer, J. E., Croughan, J., & Ratcliff, K. S. (1981). The NIMH Diagnostic Interview Schedule: Its history, characteristics, and validity. *Archives of General Psychiatry, 38,* 381–389.

Robins, L. N., Wing, J., Wittchen, H. U., Helzer, J. E., Babor, T. F., Burke, J., Farmer, A. Jablenski, A., Pickens, R., Reiger, D., Sartorius, N., & Towle, L. H. (1988). The Composite International Diagnostic Interview. *Archives of General Psychiatry, 45,* 1069–1077.

Rollnick, S., & Heather, N. (1982). The application of Bandura's self-efficacy theory to abstinence-oriented alcoholism treatment. *Addictive Behaviors, 7,* 243–250.

Rollnick, S., Heather, N., Gold, R., & Hall, W. (1992). Development of a short "Readiness to Change" Questionnaire for use in brief opportunistic interventions. *British Journal of Addictions, 87,* 743–754.

Ross, H. E., Glaser, F. B., & Germanson, T. (1988). The prevalence of psychiatric disorders in patients with alcohol and other drug problems. *Archives of General Psychiatry, 45,* 1023–1031.

Rounsaville, B. (1993). Overview: Rationale and guidelines for using comparable measures to evaluate substance abusers. In B. J. Rounsaville, F. M. Tims, A. M. Horton, Jr., & B. J. Sowder, (Eds.), *Diagnostic source book on drug abuse research and treatment* (pp. 1–10). National Institute on Drug Abuse. NIH Pub. No. 93-3508. Washington, DC: Government Printing Office.

Rounsaville, B. J., Dolinsky, Z. S., Babor, T. F., & Meyer, R. E. (1987). Psychopathology as a predictor of treatment outcomein alcoholics. *Archives of General Psychiatry, 44,* 505–513.

Rounsaville, B. J., Tims, F. M., Horton, A. M., Jr., & Sowder, B. J. (Eds.). (1993). *Diagnostic source book on drug abuse research and treatment.* National Institute on Drug Abuse. NIH Pub. No. 93-3508. Washington, DC: Government Printing Office.

Rubenstein, L., Campbell, F., & Daley, D. (1990). Four perspectives on dual disorders: An overview of treatment issues. *Journal of Chemical Dependency Treatment, 3,* 97–118.

Russell, M. (1994). New assessment tools for drinking in pregnancy: T-ACE, TWEAK, and others. *Alcohol Health and Research World, 18,* 55–61.

Russell, M., Martier, S. S., Sokol, R. J., Jacobson, S., Jacobson, J., & Bottoms, S. (1991). Screening for pregnancy risk drinking: TWEAKING the tests. *Alcoholism: Clinical and Experimental Research, 15,* 638.

Ryan, R. M., Plant, R. W., & O'Malley, S. (1995). Initial motivations for alcohol treatment: Relations with patient characteristics, treatment involvement, and dropout. *Addictive Behaviors, 20,* 279–297.

Saunders, J. B., Aasland, O. G., Babor, T. F., DeLaFuente, J. R., & Grant, M. (1993). Development of the Alcohol Use Disorders Identification Test (AUDIT): WHO collaborative project on early detection of persons with harmful alcohol consumption. *Addiction, 88,* 791–804.

Saxon, A. J., Calsyn, D. A., Haver, V. M., & DeLaney, C. J. (1988). Clinical evaluation and use of urine screening for drug abuse. *Western Journal of Medicine, 149,* 296–303.

Schafer, J., & Brown, S. A. (1991). Marijuana and cocaine effect expectancies and drug use patterns. *Jour-*

nal of Consulting and Clinical Psychology, 59, 558–565.

Schafer, J., & Fals-Stewart, W. (1993). Effect expectancies for cocaine intoxication: Initial and descending phases. Addictive Behaviors, 18, 171–177.

Schmitz, J. M., Oswald, L. M., Damin, P., & Mattis, P. (1995). Situational analysis of coping in substance abusing patients. Journal of Substance Abuse, 7, 189–204.

Schonfeld, L., Peters, R., & Dolente, A. (1993). SARA. Substance Abuse Relapse Assessment: Professional manual. Odessa, FL: Psychological Assessment Resources.

Schottenfeld, R. S. (1994). Assessment of the patient. In M. Galanter & H. D. Kleber (Eds.), The textbook of substance abuse treatment (pp. 25–33). Washington, DC: American Psychiatric Press.

Sellman, D. (1994). Alcoholism: Development of the diagnostic concept. Australian & New Zealand Journal of Psychiatry, 28(2), 205–211.

Selzer, M. L. (1971). The Michigan Alcoholism Screening Test: The quest for a new diagnostic instrument. American Journal of Psychiatry, 127, 1653–1658.

Shaffer, H., & Kauffman, J. (1985). The clinical assessment and diagnosis of addiction: Hypothesis testing. In T. E. Bratter & G. G. Forrest (Eds.), Alcoholism and substance abuse: Strategies for clinical intervention (pp. 225–258). New York: Free Press.

Shaffer, H. J., & Neuhaus, C., Jr. (1985). Testing hypotheses: An approach for the assessment of addictive behaviors. In H. B. Milkman & H. J. Shaffer (Eds.), The addictions: Multidisciplinary perspectives and treatments (pp. 87–103). Lexington, MA: Lexington Books.

Sherer, M., Haygood, J. M., & Alfano, A. M. (1984). Stability of psychological test results in newly admitted alcoholics. Journal of Clinical Psychology, 40, 855–857.

Sherman, M. F., & Bigelow, G. E. (1992). Validity of patients' self-reported drug use as a function of treatment status. Drug and Alcohol Dependence, 30, 1–11.

Siegal, H. A., Fisher, J. H., Rapp, R. C., Wagner, J. H., Forney, M. A., & Callejo, V. (1995). Presenting problems of substance abusers in treatment: Implications for service delivery and attrition. American Journal of Drug and Alcohol Abuse, 21, 17–26.

Siegel, J. M. (1986). The Multidimensional Anger Inventory. Journal of Personality and Social Psychology, 51, 191–200.

Simpson, D. D., & Joe, G. W. (1993). Motivation as a predictor of early dropout from drug abuse treatment. Psychotherapy, 30, 357–368.

Skinner, H. A. (1982). The drug abuse screening test. Addictive Behaviors, 7, 363–371.

Skinner, H. A. (1988). A model for the assessment of alcohol use and related problems. Drugs and Society, 2(2), 19–30.

Sobell, L. C., Cunningham, J. A., & Sobell, M. B. (1996). Recovery from alcohol problems with and without treatment: Prevalence in two population surveys. American Journal of Public Health, 86, 966–972.

Sobell, L. C., Kwan, E., & Sobell, M. B. (1995). Reliability of a drug history questionnaire (DHQ). Addictive Behaviors, 20, 233–241.

Sobell, L. C., & Sobell, M. B. (1986). Can we do without alcohol abusers' self-reports? Behavior Therapist, 9, 141–146.

Sobell, L. C., & Sobell, M. B. (1992). Timeline followback: A technique for assessing self-reported alcohol consumption. In R. Z. Litten & J. P. Allen (Eds.), Measuring alcohol consumption: Psychosocial and biochemical methods (pp. 41–72). Totowa, NJ: Humana Press.

Sobell, L. C., & Sobell, M. B. (1995). Alcohol consumption measures. In J. P. Allen & M. Columbus (Eds.), Assessing alcohol problems: A guide for clinicians and researchers (pp. 55–73). Treatment Handbook Series, Number 4. Bethesda, MD: National Institute on Alcohol Abuse and Alcoholism.

Sobell, L. C., Sobell, M. B., & Nirenberg, T. D. (1988). Behavioral assessment and treatment planning with alcohol and drug abusers: A review with an emphasis on clinical application. Clinical Psychology Review, 8, 19–54.

Sobell, L. C., Sobell, M. B., Toneatto, T., & Leo, G. L. (1993). What triggers the resolution of alcohol problems without treatment? Alcoholism: Clinical and Experimental Research, 17, 217–224.

Sobell, L. C., Toneatto, T., & Sobbell, M. B. (1994). Behavioral assessment and treatment planning for alcohol, tobacco, and other drug problems: Current status with an emphasis on clinical applications. Behavior Therapy, 25, 533–580.

Sokol, R. J., Martier, S. S., & Ager, J. W. (1989). The T-ACE questions: Practical prenatal detection of risk drinking. American Journal of Obstetrics and Gynecology, 160, 863–870.

Spielberger, C. D., Gorsuch, R. L., & Lushene, R. E. (1970). Manual for the State-Trait Anxiety Inventory. Palo Alto, CA: Consulting Psychologists Press.

Spielberger, C. D., Jacobs, G., Russel, S., & Crane, R. S. (1983). Assessment of anger: The State-Trait Anger Scale. J. N. Butcher & C. D. Spielberger (Eds.), Advances in personality assessment (Vol. 2, pp. 159–187). Hillsdale, NJ: Erlbaum.

Stacy, A. W., Leigh, B. C., & Weingardt, K. R. (1994). Memory accessibility and association of alcohol use and its positive outcomes. *Experimental & Clinical Psychopharmacology, 2*(3), 269–282.

Stall, R., & Biernacki, P. (1986). Spontaneous remission from problematic use of substances: An inductive model derived from a comparative analysis of the alcohol, opiate, tobacco, and food/obesity literature. *International Journal of the Addictions, 21,* 1–23.

Stasiewicz, P. R., Bradizza, C. M., & Connors, G. J. (1997). Subject-collateral reports of drinking in inpatient alcoholics with comorbid mental disorders. *Alcoholism: Clinical and Experimental Research, 21,* 530–536.

Sutker, P. B., & Allain, A. N., Jr. (1988). Issues in personality conceptualizations of addictive behaviors. *Journal of Consulting and Clinical Psychology, 56,* 172–182.

Tarter, R. E., & Hegedus, A. M. (1991). Drug Use Screening Inventory: Its application in the evaluation and treatment of alcohol and other drug abuse. *Alcohol Health and Research World, 15,* 65–75.

Tarter, R. E., Moss, H. B., Arria, A., Mezzich, A. C., & Vanyukov, M. M. (1992). The psychiatric diagnosis of alcoholism: Critique and proposed reformulation. *Alcoholism: Clinical and Experimental Research, 16,* 106–116.

Teitelbaum, L. M., & Carey, K. B. (1996). Alcohol assessment in psychiatric patients. *Clinical Psychology: Science and Practice, 3,* 323–338.

Tucker, J. A., & Gladsjo, J. A. (1993). Help-seeking and recovery by problem drinkers: Characteristics of drinkers who attended Alcoholics Anonymous or formal treatment or who recovered without assistance, *Addictive Behaviors, 18,* 529–542.

Vereby, K. (1992). Diagnostic laboratory: Screening for drug abuse. In J. Lowinsohn, P. Ruiz, R. B. Millman, & J. G. Langrod (Eds.), *Substance abuse: A comprehensive textbook* (2nd ed., pp. 425–436). Baltimore, MD: Williams & Wilkins.

Wallace, J. (1986). The other problems of alcoholics. *Journal of Substance Abuse Treatment, 3,* 163–171.

Waltman, D. (1995). Key ingredients to effective addictions treatment. *Journal of Substance Abuse Treatment, 12,* 429–439.

Wanberg, K. W., Horn, J. L., & Foster, F. M. (1977). A differential assessment model for alcoholism. *Journal of Studies on Alcohol, 38,* 512–543.

Watson, C. G., Tilleskjor, C., Hoodecheck-Schow, E. A.,

Pucel, J., & Jacobs, L. (1984). Do alcoholics give valid self-reports? *Journal of Studies on Alcohol, 45,* 344–348.

Widiger, T. A., & Smith, G. T. (1994). Substance use disorder: Abuse, dependence, and dyscontrol. *Addiction, 89,* 267–282.

Wilson, D. K., & Grube, J. (1994). Role of psychosocial factors in obtaining self-reports of alcohol use in a DUI population. *Psychology of Addictive Behaviors, 8,* 139–151.

Wilson, G. T. (1987). Cognitive processes in addiction. *British Journal of Addiction, 82,* 343–353.

Wing, J. K., Babor, T., Brugha, T., Burke, J., et al. (1990). SCAN: Schedules for Clinical Assessment in Neuropsychiatry. *Archives of General Psychiatry, 47,* 589–593.

Woolf-Reeve, B. S. (1990). A guide to the assessment of psychiatric symptoms in the addictions treatment setting. *Journal of Chemical Dependency Treatment, 3,* 71–96.

World Health Organization. (1990). *International Classification of Diseases (10th Rev.).* Geneva: World Health Organization.

Young, R. McD., & Knight, R. G. (1989). The Drinking Expectancy Questionnaire: A revised measure of alcohol related beliefs. *Journal of Psychopathology and Behavioral Assessment, 11,* 99–112

Young, R. McD., Oei, T. P. S., & Crook, C. M. (1991). Development of a drinking self efficacy scale. *Journal of Psychopathology and Behavioural Assessment, 13,* 1–15.

Zanis, D. A., McLellan, A. T., & Randall, M. (1994). Can you trust patient self-reports of drug use during treatment? *Drug and Alcohol Dependence, 35,* 127–132.

Zimmerman, M., & Coryell, W. (1987). The Inventory to Diagnose Depression (IDD): A self-report scale to diagnose major depressive disorder. *Journal of Consulting and Clinical Psychology, 55,* 55–59.

Zung, B. J. (1984). Reliability and validity of the Short MAST among psychiatric inpatients. *Journal of Clinical Psychology, 40,* 347–350.

Zywiak, W. H., Connors, G. J., Maisto, S. A., & Westerberg, V. S. (1996). Relapse research and the Reasons for Drinking Questionnaire: A factor analysis of Marlatt's relapse taxonomy. *Addiction, 91*(Supplement), S121–S130.

12

Treatment Decision Making and Goal Setting

Ronald M. Kadden

Pamela M. Skerker

For years, many substance abuse programs offered all comers a single type of treatment, in a kind of "one-size-fits-all" approach. Even though a variety of approaches were available to the field, in many cases all clients at a particular facility or clinic received the same treatment content, and for a standard length of time.

Several factors have been responsible for a shift away from that approach. One is the interest in improving treatment outcomes for substance abusers. This has led to research on typologies, to characterize subgroups of clients and develop guidelines for assigning them to the treatment modalities that would be the most beneficial for their particular needs. A related factor is the availability of treatments that can be targeted to specific problems. A variety of cognitive behavioral techniques now exist that can be used to modify particular problem behaviors, and an increasing number of medications have been developed to treat various aspects of substance abuse (e.g., craving). A third factor that has caused a shift in

thinking about the assignment of clients to treatment is the burgeoning interest in health care cost containment. This has led to the rise of "managed care" and an essentially cost-driven determination to provide the least intensive care that will get the job done. Like practitioners in most other areas of health care, substance abuse treaters were ill prepared for this development. They have been struggling to deal with the conflicts that often arise between their judgment of what seems clinically necessary and the desires (often stated as requirements) of third-party payers for less treatment.

This chapter views treatment decision making and goal setting from the perspective of clinicians who see a steady stream of new clients, must determine their unique needs, and make rational decisions so as to provide them with the most appropriate treatment at the lowest possible cost. Clinicians are now required to justify every clinical recommendation in terms of both level of care (e.g., inpatient vs. outpatient) and specific components of treatment. In this chapter, we describe the elements of the decision-making process.

We first deal with clinical considerations involved in selecting the level of care, and then with the more detailed considerations involved in determining the specific aspects of care that constitute the treatment plan. Next, there is a brief review of research that has sought to provide an empirical basis for client-treatment matching and a description of a systematic plan that has been proposed for making decisions about levels of care. Having considered levels of care and treatment planning, we then discuss the setting of goals for treatment and various means of actively engaging the client in the treatment process. We also touch upon the issue of clients who present for treatment of some other problem but are found to also have a substance use disorder. The final sections are concerned with monitoring clients' responses to treatment and utilizing that information to make midcourse modifications of the treatment plan.

UTILIZING ASSESSMENT DATA TO SELECT APPROPRIATE LEVEL OF CARE

The Institute of Medicine (1990) identified four levels of care—outpatient, intermediate, residential, and inpatient—all offering detoxification and rehabilitation services that may vary in length, intensity, setting, and treatment modality. Outpatient treatment may offer individual, couples, family, or group therapy sessions ranging from weekly (or even less often) to a few hours several times a week. At the intermediate level, partial hospital treatment offers a structured program that meets from twice a week up to daily. It can be the first level of care for some clients, avoiding the need for hospitalization, or may serve as a transition from more intensive residential or inpatient care to less intensive outpatient treatment. Evening partial hospital programs allow a person to meet job, school, family, and other daytime commitments while in treatment. At the next level, residential programs become the client's home for a week or so, providing a substance-free environment, rehabilitation services, and a tightly knit, supportive community in a nonmedical setting. Finally, inpatient treatment programs are hospital-based (in general or psychiatric hospitals) and may provide intensive medical and psychiatric services through clinicians assigned to the substance abuse program, as well as

through in-house consultants. The full range of substance abuse care levels should be kept in mind during the process of assessment, and regardless of initial placement, clients may move among the levels as needs change or various goals are met.

The assessment process may range from a brief screening in a primary-care office or at a workplace to a detailed evaluation in a specialty clinic, ideally by a clinician experienced in dual diagnosis. The literature describes a number of different assessment methods, some of which may be brief or self-administered. When screening identifies a possible problem, further assessment is indicated. This typically involves a personal interview (structured or unstructured) by a clinician, laboratory toxicology screens, and perhaps also self-administered questionnaires to further identify the unique problems and needs of the client (Miller, Westerberg, & Waldron, 1995). The areas covered should include the types of substances used, patterns of use, amounts consumed, need for detoxification, triggers for use, prior treatment, and methods used to achieve abstinence in the past. The assessment also covers other functional problem areas such as family and/or employer pressures, current legal problems, medical problems (including pregnancy and physical limitations such as vision or hearing impairment), psychiatric diagnosis, perceptual or cognitive limitations, and demographic information. The client's own perceptions and attitudes toward his or her problems and limitations are also elicited. For more comprehensive information about assessment, please refer to chapter 11.

An accepting, nonjudgmental attitude on the part of the clinician when gathering the data is vital for identifying problems and motivating the client to accept treatment recommendations. Upon completion of the initial assessment, the triage clinician typically recommends the level of care and may offer suggestions regarding the initial treatment plan, in consultation with other program staff as necessary.

There are a number of variables to be considered when deciding on the most appropriate level of care. Some of the considerations in decision making include the client's medical or psychiatric problems, past relapses and treatment failures, severity of dependence, available support system, motivation or resistance, and need for structure. Generally, the greater the severity of the problems, and the more limited the client's personal and social resources, the greater the need for more intensive treatment (Alterman, O'Brien, & McLellan, 1991; Sobell, Sobell, & Nirenberg, 1988).

Unstable major mental illness generally requires inpatient treatment, ideally in a dual-diagnosis unit. Acute or severe medical conditions are also reasons to recommend inpatient treatment. Pregnancy, while not automatically considered a problem, requires special attention not only to the mother's needs, but to the implications her substance use has on fetal development, possibly indicating the need for more intensive treatment. Another possible concern relates to the client's ability to remain substance-free in an unstructured, unsupervised setting. If not, or if the assessment reveals repeated outpatient treatment failures or lack of significant abstinent periods, then inpatient treatment is indicated, with possible consideration of long-term residential follow-up if there are many severe and chronic problems. If the assessment indicates that a client lives among substance users in an area where alcohol and drugs are readily available and openly used, is impulsive, or is mentally retarded, more intensive treatment is indicated because of its greater degree of structure and supervision.

When 24-hour care is indicated, a residential program may be satisfactory for a week or so, if the acute care medical or psychiatric services of a hospital setting are not required. However, if there is uncertainty as to whether the intensity of residential services is necessary (e.g., the client has a reasonably strong support system), then a trial in a partial hospitalization program may be initiated. In this setting, considerable structure, frequent monitoring, and fairly intensive treatment can be offered for substance use and comorbid disorders that do not require 24-hour care. Clients who can make do with even less structure and less intensive monitoring can often be served well in an outpatient setting where they are seen for group, family, or individual treatment one or more times a week. In these settings, more reliance is placed on the client's ability to function independently and on his or her support network.

Sometimes, treatment programs (or tracks within programs) are geared toward specific populations (e.g., geriatrics, adolescents, monolingual). The availability of specialized treatment programs for some populations may override other level-of-care considerations. Additional factors not to be overlooked are accessibility, the location of the program,

and transportation. The fear of going to a "bad part of town" may discourage some clients from accepting optimal treatment recommendations.

Often, what is recommended is beyond what the client is prepared to undertake. The clinician must understand that well-intended recommendations are not always accepted right away. When meeting resistance to recommendations, an alternative may be to compromise if the client is agreeable to a lower level of care. This is usually preferable to completely losing the client to treatment. If a compromise cannot be negotiated, it is important to indicate to the client that the "door will be open in the future if you change your mind." Sometimes, the client will accept the treatment at a later date, after further relapse or consequences have occurred.

A substance abuse assessment may identify suicidal thoughts, which are not uncommon in this population. These should never be discounted or dismissed as manipulative or insignificant. A thorough mental status assessment must be completed, with attention to the existence of suicidal intent, plan, lethality, and available supports. There may be a dilemma in arranging for care if the available program(s) cannot assure client safety as well as provide substance abuse treatment. Admission to an inpatient psychiatry unit may be necessary. At other times, the assurance that treatment will be provided, combined with a strong social support network, is enough for the client to contract for safety. This often requires much time and energy by the clinician but is well worth the effort when it ensures both safety and appropriate treatment.

If a client meets the legal criteria for an emergency commitment (gravely disabled or a danger to self or others), refuses treatment recommendations, and is unable or unwilling to contract for safety, then he or she must be admitted to inpatient psychiatric treatment. When the legal criteria for involuntary commitment are no longer met, the client will be given the option of continuing voluntary treatment.

UTILIZING ASSESSMENT DATA TO DEVELOP INITIAL TREATMENT PLAN

Treatment planning is what individualizes a program. The initial treatment plan may be viewed as a prioritization of problems that need immediate attention, as opposed to longer term treatment needs. Immediate needs include (a) detoxification, (b) stabilization of acute medical problems, (c) stabilization of acute psychiatric problems, and (d) elimination of hazardous substance use. If a client is physically dependent on either alcohol, a benzodiazepine, or an opioid and is at risk of severe withdrawal symptoms (seizure, vital sign fluctuation, confusion, agitation), he or she is admitted to a detoxification program. Here, the substance (or a safe and legal substitute such as methadone or a benzodiazepine) is tapered over the course of several days. Medical and/or psychiatric problems are stabilized by means of ongoing consultations and treatment as necessary. In the absence of complicating factors, detoxification can be done on an outpatient basis in close collaboration with an experienced medical provider. This is appropriate if a client is highly motivated, has a strong support system, and does not have known medical problems or a history of withdrawal complications such as seizures. When ambulatory detoxification is possible, it may provide a means of extending limited financial resources or insurance benefits.

After the initial, acute needs have been addressed, further treatment planning involves input from a multidisciplinary team. As soon after admission as practicable, the client is assessed by various disciplines. The resulting multidisciplinary database will follow the client throughout his or her treatment in the facility and provides the basis for formulating the initial treatment plan. Each discipline adds to the database as ongoing assessments are done and responses to treatment are observed. Disciplines routinely involved in this process are nursing, occupational therapy, psychology, counseling, social work, and medicine. Also included as appropriate are psychiatry, various medical specialties, dietary, dentistry, and clergy.

A clinician in solo outpatient practice, without access to a multidisciplinary team, should assess each major area and develop an appropriate treatment plan. Consultation or referral may be needed for areas beyond the practitioner's scope of practice.

The initial assessments should attempt to identify precipitating events ("triggers") that are likely to lead the client back to substance use, as well as the usual supporting consequences that would reinforce substance use once it occurred and make repeated use in similar situations more likely. The assessment process should also identify behavioral deficits that would make it difficult to implement alternative behaviors instead of substance use in high-risk situations (Sobell, Sobell, & Nirenberg, 1982). Information obtained in the assessments regarding antecedents, consequences, and behavioral deficits forms the basis for the initial treatment plan. In their functional model, Miller and Mastria (1977) organized precipitants to use and consequences of use into five life problem areas comprising social, situational, emotional, cognitive, and physiological categories, for purposes of treatment planning. Marlatt (1985) classified relapse episodes as being intrapersonal, interpersonal, or environmental in nature and identified subcategories of each of them. Regardless of the model that is used, it is imperative that all major areas be assessed to ensure that clients recognize what triggers their substance use and what consequences are likely to follow it.

Annis and Davis (1989) described use of the Inventory of Drinking Situations to assess a client's high-risk situations for drinking, and to establish a hierarchy of them from highest to lowest risk. In collaboration with the client, detailed descriptions of typical high-risk situations and the client's usual responses to them are formulated. These detailed analyses suggest intervention strategies, provide a basis for selecting treatment goals, and suggest benchmarks for assessing treatment progress. In addition to high-risk situations, treatment planning must also take into account client strengths, coping abilities, and environmental resources, to ascertain which are adequate and which need development or enhancement to support changes in response to the high-risk situations.

It is well accepted that involving the client in treatment planning is essential so that it is truly individualized. The plan is then more likely to be realistic and attainable, will provide the client with a sense of control over his or her treatment (Sobell et al., 1988), and is likely to engender greater commitment to and involvement in the treatment process (Miller & Mastria, 1977). Client involvement can also foster identification of the needs that were being met by the use of substances; then, the client and the therapist together can usually come up with a number of alternative ways to meet those needs without having to resort to substance use (Miller & Pechacek, 1987).

CLIENT-TREATMENT MATCHING

Research

Although it is now commonplace to recommend the tailoring of treatment to each client's specific needs, there is in fact little empirical support for doing so. This section reviews the status of efforts to validate this idea and then considers the American Society of Addiction Medicine (ASAM) plan for systematizing decision making about level of care.

In recent years, there has been growing interest in aptitude-treatment interactions and examining the degree to which various treatments may have differential effectiveness for certain individuals as a function of their personal characteristics (Snow, 1991). In the alcoholism field particularly, there has been interest in identifying patient characteristics that predict better (or worse) outcomes with various treatment approaches. A number of the empirical patient-treatment-matching studies that have appeared from the early 1970s were reviewed in depth by Lindstrom (1992) and summarized by Mattson et al. (1994). Successful matching to cognitive behavioral interventions has been found among clients with high psychiatric severity or sociopathy (Kadden, Cooney, Getter, & Litt, 1989); clients with less education, strong urges to drink, and high anxiety (Rohsenow et al., 1991); and clients who are able to identify their high-risk situations (Annis & Davis, 1989). Interactional group therapy (Brown & Yalom, 1977) is more beneficial for clients low in psychiatric severity or sociopathy (Kadden et al., 1989), and for clients with low urges to drink, low anxiety, or good interpersonal skills (Kadden, Litt, Cooney, & Busher, 1992). Greater intensity of treatment appears to differentially benefit those who are socially unstable (Pettinati, Meyers, Jenson, Kaplan, & Evans, 1993; Welte, Hynes, Sokolow, & Lyons, 1981), high in psychiatric severity (Pettinati et al., 1993), likely to perceive an external locus of control over what happens to them (Hartman, Krywonis, & Morrison, 1988), or behaviorally impaired due to drinking (Lyons, Welte, Brown, Sokolow, & Hynes, 1982), although in some of these studies intensity and treatment modality were confounded.

Project MATCH, a major multisite trial of matching hypotheses, has recently begun to report its findings. Although data analyses are still ongoing, at present it appears that matching to client anger is the most consistent effect. Outpatients with greater anger pretreatment reported more abstinent days and fewer drinks per drinking day following motivational enhancement treatment (MET) than after cognitive behavioral treatment (CBT) and 12-step facilitation (TSF); those low in anger fared least well if treated in MET. This effect was observed at 1 year posttreatment and again at 3 years (Project MATCH Research Group, 1998). Two additional effects were observed at 1 year only. Outpatients with few or no concomitant psychiatric problems had better outcomes if treated in TSF than in CBT (Project MATCH Research Group, 1997a). Aftercare clients with high levels of dependence on alcohol had better outcomes after TSF, while those with low dependence fared better if assigned to CBT (Project MATCH Research Group, 1997b). One effect was evident only at the 3-year assessment: Outpatients whose social network provided greater support for drinking had better outcomes after treatment in TSF, while those with low network support for drinking fared better after treatment in MET (Project MATCH Research Group, 1998).

At present, all positive matching findings that have been reported in the literature must be regarded as promising hypotheses, rather than as practical treatment assignment strategies. Before they can be recommended for widespread clinical use, they must be replicated under conditions of actual clinical practice. Furthermore, greater attention must be paid to the "causal chains" which account for the relationships between patient variables and treatment types (Longabaugh, Wirtz, DiClemente, & Litt, 1994), both to advance understanding of the matching process and to enable refinement of the treatments provided, to maximize their effectiveness for the clients who benefit from them.

ASAM Model

Given the more-or-less preliminary state of research on matching, empirically based patient placement criteria do not yet exist. Nevertheless, the rapidly evolving health-care-financing situation demands that rational client placement criteria be developed, so that clients can be assigned to levels of care that will be effective for them but will not be more intensive (read "expensive") than they require. As a result, some efforts have been made to delineate systematic patient placement criteria, although largely without the benefit of empirical research findings that support their efficacy.

The most widely known and utilized patient placement criteria are those developed by the American Society of Addiction Medicine (ASAM; Hoffman, Halikas, Mee-Lee, & Weedman, 1991). They include six dimensions for specifying the severity of clients' alcohol-related problems and four recommended levels of care. The care levels include outpatient treatment (fewer than 9 hours per week), intensive outpatient or partial hospitalization treatment involving a structured treatment program of at least 9 hours per week, medically monitored residential addiction treatment without the full resources of an acute care hospital, and medically managed inpatient treatment in a hospital setting. The six client dimensions that serve as the basis for making assignments to one of the four levels of care are: (1) current state of intoxication and the potential for life-threatening withdrawal symptoms; (2) biomedical complications that may require monitoring and/or care; (3) emotional or behavioral conditions that may affect level of care; (4) degree of treatment acceptance/resistance; (5) relapse potential; and (6) and the extent to which a client's daily environment may promote relapse or facilitate recovery. These dimensions are used to determine the initial assignment to a level of treatment, and to guide reassignment as a client's status changes during the course of treatment.

The ASAM criteria have been criticized on a number of grounds (Book et al., 1995), and an attempt to validate the psychosocial criteria (Dimensions 3–6) did not find superior treatment outcomes for alcohol- or cocaine-dependent clients who had been assigned to treatment on that basis (McKay, Cacciola, McLellan, Alterman, & Wirtz, 1997). McKay et al. concluded that the criteria could benefit from better definition of the client dimensions and from the establishment of standardized methods of assessment. They also suggested that the criteria for inpatient treatment are too broad and recommended that the inpatient level of care be used only to provide stabilization for poor prognosis clients prior to their being entered into an intensive outpatient program.

In their overviews of the ASAM criteria, Gartner and Mee-Lee (1995) and Morey (1996) suggested that matching be done not only to levels of care, but also to specific treatment modalities within each level. This suggestion appears similar to a proposal by Glaser et al. (1984) for a "core-shell" model of treatment, in which clients are assigned to specific treatment modalities as well as to levels of care. Under this model, a "core" assessment unit would evaluate all incoming clients and refer them to an appropriate level of care, selecting from among the treatment programs, providers, and modalities that constitute the "shell." Following their treatment, clients would return to the core for a follow-up assessment that would be used to construct success profiles for each treatment in the shell, thereby providing an empirical basis for making future referrals to them.

Gartner and Mee-Lee (1995) advocated the development of universally applicable patient placement criteria, perhaps based on the ASAM model, to promote the use of individualized and cost-effective treatment. They believe that broadly accepted placement criteria would provide a degree of standardization throughout the field that would make it easier to identify active treatment ingredients, identify gaps in the continuum of care, evaluate treatment outcomes, and assess the cost-effectiveness of treatment.

SETTING GOALS FOR TREATMENT

Treatment Goals for Substance Use

The primary goal of treatment is to achieve abstinence or at least to reduce the level of substance use (considerations regarding this choice of goals are discussed in the next section). If uncontrolled use continues, the client will be unable to benefit from treatment of either the substance use disorder or co-existing problems (Vuchinich, Tucker & Harllee, 1988). The first goals of treatment include identification of the antecedents and consequences of substance use, followed by acquisition of the coping and social skills needed to establish sobriety. However, in some instances, it may be necessary to focus concomitantly on other pressing problems, for if these are not resolved, then it may be unlikely that the substance use will ever change. This issue is considered in more detail in a later section.

Treatment goals should be partitioned into a series of short-term objectives that will provide the building blocks for developing necessary behaviors and skills (e.g., identifying high-risk situations, refusing offers to use drugs or to drink, managing cravings, handling anger). The goals should be clearly operationalized so that therapist and client will be able to agree as to whether or not they have been met, and they should be in small enough steps to allow for both early and ongoing success experiences (Sobell et al., 1982).

The process of setting treatment goals was described by McCrady, Dean, DuBreuil, and Swanson (1985), who provided guidelines and a structure for getting clients and clinicians working together to set goals and monitor progress toward fulfilling them. Their guidelines for goal development specify four key elements: (a) Goals should be stated in terms of the client's own behavior, so that the responsibility clearly lies with him or her, and the sense of accomplishment for successful fulfillment of them will be the client's alone; (b) goals should be measurable, so that success, or degrees of partial success, can be gauged unequivocally by the client, the treater, and significant others in the client's daily life; (c) good goals entail a certain degree of challenge and risk, which will enhance the sense of accomplishment upon fulfillment, although not so much risk that failure is likely, since that would tend to undermine the treatment process; and (d) setting time limits for completion of goals puts some pressure on clients to work toward fulfilling them and provides a framework for projecting the accomplishment of long-term goals based upon a series of short-term successes that are designed to build upon one another in an escalating sequence.

Controlled/Moderate Use Versus Abstinence Treatment Goals

The issue of selecting an appropriate drinking goal can be a difficult one. Although some clients will have come to the conclusion, prior to seeking treatment, that they must not drink any longer, many others will harbor hopes that they can continue to consume alcohol at some level (Pattison, 1985). Certainly, clients who are severely dependent should be dissuaded from hoping that they can ever drink safely again, whereas heavy drinkers without evidence of problems are likely candidates for a trial of moderate or controlled drinking. But what about the large number of people who fall between these two poles?

Miller and Muñoz (1982) began their controlled-drinking self-help guide with criteria specifying those who may or may not be appropriate for a goal of moderate drinking. They indicated that this goal is appropriate for early-stage problem drinkers who have concerns about the difficulties being caused by their drinking (but not major life crises), have experienced these problems for less than 10 years, do not consider themselves alcoholic (but worry that alcoholism may develop), have no alcoholic close relatives, and have not been physically addicted. Miller and Muñoz recommended that a controlled-drinking goal not be pursued in the presence of medical contraindications, such as liver disease, gastrointestinal problems, heart disease, other physical problems that could be worsened by even moderate drinking, or pregnancy. A controlled-drinking goal is also not recommended for those who experience a loss of control whenever they consume alcohol, have a history of physical addiction to alcohol, take prescribed medications that could interact with alcohol, or are currently abstaining successfully. Some of those who are candidates for a moderate-drinking goal might nevertheless benefit from an initial period of abstinence to repair their physical health, for psychiatric reasons (e.g., severe depression, especially with suicidality), or to achieve a period of stability before attempting moderate use.

On the other hand, some clients for whom abstinence is recommended may nevertheless insist upon a moderate-drinking goal. For such people it may be useful to agree upon a trial in which a mutually acceptable amount of alcohol (e.g., two drinks) is consumed every day without exception for a period of several weeks. Many alcohol-dependent drinkers cannot limit themselves in this way, but if the client is able to, then he or she may indeed be a candidate for a more extended trial of controlled drinking. Some clients who initially refuse a recommended goal of abstinence may revert to it on their own at a later time. For example, Hodgins, Leigh, Milne, and Gerrish (1997) provided treatment-seeking chronic alcoholics a choice of goals: either abstinence or reduced drinking. They found that initially, the participants were equally likely to choose abstinence or moderation, but by the end of 4 weeks of treatment, two thirds of them chose abstinence (especially those who were older or had more severe drinking histories). Initial goal choice was not related to treatment outcome, but those whose final choice was abstinence had better drinking outcomes in the year following treatment.

Sanchez-Craig, Wilkinson, and Davila (1995) investigated safe limits for moderate drinking among problem drinkers for whom moderation was a clinically justifiable treatment goal. They found cutoffs of 4 drinks per day and 16 drinks per week for men, and 3 drinks per day and 12 per week for women. Exceeding the per day limits was associated with continuing problems. Sanchez-Craig et al. note that the specified cutoffs apply to the social problems associated with excessive drinking, and not to the health risks of long-term use.

Clients who wish to engage in moderate use of illegal drugs should be reminded of their illegal status and encouraged to consider lifestyle changes that would eliminate all illegal activities, as part of an overall recovery plan. Here again, a client may insist upon a period of experimentation before an abstinence goal is accepted.

Since the late 1980s, a new approach has been developed that focuses less on the level of drinking or drug use than on reducing the harm caused by them. This "harm reduction" approach originated in Europe as part of the effort to reduce the spread of HIV and has since spread to the United States. It involves a public health perspective and thus tends to focus on broad strategies rather than on specific interventions for individual cases. Its goal is to minimize the harmful consequences of drug and alcohol use and, if possible, to reduce heavy use. Some of the steps fostered by this approach include needle exchange programs, designated-driver programs, pricing structures that provide incentives to consume low-alcohol beverages, and so on (Single, 1996). The harm reduction approach does not take a position regarding the alternative goals of reduced use versus total abstinence, although one assumption of the approach is that moderate drinking is an acceptable outcome.

Goal Setting in Other Areas of Life Functioning

In addition to treatment goals related to substance use, there are often other problems (sometimes a considerable number of them) that require attention. Some of these problems may be associated with substance use and may therefore put a client at risk for relapse. It is thus important to identify and attend to such collateral problems in conjunction with substance abuse treatment.

Concomitant medical or psychiatric problems require independent evaluation and treatment. If a dis-

order is substance-induced, it may remit with continued abstinence (Schuckit & Monteiro, 1988), but if it is an independent disorder it will require ongoing attention.

Some clients lack the basic coping skills to handle certain situations or thoughts which could increase their risk of relapse. These deficiencies may necessitate setting goals to enhance their ability to communicate with others, deal with criticism, refuse offers to drink or use drugs, or function better in close relationships. Clients may also need training to combat negative thinking, cope with angry feelings, make decisions, solve problems, and manage thoughts about drinking or using drugs (Monti, Abrams, Kadden, & Cooney, 1989).

Some collateral problems may require attention early in the treatment process, along with efforts to curb substance use, because the needs are so pressing that sobriety cannot be maintained, even in the short run, without their being addressed. Others may be less intense or may require a lengthy period of time to resolve and may therefore be regarded as long-term goals. The resolution of still other problems may entail the uncovering of painful affect, which in itself could pose a considerable relapse risk. It is usually better, if at all possible, to postpone the treatment of such problems until stable sobriety has been achieved, although in some cases a problem may be so intertwined with the substance use that they both must be tackled together, despite the attendant risks.

Treatment Process Goals

Certain fundamental assumptions are basic to the very process of treatment and must be met to at least some degree if anything useful is to be accomplished. These may best be viewed as therapist goals related to the viability and integrity of the treatment process.

Client motivation and cooperation with the treatment, already referred to above, must be present to at least some degree if the client is even to remain in treatment, and if anything is to be accomplished. Beyond that bare minimum, several initial therapist goals must be met if the treatment process is to be viable (McAuliffe & Albert, 1992). The therapist must recognize and acknowledge the client's discomfort associated with being in treatment and must help him or her to recognize that a certain amount of discomfort is an integral part of the process of change. Another short-term therapist goal involves efforts to resolve client denial or minimization of problems, ambivalence about change, and outright resistance to change. These are present in varying forms and degrees in most substance abuse clients. Furthermore, some clients enter treatment with the notion that they have come to "get the cure," which seems to mean that they expect treatment will be a relatively short-term process in which they can assume a passive role. They must be helped to understand the difficulty of the process (without at the same time being discouraged from continuing) and must be prepared for active participation over the long term. Finally, treatment is predicated on the existence of trust and an effective working alliance with the therapist, the development of which must be among the therapist's goals in any therapeutic encounter. In the case of group therapy, additional treatment process goals involve socialization into the group (learning its norms) and developing sufficient trust among group members so that significant issues can be broached openly in the group setting.

UTILIZING ASSESSMENT DATA TO ENGAGE THE CLIENT IN TREATMENT

It is important early in the assessment process to begin to clarify the relationship between troubling life problems and the use of substances. Schottenfeld (1994) suggested that the clinician help the client map out a "parallel chronology" that compares the development of substance use and the course of other life problems. Clients' dissatisfaction with their current situation, as well as discrepancies between their hopes or goals and current reality, is often the most effective driving force for change. It is therefore essential to identify areas of dissatisfaction and disappointment, and to explore them and their relationship to substance use in some detail. The intent of this review of problems is to heighten clients' awareness of them and of the role of substance use as a causative and/or maintaining factor (Miller & Rollnick, 1991).

It is necessary to accurately assess motivation and accept clients in their present motivational state, whatever that may be (Annis, Schober, & Kelly, 1996). This may mean settling for less ambitious initial goals than the therapist believes are indicated, or

perhaps focusing attention on an issue peripheral to substance use, to maintain a client's interest and engagement in treatment.

Miller and Rollnick (1991) described motivation as "a state of readiness or eagerness to change, which may fluctuate from one time or situation to another. This state is one that can be influenced" (p. 14). Their "motivational interviewing" techniques are particularly recommended for dealing with poorly motivated clients but can be helpful regardless of a client's motivation. Expression of empathy, rather than confrontation, is more likely to foster trust. Expressing support for the client, indicating understanding of what he or she has gone through, and expressing confidence in his or her ability to change will strengthen the therapeutic alliance and enhance client motivation. Resistance and ambivalence are common, and are best explored objectively and matter-of-factly, to avoid arousing client defensiveness (Miller & Rollnick, 1991).

If the assessment indicates that there are external obstacles such as lack of transportation, child care, or finances to cover the cost of treatment, the clinician should be familiar with and willing to suggest local resources. If a person seeking treatment has no insurance and no entitlements, referral to the local social services department or to a government-funded treatment program can eliminate the cost barrier. If a person has no transportation, some programs offer van service or bus tokens. There may also be marital or family problems. Many of these problems can be addressed through the use of a case management approach, which involves arranging and coordinating the provision of needed clinical and supportive services (Willenbring, 1996).

Withdrawal presents another potential barrier to treatment. The discomfort of withdrawal symptoms such as nausea, abdominal cramps, and muscle aches can lead to a resumption of substance use if they go unmedicated, and therefore, an attempt should be made to reduce the discomfort as much as possible.

A lengthy waiting period is a deterrent to engagement in treatment. Ideally, admission should be available immediately after initial contact, to maintain motivation. Frequently, a crisis motivates a person to seek help, and once the problem subsides, some clients may no longer be interested in treatment. If there is a waiting period, encourage the use of available supports (e.g., staying with family, daily fellowship meetings) and consider referral to another program in the area. Some programs use clinician letters or phone calls to follow up initial appointments, but care must be taken to not inadvertently breach confidentiality by leaving a message or an obvious return address.

Other methods for decreasing client resistance include encouraging family, friends, and case managers to become involved in and understand treatment. This is especially beneficial when the presenting problem is a crisis, since significant others are often affected or already involved (Barr, 1990). Of course, clinical judgment must be used when considering the involvement of others, since a client may feel pressured by family or may perceive that the clinician is taking sides with family members. Cultural differences regarding family involvement should also be considered.

For those who have had no prior treatment, McAuliffe and Albert (1992) encourage clients already in treatment to share experiences with newcomers, to help them see that treatment is relevant and that their goals are attainable. Attending 12-step programs in addition to treatment can also help maintain motivation for abstinence and for remaining in treatment.

IDENTIFYING SUBSTANCE ABUSE WHEN THE PRESENTING PROBLEM IS SOMETHING ELSE

Health care professionals must take the initiative to address substance use, regardless of what may have brought a client to their attention. Caregivers cannot assume that a person's appearance, age, or socioeconomic status exempts her or him from substance abuse. If no one asks a client about substance use, it may seem irrelevant. Some clients may be too ashamed, embarrassed, or fearful of the implications to raise the issue themselves.

Substance abuse can be a major factor even when the reason for seeking treatment appears unrelated. Serious medical or psychiatric consequences which result from substance abuse are often the reasons people seek treatment from health care professionals. Cardiac, respiratory, and gastrointestinal problems and recurring infection, trauma, depression, and psychoses are presenting problems that may be substance-related. If a substance use screening is not in-

cluded in all medical and psychiatric assessments, many cases will go undetected, and proper treatment will be delayed or not provided at all (Galanter & Kleber, 1994; Schottenfeld, 1994). A study of Boston area residents who actually believed they had alcohol-related problems revealed that many of those seen by physicians had not even been asked about alcohol use (Hingson, Mangione, Meyers, & Scotch, 1982). A hospital study in Seattle determined that almost half of nontrauma patients who abused substances had not been identified as substance abusers (Dunn & Ries, 1997). Babor (1990) advised that primary-practice health care professionals actively seek to identify substance use problems in those whom they are treating by including a routine screening among their assessments. There are several brief screening tools, some of which can be self-administered. Beyond primary care, other settings where detection may take place include emergency departments, intensive care units, medical specialties, and mental health settings.

Members of psychiatric consultation/liaison teams frequently encounter patients who are not seeking substance abuse treatment and are unaware of a problem with alcohol or drugs. This is an ideal setting for use of a screening procedure, and provides an opportunity to educate the patient about substance abuse as a means of engaging him or her in treatment (Heather, 1995).

When there have been life-threatening consequences, facing one's mortality can be a prime motivating factor in seeking or accepting treatment. However, motivation can decrease when the crisis has been resolved. Therefore, in an acute hospital setting, substance use consultation should be available as soon as a person's acute medical problems have been stabilized.

At times, people self-medicate with prescription narcotics or anxiolytics, rationalizing that it is not abuse if the medication is prescribed. Over time, they may use more than one pharmacy or health care provider to maintain an adequate supply. Repeatedly seeking pain medication, especially from different sources, can be a warning sign of substance abuse. Requesting information from other care providers may help to confirm what medications are being obtained and for what reasons. However, confidentiality laws prohibit a clinician from access to vital information that may be in the hands of others, unless the client authorizes the release of information. At the time of initial screening, the clinician must explain the importance of, and encourage the client to authorize, communication with other professionals that he or she has seen recently.

Substance abuse is a potentially serious problem with numerous consequences that can impact various areas of functioning. Therefore, health care providers should maintain a high index of suspicion of substance use in the presence of warning signs and indications from screening tools.

MONITORING RESPONSE TO TREATMENT

Treatment planning may be viewed as a continuous process in which client successes and failures provide the basis for course corrections (Sobell et al., 1982). Where there is little progress, the reasons are explored, and the treatment plan is modified accordingly. In areas of success, once new responses have been adequately practiced in a number of different situations, therapeutic attention can be shifted away from them, and more effort can be focused on remaining problems.

There are several domains in which positive responses to treatment are desired. Certainly, reduction or elimination of drinking and drug use is primary. Closely related to these are identifying and controlling the antecedents that may precede alcohol and drug use and increasing the client's perceived self-efficacy (i.e., his or her belief that he or she can achieve and maintain recovery). In addition, there are often problems in other areas of functioning that could increase the likelihood of a relapse (Vuchinich & Tucker, 1996). Finally, improvements in overall level of client functioning and sense of well-being (physical, psychological, social activities, and social support) may play a significant role in maintaining recovery (Longabaugh et al., 1994). Therefore, assessments of client progress must include the presenting problems identified at intake as well as maintain a broader focus on various aspects of overall functioning.

The monitoring of clients' responses to treatment may take several forms. The most detailed information usually comes from client self-reports to the therapist during the course of treatment. Additional information may come from daily recordings of urges to drink, actual drinking, ongoing problems, and

their antecedents (for specific examples and sample recording forms, see chapter 14 in this volume; Miller & Mastria, 1977). Clients' progress can also be monitored through assignments to practice new coping skills or problem solving in their natural environment. Careful monitoring of these assignments can provide considerable information regarding developing competencies and remaining deficiencies, which may lead to changes in emphasis, or even to changes in the overall focus of treatment. These evaluations are typically woven into the fabric of ongoing therapeutic contacts, so that there is no clear delineation between ongoing assessment and treatment.

Despite the obvious value of making treatment responsive to therapeutic process, little has been written about specific techniques for monitoring client progress, and there are few measures particularly designed for this purpose (Finney, 1995). One measure that has been adapted to meet this need is the Situational Confidence Questionnaire. During the course of treatment, clients may be requested to complete this structured assessment, in which they are asked to indicate their confidence in their ability to resist urges to drink in a variety of situations (Annis & Davis, 1989). This questionnaire provides a means of assessing changes in self-efficacy during treatment and areas of continuing low confidence that will require additional work.

The validity of self-reports can be enhanced if clients know that the information they provide will be verified. It is recommended that self-reports regarding alcohol and drug use be corroborated through the use of a breathalyzer (to estimate blood alcohol content) and urine toxicology screens. Additional information may be obtained from significant others in a client's life, such as spouse, roommate, close friend, case manager, or probation officer. Participation in recommended activities can be verified by having the client bring in physical evidence, such as a receipt, or a signature to verify attendance at AA or NA fellowship meetings.

UTILIZING ONGOING ASSESSMENT DATA TO MODIFY THE TREATMENT PLAN

Information obtained through various forms of ongoing assessment may cast new light on client problems, perhaps indicating the need for modification of treatment strategies and goals. In their review of assessment and treatment planning for substance abuse, Sobell et al. (1988) presented a plan for monitoring progress over the course of treatment, focusing on reasons for lack of progress and problems with the treatment plan. We believe that this assessment could also include evidence of progress as well as lack of it, allowing a better evaluation of the overall effectiveness of the treatment plan. The following list is an abbreviated version of the Sobell et al. evaluation questions:

- Is the client engaging in/refraining from the behaviors that are the focus of clinical attention?
- Were the antecedents/consequences of the problem behaviors correctly identified?
- Were client strengths and resources correctly identified?
- Does the client have adequate support in his or her environment?
- Are the treatment goals appropriate? Were subgoals identified in sufficiently small steps and of gradually increasing difficulty?
- Are the treatment strategies working? Does it appear that some treatment techniques are more appropriate than others with this client? Are they being properly applied by the therapist and by the client?
- Does the client understand the reasons why he or she is doing well or experiencing continued problems?
- Are the client's problems, or their consequences, serious enough to motivate the client to change?

Questions of this sort could be incorporated into scheduled periodic reviews of each case to identify areas of strength and weakness in the treatment plan.

Perhaps the most common reason for modifying treatment plans is the occurrence of persistent relapses. It has been recommended that relapse episodes be viewed as learning experiences, and that the events preceding and following the relapse be carefully analyzed to provide a basis for strengthening behaviors that would reduce the likelihood of a recurrence under similar circumstances (Miller & Mastria, 1977).

It is important to help the client understand that relapses are a common occurrence that can be viewed as an error made in the natural course of the learning process, rather than as a sign of failure or a reason to give up treatment and abandon hope (Mar-

latt, 1985). Early in treatment, clients should be provided with guidelines for coping with the immediate consequences of a relapse and for minimizing its duration and severity by getting rid of the alcohol/drug at once, removing themselves from the situation, getting help (from a sponsor, a family member, or a friend), and trying not to allow the feelings of guilt that often follow a relapse (Marlatt, 1985) provide an excuse for further substance use. After a relapse occurs, the therapist should assist the client to examine events prior to the relapse, to consider ways of avoiding a recurrence in similar circumstances, and to identify more effective coping behaviors that could be utilized in the future (McCrady et al. 1985). This process is likely to lead to a modification of the treatment plan that will strengthen coping abilities in areas of deficiency. The exact changes in the plan will depend upon the nature of the relapse situation and upon the therapist's and client's joint assessment of the weaknesses the relapse revealed. Similar principles also apply to managing continued recurrences of other problem behaviors addressed by the treatment plan.

SUMMARY

In this chapter, we have provided an overview of considerations typically involved in initial decision making about level of care, goal setting, and treatment planning, as well as monitoring the course of treatment and making midcourse adjustments. These are summarized in figure 12.1. After assessment of several key areas, a decision is made regarding the most appropriate level of care. This decision may also have to take into account the availability of needed clinical resources in the geographic area as well as limitations that may be imposed by third-party payers. After the *level* of care has been determined, the specific therapeutic interventions within that level of care must be selected. This selection will involve recommendations by the treatment provider and should include negotiations with the client based on his or her goals and expectations about treatment. Once the treatment plan has been initiated, ongoing assessment of progress and the occurrence of problems may necessitate changes in the interventions or, in some cases, perhaps a different level of care. Adjustments in the treatment plan are likely to occur sev-

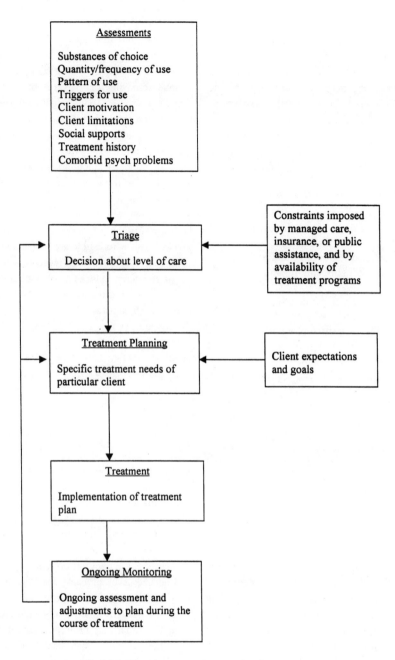

FIGURE 12.1 Key elements of treatment decision making.

eral times over the course of treatment, regardless of its success.

Many of these aspects of clinical decision making are based on clinical experience, often without the benefit of empirical validation. As the demands grow for treatments that have demonstrated efficacy, and for practitioners to provide outcome data for their clientele, it is anticipated that a body of knowledge will gradually be amassed that will provide better information on the efficacy of current treatment-planning practices and an empirical basis for improving upon them.

ACKNOWLEDGMENTS   The writing of this chapter was supported in part by NIAAA grant R01-AA09648, to Ronald Kadden, Principal Investigator. The authors wish to thank Jaime Skerker for her helpful comments on an earlier draft of this chapter.

Key References

Lindstrom, L. (1992). *Managing alcoholism: Matching clients to treatments.* Oxford: Oxford University Press.

Marlatt, G. A., & Gordon, J. R. (Eds.). (1985). *Relapse prevention: Maintenance strategies in the treatment of addictive behaviors.* New York: Guilford Press.

Miller, P. M., & Mastria, M. A. (1977). *Alternatives to alcohol abuse: A social learning model.* Champaign, IL: Research Press.

References

Alterman, A. I., O'Brien, C. P., & McLellan, A. T. (1991). Differential therapeutics for substance abuse. In R. J. Frances & S. I. Miller (Eds.), *Clinical textbook of addictive disorders* (pp. 369–390). New York: Guilford Press.

Annis, H. M., & Davis, C. S. (1989). Relapse prevention. In R. K. Hester & W. R. Miller (Eds.), *Handbook of alcoholism treatment approaches: Effective alternatives* (pp. 170–182). New York: Pergamon Press.

Annis, H. M., Schober, R., & Kelly, E. (1996). Matching addiction outpatient counseling to client readiness for change: The role of structured relapse prevention counseling. *Experimental and Clinical Psychopharmacology, 4,* 37–45.

Babor, T. F. (1990). Alcohol and substance abuse in primary care settings. In J. Mayfield & M. Grady (Eds.), *Primary care research: An agenda for the 90s* (pp. 113–124). Washington, DC: U.S. Department of Health and Human Services.

Barr, M. A. (1990). Evaluation and triage. In W. D. Lerner & M. A. Barr (Eds.), *Handbook of hospital based substance abuse treatment* (pp. 7–17). New York: Pergamon Press.

Book, J., Harbin, H., Marques, C., Silverman, C., Lizanich-Aro, S., & Lazarus, A. (1995). The ASAM and Green Spring alcohol and drug detoxification and rehabilitation criteria for utilization review. *American Journal on Addictions, 4,* 187–197.

Brown, S., & Yalom, I. D. (1977). Interactional group therapy with alcoholics. *Journal of Studies on Alcohol, 38,* 426–456.

Dunn, C. W., & Ries, R. (1997). Linking substance abuse services with general medical care: Integrated, brief interventions with hospitalized patients. *American Journal of Drug and Alcohol Abuse, 23,* 1–13.

Finney, J. W. (1995). Assessing treatment and treatment processes. In J. P. Allen & M. Columbus (Eds.), *Assessing alcohol problems. A guide for clinicians and researchers* (pp. 123–142). Bethesda, MD: National Institute on Alcohol Abuse and Alcoholism.

Galanter, M., & Kleber, H. (1994). Preface. In M. Galanter & H. D. Kleber (Eds.), *The American psychiatric press textbook of substance abuse treatment* (pp. xiii–xiv). Washington, DC: American Psychiatric Press.

Gartner, L., & Mee-Lee, D. (1995). *The role and current status of patient placement criteria in the treatment of substance use disorders: Treatment Improvement Protocol Series 13.* Rockville, MD: Center for Substance Abuse Treatment.

Glaser, F. B., Annis, H. M., Skinner, H. A., Pearlman, S., Segal, R. L., Sisson, B., Ogborne, A. C., Bohnen, E., Gazda, P, & Zimmerman, T. (1984). *A system of health care delivery* (Vols. 1–3). Toronto: Addiction Research Foundation.

Hartman, L., Krywonis, M., & Morrison, E. (1988). Psychological factors and health-related behavior change: Preliminary findings from a controlled study. *Canadian Family Physician, 34,* 1045–1050.

Heather, N. (1995). Brief intervention strategies. In R. K. Hester & W. R. Miller (Eds.), *Handbook of alcoholism treatment approaches: Effective alternatives* (pp. 105–122). Boston: Allyn & Bacon.

Hingson, R., Mangione, T., Meyers, A., & Scotch, N. (1982). Seeking help for drinking problems. A study in the Boston Metropolitan Area. *Journal of Studies on Alcohol, 43,* 273–288.

Hodgins, D. C., Leigh, G., Milne, R., & Gerrish, R. (1997). Drinking goal selection in behavioral self-management treatment of chronic alcoholics. *Addictive Behaviors, 22*(2), 247–255.

Hoffman, N. G., Halikas, J. A., Mee-Lee, D., & Weedman, R. D. (1991). *Patient placement criteria for the treatment of psychoactive substance use disorders.* Washington, DC: American Society of Addiction Medicine.

Institute of Medicine. (1990). *Broadening the base of treatment for alcohol problems.* Washington, DC: National Academy Press.

Kadden, R. M., Cooney, N. L., Getter, H., & Litt, M. D. (1989). Matching alcoholics to coping skills or interactional therapies: Posttreatment results. *Journal of Consulting and Clinical Psychology, 57,* 698–704.

Kadden, R. M., Litt, M. D., Cooney, N. L., & Busher, D. A. (1992). Relationship between role-play measures of coping skills and alcoholism treatment outcome. *Addictive Behaviors, 17,* 425–437.

Lindstrom, L. (1992). *Managing alcoholism: Matching clients to treatments.* Oxford: Oxford University Press.

Longabaugh, R., Wirtz, P. W., DiClemente, C. C., & Litt, M. (1994). Issues in the development of client-treatment matching hypotheses. In D. M. Donovan & M. E. Mattson (Eds.), Alcoholism treatment matching research: Methodological and clinical approaches. *Journal of Studies on Alcohol Monograph* (Suppl. 12), 46–59.

Lyons, J. P., Welte, J. W., Brown, J., Sokolow, L., & Hynes, G. (1982). Variation in alcoholism treatment orientation: Differential impact upon specific subpopulations. *Alcoholism: Clinical and Experimental Research, 6,* 333–343.

Marlatt, G. A. (1985). Cognitive assessment and intervention procedures for relapse prevention. In G. A. Marlatt & J. R. Gordon (Eds.), *Relapse prevention* (pp. 201–279). New York: Guilford Press.

Mattson, M. E., Allen, J. P., Longabaugh, R., Nickless, C. J., Connors, G. J., & Kadden, R. M. (1994). A chronological review of empirical studies matching alcoholic clients to treatment. In D. M. Donovan & M. E. Mattson (Eds.), Alcoholism treatment matching research: Methodological and clinical approaches. *Journal of Studies on Alcohol Monograph* (Suppl. 12), 16–29.

McAuliffe, W. E., & Albert, J. (1992). *Clean start: An outpatient program for initiating cocaine recovery.* New York: Guilford Press.

McCrady, B. S., Dean, L., DuBreuil, E., & Swanson, S. (1985). The problem drinkers' project: A programmatic application of social-learning-based treatment. In G. A. Marlatt & J. R. Gordon (Eds.), *Relapse prevention* (pp. 417–471). New York: Guilford Press.

McKay, J. R., Cacciola, J. S., McLellan, A. T., Alterman, A. I., & Wirtz, P. W. (1997). An initial evaluation of the psychosocial dimensions of the American Society of Addiction Medicine criteria for inpatient versus intensive outpatient substance abuse rehabilitation. *Journal of Studies on Alcohol, 58,* 239–252.

Miller, P. M., & Mastria, M. A. (1977). *Alternatives to alcohol abuse: A social learning model.* Champaign, IL: Research Press.

Miller, W. R., & Muñoz, R. F. (1982). *How to control your drinking.* Albuquerque: University of New Mexico Press.

Miller, W. R., & Pechacek, T. F. (1987). New roads: Assessing and treating psychological dependence. *Journal of Substance Abuse Treatment, 4,* 73–77.

Miller, W. R., & Rollnick, S. (1991). *Motivational interviewing: Preparing people to change addictive behavior.* New York: Guilford Press.

Miller, W. R., Westerberg, V. S., & Waldron, H. B. (1995). Evaluating alcohol problems in adults and adolescents. In R. K. Hester & W. R. Miller (Eds.), *Handbook of alcoholism treatment approaches: Effective alternatives* (2nd ed., pp. 61–88). Boston: Allyn & Bacon.

Monti, P. M., Abrams, D. B., Kadden, R. M., & Cooney, N. L. (1989). *Treating alcohol dependence: A coping skills training guide.* New York: Guilford Press.

Morey, L. C. (1996). Patient placement criteria. Linking typologies to managed care. *Alcohol Health and Research World, 20,* 36–44.

Pattison, E. M. (1985). The selection of treatment modalities for the alcoholic patient. In J. H. Mendelson & N. K. Mello (Eds.), *The diagnosis and treatment of alcoholism* (2nd ed., pp. 189–294). New York: McGraw-Hill.

Pettinati, H. M., Meyers, K., Jenson, J. M., Kaplan, F., & Evans, B. D. (1993). Inpatient versus outpatient treatment for substance dependence revisited. *Psychiatric Quarterly, 64,* 173–182.

Project MATCH Research Group. (1997a). Matching alcoholism treatments to client heterogeneity: Project MATCH posttreatment drinking outcomes. *Journal of Studies on Alcohol, 58,* 7–29.

Project MATCH Research Group. (1997b). Project MATCH secondary *a priori* hypotheses. *Addiction, 92,* 1671–1698.

Project MATCH Research Group. (1998). Matching alcoholism treatments to client heterogeneity: Project MATCH three-year drinking outcomes. *Alcoholism: Clinical and Experimental Research, 22,* 1300–1311.

Rohsenow, D. J., Monti, P. M., Binkoff, J. A., Leipman, M. R., Nirenberg, T. D., & Abrams, D. B. (1991). Patient-treatment matching for alcoholic men in communication skills versus cognitive-behavioral mood management training. *Addictive Behaviors, 16,* 63–69.

Sanchez-Craig, M., Wilkinson, A., & Davila, R. (1995). Empirically based guidelines for moderate drinking: 1-year results from three studies with problem drinkers. *American Journal of Public Health, 85(6),* 823–828.

Schottenfeld, R. S. (1994). Assessment of the patient. In M. Galanter & H. D. Kleber (Eds.), *The American psychiatric press textbook of substance abuse treatment* (pp. 25–33). Washington, DC: American Psychiatric Press.

Schuckit, M. A., & Monteiro, M. G. (1988). Alcoholism, anxiety and depression. *British Journal of Addiction, 83,* 1373–1380.

Single, E. (1996). Harm reduction as an alcohol-prevention strategy. *Alcohol Health and Research World, 20(4),* 239–243.

Snow, R. E. (1991). Aptitude-treatment interaction as a framework for research on individual differences in psychotherapy. *Journal of Consulting and Clinical Psychology, 59,* 205–216.

Sobell, L. C., Sobell, M. B., & Nirenberg, T. D. (1982). Differential treatment planning for alcohol abusers.

In E. Mansell Pattison & Edward Kaufman (Eds.), *Encyclopedic handbook of alcoholism* (pp. 1140–1151). New York: Gardner Press.

Sobell, L. C., Sobell, M. B., & Nirenberg, T. D. (1988). Behavioral assessment and treatment planning with alcohol and drug abusers: A review with an emphasis on clinical application. *Clinical Psychology Review, 8*, 19–54.

Vuchinich, R. E., & Tucker, J. A. (1996). Alcoholic relapse, life events, and behavioral theories of choice: A prospective analysis. *Experimental and Clinical Psychopharmacology, 4*, 19–28.

Vuchinich, R. E., Tucker, J. A., & Harllee, L. M. (1988). Behavioral assessment. In D. M. Donovan & G. A. Marlatt (Eds.), *Assessment of addictive behaviors* (pp. 51–83). New York: Guilford Press.

Welte, J. W., Hynes, G., Sokolow, L., & Lyons, J. P. (1981). Effect of length of stay in inpatient alcoholism treatment on outcome. *Journal of Studies on Alcohol, 42*, 483–491.

Willenbring, M. L. (1996). Case management applications in substance use disorders. In H. A. Siegal & R. C. Rapp (Eds.), *Case management and substance abuse treatment* (pp. 51–75). New York: Springer.

IV

Treatment

13

Enhancing Motivation for Treatment and Change

Carolina E. Yahne

William R. Miller

Imagine that a 15-year-old boy, Tommy, is sitting in your office with you. He says, "My parents are always on my back. I can't even go out with my friends without their wanting to know where I'm going, who I'm with, and when I'll be back. Now they find one joint in my drawer and they're off the wall. It's not like nobody else my age does it. Most kids do booze or weed. I wish they'd just leave me alone." How would you respond to Tommy?

In a second encounter, you listen to a 53-year-old physician, Dr. Thompson, say, "I feel like I've been railroaded. My husband's been after me about my drinking at home, and now this self-righteous 'Impaired Physician Committee' tells me I have to come here and see you or lose my license. Well, who are you to tell *me* about drugs and alcohol? Just what exactly are your qualifications?" What would you say to her?

A third conversation is with a 24-year-old man, Mr. Cervantes: "My doctor said I should come to see you. I had a routine physical because I'm in the Reserves, and there was some problem with my blood test. The doc said something about a warning that my liver isn't

working right, and that it's usually caused by drinking. It kind of took me by surprise. I'm pretty healthy, and I feel fine. But the doc thought I should talk to you." How would you proceed?

An important issue here is what you believe about Tommy, Dr. Thompson, and Mr. Cervantes, how you *think* about the problems they bring. What do your first reactions to these three people reveal about your underlying beliefs about motivation? There are, after all, many different ways of thinking about human motivation (see table 13.1), and how you conceptualize motivation directly affects how you approach change. Consider the following ways of thinking about motivation.

WHAT DO YOU BELIEVE ABOUT MOTIVATION?

Do you agree or disagree:

- Until a person is motivated to change, there is not much a practitioner can do.

TABLE 13.1 Modifiability of Client Motivation

A client's motivation is not modifiable.	Client motivation is modifiable.
The practitioner's behavior is irrelevant to a client's readiness to change.	The therapist's behavior in part determines a client's readiness to change.
Motivation is a characteristic or personality trait within the client.	Motivation is a process that happens between the client and the therapist.
Denial is the standard defense mechanism for people with addiction problems.	Readiness to change addictive behavior arises from interpersonal interaction.
Resistance is the client's problem.	Resistance is a therapist skill challenge.
A practitioner with this view may think: "You're not ready. You haven't bottomed out yet. Until you are motivated, there's nothing I can do to help you."	A practitioner with this view may think: "I'm evoking some resistance. I need to try a different approach. What could I do to help increase this person's openness to change?"
If the client is arguing with me, it is evidence of denial and lack of motivation to change.	If the client is arguing with me, it is a sign I need to shift strategies.
Contradictory beliefs about drinking are pathological and reflect denial.	Ambivalence is a normal part of change.
Motivation is a stubbornly stable pattern, consistent across situations.	Motivation is a malleable process which can change across situations.
Motivation is an individual characteristic.	Motivation changes with the environment.

- The most significant aspects of human motivation are unconscious.
- It usually takes a significant shock or crisis to motivate a person to change.
- A person's readiness for change fluctuates over time, sometimes rapidly.
- Motivation is an interpersonal interaction.
- Resistance to change arises from deep-seated defense mechanisms.
- People choose whether or not they will change.
- Motivation for change requires hitting bottom.
- Readiness for change involves a balancing of the pros and cons.
- A person's motivation depends a lot on the situation.
- Once a person is motivated to change, it is important to act quickly.
- Creating motivation for change usually requires confrontation.
- Denial is not a client problem, it is a therapist skill problem.

What is it, in your opinion, that motivates people to change? What do you think are the main motivational obstacles in treating addictions? What are your greatest frustrations in trying to help clients to change? How do you currently go about trying to motivate your clients?

WHAT RESEARCH REVEALS ABOUT MOTIVATION

Studies from the past two decades have pointed to new ways of thinking about clients' motivation for change. Persons with substance use disorders often terminate treatment early, continue to use substances during treatment, or are noncompliant with the stated requirements of the therapy, so that practitioners are led to label such clients as resistant, denying, and unmotivated. Provocative findings have challenged traditional notions that "denial" is a characteristic trait of people with substance use disorders, that it is the amount or intensity of treatment that determines how much change will occur, that motivation is a trait that individuals bring or do not bring to treatment, and that noncompliance is a function of the individual's character. Research has contributed some fascinating pieces of the puzzle, and it is a challenge to decide how to put them together.

Natural Change

The work of James Prochaska, Carlo DiClemente, and their colleagues across three decades (e.g., Prochaska & DiClemente, 1986) has highlighted a phenomenon once described as "spontaneous remission"—that many, perhaps most, people who change addictive behaviors do so on their own, with no formal treatment at all. Most smokers who have quit did so unaided by health professionals. At any given time, about 1 in 10 American adults show significant problems related to their own drinking. When interviewed some years later, most people who had drinking problems have resolved or at least substantially reduced them, and only a small minority have received formal treatment (Sobell, Sobell, & Toneatto, 1991).

What is going on here? Such "natural" change is common and appears by no means to be a spontaneous accident. Rather, research suggests, change can be described as proceeding through the sequence of predictable stages (Prochaska, DiClemente, & Norcross, 1992). Furthermore, change that happens in the context of psychotherapy appears to follow the same course. This finding suggests that therapy may be facilitating what is fundamentally a natural process of change (Sobell & Sobell, 1993).

Brief Interventions

It has been known for some time that it is possible to enhance motivation for treatment (Chafetz, 1968) and induce significant change in risky or problem drinkers with just a session or two of counseling. With impressive consistency, controlled trials of brief interventions with problem drinkers have shown a significant reduction in alcohol use, compared with the use by control groups receiving no intervention (Bien, Miller, & Tonigan, 1993). Even as little as 5–15 minutes of counseling has been found in a multinational study to suppress heavy drinking (WHO Brief Intervention Study Group, 1996).

Still more perplexing is a reasonably consistent finding from studies comparing brief intervention with various intensities of treatment for alcohol problems. Most such studies have found substantial reductions in drinking in *both* groups, with little or no difference in efficacy between brief and more extended treatment. One interpretation of this finding is that certain critical conditions that trigger change may be contained within both briefer and longer treatment approaches.

FRAMES

Searching for such common elements, Miller and Sanchez (1994; Miller & Rollnick, 1991) identified six components frequently present in brief interventions that were found to be effective in altering drinking behavior. FRAMES is an acronym for the six key components:

Feedback. Effective brief interventions provide clients with *personal* feedback regarding their individual status.

Responsibility. Effective brief interventions have emphasized personal responsibility for change and the individual's freedom of choice.

Advice. Effective brief counseling has included a clear recommendation or advice on the need for change, typically in a supportive rather than an authoritarian manner.

Menu. Often, a menu of different strategies for change is offered, providing options from which clients may choose what seems suitable to them.

Empathy. Emphasis is placed on an empathic, reflective, warm, and supportive practitioner style, which is linked with more positive treatment outcomes.

Self-efficacy. Effective brief interventions reinforce self-efficacy, the client's expectation that she or he *can* change.

The Drinker's Check-Up

How would FRAMES look in practice? A Drinker's Check-Up (DCU) was designed as an intervention to manifest the FRAMES elements (Miller & Sovereign, 1989). It consists of an assessment followed by a single counseling session in which the client is given feedback of findings in a empathic manner (Miller & Rollnick, 1991). Evaluations of the DCU have shown that it yields rapid reduction in drinking behavior relative to the drinking behavior of control groups waiting 6–10 weeks for counseling (Miller, Benefield, & Tonigan, 1993; Miller, Sovereign, & Krege, 1988). Subsequent studies evaluated the outcomes of alcoholism treatment with or without a single-session DCU upon admission, showing that drinking and related problems were substantially suppressed by the DCU when added to inpatient (Brown & Miller, 1993) or outpatient programs (Bien, Miller, & Boroughs, 1993). More recent clinical trials have supported the effectiveness of a DCU approach in counseling pregnant heavy drinkers (Handmaker, 1993), treating heroin addicts (Saunders, Wilkinson, & Phillips, 1995), and providing secondary prevention with heavy-drinking college students (Baer et. al., 1992). The Project MATCH Research Group (1993) selected the DCU as one of three treatments to be tested in a multisite randomized clinical trial which included extensive pretreatment and follow-up assessment. To provide some comparability to the other two treatments—12-step facilitation (TSF) and cognitive behavior therapy (CBT)—which were designed for 12 sessions over 12 weeks, the DCU was extended to 4 sessions offered at Weeks 1, 2, 6, and 12. The result was a manual-guided motivational enhancement therapy (MET; Miller, Zweben, DiClemente, & Rychtarik, 1992) developed specifically for Project MATCH. During the course of 12 weeks of treatment, clients randomly assigned to MET reported slightly (and significantly, in this large sample) more drinking than TSF- and CBT-treated clients. From the end of treatment (3 months) through follow-ups at 6, 9, 12, 15, and 39 months, however, outcomes of the three treatments were virtually identical. Only when outcome was defined by continuous abstinence measures (e.g., time to first drink) was there a significant difference, slightly favoring TSF over MET and CBT, which did not differ from each other (Project MATCH Research Group, 1997).

Therapist Effects

Another piece of the puzzle is found in the fact that clients' outcomes often differ substantially depending upon the therapist with whom they work (Najavits & Weiss, 1994). When one counselor resigned in a drug abuse treatment program, the caseload was randomly distributed among four other counselors. This situation offered an opportunity to study whether outcomes are affected by the particular therapist a client received by the luck of the draw. In fact, clients of two counselors showed substantial improvement, those of a third counselor showed more modest gains, and clients of the fourth counselor showed, on average, no change or deterioration on various outcome measures (Luborsky, McLellan, Woody, O'Brien, & Auerbach, 1985).

A study of problem drinkers in outpatient treatment found similar wide variability in nine therapists' success rates, ranging from 20% to 100% (Miller, Taylor, & West, 1980). This study also provided a clue as to at least one possible reason for the variation. Via one-way mirror, the nine therapists were observed while counseling and were rated on various dimensions, including their degree of therapeutic empathy as defined by Carl Rogers—the ability to reflect accurately a client's meaning and emotion through nonintrusive "active listening" (Gordon, 1970). When client outcomes were subsequently revealed by follow-up interviews, it was discovered that the degree of therapist empathy accurately predicted clients' drinking at 6 months ($r = .83$) and 12 months ($r = .67$) after treatment. Even 2 years later, therapist empathy still predicted clients' drinking levels ($r = .50$). The more empathic the counselor, the more the client changed. Valle (1981) similarly found that clients' relapse rates could be predicted from the extent to which their randomly assigned therapists manifested the interpersonal therapeutic conditions defined by Rogers. Therapist behavior was a better predictor of outcome than any client characteristic.

Further evidence on the impact of therapist skill emerged from a study in which a single counseling session was tape-recorded, and all therapist and client responses were classified by a therapy-coding system. Patterson and Forgatch (1985) had previously shown, using this coding system, that the "resistance" level of clients could be driven up and down within the same session as counselors intentionally switched back and forth between supportive/empathic and directive/confrontive styles. In the subsequent study, problem drinkers' levels of all four resistance responses were related to a single therapist response: confronting. Furthermore, the level of clients' drinking a year later was again predictable ($r = .56$, $p < .001$) from the randomly assigned therapist's level of confrontation. The more the therapist had confronted, the more the client drank (Miller et al., 1993).

Client Compliance

One more piece of the puzzle is found in what is often referred to as client compliance—the extent to which a client does what the therapist asks. It is a very common finding that in general, the longer clients continue in treatment, the better they do. In these studies, however, the length of treatment is not randomly assigned. Clients who stay longer are a self-selected minority who may differ in many ways (such as motivation) from those who leave early. Those who take their medication faithfully (even if it is a placebo) also tend to have better outcomes (Fuller et al., 1986). Voluntary involvement in Alcoholics Anonymous is also associated with better outcomes (e.g., Emrick, Tonigan, Montgomery, & Little, 1993). It appears, in fact, that recovery from alcohol problems may be associated with the extent to which an individual faithfully does *something* to get better (Miller, Westerberg, Harris, & Tonigan, 1996). Successful outcomes have also been linked to both the client's (DiClemente, Prochaska, & Gilbertini, 1985) and the therapist's (Leake & King, 1977) belief that the client will succeed.

Putting the Pieces Together

Here, then, are some intriguing findings. Many people change addictive behaviors on their own without professional help, and the process of natural change appears to be similar whether it occurs in therapy or in the natural environment. Relatively brief interventions with FRAMES elements are significantly more effective than no intervention in reducing problem drinking and appear to substantially improve the outcomes of subsequent treatment. What a therapist does interpersonally, even within the context of a single counseling session, seems to exert a substantial and long-lasting influence on whether a client will get better or worse. The extent of improvement seems to be linked to a client's believing in and actively trying a method of change.

One synthesis of these findings is that positive change is a natural process that the therapist does not own or originate but can facilitate. Enduring change can be triggered by a combination of an awareness that there is a problem and a belief that there is a way out, facilitated by a supportive and empathic therapeutic relationship. This can occur even in a single session, which is good news because the modal length of stay in substance abuse treatment is short (Ellis, McCan, Price, & Sewell, 1992). Change is usually engendered not by the therapist pushing, confronting, or directing, but by her or his listening reflectively to the client and evoking the client's own motivation for change.

MEASURING MOTIVATION

Practitioners develop hunches about a client's level of motivation or readiness to change, but these can be inaccurate and can easily become self-fulfilling

prophecies (Leake & King, 1977). Various approaches have been developed for measuring client motivation, which may help the practitioner to decide where to begin in treatment. Four measurement approaches are briefly described here.

Decisional Balance

Benjamin Franklin had his own method for making complex decisions, which involved competing motivations. He drew a line down the middle of a page and then spent time, sometimes several days, listing the pros and cons and estimating their relative importance or weights as a means of reaching a conclusion. He recommended this "moral or prudential algebra" as an aid in decision making (Janis & Mann, 1977, p. 149). Two centuries later, Janis and Mann (1977) found that people who were asked four key questions felt more secure later about decisions they had made:

1. What are the potential gains and losses for me in this choice?
2. What are the gains and losses for others in this choice?
3. What are aspects of my self-approval or -disapproval in this choice?
4. What are aspects of approval or disapproval by others in this choice (including criticism or exclusion from a group as well as being praised or obtaining prestige, admiration, and respect)?

Participants in this research who completed such a balance sheet procedure were less likely than controls to experience postdecisional distress or regret. They were also better able to implement their decision. Helping a client to construct a decisional balance sheet by simply drawing a line down the center of a piece of paper and labeling one side "Pros of Drug Use For Me" and the other side "Cons of Drug Use For Me" is a simple way to begin exploring ambivalence and measuring motivation. (Note that this balance sheet might be quite different from one drug to another.) A slightly more complicated balance sheet contains four columns. Such a decisional balance sheet might look like the one in table 13.2. The decisional balance sheet for Dr. Thompson, the physician at the opening of this chapter, might take the form of the one found in table 13.3.

TABLE 13.2 Sample Decisional Balance Sheet

Continue to smoke marijuana as before		Quit smoking pot and hashish	
Benefits	Costs	Benefits	Costs
Relax.	Smell bad at work.	No strange odor.	Feel nervous.
Forget about rape.	Can't think clearly.	Focus on tasks.	Remember being hurt.
Go with the flow.	Bad example for kids.	Make my kids proud.	Feel out of it.

Not surprisingly, the very act of constructing such a decisional balance sheet can begin to influence motivation, which is a dynamic state or process rather than a fixed trait. The balance sheet is also useful for the practitioner because it clarifies what positive and negative expectations the client has about drug use and change. It opens the door for discussion of alternative ways to achieve benefits that the client is seeking from drug use. The decisional balance sheet is a way to measure and explore ambivalence and motivation, to clarify the competing motivational factors, and to encourage the client to consider the possibility of change.

Stages of Change

Prochaska and DiClemente (1986) developed a transtheoretical model positing progressive stages of change (figure 13.1), with the idea that therapeutic interventions should be matched to the client's level of readiness. In simplest form, the stages are (a) *precontemplation*, in which a person is not considering change, often because he or she does not perceive a problem or a need to change; (b) *contemplation*, in which a person may seesaw ambivalently between changing and remaining the same, perhaps weighing the costs and benefits as in the decisional balance above; (c) *preparation*, where it is clearer that a change is needed, and the person is getting ready

or considering what to do; (d) the *action* stage, during which the person has settled on one or more steps to take and begins implementation; and (e) *maintenance*, which involves sustaining change. *Relapse* is also included as a normal part of the change process, in that most people do not maintain change on their first try and cycle through the stages several times before achieving stable change. The University of Rhode Island Change Assessment (URICA) is a 32-item self-administered questionnaire for measuring these stages of change, with strong psychometric characteristics (McConnaughy, Prochaska, & Velicer, 1983). It can be used to ask about any problem area, including problems with alcohol or other drugs.

Other instruments have been designed to identify and measure readiness for change by using the transtheoretical model. A one-page, 12-item Readiness to Change Questionnaire (RCQ; Rollnick, Heather, Gold, & Hall, 1992) taps three stages: precontemplation, contemplation, and action. It was developed for a medical population not seeking help with addiction, and therefore, the instrument avoids using problem-oriented terminology. It can therefore be used for quick administration in a busy health care setting. Heather (1995) selected patients "not ready to change" as measured by the RCQ and found that brief motivational interviewing (designed to enhance motivation for change) resulted in a significantly

TABLE 13.3 Dr. Thompson's Sample Decisional Balance Sheet

Continue to drink as before		Change my drinking	
Benefits	Costs	Benefits	Costs
Relax after work.	Husband still bugging me.	Husband more trusting.	Feel tense.
Control own time.	Risk losing license.	Keep medical license.	Lose autonomy.
Not care so much.	Have to deceive.	Not have to hide.	Feel overwhelmed.

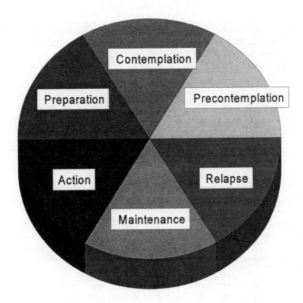

FIGURE 13.1 Stages of change. From Prochaska and DiClimente (1986).

greater reduction in drinking than did action-oriented skills-based counseling. The author recommended that problem drinkers (or at least male heavy drinkers on hospital wards) should be assessed for their stage of change readiness. The questionnaire provides a short and convenient measure of readiness to change which may be used in conjunction with brief, opportunistic interventions with excessive drinkers who are not presenting primarily with substance use concerns (Rollnick et al., 1992).

Motivational Vectors

A third approach is to sample various dimensions of motivation for change. The Stages of Change Readiness and Treatment Eagerness Scale (SOCRATES) is a 19-item paper-and-pencil measure designed specifically to assess motivation for change in problem drinking or drug use. Whereas the URICA asks questions about "my problem," SOCRATES poses questions specifically about alcohol or other drug use. Items of the SOCRATES were originally written to correspond with the stages of Prochaska and DiClemente's transtheoretical model. A series of factor analyses, however, pointed to three underlying dimensions rather than discrete stages: recognition of problem, ambivalence, and taking steps toward change. Miller and Tonigan (1996) reported test-re-

test reliability and internal consistency for these scales. Other potentially important motivational vectors include self-efficacy (DiClemente et al., 1985), outcome expectancies (Brown, 1985), specific pros and cons of change, and social support for use or abstinence (Longabaugh, Wirtz, & Clifford, 1995).

Readiness

Still simpler measures have been used to sample the single construct of readiness for change. The Readiness Ruler (see figure 13.2) is a simple scale that can be used to ask clients how ready they are for change in a particular health behavior. The scale might be used, for example, to ask about the client's motivation to change her or his use of each of several drugs. Such a visual analogue scale may range from 1 (not ready to change) to 4 (unsure) to 7 (ready to change) to 10 (trying to change). The client indicates how ready he or she is to quit or cut down on each of the drugs simply by pointing to or circling a number on the ruler.

ENHANCING MOTIVATION

Once motivation has been measured, what is the next step? Clients who are further along on readiness

Using the ruler shown below, indicate how ready you are to make a change (quit or cut down) in your use of each of the drugs shown. If you are *not at all* ready to make a change, you would circle the 1. If you are already trying hard to make a change, you would circle the 10. If you are unsure whether you want to make a change, you would circle 3, 4, or 5. If you don't use a type of drug, circle "don't use" in the box at the right.

Circle one answer for each type of drug

Types of Drugs	Not Ready to Change		Unsure			Ready to Change			Trying to Change		or: I don't use this type of drug
	1	2	3	4	5	6	7	8	9	10	
Alcohol	1	2	3	4	5	6	7	8	9	10	Don't Use
Tobacco	1	2	3	4	5	6	7	8	9	10	Don't Use
Marijuana/ Cannabis	1	2	3	4	5	6	7	8	9	10	Don't Use
Tranquilizers	1	2	3	4	5	6	7	8	9	10	Don't Use
Sedatives/ Downers	1	2	3	4	5	6	7	8	9	10	Don't Use
Steroids	1	2	3	4	5	6	7	8	9	10	Don't Use
Stimulants/ Uppers	1	2	3	4	5	6	7	8	9	10	Don't Use
Cocaine	1	2	3	4	5	6	7	8	9	10	Don't Use
Hallucinogens	1	2	3	4	5	6	7	8	9	10	Don't Use
Opiates	1	2	3	4	5	6	7	8	9	10	Don't Use
Inhalants	1	2	3	4	5	6	7	8	9	10	Don't Use
Other Drugs	1	2	3	4	5	6	7	8	9	10	Don't Use
	Not Ready to Change		Unsure			Ready to Change			Trying to Change		
	1	2	3	4	5	6	7	8	9	10	

FIGURE 13.2 Readiness Ruler.

for change (in the preparation, action, or maintenance stage) may benefit from action-oriented approaches focusing on skills and strategies for behavior change. Taking this approach with clients who are less ready for change (in the precontemplation or contemplation stage), however, is likely to elicit uncooperative responses. When confronted with the need for change, for example, an ambivalent person naturally responds with the other side of the decisional balance. This response may be misinterpreted as "denial" or "resistance," but in fact, such responses can practically be turned on and off by changes in therapist behavior (Patterson & Forgatch, 1985). How can a therapist best respond when working with less ready clients?

FRAMES: Six Components of Effective Brief Intervention

Here there are useful guidelines from research on effective brief counseling, and from the acronym FRAMES discussed earlier. These six elements will now be expanded upon with regard to therapeutic strategies.

Feedback

The *F* in *FRAMES* is personalized feedback or health-relevant information based on careful assessment. Personalized feedback should not be confused with educational information about the effects of alcohol and other drugs on people in general, which has been found to have little or no impact on substance abuse once it is established. Instead, clients are provided with personally relevant information based on an individual assessment. Such objective personal feedback may include the results of laboratory tests, or a calendar on which are recorded days of use, or measures of motivation as described above, or the more comprehensive Personal Feedback Report (Miller, Zweben, DiClemente, & Rychtarik, 1992) showing how an individual's scores compare with those of other people. Some practitioners teach their clients how to calculate standard drinks and how to use that calculation to calculate blood alcohol level. Other practitioners use carbon monoxide readings with clients who smoke. Mr. Cervantes, the client described in an opening vignette, had received feedback (liver function test values) which surprised him.

A key element of effective feedback is the client's readiness to hear it. How one *presents* feedback appears to have a potent effect on a client's ability to accept it. It can be helpful to ask a client's permission to give feedback, which can help to pave the way for taking it in, especially if it contains unexpected aspects. Of course, the information should be explained clearly, but then it is helpful to listen reflectively to the client's response to the feedback. A practitioner might respond to a client's balking at feedback by reflecting, "It sounds like these test results surprise you; they aren't what you expected." Feedback can trigger a kind of client self-reflection.

Sometimes practitioners confuse such feedback with giving the client their own opinions and impressions of the situation. Provider impressions are not what is meant by objective feedback here. Feedback should be unambiguous for learning to occur (Goldstein, Heller, & Sechrest, 1966). It should take the form of information that the client can identify as accurate, unbiased, and clear. Initial evaluation is one source of feedback, and another is systematic follow-up over time. This can be particularly useful in health care settings where people are seen periodically for various concerns. A chart note to follow up by asking about a particular topic (such as smoking or drinking) allows continued attention to a concern. Whereas a patient may not be ready to consider change at one time, readiness may be higher at a later time. A client's knowledge that you will check back with her or him in a few months seems to enhance outcome. Many studies of effective brief intervention included, as an element of research, systematic follow-up interviews that may have contributed to the achievement and maintenance of gains (cf. Bien et al., 1993; Miller & Rollnick, 1991).

Responsibility

Conveying individual responsibility with a tone of trust and respect is another common element in effective brief intervention. This involves respectfully reminding the client (and yourself) that she or he is ultimately in charge, choosing whether and how to make changes, and that no one else can take this responsibility. This tone is very different from "You are to blame and you'd better shape up." Rather, a responsibility message should convey "I respect you as a capable adult who can and will make decisions about your own future." It is up to the individual to decide what, if anything, to do with feedback. Furthermore, whatever responsibility the client has already taken can be reinforced here: "I appreciate that you followed through on your doctor's suggestion to come back in."

Issues of informed consent also relate to client responsibility. Informed consent is also a key part of rapport building. The informed-consent process in research and in treatment helps to remind both parties that the client is the one responsible for choosing about her or his own life (Edwards & Yahne, 1987; Yahne & Edwards, 1986). Clarifying the limits of confidentiality is also an essential part of informed consent. By clarifying the ground rules and structuring the interaction, the practitioner empowers the client to decide how much to disclose.

Advice

Advice, particularly if offered quickly, can be a roadblock to listening by stopping the client's momentum in discussion (Gordon & Edwards, 1995). Yet there is also a time for offering a concise expert opinion, based on objective data and presented in a manner that conveys respect for the client's ability to decide how or if to implement such advice. Clear and respectful professional advice appears to be an important component in enhancing motivation to change harmful lifestyles. The World Health Organization Brief Intervention Study Group (1996) found that after careful assessment, even relatively brief advice resulted in heavy-drinking men reducing their daily alcohol consumption by 17% more than an unadvised group.

Menu of Options

Advice to change may be more likely to be carried out if the client is offered a variety of change options, rather than a solitary solution. A menu of alternatives also increases the client's perception of personal choice and control, which promotes intrinsic motivation and can also foster optimism. One option is easily rejected, but presenting multiple options engages a client in the process of choosing among them. Furthermore, it can be helpful to consider a menu not only of change methods, but also of change goals. For example, women in recovery, when interviewed about types of services considered most helpful, ranked transportation assistance first, followed by help obtaining food, housing, clothing, recreational activities, on-site health care, and 12-step meetings (Nelson-Zlupko, Dore, Kauffman, & Kaltenback, 1996).

Empathy

Therapeutic empathy creates an environment conducive to change, instills a safe sense of being understood and accepted, and reduces defensiveness. We believe that empathy may be the most crucial of the FRAMES components. It sets the tone within which the entire communication occurs, and without it, the other components may sound like mechanical techniques. Therapist empathy has reliably predicted clients' change (or lack thereof) in drinking for as long as 2 years after treatment (Miller & Baca, 1983). The nature of the practitioner-client relationship in early sessions, even in a single session, has predicted treatment retention and outcome (Luborsky et al., 1985; Tomlinson, 1967). Carl Rogers (1959) defined accurate empathy as skillful reflective listening that clarifies and amplifies the client's own experience and meaning, without imposing the practitioner's material (cf. Gordon, 1970). Such reflective listening is not the only component of effective brief interventions, but it is a key component.

Confrontational responses from a therapist, on the other hand, tend to increase defensiveness and diminish the client's readiness to consider change. Empathy represents a conceptual opposite of confrontational strategies such as disagreeing, emphasizing negative evidence, arguing, and persuading. Confrontation elicits client resistance, which in turn is a predictor of poor outcome, whereas accurate empathy in the form of listening, reflecting, and reframing is associated with low levels of client resistance (Miller et al., 1993; Patterson & Forgatch, 1985). Thus, "resistance" from the client should be a signal to the therapist to take a different approach (Goldstein et al., 1966). In the opening vignette of Dr. Thompson, an empathic practitioner might respond, "You feel somewhat insulted at being sent in to see me, and you're wondering about my qualifications." Similarly, an empathic practitioner might respond to Tommy by saying, "Sounds as if you feel kind of frustrated by your parents' reactions."

Establishing empathy builds trust and rapport and provides a doorway through which to introduce more difficult addiction issues (Rollnick & Bell, 1991). A less emotionally charged topic may be an easier starting point than the threatening topic of addictive behavior. It may also help to clarify the client's values and sources of self-efficacy, such as any recent successes (e.g., losing weight, a child's good grades at school, qualifying for financial assistance). When a practitioner readily celebrates small victories (a client's showing a photograph of his child), the client may be more willing to explore ways to increase the likelihood of further victories, including changing addictive behavior.

Asking clients about the positive aspects of their substance use is another way to develop understanding and put a client at ease (Saunders, Wilkinson, & Allsop, 1991). Clients often come expecting to be judged, and asking, "I'd like to hear about some of the good things about your drinking" is an opener that may communicate to the client genuine interest in seeing the whole picture.

Self-Efficacy

Self-efficacy is a specific form of optimism, a "can-do" belief in one's ability to accomplish a particular task or change. Helping a client to see his or her own ability to make positive changes is crucial. To Mr. Cervantes, a practitioner who wants to affirm self-efficacy may say, "The abnormal liver test that your doctor noted is almost certainly reversible. You can bring it back to normal by changing your alcohol intake." Reminding a client of strengths and successes already demonstrated—even small ones—can be useful in boosting a sense of personal efficacy: "You made it to this meeting with me today, despite many obstacles, which tells me you can get things done when you decide to." Asked to speak about the characteristics of "good" counselors, clients said that their counselors believed in them (Nelson-Zlupko et al., 1996). As one Albuquerque client expressed it to the first author, "Thank you for believing in me until I was ready to believe in myself."

Motivational Interviewing

Motivational interviewing (Miller, 1983) was originally intended to be a prelude to treatment, to enhance client acceptance of and compliance with professional help. Indeed, as shown by research reviewed earlier, there is good evidence that outcomes of substance abuse treatment are substantially improved by adding an initial motivational interview (Bien et al., 1993; Brown & Miller, 1993; Saunders et al., 1995). An unexpected but consistent finding, however, is that motivational interviewing is also associated with behavior change when used as a stand-alone intervention. Even a relatively brief contact of a session or two often instigates change in addictive behaviors. In fact, the less motivated a client is to begin with, the greater may be the advantage in this approach (Heather, Rollnick, Bell, & Richmond, 1996).

Fundamental principles and practical procedures for motivational interviewing have been described in detail elsewhere (Miller & Rollnick, 1991; Miller et al., 1992). The five basic principles of motivational interviewing outlined by Miller and Rollnick (1991) overlap somewhat with the components of FRAMES, the common ingredients of effective brief interventions. Motivational interviewing is not so much a set of techniques as it is a style or way of being with people, helping them to resolve ambivalence and find within themselves the resources for change. The principles of motivational interviewing are defined here briefly.

Express Empathy

Paradoxically, acceptance facilitates change. The more a therapist can create an atmosphere of acceptance, the more the client may be freed to change. Conversely, confrontational approaches that empha-size the unacceptability of one's current state ("Tear them down to build them up") have a rather dreadful track record in fostering positive change.

Skillful reflective listening is fundamental in expressing empathy. When the therapist can accurately summarize the client's meaning from verbal and nonverbal communication, the client is more likely to feel understood and, indeed, to develop self-understanding. Within this context, there is nothing unusual or pathological about a person's experiencing, simultaneously, both positive and negative aspects of his or her own addictive behavior. Ambivalence is a normal experience to be explored, rather than opposed. Left unresolved, ambivalence can be immobilizing.

Develop Discrepancy

The second principle of motivational interviewing emphasizes the importance of developing within the client's awareness a growing discrepancy between the addictive behavior and more deeply held goals and values. This involves, in part, helping the client to become more aware of and to verbalize the negative consequences of his or her present course. We believe that this is most effectively done by having the client (rather than the therapist) make the argument for change. Through a variety of strategies, clients are encouraged to talk about what their current (addictive) behavior is costing them and how it is harming or inconveniencing them. This process can begin with exploring the client's most central values or life goals and then asking the client to reflect on how the addictive behavior fits into these hopes and dreams.

Avoid Argumentation

A third principle is that in general, it is unhelpful to argue with clients. Confrontation elicits defensiveness, which in turn predicts a lack of change. It is particularly countertherapeutic for the therapist to be arguing that there is a problem in need of change, while the client argues that there is no real problem or need for change. Though tempting, this is a scenario to be avoided. It is also worth observing that discrepancy can be developed effectively without the client's ever accepting a diagnostic label. Arguing about labels like *alcoholic* or *drug addict* or even "you have *a problem*" tends to get in the way of change rather than to facilitate it. Some clients enter treatment apparently ready to change, and the practitioner may begin to implement action-oriented approaches. However, practitioners should also anticipate that motivation may fluctuate during treatment. Assessment of motivation can be done at regular, repeated intervals during treatment. If motivation appears to be decreasing, therapeutic strategies should shift from action-oriented to motivation-enhancing techniques. The therapist needs to shift rather than argue. A client's defensiveness or "resistance" is a signal for the therapist to change strategies rather than to engage in combat.

Roll with Resistance

The fourth principle of motivational interviewing, rolling with resistance, encourages the practitioner to use momentum to good advantage, flexibly and creatively. Consonant with the idea of avoiding argumentation, seemingly resistant responses from the client are met not with opposition but with acceptance and an invitation to new perspectives. It may be, in fact, that "resistance" is a misleading conception here. It is less than surprising that an ambivalent person would express reluctance to change or doubts about abandoning present ways. This is nothing out of the ordinary and simply reflects part of the process of exploration as the client moves toward change. There is a sense of turning responsibility for change back to the client, who is viewed as a valuable resource in finding solutions to problems.

Support Self-Efficacy

A fifth and final principle of motivational interviewing encourages the therapist to support clients' self-efficacy, the belief that one is capable of changing. A realistically optimistic belief in the possibility of change can be a powerful instigator and motivator for change. "She believed in me," clients often say of a therapist who helped them, or "He saw that I could do it, even when I didn't think I could." Ultimately, it is the client who is responsible for choosing and carrying out personal change, but there is a very real role for hope in this process. Given the range of effective approaches available for changing addictive behaviors, such hope is warranted.

CONCLUSION

Coming full circle back to Tommy, Dr. Thompson, and Mr. Cervantes, we have discussed many ways that a practitioner might enhance their motivation for treatment and change. After reading this chapter, have your responses to the three clients in the initial vignettes shifted or expanded in any way? How might you respond to them now? Consider creatively combining components of FRAMES and principles of motivational interviewing to craft your own affirming responses such as:

> "Tommy, you seem to be a young man who values independence and making your own decisions. I'd like to hear more about what matters to you."

> "Dr. Thompson, your marriage and practicing medicine are things you really care about, and it sounds like right now you are concerned that both are in jeopardy."

> "Mr. Cervantes, I admire you for taking your health seriously. Not everyone does, you know. Maybe we should talk a little more about what the surprising news about the blood test means for you. Would that be all right with you?"

Enhancing motivation for treatment and change is a constant challenge in health care and is perhaps one of the most important parts of effective treatment. We wish you creativity, patience, and enjoyment in meeting that challenge with your own clients.

Key References

Bien, T. H., Miller, W. R., & Tonigan, J. S. (1993). Brief interventions for alcohol problems: A review. *Addiction, 88*, 315–336.

Heather, N. (1995). Brief intervention strategies. In R. K. Hester & W. R. Miller (Eds.) *Handbook of alcoholism treatment approaches: Effective alternatives* (2nd ed.). Needham Heights, MA: Allyn & Bacon.

Miller, W. R., & Rollnick, S. (1991). *Motivational interviewing: Preparing people to change addictive behavior.* New York: Guilford Press.

References

Baer, J. S., Marlatt, G. A., Kivlahan, D. R., Fromme, K., Larimer, M., & Williams, E. (1992). An experimental test of three methods of alcohol risk-reduction with young adults. *Journal of Consulting and Clinical Psychology, 60*, 9784–979.

Bien, T. H., Miller, W. R., & Boroughs, J. M. (1993). Motivational interviewing with alcohol outpatients. *Behavioural and Cognitive Psychotherapy, 21,* 347–356.

Bien, T. H., Miller, W. R., & Tonigan, J. S. (1993). Brief interventions for alcohol problems: A review. *Addiction, 88,* 315–336.

Brown, J. M., & Miller, W. R. (1993). Impact of motivational interviewing on participation and outcome in residential alcoholism treatment. *Psychology of Addictive Behaviors, 7,* 211–218.

Brown, S. A. (1985). Reinforcement expectancies and alcoholism treatment outcome after a one-year follow-up. *Journal of Studies on Alcohol, 46,* 304–308.

Chafetz, M. E. (1968). Research in the alcohol clinic of an around-the-clock psychiatric service of the Massachusetts General Hospital. *American Journal of Psychiatry, 124,* 1674–1679.

DiClemente, C. C., Prochaska, J. O., & Gilbertini, M. (1985). Self-efficacy and the stages of self-change in smoking. *Cognitive Therapy and Research, 9,* 181–200.

Edwards, W. S., & Yahne, C. E. (1987). Surgical informed consent: What it is and is not. *The American Journal of Surgery, 154*(6), 574–578.

Ellis, B. H., McCan, I., Price, G., & Sewell, C. M. (1992). The New Mexico treatment outcome study: Evaluating the utility of existing information systems. *Journal of Health Care for the Poor and Under Served, 3,* 138–150.

Emrick, C. D., Tonigan, J. S., Montgomery, H., & Little, L. (1993). Alcoholics Anonymous: What is currently known? In B. S. McCrady & W. R. Miller (Eds.), *Research on Alcoholics Anonymous: Opportunities and alternatives* (pp. 41–76). New Brunswick, NJ: Rutgers Center of Alcohol Studies.

Fuller, R. K., Branchey, L., Brightwell, D. R., Derman, R. K., Emrick, C. D., Iber, F. L., James, K. E., Lacoursiere, R. B., Lee, K. K., Lowenstam, I., Maany, I., Neiderhiser, D., Nocks, J. J., & Shaw, S. (1986). Disulfiram treatment of alcoholism: A Veterans Administration cooperative study. *Journal of the American Medical Association, 256,* 1449–1455.

Goldstein, A. P., Heller, K., & Sechrest, L. B. (1966). *Psychotherapy and the psychology of behavior change.* New York: Wiley.

Gordon, T. (1970). *Parent effectiveness training.* New York: Wyden.

Gordon, T., & Edwards, W. S. (1995). *Making the patient your partner.* Westport, CT: Auburn House.

Handmaker, N. S. (1993). *Motivating pregnant drinkers to abstain: Prevention in prenatal care clinics.* Doctoral dissertation, Albuquerque, University of New Mexico.

Heather, N. (1995). Brief intervention strategies. In R. K. Hester & W. R. Miller (Eds.), *Handbook of alcoholism treatment approaches: Effective alternatives* (2nd ed., pp. 105–122). Boston: Allyn & Bacon.

Heather, N., Rollnick, S., Bell, A., & Richmond, R. (1996). Effects of brief counseling among male heavy drinkers identified on general hospital wards. *Drug and Alcohol Review, 15,* 29–38.

Janis, I. L., & Mann, L. (1977). *Decision-making: A psychological analysis of conflict, choice, and commitment.* New York: Free Press.

Leake, G. J., & King, A. S. (1977). Effect of counselor expectations on alcoholic recovery. *Alcohol Health and Research World, 1*(3), 16–22.

Longabaugh, R., Wirtz, P. W., & Clifford, P. R. (1995). The Important People and Activities Instrument (available from Richard Longabaugh, Brown University, Center for Alcohol and Addiction Studies, 800 Butler Drive, Providence, RI 02906).

Luborsky, L., McLellan, A. T., Woody, G. E., O'Brien, C. P., & Auerbach, A. (1985). Therapist success and its determinants. *Archives of General Psychiatry, 42,* 602–611.

McConnaughy, E. A., Prochaska, J. O., & Velicer, W. F. (1983). Stages of change in psychotherapy: Measurement and sample profiles. *Psychotherapy: Theory, Research, and Practice, 20,* 368–375.

Miller, W. R. (1983). Motivational interviewing with problem drinkers. *Behavioural Psychotherapy, 1,* 147–172.

Miller, W. R. (1985). Motivation for treatment: A review with special emphasis on alcoholism. *Psychological Bulletin, 98*(1), 84–107.

Miller, W. R. (1996). Motivational interviewing: Research, practice, and puzzles. *Addictive Behaviors, 21*(6), 835–842.

Miller, W. R., & Baca, L. M. (1983). Two-year follow-up of bibliotherapy and therapist-directed controlled drinking training for problem drinkers. *Behavior Therapy, 14,* 441–448.

Miller, W. R., Benefield, R. G., & Tonigan, J. S. (1993). Enhancing motivation for change in problem drinking: A controlled comparison of two therapist styles. *Journal of Consulting and Clinical Psychology, 61,* 455–461.

Miller, W. R., & Rollnick, S. (1991). *Motivational interviewing: Preparing people to change addictive behavior.* New York: Guilford Press.

Miller, W. R., & Sanchez, V. C. (1994). Motivating young adults for treatment and lifestyle change. In G. Howard & P. E. Nathan (Eds.), *Alcohol use and misuse by young adults* (pp. 55–81). Notre Dame, IN: University of Notre Dame Press.

Miller, W. R., & Sovereign, R. G. (1989). The checkup: A model for early intervention in addictive behaviors. In T. Loberg, W. R. Miller, P. E. Nathan, & G. A. Marlatt (Eds.), *Addictive behaviors: Prevention and early intervention* (pp. 219–231). Amsterdam: Swets & Zeitlinger.

Miller, W. R., Sovereign, R. G., & Krege, B. (1988). Motivational interviewing with problem drinkers: 2. The Drinker's Check-up as a preventive intervention. *Behavioural Psychotherapy, 16,* 251–268.

Miller, W. R., Taylor, C. A., & West, J. C. (1980). Focused versus broad-spectrum behavior therapy for problem drinkers. *Journal of Consulting and Clinical Psychology, 48,* 590–601.

Miller, W. R., & Tonigan, J. S. (1996). Assessing drinkers, motivation for change: The Stages of Change Readiness and Treatment Eagerness Scale (SOCRATES). *Psychology of Addictive Behaviors, 10*(2), 81–89.

Miller, W. R., Westerberg, V. S., Harris, R. J., & Tonigan, J. S. (1996). What predicts relapse? Prospective testing of antecedent models. *Addiction, 91*(Supplement), S155–S171.

Miller, W. R., Zweben, A., DiClemente, C. C., & Rychtarik, R. G. (1992). *Motivational enhancement therapy manual: A clinical tool for therapists treating individuals with alcohol abuse and dependence.* Project MATCH Monograph Series, Vol. 2. Rockville, MD: U.S. Department of Health and Human Services and National Institute on Alcohol Abuse and Alcoholism.

Najavits, L. M., & Weiss, R. D. (1994). Variations in therapist effectiveness in the treatment of patients with substance use disorders: An empirical review. *Addiction, 89,* 679–688.

Nelson-Zlupko, L., Dore, M. M., Kauffman, E., & Kaltenback, K. (1996). Women in recovery: Their perceptions of treatment effectiveness. *Journal of Substance Abuse Treatment, 13*(1), 51–59.

Patterson, G. A., & Forgatch, M. S. (1985). Therapist behavior as a determinant for client noncompliance: A paradox for the behavior modifier. *Journal of Consulting and Clinical Psychology, 53,* 846–851.

Prochaska, J. O., & DiClemente, C. C. (1986). Toward a comprehensive model of change. In W. R. Miller & N. Heather (Eds.), *Treating addictive behaviors: Processes of change* (pp. 3–27). New York: Plenum Press.

Prochaska, J. O., DiClemente, C. C., & Norcross, J. C. (1992). In search of how people change: Applications to addictive behaviors. *American Psychologist, 47*(9), 1102–1114.

Project MATCH Research Group. (1993). Project MATCH: Rationale and methods for a multisite clinical trial matching patients to alcoholism treatment. *Alcoholism: Clinical & Experimental Research, 17,* 1130–1145.

Project MATCH Research Group. (1997). Matching alcoholism treatments to client heterogeneity: Project MATCH posttreatment drinking outcomes. *Journal of Studies on Alcohol, 58,* 7–29.

Rogers, C. R. (1959). A theory of therapy, personality, and interpersonal relationships as developed in the client-centered framework. In S. Koch (Ed.), *Psychology: The study of a science: Vol. 3. Formulations of the person and the social context* (pp. 184–256). New York: McGraw-Hill.

Rollnick, S., & Bell, A. (1991) Brief motivational interviewing for use by the nonspecialist. In W. R. Miller & S. Rollnick (Eds.), *Motivational interviewing: Preparing people to change addictive behavior* (pp. 203–213). New York: Guilford Press.

Rollnick, S., Heather, N., Gold, R., & Hall, W. (1992). Development of a short "readiness to change" questionnaire for use in brief, opportunistic interventions among excessive drinkers. *British Journal of Addictions, 87,* 743–754.

Saunders, B., Wilkinson, C., & Allsop, S. (1991). Motivational intervention with heroin users attending a methadone clinic. In W. R. Miller & S. Rollnick (Eds.), *Motivational interviewing: Preparing people to change addictive behavior* (pp. 279–291). New York: Guilford Press.

Saunders, B., Wilkinson, C., & Phillips, M. (1995). The impact of a brief motivational intervention with opiate users attending a methadone programme. *Addiction, 90,* 415–424.

Sobell, L. C., Sobell, M. C., & Toneatto, T. (1991). Recovery from alcohol problems without treatment. In N. Heather, W. R. Miller, & J. Greeley (Eds.), *Self-control and the addictive behaviours* (pp. 198–242). Sydney: Pergamon Press.

Sobell, M. B., & Sobell, L. C. (1993). *Problem drinkers: Guided self-change treatment.* New York: Guilford Press.

Tomlinson, T. M. (1967). The therapeutic process as related to outcome. In C. R. Rogers (Ed.), *The thera-*

peutic relationship and its impact. (pp. 315–335). Madison: University of Wisconsin Press.

Valle, S. K. (1981). Interpersonal functioning of alcoholism counselors and treatment outcome. *Journal of Studies on Alcohol, 42,* 783–790.

WHO Brief Intervention Study Group. (1996). A cross-national trial of brief interventions with heavy drinkers. *American Journal of Public Health, 86,* 948–955.

Yahne, C. E., & Edwards, W. S. (1986). Learning and teaching the process of informed consent. *Research In Medical Education: Proceedings of the 25th Annual Conference* (pp. 29–35). Washington, DC: Association of American Medical Colleges.

14

Behavioral and Cognitive Behavioral Treatments

Kathleen M. Carroll

Behavioral and cognitive behavioral treatments have been among the most well defined and rigorously studied of the psychosocial treatments for substance abuse and dependence, and they have a comparatively high level of empirical support across the addictions. This chapter will review their origins, their theoretical basis and application to substance use disorders, the major techniques associated with several of these approaches, and their level of empirical support.

THE BREADTH OF BEHAVIORAL AND COGNITIVE BEHAVIORAL TREATMENTS

It should be noted that behavioral and cognitive behavioral treatments do not represent a single approach to treatment. Instead, these terms encompass an extremely broad range of interventions, from "strict" behavioral interventions, where clients may be provided incentives for desired behaviors such abstinence (e.g., Higgins, Budney, Bickel, & Hughes, 1993); to approaches where behavioral principles are used in extinction paradigms for conditioned cravings for drugs (Childress et al., 1993); to cognitive behavioral approaches such as relapse prevention (e.g., Marlatt & Gordon, 1985); coping-skills training (e.g., Monti, Abrams, Kadden, & Cooney, 1989), and other broad-spectrum approaches, such as the community reinforcement approach (Hunt & Azrin, 1973), which combine behavioral principles with cognitive medication; to purely cognitive approaches (e.g., Beck, Wright, Newman, & Liese, 1991), which attempt to modify dysfunctional cognitions that may underlie substance use.

What these models have in common is a theoretical basis in learning principles: Human behavior is largely learned, and basic learning principles can be applied to change human behavior. The fundamental assumptions of these approaches include the following (Rotgers, 1996, p. 175):

1. Human behavior is largely learned rather than being determined by genetic factors (although etiology does not necessarily dictate treatment).
2. The same learning processes that create problem behaviors can be used to change them.
3. Behavior is largely determined by contextual and environmental factors.
4. Covert behaviors such as thoughts and feelings are subject to change through the application of learning principles.
5. Actually engaging in new behaviors in the contexts in which they are to be performed is a critical part of behavior change.
6. Each client is unique and must be assessed as an individual in a particular context.
7. The cornerstone of adequate treatment is a thorough behavioral assessment.

HISTORICAL ORIGINS

Early Development of Behavioral and Cognitive Behavioral Treatments

A distinction of behavioral and cognitive behavioral treatments as applied to substance use disorders is that these approaches are solidly rooted in well-established theories and principles of human behavior and are closely linked to other behavioral and cognitive behavioral treatments for a range of problems and disorders other than substance abuse. Thus, they contrast with treatments such as disease model approaches, which have developed solely within the field of substance abuse.

Behavioral Treatments

Behavioral treatments have their roots in classical behavioral theory and the pioneering work of Pavlov, Watson, Skinner, and Bandura (for excellent reviews and history, see Craighead, Craighead, & Ilardi, 1995; Rotgers, 1996). First, Pavlov's work on classical conditioning demonstrated that a previously neutral stimulus could elicit a conditioned response after being paired repeatedly with an unconditioned stimulus. Furthermore, repeated exposure to the conditioned stimulus without the unconditioned stimulus

would eventually lead to extinction of the conditioned response. The power of classical conditioning was demonstrated in drug abuse by Wikler (1971, 1973), who confirmed that opioid addicts exhibited conditioned withdrawal symptoms upon exposure to drug paraphernalia. Today, classical conditioning theory is the basis of several behavioral approaches to substance use treatment, such as cue exposure (Childress, Ehrman, Rohsenow, Robbins, & O'Brien, 1992; Childress et al., 1993), described in more detail below.

Second, Skinner's work on operant conditioning demonstrated that behaviors that are positively reinforced are likely to be exhibited more frequently. The field of behavioral pharmacology, which has convincingly demonstrated the reinforcing properties of abused substances in both humans and animals (Aigner & Balster, 1978; Bigelow, Stitzer & Liebson, 1984; Schuster & Johanson, 1974; Thompson & Pickens, 1971); is grounded in operant conditioning theory and principles. A wide range of behavioral interventions, including those which seek to provide alternate reinforcers to drugs and alcohol or to reduce reinforcing aspects of abused substances, are also based on operant conditioning theory. Examples include the Community Reinforcement Approach (CRA) of Azrin and colleagues (1976); the work of Stitzer and colleagues, which has demonstrated that methadone-maintained opioid addicts will reduce illicit drug use when incentives such as take-home methadone are offered for abstinence (Stitzer, Iguchi, Kidorf & Bigelow, 1993); and the very effective incentive systems developed by Steve Higgins and colleagues (Higgins, Budney, Bickel, Foerg, et al., 1994)—all of which are described in more detail below.

Finally, Bandura's (1977) work on modeling, which postulates that new behaviors can be acquired through observational learning and performance, is another cornerstone of behavioral approaches to substance abuse and dependence. In particular, research on the acquisition of substance use during adolescence consistently points to peer group modeling and influence (Kandel & Faust, 1975; see Kaplan & Johnson, 1992) as important factors. Many behavioral and cognitive behavioral approaches include treatment modeling and rehearsal of more effective coping strategies and behavioral alternatives to substance use. An example of the use of modeling in cognitive behavioral treatment is the group coping-skills training approach developed by Monti and colleagues (1989).

Cognitive Behavioral Treatments

Cognitive behavioral treatment (CBT), which is closely related to and grounded in behavioral theory, emphasizes the importance of the person's thoughts and feelings as determinants of behavior and reflects the pioneering work of Ellis and Beck. CBT evolved in part from dissatisfaction with strictly behavioral theory and treatment and from observations that how the individual perceived and reacted to the relationships between his or her behavior and critical events was also an important determinant of behavior (i.e., the ABC model of emotion) (Meichenbaum, 1995). In other words, the person's thoughts, feelings, and expectancies are thought to *mediate* her or his response to the environment. A key concept in CBT is *reciprocal determinism*, which emphasizes the interdependence of cognitive, affective, and behavioral processes.

In general, cognitive behavioral treatments are among the most widely used for the treatment of psychiatric disorders other than substance abuse. This group of treatments have in common strategies which help patients become aware of maladaptive cognitions and "teach them how to notice, catch, monitor, and interrupt the cognitive-affective-behavioral chains and to produce more adaptive coping responses" (Meichenbaum, 1995, p. 147).

This strategy is also the basis of the wide variety of cognitive behavioral approaches to substance use disorders. In particular, the work of Alan Marlatt and colleagues on relapse prevention (Chaney, O'Leary, & Marlatt, 1978; Marlatt, 1979; Marlatt & Gordon, 1985) stands out in the development and application of cognitive behavioral theory to the treatment of substance use disorders. Techniques which characterize this approach include the identification of high-risk situations for relapse, instruction and rehearsal of strategies for coping with those situations, self-monitoring and behavioral analysis of substance use, strategies for recognizing and coping with craving and thoughts about substance use, planning for emergencies and coping with lapses, instruction in problem-solving strategies, and focus on lifestyle balance (Carroll, 1996). Consistent with cognitive behavioral approaches for other psychiatric disorders, this approach emphasizes exposure to, practice of, and mastery of skills through rehearsal, role playing, and extrasession homework tasks (Carroll, 1996).

ETIOLOGY AND MAINTENANCE OF SUBSTANCE USE DISORDERS

Behavioral and cognitive behavioral therapies conceive of substance abuse as a complex, multidetermined behavior, with a number of etiological influences playing a role in the development of substance use disorders. These may include family history and genetic factors (particularly for substance dependence as opposed to abuse) (Cadoret, 1992; see Merikangas, Rounsaville, & Prusoff, 1992; Pickens et al., 1991); the presence of comorbid psychopathology (see Weiss, 1992); personality traits such as sensation seeking or sociopathy (see Clayton, 1992); and a host of environmental factors, including substance availability and lack of countervailing influences and rewards (see Brook, Cohen, Whitman & Gordon, 1992; Kandel & Logan, 1984). Overall, however, behavioral and cognitive behavioral therapies emphasize the reinforcing properties of substances as central to the acquisition of substance abuse and dependence. Moreover, these risk factors are seen as consistent with behavioral theories of the acquisition and maintenance of substance use. That is, substances may be abused because they are particularly rewarding to particular individuals. Examples might include individuals with a family history of alcoholism, those with comorbid depression, those with a high need for sensation seeking, those who watch and model family and friends use substances, and those who live in environments devoid of alternative reinforcers.

Behavioral factors are also seen as central to the maintenance of substance abuse and dependence once initiated. Operant conditioning factors are seen as continuing to have an important role in the maintenance of substance dependence, not only through the positive reinforcing aspects of the abused substance, but also through avoidance of withdrawal symptoms for substances with significant tolerance and withdrawal syndromes. Classical conditioning may begin to play an important role in the development of conditioned craving and withdrawal, as well as in the environmental regulation of drug-taking behavior (Rotgers, 1996). Cognitive processes, particularly expectancies of substance effects (Goldman,

Brown, & Christiansen, 1987), are also seen as important in maintaining substance abuse and dependence (e.g., "I need cocaine to get through the day"). Moreover, as the individual responds to a host of environmental, interpersonal, and intrapersonal contexts with substance use, continued substance abuse and dependence are seen as becoming an overused, overgeneralized, and maladaptive coping strategy. Hence, by the time treatment is sought (usually when the negative consequences of substance use have achieved primacy over positive effects and consequences), the individual may have few other coping responses remaining in his or her repertoire, and his or her reference group is likely to be limited to other substance-dependent individuals.

THERAPEUTIC CHANGE IN BEHAVIORAL AND COGNITIVE BEHAVIORAL TREATMENTS

Assumptions About How People Change

As noted above, behavioral and cognitive behavioral approaches posit that the same principles that may be involved in the inception or maintenance of substance abuse and dependence can be applied to change these behaviors.

For example, principles of classical conditioning are a cornerstone of cue exposure approaches (Hodgson & Rankin, 1978). Several investigators have demonstrated that repeated exposure to stimuli previously paired with substance use (e.g., handling drug paraphernalia, watching videotapes of individuals preparing and using the substance) in controlled laboratory settings has been associated with extinction of some conditioned responses to those cues, including decreases in subjective craving (Childress, Ehrman, McLellan, & O'Brien, 1988; McLellan, Childress, O'Brien, & Ehrman, 1986; Rankin, Hodgson, & Stockwell, 1983). Cognitive behavioral treatments also invoke principles of classical conditioning as they seek to decrease craving through helping the patient to understand and recognize conditioned craving, to identify his or her own idiosyncratic array of conditioned cues, or triggers, for craving, to identify means of avoiding exposure to those cues, and to learn strategies to cope effectively with craving when it does occur, without using substances, so that con-

ditioned craving is reduced and eliminated over time (Carroll, 1998).

Similarly, one of the earliest approaches to the treatment of alcohol dependence, aversive counterconditioning therapies, was also based on principles of classical conditioning. The underlying principle of these approaches was to pair an aversive experience (electric shock, induced nausea, negative images) with drinking or drinking-related stimuli, thus seeking to make drinking a negative, rather than a positive, experience (see Wilson, 1978). Although aversive counterconditioning therapies have been used for many years and with large numbers of substance users, well-controlled trials of their effectiveness have been infrequent (Childress et al. 1992).

Operant conditioning concepts are applied several ways in behavioral and cognitive behavioral treatments. A commonly used approach in behavioral treatments is the application of positive incentives for desired behaviors (such as abstinence) or negative incentives for undesired behaviors (such as continued substance use or noncompliance). Examples of negative contingencies include detoxification and termination from methadone maintenance treatment for patients who continue to use illicit drugs (e.g., McCarthy & Borders, 1985) and contracts involving notification of employers of the patient's cocaine abuse for individuals who continue to use cocaine (e.g., Anker & Crowley, 1982). Examples of positive contingencies include the incentive system developed by Higgins and colleagues to promote retention and abstinence among cocaine abusers (Higgins et al., 1991; Higgins, Budney, Bickel, Foerg, et al., 1994) and the use of available reinforcers within methadone maintenance programs (e.g., methadone take-home privileges, reduced frequency of clinic attendance, dose changes) to reduce illicit drug use within methadone maintenance programs (Stitzer et al., 1993).

Operant conditioning principles are also are used several ways in cognitive behavioral treatments. First, through a detailed examination of the antecedents and consequences of substance use, therapists attempt to develop an understanding of why the patient may be more likely to use in a given situation and to understand the role that the substance plays in his or her life. This *functional analysis* of substance use is thus used to identify the high-risk situations in which the patient is likely to use drugs and thus to provide the basis for learning more effective coping behaviors in those situations. Second, the therapist attempts to help the patient develop meaningful reinforcers alternate to drug use, that is, other activities and involvements (relationships, work, hobbies) that serve as viable alternatives to substance use and help the patient remain abstinent. Finally, a detailed examination of the consequences, both long- and short-term, of substance use is used as a strategy to build or reinforce the patients' resolve to reduce or eliminate their substance use (Carroll, 1998).

Principles of *modeling* are also used in both behavioral and cognitive behavioral treatments to help the patient learn and apply new behaviors, such as how to refuse an offer of drugs by having the patient participate in role plays with the therapist or other group members. That is, the patient learns to respond in unfamiliar, but more adaptive, ways by first watching the therapist model those new strategies and then practicing those strategies within the supportive context of the therapy hour as well as outside sessions.

Finally, principles of *cognitive change* (Beck, Rush, Shaw, & Emery, 1979) are used in many ways. An assumption of the cognitive behavioral approaches is that recognizing, monitoring, and changing maladaptive or dysfunctional beliefs that play a role in maintaining substance use can also help reduce and eliminate substance use. Examples of this approach include the work of Beck and colleagues (1991), which includes techniques such as conducting an analysis of the advantages and disadvantages of continued substance use versus discontinuation, identifying and modifying drug-related beliefs, reattribution of responsibility, thought stopping, and modifying black-and-white or catastrophic thinking.

Key Interventions in Behavioral and Cognitive Behavioral Treatments

Assessment Procedures

A thorough behavioral assessment is at the heart of behavioral and cognitive behavioral treatments. Assessment is organized around a *functional analysis* of the individual's substance use, which is simply an exploration of substance use with respect to its antecedents and consequences. Early in treatment, the functional analysis plays a critical role in helping the patient and the therapist to assess the determinants of the individual's substance use, to set goals for treat-

ment, to prioritize problems, to select the type and sequence of interventions to be used, and to monitor progress in meeting treatment goals.

Thus, applying behavioral treatments effectively requires that the patient and therapist have a thorough understanding of the following areas:

1. *What are the particular determinants of this person's substance use?* What is the severity of this person's substance use (intensity, quantity/frequency)? What are his or her individual patterns of use (weekends only, every day, binge use)? What are his or her conditioned cues, or "triggers," for substance use? Does this person use the substance by herself or himself or with other people? Where does this person buy and use substances? Where does she or he acquire the money to buy drugs? What has happened to (or within) this person before the most recent episodes of use? What circumstances were at play when the substance use began or became a problem? How does this person describe the substance and its effects on him or her? What roles, both positive and negative, does substance use play in this individual's life?

In evaluating the environmental context of the individual's substance use, therapists typically cover at least the following general domains:

a. *Social.* With whom does the individual spend most of her or his time? With whom does she or he use drugs? Does she or he have relationships with those individual outside substance use? Does the individual live with someone who is a substance abuser? How has the patient's social network changed since drug use began or escalated?

b. *Environmental.* What are the particular environmental "cues" for this patient's drug use (e.g., money, alcohol use, particular times of day, particular neighborhoods)? What is the level of this person's day-to-day exposure to these cues? Can some of these cues be easily avoided? Which are "fixed" in the individual's environment?

c. *Emotional.* Affect states commonly precede substance use or craving. These include both negative (depression, anxiety, boredom, anger) and positive (excitement, joy) affect states. Because many patients initially have difficulty linking particular states to their substance use (or do so, but only at a surface level), affective antecedents of substance use are typically more difficult to identify in the initial stages of treatment.

d. *Cognitive.* Particular sets of thought or cognitions also frequently precede substance use ("I need to escape," "I can't deal with this unless I'm high," "The hell with it," "I deserve to get high"). These cognitions often have a sense of urgency.

e. *Physical.* Desire for relief from uncomfortable physical states such as withdrawal has been implicated as a frequent antecedent of substance use. Assessing the level of the individual's tolerance or withdrawal symptoms is an essential step in planning treatment, as it also indicates the need for medical evaluation and treatment (Carroll, 1998).

Standardized diagnostic and assessment instruments that are useful in evaluating severity of substance dependence in treatment settings include the Structured Clinical Interview for *DSM-IV* (SCID; Spitzer, Williams, Gibbon, & First, 1996), the Addiction Severity Index (ASI; McLellan et al., 1992), the Form 90 (Miller & DelBoca, 1994), the TimeLine Follow-Back (Sobell & Sobell, 1992), the Drinker Inventory of Consequences (DrInC; Miller, 1992), the Cocaine Craving Questionnaire (Tiffany, Singleton, Haertzen, & Henningfield, 1993), the Cocaine Relapse Interview (McKay, Rutherford, Alterman, & Cacciola, 1996), and biological measures including the urine toxicology screen, breathalyzers, liver function tests.

2. *What skills or resources does the individual lack, and what concurrent problems may be obstacles to becoming abstinent?* Has this person been able to recognize the need to reduce the availability of substances? Has the patient been able to recognize important conditioned cues? Has he or she been able to achieve even brief periods of abstinence? Has he or she recognized events which have led to relapse? Has he or she been able to tolerate periods of craving or emotional distress without resorting to drug use? Does he or she recognize the relationship of his or her other substance use (especially alcohol) in maintaining drug dependence? Are there people in the patient's social network who do not use or supply drugs? Does he or she have a concurrent psychiatric disorder or other problems (e.g., medical, legal, familial, employment) that might confound his or her efforts to change behavior?

Standardized diagnostic and assessment instruments that evaluate clinically significant comorbid problems among substance abusers include the SCID (Spitzer et al., 1996), the ASI (McLellan et al., 1992), the California Psychological Inventory Socialization Scale (CPI-So; Megargee, 1972), and the Beck Depression Inventory (BDI; Beck et al., 1961).

3. *What skills and strengths does the individual have?* What skills or strengths has the patient demonstrated during any previous periods of abstinence? What is his or her coping style? Has he or she been able to maintain a job or positive relationships during substance use? What family/social supports and resources may be available to bolster the patient's efforts to become abstinent? How does he or she spend time when not using drugs or recovering from their effects? What was this person's highest level of functioning before using drugs? What brought this person to treatment *now?* How motivated is this individual?

Again, there are a variety of standardized instruments available for assessing these areas, including, for the assessment of motivation, the University of Rhode Island Change Assessment (URICA; DiClemente & Hughes, 1990) and the Stages of Change Readiness and Treatment Eagerness Scale (SOCRATES; Miller, 1992); for current level of substance-related coping skills, the Situational Competency Test (Chaney et al., 1978), a role-playing instrument intended to assess skill acquisition among alcoholics, which has been modified for use with other populations and settings (Abrams et al., 1991, Carroll, Nich, Frankforter, & Bisighini, in press); for self-efficacy and confidence in high-risk situations (e.g., Condiotte & Lichtenstein, 1981); and for level of social and family support, the Important People and Activities Scale (IPA; Clifford & Longabaugh, 1991).

Treatment Goals

Treatment goals in behavioral and cognitive behavioral treatments are highly individualized and typically reflect a collaborative process between patient and therapist (Morgan, 1996). Moreover, a marked contrast between these treatments and traditional disease model approaches has been the nature of treatment goals vis-à-vis substance use. Whereas traditional models have stressed complete abstinence, behavioral treatments have encompassed risk reduction goals as well as abstinence (Carey & Maisto, 1985; Morgan, 1996; Rosenberg, 1993). However, goals of moderation or risk reduction have been more typical of behavioral treatments for alcohol use disorders than among treatments for drug use and dependence disorders, in part because of the illicit nature of drug use, as well as the comparative risks and serious morbidities associated with HIV, tuberculosis, and other medical complications of many classes of drug use.

In *behavioral approaches,* treatment goals are highly focused and depend on the nature of the specific treatment approach. For example, cue exposure and extinction approaches are intended primarily to reduce reactivity to specific cues (e.g., cocaine paraphernalia) and may not generalize to other cues (e.g., affect states) nor affect other substance-related problems (Childress et al., 1992). Similarly, in contingency management approaches, researchers have generally demonstrated specificity of response to the behavior that is reinforced or punished. For example, if abstinence is reinforced, substance use generally is eliminated or reduced; conversely, if group attendance is reinforced, attendance is likely to increase, but changes in substance use may not be seen (Iguchi et al., 1996). In addition, behavioral treatments typically target a single behavior or group of behaviors; that is, contingency management protocols would be expected to reduce substance use, but have little influence on other concurrent problems. However, abstinence associated with focused behavioral treatments may lead to improvements in a number of areas, such as reductions in psychiatric symptomatology and improved social functioning.

The goals of *cognitive behavioral treatments* tend to be somewhat broader than those of "strict" behavioral approaches, and the choice of treatment goals will dictate the specific interventions implemented. For example, in broad-spectrum cognitive behavioral treatments (e.g., Azrin, 1976; Monti et al., 1989), the patient and therapist may select a wide range of target behaviors in addition to a treatment goal of abstinence or harm reduction, including improved social skills or social functioning, reduced psychiatric symptoms, reduced social isolation, and entry into the workforce.

Structure of Therapy Sessions

Behavioral and cognitive behavioral treatments are typically highly structured in comparison to other approaches for substance use disorders. That is, these treatment approaches are typically comparatively brief (12–24 weeks) and are organized closely around well-specified treatment goals. There is typically an articulated agenda for each session, and discussion remains focused around issues directly related to substance use. Progress toward treatment goals is moni-

tored closely and frequently, and the therapist takes an active stance throughout treatment.

The "typical" structure of a given session varies widely, depending on what type of behavioral approach is used. For example, in a "pure" contingency management approach, the therapist and the patient might meet infrequently, or not at all, while the contingency is in place. Alternatively, the behavioral contingency may be added to a full-spectrum treatment approach, encompassing supportive counseling, monitoring and feedback of urine toxicology or breathalyzer screen results, pharmacotherapies, and a wide array of other supportive services. More typically, behavioral and cognitive behavioral sessions take place within a regular, usually weekly, therapy "hour." In broad-spectrum cognitive behavioral approaches, sessions are often organized roughly in thirds (the 20/20/20 rule), with the first third of the session devoted to assessment of substance use and general functioning in the past week, as well as opportunity for the patient to report current concerns and problems; the second third is more didactic and devoted to skills training and practice; and the final third allows time for therapist and patient to plan for the week ahead and discuss how new skills will be implemented (Carroll, 1998). Practice of new skills outside sessions is generally seen as an integral part of treatment in cognitive behavioral therapy.

Major Techniques of the Treatments

Specific techniques vary widely with the type of behavioral or cognitive behavioral treatment used, and there are a variety of manuals and protocols available which describe the techniques associated with each approach. A brief summary of the techniques and procedures typifying the major types of behavioral and cognitive behavioral approaches referred to throughout this chapter follows.

Cue exposure approaches typically begin with a thorough assessment of cues, or stimuli, associated with conditioned craving, and with the development of a hierarchy of cues. This is followed by repeated exposure to those cues (through actual exposure to or handling of a conditioned cue, videotapes, or imagery) in a laboratory or other controlled setting which prevents the patient from having access to the substance. The patient's physiological and subjective responses to the stimuli are typically assessed both before and after each exposure session. Extinction of craving associated with a specific stimulus typically takes place in 20 sessions or fewer (Childress et al., 1993).

An example of the techniques used in *contingency management approaches* would be those described by Higgins and colleagues for their program (Budney & Higgins, 1998; Higgins & Budney, 1993; Higgins et al., 1991), which incorporates positive incentives for abstinence, reciprocal relationship counseling, and disulfiram into a Community Reinforcement Approach (CRA; Sisson & Azrin, 1989) approach. The Higgins strategy has four organizing features, which are grounded in principles of behavioral pharmacology: (a) drug use and abstinence must be swiftly and accurately detected; (b) abstinence is positively reinforced; (c) drug use results in loss of reinforcement; and (d) emphasis is on the development of reinforcers that compete with reinforcers of drug use (Higgins & Budney, 1993). In this program, urine specimens are required three times weekly. Abstinence, assessed through drug-free urine screens, is reinforced through a voucher system, where patients receive points redeemable for items consistent with a drug-free lifestyle, such as movie tickets, sporting goods, and the like, but patients never receive money directly. To encourage longer periods of consecutive abstinence, the value of the points earned by the patient increases with each successive clean urine specimen, and the value of the points is reset back to its original level when the patient produces a drug-positive urine screen or does not come in for treatment.

Cognitive behavioral approaches include a range of skills that foster or maintain abstinence. These typically include strategies for (a) reducing availability and exposure to the substance and related cues; (b) fostering resolution to stop substance use through exploring positive and negative consequences of continued use; (c) self-monitoring to identify high-risk situations and to conduct functional analyses of substance use (see figures 14.1 and 14.2); (d) recognition of conditioned craving and development of strategies for coping with craving; (e) identification of seemingly irrelevant decisions which can culminate in high-risk situations; (f) preparation for emergencies and coping with a relapse to substance use; (g) substance refusal skills; and (h) identifying and confronting thoughts about the substance. Material discussed during sessions is typically supplemented with extrasession tasks (i.e., homework) intended to foster practice and mastery of coping skills.

Broad-spectrum cognitive behavioral approaches such as that described by Monti and colleagues

Date	Situation (Include Your Thoughts and Feelings)	Intensity of Craving (1–100)	Coping Behaviors Used

FIGURE 14.1 Self-monitoring form. Reproduced from Kadden et al., 1992.

Trigger	Thoughts and Feelings	Behavior	Positive Consequences	Negative Consequences
(What sets me up to use?)	(What was I thinking? What was I feeling?)	(What did I do then?)	(What positive thing happened?)	(What negative thing happened?)

FIGURE 14.2 Functional analysis worksheet (from Kadden et al., 1992).

(1989), and adapted for use in Project MATCH (Kadden et al., 1992), expand to include interventions directed to other problems in the individual's life that are seen as functionally related to substance use, for example, general problem-solving skills, assertiveness training, strategies for coping with negative affect, awareness of anger and anger management, coping with criticism, increasing pleasant activities, enhancing social support networks, and job-seeking skills.

Active Ingredients

Behavioral and cognitive behavioral treatments, like most psychosocial therapies, realize their effects through a complex combination of common factors (treatment elements that are shared by most therapies) and unique factors. As with most therapies, outcomes for behavioral and cognitive behavioral treatments are generally thought to depend to a large extent on the effective use of common factors, including education about the nature of the disorder, a persuasive therapeutic rationale, expectations of improvement, the skill of the therapist, and the quality of the therapeutic relationship (Castonguay, 1993; Rozenzweig, 1936). However, it is also important to

note that these factors may not be a necessary condition for success in all behavioral approaches.

Unique "active ingredients" of this group of approaches depends, of course, on the specific treatment approach in question. For example, for cognitive behavioral coping-skills approaches, the active ingredients are thought to be skill acquisition and implementation; for cognitive therapies, the active ingredient is thought to be identification and modification of dysfunctional cognitions; and for cue exposure approaches, the active ingredient for extinction is repeated exposure to the conditioned stimulus under conditions incompatible with use.

The relative role and contribution of common versus specific factors to treatment outcome has in fact rarely been studied among behavioral and cognitive behavioral treatments for the addictions (DiClemente, Carroll, Connors, & Kadden, 1994). Similarly, few investigators have explicitly identified or evaluated the active ingredients of their approaches; that is, few have demonstrated that the presence of the hypothesized active ingredient is actually responsible for therapeutic change. One exception has been the elegant series of studies by Higgins and colleagues, which has demonstrated (a) that of the elements provided in their multimodal CRA approach, it was the incentive system itself that was associated with abstinence (Higgins, Budney, Bickel, Foerg, et al., 1994), and (b) that vouchers contingent on abstinence were more effective than noncontingent vouchers (Silverman et al., 1996). Similarly, preliminary evidence from work with cognitive behavioral coping-skills treatments for cocaine abusers has demonstrated that treatment-specific acquisition of skills and posttreatment skill levels were associated with better cocaine outcomes during follow-up (Carroll et al., in press).

Role of the Therapist

In behavioral and cognitive behavioral therapies, the therapeutic relationship is seen as principally collaborative. Thus, the role of the therapist is typically seen as that of a consultant, educator, and guide who can lead the patient through a functional analysis of his or her substance use, aid in identifying and prioritizing target behaviors, and consult in selecting and implementing strategies to foster the desired behavior changes.

Typical Training

A broad range of therapists can, with appropriate training and supervision, implement behavioral and cognitive behavioral treatments effectively. Typical education and training requirements for therapists implementing these treatments in controlled clinical trials have included a master's degree or higher in psychology, counseling, social work or a closely related field; several years' experience in working with a substance abuse population; familiarity with and commitment to the specific behavioral treatment they will deliver; and satisfactory completion of formal training in the approach. Therapist training in behavioral and cognitive behavioral treatments has been greatly facilitated through the wide availability of manuals for this group of approaches. Training usually involves (a) a didactic seminar which includes review of the treatment manual, viewing videotaped examples of the treatment technique, and practice exercises and (b) successful completion of several closely supervised training cases (see Carroll et al., 1994).

Personal characteristics of therapists that are associated with improved outcome specifically in behav-

ioral and cognitive behavioral treatments for the addictions have not been widely studied. However, in their classic study of psychotherapy in the context of methadone maintenance, Luborsky, McLellan, Woody, O'Brien, and Auerbach (1985) found that personal adjustment, interest in helping the patient, ability to foster a positive working alliance, and high empathy and warmth were associated with better patient outcome across therapies. In an evaluation of therapist characteristics from the large cohort of Project MATCH therapists, none of the therapist characteristics assessed (including gender, age, race, and various personality attributes) were associated with variability in outcome among patients treated by the CBT therapists (Project MATCH Research Group, in press).

Use of Relationship Elements

The quality of the therapeutic alliance has emerged as a consistent and comparatively robust predictor of positive outcome across psychotherapies of different types and with diverse clinical samples (Horvath & Luborsky, 1993; Horvath & Symonds, 1991). However, detailed studies of the relationship of the therapeutic alliance to outcome for behavioral and cognitive behavioral treatments for substance use disorders have been rare. Luborsky and colleagues (1985) found that while the purity of technique had a strong relationship to outcome for methadone-maintained opioid addicts, therapeutic alliance ratings had a far stronger correlation with outcome (across cognitive therapy, supportive-expressive therapy, and drug counseling). More recently, using the Working Alliance Inventory (Horvath & Greenberg, 1986), Connors, Carroll, DiClemente, Longabaugh, and Donovan (1997) found that the better working alliance scores were associated with improved alcohol outcomes across the Project MATCH therapies, one of which was CBT.

The complexity of the relationship between the therapeutic alliance and the delivery of active ingredients in CBT was demonstrated by data which suggested not only that the therapeutic alliance was rated as *more positive* for CBT than for clinical management (a nonspecific supportive condition that offered empathy and clinical monitoring but none of the active ingredients of CBT), but that sessions in which more of the active ingredients of CBT were delivered were also rated as having a more positive therapeutic alliance (Carroll, Nich, & Rounsaville,

1997). This finding suggests, for example, that an adequate therapeutic alliance may be necessary to provide the conditions under which specific behavioral interventions can be productively implemented. Similarly, a positive alliance may also foster greater treatment retention and thus permit more exposure by patients to active ingredients of treatment.

PATIENT CHARACTERISTICS ASSOCIATED WITH VARIABILITY IN RESPONSE TO BEHAVIORAL AND COGNITIVE BEHAVIORAL TREATMENTS

Behavioral and cognitive behavioral treatments have been designed and implemented as approaches that are highly individualized and that recognize the heterogeneity of persons with substance use disorders. Thus, they've been used successfully with a wide range of individuals.

However, comparatively few studies of behavioral and cognitive behavioral treatments have conducted detailed analyses of patient characteristics associated with variability in outcome (e.g., success profiling) or have prospectively evaluated hypothesized patient-treatment interactions. Even fewer of these studies have been replicated. Thus, it is important to note that there are few empirical data on types of individuals who are particularly well, or poorly, suited to these approaches, although variability in outcome is commonly seen.

However, some recent studies pointing to indicators of better response to behavioral interventions have emerged. Among contingency management approaches, Higgins and colleagues reported markedly improved outcomes for patients who had a significant other willing to participate in treatment compared with those who did not (Higgins, Budney, Bickel, & Badger, 1994).

For cognitive behavioral treatments, recent data from Project MATCH (Project MATCH Research Group, 1993), a multicenter trial of patient-treatment matching for alcoholics, revealed few indications of clinically significant patient-characteristic-by-treatment interactions for CBT or the other treatments evaluated (12-step facilitation and motivational enhancement therapy). However, better outcomes were

found for alcohol patients low in psychiatric severity (as measured by the ASI) when treated with 12-step facilitation as compared with CBT, although this effect tended to diminish across time (Project MATCH Research Group, 1997). Patient characteristics such as higher motivation for change were associated with better drinking outcomes across the three treatments, while higher social support for drinking and, to some extent, higher sociopathy, were associated with poorer drinking outcomes across the three treatments (Project MATCH Research Group, 1997).

Smaller, single-site studies of CBT have suggested a range of patient characteristics associated with improved outcome with respect to comparison approaches. Kadden, Cooney, Getter, and Litt (1989), in a prospective matching study, found that patients higher in sociopathy had better drinking outcomes when treated with CBT than when treated with a group interactional approach, and patients lower in sociopathy had better outcome when treated with the interactional approach. For patients higher in psychopathology, CBT was superior. For patients higher in neuropsychological impairment, the interactional therapy was superior. A 2-year follow-up indicated that these matching effects were durable (Cooney, Kadden, Litt, & Getter, 1991).

Among cocaine abusers, exploratory analyses of patient characteristics associated with treatment response have suggested better cocaine outcomes for patients higher in severity of cocaine use or higher in depressive symptoms when treated with CBT than when treated with supportive clinical management (Carroll, Nich, & Rounsaville, 1995; Carroll, Rounsaville, Gordon, et al., 1994), as well as poorer outcomes for alexithymic cocaine abusers (those who had difficulty articulating affect) when treated with CBT than when treated with clinical management (Keller, Carroll, Nich, & Rounsaville, 1995).

EMPIRICAL DATA ON THE EFFECTIVENESS OF THE MODELS

Overall, behavioral and cognitive behavioral treatments have been among the most well defined and rigorously studied of the psychosocial treatments for substance abuse and dependence, and have a comparatively high level of empirical support across the addictions. For example, in their review of cost and effectiveness data for treatments for alcohol use disorders, Holder, Longabaugh, Miller, and Rubonis (1991) included social skills training, self-control training, stress management training, and the community reinforcement approach—all broad-spectrum CBT approaches—as having good empirical evidence of effectiveness. Recent reviews of the effectiveness of treatments for drug abuse (APA Workgroup on Substance Use Disorders; Crits-Christoph & Siqueland, 1996; DeRubeis & Crits-Christoph, 1998; General Accounting Office, 1996) identified contingency management and cognitive behavioral therapy as having among the highest levels of empirical support for the treatment of opioid and cocaine dependence disorders.

Cue Exposure Approaches

While cue exposure approaches have generally been associated with reductions in some conditioned responses, the value of these procedures in producing clinically meaningful reductions in substance use has been met with only modest success to date (Childress et al., 1992; Monti et al., 1993). For example, to evaluate the utility of extinction procedures as an adjunct to drug treatment, 56 methadone-maintained addicts were randomly assigned to one of three groups: a combination group which received cognitive behavioral therapy, extinction, and relaxation training (CE); a group which received cognitive behavioral therapy and relaxation training without extinction (CT); and a group which received drug counseling alone (McLellan et al., 1986). The group which received extinction (CE) evidenced a reduction in subjective craving for opiates with repeated extinction sections. However, although both groups which received psychotherapy (CE and CT) had significantly better 6-month outcomes than the group which received drug counseling alone, the two psychotherapy groups were not significantly different from each other, a finding suggesting that the extinction procedure added no great relative benefit over the cognitive therapy plus relaxation training. The authors suggested several factors which may have undercut the power of the outpatient extinction procedure, including (a) the need for use of individualized stimuli and (b) the need to consider modifying variables such as affect or cognitive set. Similar findings have also been reported for extinction proce-

dures with cocaine patients (Childress et al., 1988), where extinction of craving to some cocaine cues has been demonstrated, but it is not yet clear whether extinction generalizes to other cues more difficult to control in laboratory/treatment settings, or whether extinction of craving has an appreciable difference on drug use (Childress et al., 1993).

Contingency Management Approaches

Because of a recognition that methadone maintenance may curtail opioid use but often has little effect on other illicit substance use, particularly cocaine use (Kosten, Rounsaville, & Kleber, 1987), a variety of contingency management approaches have been evaluated for their reduction of illicit substance use among methadone-maintained opiate addicts. Several features of standard methadone maintenance treatment (daily attendance, frequent urine monitoring, and reinforcing properties of methadone) have offered behavioral researchers the opportunity to control the reinforcers available to patients and hence to evaluate the effects of both positive and negative contingencies on outcome in methadone maintenance programs.

Several studies have evaluated negative contingency contracting, which requires specific improvements in behavior (typically submission of drug-free urines) for continued methadone treatment, with failure to improve or comply resulting in dose reduction, detoxification, or termination of treatment. Liebson, Tommasello, and Bigelow (1978) found that this procedure increased compliance with disulfiram treatment for alcoholic methadone-maintained opiate addicts. Several studies, including Dolan, Black, Penk, Rabinowitz, and DeFord (1985), McCarthy and Borders (1985), Saxon, Calsyn, Kivlahan, and Roszell (1993), and Nolimal and Crowley (1990), have demonstrated that approximately 40–60% of subjects are able to reduce or stop illicit substance use under threat of dose reduction or treatment termination. However, fully half the subjects in these studies did not reduce their substance use under these conditions and were forced to leave treatment. Often, patients who do not comply with behavioral requirements and are terminated are those with more frequent or severe polysubstance use (Dolan et al., 1985; Saxon et al., 1993). Thus, these studies demonstrate that while negative contingencies may reduce or stop illicit substance use in some methadone maintenance patients, these somewhat draconian procedures may also have the undesirable effect of terminating treatment for those more severely impaired patients who have difficulty complying and who may need treatment most (Stitzer, Bickel, Bigelow, & Liebson, 1986).

The methadone take-home privilege contingent on reduced drug use is an attractive approach, as it capitalizes on an inexpensive reinforcer which is potentially available in all methadone maintenance programs. Stitzer and colleagues (1993) did extensive work in evaluating methadone take-home privileges as a reward for decreased illicit drug use. In a series of well-controlled trials, this group of researchers demonstrated (a) the relative benefits of positive over negative contingencies (Stitzer et al., 1986); (b) the attractiveness of take-home privileges over other incentives available in methadone maintenance clinics (Stitzer & Bigelow, 1978); (c) the effectiveness of targeting and rewarding drug-free urines over other, more distal, behaviors such as group attendance (Iguchi et al., 1996); and (d) the benefits of using take-home privileges contingent on drug-free urines over noncontingent take-home privileges (Stitzer, Iguchi, & Felch, 1992).

One of the most innovative and exciting findings pertaining to the effectiveness of behavioral treatments for cocaine abuse is the recent reports of Higgins and colleagues (Budney & Higgins, 1998; Higgins, 1991, 1993; Higgins, Budney, Bickel, Foerg, et al., 1994) evaluating the combination of incentives in the form of vouchers and CRA. In a series of well-controlled clinical trials, Higgins et al. (1991, 1993) demonstrated (a) high acceptance, retention, and rates of abstinence for patients randomized to this approach (85% completing a 12-week course of treatment; 65% achieving 6 or more weeks of abstinence) relative to standard 12-step-oriented substance abuse counseling (Higgins et al., 1991, 1993); (b) no decline in rates of abstinence when less valuable incentives, such as lottery tickets, were substituted for the voucher system (Higgins & Budney, 1993); (c) the value of the voucher system itself (as opposed to other program elements) in producing good outcomes by comparing the behavioral system with and without the vouchers (Higgins, Budney, Bickel, Foerg, et al., 1994); and (d) the durability of treatment effects after cessation of the contingencies (Higgins et al., 1995). The effectiveness of this ap-

proach has also recently been replicated among cocaine-abusing methadone-maintained opioid addicts (Silverman et al., 1996).

Cognitive Behavioral Coping-Skills Approaches

Coping-skills approaches have also been widely studied and have a comparatively high level of empirical support. To date, over 25 randomized controlled trials have evaluated the effect of cognitive behavioral coping-skills treatment on substance use outcomes among adult smokers and abusers of alcohol, cocaine, marijuana, and other types of substances. Review of this body of literature suggests that across substances of abuse but most strongly for smoking cessation, there is evidence of the effectiveness of CBT compared with no-treatment control conditions. However, evidence regarding its superiority relative to discussion control conditions or other active treatments has been less consistent (Carroll, 1996). Outcomes in which CBT may hold particular promise include reducing severity of relapses when they occur (e.g.., Davis & Glaros, 1986; O'Malley et al., 1992; Supnick & Colletti, 1984); enhanced durability of effects (Azrin et al., 1996; Carroll, Rounsaville, Nich et al., 1994; O'Malley et al., 1996); and patient-treatment matching, particularly for patients at higher levels of impairment along dimensions such as psychopathology or dependence severity (e.g., Carroll, Rounsaville, Gordon et al., 1994; Kadden et al., 1989).

STRENGTHS AND WEAKNESSES

Strengths of behavioral and cognitive behavioral approaches were summarized by Rotgers (1996) and include (a) flexibility in meeting individual needs, (b) acceptability to a wide range of substance-abusing individuals seen in clinical settings, (c) solid grounding in established principles of behavior theory and behavior change, (d) an emphasis on linking science to treatment, (e) well-specified treatment goals and clear guidelines for assessing treatment progress, (f) emphasis on building self-efficacy, and (g) a comparatively strong level of empirical support. These approaches are highly flexible and can be used in a number of treatment modalities and settings, can be applied across different types of substance use with minor modifications, and are compatible with a wide range of other treatment approaches, including family therapy and pharmacotherapy. Another advantage is that these approaches have emphasized clear specification of treatment and a variety of manuals are available, thus allowing a high level of technology transfer.

Disadvantages of this group of approaches include (a) a lack of emphasis in the research evaluating these approaches on the importance of isolating and evaluating the specific active ingredients associated with behavior change; (b) comparative underutilization of these approaches outside academic treatment settings (Rotgers, 1996); (c) lack of emphasis on patient motivation and specific procedures for addressing the patient's readiness for change; and (d) a paucity of data on the patient characteristics associated with response to treatment.

SUMMARY

Behavioral and cognitive behavioral treatments have emerged in the last decade as a leading approach to the treatment of substance use disorders. Solidly grounded in well-established principles of behavior change, with strong empirical support, and applicable to a wide range of individuals with substance use disorders, these well-defined approaches should be a part of any clinician's treatment repertoire.

ACKNOWLEDGMENTS Support was provided by NIDA grants RO1 DA10679, P50-DA09241, and K02-DA00248, and NIAAA Cooperative Agreement U10 AA08430.

Key References

Childress, A. R., Ehrman, R., Rohsenow, D. J., Robbins, S. J., & O'Brien, C. P. (1992). Classically conditioned factors in drug dependence. In J. H. Lowinsohn, P. Ruiz, & R. B. Millman (Eds.), Comprehensive textbook of substance abuse (2nd ed., pp. 56–69). New York: Williams & Wilkins.

Higgins, S. T., Delaney, D. D., Budney, A. J., Bickel, W. K., Hughes, J. R., Foerg, F., & Fenwick, J. W. (1991). A behavioral approach to achieving initial cocaine abstinence. American Journal of Psychiatry, 148, 1218–1224.

Rotgers, F. (1996). Behavioral theory of substance abuse treatment: Bringing science to bear on practice. In

F. Rotgers, D. Keller, & J. Morgenstern (Eds.), Treating substance abusers: Theory and Technique (pp. 174–201). NewYork: Guilford Press.

References

Abrams, D. B., Binkoff, J. A. Zwick, W. R., Liepman, M. R., Nirenberg, T. D., Munroe, S. M., & Monti, P. M. (1991). Alcohol abusers' and social drinkers' responses to alcohol-relevant and general situations. Journal of Studies on Alcohol, 52, 409–414.

Aigner, T. G., & Balster, R. L. (1978). Choice behavior in rhesus monkeys: Cocaine versus food. Science, 201, 534–535.

American Psychiatric Association, Work Group on Substance Use Disorders. (1995). Practice guideline for the treatment of patients with substance use disorders: Alcohol, cocaine, opioids. American Journal of Psychiatry, 152(Supplement), 2–59.

Anker, A. L., & Crowley, T. J. (1982). Use of contingency contracts in specialty clinics for cocaine abuse. In L. S. Harris (Ed.), Problems of drug dependence, 1981 (NIDA Research Monograph Series No. 41, pp. 452–459). Rockville, MD: National Institute on Drug Abuse.

Azrin, N. H. (1976). Improvements in the community-reinforcement approach to alcoholism. Behavior Research and Therapy, 14, 339–348.

Azrin, N. H., Acierno, R., Kogan, E. S., Donohue, B., Besalel, V. A., & McMahon, P. T. (1996). Follow-up results of supportive versus behavioral therapy for illicit drug use. Behavior Research and Therapy, 34, 41–46.

Bandura, A. (1977). Self-efficacy: Toward a unifying theory of behavior change. Psychological Review, 84, 191–215.

Beck, A. T., Rush, A. J., Shaw, B. F., & Emery, G. (1979). Cognitive therapy of depression. New York: Guilford Press.

Beck, A. T., Ward, C. H., & Mendelson, M. (1961). An inventory for measuring depression. Archives of General Psychiatry, 4, 461–471.

Beck, A. T., Wright, F. D., Newman, C. F., & Liese, B. S. (1991). Cognitive therapy of cocaine abuse: A treatment manual. (Unpublished manuscript.)

Bigelow, G. E., Stitzer, M. L., & Liebson, I. A. (1984). The role of behavioral contingency management in drug abuse treatment. In J. Grabowski, M. L. Stitzer, & J. E. Henningfield (Eds.), Behavioral intervention techniques in drug abuse treatment (NIDA Research Monograph Series Number 46, pp. 36–52). Rockville, MD: National Institute on Drug Abuse.

Brook, J. S., Cohen, P., Whitman, M., & Gordon, A. S. (1992). Psychosocial risk factors in the transition from moderate to heavy use or abuse of drugs. In M. Glantz & R. Pickens (Eds.), *Vulnerability to drug abuse* (pp. 359–388). Washington, DC: American Psychological Association.

Budney, A. J., & Higgins, S. T. (1998). *A community reinforcement plus vouchers approach: Treating cocaine addiction.* Rockville, MD: National Institute on Drug Abuse.

Cadoret, R. (1992). Genetic and environmental factors in initiation of drug use and the transition to abuse. In M. Glantz & R. Pickens (Eds.), *Vulnerability to drug abuse* (pp. 99–113). Washington, DC: American Psychological Association.

Carey, K. B., & Maisto, S. A. (1985). A review of the use of self-control techniques in the treatment of alcohol abuse. *Cognitive Therapy and Research, 9,* 235–251.

Carroll, K. M. (1996). Relapse prevention as a psychosocial treatment approach: A review of controlled clinical trials. *Experimental and Clinical Psychopharmacology, 4,* 46–54.

Carroll, K. M. (1998). *Treating cocaine dependence: A cognitive behavioral approach.* Rockville, MD: National Institute on Drug Abuse.

Carroll, K. M., Kadden, R., Donovan, D., Zweben, A., & Rounsaville, B. J. (1994). Implementing treatment and protecting the validity of the independent variable in treatment matching studies. *Journal of Studies on Alcohol, Suppl. 12,* 149–155.

Carroll, K. M., Nich, C., Frankforter, T. L., & Bisighini, R. M. (in press). Do patients change in the ways we intend? Assessing acquisition of coping skills among cocaine-dependent patients. *Psychological Assessment.*

Carroll, K. M., Nich, C., & Rounsaville, B. J. (1995). Differential symptom reduction in depressed cocaine abusers treated with psychotherapy and pharmacotherapy. *Journal of Nervous and Mental Disease, 183,* 251–259.

Carroll, K. M., Nich, C., & Rounsaville, B. J. (1997). Contribution of the therapeutic alliance to outcome in active versus control psychotherapies. *Journal of Consulting and Clinical Psychology, 65,* 510–514.

Carroll, K. M., Rounsaville, B. J., Gordon, L. T., Nich, C., Jatlow, P. M., Bisighini, R. M., & Gawin, F. H. (1994). Psychotherapy and pharmacotherapy for ambulatory cocaine abusers. *Archives of General Psychiatry, 51,* 177–187.

Carroll, K. M., Rounsaville, B. J., Nich, C., Gordon, L. T., Wirtz, P. W., & Gawin, F. H. (1994). One year follow-up of psychotherapy and pharmacotherapy for cocaine dependence: Delayed emergence of psychotherapy effects. *Archives of General Psychiatry, 51,* 989–997.

Castonguay, L. G. (1993). "Common factors" and "nonspecific variables": Clarification of the two concepts and recommendations for research. *Journal of Psychotherapy Integration, 3,* 267–286.

Chaney, E. F., O'Leary, M. R., & Marlatt, G. A. (1978). Skill training with problem drinkers. *Journal of Consulting and Clinical Psychology, 46,* 1092–1104.

Childress, A. R., Ehrman, R. N., McLellan, A. T., & O'Brien, C. P. (1988). Conditioned craving and arousal in cocaine addiction: A preliminary report. In L. S. Harris (Ed.), *Problems of drug dependence, 1987* (NIDA Research Monograph Series No. 81, pp. 74–80). Rockville, MD: National Institute on Drug Abuse.

Childress, A. R., Ehrman, R., Rohsenow, D. J., Robbins, S. J., & O'Brien, C. P. (1992). Classically conditioned factors in drug dependence. In J. H. Lowinsohn, P. Ruiz, & R. B. Millman (Eds.), *Comprehensive textbook of substance abuse* (2nd ed., pp. 56–69). New York: Williams & Wilkins.

Childress, A. R., Hole, A. V., Ehrman, R. N., Robbins, S. J., McLellan, A. T., & O'Brien, C. P. (1993). Cue reactivity and cue reactivity interventions in drug dependence. In L. S. Onken, J. D. Blaine, & J. J. Boren (Eds.), *Behavioral treatments for drug abuse and dependence* (NIDA Research Monograph Series No. 137). Rockville, MD: National Institute on Drug Abuse.

Clayton, R. (1992). Transitions in drug use: Risk and protective factors. In M. Glantz & R. Pickens (Eds.), *Vulnerability to drug abuse* (pp. 15–51). Washington, DC: American Psychological Association.

Clifford, P. R., & Longabaugh, R. (1991). *Manual administration of the Important People and Activities Instrument.* Providence, RI: Brown University Center for Alcohol and Addiction Studies.

Condiotte, M. M., & Lichtenstein, E. (1981). Self-efficacy and relapse in smoking cessation programs. *Journal of Consulting and Clinical Psychology, 49,* 648–658.

Connors, G., Carroll, K. M., DiClemente, C. C., Longabaugh, R., & Donovan, D. (1997). The therapeutic alliance and its relationship to alcoholism treatment participation and outcome. *Journal of Consulting and Clinical Psychology, 65,* 588–598.

Cooney, N. L., Kadden, R. M., Litt, M. D., & Getter, H. (1991). Matching alcoholics to coping skills or interactional therapies: Two-year follow-up results. *Journal of Consulting and Clinical Psychol, 59,* 598–601.

Craighead, W. E., Craighead, L. W., & Ilardi, S. S. (1995). Behavioral therapies in historical perspective. In B. Bongar & L. E. Beutler (Eds.), *Comprehensive textbook of psychotherapy: Theory and practice* (pp. 64–83). New York: Oxford University Press.

Crits-Christoph, P., & Siqueland, L. (1996). Psychosocial treatment for drug abuse: Selected review and recommendations for national health care. *Archives of General Psychiatry, 53,* 749–756.

Davis, J. R., & Glaros, A. G. (1986). Relapse prevention and smoking cessation. *Addictive Behaviors, 11,* 105–114.

DeRubeis, R. J., & Crits-Christoph, P. (1998). Empirically-supported individual and group psychological treatments for adult mental disorders. *Journal of Consulting and Clinical Psychology, 66,* 37–52.

DiClemente, C., Carroll, K. M., Connors, G., & Kadden, R. (1994). Process assessment in treatment matching research. *Journal of Studies on Alcohol, Suppl. 12,* 156–162.

DiClemente, C. C., & Hughest, S. O. (1990). Stages of change profiles in alcoholism treatment. *Journal of Substance Abuse, 2,* 217–235.

Dolan, M. P., Black, J. L., Penk, W. E., Rabinowitz, R., & DeFord, H. A. (1985). Contracting for treatment termination to reduce illicit drug use among methadone maintenance treatment failures. *Journal of Consulting and Clinical Psychology, 53,* 549–551.

General Accounting Office. (1996). Cocaine treatment: Early results from various approaches. Washington, DC: Author.

Goldman, M. S., Brown, S. A., & Christiansen, B. A. (1987). Expectancy theory: Thinking about drinking. In H. T. Blane & K. E. Leonard (Eds.), *Psychological theories of drinking and alcoholism.* New York: Guilford Press.

Higgins, S. T., & Budney, A. J. (1993). Treatment of cocaine dependence through the principles of behavior analysis and behavioral pharmacology. In L. S. Onken, J. D. Blaine, & J. J. Boren (Eds.), *Behavioral treatments for drug and alcohol dependence* (NIDA Research Monograph Series, No. 137, pp. 97–121). Rockville, MD: National Institute on Drug Abuse.

Higgins, S. T., Budney, A. J., Bickel, W. K., & Badger, G. J. (1994). Participation of significant others in outpatient behavioral treatment predicts greater cocaine abstinence. *American Journal of Drug and Alcohol Abuse, 20,* 47–56.

Higgins, S. T., Budney, A. J., Bickel, W. K., Badger, G. J., Foerg, F., & Ogden, D. (1995). Outpatient behavioral treatment for cocaine dependence: One-year outcome. *Experimental and Clinical Psychopharmacology, 3,* 205–212.

Higgins, S. T., Budney, A. J., Bickel, W. K., Foerg, F. E., Donham, R., & Badger, G. J. (1994). Incentives improve outcome in outpatient behavioral treatment

of cocaine dependence. *Archives of General Psychiatry, 51,* 568–576.

Higgins, S. T., Budney, A. J., Bickel, W. K., & Hughes, J. R. (1993). Achieving cocaine abstinence with a behavioral approach. *American Journal of Psychiatry, 150,* 763–769.

Higgins, S. T., Delaney, D. D., Budney, A. J., Bickel, W. K., Hughes, J. R., Foerg, F., & Fenwick, J. W. (1991). A behavioral approach to achieving initial cocaine abstinence. *American Journal of Psychiatry, 148,* 1218–1224.

Hodgson, R. J., & Rankin, H. J. (1978). Modification of excessive drinking by cue exposure. *Behavior Research and Therapy, 14,* 305–307.

Holder, H. D., Longabaugh, R., Miller, W. R., & Rubonis, A. V. (1991). The cost effectiveness of treatment for alcohol problems: A first approximation. *Journal of Studies on Alcohol, 52,* 517–540.

Horvath, A. O., & Greenberg, L. (1986). The development of the Working Alliance Inventory. In L. S. Greenberg & W. M. Pinsof (Eds.), *The psychotherapeutic process: A research handbook,* (pp. 529–556). New York: Guilford Press.

Horvath, A. O., & Luborsky, L. (1993). The role of therapeutic alliance in psychotherapy. *Journal of Consulting and Clinical Psychology, 61,* 561–573.

Horvath, A. O., & Symonds, B. D. (1991). Relation between working alliance and outcome in psychotherapy: A meta-analysis. *Journal of Counseling Psychology, 38,* 139–149.

Hunt, G. L., & Azrin, N. H. (1973). A community reinforcement approach to alcoholism. *Behavior Research and Therapy, 11,* 91–104.

Iguchi, M. Y., Lamb, R. J., Belding, M. A., Platt, J. J., Husband, S. D., & Morral, A. R. (1996). Contingent reinforcement of group participation versus abstinence in a methadone maintenance program. *Experimental and Clinical Psychopharmacology, 4,* 1–7.

Kadden, R., Carroll, K. M., Donovan, D., Cooney, N., Monti, P., Abrams, D., Litt, M., & Hester, R. (1992). *Cognitive-behavioral coping skills therapy manual: A clinical research guide for therapists treating individuals with alcohol abuse and dependence.* (NIAAA Project MATCH Monograph Series, Vol. 3, DHHS Publication No. (ADM) 92-1895). Rockville, MD: National Institute on Alcohol Abuse and Alcoholism.

Kadden, R. M., Cooney, N. L., Getter, H., & Litt, M. D. (1989). Matching alcoholics to coping skills or interactional therapies: Posttreatment results. *Journal of Consulting and Clinical Psychology, 57,* 698–704.

Kandel, D., & Faust, R. (1975). Sequence and stages in patterns of adolescent drug use. *Archives of General Psychiatry, 32,* 923–932.

Kandel, D. B., & Logan, J. A. (1984). Patterns of drug use from adolescence to young adulthood: 1. Periods of risk for initiation, continued use, and discontinuation. *American Journal of Public Health, 74,* 660–666.

Kaplan, H. B., & Johson, R. J. (1992). Relationships between circumstances surrounding initial illicit drug use and escalation of drug use: Moderating effects of gender and early adolescent experience. In M. Glantz & R. Pickens (Eds.), *Vulnerability to drug abuse* (pp. 99–113). Washington, DC: American Psychological Association.

Keller, D. S., Carroll, K. M., Nich, C., & Rounsaville, B. J. (1995). Differential treatment response in alexithymic cocaine abusers: Findings from a randomized clinical trial of psychotherapy and pharmacotherapy. *American Journal on Addictions, 4,* 234–244.

Kosten, T. R., Rounsaville, B. J., & Kleber, H. D. (1987). A 2.5 year follow-up of cocaine use among treated opioid addicts: Have our treatments helped? *Archives of General Psychiatry, 44,* 281–284.

Liebson, I. A., Tommasello, A., & Bigelow, G. E. (1978). A behavioral treatment of alcoholic methadone patients. *Annals of Internal Medicine, 89,* 342–344.

Luborsky, L., McLellan, A. T., Woody, G. E., O'Brien, C. P., & Auerbach, A. (1985). Therapist success and its determinants. *Archives of General Psychiatry, 42,* 602–611.

Marlatt, G. A. (1979). Alcohol use and problem drinking: A cognitive-behavioral analysis. In P. C. Kendall & S. D. Hollon (Eds.), *Cognitive-behavioral interventions: Theory, research, and procedures* (pp. 319–355). New York: Academic Press.

Marlatt, G. A., & Gordon, J. R., (Eds.). (1985). *Relapse prevention: Maintenance strategies in the treatment of addictive behaviors.* New York: Guilford Press.

McCarthy, J. J., & Borders, O. T. (1985). Limit setting on drug abuse in methadone maintenance patients. *American Journal of Psychiatry, 142,* 1419–1423.

McKay, J. R., Rutherford, M. J., Alterman, A. I., & Cacciola, J. S. (1996). Development of the cocaine relapse interview: An initial report. *Addiction, 91,* 535–548.

McLellan, A. T., Childress, A. R., O'Brien, C. P., & Ehrman, R. N. (1986). Extinguishing conditioned responses during treatment for opiate dependence: Turning laboratory findings into clinical procedures. *Journal of Substance Abuse Treatment, 3,* 33–40.

McLellan, A. T., Kushner, H., Metzger, D., Peters, R., Smith, I., Grissom, G., Pettinati, H., & Argerious, M. (1992). The fifth edition of the Addiction Severity Index. *Journal of Substance Abuse Treatment, 9,* 199–213.

Megargee, E. I. (1972). *The California Psychological Inventory handbook.* San Francisco: Jossey-Bass.

Meichenbaum, D. H. (1995). Cognitive-behavioral therapy in historical perspective. In B. Bongar & L. E. Beutler (Eds.), *Comprehensive textbook of psychotherapy: Theory and practice* (pp. 140–158). New York: Oxford University Press.

Merikangas, K. R., Rounsaville, B. J., & Prusoff, B. (1992). Familial factors in vulnerability to substance use. In M. Glantz & R. Pickens (Eds.), *Vulnerability to drug abuse* (pp.75–97). Washington, DC: American Psychological Association.

Miller, W. R. (1992). *Stages of Change Readiness and Treatment Eagerness Scale (SOCRATES).* Albuquerque, New Mexico: University of New Mexico, Center on Alcoholism, Substance Abuse and Addictions.

Miller, W. R., & DelBoca, F. K. (1994). Measurement of drinking behavior using the Form 90 Family of Instruments. *Journal of Studies on Alcohol, 12* (Supplement), 112–117.

Monti, P. M., Abrams, D. B., Kadden, R. M., & Cooney, N. L. (1989). *Treating alcohol dependence: A coping skills training guide in the treatment of alcoholism.* New York: Guilford Press.

Monti, P. M., Rohsenow, D., Rubnis, A. V., Niaura, R. S., Sirota, A. D., Colby, S. M., Goddard, R., & Abrams, D. B. (1993). Cue exposure with coping skills treatment for male alcoholics: A preliminary investigation. *Journal of Consulting and Clinical Psychology, 61,* 1011–1019.

Morgan, T. (1996). Behavioral treatment techniques for psychoactive substance use disorders. In F. Rotgers, D. Keller, & J. Morgenstern (Eds.), *Treating substance abusers: Theory and technique* (pp. 202–240). New York: Guilford Press.

Nolimal, D., & Crowley, T. J. (1990). Difficulties in a clinical application of methadone-dose contingency contracting. *Journal of Substance Abuse Treatment, 7,* 219–224.

O'Malley, S. S., Jaffe, A. J., Chang, G., Rode, S., Schottenfeld, R., Meyer, R. E., & Rounsaville, B. J. (1996). Six month follow-up of naltrexone and psychotherapy for alcohol dependence. *Archives of General Psychiatry, 53,* 217–224.

O'Malley, S. S., Jaffe, A. J., Chang, G., Schottenfeld, R. S., Meyer, R. E., & Rounsaville, B. J. (1992). Naltrexone and coping skills therapy for alcohol dependence: A controlled study. *Archives of General Psychiatry, 49,* 881–887.

Pickens, R., Svikis, D., McGue, M., Lykken, D., Heston, M., & Clayton, P. (1991). Heterogeneity in the inheritance of alcoholism: A study of male and female twins. *Archives of General Psychiatry, 48,* 19–28.

Project MATCH Research Group. (1993). Project

MATCH: Rationale and methods for a multisite clinical trial matching alcoholism patients to treatment. *Alcoholism: Clinical and Experimental Research, 17,* 1130–1145.

Project MATCH Research Group. (in press). Therapist effects in three treatments for alcohol problems. *Psychotherapy Research.*

Project MATCH Research Group. (1997). Matching Alcohol Treatments to Client Heterogeneity: Project MATCH posttreatment drinking outcomes. *Journal of Studies on Alcohol, 58,* 7–29.

Rankin, H., Hodgson, R., & Stockwell, T. (1983). Cue exposure and response prevention with alcoholics: A controlled trial. *Behavior Research and Therapy, 21,* 435–446.

Rosenberg, H. (1993). Prediction of controlled drinking by alcoholics and problem drinkers. *Psychological Bulletin, 113,* 129–139.

Rotgers, F. (1996). Behavioral theory of substance abuse treatment: Bringing science to bear on practice. In F. Rotgers, D. Keller, & J. Morgenstern (Eds.), *Treating substance abusers: Theory and technique* (pp. 174–201). New York: Guilford Press.

Rozenzweig, S. (1936). Some implicit common factors in diverse methods of psychotherapy. *American Journal of Orthopsychiatry, 6,* 412–415.

Saxon, A. J., Calsyn, D. A., Kivlahan, D. R., & Roszell, D. K. (1993). Outcome of contingency contracting for illicit drug use in a methadone maintenance program. *Drug and Alcohol Dependence, 31,* 205–214.

Schuster, C. R., & Johanson, C. E. (1974). The use of animal models for the study of drug abuse. In J. Gibbens, Y. Israel, & H. Kalant (Eds.), *Research advances in alcohol and drug problems* (Vol. 1, pp. 1–31). New York: Wiley.

Silverman, K., Higgins, S. T., Brooner, R. K., Montoya, I. D., Cone, E. J., Schuster, C. R., & Preston, K. L. (1996). Sustained cocaine abstinence in methadone maintenance patients through voucher-based reinforcement therapy. *Archives of General Psychiatry, 53,* 409–415.

Sisson, R. W., & Azrin, N. H. (1989). The community reinforcement approach. In R. K. Hester & W. R. Miller (Eds), *Handbook of alcoholism treatment approaches* (pp. 242–258). New York: Pergamon Press.

Sobell, L. C., & Sobell, M. B. (1992). Timeline followback: A technique for assessing self-reported alcohol consumption. In R. Z. Litten & J. P. Allen (Eds.), *Measuring alcohol consumption: Psychosocial and biochemical methods* (pp. 41–72). Totowa, NJ: Humana Press.

Spitzer, R. L., Williams, J. B. W., Gibbon, M., & First, M. B. (1996). *Structured Clinical Interview for DSM-IV-Patient Edition (with Psychotic Screen-Version 1.0).* Washington, DC: American Psychiatric Press.

Stitzer, M. L., Bickel, W. K., Bigelow, G. E., & Liebson, I. A. (1986). Effect of methadone dose contingencies on urinalysis test results of polydrug-abusing methadone maintenance patients. *Drug and Alcohol Dependence, 18,* 341–348.

Stitzer, M. L., & Bigelow, G. E. (1978). Contingency management in a methadone maintenance program: Availability of reinforcers. *International Journal of the Addictions, 13,* 737–746.

Stitzer, M. L., Iguchi, M. Y., & Felch, L. J. (1992). Contingent take-home incentive: Effects on drug use of methadone maintenance patients. *Journal of Consulting and Clinical Psychology, 60,* 927–934.

Stitzer, M. L., Iguchi, M. Y., Kidorf, M., & Bigelow, G. E. (1993). Contingency management in methadone treatment: The case for positive incentives. In L. S. Onken, J. D. Blaine, & J. J. Boren (Eds.), *Behavioral treatments for drug abuse and dependence* (NIDA Research Monograph Series Number 137, pp. 19–36). Rockville, MD: National Institute on Drug Abuse.

Supnick, J. A., & Colletti, G. (1984). Relapse coping and problem solving training following treatment for smoking. *Addictive Behaviors, 9,* 401–404.

Thompson, T., & Pickens, R. W. (Eds.). (1971). *Stimulus properties of drugs.* New York: Appleton-Century-Crofts.

Tiffany, S. T., Singleton, E., Haertzen, C. A., & Henningfield, J. E. (1993). The development of a cocaine craving questionnaire. *Drug and Alcohol Dependence, 34,* 19–28.

Weiss, R. D. (1992). The role of psychopathology in the transition from drug use to abuse and dependence. In M. Glantz & R. Pickens (Eds.), *Vulnerability to drug abuse* (pp. 137–148). Washington, DC: American Psychological Association.

Wikler, A. (1971). Some implications of conditioning theory for problems of drug abuse. *Behavioral Science, 16,* 92–97.

Wikler, A. (1973). Dynamics of drug dependence: Implications of a conditioning theory for research and treatment. *Archives of General Psychiatry, 28,* 611–616.

Wilson, G. R. (1978). Alcoholism and aversion therapy: Issues, ethics, and evidence. In G. A. Marlatt & P. E. Nathan (Eds.), *Behavioral approaches to alcoholism* (pp. 90–113). New Brunswick, NJ: Rutgers Center for Alcohol Studies.

15

The Disease Model

Timothy Sheehan

Patricia Owen

Few would dispute the extent and severity of alcohol and drug dependence in today's society. The problem is widespread. For example, the psychiatric Epidemiological Catchment Program (Robins et al., 1984) reported an estimated 13.7% base rate of alcohol abuse and dependence in the general population. In 1992, the National Institute on Alcohol Abuse and Alcoholism (NIAAA, 1994) reported that 13.8 million Americans had problems with drinking, and in a major population survey (Reiger et al., 1990), substance abuse was identified as the largest category of mental health disorder.

The consequences of alcohol and drug dependence are serious public health problems resulting in medical conditions involving high rates of medical-surgical complications (Loveland-Cook, Booth, Blow, Gogineni, & Bunn, 1992), terminal illness, traumatic injury (Merrill, Fox, & Chang, 1993), emergency room visits (Cherpitel, 1989a, 1989b), suicide (Gomberg, 1989), and violent and homicidal behav-

ior (Pernanen, 1990; Wieczorek, Welte, & Abel, 1990). In fact, nearly one fourth of all persons admitted to general hospitals have alcohol problems or are undiagnosed alcoholics being treated for alcohol-related consequences (Lee, 1993).

Alcohol and drug dependence furthermore poses a public safety threat associated with serious automobile crashes and fatalities (Johnston, 1982). The National Institute on Alcohol Abuse and Alcoholism (1993) reported that approximately 50% of automobile crashes in 1989 were alcohol-related.

How do we explain the ravages of this problem? Can it be a simple matter of willful behavior or the results of a bad habit? How do we explain the prevalence of this problem even in the face of repeated serious personal and social consequences?

The disease model contends that alcoholism and drug dependence are not a matter of willpower nor the result of a deeply ingrained habit of recurrent excessive consumption. At the heart of the disease model is the fundamental tenet that alcohol and drug dependence is a physical illness. The disease is neither the end result nor the symptom of another disorder but a primary, progressive, chronic illness. Rather than a singular personality disorder or maladaptive learned behavior, alcohol and drug dependence involves the biological fabric of the individual and eventually impacts every phase of the afflicted person's life. As a result, the disease model represents a comprehensive explanatory concept that encompasses the social, psychological, spiritual, and biological dimensions of alcohol and drug dependence. Born from the clinical efforts of those who treated alcoholism and those who suffered from it, the disease model represents a combination of grassroots practicality and scientific endeavor.

This chapter provides a comprehensive overview of the basic tenets of the disease model, including definitions and terms, etiological hypotheses, and theoretical constructs. Treatment approaches and processes are also addressed, with careful consideration of the conceptual underpinnings of the 12 steps of Alcoholics Anonymous (1955) as a behavior change model. Historically, a form of treatment called the *Minnesota model* was developed to address the disease of alcohol and drug dependence, incorporating some of the major components of Alcoholics Anonymous (Spicer, 1993). This model was initially conceptualized at a small state hospital in Willmar, Minnesota, and was transported and fully developed at a private nonprofit residential program in Minnesota called Hazelden. From there, this model became prevalent in treatment programs across the United States, and in other countries (Fuller, 1989; Spicer, 1993). Project MATCH (Project MATCH Research Group, 1997) worked with staff at Hazelden to develop a manualized version of the Minnesota model and called it the 12-step facilitation model (Nowinski, Baker, & Carroll, 1992). The overarching feature of this model, however termed, is that it provides the vehicle by which individuals initiate pervasive, ongoing lifestyle changes that support continuous abstinence. Several recent studies have been done to define the main curative factors of the disease model in more depth (e.g., Miller & Kurtz, 1994; Morgenstern & McCrady, 1992). The purpose of this chapter is to examine the nature of alcohol and drug dependence, and its treatment, from a disease model perspective.

HISTORY AND ORIGIN: DISEASE MODEL

As early as the 18th century, Benjamin Rush, founder of modern psychiatry, described alcoholism as an illness that "resembles certain hereditary, family, and contagious diseases" (Keller, 1986, p. 27). The concept of disease is broadly defined as disregulation of homeostasis resulting in a predictable constellation of disabling symptoms. Since causes of disease are often speculative or unknown, a disease can be best understood in terms of its biological basis and symptomatic manifestations. Engels (1977) expanded the biomedical concept of disease to include psychological, cultural, and social implications affecting the individual's susceptibility and treatment response. Referring to disease as a biopsychosocial phenomenon, Engels advocated a comprehensive conceptualization of disease both to explain the multifaceted components of illness and to expand the scope of treatment to multimodel approaches.

Lewis (1994) compared alcoholism to other diseases such as essential hypertension and cardiac disease, that are not solely biological in nature and that interface with environmental risks for onset and progression. Like alcoholism, both of these medical conditions are affected by personality and lifestyle and also have genetic contributions in terms of etiology. The exact biological etiology for most chronic diseases, like alcoholism, are unknown. A biopsychosocial model of disease has greater potential for explaining and understanding disease entities while providing a broader base for effective intervention, often including behavioral or lifestyle changes.

Early Development of the Disease Model

Pioneers of the disease model (Jellinek, 1946; Silkworth, 1939); provided a theory based on traditional biological concepts of disease while stressing the psychological, spiritual, and social ramifications of both the illness and the process of recovery. Silkworth (1939) described alcohol dependence as an illness characterized by an atypical physiological reaction to alcohol that triggers a mental obsession. The mental obsession fuels a physical demand for alcohol consumption in spite of problematic consequences or strong intentions to cut back or quit altogether. Silkworth purported that alcoholics could not resume normal drinking since the root cause of the disease involved a physical allergy to alcohol.

Silkworth's early work was not limited solely to the biology of alcohol dependence. He also described the psychological aspects of craving: restlessness, irritability, and tension. Furthermore, he described the mental anguish of the alcoholic faced with an inability to reduce or stop drinking. Silkworth contended that only a pervasive personality change would alleviate the emotional turmoil and spiritual bankruptcy of the alcoholic. This transformation, described by William James as quoted in *Alcoholics Anonymous* (1955), involved a gradual yet significant change in consciousness, or a spiritual awakening.

Jellinek (1946, 1960) elaborated on the disease model by addressing its physiological dimensions, the progression of the disease, and a classification of disease typologies. Like Silkworth (1939), Jellinek (1946) contended that the alcoholic experienced an atypical response to alcohol involving an internal tension and craving that eventually led to an involuntary loss of control over drinking behavior. Jellinek hypothesized an X factor that predisposed the afflicted individual to uncontrolled drinking, in comparison to the heavy drinker. Using a survey of approximately 2,000 alcoholics, Jellinek differentiated heavy drinkers from alcoholics based on a predictable progression of symptoms.

Stages of alcoholism described by Jellinek (1946) included the symptomatic phase, the prodromal phase, the crucial phase, and the chronic phase. The prealcoholic symptomatic phase is characterized by the initial rewarding qualities of drinking behavior. The alcoholic perceives a reduction in tension as the result of drinking. Subsequently, the alcoholic's drinking progresses from occasional to more continuous relief drinking. During the symptomatic phase, there is an increase in tolerance as more alcohol is needed for its sedative effect.

As the individual engages in more continuous relief drinking, excessive quantities of alcohol are consumed, yet there may be few overt signs of intoxication. Periodically, the individual is unable to recall or account for selected intervals of time. There is no memory regarding certain behavior patterns or events. These blackouts or circumscribed periods of amnesia are symptomatic of the prodromal phase. Other concurrent progressive symptoms include drinking to feel normal, preoccupation with alcohol,

rapid consumption for relief, and lingering feelings of guilt.

In the crucial phase, the involuntary loss of control over drinking behavior becomes overt, as drinking sets off a chain reaction involving a physical demand for continued alcohol consumption. It becomes increasingly difficult to predict periods of abstinence or intoxication. The crucial phase involves hypervigilance, rationalization, and periods of remorse. There are likely to be concerted efforts to control drinking behavior by abstaining from alcohol for periods of time, changing patterns and times of drinking, or switching brands or types of alcohol consumed. The alcoholic develops a lifestyle centered on alcohol.

The chronic phase is characterized by the presentation of symptoms of the first four stages, in addition to prolonged periods of intoxication that result in ethical deterioration, severe memory dysfunction, physical traumas, and irrational fears. The chronic phase is associated with deterioration in both occupational and social functioning. During the chronic phase, the alcoholic may no longer be able to maintain interpersonal relationships or vocational productivity. Unless the alcoholic is treated, the chronic stage results in severe irreversible disability or death.

Jellinek's description of the progressive nature of the disease provides both a rationale for clinical intervention and an impetus for further research and theoretical elaboration. Jellinek (1960) was not dogmatic but contended that definitions and theories of alcoholism were likely to change as additional knowledge was gained.

Current Status of the Model

Advances in explaining the pathophysiology of alcoholism have addressed the correlation between biological dysfunction and drinking or using behavior. In particular, neurobiological and neurobehavioral explanations of addiction have been proposed in accordance with the disease model. Several researchers have continued the exploration of the progression of symptoms, as first delineated by Jellinek (1946, 1960). For example, Schuckit, Smith, Anthenelli, and Irwin (1993) studied 636 male alcoholic inpatients in a Veterans Administration hospital to determine the course of the development of their alcoholism. These researchers found a common constellation of symptoms, unfolding in a fairly consistent pattern, and concluded, "The evidence of a general progression of alcohol-related life problems is consistent with the prior research by Jellinek as well as the several additional attempts to replicate his earlier findings" (p. 790). The authors, however, were unsettled as to whether the predictable progression of symptoms actually signaled a disease and instead referred to it as a "diagnosable clinical syndrome" (p. 791).

More recent studies in the field of neurology have been able to demonstrate that alcohol and drug dependence is best characterized as a disease. In his study of molecular and cellular changes in neural function produced by chronic drug use, Hyman (1996) found that brain cells adapt to the introduction of chemicals. He suggested that the disease of addiction involves the excessive bombardment of the brain by drugs causing long-line molecular adaptations that usurp the functioning of critical pathways in the brain that control motivated behavior. Hyman (1995) concluded that "alcoholism is a brain disease that markedly impairs a person's ability to control his or her drug-seeking behavior" (p. 841).

Leshner, building on Hyman's and others' biochemical discoveries, wrote a seminal article titled, "Addiction Is a Brain Disease and It Matters" (1997). In this article, he proposed that at some point during drug use, because of drug-induced cellular adaptation, a metaphorical molecular "switch" signals a change from use or abuse to addiction. At this point, the brain becomes fundamentally altered, producing drug effects and behavior that are quite different from the "predisease" state. Leshner's article is particularly important because he stressed the importance of removing the stigma and moral overtones from the conceptualization of addiction.

In treatment, the disease model is used to teach the alcohol- or drug-dependent person that she or he has a treatable illness. While, because it is a disease, there is no blame placed on the individual, it is made clear that the patient has a responsibility for recovery—just as a person does with any other disease. The concept of alcohol and drug dependence as a disease is a foundation of the Minnesota model of treatment.

ETIOLOGY OF THE DISEASE

If addiction results from cellular adaptation, a question remains about variable predisposition. It may be that any individual who uses a particular chemical with enough regularity will develop the necessary cellular adaptation to acquire the disease. However, it may be that some people are particularly prone to (a) seeking out and ingesting chemicals and/or (b) acquiring cellular adaptation resulting from use. Research in this area has been focused on the question "If alcohol/drug dependence is genetic, what exactly is transmitted to offspring through genetic material?" Note that because alcohol is a legal and rather ubiquitous substance, most research in this area pertains to alcohol dependence (alcoholism) rather than drug dependence.

It has been hypothesized that alcoholism is the end product of a genetically linked process affecting disregulation of arousal, resulting in behavioral correlates of overactivity, anxiety, and tension (Tarter, Alterman, & Edwards, 1988). Early-stage relief drinking (Jellinek, 1960) lessens anxiety by its pharmacological effects on the noradrenergic system (Samson & Hoffman, 1995). Individuals with a genetic dysregulation of stress and emotionality may experience alcohol differently from nonalcoholics and are thus predisposed to risk (Anton, Kranzler, & Meyer, 1995).

Neurobiological theories are based on research examining the dynamics of reinforcement, tolerance, and physical dependence. In a review of the literature, Meyer (1995) cited a relationship between genetically determined neuronal sensitivity to the aversive and reinforcing effects of alcohol and the progression of alcohol dependence. Typical brain pathology associated with the reinforcing effects of alcohol intensifies the rewarding results. Tolerance to alcohol develops as the altered physiology filters the aversive qualities of excessive consumption. The reinforcing qualities of alcohol predominate as more alcohol is consumed. Neuronal dysregulation provides unreliable cues to modulate drinking behavior (Tabakoff & Hoffmann, 1988).

Since the Victorian era, alcoholism has been thought to run in families. However, these observations were rarely more than speculation, since shared environment could also explain the familial pattern (Petrakis, 1985). In 1944, Jellinek, using a review of the literature, speculated that alcoholism was not genetically transmitted but socially transmitted to vulnerable individuals. Jellinek theorized that the alcoholic inherited a physical constitution that left him or her susceptible to the social risk of alcohol dependence.

While neurobehavioral and neurobiological processes involving stress reduction or exaggerated rewarding effects may interact to create risk, additional factors are likely to play a role in the onset and maintenance of the disease (Anton et al., 1995). For instance, impulsivity is a key characteristic of many alcoholics (Babor et al., 1992; Cloninger, 1987). Serotonergic defects may result in increased impulsivity and may contribute to early onset of alcoholism in at-risk populations (Coccaro & Murphy, 1990). Likewise, alcohol craving may resemble obsessive-compulsive phenomena, where preoccupation with alcohol exists even in the absence of alcohol or related drinking cues. Thus, neurotransmitter dysregulation may play a multifaceted role in the onset, development, and progression of alcoholism (Anton et al., 1995).

While the etiology of alcoholism is multifactorial, involving culture, heredity, economics, and environmental influence, gene contribution may weigh heavily in the equation (Valliant, 1995). Since World War II, there has been mounting evidence supporting a genetic predisposition as a causal factor (Bleuler, 1955; Cotton, 1979). Researchers have relied on twin, family pedigree, and adoption studies to differentiate the effects of similar family environment and the proportional contributions of genes. For example, Cotton (1979) reviewed 39 studies on the heredity of alcoholism involving 6,251 alcoholic and 4,083 nonalcoholic families. Data from these studies indicated that alcoholics were more likely than nonalcoholics to have an alcoholic father, mother, sibling, or distant relative. Approximately one third from any of the samples studied showed that alcoholics had at least one parent who was also alcoholic.

Cadoret (1990) found a greater concordance for alcoholism among identical twins than among fraternal twins in a reevaluation of 13 published twin studies. These studies pointed to a trend suggesting that genes play a role in determining vulnerability for alcoholism and influence the frequency and quantity of drinking behavior.

In a review of adoption and twin studies from Scandinavia and the United States, Heath (1995) reevaluated the relative contributions of genes and shared environment to the development of alcoholism. Consistent evidence was found to support an important genetic influence on alcoholism risk involving men and women. Trends were identified cross-culturally and across different time intervals extending from twins born in the 1920s to twins born as late as 1967. The degree of genetic influence was also consistent in spite of different sampling methods and variability in the progression and severity of alcoholism among study subjects.

Research supporting genetic contributions to alcoholism risk provides an important dimension to the disease model. Evidence of genetic influence implies a predetermined biological vulnerability that suggests a causal link between heredity and the pathophysiology of alcohol and drug dependence. Proponents of the disease model believe that the results of such research place alcohol and drug dependence outside the realm of purely a learned behavior and instead substantiate its disease status.

MAINTENANCE OF THE DISEASE

In addition to the reinforcing qualities of alcohol that perpetuate its use (Koob & Bloom, 1988), the disease is maintained by the emergence of an elaborate defense system that essentially denies the severity of drinking or using behavior and its consequences. The defense system is characterized by attempts to minimize the amounts of alcohol or drugs consumed, rationalize problems it has engendered, and blame others for the use behavior. Intimidation, angry defensiveness, manipulation, and oppositional behavior may be used as methods to stave off intervention that disrupts access to and continued use of alcohol or other drugs (Levy, 1993; Metzger, 1988). The defense system of denial shelters the afflicted individual from reality, thereby masking harmful consequences of substance abuse and dependence. As a result, change is rarely self-initiated and is more often the result of situational stresses that provide the necessary motivation to seek assistance (FitzGerald, 1988).

One might assume that the progression of the disease into greater severity and chronicity would naturally propel an individual away from denial into reality. In fact, there are three main factors that contribute to the maintenance of the disease and the defense system: physiological changes in the individual; behavioral conditioning; and homeostatic social systems. From a physiological point of view, an individual may continue his or her use, at least in the short term, in order to avoid withdrawal symptoms and to quell craving (Beck, Wright, Newman, & Liese, 1993). However, some drugs of abuse (e.g., marijuana) do not produce extreme craving and withdrawal symptoms immediately upon discontinuation. Or for drugs that do produce immediate withdrawal symptoms, the symptoms are often short-lived and can be dealt with by medications. Rarely, however, does simple detoxification end the cycle of addiction. What may be more important—is if indeed the brain is fundamentally altered, as proposed by current neuroscientists (Hyman, 1996; Leshner, 1997)—the individual may no longer be able to experience normal reward states without chemicals. It may be that the altered brain state leads to what is termed *loss of control* (i.e., the inability to accurately predict when ingestion of a chemical will stop, once begun). In the disease model, this is a hallmark symptom.

Behavioral theorists describe alcohol and drug dependence as being maintained by reinforcement, either by the chemical itself or by stimuli in the environment prompting alcohol/drug use (Froelich & Li, 1991; Miller & Brown, 1997). Sometimes, the cues for use may be a combination of external stimuli and internal (cognitive) stimuli. For example, it is well known that addicts who return to their using environment after a long period of abstinence will experience strong feelings of craving, which make relapse more likely than if that environment is avoided. In this case, the familiar environment associated with using pairs with self-statements about desire to use or ability to cope (Beck et al., 1993). In the conceptualization of the 12-step model, this is known as the danger of "people, places, and things" associated with using in propelling a person into relapse (Nowinski, Baker, & Carroll, 1995).

Another factor that often maintains the disease is the behavior of family and friends. Families often develop defense systems around the disease, normalizing the alcohol- or drug-dependent's behavior. Partners, other family members, and friends develop their own behaviors that may inadvertently act as triggers for use or make it more likely that the using patterns will continue (Noel, McCrady, Stout, & Nelson, 1987; Wegscheider Cruse, 1989). Part of the treatment process includes helping significant others identify their own issues and behaviors surrounding the alcoholic and addict, and to make changes. Some disease model programs conceptualize or describe this as *codependency* (Morgenstern & McCrady, 1992).

An important aspect of Minnesota model treatment is teaching the individual to recognize internal and external factors that actively maintain the disease, and to make personal and lifestyle changes to address these factors. An important component of the disease model is that a patient is never fully cured; that is, because of the brain's fundamental change in how alcohol or other drugs are processed, the individual may never safely use again. This can be understood as the maintenance phase in stages-of-change theory (Prochaska, DiClementi, & Norcross, 1992), during which time the individual actively practices certain behaviors to decrease the likelihood of relapse into active addiction.

RATIONALE FOR HOW THE DISEASE MODEL OF TREATMENT FOLLOWS FROM THE THEORY

From the above discussion on the origin and maintenance of the disease, it is clear that alcohol and drug dependence is complex and multifaceted. It follows, then, that the treatment of it must also be comprehensive. By the time an individual presents with a full-blown dependency disorder, there are likely to be consequences and complications in all spheres of his or her life: biological, intrapersonal, psychosocial, and mental health.

Biologically, the person may experience withdrawal symptoms for varying lengths of time and of varying intensity. Withdrawal medications may be indicated. During this time, the person may still be physically uncomfortable and find it difficult to concentrate on standard treatment components. Craving may also be present, even after the withdrawal, again distracting the person from a focus on learning and practicing lifestyle changes. Finally, serious biomedical complications may be present stemming from the deleterious effects of the alcohol or drug use, ranging from relatively acute states (e.g., fractures or lesions from falls, fights, or accidents, out-of-control secondary diseases such as diabetes or hypertension due to alcohol/drug use) or chronic states (e.g., liver impairment, compromised cognitive functioning, acquired disease such as HIV).

From an intrapersonal standpoint there are likely to be problems with (a) treatment resistance based on denial, (b) understanding the extent and severity of the problem, and (c) initiating attitudinal and lifestyle changes consistent with continuous abstinence (Levy, 1993; Metzger, 1988). In fact, denial may be maintained to forestall the impact of the realization of how extensive the problem is and the magnitude of the changes that must be made. These intrapersonal issues are not generally viewed as an insurmountable barrier to treatment and instead often become the starting point for treatment.

From a psychosocial perspective, there are likely to be problems with (a) remorse and shame; (b) hopelessness; (c) daily coping skills involving self-assertion and stress-management, and expressing negative emotion; (d) negotiating healthy interpersonal relationships; (e) loss and unresolved grief from drinking-related issues; (f) spiritual conflict involving basic human values; and (g) vocational discord (Fitz-Gerald, 1988).

Comorbid mental health complications are relatively common (Valliant, 1995). For example, there appears to be a strong association between major depression and alcoholism. Both tend to run in families and can co-occur in the same person (Merikangas & Gelernter, 1990). In fact, the prevalence of comorbid mental health complications may be as high as one third of the substance dependence population over the life span (Robins et al., 1984). Diagnostic scrutiny is warranted to avoid (a) premature diagnosis and unnecessary treatment and (b) failure to identify and treat mental disorders that will impede treatment response and contribute to relapse (Anton et al., 1995; Liskow, Powell, Nickel, & Penick, 1990).

The sum total of biological, intrapersonal, and psychosocial and mental health implications demands a comprehensive approach. Failure to consider social and environmental support for recovery, interpersonal conflict, comorbid conditions, and psychosocial stressors results in an incomplete approach to the complexity of the disease process. Treatment methods are planned based on the individual's capacity to integrate new learning and practice newly learned behavior. Neither a singular approach nor discipline is adequate; rather, multidisciplinary team is warranted composed of counselors, physicians, nurses, psychologists, and chaplains. The Minnesota model is characterized by a holistic approach that relies on a multidisciplinary team for the assessment, planning, and delivery of treatment services. Aspects of the treatment, related to aspects of the theory, are listed below.

Physical Health Care

Physicians and nurses must ensure a safe transition from toxicity to abstinence. Symptoms are medically monitored and withdrawal protocols established to reduce seizure risk, promote physical comfort, and prevent related complications (Sheehan & Garretson, 1994). Medical conditions that have been ignored, masked, or exacerbated by excessive, recurrent consumption are diagnosed and treated. In the disease model of treatment, the goal is to stabilize the individual's physical state so that she or he can be more available for the treatment process. Stabilization is not the sole end product of treatment itself.

Mental Health Care

Psychologists identify individual differences relevant to treatment planning and continued treatment. Psychological assessment is used to measure and identify (a) intellectual functioning, (b) personality characteristics, and (c) mental disorder. Intelligence tests and neuropsychological measures are employed to evaluate cognitive skills and impairment, while objective personality tests are routinely used to identify individual traits and characteristics relevant to treatment response. Psychiatrists and psychologists work as a team in assessing, diagnosing, and treating concurrent mental health complications. Comorbid conditions are treated concurrently. Psychotherapy and nonaddictive psychotropic medications may be used. In the disease model, mental health issues are identified and addressed with the goal of helping the person understand what aspects of his or her personality (or actual disorders) may leave him or her vulnerable to relapse, as well as to identify and build on personal strengths.

Spiritual Care

Spirituality is facilitated by chaplains specially trained in clinical pastoral chemical dependence counseling. Spiritual care fosters the development of a synergistic personal belief system by aiding individuals in examining their values and standards for behavior. Spirituality provides the basis for ethical living and behavior change while addressing life's difficult questions that are not easily answered by science and reason alone. Chaplains facilitate individual pastoral counseling and group sessions and frequently provide intensive grief work for those individuals coping with losses often related to the consequences of alcohol and drug dependence. From the perspective of the disease model, people who have struggled with alcohol/drug dependency for years have often abandoned values and connections they once felt important. Finding meaning and strength beyond willpower—the power of fellowship of the group or the power of peace in a meditative state, for example—helps the person learn new ways of living without chemicals.

Chemical Dependency Counseling

Chemical dependence counselors function as primary therapists by providing the core of treatment services through a continuum of assessment, treatment planning, and individual and group counseling. Assessment and treatment entail data collection and diagnosis and include the development of treatment strategies that promote behavior change through individual and group counseling methods. The counselor coaches, mentors, and teaches by taking an active role as a change agent. Because the disease model holds that alcohol and drug dependence is a primary disorder (not a symptom of another disorder), it follows that the chemical dependency counselor is the primary caregiver on the team.

THERAPEUTIC CHANGE: ASSUMPTIONS ABOUT HOW PEOPLE CHANGE

Therapeutic change is based on three modes of intervention that build on the methodology of the 12 steps of Alcoholics Anonymous: education, therapy, and fellowship. Education provides the informational basis for self-understanding, skill training, and attitudinal changes. Individual and group therapy address the emotional conflicts that impede behavior change and promote the development of adaptive skills in coping with negative emotion. Fellowship is the interpersonal value of self-help that builds a common motivational effort to modify self-defeating behavior, gain support for ongoing change, and establish resources for continuous learning. While the Minne-

sota model was initially developed for use in a residential setting, it can be easily implemented in a hospital or outpatient setting. For outpatients, resources in the community or an adjoining residential/hospital treatment center may be used to augment outpatient resources.

KEY INTERVENTIONS IN THE MODEL

The multidisciplinary team works cooperatively to develop an individualized plan of care that is coordinated by the primary therapist (chemical dependence counselor). Counseling services use the methodology of the 12 steps of Alcoholics Anonymous to facilitate attitudinal, affective, and behavior change. Personal application of each step is measured by the parameters established in the treatment plan and is evaluated based on overt observations of anticipated changes in affect, attitude, and behavior. Treatment strategies are modified according to individual clinical needs and treatment response.

Cross-discipline key clinical processes are the avenues by which services are delivered. Each clinical process correlates with a stage of developmental change (Prochaska et al., 1992). At Hazelden, the Minnesota model is conceptualized as involving five key clinical processes: preentry, intake, assessment and care planning, care, and continuing care.

Preentry services help prepare individuals contemplating change or involvement in clinical services through educational information, emotional support, and referral.

Intake addresses the initial stage of problem recognition and transition from contemplation to taking action by identifying initial motivating factors. Intake typically (a) prioritizes presenting problems, (b) provides intervention for urgent clinical needs, and (c) facilitates transition to treatment.

Assessment and care planning entail a comprehensive evaluation of the biopsychosocial elements of the disease through an alcohol and drug assessment, a social history, a psychological evaluation, a spiritual care consultation, and a physical examination. An outcome of the assessment process is a clinical formulation that provides a comprehensive description of the clinical issues that will serve as a basis for ongoing treatment planning. Treatment planning is a highly individualized process based on the supposition that the disease is superimposed over a widely varying population. Individual differences among substance abusers include cultural influences, personality characteristics, socioeconomic backgrounds, learning styles, cognitive impairment, and psychiatric complications. As a result, treatment approaches are tailored to match the presenting clinical needs of the individual.

Care processes promote active engagement in attitude and behavior change by implementing the treatment plan. The treatment plan is a blueprint for intervention, based on a developmental approach of gradual increments of self-awareness, new learning, emotional stability, and behavior change.

Continuing care involves both ongoing care planning and specific services. A continuing-care plan entails those services necessary to facilitate adjustment to sober living posttreatment. Less intensive intervention continues, involving referral to AA, individual counseling, and in some cases, halfway house placement. Several research studies have found that AA attendance following treatment is predictive of better outcomes (Montgomery, Miller, & Tonigan, 1995; Morgenstern, LaBouvie, McCrady, Kahler, & Frey, 1997; Tonigan, Toscova, & Miller, 1996).

Assessment Procedures

Assessment of alcohol and drug abuse and dependence is an integrated process involving patient self-report, input from significant others and related sources, objective measures, and clinical observation. An important aspect of the disease model is the understanding that the patient is the primary source of information about his or her alcohol/drug history. In the disease model, the patient is treated as an intelligent, capable person in the process who is—or soon will be—responsible for choices about his or her care. There is a decided preference for believing the patient, recognizing that time and education are likely to facilitate better recall and more thorough self-report. As a result, a number of assessment methods are employed, including collateral information and, at times, drug testing, but the patient is in most cases the best source of information (Room, 1991). A systematic clinical interview is the basis for patient self-report. First, an alcohol and drug use history questionnaire is completed. The history provides an account of the type, rate, and frequency of drug and alcohol use starting chronologically from the first us-

ing episode. Next, the self-report history is reviewed with the primary therapist to aid in evaluating indicators of loss of control, continued use in spite of negative consequences, social and/or vocational dysfunction, and evidence of change in tolerance. Criteria from the fourth edition of the *Diagnostic and Statistical Manual of Mental Disorders* (*DSM-IV*; American Psychiatric Association, 1994) are formated to provide a semistructured interview allowing the clinician to assess diagnostically significant data. Frequently, the Jellinek chart, a self-administered inventory, is used to map the progression of symptoms, providing a counseling vehicle for further assessment and patient education.

Biological markers involving acute effects of alcohol toxicity (elevated liver enzymes) and/or longer term alcohol- and drug-related complications (peripheral neuropathy, secondary hypertension) are used as objective measures to help substantiate the extent and severity of alcohol and drug use.

Psychological data are employed to evaluate and describe alcohol- or drug-related symptoms. For example, neuropsychological screening results may be used to assess cognitive impairment. Other measures are used to evaluate the likelihood and nature of alcohol and drug dependence, such as the Alcohol Severity Index (ASI; McLellan, Luborsky, Woody, O'Brien, & Druley, 1983).

Treatment Ingredients, Structure, Goals, and Approaches

The clinical process of care intensively addresses the application of the 12 steps through a carefully planned treatment strategy to promote therapeutic change. Each step encompasses specific milestones that help individuals interpret and operationalize the step as a guide for living. Individual and group counseling techniques such as person-centered, cognitive behavioral, or existential approaches are employed to (a) heighten individual understanding of each step and its ramification for change; (b) reduce obstacles to continued progress; (c) resolve risk factors for relapse; and (d) mobilize potential strengths. Progress is measured by observations of attitudinal, affective, and/or behavioral change consistent with anticipated outcomes from the individual treatment plan.

Treatment approaches are designed to promote access to and participation in 12-step self-help groups posttreatment. A foundation is laid for lifelong skills that build on input and support from recovering peers as a relapse prevention strategy. Since there is no biological cure, consistent maintenance of behavior change is required to prevent relapse.

Self-Discovery

Initial treatment goals focus on recognition and acceptance of the problem. Since an elaborate defense system of denial maintains the progression of the illness, educational interventions are needed to promote self-discovery. Treatment interventions are likely to include psychoeducational services, such as bibliotherapy, group instruction, and lectures that explain the dynamics of alcohol and drug dependence. Data from the alcohol and drug assessment are used to identify self-defeating consequences such as relationship problems, vocational difficulties and medical complications. The initial stage of counseling is designed to promote acceptance of the illness, recognition of the need for help, and development of a motivational foundation for continued change. These psychological tasks or milestones assist the individual in understanding and applying Step 1 from *Alcoholics Anonymous* (1955), which reads, "We admitted we were powerless over alcohol—that our lives had become unmanageable" (p. 59).

The first step has two parts. The first phrase refers to the involuntary loss of control over alcohol and provides the rationale for continuous abstinence. The second component refers to the devastating consequences of the disease. *Unmanageability* is the term used to refer to the personal, emotional, social, and vocational problems engendered by recurrent excessive consumption.

To help personalize Step 1, the individual is given an opportunity to tell his or her story to a peer group of newly recovering individuals. The story traces major life developments beginning with formative years, first drinking episodes, and the progression of drinking behavior and its effects on interpersonal relationships, family, and vocational development. The story provides a common ground that promotes fellowship and support for change as similarities are identified. It is this process of shared fellowship that provides the basis for self-help.

Anticipated outcomes of Step 1 treatment methods typically involve (a) self-awareness concerning the extent and severity of drinking behavior and its self-defeating consequences; (b) cost-benefit analysis

of continued addictive behavior in comparison to behavior change necessary for recovery; (c) recognition that alcoholism is a disease, beyond the control of normal willpower; (d) reduction of shame and self-blame as behavior dysfunction is attributed to disease; and (e) recognition of the need for help from others in order to effect behavior change.

Self-Efficacy

The next stage in the process of care builds self-efficacy by focusing on Step 2 of Alcoholics Anonymous. Step 2 counseling emphasizes the restorative nature of recovery by facilitating hope for change. Since the control of drinking is not self-regulated, alternative resources are needed to avoid addictive behaviors. During this stage, there is an emphasis on the individual's capacity to recover by accessing resources beyond the limits of oneself. For example, treatment methods may include a daily journal of positive events, daily meditation, or reading selections from *Alcoholics Anonymous* (1955).

Alcoholics Anonymous (1939, 1955), one of the first self-help books, was written by recovering alcoholics. The first five chapters provide a hands-on approach to coping with daily stressors without drinking. The remaining chapters provide an avenue for personal identification with biographical stories of recovery. Other sources of bibliotherapy are used as well, sometimes to enrich the application of the principles of *Alcoholics Anonymous* (1955) for select populations, such as the *Dual Disorder Recovery Book* (1993) or *Women's Way Through the 12 Steps* (Covington, 1994).

It is during this stage that the concept of a Higher Power is introduced. A Higher Power represents a positive resource that potentially impacts the quality of one's life. Rather than emphasizing institutionalized belief systems or dogma, spirituality is a self-defined, highly personalized experience. For some, it is a supernatural source while for others a Higher Power may be a therapeutic support group, a counselor, or AA itself. For most, it is a combination of a spiritual understanding that helps shape and give meaning to life with the aid and support of other recovering peers.

Anticipated outcomes from Step 2 treatment activities involve the development of a realistic optimism concerning the capacity to recover by accessing available resources. There are self-reports of hope for a better quality of life and an emerging mental picture of a lifestyle free of alcohol and drugs. Emotionally, there is less cynicism and the beginnings of a stronger self-image and self-esteem. Behaviorally, the individual is typically more inclined to avoid social isolation. There is planned quiet time for reflection or meditation as a daily discipline.

Taking Action

Individual and group counseling that help facilitate transition from Step 2 to Step 3 focus on the development of trust. During this stage, behavioral recommendations may focus on social skills assignments that involve self-disclosures and risk-taking behaviors in the practice of newly learned behavioral skills. Steps 1 and 2 of Alcoholics Anonymous provide the attitudinal foundation for change through self-assessment and education, while Step 3 focuses on taking assertive action in response to newly formed or reaffirmed beliefs, expectations, and values. Step 3 of Alcoholics Anonymous reads, "Made a decision to turn our will and our lives over to the care of God *as we understood Him.*"

From a therapeutic vantage, this step signifies a number of changes. First, the individual makes a conscious decision to trust emerging values that will eventually help shape daily decisions and actions. Next, the step connotes a willingness to trust this evolving spirituality to the extent that the individual is willing to relinquish his or her dysfunctional modes of maladaptive functioning in favor of suggested methods of recovery.

It is also during this stage that introspection and self-responsibility are stressed. Early in treatment, people often blame others for the etiology or maintenance of their disease. Treatment methods are designed to help shift the focus from blame to personal responsibility. Use of AA slogans as self-statements, such as "Easy does it," are taught and reinforced to promote self-regulation of hyperarousal or reactivity to environmental cues. Treatment assignments may involve consciously applying AA slogans as a method to modulate emotionality and increase awareness of behavioral coping options. Likewise, the Serenity Prayer serves a similar function: "God grant me the serenity to accept the things I cannot change, courage to change the things I can, and wisdom to know the difference." The Serenity Prayer provides a spiritually oriented cognition that promotes realistic appraisal of potentially problematic situations. It aids in the evaluation of actions that could be constructively taken while also recognizing limitations of one's capacity to exert influence or control.

Counseling and treatment approaches associated with Step 3 are action-oriented. Counseling techniques such as cognitive restructuring are sometimes employed to challenge self-defeating attitudes, in an effort to develop and reinforce more adaptive belief systems. Likewise, behavior therapy techniques are frequently integrated with Step 3 work in terms of behavioral prescriptions for change, assertiveness training, and progressive relaxation training. These psychologically oriented techniques are applied in an effort either to assist the individual in understanding the dynamics of Step 3 or to help more concretely to apply Step 3 to everyday living.

Expected outcomes from Step 3 treatment methods can be observed in attitudinal and behavior changes such as (a) accepting and acting upon feedback from trusted resources; (b) communicating a more trusting attitude toward a process of change; (c) assessing personal needs and asserting them realistically without resorting to manipulation or aggression; (d) asking for help; (e) seeking the input of others before making decisions or acting on impulse; (f) risking the vulnerability to communicate perceptions, thoughts, and feelings to others; (g) communicating more openly and directly; (h) utilizing resources beyond oneself, such as advice of professionals, reading materials, and support from peers, to solve daily problems; (i) practicing new behavior, such as assertiveness, progressive relaxation, and social skills; (j) maintaining and initiating a personal schedule of quiet time, meditation, or inspirational reading; and (k) reducing maladaptive coping patterns, such as excessive control or self-centeredness.

In contrast, some individuals may attain an understanding of Step 3, yet have difficulties that are manifested by such attitudinal behavioral patterns as (a) openly doubting their capacity to make and maintain behavior changes; (b) expecting that circumstances, events, and/or other people will change without perceiving themselves as a catalyst; (c) believing that actions involving lifestyle changes are necessary for recovery, but doubting their personal capacity to implement these changes; (d) reporting continued anxiety and excessive worry; (e) being intermittently immobilized in making small changes in everyday behavior; (f) listening to input yet being mistrusting and slow to act on newly learned information; and (g) relying on old, maladaptive coping styles.

Specific treatment interventions are designed to reduce obstacles involving Step 3 milestones. Treatment techniques that are individually tailored to address these types of obstacles typically involve individual counseling, psychoeducational assignments, involvement in groups emphasizing assertiveness training and cognitive forms of therapy, pastoral counseling, and family conferences or topical group therapy sessions focusing on self-responsibility and the dynamics of change.

Self-Inventory

Changes that occur as the result of treatment methods associated with each of the steps are additive and self-renewing. New skills and insights are added as each step is applied to everyday living experiences. A step is never entirely finished or completed but is reaffirmed and reapplied each day. For example, Step 4 is both a renewal and an elaboration of Step 1. Step 1's emphasis on the seriousness and extent of addiction, the involuntary nature of the condition, and its harmful effects necessitates the use of psychologically oriented skills involving introspection, realistic evaluation of informational sources, self-assessment, and recognition and acceptance of human shortcomings. Step 4 builds on these milestones to expand one's conscious awareness and behavioral repertoire to engage in realistic self-appraisal of personal strengths and limitations. While Step 1's emphasis focuses on the dynamics of addiction, Step 4 has a more inclusive focus on personality and interpersonal functioning. Step 4 of Alcoholics Anonymous reads, "Made a searching and fearless moral inventory of ourselves."

While providing a format for self-assessment, Step 4 treatment methods integrate the affective changes, attitudes, and behavioral skills from Steps 1, 2, and 3. A simple formula for comprehensive self-appraisal is used to evaluate major life dimensions. Input from significant others, family, therapists, and newly recovering peers is used to help evaluate problematic traits or behavior patterns, existing strengths, and potential blocks to continued growth and change.

Treatment methods applied to Step 4 are both supportive and educational. The inventory is confidential, allowing the individual an opportunity to realize past problems and mistakes while considering strengths and personal resources. Step 4 processes often provoke negative feelings. Psychoeducational assignments may focus on readings that identify the difference between guilt and shame, or cognitive restructuring may be applied to counteract shame-provoking beliefs.

Some people have difficulty approaching their work on Step 4, perhaps because of continued excessive blaming of others, preoccupation with anger and resentments, or anxiety from painful memories. Subsequently, individualized treatment strategies are planned to address and reduce the emotional behavioral obstacles to participation in a fourth-step treatment process. For some, Step 4 may be modified by focusing more exclusively on strengths and personal resources, thereby reducing the perceived threat. For others, Step 4 can be delayed until after a more sustained period of abstinence and emotional stability.

Anticipated personality changes associated with Step 4 treatment assignments frequently involve a growing willingness to consider one's shortcomings that serve as risk factors for relapse, a more balanced self-perception of strengths and limitations, and resolution of shame and self-reproach.

Letting Go

Step 5 treatment methods provide an opportunity for catharsis by sharing the contents of the Step 4 inventory with another person. Step 5 of Alcoholics Anonymous reads, "Admitted to God, to ourselves, and to another human being the exact nature of our wrongs." Treatment methods for Step 5 include individual conferences with a trusted chaplain or spiritual adviser to lay a foundation for Step 5 self-disclosure. Step 5 is facilitated by an accepting environment where personal self-disclosures of sensitive information are shared without judgment. The process of honest disclosure is thought to be the essential therapeutic value in this treatment process. At the conclusion of the inventory, the participant is free to request feedback or engage in a dialogue regarding the inventory with the fifth-step listener.

Anticipated effects of Step 5 treatment activities usually involve a greater willingness to identify risk factors for relapse, accepting responsibility for one's own behavior change, having a greater awareness of the disease's impact on character development, reconciling with one's own spiritual beliefs and values, increasing the motivation to continue with Steps 6–

12, and often, observable relief of shame, guilt, and self-reproach.

While step work is often prescribed sequentially, different steps are applied to address varying problems. For example, an individual with significant grief and dysphoria may begin work on Step 2 as a method of developing hope prior to working on Step 1. Likewise, Step 4 work is sometimes prescribed in conjunction with Step 1 when there is considerable resentment, to facilitate an unburdening of anger and blame. The therapeutic value of each step is applied prescriptively according to the presenting needs of the individual.

Continuing Care

The initial phase of recovery is usually associated with Steps 1–5. These first steps are most closely associated with the evolution of a spiritual awakening, where the individual metaphorically wakes up to the reality of his or her situation and accepts the guidance and counsel of others to acquire the skills for sober living. These attitudes and behaviors are renewed and reinforced by Steps 6–12, which are commonly referred to as relapse prevention steps, since their focus addresses the continued elaboration of skills learned in Steps 1–5.

Posttreatment services, or continuing care, increase the quality of recovery by helping to prevent relapse. Based on variability of severity, continuing-care options are individually prescribed. One-to-one counseling and referral to a 12-step self-help support group are frequently recommended for those individuals with supportive family and social environments, employment, and relatively successful treatment response.

Many are referred to mental health professionals for the treatment of mental health complications such as unresolved childhood trauma, serious relationship dysfunction, or poorly controlled depression and anxiety. For those individuals with unstable family and social environments, prior unsuccessful treatment attempts, unresolved mental disorder, and limited vocational options, halfway house placement is recommended. Halfway house services provide continuity of care by maintaining a central focus on the disease model, application of the 12 steps, and community reintegration as a recovering person.

ROLE OF THE THERAPIST

A key treatment modality of the disease model is the mentoring relationship between a primary therapist (chemical dependence counselor) and an individual client. The relationship provides the vehicle by which coaching and counseling occur that help move the individual toward incremental behavior changes.

The training of chemical dependency counselors varies from state to state. Typically, counselors are either certified or licensed by a state regulatory agency. There is a decided preference in the field for candidates who either are recovering or have experience with 12-step programs such as Al-anon. Formal education ranges from an associate's degree to master's level preparation. Usually, the counselor has completed a certified training program and/or a supervised clinical internship in addition to educational preparation that specifically addresses the clinical dynamics of chemical dependence. Current trends support the movement of counselor-training programs to baccalaureate or master's degree programs.

The counselor plays a dynamic role by promoting change through a carefully planned agenda of intervention that builds on eclectic counseling approaches consistent with 12-step methodology. Counselors assess the extent and severity of alcohol and drug use, integrate diverse information from the multidisciplinary team, develop treatment plans, facilitate group and individual counseling, conduct family conferences, develop continuing-care plans, and coordinate related case management activities.

Counseling skills include relationship building, confrontation, emotional support, behavioral coaching, problem solving, homework assignments, and psychoeducation. Counselors often use their recovery experience to coach, role-model, and motivate.

COMMON OBSTACLES TO SUCCESSFUL TREATMENT

There are several potential obstacles to the successful delivery of the Minnesota model form of treatment. One obstacle, which can be inferred from above, is the comprehensiveness of the resources needed to implement the model as it is intended. However, if they are not available or fundable within an agency itself, creativity can be used to aggregate the resources needed from the surrounding community.

CLIENT CHARACTERISTICS

Several studies have examined the extent to which client characteristics may impede or counterindicate Minnesota model treatment. Variability of the client population is an important factor in the study of treatment response. Although research addresses this issue, there are limited studies that focus exclusively on predictive factors for treatment response to the disease model. Early efforts attempted to evaluate demographic or descriptive variables as predictors of treatment response. In terms psychopathology, women reported less problem drinking posttreatment and depressed mood as a precursor to relapse and had a higher rate of returning to abstinence following a drinking episode (Helzer et al., 1985). Negative emotional states such as depression and anxiety have been associated with posttreatment drinking (Hatsukami & Pickens, 1980; Pickens, Hatsukami, Spicer, & Svikis, 1985).

However, more recent endeavors have failed to identify predictive demographic or other standard background variables in the study of treatment response to the disease model. For example, in a study of over 1,000 men and women admitted to a disease model residential facility, Stinchfield and Owen (1998) found that variability was evenly distributed in terms of treatment outcome. Variables such as comorbid conditions, age, gender, employment, and relational support did not have predictive value for treatment outcome.

In a study of individual client types and response to different models of treatment, Project MATCH (1997) did not identify variables for treatment outcomes relevant to the disease model in terms of individual client variability. It was found that people with lower levels of psychopathology did better in the 12-step facilitation model than in the other two treatment models; the converse, however, was not true. No other demographic, mental health, alcohol severity, or other background characteristics predicted a better outcome in any of the models tested.

Morgenstern, Frey, McCrady, Labouvie, and Neighbors (1996) examined specific disease model processes and their effect on treatment outcome. Patients with a greater commitment to abstinence and stronger intentions to avoid high-risk situations achieved higher abstinence rates. Among those who did relapse, those with a greater commitment to Alcoholics Anonymous and a stronger belief in a Higher Power had less severe relapses than those who did not hold these beliefs.

Because of the nature of the Minnesota model or 12-step facilitation treatment, particular subgroups of alcoholic or drug-dependent individuals may be more likely to have a less than favorable treatment response. For example, individuals with mental disorders such as schizophrenia and related conditions or those with severe personality disorders such as borderline or antisocial are likely to have difficulty with both the relational qualities of the treatment model and its spiritual dimension. The cognitive nature of the treatment approach precludes individuals with severe cognitive dysfunction.

Because of the biopsychosocial nature of the disease model, application of select treatment modalities within or outside the Minnesota model may be indicated to address the special needs of youth, individuals with comorbid conditions, and those suffering from social instability and economic disadvantage.

EMPIRICAL DATA ON THE EFFECTIVENESS OF DISEASE MODEL TREATMENT

The disease model of treatment is one of the most widely used forms of inpatient and residential alcoholism and drug dependence treatment in the United States (Fuller, 1989; Miller et al., 1995). Perhaps because of its theoretical appeal, anecdotal evidence, or development apart from academic institutions, the disease model has not been extensively tested. In Fuller's (1989) review of alcoholism treatment outcome literature, most studies conducted were found to have methodological flaws, yet Fuller contended that from a broad perspective, the disease model of treatment is effective.

Several studies of disease-model-type programs have been published. Hazelden conducted a series of studies on its patients. Laundergan (1982) analyzed 12-month follw-up data collected on 3,638 clients treated at Hazelden between 1973 and 1975 and found that 53% of the 50% contacted reported abstinence. The low response rate compromised the accuracy of these results. Gilmore (1985) analyzed similar 12-month outcome data on 1,531 clients randomly selected for follow-up between 1978 and 1983. With a response rate of 75%, she found that 89% were abstinent or reported lower use. Higgins, Baeumler, Fisher, and Johnson (1991) analyzed 12-month outcome data on 1,655 clients treated at Hazelden in 1985 and 1986. They found that 61% were abstinent during the year after treatment. However, while the response rate was reported to be 72%, rather liberal exclusionary criteria were used. Most recently, a more rigorous Hazelden outcome study was completed, analyzing the pretreatment and posttreatment use levels of 1,083 patients treated from 1989 to 1991. At the 1-year outcome, 71% of the patients were contacted; of these, 53% reported continuous abstinence, and an additional 35% had reduced their drinking and drug use (Stinchfield & Owen, 1998).

McLellan et al. (1993) published a study reporting outcomes of patients from four private treatment centers, two inpatient and two outpatient. While the programs varied somewhat in characteristics, all four programs were based on the 12 steps of Alcoholics Anonymous, had a goal of abstinence, and utilized a multidisciplinary team to deliver services. A response rate of 94% was achieved, and patient reports were verified via urinalysis and breathalyzer. Six months after treatment, 59% were abstinent from alcohol, and 84% were abstinent from drugs during the 30-day window preceding follow-up contact. There were differences across the four programs, attributable to intensity of services. It is worth noting, however, that the two inpatient programs yielded an average abstinence rate of 71%, while the two outpatient programs averaged an abstinence rate of 48%.

Walsh and her colleagues (1991) designed a randomized study to compare the effectiveness of employee assistance program referrals to inpatient hospital treatment, or participation in Alcoholics Anonymous, or a choice of either of these two options. Ten hospitals were used as treatment sites, so consistency in model was unlikely; however, we do know that all programs were abstinence-based. Two years after treatment, 37% of those hospitalized, 16% of those assigned to Alcoholics Anonymous (with no treatment), and 17% of those given a choice reported abstinence.

Hoffmann and Harrison (1991) published a large-scale outcome report on two groups of patients followed via their outcome system, called the Chemical Abuse Treatment Outcome Registry (CATOR). Combined, over 3,000 clients, most from Minnesota-model-type treatment programs, were followed for 2 years. The response rates for the two groups were 53% and 37%. Of these, about two thirds reported abstinence for the full year after treatment. After correcting for bias and low response rate, the authors suggested that a more accurate abstinence rate for these groups was probably closer to 40%.

Recent attempts have been made to more definitively study the effectiveness of alcoholism treatment models by studying the efficacy of matching treatment approaches to specific client characteristics. The National Institute on Alcohol Abuse and Alcoholism (NIAAA), in a rigorously controlled study called Project MATCH, evaluated multisite trials of patient treatment matching. Project MATCH evaluated whether different types of clients responded differently to three different types of treatments: (a) disease model or 12-step facilitation, (b) cognitive behavioral treatment, or (c) motivational enhancement therapy. Over 12 weeks, treatment services were conducted by qualified therapists using a standard treatment protocol. Treatment outcome data revealed that (a) participants without severe psychopathology had significantly higher rates of abstinence in outpatient 12-step facilitation treatment than in cognitive behavior therapy; (b) participants in 12-step facilitation aftercare services had slightly fewer drinking episodes; and (c) 12-step facilitation outcomes were generally comparable or, in some instances, more favorable (Project MATCH Research Group, 1997).

STRENGTHS AND WEAKNESSES OF THE DISEASE MODEL

There are three main strengths of the disease model approach that directly affect clients: (a) Clients benefit not only from their counselors' input and interactions, but from their peers as well; (b) other people who are further ahead in the recovery process, even if by just a matter of a few days, provide credible and hopeful role models for the client; and (c) clients treated in the disease model become part of a support group of other recovering people that extends beyond the walls or timeline of the treatment pro- gram. By becoming familiar with and integrated into Alcoholics Anonymous groups, clients have access to support 24 hours a day, 7 days a week, in nearly every part of the world. The disease model provides a cost- free system of lifelong support through referral to a 12-step self-help group.

From a methodological perspective, a major strength of the 12-step facilitation treatment model is its holistic approach to recovery. This model is built on both a biopsychosocial and a spiritual foundation, and it has the capacity to integrate innovations as knowledge is gained regarding the nature of the ill- ness and the recovery process. The disease model serves as a conceptual umbrella which covers diverse treatment approaches, thus maximizing opportuni- ties for effective treatment. The framework of the model endorses core values that embrace the inher- ent worth and dignity of each person by recognizing the capacity to change based on education, fellow- ship, and therapy.

The model's greatest strength is also potentially its greatest limitation. Since the model relies on a multidisciplinary team, services can be time-consum- ing and costly. Some would argue that the time and money spent are a wise investment the costs are com- pared to those of continued addictive behavior. For example, in general, untreated alcoholics have health care costs at least 100% higher than nonalcoholics, and this disparity may continue for as long as 10 years before entry into treatment (Blose & Holder, 1991; Holder, Longabough, Miller, & Rubonis, 1991). Nonetheless, the model demands time, atten- tion, and effort for the principles and practices to work.

Other limitations pertain to potential problems in implementing the disease model of treatment. If too dogmatically interpreted, this form of treatment be- comes distorted and presented in a confrontive, re- ligious, or generic (rather than individualized) manner. When this occurs, the core therapeutic principles and methods of the model are obscured, and many clients are naturally resistant and unable to benefit from it.

SUMMARY

The disease model of alcoholism has evolved from theoretical innovations, clinical observations, and re- search data. As a theory or body of knowledge, it is neither static nor complete. The early work of Jelli- nek serves as a conceptual umbrella under which new dimensions or scientific findings may be added to explain the multidimensional nature of the illness. Key characteristics of disease model theory typically include an emphasis on the biological underpin- nings of addictive behavior; genetic contributions to the disease's etiology; involuntary loss of control over behavior; predictable progression of symptoms; nega- tive consequences affecting social, vocational, psy- chological, and ethical or spiritual domains; rigidly ingrained psychological defense mechanisms; and re- peated failure of attempts to reduce or control drink- ing behavior.

Abstinence is the principle prescription of the dis- ease model for recovery. Consequently, treatment implications are broad and far-reaching, ranging from specific skills training to assignments requiring major life decisions. Treatment processes provide the skills necessary to develop a lifestyle that is centered on values to help shape and give meaning to life's everyday occurrences, and to avoid, resist, or refuse alcohol in high-risk situations.

The 12-step facilitation model, or Minnesota model, is a natural outgrowth of the disease model. Twelve-step facilitation modalities are typically char- acterized by the use of a multidisciplinary team to address the biopsychosocial nature of the illness, a strong spiritual dimension, emphasis on the daily op- erationalization of the 12 steps as problem-solving and coping mechanisms, psychoeducation and bibli- otherapy, and fellowship and peer self-help in addi- tion to group and individual therapy. Posttreatment recommendations routinely involve referral to a 12- step self-help support group for relapse prevention and continuing care in addition to counseling, men- tal health services, and in some cases, extended care such as halfway house placement.

Note

Correspondence regarding this manuscript should be sent to Dr. Timothy Sheehan, Hazelden, Box 11, Cen- ter City, MN 55012. E-mail: tsheehan@hazelden.org

Key References

Morgenstern, J., & McCrady, B. S. (1992). Curative fac- tors in alcohol and drug treatment: Behavioral and disease model perspectives. *British Journal of Addiction*, 87, 901–912.

Nowinski, J., Baker, S., & Carroll, K. (1992). *Twelve step facilitation manual: A clinical research guide for therapists treating individuals with alcohol abuse and dependence*. (NIAAA Project MATCH Monograph, Vol. 1, DHHS Publication No. (ADM) 92-1893). Washington, DC: Government Printing Office.

Stinchfield, R., & Owen, P. (in press). Hazelden treatment model and outcome.

References

Alcoholics Anonymous. (1939). New York: Alcoholics Anonymous World Service.

Alcoholics Anonymous (2nd ed., new and rev.). (1955). New York: Alcoholics Anonymous World Service.

American Psychiatric Association (1994). *Diagnostic and statistical manual of mental disorders* (4th ed.). Washington, DC: Author.

Anton, R. F., Kranzler, H. R., & Meyer, R. E. (1995). Neurobehavioral aspects of the pharmacotherapy of alcohol dependence. *Neuroscience*, 3, 145–154.

Babor, T. F., Hofmann, M., DelBoca, F. K., Hesselbrock, V., Meyer, R. E., Dolinsky, Z. S., & Rounsaville, B. (1992). Types of alcoholics: 1. Evidence for an empirically-derived typology based on indicators of vulnerability and severity. *Archives of General Psychiatry*, 8, 599–608.

Beck, A. T., Wright, F. D., Newman, C. F., & Liese, B. S. (1993). *Cognitive therapy of substance abuse* (pp. 157–168). New York: Guilford Press.

Bleuler, M. (1955). Familial and personal background of chronic alcoholism. In O. Diethelm (Ed.), *Etiology of chronic alcoholism* (pp. 110–166). Springfield, IL: Charles C Thomas.

Blose, J. O., & Holder, H. D. (1991). The utilization of medical care by treated alcoholics: Longitudinal patterns by age, gender, and type of care. *Journal of Substance Abuse Treatment*, 3, 13–27.

Cadoret, R. J. (1990). Genetics of alcoholism. In R. L. Collins, K. E. Leonard, & J. S. Searles (Eds.), *Alcohol and the family: Research and clinical perspectives* (pp. 39–78). New York: Guilford Press.

Cherpitel, C. J. (1989a). Breath analysis and self-reports as measures of alcohol-related emergency room admissions. *Journal of Studies on Alcohol*, 50, 155–161.

Cherpitel, C. J. (1989b). Prediction of alcohol-related casualties: A comparison of two emergency room populations. *Drug and Alcohol Dependence*, 24, 195–203.

Cloninger, C. R. (1987). Neurogenetic adaptive mechanisms in alcoholism. *Science*, 236, 410–416.

Coccaro, E. F., & Murphy, D. L. (Eds.). (1990). *Serotonin in major psychiatric disorders*. Washington, DC: American Psychiatric Press.

Cotton, N. S. (1979). The familial incidence of alcoholism: A review. *Journal of Studies on Alcoholism*, 40, 89–116.

Covington, S. (1994). *Women's way through the 12 steps*. Center City, MN: Hazelden.

Dual disorder recovery book. (1993). Center City, MN: Hazelden.

Engels, G. L. (1977). The need for a new medical model; a challenge for biomedicine. *Science*, 196, 129–136.

FitzGerald, K. W. (1988). *Alcoholism: The genetic inheritance*. New York: Doubleday.

Froelich, J. C., & Li, T-K. (1991). Animal models for the study of alcoholism: Utility of selected lines. In F. R. George, D. Clouet, & B. Stimmel (Eds.), *Behavioral and biochemical issues in substance abuse*. New York: Haworth Press.

Fuller, R. (1989). Current status of alcoholism treatment outcome research. In L. S. Harris (Ed.), *Problems of drug dependence 1989: Proceedings of the 51st Annual Scientific Meeting* (NIDA Research Monograph 95, pp. 85–91). Rockville, MD: National Institute on Drug Abuse.

Gilmore, K. (1985). *Hazelden primary residential treatment program: 1985 profile and patient outcome* (Research Report). Center City, MN: Hazelden.

Gomberg, E. S. (1989). Suicide risk among women with alcohol problems. *American Journal of Public Health*, 79, 1363–1365.

Hatsukami, D., & Pickens, R. (1980). Depression and relapse to chemical use in individuals treated for alcoholism and drug dependence. *Research and evaluation reports*. Center City, MN: Hazelden Foundation.

Heath, A. C. (1995). Genetic influences on alcoholism risk, a review of adoption and twin studies. *Alcohol World Health and Research*, 19, 166–170.

Helzer, J. E., Robins, L. N., Taylor, J. R., Carey, K., Miller, R. H., Combs-Orme, T., & Farmer, A. (1985). The extent of long-term moderate drinking among alcoholics discharged from medical and psychiatric treatment facilities. *New England Journal of Medicine*, 312, 1678–1682.

Higgins, P., Baeumler, R., Fisher, J., & Johnson, V. (1991). Treatment outcomes for Minnesota model programs. In J. Spicer (Ed.), *Does your program measure up? An addiction professional's guide to evaluating treatment effectiveness* (pp. 93–114). Center City, MN: Hazelden.

Hoffmann, N., & Harrison, P. (1991). The Chemical Abuse Treatment Outcome Registry (CATOR): Treatment outcome from private programs. In J. Spicer (Ed.), *Does your program measure up? An addiction professional's guide to evaluating treatment effectiveness* (pp. 115–133). Center City, MN: Hazelden.

Holder, H. D., Longabaugh, R., Miller, W. R., & Rubonis, A. V. (1991). The cost effectiveness of treatment for alcoholism: A first approximation. *Journal of Studies on Alcohol, 52,* 517–540.

Hyman, S. E. (1995). A man with alcoholism and HIV infection. *Journal of the American Medical Association, 274,* 837–843.

Hyman, S. E. (1996). Initiation and adaptation: A paradigm for understanding psychotropic drug action. *American Journal of Psychiatry, 153,* 151–162.

Jellinek, E. M. (1946). Phases in the drinking history of alcoholics. *Quarterly Journal of Studies on Alcoholism, 7,* 1–88.

Jellinek, E. M. (1960). *The disease concept of alcoholism.* New Haven, CT: Hillhouse Press.

Johnston, I. R. (1982). The role of alcohol in road crashes. *Ergonomics, 25,* 921–946.

Keller, M. (1986). Old and the new in the treatment of alcoholism. In D. L. Strug, S. Priyadarsini, & M. M. Hyman (Eds.), *Alcohol interventions: Historical and sociocultural approaches* (pp. 23–40). (Alcohol Treatment Quarterly Supplement). New York: Haworth Press.

Koob, G. F., & Bloom, F. E. (1988). Cellular and molecular mechanisms of drug dependence. *Science, 242,* 715–723.

Laundergan, J. C. (1982). *Easy does it: Alcoholism treatment outcomes, Hazelden and the Minnesota model.* Center City, MN: Hazelden.

Lee, R. (1993). Preface, National Institute on Alcohol Dependence and Alcoholism. *Eighth Special Report to the U.S. Congress on Alcohol and Health.* Washington, DC: Government Printing Office.

Leshner, A. I. (1997). Addiction is a brain disease and it matters. *Science, 278,* 45–47.

Levy, M. (1993). Psychotherapy with dual diagnosis patients: Working with denial. *Journal of Substance Dependence Treatment, 10,* 499–505.

Lewis, D. C. (1994). A disease model of addiction. *American Society of Addiction Medicine,* 1–7.

Liskow, B., Powell, B. J., Nickel, E. J., & Penick, E. (1990). Diagnostic subgroups of antisocial alcoholics: Outcome at 1 year. *Comprehensive Psychiatry, 31,* 549–556.

Loveland-Cook, C. A., Booth, B. M., Blow, F. C., Gogineni, A., & Bunn, J. Y. (1992). Alcoholism treatment, severity of alcohol-related medical complications, and health services utilization. *Journal of Mental Health Administration, 19,* 31–40.

McLellan, A. T., Grissom, G. R., Brill, P., Durell, J., Metzger, D. S., & O'Brien, C. P. (1993). Private substance abuse treatments: Are some programs more effective than others? *Journal of Substance Abuse Treatment, 10,* 243–254.

McLellan, A. T., Luborsky, L., Woody, G. E., O'Brien, C. P., & Druley, K. A. (1983). Predicting response to alcohol and drug dependence treatments: Role of psychiatric severity. *Archives of General Psychiatry, 40,* 620–625.

Merikangas, K. R., & Gelernter, C. S. (1990). Comorbidity for alcoholism and depression. *Psychiatric Clinics of North America, 13,* 613–632.

Merrill, J., Fox, K., & Chang, H-H. (1993). *The cost of substance dependence to America's health care system: Report 1. Medicaid hospital costs.* New York: Center on Addiction and Substance Dependence at Columbia University.

Metzger, L. (1988). *From denial to recovery: counseling problem drinkers, alcoholics, and their families.* San Francisco: Jossey-Bass.

Meyer, R. E. (1995). Biology of psychoactive substance dependence disorders: opiates, cocaine, and ethanol. In A. F. Schatzberg & C. Nemeroff (Eds.), *Textbook of psychopharmacology* (pp. 537–556). Washington, DC: American Psychiatric Press.

Miller, W. R., Brown, J. M., Simpson, T. L., Handmaker, N. S., Bien, T. H., Luckie, L. F., Montgomery, H. A., Hester, R. K., & Tonigan, J. S. (1995). What works? A methodological analysis of the alcohol treatment outcome literature. In R. K. Hester & W. R. Miller (Eds.), *Handbook of alcoholism treatment approaches: Effective alternatives* (2nd ed., pp. 12–44). Boston: Allyn & Bacon.

Miller, W. R., & Brown, S. A. (1997) Why psychologists should treat alcohol and drug problems. *American Psychologist, 52,* 1269–1279.

Miller, W. R., & Kurtz, E. (1994). Models of alcoholism used in treatment: Contrasting AA and other perspectives with which it is often confused. *Journal of Studies on Alcohol, 55,* 159–166.

Montgomery, H. A., Miller, W. R., & Tonigan, J. S. (1995). Does Alcoholics Anonymous involvement predict treatment outcome? *Journal of Substance Abuse Treatment, 12,* 241–246.

Morgenstern, J., Frey, R. M., McCrady, B. S., Labouvie, E., & Neighbors, C. J. (1996). Examining mediators of change in traditional chemical dependency treatment. *Journal of Studies on Alcohol, 57,* 53–64.

Morgenstern, J., Labouvie, E., McCrady, B. S., Kahler, C. W., and Frey, R. M. (1997). Affiliation with Alcoholics Anonymous after treatment: A study of its therapeutic effects and mechanisms of action. *Journal of Consulting and Clinical Psychology, 65,* 768–777.

Morgenstern, J., & McCrady, B. S. (1992). Curative factors in alcohol and drug treatment: Behavioral and disease model perspectives. *British Journal of Addiction, 87,* 901–912.

National Institute on Alcohol Abuse and Alcoholism. (1993). Effects of alcohol on behavior and safety. *Eighth Special Report to the U.S. Congress on Alcohol and Health,* p. 238. Washington, DC: Government Printing Office.

National Institute on Alcohol Abuse and Alcoholism. (1994). Alcoholism and alcohol-related problems. *Alcohol Health and Research World, 18,* 243–245.

Noel, N. E., McCrady, B. S., Stout, R. L., & Nelson, H. F. (1987). Predictors of attrition from an outpatient alcoholism treatment program for alcoholic couples. *Journal of Studies on Alcohol, 48,* 229–235.

Nowinski, J., Baker, S., & Carroll, K. (1995). *Twelve step facilitation manual: A clinical research guide for therapists treating individuals with alcohol abuse and dependence.* (NIAAA Project MATCH Monograph, Vol. 1, DHHS Publication No. (ADM) 92-1893). Washington, DC: Government Printing Office.

Pernanen, K. (1991). *Alcohol in human violence.* New York: Guilford Press.

Petrakis, P. L. (1985). *Alcoholism, an inherited disease.* Washington, DC: U.S. Department of Health and Human Services.

Pickens, R., Hatsukami, D., Spicer, J., & Svikis, D. (1985). Relapse by alcohol dependencers. *Alcoholism: Clinical and Experimental Research, 9,* 244–247.

Prochaska, J. O., DiClementi, C. C., & Norcross, J. C. (1992). In search of how people change; applications to addictive behaviors. *American Psychologist, 47,* 1103–1114.

Project MATCH Research Group. (1997). Matching alcoholism treatments to client heterogeneity: Project MATCH posttreatment drinking outcomes. *Journal of Studies on Alcohol, 58,* 7–20.

Reiger, D. A., Farmer, M. E., Rae, D. S., Locke, B. Z., Keith, S. J., Judd, L. L., & Goodwin, F. K. (1990). Comorbidity of mental health disorders with alcohol and other drug abuse. *Journal of the American Medical Association, 264,* 2511–2518.

Robins, L. H., Helzer, J. E., Weissmann, M. M., Orvaschel, H., Greenberg, E., Burke, J. D., & Regire, D. A. (1984). Lifetime prevalence of specific psychiatric disorders in three sites. *Archives of General Psychiatry, 41*(10), 949–959.

Room, R. (1991). Measuring alcohol consumption in the U.S.: Methods and rationales. In W. B. Clark & M. E. Hilton (Eds.), *Alcohol in America* (pp. 26–50). Albany: State University of New York Press.

Samson, H. H., & Hoffman, P. L. (1995). Involvement of CNS catecholamines in alcohol self-administration, tolerance and dependence: preclinical studies. In H. R. Kranzler (Ed.), *The pharmacology of alcohol dependence* (pp. 121–137). New York: Springer-Verlag.

Schuckit, M. A., Smith, T. L., Anthenelli, R., & Irwin, M. (1993). Clinical course of alcohlism in 636 male inpatients. *American Journal of Psychiatry, 150,* 786–792.

Sheehan, T., & Garretson, S. (1994). Creating opportunity from crisis. *Addictions Nursing, 6,* 90–94.

Silkworth, W. D. (1939). The doctor's opinion. In *Alcoholics Anonymous* (pp. xxi–xiv). New York: Alcoholics Anonymous World Service.

Spicer, J. (1993). *The Minnesota model.* Center City, MN: Hazelden.

Stinchfield, R., & Owen, P. (1998). Hazelden's model of treatment and its outcome. *Addictive Behaviors, 23,* 669–683.

Tabakoff, B., & Hoffmann, P. L. (1988). In C. D. Chaudron & D. A. Wilkinson (Eds.), *Theories on alcoholism.* Toronto: Alcoholism and Drug Addiction Research Foundation.

Tarter, R. E., Alterman, A. I., & Edwards, K. L. (1988). Neurobehavioral theory of alcoholism. In C. D. Chaudron & D. A. Wilkinson (Eds.), *Theories on alcoholism* (pp. 73–102). Toronto: Alcoholism and Drug Addiction Research Foundation.

Tonigan, J. S., Toscova, R., & Miller, W. R. (1996). Meta-analysis of the literature on Alcoholics Anonymous: Sample and study characteristics moderate findings. *Journal of Studies on Alcohol, 57,* 65–72.

Valliant, G. E. (1995). *The natural history of alcoholism revisited.* Cambridge: Harvard University Press.

Walsh, D. C., Hingson, R. W., Merrigan, D. M., Levenson, S. M., Cupplies, L. A., Heeren, T., Coffman, G. A., Becker, C. A., Barker, T. A., Hamilton, S. K., McGuire, T. G., & Kelly, C. A. (1991). A randomized trial of treatment options for alcohol-abusing workers. *New England Journal of Medicine, 325,* 775–782.

Wegscheider Cruse, S. (1989). *Another chance: Hope and health for the alcoholic family.* Palo Alto, CA: Science & Behavior Books.

Wieczorek, W. F., Welte, J. W., & Abel, E. L. (1990). Alcohol, drugs and murder: A study of convicted homicide offenders. *Journal of Criminal Justice, 18,* 217–227.

16

Treatment Models and Methods: Family Models

Timothy J. O'Farrell

William Fals-Stewart

In the past 30 years, considerable progress has been made in the theoretical development, clinical applications, and outcome research related to marital and family treatment of alcoholism and drug abuse. A number of literature reviews have concluded that marital and family treatment produces better marital and substance use outcomes than nonfamily methods (e.g., O'Farrell, 1992; Stanton & Shadish, 1997). Furthermore, enthusiasm for understanding the role family members may play in the development, maintenance, and treatment of alcohol and other drug problems has not been limited to the research community. The popular literature on families and substance misuse has grown into an industry over the last decade, with a wide range of books describing codependency, enabling, adult children of alcoholics, and so forth appearing regularly on bookstore shelves. Additionally, different varieties of professional and self-help support groups for family members of alcoholics and addicts are now readily available in most communities.

Although alcoholism and drug abuse were historically conceptualized as an individual problem best treated on an individual basis (e.g., Jellinek, 1960), a large and growing body of research suggests that family members often play a central role in the lives of alcoholics and drug abusers (Stanton & Heath, 1997). In turn, an increasing number of researchers and clinicians have examined family factors relevant to substance use disorders, and the clinical applications of marital and family therapy have grown considerably over the last 30 years. It is now recommended that clinical practice include family members in the substance-abusing patient's treatment. In fact, the Joint Commission on Accreditation of Health Care Organizations (JCAHO) standards for accrediting substance abuse treatment programs in the United States now require that an adult family member who lives with the identified patient be included at least in the initial assessment process (Brown, O'Farrell, Maisto, Boies, & Suchinsky (1997). In this chapter, we (a) briefly describe the historical roots of family-based interventions with psychoactive substance use disorders; (b) explore the theoretical basis of family models of substance abuse etiology and maintenance; (c) examine methods of marital/family therapy in the treatment of alcoholism and drug abuse; (d) briefly summarize the empirical data on the effectiveness of family-based interventions for substance abuse; and (e) review the strengths and limitations of family treatment for substance abuse and the future research needed in this area.

HISTORICAL ORIGINS OF THE FAMILY TREATMENT MODEL AND ITS APPLICATIONS TO SUBSTANCE ABUSE

Early Developments in the Family Model of Treatment of Substance Abuse

Although it is likely that people have been listening to each other's family problems and responding with advice for as long as there have been families, only in the last century has a profession developed whose sole purpose is to deal with family-based problems (Broderick & Schrader, 1981). Formal family treatment has its roots in the social work movement of the late 1800s; charity organizations developed to aid the poor and disadvantaged routinely worked with families (Rich, 1959). However, family-based conceptualizations and treatment models for psychological and psychiatric problems as we know them today were foreshadowed by the work of the early psychoanalysts, who recognized the importance of early family relationships in shaping personality (e.g., Jung, 1910) and theorized that individual psychopathology might result from family conflict (e.g., Adler, 1917). The family therapy movement, as it is often called, began in the early 1950s, when therapists and researchers, unknown to one another at the time, began to interview families in order to understand the problems manifested by one family member (Guerin, 1976). From this practice grew the notion that family dynamics contributed to etiology and maintenance of different disorders and that addressing family dysfunction was a potentially beneficial intervention for identified patients and the family as a whole (Stanton & Heath, 1997).

Early Psychodynamic Models

In the 1930s, social workers treating alcoholic men in state mental institutions began to interview patients' spouses and found they were significantly distressed and consistently reported high levels of depression, anxiety, and somatic concerns (Lewis, 1937). The theoretical models developed to explain these observations were psychodynamically oriented, postulating that wives of alcoholics were disturbed women who resolved their neurotic conflicts by marrying alcoholic men (Whalen, 1953). These early models placed responsibility for the alcoholic's continued drinking largely on the disturbed spouse.

Early Sociological Stress Models

In the 1950s and 1960s, sociological explanatory models emerged to explain the observation that spouses of alcoholic men were psychologically distressed. Based on interviews with women attending Al-Anon meetings, Jackson (1954) suggested that symptoms observed in these wives were the result of stress from living with an alcoholic partner. Additionally, she reported that families developed and employed various coping strategies to deal with the stress created by the alcoholic family member. In contrast to the psychodynamic explanations described earlier, this stress and coping model placed responsibility for family problems with the alcoholic rather than the spouse.

Contemporary Family-Based Conceptualizations of Alcoholism and Drug Abuse

Over the last three decades, three theoretical perspectives have come to dominate family-based conceptualizations of substance use disorders (Gondoli & Jacob, 1990; O'Farrell, 1995). The best known of these and the most widely used is the *family disease model*, which views alcoholism and other drug abuse as an illness suffered not only by the alcoholic, but also by family members. The *family systems approach* applies the principles of general systems theory to families, with particular attention paid to how families maintain a dynamic balance between substance use and family functioning and how their interactional behavior is organized around alcohol or drug use. *Behavioral approaches* assume that family interactions serve to reinforce alcohol- and drug-using behavior. We will now review each of these approaches in more detail, providing (a) a brief review of their historical antecedents, (b) their current status and clinical applications, and (c) a review of relevant constructs and terms associated with each model.

The Family Disease Model

Since the founding of Alcoholics Anonymous (AA), the family unit has been one of the main foci of the disease concept of alcoholism. Several AA publications include information and advice to family members of alcoholics (e.g., Alcoholics Anonymous, 1976). AA's sister organization, Al-Anon, was founded in 1949 to assist and support family members and friends of alcoholics. The contemporary family disease model of alcoholism is perhaps best exemplified by the widely read books by Black (1982) and Wegsheider (1981), each of which describes children raised in alcoholic families and how their experiences in these families influence their adult behavior. More recently, other authors (e.g., Beattie, 1987; Schaef, 1986) have focused on how the disease of alcoholism manifests itself symptomatically in spouses and intimate partners (e.g., low self-esteem, anxiety about intimacy and separation, and enmeshment in dysfunctional relationships).

Alcoholism is viewed as a "family disease," with family members of alcoholics suffering the disease of "codependence," a term that is often used to describe the process underlying the various problems observed in the families of individuals who abuse psychoactive substances. Little consensus exists as to how the term should be defined or operationalized, but according to Schaef (1986), codependence is a disease that parallels the alcoholic disease process and is marked by characteristic symptoms (e.g., external referencing, caretaking, self-centeredness, control issues, dishonesty, frozen feelings, perfectionism, and fear); others have also attempted to define specific, identifiable symptoms of codependence (e.g., Cermak, 1986). The hallmark of codependency is enabling, which, as the term implies, is defined as any set of behaviors that perpetuates the psychoactive substance use. These include making it easier for the alcoholic or drug abuser to engage in substance use or shielding the alcoholic or drug abuser from the negative consequences often associated with drinking or drug taking.

The family disease approach typically involves separate treatment for family members without the substance-abusing patient present. Treatment often consists of psychoeducational groups about the disease concept of alcoholism and codependency; referrals to Al-Anon, Al-Ateen, or Adult Children of Alcoholics groups; and individual and group therapy to address various psychological issues. In general, the family disease approach advocates that family members should not actively intervene to try to change the substance-abusing patient's drinking or drug use but should detach and focus on themselves in order to reduce their own emotional distress and improve their own coping (Al-Anon Family Groups, 1981; Laundergan & Williams, 1993).

At present, the family disease approach has very limited research support (O'Farrell, 1995). Nevertheless, family interventions based on this model are the most commonly used in substance abuse treatment programs and have strongly influenced public perceptions of the effect of substance use on the family.

Family Systems Models

In the 1970s and 1980s, family systems approaches became increasingly influential among substance abuse treatment professionals and have since been applied to the treatment of alcoholism and drug abuse. This model suggested that a reciprocal relationship exists between family functioning and substance use, an individual's drug and alcohol use being best understood in the context of the entire family's functioning. According to family systems theory, substance abuse in either adults or adolescents often evolves during periods in which the individual family member is having difficulty addressing an important developmental issue (e.g., leaving the home) or when the family is facing a significant crisis (e.g., marital discord). During these periods, substance abuse can serve to (a) distract family members from their central problem or (b) slow down or stop a transition to a different developmental stage that is being resisted by the family as a whole or by one of its members (Stanton & Todd, 1982).

The major exponents of the application of family systems approaches to alcoholism have been Peter Steinglass and his colleagues (e.g., Steinglass, Bennett, Wolin, & Reiss, 1987). In a series of early descriptive studies of hospitalized alcoholics on a research unit, Steinglass and colleagues (Steinglass, Davis, & Berenson, 1977; Steinglass, Weiner, & Mendelson, 1971; Weiner, Tamerin, Steinglass, & Mendelson, 1971) studied the interactions between an alcoholic father and son, a pair of alcoholic bothers, and alcoholics and their spouses. Comparisons were made in the pattern of interactions when the alcoholic patients were sober and when they were intoxicated. These researchers observed certain positive changes in interactional behavior associated with drinking, which they referred to as "adaptive consequences" (Davis, Berenson, Steinglass, & Davis, 1974). More specifically, they noted that drinking stabilized family roles, allowed for expression of affect, resulted in greater intimacy among family members, and enabled family members to explore topics that they would typically avoid when sober.

In subsequent studies, Steinglass (1979, 1981) compared families with an alcoholic member who was drinking, sober, or in transition from one drinking status to another. Families in which the alcoholic was sober were the most flexible in their overall functioning (i.e., they demonstrated more flexibility during laboratory-based problem-solving tasks and had a balance between the time they spent together and time spent apart when at home). In contrast, drinking families were the most rigid in their family roles and functioning. In comparison to the other family types, families with an alcoholic member in transition from one drinking status to another were described as intermediate in their problem-solving ability and general family functioning.

The family systems approach to treating substance abuse focuses on the interactional rather than the individual level. Thus, identifying and addressing underlying family issues or processes that have necessitated the development of the substance abuse in one or more family members are crucial to therapy. From a family systems perspective, drug or alcohol use by a family member serves an important function for the family, helping to maintain the homeostasis of the family system (i.e., balance, stability, and equilibrium). It is assumed that the family's organization (i.e., structure and function) helps to maintain homeostasis and that family members will resist changes that threaten homeostasis. Thus, if a family has functioned as a stable unit with a substance-abus-

ing member, subsequent sobriety is likely to threaten homeostasis and may be resisted on some level.

In the family systems approach, therapists use a number of techniques to clarify the core issues in the family and promote changes in family interaction patterns. Therapists try to redefine roles, identify implicit and explicit rules that govern family members' behaviors, and define and reinforce boundaries between family members. In addition, once the therapist understands the function of substance abuse in the family, he or she can reframe it by explaining how the behavior has come about and what function it serves in the family (Fishman, Stanton, & Rosman, 1982).

The family systems approach has also been used to conceptualize and treat families in which adults or adolescents abuse drugs other than alcohol. Perhaps the most well developed is Stanton and Todd's (1982) use of structural-strategic therapy with heroin-addicted patients participating in methadone maintenance. These authors emphasized concrete behavioral changes, which included focus on family rules about drug-using behavior and the use of weekly urine tests to give tangible evidence of progress. Additionally, the intervention attempted to alter and interrupt repetitive family interactional patterns that maintained drug use. At 1-year follow-up, results showed that patients who participated in this family-based treatment were using illicit psychoactive drugs less frequently than patients who received nonfamily treatment consisting of methadone and individual counseling. Family systems therapy has also been used with drug-abusing adolescents (e.g., Lewis, Piercy, Sprenkle, & Trepper, 1990).

Behavioral Models

Behavioral marital and family therapy for substance abuse is an extension of the basic constructs of learning theory. The central principle is that behaviors, including drug and alcohol use, are learned and maintained through positive and negative reinforcement, which can come from familial interactions. Within the behavioral approach, social learning theory incorporates aspects of the stimulus-response models of operant and classical conditioning but expands beyond these models to include cognitive processes (chapter 14, this volume; Collins, 1990).

Early observational studies of marital communication patterns between alcoholic men and their wives lent support to the hypotheses that drinking behavior could be reinforced by family interactions. Hersen, Miller, and Eisler (1973) found that during a structured problem-solving interaction task, wives looked at their alcoholic husbands more frequently when the husbands were discussing alcohol than when they were discussing other topics, and that husbands spoke more during alcohol-related than during non-alcohol-related communications. These results suggested that spouses might actually be reinforcing alcohol use by paying more attention to alcohol-related conversations. A number of interactional studies have also reported increases in positive communication behaviors associated with alcohol consumption (e.g., Billings, Kessler, Gomberg, & Weiner, 1979; Frankenstein, 1982). Thus, despite the negative consequences that alcohol misuse may have on a dyadic relationship, these studies suggest that there are also positive changes in the relationship associated with drinking. These findings have an important treatment implication, namely, that increasing positive interactions without the presence of alcohol might serve to reduce alcohol use.

With certain exceptions, family-based behavioral treatment models have been used most frequently with alcoholic couples. Three general reinforcement patterns are typically observed in substance-abusing families: (a) reinforcement for drinking behavior in the form of attention or caretaking, (b) shielding of the alcoholic from experiencing negative consequences related to his or her drinking, and (c) punishment of drinking behavior (McCrady, 1986; McCrady & Epstein, 1995). In turn, behaviorally oriented treatment generally focusses on changing spousal or family interactions that serve as stimuli for abusive drinking or that trigger relapse, improving communication and problem-solving abilities, and strengthening coping skills that reinforce sobriety.

Two empirically supported behavioral marital therapy (BMT) approaches with alcoholic couples are O'Farrell's Antabuse contract plus BMT couples group and McCrady's work combining BMT with alcohol-focused spouse involvement. Both approaches stress that couples treatment for alcoholism must address the drinking of the alcoholic as well as the overall adjustment of the spousal system in order to be effective. Furthermore, each of these treatment packages emphasizes the importance of setting goals and practicing new ways of interacting during the treatment sessions and at home between sessions.

O'Farrell's (1993) BMT couples group program consists of 10–12 initial sessions conducted weekly with each couple and 10 weekly BMT couples group sessions. Initial sessions consist of (a) an initial interview; (b) crisis intervention for drinking or marital crises that must be resolved prior to further work; (c) negotiation of an Antabuse contract in which the alcoholic patient takes disulfiram while the spouse observes and verbally reinforces the alcoholic patient for taking the medication; (d) assessment of the drinking and relationship problems and feedback to the couple of the assessment results to increase motivation for continued treatment; and (e) preparation for participation in the couples BMT group. The BMT couples group sessions consist of 10 weekly meetings of four to five couples in which homework assignments and behavioral rehearsal are used to help couples (a) maintain abstinence and decrease arguments related to drinking by monitoring compliance with the Antabuse Contract, reviewing urges to drink, and providing crisis interventions for drinking episodes; (b) acknowledge and initiate daily caring behaviors; (c) plan shared rewarding activities; (d) learn communication skills and problem-solving strategies; and (e) plan for maintenance of therapeutic gains at the end of the group.

Noel and McCrady (1993) referred to their BMT program as "Alcohol-Focused Spouse Involvement with Behavioral Marital Therapy" (see also Epstein & McCrady, 1998; McCrady & Epstein, 1995). The program consists of interventions designed to (a) change the alcoholic's drinking behavior, (b) change the spouse's behavior that triggers and reinforces the alcoholic partner's alcohol use, and (c) enhance the dyadic relationship. Functional analysis, stimulus control, rearranging contingencies, cognitive restructuring, planning alternatives to drinking, problem solving, and posttreatment maintenance planning are used to help the alcoholic patient to stop drinking and the spouse to stop triggering and reinforcing alcohol use. BMT procedures, such as planning for fun activities, communication skills training, and negotiation and problem-solving, are used to enhance the marital relationship.

In two recent investigations, Fals-Stewart and colleagues (Fals-Stewart, Birchler, & O'Farrell, 1996;

Fals-Stewart, O'Farrell, Finneran, & Birchler, 1996) have treated drug-abusing patients and their intimate partners using BMT. They found that husbands who received BMT in addition to individual-based treatment (i.e., individual and group counseling) had better outcomes, in terms of reduced drug use and improved dyadic adjustment, than husbands assigned to receive an equally intensive individual-based treatment only.

FAMILY MODEL IN RELATION TO ETIOLOGY AND MAINTENANCE OF SUBSTANCE ABUSE

Family Model of Etiology of Substance Abuse

For centuries, philosophers have commented on the familial nature of substance abuse. However, it was not until the past few decades that Plutarch's anecdotal assertion that "drunks beget drunkards" came under careful scientific scrutiny. Numerous studies have shown that the rates of alcoholism are substantially higher in relatives of alcoholics than in relatives of nonalcoholics, children of alcoholics demonstrating a three- to fourfold increased risk for developing the disorder (e.g., Schuckit, 1987). Several major twin studies found that the concordance rate for alcoholism was significantly higher for monozygotic (i.e., identical) twins than for dizygotic (i.e., fraternal) pairs (e.g., Hrubec & Omenn, 1981). Adoption studies (i.e., the study of individuals separated soon after birth from their biological relatives and raised by nonrelative adoptive parents) indicate that individuals who had biological parents with severe alcohol problems were significantly more likely to have alcoholism themselves than if their surrogate parents were alcoholic (Goodwin, 1979).

Although these results suggest a genetic mediation of alcoholism, heredity is best used to explain an increased biological vulnerability to alcoholism. Genetic models do not explain the processes underlying the decision to begin using psychoactive substances or the pattern of use (e.g., light drinking, binge drinking). Clearly, the etiology of substance abuse is multidetermined by biological, psychological, and environmental pathways (Hesselbrock, 1986; Hill, 1994). Even given genetic factors in the development of alcoholism, there is also strong empirical

evidence of the importance of parent-child interactions and family socialization in the development of alcohol and drug abuse. For example, Harburg, Davis, and Caplan (1982) found that offspring tend to imitate their perception of their parents' drinking, particularly that of the same-sex parent. In a sample of young adult men, Clayton and Lacy (1982) found a significant positive relationship between perceived siblings' drug use and respondents' intention to use. Thus, from a social learning perspective, children are socialized by their parents and siblings peers into adult behaviors, including substance abuse.

Other investigators have examined the role of family interaction in the etiology of substance abuse. Bennett and Wolin (1990) found that transmission of alcoholism is more likely if there is continued interaction between alcoholic parents and adult children. Additionally, adult males have an increased probability of developing alcoholism if they have regular contact with the alcoholic parents of their wives. Wolin, Bennett, Noonan, and Teitelbaum (1980) demonstrated that when one or both parents in a family were alcoholics, their children were likely to have problems with alcohol misuse if family rituals—dinnertime, evening holidays, holidays, and so forth—were disrupted during the period of heaviest parental drinking. Conversely, families whose rituals remained essentially intact in spite of parental drinking were the least likely to have offspring who became alcoholic. Furthermore, Steinglass et al. (1987) reported that families that required sobriety of their members in order to participate in family rituals were less likely to experience transmission of alcoholism to their children than families in which there were no such rules.

Model of Maintenance of Substance Abuse and Framework for Treatment

As with etiology, maintenance of alcohol- and drug-using behavior is influenced by the interplay of biological, individual, environmental, interpersonal, social, and familial factors. Using a social learning framework, McCrady and Epstein (1995) described a model the provides an integrated conceptualization of these maintenance factors, which they referred to as the *S-O-R-C model* (p. 371). Drinking is conceptualized as a *response (R)* elicited by environmental *stimuli (S)*, such as time of the day or the smell of alcoholic beverages, that occur prior to drinking and are mediated by *organismic (O)* factors, such as crav-ing, withdrawal symptoms, or negative affective states (e.g., anger, depression, anxiety) and maintained by a positive *consequence (C)* of drinking, including ces-sation of withdrawal symptoms and alleviation of negative affect. As noted by the authors, this model has been applied to alcohol problems but presum-ably applies also to families in which members use other drugs.

At the family level, a variety of antecedents to and consequences of substance use can occur. Poor com-munication and problem solving, arguing, financial stressors, and nagging are often described as anteced-ents to substance use by family members. Conse-quences of drug use can be positive or negative. For example, certain behaviors by a non-substance-abus-ing spouse or other family members, such as avoid-ing conflict with the drug-abusing spouse when he or she is intoxicated, are positive consequences of substance use and can inadvertently reinforce sub-stance-using behavior. Conversely, partners' avoiding the drug user and making disapproving verbal com-ments about his or her substance abuse are among the most commonly reported negative consequences of substance use (Becker & Miller, 1976). Although these behaviors are normal reactions of family mem-bers to alcohol or drug use, they are usually counter-productive, serving as further cues for substance use. Other negative effects of substance use on the family, such as psychological and physical problems of the spouse and more behavioral and school problems among children in these environments, increase stress in the family system and may therefore lead to substance use (Moos, Finney, & Cronkite, 1990). Thus, there is a complex, reciprocal relationship be-tween the substance use and the functioning of the family.

From this social learning model of maintenance of substance abuse, McCrady and Epstein (1996) de-rived a family-involved treatment model that has five major tasks: (a) engagement of family members, pref-erably the identified substance abuser and (ideally) several other family members; (b) assessment and identification of antecedents and consequences of substance use, as well as any organismic mediating factors; (c) reduction or elimination of substance use before addressing family functioning; (d) modifica-tion of antecedents of substance use, reinforcement of consequences of substance use, and use of rein-forcement for reduction or cessation of alcohol and drug use; and (e) modification of family patterns of interaction that interfere with family functioning.

THERAPEUTIC CHANGE

The family treatments described below have been di-rected to moving the substance abuser to the action stage of initiating abstinence, to stabilizing the change in substance use and family relationships once change has begun, and to maintaining recovery and preventing relapse. Many of the methods de-scribed come from a behavioral approach because this approach has specified its interventions more fully than have other approaches and because our own work has focused on behavioral marital therapy (BMT) for alcoholism (O'Farrell, Choquette, & Cut-ter, 1998) and for drug abuse (Fals-Stewart, Birch-ler, & O'Farrell, 1996). Although behavioral approaches have been used mainly with couples and spouses, some studies have focused on broader family constel-lations (e.g., Hedberg & Campbell, 1974) or have worked with the substance abuser's parent (e.g., Ahles, Schlundt, Prue, & Rychtarik, 1983; Sisson & Azrin, 1993). Further, many of the behavioral meth-ods used with spouses and couples can be easily translated for use with dyads other than spouses or with broader family constellations (see O'Farrell, 1995, for examples).

Assumptions of the Family Model About How People Change

Our behavioral approach to couple and family ther-apy with substance abusers does not have a separate, unique set of assumptions about how people change. The model encompasses current notions about how people change in terms of a stages-of-change model. An individual can progress through a series of stages of change: (a) precontemplation, in which the indi-vidual is not concerned about changing the behavior in question; (b) contemplation, in which the individ-ual becomes concerned about and begins to consider changing the behavior; (c) action, in which the indi-vidual actually changes the behavior and stabilizes this change for an initial period; (d) maintenance, in which the behavior change remains stable; or (e) relapse, when the individual returns to the problem behavior (Prochaska & DiClemente, 1983). The family model emphasizes the role of the family in influencing an individual's progression through these various stages of change. For example, a family members' concern that individuals have an alcohol or drug problem may move the individuals from pre-contemplation, where they have little or no concern about their alcohol/drug use, into contemplation, where they begin to consider the possibility of change. Conversely, individuals who begin to become concerned about their own alcohol/drug use (contemplation) may not move to the action stage or may revert to precontemplation when a close family member encourages them to continue their current behavior, perhaps because the family member also is a heavy drinker or an illicit dug user.

Key Interventions in the Model

Assessment Procedures

In the initial interview with a substance abuser and family member(s) seeking marital or family therapy, the therapist needs to (a) determine what stage the substance abuser is in in the process of changing his or her addiction; (b) evaluate whether there is a need for crisis intervention prior to a careful assessment; and (c) orient the clients to the assessment procedures. In the initial session, the therapist's clinical interview gathers information about a series of issues. First, the therapist inquires about *the substance abuser's drinking and drug use*, especially recent quantity and frequency, whether the extent of physical dependence on alcohol or drugs requires detoxification, what led to seeking help at this time and prior help-seeking efforts, and whether the substance abuser's and family member's goal is to reduce the drinking or drug use or to abstain either temporarily or permanently. Second, the *stability of the marriage and family relationships* is examined in terms of current planned or actual separation as well as any past separations. Third, *recent family violence* and any fears of recurrence are discussed. Fourth, *current or recent suicidal ideation or behavior* of either the substance abuser or family members and any past instances of such behavior are examined. Finally, the therapist determines whether there are any *substance-abuse-related or other crises* that require immediate attention. Allowing 75–90 minutes for the initial session and including 5–10 minutes separately with each person provides sufficient time to gather the needed infor-

mation and to learn of important material (e.g., plans for separation, fears of violence) that individuals may be reluctant to share during the conjoint portion of the interview. More detailed information about the substance abuse and family relationships can be obtained in subsequent sessions.

To gather more detailed information about the substance abuse problem, we recommend certain assessment procedures. The Time Line Follow-Back Interview (Sobell & Sobell, 1996), a structured interview that uses a calendar and specialized interviewing methods, can be used to reconstruct the quantity and frequency of the substance abuser's drinking and drug use behavior during the 6–12 months prior to the interview. A breath test and a drug urine screen can detect any very recent substance use. Finally, to measure problems due to, respectively, alcohol and drug abuse, we suggest the Drinker Inventory of Consequences (Miller, Tonigan & Longabaugh, 1995) and the Addiction Severity Index (McLellan et al., 1985).

To gather more detailed information about family relationships, we use the following assessment procedures. To determine the overall level of satisfaction experienced in the relationship, we use the Dyadic Adjustment Scale (Busby, Crane, Larson & Christensen, 1995; Spanier, 1976) for couples and the Family Assessment Measure (Skinner, Steinhauer, & Santa Barbara, 1995) for other family constellations. The Conflict Tactics Scale (Straus, 1979) assesses the extent of verbal and physical abuse experienced. Among couples, we evaluate (a) steps taken toward separation and divorce with the Marital Status Inventory (Weiss & Cerreto, 1980); (b) specific changes desired in the relationship with the Areas of Change Questionnaire (Weiss & Birchler, 1975); (c) sexual adjustment (O'Farrell, Kleinke, & Cutter, 1997); and (d) communication skills, especially when talking about conflicts and problems (e.g., Murphy & O'Farrell, 1997).

After the assessment information has been gathered, the clients and therapist meet for a feedback session in which the therapist shares impressions of the nature and severity of the substance abuse and family problems and invites the clients to respond to these impressions. The first goal of the feedback is to increase motivation for treatment by reviewing in a nonjudgmental, matter-of-fact manner the quantity and frequency and the negative consequences of the substance use. The second goal of the feedback session is to prepare the clients for subsequent therapy sessions.

Typical Treatment Goals

A behavioral approach has two basic objectives in order to stabilize short-term change in the alcohol or drug problem and in the marriage and family relationships. The first goal is to eliminate abusive drinking and drug use and support the drinker's efforts to change. To this end, a high priority is changing ineffective alcohol-related interactional patterns such as nagging about past drinking and drug use but ignoring current sober behavior. Therapists can encourage abstinent alcohol or drug abusers and their families to engage in behaviors more pleasing to each other, but if they continue to talk about and focus on past or "possible" future drinking, frequently such arguments lead to renewed drinking (Maisto, O'Farrell, McKay, Connors, & Pelcovits, 1988). They then feel more discouraged than before about their relationship and the substance abuse problems, and are less likely to try pleasing each other again. The second goal is to alter general marital and family patterns to provide an atmosphere that is more conducive to sobriety. This goal involves helping the family repair the often extensive relationship damage incurred during many years of conflict over alcohol and drugs, as well as helping family members find solutions to relationship difficulties that may not be directly related to substance abuse. Finally, families must learn to confront and resolve relationship conflicts while avoiding relapse.

Typical Structure of Therapy Sessions

Once assessment is complete and initial obstacles have been overcome, the behavioral approach we use to help stabilize short-term change in the alcohol and drug problem and associated marital/family discord usually consists of 10–20 therapy sessions, each of which lasts 60–75 minutes. Sessions tend to be moderately to highly structured, with the therapist setting the agenda at the outset of each meeting. A typical session begins with an inquiry about any drinking or drug use or urges to drink or use drugs that have occurred since the last session, including compliance with any sobriety contract (see below)

that has been negotiated. The session moves from a review of homework from the previous session to considering important events of the past week. The therapist identifies a specific concern from the past week related to recovery or relationships that can be addressed in the session. The goal is to resolve the concern or to identify steps that can be taken to begin to resolve the concern. Then, the session may consider new material, such as instruction in and rehearsal of skills to be practiced at home during the week. It ends with assigning homework.

Generally, the first few sessions focus on decreasing negative feelings and interactions related to past or possible future substance abuse and on increasing positive exchanges. This focus decreases tension about substance use and builds goodwill. Both are necessary for dealing with marital/family problems and desired relationship changes in later sessions by using communication and problem-solving skills training and behavior change agreements.

Description of Major Techniques of the Treatment

Initiating Change and Helping the Family When the Substance Abuser Resists Treatment   Four marital/family therapy approaches address the difficult and all-too-common case of the substance abuser who is not yet willing to stop drinking and drugging. Three of the approaches try to help the spouse and family members to motivate the uncooperative, denying substance abuser to change. *Community reinforcement training for families* is a program for teaching the family member (usually the wife of a male substance abuser) (a) how to reduce physical abuse to herself, (b) how to encourage sobriety, (c) how to encourage seeking professional treatment, and (d) how to assist in that treatment (Sisson & Azrin, 1993). The *Johnson Institute "intervention" procedure* involves three to four educational and rehearsal sessions to prepare family members. During the intervention session itself, family members confront the substance abuser and strongly encourage entry into a substance treatment program (Liepman, 1993). The *unilateral family therapy* (UFT) approach assists the family member to strengthen his or her coping capabilities, to enhance family functioning, and to facilitate greater sobriety on the part of the substance abuser (Thomas & Ager, 1993).

UFT provides a series of graded steps the family can use prior to confrontation.

A fourth and final approach is *a group program for wives of treatment-resistant substance abusers* (Dittrich, 1993). This program tries to help wives cope with their emotional distress and concentrate on their own motivations for change rather than trying to motivate the substance abuser to change. This approach borrows many concepts from Al-Anon, by far the most widely used source of support for family members troubled by a loved one's substance abuse problem. Al-Anon advocates that family members detach themselves from the substance use in a loving way, accept that they are powerless to control the substance abuse, and seek support from other members of the Al-Anon program (Al-Anon Family Groups, 1981).

Behavioral Contracting   Written behavioral contracts, although different in many specific aspects, have a number of common elements that make them useful. The substance abuse goal is made explicit. Specific behaviors that the substance abuser and the family member(s) can do to help achieve this goal are also detailed. The contact provides daily social reinforcement for sobriety and reduces negative interactions about drinking or drugs. Finally, the agreement decreases the family member's anxiety and need to control the substance abuser.

In the *sobriety trust contract* (O'Farrell, 1995), each day at a specified time, the substance abuser initiates a brief discussion with the family member and reiterates his or her intention not to drink or use drugs that day. Then, the substance abuser asks if the family member has any questions or fears about possible drinking or drug use that day and answers the questions and attempts to reassure the family member. The family member is not to mention past drinking or any future possible drinking beyond that day. The substance abuser and the family member agree to refrain from discussing drinking or drugs at any other time, to keep the daily trust discussion very brief, and to end it with a positive statement to each other.

The *Antabuse (disulfiram) contract* adds to the sobriety trust contract daily Antabuse ingestion by the alcoholic in the presence of the family member. Antabuse (disulfiram), a drug that produces extreme nausea and sickness when the person taking the drug ingests alcohol, is widely used in treatment for persons with a goal of abstinence. Often, Antabuse therapy is not effective because the alcoholic discontinues the drug prematurely. This contract has been used by a number of investigators (e.g., Azrin, Sisson, Meyers, & Godley, 1982). It is designed to maintain Antabuse ingestion and abstinence from alcohol and to decrease alcohol-related arguments and interactions between the drinker and his or her family.

Participation in AA, NA, Al-Anon, Rational Recovery, and other self-help groups is often part of the behavioral contracts we negotiate. Weekly drug urine screens are part of the contracts for those who have current drug problems. Urine screens can provide evidence that the drug abuser is "clean" in order to reduce the family member's distrust and to facilitate the family member's reinforcement of the desirable behavior of the substance abuser. As with any other behavior that is part of a "sobriety contract," as we call the various forms of behavior contracts we use, we review attendance at self-help meetings and drug urine screen results at each therapy session.

Decreasing Family Members' Behaviors That Trigger or Reward Drinking   Noel and McCrady (1993) implemented procedures to decrease spouse behaviors that trigger or reward abusive drinking. For example, they presented an illustrative case study of a female alcohol abuser, Charlotte, and her husband, Tom. The couple identified behaviors by Tom that triggered drinking by Charlotte (e.g., drinking together after work, trying to stop her from drinking, arguing with her about drinking). Charlotte reacted by criticizing Tom until he left her alone, whereupon she would drink still more. Moreover, Tom unwittingly reinforced Charlotte's drinking by protecting her from the consequences of her drinking (e.g., by helping her to bed when she was drunk, cleaning up after her when she drank). Noel and McCrady helped the couple find mutually comfortable and agreeable methods to reverse Tom's behavior that had inadvertently promoted Charlotte's drinking. Tom decided to give up drinking. He worked hard to change his feelings that he must protect Charlotte from the negative consequences of her drinking. The therapists also taught Tom to provide positive reinforcers (such as verbal acknowledgment and going to movies and other events together) only when Charlotte had not been drinking.

Other Methods Focused on Substance Use Other major techniques, particularly in a behavioral approach, are used to promote abstinence from substance use: (a) increasing motivation for change by using the decisional matrix and the alcohol autobiography (McCrady & Epstein, 1995); (b) incorporating basic cognitive behavioral techniques (Carroll, 1998) delivered in the context of couples or family therapy so that the spouse or family members can help the alcoholic or drug abuser learn and implement such skills such as self-recording, functional analysis, and relapse prevention techniques; and (c) teaching coping skills such as problem solving, cognitive restructuring, and assertiveness (including drink refusal and assertiveness within the marriage or family relationship).

Interventions to Improve the Marital and Family Relationship Two major goals of interventions that are focused on the substance user's marital/family relationships are (a) to increase positive feeling, goodwill, and commitment to the relationship and (b) to resolve conflicts, problems, and desires for change. *Increasing positive interchanges* through increasing positive feelings and activities can build relationship satisfaction and family cohesion, thus producing a more positive family environment and reducing the risk of relapse. Methods used include increasing pleasing behaviors, planning recreational activities, and enacting core symbols of couple and family meaning. *Resolving conflicts and problems* is also important. Inadequate communication is a major problem for alcohol and drug abusers and their spouses and families (e.g., Fals-Stewart, Birchler, & O'Farrell, in press; O'Farrell & Birchler, 1987). Inability to resolve conflicts and problems can cause abusive drinking and severe marital and family tension to recur (Maisto et al., 1988). Teaching couples and families how to resolve conflicts and problems can reduce family stress and decrease the risk of relapse. Methods used include training in the communication skills of listening, expressing feelings directly, and using planned communication sessions, and in learning to negotiate and compromise and to use specific agreements to resolve conflicts and desires for change. The general sequence in teaching couples and families skills to increase positive interchanges and resolve conflicts and problems is (a) therapist instruction and modeling, (b) practice by the couple under therapist supervision, (c) assignment for homework, and (d) review of homework with further practice. O'Farrell (1993) gives more details on these procedures.

Active Ingredients of the Treatment

Data are not available on the active ingredients of any type of family-based treatment, so we will base our comments on our conceptual understanding and clinical experience of a behavioral approach. Active ingredients of a behavioral approach to marital and family therapy are based on the assumption that family members can reward abstinence and that substance abusers from happier families with better communication have a lower risk of relapse. This approach works directly to increase relationship factors conducive to sobriety. The alcoholic and the family member, often the spouse, are seen together to build support for sobriety through the use of behavioral contracting to directly reward abstinence and through work to decrease family members' behaviors that trigger or reward drinking. The treatment works to increase relationship cohesion and improve communication skills because substance abusers in more cohesive families have better treatment outcomes (Moos et al., 1990) and because arguments and conflicts from faulty communication often lead to relapse (Maisto et al., 1988). Finally, substance abusers who receive marital or family therapy often stay in treatment longer and are less likely to dropout of treatment than those who receive individually based treatment (Stanton & Shadish, 1997), probably because of encouragement by the family member to continue treatment sessions. This is important because longer outpatient treatment leads to better outcomes, especially among patients with more severe problems (e.g., Gottheil, 1992; McLellan, Arndt, Woody, & Metzger, 1993; McLellan et al., 1996; O'Farrell et al., 1998).

Role of the Therapist

Typical Training of the Therapist

A typical marital/family therapist in substance abuse has a master's degree or doctorate in psychology, social work, or counseling. Training should include courses on the nature and treatment of both substance abuse and marital and family problems, as well as supervised clinical experiences providing individual, couple, and family counseling with alcohol and drug problems. Therapists using a behavioral approach also need training in basic cognitive behavioral methods for treating substance abuse (e.g., Carroll, 1998).

Stance of the Therapist

Certain therapist attributes and behaviors are important for successful marital and family therapy with alcoholics and drug abusers. From the outset of the therapy, the therapist must structure treatment so that addressing the alcohol and drug abuse is the first priority, before attempts to help the couple or family with other problems. Many of our clients have had previous unsuccessful experiences with therapists who saw the couple in therapy without dealing with the drug and alcohol abuse. The hope that reduction in marital or family distress will lead to improvement in the substance abuse problem rarely is fulfilled. More typically, recurrent negative incidents and interactions related to ongoing substance use undermine whatever gains have been made in marital and family relationships.

Therapists must be able to tolerate and deal effectively with strong anger in early sessions and at later times of crisis. The therapist can use empathic listening to help each family member feel he or she has been heard and to insist that only one person speaks at a time. Helping defuse intense anger is important, as failure to do so often leads to a poor outcome (Gurman & Kniskern, 1978).

Therapists need to structure and take control of treatment sessions, especially the early assessment and therapy phase and, later, at times of crisis (e.g., episodes of drinking or drug use or intense family conflict). Structured therapy sessions with a relatively directive, active therapist are more effective than is a less structured mode of therapy. Many therapists' errors involve difficulty establishing and maintaining control of the sessions and responding to the myriad forms of resistance and noncompliance presented by couples and families. Therapists must steer a middle course between lack of structure and being overly controlling and punitive in response to noncompliance. Therapists need to clearly establish and enforce the rules of treatment and also acknowledge

approximation to desired behavior despite significant shortcomings.

Other therapist qualities can promote successful marital/family therapy. Therapists should empathize with each person in the therapy and not take sides favoring one person over the other on a consistent basis or join the family in scapegoating the substance abuser. Being positive and using humor constructively in therapy can contribute to patients' feeling comfortable. Practical knowledge of the financial and legal issues commonly faced by substance abusers and their families can also help. A further helpful stance, often used by therapists in BMT, is to act as educator or "coach" by teaching cognitive behavioral techniques to deal with the substance use (e.g., functional analysis, self-monitoring) or relationship issues (e.g., communication skills).

Finally, therapists need to take a long-term view of the course of change; both the alcohol or drug problem and the associated marital and family distress may be helped substantially only by repeated efforts, including some failed attempts. Such a long-term view may help the therapist encounter relapse without becoming overly discouraged or engaging in blaming and recriminations with the substance abuser and the family. The therapist should also maintain contact with the family long after the problems have apparently stabilized. Leaving such contacts to the family usually means that no follow-up contacts will occur until the family is back in a major crisis again.

Use of the Therapist-Patient Relationship to Promote Change

An important function of the therapist-patient relationship is to keep the patient and the family members coming to therapy, especially early in treatment, when risk of dropping out is high. Patients are likely to continue in therapy if they consider the therapist a knowledgeable and helpful guide to the process of substance abuse and relationship recovery. As described above, therapists who develop successful relationships with their patients have the ability to put "first things first" by giving priority to the substance use problem, to defuse and manage anger, to be fair and show an evenhanded understanding of each person's viewpoint, and to steer a steady course through the confusing emotions and family conflicts encountered in substance abuse recovery. The therapeutic relationship is strengthened when the therapist takes an active role to help clients deal with everyday problems encountered between sessions in coping with recovery, relapse, and relationships. Finally, whenever possible, it helps to have clients leave therapy sessions on a positive note, feeling as good as or better than when they arrived. This makes them want to return for the next session and promotes continued treatment.

Common Obstacles to Successful Treatment

Despite their seeming suitability for marital or family therapy, many substance abusers and their families present the therapist with substantial obstacles. A common problem encountered is pressing *substance abuse-related crises* (e.g., actual, impending, or threatened loss of job or home; major legal or financial problems) that preclude a serious and sustained focus on marital or family issues. The therapist can help the family devise plans to deal with the crisis or refer them elsewhere for such help, often after establishing a behavioral contract to support abstinence as described above. Other assessment and therapy procedures can be started when the crisis has been resolved.

Potential for violence is a common problem, in that half or more of substance abusers have engaged in domestic violence in the year before treatment (Fals-Stewart & O'Farrell, 1995; O'Farrell & Murphy, 1995). Unless the violence has been so severe that there is an acute risk of violence that could cause serious injury or could be life-threatening, BMT can generally be successful. In such cases, conflict containment is an explicit goal of the therapy from the outset, and specific steps are taken to prevent violence.

Blaming and recriminations by the spouse and family in frequent conversations about past or possible future drinking or drug use present another obstacle in couple or family sessions. It usually does not help for the therapist to interpret these actions to the family as an attempt to punish the substance abuser or sabotage his or her recovery. Overtly disapproving of the blaming behavior also does not help. These responses by the therapist tend to elicit defensiveness from the family members, who often feel the therapist is blaming them for the substance abuser's problem. A more effective approach is for the therapist to sympathetically reframe this behavior as trying to

protect the family from further substance-related problems and to suggest more constructive methods to achieve the same goal.

Multiple active substance abusers in the same family present a difficult obstacle. Couples in which both partners abuse alcohol or drugs are a good example. In contrast to couples in which only one member abuses alcohol or drugs, role conflict concerning drug use is less likely to be present when both partners abuse drugs and will not serve to motivate these partners to stop using drugs or alcohol. Additionally, depending on how much of a drinking or drug-using partnership these couples have formed, substance use may become an important shared recreational activity, and more frequent substance use may actually increase relationship satisfaction (Fals-Stewart, Birchler, & O'Farrell, in press; Wilsnack & Wilsnack, 1993).

Other common obstacles to successful treatment are comorbid psychopathology in the substance abuser and/or the family member and resistance to change in the family system and subsequent sabotaging of the treatment by family members.

CHARACTERISTICS OF CLIENTS MOST LIKELY TO RESPOND TO THE MODEL

Clients Who Are the Best Candidates for This Type of Treatment

Unfortunately, studies examining predictors of response to marital and family therapy with substance abusers are not yet available. One reason for the limited research in this area has been the general lack of heterogeneity in study samples thus far. Nonetheless, clinical experience and studies of factors that predict acceptance and completion of behavioral (Noel, McCrady, Stout, & Nelson, 1987; O'Farrell, Kleinke, & Cutter, 1986) and systems approaches to couples therapy for alcoholics (Zweben, Pearlman, & Li, 1983) provide some information on the clients most likely to benefit from such treatment. The clients most likely to accept and complete couples therapy have the following characteristics: (a) they have a high school education or more; (b) they are employed if able and desirous of working; (c) they live together or, if separated, are willing to reconcile for the duration of the therapy; (d) they are older; (e) they have more serious alcohol or drug problems of longer duration; (f) they enter therapy after a crisis, especially one that threatens the stability of the marriage or of family relationships; (g) the spouse and other family members living with the patient do not have serious alcohol and drug problems; (h) the substance abuser, the spouse, and the other family members do not have additional serious psychopathology; and (i) family violence that has caused serious injury or is potentially life-threatening is absent.

Further, evidence that the substance-abusing patient is motivated to change and to take an active role in a psychologically oriented treatment approach also suggests a potential for benefiting from BMT (O'Farrell et al., 1986). Such evidence includes contact with the treatment program personally initiated by the substance abuser and a history of successful participation in other outpatient counseling or self-help programs (as opposed to those admitted to detoxification only for relief of physical distress, without further active ongoing treatment participation). Abstinence, keeping scheduled appointments, and completing any required assignments in the initial month of outpatient treatment are process measures that seem to predict likely benefit on a clinical basis.

These characteristics may sound like those of model clients who are likely to benefit from nearly any treatment method. However, clients do not have to fit these criteria for therapists to use the treatment methods described in this chapter. Rather, the methods have to be adapted for some of the more difficult cases—generally, by going slower, individualizing the approach to a greater degree, and dealing with more varied and more frequent obstacles and resistances.

Contraindications of Treatment for Substance Abuse Based on Family Model

The main contraindications of treatment for substance abuse based on a family model relate to legal and safety issues. When there is a court-issued restraining order for the spouses not to have contact with each other, they should not be seen together in therapy until the restraining order is lifted or modified to allow contact in counseling. Some situations present concerns for the safety of participants in couple/family therapy. If the clinical assessment indicates that there is an active and acute risk of severe domestic violence that could cause serious injury or

is potentially life-threatening, it is better to treat the substance abuser and the family member(s) separately rather than together (Murphy & O'Farrell, 1996). Although domestic violence is frequent among substance abusers (Fals-Stewart & O'Farrell, 1995; O'Farrell & Murphy, 1995), most of this violence is not so severe that it precludes couples therapy. In fact, we recently showed for the first time that domestic violence, which was quite elevated among male alcoholics and their spouses in the year before BMT, decreased significantly in the first and second year after BMT and, among remitted alcoholics, returned to the levels experienced by nonalcoholic couples (O'Farrell & Murphy, 1995; O'Farrell, Van Hutton, & Murphy, in press). Another contraindication for BMT may be severe psychopathology in the substance abuser or the spouse (McCrady & Epstein, 1995). Nonetheless, our clinical experience suggests that at times, BMT is effective with such cases when it is used along with appropriate individual and psychopharmacological treatment and when the BMT sessions proceed slowly and are carefully tailored to the special needs of such clients.

EMPIRICAL DATA ON THE EFFECTIVENESS OF THE FAMILY MODEL FOR SUBSTANCE ABUSE

Empirical data on the effectiveness of the family model for treating substance abuse differ somewhat for alcoholism and drug abuse. *In terms of alcoholism,* a recent report reviewed 23 studies of marital or family therapy with alcoholics that included a control group—usually an individual treatment of some type (see O'Farrell, 1995, for details). Eight "early eclectic" studies, which were conducted primarily before 1975 and could not be easily categorized into one theoretical orientation, showed that family-based treatment was superior to individual treatment. There were 14 studies of behavioral marital/family therapy, of which 11 showed clear superiority for marital/family therapy, 2 showed mixed results with marital/family therapy superior only for some patients or some outcome measures, and 1 study showed no difference between behavioral marital/family therapy and the control group. In contrast, the one family systems study showed no difference between family systems therapy and the control group. Finally, no controlled studies have been done on the popular family disease (codependency) approach. Thus, although family systems and family disease approaches are popular and influential in the alcoholism treatment community, we do not know whether they are effective because they have not been studied. In contrast, behavioral approaches have relatively strong research support but are not yet widely used. The behavioral methods in alcoholism have been applied primarily to couples and spouses in studies of behavioral marital therapy. Support for BMT has been strengthened by recent studies showing (a) that domestic violence is reduced after BMT and (b) that alcohol-related hospital and jail costs decreased markedly after BMT, cost savings due to reduced hospitalizations/jailings being over five times more than the cost of delivering BMT (O'Farrell et al., 1996).

In terms of drug abuse, Stanton and Shadish (1997) reviewed randomized controlled outcome studies examining family/marital treatment for drug abuse. They concluded from six studies of adult drug abusers and nine studies of adolescent drug abusers that couples or family therapy (a) produces better outcomes than individual counseling, peer group therapy, and family psychoeducation and (b) is a cost-effective adjunct to methadone maintenance. In contrast with studies on alcoholism, most studies on drug abuse have focused on the relationship between drug abusers and their parents, rather than on couples and spouses. Most drug abuse studies have used a family systems rather than a behavioral approach. A notable exception is recent work showing that adding BMT to outpatient individual drug abuse treatment produced less drug use and fewer drug-related problems, better relationship outcomes, and better cost-benefit ratios and cost-effectiveness in the year after treatment than did individual treatment of similar intensity without BMT (Fals-Stewart, Birchler, & O'Farrell, 1996; Fals-Stewart, O'Farrell, & Birchler, 1997).

Strengths and Weaknesses of the Family Model of Treatment for Substance Abuse

McCrady and Epstein (1996) describe a number of strengths and weaknesses of the family model of treatment for substance abuse. The relatively strong empirical support for treatment based on the model is an important strength. Family involvement is associated with better compliance with treatment and with better treatment outcome. This approach directly aids not only substance abuse recovery but also family relationships and individual coping of family members. Recent studies extending the impact of BMT/BCT to reductions in violence (Fals-Stewart & O'Farrell, 1995; O'Farrell & Murphy, 1995) and very favorable cost-benefit results (O'Farrell et al., 1996; Fals-Stewart et al., 1997) with both alcoholics and drug abusers further extends the outcome domains that show documented improvements with this approach. A weakness of the approach is the greater complexity of the therapy given the multiple relationships and influences that must be dealt with. Working with couples and families requires specialized training and skills beyond what are typical for staff in many substance abuse treatment programs. Another weakness is that for the most part, the impact of marital/family therapy on the substance abuser's children has not been examined. A final weakness is that many studies have not included broad, heterogeneous samples, so that we have relatively little information on the effectiveness of marital/family therapy with substance abusers who are women or members of minority groups or who have serious comorbid psychiatric problems.

SUMMARY

Family models of treating alcoholism and drug abuse have evolved over the past 60 years into contemporary models consisting of behavioral, family system, and family disease approaches. A substantial research literature supports family-based treatment of both alcoholism and drug abuse. In the alcoholism research literature, behavioral approaches to couples and spouses predominate and have strong support, while in the alcoholism clinical literature family systems and family disease approaches are popular and influential but remain virtually unstudied. In the drug abuse research literature, family systems approaches to the subsystem of the addict and the parent predominate and have support; only recently have behavioral approaches to couples been studied with drug abuse. Research knowledge is limited by the absence of studies of the very popular family disease approach with alcoholics, the lack of family treatment research on alcoholics, the limited attention to couples therapy research on drug abusers, and the lack of attention to gender and ethnicity in alcoholism and drug abuse studies. Clinicians encounter family issues daily as they treat substance abuse. Family methods with empirical support are ready for clinical use so that we can improve our efforts to help substance abusers and their families.

Key References

McCrady, B. S., & Epstein, E. E. (1995). Marital therapy in the treatment of alcoholism. In A. S. Gurman & N. Jacobson (Eds.), *Clinical handbook of marital therapy* (2nd ed., pp. 369–393). New York: Guilford Press.

O'Farrell, T. J. (Ed.). (1993). *Treating alcohol problems: Marital and family interventions.* New York: Guilford Press.

Stanton, M. D., & Heath, A. W. (1997). Family and marital treatment. In J. H. Lowinson, P. Ruiz, R. B. Millman, & J. G. Langrod (Eds.), *Substance abuse: A comprehensive textbook* (3rd ed., pp. 448–454). Baltimore: Williams & Wilkins.

References

Adler, A. (1917). *The neurotic constitution.* New York: Mofatt, Yard.

Ahles, T. A., Schlundt, D. C., Prue, D. M., & Rychtarik, R. C. (1983). Impact of aftercare arrangements on the maintenance of treatment success in abusive drinkers. *Addictive Behaviors, 8,* 53–58.

Al-Anon Family Groups. (1981). *This is Al-Anon.* New York: Al-Anon Family Groups.

Alcoholics Anonymous. (1976). *Alcoholics Anonymous: The story of how many thousands of men and women have recovered from alcoholism* (3rd ed.). New York: Alcoholics Anonymous World Services.

Azrin, N. H., Sisson, R. W., Meyers, R., & Godley, M. (1982). Alcoholism treatment by disulfiram and community reinforcement therapy. *Journal of Behavior Therapy and Experimental Psychiatry,13,* 105–112.

Beattie, M. (1987). *Co-dependent no more.* Minneapolis, MN: Hazelden.

Becker, J. V., & Miller, P. M. (1976). Verbal and nonverbal marital interaction patterns of alcoholics and nonalcoholics. *Journal of Studies on Alcohol, 37,* 1616–1624.

Bennett, L. A., & Wolin, S. J. (1990). Family culture and alcohol transmission. Family culture and alcoholism transmission. In R. L. Collins, K. E. Leonard, & J. S. Searles (Eds.), *Alcohol and the family: Research and clinical perspectives* (pp. 194–219). New York: Guilford Press.

Billings, A. G., Kessler, M., Gomberg, C. A., & Weiner, S. (1979). Marital conflict resolution of alcoholic and nonalcoholic couples during drinking and nondrinking sessions. *Journal of Studies on Alcohol, 40,* 183–195.

Black, C. (1982). *It will never happen to me!* Denver, CO: Medical Administration Company.

Broderick, C. B., & Schrader, S. S. (1981). The history of professional marriage and family therapy. In A. S. Gurman & D. P. Kniskern (Eds.), *Handbook of family therapy* (pp. 5–35). New York: Brunner/Mazel.

Brown, E. D., O'Farrell, T. J., Maisto, S. A., Boies, K., & Suchinsky, R. (Eds.). (1997). *Accreditation guide for substance abuse treatment programs.* Newbury Park, CA: Sage.

Busby, D. M., Crane, D. R., Larson, J. H., & Christensen, C. (1995). A revision of the Dyadic Adjustment Scale for use with distressed and nondistressed couples: Construct hierarchy and multidimensional scales. *Journal of Marital and Family Therapy, 21,* 289–308.

Cermak, T. (1986). *Diagnosing and treating co-dependence.* Minneapolis: Johnson Institute.

Clayton, R. R., & Lacy, W. B. (1982). Interpersonal influences on male drug use and drug use intentions. *International Journal of the Addictions, 17,* 655–666.

Collins, R. L. (1990). Family treatment of alcohol abuse: Behavioral and systems perspectives. In R. L. Collins, K. E. Leonard, & J. S. Searles (Eds.), *Alcohol and the family: Research and clinical perspectives* (pp. 285–308). New York: Guilford Press.

Davis, D. I., Berenson, D., Steinglass, P., & Davis, S. (1974). The adaptive consequence of drinking. *Psychiatry, 37,* 209–215.

Dittrich, J. E. (1993). A group program for wives of treatment resistant alcoholics. In T. J. O'Farrell (Ed.), *Treating alcohol problems: Marital and family interventions* (pp. 78–114). New York: Guilford Press.

Epstein, E. E., & McCrady, B. S. (1998). Behavioral couples treatment of alcohol and drug use disorders: Current status and innovations. *Clinical Psychology Review, 18,* 689–711.

Fals-Stewart, W., Birchler, G. R., & O'Farrell, T. J. (1996). Behavioral couples therapy for male substance-abusing patients: Effects on relationship adjustment and drug-using behavior. *Journal of Consulting and Clinical Psychology, 64,* 959–972.

Fals-Stewart, W., Birchler, G. R., & O'Farrell, T. J. (in press). Drug abusing patients and their partners: Dyadic adjustment, relationship stability, and substance use. *Journal of Abnormal Psychology, 108.*

Fals-Stewart, W., & O'Farrell, T.J. (1995). *Domestic violence among drug abusing couples.* Paper presented at the Annual Convention of the Association for the Advancement of Behavior Therapy, Washington, DC.

Fals-Stewart, W., O'Farrell, T. J., & Birchler. G. R. (1997). Behavioral couples therapy for male substance abusing patients: A cost outcomes analysis. *Journal of Consulting and Clinical Psychology, 65,* 789–802.

Fals-Stewart, W., O'Farrell, T. J., Finneran, S., & Birchler, G. R. (1996). The use of behavioral couples therapy with methadone maintenance patients: Effects on drug use and dyadic adjustment. In *Convention Proceedings for the 30th Annual Association for the Advancement of Behavior Therapy Convention* (p. 492). New York: Association for the Advancement of Behavior Therapy.

Fishman, H. C., Stanton, M. D., & Rosman, B. L. (1982). Treating families of adolescent drug abusers. In M. D. Stanton & T. C. Todd (Eds.), *The family therapy of drug abuse and addiction* (pp. 335–357). New York: Guilford Press.

Frankenstein, W. (1982). *Alcohol intoxication effects on alcoholics' marital interactions for three levels of conflict intensity.* Unpublished master's thesis, Rutgers University.

Gondoli, D. M., & Jacob, T. (1990). Family treatment of alcoholism. In R. R. Watson (Ed.), *Drug and alcohol abuse prevention* (pp. 245–262). Totowa, NJ: Humana Press.

Goodwin, D. W. (1979). Alcoholism and heredity. *Archives of General Psychiatry, 36,* 57–61.

Gottheil, E. (1992). Length of stay, patient severity and treatment outcome: Sample data from the field of alcoholism. *Journal of Studies on Alcohol, 53,* 69–75.

Guerin, P. J. (1976). Family therapy: The first 25 years. In P. J. Guerin (Ed.), *Family therapy: Theory and practice* (pp. 1–24). New York: Gardner Press.

Gurman, A. S., & Kniskern, D. P. (1978). Deterioration in marital and family therapy: Empirical, clinical and conceptual issues. *Family Process, 17,* 3–20.

Harburg, E., Davis, D. R., & Caplan, R. (1982). Parent and offspring alcohol use—Imitative and aversive transmission. *Journal of Studies on Alcohol, 43,* 497–516.

Hedberg, A. G., & Campbell, L. (1974). A comparison of four behavioral treatments of alcoholism. *Journal of Behavior Therapy and Experimental Psychiatry, 5,* 251–256.

Hersen, M., Miller, P. M., & Eisler, R. M. (1973). Interactions between alcoholics and their wives. A descriptive analysis of verbal and nonverbal behavior. *Quarterly Journal of Studies on Alcohol, 34,* 516–520.

Hesselbrock, M. (1986). Alcoholic typologies: A review of empirical evaluations of common classification schemes. *Recent Developments in Alcoholism, 4,* 191–206.

Hill, S. (1994). Etiology. In J. Langenbucher, B. McCrady, W. Frankenstein, & P. Nathan (Eds.), *Annual review of addictions research and treatment* (pp. 127–148). New York: Pergamon Press.

Hrubec, Z., & Omenn, G. S. (1981). Evidence of genetic predisposition to alcohol cirrhosis and psychosis: Twin concordances for alcoholism and its biological end points by zygosity among male veterans. *Alcoholism: Clinical and Experimental Research, 5,* 207–212.

Jackson, J. (1954). The adjustment of the family to the crisis of alcoholism. *Quarterly Journal of Studies on Alcohol, 15,* 562–586.

Jellinek, E. M. (1960). *The disease concept of alcoholism.* New Haven, CT: Hillhouse Press.

Jung, C. (1910). The association method. *The American Journal of Psychology, 21,* 219–269.

Laundergan, J. C., & Williams, T. (1993). The Hazelden residential family program: A combined systems and disease model approach. In T. J. O'Farrell (Ed.), *Treating alcohol problems: Marital and family interventions* (pp. 145–169). New York: Guilford Press.

Lewis, M. L. (1937). Alcoholism and family casework. *Social Casework, 35,* 8–14.

Lewis, R. A., Piercy, F. P., Sprenkle, D. H., & Trepper, T. S. (1990). The Purdue brief family model for adolescent substance abusers. In T. Todd & M. Selekman (Eds.), *Family therapy with adolescent substance abusers.* New York: Allyn & Bacon.

Liepman, M. R. (1993). Using family member influence to motivate alcoholics to enter treatment: The Johnson Institute Intervention approach. In T. J. O'Farrell (Ed.), *Treating alcohol problems: Marital and family interventions* (pp. 54–77). New York: Guilford Press.

Maisto, S. A., O'Farrell, T. J., McKay, J., Connors, G. J., & Pelcovits, M. A. (1988). Alcoholics' attributions of factors affecting their relapse to drinking and reasons for terminating relapse events. *Addictive Behaviors, 13,* 79–82.

McCrady, B. S. (1986). The family in the change process. In W. R. Miller & N. H. Heather (Eds.), *Treating addictive behaviors: Process of change* (pp. 305–318). New York: Plenum.

McCrady, B. S., & Epstein, E. E. (1995). Marital therapy in the treatment of alcoholism. In A. S. Gurman & N. Jacobson (Eds.), *Clinical handbook of marital therapy* (2nd ed., pp. 369–393). New York: Guilford Press.

McCrady, B. S., & Epstein, E. E. (1996). Theoretical bases of family approaches to substance abuse treatment. In F. Rotgers, D. S. Keller, & J. Morgenstern (Eds.), *Treating substance abuse: Theory and technique* (pp. 117–143). New York: Guilford Press.

McLellan, A. T., Arndt, I. O., Woody, G. E., & Metzger, D. (1993). Psychosocial services in substance abuse treatment. *Journal of the American Medical Association, 269,* 1953–1959.

McLellan, A. T., Luborsky, L., Cacciola, J., Griffith, J., Evans, F., Barr, H. L., & O'Brien, C. P. (1985). New data from the Addiction Severity Index: Reliability and validity in three centers. *Journal of Nervous and Mental Disease, 173,* 412–423.

McLellan, A. T., Woody, G. E., Metzger, D., McKay, J., Alterman, A. I., & O'Brien, C. P. (1996). Evaluating the effectiveness of treatment for substance abuse disorders: reasonable expectations, appropriate comparisons. *The Milbank Quarterly, 74,* 51–85.

Miller, W. R., Tonigan, J. S., & Longabaugh, R. (1995). *The Drinker Inventory of Consequences (DrInC): An instrument for assessing adverse consequences of alcohol abuse.* Rockville, MD: National Institute on Alcohol Abuse and Alcoholism.

Moos, R. H., Finney, J. W., & Cronkite, R. C. (1990). *Alcoholism treatment: Context, process, and outcome.* New York: Oxford University Press.

Murphy, C. M., & O'Farrell, T. J. (1996). Clinical implications of recent research on marital violence among alcoholics. In W. Fals-Stewart (Chair), *Spousal violence and substance abuse.* Symposium conducted at the Annual Meeting of the American Psychological Association, Toronto.

Murphy, C. M., & O'Farrell, T. J. (1997). Couple communication patterns of maritally aggressive and nonaggressive male alcoholics. *Journal of Studies on Alcohol, 58,* 83–90.

Noel, N. E., & McCrady, B. S. (1993). Alcohol-focused spouse involvement with behavioral marital therapy. In T. J. O'Farrell (Ed.), *Treating alcohol problems: Marital and family interventions* (pp. 210–235). New York: Guilford Press.

Noel, N. E., McCrady, B. S., Stout, R. L., & Nelson, H. F. (1987). Predictors of attrition from an outpatient alcoholism treatment program for alcoholic couples. *Journal of Studies on Alcohol, 48,* 229–235.

O'Farrell, T. J. (1992). Families and alcohol problems: An overview of treatment research. *Journal of Family Psychology, 5,* 339–359.

O'Farrell, T. J. (1993). A behavioral marital therapy couples group program for alcoholics and their spouses. In T. J. O'Farrell (Ed.), *Treating alcohol problems: Marital and family interventions* (pp. 170–209). New York: Guilford Press.

O'Farrell, T. J. (1995). Marital and family therapy. In R. Hester & W. Miller (Eds.), *Handbook of alcoholism treatment approaches* (2nd ed., pp. 195–220). Boston: Allyn & Bacon.

O'Farrell, T. J., & Birchler, G. R. (1987). Marital relationships of alcoholic, conflicted, and nonconflicted couples. *Journal of Marital and Family Therapy, 13,* 259–274.

O'Farrell, T. J., Choquette, K. A., & Cutter, H. S. G. (1998). Couples relapse prevention sessions after behavioral marital therapy for alcoholics and their wives: Outcomes during three years after starting treatment. *Journal of Studies on Alcohol, 59,* 357–370.

O'Farrell, T. J., Choquette, K. A., Cutter, H. S. G., Brown, E. D., Bayog, R., McCourt, W., Lowe, J., Chan, A., & Deneault, P. (1996). Cost-benefit and cost-effectiveness analyses of behavioral marital therapy with and without relapse prevention sessions for alcoholics and their spouses. *Behavior Therapy, 27,* 7–24.

O'Farrell, T. J., Kleinke, C., & Cutter, H. S. G. (1986). Differences between alcoholic couples accepting and rejecting an offer of outpatient marital therapy. *American Journal of Drug and Alcohol Abuse, 12,* 301–310.

O'Farrell, T. J., Kleinke, C. L., & Cutter, H. S. G. (1997). A Sexual Adjustment Questionnaire for use in therapy and research with alcoholics and their spouses. *Journal of Substance Abuse Treatment, 13,* 1–10.

O'Farrell, T. J., & Murphy, C. M. (1995). Marital violence before and after alcoholism treatment. *Journal of Consulting and Clinical Psychology, 63,* 256–262.

O'Farrell, T. J., Van Hutton, V., & Murphy, C. M. (in press). Domestic violence after alcoholism treatment: A two-year longitudinal study. *Journal of Studies on Alcohol, 60.*

Prochaska, J. O., & DiClemente, C. C. (1983). Stages and processes of self-change of smoking: Toward an integrative model of change. *Journal of Consulting and Clinical Psychology, 51,* 390–395.

Rich, M. E. (1959). *A belief in people: A history of family social work.* New York: Family Service Association of America.

Schaef, A. (1986). *Codependence misunderstood/mistreated.* New York: Harper & Row.

Schuckit, M. A. (1987). Biological vulnerability to alcoholism. *Journal of Consulting and Clinical Psychology, 55,* 1–9.

Sisson, R. W., & Azrin, N. H. (1993). Community Reinforcement Training for families: A method to get alcoholics into treatment. In T. J. O'Farrell (Ed.), *Treating alcohol problems: Marital and family interventions* (pp. 34–53). New York: Guilford Press.

Skinner, H. A., Steinhauer, P. D., & Santa Barbara, J.

(1995). *Family Assessment Measure* (Version III). Toronto: Multi-Health Systems.

Sobell, L. C., & Sobell, M. B. (1996). *Timeline follow back: A calendar method for assessing alcohol and drug use (user's guide)*. Toronto: Addiction Research Foundation.

Spanier, G. (1976). Measuring dyadic adjustment: New scales for assessing the quality of marriage and similar dyads. *Journal of Marriage and the Family, 38,* 15–30.

Stanton, M. D., & Heath, A. W. (1997). Family and marital treatment. In J. H. Lowinson, P. Ruiz, R. B. Millman, & J. G. Langrod (Eds.), *Substance abuse: A comprehensive textbook* (3rd ed., pp. 448–454). Baltimore: Williams & Wilkins.

Stanton, M. D., & Shadish, W. R. (1997). Outcome, attrition, and family/couples treatment for drug abuse: A meta-analysis and a review of controlled, comparative studies. *Psychological Bulletin, 122,* 170–191.

Stanton, M. D., & Todd, T. C. (1982). *The family therapy of drug abuse and addiction.* New York: Guilford Press.

Steinglass, P. (1979). The alcoholic family in the interaction laboratory. *Journal of Nervous and Mental Disease, 167,* 428–436.

Steinglass, P. (1981). The alcoholic family at home. Patterns of interactions in dry, wet, and transitional stages of alcoholism. *Archives of General Psychiatry, 38,* 578–584.

Steinglass, P., Bennett, L., Wolin, S., & Reiss, D. (1987). *The alcoholic family.* New York: Basic Books.

Steinglass, P., Davis, D. I., & Berenson, D. (1977). Observations of conjointly hospitalized "alcoholic couples" during sobriety and intoxication: Implications for theory and therapy. *Family Process, 16,* 1–16.

Steinglass, P., Weiner, S., & Mendelson, J. H. (1971). Interactional issues as determinants of alcoholism. *American Journal of Psychiatry, 128,* 275–280.

Straus, M. A. (1979). Measuring intrafamily conflict and violence: The Conflict Tactic (CT) Scales. *Journal of Marriage and Family, 41,* 75–86.

Thomas E. J., & Ager, R. D. (1993). Unilateral family therapy with spouses of uncooperative alcohol abusers. In T. J. O'Farrell (Ed.), *Treating alcohol problems: Marital and family interventions* (pp. 3–33). New York: Guilford Press.

Wegsheider, S. (1981). *Another chance: Hope and health for the alcoholic family.* Palo Alto, CA: Science & Behavior Books.

Weiner, S., Tamerin, J. S., Steinglass, P., & Mendelson, J. H. (1971). Familial patterns in chronic alcoholism: A study of a father and son during experimental intoxication. *American Journal of Psychiatry, 127,* 1646–1651.

Weiss, R. L., & Birchler, G. R. (1975). *Areas of Change Questionnaire.* Unpublished manuscript. University of Oregon, Marital Studies Program, Eugene.

Weiss, R. L., & Cerreto, M. C. (1980). The Marital Status Inventory: Development of a measure of dissolution potential. *American Journal of Family Therapy, 8,* 80–85.

Whalen, T. (1953). Wives of alcoholics: Four types observed in a family service agency. *Quarterly Journal of Studies on Alcohol, 14,* 632–641.

Wilsnack, S. C., & Wilsnack, R. W. (1993). Epidemiological research on women's drinking: Recent progress and directions for the 1990s. In E. S. L. Gomberg & T. D. Nirenberg (Eds.), *Women and substance abuse* (pp. 62–99). Norwood, NJ: Ablex.

Wolin, S. J., Bennett, L. A., Noonan, D. L., & Teitelbaum, M. A. (1980). Disrupted family rituals: A factor in the intergenerational transmission of alcoholism. *Journal of Studies on Alcohol, 41,* 199–214.

Zweben, A., Pearlman, S., & Li, S. (1983). Reducing attrition from conjoint therapy with alcoholic couples. *Drug and Alcohol Dependence, 11,* 321–331.

17

The Therapeutic Community
Treatment Model

George De Leon

Therapeutic communities have been treating substance abusers for more than three decades. Originating as an alternative to conventional medical and psychiatric approaches, the therapeutic community (TC) has established itself as a major psychosocial treatment modality for thousands of chemically involved individuals. However, not all residential drug treatment programs are TCs, not all TCs are in residential settings, and not all programs that call themselves TCs employ the same social and psychological models of treatment. Indeed, the label *therapeutic community* is widely used, often to vaguely represent its distinct approach in almost any setting, including community residences, hospital wards, prisons, and homeless shelters. One effect of this labeling has been to cloud understanding of what the TC is as a drug treatment approach, how well it works, where it works best, and for which client it is most appropriate.

The therapeutic community is a drug-free modality that utilizes a social psychological approach to the treatment of drug abuse. Its characteristic setting is a community-based residence in urban and nonurban locales. However, TC programs have been implemented in a variety of other settings, both residential *and* nonresidential (hospitals, jails, schools, halfway houses, day treatment clinics, and ambulatory clinics). TCs offer a wide variety of services, including social, psychological, educational, medical, legal, and social advocacy. These services, however, are coordinated in accordance with the TC's basic self-help model. This chapter presents the therapeutic community as a unique social psychological approach to the treatment of substance abuse. Its model and methods are grounded in a theoretical framework that has evolved from both clinical and research experience.

Early Development of the TC Model

Therapeutic communities for addictions appeared a decade later than TCs in psychiatric hospitals pioneered by Jones (1953) and others in the United Kingdom (see Kennard, 1983; Rapoport, 1960). Emergence of the psychiatric TC is viewed within the context of what some have termed the third revolution in psychiatry, one which signaled the use of group methods and milieu therapy (Rapoport, 1960). Although the name *therapeutic community* evolved in these hospital settings, there is no clear evidence of any direct influences of psychiatric TCs on the origins and development of addiction TCs.

To date, there is no comprehensive history of the addiction therapeutic community. However, some literature does contain limited surveys of the evolution of therapeutic communities (e.g., Bratter, Bratter, & Heimberg, 1986; Brook & Whitehead, 1980; Deitch, 1974; De Leon & Ziegenfuss, 1986; Glaser, 1974; Kennard, 1983; Kooyman, 1992). TC concepts, beliefs, and practices can be traced to indirect influences of religion, philosophy, psychiatry, and the social and behavioral sciences. Immediate antecedents of the addiction TC are Alcoholics Anonymous (AA) and religious reform and temperance movements in North America, although ancient prototypes exist in all forms of communal healing and support.

Contemporary therapeutic communities for addictions derive from Synanon, founded in 1958 by Charles Dederich with other recovering alcoholics and drug addicts. Evolution of the modern addiction TC following Synanon can be readily sketched in the genealogy of programs that proliferated during the 1960 and 1970s in North America, and eventually in Europe (see, for example, Brook & Whitehead, 1980; De Leon & Ziegenfuss, 1986; Glaser, 1974; Kooyman, 1992). To a considerable extent, basic elements of the TC model and method were honed in these programs that consisted of similar designs; subscribed to shared assumptions, concepts, and beliefs; and engaged in similar practices. These commonalties may be viewed as the essential elements of the therapeutic community which make up

the theoretical framework of the TC model and method elaborated in other writings (De Leon, 1994b, 1995).

Status of the Model and Its Applications

Today, the TC modality consists of a wide range of programs serving a diversity of clients who use a variety of drugs, and who present complex social psychological problems in addition to their chemical abuse. Client differences as well as clinical requirements and funding realities have encouraged the development of modified residential TCs with shorter planned durations of stay (3, 6, and 12 months), as well as TC-oriented day treatment and outpatient ambulatory models. Correctional facilities, medical and mental hospitals, community residences, and shelter settings, overwhelmed with alcohol and illicit drug abuse problems, have implemented TC programs within their institutional boundaries. TC agencies have incorporated basic elements of the TC's drug-free philosophy and view of "right living" into education and prevention programs for schools and communities.

The TC's basic social learning model has been amplified with a variety of additional services: family, educational, vocational, medical, and mental health. Staffing composition has been altered to include increasing proportions of traditional mental health, medical, and education professionals to serve along with recovered paraprofessionals (e.g., Carroll & Sobel, 1986; De Leon, 1994b; Winick, 1990–1991). The traditional TC model described in this chapter is actually the prototype of a variety of TC-oriented programs.

Key Constructs and Terms

The TC can be distinguished from other major drug treatment modalities in two fundamental ways. First, the TC offers a systematic treatment approach guided by an explicit perspective on the drug use disorder, the person, recovery, and right living. Second, the primary "therapist" and teacher in the TC is the community itself, consisting of the social environment, peers, and staff who, as role models of successful personal change, serve as guides in the recovery process. Thus, the community is both the context in which change occurs and the method for facilitating change.

Full accounts of the perspective and method are provided in other writings (e.g., De Leon, 1994a; De Leon & Rosenthal, 1989). Briefly, substance abuse is a disorder of the whole person. Regardless of social class or primary drug differences, substance abusers share important similarities. Most reveal some problems in socialization, cognitive/emotional skills, and overall psychological development. This is evident in their immaturity, poor self-esteem, conduct and character disorder, or antisocial characteristics. Recovery is a developmental process of incremental learning toward a stable change in behavior, attitudes, and values of "right living" associated with maintaining abstinence.

The quintessential feature of the TC approach may be termed *community as method* (De Leon, 1994b). What distinguishes the TC from other treatment approaches (and other communities) is the purposive use of the peer community to facilitate social and psychological change in individuals. In a therapeutic community, all activities are designed to produce therapeutic and educational change in individual participants, and all participants are mediators of these therapeutic and educational changes.

HOW THE TC MODEL RELATES TO THEORY OF THE ETIOLOGY AND MAINTENANCE OF SUBSTANCE USE

View of Etiology of Substance Abuse

The therapeutic community views substance abuse as a disorder of the whole person. Although individuals differ in choice of substance, abuse involves some or all the areas of functioning. Cognitive, behavioral, and mood disturbances appear, as do medical problems. Thinking may be unrealistic or disorganized. Values are confused, nonexistent, or antisocial. Frequently, there are deficits in verbal, reading, writing, and marketable skills, and whether couched in existential or psychological terms, moral issues are apparent. Physical addiction or dependency must be seen in the wider context of the individual's psychological status and lifestyle. For some abusers, physiological factors may be important, but for most, these remain minor relative to the social and psychological problems that precede and the behavioral deficits that accumulate with continued substance abuse. Addiction is a symptom, not the essence of the disorder. Thus, the problem is the person, not the drug.

In the TC view, the sources of the addiction disorder are social and psychological. Typical antecedents include socioeconomic disadvantage, ineffective parenting, negative role models, and deviant social learning. Biological factors are acknowledged as important for some abusers, but only as a predisposition to use chemicals in order to induce altered mental and emotional states. Although valuable for illuminating individual differences, the biological factors and social psychological history of the individual are not considered sufficient causes nor reasons for current behavior. The emphasis is on the individuals' own contribution to their problems in the past and to their solutions in the present. Thus, regardless of the validity of historical influences, assuming responsibility for one's conduct and attitudes is the key to personal change.

View of Maintenance of Substance Abuse

Abuse of any substance is viewed as overdetermined behavior. Physiological dependency is secondary to the wide range of circumstances that influence and then gain control over an individual's drug use behavior. Invariably problems and situations associated with discomfort become regular signals for resorting to drug use. For some abusers, physiological factors may be important, but for most, these remain minor relative to the general social and psychological deficits that accumulate with continued substance abuse.

View of Right Living

Therapeutic communities adhere to certain precepts and values as essential to self-help recovery, social learning, personal growth, and healthy living. These emphasize explicit values that determine how individuals relate to themselves, peers, significant others, and the larger society. They include, for example, truth and honesty (in word and deed), the work ethic, learning to learn, personal accountability, economic self-reliance, responsible concern for others and peers ("brother's/sister's keeper"), family responsibility, community involvement, and good citizenry.

Residents reveal ill-formed personal identities, that is, how they label, perceive, and accept themselves, which relates to their history of drug use as well as to their early background. For most residents, the onset of regular drug use occurred in their early teens or even younger, and profoundly altered the course of healthy identity development. Regardless of their chronological age, they reveal an arrested stage of personal identity closer to that of adolescents.

In summary, rather than a physical disease, substance abuse is viewed as a complex social psychological disorder of the whole person, consisting of recurring negative patterns of behaving and thinking and poor emotional management. These self-defeating or destructive patterns reveal a disorder in lifestyle, self-identity, and individual function. In the TC perspective, recovery means a change in lifestyle that can be achieved only by living differently in terms not only of behaviors and attitudes but of values and beliefs. Regardless of differences in their social backgrounds, residents in TCs have lost or never acquired values to guide healthy, productive lifestyles. Learning or relearning these values requires teaching and practice in a real community that explicitly reinforces how individuals can "live right" with themselves, with others, and in society.

Rationale of How the TC Model of Treatment Follows From the Theory of Substance Abuse

Recovering people innovated the TC as a setting for individuals to learn an alternative lifestyle. Their intuitive understanding of the relevance of community as method is explicit in their perspective on the disorder, the person, transforming lifestyles, and identities. Changing the whole person requires the 24-hour-a-day setting of community life in which individuals display the full range of their behavior and attitudes. Unlike the psychotherapy hour or group therapy sessions, which sample relatively little of the individual over a long period of time, the complexity of the "whole" individual is gradually revealed in the varied situations of community life: in its social performance demands, its multiple participant roles, and relationships with others.

Community as method fosters change in the social and personal elements of identity. It provides opportunities and context for developing positive social identity in its focus on social participation, mutual responsibility, relationships based on trust, and values of right living. Community also shapes and strengthens the element of personal identity in its

emphasis on earned achievement, absolute honesty in word and in action, and learning to share private experiences. Community elements such as encounter challenge false images and foster self-objectification, in terms of personal identity, and strengthen the individual's critical self-perceptions. Of special relevance to personal identity is community acceptance of the authentically revealed individual.

THERAPEUTIC CHANGE

Assumptions of the TC Model About How People Change

The TC treatment model reflects the four views of its perspective and community-as-method approach. Disorder of the whole person means that change is multidimensional. Change must be viewed along several dimensions of behavior, perceptions, and experiences. Change is facilitated by the community, which consists of multiple interventions. Recovery unfolds as developmental social learning, which can be described in terms of characteristic stages of change. Based on its perspective, the aim of treatment is a global change in the individual to develop a positive lifestyle and personal identity. These social and psychological goals of the TC shape its treatment regimen as well as define several broad assumptions concerning its view of recovery.

Recovery as a Developmental Process

Change in the TC can be understood as a passage through stages of incremental learning. The learning that occurs at each stage facilitates change at the next, and each change reflects movement toward the goals of recovery.

Motivation

Recovery depends on pressures to change—positive and negative. Some clients, driven by stressful external pressures, seek help. Others are moved by more intrinsic factors. For all, however, remaining in treatment requires continued motivation to change. Thus, elements of the rehabilitation approach are designed to sustain motivation or detect early signs of premature termination. Although the influence of treatment depends on the person's motivation and readiness, change does not occur in a vacuum. Rehabilitation unfolds as an interaction between the client and the therapeutic environment.

Self-Help and Mutual Self-Help

Strictly speaking, treatment is not provided but made available to the individual in the TC environment, through its staff and peers and the daily regimen of work, groups, meetings, seminars, and recreation. However, the effectiveness of these elements is dependent on the individual, who must fully engage in the treatment regimen. Self-help recovery means that the individual makes the main contribution to the change process. Mutual self-help emphasizes the fact that each individual in the process contributes to change in others. The main messages of recovery, personal growth, and right living are mediated by peers through confrontation and sharing in groups, by example as role models, and as supportive, encouraging friends in daily interaction.

Social Learning

Negative behavioral patterns and attitudes and dysfunctional roles were not acquired in isolation, nor can they be changed in isolation. Therefore, recovery depends not only on what is being learned, but on how, where, and with whom learning occurs. This assumption is the basis for the community itself serving as healer and teacher. Learning occurs by doing and participating as a community member; a socially responsible role is acquired by acting the role. Changes in lifestyle and identity are gradually learned through participating in the varied roles of community life supported by people and relationships involved in the learning process. Without these relationships, newly learned ways of coping are threatened by isolation and the potential for relapse. Thus, a healthy perspective on self, society, and a life philosophy must be affirmed by a network of others to ensure a stable recovery.

Key Interventions in the Model

Assessment Procedures

Partitioning the "whole" individual into separate dimensions is a somewhat artificial device analogous to attempts at classification of the TC milieu into separate interventions. Thus, a complete assessment of change in the whole person includes both the objective behavioral dimensions and subjective changes reflected in self-perceptions and experiences. The objective dimensions are discussed for purposes of illustration.

Behavioral change can be described along four broad dimensions that reflect the TC perspective. The dimensions of community member and socialization refer to social development of the individual specifically as a member in the TC community, and generally as a prosocial participant in the larger society. The developmental and psychological dimensions refer to the evolution of individuals as unique persons in terms of their basic psychological function, personal growth, and identity. Each dimension pictures the same individual from different aspects in terms of observable behavioral indicators.

Changes in the four behavioral dimensions are assessed informally by peers on a daily basis in a variety of settings. They are also assessed formally by staff for purposes of evaluating general progress, phase graduations, job changes, or disciplinary actions. Changes in subjective domains such as self-perception, self-efficacy, and various healing experiences are assessed informally through client disclosure to peers and staff, in any setting.

Treatment Goals

The primary psychological goal is to change the negative patterns of behavior, thinking, and feeling that predispose to drug use. The main social goal is to develop a responsible, drug-free lifestyle. Stable recovery, however, depends on a successful integration of these social and psychological goals. Behavioral change is unstable without insight, and insight is insufficient without felt experience. Thus conduct, emotions, skills, attitudes, and values must be integrated to ensure enduring change in lifestyle and a positive personal and social identity.

Typical Modality for Treatment Delivery

The multidimensional view of the individual and disorder requires a multidimensional, social psychological treatment most efficiently delivered in a community-based residential setting. TC-oriented programs can be implemented in nonresidential as well as institutional settings modified for the special characteristics of the client served or the institutional boundaries.

The TC Traditional Model

Traditional TCs are similar in planned duration of stay (15–24 months), structure, staffing pattern, perspective, and rehabilitative regimen, although they differ in size (30–600 beds) and client demography. Although there is increasing diversity among contemporary TC-oriented programs, most incorporate the common components of the program model (Melnick & De Leon, in press). These can be outlined in terms of the TC *structure*, or social organization, and its *process* in terms of the individual's passage through stages of change within the context of community life. Full narrative descriptions of the TC programs are provided in other writings (e.g., De Leon & Rosenthal, 1989; De Leon & Ziegenfuss, 1986).

TC STRUCTURE: BASIC COMPONENTS

The social organization of the TC is composed of relatively few staff and stratified levels of resident peers—junior, intermediate, and senior—who constitute the community, or family, in the residence. This peer-to-community structure strengthens the individual's identification with a perceived, ordered network of others. More important, it arranges relationships of mutual responsibility to others at various levels in the program.

The daily operation of the community itself is the task of the residents, working together under staff supervision. The broad range of resident job assignments illustrates the extent of the self-help process. These include conducting all house services (e.g., cooking, cleaning, kitchen service, minor repair), serving as apprentices, running all departments, and conducting house meetings, certain seminars, and peer encounter groups.

Staff are composed of TC-trained clinicians and other human service professionals. Primary clinical staff are usually former substance abusers who themselves were rehabilitated in TC programs. Other staff consist of professionals providing medical, mental health, vocational, educational, family counseling, fiscal, administrative, and legal services.

The TC is managed by staff who monitor and evaluate client status, supervise resident groups, as-

sign and supervise resident job functions, and oversee house operations. Clinically, staff conduct therapeutic groups (other than peer encounters), provide individual counseling, organize social and recreational projects, and confer with significant others. They decide matters of resident status, discipline, promotions, transfers, discharges, furloughs, and treatment planning.

The new client enters a setting of upward mobility. Resident job functions are arranged in a hierarchy according to seniority, clinical progress, and productivity. Job assignments begin with the most menial tasks (e.g., mopping the floor) and lead vertically to levels of coordination and management. Indeed, clients come in as patients and can leave as staff. This social organization of the TC reflects the fundamental aspects of its rehabilitative approach, work as education and therapy, mutual self-help, peers as role models, and staff as rational authorities.

Work as Education and Therapy

In the TC, work mediates essential educational and therapeutic effects. Work and job changes have clinical relevance for substance abusers in TCs, most of whom have not successfully negotiated the social and occupational world of the larger society. Vertical job movements carry the obvious rewards of status and privilege. However, lateral job changes are more frequent, providing exposure to all aspects of the community. Typically, residents experience many lateral job changes that enable them to learn new skills and to negotiate the system. This increased involvement also heightens their sense of belonging and strengthens their commitment to the community.

Mutual Self-Help

The essential dynamic in the TC is mutual self-help. The day-to-day activities of a TC are conducted by the residents themselves. In their jobs, groups, meetings, recreation, and personal and social time, it is residents who continually transmit to each other the main messages and expectations of the community.

Peers as Role Models

Peers as role models and staff as role models and rational authorities are the primary mediators of the recovery process. Members who demonstrate the expected behaviors and reflect the values and teachings of the community are viewed as role models. This is illustrated in two main attributes.

Resident role models "act as if." They behave as the person they should be, rather than as the person they have been. Despite resistance, perceptions, or feelings to the contrary, they engage in the expected behaviors and consistently maintain the attitudes and values of the community. These include self-motivation, commitment to work and striving, positive regard for staff as authority, and an optimistic outlook toward the future. In the TC view, acting as if is not just an exercise in conformity but an essential mechanism for more complete psychological change. Feelings, insights, and altered self-perceptions often follow rather than precede behavior change.

Role models display responsible concern. This concept is closely akin to the notion of "I am my brother's/sister's keeper." Showing responsible concern involves willingness to confront others whose behavior is not in keeping with the rules of the TC, the spirit of the community, or the knowledge that is consistent with growth and rehabilitation. Role models are obligated to be aware of the appearance, attitude, moods, and performance of their peers, and to confront negative signs in these. In particular, role models are aware of their own behavior in the overall community and the process prescribed for personal growth.

Staff as Rational Authorities

Staff foster the self-help learning process through their managerial and clinical functions described above and in their psychological relationship with the residents as role models, parental surrogates, and rational authorities. TC clients often have had difficulties with authorities, who have not been trusted or perceived as guides and teachers. Thus, they need a successful experience with an authority figure who is viewed as credible (recovered), supportive, corrective, and protective in order to gain authority over themselves (personal autonomy). Implicit in their role as rational authorities, staff provide the reasons for their decisions and explain the meaning of consequences. They exercise their powers to teach and guide, facilitate and correct, rather than to punish, control, or exploit.

COMPONENTS OF A GENERIC TC PROGRAM MODEL

The perspective and approach of the traditional TC provide the conceptual basis for defining the basic components of a *generic* TC program model, which can be adapted for special populations and various settings, both residential and nonresidential.

Community Separateness

TC-oriented programs have their own names—often innovated by the clients—and are housed in a space or locale separated from other agency or institutional programs or units and generally from the drug-related environment. In the residential settings, clients remain away from outside influences 24 hours a day for several months before earning short-term day-out privileges. In the nonresidential "day treatment" settings, the individual is in the TC environment for 4–8 hours and then is monitored by peers and family. Even in the least restrictive outpatient settings, TC-oriented programs and components are in place. Members gradually detach from old networks and relate to drug-free peers in the program.

A Community Environment

The inner environment of a TC facility contains communal space to promote a sense of commonality and collective activities (e.g., groups, meetings). Walls display signs which state in simple terms the philosophy of the program, the messages of right living and recovery. Corkboards and blackboards identify all participants by name, seniority level, and job function in the program. Daily schedules are also posted. These visuals display an organizational picture of the program that the individual can relate to and comprehend, factors which promote affiliation.

Community Activities

To be effectively utilized, treatment or educational services must be provided within a context of the peer community. Thus, with the exception of individual counseling, all activities are programmed in collective formats. These include at least one daily meal prepared, served, and shared by all members; a daily schedule of groups, meetings, and seminars;

team job functions; and organized recreational/leisure time, ceremonies, and rituals (e.g., birthdays, phase/progress graduations).

Staff Roles and Functions

The staff are a mix of recovered professionals and other traditional professionals (e.g., medical, legal, mental health, and educational) who must be integrated through cross-training that is grounded in the basic concepts of the TC perspective and community approach. Professional skills define the function of staff (e.g., nurse, physician, lawyer, teacher, administrator, caseworker, clinical counselor). Regardless of professional discipline or function, however, the generic *role* of all staff is that of community member who, rather than providers and treaters, are rational authorities, facilitators, and guides in the self-help community method.

Peers as Role Models

Members who demonstrate the expected behaviors and reflect the values and teachings of the community are viewed as role models. Indeed, the strength of the community as a context for social learning relates to the number and quality of its role models. All members of the community are expected to be role models: roommates; older and younger residents; and junior, senior, and directorial staff. Therapeutic communities require these multiple role models to maintain the integrity of the community and ensure the spread of social learning effects.

A Structured Day

The structure of the program relates to the TC perspective, particularly the view of the client and recovery. Ordered, routine activities counter the characteristically disordered lives of these clients and distract from negative thinking and boredom, factors which predispose to drug use. Structured activities of the community facilitate learning self-structure for the individual in time management, planning, setting and meeting goals, and, in general, accountability. Thus, regardless of its length, the day has a formal schedule of varied therapeutic and educational activities with prescribed formats, fixed times, and routine procedures.

Work as Therapy and Education

Consistent with the TC's self-help approach, all clients are responsible for the daily management of the facility (e.g., cleaning, activities, meal preparation and service, maintenance, purchasing, security, coordinating schedules, preparatory chores for groups, meetings, seminars). In the TC, the various work roles mediate essential educational and therapeutic effects. Job functions strengthen affiliation with the program through participation, provide opportunities for skill development, and foster self-examination and personal growth through performance challenge and program responsibility. The scope and depth of client work functions depend upon the program setting (e.g., institutional vs. freestanding facilities) and client resources (levels of psychological function, social and life skills).

Phase Format

The treatment protocol, or plan of therapeutic and educational activities, is organized into phases that reflect a developmental view of the change process. Emphasis is on incremental learning at each phase, which moves the individual to the next stage of recovery.

TC Concepts

There is a formal and informal curriculum focused on teaching the TC perspective, particularly its self-help recovery concepts and view of right living. The concepts, messages, and lessons of the curriculum are repeated in the various groups, meetings, seminars, and peer conversations, as well as in readings, signs, and personal writings.

Peer Encounter Groups

The main community or therapeutic group is the encounter, although other forms of therapeutic, educational, and support groups are utilized as needed. The minimal objective of the peer encounter is similar in TC-oriented programs: to heighten individual awareness of specific attitudes or behavioral patterns that should be modified. However, the encounter process may differ in degree of staff direction and intensity, depending on the client subgroups (e.g., adolescents, prison inmates, the dually disordered).

Planned Duration of Treatment

The optimal length of time for full program involvement must be consistent with TC goals of recovery and its developmental view of the change process. How long the individual must be program-involved depends on his or her phase of recovery, although a minimum period of intensive involvement is required to ensure internalization of the TC teachings.

Continuity of Care

Completion of primary treatment is a stage in the recovery process. Aftercare services are an essential component in the TC model. Whether implemented within the boundaries of the main program or separately as in residential or nonresidential halfway houses, or ambulatory settings, the perspective and approach guiding aftercare programming must be continuous with that of primary treatment in the TC. Thus, the views of right living and self-help recovery and the use of a peer network are essential to enhancing appropriate use of vocational, educational, mental health, social, and other typical aftercare or reentry services.

TC Process: Basic Program Elements

The recovery process may be defined as interaction between treatment interventions and client change. Unlike other treatment approaches, however, the TC is a community milieu whose daily regimen consists of structured and unstructured activities and social intercourse occurring in formal and informal settings. All of these constitute the treatment interventions in the process. These activities may be grouped into three main elements: therapeutic educative, community enhancement, and community and clinical management.

Therapeutic Educative Activities

These consist of various group and individual counseling. They promote expression of emotions, divert negative acting out, permit ventilation of feeling, and resolve personal and social issues. They increase communication and interpersonal skills, examine and confront behavior and attitudes, and offer instruction in alternate modes of behavior.

There are four main forms of group activity in the TC: encounters, probes, marathons, and tutorials. These differ somewhat in format, objectives, and method, but all attempt to foster trust, personal disclosure, intimacy, and peer solidarity to facilitate therapeutic change. The focus of the encounter is behavioral. Its approach is confrontation, and its objective is to modify negative behavior and attitudes directly. Probes and marathons have as their primary objective significant emotional change and psychological insight. Tutorial groups stress learning of skills. With the exception of the encounter, which is peer-led, the groups are conducted by staff assisted by senior peers.

The four main groups are supplemented by a number of ad hoc groups that convene as needed. These vary in focus, format, and composition. For example, gender-, ethnic-, or age-specific theme groups may utilize encounter or tutorial formats. Additionally, sensitivity-training, psychodrama, conventional-Gestalt, emotionality, relapse-prevention, and 12-step groups are employed to varying extents.

One-to-one counseling balances the needs of individuals with those of the community. Peer exchange is ongoing and constitutes the most consistent form of informal counseling in TCs. Staff counseling sessions are both formal and informal and usually conducted as needed. The staff counseling method in the TC is not traditional, as is evident in its main features: transpersonal sharing, direct support, minimal interpretation, didactic instructions, and concerned confrontation.

Community Enhancement Activities

These facilitate the individual's assimilation into the community and strengthen the community's capability to teach and to heal. They include the four main facilitywide meetings. The morning meeting, seminars, and the house meeting are held each day, and the general meeting is called when needed.

Morning meetings convene all residents of the facility and the staff on the premises after breakfast to initiate the day's activities with a positive attitude, to motivate residents, and to strengthen unity. This is accomplished through a planned program of recitation of the TC philosophy, songs, readings, and skits conducted by peers. This meeting is particularly important in that most residents of TCs have never adapted to the routine of an ordinary day.

Seminars convene every afternoon, usually for 1 hour. The seminar collects all the residents together at least once during the working day. Most seminars are conducted by residents, although sometimes led by staff and outside speakers. Of the various meetings and groups in the TC, the seminar is unique in its emphasis on listening, speaking, and conceptual behavior.

House meetings convene nightly after dinner, usually for 1 hour, and are coordinated by a senior resident. The main aim of these meetings is to transact community business, although they also have a clinical objective. In this forum, social pressure is judiciously employed to facilitate individual change through public acknowledgment of positive or negative behaviors by certain individuals or subgroups.

General meetings convene only when needed, usually to address negative behavior, attitudes, or incidents in the facility. These meetings, conducted by staff, are designed to identify problem people or conditions or to reaffirm motivation and reinforce positive behavior and attitudes in the community.

Community and Clinical Management

These activities maintain the physical and psychological safety of the environment and ensure that resident life is orderly and productive. They protect the community as a whole and strengthen it as a context for social learning. The main activities—privileges, disciplinary sanctions, and surveillance—have both management and clinical relevance in the model.

In the TC, privileges are explicit rewards that reinforce the value of achievement. Privileges such as job promotions, furloughs, room privacy, and peer leadership roles are accorded by overall clinical progress in the program. Displays of inappropriate behavior or negative attitude can result in loss of privileges, which can be regained by demonstrated improvement. Because privilege is equivalent to status in the vertical social system of the TC, loss of even small privileges is a status setback that is particularly painful for individuals who have struggled to raise their low self-esteem. Moreover, since substance abusers often cannot distinguish between privilege and entitlement, the privilege system in the TC teaches that productive participation or membership in a family or community is based on an earning process. Finally, privileges provide explicit feedback in the learning process. They are one of the tangible rewards that are contingent on individual change. This concrete feature of privilege is particularly suitable for individuals with histories of performance failure or incompleteness.

Therapeutic communities have their own specific rules and regulations that guide the behavior of residents and the management of facilities. The explicit purpose of these is to ensure the safety and health of the community; however, their implicit aim is to train and teach residents through the use of discipline.

In the TC, social and physical safety are prerequisites for psychological trust. Thus, disciplinary sanctions are invoked against any behavior that threatens the safety of the therapeutic environment. For example, breaking one of the TC's cardinal rules—such as no violence or threat of violence—can bring immediate expulsion. Even threats as minor as the theft of a toothbrush or a book must be addressed.

The choice of sanction depends on the severity of the infraction, time in the program, and history of infractions. For example, verbal reprimands, loss of privileges, or speaking bans may be selected for less severe infractions. Job demotions, loss of residential time, and expulsion may be invoked for more serious infractions.

Although often perceived as punitive, the basic purpose of contracts is to provide a learning experience by compelling residents to attend to their own conduct, to reflect on their own motivation, to feel some consequence of their behavior, and to consider alternate forms of acting under similar situations.

Contracts also have important community functions. The entire facility is made aware of all disciplinary actions. Thus, contracts deter violations. They provide vicarious learning experiences for others. As symbols of safety and integrity, they strengthen community cohesiveness.

The TC's most comprehensive method for assessing the overall physical and psychological status of the residential community is the house run. Several times a day, staff and senior residents walk through the entire facility from top to bottom, examining its overall condition. This single procedure has clinical implications as well as management goals. House runs provide global "snapshot" impressions of the facility: its cleanliness, planned routines, safety procedures, morale, and psychological tone. They illuminate the psychological and social functioning of individual residents and peer collections. House runs provide observable, physical indicators of self-management skills, attitudes toward self and the program, mood and emotional status, and the residents' (and staff's) general level of awareness of self and the physical and social environment.

Most TCs utilize unannounced random urine testing or incident-related urine-testing procedures. Residents who deny the use of drugs or refuse urine testing on request are rejecting a fundamental expectation in the TC, which is to trust staff and peers enough to disclose undesirable behavior. The voluntary admission of drug use initiates a learning experience, which includes exploration of conditions precipitating the infraction. Denial of actual drug use, either before or after urine testing, can block the learning process and may lead to termination or dropout.

When positive urine is detected, the action taken depends on the drug used, time and status in the program, previous history of drug and other infractions, and locus and condition of use. Actions may involve expulsion, loss of time, radical job demotion, or loss of privileges for specific periods. Review of the "triggers" or reasons for drug use is also an essential part of the action taken.

Active Ingredients of the Treatment

All activities/interventions of the social environment (e.g., the structure and process components) are designed to produce therapeutic and educational change in individual participants, and all participants are mediators of these therapeutic and educational changes. The interrelationship among these activities provides "global intervention" of the community, which results in individual social and psychological change. The efficacy of this global intervention, however, depends on the individual's participation in the program. Participation means that the individual engages in and learns to use all of the elements of the community as tools for self-change. Therefore the overarching aim of treatment is sustaining individuals' full participation in the community in order to achieve their goals of lifestyle and identity change. And participation is the most comprehensive measure of change.

Thus, the "active treatment ingredients" of the TC approach are contained in the relationship between the individual and the community. These ingredients are defined in terms of four interrelated components of community as method: (a) the community context, which consists of peer and staff relationships and daily regimen of planned activities (meetings, groups, individual peer and staff counseling, work, meals, recreation); (b) the community's expectations, which consist of the explicit standards and implicit demands for individual participation in, and use of, its context; (c) community assessment, which consists of peers' and staff's formal and informal observations of the individual's progress in meeting community expectations; and (d) community responses to assessment, which consist of various forms of feedback, instruction, positive and negative sanctions, and consequences. It is in striving to meet community expectations and standards for participation that the individual achieves his or her social and psychological goals.

Role of the Therapist

The social environment, consisting of daily regimen of activities, provides residents with myriad social learning opportunities. It is staff, however, who are responsible for sustaining an environment that enhances the self-help learning process for a single resident and/or the entire community.

Therapist Training

Staff composition in the TC consists of a mix of traditional and nontraditional professionals in a variety of clinical, management, administrative, and supportive service positions. Treatment program personnel are directly responsible for the day-to-day clinical and operational activities of the residential facility. Nontraditional professionals generally have recovery experience as well as formal training in human services. Traditional professional staff consists of social workers, psychologists, psychiatrists, and nurses, some with recovery experience. Regardless of their background, all staff must be integrated through cross-training in the basic concepts of the perspective, community approach, program model, and methods of the TC in order to ensure effective implementation of the program.

Stance of Therapist

The primary counseling staff in the standard TC does not routinely engage in formal psychotherapy, although they may use some conventional psychotherapy techniques and typical therapeutic effects often occur such as emotional breakthroughs and powerful insights. However, counselors are discouraged from using conventional therapeutic language or methods and from conceptualizing themselves as therapists.

Therapeutic counseling sessions may be conducted directly with the resident in planned private conversations. These generally address crisis events in the resident's family life or personal issues of particular sensitivity, such as motivation, psychological symptoms, sexual orientation, sexual abuse, past violence. The goal of these sessions is resolution of issues that threaten the resident's commitment or ability to remain in the peer community. Staff primarily advises, supports and instructs, and in some cases refers the resident to mental health therapists or other service professionals. Thus, counseling in the standard TC is both part of the therapeutic process and reinforces the community as the method in the therapeutic process (The *modified* TC programs for dually disordered populations, however, have successfully incorporated conventional psychotherapists and therapeutic strategies into the community approach [see De Leon, 1993b, 1997].)

Therapist/Patient Relationship and the Change Process

Staff role distinctions in the TC can be contrasted with mental health treatment and human service providers in conventional treatment settings. For example, among case managers, counselors, and therapists in other settings, the relationship between client and staff is viewed as the primary therapeutic alliance. In the TC, the essential therapeutic alliance is the client's relationship with the peer community. Primary treatment staff assume various roles to enhance this relationship. Four main staff roles can be identified: facilitator/guide, rational authority, counselor/therapist, and community manager. Although these roles obviously merge, interchange, and overlap constantly, each is recognizable in its distinct characteristics

and emphasis, and each impacts the individual resident and the community in different ways.

Common Obstacles to Successful Treatment

A majority of admissions fail to complete the full course of treatment. Although research shows that many of these noncompleters show benefits, the global social and psychological goals of the TC are not fully realized. Thus, the obstacles to successful treatment are the factors which contribute to premature dropout. Though not fully understood, some of these factors associated with characteristics of the client and implementation of the treatment protocol are briefly listed:

- *Client suitability.* Many substance abusers who enter TCs cannot tolerate the structured regimen and demands of these programs.
- *Client motivation.* Client motivation continually fluctuates during the course of the residential stay. Thus, there is constant emphasis on sustaining motivation—particularly in the early phases of treatment.
- *Conflicts.* The intensity of community life in the TC fosters conflict between residents, and between residents and staff.
- *External pressures.* Residents in TCs often experience pressures from family or employers to leave treatment prematurely.
- *Flight into health.* Most admissions to TCs show improvements within the first 3 months of treatment, which may paradoxically stimulate many to leave prematurely.
- *Environmental risk.* Recent research indicates that TC programs vary in their adherence to essential elements of the model. In particular, differences in the internal and surrounding environment of the program may contribute to dropout (Jainchill, Messina, & Yagelka, 1997).
- *Staff training.* Staff require an understanding of the theory and rationale for the treatment protocol. Recovered staff with TC experience are often inflexible in their response to individual differences. Their clinical skills and knowledge may be limited by their narrow experience and training rather than conceptual understanding of the TC approach. Conversely, traditionally trained human services professionals in TCs lack experience with personal recovery and are limited by concepts, language,

and perspectives of their professional training. In particular, they have difficulty acclimating to the primacy of the peer community as the method for treatment.

- *Funding policy.* Recent changes in health care policy have resulted in shorter planned durations of treatment. These changes impose limits in implementing the TC treatment protocol based upon its perspective.

CHARACTERISTICS OF CLIENTS MOST LIKELY TO RESPOND TO THE MODEL

Social and Psychological Profiles

Residents in traditional programs are usually men (70–75%), but admissions of women have been increasing in recent years. Most community-based TCs are integrated across gender, race/ethnicity, and age, although the demographic proportions differ by geographic regions and in certain programs. In general, Hispanics, Native Americans, and patients under 21 years of age represent smaller proportions of admissions to TCs.

About half of all admissions are from broken homes or ineffective families. A large majority have poor work histories and have engaged in criminal activities at some time in their lives. Among adult admissions less than one third have been employed full time during the year before treatment, more than two thirds have been arrested, and 30–40% have had prior drug treatment histories (e.g., De Leon, 1984; Hubbard, Rachal, Craddock, & Cavanaugh, 1984; Simpson & Sells 1982).

Among adolescents, 70% have dropped out of school, and more than 70% have been arrested at least once or involved with the criminal justice system. More have histories of family deviance, fewer have had prior treatment for drug use (De Leon & Deitch 1985; Holland & Griffen 1984), but more of the younger adolescents have had treatment for psychological problems (Jainchill, 1997). Approximately 30% of adult admissions and 50–70% of adolescent admissions to long-term residential TCs are criminal justice referrals, although some TC programs exclusively serve criminal justice referrals (De Leon, 1993a; Jainchill, 1997; Tims, De Leon, & Jainchill, 1994).

The majority of TC admissions have histories of multiple drug use including marijuana, opiates, alcohol, and pills, although in recent years most report cocaine/crack as their primary drug of abuse. Research has documented that individuals admitted to TCs reveal a considerable degree of psychosocial dysfunction in addition to their substance abuse. Although clients differ in demography, socioeconomic background, and drug use patterns, psychological profiles obtained with standard instruments appear remarkably uniform, as evident in a number of TC studies (e.g., Biase, Sullivan, & Wheeler, 1986; Brook & Whitehead, 1980; De Leon, 1976, 1980, 1984, 1989; Holland, 1986; Kennard & Wilson 1979; Zuckerman, Sola, Masterson, & Angelone, 1975).

Psychological profiles reveal drug abuse as the prominent element in a picture that mirrors the features of both psychiatric and criminal populations. For example, the character disorder characteristics and poor self-concept of delinquent and repeated offenders are present, along with the dysphoria and confused thinking of emotionally unstable or psychiatric populations. These profiles vary little across age, sex, race, primary drug, or admission year and are not significantly different from those of drug abusers in other treatment modalities.

Recent studies indicate that over 70% of admissions reveal a lifetime nondrug psychiatric disorder in addition to substance abuse or dependence. One third have a current or continuing history of mental disorder in addition to their drug abuse. The most frequent nondrug diagnoses are phobias, generalized anxiety, psychosexual dysfunction, and antisocial personality. There are only a few cases of schizophrenia, but lifetime affective disorders occurred in over one third of those studied (De Leon, 1993a; Jainchill, 1989, 1994; Jainchill, De Leon, & Pinkham 1986). Thus, drug abusers who come to the TC do not appear to be mentally ill, as do patients in psychiatric settings, nor are they simply hard-core criminal types. However, they do reveal a considerable degree of psychological disability.

Clients Who Are Best Candidates for Long-Term Residential TCs

There is no typical profile of the substance abusers who succeed in residential therapeutic communities. However, the need for long-term treatment in TCs is based on clinical and research experience. The clinical indicators of long-term residence in TCs can be briefly summarized across five main domains:

1. *Health and social risk status.* Most abusers who seek treatment in the TC experience acute stress. They may be in family or legal crisis or at significant risk to harm themselves or others, so that a period of residential stay is indicated. However, clients suitable for long-term residential treatment reveal a more chronic pattern of stress that induces treatment seeking and, when relieved, usually results in premature dropout. They require longer term residential treatment because they are a constant risk threat, and they must move beyond relief seeking to initiate a genuine recovery process.

2. *Abstinence potential.* In the TC's view of substance abuse as a disorder of the whole person, abstinence is a prerequisite for recovery. Among chronic users, the risk of repeated relapse can subvert any treatment effort, regardless of the modality. Thus, the residential TC is needed to interrupt out-of-control drug use and to stabilize an extended period of abstinence in order to facilitate a long-term recovery process.

3. *Social and interpersonal function.* Inadequate social and interpersonal function not only results from drug use but often reveals a more general picture of immaturity or an impeded developmental history. Thus, a setting such as the TC is needed—it focuses upon the broad socialization and/or habilitation of the individual.

4. *Antisocial involvement.* In the TC view, the term *antisocial* also suggests characteristics which are highly correlated with drug use. These include behaviors such as exploitation, abuse and violence, attitudes of mainstream disaffiliation, and the rejection or absence of prosocial values. Modification of these characteristics requires the intensive resocialization approach of the TC setting.

5. *Suitability for the TC.* A number of those seeking admission to the TC may not be ready for treatment in general or suitable for the demands of a long-term residential regimen. Assessment of these factors at the time of admission provides a basis for treatment planning in the TC, and sometimes for appropriate referral. Some indicators of motivation, readiness, and suitability for TC treatment are acceptance of the severity of drug problem; acceptance of the need for treatment ("can't do it alone"); willingness to sever ties with family, friends, and current lifestyle while in treatment; and willingness to surrender a private life and to meet the expectations of a structured community. Although motivation, readi-

ness, and suitability are not criteria for admission to the TC, the importance of these factors often emerges after entry into treatment, and if they are not identified and addressed, they are related to early dropout (De Leon, 1993a; De Leon & Jainchill, 1986; De Leon, Melnick, Kressel, & Jainchill, 1994).

Overall, the picture that residents present when entering the TC is one of health risk and social crises. Drug use is currently or recently out of control; individuals reveal little or no capacity to maintain abstinence on their own; social and interpersonal function is diminished; and their drug use either is embedded in or has eroded to a socially deviant lifestyle. Although individuals may differ in the severity, extent, or duration of the problems in each area, all require the residential TC to initiate change. As elaborated below, however, clients' levels of motivation and readiness to change and their perceived need for residential TCs are overarching indicators for this treatment approach.

Contraindications for Residential TC Treatment

Traditional TCs maintain an open-door policy with respect to admission to residential treatment. This understandably results in a wide range of treatment candidates, not all of whom are equally motivated, ready, or suitable for the demands of the residential regimen. Relatively few are excluded, because the TC policy is to accept individuals who elect residential treatment—regardless of the reasons influencing their choice. However, there are two major guidelines for excluding clients: suitability and community risk. As discussed above, suitability refers to the degree to which the client can meet the demands of the TC regimen and integrate with others. This includes participation in groups, fulfilling work assignments, and living with minimal privacy in an open community, usually under dormitory conditions. Community risk refers to the extent to which clients present a management burden to the staff or pose a threat to the security and health of the community or others.

Specific exclusionary criteria most often include histories of arson, suicide, and serious psychiatric disorder. Psychiatric exclusion is usually based on a documented history of psychiatric hospitalizations or prima facie evidence of psychotic symptoms on interview (e.g., frank delusions, thought disorder, hallucinations, confused orientation, or signs of serious affect disorder). Generally, clients on regular psychotropic regimens are excluded because use of these usually correlates with chronic or severe psychiatric disorder. Also, regular administration of psychotropic medication, particularly in the larger TCs, presents a management and supervisory burden for the relatively few medical personnel in these facilities. There are examples of integrating into mainstream TCs some clients requiring psychiatric medication (Carroll & Sobel, 1986). And as discussed in the last section, modified TCs for mentally ill chemical abusers requiring medication have been successfully implemented.

Clients requiring medication for medical conditions are acceptable in TCs, as are handicapped clients or those who require prosthetics, providing they can meet the participatory demands of the program. Because of concern about communicable disease in a residential setting, TCs require tests for conditions such as tuberculosis and hepatitis prior to entry into the facility or at least within the first weeks of admission.

Policy and practices concerning testing for HIV status and management of AIDS or AIDS-related complex (ARC) have recently been implemented by most TCs. These emphasize voluntary testing, with counseling, special education seminars on health management and sexual practices, and special support groups for residents who are HIV-positive or have a clinical diagnosis of AIDS or ARC (De Leon, 1997; McKusker & Sorensen, 1994).

EFFECTIVENESS: EMPIRICAL DATA

A substantial evaluation literature documents the effectiveness of the TC approach in rehabilitating drug abusers (e.g., Condelli & Hubbard, 1994; De Leon, 1984, 1985; Hubbard et al., 1989; Institute of Medicine, 1990; Simpson & Curry, 1997; Simpson & Sells, 1982; Tims et al., 1994; Tims & Ludford, 1984). The main findings on short- and long-term posttreatment follow-up status from single program and multiprogram studies are now briefly summarized.

Success and Improvement Rates

Significant improvements occur on separate outcome variables (drug use, criminality, and employ-

ment) and on composite indices for measuring individual success. Maximum to moderately favorable outcomes (based on opioid, nonopioid, and alcohol use; arrest rates; retreatment and employment) occur for more than half of the sample of completed clients and dropouts (De Leon, 1984; Hubbard et al., 1989; Simpson & Sells, 1982).

There is a consistent positive relationship between time spent in residential treatment and posttreatment outcome status. For example, in long-term TCs, success rates (on composite indices of no drug use and no criminality) at 2 years posttreatment approximate 90%, 50%, and 25%, respectively, for graduates/completers and dropouts who remain more than and less than 1 year in residential treatment. Improvement rates over pretreatment status approximate 100%, 70%, and 40%, respectively (De Leon, Wexler, & Jainchill, 1982).

In a few studies that investigated psychological outcomes, results uniformly showed significant improvement at follow-up (e.g., Biase et al., 1986; De Leon, 1984; Holland, 1983). A direct relationship has been demonstrated between posttreatment behavioral success and psychological adjustment (De Leon, 1984; De Leon & Jainchill, 1981–1982).

Retention

Dropout is the rule for all drug treatment modalities. For therapeutic communities, retention is of particular importance because research has established a firm relationship between time spent in treatment and successful outcome. However, most admissions to therapeutic community programs leave residency, many before treatment influences are presumed to be effective.

Research on retention in TCs has been increasing in recent years. Reviews of TC retention research are contained in the literature (e.g., De Leon, 1985, 1991; Lewis, McCusker, Hindin, Frost, & Garfield, 1993). Studies focus on several questions, including retention rates and client predictors of dropout. The key findings from these may be briefly summarized:

Retention Rates

Dropout is highest (30–40%) in the first 30 days of admission and declines sharply thereafter (De Leon & Schwartz 1984). This temporal pattern of dropout is uniform across TC programs (and other modalities). In long-term residential TCs, completion rates average 10–20% of all admissions. One-year retention rates range from 15% to 30%, although more recent trends suggest gradual increases in annual retention compared to the period before 1980 (De Leon, 1989).

Predictors of Dropout

There are no reliable client characteristics that predict retention, with the exception of severe criminality and/or severe psychopathology, which are correlated with earlier dropout. Recent studies point to the importance of dynamic factors in predicting retention in treatment, such as perceived legal pressure, motivation and readiness for treatment (e.g., Condelli & De Leon, 1993; De Leon, 1993a; De Leon & Jainchill, 1986; Hubbard et al., 1989; Schoket, 1992; Siddiqui, 1989).

Only a few studies have assessed self-reported reasons for leaving treatment prematurely. Findings from these suggest the importance of client perception factors as reasons for early dropout. These mainly reflect low readiness for treatment in general or perceived unsuitability for the TC life in particular (e.g., De Leon, 1993a; De Leon & Wexler, 1983). While a legitimate concern, retention should not be confused with treatment effectiveness. Therapeutic communities are effective for those who remain long enough for treatment influences to occur.

The outcome studies reported were completed on an earlier generation of chemical abusers, primarily opioid addicts. Since the early 1980s, however, most admissions to residential TCs have been multiple drug abusers, primarily involved with cocaine, crack, and alcohol, with relatively few primary heroin users. Studies in progress evaluate the effectiveness of the TC for the recent generation of abusers (Hubbard et al., 1970; National Treatment Improvement Evaluation Study, 1997). Although still preliminary, these studies confirm the effectiveness of modified TCs for special populations of substance abusers, such as those with co-occurring mental illness (e.g., Sacks, De Leon, Bernhardt, & Sacks, 1997), adolescents (Jainchill, 1997), and inmates in state correctional facilities (e.g., Graham & Wexler, 1997; Lipton, 1995; Lockwood, Inciardi, Butzin, & Hooper, 1997; Wexler & Lipton, 1993).

Current Modifications of the TC Model

Most community-based traditional TCs have expanded their social services or have incorporated new interventions to address the needs of their diverse admissions. In some cases, these additions enhance but do not alter the basic TC regimen; in others, they significantly modify the TC model itself.

FAMILY SERVICES APPROACHES

The participation of families or significant others has been a notable development in TCs for both adolescents and adults. Some TCs offer programs in individual- and multiple-family therapy as components of their adolescent, nonresidential, and (more recently) short-term residential modalities. However, most traditional TCs do not provide a regular family therapy service because the individual in residence rather than the family unit is viewed as the primary target of treatment. Thus, family psychoeducational and participation activities and support groups are offered to enhance the TC's rehabilitative process for the residential client by establishing an alliance between significant others and the program.

PRIMARY HEALTH CARE AND MEDICAL SERVICES

Although funding for health care services remains insufficient for TCs, these agencies have expanded services for the growing number of residential patients with sexually transmitted and immune-compromising conditions, including HIV seropositivity, AIDS, syphilis, hepatitis B, and, recently, tuberculosis. Screening, treatment, and increased health education have been sophisticated, both on site and through links with community primary-health-care agencies.

Aftercare Services

Currently, most long-term TCs have links with other service providers and 12-step groups for their graduates. However, the TCs with shorter term residential components have instituted well-defined aftercare programs both within their systems and through links with other non-TC agencies. There are limits and issues concerning these aftercare efforts because of discontinuities between the perspectives of the TC and other service agencies. These are outlined along with a fuller discussion of aftercare in TCs in other writings (De Leon, 1990–1991).

Relapse Prevention Training

Based on their approach to recovery, traditional TCs have always focused on the key issues of relapse throughout all the stages of the program. Currently, however, a number of TCs include special workshops on relapse prevention training (RPT), using curriculum, expert trainers, and formats developed outside of the TC area (e.g., Marlatt, & Gordon, 1985). These workshops are offered as formal additions to the existing TC protocol, usually in the reentry stage of treatment. However, some programs incorporate RPT workshops into earlier treatment stages, and in a few others, RPT is central to the primary treatment protocol (e.g., Lewis & Ross, 1994). Clinical impressions supported by preliminary data of the efficacy of RPT within the TC setting are favorable, although rigorous evaluation studies are still in progress (McCusker & Sorensen, 1994).

12-Step Components

Historically, TC graduates were not easily integrated into AA meetings for a variety of reasons (see De Leon, 1990–1991). In recent years, however, there has been a gradual integration of AA/NA/CA (Cocaine Anonymous) meetings during and following TC treatment because of the wide diversity of users socially and demographically and the prominence of alcohol use regardless of the primary drug. The common genealogical roots found in TCs and the 12-step groups are evident to most participants in these, and the similarities in the self-help view of recovery far outweigh the differences in specific orientation. Today, 12-step groups may be introduced at any stage in residential treatment but are considered mandatory in the reentry stages of treatment and in the aftercare or continuance stages of recovery after leaving the residential setting.

Mental Health Services

Among those seeking admission to TCs, increasing numbers reveal documented psychiatric histories (e.g., De Leon, 1989; Jainchill, 1989; Jainchill et al.,

1986). Certain subgroups of these patients are treated within the traditional TC model and regimen, which requires some modification in services and staffing. For example, psychopharmacological adjuncts and individual psychotherapy are used for selected patients at appropriate stages in treatment. Nevertheless, the traditional community-based TC models still cannot accommodate substance-abusing patients with serious psychiatric disorders. As described in recent literature (De Leon, 1997), these primary psychiatric substance-abusing individuals require specially adapted forms of the TC model.

Multimodal TC and Patient-Treatment Matching

Traditional TCs are highly effective for a certain segment of the drug abuse population. However, those who seek assistance in TC settings represent a broad spectrum of patients, many of whom may not be suitable for a long-term residential stay. Improved diagnostic capability and assessment of individual differences have clarified the need for options other than long-term residential treatment.

Many TC agencies are multimodality treatment centers, which offer services in their residential and nonresidential programs depending on the clinical status and situational needs of the individual. The modalities include short- (less than 90 days), medium- (6–12 months), and long-term (1–2 years) residential components and drug-free outpatient services (6–12 months). Some TCs operate drug-free day treatment and methadone maintenance programs. Assessments attempts to match the patient to the appropriate modality within the agency. For example, the spread of drug abuse in the workplace, particularly cocaine use, has prompted the TC to develop short-term residential and ambulatory models for employed, more socialized patients.

To date, the effectiveness of TC-oriented multimodality programs has not been systematically evaluated, although several relevant studies are currently under way. Of particular interest are the comparative effectiveness and cost-benefits of long- and short-term residential treatment. Thus far, however, there is no convincing evidence supporting the effectiveness of short-term treatment in any modality, residential or ambulatory. More detailed descriptions of the applications and modifications of the TC model are provided elsewhere (De Leon, 1997).

STRENGTHS AND WEAKNESSES OF
THE MODEL FOR SUBSTANCE ABUSE

Although TCs have been successfully treating substance abusers for some 30 years, an explicit theoretical framework of the model and method is a recent development. The strengths and weaknesses of the TC approach are based on clinical experience supported by developing research. Not unexpectedly, some of the strengths of the TC are also its weaknesses.

Strengths

The TC remains the treatment of choice for the severe, antisocial, or socially disaffiliated substance abuser. For this population of substance abusers, the goals of lifestyle and identity change remain paramount but require long-term treatment involvement, regardless of changes in health care policy. Nevertheless, the model has also proved to be generalizable, evident in the current adaptations for special populations and settings. Studies in progress confirm the effectiveness of modified TCs for special populations of substance abusers such as those with co-occurring mental illness (e.g., Sacks et al., 1997), adolescents (Jainchill, Bhattacharya, & Yagelka, 1995), and inmates in state correctional facilitates (e.g., Lipton, 1995; Lockwood et al., 1997; Wexler & Graham, 1994; Wexler, Falkin, & Lipton, 1990).

The TC model is the best example of an effective self-help, recovery-oriented approach to the treatment of substance abuse. Contrasted with conventional medical and mental-health-oriented approaches, the model underscores the importance of empowering the individual in the change process, the use of peer communities as a method of facilitating change, and the reality of achieving long-term, sustained changes.

Weaknesses

The TC approach is inherently limited in its responsivity to individual differences. Although the individual is the constant focus of the TC, the structure and process elements of a peer community as method approach are relatively inflexible in meeting the unique needs of individuals. Thus, in TC programs, there is a constant tension between the needs of the individual and those of the community, which, however, must ultimately resolve in favor of the individual.

The TC model appears most appropriate only for certain subgroups of substance abusers, notably the most serious users, and those who are socially deviant. In the past, the traditional addiction TC was clearly not appropriate for well-socialized addicts, or for those with serious psychiatric illness. Thus, the generality of effectiveness remains to be fully documented.

More generally, the TC is a high-demand treatment that appears appropriate for clients who are highly motivated and ready to change, and who perceive the TC environment as suitable. The contribution of these selection factors has tended to cloud interpretations of effectiveness.

The TC model has assumed that the issues of aftercare are adequately addressed in the reentry stage of the residential program. Thus, until recently, the model has not provided for well-developed aftercare networks to maintain treatment gains. The pressure of cost containment has further challenged the relevancy of the long-term residential model and has underscored distinctions between primary treatment and aftercare.

The TC illustrates the complexity of a community as method model of treatment. Multiple interventions—formal and informal—address multiple dimensions of the individual in a process of change, defined as a dynamic interaction between the individual and the community. Empirical research on such a complex model is difficult to implement. Abstracting the "active treatment elements" of the TC process poses methodological challenges similar to those in researching villages or family systems. Nevertheless, several decades of research have established firm evidence of the effectiveness of the model. And the recent development of a theoretical framework is guiding current research into the treatment process.

SUMMARY

The TC is a powerful social psychological alternative to pharmacological treatments of substance abuse and related problems. It provides a comprehensive approach guided by an explicit perspective. The TC is oriented to recovery, not simply abstinence or symptom reduction. It stresses and provides the setting for individuals to change lifestyles and identities. Thus, it remains the treatment of choice for the severe drug abuser: the unhabilitated, the antisocial, the socially disaffiliated, and many adolescents. However, it is also adaptable to many settings and populations. Finally, though the TC model is systematic and structured, it can integrate various effective elements of other approaches, such as family therapy, relapse prevention, and mental health.

The increasing diversity of TC-oriented programs for special populations and the integration of staff and various treatment and service components from other approaches pose both challenge and opportunity to the therapeutic community. Continued modification and adaptability of TC programs contain the risk of dilution of a basic model, which has proved its effectiveness. Conversely, these developments also portend the evolution of a generic TC approach useful for a wide diversity of populations and problems.

Key References

De Leon, G. (1994). Therapeutic communities. In M. Galanter & H. D. Kleber (Eds.). *The American Psychiatric Press textbook of substance abuse treatment* (pp. 391–414). Chicago: American Psychiatric Press.

De Leon, G. (1995). Therapeutic communities for addictions: A theoretical framework. *International Journal of the Addictions, 30*, 1603–1649.

De Leon, G. (1997). *Community as method: Therapeutic communities for special populations and special settings.* Westport, CT: Greenwood Press.

References

Biase, D. V., Sullivan, A. P., & Wheeler, B. (1986). Daytop miniversity—Phase 2: College training in a therapeutic community: Development of self-concept among drug free addict/abusers. In G. De Leon & J. Ziegenfuss, Jr. (Eds.), *Therapeutic communities for addictions: Readings in theory, research and practice* (pp. 121–130). Springfield, IL: Charles C Thomas.

Bratter, T. E., Bratter, E. P., & Heimberg, J. F. (1986). Uses and abuses of power and authority within the American self-help residential therapeutic community: A perversion or a necessity? In G. De Leon & J. T. Ziegenfuss (Eds.), *Therapeutic communities for addictions: Readings in theory, research and practice* (pp. 191–208). Springfield, IL: Charles C Thomas.

Brook, R. C., & Whitehead, I. C. (1980). *Drug-free therapeutic community.* New York: Human Sciences Press.

Carroll, J. F. X., & Sobel, B. S. (1986). Integrating mental health personnel and practices into a therapeutic community. In G. De Leon & J. T. Ziegenfuss (Eds.), *Therapeutic communities for addictions: Readings in theory, research and practice* (pp. 209–226). Springfield, IL: Charles C Thomas.

Condelli, W. S., & De Leon, G. (1993). Fixed and dynamic predictors of client retention in therapeutic communities. *Journal of Substance Abuse Treatment, 10*, 11–16.

Condelli, W. S., & Hubbard, R. L. (1994). Client outcomes from therapeutic communities. In F. M. Tims, G. De Leon, & N. Jainchill (Eds.), *Therapeutic community: Advances in research and application* (NIDA Research Monograph, NIH Publication No. 94-3633, pp. 80–98). Rockville, MD: National Institute on Drug Abuse.

Deitch, D. A. (1974). Treatment of drug abuse in the therapeutic community: Historical influences, current considerations, and future outlooks. *National Commission on Marihuana and Drug Abuse* (Vol. 4, pp. 158–175).Washington, DC: Government Printing Office.

De Leon, G. (1976). *Psychological and socio-demographic profiles of addicts in the therapeutic community.* (Final report of project activities under National Institute of Drug Abuse Grant No. DA-00831). Rockville, MD: National Institute on Drug Abuse.

De Leon, G. (1980). *Therapeutic communities: Training self evaluation.* (Final report of project activities under National Institute of Drug Abuse Grant No. 1H81-DAO). Rockville, MD: National Institute on Drug Abuse.

De Leon, G. (1984). *The therapeutic community: Study of effectiveness.* Treatment Research Monograph Series, DHHS Publication No. (ADM) 85-1286. Rockville, MD: National Institute on Drug Abuse.

De Leon, G. (1985). The therapeutic community: Status and evolution. *International Journal of the Addictions, 7*, 823–844.

De Leon, G. (1989). Therapeutic communities for substance abuse: Overview of approach and effectiveness. *Psychology of Addictive Behaviors, 3*(3), 140–147.

De Leon, G. (1990–1991). Aftercare in therapeutic communities. *International Journal of the Addictions, 25*(9A–10A), 1229–1241.

De Leon, G. (1991). Retention in drug-free therapeutic communities. In R. W. Pickens, C. G. Leukefeld, & C. R. Schuster (Eds.), *Improving drug treatment* (National Institute on Drug Abuse Research Monograph #106). Rockville, MD: National Institute on Drug Abuse.

De Leon, G. (1993a). Cocaine abusers in therapeutic community treatment. In F. M. Tims (Ed.), *Cocaine treatment: Research and clinical perspectives* (NIDA Publication No. 93-3639, pp. 163–189). Washington, DC: Government Printing Office.

De Leon, G. (1993b). Modified therapeutic communities for dual disorder. In J. Solomon, S. Zimberg, & E. Shollar (Eds.), *Dual diagnosis: Evaluation, treatment, training, and program development* (pp. 147–170). New York: Plenum Press.

De Leon, G. (1994a). A recovery stage paradigm and therapeutic communities. *Proceedings of the Therapeutic Communities of America 1992 Planning Conference, Paradigms: Past, Present and Future, Chantilly, Virginia* (pp. 116–122). Edited and Published by Manisses Communications Group, Providence, RI.

De Leon, G. (1994b). Therapeutic communities. In M. Galanter & H. D. Kleber, (Eds.), *The American psychiatric press textbook of substance abuse treatment* (pp. 391–414). Chicago: American Psychiatric Press.

De Leon, G. (1995). Therapeutic communities for addictions: A theoretical framework. *International Journal of the Addictions, 30,* 1603–1649.

De Leon, G. (Ed.). (1997). *Community as method: Therapeutic communities for special populations and special settings.* Westport, CT: Greenwood Press.

De Leon, G., & Deitch, D. (1985). Treatment of the adolescent substance abuser in a therapeutic community. In A. Friedman & G. Beschner (Eds.), *Treatment services for adolescent substance abusers* (DHHS Publication No. (ADM) 85-1342, pp. 216–230), Rockville MD: National Institute of Drug Abuse.

De Leon, G., & Jainchill, N. (1981–1982). Male and female drug abusers: Social and psychological status 2 years after treatment in a therapeutic community. *American Journal of Drug and Alcohol Abuse, 8,* 465–497.

De Leon, G., & Jainchill, N. (1986). Circumstances, motivation, readiness and suitability (CMRS) as correlates of treatment tenure. *Journal of Psychoactive Drugs, 8,* 203–208.

De Leon, G., Melnick, G., Kressel, D., & Jainchill, N. (1994). Circumstances, motivation, readiness and suitability (The CMRS Scales): Predicting retention in therapeutic community treatment. *American Journal of Drug and Alcohol Abuse, 20,* 495–515.

De Leon, G., & Rosenthal, M. S. (1989). Treatment in residential therapeutic communities. In T. B. Karasu (Ed.), *Treatments of psychiatric disorders* (Vol. 2). Washington, DC: American Psychiatric Press.

De Leon, G., & Schwartz, G. (1984). Therapeutic communities: What are the retention rates? *American Journal of Drug and Alcohol Abuse, 10,* 267–284.

De Leon, G., & Wexler, H. (1983). *Perceived quality of adjustment 5 years after therapeutic community treatment.* Paper presented at the American Psychological Association convention, Los Angeles.

De Leon, G., Wexler, H., & Jainchill, N. (1982). Success and improvement rates 5 years after treatment in a therapeutic community. *International Journal of Addictions, 17,* 703–747.

De Leon, G., & Ziegenfuss, J. (Eds.). (1986). *Therapeutic communities for addictions: Readings in theory, research and practice.* Springfield, IL: Charles C Thomas.

Glaser, F. B. (1974). Some historical and theoretical background of a self-help addiction treatment program. *American Journal of Drug and Alcohol Abuse, 1,* 37–52.

Graham, W. F., & Wexler, H. K. (1997). The amity therapeutic community program at Donovan prison: Program description and approach. In G. De Leon (Ed.), *Community as method: Therapeutic communities for special populations and special settings.* Westport, CT: Greenwood Press.

Holland, S. (1983). Evaluating community based treatment programs: A model for strengthening inferences about effectiveness. *International Journal of Therapeutic Communities, 4,* 285–306.

Holland, S. (1986). Measuring process in drug abuse treatment research. In G. De Leon & J. T. Ziegenfuss (Eds.), *Therapeutic communities for addictions: Readings in theory, research and practice* (pp. 169–181). Springfield, IL: Charles C Thomas.

Holland, S., & Griffen, A. (1984). Adolescent and adult drug treatment clients: Patterns and consequences of use. *Journal of Psychoactive Drugs, 16,* 79–90.

Hubbard, R. L., Craddock, S. G., Flynn, P. M., Anderson, J., & Etheridge, R. M. (1970). Overview of 1-year follow-up outcomes in the drug abuse treatment outcome study (DATOS). *Psychology of Addictive Behavior* (Special Issue), *11*(4), 261–278.

Hubbard, R. L., Marsden, M. E., Rachal, J. V., Harwood, J. J., Cavanaugh, E. R., & Ginzburg, H. M. (1989). *Drug abuse treatment: A national study of effectiveness.* Chapel Hill: University of North Carolina Press.

Institute of Medicine. (1990). *Treating drug problems: A study of the evolution, effectiveness, and financing of public and private drug treatment systems.* Report by the Institute of Medicine Committee for the Substance Abuse Coverage Study, Division of Health

Care Services. Washington, D.C: National Academy Press.

Jainchill, N. (1989). *The relationship between psychiatric disorder, retention in treatment, and client progress, among admissions to a residential, drug free modality.* Unpublished doctoral dissertation. Ann Arbor, MI: UMI Dissertation Information Service.

Jainchill, N. (1994). Co-morbidity and therapeutic community treatment. In F. M. Tims, G. De Leon, & N. Jainchill (Eds.), *Therapeutic community: Advances in research and application* (NIDA Research Monograph #144, NIH Publication No. 94-3633, pp. 209–231). Rockville, MD: National Institute on Drug Abuse.

Jainchill, N. (1997). Therapeutic communities for adolescents: The same and not the same. In G. De Leon (Ed.), *Community as method: Therapeutic communities for special populations and special settings* (pp. 161–178). Westport, CT: Greenwood Press.

Jainchill, N., Bhattacharya, G., & Yagelka. J. (1995). Therapeutic communities for adolescents. In E. Rahdert & D. Czechowicz, (Eds.), *Adolescent drug abuse: Clinical assessment and therapeutic interventions* (pp. 190–217). (NIH Publication no. 95-3908). Rockville, MD: National Institute on Drug Abuse.

Jainchill, N., De Leon, G., & Pinkham, L. (1986). Psychiatric diagnoses among substance abusers in the therapeutic community. *Journal of Psychoactive Drugs, 8*, 209–213.

Jainchill, N., Messina, M., & Yagelka, J. (1997). *Development of a treatment environment risk index (TERI).* Unpublished manuscript. New York: Center for Therapeutic Community Research at NDRI, Inc.

Jones, M. (1953). *The therapeutic community: A new treatment method in psychiatry.* New York: Basic Books.

Kennard, D. (1983). *An introduction to therapeutic communities.* London: Routledge & Kegan Paul.

Kennard, D., & Wilson, S. (1979). The modification of personality disorders in a therapeutic community for drug abusers. *British Medical Journal of Psychiatry, 52,* 215–221.

Kooyman, M. (1992). *The therapeutic community for addicts: Intimacy, parent involvement and treatment outcome.* Rotterdam: Universities Drukkerij.

Lewis, B. F., McCusker, J., Hindin, R., Frost, R., & Garfield, F. (1993). Four residential drug treatment programs: Project IMPACT. In J. A. Inciardi, F. M. Tims, & B. W. Fletcher (Eds.), *Innovative approaches in the treatment of drug abuse: Program models and strategies* (pp. 45–60). Westport, CT: Greenwood Press.

Lewis, B. F., & Ross, R. (1994). Retention in therapeutic communities: Challenges for the Nineties. In F. M. Tims, G. De Leon, & N. Jainchill (Eds.), *Therapeutic community: Advances in research and applications* (NIDA Research Monograph No. 144, NIH Publication no. 94-3633). Rockville, MD: Government Printing Office.

Lipton, D. (1995). *The effectiveness of treatment for drug abusers under criminal justice supervision.* Presentation at the annual Conference on Criminal Justice Research and Evaluation, What to Do About Crime, Sponsored by the National Institute of Justice, the Bureau of Justice Assistance, and the Office of Juvenile Justice and Delinquency Prevention, Washington, DC.

Lockwood, D., Inciardi, J. A., Butzin, C. A., & Hooper, R. M. (1997). The therapeutic community continuum in corrections. In G. De Leon (Ed.), *Community as method: Modified therapeutic communities for special populations and special settings* (pp. 87–96). Westport, CT: Greenwood Press.

Marlatt, G. A., & Gordon, J. R. (Eds.). (1985). *Relapse prevention.* New York: Guilford Press.

McKusker, J., & Sorensen, J. L. (1994). HIV and therapeutic communities. In F. M. Tims, G. De Leon, & N. Jainchill (Eds.), *Therapeutic community: Advances in research and application* (NIDA Research Monograph, NIH Publication No. 94-3633, pp. 232–258). Washington, DC: Government Printing Office.

Melnick, G., & De Leon, G. (in press). Clarifying the nature of therapeutic community treatment: A survey of essential elements. *Journal of Substance Abuse Treatment.*

National Treatment Improvement Evaluation Study. (1997, September). *Preliminary report: The persistent effects of substance abuse treatment—One year later.* Rockville, MD: U.S. Department of Health and Human Services, Substance Abuse and Mental Health Services Administration, Center for Substance Abuse Treatment.

Rapoport, R. N. (1960). *Community as doctor.* Springfield, IL: Charles C Thomas.

Sacks, S., De Leon, G., Bernhardt, A. I., & Sacks, J. Y. (1997). A modified therapeutic community for homeless mentally ill chemical abuse clients. In G. De Leon (Ed.), *Community as method: Modified therapeutic communities for special populations and special settings* (pp. 17–37). Westport, CT: Greenwood Press.

Schoket, D. (1992). *Circumstances, motivation, readiness and suitability for treatment in relation to retention in a residential therapeutic community: Secon-*

dary analysis. Unpublished doctoral dissertation, City University of New York, New York City.

Siddiqui, Q. (1989). *The relative effects of extrinsic and intrinsic pressure on retention in treatment*. Unpublished doctoral dissertation. City University of the City, New York City.

Simpson, D. D., & Curry, S. J. (Eds.). (1997). (Special Issue) Drug abuse treatment outcome study. *Psychology of Addictive Behaviors, 11.*

Simpson, D. D., & Sells, S. B. (1982). Effectiveness of treatment for drug abuse: An overview of the DARP research program. *Advances in Alcohol and Substance Abuse, 2,* 7–29.

Therapeutic community research facts: What we know. *Therapeutic Communities of America News,* (1988, Summer). pp. 1–2.

Tims, F. M., De Leon, G., & Jainchill, N. (Eds.). (1994). *Therapeutic community: Advances in research and application* (NIDA Research monograph, NIH Publication No. 94-3633). Rockville, MD: Government Printing Office.

Tims, F. M., & Ludford, J. P. (Eds.). (1984). *Drug abuse treatment evaluation: Strategies, progress, and prospects* (NIDA Research monograph, DHHS Publica-

tion No. (ADM) 84-1329). Rockville, MD: National Institute on Drug Abuse.

Wexler, H. K., Falkin, G. P., & Lipton, D. S. (1990). Outcome evaluation of a prison therapeutic community for substance abuse treatment. *Criminal Justice and Behavior, 17,* 71–92.

Wexler, H. K., & Graham, W. (1994). *Prison-based therapeutic communities for substance abusers: Retention, re-arrest, and re-incarceration.* Paper presented at American Psychological Association convention, Los Angeles.

Wexler, H. K., & Lipton, D. S. (1993). From REFORM to RECOVERY: Advances in prison drug treatment. In J. Inciardi (Ed.), *Drug treatment and criminal justice* (Sage Criminal Justice System Annuals, Vol. 29). Newbury Park, CA: Sage Publications.

Winick, C. (1990–1991). The counselor in drug abuse treatment. *International Journal of the Addictions 25,* 1479–1502.

Zuckerman, M., Sola, S., Masterson, J., & Angelone, J. V. (1975). MMPI patterns in drug abusers before and after treatment in therapeutic communities. *Journal of Counseling and Clinical Psychology, 43,* 286–296.

18

Self-Help Groups for Addictions

Joseph Nowinski

Individuals with substance abuse problems pursue many different paths in their efforts to deal with the problem. Data suggest that many are able to reduce, control, or stop alcohol or drug use without resorting to either formal treatment or self-help groups (Price, Cottler, & Robins, 1991; Sobell, Sobell, & Toneatto, 1991). In general, it is a desire to deal with the psychosocial consequences of substance abuse, as opposed to a desire to reduce use per se, that appears to motivate help seeking (Marlatt, Tucker, Donovan, & Vuchinich, 1997), and most substance abusers who do seek help tend to seek medical care prior to availing themselves of formal substance abuse treatment or self-help (Pokorny, Kanas, & Overall, 1981). Still, a significant number of substance abusers do turn to professional treatment and/or self-help groups at some point in their efforts to stop or control use.

This chapter will discuss the major self-help organizations currently available as resources for persons who are troubled by addictive behaviors. Practitioners who are asked to help individuals overcome addictions are increasingly confronted with the need not only to be aware of such community-based resources, but also to actively facilitate patients' utilization of them as an adjunct to professional treatment. The pressure to augment formal treatment with self-help comes both from patients themselves and from third-party payers who are interested in cost-effectiveness. In this age of managed care, the professional therapist or treatment program cannot reasonably expect to be the sole source of therapeutic efforts. With this in mind, this chapter will attempt to educate the practitioner regarding the most popular self-help groups that are available, the key elements of self-help as it pertains particularly to the addictions, and how to effectively facilitate patients' utilization of these programs. We must appreciate, however, that an individual's decision to turn to a self-help group, much like the decision to seek formal treatment, is not likely to be an act of *first* resort in the process of his or her efforts to deal with a substance abuse problem. Rather, as noted above, the data suggest that such decisions are typically preceded by significant psychosocial consequences of substance abuse.

EARLY DEVELOPMENT OF THE SELF-HELP MOVEMENT FOR ADDICTIONS

The modern self-help movement for addictive behaviors had its origins in the Oxford Groups, which were a precursor to Alcoholics Anonymous. The Oxford Group was an international, nondenominational, and theologically conservative evangelical organization whose stated goal was to instill in its members what it considered fundamental Christian precepts (Kurtz, 1988). The Oxford Group meetings that were attended by Bill Wilson and other alcoholics inspired him not only with the members' kindness but with their emphasis on spiritual renewal and fellowship as keys to personal transformation.

Alcoholics Anonymous (AA) eventually evolved from the Oxford movement, taking with it the Oxford emphasis on fellowship and faith (as opposed to self-determinism), on the virtues of taking one's "moral inventory" and making amends to others harmed by one's faults (including addiction), on public confession or "sharing" of one's experiences, and on service to others as cornerstones of sobriety. What differentiated AA from the Oxford movement was its less dogmatic, more pluralistic view of the concept of God, which AA reframed as a "Higher Power." Thus, AA became an organization which, while emphasizing the need for faith, as well as the importance of humility as a condition for recovery from addiction, could be receptive to a much a greater diversity of spiritual beliefs.

It is noteworthy that from its beginnings, AA and the 12-step movement did not regard alcoholism as primarily a medical illness so much as a spiritual and psychological one. All of the early influences on Bill Wilson and his colleagues, and subsequently on AA, were either spiritual—as embodied, for example, in the Oxford Groups—or psychological. Wilson specifically cited the writings of the psychologist William James and the psychiatrist Carl Jung as being influential in the conceptual development of AA.

CURRENT STATUS OF THE SELF-HELP MOVEMENT

AA and its 12-step program of recovery from alcoholism (Alcoholics Anonymous [AA], 1952, 1976) appear to have represented an idea whose time had come. Following the success of AA, a number of similar groups, based on the same 12-step model of recovery, emerged, including Al-Anon (1966) for family members of alcoholics and Narcotics Anonymous (1987) for drug abusers. Meanwhile, those wishing to return to a more Oxford-like Christian Fundamentalist fellowship formed religiously based fellowships such as the Calix Society (Calix, undated) and Overcomers Outreach (1988; Bartosch & Bartosch, 1985). Of these organizations, AA remains by far the most ubiquitous, with approximately 89,000 registered groups (AA, 1993) and over 1.7 million members (AA, 1990a) worldwide.

Following on the popular success of AA, a virtual "12-step movement" emerged (Room, 1993), so that by 1988, it was estimated that there were approximately 125,000 separate chapters of various 12-step groups in this country and abroad (Madara & Meese, 1988). This movement now extends well beyond the issues of alcoholism and drug addiction and includes 12-step fellowships for "emotional addiction" (Emotions Anonymous, 1978), "food addiction" (Overeaters Anonymous, 1980), and "sex addiction" (Augustine Fellowship, 1986), to name a few.

Returning to the problem of substance abuse and addiction, a number of secular self-help organizations have also emerged in recent years, including Self-Management and Recovery Training, or S.M.A.R.T. (1996); Rational Recovery, or RR (Trimpey, 1992); Women for Sobriety (1993a, 1993b); Moderation Management (1996); and Secular Organizations for Sobriety, or SOS (undated a, undated b). These groups, as well as the various 12-step groups, all aim to help individuals overcome alcohol or drug problems. They differ significantly, however, with respect to philosophy, strategies, and organization.

A CLASSIFICATION OF "SELF-HELP" GROUPS

A closer examination of this plethora of groups and organizations suggests that the generic use of term *self-help* in itself requires some clarification. According to the steps and traditions of Alcoholics Anonymous, for example, attempting to overcome alcoholism through *self*-help is precisely the problem. Following on the example set by the Oxford Groups, 12-step programs like AA, NA, and the others cited above explicitly advocate forgoing *self*-help and an exclusive reliance on willpower (i.e., radical self-determination) in favor of *group* help (i.e., fellowship) plus faith in some Higher Power as a means of conquering addiction.

The term *mutual help* has been suggested as perhaps being more descriptive than *self-help* (Mc-Crady, personal communication, 1996), for the simple reason that most of the groups and programs discussed here rely heavily on support and counsel from fellow sufferers. As we will see, the "self-help" movement is in reality more pluralistic than that label implies. Not all "self-help" groups for addictions, for example, are equally democratic in organization, nor are all based in this tradition of advice derived from the common experience of members who have struggled with the same problem.

Anthropologists and sociologists have used terms such as *folk*—as, for example, in referring to folk medicine—(Borkman, 1990) and *informal help* (Powell, 1990) to denote the difference between help that is delivered by trained individuals (i.e., "professional" help) and help which is based primarily in common wisdom that is derived from accumulated experience. This distinction has clear application to 12-step groups such as AA, as well as to some secular programs, such as Women for Sobriety, which operate on these principles of peer assistance and common wisdom. Bill Wilson, cofounder of AA, referred to this stream of common wisdom as the "group conscience" (Bill W., 1948/1992) and described it this way:

> We believe that every AA group has a conscience. It is the collective conscience of its own membership. Daily experience informs and instructs this conscience. When a customary way of doing things is definitely proved to be the best, then that custom forms into AA tradition. (p. 24)

Although relying in many ways on a fund of knowledge similar to what is the basis of folk medicine, groups such as AA and Women for Sobriety are much more organized than the relatively unstructured systems which terms like *folk medicine* and *informal help* connote.

Not all self-help groups share this same tradition of basing their programs on the accumulated experience of peers. Some, such as S.M.A.R.T. Recovery (1996) and Rational Recovery (Trimpey, 1992), are

based not so much on common wisdom and support from fellow sufferers as on social science and psychology. Unlike pure peer-support groups such as AA, these programs are in fact professionalized to varying degrees. Rational Recovery (RR) offers professionally conducted courses and discussion groups through a national network of Rational Recovery Centers for a fee (Rational Recovery Systems, undated). Rational Recovery also states that it "is definitely not a 'support' group" (L. Trimpey, 1996) but a treatment program whose basis is the Addictive Voice Recognition Technique (Trimpey, undated).

S.M.A.R.T. Recovery programs also utilize professionally facilitated groups, though in this case the facilitators are volunteers. Still, S.M.A.R.T. trainers are professionals who must go through a standardized training. They do not emerge as natural leaders from the context of a fellowship of peers. S.M.A.R.T. Recovery employs techniques derived from cognitive behavioral therapies, and its content clearly represents the work of behavioral science professionals (S.M.A.R.T., 1996).

This writer has used the term *fellowship* (Nowinski, 1996; Nowinski & Baker, 1992) when referring specifically to 12-step groups. However, this label would also seem appropriate to denote those mutual help organizations, like Women for Sobriety, that are founded on the principles of peership and that are intentionally nonprofessional. The term *guided self-help*, in contrast, could more accurately describe those programs, like S.M.A.R.T. Recovery, that rely to a greater or lesser extent on trained professionals to deliver their programs. The reader may find this distinction useful both in understanding the dynamics of the various groups discussed here and when recommending them to patients.

A second useful distinction among mutual help organizations concerns the issue of *spirituality*. Clearly, some mutual help organizations, such as AA and its fellow 12-step fellowships, deliberately advocate some form of spiritual belief in the form of a Higher Power and consider such a belief vital to recovery. Granted, AA defines this Higher Power so loosely that the group itself as opposed to a deity is acceptable as one's Higher Power, as the following excerpt from *Twelve Steps and Twelve Traditions* (AA, 1952) indicates:

> You can, if you wish, make A.A. itself your "higher power." In this respect they are certainly

a power greater than you, who have not even come close to a solution. (p. 27)

Alcoholics Anonymous is sometimes taken for a religious organization, which it clearly is not. In fact, AA moved away from the Oxford Groups, where it had its beginnings, for this very reason. This caveat notwithstanding, most 12-step fellowships differ from what we could call their *secular* counterparts in the extent to which spirituality is integral to their philosophy. In general, people who elect to go to 12-step groups are at the very least more amenable to some form of spiritual belief than those who prefer other groups. Some of these groups, such as Secular Organizations for Sobriety, specifically state in their literature that they are intentionally nonreligious:

S.O.S. is not a spin-off of any religious or secular group. There is no hidden agenda, as S.O.S. is concerned with achieving and maintaining sobriety (abstinence), not religiosity. (SOS, undated a, p. 3)

Other mutual help groups, such as Women for Sobriety, do not reject spirituality and the idea of a Higher Power so much as they leave it out of their programs. For example, Women for Sobriety summarizes its philosophy as follows:

The WFS program is based upon metaphysical philosophy. The Fifth Statement, "I am what I think," is the entire basis for the program. (Kirkpatrick, 1982, p. 2)

In its literature, Women for Sobriety (WFS) suggests there is no inherent incompatibility with utilizing both WFS *and* AA as aids to sustaining one's recovery. Rather, WFS emphasizes the need for women to turn to other women as peers who can best understand their experience and support their recovery.

This dimension—of spiritual versus secular—is also useful with respect to understanding mutual help groups and referring patients to them.

A third dimension which is relevant when classifying mutual help groups concerns their stated *goals*. For virtually every program described here, with the exception of Moderation Management (1996), the goal is *abstinence* from the use of alcohol or drugs. In contrast, Moderation Management (MM), as the name implies, seeks to teach skills needed to *control*

drinking. In its literature, MM describes itself as being "for people who want to reduce their drinking" (MM, 1996, p. 1).

The above classification schema is summarized in table 18.1, which lists a number of the more popular mutual help organizations.

OVERVIEW OF MUTUAL HELP GROUPS

In this section we will examine some of the more popular mutual help groups, following the above classification schema.

Spiritual Fellowships

Clearly, the 12-step fellowships are the most ubiquitous of the spiritually based mutual help programs. They include Alcoholics Anonymous, Narcotics Anonymous, and Cocaine Anonymous (CA) for substance abusers, as well as the collateral fellowships of Al-Anon, Al-Ateen, and Nar-Anon, which were established by and for the benefit and support of significant others of substance abusers. All of these fellowships are modeled closely after the 12 steps of Alcoholics Anonymous. Also included among the spiritual fellowships are the Calix Society and Overcomers Outreach.

Alcoholics Anonymous

In 1992, Alcoholics Anonymous, by far the largest mutual help program for substance abusers, had 89,000 groups registered worldwide (AA, 1993). This represented an increase of some 2,000 groups over a period of only 3 years (AA, 1990a). Moreover, these statistics may actually understate the size of this fellowship, since it is not a requirement of AA that every group register itself with the central office, and it is common knowledge within the fellowship that quite a few groups opt not to register, preferring to grow solely by word of mouth.

In an independent national survey, 3.1% of the adult population indicated that they had *ever* been to an AA meeting, and 1.5% indicated they had been to one *in the past year* (Room & Greenfield, 1991). These prevalence data were roughly three times as great as AA's own estimates of its prevalence based on contemporaneous membership surveys (AA, 1990a). Because of its size, its organization, and its influence

TABLE 18.1 Classification of Mutual Help Organizations

Fellowships		Guided self-help groups
Spiritual	Secular	
Alcoholics Anonymous	Secular Organizations for Sobriety	S.M.A.R.T. Recovery
Narcotics Anonymous	Women for Sobriety	Rational Recovery
Cocaine Anonymous		Moderation Management[a]
Calix Society		
Overcomers Outreach		

[a]Moderation Management states that its goal is to help individuals reduce drinking; all others state that abstinence is the goal.

on society as a whole, AA has been described as more than a mutual help program. At least one sociologist has made the case that AA and its 12-step program could be considered a *social movement* (Room, 1993).

The 12 steps of Alcoholics Anonymous are presented in table 18.2. Narcotics Anonymous, Al-Anon, and other 12-step programs all advocate following these same steps as a program of recovery, the ideal result of which is a "spiritual awakening" (Step 12). This is significant, because the 12-step program is *not* merely a program for staying sober. The founders of AA (and other 12-step programs) regarded addiction as a part of a larger spiritual crisis and therefore viewed recovery as a process of spiritual renewal, only part of which is staying sober. The process via which this spiritual renewal is achieved is a gradual one:

> No one among us has been able to maintain anything like perfect adherence to these principles. We are not saints. The point is, that we are willing to grow along spiritual lines. The principles we have set down are guides to progress. We claim spiritual progress rather than spiritual perfection. (AA, 1976, p. 60)

This conceptualization of recovery as primarily a process of spiritual growth (and therefore of alcoholism as primarily a spiritual malady) is unique to 12-step programs. For them, recovery is *not* merely staying sober. On the contrary, 12-step fellowships have

TABLE 18.2 The 12 Steps of Alcoholics Anonymous

Step 1	We admitted we were powerless over alcohol—that our lives had become unmanageable.
Step 2	Came to believe that a Power greater than ourselves could restore us to sanity.
Step 3	Made a decision to turn our will and our lives over to the care of God *as we understood him.*
Step 4	Made a searching and fearless moral inventory of ourselves.
Step 5	Admitted to God, to ourselves, and to another human being the exact nature of our wrongs.
Step 6	Were entirely ready to have God remove all these defects of character.
Step 7	Humbly asked Him to remove our shortcomings.
Step 8	Made a list of all persons we had harmed, and became willing to make amends to them all.
Step 9	Made direct amends to such people wherever possible, except when to do so would injure them or others.
Step 10	Continued to take personal inventory and when we were wrong promptly admitted it.
Step 11	Sought through prayer and meditation to improve our conscious contact with God *as we understood him,* praying only for knowledge of His will for us and the power to carry that out.
Step 12	Having had a spiritual awakening as the result of these steps, we tried to carry this message to alcoholics and to practice these principles in all our affairs.

Note. From Alcoholics Anonymous (1976).

a name for someone who stays sober without pursuing a program of spiritual renewal: the "dry drunk" (Solberg, 1983).

The founders of AA (and other 12-step programs), then, regarded addiction as a part of a larger spiritual crisis and regarded recovery as a process of spiritual renewal, only part of which is staying sober. This process begins with admitting that one's efforts to control drinking have failed and that as a result, life has become unmanageable (Step 1). This is also commonly referred to as *acceptance* within the 12-step culture. *Acceptance* was defined by the psychiatrist Harry Tiebout (who was in fact Bill Wilson's therapist) as follows:

Acceptance appears to be a state of mind in which the individual accepts rather than rejects or resists: he is able to take things in, to go along with, to cooperate, to be receptive. Contrariwise, he is not argumentative, quarrelsome, irritable, or contentious. It is necessary to point out that no one can tell himself or force himself wholeheartedly to accept anything. One must have a *feeling—conviction*—otherwise acceptance is not wholehearted but halfhearted with a large element of lip service. (Tiebout, 1953, p. 60)

When working with clients who are involved in a 12-step program, the practitioner should understand that resistance to the above idea of acceptance is essentially what is meant by the term *denial*. The first step asks that the individual do more than recognize that she or he has a drinking problem; it asks that he or she humbly accept on this emotional level the reality that personal efforts to control drinking have failed and that life has become unmanageable. This level of acceptance implies a degree of openness to change. Newcomers to AA and other 12-step groups can expect to be confronted sooner or later on this issue of acceptance.

The second and third steps of the 12-step program are often linked together through the concept of *surrender*. Surrender follows from acceptance and has been conceptualized as a readiness to change:

After an act of surrender, the individual reports a sense of unity, of ended struggles, of no longer divided inner counsel. He knows the meaning of inner wholeness and, what is more, he knows from immediate experience the feeling of being wholehearted about anything. He recognizes for the first time how insincere his previous protestations actually were. (Tiebout, 1953, p. 65)

Resistance to the above idea of surrender, like resistance to acceptance, is also part of what is meant by *denial* in the context of 12-step groups. On a practical level, the newcomer to AA will be asked in time to "surrender" to the program. The practitioner should understand that this means embracing the 12-step program and following the traditions and the counsel of fellow members. Surrender, like true acceptance, represents the resolution of any inner doubts about whether one can control drinking and represents a willingness to take whatever action is necessary in order to stay sober.

Alcoholics Anonymous and other 12-step meetings vary in format. *Open meetings*, for example, are defined as ones which may be attended by persons who do not necessarily acknowledge that they have an alcohol (or drug) problem, as well as by those men and women who are willing to admit that they have a drinking (or drug) problem. Thus, open meetings are appropriate for clients who are undecided about whether they have a problem with alcohol. In contrast, *closed meetings* are to be attended only by men and women who acknowledge a problem and have the "desire to stop drinking" that is cited in AA literature as the sole "requirement" for membership in the fellowship (AA, 1952, p. 139).

Meetings typically last from 1 hour to an 1½ hours. Each has a chairperson, who is elected by the membership, and a secretary. The chairperson and the secretary change periodically, though in keeping with the AA tradition of decentralization, there is no set standard.

Meetings are governed by established rules of etiquette. These are primarily transmitted orally to newcomers. Most important of these is the rule of anonymity. Members typically identify themselves by their first names only. In addition, members are strongly encouraged to regard everything that is said in an AA meeting as confidential. Additional rules of etiquette include not interrupting or questioning a speaker, respecting one's right not to speak (i.e., "passing"), and avoiding dual relationships with members of the group. That is not to say that AA members do not socialize with one another; on the contrary, socializing before and after meetings is commonplace, as are various AA social events. However, dating among members of the same group is discouraged, as is any romantic involvement at all during one's first year of AA participation.

Several types of meetings are described below. Keep in mind that each type can be either "open" or "closed." For instance, an AA meeting schedule may list a number of "open speaker" and "closed speaker" meetings.

Speaker Meetings At speaker meetings, which are highly recommended for newcomers as well as for those who are undecided about whether they have a problem, members of the group as well as occasional "guest speakers" relate the story of their addiction and recovery. The format of these meetings is as follows: *how things were, what happened, and how things are now.* These are basically tales of addiction and renewal. This is perhaps the strongest tradition within AA and other 12-step fellowships and can be traced to the Oxford Groups with their emphasis on public confession as a spiritual path.

Storytelling accomplishes several things, beginning with creating a bond of commonality—of shared experience—among the members of the group. Despite their outward differences in form, the *process* of addiction is remarkably similar across stories and promotes identification and bonding. The newcomer to AA is strongly encouraged to "identify, not compare."

Storytelling also helps members to maintain their memories of the consequences that are associated with substance abuse and addiction. AA believes that any tendency to forget the unpleasant past is dangerous. Fading memories of negative consequences associated with alcohol abuse can effectively undermine one's motivation to stay sober and to stay active in the fellowship. One suggested method for staying sober is "remembering your last drunk" (AA, 1975). Advice such as this, as well as relating personal histories (so-called drunkalogs) are therefore intended not to glorify substance abuse but to keep the memory of its consequences alive.

Discussion Meetings The format in discussion meetings is to select a topic (e.g., gratitude, self-centeredness, resentments) and share thoughts about it. Typically, either the chairperson selects the topic or the members do so in rotation. Sometimes, the topic is a reading from the Big Book or another AA publication.

Step Meetings In step meetings, the format is to read one of the 12 steps and for members to share their thoughts about how they as individuals are "working" that step: how they are attempting to implement it in their day-to-day lives, as the 12th step advises them to do. Through attending step meetings, newcomers have an opportunity to learn how others have interpreted the steps and how they relate to lifestyle and attitude changes that are associated with "recovery" versus merely staying sober. Some step meetings limit themselves to the first 3 steps, whereas others include all 12 steps as topics for reflection and discussion.

Specialty Meetings In addition to the above generic types of meetings, there are also a growing number of specialty meetings, for example, men's meetings and women's meetings, meetings for gays and lesbians, meetings for professionals, and meetings for specific ethnic groups. To the extent that participation in such groups facilitates identification and bonding, newcomers may find them useful.

Narcotics Anonymous, Cocaine Anonymous, Nicotine Anonymous

Narcotics Anonymous (NA), Cocaine Anonymous (CA), and Nicotine Anonymous, as their names imply, are 12-step fellowships modeled closely after AA. All are spiritually based fellowships that are open to those who wish to recover from substance abuse using the 12-step model. Narcotics Anonymous has published its own version of the "AA Big Book" (*Alcoholics Anonymous*), titled *Narcotics Anonymous* (1987). It includes the same 12-step program used by AA, merely substituting the word *narcotics* for *alcohol*, as well as stories of recovery that are very similar in theme to those that make up the second half of *Alcoholics Anonymous*. Like the other 12-step programs, such as Cocaine Anonymous and Nicotine Anonymous, NA follows the same traditions and is organized the same way that AA is.

Their inherent compatibility facilitates the use of several programs concurrently by persons who abuse multiple psychoactive substances. For example, it is not uncommon to find someone attending AA, NA, and Nicotine Anonymous meetings concurrently.

Al-Anon, Nar-Anon, Alateen, and Alatot No discussion of spiritually based mutual help fellowships for substance abusers would be complete without some mention of Al-Anon, Nar-Anon, Alateen, and Alatot. These companion fellowships to AA, NA, and other 12-step fellowships for substance abusers were established by and for concerned significant others of alcohol abusers. They parallel AA, using the same AA 12-step program, which begins with admitting one's own powerlessness over a loved one's addiction (Step 1).

Al-Anon reports that it has 30,000 known groups worldwide (Al-Anon Family Groups, 1996). Of Al-Anon members, 85% are female (Al-Anon Family Groups, 1993), compared to 35% of AA members (AA, 1993). Of AA members, 56% are between the ages of 30 and 50 (AA, 1993) as are 57% of Al-Anon members (Al-Anon Family Groups, 1996). These data suggest that demographically as well as philosophically these two self-help programs do indeed complement one another.

The objective of Al-Anon and the related fellowships like Nar-Anon is *caring detachment* (Al-Anon Family Groups, 1985; Carolyn W., 1984; Nowinski, in press). Caring detachment, much like the concept of recovery itself, is complex but consists in part in allowing the substance abuser to experience the natural consequences of his or her substance abuse, and to focus on one's mental health and spiritual growth as opposed to becoming preoccupied with the substance abuser. Caring detachment is thought to help restore balance in relationships and families—a balance that is disrupted when one member falls victim to addiction.

Overcomers Outreach, Calix Society Alcoholics Anonymous and the other 12-step fellowships have been deliberately nondenominational since their inception. Overcomers Outreach (OO), founded in 1985 (Overcomers Outreach, 1988, undated) and the Calix Society, founded in 1947 (Calix Society, undated a, b), were founded by and for Christians and Catholics, respectively. These spiritual fellowships do not limit themselves to problems of alcohol or drug abuse but state that they are open to men and women suffering from any form of addictive behavior, from alcoholism to sexual addiction. They are much smaller than AA and the other nondenominational 12-step fellowships. Calix, for example, lists a total of 42 chapters in the United States, 3 in Canada, and 29 in Great Britain (Calix, 1995). Overcom-

ers Outreach reports "approximately 1,000" groups (Overcomers Outreach, 1988) worldwide.

Overcomers Outreach and Calix do not view themselves as competitive with or incompatible with AA; rather, they view themselves as complementary to AA, but as offering programs that place greater emphasis on Christian or Catholic doctrine than AA itself does. For example, Overcomers Outreach defines itself as follows:

> Overcomers Outreach groups are not intended to replace Alcoholics Anonymous, Al-Anon, etc. but are designed to be a supplement from the Christian perspective where A.A.'s 12 Steps to recovery are directly related to their corresponding Scriptures. (Overcomers Outreach, 1988, p. 2)

In its traditions and its structure, Overcomers Outreach remains faithful to the principles of AA. It is, for example, intentionally nonprofessional, subscribes to the principle of anonymity, and so on. Therefore, participation in AA is not at all inconsistent or incompatible with participation in Overcomers Outreach. The essential difference lies in OO's identification of Jesus Christ as *the* Higher Power and its reliance on Christian faith for its spiritual foundation. Table 18.3 summarizes the way in which Overcomers Outreach relates Scripture to the twelve steps of Alcoholics Anonymous.

A perusal of table 18.3 reveals some of the early roots of AA in the Oxford Groups, especially the emphasis on confessing one's faults and sins to others, as well as on personal humility.

The Calix Society, like OO, recognizes the 12-step program of AA as "the best therapy for those afflicted with the disease of alcoholism" (Calix, undated a). It, too, however, bases its existence on the need for some to connect themselves to a more dogmatic spirituality. Thus:

> For Catholics . . . something more is needed. They realize that the A.A. program advocates recourse to a "higher power" and God, but they also know that A.A. is necessarily nondenominational. Having been raised in a Church rich in tradition, dogma and ritual, these recovering alcoholics begin to yearn once again for the faith they probably have neglected or abandoned. (Calix Society, undated a, p. 1)

TABLE 18.3 Christian Scripture Correlates of the 12 Steps of AA

AA step	Scripture correlates
Step 1	We felt we were doomed to die and saw how powerless we were to help ourselves; but that was good, for then we put everything into the hands of God, who alone could save us. (2 Corinthians 1:9)
Step 2	A man is a fool to trust himself! But those who use God's wisdom are safe. (Proverbs 28:26)
Step 3	Trust in the Lord completely; don't ever trust yourself. In everything you do, put God first, and he will direct you and crown your efforts with success. (Proverbs 3:5–6)
Step 4	Let us examine ourselves and repent and turn again to the Lord. Let us lift our hearts and our hands to Him in heaven. (Lamentations 3:40–41)
Step 5	Admit your faults to one another and pray for each other so that you may be healed. (James 5:16)
Step 6	So give yourselves humbly to God . . . then, when you realize your worthlessness before the Lord, He will lift you up, encourage and help you. (James 4:7–10)
Step 7	But if we confess our sins to Him, He can be depended on to forgive us and to cleanse us from every wrong. (John 1:9)
Step 8	If you are standing before the altar . . . and suddenly remember that a friend has something against you, leave your sacrifice there and go and be reconciled . . . and then come and offer your sacrifice to God. (Matthew 5:23–24)
Step 9	You can pray for anything, and if you believe, you have it; it's yours! But when you are praying, first forgive anyone you are holding a grudge against, so that your Father in heaven will forgive you your sins too. (Mark 11:24–25)
Step 10	But how can I ever know what sins are lurking in my heart? Cleanse me from these hidden faults. And keep me from deliberate wrongs; help me to stop doing them. Only then can I be set free of guilt! (Psalm 19:12)
Step 11	If you want better insight and discernment, and are searching for them as you would for lost money or hidden treasure, then wisdom will be given you, and knowledge of God Himself; you will soon learn the importance of reverence for the Lord and of trusting Him. (Proverbs 2:3–5)
Step 12	Quietly trust yourself to Christ your Lord and if anybody asks why you believe as you do, be ready to tell him, and do it in a gentle and respectful way. (1 Peter 3:15)

Note. From Overcomers Outreach (1988).

Calix meetings utilize the 12 steps of Alcoholics Anonymous but also rely on the participation of volunteer priests to help members interpret and work the steps in ways consistent with Catholic dogma.

Secular Fellowships

Secular fellowships are organized along the same lines—most notably being intentionally nonprofessional and decentralized—as the spiritual fellowships. However, they do not advocate any theistic belief. More than merely nondenominational, the secular fellowships eschew belief in any "higher power" as necessary for recovery from addiction. The primary secular fellowships for the addictions include Secular Organizations for Sobriety and Women for Sobriety.

Secular Organizations for Sobriety

Secular Organizations for Sobriety (SOS) was founded in 1985 by James Christopher, an individual who had been sober since 1978, initially achieving sobriety with the help of AA (Christopher, 1988, 1989). Later, Christopher decided that the spiritual nature of AA and other 12-step fellowships was either unnecessary or counterproductive:

Studies of religions and cults have consistently proved that people tend to convert at times of great stress or failure in their lives. These are the times when promises of enlightenment and cures for pain are most appealing. People don't look for proof or evidence or even coherence in belief. They see someone throwing them a life-preserver, and they grab it. Put in this context, it is easy to scc why the religious fervor that permeates AA's meetings and literature has gone unchallenged for so long. (SOS, undated b, p. 1)

Though secular in its approach, SOS, like AA, advocates abstinence as the only viable goal for alcoholics and addicts:

> To break the cycle of denial and achieve sobriety, we first acknowledge that we are alcoholics and addicts. We reaffirm this truth daily and accept without reservation the fact that, as clean and sober individuals, we cannot and do not drink or use, no matter what. (SOS, undated a, p. 3)

SOS reports that as many as 96% of its members have had prior involvement with AA, and that 70% describe themselves as atheists or agnostics (SOS, 1996), suggesting that SOS is primarily a self-selected group of individuals who have left AA but who are nonetheless interested in group support to sustain their recovery.

Like other fellowships, SOS is decentralized to a considerable degree. Though guided by a shared philosophy, SOS groups, like all AA groups, are each self-supporting. The approach taken to maintaining sobriety is a highly pragmatic one. However, it should be pointed out that 12-step fellowships are also prag-

matic. Table 18.4 compares some of the advice offered by SOS (undated c) to that offered by AA (1975).

A perusal of table 18.4 suggests that SOS and AA share a great deal on the pragmatic level. Their differences appear to lie primarily in whether spiritual faith is necessary for sustained recovery.

Women for Sobriety

Women for Sobriety (WFS) describes itself as "an organization whose purpose is to help all women recover from problem drinking through the discovery of self, gained by sharing experiences, hopes and encouragement with other women in similar circumstances" (Women for Sobriety [WFS], undated b, p. 3). WFS sees itself and AA as "complementary" but strongly advocates that women involved in AA also attend WFS since it believes that women have special needs that cannot be satisfactorily met through AA (Kirkpatrick, 1982):

> The problems of most women are tied to the male-female relationship, and these problems cannot be talked about or thoroughly explored in a mixed group. Too often in mixed groups the men dominate and the women have little chance to express themselves or to speak about what is truly bothering them. (Kirkpatrick, 1982, p. 2)

TABLE 18.4 Comparison of Advice Offered by SOS and AA

SOS	AA
Attend as many SOS meetings as you can. Take what you can use from these and leave the rest.	Sometimes an AA member will talk about the various parts of the program in cafeteria style—selecting what he likes and letting alone what he does not want.
Get names and phone numbers from other sober alcoholics/addicts at meetings. Use these phone numbers. Practice calling people when you're feeling okay so that you'll be able to call more easily when you're in need of help.	When we stopped drinking, we were told repeatedly to get AA people's telephone numbers and, instead of drinking, to phone these people. Once the first call is made, it is much, much easier to make another when it is needed.
Try putting some simple structure into your life: get up and get dressed at a regular time, take a walk before or after dinner. Be gentle with yourself. Sobriety skills aren't developed overnight.	When we first stopped drinking many of us found it useful to look back at the habits surrounding our drinking and, whenever possible, to change a lot of the small things connected with drinking.
Choose to stay sober one day at a time.	We have found it more realistic—and more successful—to say, "I am not taking a drink *just for today*."
Keep plenty of mineral water, soda, and/or fruit juices on hand.	Many of us have learned that something sweet-tasting, or almost any nourishing food or snack, seems to dampen a bit the desire for a drink.

Note. From SOS (undated c) and AA (1975).

The above notwithstanding, it should be noted that AA and other 12-step fellowships have seen their greatest rate of growth in recent years among women (AA, 1990b), including women-only groups. This degree of acceptance of AA on the part of women led one reviewer to conclude, "I now believe that A.A., a fellowship originally designed by and composed primarily of men, appears equally or more effective for women than for men" (Beckman, 1993, p. 213).

WFS subscribes to the same guidelines (confidentiality, nonprofessionalism, decentralized and self-supporting, etc.) that govern other mutual help fellowships. WFS also advocates abstinence from alcohol and drugs as the desired result of recovery. It seeks to help women achieve this through group support. WFS describes its meetings as "a conversation in the round" (WFS, 1993a, p. 1). The groups are small (a size of 6–10 is recommended) and last a maximum of an hour and a half. They are run by a "moderator" who is not a trained professional but a woman in recovery who is well versed in the WFS philosophy. The moderator opens the meeting and reads the "13 statements" of WFS (1993a). These statements, listed in table 18.5, form the basis of the WFS New Life Acceptance Program (WFS, 1993a).

This New Life Acceptance Program clearly implies that problems of self-esteem and self-acceptance lie at the heart of substance abuse problems in women; conversely, recovery involves a process of gaining self-acceptance through active involvement in WFS. This view is further affirmed in WFS literature, which states: "Guilt, depression, low (or no) self-esteem are the problems of today's woman and dependence upon alcohol temporarily masks her real needs, which are for a feeling of self-realization and self-worth" (WFS, undated a, p. 1).

The strategies for change that WFS favors include positive reinforcement through support, approval, and encouragement; positive thinking as emphasized in its New Life Acceptance Program; and taking care of one's physical health.

Guided Self-Help Groups

We turn now to a consideration of those groups which offer guided self-help. As opposed to the fellowships, these programs all rely on the use of trained leaders or facilitators. They are more centralized than the fellowships. In addition, some (but not all) of the guided self-help programs charge fees for their services. The programs we will examine include S.M.A.R.T. Recovery, Rational Recovery, and Moderation Management.

S.M.A.R.T Recovery

S.M.A.R.T. Recovery is "an abstinence-based, not-for-profit organization with a sensible self-help program for people having problems with drinking and using" (S.M.A.R.T. Recovery, 1996, p. 2). In its

TABLE 18.5 The Women for Sobriety New Life Acceptance Program

1. I have a life-threatening problem (that once had me).
2. Negative thoughts destroy only myself.
3. Happiness is a habit I will develop.
4. Problems bother me only to the degree I permit them to.
5. I am what I think.
6. Life can be ordinary or it can be great.
7. Love can change the course of my world.
8. The fundamental object of life is emotional and spiritual growth.
9. The past is gone forever.
10. All love given returns.
11. Enthusiasm is my daily exercise.
12. I am a competent woman and have much to give life.
13. I am responsible for myself and my actions.

Note. From Women for Sobriety (1993a).

TABLE 18.6 S.M.A.R.T. Recovery: Key Areas of Awareness and Change

Key area	Topics/exercises
Building motivation	Building Motivation Am I Hooked Yet? Do I Have to Quit?
Coping with urges	Coping With Urges Recognizing and Resisting Urges New Ways to Cope Stopping an Addiction Catch the Wave Refusing that First Drink S.M.A.R.T. Reality Check
Problem solving	Problem Solving Rational-Emotive Therapy's A-B-C Theory of Emotional Disturbance The ABCs of Gaining Independence From Addictive Behavior Exchange Vocabulary Rational Beliefs to Increase Frustration Tolerance Confidence-Building and Anxiety-Reducing Rational Beliefs Anger-Reducing Rational Beliefs Some Methods for Managing Anger Forward Steps to Recovery Backward Steps Into Addictive Behaviors
Lifestyle changes	Lifestyle Change Our Beliefs Affect Our Socializing Ten Rational Beliefs About Decision Making Self-help recovery homework suggestions

Note. From S.M.A.R.T. Recovery (1996).

conceptualization of alcoholism and addiction, S.M.A.R.T., much as does Women for Sobriety, emphasizes that people drink or use drugs as a means of coping. However, both drinking and using in turn create problems. Accordingly, the S.M.A.R.T. program emphasizes building alternative coping skills as the key to recovery.

S.M.A.R.T. issues a standard meeting outline that begins with a general welcoming with special attention paid to newcomers. Members are asked next to share something positive that they have learned or done as a result of attending meetings. Members are then polled to see who, if anyone, may need some extra time to deal with concerns or problems. The bulk of the hour-and-a-half meeting time is then devoted to a discussion of one of S.M.A.R.T. Recovery's main themes using one of the structured exercises that have been developed by S.M.A.R.T. Recovery. These themes and associated exercises are presented in table 18.6.

S.M.A.R.T. Recovery makes extensive use of cognitive behavioral theory and technique as set forth in rational-emotive therapy (Ellis & Harper, 1975). Meetings end with each member being asked to say something about what he or she intends to do in the coming week to support his or her recovery ("homework"). Following the end of the formal meeting, members are encouraged to socialize and exchange phone numbers. S.M.A.R.T. Recovery, like most of the programs described here, relies on voluntary contributions from members to support itself. Like other guided self-help programs, it uses trained professionals to run meetings; these individuals, however, are not paid for their services.

Rational Recovery

Rational Recovery (RR) is a guided self-help program based on the addictive voice recognition technique (AVRT) that was developed by Jack Trimpey (1992, 1996). Training in AVRT as well as RR materials are offered by Rational Recovery Systems, Inc., for a fee. In its advertising, RR makes the following claim: "AVRT shows that the *sole cause* of addiction is the

Addictive Voice—the thinking and feeling that supports your use of alcohol or other drugs. By learning to recognize your Addictive Voice, you can completely recover from any substance addiction in a mercifully brief time" (Rational Recovery Systems [RRS], undated, p. 1).

Rational Recovery is fundamentally a cognitive behavioral approach which frames addiction in terms of an internal conflict between a primitive "beast brain," which craves the substance one is addicted to, and a "healthy adult brain," whose goal is to stay in control of one's behavior and abstain from substance use (Trimpey, undated). RR does not view the cravings associated with the beast brain as physiological so much as psychological. Addictive drinking or using is thought to be the result of the irrational belief of this beast brain: "It views alcohol or drugs as necessary to survival" (Trimpey, undated, p. 2).

The Rational Recovery program seeks to help individuals overcome addiction through teaching them the addictive voice recognition technique, which involves learning to separate the irrational beliefs associated with the beast brain from one's rational consciousness: one's "neocortical authority" (Trimpey, undated, p. 2).

One may learn AVRT through reading Rational Recovery Systems, Inc., literature, or through attending one of its Rational Recovery Centers, which are described as offering "a unique service for substance addiction that is intended to *replace* addiction treatment and extended recovery group involvement" (RRS, undated, p. 5). Thus, it appears that in contrast to the other programs described here, RR does *not* advocate ongoing involvement in a mutual help program. In fact, RR describes its groups in this way: "RR groups are lay-led discussion groups centering around AVRT. Long-term involvement is discouraged unless in a leadership role" (RRS, undated, p. 4).

In summary, RR is based in a cognitive behavioral view of addiction as an internal process in which rational beliefs prevail over irrational cravings and result in sobriety. The key is to learn the addictive voice recognition technique (i.e., to reframe cravings, thoughts, and emotions associated with substance use as artifacts of a "beast brain"). RR does not, however, identify itself with other mutual help programs, stating instead, "RR is definitely *not* a 'support' group. We only teach people how to quit addictions in a mercifully brief period of time" (Trimpey, 1997, personal communication).

Moderation Management

Moderation Management (MM; Kishline, 1996) is the sole program for substance abusers which openly advocates moderation as a long-term goal as opposed to abstinence (MM, 1996). This program, which emphasizes progressive changes in lifestyle to support moderation, does recommend abstinence initially (for 30 days), presumably as a litmus test for moderation. MM indicates that it "is not for alcoholics or chronic drinkers" but "is intended for problem drinkers who have experienced *mild to moderate* levels of alcohol-related problems" (MM, 1996, p. 2).

It appears that it is only through an accurate self-assessment can one decide the difference between "mild to moderate" and "severe" consequences of substance abuse. Alcoholic Anonymous also suggests a "test period" as an aid to self-diagnosis:

> We do not like to pronounce any individual as alcoholic, but you can quickly diagnose yourself. Step over to the nearest barroom and try some controlled drinking. Try to drink and stop abruptly. Try it more than once. It will not take long for you to decide, if you are honest with yourself about it. (AA, 1976, p. 31)

AA and other abstinence-based mutual help programs essentially use the same empirical definition of addiction, summarized in *Alcoholics Anonymous* (1976):

> We have seen the truth demonstrated again and again: "Once an alcoholic, always an alcoholic." *Commencing to drink after a period of sobriety, we are in a short time as bad as ever.* (p. 33)

Moderation Management also seeks to use an empirical definition: It is for those individuals who do *not* quickly find themselves returning to their pre-abstinence level of substance use following a period of sobriety, and who can sustain moderate use. The clinically relevant question then becomes: After how many failures at moderation is moderation no longer a viable goal?

The Moderation Management program, much like that of S.M.A.R.T. Recovery, utilizes a cognitive behavioral model of addiction. The MM "nine step" program for moderation (see table 18.7) includes many strategies for change that are drawn from the cognitive behavioral literature. MM also recom-

TABLE 18.7 The Moderation Management Nine-Step Program

1. Attend MM meetings and learn about the program of Moderation Management.
2. Abstain from alcoholic beverages for 30 days and complete Steps 3 through 6 during this time.
3. Examine how drinking has affected your life.
4. Write down your priorities.
5. Take a look at how much, how often, and under what circumstances you used to drink.
6. Learn the MM guidelines and limits for moderate drinking.
7. Set moderate drinking limits and start weekly "small steps" toward positive lifestyle changes.
8. Review your progress and update your goals.
9. Continue to make positive lifestyle changes, attend meetings for ongoing encouragement and support, and help newcomers to the group.

Note. From Moderation Management (1996).

mends a number of self-help books, all of which offer many cognitive behavioral strategies for moderation. The primary difference between MM and S.M.A.R.T. appears to lie not so much in their techniques as in their respective goals (i.e., moderation versus abstinence).

INTEGRATING MUTUAL HELP GROUPS WITH PROFESSIONAL PRACTICE

Practitioners can approach the issue of integrating mutual help into a comprehensive treatment plan in one of two ways, the first of which could be called *passive facilitation*. In this approach, the therapist may recognize the usefulness of a mutual help program—say, AA and/or Al-Anon—as an adjunct to treating a substance abuser and his or her significant other. The therapist may earnestly recommend attendance at meetings and may go so far as to provide the patient with a current meeting schedule. Follow-up on this therapeutic recommendation, however, under the passive approach, is typically limited to asking the patient if she or he has gone to any meetings and if so how she or he reacted to it. Attendance may be reinforced; on the other hand, *working through resistance to attendance* is rarely identified as an additional treatment goal.

In the second approach, *active facilitation*, the therapist in effect makes active involvement in one more mutual help groups an integral part of the treatment plan. In other words, compliance with the recommendation that the client utilize a mutual help group is a separate treatment goal. The therapist

intentionally and consistently employs interventions (reinforcement, role playing, etc.) designed to achieve that goal. The extra clinical effort required by the active facilitation approach can be justified in part by findings which suggest that compliance with recommended treatment protocols is generally correlated with more positive treatment outcomes (Cowen, Jim, Boyd, & Gee, 1981; Horwitz & Horwitz, 1993).

In order to be an effective active facilitator, the therapist must first be much more knowledgeable about the mutual help group being referred to than is necessary under a passive approach. The therapist must have a good understanding of the philosophy, goals, and structure of the fellowship or program that is being utilized in order to understand the specific nature of any patient resistance that may arise.

In addition to a clear understanding of the workings of the mutual help group that is being integrated into the treatment plan, the active facilitator is aware of the process which is associated with active involvement in mutual help, and she or he devotes a good amount of therapeutic time and effort to guiding that involvement. Resistance to involvement is identified by the active facilitator as something to be worked through with the patient. This process, whose goal is bonding with the group, typically proceeds through several stages, as described below.

Mutual Help Group Involvement and the Process of Bonding

The goal of active facilitation is the bonding of the patient to a mutual help group as an integral part of treatment and an independent treatment goal. The process of bonding typically proceeds through several stages, as described below.

Attendance

Bonding to a mutual help group obviously begins with attendance. Not surprisingly, resistance often is most evident at this very point. In this regard, it is very helpful if the therapist is familiar with the *format* and the *ground rules* of the mutual help group that the client is being referred to. Knowing in advance what to expect when one walks into a meeting—be it an AA meeting, a S.M.A.R.T. Recovery meeting, a Women for Sobriety, or a Moderation Management meeting—combined with knowing the client's psychodynamics puts the therapist in a position to anticipate issues and thereby help the client overcome anticipatory anxiety.

Clients who experience social anxiety, who express exceptional shame about their substance abuse, or who worry about potential exposure may hesitate to take even the first step toward utilizing a mutual help group, which is to get to a meeting. These worries can often be dealt with if the client is educated by the therapist as to what to expect. Role playing around potential issues (e.g., "Let's practice how you would introduce yourself") would be another way to desensitize anxiety. Similarly, problem solving around accessibility issues (e.g., child care, transportation) can facilitate the process of involvement. Finally, the therapist can make specific suggestions (e.g., "Just go and listen the first few times") as a means of helping a client get started on using mutual help.

Identification

Another step in the bonding process is taken when the newcomer to a mutual help group begins to *identify* with other members of the group. "Identify, don't compare" is the advice often given to the AA newcomer. The therapist can expect to encounter some resistance, and the more that resistance can be worked through, the more the client can be expected to begin to bond with the self-help group of choice.

Most often, client resistance at this stage takes the form of drawing *contrasts* between himself or herself and others in the group. These contrasts may be based on age, education, religiosity, income, and even interests. The motivation behind drawing these contrasts quickly becomes apparent: The client is emphasizing differences in order to justify not identifying with the group. She or he is resisting the bonding process. For example, instead of identifying with what has been aptly called the "core story" (Fowler, 1993) of Alcoholics Anonymous—a story which involves a journey from powerlessness and hopelessness to empowerment and renewal through commitment to "a new community of interpretation and action" (Fowler, 1993, p. 116)—the resistant client may reject the notion of powerlessness out of hand and cling to the idea that willpower alone will still succeed, in the face of ample evidence that this has not been the case. As Fowler (1993) pointed out, however, "There is a kind of power that issues from acknowledged powerlessness" (p. 116). That power has its roots in collective identification and bonding and a willingness to trust in the collective wisdom of those who have made the same journey. To the extent that the therapist can help the resistant client identify with key elements of other members' stories, she or he also helps indirectly to empower the client. This is true regardless of what mutual help group is involved, since all of them implicitly assume that willpower is not enough and that group support is a key to sustaining sobriety.

Participation

Once a newcomer has gotten to the point where she or he is attending meetings and beginning to identify with others, bonding can be further facilitated by encouraging active participation.

Networking   Networking is an important part of all mutual help groups. Virtually all of the groups discussed here, with the possible exception of Rational Recovery (which discourages long-term involvement), encourage members to build a support network by establishing contact with other members on a regular basis. Alcoholics Anonymous (1975) calls this *telephone therapy*. The therapist should encourage this as well, justifying it as SOS (undated c) suggests: as a means of establishing a social safety net in advance of the actual need for one. Through telephone and personal contact (before or after meetings), the newcomer begins to make new friends and establish himself or herself in a new peer group—

one that is moving away from substance abuse toward a healthier lifestyle.

Sponsorship The concept of sponsorship appears unique to 12-step fellowships. The role of the sponsor could be described as that of guide and/or mentor. The relationship to the sponsor is especially important for the newcomer. Without a sponsor, the client is apt to turn to the therapist for advice and support when that advice and support could be obtained through the mutual help group. The therapist should therefore consistently encourage and coach the client to find an initial ("temporary") sponsor. This should be someone who is of the same sex as the client, who is active in the fellowship, who has established some sobriety, who leads what the client perceives to be a healthy lifestyle, and whom the client respects. The newcomer should be advised to use this sponsor for the first year of sobriety and then to consider changing sponsors. This is consistent with AA tradition.

In judging whether the newcomer-sponsor relationship is working, the therapist should inquire as to how often the newcomer speaks to the sponsor (this should be often) and whether the sponsor is making specific suggestions about meetings, coping with urges, dealing with emotions, and so on. The sponsor is not a therapist; on the other hand, a good sponsor has much wisdom to share. Developing a relationship with a sponsor constitutes an important step toward bonding with the larger fellowship.

Rituals and Traditions Rituals and traditions have always been a vehicle whereby the individual bonds to a group. It is not surprising, therefore, that many mutual help groups deliberately incorporate rituals and traditions into their programs. Women for Sobriety, for example, begins each meeting by reading the 13 statements of its "new life" program, then asks members to "stroke" themselves, and ends each meeting by joining hands and reciting the WFS motto: "We are capable and competent, caring and compassionate, always willing to help another, bonded together in overcoming our addictions" (WFS, 1993b, p. 1). S.M.A.R.T. Recovery meetings incorporate a ritual wherein members share "successes" from the week before.

Twelve-step fellowships are replete with rituals and traditions which bond members together. The newcomer who is ambivalent about the group can be expected to be uncomfortable with such things and reluctant to wholeheartedly participate in them. Typical rituals include reciting the Serenity Prayer, acknowledging and celebrating members' "anniversaries" of sobriety, storytelling, and so on. Other traditions that newcomers can take part in include doing what is called "service work": setting up chairs, making coffee, cleanup. These simple contributions to the group can also help to bond the newcomer to it over time and should be encouraged. Newcomers who are socially shy and inclined to be quiet listeners at meetings can begin to bond through volunteering for service work. Because AA and its sister 12-step fellowships are intentionally decentralized, many individual groups develop unique rituals and traditions. The therapist is likely to hear of these from the newcomer who reports back on his or her latest experiences with the group. By understanding the important role that these rituals and traditions play in cementing the relationship to the group, and by encouraging the newcomer to "give it a try" and "keep an open mind," the therapist can play a significant role in transferring the locus of therapeutic change from the client-therapist relationship to the client-group relationship.

EFFECTIVENESS OF MUTUAL HELP

Probably the best studied of the self-help groups is Alcoholics Anonymous, which conducts triennial surveys of its own membership. Other mutual help groups do not do so. According to its most recent survey (AA, 1993), 35% of active members had been sober for over 5 years, and another 34% of active members had been sober between 1 and 5 years. A prior survey (AA, 1990b) reported that 40% of AA newcomers who remained active in the fellowship for 1 year stayed sober for a second year.

There is also some evidence that stronger bonding to the program promotes recovery. For example, a meta-analysis of studies of AA concluded that "AA members who 'work the program' are more likely to have a better status with respect to their drinking behavior" (Emrick, Tonigan, Montgomery, & Little, 1993, p. 27). In this regard, "working the program" means attending meetings regularly, getting a sponsor, leading a meeting, and doing service work.

As encouraging as the above data may seem, it is important to qualify them. Although there is evidence that individuals who actively work the AA program have a promising outcome with respect to drinking, 60% of individuals cease their involvement in AA within a year (AA, 1990b). This in effect suggests that AA "works for those who work it" at the same time that it suggests that only a minority of those who give AA a try stay with it.

The overwhelming majority of outcome research reports on the overall effectiveness of a single treatment *model*, and/or on the comparative effectiveness of two or more competing models, for example, cognitive behavioral treatment versus 12-step facilitation versus motivational enhancement therapy (Project MATCH Research Group, 1997). Some analyses of treatment outcome studies have suggested that overall, a cognitive behavioral approach is most efficacious (Miller et al., 1995), whereas others have reported that alternate treatments can be equally effective (Project MATCH Research Group, 1997). It must be noted, however, that these are studies not of mutual help but of professionally delivered treatments with differing theories and treatment strategies.

Hard data on the effectiveness of mutual help groups is limited and also hampered by methodological pitfalls. For example, because of the diversity within AA and other 12-step fellowships, it is all but impossible to establish a "standard dose" of treatment. All mutual help programs lay claim to being effective, and no doubt all do work for some people. Exactly how effective they are in general at reducing substance abuse over the long run, however, remains largely an unanswered question.

Key References

Alchoholics Anonymous. (1981). *Twelve steps and twelve traditions*. New York: Alcoholics Anonymous World Services.

S.M.A.R.T. Recovery. (1996). *S.M.A.R.T. recovery: Self-management and recovery training: Member's manual*. Beachwood, OH: S.M.A.R.T. Recovery Self-Help Network.

Narcotics Anonymous. (1987). *Narcotics Anonymous* (4th ed.). Van Nuys, CA: Narcotics Anonymous World Service Office.

References

Al-Anon. (1966). *Al-Anon family groups*. New York: Al-Anon Family Group Headquarters.

Al-Anon Family Groups. (1985). *Al-Anon faces alcoholism* (2nd ed.). New York: Al-Anon Family Group Headquarters.

Al-Anon Family Groups. (1993). *Al-Anon family groups 1993 survey*. Virginia Beach, VA: Al-Anon Family Group Headquarters.

Al-Anon Family Groups. (1996). *Fact sheet for professionals*. Virginia Beach, VA: Al-Anon Family Group Headquarters.

Alcoholics Anonymous. (1952). *Twelve-steps and twelve traditions*. New York: Alcoholics Anonymous World Services.

Alcoholics Anonymous. (1975). *Living sober: Some methods A.A. members have used for not drinking*. New York: Alcoholics Anonymous World Services.

Alcoholics Anonymous. (1976). *Alcoholics Anonymous: The story of how many thousands of men and women have recovered from alcoholism* (3rd ed.). New York: Alcoholics Anonymous World Services.

Alcoholics Anonymous. (1990a). *Alcoholics Anonymous 1989 membership survey*. New York: Alcoholics Anonymous World Services.

Alcoholics Anonymous. (1990b). *Comments on A.A.'s triennial surveys*. New York: Alcoholics Anonymous World Services.

Alcoholics Anonymous. (1993). *Alcoholics Anonymous 1992 membership survey*. New York: Alcoholics Anonymous World Services.

Augustine Fellowship. (1986). *Sex and love addicts anonymous*. Boston: Augustine Fellowship, Sex and Love Addicts Anonymous Fellowship-Wide Services.

Bartosch, B., & Bartosch, P. (1985). *Guidebook for Overcomers Outreach 12 step support groups*. Anahein, CA: Overcomers Outreach.

Beckman, L. J. (1993). Alcoholics anonymous and gender issues. In B. S. McCrady & W. R. Miller (Eds.), *Research on Alcoholics Anonymous: Opportunities and alternatives*. New Brunswick, NJ: Rutgers University Press.

Bill, W. (1948/1992). Tradition two. *AA Grapevine* (Feb. 1992), pp. 24–25.

Borkman, T. J. (1990). Experiential, professional, and lay frames of reference. In T. J Powell (Ed.), *Working with self-help*. Silver Spring, MD: National Association of Social Workers Press.

Calix Society. (1995). *Directory of Calix units*. Minneapolis: Author.

Calix Society. (undated a). *Calix: What and why*. Minneapolis: Author.

Calix Society. (undated b). A word for the problem drinker! Minneapolis: Author.

Carolyn W. (1984). *Detaching with love*. Center City, MN: Hazelden.

Christopher, J. (1988). *How to stay sober: Recovery without religion.* Buffalo, NY: Prometheus.

Christopher, J. (1989). *Unhooked: Staying sober and drug free.* Buffalo, NY: Prometheus.

Cowen, M., Jim, L. K., Boyd, E. L., & Gee, J. P. (1981). Some possible effects of patient noncompliance. *Journal of the American Medical Association, 245,* 1121.

Ellis, A., & Harper, R. (1975). *A new guide to rational living.* North Hollywood, CA: Wilshire.

Emotions Anonymous. (1978). *Emotions Anonymous.* St. Paul, MN: Emotions Anonymous International.

Emrick, C. D., Tonigan, J. S., Montgomery, H., & Little, L. (1993). Alcoholics Anonymous: What is currently known? In B. S. McCrady & W. R. Miller (Eds.), *Research on Alcoholics Anonymous: Opportunities and alternatives.* New Brunswick, NJ: Rutgers University Press.

Fowler, J. W. (1993). Alcoholics Anonymous and faith development. In B. S. McCrady & W. R. Miller (Eds.), *Research on Alcoholics Anonymous: Opportunities and alternatives.* New Brunswick, NJ: Rutgers University Press.

Horwitz, R. I., & Horwitz, S. M. (1993). Adherence to treatment and health outcomes. *Archives of Internal Medicine, 153,* 1863–1868.

Kirkpatrick, J. (1982). A self-help program for women alcoholics. *Alcohol and Research World* (Summer), pp. 1–2.

Kishline, A. (1996). *Moderate drinking: The Moderation Management guide for people who want to reduce their drinking.* New York: Crown.

Kurtz, E. (1988). *A.A.: The story.* New York: Harper/Hazelden.

Madara, E., & Meese, A. (Eds.). (1988). *The self-help sourcebook: Finding and forming mutual aid self-help groups* (2nd ed.). Denville: New Jersey Self-Help Clearinghouse.

Marlatt, G. A., Tucker, J. A., Donovan, D. M., & Vuchinich, R. E. (1997). Help-seeking by substance abusers: The role of harm reduction and behavioral-economic approaches to facilitate treatment entry and retention. In L. S. Onken, J. D. Blaine, & J. J. Boren (Eds.), *Beyond the therapeutic alliance: Keeping the drug-dependent individual in treatment* (pp. 44–84). National Institute on Drug Abuse Research Monograph 165. DHHS Pub. No. 97-4142. Rockville MD: National Institute on Drug Abuse.

Miller, W. R., Brown, J. M., Simpson, T. L., Handmaker, N. S., Bien, T. H., Montgomery, H. A., Hester, R. K., & Tonigan, J. S. (1995). What works? A methodological analysis of the alcohol treatment outcome literature. In R. K. Hester & W. R. Miller (Eds.), *Handbook of alcoholism treatment approaches: Effective alternatives* (2nd ed.). Boston: Allyn & Bacon.

Moderation Management. (1996). *For people who want to reduce their drinking.* Ann Arbor, MI: Author.

Narcotics Anonymous. (1987). *Narcotics Anonymous* (4th ed.) Van Nuys, CA: Narcotics Anonymous World Service Office.

Nowinski, J., & Baker, S. (1992/1998). *The twelve-step facilitation handbook: A systematic approach to early recovery from alcoholism and addiction.* San Francisco: Jossey-Bass.

Nowinski, J. (1996). Facilitating 12-step recovery from substance abuse and addiction. In F. Rotgers, D. S. Keller, & J. Morgenstern (Eds.), *Treating substance abuse: Theory and technique.* New York: Guilford Press.

Nowinski, J. (1998). *Substance abuse and family recovery: A twelve-step guide for treatment.* Thousand Oaks, CA: Sage.

Overcomers Outreach. (1988). *The 12 Steps . . . with their corresponding scriptures!* Anaheim, CA: Author.

Overcomers Outreach. (undated). *Overcomers outreach: A Christ-centered 12-step recovery program addressing addictions and compulsions.* Anaheim, CA: Author.

Overeaters Anonymous. (1980). *Overeaters Anonymous.* Torrance, CA: Author.

Pokorny, A. D., Kanas, T., & Overall, J. E. (1981). Order of appearance of alcoholic symptoms. *Alcoholism: Clinical and Experimental Research, 5,* 216–220.

Powell, T. J. (1990). Self-help, professional help, and informal help. In T. J. Powell (Ed.), *Working with self-help.* Silver Spring, MD: National Association of Social Workers Press.

Price, R. K., Cottler, L. B., & Robins, L. N. (1991). Patterns of drug abuse treatment utilization in a general population. In L. Harris, (Ed.), *Problems of drug dependence.* National Institute on Drug Abuse Research Monograph 105. DHHS Pub. No. (ADM)91-1753. Washington, DC: Government Printing Office.

Project MATCH Research Group. (1997). Matching alcoholism treatment to client heterogeneity: Project MATCH posttreatment drinking outcomes. *Journal of Studies on Alcohol, 58,* 7–29.

Rational Recovery Systems. (undated). *What's the shortest route between addiction and recovery?* Lotus, CA: Author.

Room, R. (1993). Alcoholics Anonymous as a social movement. In B. S. McCrady & W. R. Miller (Eds.), *Research on Alcoholics Anonymous: Opportunities and alternatives.* New Brunswick, NJ: Rutgers University Press.

Room, R., & Greenfield, T. (1991). *Alcoholics Anonymous, other 12-Step movements and psychotherapy in* the U.S. population, 1990. (Working Paper F281). Berkeley, CA: Alcohol Research Group, Medical Research Institute of San Francisco.

Secular Organizations for Sobriety. (1996, Summer). SOS International Newsletter, 9(2), 1–2.

Secular Organizations for Sobriety. (undated a). Secular Organizations for Sobriety: A self-empowerment approach to recovery. Buffalo, NY: Author.

Secular Organizations for Sobriety. (undated b). The sobriety priority. Buffalo, NY: Author.

Secular Organizations for Sobriety. (undated c). Recovery for family and friends of alcoholics and addicts. Buffalo, NY: Author.

S.M.A.R.T. Recovery. (1996). S.M.A.R.T. Recovery: Self-management and recovery training; Member's manual. Beachwood, OH: S.M.A.R.T. Recovery Self-Help Network.

Sobell, L. C., Sobell, M. B., & Toneatto, T. (1991). Recovery from alcohol problems without treatment. In N. Heather, W. R. Miller, & J. Greeley, (Eds.), Self-control and addictive behaviors (pp. 192–242). New York: Macmillan.

Solberg, R. J. (1983). The dry drunk syndrome (pamphlet). Center City, MN: Hazelden Foundation.

Tiebout, H. M. (1953). Surrender versus compliance in therapy with special reference to alcoholism. Quarterly Journal of Studies on Alcohol, 14, 58–68.

Trimpey, J. (1992). The small book: A revolutionary alternative for overcoming alcohol and drug dependence. New York: Delacorte.

Trimpey, J. (1996). Rational reccovery: The new cure for substance addiction. New York: Pocket Books.

Trimpey, J. (undated). AVRT in a nutshell. Lotus, CA: Lotus Press.

Women for Sobriety. (1993a). Welcome to WFS and the new life program. Quakertown, PA: Author.

Women for Sobriety. (1993b). Who we are. Quakertown, PA: Author.

Women for Sobriety. (undated a). Are you a woman who drinks to cope? Quakertown, PA: Author.

Women for Sobriety. (undated b). Women and addictions: A way to recovery. Quakertown, PA: Author.

19

Pharmacotherapies

Wayne S. Barber
Charles P. O'Brien

Intuitively, one might seek a solution to the problems of chemical dependence in molecules that oppose the actions of the offending agents of addiction—if you will, as *antidotes* to substances of misuse. And there are a number of appealing targets for pharmacological attack. In theory, then, should a compound be developed that blocks the effect of an addicting agent, whether at a specific receptor site or more centrally at a locus of reinforcement, one's opportunity to develop or maintain the addicted state could be reduced or even eliminated. Yet this has not proved to be so. As an example, naltrexone, which effectively blocks opiate effects at the μ-receptor, has found minimal acceptance among those who have become opiate-dependent, most likely because of reluctance to forsake the euphoric reward they find in substance use. While most can attain abstinence with comparative ease, with or without medical support, few can sustain it, succumbing instead to the multiple pressures that foster relapse.

Alternatively, research efforts might focus on the reduction of drug craving, acknowledging the remarkable tensions that drive the experienced substance user to "pick up." This line of inquiry has been pursued vigorously in an effort to thwart the seductive impact of crack cocaine on those devoted to its immediate reward, recognizing the significant influence of craving in maintaining dependent cocaine use. Current studies utilizing positron emission tomography (PET) scans seek to expose those dynamic neurophysiological processes central to the craving experience, with hopes that determining an anatomic locus, with the attendant biochemical interactions that subserve this phenomenon, will enable the development of compounds that can oppose it. Even with the sense of promise that underlies such investigation, there remains a healthy skepticism that the social and psychological pressures which support drug seeking and drug use cannot be countered by an attack on craving alone.

Thus far, the greatest success in the effort to medicate the disorders of drug addiction has been found in compounds that substitute for the addicting substance by providing modest reinforcement just sufficient to mollify drug craving and prevent the discomfort of withdrawal, while producing blockade of those subjective effects sought from the primary agent of abuse. Thus, methadone may be utilized in maintenance programs which permit the addict to return to a life of useful function without risking full exposure to the biopsychosocial pressures which promote return to addictive use.

Such cautious statements are not intended to discourage the quest to identify compounds that can safely medicate these distinct events in the addictive cycle. On the contrary, we wish to describe lines of inquiry that have explored the benefit of many varied medications in the treatment of the addictions and give promise of even greater successes with discoveries yet to follow. Yet such efforts must be understood in a broader awareness that addiction is fundamentally a disorder of behavior, comprising of compulsive drug seeking and poorly controlled use, and best addressed by an integrated program of medical, psychological, and social services. The damaging psychosocial consequences of years of dependent use require time and patience to remediate and repair. Behavior patterns encoded during thousands of drug ingestions are not eliminated simply by detoxification, nor are they substantially assuaged even during the early months of rehabilitation. Thus, the chronic, relapsing nature of this illness holds the recovering addict in continuing jeopardy of relapse, as he or she seeks to develop and refine those tools of self-management so crucial to the maintenance of recovery. Medications which can smooth the patient's passage through the dangers and discomforts of detoxification and entry into rehabilitation or deter his or her return to dependent use can play a critical role in the patient's continuation in treatment and commitment to recovery.

POTENTIAL THERAPEUTIC TARGETS OF MEDICATIONS

Good clinical care requires a clear-thinking awareness of the varied components of the addiction experience, coupled with focused efforts to crisply define the targets of one's specific therapeutic efforts. The detoxification treatment of withdrawal (those drug-opposite effects released by drug absence) centers on substitution of long-acting, cross-tolerant compounds for the substance of abuse, administered in a scheduled taper of dosage that permits homeostatic re-equilibration toward the original drug-naive state. Supportive care may include medications that reduce assorted discomforts that may be part of this restorative process. Toxic use may require aggressive intervention to counter the effects of noxious intoxication or the more serious dangers of acute overdose. The behaviors of compulsive use may be countered through medication effects which reduce the subjective or rewarding effects of substance use or dampen the impact of drug craving. Those biological pressures which promote release might be challenged by suppressing the experience of drug craving.

Since comorbid conditions may challenge a patient's capacity to address the tasks of recovery, specific medical treatment should be pursued whenever indicated. Yet it is important that one remain cautiously aware that several major psychiatric disorders may be mimicked by substance use and/or withdrawal. In many instances, the consideration of specific pharmacological treatment for these conditions would best be delayed while observing for their spontaneous remission as part of the process of recovery.

It is the intent of this chapter to explore what is known regarding effective specific pharmacological treatments of the varied problem states encountered with the major substances of abuse, and to describe additional avenues of research which may bear fruit in the not too distant future.

ALCOHOL

The Roman philosopher Seneca once sought to distinguish a "man who is drunk" from one who "has no control over himself . . . who is accustomed to get drunk, and is a slave to the habit" (O'Brien & Chafetz, 1991, pp. 88–89). Two millennia later, the problems of alcohol persist and continue to command our attention. Until recently, pharmacological approaches to the treatment of alcoholism focused on detoxification, finding little to offer during the long-term psychosocial adjustments required of the alcoholic during rehabilitation. But during the past decade, there has been increasing interest in the prospect of reducing craving, consumption, and reward through psychotropic approaches in support of the comprehensive biopsychosocial treatment of this multifaceted illness. Several medications have already shown themselves to be effective in this regard, and there is reason to expect that more are on the way.

Alcohol's Pharmacolgical Effects

In recent years, there has been mounting evidence that ethyl alcohol exerts major effects on certain ion channel-receptor complexes, most prominently N-methyl-D-aspartate (NMDA) and γ-aminobutyric acid (GABA$_A$). While these ion fluxes are thought to be substantially relevant to alcohol's intoxicating, amnesic, and ataxic effects, there are no indications that they contribute to the phenomena of craving or reinforcement (O'Brien, Eckardt, & Linnoila, 1995). In contrast, there is substantial evidence that the crucial triggers of relapse are mediated through the endogenous opioid system, and that medications specifically targeted toward suppressing opioid expression can be of substantial benefit to an alcoholic's establishment and maintenance of recovery (O'Brien et al., 1995). Meanwhile, research efforts continue to consider the participation of other neurotransmitter systems in the quest for comprehensive understanding of alcohol's full biochemical effect. In this section, we shall survey those medications currently in use for the several components of detoxification treatment, as well as those found effective or promising in the process of rehabilitation.

Treatment of Toxic Consequences of Use

Physicians have long been involved with the acute problems presented by toxic alcohol ingestion. Whether confused, combative, or comatose, this patient is still best served by supportive and symptomatic treatments not specifically focused on the biochemistry of alcoholism. Safe harbor has not been found in extensive trials with naloxone, GABA antagonists, or high doses of amphetamines or caffeine. Good airway maintenance, support of vital signs, assessment of psychiatric status including risk for suicide, and attentive observation during hepatic processing of elevated blood levels are the core of proper treatment. Of course, careful diagnostic attention should be directed toward the search for contributing medical illnesses, concurrent use of illicit substances, and pathological medical consequences of excessive alcohol intake, both acute and enduring. One should be particularly attentive to the possibility of concurrent hypoglycemia, initiating glucose replacement only after pretreatment with thiamine 100 mg IM to avoid the risk of precipitating the emergence of the Wernicke-Korsakoff syndrome (WKS).

Treatment of Withdrawal

While proportionately few patients encounter serious medical difficulties during withdrawal, most will find the course softened by specific pharmacological treatments available for detoxification, that process of clearing alcohol from the body while permitting readjustment of all systems to functioning in the absence of alcohol. One in twenty will experience significant medical distress comprising of tremulousness, tachycardia, diaphoresis, restlessness, and even alcohol-withdrawal-based seizures. Malnutrition, electrolyte imbalance, infection, gastritis, or traumatic injury may contribute to the severity of the patient's condition. While good nursing care alone greatly reduces the severity of the syndrome, specific medical interventions are sometimes required. In most cases, outpatient detoxification is as effective as hospitalization yet at far less cost (Hayashida et al., 1991), although there are four general conditions that mandate inpatient treatment: (a) the demonstrated inability to discontinue use despite appropriate outpatient treatment, (b) the concomitant presence of medical or psychiatric conditions warranting close observation, (c) an inadequate psychosocial support system, and (d) the necessity to interrupt a living situation that strongly reinforces substance abuse.

Uncomplicated Medical Detoxification

The major objective of the pharmacological treatment of withdrawal is the prevention of seizures, delirium, and arrhythmias. As the suppression of anxiety, restlessness, tremor, and insomnia is important to patient comfort, relief of these symptoms will increase patients' retention in treatment and enhance their chance for successful recovery. The basic pharmacological principle assumes the rapid substitution for alcohol with a cross-tolerant drug which can then be tapered in measured dosage over the next several days. Most clinicians regard the various benzodiazepines (BZD) as the treatment of choice for detoxification of alcohol in the absence of concurrent sedative abuse, largely based on their smooth efficacy, modest risk for escalating dependency, and greater index of safety. Barbiturates, which are equally cross-tolerant with alcohol but have a poor margin of safety regarding respiratory depression, may be held in reserve for nonresponsive cases or situations of mixed dependence on alcohol and sedatives.

The manner of detoxification and the selection of specific BZD vary between clinicians and programs but generally fall into one of two categories of tapered support:

1. *Symptom-triggered dosing*, monitored by standardized, semiquantitative severity assessment scales such as the Modified Selective Severity Assessment (MSSA) or the Clinical Institute Withdrawal Assessment for Alcohol scale–revised (CIWA-Ar) (Sullivan, Sykora, Schneiderman, Naranjo, & Sellers, 1989), which track perturbations of vital signs, tremor, cognitive responsiveness, and motor restlessness as an index of physiological instability. Selection of a specific BZD then varies with the following factors:

a. *Long-acting BZDs* such as chlordiazepoxide (Librium), diazepam (Valium), and clonazepam (Klonopin) may be begun in loading doses that substantially self-taper through their production of active metabolites that sustain a gradually dwindling blood level over several days without continued dosing. Such a program is more popular in inpatient settings, where attentive medical care and patient monitoring can be assured.

b. *Short-acting BZDs* comprising lorazepam (Ativan), oxazepam (Serax), and temazepam (Restoril), which produce no active metabolites, are hence less likely to yield toxic accumulations that may be particularly hard to monitor in an outpatient setting. Responsible outpatient detoxification will require that the patient attend the clinic daily over 5–10 days for ongoing clinical evaluation, management of BZD pharmacotherapy, and the dispensing of vitamins.

2. *Scheduled sedative administration* using fixed schedules of medication administration under rather general guidelines is appropriate only to inpatient settings. Properly conducted, this format provides safe and adequate care while requiring less staff involvement, but at the cost of longer hospital stays and frequent oversedation.

Symptomatic Relief of Adrenergic Overflow

Some clinicians seek to further reduce patient distress with the use of α-adrenergic agonists such as clonidine (Catapres) or lofexidine (available in the UK, in clinical trials in United States). Acting at the autoreceptor, these drugs can moderate adrenergic symptoms, but at the risk of unwanted hypotension. Others employ β-blockers such as propranolol (Inderal) or atenolol (Tenormin) seeking to reduce craving and the duration of withdrawal. Some challenge this practice with the concern that such treatment masks the presence of tremor and cardiovascular indicators of withdrawal severity that must be observed in order to properly titrate withdrawal medication (Jaffe, Kranzler, & Ciraulo, 1992).

Alcoholic Hallucinosis

An occasional patient will present with nonthreatening, ego-dystonic, and usually auditory hallucinations, accompanied by more intense expression of the withdrawal signs and symptoms characteristic of uncomplicated withdrawal. Inpatient treatment, including augmented dosing of the BZD of choice, is generally sufficient care. Once withdrawal symptoms have stabilized, hallucinations have ceased, or the patient falls asleep, one may return to the protocol employed for the uncomplicated state. The use of phenothiazines is to be avoided given the risks of hypotension and lowered seizure threshold (Jaffe et al., 1992).

Delirium Tremens

This toxic psychosis, characterized by extreme agitation, threatening ego-syntonic hallucinations (visual > auditory > tactile in frequency of occurrence), and marked physiological destabilization, merits prompt hospitalization in a full-service medical facility providing fluid replacement, vitamin supplementation, full medical monitoring, and seizure precautions in a quiet setting without disturbing stimulation. Haloperidol may be needed for control of the psychosis, with a dosage range of 0.5–2.0 mg IM every 2 hr until hallucinations and agitation have sufficiently subsided or the maximum of five doses has been given. Special attention should be directed to the monitoring of fluid intake and output, electrolyte shifts, risk of cardiac arrhythmias, and appearance of WKS (Jaffe et al., 1992).

Related Pharmacological Management Issues

Thiamine depletion, caused by compromised nutrition and impaired intestinal absorption, mandates replacement, given 100 mg PO or IM daily over 10–30 days. One must be alert to begin this treatment prior to the giving of glucose, which when given prematurely can precipitate the emergence of WKS.

Potassium depletion can realistically be encountered and contribute to fatigue, muscle weakness, and the appearance of cardiac arrhythmias. This depletion can be readily reversed with potassium chloride supplementation until normal oral intake of food has been attained.

Withdrawal seizures can occur between 24 and 48 hr following the onset of a falling blood-alcohol concentration. These are typically grand mal and nonfocal and rarely more than two in number. Seizures occurring outside this window or in an atypical presentation should alert one to seek other causes, most frequently concomitant dependence on BZDs. The use of phenytoin is discouraged, since parenterally it is poorly absorbed and slow to establish therapeutic blood levels (Alldredge, Lowenstein, & Simon, 1989). Moreover, it has not been demonstrated to affect withdrawal seizures in laboratory animals. The clinician's BZD of choice should provide sufficient treatment unless the patient is simultaneously withdrawing from BZDs, in which case phenobarbital is to be preferred.

Total body *magnesium depletion* in the face of normal serum concentration could account for the lethargy, weakness, and decreased seizure threshold common in the withdrawal state, although many clinicians view this as a distributional phenomenon not requiring supplementation.

Treatment During Rehabilitation

Anticraving Agents

Beginning with animal observations that alcohol increases endogenous opioid activity, and that opioid blockers reduce alcohol consumption in ethanol-preferring rats and monkeys, formal studies of this phenomenon in humans was undertaken, utilizing the long-acting μ/δ-antagonist naltrexone (Revia). The Philadelphia Study found significant reductions in rate of relapse, drinking days, alcohol craving, and the subjective experiencing of an alcoholic "high" (Volpicelli, Alterman, Hayashida, & O'Brien, 1992). Confirmatory studies in New Haven yielded similar findings, with a marked decrease in drinking days and alcohol consumption (O'Malley et al., 1992).

These and subsequent studies revealed remarkable safety from toxicity or meaningful side effects at the standard dose of 50 mg/day. Nausea and vomiting were the more common complaints, followed by headache, anxiety, diminished energy, depressed mood, skin rashes, and blunted alertness. As these side effects typically resolve spontaneously within a few days, such symptoms may represent a mild withdrawal response to the blockade of endogenous opioid stimulation. While hepatotoxicity has been seen at dosages many times this therapeutic level, there has been no evidence of reactively elevated liver enzymes in the many populations of treated subjects observed over several decades. Reports of anticipated dysphoria or neuroendocrine change have been minimal (Berg, Pettinati, & Volpicelli, 1996).

Drug-Drug Interactions   Since a 50-mg dose will competitively inhibit the effects of intravenous heroin for 1–3 days, careful inquiry should be made regarding the possible concomitant use of opioids. One should also be watchful that patients do not attempt to override the opioid blockade by self-administering high doses of alcohol and/or opioids which might yield life-threatening results should they remain in the body beyond the duration of naltrexone's clinical effects. Clinical experience reveals no difficulty when taken concurrently with disulfiram or common psychotropics at usual dosages.

Clinical Treatment   For the treatment of alcoholism, 50 mg/day PO is sufficient. Experience suggests that patients should be maintained at this level for 6 months or longer to provide sufficient time to establish sturdy psychosocial tools to maintain recovery in the absence of this maintenance support. One should initiate treatment with 25 mg/day PO for the first 2 days to minimize the intrusion of initial side effects. Preliminary clinical laboratory testing should include urine screen for opioids, hepatic profile (aspartate aminotransferase [AST], alanine aminotransferase [ALT], γ-glutamyltransferase [GGT], and bilirubin), hepatitis screen, complete blood count, and, when applicable, pregnancy testing. Treatment should not be initiated when a transaminase level is found to be >3 times the upper limit of normal. Periodic retesting of liver function is suggested, especially for patients older than 40. The use of naltrexone is contraindicated in the setting of acute hepatitis, liver failure, or any other condition causing significant hepatocellular dysfunction, as indicated by an elevated bilirubin (Berg et al., 1996). Because very high doses of naltrexone used in clinical trials of obese patients resulted in increased liver enzymes, the package insert warns about the possibility of liver damage. In reality, naltrexone is not dangerous to the liver. Naltrexone is metabolized in the liver and usually results in improved liver function because patients drink less alcohol. It is imperative that patients be detoxified from all substances of abuse prior to initiating this treatment. Accordingly, a naloxone challenge may be indicated should a patient seem not to be candid regarding possible current opioid use.

Sensitizing Agents

Until the recent Food and Drug Administration (FDA) approval of naltrexone in the treatment of alcoholism, disulfiram (Antabuse) was the only available medication for use in the maintenance of recovery. By inhibiting aldehyde dehydrogenase, an enzyme in the pathway responsible for the metabolism of ethanol, it promotes an aversive response upon the ingestion of alcohol. The consequent accumulation of acetaldehyde produces generalized physical discomfort, including vasodilation, headache, tachycardia, pronounced diaphoresis, hypotension, nausea, vomiting, generalized weakness, vertigo, and confusion. Adverse effects are common, through the inhibition of several enzyme systems. Drug-drug interactions include the reduced clearance of all BZDs except lorazepam, oxazepam, and temazepam and the tricyclics imipramine and desipramine, leading to an increase in their elimination half-lives (Jaffe et al., 1992).

The most carefully controlled and credible studies regarding disulfiram's efficacy find it lacking, yielding an effect no better than that obtained with placebo (Fuller et al., 1986). Nonetheless, disulfiram may be of benefit to healthy, motivated patients who are able to understand the consequences of their drinking while so medicated and wish to utilize this aversive support to their commitment to sobriety. The appropriate maintenance dose is 250 mg/day.

Pharmacotherapy Directed at Comorbid Conditions

Major Depression Aware that ethanol produces effects in serotonergic pathways, researchers have explored the use of serotonergic antidepressants as possible inhibitors of alcohol's subjective reward or of a patient's alcoholic cravings. No studies to date have supported the efficacy of these classes of drugs for this purpose. Nonetheless, several studies have demonstrated improved mood in depressed alcoholics treated with imipramine or fluoxetine, while more recently, desipramine has proved effective for depressed outpatients recovering from alcohol dependence. While preliminary reports of open trials from each of these research teams hinted of a specific benefit in reducing drinking, this was not sustained in the final analysis of more stringently controlled trials. Accordingly, while some argue compellingly for the use of serotonergic antidepressants to relieve depression secondary to a heavy use of alcohol, there is no convincing evidence that these medications will reduce alcohol use, whether or not the patient is currently depressed (Litten & Allen, 1995).

Anxiety States Four studies have addressed the question of benefit to anxious alcoholics by treatment with buspirone, a serotonin 1_A partial agonist. While three of these studies variously described diminished anxiety, reduced craving, reduced drinking, and enhanced treatment retention, the more carefully designed study found no difference between buspirone and placebo in the treatment of anxiety or alcohol dependence. Significantly, this was the only study that did not provide psychosocial treatment to the cohort (Litten & Allen, 1995).

Failures and Hangers-on

Extensive investigation of lithium in a multicenter VA study found it to be no more effective than placebo, regardless of the presence of depression. Likewise, dopamine and serotonin precursors augmented with carbidopa failed to demonstrate benefit. The $GABA_A$ receptor agonist acamprosate claimed efficacy in two controlled studies for the treatment of alcoholism, and further controlled clinical trials are warranted. Two separate trials of bromocriptine, a relatively nonspecific D_2 dopamine receptor agonist, proved contradictory. In a recent double-blind study, tiapride, a D_2 receptor antagonist, halved the consumption of alcohol and doubled the number of abstinent days. The size of the claimed therapeutic effect clearly warrants further investigation. Finally, γ-hydroxybutyrate, an endogenous sedative thought by some to mimic alcohol's reinforcing effects, seemed to reduce alcohol use, but only after 2 months of treatment (O'Brien et al., 1995). These encouraging results deserve to be confirmed.

OPIOIDS

Opium, smoked for centuries in the pursuit of pleasure, was quickly recognized as providing relief of subjective discomfort. Once morphine was isolated in the early 1800s as the most potent ingredient of the opium poppy, its efficacy as an oral analgesic was quickly established. Of course, the arrival of the hypodermic syringe midcentury found it to be even more powerful when administered parenterally. As the quest for even greater efficacy provided heroin—a morphine derivative that was far more potent and rapid acting—it became the substance sought on the streets.

By the turn of the 19th century, heroin was well known as a drug of addiction, competing with cocaine and opiates in patent medicines for popularity. Societal pressures demanded that the use of such drugs be outlawed, prompting passage of the Harrison Narcotics Act in 1914 and its aggressive implementation following World War I. The federal facilities required to house and treat this new class of criminals afforded an opportunity to study the behaviors of opiod addicts in a controlled setting. It was soon noted that withdrawal, while physiologically turbulent, uniformly proceeded to prompt and safe completion. Yet an intense desire to return to use remained and was usually acted upon shortly following release from incarceration. Clearly, behavioral issues were strongly at play.

As the urbanization of America advanced, active heroin use became concentrated in the major cities, supported by enhanced routes of transportation developed in the wake of World War II. With the adoption of mandatory minimum sentencing in the 1950s, forces favoring punishment were at loggerheads with efforts to provide medical treatment. In this context, Vincent Dole in New York City espoused a belief that opiate addiction was in fact a metabolic disorder—if you will, a deficiency disease involving an inadequate capacity to manufacture intrinsic opiates, so that the potential addict would seek to satisfy her or his needs through external sources (Dole & Nyswander, 1967). Of course, such a disor-

der would become apparent only in those who were predisposed, had access, and were inclined to look outside themselves for comfort.

Dole and his colleague Marie Nyswander were aware of the German development during World War II of methadone, as a longer acting opiate analgesic. In contrast to morphine and heroin, it is well absorbed orally, so that its administration by this route delays its action and tempers its effect; thus limiting *its* euphoric reward and the consequent risk of respiratory depression, while suppressing withdrawal and blocking the anticipated effect of subsequent self-administration.

Thus was born the concept of methadone maintenance (Dole & Nyswander, 1965), soon to lead to the implementation of dedicated clinics throughout the nation—with treatment that greatly improved the quality of life for patients and those upon whom their lives impacted, although it did not fully spare the addict from the tentacles of the disease.

As the exploration into opiate effects swiftly advanced, several important studies gave support to Dole's concept of a deficiency disorder. The discovery of the opiate receptor and its endogenous opiate system in 1973 (Pert & Snyder, 1973) provided a mechanism for explaining such a disease state. Chemical determinations of endogenous blood levels found significant elevations in children with a propensity toward respiratory depression that could be suppressed by naloxone, indicating the presence of an opiod-mediated mechanism. Preoperative levels of endogenous opioids were found to correlate with a patient's subsequent requirement for analgesic relief (O'Brien, 1992). Stress was found to induce an increase in endogenous opiod production in laboratory animals, providing a model to explain the prevalence of post-traumatic stress disorder (PTSD) in patients with baseline low levels of endogenous opiod activity (O'Brien, 1992).

It is thus conceivable that one's susceptibility to opiate dependence is in part determined by innate activity of the endogenous opioid system, although there are as yet no human data to support this hypothesis. Since not all opioid abuse advances to dependence, as demonstrated by the proportion of American soldiers who did not resume their dependent use upon returning home from Vietnam, perhaps those who remained addicted were those who were constitutionally primed. Of course, the possibility remains that a more permanent requirement for opioid supplementation could be *created* in certain individuals by the chronic administration of opiate drugs. For them, living without an externally enhanced opiate supply might become difficult, or even impossible. Either of these two scenarios provides support for the concept of maintenance treatment.

Maintenance Treatments

Given this history, it is not beyond understanding that agonist maintenance therapy has become the most reliable and durable treatment of heroin addiction. The goals of such an approach are to discourage use while facilitating the extinction of classically conditioned drug craving.

Methadone maintenance is based on two essential pharmacological principles: (a) protecting against withdrawal and (b) reducing the effects of self-administered opiates through the mechanism of cross-tolerance. When opioids are given orally, hence slowly absorbed, the onset of their effects is quite gradual, and euphoria and sedation are largely avoided. With skillful dosing there is no interference with normal activities such as working, attending school, or taking care of a family. The relatively high and stable opioid maintenance dose produces cross-tolerance to additional opiates, thus reducing their rewarding effects.

Dosing of methadone begins with 20–30 mg daily, followed by increases of 5–10 mg every 2–3 days until the patient no longer complains of withdrawal discomfort. Better compliance has been found in dosage ranges exceeding 60 mg/day, although current environments well supplied with high-purity heroin find many patients require > 100 mg/day to block the effect of available street drug. During the period of stabilization of dosing, most patients continue to use but with less intensity and regularity.

Methadone aids in the rehabilitation of opiate addicts in several ways: (a) by producing a more level and stable physiological state, less disruptive to the homeostatic balance of the organism than the multiple daily dosing required by shorter acting heroin; (b) by diminishing the potential reward of the street drug, permitting the diminution of those habits maintaining compulsive heroin use; (c) by freeing the addict sufficiently from drug seeking and the cycles of use to become more available to the benefits of psychotherapy; and (d) by permitting the opportunity for greater attention to personal needs, including medical care, diet, and interpersonal relationships.

A large body of research has shown that methadone maintenance is most successful when coupled with a variety of therapeutic services, including regular client contact and urine drug monitoring (Cooper, 1989). Employed in this manner, it is widely regarded as the best treatment for the greatest number of patients struggling with opioid dependence.

As with any treatment, the use of methadone poses certain problems: (a) Methadone produces physical dependence, more than satisfying the urges of most street users; drug diversion must be impeded by dispensing in an oral format not amenable to injection, with watchful supervision over the patient's act of ingestion, and (b) detoxification from methadone takes significantly longer than detoxification from heroin; patients express many complaints of their prolonged discomfort during this process, even though the intensity of specific symptoms is generally less.

Intuitive reasoning suggests that years of treatment would harmfully suppress endogenous opioid production, yet studies fail to find evidence of problems even in patients maintained for many years (O'Brien, Terenius, Nyberg, McLellan, & Eriksson, 1988). Greater concern surrounds the clinical observation that patients tend to have difficulty achieving stable drug-free status after extended treatment with methadone, so that many patients choose to continue with substitution treatment indefinitely. Fortunately, studies of long-term treatment have found no evidence of toxic effects from prolonged use (Kreek, 1978).

LAAM (l-α-acetylmethadol), originally synthesized in the search for longer duration pain relief, is now employed as an alternative to substitution therapy with methadone, since its longer duration of action permits less frequent dosing, thus reducing the risk of diversion of take-home doses. Compared with methadone, LAAM produces less euphoria, hence possesses lower abuse potential. However, this advantage of longer duration is countered by delays in onset, requiring an initial period of uncomfortable adjustment which discourages some experienced methadone users. Accordingly, many programs first stabilize their patients with methadone, later transferring to LAAM in a ratio of 6:5 over methadone.

Standard dosing utilizes a three times weekly schedule, with the Friday dose increased by 20–40%. Most heroin users are begun on 20–40 mg qod, gradually increasing by 10 mg weekly until cravings and withdrawal symptoms have been successfully suppressed. One must take care that 2-day doses of LAAM never exceed 120 mg. Those with low opioid usage should be titrated cautiously, given LAAM's delayed onset of action. Once stabilized, many patients report full suppression for as long as 72 hr, while experiencing less sedation, euphoria, or nodding than with methadone.

Buprenorphine (a partial agonist/antagonist) presents with a different twist. As a partial agonist with a compelling affinity for the μ-receptor, it is sufficiently stimulating to satisfy craving and block withdrawal, while by its avid occupancy of the receptor site, it blocks the effect of street opioids that the addict may choose to self-administer. Thus, buprenorphine blends the strengths of methadone *and* naltrexone in an alliance of effects that may prove even more effective (a) as a *weak agonist*, thereby satisfying cravings and blocking withdrawal, two crucial contributors to reinforcement; yet lacking that intensity of opiod stimulation which can induce respiratory depression; (b) as an *antagonist*, preferentially occupying the μ-receptor, thereby blocking any stimulation by more potent street drugs that the addict may self-administer; (c) effectively *absorbed sublingually* (but not if swallowed), permitting convenient, noninvasive, observed administration; and (d) providing *long duration* of action, affording smooth and stable control which prevents the vicissitudes of extreme physiological and/or psychological variations. Moreover, even when its use is abruptly discontinued, withdrawal symptoms are minimal.

Buprenorphine maintenance with a *sublingual dose of 8 mg* daily compares well with 30–60 mg daily methadone with respect to treatment retention, medication compliance, adherence to a counseling regimen, and the frequency of opioid-positive urines (Johnson, Jaffe, & Fudala, 1992). Currently under study in a combined formulation with naloxone to discourage diversion, it has yet to be approved by the FDA for administration in maintenance treatment.

Discouraging Use Through Blockade: Opiate Antagonist Treatment

We indicated at the outset that the benefits of blockade to discourage use are more implied than real. The synthesis of naltrexone in 1963 provided an opportunity to test the efficacy of a seemingly perfect antidote: a molecule with such compelling affinity for the μ-receptor that it could block virtually all the effects of usual doses of opiates, including heroin; hence, further use would be abandoned. Would that this were so. Trials with detoxified street addicts found little enthusiasm for naltrexone since "it keeps you from getting high." Without any reinforcement, few were sufficiently motivated to persist with their treatment.

Nonetheless, antagonist maintenance does have its role in the treatment of a subgroup of highly motivated patients: those who find compelling psychosocial rewards in resisting a return to use. Skilled professionals such as physicians or pharmacists, especially those whose work requires them to have access to controlled substances, embrace this treatment with particular interest since it permits the continuation of their careers. Extended studies of federal probationers on work release find rehabilitation success rates on naltrexone blockade equal to that of inmates without a drug history (Brahen, Henderson, Capone, & Kordal, 1984). A recent controlled study of federal probationers (Cornish et al., 1997) found a 50% reduction in reincarceration rate for parolees randomly assigned to naltrexone compared to controls.

Naltrexone has clinical activity in blocking the effects of administered opiates for as long as 72 hr. It is well absorbed when given orally and does not demonstrate tolerance to its antagonism of opiate effects. Since it is not a controlled substance, it can be prescribed or administered by any licensed physician. For the management of highly motivated patients, naltrexone can play an important role in a comprehensive treatment program.

A necessary first step in antagonist treatment is effective detoxification from current opiate use, using one of the several methods described below. Users of heroin require 4–5 days, and those on methadone almost twice as long. Before initiating antagonist maintenance treatment, a naloxone challenge test is indicated to rule out residual dependence. A positive response indicates a delay of at least 24 hr before testing again.

Once the system is opiod-free, naltrexone may be employed for relapse prevention, beginning with a dose of 25 mg PO, repeated in 1 hr if no problem side effects occur. One may then continue with 50 mg daily, with the option of switching to dosing three times weekly when circumstance permit (Monday–Wednesday–Friday: 100 mg–100 mg–150 mg). Compliance is maintained by monitoring of ingestion and confirming expected progress in treatment according to the patient's engagement in psychotherapy, performance on the job, and the absence of drug positive urine screens.

Side effects are mild and infrequent, usually limited to abdominal discomfort, headache, and mildly increased blood pressure, possibly due to opioid withdrawal. Those who experience persisting abdominal distress should remain on a schedule of daily dosing. There are no known medical risks for a healthy patient taking naltrexone. Laboratory findings in large trials give no evidence of significant abnormalities despite the generally compromised health of addicted individuals. While experimental dosing well outside the therapeutic range has resulted in elevated transaminase levels, even these changes were transient and reversible upon discontinuation of the medication. Notwithstanding, opiate-addicted persons with liver failure should not be treated with naltrexone. Patients presenting with AST or ALT > two times the upper limit of normal should not start the medication, and treatment should be discontinued in any patient whose levels exceed three times normal. No data are yet available for pregnant woman or for children. No significant drug-drug interactions have been identified.

Special attention should be paid to the need for treatment of pain. Patients should discontinue treatment several days in advance of elective surgery should opiate medication need to be administered. In emergencies, it is best to use nonopioid anesthesia and postoperative pain medication, although if necessary, it would be possible to override naltrexone blockade with carefully supervised higher opiate dosing.

Detoxification

This description of the methods used for detoxification from chronic opioid use has been intentionally left to the end of this section since its fundamental concepts are best described in the previous discussions of agonist and antagonist maintenance. This is not meant to understate its position of central importance in the pharmcopeia of addiction management. Medication for detoxification should never be prescribed by a cookbook approach, but by thoughtful titration in concert with careful patient observation. Patient reports are commonly unreliable and

sometimes intentionally deceitful. One must remain particularly alert to the risks of multiple dependencies with their complex biological interactions.

Detoxification can be approached in several different ways, varying with the philosophies and capabilities of individual programs: Unassisted or "cold turkey" detoxification depends upon a safe and supportive setting that is prepared to guide the addict through a significantly uncomfortable but not life-threatening several days in the absence of specific pharmacological treatment. For dependence on heroin, this takes 4–5 days, and for methadone somewhat longer. Benzodiazepines on an as-needed basis may be offered to reduce muscle cramping and agitation.

Substitution detoxification customarily utilizes methadone as an opiate agonist, as described above, providing a relatively smooth and predictable withdrawal. This medication can be administered for purposes other than pain management only in specially licensed facilities. One typically begins with a dose of 10 mg PO which usually proves sufficient to suppress withdrawal. Most patients will require a repeat of this dosage two to three times further throughout the first day, then tapering by 5 mg over a 5–6 day period. Minimal withdrawal symptoms will still be noticed during this detoxification phase, as well as over the ensuing 1–2 weeks. Many programs begin with an extended methadone stabilization period for up to 3 months leading to explicit detoxification, feeling this reduces the frequency of relapse.

Nonopioid detoxification, usually employing clonidine (Catapres), has been widely espoused as an alternative to substitute dosing with narcotics (Gold, Redmond, & Kleber, 1979), especially since it can be done in any traditional medical setting without a special license. Several lines of evidence converge to suggest that a major component of the opiate withdrawal syndrome is rebound central adrenergic hyperactivity. Clonidine activates autoreceptors in the locus coeruleus, producing presynaptic inhibition of adrenergic outflow. Careful study indicates clonidine can be most successfully employed on an inpatient basis, perhaps because of the relative absence of cues triggering an urge to pick up. On an outpatient basis, it appears to be most effective for well-motivated opioid addicts who are willing to tolerate some discomfort. Target symptoms include nausea, vomiting, abdominal cramps, diaphoresis, tachycardia, and hypertension. It does not alleviate the generalized aches, anxiety, restlessness, insomnia, and opioid cravings so characteristic of withdrawal. The most frequent side effects, although usually mild, are sedation, hypotension, and fainting.

The typical dosage regimen begins with 0.1–0.2 mg three to four times daily, raised to a total of 1–2 mg/day as required. Gradual withdrawal then proceeds by taper over a 6- to 10-day period. It is essential that blood pressure be regularly monitored for the possible development of significant hypotension.

Other techniques espoused as effective include a combined naltrexone and clonidine detoxification conducted over 4–5 days (Stine & Kosten, 1992), said to limit patient discomfort to restlessness, insomnia, and muscle cramps, while simultaneously permitting initiation of naltrexone maintenance. Rapid detoxification under anesthesia (methohexital or midazolam) with naltrexone is claimed to precipitate quick and manageable abstinence (Loimer, Lenz, Schmid, & Presslich, 1991), although there remains substantial concern about the medical risks, not to mention a precipitous entry into the rehabilitation phase without adequate psychological preparation. There is no evidence that a particular method of detoxification produces a better outcome over the long term. Without maintenance treatment, most of the detoxified opiate addicts relapse within 6 months, no matter what kind of detoxification was performed.

Naloxone, a short-acting opiate antagonist, has value in the treatment of overdose as well as for the diagnosis of physical dependence on opioid drugs. While poorly absorbed from the gut, it is rapidly metabolized when given parenterally, yielding a prompt but brief effect of opioid blockade. In the event of opioid-induced respiratory depression, airway support should be paired with naloxone hydrochloride 0.01 mg/kg intravenously to reverse the effect. A positive diagnosis of opioid dependence is indicated when brief, immediate withdrawal occurs following subcutaneous or intramuscular injection in the dosage range of 0.4–0.8 mg. This effect is short-lived, ending in less than 1 hr.

NICOTINE

Following decades of contentious dispute, the debate over harm caused by cigarette smoking and the role of nicotine addiction in maintaining smoking behaviors has finally been put to rest. Recognizing that nearly half a million American lives are lost yearly to exposure to tobacco products (Rose, 1996), while an even greater number find their lifestyle compromised by compulsive use, public opinion has shifted to make nicotine addiction a major target of political concern.

Although the incidence of smoking was all but halved over the quarter century following the Surgeon General's first report, use has now held steady for almost a decade, reflecting the intransigence of the habit in this subset of the smoking population. That they have been entrapped by their dependence is supported by data regarding their struggle to stop. While one third of America's smokers seek to quit in any given year, fewer than 7% will abstain for a full year, and the majority will return to smoking within 3 days (Henningfield, Schuh, & Jarvik, 1995). This is indeed a persuasive addiction.

Delivery System

Central to our understanding of the nature of this process is an appreciation of the efficiency of the delivery system. Each inhalation of cigarette smoke provides an intense concentration of ionized nicotine to the alveoli, carried by adhesive tars that ensure its presentation to the mucosal surface. Rapidly diffused into the pulmonary circulation, it becomes instantaneously available to brain tissue, prior to any meaningful dilution by peripheral distribution. And it leaves as abruptly as it arrived. Such brief spikes of intense stimulation provide as swift and powerful an induction of a drug-dependent state as has yet been found (Volkow, Ding, Fowler, & Wang, 1996).

Pharmacological Effects

While nicotine's effects on peripheral ganglia and the neuromuscular junction have long been recognized, it is now acknowledged that reinforcement occurs through the drug's pharmacodynamic interactions with central nicotinic cholinergic receptors in the ventral tegmentum, culminating in dopaminergic neurons of the nucleus accumbens (Rose, 1996), just as for every other known agent of addiction. Tolerance is rapidly acquired and, following an overnight washout, even more swiftly reacquired with each new smoking day (Henningfield et al., 1995). This phenomenon—tachyphylaxis—may contribute to the smoker's disappointment with alternative nicotine delivery systems. The signs and symptoms of withdrawal ensue within several hours following the latest cigarette, primarily displayed as increased craving, anxiety, irritability, and appetite associated with decreased heart rate and cognitive acuity (Hughes, 1996). This experience is described as ranging from generally unpleasant to frequently intolerable. Urges to renew smoking may recur for many years (Henningfield et al., 1995). Behavioral mechanisms contribute to this high relapse rate. Conditioning is especially powerful because of almost instantaneous reward from smoked nicotine (Haxby, 1995). And smoking rituals provide powerful cues that become conditioned stimuli. When nicotine's effect on mood and cognition is perceived as positive, repetition of the experience will be sought. Nicotine withdrawal's robust effect on weight gain, clearly established as a consequence of smoking (Eisen, Lyons, Goldberg, & True, 1993), can be a strong deterrent to abstinence. It should be clear that a comprehensive treatment program is required to address these multivariate factors.

Treatment

Most contemporary treatment programs combine behavioral therapies with pharmacological support of withdrawal. Behavioral strategies currently in favor include health education, self-management tactics such as self-monitoring and cue extinction, and relapse prevention training. The virtues of cognitive behavioral therapy have frequently been emphasized. Largely abandoned as proven to be ineffective include the tactics of nicotine fading, sequential filtration, acupuncture, hypnosis, and the aversive experience of rapid smoking (Haxby, 1995).

The goal of any detoxification treatment is reduction of withdrawal discomfort sufficient that the patient can concentrate on the tasks of acquiring durable tools of recovery. While nicotine replacement does not appear to shorten withdrawal, it can substantially reduce the severity of symptoms to much more tolerable levels, approximating the degree of discomfort ordinarily encountered in the second or third month of cold turkey abstinence (Henningfield et al., 1995). The objectives of such replacement therapy include (a) reduced intensity of withdrawal symptoms, (b) partial satiation of craving through the satisfaction of tolerance, and (c) partial satisfaction of those effects the individual may seek to repeat

through the act of smoking. Several formats for alternative nicotine delivery have been employed.

Nicotine polacrilex was the first replacement delivery system to become generally available in this country. Approved by the FDA in 1984 in a 2-mg chewable formulation, it is now also available in a 4-mg dose that significantly improves quit rates. Since nicotine in solution can be absorbed only in a basic medium, it is imperative that the patient be instructed to avoid the ingestion of acidic beverages (coffee, tea, soft drinks, fruit juices) prior to chewing. When it is properly administered, blood levels rise substantially within 30 min to $\frac{1}{3}$–$\frac{1}{2}$ those achieved through smoking (Hughes, 1996). Recent studies indicate a fixed schedule of administration is more effective than polacrilex chewed *ad libitum* (Haxby, 1995; Hughes, 1996), perhaps because it improves compliance. Common side effects of objectionable taste, difficulty chewing, and stomach upset tend to compromise compliance (Rose, 1996).

The transdermal patch was first approved by the FDA late in 1991, several dosage strengths having arrived on the market since. Intended to achieve and maintain steady-state blood levels within 2 days, they yield plasma levels roughly similar to those encountered in the trough of smoking, just prior to initiating the next cigarette (Rose, 1996). Side effects are limited to erythema at the site of application, which can be minimized by varying the position of the patch, and initial insomnia, which usually clears rapidly. Sixteen-hour patches are available, intended to reduce insomnia, but they have proved to be no more effective in supporting sleep, with the drawback of lessened protection against craving for the first cigarette the next morning. While caution is advised for those with a history of coronary artery disease, research indicates that use of the patch, even in high-dose regimens (44 mg/day), does not produce increased risk over that of continued smoking (Benowitz, Zevin, & Jacob, 1997). Patients with unstable coronary artery disease should be advised not to begin patch therapy. Compliance with patch treatment is substantially better than that with nicotine polacrilex (Rose, 1996).

Clinical investigators differ in their preference of patch dosage, duration of use, and choice of associated behavior therapy. The most common recommendation is for an initial dosage of 22 mg daily during the first 4 weeks, followed by 2–4 weeks of graduated taper. Studies employing higher dosage protocols for heavy smokers demonstrate dose-response relationships in providing symptomatic relief from withdrawal, but no difference in long-range abstinence, and at the cost of an increase in side effects. Investigators have sought in vain to predict dosage requirements based upon subject's customary cigarettes per day or baseline levels of nicotine's more stable metabolite, cotinine. Most now advocate the individualization of nicotine dosing based on the principles of therapeutic drug monitoring, especially for those patients begun on high-dose regimens (Gourley, Benowitz, Forbes, & McNeil, 1997).

Meta-analyses indicate the use of either nicotine polacrilex or transdermal patches can double quit rates (Fiore, Smith, Jorenby, & Baker, 1994; Silagy, Mant, Fowler, & Lodge, 1994). Some investigators advocate combining the gum and patch, seeking even better outcomes (Silagy et al, 1994). Both are relatively effective in relieving the withdrawal symptoms of drowsiness, difficulty concentrating, and irritability (Rose, 1996). While craving is little affected in the early stages, later weeks find replacement provides substantial amelioration (Faberstrom, Schneider, & Lunell, 1993). The most common duration of detoxification treatment is 8 weeks, acknowledging that particularly resistant smokers may require extended maintenance. While it seems intuitive that associated psychotherapeutic support would assist recovery, carefully conducted studies have yielded conflicting results (Dale, Hunt, & Offord, 1995; Jorenby et al., 1995). Nonetheless, most investigators advocate concomitant behavior therapy, and some feel only cognitive behavioral therapy is of proven efficacy (Hughes, 1996).

Alternative Delivery Vehicles

Although not yet approved for general clinical use, two additional delivery formats are currently in active investigation. A nicotine nasal spray, administered 0.5 mg of nicotine to each nostril in response to the urge to smoke, shows evidence of relieving craving more quickly than either gum or patch (Henningfield et al., 1995; Rose, 1996). It appears to be most effective with more highly dependent smokers (Rose, 1996). More recently, inhalers, which deliver vaporized nicotine base at 13% the strength of cigarette smoke, have been found particularly effective in damping the intense cravings of the first abstinent week (Hughes, 1996). While requiring many more puffs to approach the delivery of a cigarette, they produce upper airway sensations that resemble those of smoking, possibly of benefit to those who depend upon this experience. Their advantage of self-titration is somewhat offset by side effects of throat irritation and coughing (Rose, 1996). Recent studies indicate that the abuse liability of both spray and inhaler is substantially lower than that of cigarettes (Schuh, Schuh, Henningfield, & Stitzer, 1997).

Other Pharmacologic Approaches

In previous years, over-the-counter compounds have utilized silver acetate for its aversive distaste effect to deter continued smoking. Given poor patient compliance and absence of benefit in placebo-controled trials (Haxby, 1995), the FDA removed it from the market as ineffective and of unproven safety. Lobeline, a weak nicotine receptor agonist, has not been found to be effective (Haxby, 1995; Henningfield et al., 1995). The relief of physiological dimensions of withdrawal expected from clonidine has not been forthcoming, affording benefit only to women with no alteration of quit rates (Haxby, 1995; Henningfield et al., 1995; Rose, 1996). Some claim greater promise in the nicotine receptor antagonist mecamylamine, marketed as an antihypertensive, which, combined with patch treatment, has improved abstinence threefold (Rose, 1996), but at the cost of troublesome side effects, including sedation, hypotension, and syncope (Henningfield et al., 1995).

Since many subjects report that smoking relieves anxiety and/or depressed mood, studies have explored the potential benefit of both antianxiety medication and antidepressants. Benzodiazepines have not been effective (Haxby, 1995). While earlier studies suggested that buspirone modified the withdrawal experience, a subsequent randomized, placebo-controlled trial failed to demonstrate an effect (Haxby, 1995). Tricyclics proved ineffective while exacerbating the weight gain of withdrawal (Haxby, 1995). The response to fluoxetine and related serotonin-specific reuptake inhibitors (SSRIs) was equivocal (Haxby, 1995).

Comorbid Psychiatric Conditions

Over the past 15 years, clinical investigators have become progressively aware of a significant relationship between smoking and several common psychiatric disorders. The diagnoses of major depression, schizophrenia, generalized anxiety disorder, and/or other substance use disorders apply to more than one third of all smokers (Breslau, Kilbey, & Andreski, 1991), predicting a poorer outcome in achieving abstinence. A carefully crafted prospective study found disproportionately high relapse rates in recovering alcoholics and subjects with past diagnoses of either major depression or bipolar disorder (Glassman, 1993). It has been established that 50% of all psychiatric patients smoke (Glassman, 1993), twice the rate found in the general population. Three quarters of once-depressed smokers experienced the return of depressive mood during their first week of withdrawal (Glassman et al., 1993). Thus, the evidence strongly suggests that major depression, especially when recurrent, amplifies both the likelihood of smoking and difficulty in stopping. Moreover, it is equally clear that for those with such a history, abstinence can induce the onset of severe depressive relapse (Glassman et al., 1993). Plainly, particular care must be exercised while providing smoking cessation therapy to patients who have been depressed.

Although the nature of the relationships is less clear, there are also demonstrable associations between both cigarette smoking and generalized anxiety disorder, and between cigarette smoking and alcoholism (Glassman & Covey, 1995). And recovering alcoholics with a past history of depression are rarely able to give up smoking (Glassman & Covey, 1995).

Of all the nosological groups, by far the greatest proportion of smokers is found in those diagnosed with chronic schizophernia (Glassman & Covey, 1995). While the specifics of the relationship have yet to be established, it is known that negative symptoms are exacerbated during smoking withdrawal (Glassman & Covey, 1995), the administration of nicotine reverses this (Glassman, 1993), and the requirement for neuroleptic medication is greater in the 90% of chronic schizophrenics who smoke (Glassman & Covey, 1995). It has been suggested that their nicotine intake per puff is significantly greater than that of other smokers (Olincy, Young, & Freedman, 1997). As one then might suspect, their success in smoking cessation is negligible (Glassman & Covey, 1995).

Bupropion (Zyban)

While exploring the possible usefulness of antidepressant medication in alleviating nicotine withdrawal, it began to appear that buproprion had specific utility not only for easing depressed mood but for enhancing smoking cessation itself (Ferry & Burchette, 1994; Hurt et al., 1997). Recently approved by the FDA for this indication, it was shown to significantly improve quit rates in two placebo-controlled, double-blind trials of non-depressed subjects, including some concurrently receiving transdermal patch therapy. Current dosage recommendations are for 150 mg for 3 days followed by 150 mg bid thereafter, to begin at least 1 week prior to the intended quit date in order to achieve steady-state dynamics. Continuation of treatment is indicated for at least 7–12 weeks.

Drug-Drug Interactions

The benzopyrenes in smoke are powerful inducers of the P_{450} hepatic enzyme systems (Hughes, 1996). Accordingly, smokers have higher requirements for some medications and, in abstinence, need adjustment. Medications known to be so affected include the antidepressants imipramine, desipramine, clomipramine, and doxepine; the antipsychotics clozepine, fluphenazine, and haloperidol; and the benzodiazepines desmethyldiazepam and oxazepam (Hughes, 1996). Caffeine concentrations increase 250% upon smoking cessation (Hughes, 1996). Should patients seek to discontinue coffee concomitantly with smoking, they should be made aware of the caffeine abstinence syndrome.

Future Considerations

It is apparent there is much yet to be known regarding the effects of nicotine on the central nervous system, especially its influence on addictive illness as well as other psychiatric disorders. Of particular interest is the recently described finding in rodent models suggesting that the nicotine-induced release of endogenous opioids may be a factor in nicotine dependence (Malin et al., 1996a, 1996b), just as it appears to be for alcoholism (O'Malley et al., 1992; Volpicelli et al., 1992). Perhaps opiate antagonists could prove useful in diminishing nicotine reinforcement of smoking behaviors. Meanwhile, current efforts continue to focus on refining our awareness of specific interactions with the intent to improve the individualization of smoking-cessation strategies.

COCAINE

The unfolding of yet another cycle of cocaine popularity over the past two decades has generated active exploration of its biological effects, taking advantage of recent advances in technology. As in previous epidemics, early enthusiasm for its presumed safety as a sophisticated euphoriant yielded quickly to renewed awareness of its remarkable potential for harm, by both its toxic effects and the likelihood of addiction. With the arrival of inexpensive crack in the mid-1980s came the greater threat of easy street availability coupled with a delivery system optimally primed to promote rapid dependence. Thus, despite a significant decline in recreational use over the past decade, the incidence of regular use has greatly intensified, yielding the multiple consequences of more users who become addicted, more disrupted lives, more serious medical consequences, and greater social disruption by associated criminal behaviors.

As of this writing, effective medical treatment of cocaine dependence continues to be supportive, devoted to managing the vicissitudes of acute intoxication, responding to the discomforts of early abstinence, and providing substantive training in the tools of recovery. Nonetheless, widespread concern with the personal, social, and economic consequences of cocaine use continue to drive intense efforts to find pharmacological solutions to this international problem. Important targets of pharmacological treatment are those experiences which support continued use or predispose to relapse, craving, and reward.

Cocaine's physiological effects occur in multiple areas. Medical problems are caused by its actions as a sympathomimetic agent producing systemic hypertension through a combination of tachycardia and increased peripheral resistance, sometimes eventuating in myocardial infarction or cerebral vascular accident; by its anesthetizing of the cardiac conduction system, producing life-threatening dysrhythmias and sudden death; by increased heat production through skeletal muscle activity, coupled with a restriction in heat loss due to peripheral vasoconstriction, yielding hyperthermia; and in higher doses leading to seizures and/or toxic encephalopathy through heightened central stimulation.

Behavioral effects come from its action as a psychostimulant, producing euphoria, a sense of enhanced energy and clarity of thought, increased locomotor activity, and occasional paranoid psychotic

thinking and behavior. These latter effects are thought to be produced by the blocking of presynaptic reuptake of norepinephrine (NE), serotonin, and dopamine (DA), prolonging the action of these neurotransmitters upon their receptors. Accordingly, the search for a pharmacological solution to the problems of cocaine use and dependence have focused especially on interactions at these receptors.

As of this writing, no drug has been found that significantly reduces cocaine use; yet recent advances have sharpened research focus on several promising targets. In expectation there will be agents of specific utility in the not too distant future, it may be helpful to summarize the history of salient developments to date.

Monaminergic Receptors

Norepinephrine

Appreciation of the dysphoric mood following discontinuation of cocaine use provided the rationale for clinical trials with antidepressants, reasoning that by decreasing withdrawal dysphoria, one might reduce pressures toward relapse. Trials with desipramine (DMI) in the early 1980s claimed facilitation of early abstinence (Gawin et al., 1989), although laboratory-based investigation found no reduction in self-administration by human subjects despite alterations in the subjective effects described with use (Witkin, 1994). All subsequent placebo-controlled, double-blind trials found DMI to be ineffective in the treatment of cocaine dependence (Mendelson & Mello, 1996), although one demonstrated improvement in psychiatric status (Arndt, Dorozynsky, Woody, McLellan, & O'Brien, 1992).

Serotonin

As it became clarified that DMI primarily influenced NE reuptake, attention was directed toward serotonergic compounds, given growing recognition of cocaine's intense binding to the serotonin uptake site (Ritz, Lamb, Goldberg, & Kuhar, 1987). Yet, no compounds have been found to show particular promise. Preclinical investigation of specific serotonin receptor antagonists such as ritanserin yielded contradictory results, while a recent clinical trial found no ritanserin effect in blocking cue-elicited cocaine dependence (Ehrman, Robbins, Cornish, Childress, & O'Brien,

1996). Studies of the serotonin reuptake inhibitors fluoxetine (Mendelson & Mello, 1996) and sertraline (Witkin, 1994) have failed to demonstrate an effect in reducing cocaine dependence.

Dopaminergic Receptors

The discovery of multiple dopamine (DA) receptor sites and of compounds that selectively interact with them made it pertinent to search for more particular and specific targets of cocaine's actions, seeking to identify those effects instrumental to the initiation and maintenance of addiction (Witkin, 1994).

An early theoretical approach postulated that the prolonged use of cocaine depleted DA (Dackis & Gold, 1985), producing anergia, anhedonia, depressed mood, and (with abstinence) marked craving, possibly constituting a withdrawal syndrome related to disturbances in DA function (Gawin & Kleber, 1986). Perhaps pharmacotherapies which increased DA activity would alleviate mood disturbances, promoting withdrawal, and thereby reducing craving and the risk of relapse. Yet subsequent inpatient studies, without the customary conditioned cues of the using environment, found minimal evidence of this putative state (Satel et al., 1991).

In recent years, it has become apparent that with cocaine, as with all other agents of addiction, reinforcement occurs in dopaminergic neurons of the nucleus accumbens (Kornetsky & Porrino, 1992), a finding which insists upon exploration of potential agonists and antagonists at that site. Earlier self-administration studies pointed to a prominent role for the postsynaptic receptor.

Dopamine Antagonists

As evidence developed linking the blockade of DA reuptake to the behavioral effects of cocaine (Ritz et al., 1987), it was rational to speculate that excessive accumulation of DA might be responsible. Thus, it was undertaken to counter this at the postsynaptic receptor with an agent that opposed DA's effects. Nonetheless, compounds designed to antagonize the postsynaptic receptor, including haloperidol and flupenthixol, were found to be clinically ineffective and associated with unpleasant to potentially dangerous side effects, particularly with repeated administration (Witkin, 1994).

Dopamine Agonists

Substantial effort has been devoted to developing effective substitution therapy. Early studies with methylphenidate were disappointing since only those with concomitant attention deficit disorder demonstrated benefit (Gawin, Riordin, & Kleber, 1985). Specific D_2 antagonists bromocriptine (Witkin, 1994) and pergolide (Malcolm, Butto, Philips, & Ballenger, 1991) were investigated as potential antidotes to crash and craving but were abandoned because of contradictory results and problem side effects (Witkin, 1994). Considerable attention has been paid to amantadine, an anti-Parkinsonian medication with complex pharmacological effects, including those which increase DA concentrations at the synapse. Yet, despite early enthusiasm (Alterman et al., 1992; Witkin, 1994), a recent double-blind, placebo-controlled trial found it not only to be ineffective in the treatment of cocaine dependence but possibly contributing to a rebound increase in cocaine use following discontinuation of this agent (Kampman et al., 1996).

Recent reports of a dissociation between actions of D_1 and D_2 receptors in rats suggest a specific target for further medication development. D_2-like agonists were found to increase craving and aggravate addiction, thus discouraging further exploration of compounds that interact with this site. D_1-like agonists did not (Self, Barnhard, Lehman, & Nestler, 1996). Instead, they prevented cocaine-primed reinstatement of use (Rothman et al., 1989). These findings offer cautious hope of finding an anticraving agent analogous to naltrexone's efficacy for alcoholism.

Dopamine Reuptake Inhibitors

As studies showed that cocaine's behavioral effects correlate directly with its blockade of the reuptake of DA (Ritz et al., 1987), investigators were encouraged to search for compounds which act upon this presynaptic receptor. The expectation was that partial agonists occupying this site could mimic the effects of cocaine, yet with greatly reduced intensity, thus preventing the behavioral effects of cocaine. Mazindol, marketed as a short-term anorectic and pharmacologically similar to cocaine, was reported to reduce cocaine intake and craving in open trials of methadone-maintained patients. Yet animal studies suggested the likelihood of mutual exacerbation of cocaine's toxicity (Witkin, 1994).

GBR 12909

This piperazine derivative, originally intended as an antidepressant, has been shown to preferentially bind to the dopamine transporter (DAT) with 500 times the affinity of cocaine, thus blocking cocaine's effects (Rothman et al., 1989). Since it totally substitutes for cocaine in discrimination studies and selectively decreases self-administration by rhesus monkeys (Glowa et al., 1995), it bodes well for a similar effect in discouraging cocaine use in humans. Moreover, its reported slower onset of action diminishes the extent of a euphoric reinforcement, while prolonging its duration of activity. Subsequent work implies its promise may extend beyond that of maintenance treatment. Revisiting the DA depletion hypothesis, it may be postulated that DAT upregulation in cocaine addiction leads to reactive DA depletion in abstinence. Perhaps long-term treatment with GBR 12909 would return DAT densities to normal, thus bypassing the withdrawal symptoms of DA depletion during abstinence (Tella, Landenheim, Andrews, Goldberg, & Cadet, 1996). PPT [2-propanoyl-3-(-4-toyl)-tropane], currently under study in rhesus monkeys, is described as producing an effect similar to that of GBR 12909 at the DAT (Nader, Grant, Davies, Mach, & Childer, 1997). Both compounds are currently being studied for safety and efficacy in human subjects.

Agents with Other Putative
Mechanisms of Action

Opioid-Medicated Effects

It has been speculated that endogenous opioid systems in the brain may be involved in the reinforcing effects of cocaine in a manner similarly to those hypothesized with alcohol. If true, this could provide a single therapeutic approach to the management of both heroin and cocaine. Yet initial enthusiasm for buprenorphine in preclinical investigation was soon countered by evidence that the effect was insufficiently specific, lacked a good dose-response curve, and was not enduring. Subsequent human studies have been less than convincing (Witkin, 1994).

Antikindling Effects

Following work claiming that cocaine kindled seizures in animal models, open clinical trials suggested that carbamazepine could reduce both cocaine craving and cocaine use, as measured by a decrease in cocaine-positive urines over a brief span. Yet subsequent trials found it to be no better than placebo (Cornish et al., 1995; Malin et al., 1996a).

Thus, while no strong argument can be made for benefit from currently available medications in the reduction of cocaine use, recent research has targeted two areas of particular promise for medication development:

- Maintenance treatment via substitution therapy with compounds such as GBR 12909 or PPT
- D_1 agonists and D_1 antagonists reported in animal models to inhibit reinstatement of cocaine self-administration.

SEDATIVES/HYPNOTICS

These oft prescribed and sometimes abused medications form the final group of agents which respond to specifically targeted pharmacological interventions, largely those which employ like or cross-tolerant compounds to ameliorate the discomforts of withdrawal.

Benzodiazepines

Safe clinical management of the use or abuse of these compounds requires an awareness of the concept of differential tolerance. Since an individual will develop tolerance separately to the various biological effects of an agent, a discrepancy may exist between tolerance acquired for euphoric effects and that for effects on vital functions, such as respiration or blood pressure. Tolerance is quickly established for the sedating effects of benzodiazepines, more slowly toward respiratory depression, and minimally with respect to BZD-induced memory loss. Accordingly, the window of safety narrows somewhat with extended use, especially when forgetful insomniacs may unknowingly repeat their dose of hypnotic. Fortunately, a competitive antagonist, flumazenil, is available for IV infusion in cases of accidental or intentional overdose.

Detoxification may be accomplished through substitution with a like or cross-tolerant long-acting compound administered in a scheduled taper. Chlordiazepoxide or clonazepam are those most commonly employed. While the great majority of BZD users continue with their prescribed therapeutic dosage, regular use beyond 4 months finds the patient prone to withdrawal symptoms upon discontinuation. In general, the withdrawal state is one of drug-opposite effects, centering on CNS hyperarousal. First to appear is profound rebound anxiety and insomnia, accompanied by general restlessness. Tremor, sweating, anorexia, and myoclonus are often noted. Tachycardia, hypertension, and agitation may also be seen. Later developments can include confusion, depersonalization, perceptual distortions, paresthesia, hyperacusis, and photophobia. While rare, seizures can occur during the early withdrawal period, typically within 3 days of discontinuation of drug use. Seizure risk is increased substantially by the concomitant use of other sedating agents, particularly ethanol. Abrupt termination of administration is never wise; rather, gradual taper over several weeks is preferred. On occasion, propranolol has been used to assuage autonomic excitation. Sedating tricyclic antidepressants may be employed to assist sleep.

Escalating or high-dose dependence presents far more serious issues of management. Whether begun as street use to augment the potential high of methadone or curb the crash after cocaine, or combined with alcohol or other sedatives in attempted self-medication of anxiety or depression, it constitutes dependent use with the attendant risks of multiple substance abuse and addictive behavior. The likelihood of seizure is more pronounced, and the risk of fatal respiratory depression greatly increased, particularly when combined with barbiturates. Assessment for inpatient management is indicated, with the prospect of a troublesome detoxification treated with long-acting BZDs or phenobarbital, and active supportive management.

Other Agents

While no longer so frequently seen, dependence on barbiturates, glutethimide, and ethchlorvynol can still be encountered, usually abused in combination with other agents. Because the tolerance to euphoria occurs more rapidly and extensively than tolerance to brain stem depressant effects, the use of these agents

engenders far greater risk and commonly requires carefully supervised inpatient treatment.

AGENTS RESPONDING TO SPECIFIC SUPPORTIVE INTERVENTIONS

Hallucinogens

Since the early 1990s, use of these agents by young people has again been on the rise. The temporary alteration of thought, perception, and mood which they induce does not commonly bring users to medical attention. Yet patients will occasionally present with complaints of panic anxiety as part of a "bad trip." Reassurance and a calm atmosphere usually provide sufficient treatment, although low doses of BZDs may be employed to mute dysphoria. Phencyclidine (PCP, angel dust) deserves special mention because its reinforcing qualities readily promote abuse, especially when rapidly administered by smoking. Psychotic thinking generated by lower doses advances to hallucinations as use increases and sometimes progresses to hostile or assaultive behavior. On occasion, the degree of agitation may warrant BZDs given by IV titration, or even haloperidol if driven by psychotic ideation. One should avoid using anticholinergic antipsychotics such as chlorpromazine or thioridizine, which may augment the delirium. PCP's dose-related anesthetic effects lead to stupor and coma in heavy abusers, accompanied by muscular rigidity, rhabdomyosis, and hyperthermia. Early signs of intoxication in those with a history of PCP use warn of the need for emergency care. No receptor antagonist is known.

Cannabis

Marijuana, hemp, hash, and pot are all names for this controversial drug. Since the 1970s, it has been known to be capable of producing physical dependence (Jones, Benowitz, & Herning, 1981), but most users take it occasionally and do not develop withdrawal symptoms. Specific cannabinoid receptors have been identified throughout the brain, and their density and widespread location suggest that they may play an important, yet unknown, role in brain function (Devane, Dysanz, Johnson, Melvin, & Howlett, 1988). An endogenous ligand has been identified (Devane et al., 1992). A withdrawal syn-

TABLE 19.1 Clinical Uses of Pharmacological Agents for the Treatment of Addictive Illnesses

	Opioids	Alcohol	Nicotine	Cocaine	Benzodiazepines
Emergency antidote	Naloxone				Flumazenil
Prevents effect	Naltrexone				
Provides moderate effect while deterring withdrawal	Methadone LAAM		Nicotine		
Provides weak effect while deterring withdrawal	Buprenorphine			GBR 12909? PPT?	
Diminishes effect	Receptor agonist	Naltrexone	Mecamylamine?	D₁ agonists	
Detoxification—Minimizing withdrawal discomfort	Methadone	Benzodiazepines Phenobarbital			Benzodiazepines Phenobarbital
Detoxification—Reducing withdrawal discomfort	Naltrexone plus clonidine				
Aversive deterrent		Disulfiram	Silver acetate		

TABLE 19.1 Clinical Uses of Pharmacological Agents for the Treatment of Addictive Illnesses

(Row labels, left-most column)
Emergency antidote — Receptor antagonist
Prevents effect — Receptor antagonist
Provides moderate effect while deterring withdrawal — Receptor agonist
Provides weak effect while deterring withdrawal — Partial receptor agonist
Diminishes effect — Receptor agonist
Detoxification—Minimizing withdrawal discomfort — Long acting cross tolerant agent
Detoxification—Reducing withdrawal discomfort — Receptor blockade plus sympathomimetic damping
Aversive deterrent — Noxious agent

drome typical of that seen with other sedatives has been described by heavy users, comprising heightened tension and anxiety, restlessness, sleep disturbance, and changes in appetite (Wiesbeck et al., 1996). Recent reports in rodent models identified a diminution of corticotropin-releasing factor (CRF) release in the amygdala in response to stimulation with a marijuana-like ligand, similar to that seen with other agents of abuse. Blocking of the cannabinoid receptor in marijuana-dependent rats yielded a pronounced increase in CRF release, accompanied by behavior patterns characteristic of withdrawal (Rodriguez de Fonseca, Carrera, Navarro, Koob, & Weiss, 1997). Given recent data indicating a renewed increase in marijuana use by young high school students (Johnston, O'Malley, & Bachman, 1997) and persuasive evidence that chronic use impairs skills related to attention, memory, and learning (Pope & Yurgelun-Todd, 1996), investigators have intensified their efforts to identify pharmacological agents that could assist in the management of cannabis dependence.

SUMMARY AND CONCLUSIONS

Addictive disorders have complex etiologies involving genetic, social, cultural, and even political influences. Treatment approaches using a biopsychosocial approach are clearly the most effective. Medications have been shown to aid in the rehabilitation of persons dependent on alcohol, nicotine, and opiates. Table 19.1 summarizes the clinical uses of pharmacological agents discussed in this chapter.

Persons dependent on any drug may have coexisting psychiatric disorders that also require medication. In all cases, however, the medication works best within the context of a comprehensive rehabilitation program that addresses psychological, social, medical, familial, legal, occupational, and other problems typically present in a patient suffering from an addiction.

Key References

Mendelson, H. J., & Mello, N. K. (1996). Management of cocaine abuse and dependence. *New England Journal of Medicine, 334,* 965–972.

O'Brien, C. P., Eckardt, M. J., & Linnoila, V. M. I. (1995). Pharmacotherapy of alcoholism. In F. E. Bloom & D. J. Kupfer (Eds.), *Psychopharmacology:*

The fourth generation of progress (pp. 1745–1755). New York: Raven Press.

Rose, J. E. (1996). Nicotine addiction and treatment. *Annual Review of Medicine, 47,* 493–507.

References

Alldredge, B. K., Lowenstein, D. H., & Simon, R. P. (1989). Placebo-controlled trial of intravenous diphenylhydantoin for short-term treatment of alcohol withdrawal seizures. *American Journal of Medicine, 87,* 645–648.

Alterman, A. I., Droba, M., Antelo, R. E., Cornish, J., Sweeney, K. K., Parikh, G. A., et al. (1992). Amantadine may facilitate detoxification of cocaine addicts. *Drug and Alcohol Dependence, 31,* 19–29.

Arndt, I. O., Dorozynsky, L., Woody, G. E., McLellan, A. T., & O'Brien, C.P. (1992). Desipramine treatment of cocaine dependence in methadone-maintained patients. *Archives of General Psychiatry, 49,* 888–893.

Benowitz, N. L., Zevin, S., & Jacob, P. (1997). Sources of variability in nicotine and cotinine levels with the use of nicotine nasal spray, transdermal nicotine, and cigarette smoking. *British Journal of Clinical Pharmacology, 43,* 259–267.

Berg, B. J., Pettinati, H. M., & Volpicelli, J. R. (1996). A risk-benefit assessment of naltrexone in the treatment of alcohol dependence. *Drug Safety, 15,* 274–282.

Brahen, L. S., Henderson, R. K., Capone, T., & Kordal, N. (1984). Naltrexone treatment in a jail work-release program. *Journal of Clinical Psychiatry, 45,* 49–52.

Breslau, N., Kilbey, N., & Andreski, P. (1991). Nicotine dependence, major depression, and anxiety in young adults. *Archives of General Psychiatry, 48,* 1069–1074.

Cooper, J. R. (1989). Methadone treatment and acquired immunodeficiency syndrome. *Journal of the American Medical Association, 262,* 1664–1668.

Cornish, J. W., Maany, I., Fudala, P. J., Neal, S., Poole, S. A., Volpicelli, P., et al. (1995). Carbamazepine treatment for cocaine dependence. *Drug and Alcohol Dependence, 38,* 221–227.

Cornish, J. W., Metzger, D., Woody, G. E., Wilson, D., McLellan, A. T., Vandergrift, B., et al. (1997). Naltrexone pharmacotherapy for opioid dependent federal probationers. *Journal of Substance Abuse Treatment, 14(6),* 529–534.

Dackis, C. A., & Gold, M. S. (1985). New concepts in cocaine addiction: The dopamine depletion hypothesis. *Neuroscience and Behavioral Development, 9,* 467–477.

Dale, L. C., Hunt, R. D., & Offord, K. P. (1995). High dose nicotine patch therapy: Percentage of replacement and smoking cessation. *Journal of the American Medical Association, 274,* 1353–1358.

Devane, W.A., Dysanz II, F. A., Johnson, M. R., Melvin, L. S., & Howlett, A. C. (1988). Determination and characterization of a cannabinoid receptor in rat brain. *Molecular Pharmacology, 34,* 605–613.

Devane, W. A., Hanus, L., Brever, A., Pertwee, R. G., Stevenson, L. A., Griffin, G., et al. (1992). Isolation and structure of a brain constituent that binds to the cannabinoid receptor. *Science, 258,* 1946–1949.

Dole, V. P., & Nyswander, M. (1965). A medical treatment for diacetylmorphine (heroin) addiction: A clinical trial with methadone hydrochloride. *Journal of the American Medical Association, 193,* 80–84.

Dole, V. P., & Nyswander, M. (1967). Heroin addiction—A metabolic disease. *Archives of Internal Medicine, 120,* 19–24.

Ehrman, R. N., Robbins, S. J., Cornish, J. W., Childress, A. R., & O'Brien, C. P. (1996). Failure of ritanserin to block cocaine cue reactivity in humans. *Drug and Alcohol Dependence, 42,* 167–174.

Eisen, S. A., Lyons, M. J., Goldberg, J., & True, W. R. (1993). The impact of cigarette and alcohol consumption on weight and obesity: An analysis of 1911 monozygotic male twin pairs. *Archives of Internal Medicine, 153,* 2457–2463.

Faberstrom, K., Schneider, N. G., & Lunell, E. (1993). Effectiveness of nicotine patch and nicotine gum as individual vs. combined treatments for tobacco withdrawal symptoms. *Psychopharmacology, 111,* 271–277.

Ferry, L. H., & Burchette, R. J. (1994). Efficacy of buproprion for smoking cessation in nondepressed smokers. *Journal of Addictive Diseases, 13,* A9.

Fiore, M. C, Smith, S. S., Jorenby, D. E., & Baker, T. B. (1994). The effectiveness of the nicotine patch for smoking cessation: a meta-analysis. *Journal of the American Medical Association, 271,* 1940–1946.

Fuller, R. K., Branchey, L., Brightwell, D. R., Derman, R. M., Emrick, C. D., Iber, F. L., et al. (1986). Disulfiram treatment of alcoholism: A Veterans Administration cooperative study. *Journal of the American Medical Association, 256,* 1449–1455.

Gawin, F. H., & Kleber, H. D. (1986). Abstinence symptomatology and psychiatric diagnosis in cocaine abusers: Clinical observations. *Archives of General Psychiatry, 43,* 107–113.

Gawin, F. H., Kleber, H. D., Byck, R., Rounsaville, B. J., Kosten, T. R., Jatlow, P. I., et al. (1989). Desipramine facilitation of initial cocaine abuse. *Archives of General Psychiatry, 46*(2), 117–121.

Gawin, F. H., Riordin, C., & Kleber, H. D. (1985). Methylphenidate treatment of cocaine abusers without attention deficit disorder: A negative report. *American Journal of Drug and Alcohol Abuse, 11,* 193–197.

Glassman, A. H. (1993). Cigarette smoking: Implications for psychiatric illness. *American Journal Psychiatry, 150,* 546–553.

Glassman, A. H., & Covey, L. S. (1995). Nicotine dependence and treatment. In R. Michels, A. M. Cooper, & S. B. Guze (Eds.), *Psychiatry, 116* (pp. 1–10). New York: Lippincott-Raven.

Glassman, A. H., Covey, L. S., Dalack, G. W., Stetner, F., Rivelli, S. K., Fleiss, J., et al. (1993). Smoking cessation, clonidine, and vulnerability to nicotine among dependent smokers. *Clinical Pharmacological Therapies, 54,* 670–679.

Glowa, J. R., Wojnicki, F. H. E., Matecka, D., et al. (1995). Effects of dopamine reuptake inhibitors on food- and cocaine-mediated responding: 1. Dependence on unit dose of cocaine. *Experimental and Clinical Psychopharmacology, 3,* 219–231.

Gold, M. S., Redmond, D. E., & Kleber, H. D. (1979). Noradrenergic hyperactivity in opiate withdrawal supported by clonidine reversal of opiate withdrawal. *American Journal of Psychiatry, 136,* 100–102.

Gourley, S. G., Benowitz, N. L., Forbes, A., & McNeil, J. T. (1997). Determinants of plasma concentrations of nicotine and cotinine during cigarette smoking and transdermal nicotine treatment. *European Journal of Clinical Pharmacology, 51,* 407–414.

Haxby, A. G. (1995). Treatment of nicotine dependence. *American Journal of Health-Systems Pharmacology, 52,* 265–281.

Hayashida, M., Alterman, A. I., McLellan, A. T., O'Brien, C. P., Purtill, J. J., & Volpicelli, J. R. (1991). Comparative effectiveness of treatment for alcohol problems: A first approximation. *Journal of Clincal Studies of Alcohol, 52,* 517–540.

Henningfield, J. E., Schuh, L. M., & Jarvik, M. E. (1995). Pathophysiology of tobacco dependence. In F. E. Bloom & D. J. Kupfer (Eds.), *Psychopharmacology: The fourth generation of progress* (pp. 1715–1719). New York: Raven Press.

Hughes, J. R. (1996). An overview of nicotine use disorders for alcohol/drug abuse clinicians. *American Journal of Addictions, 5,* 262–274.

Hurt, R. D., Sachs, D. P., Glover, E. D., Offord, K. P., Johnston, J. A., Dale, L. C., et al. (1997). A comparison of substained-release buproprion and placebo for smoking cessation. *New England Journal of Medicine, 337*(17), 1195–1202.

Jaffe, J. H., Kranzler, H. R., & Ciraulo, D. A. (1992). Drugs used in the treatment of alcoholism. In J. H.

Mendelson & M. K. Mello (Eds.), *Medical diagnosis and treatment of alcoholism* (pp. 431–161). New York: McGraw-Hill.

Johnson, R. E., Jaffe, J. H., & Fudala, P. J. (1992). A controlled trial of buprenorphine treatment for opiod dependence. *Journal of the American Medical Association, 267,* 2750–2755.

Johnston, L. D., O'Malley, P. M., & Bachman, J. G. (1997). *National Survey Results on Drug Use from the Monitoring The Future Study, 1975–1995* (NIH Publication No. 98-4140). Washington, DC: Government Printing Office.

Jones, R. T., Benowitz, N. L., & Herning, R. I. (1981). Clinical review of cannabis tolerance and dependence. *Journal of Clinical Pharmacology, 21,* 143S–152S.

Jorenby, D. E., Smith, S. S., Fiore, M. C., Hurt, R. D., Offord, K. P., Croghan, I. T., et al. (1995). Varying nicotine patch dose and type of smoking cessation counseling. *Journal of the American Medical Association, 274,* 1347–1352.

Kampman, K., Volpicelli, J. R., Alterman, A., Cornish, J., Weinrieb, R., Epperson, L., et al. (1996). Amantadine in the early treament of cocaine dependence: A double-blind, placebo-controlled trial. *Drug and Alcohol Dependence, 41,* 25–33.

Kornetsky, C., & Porrino, L. J. (1992). Brain mechanisms of drug-induced reinforcement. In C. P. O'Brien & J. H. Jaffe (Eds.), *Addictive states* (pp. 59–77). New York: Raven Press.

Kreek, M. J. (1978). Medical complications in methadone patients. *Annals of the New York Academy of Science, 311,* 110–134.

Litten, R. Z., & Allen, J. P. (1995). Pharmacotherapy for alcoholics with collateral depression or anxiety: An update of research findings. *Experimental and Clinical Psychopharmacology, 3,* 87–93.

Loimer, N., Lenz, K., Schmid, R., & Presslich, O. (1991). Technique for greatly shortening the transition from methadone to naltrexone maintenance of patients addicted to opiates. *American Journal of Psychiatry, 148,* 933–935.

Malcolm, R., Butto, B. R., Philips, J. D., & Ballenger, J. C. (1991). Pergolide mesylate treatment of cocaine withdrawal. *Journal of Clinical Psychiatry, 52,* 39–40.

Malin, D. H., Lake, J. R., Payne, M. C., Short, P. E., Carter, V. A. Cunningham, T.S., et al. (1996a). Nicotine alleviation of nicotine abstinence syndrome is naloxone-reversible. *Pharmacology, Biochemistry and Behavior, 53,* 81–85.

Malin, D. H., Lake, J. R., Short, P. E., Blossman, J. B., Lawless, B. A., Schopen, C. K., et al. (1996b). Nicotine abstinence syndrome precipitated by an analog of neuropeptide FF. *Pharmacology, Biochemistry and Behavior, 54,* 581–585.

Nader, M. A., Grant, K. A., Davies, H. M. L., Mach, R. H., & Childer, S. R. (1997). The reinforcing and discriminative effects of the novel cocaine analogue 2-propanoyl-3-(4-toyl)-tropane in rhesus monkeys. *Journal of Pharmacology and Experimental Therapeutics, 280,* 541–550.

O'Brien, C. P. (1992). Opioid addiction. In A. Herz (Ed.), *Handbook of experimental pharmacology* (pp. 803–823). Heidelberg: Springer-Verlag.

O'Brien, C. P., Terenius, L. Y., Nyberg, F., McLellan, A. T., & Eriksson, I. (1988). Endogenous opioids in cerebrospinal fluid of opiod-dependent humans. *Biological Psychiatry., 24,* 649–662.

O'Brien, R., & Chafetz, M. (1991). *The encyclopedia of alcoholism* (2nd ed.). New York: Facts on File.

Olincy, A., Young, D. A., & Freedman, R. (1997). Increased levels of the nicotine metabolite cotinine in schizophrenic smokers compared to other smokers. *Biological Psychiatry, 42,* 1–5.

O'Malley, S. S., Jaffe, A. J., Chang, G., Schottenfeld, R. S., Meyer, R. E., & Rounsaville, B. (1992). Naltrexone and coping skills therapy for alcohol dependence: a controlled study. *Archives of General Psychiatry, 49,* 881–887.

Pert, C. B., & Snyder, S. H. (1973). Opiate receptor; demonstration in nervous tissue. *Science, 179,* 1011–1014.

Pope, H. G., & Yurgelun-Todd, D. (1996). The residual cognitive effects of heavy marijuana use in college students. *Journal of the American Medical Association, 275*(7), 521–527.

Ritz, M. C., Lamb, R. J., Goldberg, S. R., & Kuhar, J. F. (1987). Cocaine receptors on dopamine transporters are related to self-administration of cocaine. *Science, 237,* 1219–1223.

Rodriguez de Fonseca, F., Carrera, M. R. A., Navarro, J., Koob, G. F., & Weiss, F. (1997). Activation of corticotropin-releasing factor in the limbic system during cannabinoid withdrawal. *Science, 276,* 2050–2054.

Rothman, R. B., Mele, A., Reid, A. A., Akunne, H., Greig, N., Thurkauf, A., et al. (1989). Tight binding dopamine reuptake inhibitors as cocaine antagonists: A strategy for drug development. *Federation of European Biochemical Societies letter, 257,* 341–344.

Satel, S. L., Price, L. H., Palumbo, J. M., McDougle, C. J., Krystal, J. H., Gawin, F. H., et al. (1991). Clinical phenomenology and neurobiology of cocaine abstinence: a prospective inpatient study. *American Journal of Psychiatry, 148,* 1712–1716.

Schuh, K. J., Schuh, L. M., Henningfield, J. E., & Stitzer, M. L. (1997). Nicotine nasal spray and vapor inhaler: Abuse liability assessment. *Psychopharmacology, 130,* 352–361.

Self, D. W., Barnhart, W. J., Lehman, D. A., & Nestler, E. J. (1996). Opposite modulation of cocaine-seeking behavior by D₁- and D₂-like dopamine receptor agonists. *Science, 271,* 1586–1589.

Silagy, C., Mant, D., Fowler, G., & Lodge, M. (1994). Meta-analysis on efficacy of nicotine replacement therapies in smoking cessation. *Lancet, 343,* 139–142.

Stine, S. M., & Kosten, T. R. (1992). Use of drug combinations in treatment of opioid withdrawal. *Journal of Clinical Psychopharmacology, 12,* 203–209.

Sullivan, J. T., Sykora, K., Schneiderman, J., Naranjo, C. A., & Sellers, E. M. (1989). Assessment of alcohol withdrawal: The revised clinical institute withdrawal assessment for alcohol scale (CIWA-Ar). *British Journal of Addiction, 84,* 1353–1357.

Tella, S. R., Landenheim, B., Andrews, A. M., Goldberg, S. R., & Cadet, J. L. (1996). Differential reinforcing effects of cocaine and GBR-12909: Biochemical evidence for divergent neuroadaptive changes in the mesolimbic dopaminergic system. *Journal of Neuroscience, 16,* 7416–7427.

Volkow, N. D., Ding, Y. S., Fowler, J. S., & Wang, G. J. (1996). Cocaine addiction: Hypothesis derived from imaging studies with PET. *Journal of Addictive Diseases, 15,* 55–71.

Volpicelli, J. R., Alterman, A. I., Hayashida, M., & O'Brien, C. P. (1992). Naltrexone in the treatment of alcohol dependence. *Archives of General Psychiatry, 49,* 876–880.

Wiesbeck, G. A., Schukit, M. A., Kalmijin, J. A., Tipp, J. E., Bucholz, K. K., & Smith, T. L. (1996). An evaluation of the history of a marijuana withdrawal syndrome in a large population. *Addiction, 91,* 1469–1478.

Witkin, J. M. (1994). Pharmacotherapy of cocaine abuse: Preclinical development. *Neuroscience and Biobehavioral Reviews, 18,* 121–142.

20

Relapse Prevention: Maintenance of Change After Initial Treatment

Lori A. Quigley

G. Alan Marlatt

Early research on the effectiveness of treatment for substance use focused on resumption of substance use as the primary outcome variable (Hunt, Barnett, & Branch, 1971). Regardless of the amount, duration, or consequences of use, any posttreatment use was considered a "relapse" and tantamount to treatment "failure." Thus, two outcomes were possible: treatment success, defined as complete and continuous abstinence, and treatment failure, defined as any posttreatment use. As research in this field has progressed, a variety of outcomes associated with improved status, yet short of complete and total abstinence, have been acknowledged, and there is greater acceptance of diverse pathways toward improvement (Miller, 1996). Even so, return to problematic use continues to be a challenge in the addictive behaviors treatment field.

Rates for the resumption of substance use following abstinence-oriented treatment are uniformly high across addictive behaviors. In an early study by Hunt and colleagues (Hunt et al., 1971), roughly two thirds of individuals who received treatment for smoking cessation, alcohol abuse, or heroin addiction returned to substance use within 3 months of treatment. A much smaller percentage remained continuously abstinent through 1-year posttreatment (less than 35% for alcohol use and less than 25% for smoking and heroin use). For a large proportion of individuals treated for addictive behavior, resumption of substance use is the most likely outcome. This high rate of relapse following treatment is likely to lead to a continuous "revolving door" back into treatment.

Regardless of the method used to achieve abstinence or a reduction in substance use, relapse prevention (RP; Marlatt & Gordon, 1985) techniques can be utilized to maintain changes attained during the course of treatment. Skills to decrease the probability of a return to maladaptive substance use can be taught to clients regardless of the methods employed to achieve initial abstinence or moderation. The goals of RP are twofold. The first goal is to prevent a lapse or initial return to substance use (or transgression of one's goal) so that a full-blown relapse, defined as return to problematic use, is less likely. The second goal is successful management of relapse episodes, if they do occur, to prevent exacerbation or continuation of maladaptive substance use. RP techniques may also be utilized to facilitate initial changes in addictive behaviors.

Marlatt and Gordon's (1985) RP approach was originally developed as a maintenance program for individuals who had undergone treatment to moderate or discontinue substance use. It was developed to extend and enhance therapeutic gains and to reduce the possibility of recycling back through treatment. Rather than viewing those who experience initial lapse episodes as "treatment failures" who are victims of an underlying disease process, the RP approach views such episodes as errors or temporary setbacks that might be expected from someone who is in the process of learning new coping behaviors. Viewed in this way, these episodes may provide valuable lessons in preventing future episodes. Lapses to use, and relapses, therefore, are part of a learning process rather than a final outcome of treatment. Attributions for a return to substance use which involve uncontrollable causes may lead to a return to problematic use and to demoralization on the part of clients as well as treatment providers. In a recent prospective alcohol treatment outcome study, Miller, Westerberg, Harris, and Tonigan (1996) found that endorsement of a disease model of alcoholism was strongly predictive of relapse by 6 months. This suggests that the way clients conceptualize their substance-related problems, including their attributions of controllability, may play a key role in successful behavior maintenance.

Although the RP model was developed primarily as a maintenance program, it is also utilized as a strategy for the initiation of behavior change. RP strategies may be used in conjunction with other initiation strategies designed to enhance motivation for change such as motivational interviewing (Miller & Rollnick, 1991) or even disease model approaches. RP approaches were initially developed with substance-related behaviors (e.g., smoking, drinking, heroin use) and other impulse control problems (e.g., gambling, pedophilia) in mind.

Within the area of addictive behaviors, recent applications have included programs which are developed for groups lower in problem severity (Marlatt et al., 1998) and which address other problems of impulse control, including obesity (Fremouw & Damer, 1992), other forms of disordered eating (Orimoto & Vitousek, 1992; Rankin, 1989), and sexual deviance (Marshall, Hudson, & Ward, 1992). RP techniques have also been combined with other forms of therapy in behavioral marital therapy (McCrady, 1993; O'Farrell, 1993) and treatment for depression (Wilson, 1992), schizophrenia (Kavanagh, 1992), panic disorder (Brown & Barlow, 1992), obsessive-compulsive disorders (Emmelkamp, Kloek, & Blaauw, 1992), chronic pain (Nicholas, 1992), marital distress (Truax & Jacobson, 1992), social competence (Azar, Ferguson, & Twentyman, 1992), and stuttering (Andrews, 1992).

THE RP MODEL AND LINKAGE TO THEORY OF ETIOLOGY AND MAINTENANCE OF SUBSTANCE USE

Marlatt and Gordon's RP model is based on an "addictive behaviors model," with its roots primarily in social learning theory in conjunction with social and cognitive psychology (Bandura, 1977; Lang & Marlatt, 1982; Mackay, Donovan, & Marlatt, 1991; Marlatt & Gordon, 1985). Addictive behaviors, from this standpoint, develop as acquired or overlearned habits. To the extent that a substance is used to cope with unpleasant situations, experiences, or emotions, the behavior may also be viewed as a learned maladaptive coping strategy. Such habits may be learned through a combination of both classical and operant conditioning processes, which may not be under the individual's direct control. Individuals struggling with addictive behaviors, therefore, are not held accountable for the development of an addiction, just as they are not held responsible for their learning histories.

The model assumes a biopsychosocial etiology, the specific determinants of which may vary greatly among individuals. Such influences may include biological and genetic vulnerabilities, environmental and/or situational factors, family history of substance use, substance use by peers, early experience with substances, and beliefs and expectancies about the effects of a substance. Social and societal influences may play a large role in the development of addictive behaviors. Within the RP model, individuals who struggle with addictive behavior patterns are not viewed as categorically different ("alcoholic" or not) from those who do not. Rather, they are viewed as being at a different place along a continuum from nonuse and nonproblem use to severe problem use.

The RP model views the development of addictive behaviors as multiply determined and maintained. However, the factors involved in the development of potentially harmful habits may not necessarily be the same factors involved in their maintenance. Maintenance of substance use may be primarily driven by the drug's short-term reinforcing effects. A drug's predictability in providing some relief, if only temporarily, to an individual who has not developed alternative ways of handling unpleasant situations or emotions may foster continued reliance on drug taking as an attempt to cope. Perceived lack of alternative coping strategies combined with low self-efficacy (Bandura, 1977; Marlatt, Baer, & Quigley, 1995), or confidence in one's ability to effectively carry out alternative coping strategies, may serve to maintain a maladaptive pattern of substance use. An individual may not have developed skills to perform more appropriate, less harmful behaviors or may lack confidence in his or her ability to perform a more appropriate behavior successfully.

Not all addictive behaviors develop as maladaptive coping responses that may have their origin in skill deficits. Use of psychoactive substances, particularly the use of alcohol, is generally a socially accepted practice among adults in many societies. Alcohol use, for example, in addition to its reinforcing pharmacological effects, is also reinforced socially. Potentially problematic behaviors may become incorporated into an individual's lifestyle with little forethought as to possible risks or negative long-term consequences. Some short-term negative consequences may be accepted as a small price to pay for the benefits derived from the drug-taking behavior. Until such negative consequences begin to accrue, or more serious consequences occur, individuals may not be motivated to examine and/or change their behavior. Maladaptive substance use is not viewed as a symptom of an underlying disease, although it is acknowledged that substance habits may result in serious health consequences or disease

states (e.g., cirrhosis). The substance-taking behavior itself is not a disease.

HOW THE RP TREATMENT APPROACH FOLLOWS FROM THE RP THEORY OF SUBSTANCE ABUSE

Regardless of the factors involved in the development or maintenance of substance use problems, RP strategies may be used to minimize the likelihood of continued maladaptive substance use. RP is a compensatory model (Brickman et al., 1982); that is, regardless of the factors leading to a problem, an individual can compensate by assuming personal responsibility for behavior change (Marlatt & Gordon, 1985). In this self-management model, an individual may learn to identify the determinants of his or her own problem substance use and develop strategies to affect successful behavior change.

As a self-management approach, the RP model considers the individual (rather than a higher power or a group) to be the responsible agent of change. The individual is taught skills and strategies to recognize and successfully navigate the situations which may have led to relapse in the past. Essentially, treatment utilizing the RP approach is empowering and trains individuals to act as their own therapists with regard to managing their addictive behavior patterns.

KEY CONSTRUCTS AND TERMS IN THE RP TREATMENT MODEL

Following initial abstinence or attainment of the individual's goals, sooner or later the client will encounter a *high-risk situation*, defined as any situation that poses a threat for resumed or excessive substance use. High-risk situations can be classified as having either intrapersonal or interpersonal determinants (Cummings, Gordon, & Marlatt, 1980; Marlatt & Gordon, 1980). In an analysis of over 300 initial relapse episodes involving return to cigarette, alcohol, or heroin use, or to overeating or gambling, three primary events emerged which classified over 70% of initial relapse episodes as retrospectively assessed (Cummings et al., 1980). Negative emotional states, classified as intrapersonal determinants, such as anger, boredom, anxiety, frustration, and depression, accounted for about 35% of relapse trigger episodes.

Two types of interpersonal determinants were other primary determinants of initial lapses. Interpersonal conflict and social pressure accounted for 16% and 20% of trigger episodes, respectively. Interpersonal conflict involved ongoing conflictual relationships (e.g., tension in marital relationship) or recent conflict with another person (e.g., argument with a co-worker). Social pressure included both direct verbal persuasion by another to engage in the discontinued behavior (or to exceed one's established limit) and indirect pressure, such as being in the company of others who are engaging in the same behavior.

The remaining initial relapse situations were classified as negative physical states (3%), positive emotional states (4%), testing personal control (5%), and urges and temptations (8%)(all intrapersonal determinants) and positive interpersonal emotional states (interpersonal). The reliability and validity of this relapse taxonomy has been recently evaluated by three research teams (Lowman, Allen, Stout, & The Relapse Research Group, 1996) and is discussed in the section below, which addresses empirical support for the RP model. The clinical utility of Marlatt's relapse taxonomy is to provide a framework for understanding a client's unique situation and characteristics that may serve as proximal determinants for relapse so that treatment is appropriately planned (Marlatt, 1996).

A COGNITIVE BEHAVIORAL MODEL OF RELAPSE

Figure 20.1 presents Marlatt's model of the relapse process. When a high-risk situation is encountered, an individual may or may not invoke the use of a cognitive or behavioral *coping response* in an attempt to deal with the situation without using the undesired substance (or exceeding a limit for that substance). If a coping response is utilized effectively, the individual is likely to respond with increased *self-efficacy* to cope successfully with future similar situations (Marlatt et al., 1995).

Alternatively, the individual may be unable or unwilling to cope with the high-risk situation. In this case, there may be a skill deficit on the part of the individual, the performance of a learned coping response may be blocked due to anxiety brought on by the situation, or the situation may not be recognized as being a risky one until it is too late to initiate an appropriate coping response. If this occurs, a decrease in self-efficacy is likely to occur, often characterized as a feeling of hopelessness about ever being able to manage substance-related behavior. The probability of lapsing is increased to the extent that decreased self-efficacy is combined with *positive outcome expectancies* for the initial effects of substance use. Positive outcome expectancies are the short-term positive effects or immediate gratification one anticipates receiving through use of the substance.

A *lapse*, or initial return to substance use or transgression of one's goal, may follow from the inability to cope with a high-risk situation and associated lowered self-efficacy (Marlatt et al., 1995). Whether a lapse precipitates a *relapse*, usually defined as a return to maladaptive or pretreatment levels of substance use, appears to be determined in part by one's reaction to and attributions for the initial lapse. Individuals can experience strong negative reactions to their transgression of a goal or initial episode of non-abstinence, particularly when they have personally committed to a goal of moderation or abstinence. The magnitude of this *abstinence violation effect* (AVE) or *goal violation effect* (GVE; Marlatt & Gordon, 1985) in the case of a moderation goal is likely to influence the probability that this initial transgression will precipitate a full-blown relapse.

The AVE is conceptualized as the interplay of two cognitive affective elements: *cognitive dissonance* (Festinger, 1964) and a negative *self-attribution* effect. Cognitive dissonance, as theorized by Festinger (1964), arises when one's behaviors are not congruent with one's self-image or beliefs about oneself. When an individual who has made a commitment to a goal of abstinence uses the forbidden substance, cognitive dissonance may result, as the drug-taking behavior is incongruent with the new self-image of an "abstainer." Cognitive dissonance is presumed to involve an internal conflict involving guilt ("I did a forbidden thing") which individuals are motivated to resolve. The individual may resolve this conflict either by providing a rationalization for the behavior ("I was overwhelmed by the situation and therefore not responsible for my behavior"), thereby maintaining her or his self-image, or by changing the self-image to be congruent with her or his behavior ("I guess this just proves I'm a drunk after all"). Recognition of the inherent difficulties of a situation, coupled with an awareness of coping deficits, may serve to motivate an individual to learn how to better pre-

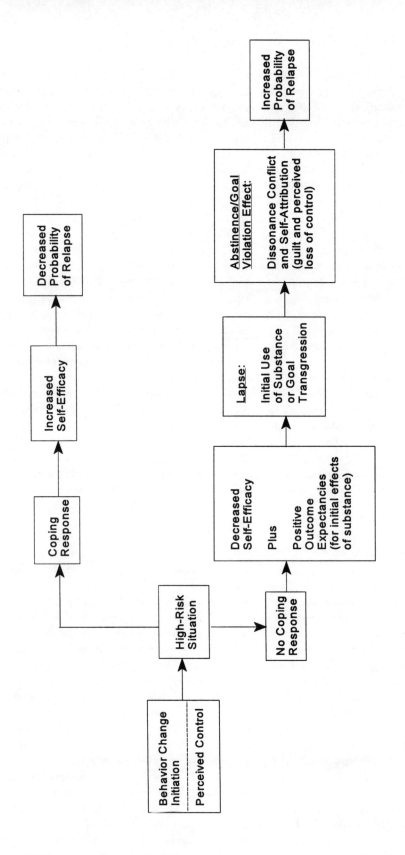

FIGURE 20.1 A cognitive behavioral model of the relapse process.

pare for future situations and to get back "on the wagon" or moderation plan. Self-attributions for a lapse that do not acknowledge the inherent challenges of the high-risk situation but that are largely personalized and negative ("I'm a failure; I have no willpower and can't control my drinking") may lead to lowered expectations for future success at behavior change. Resolution of cognitive dissonance by changing one's self-image to be congruent with a behavioral transgression (e.g., "This proves I am an addict") may precipitate continued use and increase the probability of full-blown relapse.

THERAPEUTIC CHANGE

Assumptions of the RP Model of How People Change and Key Interventions

Because the RP model is rooted in behavior theory, it focuses on the "unlearning" of maladaptive associations and behaviors and on learning more adaptive behaviors. Behavior change efforts are facilitated by sharing with clients an understanding of the theoretical model and the assumptions underlying the RP approach. Metaphors are recommended to clarify the process of behavior change (Marlatt & Fromme, 1987). As an example, the transition from problem substance use to nonuse may be viewed metaphorically as a journey. Three main phases are involved: preparation, departure, and taking the journey itself. Different strategies are employed during each phase of this journey.

Preparing for the Journey

Strategies related to preparation for the journey are utilized with those who have not yet embarked on a behavior change process. These techniques are designed to assess motivation, commitment, and self-efficacy for change. Initial motivation should be assessed early in the process and enhanced if necessary to ensure adequate strength of motivation to affect successful behavior change.

Those considering a behavior change (for addictive or other behaviors) often have ambivalent feelings about quitting (as well as continuing) the problematic behavior. To address this ambivalence, the *decision matrix exercise* (Marlatt & Gordon, 1985) is designed to lead a client through a discussion of the

benefits and costs of both changing and not changing the behavior. A decision matrix assesses the benefits and costs which are both immediate and delayed and is used to build motivation for behavior change and to identify potential barriers. In addition to identifying common motivators for change (e.g., improved health), this technique is useful in identifying idiosyncratic motivations for use or quitting. Such idiosyncratic beliefs, when inaccurate, may be challenged by the therapist. An example of a completed decision matrix is presented in figure 20.2.

Some clients keep a copy of the decision matrix to refer to, especially during times when motivation may be waning, in order to provide themselves with a reminder of the reasons for embarking on the journey. The salience of these reasons may shift over time as various successes, setbacks, and challenges occur throughout the behavior change process. Additional motivational enhancement strategies such as those described by Miller and Rollnick (1991) may be used to further sustain behavior change efforts.

Another area to assess is the client's self-image as a drug user or drinker. Clients often have a difficult time thinking of themselves as other than an "addict" or "alcoholic" and may either feel shame or stigma or perhaps have an overly romanticized view of this lifestyle. To heighten awareness of self-image, clients can provide a *historical autobiography* of their drug or alcohol use. This autobiography should include descriptions of alcohol or substance use in their families of origin and the reasons for initiating substance use, along with the feelings, experiences, and persons associated with use. Clients are also encouraged to write a description of themselves as a nonuser or as a moderate drinker or nondrinker. To this end, clients may benefit from imagery and covert-modeling techniques geared to the development a new self-image.

A person who is very motivated to change an addictive behavior but who believes that he or she lacks the skills and abilities to carry this out may experience low self-efficacy, often in response to previous quit or moderation attempts that failed. For successful habit change in the addictions domain, efficacy can best be evaluated by assessing the client's degree of confidence and skill level in successfully managing not to lapse in a variety of risky situations. The Situational Confidence Questionnaire (SCQ-39; Annis & Graham, 1988) provides such an assessment for alcohol use, and the Substance Abuse Relapse

	Immediate Consequences		Delayed Consequences	
	Positive	Negative	Positive	Negative
To Stop/ Moderate Drinking	Spouse/family & employer approval Financial gain Enhanced self- efficacy	Denial of gratification Disapproval from drinking buddies Self-consciousness when others are drinking Withdrawal discomfort Increased irritability or boredom	Improved health Improved relationships with family Financial gain Enhanced self-control and self-esteem Increased career potential	Denial of gratification associated with drinking
To Continue Drinking	Immediate gratification Withdrawal discomfort Maintain self-image and status with drinking buddies	Low self-control and self-esteem Negative physical effects Family tension Social disapproval Financial loss	Continued gratification	Increased health risks Job/financial loss Decreased self-control and self-esteem Family disapproval

FIGURE 20.2 Decision matrix for alcohol moderation/cessation.

Assessment (SARA; Schoenfeld, Peters, & Dolente, 1993) is used for alcohol and other substances. The SCQ-39 assesses strategies that a client would employ in high-risk situations and ratings of confidence in executing coping behaviors. The SARA can be used to assess coping skills and situations likely to lead to relapse based on a client's substance use behavior chain. Both measures can be used to identify situations in which self-efficacy is low and areas where skills training is needed. Prior to the initiation of behavior change, skills can be taught that enhance efficacy for change.

There are several general strategies used within the RP framework. First, clients are treated as consulting partners, rather than as patients in a "one-down" role, and are encouraged to assume shared responsibility for treatment and more objectivity regarding the substance problem. Meetings with the therapist are presented as opportunities to engage in a productive and objective discovery process rather than as a confessional session. Second, goal setting, which breaks longer term objectives down to a schedule of realistic subgoals, also enhances client self-efficacy. Third, role-playing tasks are used to practice newly acquired coping skills. Fourth, change in self-image is

facilitated by emphasizing that clients are capable of successful behavior change.

Before embarking on the behavior change journey, clients are encouraged to *self-monitor* their drinking or drug-taking behavior. Clients may be asked to keep a log of all aspects of their current drug-taking episodes, including type and quantity consumed, time of day, where they were and with whom, and their mood state. Any positive or negative experiences associated with the episode are recorded in this self-monitoring log. This log enables therapists and clients to identify the functional role of substance use as well as triggers (moods, persons, or places) which may present the highest risk for resumed use. In addition, a more comprehensive assessment of drug use situations may be beneficial to develop safer navigational routes for the impending journey. The Inventory of Drinking Situations (IDS; Annis, 1982) provides such an assessment for drinkers by self-report of the frequency with which the client drank heavily over the past year in various situations. The IDS was derived from Marlatt's taxonomy of relapse situations (Marlatt & Gordon, 1980, 1985). Contexts involving higher frequency of heavy use in the past may be presumed to present the highest risk for future drinking. Assessment of *relapse fantasies* may also provide clues regarding potential risks.

Departure

In the behavior change process, the quit date or the day starting treatment may be viewed as a departure day. Many procedures can be used to help initiate cessation, or change, but the RP model favors those that encourage personal responsibility and self-agency. The choice of how to stop, whether gradual reduction, detoxification, or abrupt "cold turkey," is made by considering clients' beliefs about what will be best given their unique situations. Pros and cons of each method should be discussed with clients before decisions are made. Clients are encouraged to set a "date of departure" for their journey or quit date. This date should be carefully chosen so as to not coincide with stressful life events (stormy weather) and to allow adequate time for preparation, including the enlistment of social support and acquisition of skills needed for the journey. Adjustments to the environment through *stimulus control* procedures to remove cues associated with prior maladaptive substance use (e.g., discarding drug use paraphernalia) are necessary for a successful launching. In addition, planning substitute activities and stocking up on nonharmful substances may facilitate the departure. A well-plotted course is a key feature of a successful journey. The moment of departure may be marked by an individualized *departure ceremony* in recognition of the commitment made and the destination of a healthier lifestyle.

The Journey

Despite a well-chosen course and fair weather upon departure, events occur once en route which can challenge the less seasoned traveler. The prepared traveler is informed about the possibility of inclement weather, engine problems, or flat tires (i.e., possible lapses en route) and other navigational challenges and must plan accordingly. Even the most well-prepared individual is likely to encounter difficult situations once behavior change is initiated. Relapse rates are particularly high during the first 3 months of behavior change. For this reason, clients need to be warned about the importance of remaining vigilant and equipped for this possibility. Challenging situations include the following: coping with temptation to use; coping with initial use of the substance (or transgression of moderation goal); the abstinence (or goal) violation effect; and ineffective decision making.

The first few days of behavior change are particularly risky in terms of giving in to *cravings* or *urges* to resume substance use. Cravings often are mediated cognitively by the subjective value or importance of the immediate positive effects one expects from engaging in the addictive behavior. An urge represents an intention to engage in a behavior to gratify or satisfy craving. Thus, both urges and cravings are mediated by positive *outcome expectancies* for the immediate effects of the substance or the benefits anticipated from indulgence in the drug-taking behavior. These outcome expectancies develop from several potential sources: (a) classical conditioning, in which drug cues serve as conditioned stimuli for a conditioned craving response; (b) exposure to high-risk situations coupled with low self-efficacy for coping; (c) physical dependence or withdrawal; (d) personal and cultural beliefs about expected effects of substance or behavior; and (e) environmental settings where consumption takes place (Marlatt, 1985a).

Because positive outcome expectancies for the effects of a substance may play an influential role in the relapse process, these expectancies should be assessed early in treatment. Individuals may have come to rely on a substance to modulate mood or behavior due to their beliefs about the effects of that substance. For example, a person who drinks to become less anxious in social situations may experience the need to use alcohol in a variety of situations that evoke social anxiety. Reliance on a substance due to beliefs about the effects of the substance (rather than the actual pharmacological effects) is closely related to psychological dependency. Positive and negative outcome expectancies regarding both continuation and cessation of substance use should be assessed. This information may help a client identify reasons for substance use. For some clients, a relationship between psychiatric symptoms and substance use may become apparent.

Measures to explore clients' substance-related expectancies include the Comprehensive Effects of Alcohol scale (CEOA; Fromme, Stroot, & Kaplan, 1993), the Effects of Drinking Alcohol scale (EDA; Leigh, 1987, 1989), the Alcohol Effects Questionnaire (AEQ; Rohsenow, 1983), the AEQ-3 (George et al., 1995), and the Alcohol Expectancy Questionnaire (Brown, Christiansen, & Goldman, 1987) for alcohol-related expectancies. Fewer measures exist for assessing expectancies for other drugs; however, a section of the SARA (Schoenfeld et al., 1993) can be used to assess prominent emotions anticipated after substance use (see also chapter 11 in this volume).

To counter urges and cravings, the therapist educates the client about the immediate and longer term effects of engaging in the addictive behavior. Many individuals perceive their cravings to be physiologically based. Urges and cravings can be reframed as a cognition-based desire for immediate gratification, rather than a biological need. Clients are then encouraged to pursue healthier means of gratification (e.g., exercise or massage) to assuage their urges. In addition, clients are instructed to externalize their urges to use ("I am experiencing a craving for a drink") rather than to identify with them ("I need a drink"). Development of a sense of detachment from cravings allows a client to more objectively observe this process and invoke the use of cognitive and behavioral coping strategies. For a client who believes that the strength of cravings will continue to increase over time until he or she succumbs to them, a therapist can point out that over time, cravings, like an ocean wave, will build in intensity, peak, and eventually subside. The client's challenge, therefore, is to learn to ride out these waves of craving without "wiping out." This is a technique metaphorically described as *urge surfing* (Marlatt, 1985a, 1994).

Dealing with a Lapse

The second navigational challenge is responding to and coping with lapses. Coping with lapses has both behavioral and cognitive affective elements. On the behavioral end, clients develop a specific, preplanned course of action to follow in the event of substance use. This can be outlined on a reminder card to be carried with the individual at all times and includes coping strategies such as leaving the area, engaging in an alternative activity, or asking for help from others in a crisis situation. An individual who has just lapsed should be encouraged to remain calm and not give in to feelings of guilt or self-blame for the incident. Such feelings are framed as a normal reaction to lapse, to avoid the escalation of the substance use. By renewing the commitment to the orig-

inal goal, making an immediate recovery plan, and reviewing the events leading up to the lapse, an individual is in a position to learn valuable information about his or her high-risk situations and potential areas for learning effective coping strategies.

Feelings of guilt and attributions of self-blame or uncontrollability for a lapse are characteristics of the abstinence violation effect (AVE) described earlier. This reaction, though normal, is likely to occur when one has previously made a strong commitment to a goal of abstinence and has experienced a slip or lapse. The magnitude of the reaction is related to several factors, including the strength of the prior commitment and the amount of time or effort invested in the goal. The stronger the magnitude of the AVE, the greater the likelihood of exacerbation following an initial lapse (Curry, Marlatt, & Gordon, 1987; Marlatt, 1985a).

Several strategies can assist a client who is struggling with the cognitive affective aftermath of a lapse. At the earliest opportunity, the lapse should be debriefed with the therapist through an in-depth exploration of the lapse situation. The lapse can be reframed as a mistake, a valuable learning opportunity rather than a failure experience. Attributions and cognitive distortions (such as catastrophizing) related to the lapse are assessed. If necessary, the therapist gently challenges these attributions and distortions. The lapse can be reattributed to the riskiness of the situation (rather than client self-attribution of blame), and to inadequate coping ability rather than to inadequate effort. Clients experiencing a lapse should be encouraged to renew their commitment and motivation to the target goal. These techniques increase the likelihood of successfully coming away from a lapse experience without risk of exacerbation to a relapse. In some cases, so much is learned from a lapse experience that the individual ends up ahead in overall improvement; this type of lapse can be viewed as a "prolapse."

Many times, the events leading up to a lapse are preventable. After a lapse, a therapist helps the client process the events leading up to and including the decision to use. A microanalysis of these events sometimes reveals "minidecisions" leading up to the lapse episode. These "minidecisions" are often discounted by the individual during the actual course of events leading up to a lapse. In a retrospective analysis of these decisions, however, a covert planning process leads to a "setup" for lapsing. These minidecisions, or *seemingly irrelevant decisions* (SIDs), set the stage for a lapse by placing the individual in a high-risk situation. An example would be the case of an alcoholic in abstinence-based treatment who "decides" to go to a bar "just to visit his old friends and watch TV," and ends up giving in to social pressure to drink. The lapse which results appears to be justified to both the individual and others, which serves to minimize the personal responsibility an individual will decide to accept responsibility for the lapse. To avoid this, RP therapists encourage clients to explore the earliest decisions leading off course to teach better decision making and recognition of some decisions as "red-flagged" choice points for relapse (Marlatt, 1985a).

Lifestyle Balance

Decisions which lead one to be dangerously close to the precipice of a lapse are more likely to occur when the one's lifestyle is unbalanced. A *balanced lifestyle* is one in which an individual's daily activities contain a sufficient pattern of enjoyable activities and coping resources to balance out the impact of daily and ongoing life stressors. When stressors outweigh one's coping resources, one may rely on and justify the addictive behavior as an attempt to restore some (temporary) sense of balance (e.g., "I deserve to get high after the day I've had"). To the extent that clients are unaware of other outlets for stress reduction, they are more likely to resume the addictive behavior.

Helping a client to achieve a balanced lifestyle is an important component of RP. A balanced lifestyle is one in which external demands and activities (the shoulds) do not outweigh the activities which bring self-fulfillment and pleasure (the wants) (Marlatt, 1985b). To determine the degree of lifestyle imbalance, several assessment techniques are available. The Life Experiences Survey (Sarason, Johnson, & Siegel, 1978) assesses major life events. In addition, an assessment of typical workday and weekend activities can be conducted with a client's rating of where along a "want-should" continuum an activity falls. The Daily Want-Should Tally Form (Marlatt, 1985b) is one format for such an assessment which also includes an assessment of daily satisfaction.

As an assessment of pleasurable daily events, clients can be asked about their leisure time activities. Many clients have cast recreational activities by the wayside as their substance-related activities increased. For others, recreational activities have become strongly associated with use of the problem substance. Activities such as physical exercise and meditation can help restore balance and have been associated with reductions of addictive behaviors (Murphy, Pagano, & Marlatt, 1986). These activities may decrease a client's perception of self-deprivation and need for self-indulgence.

ASSESSMENT PROCEDURES

Throughout the discussion of RP techniques, we have referred to various instruments that are utilized in treatment-related assessment. In this section, we will focus on initial assessment of the client. During the first session, an overview of the RP approach is provided by the therapist, and a history of the problem behavior is solicited. A detailed assessment of substance use and substance-related risk behaviors is conducted. Initial use and last period of use are obtained, including the typical quantity and frequency and pattern of use, the route of administration (oral, smoked, inhaled, or injected), the length of the typical run, and the largest amount of the substance taken in the recent past. Symptoms of physical dependence should also be assessed. If an individual is moderately to severely physically dependent on a substance, a monitored detoxification may be in order.

Information about past use of a substance also provides valuable information to guide treatment. A client is asked about the heaviest period of use, the quantity and frequency of use during that time, and the longest period of abstinence from each problem substance. A treatment history should also be obtained, including aspects of previous treatment the client found to be most and least useful. A detailed assessment of consequences and risk behaviors is also conducted. This assessment covers interpersonal, occupational and/or academic, legal, financial, and health-related risks and consequences and those related to the general psychological well-being of the client. An assessment of motivation and commitment to change and substance-related outcome expectancies is conducted, utilizing some of the techniques discussed previously (e.g., decision matrix, autobiography). Other psychiatric symptomatology is also assessed, as many individuals struggling with substance abuse are also comorbid for other psychiatric disorders. Treatment within the RP model may be tailored to the unique needs of dually diagnosed clients.

TYPICAL TREATMENT GOALS

According to the RP model, the client chooses whether to pursue a goal of abstinence or moderation. The therapist can offer guidance as this decision is made and recommend abstinence if the client's situation contraindicates any alcohol or substance use. Although an abstinence goal may be more appropriate for a particular client, if the client is unwilling to commit to abstinence but is willing to work toward moderation, then this decision should be honored by the therapist. From a harm reduction perspective (Marlatt, 1998; Marlatt & Tapert, 1993), reductions from abusive to moderated use of a substance are steps in a more healthful direction and should be reinforced by the therapist. The choice of treatment goal can be revisited during the course of therapy, since clients experiencing setbacks while pursuing a moderation goal may decide that abstinence might be more easily attained. It is interesting that in one treatment outcome study, about a quarter of the clients were found to be continuously abstinent for 12 months despite receiving treatment which was oriented toward drinking moderation (Miller, Leckman, Delaney, & Tinkcom, 1992).

THE ROLE, TRAINING, AND STANCE OF THE THERAPIST

Training in the RP model varies from reading clinical literature, to workshop attendance, to participation in certification programs. In addition to a solid background in mental health and in the physiological processes and biochemical effects of substance use, a strong foundation in behavioral theory and clinical supervision is recommended for those who wish to incorporate RP strategies into their clinical work.

Firm grounding in behavior theory and behavior therapy best enables a counselor or therapist to assist a client in evaluating emotional states and situations which are likely to lead to or maintain maladaptive

substance use, as well as positive and negative consequences associated with this use. Supervision from a colleague who is proficient with these strategies will be invaluable for therapists beginning to incorporate these techniques into their clinical repertoire.

As described previously, the therapist adopts a collegial stance with respect to the client. This is in contrast to a "top-down" doctor-patient relationship, in which a client is less likely to accept personal responsibility for treatment and expects treatment to be administered by the "expert" to a passive "patient." A collegial relationship allows both client and therapist to observe the change process from an objective perspective and allows both to analyze client data with some detachment.

COMMON OBSTACLES TO SUCCESSFUL TREATMENT

There are several obstacles to successful treatment. One of the most common is that a client who has lapsed may experience so much shame associated with the abstinence violation effect that he or she may not return for the next session. In this case, the therapist is encouraged to take an active role in pursuing the client in order to normalize the client's emotional reaction to the lapse and to assist the client in getting back on track toward the goal.

Other barriers to successful treatment include ambivalence and environmental stressors. Motivational ambivalence may be managed by a review of a client's original decision matrix, which serves as a reminder of the reasons for pursuing behavior change and increases motivation for change. Unforeseen environmental stressors leading to lapses may also threaten treatment success.

CHARACTERISTICS OF CLIENTS MOST LIKELY TO RESPOND TO THE MODEL

Controlled clinical trials of the RP model reviewed by Carroll (1996) have shown the relative effectiveness of RP over more insight-oriented or interpersonal forms of therapy for individuals who were greater in global psychopathology or sociopathy or who had a higher level of severity of substance use.

RP has not been shown to be contraindicated for any specific client group. However, as with other forms of therapy, individuals who have cognitive impairments may require adaptation of RP strategies to facilitate therapeutic change.

EMPIRICAL DATA ON THE EFFECTIVENESS OF THE RP MODEL

Evaluation of Marlatt's Relapse Taxonomy

An evaluation of the reliability and predictive validity of Marlatt's relapse taxonomy was conducted by the Relapse Replication and Extension Project (RREP; Allen et al., 1996). This project involved research teams at three sites and evaluated relapse precipitants utilizing both prospective and retrospective indices. The results of the RREP provided moderate support for the reliability of Marlatt's relapse category taxonomy (Longabaugh, Rubin, Stout, Zywiak, & Lowman, 1996). The taxonomy was most reliable for the classification of negative emotional states, testing personal control, negative physical states, and social pressure. Categories which were less reliably classified included interpersonal conflict, both intraindividual and interpersonal enhancement of positive emotional states, and urges and temptations. The relapse taxonomy provided limited predictive validity when utilized to predict first episode of heavy drinking (drinking to a blood alcohol level of 0.10 ml/dl) from clients' retrospective reports of pretreatment relapse episodes (Stout, Longabaugh, & Rubin, 1996). This is not surprising if relapse is to be viewed not as a static but as a dynamic process (Marlatt, 1994). In general, the research literature is useful for the identification of distal determinants of relapse which the skillful clinician should bear in mind.

Evaluation of the RP Model

Carroll conducted a review of controlled clinical trials of Marlatt and Gordon's (1985) RP Model (Carroll, 1996). Only studies were reviewed which reported substance use as a primary outcome variable and which specifically evaluated the effectiveness of RP as either the primary form or a component of substance abuse treatment relative to no treatment, minimal treatment, or alternative treatments.

Twenty-four studies were reviewed which met these criteria. Of these, 12 were based on smoking cessation, 6 on treatment for alcohol problems, 1 on marijuana, 3 on cocaine, and 2 on treatment for other substances.

When compared to no-treatment control groups, RP-based treatments fared positively at both posttreatment and follow-up periods of up to 1 year. Relative to minimal treatment controls (including attention controls and standard treatment), only half of the RP treatments were shown to be significantly more effective in the immediate posttreatment period. However, for studies which included longer research follow-up evaluations, RP generally fared more positively, as evidenced by such outcomes as lower relapse rates and continued improvement over time relative to minimal treatment controls. This "delayed emergent effect" (Carroll, 1996) is consistent with learning theory upon which RP strategies are based, where improvement may reflect acquisition of and greater facility with coping skills over time. RP was comparable to alternative psychotherapies (e.g., interpersonal psychotherapy and a 12-step recovery support group) at both posttreatment and follow-up (Carroll, 1996). However, interaction effects favoring RP for more severely impaired clientele were observed. Participants who had greater psychopathology, sociopathy, or severity of substance use tended to fare better when treated with RP. There were no differential treatment effects for those lower in impairment in these domains.

Thus, the literature demonstrates treatment effectiveness of RP when compared to no treatment, similar short-term but greater long-term improvement when compared to minimal treatments indicating an emergent treatment effect, and comparable effectiveness to alternative therapies for those at a lower level of impairment. More severely impaired substance abusers may differentially benefit from RP over alternative therapeutic approaches.

A recent controlled clinical trial evaluated the effectiveness of RP compared with discussion-only and no-additional-treatment control groups for a sample of 60 severely alcohol dependent men (Allsop, Saunders, Phillips, & Carr, 1997). Those receiving the RP treatment had greater increases in pre- and posttreatment self-efficacy relative to the discussion-only control group. Those receiving RP also had a significantly higher probability of total abstinence and a longer survival time to initial lapse than both control groups. These effects were significant at 6 months posttreatment, but the effects diminished by 12 months posttreatment.

Strengths and Weaknesses of the RP Model for Treatment of Substance Abuse

A great strength of the RP model is its intuitive appeal to therapists and clients. The model has been widely adopted by practictioners working with substance abusers, and adaptations have been made to this model for different clinical problems. As the substance abuse treatment field is continuously evolving, controlled clinical trials may lead to refinement of the model and greater emphasis on one or more components for successful treatment outcome.

SUMMARY

The RP model and approach was developed in response to the high rate of resumed substance use among treated individuals (Marlatt & Gordon, 1985). The model has its roots in social learning theory and draws upon cognitive and behavioral treatment approaches. In this model, substance misuse is understood as resulting from maladaptive learning rather than to a disease process. Treatment strategies developed within this framework, therefore, focus on the unlearning of maladaptive substance use patterns and the learning of new and adaptive coping patterns.

RP has two main goals: the prevention of initial use following treatment (or the prevention of goal transgressions in the case of a moderation goal) and the successful management of lapse and relapse episodes so that harm is minimized if and when these occur. Preventing initial use involves the identification of situations which present a high risk for resumed use and the teaching of effective coping strategies to successfully manage such situations. Strategies for lifestyle balance are also viewed as key components in reducing the likelihood of resumed use. In the event of a lapse or relapse, an RP therapist can help a client to identify situational challenges and skill deficits that may be addressed through treatment so that future lapses are less likely.

Despite few well-controlled studies evaluating its effectiveness, the RP approach has been widely adopt-ed by treatment providers, perhaps due to its intuitive appeal. More research is needed to further refine the RP model and its clinical applications.

Key References

Dimeff, L. A., & Marlatt, G. A. (1995). Relapse prevention. In R. K. Hester & W. R. Miller (Eds.), *Handbook of alcoholism treatment approaches: Effective alternatives* (2nd ed., pp. 176–194). Boston: Allyn & Bacon.

Marlatt, G. A., & Gordon, J. R. (Eds.). (1985). *Relapse prevention: Maintenance strategies in the treatment of addictive behaviors.* New York: Guilford Press.

Wilson, P. H. (Ed.). (1992). *Principles and practice of relapse prevention.* New York: Guilford Press.

References

Allsop, S., Saunders, B., Phillips, M., & Carr, A. (1997). A trial of relapse prevention with severely dependent male problem drinkers. *Addiction, 92,* 61–73.

Andrews, G. (1992). Stuttering. In P. H. Wilson (Ed.), *Principles and practice of relapse prevention* (pp. 349–365). New York: Guilford Press.

Annis, H. M. (1982). *Inventory of drinking situations.* Toronto: Addiction Research Foundation.

Annis, H. M., & Graham, J. M. (1988). *Situational Confidence Questionnaire (SCQ-39): User's guide.* Toronto: Addiction Research Foundation.

Azar, S. T., Ferguson, E. S., & Twentyman, C. T. (1992). Social competence: Interventions with children and parents. In P. H. Wilson (Ed.), *Principles and practice of relapse prevention* (pp. 322–348). New York: Guilford Press.

Bandura, A. (1977). Self-efficacy: Toward a unifying theory of behavior change. *Psychological Review, 84,* 191–215.

Brickman, P., Rabinowitz, V. C., Karuza, J. Coates, D., Cohn, E., & Kidder, L. (1982). Models of helping and coping. *American Psychologist, 37,* 368–384.

Brown, S. A., Christiansen, B. A., & Goldman, M. S. (1987). The Alcohol Expectancy Questionnaire: An instrument for the assessment of adolescent and adult expectancies. *Journal of Studies on Alcohol, 48,* 483–491.

Brown, T. A., & Barlow, D. H. (1992). Panic disorder and panic disorder with agoraphobia. In P. H. Wilson (Ed.), *Principles and practice of relapse prevention* (pp. 191–212). New York: Guilford Press.

Carroll, K. M. (1996). Relapse prevention as a psychosocial treatment: A review of controlled clinical trials. *Experimental and Clinical Psychopharmacology, 4,* 46–54.

Cummings, C., Gordon, J., & Marlatt, G. A. (1980). Relapse: Strategies of prevention and prediction. In W. R. Miller (Ed.), *The addictive behaviors.* Oxford, UK: Pergamon Press.

Curry, S., Marlatt, G. A., & Gordon, J. R. (1987). Abstinence violation effect: Validation of an attributional construct with smoking cessation. *Journal of Consulting and Clinical Psychology, 55,* 145–149.

Dimeff, L. A., & Marlatt, G. A. (1995). Relapse prevention. In R. K. Hester & W. R. Miller (Eds.), *Handbook of alcoholism treatment approaches: Effective alternatives* (2nd ed., pp. 176–194). Boston: Allyn & Bacon.

Emmelkamp, P. M. G., Kloek, J., & Blaauw, E. (1992). Obsessive-compulsive disorder. In P. H. Wilson (Ed.), *Principles and practice of relapse prevention* (pp. 214–234). New York: Guilford Press.

Festinger, L. (1964). *Conflict, decision and dissonance.* Stanford, CA: Stanford University Press.

Fremouw, W., & Damer, D. (1992). Obesity. In P. H. Wilson (Ed.), *Principles and practice of relapse prevention* (pp. 69–84). New York: Guilford Press.

Fromme, K., Stroot, E. A., & Kaplan, D. (1993). Comprehensive effects of alcohol: Development and psychometric assessment of a new expectancy questionnaire. *Psychological Assessment, 5,* 19–26.

George, W. H., Frone, M. R., Cooper, M. L., Russell, M., Skinner, J. B., & Windle, M. A. (1995). A revised alcohol expectancy questionnaire: Factor structure and confirmation and invariance in a general population sample. *Journal of Studies on Alcohol, 56,* 177–185.

Hunt, W. A., Barnett, L. W., & Branch, L. G. (1971). Relapse rates in addiction programs. *Journal of Clinical Psychology, 27,* 455–456.

Kavanagh, D. J. (1992). Schizophrenia. In P. H. Wilson (Ed.), *Principles and practice of relapse prevention* (pp. 157–190). New York: Guilford Press.

Lang, A. R., & Marlatt, G. A. (1982). Problem drinking: A social learning perspective. In R. J. Gatchel, A. Baum, & J. E. Singer (Eds.), *Handbook of psychology and health: Vol. 1. Clinical psychology and behavioral medicine: Overlapping disciplines* (pp. 121–169). Hillsdale, NJ: Erlbaum.

Leigh, B. C. (1987). Beliefs about the effects of alcohol and self and others. *Journal of Studies on Alcohol, 48,* 467–475.

Leigh, B. C. (1989). Confirmatory factor analysis of alcohol expectancy scales. *Journal of Studies on Alcohol, 50,* 268–277.

Longabaugh, R., Rubin, A., Stout, R. L., Zywiak, W. H., & Lowman, C. (1996). The reliability of Marlatt's taxonomy for classifying relapses. *Addiction, 91*(Suppl.), S73–S78.

Lowman, C., Allen, J., Stout, R. L., & the Relapse Research Group. (1996). Replication and extension of Marlatt's taxonomy of relapse precipitants: Overview of procedures and results. *Addiction, 91* (Suppl.), S51–S71.

Mackay, P. W., Donovan, D. M., & Marlatt, G. A. (1991). Cognitive and behavioral approaches to alcohol abuse. In R. J. Frances & S. I. Miller (Eds.), *Clinical textbook of addictive disorders: The Guilford substance abuse series.* (pp. 452–481). New York: Guilford Press.

Marlatt, G. A. (1985a). Cognitive assessment and intervention procedures for relapse prevention. In G. A. Marlatt & J. R. Gordon (Eds.), *Relapse prevention: Maintenance strategies in the treatment of addictive behaviors* (pp. 201–279). New York: Guilford Press.

Marlatt, G. A. (1985b). Lifestyle modification. In G. A. Marlatt & J. R. Gordon (Eds.), *Relapse prevention: Maintenance strategies in the treatment of addictive behaviors* (pp. 280–348). New York: Guilford Press.

Marlatt, G. A. (1994). Addiction, mindfulness, and acceptance. In S. C. Hayes, N. S. Jacobson, V. M. Follette, & M. J. Dougher (Eds.), *Acceptance and change: Content and context in psychotherapy* (pp. 175–197). Reno, NV: Context Press.

Marlatt, G. A. (1996b). Lest taxonomy become taxidermy: A comment on the relapse replication and extension project. *Addiction, 91*(Suppl.), S147–S153.

Marlatt, G. A. (Ed.). (1998). *Harm reduction: Pragmatic strategies for managing high-risk behaviors.* New York: Guilford Press.

Marlatt, G. A., Baer, J. S., Kivlahan, D. R., Dimeff, L. A., Larimer, M. E., Quigley, L. A., Somers, J. M., & Williams, E. (1998). Screening and brief intervention for high-risk college student drinkers: Results from a two-year follow-up assessment. *Journal of Consulting and Clinical Psychology, 66,* 604–615.

Marlatt, G. A., Baer, J. S., & Quigley, L. A. (1995). Self-efficacy and addictive behavior. In A. Bandura (Ed.), *Self-efficacy in changing societies* (pp. 289–315). New York: Cambridge University Press.

Marlatt, G. A., & Fromme, K. (1987). Metaphors for addiction. *Journal of Drug Issues, 17,* 9–28.

Marlatt, G. A., & Gordon, J. R. (1980). Determinants of relapse: Implications for the maintenance of behavior change. In P. O. Davidson & S. M. Davidson (Eds.), *Behavioral medicine: Changing health lifestyle* (pp. 410–452). New York: Brunner/Mazel.

Marlatt, G. A., & Gordon, J. R. (Eds.). (1985). *Relapse prevention: Maintenance strategies in the treatment of addictive behaviors.* New York: Guilford Press.

Marlatt, G. A., & Tapert, S. F. (1993). Harm reduction: Reducing the risks of addictive behaviors. In J. S. Baer, G. A. Marlatt, & R. McMahan (Eds.), *Addic-*

tive behaviors across the lifespan (pp. 243–273). Newbury Park, CA: Sage.

Marshall, W. L., Hudson, S. M., & Ward, T. (1992). Sexual deviance. In P. H. Wilson (Ed.), *Principles and practice of relapse prevention* (pp. 235–254). New York: Guilford Press.

McCrady, B. S. (1993). Relapse prevention: A couples-therapy perspective. In T. J. O'Farrell (Ed.), *Treating alcohol problems: Marital and family interventions* (pp. 327–350). New York: Guilford Press.

Miller, W. R. (1996). What is relapse? Fifty ways to leave the wagon. *Addiction, 91*(Suppl.), S15–S27.

Miller, W. R., Leckman, A. L., Delaney, H. D., & Tinkcom, M. (1992). Long-term follow-up of behavioral self-control training. *Journal of Studies on Alcohol, 53,* 249–261.

Miller, W. R., & Rollnick, S. (1991). *Motivational interviewing: Preparing people for change in addictive behaviors.* New York: Guilford Press.

Miller, W. R. Westerberg, V. S., Harris, R. J., & Tonigan, J. S. (1996). What predicts relapse? Prospective testing of antecedent models. *Addiction, 91*(Suppl.), S155–S171.

Murphy, T. J., Pagano, R. R., & Marlatt, G. A. (1986). Lifestyle modification with heavy alcohol drinkers: Effects of aerobic exercise and meditation. *Addictive Behaviors, 11,* 175–186.

Nicholas, M. K. (1992). Chronic pain. In P. H. Wilson (Ed.), *Principles and practice of relapse prevention* (pp. 255–289). New York: Guilford Press.

O'Farrell, T. J. (1993). Couples relapse prevention sessions after a behavioral marital therapy couples group program. In T. J. O'Farrell (Ed.), *Treating alcohol problems: Marital and family interventions* (pp. 305–326). New York: Guilford Press.

Orimoto, L., & Vitousek, K. B., (1992). Anorexia nervosa and bulimia nervosa. In P. H. Wilson (Ed.), *Principles and practice of relapse prevention* (pp. 85–127). New York: Guilford Press.

Rankin, H. (1989). Relapse and eating disorders: The recurring illusion. In M. Gossop (Ed.), *Relapse and addictive behavior* (pp. 86–95). New York: Tavistock/ Routledge

Rohsenow, D. J. (1983). Drinking habits and expectancies about alcohol's effects for self versus others. *Journal of Consulting and Clinical Psychology, 51,* 752–756.

Sarason, I. G., Johnson, J. H., & Siegel, J. M. (1978). Assessing the impact of life changes: Development of the Life Experiences Scale. *Journal of Consulting and Clinical Psychology, 46,* 932–946.

Schoenfeld, L., Peters, R., & Dolente, A. (1993). *Substance Abuse Relapse Assessment: Professional manual.* Odessa, FL: Psychological Assessment Resources.

Stout, R. L., Longabaugh, R., & Rubin, A. (1996). Predictive validity of Marlatt's relapse taxonomy versus a more general relapse code. *Addiction, 91*(Suppl.), S99–S110.

Truax, P., & Jacobson, N. (1992). Marital distress. In P. H. Wilson (Ed.), *Principles and practice of relapse prevention* (pp. 290–321). New York: Guilford Press.

Wilson, P. H. (1992). Depression. In P. H. Wilson (Ed.), *Principles and practice of relapse prevention* (pp. 128–156). New York: Guilford Press.

21

Treatment of Drug and Alcohol Abuse: An Overview of Major Strategies and Effectiveness

John P. Allen

Raye Z. Litten

The chapters in this section of the text describe several approaches to the treatment of substance abuse problems. While these strategies differ significantly from each other, nevertheless, each has demonstrated efficacy. In this overview chapter we will briefly summarize key information from the chapters. With the exception of the section dealing with medications, references will not be provided here since the citations are given in full in the underlying text chapters.

THE DISEASE MODEL STRATEGY

Of the approaches presented, the oldest is the disease model. It conceptualizes alcohol and drug dependence as chronic physical illnesses. Dependence is viewed not as symptomatic of another psychiatric condition but as a primary problem with biological, emotional, and spiritual underpinnings and presenting features. This theorization of substance dependence is largely congruent with tenets of Alcoholics Anonymous (AA) itself, other AA-based peer support groups, and the so-called Minnesota model.

A key aspect of the disease model is the notion that dependence is progressive. Based on retrospective accounts of AA members, Jellinek, an early alcoholism researcher, identified four stages in its development. In the symptomatic phase, there is an increase in tolerance and drinking to relieve tension. The prodromal phase is characterized by drinking with greater frequency and quantity. "Blackouts" are the hallmark feature of the prodromal stage. The crucial phase is marked by loss of control and recurrent efforts both to limit drinking and to rationalize it when it occurs. At this point, the alcoholic's lifestyle centers on alcohol consumption. The chronic phase includes prolonged periods of intoxication, deterioration in behavioral and ethical functioning, and substantial physical and cognitive loss.

A key feature of the disease model, and one which distinguishes it from more contemporary approaches, is its emphasis on "denial." The alcoholic is believed to have an elaborate system of personality defenses against acknowledgment of the severity and consequences of drinking. Denial of the problem makes self-motivated change difficult. A major goal of treatment, therefore, is to reduce denial and resistance to change.

Because dependence is viewed as such a pervasive phenomenon, treatment must be comprehensive and directed toward fundamental change in biological, interpersonal, emotional, and spiritual functioning. In fact, a multidisciplinary team is needed since major change must occur in very different spheres of life functioning. In addition to ensuring the safety of the withdrawal process, physicians and nurses address physical pathology that may have been prompted by or ignored during the period of heavy drinking. Comprehensive psychological assessment identifies patient traits and characteristics relevant to response to treatment. Since spirituality is posited as an important feature of the disease, chaplains also play a salient role in treatment. They assist the patient in examining value systems, coping with guilt, and dealing with loss. Finally, counselors, often recovering people themselves, play a key role in treatment planning in treatment.

While there has been little research on efficacy of treatments based on the disease model, it is very likely the most common approach assumed by treatment facilities in the United States. There appear to be several reasons. The approach is quite comprehensive and has inherent appeal to recovering alcoholics and staff with medical backgrounds who conceptualize behavioral phenomena in disease constructs. The model is older than most others. Also, the disease model has incorporated many of the treatment techniques developed by newer, learning-theory-based strategies. Unfortunately, this approach tends to be quite labor-intensive and costly. Research on its efficacy is clearly warranted.

PEER SUPPORT GROUPS

AA is the largest and most widely known self-help group for treating persons with alcohol or, for that matter, other behavioral problems. Approximately 3% of the adult population of the United States has at some time attended an AA meeting, and half of these have attended during the past year. Narcotics Anonymous (NA) was established to parallel AA in

philosophy and content and to assist individuals suffering drug problems. A number of other 12-step programs have also arisen that focus on the unique needs of particular kinds of clients, such as those sharing common religious or philosophical beliefs. So, too, a variety of types of family member support groups have developed, often incorporating a philosophy similar to that of AA. Finally, the 12-step philosophy has inspired other types of programs dealing with nonsubstance abuse but addictionlike problems. While AA, NA, and several related programs are spiritual in nature, "secular" self-help programs also exist. These include Women for Sobriety, Secular Organizations for Sobriety, S.M.A.R.T. Recovery, and Rational Recovery.

Nowinski's chapter discusses how therapists can integrate peer support groups into formal treatment. This seems to be a rather original topic in the literature since at least in some instances in the past, relations between professionals and peer support groups have been characterized by distrust. To actively facilitate client participation in a self-help group requires that the therapist have a solid grasp of the philosophy, goals, and nature of the self-help program and expend time and effort guiding the client toward involvement in it. In particular, consistency across the client's, therapist's, and group's views on abstinence versus moderation as the goal of treatment is important. Often, the self-help group and the therapist espouse total abstinence. If the client feels that moderation is an appropriate goal, the therapist might review previous attempts at moderation and evaluate how successful they have been.

The therapist should also be aware of the "steps," or sequential tasks, of the self-help program. Using AA as his primary example, Nowinski reviews the first three steps and discusses in some detail how the therapist can reinforce progress in achieving them.

While he recommends that the therapist facilitate the client's involvement in the first three steps of AA, Nowinski suggests that the sponsor, a more experienced AA member chosen by the client to serve as his or her personal AA resource and experiential mentor, assist in achieving the other nine steps.

The therapist can also perform a variety of activities to encourage the client to "bond" with the self-help group. These include fostering involvement by reducing worries or shame over participation and by describing in advance the format of sessions or, in the case of AA, explaining the different types of sessions, such as speaker meetings, step meetings, and discussion meetings. The therapist can also reduce anxiety by strategies such as encouragement, practical suggestions, and role play of basic participation skills surrounding meeting activities, such as how to introduce oneself. Helping the patient become integrated with the self-help group may also take the form of helping him or her to identify with other participants and begin networking with them outside sessions. These strategies should facilitate establishment of a positive peer group, aid the patient in selecting and working with a sponsor, and reinforce acceptance of various group customs and traditions of the group.

In particular, AA has proved quite popular in the United States, and results from Project MATCH suggest that attendance at AA, and more especially personal involvement in the program, is associated with more favorable treatment outcome, regardless of the formal treatment to which the patient was assigned. Nevertheless, a causal link between AA and favorable treatment outcome has yet to be established. One would also hope that alternative peer support groups would propagate to assist recovering alcoholics who do not readily affiliate with AA or ascribe to its tenets.

ENHANCING TREATMENT MOTIVATION

One of the strongest predictors of days of abstinence and reduction of level of alcohol consumption on days when Project MATCH outpatients did drink was motivation, and indeed, substance abuse treatment counselors seem to ascribe success of patients in treatment to motivational factors. In their chapter, Yahne and Miller discuss several procedures for assessing motivation, suggest strategies for enhancing motivation, and allude to its role in brief intervention for alcohol problems.

Four procedures for evaluating motivation are described. The "decisional balance" approach involves asking patients to list the advantages (benefits) of substance abuse for them in one column on a piece of paper and the disadvantages (costs) in an adjoining column. The authors note that this exercise may itself influence motivational factors and serve as a basis for direct discussion with the patient.

Second, a standardized instrument, such as the University of Rhode Island Change Assessment (URICA), may be used. Subscale scores on the URICA help the counselor determine patients'

"readiness" to change by assessing their standing in five putative stages in the change process. The stages range from precontemplation, in which the patient is unconcerned about the problem, through stages dealing with active consideration of the problem and needs for action to resolve it, concrete corrective actions, and sustenance of efforts to keep the problem at bay.

A third technique for assessing motivation is the psychometric instrument Stages of Change Readiness and Treatment Eagerness Scale (SOCRATES), the content of which differs from that of URICA by being specific to substance abuse. It assesses three motivational vectors: recognition of the problem, ambivalence, and taking steps toward change.

Rollnick and his colleagues have also developed a "Readiness Ruler," a visual-analogue, continuous scale that allows patients to indicate on a line their degree of motivation from 1 (not ready to change) to 10 (trying to change).

One of the most encouraging developments in treatment of alcoholism has been recognition that even fairly brief interventions varying, from as short as 5 minutes to four sessions, can result in substantial change for at least "at-risk," early-stage problem drinkers. Granted the low cost of brief intervention, its effectiveness, and the high prevalence of alcohol abuse as a public health problem, greater attention should be given to incorporating brief intervention into general medical practice.

Miller and his colleagues have argued that there are six elements which underlie the effectiveness of these interventions and even apparently of more extended treatments.

The chapter concludes by offering additional recommendations for the therapeutic style that a counselor should adopt in interviewing patients. These include expressing empathy and listening in a reflective, nonjudgmental way; helping the patient become more aware of the discrepancy between addictive behavior and personal goals and values; avoidance of argumentation; encouraging adoption of new perspectives; and reinforcing the patient's belief that he or she is capable of changing.

BEHAVIORAL AND COGNITIVE BEHAVIORAL TREATMENTS

Strategies for effecting behavioral change based on learning theory are employed for treating a host of psychological problems including substance abuse. Fundamental learning principles allow for initiation and regulation not only of overt behaviors, such as taking illicit drugs or drinking excessively, but also of covert behaviors such as the urge to drink and cognitive expectancies that use of alcohol and drugs will lead to positive consequences such as pleasure, relief of tension, enhanced mood, and so on.

Specific interventions derive from various behavioral theories, most notably classical conditioning, operant conditioning, modeling, and social learning theory. Cue exposure, for example, is an extension of classical conditioning since it instantiates an extinction paradigm in which the patient is presented with conditioned stimuli of substance use without pairing to unconditioned stimuli. In time, the conditioned response of craving and its biological correlates diminishes. To the extent that craving may lead to actual use of the substance, its diminution should assist in maintaining abstinence.

A variety of contingency management approaches have been employed in treatment of drug and alcohol abuse. These strategies involve providing positive reinforcers for nonuse or punishments for use. Imitation and practice of drink refusal skills represent an application of Bandura's theory of behavioral modeling.

More recent approaches include helping the patient to manage moods or change cognitions that might lead to substance abuse.

In her chapter, Carroll also emphasizes the key role of functional analysis in developing a treatment plan. The therapist must understand the full topography of the problem before developing a strategy to remediate it. This includes identification of the stimuli for, conditions for, and consequences of use, as well as features of the patient's social, emotional, cognitive, and physical environment that bear on use.

Beyond clinical interview, several standardized instruments may assist in the functional analysis. These include the Time-Line Follow Back, Drinker Inventory of Consequences, Cocaine Craving Questionnaire, and Cocaine Relapse Interview.

In addition to determining the pattern of abuse and the stimuli that elicit and reinforce it, it is extremely important that the therapist delineate the patient's deficits and assets in skills to cope with these stimuli. Finally, assessment includes determination of the patient's current motivation to change. The

URICA and the SOCRATES are recommended for this.

Several features characterize behavioral and cognitive behavioral therapies. In that patients may be "at-risk" drinkers rather than physically dependent on alcohol, moderation may be the goal of treatment. Nevertheless, with illicit drugs, abstinence is more commonly the measure of success. The goals of this family of interventions tend to be quite specific and may include attendance at treatment sessions, completion of extratherapy assignments, or reduced use.

Unlike disease model approaches, behavioral interventions are generally brief and targeted. Treatment is typically conducted in weekly outpatient sessions. The first third of the hour therapy session reviews recent substance use and overall functioning. The second third is typically didactic and includes skills training and practice. The final third is devoted to planning for the week ahead and discussing how the new skills will be implemented.

Carroll then describes several major learning-based types of treatment and discusses the nature of their active components (i.e., the specific factors which elicit desired positive change). She concludes her chapter by presenting results of several controlled clinical trials of treatment efficacy.

FAMILY MODELS OF TREATMENT

For the most part, O'Farrell and Fals-Stewart organize their presentation on family treatments for substance abuse around three major models.

The "family disease model" views substance abuse as an illness suffered by family members as well as by the index case. In its philosophy of substance abuse, Al-Anon typifies the family disease model. *Codependence* is a major construct of this view. Codependence is believed to parallel substance dependence as a disease and refers to family reactions to substance abuse. These may include control issues, external referencing, fear, and emotional blunting. Codependence often includes "enabling," the constellation of behaviors by significant others that, often unwillingly, reinforce abuse. Enabling involves shielding the client from the natural negative consequences of substance abuse that might have deterred it in the future.

Under the family disease model, treatment of family members is generally conducted separately from that of the index patient. The emphasis is on helping them resolve their own problems rather than on actively intervening with the abuser.

The "family systems model" assumes a reciprocal relationship between the family's functioning and the substance abuse. Substance abuse may distract family members from directly confronting other problems such as marital discord on leaving home. Curiously, interactional behaviors, such as emotional expression, may actually improve during periods of heavy drinking.

Therapy entails treating the family as a unit rather than focusing on the individual with the abuse problem. Therapy is designed to redefine roles and personal boundaries as well as to identify the interplay between substance abuse and family functioning.

"Behavioral models" are the most heavily researched of the treatments discussed in the chapter. Such approaches incorporate constructs of learning theory. Family interactions are believed to provide positive and negative reinforcers for substance abuse. In some instances, positive interactions may actually reinforce abuse. McCrady notes, for example, that caretaking or attention may reinforce drinking behaviors.

Behavioral marital therapy emphasizes setting goals related to drinking and modeling more effective ways of responding to drinking or modifying the stimuli that may prompt drinking. It also includes training in new ways of interacting and communicating with each other.

Therapy is usually conducted on an outpatient basis in a series of weekly sessions. Assessment procedures precede formal intervention. Initially, a determination is made about whether the patient requires detoxification. This is done primarily by evaluating recent quantity and frequency of alcohol consumption and degree of physical dependence. The Time-Line Follow Back, breath analysis, and drug urine screening may assist in assessing recent use patterns. The Drinker Inventory of Consequences and Addiction Severity Index may aid in determining severity of adverse effects of substance abuse. Earlier attempts at treatment are also reviewed, as well as the extent to which the patient and his or her family are motivated for achieving goals of moderation or abstinence.

Quality and stability of family relationship are evaluated by use of a large battery of psychometric instruments identified by the authors.

Feedback on results of the assessment procedures enhances treatment motivation and allows for development of treatment goals.

Several major strategies of marital family therapy are described. Particular attention is given to behavioral contracting. Contracts are written and focus on specific behaviors. Commonly employed are the "sobriety trust contract," involving a daily affirmation by the patient of the intention to not use alcohol or drugs that day, as well as including an opportunity to resolve family members' concerns over efforts to refrain from use. The contract also provides that this will be the only time during which substance abuse will be discussed.

Disulfiram contracts involve the patient's agreement to take the medication daily in the presence of a family member. Other behavioral contracts may focus on participation in peer support recovery groups as well as submission to drug urine screens.

A variety of interventions to improve marital and family relationships are described. Patients who may be expected to be ideal candidates for marital family therapy seem to be better educated, employed, cohabiting, older, and more seriously involved with substance abuse. A stable, nonviolent, nonabusing home environment is also believed to have positive prognostic significance. Patients who are more motivated to change, often following a recent crisis, are also likely to do better.

THERAPEUTIC COMMUNITY TREATMENT

A very different approach to treatment of substance abuse, especially drug abuse, is the therapeutic community. These programs are drug-free and incorporate a social psychological strategy for achieving behavior change. While traditionally therapeutic communities were stand-alone residential programs lasting perhaps up to 2 years, because of funding realities and variations in the clients now served, their application has now extended to a variety of other settings, including outpatient and day treatment centers. Many of these modified therapeutic communities are characterized by shorter lengths of stay.

A distinguishing feature of this type of intervention is that the change agent is seen as the community itself rather than a specific person. The social environment, as well as peer and staff role models, is seen as the active component of behavior change. All activities in the therapeutic community are purposively designed to produce change, and all participants in the program are mediators of change.

The therapeutic community model envisions substance abuse as a disorder of the whole person rather than as simply a dysfunctional habit. While differing in peripheral ways such as demographics, all substance-dependent patients are believed to reveal an arrested state of personal identity not unlike that of adolescents.

Recovery and maintenance of abstinence are seen as a developmental process to achieve attitudes and values of "right living," truth, adherence to the work ethic, accountability, responsibility, self-reliance, and so on.

Recovery proceeds through a series of stages of incremental learning, with each stage building on the previous one and advancing the client to the goal of recovery. Patient motivation is important, as are self-help and mutual help. Proponents of the model believe that negative behavioral and attitudinal roles are best modified by participating in the therapeutic community as a socially responsible participant.

Assessment is comprehensive in that it considers objective behavioral dimensions as well as self-perceptions. Rather than relying on psychometric measures, assessment is done primarily by peers and staff on a daily basis and in a variety of settings.

Physical features of the therapeutic community are seen as important aids to the change process and establishment of a sense of commonality with other members. The programs are housed separately from other institutional programs and are given names. Tenets of program philosophy are posted on wall display signs. Daily schedules and member status information are also displayed on cork boards or blackboards.

While the staff includes traditional professionals (such as physicians and mental health providers), all staff function as members of the community who serve to facilitate and guide the self-help community methods.

The program is highly structured and includes strong components of work (e.g., facility maintenance and program management) and education. Confrontive encounter groups are designed to heighten individual awareness of attitudes or behaviors that should be modified.

De Leon notes that a majority of admissions fail to complete the full course of treatment. He offers several possible reasons. Some involve client characteristics like low tolerance for structure and inadequate motivation. Others involve external factors like familial pressures, staff inadequacies, and funding limitations.

While these communities maintain a generally "open-door" policy for admission, patients who seem unable to meet the demands of the intensive regimen or who would appear to pose a risk to other participants are generally excluded.

MEDICATIONS

Over the past decade, research activity on medications development for alcoholism and drug treatment has burgeoned. The fruits of this effort have been particularly recognized by the Food and Drug Administration (FDA) approval of several pharmacological agents for alcohol, opiate, and nicotine dependence.

The two most promising agents for treating alcohol dependence are naltrexone and acamprosate. Each has now been approved in over 15 countries.

Naltrexone, an opioid antagonist, was first approved for alcoholism treatment in the United States in December 1994. This approval was based on results of two clinical trials (O'Malley et al., 1992; Volpicelli, Alterman, Hayashida, & O'Brien, 1992). These 3-month studies demonstrated that naltrexone treatment leads to reduction in both frequency and amount of drinking by alcoholics. Interestingly, the type of psychosocial intervention which it accompanies seems to influence treatment outcome from naltrexone. O'Malley et al. (1992) found that alcoholics treated with naltrexone and weekly supportive therapy emphasizing abstinence enjoyed a high rate of abstinence, while naltrexone-treated patients receiving weekly coping-skills/relapse-prevention therapy achieved lower rates of relapse to heavy drinking if they did sample alcohol.

O'Malley et al. (1996) followed the patients after naltrexone treatment ceased. Some residual effect of naltrexone was evident for an additional 4 months. At the end of the 6-month follow-up period, patients treated with naltrexone were found less likely to meet the criteria for alcohol dependence or abuse than placebo-treated patients.

Two studies indicate that patient compliance is essential for naltrexone to be efficacious. Volpicelli et al. (1997) replicated their earlier naltrexone project while employing a more diverse population of alcoholics and utilizing a less intense psychosocial intervention. In contrast to results of their earlier study, across the board, naltrexone produced only modest effects in reducing alcohol consumption. However, among compliant patients (i.e., those who took the medication at least 90% of the time), it proved far more effective than placebo, reducing the number of days drinking (3% versus 11%) and preventing relapse to heavy drinking (14% versus 52%).

Similarly, Chick et al. (1992; Litten & Fertig, 1996) found that while, in general, 3 months of naltrexone treatment failed to yield significant difference from placebo, naltrexone compliance (based on correct pill count on at least 80% of patient return visits) was associated with benefits in both frequency and level of drinking.

Acamprosate has also demonstrated effectiveness in treating alcoholism. Lipha Pharmaceuticals conducted 11 independent trials, employing over 3,000 alcohol-dependent patients. Analyses of the pooled data indicated that patients treated with it were twice as likely to remain abstinent than those treated with placebo (Mann, Chabac, Lehert, Potgieter, & Henning, 1995). Results of several of these independent trials have now been published. These include multisite, 6- to 12-month trials in France (Paille et al., 1995), in Germany (Sass, Soyka, Mann, & Zieglgansberger, 1996), in Austria (Whitworth et al., 1996), and in the Netherlands, Belgium, and Luxembourg (Geerlings, Ansoms, & van den Brink, 1997). All of the studies showed an increase in complete abstinence for acamprosate-treated subjects.

Acamprosate is well tolerated, the most common side effect being diarrhea. The mechanism underlying its action remains unknown, although recent research indicates it blocks the glutamate receptor (Spanagel & Zieglgansberger, 1997).

Although disulfiram has been available for 50 years, surprisingly few well-designed studies have been conducted. The most rigorous study was performed by Fuller et al. (1986). This was a nine-site VA trial that included 605 alcohol-dependent patients. Although neither abstinence rate nor time to first drink distinguished the disulfiram and placebo groups, disulfiram patients who did sample alcohol drank on fewer days.

A variety of studies have suggested that good compliance improves disulfiram's contribution to treatment outcome (Allen & Litten, 1992). For example, Chick et al. (1992) found that when disulfiram intake was observed, patients assigned to the drug experienced fewer days drinking and consumed less alcohol than did those on placebo.

Perhaps most intriguing, preliminary studies have indicated that patients with concurrent cocaine and alcohol problems reduced both their alcohol and cocaine intake as a function of disulfiram treatment (Carroll et al., 1993; Higgins, Budney, Bickel, Hughes, & Foerg, 1993).

Finally, antidepressant and anxiolytic medications may be useful in treating alcoholics suffering comorbid depression and anxiety disorders. Mason, Kocsis, Ritivo, and Cutler (1996) and McGrath et al. (1996) have reported that the tricyclic antidepressants desipramine and imipramine reduce depressive symptoms and, to some extent, drinking behavior. Recently, Cornelius et al. (1997) showed that fluoxetine, a selective serotonin reuptake inhibitor (SSRI), ameliorates depression and reduces frequency and amount of drinking in inpatients suffering major depression and alcohol dependence. Interestingly, the SSRIs have not demonstrated a high degree of efficacy in reducing drinking by alcoholics who are not depressed.

Buspirone, a partial 5-HT$_{1A}$ agonist, appears effective in reducing anxiety symptoms and increasing treatment retention in subjects suffering from alcoholism and an anxiety disorder (Litten, Allen, & Fertig, 1996; Malec, Malec, & Dongier, 1996). However, it does not appear to have a primary effect on drinking outcome (Kranzler et al., 1994; Malec, Malec, Gagne, & Dongier, 1996; Malcolm et al., 1992).

Progress in treating opiate addiction with medications has also been made. Several approaches have been developed to detoxifying opiate dependent patients (Meandziga & Kosten, 1994). These include slow methadone withdrawal, therapy with clonidine (an alpha 2-adrenergic agonist that reduces sympathetic activity), clonidine/naltrexone treatment, and buprenorphine detoxification. An advantage of buprenorphine, a long-acting partial opioid agonist/antagonist, is that it partially mitigates withdrawal symptoms.

Methadone, L-alpha-acetylmethadol (LAAM), and naltrexone have been approved in the United States to treat opiate dependence. In this regard, methadone, a long-acting opioid agonist, is the most effective and safe pharmacological maintenance treatment (Litten, Allen, Gorelick, & Preston, 1997). It reduces subjective effects of heroin and other illicit opiates, through a mechanism of cross-tolerance. It also diminishes crime and needle sharing, thus reducing risk of AIDS. In order for methadone to be fully effective, patients must be adequately dosed, monitored closely for medical problems, and provided psychosocial therapy (McLellan, Arndt, Metzger, Woody, & O'Brien, 1993).

LAAM, another opioid agonist, approved in the United States in 1993, is similar to methadone. The main difference is that LAAM is administered only every 3 days in contrast to methadone, which is given daily. A disadvantage of LAAM is the long time required to achieve initial stabilization, thus increasing relapse risk (Jaffe, 1995; Herman, Vocci, Bridge, & Litten, 1996).

Naltrexone would seem to be an ideal medication since it blocks opioid receptor sites, thus preventing activation by heroin and other illicit opiates. However, unlike its role in alcoholism treatment, naltrexone has not proved very successful in treating opiate dependence, most likely due to poor patient compliance (Jaffe, 1995; O'Brien & McLellan, 1996). Nonetheless, naltrexone therapy appears useful for individuals highly motivated to quit. Health care professionals, business executives, and probationers are among these (Meandziag & Kosten, 1994).

Finally, buprenorphine reduces heroin use, blocks subjective and physiological effects of other opiates, and augments treatment retention (Bickel et al., 1988; Johnson, Jaffe, & Fudala, 1992; Strain, Stitser, Liebson, & Bigelow, 1994). The agent is safe and less liable to abuse potential than methadone and can be withdrawn or tapered with relative ease (Litten et al., 1997). Buprenorphine is expected to be approved by the FDA in the near future.

New pharmacological agents and devices have recently been developed to curb smoking. This topic of research activity reflects concern over the large number of cigarettes smokers in America, currently over 60 million. Nicotine remains the most heavily used drug in America.

Several studies have shown that the nicotine replacement increases abstinence rates by occupying the nicotine receptors and thus reducing craving (Hughes et al., 1991; Keenan, Jarvik, & Henning-

field, 1994; Rose, Levin, Behm, Adivi, & Schur, 1990; Schneider et al., 1996; Transdermal Nicotine Study Group, 1991). Nicotine replacement is now readily available in different forms as an adjunct treatment to stop smoking. These include nicotine polacrilex (nicotine gum), transdermally delivered nicotine (nicotine patch), and nasal nicotine spray. All have been approved by the FDA, with the nicotine gum and the nicotine patch now being sold over the counter.

Recently, bupropion (Zyban), a medication approved to treat depression under the trade name Wellbutrin, has been approved by the FDA. The sustained-release form of bupropion has been efficacious in increasing abstinence rates (Glaxo Wellcome, 1997). The mechanism of this "anticraving" agent is still unknown. It may be related to the drug's ability to block neuronal uptake of dopamine, a neurotransmitter believed to be involved in the positive reinforcement of smoking.

In contrast to the success in alcohol, opiate, and nicotine dependence, no medication has consistently shown efficacy in the treatment of cocaine addiction. A range of pharmacological agents have been investigated, including stimulants, antidepressants, cocaine antagonists, dopaminergic agents, serotonergic medications, opioid agents, and anticonvulsants (Litten et al., 1997; Mendelson & Mello, 1996). Several areas of research are currently being pursued. First, medications are being investigated that bind specifically to the dopamine transporter but do not cause stimulatory effects similar to cocaine (Giros, Jaber, Jones, Wightman, & Caron, 1996; Volkow et al., 1997). Second, new agents that bind specifically to subtype dopamine receptors are being explored. Dopaminergic agents have profound effects on cocaine-seeking behavior (Self, Barnhart, Lehman, & Nestler, 1996). Finally, progress has been made in developing cocaine antibodies and other agents that alter pharmacokinetics of cocaine once it is ingested (Rocio et al., 1995).

Unfortunately, no medications are yet available to treat patients suffering abuse of other drugs, such as marijuana, anabolic steroids, phencyclidine (PCP), and inhalants (Wilkins & Gorelick, 1994). The mainstay treatments consist of psychosocial therapies and pharmacological intervention to at least alleviate the drug-induced medical and psychiatric symptoms.

CONCLUSION

The treatments discussed in this chapter reflect the rich diversity of strategies available for treating patients with alcohol and drug abuse problems. The approaches differ along several dimensions, including the importance that patient motivation is assumed to have in determining outcome; the extent to which abuse is seen as fairly endogenous or characterological to the patient versus simply an acquired, counterproductive behavioral pattern; the role of assessment (especially psychometric procedures) in establishing a treatment plan; the amount of responsibility that the patient personally bears in resolving the problem; the intensity of treatment required; the desirability of participation by others in treatment; and the role of the therapist.

Despite their diversity, research evidence exists in varying degrees suggesting that each of the strategies may be effective. Therapists and patients thus now have a broad range of choices in their attempts to resolve substance abuse problems. Future research on treatment should aid in identifying the "active ingredients" of the various options and, perhaps, eventually allow reasoned integration across approaches. So, too, it should ultimately be possible to determine under which conditions a particular intervention should be chosen. By describing and documenting the key features of current strategies, the authors of chapters in this section of the text have advanced these goals.

Key References

Keenan, R. M., Jarvik, M. E., & Henningfield, J. E. (1994). Management of nicotine dependence and withdrawal. In N. S. Miller (Ed.), *Principles of addiction medicine* (Section XI, Chapter 7, pp. 1–11). Chevy Chase, MD: American Society of Addiction Medicine.

Litten, R. Z., Allen, J., & Fertig, J. (1996). Pharmacotherapies for alcohol problems: A review of research with focus on developments since 1991. *Alcoholism: Clinical and Experimental Research, 20,* 859–876.

O'Malley, S. S., Jaffe, A. J., Chang, G., Schottenfeld, R. S., Meyer, R. E., & Rounsaville, B. (1992). Naltrexone and coping skills therapy for alcohol dependence: A controlled study. *Archives of General Psychiatry 49,* 881–887.

References

Allen, J. P., & Litten, R. Z. (1992). Techniques to enhance compliance with disulfiram. *Alcoholism: Clinical and Experimental Research, 16,* 1035–1041.

Bickel, W. K., Stitzer, M. L., Bigelow, G. E., Liebson, I. A., Jasinski, D. R., & Johnson, R. E. (1988). A clinical trial of buprenorphine: Comparison with methadone in the detoxification of heroin addicts. *Clinical Pharmacology and Therapeutics, 43,* 72–78.

Carroll, K., Ziedonis, D., O'Malley, S., McCance-Katz, E., Gordon, L., & Rounsaville, B. (1993). Pharmacologic interventions for alcohol- and cocaine-abusing individuals. *American Journal on Addictions, 2,* 77–79.

Chick, J., Gough, K., Falkowski, W., Kershaw, P., Hore, B., Mehta, B., Ritson, B., Ropner, R., & Torley, D. (1992). Disulfiram treatment of alcoholism.*British Journal of Psychiatry, 161,* 84–89.

Cornelius, J. R., Salloum, I. M., Ehler, J. G., Jarrett, P. J., Cornelius, M. D., Perel, J. M., Thase, M. E., & Black, A. (1997). Fluoxetine in depressed alcoholics: A double-blind placebo-controlled trial. *Archives of General Psychiatry, 54,* 700–705.

Fuller, R. K., Branchey, L., Brightwell, D. R., Derman, R. M., Emrick, C. D., Iber, F. L., James, K. E., Lacoursiere, R. B., Lee, K. K., Lowstam, I., Maany, I., Neiderhiser, D., Nocks, J. J., & Shaw, S. (1986). Disulfiram treatment of alcoholism: A Veterans Administration cooperative study. *Journal of the American Medical Association, 256,* 1449–1455.

Geerlings, P. J., Ansoms, C., & van den Brink, W. (1997). Acamprosate and prevention of relapse in alcoholics. *European Addiction Research, 3,* 129–137.

Giros, B., Jaber, M., Jones, S. R., Wightman, R. M., & Caron, M. G. (1996). Hyperlocomotion and indifference to cocaine and amphetamine in mice lacking the dopamine transporter. *Nature, 379,* 606–612.

Glaxo Wellcome. (1997). *Use of bupropion hydrochloride in smoking cessation therapy.* Research Triangle Park, NC: Author.

Herman, B. H., Vocci, F., Bridge, P., & Litten, R. Z. (1996, September). *Medications development for opiate, cocaine, and alcohol dependence.* Paper presented for American Academy of Child and Adolescent Psychiatry, Philadelphia.

Higgins, S. T., Budney, A. J., Bickel, W. K., Hughes, J. R., & Foerg, F. (1993). Disulfiram therapy in patients abusing cocaine and alcohol. *American Journal of Psychiatry, 150,* 675–676.

Hughes, J. R., Gust, S. W., Keenan, R., Fenwick, J. W., Skoog, K., & Higgins, S. T. (1991). Long-term use of nicotine vs placebo gum. *Archives of Internal Medicine, 151,* 1991–1998.

Jaffe, J. H. (1995). Pharmacological treatment of opioid dependence: Current techniques and new findings. *Psychiatric Annals, 25,* 369–375.

Johnson, R. E., Jaffe, J. H., & Fudala, P. J. (1992). A controlled trial of buprenorphine treatment for opioid dependence. *Journal of the American Medical Association, 267,* 2750–2755.

Keenan, R. M., Jarvik, M. E., & Henningfield, J. E. (1994). Management of nicotine dependence and withdrawal. In N. S. Miller (Ed.), *Principles of addiction medicine* (Section XI, Chapter 7, pp. 1–11). Chevy Chase, MD: American Society of Addiction Medicine.

Kranzler, H. R., Burleson, J. A., Del Boca, F. K., Babor, T. F., Korner, P., Brown, J., & Bohn, M. J. (1994). Buspirone treatment of anxious alcoholics: A placebo-controlled trial. *Archives of General Psychiatry, 51,* 720–731.

Litten, R. Z., Allen, J., & Fertig, J. (1996). Pharmacotherapies for alcohol problems: A review of research with focus on developments since 1991. *Alcoholism: Clinical and Experimental Research, 20,* 859–876.

Litten, R. Z., Allen, J. P., Gorelick, D. A., & Preston, K. (1997). Experimental pharmacological agents to reduce alcohol, cocaine, and opiate use. In N. S. Miller (Ed.), *The principles and practice of addictions in psychiatry* (pp. 532–567). Philadelphia: Saunders.

Litten, R. Z., & Fertig, J. (1996). International update: New findings on promising medications. *Alcoholism: Clinical and Experimental Research, 20*(Suppl.), 216A–218A.

Malcolm, R., Anton, R. F., Randall, C. L., Johnston, A., Brady, K., & Thevos, A. (1992). A placebo-controlled trial of buspirone in anxious inpatient alcoholics. *Alcoholism: Clinical and Experimental Research, 16,* 1007–1013.

Malec, T. S., Malec, E. A., & Dongier, M. (1996a). Efficacy of buspirone in alcohol dependence: A review. *Alcoholism: Clinical and Experiment Research, 20,* 853–858.

Malec, E., Malec, M. A., Gagne, M. A., & Dongier, M. (1996b). Buspirone in the treatment of alcohol dependence: A placebo-controlled trial. *Alcoholism: Clinical and Experiment Research, 20,* 307–312.

Mann, K., Chabac, S., Lehert, P., Potgieter, A., & Henning, S. (1995, December). *Acamprosate improves treatment outcome in alcoholics: A polled analysis of 11 randomized placebo controlled trials in 3338 patients.* Poster presented at the annual conference of the American College of Neuropsychopharmacology, Puerto Rico.

Mason, B. J., Kocsis, J. H., Ritvo, E. C., & Cutler, R. B. (1996). A double-blind placebo-controlled trial of desipramine in primary alcoholics stratified on the presence or absence of major depression. *Journal of the American Medical Association, 275,* 1–7.

McGrath, P. J., Nunes, E. V., Stewart, J. W., Goldman, D., Agosti, V., Ocepek-Welikson, K., & Quitkin, F. M. (1996). Imipramine treatment of alcoholics with primary depression: A placebo-controlled clinical trial. *Archives of General Psychiatry, 53,* 232–240.

McLellan, A. T., Arndt, I. O., Metzger, D. S., Woody, G. E. & O'Brien, C. P. (1993). The effects of psychosocial services in substance abuse treatment. *Journal of American Medical Association, 260*(15), 1953–1959.

Meandzija, B., & Kosten, T. R. (1994). Pharmacologic therapies for opioid addiction. In N. S. Miller (Ed.), *Principles of addiction medicine* (Section XII, Chapter 4, pp. 1–5). Chevy Chase, MD: American Society of Addiction Medicine.

Mendelson, J. H., & Mello, N. K. (1996). Management of cocaine abuse and dependence. *New England Journal of Medicine, 334,* 965–972.

O'Brien, C. P., & McLellan, A. T. (1996). Myths about the treatment of addiction. *Lancet, 347,* 237–240.

O'Malley, S. S., Jaffe, A. J., Chang, G., Rode, S., Schottenfeld, R., Meyer, R. E., & Rounsaville, B. (1996). Six month follow-up of naltrexone and psychotherapy for alcohol dependence. *Archives of General Psychiatry, 53,* 217–224.

O'Malley, S. S., Jaffe, A. J., Chang, G., Schottenfeld, R. S., Meyer, R. E., & Rounsaville, B. (1992). Naltrexone and coping skills therapy for alcohol dependence: A controlled study. *Archives of General Psychiatry, 49,* 881–887.

Paille, F. M., Guelfi, J. D., Perkins, A. C., Royer, R. J., Steru, L., & Parot, P. (1995). Double-blind randomized multicentre trial of acamprosate in maintaining abstinence from alcohol. *Alcohol and Alcoholism, 30,* 239–247.

Rocio, M., Carrera, A., Ashley, J. A., Parsons, L. H., Wirsching, P., Koob, G. F., & Janda, K. D. (1995). Suppression of psychoactive effects of cocaine by active immunization. *Nature, 378,* 727–730.

Rose, J. E., Levin, E. D., Behm, F. M., Adivi, C., & Schur, C. (1990). Transdermal nicotine facilitates smoking cessation. *Clinical Pharmacology and Therapeutics, 47,* 323–330.

Sass, H., Soyka, M., Mann, K., & Zieglgansberger, W. (1996). Relapse prevention by acamprosate: Results from a placebo-controlled study on alcohol dependence. *Archives of General Psychiatry, 53,* 673–680.

Schneider, N. G., Olmstead, R., Nisson, F., Mody, F. V., Franzon, M., & Doan, K. (1996). Efficacy of a nicotine inhaler in smoking cessation: A double-blind, placebo-controlled trial. *Addiction, 91*, 1293–1306.

Self, D. W., Barnhart, W. J., Lehman, D. A., & Nestler, E. J. (1996). Opposite modulation of cocaine-seeking behavior by D_1- and D_2-like dopamine receptor agonists. *Science, 271*, 1586–1589.

Spanagel, R., & Zieglgansberger, W. (1997). Anti-craving compounds for ethanol: New parmacological tools to study addictive processes. *Trends in Pharmacological Sciences, 18*, 54–59.

Strain, E. C., Stitzer, M. L., Liebson, I. A., & Bigelow, G. E. (1994). Comparison of buprenorphine and methadone in the treatment of opioid dependence. *American Journal of Psychiatry, 151*, 1025–1030.

Transdermal Nicotine Study Group. (1991). Transdermal nicotine for smoking cessation: Six-month results from two multicenter controlled clinical trials. *Journal of American Medical Association, 266*, 3133–3138.

Volkow, N. D., Wang, G. J., Fischman, M. W., Foltin, R. W., Fowler, J. S., Abumrad, N. N., Vitkun, S., Logan, J., Gatley, S. J., Pappas, N., Hitzemann, R., & Shea, C. E. (1997). Relationship between subjective effects of cocaine and dopamine transporter occupancy. *Nature, 386*, 827–830.

Volpicelli, J. R., Alterman, A. I., Hayashida, M., & O'Brien, C. P. (1992). Naltrexone in the treatment of alcohol dependence. *Archives of General Psychiatry, 49*, 876–880.

Volpicelli, J. R., Rhines, K. C., Rhines, J. S., Volpicelli, L. A., Alterman, A. I., & O'Brien, C. P. (1997). Naltrexone and alcohol dependence: Role of subject compliance. *Archives of General Psychiatry, 54*, 737–742.

Whitworth, A. B., Fischer, F., Lesch, O. M., Nimmerrichter, A., Oberbauer, H., Platz, T., Potgieter, A., Walter, H., & Fleischhacker, W. W. (1996). Comparison of acamprosate and placebo in long-term treatment of alcohol dependence. *Lancet, 347*, 1438–1442.

Wilkins, J. N. & Gorelick, D. A. (1994). Pharmacologic therapies for other drugs and multiple drug addiction. In N. S. Miller (Ed.), *Principles of addiction medicine* (Section XII, Chapter 6, pp. 1–6). Chevy Chase, MD: American Society of Addiction Medicine.

V

Practice Issues

22

Legal and Ethical Issues

Frederick B. Glaser
David G. Warren

There are things that one does, and
there are things that one does not do.
—Yiddish Proverb

Clinical encounters consistently raise ethical, legal, and moral questions. Value judgments are an integral and unavoidable aspect of the therapeutic situation. To make a sharp distinction between clinical situations and ethical, legal, and/or moral situations is not tenable. "Implied in therapy," notes one commentator, "are beliefs about human nature, pathology, how people should live, and the assumption that the therapist is an ethical person" (Woody, 1990, p. 134). Consider the following fictional vignettes:

- Joan, a 31-year-old secretary, seeks therapy for depression. In the course of the initial interview, she reveals she has recently learned that she is HIV-positive. However, she is afraid to inform her companion. They have lived together for 10 years and have never used condoms.
- Ralph, a 47-year-old accountant, is referred to outpatient alcohol treatment by his employer. Ralph comes to his therapy group visibly intoxicated, registering a blood alcohol level of 263 mg/100 ml on a breathalyzer (more than three

times the legal limit in his jurisdiction). The clinician knows that Ralph always drives to the treatment facility.
- Mark, a 23-year-old unemployed man, is referred to treatment by his probation officer following his arrest for possession of cocaine. Initially guarded in treatment, Mark develops a positive relationship with his therapist and gradually begins to divulge more of his drug history and drug use pattern. He acknowledges that he continues to sell drugs on occasion as a means to obtain money. Mark's probation officer contacts his therapist regularly for updates on Mark's progress. The therapist has an appropriately endorsed release from Mark to speak with the probation officer.
- Maria, a 58-year-old widow, is an episodic drinker who is self-referred to treatment. She reports that she has been abstinent for the last 6 weeks. Maria has a daily responsibility for the care of her two granddaughters while her daughter works. The children are 1 and 3 years old. She tells her therapist that she occasionally

"loses her temper" with the children, but only when she is hung over after a heavy drinking bout. She denies ever drinking while caring for the children.

In contemporary therapeutic practice, situations like these are common. They raise important questions about what the therapist should do. Such questions are not easy to answer but, at the same time, are very important. The safety and well-being of both the client and other persons may be significantly dependent on whether and how the therapist decides to deal with them. This chapter will attempt to provide a basis for considering and working through the ethical, legal, and moral dilemmas raised by these and other clinical situations.

Ethics and the law have to do with right conduct. They provide guidance as to what one ought to do under many different circumstances. In this regard, they are related to morality. The *Oxford English Dictionary* defines ethics as "the science of morals" and moral(s) as "of or pertaining to the distinction between right and wrong . . . in relation to the actions . . . of responsible beings; ethical" (*Oxford English Dictionary*, Vol. 3, p. 312; Vol. 6, p. 653). According to *Black's Law Dictionary* (6th ed., 1990), "Law, in its generic sense, is a body of rules of action or conduct prescribed by controlling authority and having binding legal force" (p. 884). Generally speaking, ethics and morals are the guides for right conduct, and law is the enforcement of right conduct.

Concerns about right conduct are among the oldest and most persistent of human concerns. The Code of Hammurabi, the Ten Commandments, and the oath of Hippocrates have long been with us and are still actively debated today. But codes of conduct are not necessarily ancient. The Nuremberg code, which is the most pertinent ethical guideline in research on human subjects, was formulated only 50 years ago (Shuster, 1997). Legislative bodies, professional organizations, and judicial jurisdictions constantly update existing codes and formulate new ones. Guidelines for conduct are not lacking, and keeping up with their provisions is not an easy task.

Although for purposes of discussion we will treat ethical and legal issues separately, in reality they are closely related. Laws are often based upon ethical considerations, and ethical and moral conduct is usually consonant with the law. But conflicts may arise between ethics and the law. That ethical conduct may be illegal is an element of the tradition of civil disobedience exemplified by Thoreau, Gandhi, and Martin Luther King, Jr. In medicine, one may cite the current controversy around physician-assisted suicide, apparently widely practiced but technically illegal in most jurisdictions. In substance abuse, many have felt it ethically imperative to mount needle exchange programs to reduce the spread of intravenously transmitted HIV infection despite state and/or local laws restricting access to "paraphernalia."

That legally sanctioned behavior may be unethical is exemplified by the Nuremberg trials following World War II, in which the plea of many defendants that their conduct conformed to the legalities of National Socialist Germany was not accepted by the tribunal as a mitigating factor in actions construed as "crimes against humanity." A more contemporary example is the continuing controversy surrounding the application of the death penalty, especially in cases involving women and minors. In medicine, many states have legislatively adopted lethal injection as their means of execution, but physicians often feel it is unethical or immoral and will not participate. In substance abuse, the ethical propriety of withholding information critical to a criminal investigation on the grounds that federal confidentiality laws prohibit its release has been an issue. In the 1994 revision of their book *Ethics for Addiction Professionals*, Bissell and Royce (1994) stated:

> Whether or not a given behavior is legal or illegal does not determine whether or not it is ethical. There are good laws and bad laws. Sometimes the courts are able to render justice, at other times they cannot. For example, physicians attempting to protect themselves from malpractice suits may sometimes perform unnecessary procedures. Addiction professionals may feel torn between the need to protect themselves or their institution from litigation and the desire to spare the patient unneeded discomfort or expense. (pp. 1–2)

What constitutes right behavior is deeply imbedded in culture and philosophy and hence changes across time and place, as do culture and philosophy. "The Law" is frequently deferred to as universal and immutable; yet, for example, laws in the two contiguous areas of Canada and the United States have evolved in very different ways, and laws are very different in different Canadian provinces and in different states of the United States. Even within jurisdictions, ethical and legal guidelines are neither complete (they do not cover all situations) nor consistent (they may contradict each other) nor permanent (both courts and legislatures continually make and revise laws). Ethical and legal precepts are constantly challenged, debated, interpreted, and modified (Spring, Lacoursiere, & Weissenberger, 1997).

To discuss in any detail morality, which involves the relative adjudication of values and (as noted) is closely related to ethics and to the law, would go beyond the purpose of this chapter. Suffice it to say here that in the health care professions generally and in the field of substance abuse in particular, there has been a determined attempt to brand moral considerations as antiquated and irrelevant, and to propose that standard clinical practice is grounded in a totally objective and morally neutral science. We view such a position as not only misguided but naive in the extreme, and ultimately dangerous. The example of the atomic scientists who ultimately came to regard their work as morally repugnant should have exploded for all time the myth of a science exempt from moral considerations. Interested readers are referred to recent works on morality (Midgley, 1991; Wilson, 1993); the latter deals specifically with the moral aspects of substance abuse.

Neither this chapter nor ethical and legal guidelines themselves can necessarily provide an infallible guide to right conduct for a specific therapist in a particular situation at a given place and time. While science, at least in the view of some, searches for and on occasion discovers the immutable principles of nature, ethical, moral, and legal discourse is an ongoing process that rarely reaches any ultimate conclusions. Accordingly, the informed reader will view with skepticism whatever advice may be offered in what follows and will apply it creatively to the unique circumstances in which he or she practices. At the close of this chapter we will offer some guidelines for resolving the legal, ethical, and moral dilemmas that arise in the course of therapeutic practice.

LEGAL ISSUES FACING PRACTITIONERS

Providing Respect to Others: The Duty of Confidentiality

All health care providers are to varying degrees familiar with the duty of confidentiality. It is bred into professional training and bolstered by professional codes of ethics as well as state and federal laws, institutional protocols, and social mores. Confidentiality has become commonly accepted as a fundamental "patient's right," grounded in the legal principle of privacy and the ethical principle of autonomy. In the case of therapists in federally assisted substance abuse programs, there is a detailed federal rule (42 Code of Federal Regulations, Part 2) that spells out in great detail requirements for the confidentiality of patient records. The provisions of the code are discussed below.

Numerous dilemmas arise for all therapists in attending to the duty of confidentiality. Some of these are highlighted by the vignettes regarding the cases of Joan, Ralph, Mark, and Maria presented at the beginning of this chapter. They will be discussed in some detail in the appropriate section on ethical considerations that follows. In this way, both the legal and ethical aspects of these cases, which as noted are not readily separable, can be discussed at the same time.

In general, however, a therapist's responsibility to patients with regard to confidentiality is not as straightforward as it appears. It is easy to give allegiance to confidentiality but more difficult to follow it in practice. The legal duty is not always clear because there are numerous exceptions created by differing state laws and conflicting court decisions. Even if a therapist is knowledgeable about the law, new legal interpretations and changes are continually occurring. Even if a therapist is especially conscientious about respecting a patient's privacy, there are often administrative and practical barriers. A further complication sometimes is a patient's own disregard for the right of privacy.

Confidentiality in the Health Care Setting

There is an innate sensitivity in therapists about maintaining a modicum of privacy in the therapeutic environment. Each of us in our sometime role as a patient expects to be treated with personal respect both for our bodies and our backgrounds. Therefore, nearly every health care facility provides physical surroundings designed to promote personal security, such as soundproofed rooms for history taking and psychotherapy, changing rooms, and closed examination rooms. Health care facilities also take detailed precautions to maintain security for patient records.

A considerable amount of information is learned about patients in the course of taking histories and doing physical and mental examinations. Neither providers nor patients generally expect these facts and observations to become public information. We take for granted the ethical responsibility to maintain confidentiality in the health care setting, and in standard clinical situations, confidentiality is usually provided. But many clinical situations are not "standard." For example, the situations outlined in the vignettes all raise important issues regarding confidentiality, and they are by no means unusual.

The General Law of Confidentiality

There are two components of the principle of privacy, which underpins the laws and regulations governing patient confidentiality in the therapeutic environment. First, the principle of privacy as it relates to the body requires that therapists seek the patient's authorization before touching the patient. To touch without such authorization is, technically, battery. Authorization to touch, or to otherwise examine the patient, is termed *informed consent*. Such consent is, for example, routinely obtained in writing prior to any invasive surgical procedure. For counseling and psychotherapy, the patient's consent is often provided either orally or by the patient's actions (implied consent), such as continuing to attend sessions and to engage in therapeutic activities.

Second, the principle of privacy as it relates to the patient's background requires that a therapist maintain records and other information about patients in an appropriately confidential manner. The law of confidentiality with respect to written records is embodied in a variety of federal and state statutes as well as court decisions. Fundamentally, the law holds that a patient's records should be seen only by those necessarily involved in the patient's care and treatment, and that a therapist should not ordinarily reveal information obtained in the course of the therapist-patient relationship.

There are exceptions that permit or require disclosure of patient information, based on the nature of the information (e.g., communicable diseases and child abuse must be reported in most jurisdictions), the setting (e.g., in a teaching hospital, medical records are permissibly used in teaching and research as well as treatment), the use of the information (it can be subpoenaed for litigation), and other situations (state laws provide specific requirements for disclosure). Above all, a patient can authorize the disclosure or can waive the right of confidentiality, either expressly (e.g., consent forms routinely contain a provision for disclosure for insurance purposes) or impliedly (when the patient files a lawsuit).

The Federal Regulations: Confidentiality in Substance Abuse Treatment

For therapists who work in federally assisted alcohol and drug treatment programs, the rules of confidentiality of patient information are uniquely stringent. They are comprehensively prescribed by federal regulations. This makes it both easier and more problematic for the therapist. The regulations are comprehensive and spell out nearly all circumstances, but they are also inflexible and unusually detailed. Some might say that they are excessively restrictive, making referrals and interprofessional communications more difficult.

The addiction field generally is very well aware of the federal regulations and in fact urged their original adoption in the early 1970s. The intent of the regulations is to combat the presumed stigma that is associated with alcohol and drug problems and that is thought to discourage individuals from seeking treatment. The method is to cover treatment programs with secrecy, restricting disclosure of nearly all information about persons participating in the program. The regulations in general go beyond traditional rules of confidentiality and even beyond existing legal precedents; for example, they do not take into account the duty to warn (discussed below).

The federal regulations on confidentiality apply to all programs that are "federally assisted." Thus, program that are purely private in nature (and in which the costs to the patient for treatment are *not* covered by federal insurance programs) are not governed by these regulations. A working knowledge of the general points contained in the federal regulations, including the technical definition of *federally assisted*, is essential for any therapist. The general rules are summarized in table 22.1.

For the therapist in a private health care setting or private practice, then, there is a general expectation of confidentiality, albeit with some exceptions to the rule. For the therapist working in a federally assisted substance abuse program, however, there is the added problem of the observance of the specific federal regulations on confidentiality. This must be

TABLE 22.1 Summary of the Provisions of the Federal Regulations on Confidentiality for Substance Abuse Programs

The records or other information concerning any patient in a federally assisted alcohol or drug abuse program shall not be disclosed, except as stated in the rule, regardless of any other federal or state laws.

Disclosure means any communication about a patient, including verification of information already known by the inquirer, and records, whether or not they are in writing.

A patient is any person who has applied for, participated in, or received an interview, counseling, or any other service, including an evaluation after a criminal arrest. Every patient admitted to a program must be given a written summary of the federal regulations.

A program is defined as federally assisted if it receives federal funds in any form, has federal tax exempt status, is authorized by the federal government (e.g., licensed to provide methadone or certified for Medicare), or is conducted directly by the federal government (e.g., an employee assistance program in a federal agency).

Hospitals and other general medical facilities are considered "programs" if they have an "identified" unit or staff which specializes in substance abuse services. Some emergency rooms consider themselves"programs" because of an unexpected court ruling in 1989 which narrowly interpreted the regulations.

Many program managers and even legal advisers have also read the regulations narrowly. The regulations themselves are written in a very restrictive manner and invite literal interpretation. There are, however, exceptions to the general rule that permit limited disclosures with patient consent and a few without patient consent. The examples are described specifically in the regulations and relate to the following situations:

1. Written patient consent (a detailed model consent form is included in the regulations)
2. Information to third-party payers and funding sources (only with patient consent)
3. Reports to employers (only with patient consent)
4. Reports to the criminal justice system (only with patient consent)
5. Reporting of aggregated program data or nonidentifying case histories
6. Communication made to other staff members
7. Reporting patient admissions to a central registry to prevent multiple patient enrollment
8. Immediate medical emergency of the patient or another individual
9. Subpoenas and court-ordered disclosures (the grounds and scope are limited by the regulations)
10. Requesting law enforcement assistance for patient crimes on program premises or against program personnel
11. Scientific research (safeguards are provided by the regulations)
12. Audits and evaluations, provided the inspectors certify confidentiality
13. Reporting of child abuse and neglect, if required by state law
14. Qualified service organizations (i.e., outside agencies contracted to perform vocational counseling, data processing, accounting, legal services, urinalysis, etc.) provided the organizations certify confidentiality

done in a way that promotes good care as well as patient trust in the program.

To walk this tightrope requires a clear understanding of the regulations and a pragmatic application of their perhaps overly stringent provisions. Therapists are well advised to study the regulations and legal explanations of them in order to understand them and to avoid mistakes. Every facility should make copies available to therapists and clients who request them. In many instances in which dilemmas arise, therapists may wish to seek legal advice as to the meaning of the regulations within the context of applicable local and state laws. Violating the regulations is punishable by a fine of up to $500 for a first offense or up to $5,000 for each subsequent offense.

LEGAL ISSUES FACING CLIENTS

As policymakers have come to appreciate the significance of substance abuse and have attempted to address some of the problems it poses, federal and state statutes and regulations have become increasingly germane to the field. They create rights and responsibilities for individuals both within the treatment setting and in other settings. In this section, we will summarize some of the more significant legal issues and current legal trends. But (as noted above) regulations may vary considerably from one jurisdiction to another, and because they are subject to change (often quite sudden change), generalization to a particular set of circumstances may be hazardous. The laws and regulations pertinent to substance abuse are also highly detailed and can be covered herein in only a general way. For any therapist whose clients have legal issues, a thorough knowledge of what is locally relevant, or consultative access to a source of such knowledge, is indispensable.

General Provisions

With regard to alcohol, it is illegal in most jurisdictions for individuals under the age of 21 to purchase, possess, or use beverage alcohol. Previously, the age provisions varied from state to state, but with the threatened forfeiture of funds from the federal highway trust, all 50 states have raised the minimum drinking age to 21. Most jurisdictions formerly had legal prohibitions against public intoxication that could result in various penalties, including imprisonment. With the rise of interest in treating alcohol problems as a therapeutic rather than a criminal matter, public intoxication laws have largely been taken off the books. Disorderly conduct while under the influence of alcohol, however, remains a criminal offense in most jurisdictions.

With regard to narcotics and other drugs, their possession and use, irrespective of age or other parameters, is prohibited except for medical reasons. Laws regarding cannabis (marijuana) tend to be more variable than for other drugs. Two states have recently passed referenda making cannabis preparations available by prescription, raising an issue of conflict between federal and state regulations. In recent years, laws in some jurisdictions have been enacted against possession with intent to sell, specifying the amounts (usually large) that permit such a charge to be lodged.

State statutes regarding the operation of a motor vehicle under the influence of alcohol or drugs are a patchwork of different standards and enforcement procedures. Some use the term *driving while impaired* or *intoxicated* (DWI), while others speak of *driving under the influence* (DUI). All of them prohibit the operation of motor vehicles while under the influence of an intoxicant, narcotic, or hallucinogenic to the extent that the driver's "normal faculties" are impaired. All of them also prohibit driving with an unlawful blood alcohol level; many states specify a level of 100 mg/100 ml or higher, but others have recently lowered this level to 80 mg/100 ml.

Many states have enacted "zero tolerance" levels for drivers under age 18; that is, any detectable level of blood alcohol in such an individual will trigger the specified legal sanctions. In the wake of some highly publicized cases, the U.S. Department of Transportation issued Drug and Alcohol Testing Rules that came into effect on January 1, 1995, covering employers with at least 50 drivers who have commercial licenses.

Workplace Laws and Regulations

Since substance abusers in treatment may also be employed, therapists should develop an understanding of the rules and regulations that apply to them in the workplace. Current alcoholics and rehabilitated drug abusers are protected by the Americans with Disabilities Act (ADA). But current illegal drug users and employees who use alcohol on the job are not protected; employers are free to take reasonable disciplinary actions against such employees, and the employees cannot enter rehabilitation programs to escape consequences. A major complication of this law is that court interpretations of "current drug use" are inconclusive at this time. Employee Assistance Programs (EAPs) generally encourage entry into rehabilitation programs as an alternative to dismissal. Employer-mandated drug and alcohol tests are generally allowed under the ADA.

Provisions of the Family and Medical Leave Act (FMLA) also apply to drug and alcohol problems. The Drug-Free Workplace Act of 1988 (DFWP) applies to all federal grant recipients and those businesses having contracts with the federal government worth more than $25,000. While the act neither requires nor prohibits drug testing of employees, testing is subject to the laws of the various states and to specific federal laws governing the transportation industry. State laws may provide for such activities as mandated testing for certain employees (e.g., school bus drivers) for specified drugs, denial of unemployment benefits, and denial of workmen's compensation benefits to employees who are injured on the job as a result of using illegal drugs or alcohol or who tested positive for illegal drugs or alcohol. The National Labor Relations Act governs development of a DFWP in a workplace subject to a "private sector" collective bargaining agreement, including drug testing components.

Drug Testing

Guidelines of the National Institute on Drug Abuse regulate drug testing undertaken pursuant to federal law. But the drug-testing component of a DFWP may be subject to state statute as well. Different states have taken different approaches. Some recognize an employer's right to require testing as part of a DFWP, while others do not. In most states, employers are free to test employees and applicants for jobs for drugs and alcohol, and most state laws on testing simply regulate or limit tests in some way rather than prohibiting them. No state prohibits *all* workplace drug testing. But some state statutes require reasonable cause for testing (as opposed to routine testing), and some prohibit random testing.

Existing federal and state statutes do not answer all the legal and ethical questions that are posed by drug testing, and they pose many others. For example, defense attorneys commonly raise scientific and procedural questions about testing when workers are discharged or disciplined. When and how was the test performed? How reliable was the procedure? Was the employee's freedom in some way abridged by inappropriate employer conduct? Many of these issues are discussed in current guidebooks, such as the *Attorney's Guide to Drugs in the Workplace* (Denenberg & Denenberg, 1996).

Other Issues

Some states have a human rights act or antidiscrimination law that covers individuals with physical or mental disabilities. Most state statutes, however, mirror the Americans with Disabilities Act in providing that a current drug abuser or someone who uses alcohol on the job is not a qualified individual with a disability. Recent federal legislation eliminates drug addiction and alcoholism as a basis for social security and supplemental security income disability benefits. Some professionals in the treatment community have decried this action as damaging to the stability of treatment programs. Others have seen it as a call for more effective prevention programs.

Therapists may encounter clients such as physicians, nurses, and pharmacists who have run afoul of the federal or state laws governing the use of controlled substances. These laws permit the medical use of listed drugs such as opiates, cocaine, barbiturates, amphetamines, and other drugs, but under tightly regulated conditions. Both the federal Drug Enforcement Agency (DEA) and professional licensing boards aggressively monitor this area. Therapists having such clients are well advised to become familiar with the provisions of the relevant laws and regulations in their jurisdictions.

Most jurisdictions also have laws against the possession of "paraphernalia," that is, equipment that is employed for the self-administration of drugs, such as needles and syringes. Whatever surface validity such provisions may have, their deterrent value is doubtful, and in some jurisdictions they have been used to impede the development of needle and syringe exchange programs. Such programs are designed to prevent the spread of infectious diseases among users, especially AIDS. Individuals are provided with sterile injection equipment if they hand in used equipment.

In general, persons with alcohol or drug problems are not legally required to undergo treatment. But a person under the influence of alcohol or drugs who commits a crime may be required by a court to undergo treatment. Caution should be exercised when this occurs. Recent (1997) decisions in three judicial districts have held that mandatory referral to Alcoholics Anonymous (AA) as the sole treatment option is a violation of the separation of church and state provisions of the First Amendment to the Constitution: *Griffin v. Coghlin* in the New York State Court of Appeals, *Kerr v. Farrey and Lind* in the U.S. Court of Appeals for the Seventh Circuit (Wisconsin, Illinois, and Indiana), and *Warner v. Orange County Department of Probation* in the U.S. Court of Appeals for the Second Circuit (New York, Connecticut, and Vermont). But this difficulty is readily mitigated if non-AA treatment options are made available and the patient is permitted to choose the kind of assistance he or she prefers.

There are some programs, such as the federal Treatment Alternatives to Street Crime (TASC), that systematically divert alcohol and drug offenders from the judicial to the therapeutic system. The creation of drug courts is a similar effort in which therapists and court officials are brought together to provide assistance to clients. In instances of substance abuse, as in instances of mental illness, there have been many attempts to mitigate criminal responsibility when a crime has been committed under the influence of alcohol or drugs. In general, however, the courts have not accepted such a defense (cf. Fingarette, 1979).

ETHICAL ISSUES FACING PRACTITIONERS

The Duty of Care

Important ethical issues can be generated when one person asks another for help. What constitutes right behavior for the person to whom such a request is addressed? Or to put it in other terms, what is the duty of care that is generated by such a request?

A logical first step in deciding whether to respond to a request for help is to determine precisely what it is the helper is being asked to do. This is often not immediately apparent and may require some exploration. One team of investigators found that there were significant differences between what the patient actually wanted and what the therapist thought the patient wanted (Lazare, Eisenthal, & Wasserman, 1975). There has been little subsequent study of this issue, but long experience suggests that such differences in perception continue to obtain.

Once the help seeker's request has been clarified, the issue is whether a duty of care exists to respond to it. An important element of this calculus has to do with the appropriateness of the request. Therapists are not omnipotent. Not every therapist can respond appropriately to every request for help. If the request for help is inappropriate, it should be renegotiated. If this cannot be accomplished, help may appropriately be declined. Ideally, one would then redirect the help seeker to a more appropriate source of assistance. But even when this is not possible, it is ethically imperative not to accede to requests for help that one realistically is not able to provide, or that one believes are inappropriate to provide.

Even if the request for assistance has been clarified and realistic goals have been set that are mutually agreeable to client and clinician, there are further issues to take into account in determining the nature and extent of the duty of care. Among these are conceptual issues. How both the help seeker and the help provider construe the nature of the problem to be dealt with in treatment may affect what they both understand to be the duty of care.

Alcohol and drug problems can be understood in a variety of ways (Brower, Blow, & Beresford, 1989; Miller & Kurtz, 1994; Siegler & Osmond, 1968; Siegler, Osmond, & Newell, 1968). For example, in a pure medical model, the individual is seen as having fallen ill through no fault of his or her own. In a moral model, the individual is seen as deliberately choosing to behave badly. The role of the helper varies accordingly. In the medical model, the principal responsibility for dealing with the patient's behavior belongs to the helper, while in the moral model the principal responsibility belongs to the person being helped (cf. Brickman et al., 1982). In other models, the responsibilities are differently divided.

Perhaps because the way they conduct therapy seems natural to them, therapists often do not explicitly reflect upon the assumptions and implications of their clinical methods. They would do well to study the options that are available in terms of models of alcohol and drug problems, and to determine which of them most closely approximates their own practice. Only with a thorough understanding of his or her own conceptual framework can a therapist truly gauge what duty of care he or she owes in agreeing to try to help a given patient. A concurrent advantage to such reflection is that it enables one to determine whether there is congruence between the patient's expectations of the therapeutic situation and one's own (Brickman et al., 1982). If there is not, the likelihood of a positive result is greatly diminished.

The Undistributed Duty of Care

Let us assume (a) that what the patient is requesting has been clarified, (b) that the therapist agrees that the request is reasonable, and (c) that the patient and therapist are operating within compatible conceptualizations of the presenting problem. Under these circumstances, it is reasonable for the therapist to undertake a duty of care to the patient. It now becomes important to understand that duties of care may differ importantly in terms of their object. That is, one must consider to whom the duty of care is owed.

The duty of care is often viewed as being owed exclusively to the individual who has requested help and who is the recipient of care, that is, the patient or client. In such instances one may speak of an undistributed duty of care. As ethical, legal, and moral reflection upon the therapeutic situation has evolved over time, however, the issue of to whom the duty of care is owed has become increasingly complex. While there are indeed situations in which the duty of care is owed exclusively to the designated patient, there are also situations in which it is owed at least in part, and sometimes entirely, to some other individual or entity. In such situations, one may speak of a partially or wholly distributed duty of care, in contrast to an undistributed duty of care.

If a patient presenting for treatment has symptoms that are largely self-regarding, it may be reasonable to conclude that he or she is owed an undistributed duty of care. That is, in such an instance, the therapist can focus his or her therapeutic attention almost exclusively upon the patient. An example would be the development of a social phobia in an unmarried individual. In such a case ethical, legal, and/or moral dilemmas are less probable, though still possible. For example, if a therapist provides only psychoanalytically oriented psychotherapy, but the possibility exists that behaviorally oriented therapy will be more effective in this particular instance, a dilemma may arise regarding referral. And concern about possible sexual involvement of therapists and their patients is not mitigated by an undistributed duty of care.

The Partially Distributed Duty of Care

Where there is a partially distributed duty of care—that is, where the duty of care is owed in part to some other individual or entity—ethical, legal, and/or moral dilemmas are very likely to arise. This is especially so if the therapist-client interaction falls within the scope of the federal confidentiality guidelines. The case of Joan, outlined in the first paragraph of this chapter, illustrates what may be a partially distributed duty of care.

The client has sought help for depression. But she has also indicated that she is HIV-positive, that she has not revealed this information to her companion, and that they engage in unprotected sexual relations. The companion is presumably therefore at high risk of contracting an HIV infection or, if he has already done so, of delaying the institution of treatment. The dilemma arises whether the therapist, now in possession of this information, thereby owes a duty of care to the client's companion, as well as to the client. From a legal standpoint, there is at least the theoretical possibility of a future liability suit from the companion.

If it is concluded that the therapist owes a duty of care to Joan's companion, several difficult options present themselves. In many jurisdictions, the reporting of HIV infections to the local health authorities is mandatory. However, carrying the investigation to the positive person's sexual contacts is often done only where they are indiscriminate, and that does not appear to be the case in this instance. Further complicating the issue is that, while a spouse is often covered by mandatory reporting statutes, a long-term companion is often not covered. What is to be done?

The therapist could encourage the patient to be open with her companion and subsequently take her at her word that she has told him. Or the therapist could seek the client's permission to tell her companion about her HIV infection. Or if the client refuses either to tell her companion or to permit the therapist to do so, the therapist could break confidentiality and warn the companion, justifying this action on the grounds of the threat to the companion's life. But breaking confidentiality for any reason is often viewed as ipso facto unethical and may be illegal, particularly under the federal confidentiality statue for substance abusers, which does not appear to recognize the duty to warn (see table 22.1).

The duty of a therapist to warn others who may be in danger from a patient under care was raised by the *Tarasoff* case and others (Curran, 1975; Dickens, 1986; Eberlein, 1980). Tarasoff was a young woman who was threatened with death and was subsequently murdered by a patient (not in this case a substance abuser) who was under care. His caregivers, who were aware of his threats, were found liable for not directly warning Tarasoff and her family of the danger she was in. The therapists *did* alert the local police, who detained the future murderer briefly but let him go; the court ruled that this action was insufficient to protect the therapists from liability. A critical element of the *Tarasoff* decision was that the patient's caregivers were aware of the specific persons (Tarasoff and her family) who would be harmed if the patient's threats were carried out. Courts making rulings prior to the promulgation of the federal confidentiality statutes have generally insisted that nondisclosure in the therapeutic situation must yield to the "supervening interest of society," and that therapists are expected to act as "agents of society dutybound to control potentially disruptive forces" (Fleming & Maximov, 1974, pp. 1033, 1035–1036).

Joan's case is not unique in raising ethical dilemmas related to a partially distributed duty of care. In any case in which it becomes apparent that the duty of care is owed in part to someone other than the patient, a dilemma arises because of the countervailing requirement of confidentiality. Each of the case examples given at the beginning of this chapter illustrates this point.

In the case of Ralph, the intoxicated accountant who always drives to treatment sessions and who currently has a blood alcohol level well in excess of the permitted legal limit, the therapist may also have a duty of care to the person or persons who could be injured by Ralph as he attempts to drive home. This is not only an ethical but a legal question. Case law precedents in many jurisdictions make it likely the therapist would be held legally and financially liable for any damages caused by Ralph. Some jurisdictions have server liability laws which hold that those who purvey alcoholic beverages to intoxicated persons are similarly liable. While these laws do not specifically apply to therapists, the general principle could be viewed as applicable.

As with Joan, there are several options with regard to Ralph. He might be persuaded to remain under the surveillance of the therapist until his blood alcohol level reverts to normal; given its elevated status, this would take a long time. Alternatively, he could be persuaded to leave his car at the facility and be driven home by a friend or a taxi. Some companies have contracted with private providers to make this service available to their employees as a benefit, with no cost to the employee.

Should such options not be feasible, the alternatives become far more problematic. One that is frequently exercised is not to interfere with the patient's leaving the treatment setting but to inform the police immediately upon his departure. However, liability could be incurred if the police find the intoxicated individual too late or fail to locate him or her at all. Alternatively, the police could be asked to come to the treatment setting and discuss the matter directly with the patient. Either action involves a breach of confidentiality if carried out without the patient's explicit consent, which is unlikely to be granted in such circumstances.

Forcible restraint of the intoxicated individual and/or confiscation of his or her keys often becomes the sole remaining option and is itself illegal. The authors are aware of cases in which therapists and facilities pursuing this course of action have been sued by patients. The courts have generally found the therapists and/or their institutions guilty of unlawful restraint but have assessed nominal penalties (e.g., $1). Given the enormous sums that can be involved in liability settlements, this may be considered on balance a satisfactory outcome.

Let us move on to the case of Mark, who is on probation for possession of cocaine. His therapist, who knows that Mark is occasionally selling cocaine, has an "appropriately endorsed" release of information from the patient to talk to his probation officer. The therapist considers providing this information to Mark's probation officer. But he is concerned that if he does so, he may be breaching confidentiality; moreover, the patient's probation may be violated and the patient incarcerated.

One could posit that the therapist owes a duty of care to those to whom his client may sell an illegal and dangerous, even potentially fatal, drug. In a recent and highly publicized case, the celebrity father of a drug abuser who died of an overdose has publicly pursued his son's alleged provider through the mass media, by implication holding the provider at least partly responsible for his son's death. Alternatively, the duty to warn might be construed as requiring the therapist to take action.

On the other hand, a drug user, unlike the companion of Joan in the first example or those who could be injured by the intoxicated Ralph in the second example, is actively and deliberately participating in an enterprise known to be illegal, dangerous, and even potentially fatal. To what extent does this vitiate the duty of care that may be owed by Mark's therapist to these individuals, if at all? In common practice in the substance abuse field, the purchase and/or sale of illegal drugs by clients is not reported to enforcement officials, perhaps because the behavior is considered largely involuntary.

Under the federal confidentiality statute, a substance abuse therapist may, with appropriate consent, make reports to the criminal justice system. Indeed, the statute helpfully provides a model form for the release of information. However, "the consent form must be recognized for what it is: nothing more than evidence that informed consent has been obtained. Virtually the only way to obtain informed consent is through a conversation" (Vaccarino, 1978). That is, the therapist and the patient must have discussed the release of information in detail, until the therapist is satisfied the patient has a clear and exact understanding of how sensitive information provided to the therapist will be dealt with.

Patients have testified in subsequent legal actions that they signed a consent form as a matter of routine, and that those who obtained the written consent failed to have such a crucial conversation with them. In some cases, courts have agreed with the patient: "The over-riding importance of the conversation cannot be minimized. . . . Informed consent should always be viewed in terms of the direct discussion between the [therapist] and the patient" (Vaccarino, 1978, p. 455). It seems unlikely that Mark's therapist had specifically stated he would report Mark to his probation officer if he learned the patient was selling drugs. Under those circumstances, Mark would not be likely to have divulged this information. Therefore, despite "an appropriately endorsed release from Mark to speak with the probation officer," one could conclude that informed consent on this point does not exist, and that divulging the information does constitute a legal breach of confidentiality.

Finally, there is the consideration that if Mark's freedom were abrogated by the therapist's disclosure, Mark's therapy would end. The therapist's perception of the likelihood that Mark would benefit from therapy could therefore become a factor in the calculus leading to a decision as to what to do. Beyond this, the therapist may take into account the financial implications of Mark's loss to therapy. If, as can happen, the income from Mark's treatment represents a significant portion of the therapist's income, the therapist should be appropriately cautious that this factor does not unduly influence his decision.

In the final case vignette of Maria, a 58-year-old widow who is self-referred to treatment for episodic drinking, the therapist has learned that she has daily responsibility for the care of her young granddaughters. Maria admits to having lost her temper on occasion with the children as a consequence of her drinking. But she reports she has been abstinent for 6 weeks and denies that she drinks while she is caring for the children; her loss of temper, she says, occurs only when she has been hung over from a heavy drinking bout.

Once again, the duty of care that the therapist owes to Maria may be partially distributed; it may be owed in part to Maria's grandchildren and to their mother. The children may be in danger. What is involved in Maria's episodes of loss of temper? It is possible that physical abuse of the children may have occurred, or could occur, especially if Maria is drinking actively while the children are in her care.

To be sure, she has stated that she does not drink under these circumstances, and in general, the self-report of persons who use alcohol excessively is valid (Babor, Stephens, & Marlatt, 1987). But such validity may be compromised when there are direct and certain consequences of what is reported, and it is generally understood that reporting child abuse to the relevant authorities is legally mandatory in most jurisdictions. Further, loss of temper during a hangover cannot reasonably be considered devoid of the possibility of physical abuse on a prima facie basis.

Certainly, the therapist needs to explore with Maria the details of her interaction with her granddaughters. But this may well leave the issue unresolved. Permission could be sought from Maria to discuss details of her case with her daughter; seeking collateral information is a commonplace of clinical practice in the addiction field generally. However, to raise the issue of possible child abuse with Maria's daughter without indicating explicitly in the conversation with Maria preceding the collateral interview that this will be done vitiates informed consent (see the discussion on informed consent in the case of Mark above).

It is not beyond the realm of possibility that Maria might agree to an explicit discussion with her daughter regarding whether physical abuse had occurred or was likely to occur. This would smooth the way for the collateral interview but might not resolve the issue. The possibility exists that Maria and her daughter will collaborate in covering up the physical abuse of the children, out of her daughter's loyalty to Maria or for other reasons. If at the close of the collateral interview the therapist continues to feel in doubt regarding the facts of the case, it may be necessary to set the wheels in motion for an independent evaluation by an external agency.

Once again, this therapeutic situation raises a dilemma with regard to the issue of breach of confidentiality. The current federal confidentiality statute covering substance abusers in treatment does provide for the reporting of child abuse where state law makes this mandatory. But this does not necessarily resolve the ethical dilemma in this particular case. As noted at the beginning of the chapter, what is legal is not necessarily ethical, and vice versa. If a blanket assurance of confidentiality has been issued, or appears to have been issued, and is then violated, an ethical problem exists. There is also the issue of potential future child abuse. Laws in general become operative only when an action has occurred, not because it might occur. It could be argued that if the mother of the children has been made aware of the possibility of physical abuse, any duty of care to the children in this regard has been discharged, since protecting the children has now become the mother's responsibility. Perhaps the reader will find these arguments persuasive; perhaps not. The authors do not find them so.

Our detailed consideration in this section of the four fictitious case vignettes presented at the outset has yielded a quite consistent finding with major legal, ethical, and moral implications. In many therapeutic situations, the therapist will discover that he or she owes a duty of care not only to the designated patient but to other individuals or entities as well. We have termed this a *partially distributed duty of care*. The case examples do not exhaust all of the circumstances in which a partially distributed duty of care may arise.

The degree to which therapists are ethically obliged to consider the welfare of persons or entities other than their patients or clients must always be a matter of judgment in each individual case. The overriding ethical principle, we believe, is that all individuals have a substantial level of responsibility for other individuals. Therapy is not apart from life but is an integral part of life. As life itself is subject to legal and ethical constraints, so therapy must be similarly subject to such constraints. Legal and ethical concerns do not stop at the therapist's door. Individuals in our society are highly interdependent; the actions of anyone may affect everyone, and any action of any individual is virtually certain to affect others in a significant manner. Therapeutics must take this into account. The principle of responsibility for others, after all, is not really a new idea. In the fourth chapter of Genesis, Cain asks whether he is his brother's keeper. The response is generally interpreted as being in the affirmative.

In addition to showing that a partially distributed duty of care often comes into being in the therapeutic situation, the case examples also show that this kind of duty of care often comes into conflict with the principle of confidentiality. This is particularly so with regard to the provisions of the current federal regulations regarding the treatment of persons with problems related to drugs or alcohol. They project a high level of confidentiality, approaching the absolute. We surmise that the purpose of such a high standard is to encourage prospective clients to enter treatment. That high levels of confidentiality assurance would accomplish this desirable end is certainly possible, though to our knowledge no empirical data are available to support it.

Few, however, would disagree that confidentiality as a general principle is a critical component of the therapeutic situation, and that its protection requires vigilance and energy on the part of therapists. Program directors as well as therapists have been incarcerated on occasion when they refused to back down on protecting the confidentiality of their program records, and we applaud their highly principled actions. There have also been egregious instances of the violation of confidentiality, particularly in the political arena; it is manifestly a principle that requires ethical and legal protection, at least to some degree.

Thus, in situations in which the duty of care is partially distributed, it is likely that the therapist's ethical responsibility to a person other than the designated patient will come into conflict with the therapist's ethical responsibility to maintain confidentiality. Under these circumstances, the therapist faces an ethical dilemma, which arises "when two or more values, principles, or obligations conflict and uncertainty prevents [an] intuitive response" (Woody, 1990, p. 133). Nor are therapeutic situations in which there is an undistributed duty of care (see above) or a wholly distributed duty of care (see below) devoid of such dilemmas. The question then becomes how one goes about solving ethical dilemmas. This will be the subject of the next major section of the chapter.

The Wholly Distributed Duty of Care

Before proceeding to that discussion, however, it is necessary to mention a final variant of the distribution of the duty of care. Thus far, we have discussed situations in which the duty of care (a) is owed wholly to the designated patient and (b) is owed partly to the designated patient and partly to other individuals and/or institutions. We have now to consider situations in which the duty of care (c) is owed, at least in theory, not at all to the individual who is the subject of the clinician's attentions but entirely to another individual or, more commonly, an institution.

This third situation, which may be termed a *wholly distributed duty of care*, occurs when the clinician is acting at the behest of (and commonly in the employ of) a third party. A person who is at other times a caregiver may examine individuals on behalf of a court of law, for example, to determine competency to stand trial. Under such circumstances, it may seem to the individual being examined that he or she is being cared for by a helping professional as he or she would ordinarily be. But this is not the case.

It is crucial under such circumstances for the individual being dealt with by the therapist to understand that the helping professional is an agent of the court or of another institution and is not the individual's personal agent, and that the professional's conclusions may be contrary to the individual's interest. Another way of saying this is that informed consent under such circumstances is crucial. Failure to provide a precise understanding of the agency of the clinician—that is, in whose interest he or she is acting—constitutes an unacceptable level of deception.

Similar circumstances apply when the caregiver is in the employ of a company, such as an employee assistance program or, as is increasingly common, a managed-care organization. In a typical situation, an individual may meet with a professional employed by a managed-care organization whose assignment is to determine whether the organization should provide care to the individual. Serious concerns have already surfaced that professionals in these circumstances may base their therapeutic decisions not upon the needs of the individual but on the profit margin of the organization.

Such situations seem to be relatively straightforward. One simply informs the individual of the facts of the situation and then proceeds. Once again, however, the matter is more complex than it may appear. There is evidence that irrespective of what individuals may be told in a discussion on informed consent, they nevertheless persist in believing that a clinician will invariably act in their interest (Appelbaum, Roth, & Lidz, 1983). Being dealt with by a clinician in the employ of a third party is sufficiently similar to the more common therapeutic situation so that this misconception may be quite frequent.

This similarity may have implications for the therapist, too. He or she may be lulled into a suspension of responsibilities to the third party and revert to acting on behalf of the patient. Indeed, it is difficult to accept that some allegiance is not owed to the patient, even under these circumstances. With the projected growth of managed care and of group rather than individual practice situations, the opportunity to explore the legal, ethical, and moral implications of a wholly distributed duty of care is likely to be much greater in the future.

RESOLVING ETHICAL DILEMMAS

As we have tried to show, ethical, legal, and moral dilemmas are a common feature of clinical situations. Moreover, such dilemmas arise not necessarily because therapists fail to behave appropriately (though this may happen), but because they are inherent in the therapeutic situation itself. This being so, it becomes important to understand how to proceed toward a solution to a given ethical dilemma that represents the best compromise between the competing laws, regulations, values, principles, or obligations involved.

Precisely because there is always something to be said in favor of either of the horns of an ethical dilemma, resolving such situations is not an easy process. And for the same reason, whatever solution is reached will often be less than completely satisfactory. A knowledgeable commentator has observed, "It seems that any decision we make will violate one or another value which we hold dear" (Hundert, 1987, p. 839). He goes on to explain:

> Unfortunately, the many values that bear on any given dilemma are what philosophers call "incommensurable." That is, it is impossible to quantify just how much one value (say, social welfare or telling the truth) is "worth" in terms of another value (say, individual liberty or relief from suffering). Yet, as we choose among possible actions, we are often forced to balance one incommensurable value against another, to balance a patient's individual liberty against social welfare, to balance our standards of truth-telling against the relief of suffering. (p. 839)

Woody (1990) has proposed a "pragmatic model" for resolving ethical concerns in clinical practice. She suggests that there are five "decision bases" or sources of information regarding right conduct that therapists should consult in the process of arriving at the best solution: (a) theories of ethics, (b) professional codes of ethics, (c) professional theoretical premises, (d) the sociolegal context, and (e) the personal/professional identity. Her fundamental suggestion is that each of these five decision bases should be systematically plumbed for all of the information it can yield that is relevant to the specific case, and that all of this relevant information should then be weighed and balanced in arriving at the best solution. She helpfully provides examples of actual cases in which this approach proved effective in formulating a resolution of an ethical dilemma.

Yet she candidly admits that the use of these guidelines does not eliminate all difficulties. Each of the "decision bases" may provide conflicting information. She notes, for example, that "there are several theories of ethics, and a given decision is likely to vary depending on which theory is used" (p. 134). She recognizes that a given therapist may be a member of more than one professional organization, each of which may have its own ethical code, and that "the various codes may not mesh on some issues" (p. 138). Different professional theories "will offer diverse and contradictory positions on how to serve the client's welfare" and often "are largely unvalidated hypotheses" (p. 139). They also "take diverse positions on the personhood and personal influence of the therapist versus neutrality and technical competence" (p. 143). While expressing the hope that her theoretical model "will promote increased objectivity," she concludes that "In the final analysis we are left with the messy reality that clinical decision making consists of an unpredictable mix of intuition and rationality" (p. 144).

As may well be imagined, it is often more difficult to negotiate these troubled waters alone than it would be in the company of a knowledgeable pilot. In many locations, experienced ethicists are available for consultation, and many institutions have ethics committees that are well versed in the resolution of dilemmas of this kind. Their help can be sought and may be useful. The same may be said for lawyers who specialize in health law. Ultimately, though, the inherent ethical difficulties in clinical situations will remain. It may be the case, as the epigraph to this chapter would have it, that "there are things that one does, and there are things that one does not do," but in the therapeutic situation, it is not always an easy matter to tell the difference.

Note

The opinions expressed in this chapter are those of the authors and not necessarily those of the editors. The authors would like to thank Barbara McCrady, Elizabeth Epstein, and Renee Willis for their constructive comments on earlier drafts of the chapter.

Key References

Bissell, L., & Royce, J. E. (1987). *Ethics for addiction professionals* (2nd ed.). Center City, MN: Hazelden.

Spring, R. L., Lacoursiere, R. B., & Weissenberger, G. (1997). *Patients, psychiatrists, and lawyers: Law and the mental health system* (2nd ed.). Cincinnati, OH: Anderson.

Woody, J. D. (1990). Resolving ethical concerns in clinical practice: Toward a pragmatic model. *Journal of Marital and Family Therapy, 16,* 133–150.

References

Appelbaum, P. S., Roth, L. H., & Lidz, C. (1983). The therapeutic misconception: Informed consent in psychiatric research. *International Journal of Law and Psychiatry, 5,* 319–29.

Babor, T. F., Stephens, R. S., & Marlatt, G. A. (1987). Verbal report methods in clinical research on alcoholism: Response bias and its minimization. *Journal of Studies on Alcohol, 48,* 410–424.

Bissell, L., & Royce J. E. (1994). *Ethics for addiction professionals* (2nd ed.). Center City, MN: Hazelden.

Brickman, P., Rabinowitz, V. C., Karuza, J., Coates, D., Cohn, E., & Kidder, L. (1982). Models of helping and coping. *American Psychologist, 37,* 368–384.

Brower, K. J., Blow, F. C., & Beresford, T. P. (1989). Treatment implications of chemical dependency models: an integrative approach. *Journal of Substance Abuse Treatment, 6,* 147–157.

Curran, W. J. (1975). Law-medicine notes: confidentiality and the prediction of dangerousness in psychiatry. *New England Journal of Medicine, 293,* 285–286.

Denenberg, T. S., & Denenberg, R. V. (Eds.). (1996). *Attorney's guide to drugs in the workplace.* Chicago: American Bar Association.

Dickens, B. M. (1986). Legal issues in medical management of violent and threatening patients. *Canadian Journal of Psychiatry, 31,* 772–780.

Eberlein, L. (1980). Legal duty and confidentiality of psychologists: Tarasoff and Haines. *Canadian Psychologist, 21,* 49–58.

Fingarette, H. (1979). How an alcoholism defense works under the ALI Insanity test. *International Journal of Law and Psychiatry, 2,* 299–322.

Fleming, J. G., & Maximov, B. (1974). The patient or his victim: The therapist's dilemma. *California Law Review, 62,* 1025–1068.

Hundert, E. M. (1987). A model for ethical problem solving in medicine, with practical applications. *American Journal of Psychiatry, 144,* 839–846.

Lazare, A., Eisenthal, S., & Wasserman, L. (1975). The customer approach to patienthood: Attending to patient requests in a walk-in clinic. *Archives of General Psychiatry, 32,* 553–558.

Midgley, M. (1991). *Can't we make moral judgments?* New York: St. Martin's Press.

Miller, W. R., & Kurtz, E. (1994). Models of alcoholism used in treatment: Contrasting AA and other perspectives with which it is often confused. *Journal of Studies on Alcohol, 55,* 159–166.

Shuster, E. (1997). Fifty years later: the significance of the Nuremberg code. *New England Journal of Medicine, 337,* 1436–1440.

Siegler, M., & Osmond, H. (1968). Models of drug addiction. *International Journal of the Addictions, 3,* 3–24.

Siegler, M., Osmond, H., & Newell, S. (1968). Models of alcoholism. *Quarterly Journal of Studies on Alcohol, 29,* 571–591.

Spring, R. L., Lacoursiere, R. B., & Weissenberger, G. (1997). *Patients, psychiatrists, and lawyers: Law and the mental health system* (2nd ed.). Cincinnati: Anderson.

Vaccarino, J. M. (1978). Consent, informed consent, and the consent form. *New England Journal of Medicine, 298,* 455.

Wilson, J. Q. (1993). *The moral sense.* New York: Free Press.

Woody, J. D. (1990). Resolving ethical concerns in clinical practice: A pragmatic model. *Journal of Marital and Family Therapy, 16,* 133–150.

23

Credentialing, Documentation, and Evaluation

Theresa B. Moyers
Reid K. Hester

There are two conflicting aspects to a discussion of credentialing, documentation, and evaluation. On the one hand, these topics are typically not as interesting as the clinical material our clients bring to therapy. On the other hand, they are, in a number of ways, helpful in improving the effectiveness of the interventions we use with clients. Our goal in this chapter is to provide a road map to understanding these topics and to help locate additional resources to pursue credentialing, improve documentation, and/or improve the effectiveness of treatment with evaluation.

CREDENTIALING FOR TREATMENT OF SUBSTANCE USE DISORDERS

Like most complex and devastating health problems, the treatment of addiction draws upon a variety of professions including physicians, psychologists, social workers, and counselors. Unlike most other health problems, the treatment of substance abuse has also been powerfully influenced by recovering substance abusers, and intervention by paraprofessionals is still an accepted standard of care in many settings. Recent changes, including legal consequences for malpractice as well as pressure from third-party payers, have stimulated a need for treatment providers in the addictions field to demonstrate proficiency in the specific treatment they provide. While it was previously possible to practice safely under the umbrella of a professional degree in a related field or even the hard-won experience of recovering from an addiction, it is now prudent for providers to obtain credentials indicating a standard of specific competence in the treatment of chemical dependency. The following is a brief overview of the manner in which various professionals currently obtain documentation of such competence.

Physicians

There currently is not a board-certified medical specialty for addictions, although there are plans to establish a board of addiction medicine. At this time, physicians wishing to show proficiency in the treatment of substance abuse may sit for a certification examination through the American Society for Addiction Medicine (ASAM). Certification requires successful completion of a national examination, one year's full-time involvement in the field of alcoholism and other drug dependencies, and 50 hours of continuing education (CE) pertaining to alcoholism and drug treatment. In addition to ASAM certification, a specialty certification in addiction psychiatry is available through the American Psychiatric Association.

Psychologists

Likewise, psychologists do not have a board specialty for addictive behaviors. There are plans to add an addictions specialty to the American Board of Professional Psychology (ABPP) diplomate examinations. This would be intended to demonstrate advanced clinical competence. Currently, doctoral-level psychologists wishing to show competence in the treatment of addictions may obtain a Certificate of Proficiency in the Treatment of Alcohol and Other Psychoactive Substance Use Disorders, developed by the College of Professional Psychology of the American Psychological Association. This Certificate is designed to show entry-level proficiency. It requires successful completion of a national examination and documented experience treating addictions for one year.

Counselors

Counselors are not defined by their educational backgrounds as are other disciplines. Depending on the state, individuals may or may not need a specific educational degree to call themselves counselors. Typically, a counselor is someone who has either education or experience in a health-related field.

There are several routes available for counselors who wish to show proficiency in the treatment of addictive behaviors. State licensure laws are highly variable and may demand as little as 1 year of supervised experience and 120 hours of classroom instruction or as much as 3 years of supervised experience and 450 hours of classroom instruction for an entry-level license. Some states do not require a license for counselors wishing to provide substance abuse treatment.

In addition to state licensure, there are two national organizations which certify competency for addiction counselors. The International Certification Reciprocity Consortium (ICRC) issues certification for three types of practitioners: (a) alcohol and drug counselors, (b) clinical supervisors, and (c) prevention specialists. Alcohol and drug counselors need 3 years of supervised experience, 270 hours of education, and 300 hours of training specifically related to the 12 core functions of substance abuse treatment. The National Association of Alcohol and Drug Abuse Counselors (NAADAC) also certifies three different levels of providers: (a) National Certified Addictions Counselor Level I, which requires 3 years' supervised experience; (b) National Certified Addictions Counselor Level II, which requires a baccalaureate degree, 5 years' experience, and 450 classroom hours in substance abuse content; and (c) Master Addictions Counselor, which requires a master's degree, 2 years' postmaster's experience, and 550 classroom hours of substance abuse content. NAADAC certification requires counselors to pass an examination specific to each level.

Counselors will probably choose between these two organizations depending on the requirements of their state licensing board; many state boards borrow the exams from either the ICRC or the NAADAC as their entry-level examination. Membership in one organization does not preclude membership in the other, and each offers particular benefits which may be of interest to specific applicants.

Social Workers

At this time, there is no organization which certifies proficiency for social workers for the treatment of addictive behaviors. Social workers wishing to focus their clinical activities in this area are eligible to obtain both licensure through states boards and certification through either the ICRC or the NAADAC.

DOCUMENTATION

Many therapists consider record keeping one of the banes of their existence. Why bother to keep detailed notes on interactions with clients when the grist of clinical work should take precedence? Clinicians often feel that they are forced to make a choice between writing notes about their clients and seeing them. This dilemma has intensified with the avalanche of documentation often required by managed-care organizations and accrediting agencies. That said, there are some compelling reasons to document what we do.

Written documentation of client contacts forms a record which serves at least three functions. First, and most important, a written record allows the clinician to provide consistent treatment. Second, documentation is a legal record to provide evidence in the event that there is some question about the type or quality of care clients have received. Finally, the chart provides a yardstick for certifying agencies (e.g., Joint Commission on Accreditation of Health Care Organizations [JCAHO] and National Committee on Quality Assurance) and managed-care organizations to assess the quality of care given by the organization as a whole as well as individual practitioners.

In general, all client contacts which lead to meaningful clinical interactions should be documented with a chart note. This would include, for example, phone calls and consultations with other professionals about the client's care but would not include a simple phone call to cancel and reschedule an appointment. The intent of the documentation is to provide an ongoing record of the client's progress as well as any information which would be needed in the event that another professional should undertake care of the client. Chart notes should include an assessment, a treatment plan, a discharge summary, and notes for each client contact. Specific requirements for therapists treating substance-dependent clients are discussed below.

Assessment

A thorough assessment is necessary to discover the extent and severity of substance use as well as client problems and functioning in other domains which may influence treatment. At a minimum, the assessment should contain an introduction to the relevant demographic information about the client and a clear picture of the addiction, including consequences of use in all life domains, dependence or medical sequelae, and some measure of consumption. In addition, an assessment interview should yield a diagnosis from a formal coding system such as *DSM-IV* (American Psychiatric Association, 1994) or *ICD-9* (World Health Organization, 1980). A more complete assessment would include evaluation for comorbid psychiatric disorders known to be more common in this population, including mood disorders and antisocial personality disorder, as well as a determination of suicidal and homicidal risk.

Assessment standards from JCAHO for 1997–1998 state that all clients receiving treatment for chemical dependency should, in addition to a standard assessment, have specific items relating to substance abuse addressed. (See table 23.1 for examples of the intent of these standards.)

Such documentation is difficult even under conditions where substance use is recent, the interviewer is skilled, the client is highly functional, and the client is prepared to discuss his or her substance abuse openly. A more typical clinical scenario is one in which the client's substance use has spanned many years, perhaps with a variety of different drugs. There may be medical, legal, and social consequences of this use, and the client may be forgetful, irritable, or dishonest when reporting his or her history. The interviewer may have limited interest in the goal of assessment, perhaps viewing it as a hurdle prior to the honest work of therapy. Furthermore, the time allotted to complete substance abuse assessments is typically limited.

Within this more typical scenario, the value of a structured assessment instrument becomes obvious. Structured assessments ensure that important information will not be disregarded or forgotten. They provide an efficient method for gathering a large number of data in a limited time, and they often have the added advantage of yielding standardized indicators of client functioning which can be used as follow-up measures after treatment completion. Allen and Columbus (1995) profiled many such standardized instruments as well as data on reliability and validity for each in an excellent sourcebook provided free of charge by National Institute on Alcohol Abuse and Alcoholism and includes self-report questionnaires and structured clinical interviews (see

TABLE 23.1 Joint Commission on Accreditation of Health Care Organizations: Intent of Special Assessment of Individuals in Chemical Dependency Programs and Services

Factors assessed and considered in providing services to the individual served include
— Identifying the physical, emotional, behavioral, and social functioning of the individual before the onset of chemical dependency.
— Evaluating the effects that chemical dependency has had on each individual's physical, emotional, and social well-being.
— Evaluating patterns of use, for example, continuous, episodic, or binge use.
— Identifying consequences of use, for example, legal problems, divorce, loss of friends, job-related incidents, financial difficulties, blackouts, and memory impairment.
— Assessing the history of physical problems associated with chemical dependency to help substantiate the diagnosis, to anticipate potential medical problems related to chemical withdrawal management, to identify the individual's level of function, and to help the individual who is minimizing the physical consequences of dependence.
— Assessing information about the use of alcohol or other drugs by family members to enhance understanding of the individual's behavioral dynamics and help determine the potential for extended-family support, as well as the impact of family circumstances on treatment.
— Assessing each individual's spiritual orientation, which may relate to the dependency in terms of how the individual views himself or herself as an individual of value and worth. Spiritual orientation is not considered synonymous with an individual's relationship with an organized religion.
— Assessing any previous treatment and response to the treatment to see whether the individual responded appropriately to the treatment and if expected outcomes were achieved. If not, what revisions were made, if any?
— Assessing whether the individual has experienced a history of abuse (including physical or sexual abuse as either the abuser or the abused) that may affect the individual's ability to address his or her dependence.

Note. From *Comprehensive Accreditation Manual for Behavioral Health Care 1997–98.* (1996). Used with permission of the Joint Commission on Accreditation of Health Care Organizations. JCAHO, Oakbrook, IL.

also chapter 11). The specific instrument selected will be determined by the needs of the practitioner, the agency or hospital, and the client populations served.

Treatment Plan

A treatment plan is any written document which specifies the interventions that will be used to address symptoms identified in the assessment. For chemical dependency, every treatment plan should include goals of change in drinking and/or drug use, problems achieving initial abstinence or moderation of consumption, relapse prevention, and maintenance of abstinence or return to nonharmful use. Additional components directly related to substance abuse that may require notation include craving and urges, social pressures to use, and skills training. A variety of other concerns may be addressed in a chemical dependency treatment plan when appropriate, including cognitive testing, therapy with family members, vocational rehabilitation, and recreational enrichment. When comorbid psychiatric disorders are identified in the treatment plan, specialists may be designated to address these issues.

A treatment plan should list specific behavioral goals for the problems identified, criteria for determining success, and an estimated time frame for completion. It should reflect collaboration with the client and should include his or her unique problems, perceptions, and solutions.

For those working in JCAHO-accredited settings (e.g., hospitals), there are standards for formulating treatment plans, but they do not have components specific to treating substance abuse. In general, these standards require that the treatment provider involve other members of the multidisciplinary team such as dietitians, recreational therapists, mental health providers, and family members, when appropriate. There is also an emphasis on periodic review and revision of the treatment plan at timely intervals (Joint Commission on Accreditation of Healthcare Organizations, 1996).

As with assessment, the task of writing a treatment plan can sometimes be seen as a time-consuming paperwork hurdle before beginning urgently needed treatment. Nevertheless, treatment plans written by experienced clinicians often reflect the unique needs and qualities of the client so vividly that the client can be "seen" by the reader. One exercise for the novice writer of treatment plans is to imagine that other providers are reading the plan and trying to identify the client from his or her notations (i.e., "name that client"). This may help to bring the unique characteristics of the client to the document, reflecting the careful thought the clinician has actually given to the problems he or she is treating.

Discharge Summary

The discharge summary provides a concise summary of the client's problems and the treatment provided. It also describes any recommended future care. It is written at the point that the provider or program no longer maintains active responsibility for care of the client (i.e., when treatment has ended). It should serve as a reference for future providers who may need to examine a history of several hospitalizations or treatment episodes.

Confidentiality

Many clients expect a shroud of confidentiality to surround their treatment for substance abuse. They expect providers to honor their ethical and legal obligations regarding privacy of the therapeutic interaction. However, this shroud of privacy can be pierced by others outside the therapeutic relationship. Insurance and managed-care organizations may demand specific information about the treatment plan and diagnoses. By using their insurance benefits, clients relinquish their right to keep such information private from these organizations. Clients may not understand this, and it is the therapist's obligation to educate clients before any confidential information is discussed. Clients wishing to protect their privacy may choose to pay for their treatment themselves.

Legal Obstacles to Maintaining Confidentiality

There are certain circumstances in which a provider can be compelled to release confidential information against the wishes of the client. If the provider believes that clients are a genuine risk either to themselves or to another person, he or she is legally obligated to attempt to prevent harm. This may include informing authorities of such a risk, thereby violating confidentiality. Similarly, in many states, if the provider has a reasonable suspicion that a child is endangered, this must be reported. Naturally, it is prudent to include clients as much as possible in the process when such disclosures must be made.

Finally, providers may be compelled to release confidential information when presented with a subpoena. Laws vary among states, and providers usually consult with an attorney before complying with subpoenas. Nevertheless, this, along with the other limits of confidentiality, should be discussed with clients before beginning treatment.

Confidentiality of Clients Participating in Treatment Outcome Studies

Clients who participate in federally funded treatment outcome studies have additional protections of privacy provided by a confidentiality certificate. A confidentiality certificate is issued by the funding institute (e.g., National Institute on Alcohol Abuse and Alcoholism) to the principal investigator of the study. The certificate authorizes those therapists and researchers connected to the study to withhold the names and identifying characteristics of study participants. The Public Health Service Act (42 U.S.C) states, "Persons so authorized to protect the privacy of such individuals may not be compelled in any Federal, State, or local, civil, criminal, administrative, legislative, or other proceedings to identify such individuals." This protection of confidentiality is permanent.

EVALUATION

Providing treatment without evaluating the outcome is like playing golf in the fog. The practitioner can marvel at the power of his or her swing and how well the ball has left the head of the club but still have no idea if the ball is anywhere near the hole or even on the fairway. Evaluation tells the provider whether the ball ended up on the fairway or in the rough.

Types of Evaluation

There is a range of intensity and complexity in the continuum of evaluation efforts. At one end are individual practitioners who consistently follow up with their clients after therapy is completed. Within institutions, evaluation might involve programwide follow-up of clients after treatment. More systematic evaluations include quality assurance (QA) and formal treatment outcome research.

QA is a reciprocal process of assessing client outcomes and then using those outcomes in a feedback loop to enhance treatment within the program. Areas of investigation are typically chosen if they are high-risk, high-volume, or problem-prone. QA results, because they are intended for institutional improvement, should not be published without prior review by an institutional review board (IRB) and the consent of the participants involved.

Formal substance abuse treatment research usually, but not always, involves more detailed evaluation of outcomes and must survive IRB review prior to implementation. While the results can be used to improve treatment within a specific program, as QA does, they are also typically published to contribute to the body of scientific knowledge. Because of the overlap in these two activities, practitioners with expertise in research and substance abuse are ideally suited for planning and implementing QA activities and treatment research.

Outcome Measures in Evaluation

Although abstinence has traditionally been the "gold standard" in evaluating substance abuse treatment, relying on it as a single or primary measure of effectiveness is fraught with difficulty. First, complete abstinence constitutes an unrealistic and unhelpful standard of success. Since the treatment literature consistently documents very low abstinence rates even with the best treatment available (Miller et al., 1995), providers do themselves a disservice by not using a continuum of success to evaluate client outcomes. Furthermore, clients may moderate their drinking or drug use in a variety of ways that reduce harm to themselves and others without totally abstaining. The use of continuous measures is a more sensitive measure of treatment success. For example, the number of drinks per drinking day in the month prior to follow-up will provide a more accurate picture of outcome than simply determining if the client has maintained abstinence or not.

Second, measuring treatment effectiveness using *only* consumption belies the complexity of the recovery process. Clients may improve along a variety of dimensions, including alcohol and/or drug use, psychological functioning, vocational status, familial and social functioning, and physical health. Assessment in a variety of domains gives a more complete picture of the client's substance use, the consequences of it, and the helpfulness of treatment.

There are a variety of instruments to help providers collect outcome data (Allen & Columbus, 1995). Some require relatively little effort, although most are comprehensive enough to answer research and programmatic questions about outcomes. Typically, these measures are linked to the pretreatment evaluation. Ideally, both assessment and follow-up instruments should be selected prior to treatment. However, even without such forethought, a variety of interesting questions can be answered when clients return for follow-up after completing treatment. It also gives the therapist an opportunity to offer additional and/or different treatment if the client's outcomes are unsatisfactory.

CONCLUSION

Credentialing, documentation, and evaluation, while all involving paperwork, provide benefits to clients, structure to the treatment process, and protection for the provider. Credentialing provides some assurance to clients that providers are competent to deliver the treatments they offer. Documentation in the form of assessment and treatment planning helps the provider conceptualize the case and provides a record of treatment efforts. Evaluation helps providers and programs alike know the impact of their efforts and can inform them about the types of clients with whom they are most successful.

RESOURCE LIST

American Psychological Association, College of Professional Psychology, 750 First St. NE, Washington, DC 20002-4242; 202-336-6100; 202-336-5797 (fax); E-mail apacollege@apa.org; web site: www.apa.org.

American Society of Addiction Medicine, 4601 N. Park Ave., Suite 101, Upper Arcade, Chevy Chase, MD 20815.

International Certification Reciprocity Consortium, 3725 National Dr., Suite 213, Raleigh, NC 27612; 919-781-9734; 919-781-3186 (fax).

Joint Commission on Accreditation of Healthcare Organizations, One Renaissance Blvd., Oakbrook Terrace, IL 60181.

National Association of Alcohol And Drug Abuse Counselors, Certification Commission, 1911 N. Fort Myer

Dr., Suite 900, Arlington, VA 22209; 1-800-548-0497; 1-800-377-1136 (fax); E-mail naadac@internet mci.com.

National Committee on Quality Assurance, 2000 L St. NW, Suite 500, Washington, DC 20036; 202-955-3500; 202-955-3599 (fax).

References

Allen, J., & Columbus, M. (Eds.). (1995). *Assessing alcohol problems: A guide for clinicians and researchers.* Bethesda, MD: National Institute on Alcohol Abuse and Alcoholism.

American Psychiatric Association. (1994). *Diagnostic and statistical manual of mental disorders* (4th ed.). Washington, DC: Author.

Joint Commission on Accreditation of Healthcare Organizations. (1996). *Comprehensive accreditation manual for behavioral health care 1997–98.* Oakbrook, IL: Author.

Miller, W. R., Brown, J. M., Simpson, T. L., Handmaker, N. S., Bien, T. H., Luckie, L. F., Montgomery, H. A., Hester, R. K., & Tonigan, J. S. (1995). What works? A methodological analysis of the alcohol treatment outcome literature. In *Handbook of alcoholism treatment approaches: Effective alternatives* (2nd ed., pp. 12–44). Needham Heights, MA: Allyn & Bacon.

World Health Organization. (1980). *ICD 9 CM: International classification of diseases 9th revision clinical modification.* Ann Arbor, MI: Commission on Professional and Hospital Activities.

24

Interfaces between Substance Abuse Treatment and Other Health and Social Systems

Susan J. Rose

Allen Zweben

Virginia Stoffel

The purpose of this chapter is to develop a framework for examining the issues surrounding the interrelationships of the wide variety of service settings encountered by substance abusers. It familiarizes the reader with the multiplicity of needs experienced by persons with substance-use-related problems, analyzes the challenges to the current system of service provision presented by these complex needs, identifies the barriers to coordinated care, and suggests areas for further development of "best practice" with persons abusing alcohol and other drugs.

In part as a result of using a broader definition of alcoholism and drug abuse, more persons with substance use problems are being identified at earlier stages and from a greater variety of sources. For example, persons abusing alcohol and drugs can be identified in child protection programs, voluntary family support agencies, employee assistance programs, health maintenance organizations, inpatient and outpatient psychiatric facilities, public financial support programs, and vocational rehabilitation settings. The multiplicity of needs experienced by persons abusing a range of substances, as well as public and private treatment innovation initiatives, have been the driving forces behind a more coordinated system of care. However, the development of such systems, in which diverse settings with diverse goals must interact, requires reaching better consensus on problem definition, goals, procedures, methods, referral pathways, and available resources.

DESCRIPTION OF NETWORK OF AGENCIES WITH WHICH SUBSTANCE ABUSERS INTERFACE

The boundaries of the alcohol or drug abuse (AODA) service system frequently overlap with those of other, related systems, including but not limited to child protection systems, primary health care providers, social service systems, criminal justice institutions, vocational rehabilitation programs, health insurance companies, and the substance abuse treatment system. A beginning description of some of the types of agencies with which substance abusers come in contact is necessary to understand the scope of their treatment needs and the complications of coordinating these services.

Child protection systems are designed to identify children at risk of abuse or neglect, and to provide for their safety through a continuum of services from prevention to reunification and adoption. These systems are charged with the protection of minor children from further harm in their immediate environments, reducing the risk of future harm to their safety through preventing further maltreatment, improving parental functioning, or removing to permanent substitute homes children who are adjudicated as being unable to ever live safely with their birth families (Downs, Costin, & McFadden, 1996).

Primary health care providers include providers of both physical and behavioral health care (mental health), and the venues of their practice can be categorized into acute, subacute, and long-term settings. Acute settings are primarily emergency rooms, hospital units, 24-hour beds, crisis lines, and outreach units. Subacute settings include hospitals, ambulatory care programs, day treatment programs, intensive outpatient programs, in-home programs, mental health centers, and individual practitioners. Long-term settings are primarily mental health centers, residential care units or institutions, and practitioners' offices. Medications are used for physical and severe mental health disorders, or for more time limited mood disorders arising from adjustment problems or acute trauma.

Nonmedical, community-based agencies constitute the bulk of the *social services system*. These social service agencies provide counseling, support, advocacy, concrete resources, housing assistance, and a variety of needed services for people to maintain themselves in the community. Persons seeking help from these settings often do so for a full range of family, individual or marital problems or for other life adjustment difficulties.

The *legal system* is a complex array of levels of retribution and rehabilitation initiatives. The balance between these two approaches drives a range of options for offenders, from the least restrictive forms of court supervision to the most restrictive: incarceration in federal penitentiaries. Least restrictive alternatives include court-mandated education, diversion programs, and some types of intermediate sanctions (means-based fines, community service, restitution, day reporting centers, court-mandated outpatient treatment, etc.). More intrusive and restrictive alternatives include intensive supervision of probation, curfews or house arrest, halfway houses or work release centers, boot camps, and incarceration for varying amounts of time and in detention centers, jails, or prisons with varying degrees of security.

Vocational rehabilitation programs emphasize work preparation, job-seeking skills, and matching workers with disabilities to jobs which fully utilize their talents. Employment is used as a key variable in determining successful treatment outcomes for drug abuse rehabilitation programs (Platt, 1995).

Health insurance companies, responding to the devolution of responsibility and financing of services from federal to state auspices, have been a critical influence in the development of a model of coordination among treatment systems, as a way to hold down the escalating costs of physical and behavioral health care. As both private and public systems of care have continued to migrate toward the use of managed care methods, appropriate frequency, and intensity and a continuum of care have been emphasized as the standard for best practice (Rose & Keigher, 1996). To progress toward this goal, health care insurance companies have partnered with health maintenance organizations (HMOs), managed care companies (MCOs), and other, more innovative strategies. The results have been sometimes awkward attempts at coordination among settings with disparate goals, procedures, theoretical orientations, and methods.

Substance abuse practitioners have often found themselves in the middle of these changes in the health care insurance industry, having to master a complex set of requirements for precertification of substance abuse treatment. These precertification requirements are unique to specific insurance plans and often make it more difficult to plan treatment across a variety of clients with individual service needs. Thus, length of inpatient and outpatient care can be dictated by the quality of the insurance coverage, rather than by a standard of best practice among professional caregivers.

The current *alcohol and drug treatment system* is not a unitary entity, but a collection of types of services. It includes social and medical model detoxification programs, short- and long-term treatment programs, methadone maintenance programs, long-term therapeutic communities, and self-help adjunct programs (Center for Substance Abuse Treatment [CSAT], 1994a). These services themselves maintain variation in treatment goals and philosophies regarding abstinence as a prerequisite or as a long-term goal of treatment. There is also wide variation in practitioner requirements among service settings, including physicians, psychiatrists, psychologists, social workers, nurses, certified alcoholism counselors, other rehabilitation therapists, and recovering paraprofessionals. Medication is used primarily to treat the complications of addiction, and most programs attempt to end a patient's use of all medications within a prescribed period of time. Central to the growing treatment system are consumer-developed self-help groups, such as Alcoholics Anonymous (AA), Narcotics Anonymous (NA), Cocaine Anonymous, and Rational Recovery, that serve as an important adjunct to professional treatments.

As substance abusers increasingly use and come in contact with many nonspecific settings in the complex public and private service system, critical challenges to coordination can occur between persons seeking help and providers. In particular, how an individual identifies his or her problem is not always consistent with how a service provider might identify the same problem. A young mother in the child welfare system might see her problem as how to have her child returned to her care, while the court might interpret the problem as how to keep her from further court involvement, and the social service agency might view the problem as how to strengthen her coping abilities. These multiple perspectives must be taken into account in the definition utilized by settings in identifying substance use problems, the intervention modalities employed to detect and treat substance use problems, and the strategies used to effect a referral to other settings. In addition, the barriers presented by particular definitional perspectives, inconsistent goals established in relation to care, the level of client choice in the establishment and implementation of treatment goals, and the resources available to meet these goals need explication.

EXAMINING THE SERVICE NETWORK FOR TREATING SUBSTANCE USE PROBLEMS

Innovations in substance abuse treatments are leading to the adoption of a broader definition of substance use problem behaviors (Institute of Medicine, 1990). Inherent in these innovations is a recognition that persons can be placed on a continuum of problem behaviors stemming from their substance use, ranging from those with severe difficulties (e.g., medical, psychiatric, and legal complications) to those with mild or moderate difficulties (e.g., interpersonal stress). Nonspecialized community agencies that interact with substance abusers need to have available a repertoire of strategies to address the diverse treatment needs of these persons. These strategies include methods of screening and assessment of problem behaviors, use of brief intervention methods, and referral compliance techniques for those with more serious problems.

The first component to consider in assessing the service network is what definitional parameters are used to identify alcohol and drug problems. Nonspecialized settings should have established criteria for determining which individuals are suitable for intervention in the nonspecialized setting and which persons might more appropriately be served in a specialized facility. The development of such criteria implies that the agency has the capacity to make distinctions among individuals with varying levels of severity of their alcohol or drug problems (Cooney, Zweben, & Fleming, 1995). Individuals identified as having mild or moderate levels of severity might be suitably treated by agency staff trained in brief intervention modalities, while those with more severe problems might more properly be referred to specialist facilities (Zweben & Barrett, 1997).

The second component to consider is what intervention modalities have been incorporated into the practice protocols of the agency professionals. Recent developments in substance use research suggest that brief interventions are a viable, cost-effective alternative to more extensive specialized methods of treating individuals who have lower levels of problem severity stemming from drinking or drug use (Zweben & Fleming, in press). Brief interventions have been employed in a variety of nonspecialized settings such as employee assistance programs (EAPs), emergency rooms, and criminal justice programs, to treat nondependent drinkers and other drug-using populations (Zweben & Fleming, in press). They can also be employed to enhance the motivation of more severely dependent users to engage in specialized treatments.

The third component to consider is what kinds of strategies nonspecialized settings use to effect compliance with referral to more specialized substance use treatment programs. In this country, failure rates for referrals to alcohol treatment programs range from 70% to 90% (Babor, Ritson, & Hodgson, 1986; Soderstrom & Cowley, 1987; Stephen, Swindle, & Moos, 1992). In British substance abuse treatment programs, the rate of dropout after only one session is about 44% (Rees, Beech, & Hore, 1984; Thom et al., 1992). Substance abusers have multiple needs that are difficult to address through the auspices of one single setting, and these settings are not always able to effect a referral when specific services outside their capabilities are required (Institute of Medicine, 1990). Effective referral compliance strategies must be implemented when persons with more severe dependence are identified and referred to specialized treatment settings. Failure to move toward resolution of these differences can act as a barrier to effective referrals and coordination of care.

BARRIERS TO COORDINATING CARE BETWEEN COMMUNITY AND SPECIALIZED SETTINGS

A significant barrier to coordinated care is that some practitioners in nonspecialized settings have maintained restrictive views of alcohol and drug problems despite the introduction of new paradigms into the substance abuse field. From this more restrictive perspective, substance abuse is considered a degenerative disorder, and the course of the "illness" is expected to progressively worsen unless total abstinence is achieved and sustained. In this "disease" model, single violations of abstinence (e.g., 1–2 drinks) would be tantamount to relapse. At the same time, clients are seen as "powerless" to regulate their own problem behaviors, and therefore, reliance is placed on self-help groups such as AA or NA fellowship. In these programs, clients are requested to perform a variety of tasks (e.g., 12 steps) necessary for maintaining an abstinent lifestyle.

Other practitioners have moved away from medical models and toward a public health perspective on alcohol and drug problems. In the latter model, clients are viewed as having varying levels of severity of alcohol or drug problems with differing medical and psychosocial needs and individual and social coping resources. Individuals seeking help for their alcohol or drug problems are given the opportunity of *choosing* from a continuum of treatment modalities available that are relevant to their individual

needs. Once clients are engaged in a particular treatment, efforts are made to involve them in all aspects of decision making about their treatment goals and action plan. Depending upon the severity of substance use problems and the preferences of clients, treatment might be aimed at "problem-free drinking," reducing harmful consequences of the abuse (e.g., engaging in a needle exchange program), or total abstinence. In addition, in this model, an episode of drinking or drug use is considered "normative" and does not necessarily constitute a total relapse or treatment failure.

Specialized settings which mandate abstinence as a condition for treatment participation (e.g., probation and parole agencies) and request regular AA attendance may be in conflict with referral sources which promote client choice and individualized treatment goals. Nonspecialized programs which view relapse as a rationale for discontinuation of services (e.g., family support programs) may be in conflict with those treatment settings which promote harm reduction as a goal or which view relapse as a "normative" aspect of the recovery process (cf. Austin, Bloom, & Donahue, 1992). For example, some social service agencies require the client to stop drinking before family counseling can begin, and they negotiate differences between client and practitioner concerning how the problem behaviors will be addressed in the treatment situation. An additional example from our own drinking checkup program is that it has been difficult to secure referrals from court (e.g., DWIs) and EAPs because of our willingness to consider moderate drinking a goal for participants. Clients themselves will be reluctant to participate in treatment where there are serious disparities between referral source and specialist practitioner with regard to the above issues.

A third barrier is the availability of resources within the setting and within the community to address a continuum of care for persons with substance-abuse-related problems. Relevant treatment modalities are not always available for persons who are identified along the continuum of substance-use-related difficulties, despite the ability to effect a referral or develop common goals in relation to substance use. This has become an increasingly problematic issue in nonurbanized areas with only limited resources devoted to substance abuse. For example, in Tennessee, in 1995, it was estimated that only 36% of the state had any coverage for alcohol or substance abuse treatment ("Switch To Managed Care,"

1995). In other areas, only limited aspects of a continuum of care may be available. It may be only an AA group, or a family service agency, or an outpatient mental health center available within a 30-mile radius.

The dilemmas and barriers inherent in the coordination of multiple agencies with which persons with substance use problems interact can be described for a variety of service systems. The child protection services system, however, is particularly emblematic and merits more detailed analysis. It highlights in particular the difficulties in trying to coordinate care among systems with different definitions of substance use problems, different intervention methods, and different goals and resources.

CHILD PROTECTION SERVICES

Substance abusers interact with this system at all levels: prevention, family support, investigation, case planning, in-home services, substitute care, and adoption. They can come into contact with the system either through bearing a child with alcohol or drug exposure, through evidence of substance abuse as a contributing factor to initial allegations of child abuse and neglect, or through a caretaker's inability to keep a child at home safely.

Estimates of the incidence of substance abuse in the 2.9 million reports of child maltreatment filed annually in this country have ranged from 25% to 84% (Leonard & Jacob, 1988; Tracy, Green, & Bremseth, 1993) with an average estimate of 26% (Daro & McCurdy, 1994). Approximately 10 million children are living in households with an adult substance abuser, and 675,000 children annually are seriously maltreated by substance-abusing caretakers (Daro & Mitchell, 1989).

The agreement of child protection systems on a definition used to identify substance use problems among parents is not consistent across jurisdictions. Alcohol and substance use are identified as problems by child protection workers when they interfere with the parents' ability to care for a child, both at the time of an initial allegation and when assessing readiness for reunification of a child with her or his family. Child abuse and neglect are suspected to be more likely in families with a substance-abusing parent (Daro, 1988; Gelles & Cornell, 1990; Starr, 1982; Straus, 1980; Wolock & Horowitz, 1979). In particular, substance abuse is viewed as a triggering

event in incidents of sexual abuse (Smith & Kunjukrishman, 1985) and physical abuse, and as a factor in chronic neglect (Leonard & Jacob, 1988).

While some child protection authorities have taken the position that any evidence of prenatal exposure or use of illegal substances is prima facie evidence of maltreatment (Roberts, 1990), such connections have yet to be demonstrated. It is estimated that 5 million women of childbearing age—and more specifically, 27% of women aged 18–25—used alcohol or illicit drugs in 1988 (National Institute on Drug Abuse, 1992; U.S. Government Accounting Office, 1990). One study of hospital discharges reported an estimate of 38,000 drug-exposed babies born in 1987, representing a 361% increase in number of drug-exposed newborns between 1979 and 1987 (Dicker & Leighton, 1991). Other studies have estimated the number to be closer to 300,000 (Chasnoff, 1992). The percentage of children born with some type of illegal substance exposure in utero has been variably estimated to be between 2% and 11% (American Academy of Pediatrics, 1990; Besharov, 1989; Chasnoff, 1989).

However, more children are born alcohol-exposed than drug-exposed, and the consequences can be more profound (Barth, 1993a). The risk of fetal alcohol syndrome (FAS) in an alcohol user's pregnancy has been estimated at 10% (Rossett & Weiner, 1984; Sokol & Abel, 1992). The cost of providing care for one drug-exposed child with some significant physiological or neurological impairment is estimated at $750,000 over the lifetime of the child, and the cost for one residential treatment episode for a substance-abusing mother and her children is about $40,000 (Barth, 1993b).

Despite the reality that child protection services and substance abuse treatment are overlapping areas of practice, child welfare workers continue to have limited training in screening for substance abuse problems, in determining the level of risk posed to minor children, or in offering any intervention besides referral to specialized programs (Tracy & Farkas, 1994). Tracy (1994) reported that child welfare workers even doubt their right to ask parents about their substance use because the workers lack the necessary interviewing and assessment skills in this area.

Child protection workers are commonly called upon to make a referral to a more specialized treatment setting for substance users, due to court orders for such treatment or the recognition of the parents themselves of the role of substance abuse in their inability to care for their children. Unwanted pregnancy can be one of the first unintended consequences of problem drinking or illegal drug use (Ewing, 1991), and for some substance-abusing mothers, the birth of a drug-exposed baby or the removal of their children can be a powerful incentive to enter treatment. For others, the anger over a child's placement, the guilt about delivering a drug-exposed baby, or the stress of the baby's condition can diminish already limited parenting skill and lead to increased use or resumption of use (Freier, Griffith, & Chasnoff, 1991). Specific referral compliance strategies, however, continue to be the reliance on the authority of the court to effect the referral.

Significant barriers to any coordination between child protection agencies and other systems are a narrow view of substance use and conflicting goals. Conflicting goals between the child protection system and the substance abuse treatment system revolve around the problems of treating caretakers while protecting dependent children from harm. This conflict can best be seen by the role of relapse. While relapse can be seen as an expectable part of a substance abuse disorder, it raises significant questions for the care and safety of dependent children.

Confidentiality is also a significant factor reducing pathways to collaboration and cooperation between child protection and substance abuse treatment systems. Increasing attempts to institute charges against women who give birth to drug-exposed babies have resulted in substance-abusing pregnant women not seeking prenatal care or not reporting their use for fear of prosecution, placing the child at even greater risk. Further, the criminalization of substance use during pregnancy has raised ethical questions about physicians' obligation to report suspected child maltreatment if such a report is likely to result in the incarceration of the mother.

The resources necessary to encourage coordination between child protection systems and substance abuse treatment programs are limited. Successful programs for substance abusers in child protection take into account both the parent's recovery goals of sobriety and the family's goals of protecting and caring for the child's well-being (Tracy & Farkas, 1994). Home-based family preservation programs serve only a small percentage in the child protection system, an estimated 20,000 children (Barth, 1993a), and have been reported to be least effective with substance-abusing families (Spaid & Fraser, 1991). There are also few programs that provide for residential units for women and their children in various stages of recovery; however, these may be further developed by the move toward more integrated systems of care conceptualized under block granting for states.

There are two major categories of circumstances which might cause a substance abuse practitioner to initiate a report to child protection authorities. First, anytime alcohol use interferes with parents' ability to care for the physical and emotional needs of their child, compromising the child's safety and resulting in neglect of the child, authorities should be contacted to investigate the risk. An example of such behaviors might be a parent's engaging in alcohol or drug-taking binges away from the home and leaving the child alone for days at a time. Another situation might be when a parent drinks at home and fails to feed, clothe, or attend to the child for long periods of time. An additional scenario might be when a parent endangers the safety of the child by engaging in dangerous activities while drinking (driving or passing out while smoking).

A second major category of concern that would warrant protective service intervention is anytime parents exploit their child in order to use or maintain their own substance abuse habit, resulting in misuse or abuse of the child. This would include having children steal drugs or alcohol, requiring children to work or prostitute themselves for money to obtain drugs or alcohol, or giving alcohol or drugs to children to use.

In considering making a request for investigation by protective service authorities, practitioners must consider the age and vulnerability of the child, family and community resources available to the individual, and the specific laws about reporting child abuse and neglect in their community. When a protective service concern arises in the course of treating an individual with substance-abuse-related problems, this concern should first be discussed with the individual with emphasis placed on the consequences of the substance abuse behavior for the safety of the child.

PRIMARY HEALTH CARE PROVIDERS

Research findings indicate that drug and alcohol problems play a significant role in a large number of cases seen in primary health care settings. Nowhere is the problem more evident than in emergency rooms of general hospitals (Institute of Medicine, 1990). Alcohol use has been implicated in injuries resulting from automobile collisions, falls, fires, homicides, assaults, suicide attempts, and near drowns (National Institute on Alcohol Abuse and Alcoholism [NIAAA], 1990). Approximately 40% of individuals treated for head injuries in emergency room settings have been previously treated for alcohol problems (Stephens-Cherpitel, 1988). About 50% of admissions of Level I trauma centers have been found to be legally intoxicated, and a substantial proportion of those found with positive blood alcohol levels experience some degree of alcohol-related problems (Soderstrom & Crowley, 1987). Within an inpatient medical setting, about 20–25% of those being treated for trauma have been found to have alcohol-related difficulties (Waller, 1988). Similarly, there has been an association between alcohol use and a variety of medical problems, including gastrointestinal disorders (e.g., peptic ulcer), hypertension, and orthopedic problems such as fractures (Institute of Medicine, 1990). For these reasons, the Institute of Medicine (1990) recommended that alcohol screenings be conducted for persons coming to medical settings and that depending upon the seriousness of the problems, either a brief intervention or a referral for specialized intervention be offered.

Despite the connection between substance use problems and medical disorders, there has been a significant lack of routine alcohol- and drug-screening programs in primary-care health settings. For example, it has been revealed that only 55% of Level I trauma centers regularly obtain blood alcohol levels in their patients and that only a few centers routinely provide referrals for alcohol problems (Soderstrom & Cowley, 1987). Similarly, alcohol use by pregnant women is not routinely identified despite the harm associated with the drinking (Serdula, Williamson, Kendrick, Anda, & Byers, 1991).

Primary-care settings that strive to provide routine screenings have had difficulty in fulfilling their referral compliance goals (Stephen et al., 1992, cited in Cooney et al., 1995). Data obtained from the Veterans Administration show that 10% of individuals identified as having alcohol problems actually enroll in specialist treatment programs (Stephen et al., 1992). Similar findings have been observed in non-VA medical facilities. A study conducted by the Addiction Research Foundation in Toronto, Canada, found that only 14% of identified hazardous drinkers

agreed to participate in specialized treatment (cited in Babor et al., 1986).

The low rates of compliance among primary-care patients has led to the use of referral compliance methods in combination with screening methods in these health care settings (Cooney et al., 1995). Strategies such as feedback and advice incorporated into a 15–30 minute health promotion interview have proved to be effective with primary-care patients (cf. Elvy, Wells, & Baird, 1988; Fleming, Cotter, & Talboy, 1997; Goldberg, Millen, Richard, Psaty, & Ruch, 1991). In a recent study conducted in primary-care settings, Fleming, Barry, Manwell, Johnson, and London (1997) showed that combining screening with a brief intervention approach can result in 10–30% reduction in alcohol use among patients seen in these settings.

From a systems perspective, failure to provide adequate screening and referral in primary-care health settings can be attributed to a number of factors. Despite available evidence, payees such as insurance companies and health care maintenance organizations are not convinced that providing screening and intervention for substance use problems will reduce health care utilization and related costs (Zweben & Fleming, in press). Consequently, financial incentives are not offered to providers for undertaking the training in standardized screening and intervention protocols for alcohol and drug problems that are currently available to providers (cf. NIAAA, 1995, 1990). Providers that are familiar with the standardized referral protocols are reluctant to employ these techniques without receiving additional compensation from payees.

"Carve-outs" serve as an another impediment to the development and implementation of secondary prevention programs in primary-care settings. In many managed care settings, providers are required to send individuals with alcohol or drug problems to outside settings (i.e., carve-outs) that provide standalone treatment for substance use problems.Often these carve-outs are located at quite a distance from the primary-care setting, and there is little communication between the referral source and the specialized treatment setting. Lacking financial incentives and busy with everyday clinical concerns, providers often fail to find the time to follow up on referrals to specialized treatment programs. The lack of communication between primary-care provider and specialist practitioner can impact negatively on referral compliance rates. As indicated earlier, the majority of these referrals fail to enter or remain in these specialized treatment programs.

There are a number of circumstances in which a practitioner might initiate collaboration with a primary-care physician. First, when an individual is experiencing symptoms of alcohol or drug withdrawal, a primary-care physician should make a determination whether the person requires detoxification in an inpatient or outpatient setting before participating in behavioral treatment. Second, when individuals afflicted with medical complications resulting from the substance use problems (such as gastrointestinal, cardiovascular, and hematological diseases), a primary-care physician should treat these disorders either prior to or during the course of behavioral treatment. Third, when individuals are receiving medications for psychiatric diagnoses (such as depression, affective disorders, and anxiety), a primary-care physician should monitor the dosage levels of these medications to handle side effects.

Recently, it has been recommended that primary-care collaboration is necessary when a pharmacotherapy component has been added to behavioral treatment. Medications such as acamprosate and naltrexone have been found to be effective with substance-abusing populations, especially when combined with behavioral treatment (Carroll, 1997). Such medications have been employed to address some of problems related to relapse, including dysphoria and cravings/urges for alcohol. Primary-care physicians must assess the suitability of clients for these medications as well as be responsible for their medical management while receiving them. This requires a complete medical examination to rule out clients who may experience adverse consequences from the drug. For example, individuals with renal disease, hepatic failure, and diabetes are routinely excluded from receiving acamprosate. Medical management of these clients entails reviewing serum chemistry panels and assessing side effects resulting from the medication.

SOCIAL SERVICE SETTINGS

The social service system consists of a variety of nonmedical, nonhospital-based, community-based private for-profit and not-for-profit social agencies. These systems employ persons from many disciplines and include crisis lines, outreach units, day treatment programs, intensive outpatient programs, in-home programs, family service centers, community mental health centers, and individual practitioners. Persons seeking help from these settings often do so for less severe substance use problems; for a full range of family, individual, or marital problems that are related to their substance use; or for other life adjustment difficulties exacerbated by substance use. Such clients may or may not relate these life difficulties to their substance use.

Identification of substance use in social service settings is hampered by this inability to connect substance use with life problems. Nondependent problem drinkers in voluntary social service settings focus on issues which initially brought them into the setting, such as marital conflict, domestic violence, and employment problems, and do not make a connection between their alcohol use and psychosocial issues (Cooney, Zweben, & Fleming, 1995; Zweben & Barrett, 1997). Shaw, Cartwright, Spratley, and Harwin (1978) reported that only 9% of nondependent problem drinkers in social service settings were able to acknowledge their drinking as a primary problem. Even among the more dependent population, frequent heavy drinkers with higher incomes and educational levels are less likely to report both dependence symptoms and alcohol-use-related consequences than those with lower incomes and less education (U.S. Department of Health and Human Services [DHHS], 1993).

Compounding the problem of the lack of awareness of substance abuse is the lack of adequate screening and identification of these problems at intake. Even when presented with clients with substance use difficulties, practitioners in social service settings do not define them as the problem. In a study of 100 cases from four different agencies, only 5 cases were identified as containing a substance abuse problem, despite subsequent interviews that revealed 39 of the cases had some level of substance abuse (Kagle, 1987).

Other than for more severe alcohol dependence, screening for substance abuse has not been a usual part of agency practice. Googins (1984) reported that only 40% of social service agencies included questions about an individual's drinking history (or that of family members) in their intake procedures.

While there are a number of screening instruments available for use among professionals in secondary settings, professionals are not always knowledgeable or trained in their use (Van Wormer, 1987).

When a referral is made by a social service agency, it is typically to a more conventional treatment facility, which usually requires a commitment to abstinence, regular attendance at self-help groups, and participation in an intensive treatment regimen that includes alcohol and drug education and group therapy. Many of the nondependent users who approach social service settings for care are not ready to undergo the rigorous demands or expectations made of participants in traditional treatment programs, which may not be applicable to the range of issues encountered by them.

Providers in more specific substance abuse settings should consider initiating referrals to social service agencies in the community when any family, legal, employment, or financial issues are identified in either assessment or ongoing treatment phases of contact. Practical questions should be raised early about the need for additional social services, and clinicians should specifically ask about concrete needs. Additionally, during the end phase of treatment, providers must also explore what family, legal, vocational, or financial problems have not been resolved despite resolution of the substance-related problems and must consider referral to community social service agencies as part of discharge planning.

LEGAL SYSTEM

Substance abusers often come into contact with the legal system as a result of their substance use. Legal problems may include driving while intoxicated or under the influence (DWI, DUI) offenses, possession or sale of controlled substances, acts of violence while intoxicated, or disorderly conduct. Some persons with substance use problems can be motivated to seek treatment by their contact with the legal system; however, treatment services during incarceration are limited.

The criminal justice system has extensive contact with substance abusers, as criminal populations are disproportionally involved in the use and abuse of both alcohol and illegal drugs (Shaffer, Nurco, & Kinlock, 1984), both in the incarcerated, probation-

ary, and diversionary populations. These offenders have extensive involvement with drugs and alcohol, both prior to and during the commission of crimes (U.S. Bureau of Justice Statistics, 1990). Many offenders who are addicted to drugs and alcohol then become readdicted within a short period of time after release from correctional supervision (Maddux & Desmond, 1981).

Services within the criminal justice system aimed at substance abusers include efforts both within the criminal justice institutions and through limited access to community-based agencies. Community-based initiatives include prevention and early identification programs (e.g., Drug Abuse Resistance Education [DARE]), community-based residential programs as an alternative to revocation for probation and parole violators, day reporting centers providing substance abuse treatment of varying intensities by public or private treatment agencies, home confinement or curfews that allow substance abusers release to seek treatment from community programs, and self-help groups in a community setting. Initiatives within the criminal justice system itself include substance abuse programs offered by probation or corrections agencies on-site, specialized substance abuse caseloads in probation and parole agencies, and self-help groups offered within a justice institution.

The problem of how substance use problems are defined is significant when criminal justice institutions attempt to coordinate with other treatment systems. Just the use of most substances is illegal, either by virtue of the substance itself or the age and status of the user (e.g., the use of alcohol by minors or the use of alcohol while driving a vehicle). Thus, substance use at any level is defined as a crime, requiring legal sanctions, treatment being secondary to the system goal of deterrence and punishment.

The impact of differing goals is problematic in attempts to coordinate substance abuse treatment with any aspect of the legal system. The emphasis in the criminal justice system on punishment as a goal leads to more specific goal of incapacitation or restricting the offender's opportunity to engage in further use. Because a number of substances are illegal in and of themselves, one-time use can result in such restriction. This goal of no use or immediate and total abstinence is often incompatible with substance abuse programs that have controlled use or reduced amount of consumption as a goal. It is clearly in conflict with treatment programs that view relapse or periodic, episodic use as an expectable stage in the recovery process. This conflict makes it problematic at best for a substance abuser to be open in revealing the extent and frequency of his or her use to clinicians who are often required to report to criminal justice officers about their progress.

Rehabilitation approaches in the criminal justice system are less common and depend on several key ingredients, the first being a reliable assessment of the offender's needs and some means of responding to the needs identified from this assessment (CSAT, 1994a). Lurigio and Swartz (1994) reported that difficulties in evaluation and treatment of substance-abusing offenders in urban environments were related to the movement of participants as well as the need for multiagency involvement. Urinanalysis screens are often the first step in an assessment as well as a means of providing information about relapses during ongoing treatment and continuing care. Their limitation as a diagnostic tool is in their exclusive use, as they measure only recent use and provide little information about extent, history, or other important assessment variables.

Referral compliance is effected in legal systems through a series of coercive methods relative to the magnitude of the offense related to the substance use. While this type of coercion is unique to legal systems and may be viewed as counter to best practice methods, Gostin (1991) suggested that such mandatory treatment enhances reduction in morbidity, mortality, and the criminality associated with substance abuse.

The availability of resources continues to be a significant barrier to coordination of care for substance users in the criminal justice system. Probation and parole agencies are faced with increasing numbers of offenders under supervision who have been ordered to comply with outpatient substance abuse treatment, but for whom limited or no treatment is available (CSAT, 1994a; Falkin, Prendergast, & Anglin, 1994). In addition to the magnitude of the demand for services in this population, the complexity of treatment issues for substance abusers involved in the criminal justice system is also an obstacle to coordination. Many providers outside the legal system cite security and safety as reasons for not offering services to substance-abusing offenders, restricting availability of care even further (Petersilia, 1990).

VOCATIONAL REHABILITATION SYSTEMS AND THE EMPLOYMENT SETTING

Vocational rehabilitation programs emphasize work preparation, job-seeking skills, and matching workers with disabilities to jobs which fully utilize their talents. Employment is used as a key variable in determining successful treatment outcomes for drug abuse rehabilitation programs (Platt, 1995). Employment problems are common for persons with substance use disorders, yet comprehensive vocational services are not readily available to them (Schottenfeld, Pascale, & Sokolowski, 1992). Comprehensive rehabilitation programs report that alcohol-related injuries account for up to 79% of rehabilitation patients (Hubbard, Everett, & Kahn, 1996), with preinjury prevalence of alcohol dependence reported in from 29% to 68% of persons with head injuries (Ruff et al., 1990). For persons with spinal cord injuries, preinjury levels of alcohol and drug problems were found to be similar at postinjury, ranging from 17% to 79% (Heinemann, 1991; Heinemann, Goranson, Ginsburg, & Schnoll, 1989). Access to pain and spasticity medications, combined with the experience of pain, spasticity, depression, and frustration, may contribute to abuse of prescription medications by the person with a spinal cord injury (Hubbard et al., 1996).

In addition to vocational rehabilitation programs, business- and industry-based programs for prevention, detection, and referral for workers and family members with problems related to substance abuse are prevalent. Employee assistance programs have been in place since the 1970s to deal with the total spectrum of problems which might impact workers, including substance abuse, family and marital, legal, psychiatric, and financial problems (Roman & Blum, 1993). Employees may self-refer to the EAP, be referred by a work peer, or be referred by a supervisor due to absenteeism or poor work performance. After making a referral, EAP personnel may be involved in posttreatment aftercare, follow-up, and working with managed-care personnel to recommend cost-effective and quality programs. More intensive follow-up has been shown to significantly reduce substance abuse disability costs, treatment cost, and further hospitalizations (Erfurt & Foote, 1988).

Persons with substance use disorders interact with vocational rehabilitation systems in a variety of ways.

Problems with performance, productivity, absenteeism, and supervisory relationships may capture the attention of the employer and precipitate an employee assistance program referral. Although the frontline approach may involve monitoring performance and require that the individual complete a substance abuse treatment program, should the problem get worse and the individual lose his or her job, more formalized vocational rehabilitation intervention may be indicated. Persons with physical or mental disabilities may be involved in the vocational rehabilitation system due to their identified disability, and the substance use disorder may be uncovered over time. A comprehensive substance abuse treatment program might regularly address vocational issues and involve clients in vocational programs aimed at stabilizing their function at work as part of the treatment approach.

Screening and assessment for substance use disorders is not commonly included in the vocational rehabilitation process, unless identified as a problem in the initial referral process. Identification of alcohol abuse in clients with chronic mental illness and physically induced trauma by rehabilitation counselors was found by Ingraham, Kaplan, and Chan (1992) to be underestimated. In a content analysis of the rehabilitation literature, only 20 of 1,743 articles addressed alcohol and drug abuse issues, primarily in traditional vocational rehabilitation programs (Benshoff, Janikowski, Taricone, & Brenner, 1990). Identification of substance use disorders in vocational rehabilitation program participants in an adult prison release program was identified as a key variable in success on parole, with emphasis placed on acquisition of marketable job skills and psychological counseling for substance use disorders while incarcerated (Anderson, Schumacker, & Anderson, 1991).

Goals of the workplace via EAPs and vocational rehabilitation programs typically focus in two directions: one toward job placement and stability, and the other toward abstinence or involvement in substance abuse treatment. Although these goals can be consistent with one another, they may be emphasized differently by the system measuring outcome (Roman & Blum, 1993).

Referral compliance strategies related to alcohol and other drug specialized treatment services are enhanced when involvement in vocational rehabilitation services is a condition of continued employment. The complexity of issues around referral and treatment compliance in a program where substance abuse problems were addressed in an integrated supported employment program found that monitoring compliance, lack of funding and appropriate treatment, withdrawal of services for noncompliance, and problems with family support and transportation were identified as issues (Groah, Goodall, Kreutzer, & Sherron, 1990).

For example, a supported employment program at the University of Virginia for individuals with traumatic brain injury found that an education program identifying risks and consequences of substance abuse, an emphasis on abstinence to help those with memory problems, and providing medical and psychological reasons for abstinence to be important aspects of the substance abuse treatment component.

Employment problems are common for persons with substance use disorders, yet comprehensive vocational services are not readily available to them (Schottenfeld et al., 1992). A comprehensive substance abuse treatment program might regularly address vocational issues and involve its clients in vocational programs aimed at stabilizing their functioning at work as a part of the treatment approach.

DISCUSSION: TOWARD THE DEVELOPMENT OF A BEST PRACTICE MODEL

In the search for best practice models, multiple forces are driving the trend toward coordination among systems that interact with substance abusers. First is an awareness of the increasing magnitutde of the population of persons abusing a wide range of substances. As the definitional parameters for substance abuse increase, more persons are included in the population of concern. Second is the variety of settings with which these persons interact. As greater recognition develops of the continuum of severity of problems experienced by persons using substances, more service systems are developing methods of identifying persons with a range of substance use problems among their target populations. Third is the incursion of managed-care methods into both the private and public care systems that emphasize coordinated systems and a continuum of care. The need to develop more cost-conscious methods of care in line with the principle of parsimony (the least treatment necessary is the best treatment) argues for incorporating brief interventions into standard practice protocols (and evaluating their effectiveness) for treating persons with the full range of substance use problems.

Minimally, the components of such a coordinated system of care must include (a) a network with a continuum of care for persons with all levels of substance use problems, (b) the development of staff skills in screening for substance use problems and motivational enhancement for treatment and referral, (c) methods of coordinating this care among settings, and (d) the incorporation of brief interventions in all settings.

First, a network of care must be able to accommodate various levels of severity and disability, motivation, and compliance as well as different goals in relation to abstinence. This continuum of care must include acute stabilization systems for a range of substance-abuse-related problems, including psychiatric, financial, child care, and legal. Continuity of care must be established between programs and components, as well as over time.

Second, all treatment contacts with persons in nonspecialized settings should include basic screening for substance use problems, most especially all frontline staff should be trained in the use of these screening methods (CSAT, 1994b). This type of training must be clearly connected to the primary purpose of the setting and the awareness of how undiagnosed and untreated substance abuse problems can prevent the attainment of the more primary goal of the setting (i.e., the protection of children, the amelioration of symptoms of a specific mental disorder, the reduction of reoffending, the completion of vocational training, the reduction of physical symptomatology, or the maintenance of financial stability).

In child protection agencies, more easily administered screening instruments (e.g., Michigan Alcoholism Screening Test [MAST]) can be used routinely in investigations of allegations of abuse and neglect. More objective safety assessment instruments are being developed in a number of child welfare jurisdictions (e.g., Child Well-Being Scales), and it would be consistent with these methods to add screening for substance use problems.

In primary-care settings, methods of screening and brief intervention could easily be incorporated into daily routines of medical practices delivered by a physician or intervention specialist such as a nurse, health educator, and physician assistant and are consistent with secondary prevention activities carried out in relation to other medical conditions such as diabetes, hypertension, and depression.

In criminal justice systems, assessment and screening should occur at pretrial hearings, as well as at admission to incarceration. Judges could be advised about the substance abuse treatment options and encouraged to consider them during these hearings.

Third, coordination of ongoing care requires more systemic change. Linkages between systems can occur through joint training (e.g., child protection workers and probation officers), the development of joint protocols between related agencies (i.e., social service and mental health), and institution of specific procedures to facilitate referrals at an institutional level (e.g., common intake forms). The development of a communitywide care management team has been attempted in child welfare (i.e., "wrap around services") and might be successfully utilized in the treatment of adult substance abusers.

Fourth, incorporating brief interventions into standard practice protocols for treating persons with the full range of substance-use-related problems should be encouraged. Increased use of brief interventions provides more targeted treatment and increases the gatekeeping function of practitioners in specialized and nonspecialized settings. In nonspecialized settings such as hospitals, EAPs, and child welfare systems, brief intervention can also serve as a case-finding technique, reducing barriers to care by identifying and treating alcohol use problems complicating the primary focus of care.

The lack of education about specific methods and the rationale for the use of brief interventions acts as a barrier to their use by practitioners in nonspecialized settings. Empirical evidence that addresses the effectiveness and implementation of brief interventions should be included not just in professional journals specific to the field of alcoholism treatment, but also in professional journals with a more generalized audience (e.g., child welfare, mental health, criminal justice, public welfare, women's issues, gerontology, and health). Such material might also be included through in-service training workshops for persons in nonspecialized settings. The focus of such education and training should be on a public health approach with an emphasis on primary prevention and the early intervention aspects of secondary prevention.

CONCLUSIONS

The practice environment has moved beyond individual systems of care. Encouraged by the incentives for coordination offered by managed-care organizations, private agencies are partnering with related providers in order to position themselves to accept referrals from funders of physical and behavioral health care. At the public level, grants for new programs more commonly require evidence of coordination with other providers as a consideration for funding. Thus, administrators and practitioners who wish to have a voice in how these systems are to be coordinated must take the lead in the design of these systems or find themselves adapting to systems designed primarily by health insurance companies.

Providers in both specialized and nonspecialized settings have a unique opportunity to improve the care of individuals with alcohol or drug problems through development of and participation in coordinated systems of care. While these systems must recognize the diversity of approach of the individual agencies, they must also strive to reach consensus on compatible goals, methods, and policies. These are complex issues, requiring open discussion at both the practitioner and the systemic level.

The challenges of coordination are complex, but the consequences of the lack of coordination are profound for both clients and providers. The impact of increasing costs coupled with less than adequate treatment demands the investment of time and money to develop the knowledge and skill necessary to coordinate the care of the growing number of persons with substance-use-related problems.

Key References

Barth, R. P., Pietrzak, J., & Ramler, M. (1993). *Families living with drugs and HIV: Intervention and treatment strategies.* New York: Guilford Press.

Cooney, N. L., Zweben, A., & Fleming, M. F. (1995). Screening for alcohol problems and at-risk drinking in healthcare settings. In R. K. Hester & W. R. Miller (Eds.), *Handbook of alcoholism treatment approaches* (2nd ed., pp. 45–60). Boston: Allyn & Bacon.

Groah, C., Goodall, P., Kreutzer, J. S., & Sherron, P. (1990). Addressing substance abuse issues in the context of a supported employment program. *Cognitive Rehabilitation, 8*(4), 8–12.

References

American Academy of Pediatrics, Committee on Substance Abuse. (1990). Drug-exposed infants. *Pediatrics 86*(4), 639–642.

Anderson, D. B., Schumaker, R. E., & Anderson, S. L. (1991). Releasee characteristics and parole success. *Journal of Offender Rehabilitation, 17*(1–2), 133–145.

Austin, J., Bloom, B., & Donahue, T. (1992). *Female offenders in the community: An analysis of innovative strategies and programs.* San Francisco: National Council on Crime and Delinquency.

Babor, T. F., Ritson, E. B., & Hodgson, R. J. (1986). Alcohol-related problems in the primary health care setting: A review of early intervention strategies. *British Journal of Addiction, 81,* 23–46.

Barth, R. (1993a). Rationale and conceptual framework. In R. P. Barth, J. Pietrazak, & M. Ramler (Eds.), *Families living with drugs and HIV: Interventions and treatment strategies.* (pp. 3–17). New York: Guilford Press.

Barth, R. (1993b). Shared family care: Child protection without parent-chld separation (pp. 272–295). In R. P. Barth, J. Pietrazak, & M. Ramler (Eds.), *Families living with drugs and HIV: Intervention and treatment strategies.* New York: Guilford Press.

Benshoff, J. J., Janikowski, T. P., Taricone, P. F., & Brenner, J. S. (1990). Alcohol and drug abuse: A content analysis of the rehabilitation literature. *Journal of Applied Rehabilitation Counseling, 21*(4), 9–12.

Besharov, D. (1989). The children of crack: Will we protect them? *Public Welfare, 47,* 7–11.

Carroll, K. M. (1997). Integrating psychotherapy and pharmacotherapy to improve drug abuse outcomes. *Addictive Behaviors, 2,* 233–246.

Center for Substance Abuse Treatment. (1994a). *Assessment and treatment of patients with coexisting mental illness and alcohol and other drug abuse.* Washington, DC: Public Health Service, Substance Abuse and Mental Health Services Administration.

Center for Substance Abuse Treatment. (1994b). *Improving treatment for drug-exposed infants.* Washington, DC: Public Health Service, Substance Abuse and Mental Health Services Administration.

Chasnoff, I. J. (1989). Cocaine, pregnancy, and the neonate. *Women and Health, 15*(3), 23–35.

Chasnoff, I. J. (1992). Drug use in pregnancy: Parameters of risk. *Pediatric Clinics of North America, 35,* 1403.

Cooney, N. L., Zweben, A., & Fleming, M. F. (1995). Screening for alcohol problems and at-risk drinking in healthcare settings. In R. K. Hester & W. R. Miller (Eds.), *Handbook of alcoholism treatment approaches* (2nd ed., pp. 45–60). Boston: Allyn & Bacon.

Daro, D. (1988). *Confronting child abuse.* New York: Free Press.

Daro, D., & McCurdy, K. (1994). *Current trends in child abuse reporting and fatalities: NCPCA's 1993 annual fifty state survey.* Chicago: National Committee for Prevention of Child Abuse.

Daro, D., & Mitchell, L. (1989). *Child abuse fatalities continue to rise: Results of the 1988 annual fifty state survey* (Fact Sheet #14). Chicago: National Committee for Prevention of Child Abuse.

Dicker, M., & Leighton, E. A. (1991). Trends in diagnosed drug problems among newborns: United States, 1979–1987. *Drug and Alcohol Dependence,* 28 (August), 151–165.

Downs, S. W., Costin, L. B., & McFadden, E. J. (1996). *Child welfare and family services: Policies and practice.* White Plains, NY: Longman.

Elvy, G. A., Wells, J. E., & Baird, K. A. (1988). Attempted referral as intervention for problem drinking in the general hospital. *British Journal of Addiction,* 83, 83–89.

Erfurt, J. C., & Foote, A. (1988). The impact of intensive in-plant followup on EAP effectiveness and relapse prevention. *Research Track,* 17th Annual AL-MACA Conference, Los Angeles, 1–7.

Ewing, H. (1991, April 19). *Management of the pregnant alcoholic/addict.* Paper presented at the American Society of Addictions Medicine Scientific Conference, Boston, Massachusetts.

Falkin, G. P., Prendergast, M., & Anglin, M. D. (1994). Drug treatment in the criminal justice system. *Federal Probation,* 58(3), 31–36.

Fleming, M., Cotter, F., & Talboy, E. (1997). *Training physicians in techniques for alcohol screening and brief intervention.* Washington, DC: U.S. Dept. of Health and Human Services, Public Health Services, National Institute of Health, National Institute on Alcohol Abuse and Alcoholism.

Fleming, M. F., Barry, K. L., Manwell, L. B., Johnson, C., & London, R. L. (1997). Brief physician advice for problem drinkers: A randomized controlled trial in community based primary care practices. *Journal of the American Medical Association,* 277(13), 1039–1045.

Freier, M. C., Griffith, D. R., & Chasnoff, I. J. (1991). In utero drug expose: Developmental follow-up and maternal-infant interaction. *Seminars in Perinatology,* 15(4), 310–316.

Gelles, R. J., & Cornell, C. P. (1990). *Intimate violence in families* (2nd ed.). Newbury Park, CA: Sage.

Goldberg, H. I., Millen, M., Richard, K. R., Psaty, B. M., & Ruch, B. P. (1991). Alcohol counseling in a general medical clinic. *Medicine Care,* 7, JS49–JS56.

Googins, B. (1984). Avoidance of the alcoholic client. *Social Work,* 29(2), 161–166.

Gostin, L. O. (1991). Compulsory treatment for drug-dependent persons: Justifications for a public health approach to drug dependency. *Milbank Quarterly,* 69, 561–593.

Groah, C., Goodall, P., Kreutzer, J. S., & Sherron, P. (1990). Addressing substance abuse issues in the context of a supported employment program. *Cognitive Rehabilitation,* 8(4), 8–12.

Heinemann, A. W. (1991). Substance abuse and spinal cord injury. *Paraplegia News* (July), 16–17.

Heinemann, A. W., Goranson, N., Ginsburg, K., & Schnoll, S. (1989). Alcohol use and activity patterns following spinal cord injury. *Rehabilitation Psychology,* 34, 191–205.

Hubbard, J. R., Everett, A. S., & Kahn, M. A. (1996). Alcohol and drug abuse in patients with physical disabilities. *American Journal of Drug and Alcohol Abuse,* 22, 215–231.

Ingraham, K., Kaplan, S., & Chan, F. (1992). Rehabilitation counselors' awareness of client alcohol abuse patterns. *Journal of Applied Rehabilitation Counseling,* 23(3), 18–22.

Institute of Medicine. (1990). *Broadening the base of treatment for alcohol problems.* Washington, DC: National Academy Press.

Kagle, J. D. (1987). Secondary prevention of substance abuse. *Social Work,* 32, 446–448.

Leonard, K. E., & Jacob, T. (1988). Alcohol, alcoholism, and family violence. In V. B. Van Hasselt, R. I. Morrison, & A. S. Bellack (Eds.), *Handbook of family violence* (pp. 139–154). New York: Plenum Press.

Lurigio, A. J., & Swartz, J. (1994). Life at the interface: Issues in the implementation and evaluation of a multiphased, multiagency jail-based treatment program. *Evaluation and Program Planning,* 17, 205–216.

Maddux, J. F., & Desmond, D. P. (1981). *Careers of opioid users.* New York: Praeger.

National Institute on Alcohol Abuse and Alcoholism. (1990). *Alcohol and health: Seventh Special Report to the U.S. Congress.* Washington, DC: U.S. Department of Health and Human Services.

National Institute on Alcohol Abuse and Alcoholism. (1995). *The physician's guide to helping patients with alcohol problems.* Washington, DC: U.S. Department of Health and Human Services, National Institutes of Health, NIH Publication No. 95-3769.

National Institute on Drug Abuse. (1992). *National household survey on drug abuse: Highlights, 1991* (DHHS Publications No. ADM 91-1681). Rockville, MD: Author.

Petersilia, J. (1990). Conditions that permit intensive supervision programs to survive. *Crime and Delinquency* 36(1), 126–145.

Platt, J. J. (1995). Vocational rehabilitation of drug abusers. *Psychological Bulletin, 117,* 416–433.

Rees, E. W., Beech, H. R., & Hore, B. D. (1984). Some factors associated with compliance in treatment of alcoholism. *Alcohol and Alcoholism, 19,* 303–307.

Roberts, D. E. (1990). Drug addicted women who have babies. *Trial* (April), 56–61.

Roman, P. M., & Blum, T. C. (1993). Dealing with alcohol problems in the workplace. In M. Galanter (Ed.), *Recent developments in alcoholism: Vol. 11. Ten years of progress* (pp. 473–491). New York: Plenum Press.

Rose, S. J., & Keigher, S. M. (1996). Managing mental health: Whose responsibility? *Health and Social Work, 21(1),* 76–80.

Rossett, H., & Weiner, L. (1984). *Alcohol and the fetus: A clinical perspective.* New York: Oxford University Press.

Ruff, R. M., Marshall, L. G., Kauber, M. R., Blunt, B. A., Grant, I., Foulkes, M. A., Eisenberg, J., Jane, J., & Marmarou, A. (1990). Alcohol abuse and neurological outcome of the severely head injured. *Journal of Head Trauma Rehabilitation, 5(3),* 21–31

Schottenfeld, R. S., Pascale, R., & Sokolowski, S. (1992). Matching services to needs: Vocational services for substance abusers. *Journal of Substance Abuse Treatment, 9,* 3–8.

Serdula, M., Williamson, D. F., Kendrick, J. S., Anda, R. F., & Byers, T. (1991). Trends in alcohol consumption by pregnant women: 1985–1988. *Journal of the American Medical Association, 265(7),* 876–879.

Shaffer, J. E., Nurco, D. N., & Kinlock, T. W. (1984). A new classification of narcotic addicts based on type and extent of criminal activity. *Comprehensive Psychiatry, 25,* 315–328.

Shaw, S., Cartwright, A., Spratley, T., & Harwin, J. (1978). *Responding to drinking problems.* Baltimore, MD: University Park Press.

Smith, S. M., & Kunjukrishnan, R. (1985). Child abuse: Perspectives on treatment and research. *Psychiatric Clinics of North America, 32,* 685–694.

Soderstrom, C. B., & Cowley, R. A. (1987). A national alcohol and trauma center survey. *Archives of Surgery, 122,* 1067–1071.

Sokol, R. J., & Abel, E. L. (1992). Risk factors for alcohol-related birth defects: Threshold, susceptibility,

and prevention. In T. B. Sonderegger (Ed.), *Perinatal substance abuse* (pp. 90–103). Baltimore: Johns Hopkins University Press.

Spaid, W. M., & Fraser, M. (1991). The correlates of success/failure in brief and intensive family treatment: Implications for family preservation services. *Children and Youth Services Review, 13,* 77–99.

Starr, R. H. (1982). A research-based approach to the prediction of child abuse. In R. H. Starr (Ed.), *Child abuse prediction* (pp. 105–134). Cambridge, MA: Ballinger.

Stephen, M., Swindle, R. W., & Moos, R. H. (1992). Alcohol screening in the Department of Veteran Affairs medical centers. In R. E. Parry (Ed.), *Screening for alcoholism in the Department of Veteran Affairs.* Washington, DC: Department of Veteran Affairs.

Stephens-Cherpitel, C. J. (1988). Drinking patterns and problems associated with injury status in emergency room admissions. *Alcoholism: Clinical and Experimental Research, 12(1),* 105–110.

Straus, M. A. (1980). Stress and physical abuse. *Child Abuse and Neglect, 4,* 75–88.

Switch to managed care tricky. (1995, July 13). *Chicago Tribune,* Section 1, p. 1.

Thom, B., Brown, C., Drummond, C., Edwards, G., Mullan, M., & Taylor, C. (1992). Engaging patients with alcohol problems in treatment: The first consultation. *British Journal of Addiction, 87,* 601–611.

Tracy, E. M. (1994). Maternal substance abuse: Protecting the child, preserving the family. *Social Work, 39(5),* 534–540.

Tracy, E. M., & Farkas, K. J. (1994). Preparing practitioners for child welfare practice with substance-abusing families. *Child Welfare, 73(1),* 57–68.

Tracy, E. M., Green, R. K., & Bremseth, M. D. (1993). Meeting the environmental needs of abused and neglected children: Implications from a statewide survey of supportive services. *Social Work Research and Abstracts, 29(2),* 21–26.

U.S. Bureau of Justice Statistics. (1990). *Bureau of Justice Statistics data report, 1989.* Washington, DC: U.S. Department of Justice.

U.S. Bureau of Justice Statistics. (1993). *Survey of state prison inmates, 1991.* Washington, DC: U.S. Department of Justice

U.S. Department of Health and Human Services. (1993). *Eighth special report to the U.S. Congress on alcohol and health.* Washington, DC: Government Printing Office, ADM 291-91-003, NIH Publication No. 94-3699.

U.S. Government Accounting Office. (1990). *Drug-exposed infants: A generation at risk.* Washington, DC: Author.

Van Wormer, K. (1987). Social work and alcoholism counseling. *Social Casework, 68*(7), 426–432.

Waller, J. (1988). *Diagnosis of alcoholism in the injured patient.* Paper presented at the NIAAA conference on Post-Injury Treatment of Patients with Alcohol-Related Trauma, Washington, DC.

Wolock, I., & Horowitz, B. (1979). Child maltreatment and material deprivation among AFDC-recipient families. *Social Service Review, 53*, 175–194.

Zweben, A., & Barrett, D. (1997). Facilitating compliance in alcoholism treatment. In B. Blackwell (Ed.), *Treatment compliance and the therapeutic alliance* (pp. 277–293). New York: Gorgon & Breach.

Zweben, A., & Fleming, M. D. (in press). Brief intervention for alcohol and drug problems. In J. Tucker, D. M. Donovan, & G. B. Marlatt (Eds.), *Changing addictive behaviors: Moving beyond therapy assisted change.* New York: Guilford Press.

VI

Issues in Specific Populations

25

Treatment of Persons with Dual Diagnoses of Substance Use Disorder and Other Psychological Problems

Richard N. Rosenthal

Laurence Westreich

The practical textbook on the treatment of addictive disorders should include a chapter on dual diagnosis because of the historical disconnection between the organized mental health delivery system, its attendant public and private services, the professional training programs that fuel them, and the traditional addiction treatment system that serves patients with addictive disorders. As a result, clinicians are typically undereducated in one of the two clinical domains. Patients with both addictive disorders and other mental disorders are frequently underdiagnosed and almost certainly undertreated. In addition, the lack of attention to addiction treatment in the training of mental health professionals and of appropriate attention to mental disorders in training addiction professionals, as well as the fact that many reimbursement methodologies reinforce a tradition of singular diagnosis, all contribute to nontreatment of even recognized disorders. The current dichotomy is a result of history, politics, expedience, economics, cultural traditions, and belief systems and its not due

to rational scientific distinctions in biological vulnerability, chronicity, psychosocial impairment, or potential for treatment.

Detailed coverage of the topic of comorbidity could easily fill an entire book. Therefore, this chapter will attempt to address important concepts that the authors believe are important to the clinical approach to patients with substance use disorders (SUDs) and to provide sufficient factual information to reinforce acceptance and retention of those concepts. For the heuristic goals of this chapter, the set of mental disorders not related to substance use needs to be characterized. Previous attempts have called these disorders *functional* as contrasted to *organic*, or *other mental disorders*. This chapter will simply call those disorders *non-substance-related (NSR) mental disorders*.

OVERVIEW

As the bulk of the addiction treatments supplied by the mental health delivery system in the first half of the 20th century were psychodynamic in nature, the focus upon the continued failure to regain control of addictive behavior led dynamic theorists to conceptualize the addict as having a personality structure that generally precluded analytic treatment. With the failure of traditionally applied psychotherapy to treat addiction, the concept of *addictive personality* was developed, characterizing this population as having poor frustration tolerance, manipulativeness, insincerity, and superego lacunae. This attitude among the trendmakers in mental health led to a further disenfranchisement of the addicted population from the mental health delivery system. In self-fulfilling terms, there arose a widespread belief that since addicts were not treatable by the analytic method, they therefore were not treatable. This is a bias that persists to this day both in the mental health domain and in the general public. Mental health workers have tended to look at substance use disorders as bad behavior that complicates the treatment of other mental disorders, rather than as independent disorders requiring specific treatment by knowledgeable practitioners.

The emergence of self-help groups gave first to alcoholics and then to other substance-dependent people an approach attained by trial and error to achieve and maintain abstinence. The self-help philosophy underscored much of the approach of the professional addiction treatment community. Over time, these approaches provided a philosophical view about addiction that was different from the view within the mental health delivery system. Based on an expanding knowledge and philosophical base, these alcohol and substance dependence treatment systems developed educational and professional licensure pathways that were by and large in parallel with, but separate from, the traditional mental health training pathways. At present, regulatory agencies are stabilizers of a nonunified view of addiction and mental disorder, due to the typical pattern of licensing programs and paying for treatment of either chemical dependence or NSR mental disorders, but not both.

INCIDENCE AND PREVALENCE

General Epidemiology

Prevalence rates of both mental disorders and substance use disorders are much higher than clinicians typically believe. Derived from a nationally representative sample of 8,098 persons in the community, the National Comorbidity Survey (NCS) lifetime prevalence rate of all *DSM-III-R* (American Psychiatric Association [APA], 1987) alcohol, drug, and mental (ADM) disorders is 48.0%, and the 12-month prevalence is 29.5% (Kessler et al., 1994). The 48% ADM disorder prevalence includes disorders such as simple phobias and mild adjustment disorders that tend to be self-limited and generate little clinical attention.

The NCS lifetime prevalence for any substance use disorder is 26.6%, for other mental disorders is 21.4%, and for both disorders is 13.7%. Of the 48% of the U.S. population with lifetime ADM disorders, less than half (21%) will have only one disorder, whereas 27% will have two or more disorders (Kessler et al., 1994). In any year, the prevalence rate for comorbid substance use and other mental disorders is 2.7% (Kessler et al., 1994), of which fewer than half receive any treatment (Kessler et al., 1996). Of the population with 12-month severe disorders (psychosis, mania, or needing hospitalization), 89.5% had three or more lifetime ADM disorders (14% of the sample). The high prevalence rate of psychiatric morbidity is therefore concentrated in about one sixth of the population with three or more comorbid disorders. Yet, among this group, fewer than half ever have specialty mental health or addiction treatment (Kessler et al., 1994). From a utilization/costs perspective, comorbid disorders of patients are underrecognized and undertreated, yet those that are treatment seeking use a disproportionately large share of available treatment resources. It is thus important to focus on this population, not only because of the historical difficulty in entering and maintaining these patients in treatment, but also because of the obvious economic impact this subpopulation has compared with patients with only a single ADM disorder.

Data from the Epidemiologic Catchment Area Study (ECA) of the National Institute of Mental Health, a non-treatment-seeking community sample, have been used to estimate U.S. population lifetime prevalence rates for *DSM-III* (APA, 1980) Axis I mental disorders (affective, anxiety, and schizophrenia) and antisocial personality disorder, for alcohol abuse and dependence, and for other substance abuse and dependence (Regier et al., 1990). Among persons with addictive disorders, any comorbid mental disorder occurs at greater than expected rates, with 37% lifetime prevalence for alcohol abuse/dependence and 53% for other drug abuse or dependence. ECA data also demonstrate that a history of mental disorder increases lifetime odds ratios for any alcohol or drug disorder to 2.7 over normal risk values (Regier et al., 1990) and 10–20 times greater than expected for patients with schizophrenia, mania, or antisocial personality disorder (Boyd et al., 1984). Thus, NSR psychopathology is a risk factor for substance abuse.

Comorbidity in Treatment-Seeking Samples

Househould sample prevalence rates are compelling enough from the epidemiological point of view, but the rates of comorbidity in treatment-seeking populations are even higher. The highest rates of comorbid disorders are typically found in institutional populations such as hospital inpatient and outpatient psychiatric units, substance abuse treatment programs, and jails (Hien, Zimberg, Weisman, First, & Ackerman, 1997; Jordan, Schlenger, Fairbank, & Caddell, 1996; Kokkevi & Stefanis, 1995; Regier et al., 1990).

Surveys of inpatient and outpatient psychiatric facilities indicate that 20–50% of psychiatric patients have concurrent problems with alcoholism or substance abuse (Galanter, Castaneda, & Ferman, 1988). There is a high rate of alcohol and substance abuse among patients hospitalized with psychiatric disorders (Fernandez-Pol, Bluestone, & Mizruchi, 1988; Fischer, Halikas, Baker, & Smith, 1975; Richard, Liskow, & Perry, 1985), a rate that may be inflated due to higher rates of treatment-seeking among patients with comorbidity (Berkson, 1946). In a study of public hospital psychiatric inpatients, 55.9% had current psychoactive substance use disorders (Lehman, Myers, Corty, & Thompson, 1994). The most common substances used by patients in psychiatric treatment are nicotine, alcohol, marijuana, and cocaine. The reported rates vary from 30% to 70%, and are highest in populations with most acuity or severity.

In those patients seeking treatment in addiction treatment centers, there is wider variation in reports of concurrent mental illness, including reports that seem low when compared to epidemiological samples. One reason for these lower rates is that certain settings (e.g., traditional therapeutic communities) typically screen out patients with severe mental illness or in need of psychotropic medication. For example, rates have been found for bipolar disorder as low as 2–4% in alcoholic inpatients (Hesselbrock, Meyer, & Keener, 1985; Lydiard, Brady, Ballenger,

Howell, & Malcolm, 1992). In addiction treatment settings, there are high comorbidity rates for Axis II disorders. Kranzler, Satel, and Apter (1994) found among cocaine-dependent inpatients that 70% met criteria for at least one Axis II diagnosis; the mean number of Axis II diagnoses among these patients was 2.54. The most common Axis II diagnosis was borderline (34% of all patients), followed by antisocial and narcissistic (each 28%), avoidant and paranoid (each 22%), obsessive-compulsive (16%), and dependent (10%).

Specific Mental Disorders

Table 25.1 summarizes ECA data for lifetime prevalence of SUD in persons with various Axis I NSR mental disorders.

Depression and SUD

Up to 40% of mixed groups of substance abusers have concurrent *DSM-III* Axis I diagnoses in addition to drug and alcohol dependence (Mirin, Weiss, Michael, & Griffin, 1988; O'Brien, Woody, & McLellan, 1984). Conversely, subgroups of the population (e.g., young adult males) with moderate to severe depressive disorders have substance abuse in 44–48% of cases (Schuckit, 1985). These rates of substance abuse co-occurring with depression are in excess of the 1-month (3.8%) and the lifetime (16.4%) prevalence rates of substance use disorders in the general population, or the 9.3% 1-month prevalence rate of substance abuse disorders in males aged 18–24 years, as estimated from ECA data (Regier et al., 1988). Similarly, the lifetime prevalence rate of major depression is clearly overrepresented among patients with substance use disorders who seek addiction treatment (24.3%) compared with the 5.8% lifetime prevalence of major depression in the general population (Regier et al., 1988; Ross, Glaser, & Germanson, 1988). Major or minor depression also appears to be a risk factor for increased cocaine abuse in a 2.5-year follow-up study of 268 opioid addicts, as those with increased cocaine abuse at follow-up were more likely to have depressive disorders (Kosten, Rounsaville, & Kleber, 1987).

Bipolar Disorder and SUD

Of all Axis I disorders, bipolar disorder is the most likely to co-occur with substance use disorders. The

TABLE 25.1 Lifetime Prevalence of SUD in Persons with Axis I NSR Mental Disorders

	Any substance		Alcohol diagnosis		Other drug diagnosis	
Major depression	27.2%	1.9[a]	16.5%	1.3[a]	18.0%	3.8[a]
Bipolar I disorder	60.7%	7.9	46.2%	5.6	40.7%	11.1
Schizophrenia	47.0%	4.6	33.7%	3.3	27.5%	6.2
Anxiety disorders	23.7%	1.7	17.9%	1.5	11.9%	2.5
Panic disorder	35.8%	2.9	28.7%	2.6	16.7%	3.2
Phobia	22.9%	1.6	17.3%	1.4	11.2%	2.2
Obsessive-compulsive	32.8%	2.5	24.0%	2.1	18.4%	3.7

Note. Adapted from Regier et al. (1990).

[a]This column lists odds ratios.

ECA estimate of the lifetime prevalence of any substance abuse or dependence among persons with any bipolar disorder (I & II) is 56.1% and with Bipolar I disorder is 60.7% (Regier et al., 1990). This high comorbidity rate has been demonstrated in clinical samples (Brady, Casto, Lydiard, Malcolm, & Arana, 1991; Miller, Busch, & Tanenbaum, 1989; Reich, Davies, & Himmelhoch, 1974; Winokur et al., 1995). Patients with harder-to-treat subtypes of bipolar disorder (e.g., mixed, rapid-cycling) are more likely to have substance use disorders (Brady & Sonne, 1995; Calabrese & Delucci, 1990; Keller et al., 1986). Antisocial personality disorder is the only NSR mental disorder with a documented higher rate of comorbid substance use disorder than bipolar disorder.

Personality Disorder and SUD

Helzer and Pryzbeck (1988) reported from ECA data a strong risk relationship of alcoholism for antisocial personality disorder (ASPD), with a lifetime ASPD prevalence of 15% in alcoholic men compared with 4% in nonalcoholic men. ASPD and antisocial behavior are frequent in individuals with alcoholism and occur three times more frequently in males than in females (48% vs. 15%). In a sample of 716 treatment-seeking opioid abusers, the most common NSR diagnosis was ASPD, seen in 25.1% (Brooner, King, Kidorf, Schmidt, & Bigelow, 1997). In families where there is both ASPD and alcoholism in one or both biological parents, the risk for alcoholism in the offspring increases over that for either disorder alone. Rounsaville et al. (1991) reported that 32.9% of treatment-seeking cocaine abusers met DSM-III-R criteria for ASPD. Among 50 patients hospitalized for

cocaine dependence, Weiss, Mirin, Griffin, Gunderson, and Hufford (1993) found that 74% had at least one personality disorder, of which 69% of Axis II diagnoses remained relatively stable independent of current drug use patterns. Resnick and Resnick (1986) emphasized the borderline or narcissistic personality organization of many compulsive cocaine users.

Schizophrenia and SUD

Longitudinal studies have shown that young adults (aged 18–30) with schizophrenia and related disorders commonly abuse drugs and alcohol (25–60%) (Test, Knoedler, Allness, & Burke, 1985; Test, Wallisch, Allness, & Ripp, 1989). These high rates of substance abuse co-occurring with schizophrenia exceed the 3.8% 1-month and the 16.4% ECA lifetime prevalence rates of substance use disorders in the general population, or the 9.3% 1-month prevalence rate of substance use disorders in males aged 18–24 years (Regier et al., 1988). Compared with the lifetime prevalence of schizophrenia in the general population (1.3%), among patients with substance use disorders seeking addiction treatment the lifetime prevalence rate of schizophrenia is overrepresented (7.4%) (Regier et al., 1988; Ross et al., 1988). Among psychiatric inpatients, stimulants such as cocaine and amphetamines are more likely to have been abused by schizophrenia patients than by other diagnostic groups (Richard et al., 1985; Treffert, 1978).

Panic Disorder and SUD

From ECA estimates, persons with panic disorder have a 35.8% lifetime prevalence of any substance disorder (Regier et al., 1990). From NCS estimates, in any 12-month period 16% of people with panic disorder have a substance use disorder (Kessler et al., 1996). Alcohol treatment settings have yielded lifetime prevalence rates of panic disorder from 2% to 21%, again, generally higher than prevalence of panic disorder from epidemiological samples of the general population, where the rates are 1.4–3.5% (Kessler et al., 1994). Interestingly, although the lifetime panic disorder prevalence rates for women are about twice those for men in general population samples, male relatives of agoraphobics are at increased risk for alcohol disorder, whereas female relatives are at increased risk for agoraphobia. ECA data also show an increased risk of panic disorder in cocaine abusers (Anthony, Tien, & Petronis, 1989), and cocaine has been implicated in precipitating panic disorder (Aronson & Craig, 1986).

Posttraumatic Stress Disorder and SUD

Among substance abusers, substance abuse appears to be a predisposing factor for the development of posttraumatic stress disorder (PTSD) (Cottler, Compton, Mager, Spitznagel, & Janca, 1992) and is a common comorbid diagnosis (Hyer, Leach, Boudewyns, & Davis, 1991). Clinical samples of substance abusers have demonstrated high rates of comorbid PTSD symptoms both among male veterans (McFall, Mackay, & Donovan, 1991) and civilian women (Kovatch, 1986), although women have twice the risk of men of developing PTSD (Kessler et al., 1994). PTSD appears both to increase the risk for relapse in patients with substance use disorders and to be associated with poorer treatment outcome, but this has not been well documented (Brown & Wolfe, 1994).

Attention Deficit Hyperactivity Disorder and SUD

In adult patients with attention deficit hyperactivity disorder (ADHD), several studies have demonstrated an elevated, even doubled, risk of substance use disorders compared with the general population (Biederman et al., 1993, 1995). In ADHD adults, lifetime alcohol use disorders range from 17% to 45%, and other substance use disorders range from 9% to 30% (Biederman et al., 1993). Wilens, Spenser, and Biederman (1994) found in reviewing studies of adult and adolescent patients with substance use disorders that

ADHD was found in 23% of the combined sample. ADHD typically has an earlier onset than substance use disorder, but both predominate in males, tend to run in families, appear to have a genetic component, and share high rates of comorbidity with antisocial personality and mood and anxiety disorders (Biederman, Newcorn, & Sprich, 1991; Wilens, Biederman, Spenser, & Frances, 1994).

CONCEPTUALIZING PROBLEMS OF THE DUALLY DIAGNOSED

Extrinsic/Systemic Problems

The largest current problem for patients with comorbid substance use and other mental disorders is the lack of integrated treatment systems at the national, state, and local levels that could provide for comprehensive diagnosis and appropriate, integrated treatments. The fourth edition of the *Diagnostic and Statistical Manual* (*DSM-IV*; APA, 1994) classifies drug addiction as a series of diagnosable mental disorders, yet most treatment for patients with concurrent substance use and mental disorders is not delivered in a specialty mental health or even an addiction setting (Narrow, Regier, Rae, Manderscheid, & Locke, 1993).

Due to traditional gaps in the training of clinicians, diagnoses of comorbid substance use disorders are frequently missed in patients presenting acutely with symptoms of a mental disorder. Patients complaining of mental symptoms do not usually offer information about patterns of alcohol and drug use. A study of 75 patients admitted to an acute psychiatric inpatient ward (Ananth, Vandeater, Kamal, & Brodsky, 1989) demonstrated the potential for missing a dual-diagnosis problem. When initially evaluating the patients, the emergency departments made 4 drug abuse/dependence diagnoses, while 29 diagnoses were made on the inpatient service. By carefully reevaluating the patients using the Diagnostic Interview Schedule (DIS), researchers made 187 drug abuse/dependence diagnoses (i.e., many of the 75 patients met criteria for abuse/dependence involving more than one substance). The authors attributed their success in making the previously missed diagnoses of substance abuse/dependence to structured history and physical examinations and the time lapse between the initial diagnoses and their own "second look" at the patients.

Dual-Diagnosis Concept: Clinically Inadequate

Dual diagnosis is frequently a misnomer, given the high rates of patients comorbid for three or more lifetime ADM disorders (Kessler et al., 1994). Commonly, these patients have three and four or more current diagnoses, including multiple other medical conditions. Recent popularization of the dual-diagnosis concept has led to increased recognition in the field but also to increased reductionism. When considering treatment alternatives, labels like *MICA (mentally ill chemical abuser), SAMI (substance-abusing mentally ill)*, or *CoAMD (co-occurring addiction and mental disorder)* do not adequately describe the breadth and depth of clinical presentations and problems of patients with mental disorders in the context of substance abuse or dependence. The *dual-diagnosis patient* is a deceptive concept because it implies a clinical category that has internal consistency. As we build a differential therapeutics, treatments should become more, not less, specific. Therefore, the dual-diagnosis concept is reductionistic and adds no specificity in exchange for a loss in descriptive resolution. Clinicians know intuitively that specific treatment will differ substantively in organization, content, and timing for a married Caucasian male suburban corporate executive with a panic disorder and alcohol abuse, from that of a homeless 17-year-old African-American inner-city girl who is a high school dropout and who suffers from both schizophrenia and crack cocaine dependence. Yet each has a "dual diagnosis."

Limitations of Traditional Models of Addictive Disorders

Many of the mental health and chemical dependency models contain some serious limitations. It is vital, however, to find the right words to communicate between domains that have separate philosophical structures, languages, and worldviews. The mental health and chemical dependency systems typically have several groups of providers (mental health, alcoholism, substance abuse) who have been trained within separate guilds, each having an intrinsic and often disparate philosophy and technical language. It is imperative that clinicians attempting to understand the diagnosis and treatment of patients with comorbid mental disorder and addiction get

"the big picture." In order to do this, clinicians must expand their repertoire of concepts and language beyond what they learned during training.

Self-Medication Hypothesis The traditional mental health model of addictive disorders was based upon psychodynamic explanations, such as bolstering ego defenses, reducing painful affects, and quelling intolerable rage. The self-medication hypothesis, first put forth by Freud in 1884 (1974) and explored by other psychoanalytic thinkers (Khantzian, 1985, 1990; Rado, 1933), postulates that the choice of drugs that a person abuses is based upon the drug's specific ability to modulate intense painful affects or impulses. It has been argued that self-medication cannot be validated as an explanation of drug abuse because addicts continue to use drugs and alcohol in spite of the worsening of substance-induced psychiatric symptoms (Miller & Fine, 1993). This reasoning does not rule out self-medication as an etiological factor in addiction, with the initiation of compulsive use in spite of negative states or consequences being a hallmark of the disorder. Although self-medication may be an etiological pathway for substance use disorders, psychodynamic interpretations of addictive behaviors alone are not sufficient to stop the addictive process.

Disease Model of Chemical Dependency A popular model that is of heuristic value and has become associated with mainstream chemical dependence treatment is the disease model of addiction, a model and operating philosophy quite different from traditional psychodynamic and psychobiological theories. The proponents of the disease concept of addiction thought that it was an error to consider alcoholism a symptom of another disorder. The model stresses that chemical addiction is a chronic, relapsing, and progressive illness. Rather than being the fault of the patient, the disease becomes the responsibility of the patient; that is, the patient needs to work with the treating clinician to maintain sobriety or else the disease will sicken the patient, cause dysfunction and disability, and ultimately prove fatal. This approach offers patients a diagnosis rather than name calling or blaming and is one remedy to unilateral application of the moral model of addiction (see below). The disease model brings addiction treatment into closer apposition with evolving psychiatric modes of treatment, and makes things more concrete and structured for the providers of treatment. (See chapter 15 for a more comprehensive explication of the model.)

A number of problems exist with the disease model. It does not conform to Koch's Postulates of a classical disease. The definition, while useful to characterize a process, is phenomenologically vague. The model is often attributed to Jellinek (1952), yet his approach to alcoholism explicated several typologies that differed in onset, severity, pattern, and chronicity of use. Further, the understanding by patients with addictive disorders that they have a chronic illness can become a factor in their demoralization. Similarly, patients can use the disease concept for secondary gain, to rationalize maintenance of substance use, to resist change, and to avoid responsibility for bad behavior.

It is important to understand that the disease model is just that, a model, and can impede the development of differential therapeutics for substance use disorders if taken too concretely. Treatments derived from reductionistic and idealized models have the suggestion of panacea (e.g., 28-day inpatient rehabilitation). This Procrustean tendency has been in part responsible for the difficulty we face today in treating patients with comorbid addictive and mental disorders. For example, one common belief about treatment from within the chemical dependency/disease model domain is that a patient who is still using a substance of abuse is not yet ready for treatment. While this strategy may increase the efficiency of staff effort in a selected population, it ignores current thinking on motivation (Osher & Kofoed, 1989; Prochaska & DiClemente, 1984), considering only people in the "action" or "active treatment" category to be "patients" (see "Stages of Treatment" below). It is also likely that a high percentage of those deemed "not motivated for treatment" by traditional methods have comorbid mental disorders. In contrast, patients with comorbid severe disorders are able to be retained in integrated outpatient treatment that focuses upon "precontemplation and contemplation" or "persuasion and engagement" and uses sobriety as a goal rather than as a prerequisite of treatment (Hellerstein, Rosenthal, & Miner, 1995; Ries & Comtois, 1997; Ziedonis & Fisher, 1996).

The Moral Model and Countertransference   The moral model essentially blames the patient for the addiction. The model uses the concepts of moral responsibility and willpower to imply that people who are addicted, rather than being trapped in a cycle of reinforced behaviors, are free to stop by choice. Thus, addicts are deemed morally bankrupt because they choose to continue socially unacceptable actions. Name calling ("dope fiend") and blaming are responses that fall within the moral model of addiction. This is a posture that the general population adopts out of tradition, ignorance, and fear, and that clinicians adopt partly out of cultural identity and through countertransference feeling. These attitudes serve a defensive purpose that allows people to avoid uncomfortable feelings and impulses. In clinicians, the moral model may become a justification for acting on their own frustration and disappointment with patients' failure to meet treatment objectives. Thus, the moral model must be held up for scrutiny when it is invoked. Interventions based on this model may add to the patients' already significant levels of self-loathing and demoralization.

Problems Intrinsic to Patients with Comorbid Disorders

Effects of Comorbidity on Trajectory of Illness

The rates of relapse to substance abuse or exacerbation of mental disorder are higher in patients with comorbidity (Renz, Chung, Fillman, Mee-Lee, & Sayama, 1995). According to data from the National Comorbidity Survey (Kessler et al., 1994; Warner, Kessler, Hughes, Anthony, & Nelson, 1995), the 12-month prevalence for any substance use disorder is 11.3% (drug dependence alone, 2.8%), yet only 19% of patients with alcohol dependence and 25% with other substance dependence are in treatment in a year (Warner et al., 1995). Psychiatric comorbidity tends to drive up service utilization. For example, co-occurring anxiety or depressive disorders increase the rate of some sort of treatment of alcoholics to 41% and other drug disorders to 63% in 1 year (Warner et al., 1995). Young patients with substance abuse and schizophrenia spend much of their time admitted to inpatient services and have more frequent but shorter stays than patients with schizophrenia and no substance abuse (Richardson, 1985).

The Effect of Concurrent NSR Mental Disorders on the Outcome of Addiction Treatment   Among alcoholics, those with psychiatric symptoms (mood lability, depression, dysphoria) have a higher suicide rate (Berglund, 1984), and comorbid psychiatric diagnoses generally predict a poorer treatment outcome at 1 year (Rounsaville, Dolinsky, Babor, & Meyer, 1987). More specifically, concurrent antisocial personality disorder generally predicts lower treatment retention and a poorer addiction treatment outcome (Alterman & Cacciola, 1991; Kranzler, Del Boca, & Rounsaville, 1996; Leal, Ziedonis, & Kosten, 1994; Schuckit, 1985). The presence of psychotic symptoms in patients with addictive disorders is associated with poorer outcome for substance abuse treatment, and the degree of psychiatric impairment is more predictive of drug abuse treatment outcome than any other pretreatment factor, including substance abuse severity (Kosten, Rounsaville, & Kleber, 1985; LaPorte, McLellan, O'Brien, & Marshall, 1981; McLellan, Luborsky, Woody, O'Brien, & Druley, 1983; O'Brien et al., 1984). In opioid abusers, psychiatric comorbidity is also associated with a more severe substance use disorder (Brooner et al., 1997). In light of the high risks for psychiatric comorbidity and the impact of that comorbidity upon addiction treatment outcome, all addicted patients should be screened for other NSR mental disorders.

Comorbid personality disorders have been recognized increasingly as an important variable in the trajectory and treatment of chronic substance abuse. Nace, Davis, and Gaspari (1991) found at least one *DSM-III-R* personality disorder in 57% of treatment-seeking substance abusers. Personality disorders seem particularly crucial in accounting for high treatment dropout and relapse rates (Nace, Saxon, & Shore, 1986). Alcoholics with ASPD have an earlier onset of alcoholism, more polysubstance abuse, and poorer prognosis (Stabenau, 1984). Sociopathy among substance abusers is associated with high treatment dropout and poorer treatment outcome (Leal et al., 1994; Woody, McLellen, Luborsky, & O'Brien, 1985). For example, Woody et al. (1984) found that the presence of antisocial personality disorder in opioid addicts predicted poor outcome in either supportive expressive or cognitive behavioral psychotherapy during methadone maintainance treatment. More recently, Nace and Davis (1993) demonstrated differential 1-year follow-up outcomes by presence of personality disorder with respect to decreases in types of abused substances and degree of life satisfaction in 100 substance abuse patients.

Substance Abuse Affects the Course of NSR Mental Disorders In patients with chronic mental illness, drug and alcohol abuse negatively affect appropriate behavior and are associated with poorer psychiatric treatment outcome (McCarrick, Manderscheid, & Bertolucci, 1985; Pepper & Ryglewicz, 1984). Drug abuse is significantly associated with an increased rate of rehospitalization in patients with schizophrenia (Craig, Lin, El-Defrawi, & Goodman, 1985) and bipolar disorder (Brady, Casto, et al., 1991). In patients with schizophrenia, alcohol and other substance abuse both decrease global functioning (Kovasznay et al., 1997) and increase the risk for tardive dyskinesia (Bailey, Maxwell, & Brandabur, 1997; Dixon, Weiden, Haas, & Sweeney, 1992). Heavy cannabis use is associated with earlier and more frequent psychotic relapse in schizophrenia (Linszen, Dingemans, & Lenior, 1994). Similarly, bipolar disorder patients with comorbid substance use disorders, compared to those without, have more hospital admissions (Brady, Casto, et al., 1991; Reich et al., 1974), shorter time to relapse (Tohen, Waternaux, & Tsuang, 1990), an earlier mood disorder onset, more dysphoria, and worse clinical course (Sonne, Brady, & Morton, 1994), including a poorer response to lithium (Albanese, Bartel, Bruno, Morgenbesser, & Schatzberg, 1994). Concurrent alcohol dependence is associated with increased suicidality among depressed patients (Cornelius et al., 1995). Patients with borderline personality disorder and antisocial personality disorder have an increased vulnerability to the development of affective instability and psychosis (Fyer, Frances, Sullivan, Hurt, & Clarkin, 1988; Schuckit, 1985) and are at high risk for substance use disorders (Kessler et al., 1994) that clinicians recognize as complicating the clinical course. Clinically unrecognized addictive disorders may account for many of the dramatic events in the treatment of these patients.

ISSUES IN ASSESSMENT

Understanding Dual Diagnosis

Since patients dually diagnosed with mental illness and addiction typically present for treatment with a confusing array of psychiatric symptoms and physical findings, the clinician must begin the assessment with an open mind to possible diagnoses. Although a working diagnosis or set of diagnoses should be decided upon as soon as possible, the clinician should remain wary of premature closure, which can subject the patient to incorrect and potentially harmful treatment. Using knowledge of *DSM-IV*, experience with common presentations of the dually diagnosed, and the necessary patience in waiting for drug-induced syndromes to clear, the astute clinician can efficiently diagnose and treat the dually diagnosed patient.

Given the potentially disastrous implications of missing a connection between psychiatric symptoms and substance use, clinicians should use probing questions and diagnostic patience. Having diagnosed co-occurring mental illness and addictive disorder, the clinician is faced with the task of understanding the interactions, if any, between the two or more conditions. In order to clarify the relationship between substance use and psychological symptoms, the clinician should assess (a) when mental symptoms first occurred and, if an exacerbation, when they began again; (b) when symptoms of SUD first occurred, whether the symptoms preceded the onset of substance abuse (Schuckit & Hesselbrock, 1994), and if a relapse, when they began again; (c) what subjective effects use of substances has on mental symptoms (relief, exacerbation); (d) what effects upon mental symptoms cessation (if any) of drug use has; and (e) what effects amelioration of psychiatric symptoms has on patterns of substance use. In a paradigm for understanding interactions between NSR mental disorders and SUDs, Weiss and Collins (1992) outlined five major patterns of interaction (table 25.2). Although few patients fall clearly into one demarcated category, the exercise of considering phenomenology, time course, and etiology will help the clinician derive the most efficacious treatment.

The first interaction, predisposition/risk, has been documented above in the epidemiological data from the ECA (Regier et al., 1990) and the NCS (Kessler et al., 1994) studies. Earlier onset of bipolar disorder is seen in patients who develop SUDs compared to those who do not, suggesting that an earlier age of onset may put individuals at risk for SUDs (Dunner & Feinman, 1996). Another potential way for the increased vulnerability for drug abuse to manifest is through self-medication of states related to mental disorders. For example, negative symptoms in schizophrenia may predispose affected individuals to subsequent substance use disorders (Schneier & Siris, 1987): Amphetamine has been shown to markedly improve the anhedonia, anxiety, and hypochondriasis seen in negative-symptom schizophrenia patients (Cesarec & Nyman, 1985), and negative symptoms are acutely and significantly reduced in schizophrenia patients who have used cocaine (Serper et al., 1995). The data suggest that abuse of stimulants in this population might be quite directed.

Dysphoria has been implicated as a prime cause of relapse in substance abusers (Litman, Stapleton, Oppenheim, Peleg, & Jackson, 1983; Marlatt & Gordon, 1985), and one report suggests that patients with co-occurring seasonal dysphoria and cocaine abuse demonstrate fluctuations in cocaine craving that par-

TABLE 25.2 NSR-SUD Interaction Models

Interaction	Example
NSR psychopathology (Axis I/Axis II) as a risk factor for substance use disorder	The depressed patient who "treats" dysphoria with an illicit substance such as cocaine
Psychiatric symptoms developing in the course of a chronic intoxication and following the course of the substance use	The cocaine user who experiences paranoia while using the substance, and whose symptoms remit with cessation of drug use
Psychiatric disorder which occurs as a consequence of substance use but persists after cessation of substance use	Panic attacks which are triggered by cocaine use, and which persist long after abstinence from cocaine has been achieved
Substance abuse and psychiatric symptomatology meaningfully linked over time	Anorexia nervosa patient who finds cocaine a perfect mood enhancer and anorectic agent
No relationship between substance abuse and psychiatric symptomatology	The depressed alcoholic whose symptoms do not remit with prolonged abstinence from alcohol

Note. Adapted from Weiss and Collins (1992).

allel their cyclic changes in mood (Satel & Gawin, 1989). In patients with comorbid cocaine abuse and depression, it is often unclear whether the depressive symptomatology is a result of the neurotoxic and social effects of cocaine use or antedated the development of the substance abuse disorder. The specific affect that is purportedly modulated by cocaine is depression/dysphoria (Khantzian, 1985). Weiss, Mirin, Michael, and Sollogub (1986) described concurrent DSM-III affective disorders in 53.5% of a group of cocaine abusers comprising a depressed subgroup, who valued the euphorigenic effects, and a bipolar/cyclothymic subgroup, who augmented hypomanic symptoms or alleviated depressive symptoms. Patients with schizophrenia have reported that cocaine use decreases dysphoria and increases sociability (Dixon, Haas, Weiden, Sweeney, & Francis, 1991).

The second interaction described by Weiss and Collins (1992) is substance-induced disorders which are typically self-limited: mood, anxiety, and other disorders that are independent of NSR psychiatric illnesses and typically follow the time course of intoxication or withdrawal. There are factors (family history, temperament, affect/anxiety regulation) that may increase a person's vulnerability to the development of transient mental symptoms in the context of substance use disorders, without the person's having a diagnosable NSR disorder. For example, in Caucasian populations, certain dopamine transporter genotypes may predispose to paranoia in the context of cocaine use (Gelernter, Kranzler, Satel, & Rao, 1994).

In addition to substance-induced disorders, drugs of abuse can also exacerbate the symptoms of underlying mental disorders, often in a self-limited way, without causing a full-blown relapse of the NSR disorder. Compared to schizophrenia patients without SUDs, substance abuse in schizophrenia is correlated with an increase in hallucinations (Sokolski et al., 1994) and thought disorder (Cleghorn et al., 1991). Prevalence rates for auditory hallucination are higher in schizophrenia patients who abuse crack than in those who do not (Rosenthal, Hellerstein, & Miner, 1992a). Also supporting a vulnerability model, schizophrenia patients are differentially sensitive to methylphenidate-induced increases in thought disorder compared to normals (Levy et al., 1993).

The third interaction is initiation: Chronic substance use may precipitate NSR psychiatric illness in patients with an underlying diathesis including mania (Strakowski, Tohen, Stoll, Faedda, & Goodwin, 1992), panic disorder (Aronson & Craig, 1986), or schizophrenia (Linszen et al., 1994; McLellan, Woody, & O'Brien, 1979; Sevy, Kay, Opler, & van Praag, 1990; Turner & Tsuang, 1990). Chronic substance use may also precipitate a DSM-IV persisting substance-induced disorder such as alcoholic hallucinosis, which, although substance-induced, is not self-limited and continues indefinitely after cessation of substance use.

The fourth interaction is altered trajectory: Patients with NSR mental disorders may benefit from the effects of abused drugs in such a way that the trajectory of the illness is modified. For example, as patients with negative symptoms in schizophrenia may achieve some diminution of anhedonia, amotivation, akinesia, and social withdrawal through the use of stimulants (Rosenthal, Hellerstein, & Miner, 1994), stimulants may cause changes in the temporal stability of negative symptoms (Lysaker, Bell, Bioty, & Zito, 1997).

Fifth, there may be instances where substance use and other mental disorders, although present concurrently, are not meaningfully interrelated.

Conducting a Differential Diagnosis

Differential diagnosis involves examination of a complex relationship between substance abuse and psychiatric symptoms. In the DSM-IV (APA, 1994), most diagnosis is polythetic (i.e., made by identifying a threshold number of symptoms from a list rather than fitting criteria to a specific symptom that all members of the diagnostic category have). Frequently, chronologically primary and secondary diagnoses cannot be established during the initial evaluation. Patients with substance use disorders may present retrospective falsification or distortion of personal history, so the clinician should obtain collateral history from significant others, if possible. Establishing a primary and secondary diagnosis may be helpful to planning treatment, as the clinical picture tends to run the course of the primary disorder (Brown et al., 1995; Schuckit, 1985). For example, patients with primary alcoholism have significantly fewer episodes of affective disorder than bipolar patients with secondary alcoholism (Winokur et al., 1995).

Cross-Sectional Analysis: Insufficient for Making DSM-IV Diagnoses

Most diagnostic categories in *DSM-IV* have specified intervals over which the symptoms must occur in order to reach threshold. Therefore, cross-sectional analysis is insufficient for making *DSM-IV* diagnoses without information about interval and duration in a historical context. This is of specific importance when attempting to understand the nature of mental symptoms in the context of substance abuse. Therefore, diagnoses may have to be made over time, with serial treatment contacts that clarify the relationship of the onset and persistence of mental symptoms to the intervals over which substance abuse took place.

Standardized assessment provides a more comprehensive appraisal of multiple substance abuse than routine clinical procedures (Ananth et al., 1989; Rosenthal et al., 1992a). In a set of studies on an inpatient dual-diagnosis unit, diagnoses of *DSM-III-R* substance abuse/dependence in schizophrenia patients revealed 10.9% abusing or dependent upon three or more substances by retrospective chart review, 16.0% by routine clinical methods, and fully 90.0% using structured research interviews (Rosenthal et al., 1992a). Even the use of a simple rating scale of alcohol and substance use severity from 1 (none) to 5 (extremely severe) increases the ability of clinicians to make distinctions between presence or absence of current substance-related problems, with reasonable concurrent validity with more comprehensive instruments (Carey, Cocco, & Simons, 1996.)

Substance-Induced Disorders

In attempting to elucidate the causes of mental symptoms in patients with histories of concurrent substance use disorders, the clinician must differentiate symptoms due to the effects of substances from those intrinsic in NSR mental disorders. Intoxication or withdrawal states due to substances of abuse frequently cause symptoms of mood, anxiety, psychotic, and/or personality disorders. In the acute care setting, it is often difficult to ascertain the time of onset of either symptoms of psychosis or substance use disorders, making definitive NSR/substance-induced diagnoses restricted (Kane & Selzer, 1991; Rosenthal, Hellerstein, & Miner, 1992b; Shaner et al., 1993). In a study of 435 patients admitted to an inner-city hospital with psychiatric diagnoses, researchers using a structured interview (SCID) found that 53.6% of the subjects had no freestanding psychiatric disorder outside the addiction problem (i.e., presenting psychiatric symptoms were directly related to substance abuse) (Lehman et al., 1994).

Careful history taking, as well as medical, neurological, and toxicological screening are essential to elucidate causes of symptoms as being due to direct actions of drugs, drug withdrawal, independent medical problems, or medical ramifications of substance abuse. Every patient assessed for mood, anxiety, cognitive, stress, relationship, or job-related problems should be asked about alcohol and other substance use patterns. Patients who are seen with new-onset complaints of mental symptoms should have a medical screening and physical examination in the absence of a clear prior history of mental disorder without concurrent substance abuse or dependence. Many mental symptoms can be induced by intoxication with a substance of abuse or its withdrawal in a habituated person.

The way in which symptoms change with cessation of drug use may also provide an important clue to the etiology of those symptoms. In a recent inpatient study, 40% of 171 males recently detoxified from alcohol experienced multiple anxiety symptoms and had significantly elevated levels of state anxiety at admission ($\geq$ 75th percentile) that typically returned to the normal range by the second week of treatment (Brown, Irwin, & Schuckit, 1991). This is not the typical course for generalized anxiety disorder, and only 4% fulfilled criteria for generalized anxiety symptoms after 3 months' sobriety (Schuckit, Irwin, & Brown, 1990).

Psychosis and Substance Use Disorders

There is an underrecognized clinical population of patients who present with psychotic symptoms and a history of substance abuse but who do not meet criteria for NSR mental disorders. These patients are typically treated acutely as if they had an NSR mental illness (Szuster, Schanbacher, McCann, & McConnell, 1990). Substance-abusing patients demonstrate acute psychotic symptoms due to direct effects of substance abuse (Brady, Lydiard, Malcolm, & Ballenger, 1991; Satel, Southwick, & Gavin, 1991; Szuster et al., 1990), independent NSR mental disorders

(Weiss & Collins, 1992), or some combination of the two (Rosenthal et al., 1994). Recent evidence suggests that even among patients with psychotic symptoms and concurrent substance use disorders, there are patient characteristics such as formal thought disorder or bizarre delusions that significantly predict a diagnosis of schizophrenia, while intravenous cocaine abuse and a history of drug detoxification or methadone maintenance predict substance-induced delusional disorder or hallucinosis (Rosenthal & Miner, 1997). The default assumption regarding acutely presenting patients with substance use disorders and psychotic symptoms should be that the symptoms are substance-induced until otherwise demonstrated. This strategy reduces the potential harm of untreated withdrawal states (Becker & Hale, 1993; Brown, Anton, Malcolm, & Ballenger, 1988) or the unnecessary exposure to neuroleptic treatment of patients differentially sensitive to adverse effects (Olivera, Kiefer, & Manley, 1990; Ziedonis, Kosten, & Glazer, 1992).

Mood Disturbance and Substance Use Disorders

Similarly, mood symptoms, especially depressive-spectrum symptoms, are exceedingly common in substance use disorders and are commonly diagnosed and treated by unsophisticated clinicians as primary mood disorders. The ability of commonly abused drugs to induce mood syndromes that resemble functional psychiatric disorders is well documented, especially with respect to alcohol-induced mood disorders. Frequently, there is a decrease in the intensity of depressive mood once sobriety is established (Brown & Schuckit, 1988; Brown et al., 1995; Dorus, Kennedy, Gibbons, & Ravi, 1987). Dorus and colleagues (1987) found that 66% of 50 alcoholic subjects had Beck Depression Inventory scores (BDI) greater than 17 within 24 hours of the last drink. At 24 days after cessation of alcohol, only 16% had BDI scores greater than 17. Substance abusers may have a substance-induced mood disorder or concurrent NSR major depression, or both. A subclass of patients with substance use disorders and mood symptoms have a complex picture: a chronic low-grade mood disorder such as dysthymia or atypical depression, which may predispose the patient to develop alcohol dependence, in which an even more intense depressive syndrome is induced.

Stimulant-Induced Depression

Clinical observation shows that stimulant abusers exhibit symptoms of depressive disorders that may be different from major depression or dysthymia. Post, Kotin, and Goodwin (1974) administered intravenous cocaine to patients who had major depression and found that this caused first euphoria, then dysphoria, demonstrating the ability of cocaine to directly cause symptoms of a mood disorder. Gawin and Kleber (1986) described a three-phase sequence of post-cocaine-abstinence symptomatology, where DSM-III diagnoses of primary depressive disorders were given only if symptoms were persistent beyond 10 days of sobriety. Cross-sectional analysis of symptoms in the first 6 days (crash phase) of cocaine abstinence led to a diagnosis consistent, except for duration of symptoms, with melancholic depression in 70% of the subjects. However, with a 10-day cutoff, depression was diagnosed in 33% of the subjects: 13% major depression and 20% dysthymia, each clearly higher than the rate of depression in the general population. The investigators suggested that primary diagnoses of psychiatric disorder are suspect in cocaine abusers because protracted, binge-independent syndromes could still be secondary to cocaine abuse (Gawin & Kleber, 1986). Similarly, Weiss, Griffin, and Mirin (1989) found a diagnosis of major depression in 13% of 149 hospitalized cocaine abusers but also found that depressive symptoms correlated less well with a diagnosis of major depression after 2–4 weeks of cocaine abstinence.

Substance-Induced Personality Changes and Independent Personality Disorders

Although clinicians who treat addictions are well aware of the changes that occur in the interpersonal functioning and lifestyle of people who develop substance use disorders, the diagnosis of substance-induced personality disorder is used infrequently. As the patient becomes involved in the drug lifestyle, he or she begins to change priorities, shifting interpersonal values from egalitarian to utilitarian. As more time and energy are spent in obtaining money to procure drugs and deceiving others, there is an increase in interpersonal exploitiveness, often with the onset of "street" behavior, crime, and so on. Interestingly, 33% of treatment-seeking cocaine abusers in a study by Rounsaville and colleagues (1991) met DSM-III-R criteria for antisocial personality disorder (ASPD), but only 8% met the diagnosis by more restrictive Research Diagnostic Criteria (Spitzer, Endicott, & Robins, 1978), where ASPD symptoms that are clearly due to substance abuse are excluded. Among 37 of 50 cocaine-dependent inpatients that met criteria for *DSM-III-R* (APA, 1987) personality disorders, 19% had personality diagnoses that were made exclusively under conditions of drug use (Weiss et al., 1993.)

Patients who come to therapists or treatment centers with mood lability and suicidal ideation, and who are manipulative, needy, demanding, dysphoric, and impulsive, are frequently labeled *borderline*. As with other diagnoses, the clinician must make careful assessments to make a primary diagnosis of *DSM-IV* borderline personality disorder (BPD). Many patients with alcohol or substance abuse disorders can look quite labile, dysphoric, and impulsive when in a state of chronic intoxication and acute crisis, and they frequently have high-intensity mood disorder symptoms (Rosenthal et al., 1992a). They can have mixed personality disorders, or BPD with a concomitant panic, anxiety, or major depressive disorder, which may be missed without rigorous diagnostic thinking. Patients with BPD often regress under stress when they increase their alcohol or drug intake. This further disinhibits an already impulsive person and often increases the sense of crisis, dysphoria, and suicidality.

Comorbidity of Alcohol Use Disorders and Other SUDs

Currently, mixed addictions are common, and this is certainly true of patients with comorbid other mental disorders as well. Traditionally, there was a conceptual distinction between "alcoholism" and "drug addiction." Today, it is clear that alcoholism and substance dependence cross all social strata, and that distinctions between legal/illegal use and type of personality are insufficient to explain addiction. On balance, it is important to note that over half of the alcoholics (56.3%) and about 30% (29.5%) of drug abusers in the community have no other mental disorders. However, 20.7% of people with alcohol abuse and dependence have a lifetime prevalence of drug abuse, and about 46% of drug abusers have a lifetime prevalence of alcohol abuse or dependence (Regier et al., 1990). Combined alcohol and other drug abuse is the norm for chemically dependent patients under 35 years of age (State of New York, 1991). Models for discrete alcoholism and substance abuse treatments are increasingly seen as inadequate. There is an appropriate movement in many state governments to consolidate the provision of alcohol and drug treatment services.

TREATMENT

Reductionism and the Philosophy of Treatment Design

In recovery language, once you are a pickle, there is no going back to being a cucumber. It is important that clinicians not assume that appropriate treatment is a sort of undoing of first causes. A complex etiology of substance dependence does not necessarily imply that the treatment of choice must address etiological factors. This may be why earlier psychodynamic attempts at treating conditions assumed to be underlying the addictions frequently resulted in failure. In the staging of treatment, attenuating current pathological behavior may be more important than addressing predisposing conditions.

Reductionism Applied to Comorbid Psychiatric and Addictive Disorders

Clinicians tend to use treatment approaches based upon etiological models generated from their own traditional treatment domain, either mental health or chemical dependence. As a result, the patient with a chronic mental disorder may do poorly in traditional substance abuse treatment that tends to be intolerant of inappropriate or bizarre behavior (LaPorte et al., 1981; McLellan et al., 1983). Traditional forms of substance abuse treatment, such as those seen in therapeutic communities and drug rehabilitation programs, can be very structured and confrontational, with intense group interaction and display of affect (Rosenthal, 1984). This treatment is likely to be unsuitable for a patient with a severe disorder such as schizophrenia, given the association of both high expressed emotion and relapse (Vaughn & Leff, 1976) and intensive treatment and poorer long-term adjustment (Drake & Sederer, 1986) in schizophrenia. Conversely, patients with substance use disorders often do poorly in a traditional psychiatric milieu, where there is a more permissive environment (Pinsker, 1983). Substance abuse treatment programs more rigidly control the environment because these patients have a high incidence of personality disorders (Kessler et al., 1994; Miller & Ries, 1991) and/or characteristics, that resemble pathological character traits (Miller & Fine, 1993). Therefore, patients with manipulativeness, impulsivity, interpersonal exploitiveness, and poor frustration tolerance are generally taxing for staff to treat in a permissive environment where they can disrupt a therapeutic milieu.

Bottom-Up: More Effective Than Top-Down

If one considers the wide variety of comorbidity and severity in thinking about differential therapeutics for patients with comorbid disorders, it should be clear that one standard approach will not serve all patients, although traditional approaches have been programmatic ("top-down"). It is becoming clearer that it is not sensible to attempt programmatic approaches to treatment matching, but that "bottom-up" planning of individual services based upon the severity and phasing of a patient's problems (see "Sequencing of Treatment" below) has merit. Accurate diagnosis is of paramount importance because of the obvious implications for treatment planning and prognosis. Within the diagnostic frame, one can then explore what patient characteristics (e.g., demographics, symptoms, behaviors) are correlated with the best outcome of specific interventions.

Typology by Problem Severity

Another critical factor for framing clinical intervention is problem severity. Although treatment matching for alcoholism alone seems to have little impact on general outcomes of outpatient treatment (Project Match Research Group, 1997), the severity of psychiatric pathology has a significant impact on substance abuse treatment outcome and is specifically related to treatment selection.

High-psychiatric-severity cases may respond less well to standard care due to a failure to provide adequate "doses" of treatment services for their multiple problems (Alterman, McLellan, & Shifman, 1993). McLellan et al. (1983) evaluated 722 addicted subjects at their 6-month follow-up after treatment in six different rehabilitation programs. When the patients were separated into groups with low, medium, and

high psychiatric severity based on the psychiatric severity scale of the Addiction Severity Index (ASI; McLellan, Luborsky, Cacciola, & Griffith, 1985), it revealed that although treatment selection had no impact on outcome for the groups with low and high psychiatric severity, for those in the group with medium psychiatric severity outcome was heavily affected by the choice of treatment program. More recently, McLellan and colleagues (1997) demonstrated that patients in private addiction treatment programs matched to a minimum of three professional sessions directed at important family, employment, or psychiatric problems stayed longer in treatment, were more likely to complete treatment, and had better treatment outcomes. Another study of dually diagnosed outpatients in an integrated program with severity-based treatment phases demonstrated that cases with high total severity (psychiatric symptoms, substance abuse, level of dysfunction) typically receive more case management and medication services (Ries & Comtois, 1997).

A simple typology model, suggested to the first author by Stephan Larkin of the New York State Office of Mental Health, can assist the clinician in the overall assessment of and treatment planning for patients presenting with both mental symptoms and a substance abuse history (Rosenthal, 1993), but it is no substitute for the hard work of elucidating accurate diagnoses. The model assigns the patient to one of four categories based upon severity of mental disorder and severity of the substance use disorder (table 25.3; see also Ries, 1993). A simple instrument such as the four-dimensional Case Manager Rating Form (Comtois, Ries, & Armstrong, 1994), which rates severity of psychiatric symptoms and substance abuse symptoms (as well as functional disability and treatment noncompliance) on a 0–6 anchored scale, can be used to make high- and low-severity attributions. Other models have attempted to categorize clinically useful subtypes by differentiating chronologically primary and secondary disorders with the notion that the overall course of illness tends to run with the primary disorder (Hien et al., 1997; Schuckit, 1985). A new, unpublished model by Minkoff and Rossi (1997) attempts to integrate stages of treatment (see "Sequencing of Treatment" below) into a four-box model, and it is probable that future guidelines for care will develop this approach.

Patients in the high-NSR-psychopathology–high-substance-severity category are typically those with

TABLE 25.3 Four-Box Severity Model

	High NSR psychopathology	Low NSR psychopathology
High substance severity		
Diagnostic categories	Mentally ill chemical abusers: schizophrenia, schizoaffective, bipolar, deteriorated personality disorders, and polysubstance abusers	Primary substance use disorders ± personality disorders; substance-induced disorders; toxic/withdrawal psychoses; mood and anxiety disorders
Characteristic behaviors	Chronic psychosis with exacerbations: deteriorated social skills, cognitive impairment, agitated, bizarre, grandiose	More "street smart," labile, manipulative, drug seeking; primary or secondary sociopathy; work and legal problems
Substance abuse patterns	Severe functional psychopathology and persistent severe drug dependence	Persistent substance dependence or severe abuse/binging behavior
Level of functioning	Very low functioning, homeless, severely and persistently mentally ill (SPMI)	Fair functioning when sober; may be disenfranchised from family, community
Structure/support need	Great need for support, esteem, safety	Structure most useful
Stress tolerance	Poor stress tolerance	Varying stress tolerance
Treatment strategies	Mentally ill chemical abuser (MICA) unit for acute stabilization, detoxification, medication; form alliance, easy early goals, longer view toward abstinence, recovery; repeat simple recovery concepts; engage and persuade, attention to reengagement	Detoxification; TC or rehab model with clear contract; intensive, supportive, reality; cut through denial; offer substitutive behaviors; use leverage to enforce goal; cognitive behavior therapy, psychoeducation
Treatment problems	Disorganization, poor judgment, denial are major obstacles; multiple relapses; low social support/housing	Impulsivity/compulsivity is major problem; multiple relapses
Low substance severity		
Diagnostic categories	Severe psychiatric disorders and substance abuse/misuse	Low degree of functional impairment e.g., dysthymia, phobias, Cluster "C" personality disorder, substance-induced disorders
Characteristic behaviors	Psychopathology exacerbated by substance abuse, some MICA	Consistent low-level interpersonal or vocational problems, or acute crisis
Substance abuse patterns	Low-grade use; binging during exacerbations of mental disorder	Chronic low-level abuse, or chronic episodic binging
Level of functioning	Wide range of function, susceptible to decreases during episodes of drug use	Variable, usually moderate to high
Structure/support need	Much support and structure needed	Structure useful
Stress tolerance	Fair to poor stress tolerance	Good to fair stress tolerance
Treatment strategies	Stabilization of acute decompensation, detox if needed, compliance with psych meds, education about effects of abused drugs; confront only when indicated; skills training including relapse prevention	Can make use of structured intervention with confrontation, reality-based orientation; contingency management useful; supportive or insight-oriented therapy as indicated; make maladaptive behavior ego-dystonic
Treatment problems	Denial of drug abuse, contributing to noncompliance with treatment and relapse of NSR disorder	Rigidity of character defenses and capacity to postpone consequences, interfering with treatment, engagement

Note. Adapted from Rosenthal (1993).

diagnoses of substance dependence and severe NSR disorders, such as schizophrenia, bipolar disorder, or other psychotic disorders, or Cluster A and B personality disorders, such as borderline, schizotypal, or antisocial with severe deterioration in psychosocial functioning. The drug use is of high severity and contributes to chronic impairment in psychosocial functioning, cognitive disorganization, and noncompliance with treatment. This group usually needs inpatient hospitalization in specialized units for acute stabilization, medical detoxification, and initiation of pharmacotherapy for NSR mental disorders (Axis I), as well as some form of structured, integrated psychiatric and substance abuse treatment for subacute treatment, prophylaxis of relapse, and longer term maintenance. Family involvement for patient support and for family psychoeducation should be started in the acute phase. Case management (see below) is often necessary for outreach and engagement in outpatient treatment. Sobriety is typically a goal of treatment, which is conducted with a harm reduction model. Patients, once engaged in treatment, benefit from integrated treatment consisting of substance abuse counseling, medication management, psychoeducation about mental illness and drugs of abuse, relapse prevention skills training, self-help groups, and peer support. Later treatment focuses upon recovery of psychosocial function, relapse prevention, and vocational rehabilitation, if warranted.

High-NSR-psychopathology–low-substance-severity patients have severe mental disorders needing intensive mental health services but have lower intensity of substance-related dysfunction, often fulfilling abuse criteria. Patterns often show binging during periods of exacerbation of a primary NSR mental disorder with superimposed substance-induced disorders. Acute exacerbations of the mental disorder are best treated with inpatient, partial hospital, or intensive outpatient psychiatric treatment. In the subacute phase, where the patient becomes engaged in treatment, he or she can be treated in an integrated dual-diagnosis day-treatment–outpatient group or, if the patient is reasonably well integrated, an addiction recovery program that operates in close parallel with the mental health services. In either case, the patient must receive psychoeducation about mental illness and drugs of abuse, medication management, support for medication compliance, addiction counseling services, support to attend self-help groups, relapse

prevention work, and peer support. Case management services can be useful with disorganized patients.

Low-NSR-psychopathology–high-substance-severity patients are typical of the patients with substance dependence seen in addiction treatment programs. Patients are not free of psychopathology, but their higher baseline level of functioning allows them to make use of the more structured and confrontational environment of addiction treatment settings. These patients often have substance-induced mood, anxiety, personality, and brief psychotic disorders superimposed upon primary personality, mood, and anxiety disorders, but their baseline functioning is not severely impaired when the substance use disorder is in remission. When in crisis, they may need medically managed inpatient admission for detoxification. These patients tend to be able to make use of the standard array of phase-specific addiction treatment services, but it is likely that psychosocial functioning is increased by proper attention to problem areas other than substance use disorders, including treatment of comorbid NSR mood and anxiety disorders.

Patients in the low-NSR-psychopathology–low-substance-severity category are higher functioning at baseline and show less psychosocial impairment due to either substance misuse/abuse or concurrent mental disorders such as dysthymia, generalized anxiety, adjustment disorders, situational stress, and Cluster C and less severe cluster B personality disorders. These patients often present to private clinicians and to outpatient clinics for treatment, usually with a complaint related either to a single diagnostic focus or to another problem area, such as their relationship or job. Because of lower overall severity, these patients respond robustly to interventions aimed at increasing motivation toward abstinence, to cognitive approaches, to medication for low-severity comorbid NSR disorders, and to dynamic therapies, once concrete methods for maintaining sobriety have been established.

Although the four-box model generalizes pathology into high and low severity, a dichotomous approach has been developed with SUD treatment populations that also attends to severity of psychopathology and SUD. There is recent evidence of validity for a multidimensional typology of alcohol (Babor et al., 1992) and cocaine dependence (Ball, Carroll, Babor, & Rounsaville, 1995) based upon Type B having higher premorbid risk factors (family history, childhood behavior problems, personality, age of onset), higher dependence/abuse severity, more psychosocial impairment, more antisocial behavior, and higher psychiatric comorbidity than Type A.

Current Treatment Modalities and Settings for the Dually Diagnosed

Because the clinical experience of individuals who have focused upon treatment of comorbid substance use and mental disorders far outweighs the extent of empirical research on specific inteventions for specific comorbid disorders, most of what is recommended in this section has an experiential/rational basis and has yet to be validated scientifically. Nonetheless, it should be clear that no one programmatic approach by either substance abuse treatment or mental health systems will suffice to adequately address comorbid disorders. This places the onus upon the clinician to derive the best fit of clinical services and treatments with the highest degree of integration possible for patients. This will often require creativity and flexibility on the part of the clinician, with occasional chafed egos resulting from contact with systems that will not move to address the real clinical problems.

Acute/Short-Term Issues

For acutely ill patients, the appropriate intensity of services will depend upon the presenting severity of illness, as well as other factors such as medical risk or need for protection from self- or other-directed harm.

Special-purpose dual-diagnosis inpatient units generally serve to perform a sophisticated differential diagnostic evaluation of the high-severity patient, detoxify the patient from drugs and alcohol, stabilize the patient's acute mental disorder using psychotropic medications if indicated, engage the patient in early sobriety, and make recommendations about further treatment. Rediagnosis may be made after resolution of acute symptoms. Hospitalization provides a concrete interruption of the patient's daily routine, vocational or educational milieu, and interpersonal relationships, any or all of which may be contributing to the maintenance of the patient's addictive behavior. Follow-up recommendations may include combinations of services in the community, such as partial hospitalization, outpatient psychiatric

treatment, outpatient alcohol/drug counseling, and self-help groups. Provided there is an appropriate diagnostic evaluation that assesses the impact of the NSR mental disorder upon the addiction treatment, patients with lower severity mental disorders may be treated on detoxification inpatient units, if that level of care is necessary, and transitioned to residential, partial hospital, or intensive outpatient treatment.

Some patients may not need the protection of a 24 hour medically managed unit and thus can be treated for mild exacerbations of NSR illness and acute relapse to SUD or crisis states in the context of partial hospital or intensive outpatient treatments. These patients usually have some type of community structure in the form of an interested and supportive family, a structured living environment, and/or a vocational endeavor. The extent to which the services are provided by staff who are cross-trained in addictions and NSR disorder treatment and who are comfortable rendering medication management, outpatient withdrawal management, engagement into recovery work, psychoeducation about drugs of abuse and mental illness, cognitive behavioral approaches is the extent to which a single program can optimally address the range of typical problems of dually diagnosed patients.

Longer Term Issues

Therapeutic Community for High-Severity Disorders   Patients who are unable to make use of outpatient treatment are often referred to residential therapeutic communities (TC). Only complete removal from an environment that supports substance abuse, coupled with a long-term (6-month to 2-year) commitment to total immersion in a peer-supported substance-dependence-treatment milieu is believed to have sufficient effect on the addict to allow him or her to return to sober living in the community. Many TCs have transitional programs that allow the patient in later stages of treatment to work in the community or continue educational pursuits. Although opiate addicts are the stereotypical residents of a therapeutic community, trends over the past decade indicate that crack and cocaine addicts have been populating many of the beds in these programs (see chapter 17).

When psychiatric patients are treated for substance abuse in the highly controlled environment of a traditional therapeutic community, those with severe mental illness have poor outcomes (McLellan et al., 1983). Drug rehabilitation programs typically lack the clinical resources to manage aberrant behavior, and they typically screen out patients who have histories of suicidal behavior and those who need psychoactive medications. In many therapeutic community settings, substance abuse treatment employs confrontational techniques in the context of heated group interaction and strong displays of affect (Rosenthal, 1984). There is an association between high exposure to expressed emotion and relapse in schizophrenia (Vaughn & Leff, 1976). Therefore, confrontational or uncovering approaches (Drake & Sederer, 1986) may exacerbate symptoms in patients with psychotic disorders, rendering the classical TC less appropriate for dual-diagnosis patients with more severe disorders.

However, integration of mental health services can make a difference in the TC setting, as demonstrated by two recent studies. Carroll and McGinley (1997) demonstrated that while higher psychopathology was inversely related to treatment outcome, the use of enhanced mental health staffing in a TC with addicts who had severe mental disorders contributed to significant treatment benefits at 6 months. For patients with NSR mood and psychotic disorders, Westreich, Galanter, Lifshutz, Metzger, and Silberstein (1996) demonstrated 33% program completion rates in a residential drug-free TC located in a homeless shelter. In this TC model, community confrontation of "bad" behavior was modulated to the capacity of the resident to tolerate it. Therapeutic communities fare better with patients with personality disorders, who are probably a large percentage of the patients seeking treatment; nonetheless, the overall dropout rate from TC treatment in the first 30 days has been relatively high.

Sequencing of Treatment

Two traditional approaches to treating dually diagnosed persons are serial treatment, where either the NSR mental disorder or substance use disorder is addressed first, and parallel treatment, where both disorders are addressed concurrently, but typically without formal interaction of the clinicians or programs involved. Generally, neither approach represents a well-reasoned treatment strategy; both are the result either of lack of coordination of local mental health and substance abuse provider systems or of limitations of the treating clinicians. Clinicians' belief that

one form of treatment must come first may be due to an insufficiently broad understanding of addictions and mental disorders treatment. However, in certain cases, there may be a strategic reason to pursue a serial approach to treatment.

For example, with PTSD, both serial and concurrent models have been applied. Reduction in PTSD symptoms might decrease risk for relapse by decreasing dysphoric states, but proponents of serial treatment believe that stable sobriety must be achieved before the PTSD is addressed (Brinson & Treanor, 1988; Roy, 1984; Moyer, 1988). Advocates for concurrent approaches state that the risk of substance use relapse is reduced when the traumatic events are addressed earlier in treatment (Bollerud, 1990). Not yet addressed in the literature are differential treatment models based on the sequencing in which the PTSD and the SUD developed.

Integrated Treatment

Patients with a substance use disorder and a co-occurring severe mental illness such as schizophrenia have difficulty being treated adequately within the format of traditional provider systems, and it is reasonable and important to investigate combining and integrating services to these patients (Drake, Mueser, Clarke, & Wallach, 1996; Rosenthal et al., 1992b). Early studies suggested that treatment with a dual focus was beneficial for certain diagnostic groups with respect to maintenance of level of function (Kofoed, Kania, Walsh, & Atkinson, 1986) and decreased rates of readmission to hospital (Hellerstein & Meehan, 1987). Recent models of integrated treatment synthesize traditional mental health and addiction counseling into an approach that appears seamless to patients with respect to philosophical underpinnings, treatment approach, and psychoeducational content (Minkoff, 1989; Ries, 1993; Rosenthal et al. 1992b). In dually diagnosed patients with severe disorders, service integration has an important retention effect, and patients who remain in treatment improve (Hellerstein et al., 1995). In dually diagnosed patients with less severe disorders, coordinated psychiatric services and addiction rehabilitation services also may lead to better outcome (McLellan et al., 1997).

Stages of Treatment and States of Change

Recently, two groups have described the change process as occurring in stages. Prochaska and DiClemente (1984, 1986; Prochaska, DiClemente & Norcross, 1992), focusing on the treatment of substance use disorders, have suggested that individuals progress through five stages of motivational readiness to change: precontemplation, contemplation, preparation, action, and maintenance. In the precontemplation stage, the person is generally underaware of a problem and has no intention to change the behavior. In the contemplation stage, the person is aware of the problem but is not ready to make a decision and may weigh the pros and cons of the addictive behavior. In the preparation stage, the person intends to stop the addictive behavior and may have taken preliminary steps, such as cutting down on drug use and mapping out a treatment program that makes sense. In the action stage, people commit time and energy to modifying their behavior and their environment to support the achievement of a targeted goal. Maintenance is the stage of relapse prevention, where stabilization of behavioral change and integration of the methods of maintenance of recovery occur; it lasts indefinitely after the action stage.

Paralleling the work of Prochaska and his colleagues, Osher and Kofoed (1989) described five treatment phases for the severely mentally ill patient with SUD: engagement, persuasion, active treatment, maintenance, and relapse prevention. In this model, engagement is an early-stage intervention to motivate the patient toward contact with the provider and is most appropriate to the precontemplation stage. In the persuasion stage, appropriate to the contemplation stage, the therapist focuses on motivating the patient to realize that there is a problem which needs both professional intervention and the participation of the patient. Active treatment focuses on both the preparation and action stages, and in severely mentally ill patients, the achievement of stable sobriety may take an extended period of time. Relapse prevention uses techniques that are appropriate to the maintenance stage.

Attempting to use the treatment methods appropriate for a later stage while the person is at an earlier stage results in a therapist-patient mismatch. For example, while the patient is in the stage of precontemplation, vigorous use of injunction and confrontation typical of the contemplation/persuasion stage, rather than engagement, typically results in a rupture of the therapeutic alliance and the development of an "ex-patient." With dual-diagnosis patients, retention in treatment is often half the battle. Treatment that provides interventions appropriate to the patient's stage of readiness to change is likely to result in a higher rate of retention and, thus, better outcome. Several instruments have been used to determine the patient's current motivational stage. McHugo, Drake, Burton, and Ackerson (1995) derived a psychometrically reliable and valid scale that operationalizes eight stages based upon patient behaviors such as frequency of clinical contact, quantity of drug use, and timing of recovery milestones. The Recovery Attitude and Treatment Evaluator Questionnaire (RAATE-QI; Smith, Hoffman, & Nederhoed, 1995) measures five dimensions used for treatment matching in dual-diagnosis patients: motivation/denial, resistance to continuing care, biomedical acuity, psychiatric acuity, and environmental support status.

Recovery Is Nonlinear:
The Virtue of Persistence

In dual-diagnosis patients, the recovery process is not linear, and exacerbations of both disorders are episodic. Patients often cycle repeatedly through different phases of treatment. When they come back into contact with health care providers, they may be in an earlier motivational stage or even in denial that a problem really exists. In contrast to conventional wisdom, if treatment can "stay with" the patient over time attenuation of both the substance use and the mental disorders is possible (Hellerstein et al., 1995). With the more severe disorders, the time frame of recovery often needs to be extended. Patients with comorbid severe mental illness and substance use disorders may need more than 2 years to gain stable sobriety (Drake, McHugo, & Noordsy, 1993).

Integrating Psychological Therapies

There is no one-size-fits-all treatment for dual-diagnosis patients because there is little homogeneity within diagnostic sets, and even less across the many permutations of possible diagnoses of substance use and other mental disorders. Treatment must be individualized to the problem severity of the patient, rather than relying upon program-driven or philosophy-driven approaches to care. Supportive treatment components, common factors of all therapies (Pinsker, Hellerstein, Rosenthal, Muran, & Winston, 1996), are the basis for the approach with dually diagnosed patients. Practically speaking, elements of supportive therapy, cognitive behavioral measures, and behavioral reinforcement techniques can be integrated into individualized treatment. Even in dynamically based psychotherapies, elements of relapse prevention (Marlatt & Gordon, 1985) should be structured into the therapy to arm patients with a range of choices and behaviors to mobilize in the context of internal and external triggers to use. Most dual-diagnosis patients benefit from both interpersonal support and cognitive restructuring in the form of new information and skills building. Cognitive behavioral therapies teach patients how to cope with strong affects and how to promote or repair adaptive skills such as problem solving or substance refusal skills. For psychotherapy with these patients, nonpunitive confrontation and support without being overresponsible (enabling) or fostering regression are therapeutic challenges.

Timing of intervention is important with dual-diagnosis patients, both on the macro level (see "Stages of Change" above) and in the interpersonal process between therapist and patient. For example, patients who are depressed usually have decreased energy and concentration to put into the work of recovery. The rate of remission of depressive symptoms is consistent with the primary diagnosis in that symptoms remit more rapidly among patients with primary alcoholism than among those with primary affective disorder (Brown et al., 1995), a difference that affects when the patient will be able to make use of more intensive and complex information and emotional processes. In patients with SUD and bipolar disorder, because of initial difficulties internalizing the cognitive strategies, a 12-week course of relapse prevention group therapy had to be extended to 20 weeks in order to demonstrate significant effects upon drug use (Weiss et al., 1997). Typically, in addicted patients who have the psychological-mindedness and ego development to make use of it, psychodynamic treatment may be useful in later stages of treatment, when the patient has developed a concrete method of maintaining sobriety and a firm working alliance with the therapist, so that the anxiety-provoking procedures of expressive treatment do not lead to relapse (Kaufman & Reoux, 1988).

Certain interventions work better with some populations of persons comorbid for substance use disorders and other mental disorders than with others. For example, there is good reason to expect that contingency management can work reasonably well with a patient who has something to lose. For a 45-year-old married patient with children who has a mortgage on the house, is active in community activities, and belongs to the country club, sending a letter to the chairman of the board of the brokerage firm where the patient is a vice president at the next urine toxicology positive for cocaine is likely to be an effective intervention. In contrast, for the homeless, crack-dependent 18-year-old patient who has schizophrenia, but no relatives or friends, the problem is less what she has to lose than where therapeutic leverage can be applied at all. This latter patient is more likely to respond to positive reinforcement. Nonetheless, in spite of a lack of studies demonstrating its effectiveness, contingency management of payee benefits appears to be in widespread practice (Ries & Dyck, 1997).

Motivational enhancement techniques, initially used for higher functioning problem drinkers (Miller & Rollnick, 1991), have been used in the treatment of more severely ill dual-diagnosis patients (Ziedonis & Fisher, 1996). Ziedonis and Trudeau (1997) described a motivation-based treatment model (MBT) for dual-diagnosis patients that includes interventions specifically targeted to the motivational stages of change (Prochaska & DiClemente, 1984) described above. For example, in MBT, low-motivation patients have harm reduction goals, whereas high-motivation patients have abstinence as a goal. Motivational enhancement techniques (Miller, Zweben, DiClemente, & Rychtarik, 1992; see also chapter 13) are used in the precontemplation, contemplation, and preparation stages.

Integrating Pharmacotherapies

Differential diagnosis is essential to achieve maximum clarity about which syndromes are independent mental disorders that need medication for acute or subacute stabilization, and which arise in the context of substance use. Without that clarity, inappropriate medicating as well as over- or undermedicating are likely. Given the clinical complexities in managing comorbid mental disorders among substance abusers, there is an increasing role for psychiatrists to collaborate in addiction treatments conducted by other professionals (see chapter 19).

Basic principles of pharmacotherapy for dually diagnosed patients are: (a) Do not provide pharmacological treatments for substance-induced disorders acutely, except for safety or medical management reasons; (b) treat all treatable NSR mental disorders, avoiding, if possible, medications with a high abuse liability; (c) use parsimony in choosing and dosing medications, but don't undertreat; (d) syndromes are less risky to treat than symptoms; and (e) psychoeducation and support for compliance are critical.

When considering pharmacotherapy for patients with substance use disorders, medication-responsive comorbid disorders, if not acute and substance-induced, should be treated. At least 3 weeks of abstinence from alcohol appears to be necessary to consistently differentiate the groups with dual diagnoses into primary and secondary (substance-induced) on the basis of current depressive symptoms (Brown et al., 1995). However, the initial treatment of a substance-induced mood disorder is detoxification and support. Clinicians can use the dysphoria and anxiety associated with drug use to motivate engagement in treatment and attainment of sobriety.

In actual practice, disorders that are substance-induced but persist more than a month or so after cessation of substance use may respond to medication. The timing of the intervention is dependent upon the type of symptoms, their severity, their effects upon general quality of life, and, more specifically, capacity to maintain sobriety. Use of psychotropic medications with low abuse liability, such as neuroleptics for persisting hallucinosis or serotonin reuptake blockers for persisting depression, is less risky to sobriety than using medications with high abuse liability such as benzodiazepines for anxiety disorders or stimulants for ADHD. For example, low-grade depressive symptoms may persist months after cessation of alcohol or cocaine. As stated earlier, if one finds that the depression predated the onset of the addictive disorder, as in primary dysthymia, then the disorder should be treated. If the disorder is secondary but persists for weeks to months despite sobriety and some recovery, and if the symptoms are of sufficient intensity to interfere with the recovery process, then it may be treated. However, in SUD patients, the medication of individual symptoms (e.g., anxiety, dysphoria, or insomnia) is potentially more risky than medicating clusters of symptoms that meet syndromal criteria (e.g., panic disorder or major depression), even if secondary.

Pharmacotherapy is typically only one of several treatment modes that is essential for the stabilization and recovery of patients with NSR mental disorders and SUD. As with the pharmacotherapy of substance use disorders, the efficacy of pharmacotherapy of comorbid NSR disorders is likely to be increased in the context of appropriate psychosocial interventions, including those that increase medication compliance (Volpicelli et al., 1997). Core principles that serve to frame the basis of pharmacological treatment of dual-diagnosis patients are listed in table 25.4 (see Gastfriend, 1993).

Pharmacotherapy of SUD

Pharmacotherapy of SUD is covered in detail in chapter 19 and will be described here only briefly. Medication of SUD can follow by several strategies: (a) substitution, using agonists during detoxification or maintenence (e.g., opioid or nicotine replacement); (b) blocking the effects of drugs with antagonists (e.g., naltrexone); (c) contingency management through aversive agents (e.g., disulfiram); (d) use of agents that reduce craving; (e) use of medications for comorbid NSR or substance-induced disorders; (f) use of medications for comorbid medical disorders (Wilkins, 1997); and (g) use of agents that reduce constitutional vulnerability (e.g., impulsivity, negative symptoms) to drug use. The main problem with pharmacotherapy in SUDs is similar to other modes of treatment, namely, compliance with the regimen. Methadone maintenance programs exist both as hospital-based and freestanding private clinics in the community with more than 150,000 slots for opiate-dependent people (National Institute on Drug Abuse, 1995). Although methadone maintenance remains controversial even after decades of documented positive treatment outcomes (Ball & Ross, 1991; Condelli & Dunteman, 1993), it is a mainstay for thousands of well-functioning people with intractable opiate dependence. There is high psychopathology among opioid-dependent persons, demonstrated in both epidemiological (Kessler et al., 1994) and clinical samples (Rounsaville, Weissman, Kleber et al., 1982; Rounsaville, Weissman, Crits-Cristoph et al., 1982), and it is clear that diagnosed NSR mental disorders can and should be treated pharmacologically in this population, where appropriate (Nunes et al., 1995).

Compared with opioid substitution pharmacotherapy, there are no effective substitutive medications for alcohol or stimulant dependence. Other types of medications may support sobriety in the context of psychosocial treatment. The opiate antagonist

TABLE 25.4 Key Elements of a Dual-Diagnosis Pharmacotherapy Contract

1. Medication is part of a rational psychosocial treatment package and will be discontinued if other primary treatment elements are neglected.

2. Medication is not a substitute for the work of recovery.

3. Urine or blood testing may be required on demand to provide objective clinical data on the course of addiction treatment, or to determine if there are adequate blood levels of prescribed medication.

4. Medication will be used only as prescribed. Any need for changes must first be discussed with the physician. A unilateral change in medication by the patient is often an early sign of relapse.

5. The purpose of medication is to treat disorders characterized by predetermined target symptoms. If medication proves ineffective, it will be discontinued.

6. Once target symptoms remit, a process of dose tapering may be initiated to determine the minimum dose (including discontinuation) necessary to maintain healthy function.

7. Medication may not be necessary on a long-term basis.

Note. Adapted from Gastfriend (1993).

naltrexone has shown utility in the treatment of alcohol dependence (Volpicelli et al., 1997). Disulfiram (Antabuse) can be used as an aversive support for sobriety from alcohol in patients with NSR mental disorders who can (a) understand the risks of concurrent alcohol use; (b) responsibly avoid contact with any alcohol-containing substance, like hair spray or after-shave; and (c) withstand impulses to use alcohol. Therefore, patients with cognitive impairment or impaired judgment due to severe mental illness are less suitable candidates. There are no medications that have been demonstrated to reliably reduce drug craving that are not based on the substitution model.

Pharmacotherapy of Mood Disorders

According to Marlatt and Gordon (1985) and Litman et al. (1983), dysphoric mood related to depression, loneliness, anger, or frustration is the most common precipitant of relapse in addictive disorders. In patients with alcohol dependence and major depression, the tricyclic antidepressants imipramine (McGrath et al., 1996) and desipramine (Mason, Kocsis, Ritvo, & Cutler, 1996) are effective in treating the mood disorder but have equivocal effects on drinking behavior. A recent placebo-controlled study by Cornelius and colleagues (1997) demonstrated the efficacy of fluoxetine in reducing not only mood symptoms in depressed alcoholics, but also the frequency and amount of drinking. Since persisting depression can interfere with the process of recovery and psychosocial rehabilitation, once a substance-induced

disorder is ruled out mood disorders should be treated. In the absence of a comorbid mood or anxiety disorder, fluoxetine probably should not be used to maintain abstinence or reduce drinking in high-risk/severity (Type B) alcoholics, as it has been demonstrated to result in poorer drinking-related outcomes than placebo treatment (Kranzler, Burleson, Brown, & Babor, 1996).

Depression and dysphoria are common in cocaine-abusing patients (Gawin & Kleber, 1986; Nunes, Quitkin, & Klein, 1989; Weiss et al., 1986) and are associated with poorer substance abuse treatment outcome (Hodgins, el-Guebaly, & Armstrong, 1995; LaPorte et al., 1981; Woody, O'Brien, & Rickels, 1975). Depression appears to be a risk factor for increased cocaine abuse in opioid addicts, as those with increased cocaine abuse at 2.5 year follow-up were more likely to have depressive disorders (Kosten et al., 1987). In the laboratory, Childress and colleagues (1994; Childress, McLellan, Natale, & O'Brien, 1987) have demonstrated that negative mood states can elicit both conditioned withdrawal and craving and, when these are induced, can trigger drug use in substance abusers. The inability to self-soothe a dysphoric state also has implications for relapse in that after cocaine cue exposure, cocaine-dependent subjects who are unable to reduce their arousal/craving have a higher risk of treatment failure (Margolin, Avants, & Kosten, 1994).

Concurrent mood disorder was an important predictor of poor treatment outcome in one controlled study (Ziedonis & Kosten, 1991), but of good outcome in another (Carroll, Nich, & Rounsaville,

1995). Several recent studies, while not finding significant overall effects of antidepressant medications for cocaine abuse, have found that patients who were depressed were more likely to respond (Margolin et al., 1995; Nunes et al., 1995; Ziedonis & Kosten, 1991). Patients who respond to antidepressants may be those who abuse cocaine in an attempt to self-medicate dysphoria or depression (Kosten, 1989). In addition, SUD patients whose depressive symptoms are not due to primary depression may also have a differential response to tricyclic medication (Nunes et al., 1995). In all, patients with cocaine-induced dysphoria who present with depressive mood may be more constitutionally vulnerable to the mood-modulating effects of external reinforcers and therefore, may benefit from medication for mood disorder. Similarly, in bipolar disorder patients, there is a higher probability of remission of an alcohol use disorder than in primary alcoholism patients without bipolar disorder (Winokur et al., 1995).

Pharmacotherapy of Anxiety Disorders

Anxiety symptoms are very common in SUD patients. The traditional addictions approach has been to support the patient through anxious times by having the patient go to self-help meetings; talk to a sponsor, loved one, or friend; or engage in distracting behaviors. Clinicians have appropriate concerns that reducing some of the dysphoria early in treatment may decrease motivation amd engagement in the work of recovery. The prevailing attitude has been that anxiety in SUD is related to intoxication or withdrawal states and abates over time with continued sobriety. Although this is true in many instances (Brown et al., 1991), in others, there are co-occurring primary anxiety disorders that, left untreated, interfere with recovery by either increasing the risk of relapse or decreasing the patient's ability to participate in psychosocial rehabilitation (e.g., social phobia reducing participation in therapeutic groups). Clearly, psychotherapeutic interventions focused upon direct anxiety reduction and developing coping skills are first-line interventions in this population, including those with panic or PTSD symptoms. The primary pharmacotherapy guidelines in this case are safety, efficacy, and low abuse liability. Once the commitment is made to pharmacotherapy of anxiety, corollary psychoeducational treatment components should underscore that the patient's drugs of abuse make poor overall anxiolytics, and psychosocial interventions should include those that increase medication compliance. Kranzler (1996), in a review of placebo-controlled trials, suggested that the use of the non-benzodiazepine anxiolytic buspirone in anxious alcoholics for a minimum of 4–6 weeks at a substantial dose helps with treatment retention and reduces both anxiety symptoms and heavy drinking. Panic disorder is responsive to many medications with low abuse liability, such as serotonin selective reuptake blockers and imipramine, as well as those with high abuse liability, such as alprazolam. Unless other methods have repeatedly failed to address concurrent severe anxiety, the use of benzodiazepines, except for control of acute withdrawal or psychotic agitation, is probably ill advised in patients with SUD because of the high liability for abuse and the potential for dangerous synergistic effects (e.g., overdose) with alcohol and other sedative hypnotics.

Pharmacotherapy of Psychotic Disorders

Because intoxication or withdrawal can induce psychotic states or exacerbate preexisting psychotic disorders, acute psychosis is best handled symptomatically with safety the primary concern. This means using sedative medications such as lorazepam for psychotic agitation and deferring the use of antipsychotic medication until the clinical picture is clearer (see "Psychosis and Substance Use Disorders" above). The time course of psychosis that is substance-induced generally follows the activity or withdrawal cycle of the type and amount of the drug used. For example, with the short action of cocaine, cocaine delusional disorder rarely lasts more than a few days, whereas the chronic use of amphetamine (a longer acting drug) may induce delusions that may take weeks to clear. Once a presumptive diagnosis of an NSR psychotic disorder or a substance-induced persisting psychosis is made, then treatment with an antipsychotic medication is warranted. In patients with severe mental disorders and SUDs, compliance with medication is essential for stabilization and recovery. Even with medication compliance, persisting psychosis is not infrequent in schizophrenia and other psychotic disorders and typically interferes with the process of recovery. Because negative symptoms may increase the risk for substance abuse (Rosenthal et al., 1994; Schneier & Siris, 1987), newer, atypical antipsychotics such as clozapine and olanzepine that appear to have higher efficacy on negative symptoms may be of differential value in substance-abusing schizophrenia patients (Buckley, Thompson, Way, & Meltzer, 1994).

OTHER UNIQUE ISSUES IN TREATING THE DUALLY DIAGNOSED

Continuity of Care

Because of their often confusing presentations, dually diagnosed patients must have continuity of care over time and across disciplines. The chronic, progressive, and relapsing nature of both NSR and SUDs makes continuity of care imperative for maintenance of therapeutic gains. If possible, treatment should be delivered in an integrated manner, especially for severely mentally ill patients (see "Chronically Mentally Ill Substance Abusers" below) (Hellerstein et al., 1995; Minkoff, 1989; Ries, 1993; Rosenthal et al., 1992b). Parallel but not integrated delivery of services is associated with a rapid and statistically significant decrease in treatment retention of patients with severe mental illness and substance use disorders (Hellerstein et al., 1995). By combining psychiatric and addiction treatment, the patient participates in a sensible diagnosis and treatment plan that has the potential for addressing his or her problems.

Case Management: Singular Responsibility in a Team Approach

Case management is a procedure whose utility in dual-diagnosis patients increases with illness severity. No one provider typically supplies all of the necessary services that will stabilize a seriously ill dual-diagnosis patient in the community. In case management, one person in the network of different clinicians/programs that provide services to a particular patient takes responsibility for coordinating the treatment plan, communicating across providers, and creating an overview of the case. Case management can most easily be done within institutional settings but can also be done in the community, provided all clinicians participate. In this way, a team is created that works in concert to provide the range of services deemed appropriate for a particular patient's care. An additional advantage is that clinicians isolated by

niche are exposed over time to the knowledge and practice of clinicians in other domains, often a useful learning experience. In the public service system that generally treats the high-substance-abuse-severity–high-psychopathology patient, a specialized form of case management has been generated. Case managers steer the patient among various mental health, addiction, medical, housing, and entitlement services, serving in an ombudsman capacity with agencies, and providing on-the-fly clinical support. A major focus is upon early intervention in drug abuse relapse (i.e., locating patients, escorting them to 12-step meetings, detoxification or other services as necessary, and intervening to support sobriety).

Social and Environmental Needs, Including Issues of the Homeless

In order to recover from a major mental illness and an addictive disorder, the dually diagnosed person needs, at a minimum, a safe, drug-free living environment, a reasonable means of support, and supportive social contacts. Unfortunately, these seemingly simple needs often go unmet for the person at the lowest end of the socioeconomic scale, who may have drifted there by virtue of serious coexisting disorders.

Herman, Galanter, and Lifshutz (1991) found that 46 of 100 patients admitted to the Bellevue Dual-diagnosis Unit had been homeless (living in shelters, missions, public buildings, streets, or parks) on the day prior to inpatient admission. Interestingly, 34 had been homeless a majority of the time in the 2 months prior to admission, and 27 had been homeless a majority of the time in the 2 years prior to admission. Homeless persons were more likely to attend "self-help" groups such as AA than nonhomeless persons. The authors recommended specific psychiatric outreach and the introduction of self-help groups into the shelter system.

A safe living environment and the routine of work or school promote stable recovery of dually diagnosed patients. The traditional mental health service system, however, has been separate, both organizationally and financially, from such social service concerns. This separation, in addition to its arbitrary and artificial nature, ignores the realities of treating a severely ill dually diagnosed population.

A successful program, housed inside a homeless shelter, concentrated on the treatment of severely mentally ill men who both were also homeless and had substance use disorders (Westreich et al., 1996). The relatively high treatment completion rate (33%) and low incidence of drug use could be attributed to the program's sophisticated care and—perhaps as important—its provision of a supportive home. Although relatively expensive in the short term, such programs may prevent future emergency department visits and hospital admissions, reducing long-term costs. Although the validity of this cost offset argument has been demonstrated for the addicted population (Lewis & Kleinenberg, 1994), the scientific community still awaits such a well-documented demonstration for the dually diagnosed person.

Potential Problems in Utilizing 12-Step Programs

Self-Help Groups

Thousands and thousands make use of Alcoholics Annonymous (AA) and other self-help groups in order to achieve and maintain sobriety, often without other professional contact. There are probably more patients than qualified clinicians to treat them, and a large percentage of people with SUDs and/or NSR mental disorders are never treated in a clinical setting (Kessler et al., 1996; Narrow et al., 1993). To the extent that dually diagnosed patients are deemed able to make use of self-help recovery groups in the community, they should be supported by clinicians.

Although peer-led groups like AA are often the mainstay of treatment for the addicted person, the groups do have a potential pitfall for persons with an NSR mental illness. Psychiatric medications have at times been an issue for people attending AA. All abused psychoactive substances are considered harmful by AA, because of both concerns about developing new addictions and concern about medications interfering with true recovery. AA's official policy on medications, as stated in the AA booklets "To The Doctor" and "The AA Member and Medications," is to avoid interference with the legitimate prescription of medications. Most AA members adhere to this policy and, in the best tradition of AA, endeavor to have no opinion on matters not directly related to their fellow AA member's alcoholism. Unfortunately, over-zealous self-help members may pressure the person taking psychiatric medications to stop taking medication, with predictable clinical results.

The AA member who is prescribed psychiatric medications should carefully review with his or her prescribing doctor the addiction liability of each medication. Although most AA groups and AA members are open-minded about psychiatric medication, if a member is criticized for taking these medications alternative meetings should be sought. Originating in the early 1980s, self-help groups such as Dual Recovery or Double Trouble operate on a 12-step model but are inclusive of mental disorders other than addiction. One of the clear advantages of these self-help groups is that they offer to patients with severe mental disorders a chance to "fit in" without having to disclose a psychiatric disability where it may not be understood or having to feel deceptive by not revealing a significant impediment to recovery. Dual recovery groups are by design more comfortable with the concept of psychoactive medication than traditional 12-step meetings. At times, it may be beneficial to counsel dual-diagnosis patients who go to regular 12-step meetings not to discuss their mental illness and medication, and to "take what you need and leave the rest."

Chronically Mentally Ill Substance Abusers

A large measure of clinical difficulty and financial pressure on society is found in a subset of the 14% of the population with three or more lifetime comorbid disorders, among whom are the severely and persistently mentally ill (SPMI). In a study of substance abuse among the chronically mentally ill, Drake and Wallach (1989) interviewed 187 chronically mentally ill persons and found that the dually diagnosed patients, compared to those who were only mentally ill, were younger, more likely to be male, less able to maintain stable housing and financial stability, and more likely to evidence hostility, suicidal thoughts, and medication noncompliance.

The SPMI population has been poorly served by both the traditional mental health care system and the traditional substance abuse treatment system. Although managed-care organizations have also often found this population difficult to treat with a sensible amount of financial risk, new carve-out designations for the SPMI population may prove beneficial over the long term. By carving out this population from traditional capitation contracts and shifting responsibility to government or an appropriately funded private system, managed-care organizations may do a service by officially recognizing the very different needs of the SPMI population from those of other groups of people.

Integrated Treatment for Severe Mental Illness

One simple model of treatment that has established efficacy for severely mentally ill patients with SUDs is the combined psychiatric and addictive disorder, or COPAD, model. The treatment model consists of substance abuse counseling, supportive group psychotherapy (Rosenthal, in press), psychiatric medication management, and ad hoc crisis intervention, all integrated philosophically and geographically into two group therapy sessions per week. Individual sessions with the psychiatrist are provided ad libitum for medication problems and so on. The persuasion and active treatment phases of dual-diagnosis treatment as conceptualized by Osher and Kofoed (1989) are combined in the COPAD treatment (Hellerstein et al., 1995; Rosenthal et al., 1992b), along with the engagement phase (Drake, Bartels, Teague, Noordsy, & Clark, 1993). Interventions at crisis points for schizophrenia patients with substance use disorders must typically be aimed at engagement and persuasion (Lehman, Herron, Schwartz, & Myers, 1993).

This model demonstrates strong retention effects simply due to integrating services. Compared to a parallel treatment group that received addiction and psychiatric services in different locations, at 4 months 69.6% of patients in integrated treatment remained in treatment, compared to only 37.5% in the nonintegrated treatment (Hellerstein et al., 1995). Patients retained in treatment had significant reductions in both psychiatric and substance use symptom severity. The success of COPAD was directly linked to the coordination of addiction and psychiatric care, delivered by the same clinicians in the same physical space. By having an ongoing long-term relationship with the patients, the clinicians were able to assess each presenting complaint in the context of their previous observations and accurately decide if the symptoms warranted supportive psychotherapy, medication adjustment, or hospitalization. Patients who failed to engage in treatment had significantly more days in the hospital than those who began treatment, and failure to engage was strongly related to return to a controlled environment (Hellerstein et al., 1995).

Assertive Case Management for High-Severity Cases

Assertive community treatment (ACT) programs are based on a model pioneered by Stein and Test (1980; Olfson, 1990) for community treatment of seriously mentally ill patients. ACT programs (Olfson, 1990) have interdisciplinary staffs, generally directed by a psychiatrist, that provide community-based treatment for chronic psychiatric patients, focusing on issues of daily living, basic material needs, and case management, with a significant degree of outreach in the community. In particular, such services provide frequent off-site visits, 24-hour-per-day availability, continuity of care, and assertive offering of treatment when patients begin to relapse. Drake, McHugo, and Noordsy (1993) found that 61% of substance abusers with schizophrenia achieved stable (> 6-month) remission from alcoholism at 4-year outcome in an integrated treatment program that included assertive case management. In another study, 42 patients with *DSM-IV* schizophrenia and substance dependence were randomized to a control group of integrated outpatient treatment or an experimental group of integrated treatment including a reduced form of ACT called *targeted assertive outreach (TAO)*. At 4 months, control subjects showed 27% diminution in positive symptom severity compared to 51% for those receiving TAO services (community visits from team staff members; crisis intervention and assertive outreach to support treatment compliance, medication use, and attendance at scheduled appointments; and direct support of attendance at 12-step programs) (Rosenthal, Hellerstein, & Miner, 1997).

Targeted Assertive Outreach

TAO differs from other case management models by (a) reliance on in vivo assistance and training of patients; (b) utilizing assertive case management staff who are providers and not just brokers of aspects of the service package; (c) heavy emphasis upon staff teamwork; (d) maintaining a 1:10–15 staff-to-patient ratio; (e) ensuring that no team has a caseload greater than 60 patients so that every worker can be acquainted with every patient; (f) maintaining a long-term commitment to patients that they can use the services as long as needed (Bond, 1990); (g) 24-hour availability of team members; and (h) a clinical supervisor who is also on the team. As stated above, recovery is understood to be nonlinear. Therefore, the TAO team assists patients as they cycle through initial and subsequent engagement phases of treatment (Ridgely, 1991). TAO focuses upon "rerecruitment" at points where the patient is most likely to have an exacerbation of illness, and TAO therapists use their knowledge of the COPAD treatment (including drug counseling, psychoeducation, and supportive psychotherapy) to motivate and rerecruit subjects into more active treatment. Assertive community treatment with an explicit focus upon engagement and stabilization has been successful in maintaining dually diagnosed patients in long-term treatment (Drake, McHugo, & Noordsy, 1993). As much attrition in treatment results from early dropout of mixed-syndrome male schizophrenia patients (Miner, Rosenthal, Hellerstein, & Muenz, 1997), they especially may benefit from these services. Preliminary outcome data suggest that over and above the gains resulting from integration of addiction and mental health services, there is a differential effect of adding TAO-type services on psychiatric and alcohol symptom severity (Rosenthal et al., 1997).

Interfacing with Mental Health Professionals

There has been a long-standing split between workers in psychiatry and workers in substance abuse. Substance abuse workers have believed that mentally ill patients are too difficult to treat with the confrontational methods of the therapeutic communities and group therapies. In the traditional "drug-free" substance abuse treatment, there is no place for psychotropic medications. Psychiatric practitioners have shied away from patients with substance abuse disorders as too manipulative, noncompliant, challenging, and frustration-intolerant. Because of this split between substance abuse and mental illness theory (Miller & Gold, 1992), funding and research patterns have petrified the field into two camps. The dual-diagnosis patient has traditionally been excluded from treatment in both communities. The care and treatment of dually diagnosed patients have recently become a more legitimate (and better funded) field of study within psychiatry. A broad and

flexible understanding of substance abuse theory and psychiatry is necessary for the competent treatment of dually diagnosed patients.

Access to just such an understanding is described in a demonstration project described by Minkoff (1989). In this model of treatment for addicted people with psychosis, traditional psychiatric treatment is blended with chemical dependency treatment and the principles of AA. Both the psychiatric and the addiction conditions are assigned separate legitimacy from the standpoint of treatment, and specific efforts are made to educate treating professionals in any areas of deficiency. Addiction professionals are taught about mental illness and the prescription of psychoactive medications as opposed to the abuse of licit and illicit psychoactive substances. Mental health professionals are educated about the usefulness of self-help groups and about helpful prescribing practices for the dually diagnosed.

In summary, *collaboration* should by the watchword for addiction clinicians and mental health professionals treating the dually diagnosed person. Ideally, the artificial distinctions between service delivery domains will break down as knowledge of the interactions between addiction and mental illness suffuses the education of health care workers. Staff that are cross-trained in treatment of addictions and NSR mental disorders will be best positioned to deliver comprehensive care. Also valuable is cooperation with sponsors and members from peer-led groups who, although they may lack professional training, often bring a wealth of practical knowledge to their efforts to assist their peers.

Committing a Patient

Laws vary from state to state regarding the commitment of mentally ill and addicted persons, and the clinician must know local statutes. However, a few common themes should be considered while considering an involuntary commitment to treatment. Although states do not permit the involuntary commitment of an addicted person for treatment of addiction, all states permit the involuntary commitment of a person who is an acute danger to self or others. Although continued addiction is often self-destructive and has even been called "a suicidal flight from disease" (Menninger, 1938), most states do not recognize addiction per se as a reason for withholding a person's freedom and committing him or her to treatment. Although many addiction professionals would agree with the necessity of mandated addiction treatment for some populations (Platt, Buhringer, & Kaplan, 1988), few practical programs exist.

The person who puts self or others in immediate danger because of a mental disorder must be detained and kept safe, regardless of etiology. But this sort of emergency hold can be justified only briefly while, for example, a person intoxicated with alcohol "sleeps it off" or a person who is agitated and threatening after using phencyclidine (PCP, "angel dust") is sedated and allowed to recompensate to his or her baseline mental state.

When the question of commitment to longer term treatment arises, the clinician must examine the patient with an eye to finding mental illness other than addiction that meets legal criteria for commitment to treatment. For instance, a person with impaired judgment due to chronic paranoid schizophrenia could benefit from involuntary commitment, while a person with impaired judgment due to cocaine intoxication may need a brief holding period until the intoxication has passed. The person with a documented mental illness can, in most states, be held involuntarily if the clinician can show that discharge from a hospital is likely to result in danger to the patient or others immediately or within some defined period of time.

Dealing with Emergencies

Emergency situations with the dually diagnosed patient are fraught with all the risk factors of each separate disorder. Most worrisome is the suicide attempt or parasuicidal action that often heralds the arrival of the dually diagnosed patient in the emergency department or admission unit. Because addiction is a clear risk factor for completed suicide (Adams, 1985), and conditions like schizophrenia, major depression, and bipolar disorder (Breier, Schreiber, Dyer, & Pickar, 1991) also increase the likelihood of a suicidal act, clinicians must make especially careful treatment and disposition plans for the dually diagnosed patient. Patients presenting to the emergency service with a history of alcohol or drug abuse, depressed mood, and suicidal ideation or intent must be assessed carefully. A study of 133 suicides under age 30 years found that 53% had a principal psychiat-

ric diagnosis of substance abuse, and 24% had an additional diagnosis of atypical depression, psychosis, or adjustment disorder with depressed mood (Fowler, Rich, & Young, 1986). In a recent review, Murphy and Wetzel (1990) reported that although the lifetime risk of 2.0–3.4% for suicide in conservatively diagnosed alcoholics is apparently small, the risk for suicide in this group is 60–120 times that of the non-psychiatrically ill and accounts for about 25.0% of all suicides. In another study, 34 of 50 alcoholic suicides had depression that was mostly secondary to alcoholism (Murphy, Armstrong, Hermele, Fischer, & Clendenin, 1979). Clearly, a depressed mood in the context of drug and alcohol abuse increases the already large proportionate risk of suicide (Berglund, 1984).

The clinician should track prior history as one indicator of acute suicidal risk in substance abusers. For example, there are those patients who make suicidal threats or actions only when intoxicated. Often, patients with this pattern will respond to several hours of observation and no longer evince suicidal symptoms when they sober up. Another pattern of state-dependent suicidal risk in alcoholics is analogous to that observed in patients recovering from major depression. In this pattern, the patient becomes more capable of acting on the suicidal impulse after becoming sober and has more cognitive tools with which to assess his or her current life condition, becomes demoralized or despairing, and acts.

The psychotic break, especially the first psychotic break for a schizophrenia patient, must be considered a potentially dangerous time for suicidal behavior because the patient may recognize the loss of control over his or her thinking processes and the lifetime implications of the loss. The disinhibiting effects of substances of abuse can only add to the danger of committing an impulsive self-destructive act. Similarly, substance abuse among patients with bipolar disorder increases the suicide risk.

Behavioral control of an agitated or dangerously psychotic dual-diagnosis patient should be established with sedative/hypnotic medications such as diazepam (Valium and others), lorazepam (Ativan and others), or clonazepam (Klonopin). The addition of antipsychotic medications such as haloperidol (Haldol) and Prolixin (fluphenazine) can add substantially to the antiagitation effect of the sedative/hypnotics but exposes the patient to the risks of side effects and the dangerous interactions with street drugs associated with the antipsychotic medications.

Since antipsychotic medications have an acute sedative effect but a delayed onset of antipsychotic effect, they are generally reserved for those patients known to have a freestanding psychiatric disorder not caused by a substance of abuse.

A common emergency in the dually diagnosed patient is relapse to the substance of abuse, often associated with the recurrence of psychiatric symptoms. A brief "slip" or even a longer term relapse to the substance abuse should be framed as a learning experience in which the addict learns yet another cue or inciting factor to use of the illicit substance. By carefully reviewing the events leading up to the slip, the clinician can often help the patient identify dangerous situations, attitudes, or even objects that can be avoided in the future.

It is exceedingly important that clinicians be thoroughly familiar with typical intoxication and withdrawal syndromes (see chapters 4–10). Clearly, appropriate supervision can lead to emergency room treatment and prompt resolution of psychiatric symptomatology in patients who present with mental symptoms solely due to drugs of abuse (e.g., due to alcohol withdrawal or acute anxiety in cocaine intoxication). This capacity to discriminate substance-induced symptoms is important to reduce the number of false-positive identifications of patients as mentally ill chemical abusers and to direct those that might have been diagnosed as such to more appropriate treatment facilities. Admitting too many patients without treatable acute mental disorders to services for the psychiatrically ill stresses those systems by increasing turnover rates, demoralizing staff, and so on.

SUMMARY

Patients with both SUDs and NSR mental disorders are frequently underdiagnosed and almost certainly undertreated. The prevalence rates of comorbidity of both disorders have been much higher than clinicians typically believe. Because of both the inadequate training of clinicians and the structure of program licensure, when comorbidity is recognized as complicating the clinical picture most current treatment is delivered in a sequential or concurrent style that is less than optimal for supporting recovery from both illnesses. Recent evidence suggests that integrating addiction and mental health services supports treatment retention and recovery from both SUDs

and NSR mental disorders. The relationships between SUDs and NSR mental disorders are complex, and there is evidence supporting the existence of many forms of interaction. Until a differential trajectory of illness based upon order of onset is better articulated, treatments should be based upon clinical characteristics that already have known impact on outcome, including severity of illness, motivational state, cognitive capacity, medication responsivity, and chronicity. Therefore, treatments should be individualized to the individual patient's problem set. When systemic roadblocks to this type of treatment are bypassed, even patients with chronic and severe disorders can establish a reasonable path of recovery.

Key References

Kessler, R. C., McGonagle, K. A., Zhao, S., Nelson, C. B., Hughes, M., Eshelman, S., Wittchen, H. U., & Kendler, K. S. (1994). Lifetime and 12-month pevalence of DSM-III-R psychiatric disorders in the United States: Results from the National Comorbidity Study. *Archives of General Psychiatry, 51*, 8–19.

Regier, D. A., Farmer, M. E., Rae, D. S., Locke, B. Z., Keith, S. J., Judd, L. L., & Goodwin, F. K. (1990). Comorbidity of mental disorder with alcohol and other drug abuse. Results from the Epidemiologic Catchment Area (ECA) Study. *Journal of the American Medical Association, 264*, 2511–2518.

Schuckit, M. A., & Hesselbrock, V. (1994). Alcohol dependence and anxiety disorders: What is the relationship? *American Journal of Psychiatry, 151*, 1723–1734.

References

Adams, K. S. (1985). Attempted suicide. *Psychiatric Clinics of North America, 8*, 183–201.

Albanese, M., Bartel, R., Bruno, R., Morgenbesser, M. W., & Schatzberg, A. F. (1994). Comparison of measures used to determine substance abuse in an inpatient psychiatric population. *American Journal of Psychiatry, 151*, 1077–1078.

Alterman, A. I., & Cacciola, J. S. (1991). The antisocial personality disorder diagnosis in substance abusers: Problems and issues. *Journal of Nervous and Mental Disease, 179*, 401–409.

Alterman, A. I., McLellan, A. T., & Shifman, R. B. (1993). Do substance abuse patients with more psychopathology receive more treatment? *Journal of Nervous and Mental Disease, 181*, 576–582.

American Psychiatric Association. (1980). *Diagnostic and statistical manual of mental disorders* (3rd ed.). Washington, DC: Author.

American Psychiatric Association. (1987). *Diagnostic and statistical manual of mental disorders* (3rd ed., Rev.). Washington, DC: Author.

American Psychiatric Association. (1994). *Diagnostic and statistical manual of mental disorders* (4th ed.). Washington, DC: Author.

Ananth, J., Vandeater, S., Kamal, M., & Brodsky, A. (1989). Missed diagnosis of substance abuse in psychiatric patients. *Hospital and Community Psychiatry, 40,* 297–299.

Anthony, J. C., Tien, A. Y., & Petronis, K. R. (1989). Epidemiologic evidence on cocaine use and panic attacks. *American Journal of Epidemiology, 129,* 543–549.

Aronson, T. A., & Craig, T. J. (1986). Cocaine precipitation of panic disorder. *American Journal of Psychiatry, 143,* 643–645.

Babor, T. F., Hofman, M., DelBoca, F. K., Hesselbrock, V., Meyer, R. E., Dolinski, Z. S., & Rounsaville, B. (1992). Types of alcoholics: 1. Evidence for an empirically derived typology based upon indicators of vulnerability and severity. *Archives of General Psychiatry, 49,* 599–608.

Bailey, L. G., Maxwell, S., & Brandabur, M. M. (1997). Substance abuse as a risk factor for tardive dyskinesia: a retrospective analysis of 1,027 patients. *Psychopharmacology Bulletin, 33,* 177–181.

Ball, J. C., & Ross, A. (1991). *The effectiveness of methadone maintenance treatment: Patients, programs, services and outcomes.* New York: Springer-Verlag.

Ball, S. A., Carroll, K. M., Babor, T., & Rounsaville, B. J. (1995). Subtypes of cocaine abusers: Support for a Type-A Type-B distinction. *Journal of Consulting and Clinical Psychology, 63,* 115–124.

Becker, H. C., & Hale, R. L. (1993). Repeated episodes of ethanol withdrawal potentiate the severity of subsequent withdrawal seizures: An animal model of alcohol withdrawal "kindling." *Alcoholism: Clinical & Experimental Research, 17,* 94–98.

Berglund, M. (1984). Suicide in alcoholism, A prospective study of 88 suicides: 1. The multidimensional disgnosis at first admission. *Archives of General Psychiatry, 41,* 888–891.

Berkson, J. (1946). Limitations of four-fold tables to hospital data. *Biomet Bulletin, 35,* 47–53.

Biederman, J., Faraone, S. V., Spencer, T., Wilens, T., Norman, D., Lapey, K. A., Mick, E., Lehman, B. K., & Doyle, A. (1993). Patterns of psychiatric comorbidity, cognition, and psychosocial functioning in adults with attention deficit hyperactivity disorder. *American Journal of Psychiatry, 150,* 1792–1798.

Biederman, J., Newcorn, J., & Sprich, S. (1991). Comorbidity of attention-deficit hyeractivity disorders with conduct, depressive, anxiety and other disorders. *American Journal of Psychiatry, 148,* 564–577.

Biederman, J., Wilens, T., Mick, E., Milberger, S., Spenser, T. J., & Faraone, S. V. (1995). The psychoactive substance use disorders in adults with attention-deficit hyperactivity disorder (ADHD): Effect of ADHD and comorbidity. *American Journal of Psychiatry, 152,* 1652–1658.

Bollerud, K. (1990). A model for the treatment of trauma-related syndromes among chemically dependent inpatient women. *Journal of Substance Abuse Treatment, 7,* 83–87.

Boyd, J. H., Burke, J. D., Gruenberg, E., Holzer, C. E., Rae, D. S., George, L. K., Karno, M., Stoltzman, R., McEvoy, L., & Nestadt, G. (1984). Exclusion criteria of DSMIII—A study of co-occurrence of hierarchy-free syndromes. *Archives of General Psychiatry, 41,* 983–989.

Brady, K., Casto, S., Lydiard, R. B., Malcolm, R., & Arana, G. (1991). Substance abuse in an inpatient psychiatric sample. *American Journal of Drug and Alcohol Abuse, 17,* 389–397.

Brady, K. T., Lydiard, R. B., Malcolm, R., & Ballenger, J. C. (1991). Cocaine-induced psychosis. *Journal of Clinical Psychiatry, 52,* 509–512.

Brady, K. T., & Sonne, S. C. (1995). The relationship between substance abuse and bipolar disorder. *Journal of Clinical Psychiatry, 56* (Suppl. 3), 19–24.

Breier, A., Schreiber, J. L., Dyer, J., & Pickar, D. (1991). National Institute of Mental Health longitudinal study of chronic schizophrenia: Prognosis and predictors of outcome. *Archives of General Psychiatry, 48,* 239–246.

Brinson, T., & Treanor, V. (1988). Alcoholism and post-traumatic stress disorder among combat Vietnam veterans. *Alcoholism Treatment Quarterly, 5,* 65–82.

Brooner, R. K., King, V. L., Kidorf, M., Schmidt, C. W., Jr., & Bigelow, G. E. (1997). Psychiatric and substance abuse comorbidity among treatment-seeking opiod abusers. *Archives of General Psychiatry, 54,* 71–80.

Brown, M. E., Anton, R. F., Malcolm, R., & Ballenger, J. C. (1988). Alcohol detoxification and withdrawal seizures: Clinical support for a kindling hypothesis. *Biological Psychiatry, 23,* 507–514.

Brown, P. J., & Wolfe, J. (1994). Substance abuse and post-traumatic stress disorder comorbidity. *Drug and Alcohol Dependence, 35,* 51–59.

Brown, S. A., Inaba, R. K., Gillin, J. C., Schuckit, M. A., Stewart, M. A., & Irwin, M. R. (1995). Alcoholism and affective disorder: Clinical course of depressive symptoms. *American Journal of Psychiatry, 152,* 45–52.

Brown, S. A., Irwin, M., & Schuckit, M. A. (1991). Changes in anxiety among abstinent male alcoholics. *Journal of Studies on Alcohol, 52,* 55–61.

Brown, S. A., & Shuckit, M. A. (1988). Changes in depression among abstinent alcoholics. *Journal of Studies on Alcohol, 49,* 412–417.

Buckley, P., Thompson, P., Way, L., & Meltzer, H. Y. (1994). Substance abuse among patients with treatment-resistant schizophrenia: Characteristics and implications for clozapine therapy. *American Journal of Psychiatry, 151,* 385–389.

Calabrese, J. R., & Delucci, G. A. (1990). Spectrum of efficacy of valproate in 55 patients with rapid-cycling bipolar disorder. *American Journal of Psychiatry, 147,* 431–434.

Carey, K. B., Cocco, K. M., & Simons, J. S. (1996). Concurrent validity of clinician's ratings of substance abuse among psychiatric outpatients. *Psychiatric Services, 47,* 842–847.

Carroll, J. F. X., & McGinley, J. J. (1997). From the field: Providers can treat dually diagnosed in mainstream settings. *Alcoholism and Drug Abuse Weekly,* 9(26), 5.

Carroll, K. M., Nich, C., & Rounsaville, B. J. (1995). Differential symptom reduction in depressed cocaine abusers treated with psychotherapy and pharmacotherapy. *Journal of Nervous and Mental Disease, 183,* 251–259.

Cesarec, Z., & Nyman, A. K. (1985). Differential response to amphetamine in schizophrenics. *Acta Psychiatrica Scandinavica, 71,* 523–538.

Childress, A. R., Ehrman, R. N., McLellan, A. T., MacRae, J., Natale, M., & O'Brien, C. P. (1994). Can induced moods trigger drug-related reponses in opiate patients. *Journal of Substance Abuse Treatment, 11,* 17–23.

Childress, A. R., McLellan, A. T., Natale, M., & O'Brien, C. P. (1987). Mood states can elicit conditioned withdrawal and craving in opiate abuse patients. *Problems of Drug Dependence, 1986,* NIDA Research Monograph 76, 137–144.

Cleghorn, J. M., Kaplan, R. D., Szechtman, B., Szechtman, H., Brown, G. M., & Franco, S. (1991). Substance abuse in schizophrenia: Effects on symptoms but not on cognitive functions. *Journal of Clinical Psychiatry, 52,* 26–30.

Comtois, K. A., Ries, R., & Armstrong, H. E. (1994). Case manager ratings in a dual diagnosis program for the severely mentally ill. *Hospital and Community Psychiatry, 45,* 568–573.

Condelli, W. S., & Dunteman, G. H. (1993). Exposure to methadone programs and heroin use. *American Journal of Drug and Alcohol Abuse, 19,* 65–78.

Cornelius, J. R., Salloum, I. M., Ehler, J. G., Jarrett, P. J., Cornelius, M. D., Perel, J. M., Thase, M. E., & Black, A. (1997). Fluoxetine in depressed alcoholics: A double-blind, placebo-controlled trial. *Archives of General Psychiatry, 54,* 700–705.

Cornelius, J. R., Salloum, I. M., Mezzich, J., Cornelius, M. D., Fabrega, H., Ehler, J. G., Ulrich, R. F., Thase, M. E., & Mann, J. J. (1995). Disproportionate suicidality in patients with comorbid major depression and alcoholism. *American Journal of Psychiatry, 152,* 358–364.

Cottler, L. B., Compton, W. M., Mager, D., Spitznagel, E. L., & Janca, A. (1992). Post-traumatic stress disorder among substance users from the general population. *American Journal of Psychiatry, 149,* 664–670.

Craig, T. J., Lin, S. P., El-Defrawi, M. H., & Goodman, A. B. (1985). Clinical correlates of readmission in a schizophrenic cohort. *Psychiatric Quarterly, 57,* 5–10.

Dixon, L. D., Haas, G., Weiden, P. J., Sweeney, J., & Francis, A. (1991). Drug abuse in schizophrenia patients: Clinical correlates and reasons for use. *American Journal of Psychiatry, 148,* 224–230.

Dixon, L., Weiden, P. J., Haas, G., & Sweeney, J. (1992). Increased tardive dyskinesia in alcohol abusing schizophrenic patients. *Comprehensive Psychiatry, 33,* 121–122.

Dorus, W., Kennedy, J., Gibbons, R. D., & Ravi, S. D. (1987). Symptoms and diagnosis of depression in alcoholics. *Alcoholism: Clinical and Experimental Research, 11,* 150–154.

Drake, R. E., Bartels, S. J., Teague, G. B., Noordsy, D. L., & Clark, R. E. (1993). Treatment of substance abuse in severely mentally ill patients. *Journal of Nervous and Mental Disease, 181,* 606–611.

Drake, R. E., McHugo, G. J., & Noordsy, D. L. (1993). Treatment of alcoholism among schizophrenic outpatients: 4-year outcomes. *American Journal of Psychiatry, 150,* 328–329.

Drake, R. E., Mueser, K. T., Clark, R. E., & Wallach, M. A. (1996). The course, treatment, and outcome of substance disorder in persons with severe mental illness. *American Journal of Orthopsychiatry, 66,* 42–51.

Drake, R. E., & Sederer, L. I. (1986). Inpatient psychosocial treatment of chronic schizophrenia: Negative effects and current guidelines. *Hospital and Community Psychiatry, 37,* 897–901.

Drake, R. E., & Wallach, M. A. (1989). Substance abuse among the mentally ill. *Hospital and Community Psychiatry, 40,* 1041–1046.

Dunner, D. L., & Feinman, J. (1996). The effect of substance abuse on the course of bipolar disorder. *Biological Psychiatry, 39,* 617.

Fernandez-Pol, B., Bluestone, H., & Mizruchi, M. S. (1988). Inner-city substance abuse patterns: A study of psychiatric inpatients. *American Journal of Drug and Alcohol Abuse, 14,* 41–50.

Fischer, D. E., Halikas, J. A., Baker, J. W., & Smith, J. B. (1975). Frequency and patterns of drug abuse in psychiatric patients. *Diseases of the Nervous System, 36,* 550–553.

Fowler, R. C., Rich, C. L., & Young, D. (1986). San Diego suicide study: 2. Substance abuse in young cases. *Archives of General Psychiatry, 43,* 962–965.

Freud, S. (1974). Uber Coca. In R. Byck (Ed.), *Cocaine papers: Sigmund Freud.* New York: Stonehill.

Fyer, M. R., Frances, A. J., Sullivan, T., Hurt, S. W., & Clarkin, J. (1988). Suicide attempts in patients with borderline personality disorder. *American Journal of Psychiatry, 145,* 737–739.

Galanter, M., Castaneda, R., & Ferman, J. (1988). Substance abuse among general psychiatric patients: Place of presentation, diagnosis, and treatment. *American Journal of Drug and Alcohol Abuse, 14,* 211–235

Gastfriend, D. R. (1993). Pharmacotherapy of psychiatric syndromes with comorbid chemical dependency. *Journal of Addictive Disease, 12,* 155–170.

Gawin, F. H., & Kleber, H. D. (1986). Abstinence symptomatology and psychiatric diagnosis in cocaine abusers: Clinical observations. *Archives of General Psychiatry, 43,* 107–113.

Gelernter, J., Kranzler, H. R., Satel, S. L., & Rao, P. A. (1994). Genetic association between dopamine transporter protein alleles and cocaine-induced paranoia. *Neuropsychopharmacology, 11,* 195–200.

Hellerstein, D. J., & Meehan, B. (1987). Outpatient group therapy for schizophrenic substance abusers. *American Journal of Psychiatry, 144,* 1337–1339.

Hellerstein, D. J., Rosenthal, R. N., & Miner, C. R. (1995). A prospective study of integrated outpatient treatment for substance-abusing schizophrenic patients. *American Journal on Addictions, 4,* 33–42.

Helzer, J. E., & Pryzbeck, T. R. (1988). The co-occurrence of alcoholism with other psychiatric disorders in the general population and its impact on treatment. *Journal of Studies on Alcohol, 49,* 219–224.

Herman, M., Galanter, M., & Lifshutz, H. (1991). Combined substance abuse and psychiatric disorders in homeless and domiciled patients. *American Journal of Drug and Alcohol Abuse, 17,* 415–422.

Hesselbrock, M. N., Meyer, R. E., & Keener, J. J. (1985). Psychopathology in hospitalized alcoholics. *Archives of General Psychiatry, 42,* 1050–1055.

Hien, D., Zimberg, S., Weisman, S., First, M., & Ackerman, S. (1997). Dual-diagnosis subtypes in urban substance abuse and mental health clinics. *Psychiatric Services, 48,* 1058–1063.

Hodgins, D. C., el-Guebaly, N., & Armstrong, S. (1995). Prospective and retrospective reports of mood states before relapse to substance use. *Journal of Consulting and Clinical Psychology, 63,* 400–407.

Hyer, L., Leach, P., Boudewyns, P. A., & Davis, H. (1991). Hidden PTSD in substance abuse in-patients among Vietnam veterans. *Journal of Substance Abuse Treatment, 8,* 213–219.

Jellinek, E. M. (1952). Phases of alcohol addiction. *Quarterly Journal of Studies on Alcohol, 13,* 673–684.

Jordan, B. K., Schlenger, W. E., Fairbank, J. A., & Caddell, J. M. (1996). Prevalence of psychiatric disorders among incarcerated women: 2. Convicted felons entering prison. *Archives of General Psychiatry, 53,* 513–519.

Kane, J. M., & Selzer, J. (1991). Considerations on "organic" exclusion criteria for schizophrenia. *Schizophrenia Bulletin, 17,* 69–73.

Kaufman, E., & Reoux, J. (1988). Guidelines for the successful psychotherapy of substance abusers. *American Journal of Drug and Alcohol Abuse, 14,* 199–209.

Keller, M. B., Lavori, P. W., Coryell, W., Andreasen, N. C., Endicott, J., Clayton, P. J., Klerman, G. L., & Hirschfeld, R. M. A. (1986). Differential outcome of pure manic, mixed/cycling, and pure depressive episodes in patients with bipolar illness. *Journal of the American Medical Association, 255,* 3138–3142.

Kessler, R. C., McGonagle, K. A., Zhao, S., Nelson, C. B., Hughes, M., Eshelman, S., Wittchen, H. U., & Kendler, K. S. (1994). Lifetime and 12-month pevalence of DSM-III-R psychiatric disorders in the United States: Results from the National Comorbidity Study. *Archives of General Psychiatry, 51,* 8–19.

Kessler, R. C., Nelson, C. B., McGonagle, K. A., Edlund, M. J., Frank, R. G., & Leaf, P. J. (1996). The epidemiology of co-occurring addictive and mental disorders: Implications for prevention and service utilization. *American Journal of Orthopsychiatry, 66,* 17–31.

Khantzian, E. J. (1985). The self-medication hypothesis of addictive disorders: Focus on heroin and cocaine dependence. *American Journal of Psychiatry, 42,* 1259–1264.

Khantzian, E. J. (1990). Self-regulation and self-medication factors in alcoholism and addictions: Similarities and differences. In M. Galanter (Ed.), *Recent developments in alcoholism* (Vol. 8). New York: Plenum Press.

Kofoed, L., Kania, J., Walsh, T., & Atkinson, R. M. (1986). Outpatient treatment of patients with substance abuse and coexisting psychiatric disorder. *American Journal of Psychiatry, 143,* 867–872.

Kokkevi, A., & Stefanis, C. (1995). Drug abuse and psychiatric comorbidity. *Comprehensive Psychiatry, 36,* 329–337.

Kosten, T. R. (1989). Pharmacotherapeutic interventions for cocaine abuse: Matching patients to treatments. *Journal of Nervous and Mental Disease, 177,* 379–389.

Kosten, T. R., Rounsaville, B. J., & Kleber, H. D. (1985). Concurrent validity of the Addicition Severity Index. *Journal of Nervous and Mental Disease, 171,* 606–610.

Kosten, T. R., Rounsaville, B. J., & Kleber, H. D. (1987). A 2.5-year follow-up of cocaine use among treated opioid addicts. *Archives of General Psychiatry, 44,* 281–284.

Kovasznay, B., Fleischer, J., Tananberg-Karant, M., Jandorf, L., Miller, A. D., & Bromet, E. (1997). Substance use disorder and the early course of illness in schizophrenia and affective psychosis. *Schizophrenia Bulletin, 23,* 195–201.

Kovatch, J. (1986). Incest as a treatment issue for alcoholic women. *Alcoholism Treatment Quarterly, 3,* 1–15.

Kranzler, H. R. (1996). Evaluation and treatment of anxiety symptoms and disorders in alcoholics. *Journal of Clinical Psychiatry, 57*(Suppl. 7), 15–21.

Kranzler, H. R., Burleson, J. A., Brown, J., & Babor, T. F. (1996). Fluoxetine treatment seems to reduce the beneficial effects of cognitive-behavioral therapy in type B alcoholics. *Alcoholism: Clinical and Experimental Research, 20,* 1534–1541.

Kranzler, H. R., Del Boca, F. K., & Rounsaville, B. J. (1996). Comorbid psychiatric diagnosis predicts three-year outcomes in alcoholics: A posttreatment natural history study. *Journal of Studies on Alcohol, 57,* 619–626.

Kranzler, H. R., Satel, S., & Apter, A. (1994). Personality disorder and associated features in cocaine-dependent inpatients. *Comprehensive Psychiatry, 35,* 335–340.

LaPorte, D. J., McLellan, A. T., O'Brien, C. P., & Marshall, J. R. (1981). Treatment response in psychiatrically impaired drug abusers. *Comprehensive Psychiatry, 22,* 411–419.

Leal, J., Ziedonis, D., & Kosten, T. (1994). Antisocial personality disorder as a prognostic factor for pharmacotherapy of cocaine dependence. *Drug and Alcohol Dependence, 35,* 31–35.

Lehman, A. F., Herron, J. D., Schwartz, R. P., & Myers, C. P. (1993). Rehabilitation for adults with severe mental illness and substance use disorders: A clinical

trial. *Journal of Nervous and Mental Disease, 181,* 86–90.

Lehman, A. F., Myers, C. P., Corty, E., & Thompson, J. W. (1994). Prevalence and patterns of "dual-diagnosis" among psychiatric inpatients. *Comprehensive Psychiatry, 35,* 106–112.

Levy, D. L., Smith, M., Robertson, D., Jody, D., Lerner, G., Alvir, J., Geisler, S. H., Szymanski, S. R., Gonzalez, A., Mayerhoff, D. I., Lieberman, J. A., & Mendell, N. R. (1993). Methylphenidate increases thought disorder in recent onset schiophrenics, but not in normal controls. *Biological Psychiatry, 34,* 507–514.

Lewis, D. C., & Kleinenberg, E. M. (1994). Researchers and health care reform (editorial). *Alcoholism: Clinical and Experimental Research, 18,* 771–773.

Linszen, D. H., Dingemans, P. M., & Lenior, M. E. (1994). Cannabis abuse and the course of recent-onset schizophrenic disorders. *Archives of General Psychiatry, 51,* 273–279.

Litman, G., Stapleton, J., Oppenheim, A. N., Peleg, M., & Jackson, P. (1983). Situations related to alcoholism relapse. *British Journal of Addiction, 78,* 381–389.

Lydiard, R. B., Brady, K., Ballenger, J. C., Howell, E. F., & Malcolm, R. (1992). Anxiety and mood disorders in hospitalized alcoholic individuals. *American Journal on Addictions, 1,* 325–331.

Lysaker, P. H., Bell, M. D., Bioty, S. M., & Zito, W. S. (1997). Cognitive impairment and substance abuse history as predictors of the temporal stability of negative symptoms in schizophrenia. *Journal of Nervous and Mental Disease, 185,* 21–26.

Margolin, A., Avants, S. K., & Kosten, T. R. (1994). Cue-elicited cocaine craving and autogenic relaxation. Association with treatment outcome. *Journal of Substance Abuse Treatment, 11,* 549–552.

Margolin, A., Kosten, T. R., Avants, S. K., Wilkins, J., Ling, W., Beckson, M. l., Arndt, I. O., Cornish, J., Ascher, J. A., Li, S-H., & Bridge, P. (1995). A multicenter trial of bupropion for cocaine dependence in methadone-maintained patients. *Drug and Alcohol Dependence, 40,* 125–131.

Marlatt, G. A., & Gordon, J. R. (1985). *Relapse prevention: Maintenance strategies in the treatment of addictive behaviors.* New York: Guilford Press.

Mason, B. J., Kocsis, J. H., Ritvo, C. E., & Cutler, R. B. (1996). A double-blind placebo-controlled trial of desipramine for primary alcohol dependence startified on the presence or absence of major depression. *Journal of the American Medical Association, 275,* 761–767.

McCarrick, A. K., Manderscheid, R. W., & Bertolucci, D. E. (1985). Correlates of acting-out behaviors among young adult chronic patients. *Hospital and Community Psychiatry, 36,* 848–853.

McFall, M. E., Mackay, P. W., & Donovan, D. M. (1991). Combat-related post-traumatic stress disorder and severity of substance abuse in Vietnam veterans. *Journal of Studies on Alcohol, 53,* 357–362.

McGrath, P. J., Nunes, N. V., Stewart, J. W., Goldman, D., Agosti, V., Ocepek-Welikson, K., & Quitkin, F. M. (1996). Imipramine treatment of alcoholics with major depression: A placebo-controlled trial. *Archives of General Psychiatry, 53,* 232–240.

McHugo, G. J., Drake, R. E., Burton, H. L., & Ackerson, T. H. (1995). A scale for assessing the stage of substance abuse treatment in persons with severe mental illness. *Journal of Nervous and Mental Disease, 183,* 762–767.

McLellan, A. T., Grissom, G. R., Zanis, D., Randall, M., Brill, P., & O'Brien, C. P. (1997). Problem-service matching in addiction treatment: A prospective study in 4 programs. *Archives of General Psychiatry, 54,* 730–735.

McLellan, A. T., Luborsky, L., Cacciola, J., & Griffith, J. (1985). New data from the Addiction Severity Index: Reliability and validity in three centers. *Journal of Nervous and Mental Disease, 173,* 412–423.

McLellan, A. T., Luborsky, L., Woody, G. E., O'Brien, C. P., & Druley, K. A. (1983). Predicting response to alcohol and drug abuse treatments: Role of psychiatric severity. *Archives of General Psychiatry, 40,* 620–625.

McLellan, A. T., Woody, G. E., & O'Brien, C. P. (1979). Development of psychiatric illness in drug abusers: Possible role of drug preference. *New England Journal of Medicine, 301,* 1310–1314.

Menninger, K. (1938). *Man against himself.* New York: Harcourt, Brace & World.

Miller, F. T., Busch, F., & Tanenbaum, J. H. (1989). Drug abuse in schizophrenia and bipolar disorder. *American Journal of Drug and Alcohol Abuse, 15,* 291–295.

Miller, N. S., & Fine, J. (1993). Current epidemiology of comorbidity of psychiatric and addictive disorders. *Psychiatric Clinics of North America, 16,* 1–10.

Miller, N. S., & Gold, M. S. (1992). The psychiatrist's role in integrating pharmacological and nonpharmacological treatments for addictive disorders. *Psychiatric Annals, 22,* 437–440.

Miller, N .S., & Ries, R. K. (1991). Drug and alcohol dependence and psychiatric populations: The need for diagnosis, intervention and training. *Comprehensive Psychiatry, 32,* 268–276.

Miller, W. R., & Rollnick, S. (1991). *Motivational interviewing: Preparing people to change addictive behavior.* New York: Guilford Press.

Miller, W. R., Zweben, A., DiClemente, C. C., & Rychtarik, R. G. (1992). *Motivational enhancement therapy manual.* US Department of Health and Human Services, Publication No. (ADM):92-1894, Rockville, MD.

Miner, C. R., Rosenthal, R. N., Hellerstein, D. J., & Muenz, L. R. (1997). Prediction of non-compliance with outpatient treatment referral in substance-abusing schizophrenics. *Archives of General Psychiatry, 54,* 706–712.

Minkoff, K. (1989). An integrated treatment model for dual diagnosis of psychosis and drug addiction. *Hospital and Community Psychiatry, 40,* 1031–1036.

Minkoff, K., & Rossi, A. (1997). Treatment Interventions by phase of recovery and type of dual diagnosis. In K. Minkoff (Chair), *Clinical standards and workforce competencies project. co-occurring mental and substance disorders (dual diagnosis) panel annotated bibliography.*

Mirin, S. M., Weiss, R. D., Michael, J., & Griffin, M. L. (1988). Psychopathology in substance abusers. *American Journal of Drug and Alcohol Abuse, 14,* 139–157.

Moyer, M. A. (1988). Acheiving successful chemical dependency recovery in veteran survivors of traumatic stress. *Alcoholism Treatment Quarterly, 4,* 19–34.

Murphy, G. E., Armstrong, J. W., Hermele, S. L., Fischer, J. R., & Clendenin, W. W. (1979). Suicide and alcoholism: Interpersonal loss confirmed as a predictor. *Archives of General Psychiatry, 36,* 65–69.

Murphy, G. E., & Wetzel, R. D. (1990). The lifetime risk of suicide in alcoholism. *Archives of General Psychiatry, 47,* 383–391.

Nace, E. P., & Davis, C. W. (1993). Treatment outcome in substance abusing patients with a personality disorder. *American Journal on Addictions, 2,* 26–33.

Nace, E. P., Davis, C. W., & Gaspari, J. P. (1991). Axis II comorbidity in substance abusers. *American Journal of Psychiatry, 148,* 118–120.

Nace, E. P., Saxon, J. J., & Shore, N. (1986). Borderline personality disorder and alcoholism treatment: A one-year follow-up study. *Journal of Studies on Alcohol, 47,* 196–200.

Narrow, W. E., Regier, D. A., Rae, D. S., Manderscheid, R. W., & Locke, B. Z. (1993). Use of services by persons with mental and addictive disorders. *Archives of General Psychiatry, 50,* 95–107.

National Institute on Drug Abuse International Program. (1995). *Methadone maintenance treatment: Translating research into policy.* Bethesda, MD: U.S. Public Health Service.

Nunes, E. V., McGrath, P. J., Quitkin, F. M., Ocepek-Welikson, K., Stewart, J. W., Koenig, T., Wager,

S., & Klein, D. F. (1995). Imipramine treatment of cocaine abuse: Possible boundaries of efficacy. *Drug and Alcohol Dependence, 39,* 185–195.

Nunes, E. V., Quitkin, F. M., & Klein, D. F. (1989). Psychiatric diagnoses in cocaine abuse. *Psychiatry Research, 28,* 105–114.

O'Brien, C. P., Woody, G. E., & McLellan, A. T. (1984). Psychiatric disorders in opioid-dependent patients. *Journal of Clinical Psychiatry, 45*(12, Sec. 2), 9–13.

Olfson, M. (1990). Assertive community treatment: An evaluation of the experimental evidence. *Hospital and Community Psychiatry, 41,* 634–641.

Olivera, A. A., Kiefer, M. W., & Manley, N. K. (1990). Tardive dyskinesia in psychiatric patients with substance abuse disorders. *American Journal of Drug and Alcohol Abuse, 16,* 57–66.

Osher, F. C., & Kofoed, L. L. (1989). Treatment of patients with psychiatric and psychoactive substance abuse disorders. *Hospital and Community Psychiatry, 40,* 1025–1030.

Pepper, B., & Ryglewicz, H. (1984). The young adult chronic patient and substance abuse. *Tie Lines Bulletin, 1,* 1–5.

Pinsker, H. (1983). Addicted patients in hospital psychiatric units. *Psychiatric Annals, 13,* 619–626.

Pinsker, H., Hellerstein, D. J., Rosenthal, R. N., Muran, J. C., & Winston, A. (1996, May). *Supportive therapy, common factors, and eclecticism.* Presented at 149th Annual Meeting of American Psycahiatric Association, New York.

Platt, J. J., Buhringer, G., & Kaplan, B. S. (1988). The prospects and limitations of compulsory treatment for drug addiction. *Journal of Drug Issues, 18,* 505–524.

Post, R. M., Kotin, J., & Goodwin, F. K. (1974). The effects of cocaine on depressed patients. *American Journal of Psychiatry, 131,* 511–517.

Prochaska, J. O., & DiClemente, C. C. (1984). *The transtheoretical approach: Crossing traditional boundaries of therapy.* Homewood, IL: Dorsey.

Prochaska, J. O., & DiClemente, C. C. (1986). Towards a model of change. In W. R. Miller & N. Heather (Eds.), *Treating addictive behaviors: Processes of change* (pp. 3–27). New York: Plenum Press.

Prochaska, J. O., DiClemente, C. C., & Norcross, J. C. (1992). In search of how people change. Applications to addictive behaviors. *American Psychologist, 47,* 1102–1114.

Project Match Research Group. (1997). Matching alcoholism treatments to client heterogeneity: Project match posttreatment drinking outcomes. *Journal of Studies on Alcohol, 58,* 7–29.

Rado, S. (1933). Psychoanalysis of pharmacothymia. *Psychoanalytic Quarterly, 2,* 1–23.

Regier, D. A., Boyd, J. H., Burke, J. D., Rae, D. S., Myers, J. K., Kramer, M., Robins, L. N., George, L. K., Karno, M., & Locke, B. Z. (1988). One-month prevalence of mental disorders in the United States. *Archives of General Psychiatry, 45,* 977–986.

Regier, D. A., Farmer, M. E., Rae, D. S., Locke, B. Z., Keith, S. J., Judd, L. L., & Goodwin, F. K. (1990). Comorbidity of mental disorder with alcohol and other drug abuse: Results from the Epidemiologic Catchment Area (ECA) Study. *Journal of the American Medical Association, 264,* 2511–2518.

Reich, L. H., Davies, R. K., & Himmelhoch, J. M. (1974). Excessive alcohol use in manic-depressive illness. *American Journal of Psychiatry, 131,* 83–86.

Renz, E. A., Chung, R., Fillman, T. O., Mee-Lee, D., & Sayama, M. (1995). The effect of managed care on the treatment outcome of substance use disorders. *General Hospital Psychiatry, 17,* 287–292.

Resnick, R. B., & Resnick, E. B. (1986). Psychological issues in the treatment of cocaine abuse. In L. S. Harris (Ed.), *Problems of drug dependence 1985. NIDA Research Monograph, 67.* Rockville, MD.

Richard, M. L., Liskow, B. I., & Perry, P. J. (1985). Recent psychostimulant use in hospitalized schizophrenics. *Journal of Clinical Psychiatry, 46,* 79–83.

Richardson, M. A. (1985). Treatment patterns of young schizophrenic patients in the era of deinstitutionalization. *Psychiatric Quarterly, 57,* 243–249.

Ridgely, M. S. (1991). Creating integrated programs for severely mentally ill persons with substance disorders. In K. Minkoff & R. E. Drake (Eds.), *Dual diagnosis of major mental illness and substance disorder. New Directions for Mental Health Services, 50,* 29–41. San Francisco: Jossey-Bass.

Ries, R. (1993). Clinical treatment matching models for dually diagnosed patients. In Psychiatric Clinics of North America 16: N. S. Miller (Ed.), *Recent advances in addictive disorders* (pp. 167–175). Philadelphia: Saunders.

Ries, R. K., & Comtois, K. A. (1997). Illness severity and treatment services for dually diagnosed severely mentally ill outpatients. *Schizophrenia Bulletin, 23,* 239–246.

Ries, R. K., & Dyck, D. G. (1997). Representative payee practices of community mental health centers in Washington state. *Psychiatric Services, 48,* 811–814.

Rosenthal, M. S. (1984). Therapeutic communities—A treatment alternative for many but not all. *Journal of Substance Abuse Treatment, 1,* 55–58.

Rosenthal, R. N. (1993). *Mental illness/chemical addiction: A guide to emergency services assessment and treatment*. Albany, NY: State Office of Mental Health, Division of Clinical Support Systems.

Rosenthal, R. N. (in press). Group treatments for schizophrenic substance abusers. In D. W. Brook & H. I. Spitz (Eds.), *The group psychotherapy of substance abuse*. Washington, DC: American Psychiatric Press.

Rosenthal, R. N., Hellerstein, D. J., & Miner, C. R. (1992a). Integrated services for treatment of schizophrenic substance abusers: Demographics, symptoms and substance abuse patterns. *Psychiatric Quarterly, 63*, 3–26.

Rosenthal, R. N., Hellerstein, D. J., & Miner, C. R. (1992b). A model of integrated services for outpatient treatment of patients with cormorbid schizophrenia and addictive disorders. *American Journal on Addictions, 1*, 339–348.

Rosenthal, R. N., Hellerstein, D. J., & Miner, C. R. (1994). Positive and negative syndrome typology in schizophrenic patients with psychoactive substance use disorders. *Comprehensive Psychiatry, 35*, 91–98.

Rosenthal, R. N., Hellerstein, D. J., & Miner, C. R. (1997, May). *Effects of targeted assertive outreach in patients with schizophrenia and substance use disorders*. New Research Program and Abstracts, American Psychiatric Association 150th Annual Meeting, San Diego.

Rosenthal, R. N., & Miner, C. R. (1997). Differential diagnosis of substance-induced psychosis and schizophrenia in patients with substance use disorders. *Schizophrenia Bulletin, 23*, 187–193.

Ross, H. E., Glaser, F. B., & Germanson, T. (1988). The prevalence of psychiatric disorders in patients with alcohol and other drug problems. *Archives of General Psychiatry, 45*, 1023–1031.

Rounsaville, B. J., Anton, S. F., Carroll, K., Budde, D., Prusoff, B. A., & Gawin, F. (1991). Psychiatric diagnoses of treatment-seeking cocaine abusers. *Archives of General Psychiatry, 48*, 43–51.

Rounsaville, B. J., Dolinsky, Z. S., Babor, T. F., & Meyer, R. E. (1987). Psychopathology as a predictor of treatment outcome in alcoholism. *Archives of General Psychiatry, 44*, 505–513.

Rounsaville, B. J., Weissman, M. M., Crits-Christoph, K., Wilber, C., & Kleber, H. (1982). Diagnosis and symptoms of depression in opiate addicts: Course and relationship to treatment outcome. *Archives of General Psychiatry, 39*, 151–156.

Rounsaville, B. J., Weissman, M. M., Kleber, H., & Wilber, C. (1982). The heterogeneity of psychiatric disorders in treated opiate addicts. *Archives of General Psychiatry, 39*, 161–166.

Roy, R. E. (1984). Alcohol misuse and post-traumatic stress disorder. *Journal of Studies on Alcohol, 45*, 285–287.

Satel, S. L., & Gawin, F. H. (1989). Seasonal cocaine abuse. *American Journal of Psychiatry, 146*, 534–535.

Satel, S. L., Southwick, S. M., & Gawin, F. H. (1991). Clinical features of cocaine-induced paranoia. *American Journal of Psychiatry, 148*, 495–498.

Schneier, F. R., & Siris, S. G. (1987). A review of psychoactive substance abuse in schizophrenia. *Journal of Nervous and Mental Disease, 175*, 641–652.

Schuckit, M. A. (1985). The clinical implications of primary diagnostic groups among alcoholics. *Archives of General Psychiatry, 42*, 1043–1049.

Schuckit, M. A., & Hesselbrock, V. (1994). Alcohol dependence and anxiety disorders: What is the relationship? *American Journal of Psychiatry, 151*, 1723–1734.

Schuckit, M. A., Irwin, M., & Brown, S. A. (1990). The history of anxiety symptoms among 171 primary alcoholics. *Journal of Studies on Alcohol, 51*, 34–41.

Serper, M. R., Alpert, M., Richardson, N., Dickson, S., Allen, M., & Werner, A. (1995). Clinical effects of recent cocaine use in acute schizophrenia. *American Journal of Psychiatry, 152*, 1464–1469.

Sevy, S., Kay, S. R., Opler, L. A., & van Praag, H. M. (1990). Significance of cocaine history in schizophrenia. *Journal of Nervous and Mental Disease, 178*, 642–648.

Shaner, A., Khalsa, M. E., Roberts, L., Wilkins, J., Anglin, D., & Hsieh, S. C. (1993). Unrecognized cocaine use among schizophrenic patients. *American Journal of Psychiatry, 150*, 758–762.

Smith, M. B., Hoffmann, N. G., & Nederhoed, G. (1995). The development and reliability of the Recovery Attitude and Treatment Evaluator Questionnaire I (RAATE-QI). *International Journal of the Addictions, 30*, 147–160.

Sokolski, K. N., Cummings, J. L., Abrams, B. I., DeMet, E. M., Katz, L. S., & Costa, J. F. (1994). Effects of substance abuse on hallucination rates and treatment responses in chronic psychiatric patients. *Journal of Clinical Psychiatry, 55*, 380–387.

Sonne, S. C., Brady, K. T., & Morton, W. A. (1994). Substance abuse and bipolar affective disorder. *Journal of Nervous and Mental Disease, 182*, 349–352.

Spitzer, R. L., Endicott, J., & Robins, E. (1978). Research diagnostic criteria—rationale and reliability. *Archives of General Psychiatry, 35*, 773–782.

Stabenau, J. R. (1984). Implications of family history of alcoholism, antisocial personality, and sex differences in alcohol dependence. *American Journal of Psychiatry, 141*, 1178–1182.

State of New York Division of Alcoholism and Alcohol Abuse. (1991). *Comparative estimates of the size of alcohol and drug problems in New York State.* Albany, NY: Author.

Stein, L. I., & Test, M. A. (1980). Alternative to mental hospital treatment: 1. Conceptual mode, treatment program, and clinical evaluation. *Archives of General Psychiatry, 37,* 392–397.

Strakowski, S. M., Tohen, M., Stoll, A. L., Faedda, G. L., & Goodwin, D. C. (1992). Comorbidity in mania at first hospitalization. *American Journal of Psychiatry, 149,* 554–555.

Szuster, R. R., Schanbacher, B. L., McCann, S. C., & McConnell, A. (1990). Underdiagnosis of psychoactive-substance-induced organic mental disorders in emergency psychiatry. *American Journal of Drug and Alcohol Abuse, 16,* 319–327.

Test, M. A., Knoedler, W. H, Allness, D. J., & Burke, S. S. (1985). Characteristics of young adults with schizophrenic disorders treated in the community. *Hospital and Community Psychiatry, 36,* 853–858.

Test, M. A., Wallisch, L., Allness, D. J., & Ripp, K. (1989). Substance use in young adults with schizophrenic disorders. *Schizophrenia Bulletin, 15,* 465–476.

Tohen, M., Waternaux, C. M., & Tsuang, M. T. (1990). Outcome in mania: A four-year prospective follow-up of 75 patients utilizing survival analysis. *Archives of General Psychiatry, 47,* 1106–1111.

Treffert, D. A. (1978). Marijuana use in schizophrenia: A clear hazard. *American Journal of Psychiatry, 135,* 1213–1215.

Turner, W. M., & Tsuang, M. T. (1990). Impact of substance abuse on the course and outcome of schizophrenia. *Schizophrenia Bulletin, 16,* 87–95.

Vaughn, C. E., & Leff, J. P. (1976). The influence of family and social factors on the course of psychiatric illness. *British Journal of Psychiatry, 129,* 125–137.

Volpicelli, J. R., Rhines, K. C., Rhines, J. S., Volpicelli, L. A., Alterman, A. I., & O'Brien, C. P. (1997). Naltrexone and alcohol dependence: Role of subject compliance. *Archives of General Psychiatry, 54,* 737–742.

Warner, L. A., Kessler, R. C., Hughes, M., Anthony, J. C., & Nelson, C. B. (1995). Prevalence and correlates of drug use and dependence in the United States. *Archives of General Psychiatry, 52,* 219–229.

Weiss, R. D., Collins, D. A. (1992). Substance abuse and psychiatric illness, the dually diagnosed patient. *American Journal on Addictions, 2,* 93–99.

Weiss, R. D., Griffin, M. L., & Mirin, S. M. (1989). Diagnosing major depression in cocaine abusers: The use of depression rating scales. *Psychiatry Research, 28,* 335–343.

Weiss, R. D., Mirin, S. M., Griffin, M. L., Gunderson, J. G., & Hufford, C. (1993). Personality disorders in cocaine dependence. *Comprehensive Psychiatry, 34,* 145–149.

Weiss, R. D., Mirin, S. M., Michael, J. L., & Sollogub, A. C. (1986). Psychopathology in chronic cocaine abusers. *American Journal of Drug and Alcohol Abuse, 12,* 17–29.

Weiss, R. D., Najavits, L., Greenfield, S., Soto, J., Wyner, D., & Tohen, M. (1997, June). *Relapse prevention group therapy for patients with coexisting bipolar disorder and substance use disorder.* Society for Psychotherapy Research, Abstracts of the 28th Annual Meeting, Geilo, Norway.

Westreich, L., Galanter, M., Lifshutz, H., Metzger, E. J., & Silberstein, C. (1996). A modified therapeutic community for the dually diagnosed. Greenhouse Program at Bellevue Hospital. *Journal of Substance Abuse Treatment, 13,* 533–536.

Wilens, T. E., Biederman, J., Spenser, T. J., & Frances, R. J. (1994). Comorbidity of attention-deficit hyperactivity and psychoactive substance use disorders. *Hospital and Community Psychiatry, 45,* 421–435.

Wilens, T. E., Spenser, T. J., & Biederman, J. (1994). Attention deficit disorder with substance abuse. In T. Brown (Ed.), *Subtypes of attention deficit disorder in children, adolescents and adults.* Washington, DC: American Psychiatric Press.

Wilkins, J. N. (1997). Pharmacotherapy of schizophrenia patients with comorbid substance abuse. *Schizophrenia Bulletin, 23,* 215–228.

Winokur, G., Coryell, W., Akiskal, H. S., Maser, J. D., Keller, M. B., Endicott, J., & Mueller, T. (1995). Alcoholism in manic-depressive(bipolar) illness: Familial illness, course of illness, and the preimary-secondary distinction. *American Journal of Psychiatry, 152,* 365–372.

Woody, G. E., McLellan, A. T., Luborsky, L., & O'Brien, C. P. (1985). Sociopathy and psychotherapy outcome. *Archives of General Psychiatry, 42,* 1081–1086.

Woody, G. E., McLellan, A. T., Luborsky, L., O'Brien, C. P., Blaine, J., Fox, S., Herman, I., & Beck, A. T. (1984). Severity of psychiatric symptoms as a predictor of benefits from psychotherapy: The Veterans Administration-Penn study. *American Journal of Psychiatry, 141,* 1172–1177.

Woody, G. E., O'Brien, C. P., & Rickels, K. (1975). Depression and anxiety in heroin addicts. *American Journal of Psychiatry, 32,* 411–414.

Ziedonis, D., & Fisher, W. (1996). Motivation-based assessment and treatment af substance abuse in patients with schizophrenia. *Directions in Psychiatry, 16*, 1–7.

Ziedonis, D. M., & Kosten, T. R. (1991). Depression as a prognostic factor for pharmacological treatment of cocaine dependence. *Psychopharmacology Bulletin, 27*, 337–343.

Ziedonis, D. M., Kosten, T. R., & Glazer, W. M. (1992, May 2–7). The impact of drug abuse on psychotic outpatients. American Psychiatric Association 145th Annual Meeting, New Research Program and Abstracts, p. 103.

Ziedonis, D. M., & Trudeau, K. (1997). Motivation to quit using substances among individuals with schizophrenia: Implications for a motivation-based treatment model. *Schizophrenia Bulletin, 23*, 229–238.

26

Age-Limited Populations: Youth, Adolescents, and Older Adults

Pilar M. Sanjuan

James W. Langenbucher

Historically, addictions research and treatment have focused on individuals in early or middle adulthood, ignoring both adolescents and older adults. Yet youth and the elderly differ from other substance users in a variety of meaningful ways, including patterns of use, course, and consequences; the presence of unique risk factors; and the need for special assessment and treatment measures. Adolescence is a critical period for intervention if we are to prevent future health problems as well as the exponential increase in other consequences associated with continued substance abuse. Older adults are an essential group to target as well, since we can expect an increase in the number of older adults needing treatment as the population ages. Therefore, it would be useful to foster better understanding of geriatric and adolescent substance abuse issues so that they can be better considered in future policy initiatives.

The definition of substance abuse remains somewhat controversial (Langenbucher & Martin, 1996). For the purpose of this chapter, the term *abuse* is employed in reference to the diagnoses of both abuse and dependence in the fourth edition of the *Diagnostic and Statistical Manual of Mental Disorders* (American Psychiatric Association [APA], 1994). *Use* refers to any subthreshold level of drug use. When discussing adolescents and the elderly, we are often talking more about abuse than frank dependence.

ADOLESCENTS

Description

Epidemiology and Patterns of Use

The distinction between use and abuse is particularly important in adolescent groups. Youthful experimentation is common; most adolescents use psychoactive substances at some point but do not develop significant problems. For some, though, this use becomes habitual and hazardous (Tarter, 1990). Table 26.1

shows percentages of nonexperimental use (use six or more times) for high school students. Many of these drugs are used simultaneously or within the same period of time. Alcohol and tobacco are the most frequent combination among first-year college students (Martin, Clifford, & Clapper, 1992), followed by alcohol and marijuana, tobacco and marijuana, and then alcohol and hallucinogens. Estimates of the rates of substance abuse and dependence among adolescents in the general population vary from 2% found in a sample aged 9–18 (Kandel et al., 1997) to 6% in a sample aged 14–18 (Rohde, Lewinsohn, & Seeley, 1996). Rohde et al. (1996) found that an additional 17% had alcohol symptoms or other alcohol problems but did not meet *DSM-IV* criteria for a diagnosis.

Recent epidemiological studies show changes in adolescent drug use trends in recent years and challenge some stereotypes that emerged in earlier research. Lifetime use of multiple drugs is very common among adolescent alcohol abusers, and male and female alcohol users share quite similar poly-

drug use patterns (Martin, Arria, Mezzich, & Bukstein, 1993). Nevertheless, male secondary-school students are more likely to use drugs and to use them more frequently than their female classmates, although this difference has declined since 1975 (Johnston, O'Malley, & Bachman, 1995).

Gender roles appear to mediate the difference in drug use between girls and boys more strongly than biological sex, and it may be that the merging of gender roles in recent years is responsible for the growing similarity in drug use among male and female adolescents (Huselid & Cooper, 1994). On the other hand, persisting gender roles may be responsible for some sex differences in use patterns. For example, adolescent girls concerned about their weight start smoking at higher rates than boys with weight concerns or female nondieters (French, Perry, Leon, & Fulkerson, 1994); thus, weight control may contribute to the higher rates of tobacco smoking and stimulant use we now observe among teenage girls.

In terms of other demographic findings, the difference between rates of drug use for urban and rural

TABLE 26.1 1994 Percentages of Nonexperimental Use[a] Among Students

Drug	8th grade	10th grade	12th grade
Alcohol (consumed)	29.2	47.1	61.5
Alcohol intoxication	7.4	20.1	36.3
Cigarettes[b]	11.8	18.9	22.6
Marijuana	7.7	17.1	23.9
Other hallucinogens	1.2	2.6	4.6
LSD	1.0	2.2	4.2
Cocaine	1.0	1.3	2.2
Crack	0.7	0.5	1.1
Stimulants	3.2	5.0	5.7
Inhalants	5.1	4.6	5.1
Tranquilizers	0.8	1.3	1.8
Heroin	0.6	0.4	0.4
Other opiates[c]	—	—	2.1
PCP[c]	—	—	1.1
Steroids	0.5	0.6	1.1

Note. From *National Survey Results on Drug Use from the Monitoring the Future Study, 1975–1994: Vol. 1. Secondary School Students* (pp. 44–46, 51), by L. D. Johnston, P. M. O'Malley, and J. G. Bachman (1995). Washington, DC: US Government Printing Office (NIH Publication No. 95-4026). Adapted with permission.

[a]Used more than five times in their lifetime.

[b]Percentage of students who used regularly in their lifetime.

[c]12th grade only.

youth has decreased over the years and at this point is quite small (Donnermeyer, 1992; Johnston et al., 1995). African-American youths have lower rates of substance use than Caucasians and Latinos (Johnston et al., 1995). However, caution must be used when interpreting results from such groupings, since important cultural and economic differences exist between ethnic subgroups of these populations (Gilbert & Alcocer, 1988; Harper, 1988), which can render race- or language-based distinctions somewhat arbitrary. Moreover, there is evidence that Latina females have lower levels of alcohol consumption than Latino males or Caucasian females, which may serve to mask the severity of male Latino consumption. A similar phenomenon could be occurring among African-Americans. It is also important to note that most surveys of drug use among adolescents are based on school populations and so do not take into account teenagers who have dropped out of school or who were absent the day of data collection.

Unique Risk and Protective Factors

Risk factors are individual attributes, characteristics, situational conditions, or environmental contexts that increase the probability of drug abuse. Protective factors, on the other hand, are individual attributes, characteristics, situational conditions, or environmental contexts that inhibit, reduce, or buffer the probability of drug abuse (Clayton, 1992). A great deal of research has been aimed at identifying individual factors or clusters of factors and at deconstructing their roles in the initiation of substance use. Research has also concentrated on risk and protective factors that are specific to problem use or abuse among adolescents. This impressive volume of research has resulted in a wide variety of theories as well as an abundance of potential risk and protective factors, many of which can be viewed as steps on a pathway to increased risk.

In one of the earlier studies, Bry, McKeon, and Pandina (1982) demonstrated that drug use and drug abuse were more likely and more severe with the increasing number of risk factors to which the individual has been exposed. This has become known as the *multiple-risk-factor model*. Although seemingly simplistic, this model may be one of the most stable findings in the risk factor research. The ratio of the number of risk factors to the number of protective factors can provide a good idea of whether an adolescent is at risk for future substance abuse problems. The goal of prevention or treatment efforts would then be to decrease the number of risk factors while increasing the number of protective factors. The multiple-risk-factor idea has been expanded by several researchers to develop risk and protective factor indices, which together constitute a "vulnerability" index that predicts both initiation of drug use and future drug problems (Newcomb & Felix-Ortiz, 1992). However, at this point, these models are less transferable to clinical methods.

Another promising early contribution is problem behavior theory (Jessor, 1987), in which substance use by adolescents is characterized as one of several deviant behaviors that occur together. Susceptibility to this syndrome results from the interaction of the person and the environment.

Peer cluster theory (PCT; Oetting & Beauvais, 1987) is another important contribution. Instead of attributing the strong association between an adolescent's use of substances and the drug use of their peers to social pressure to use drugs, PCT outlines a more complex mechanism with two main components: peer selection and peer influence. Peer selection is a process by which adolescents seek out and form friendships with similar individuals; in peer influence, individuals in a peer group reciprocally model drug use behavior. Psychological and social characteristics of adolescents determine susceptibility to drug use and the probability of joining drug-using peer clusters and may contribute to the likelihood of the peer cluster moving toward further drug involvement.

Risk and protective factors do not function in isolation; they often interact. For example, Chassin, Curran, Hussong, and Colder (1996) studied the relation of parental alcoholism to adolescent substance use over time. They were interested in whether parental alcoholism effects could be partially explained by parental affective or antisocial personality disorder, as well as in whether these parental disorders exerted their effects through changes in parental monitoring and adolescent stress, emotionality, sociability, negative affect, and associations with drug-using peers. The results of their structural model are illustrated in figure 26.1. It is clear that the factors act upon each other, and it is this interaction together with direct effects that results in initial substance use (intercept) and escalation (slope). For example, alcoholism in the biological father was the

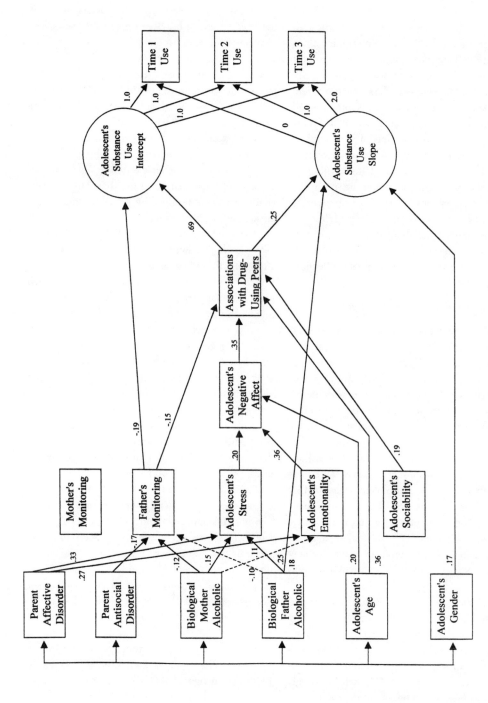

FIGURE 26.1 Final structural model. Standardized path coefficients are shown. For solid lines, $p < .05$; for dashed lines, $p < .10$, χ^2 (62, $N = 316$) = 88.6, $p = .01$, Tucker-Lewis Fit Index = .95, Comparative Fit Index = .98. *Note.* From "The Relation of Parent Alcoholism to Adolescent Substance Use: A Longitudinal Follow-Up Study," by L. Chassin, P. J. Curran, A. M. Hussong, & C. R. Colder (1996) *Journal of Abnormal Psychology, 105*(1), p. 77. Copyright 1996 by the American Psychological Association, Inc. Reprinted with permission.

only parental disorder that had a direct effect on escalation of use. However, alcoholism in the biological father also has indirect effects through adolescent's stress, and to some extent through father's monitoring, on both initiation and escalation of use.

There have been several attempts to classify risk and protective factors into more manageable categories. Pandina (1996) has constructed a list of risk and protective factors with the intention of identifying factors with strong empirical support and consolidating related factors into more general categories (see table 26.2). For example, anxiety and negative affect are represented by the broader "emotional profile." The risk and protective factors are further separated into biological, psychological/behavioral, and social/environmental factors, representing the biopsychosocial aspect of the process.

Although risk and protective factors can exert their effects in a variety of ways that are not completely understood at this time, there are some general characteristics that have been identified consistently across studies (Pandina, 1996). However, linear models of how these factors work may not be sufficient and do not capture the complexity involved. Risk and protective factors can be cumulative or synergistic. They may differ qualitatively and quantitatively; thus, risk and protective factors that seem to be opposite ends of the same continuum (such as conventional values) may behave differently depending upon whether they are acting as risk or protective factors. Furthermore, risk and protective factors each vary in importance across individuals or groups. For example, high IQ seems to operate as protective in some groups and as risk in others. Dif-

TABLE 26.2 Classification Schema for Risk/Protective Factors

Classes of factors	Factors
Biological (genetic and constitutional)	Genetic profile Sensory processing disturbances Neurocognitive alterations Personal history of affective disorders, impulse disorders Family history of alcoholism, drug abuse Family history of impulse disorders (e.g., conduct disorder, antisocial personality) Family history of affective disorders and emotional disturbance (e.g., depression, anxiety)
Psychological and behavioral (internal processes, behavioral action profiles and repertoire, and interpersonal interactional styles)	Personality styles (e.g., sensation seeking, novelty seeking, harm avoidance, reinforcement sensitivity) Emotional profile Self-regulation style (e.g., coping repertoire) Behavioral competence Self-efficacy/self-esteem Positive and negative life events/experiences Attitudes, values, beliefs regarding drug use
Social and environmental (familial interactions, peer interactions, institutional interactions, social/institutional structures)	Structure/function of family supports Parenting styles Opportunities for development of basic competencies Peer affiliations Economic and social (including educational) opportunities General social support structure Availability of prosocial activities in relevant socioenvironmental structures (e.g., schools, communities, workplace) Strength and influence of the faith community Social norms, attitudes, and beliefs related to drug use Availability and projected attractiveness of drugs and drug use Economic and social incentives of drug trafficking.

Note. From *Risk and Protective Factor Models in Adolescent Drug Use: Putting Them to Work for Prevention* (tables 8–11), by R. J. Pandina (1996). Paper presented at the National Conference on Drug Abuse Prevention Research, Washington, DC. Adapted with permission.

ferent factors also fluctuate in influence at different times during the life cycle and vary in significance for the emergence of drug use stages and outcomes. The more extensively studied stage has been acquisition, which consists of priming, initiation, and experimentation. Less well examined, but equally important, are the maintenance stage (habit formation, dependence, and obsessive-compulsive use) and the control stage (problem awareness, interruption/suspension, and cessation). Risk and protective factors are likely to act differently at each of these stages. Furthermore, research has indicated that many factors operate differentially by age group (Scheier, Newcomb, & Skager, 1994). There has not been much focus on the fact that drug use is a continuum that is somewhat normally distributed. Most adolescents do not fall at either extreme: complete abstinence or heavy use. A recent investigation by Schedler and Block (1990) revealed that those at either tail of the distribution are likely to have psychological problems as adults, although those adolescents who use heavily had significantly more problems than those who abstained altogether. This indicates that it might not be as useful to study initiation, which seems to be normative, as to study the transition to heavy use. Additionally, little attention has been given to whether risk factors operate equally for all substances or if they might function differently for different drugs, such as cigarette smoking versus cocaine use. Overall, perhaps the most significant characteristic of risk and protective factors is that they are subject to change and can be reduced or induced. This indicates that the quantity of risk and protective factors in an individual is an excellent target for intervention.

Course

Adolescents with alcohol problems differ from adults in the occurrence and the order of onset of symptoms. Alcohol-dependent youths are much less likely to experience withdrawal than adults with dependence diagnoses, due to the limited time span during which teenagers have been using alcohol heavily. Furthermore, tolerance to alcohol is less specific to a dependence diagnosis in youths, suggesting that an increase in alcohol consumption may be a common developmental occurrence for adolescents. Other symptoms of abuse and dependence used in DSM-IV are also less applicable to younger problem drink-

ers. For example, "continued drinking despite a medical problem" is much less prevalent than "drinking despite psychological problems," and job trouble is less likely to occur since many adolescents do not work, (Martin, Kaczynski, Maisto, Bukstein, & Moss, 1995). Martin, Langenbucher, Kaczynski, and Chung (1996) identified three broad stages of alcohol problems in adolescents broadly sampled for all levels of alcohol involvement. The first stage was characterized by "heavy and heedless drinking" consisting of tolerance, drinking more or longer than intended, and much time spent using alcohol (dependence symptoms), as well as repeated intoxication resulting in a failure to meet role obligations and social and interpersonal problems due to drinking (abuse symptoms). The second stage, characterized by "psychological dependence," included repeated attempts to cut down or stop using, reduced social and recreational activities in favor of drinking, and continued drinking despite physical or psychological problems (dependence symptoms); hazardous use and legal problems (abuse symptoms); and persistent or recurrent blackouts (an experimental domain). Stage 3 was represented by withdrawal (a dependence symptom). The evidence that abuse symptoms do not necessarily precede dependence symptoms in adolescents suggests limitations in the application of DSM-IV criteria for this population.

A clear pathway is discernible in adolescents from the use of licit to illicit substances. A number of studies, including Chen and Kandel (1995), Kandel and Logan (1984), Kandel, Yamaguchi, and Chen (1992), Raveis and Kandel (1987), and Yamaguchi and Kandel (1984a, 1984b), indicate that adolescent drug use begins with beer and wine, progresses to hard liquor and cigarettes, then to marijuana, and then to other illicit substances. Adolescents who have used drugs in a later class, such as other illicit substances, have usually already been through earlier classed drugs, such as marijuana. However, use of an earlier drug class, such as marijuana, does not necessarily result in progression to the use of drugs in later classes, such as other illicit substances. Among females, cigarettes play a more important role in the initiation of illicit drug use and can precede the use of marijuana without the use of alcohol. After using either alcohol, marijuana, or other illicit drugs, some adolescents veer to the use of prescription drugs (with or without medical authorization). Initiation to alcohol is usually completed by age 18, to cigarettes by age 19, to marijuana by age 20, and to hallucinogens by age 21. In general, the use of alcohol and cigarettes increases sharply during adolescence, stabilizes in the late teens, and declines slightly in the late 20s. Overall, marijuana use peaks at age 19, stabilizes for 4–5 years, and then, at ages 23–24, begins a continuous decline. In a sample of secondary-school students, Bailey (1992) found that use of illicit substances was predicted more by the rate of progression from lighter use to heavier use than by the actual level of alcohol and cigarette use.

The use of illicit drugs is less stable than the use of alcohol and cigarettes, and those who continue, as they age, to use illicit substances do so at lower levels of intensity than those of younger age (Chen & Kandel, 1995). The majority of adolescents eventually stop using most drugs in adulthood, a phenomenon known as *maturing out*. While age of onset is frequently identified as a predictor of whether an adolescent will progress to "heavier" drug use, it is not necessarily associated with whether or not individuals will moderate alcohol use or mature out of illicit substance use by age 30 (Labouvie, Bates, & Pandina, 1997). Maturing out is best conceptualized as a developmental transition from adolescence to adulthood. As individuals enter their late 20s, they acquire a greater personal responsibility for their futures, cut down on behaviors that impede the pursuit of personal goals, and perceive long-term romantic commitment and parenthood as more important (Labouvie, 1996). At this point, it is difficult to predict which groups of adolescents are more likely to successfully mature out of substance use; however, it is likely that those factors that make the other elements of the transition to adult roles more difficult will also negatively affect substance use trajectories.

Consequences

With respect to adolescent substance use and abuse, consequences are far more difficult to identify than risk factors. The risk factors for drug use described above are likely to interact with actual substance use, working synergistically to produce negative outcomes. It is difficult to find evidence for many problems that seem to be obvious consequences of use, such as educational impairment or social problems (see Newcomb, 1987, for a review of a variety of theories not yet supported empirically). One conclusion is that substance use during adolescence that is not carried into adulthood does not have as many primary consequences as was once believed. Further research is clearly needed before a comprehensive understanding of teenage drug use consequences is possible. It is known, though, that some adolescents continue drug abuse into adulthood, where there are more negative outcomes that are much better understood.

Exceptions do exist to the paucity of documented consequences of adolescent drug use. Injuries and fatalities resulting from driving while intoxicated are perhaps the most intensely researched of these. Youths are overrepresented among drunk drivers involved in automobile accidents, possibly due to their inexperience in driving combined with increased risk-taking behaviors (Augustyn & Simons-Morton, 1995). The combination of risk taking with substance use also results in an increase in other physically injurious accidents among youth (Arria, Tarter, & Van Thiel, 1991).

Some other possible health-related consequences of teenage drug use have been identified. It is known that alcohol use impairs the body's ability to utilize nutrients, and heavy use in adolescence suppresses levels of growth hormones, increases production of adrenal hormones, decreases testosterone levels, and increases availability of estrogen. These changes may lead to developmental deficits among youths who drink heavily (Arria et al., 1991). Just how heavy use must be to cause permanent and pathological damage is not currently known.

Substance use is a risk factor for suicide among youths (Fowler, Rich, & Young, 1986). Alcohol is more often implicated as a factor in suicide than other drugs, particularly when the drinker is depressed or has a conduct disorder (Crumley, 1990). Death or, in some cases, brain damage can occur from accidental overdoses with a number of substances of abuse. Adolescents, a group less experienced with drugs such as alcohol and more likely to be careless, may be at an increased risk of overdosing. Risk-taking and thrill-seeking behavior, possibly enhanced by substance use, also results in increased exposure to sexually transmitted diseases, and although intravenous drug use is not as common among adolescents, it is associated with increased exposure to HIV, hepatitis, and other viral as well as bacterial infections (Adger & DeAngelis, 1994). Intranasal cocaine use is more common among adolescents, and recent research indicates that this (and presumably intranasal use of other drugs as well) is a probable route of transmission for hepatitis C (Conry-Cantilena et al., 1996).

Neurological damage from adolescent substance use is less prominent than it is in adults, probably due to shorter exposure to drugs. However, heavy and consistent use of inhalants can result in neurological, renal, and hepatic damage (Blanken, 1993). While less clear, research has suggested that LSD use can exacerbate preexisting psychiatric disorders, cause posthallucinogen perceptual disorder (i.e., "flashbacks"), and possibly lead to major depressive disorders (Schwartz, 1995). PCP use can exacerbate or trigger a psychotic episode in schizophrenics and individuals predisposed to schizophrenia (Weiss & Millman, 1991). PCP use also causes short-term neurological impairment lasting beyond the euphoric effects of the drug. However, conclusive evidence of long-term neurological damage from PCP has not been found (Bates & Convit, in press).

Adolescents with substance abuse and dependence often suffer from comorbid psychiatric disorders. These patients are commonly referred to as *dual-diagnosis* or *mentally ill chemical abusers* (MICA). It is difficult to determine whether these comorbid disorders are consequences of use, risk factors, or merely disorders that surfaced during the same developmental stage as substance use. Adolescence is often the period of onset for many psychiatric illnesses in patients who do not have concurrent problems with psychoactive substances. Conduct and mood disorders are the most prevalent diagnoses concurrent with substance abuse and dependence (Kaminer, 1991; Kandel et al., 1997; Rohde et al., 1996). Adolescents with dual diagnoses may be at increased risk for future problems. Substance abusing youths with comorbid conduct disorders have been found to be more likely to drop out of substance abuse treatment programs (Kaminer, Tarter, Bukstein, & Kabene, 1992) and to have elevated rates of academic problems (Lewinsohn, Rohde, & Seeley, 1995).

Assessment and Treatment Issues

Assessment

The evaluation of substance use and abuse in adolescents can be difficult for three reasons. First, most of the instruments designed specifically for youth have fairly thin empirical bases, and adult measures adapted for use with adolescents usually have not been tested for reliability or validity with this population. Second, there is more ambiguity about what constitutes problem use in adolescents. Some argue that any use is a problem, while others feel that a certain amount of substance use is developmentally normal for teenagers. Third, some youth present with problems unique to their developmental stage, such as conflict with family members or distress in school. Instruments for the evaluation of adolescent substance use and abuse must be sensitive to the unique problems of substance use in adolescents.

The purpose of screening is to detect possible problems and identify potential cases (Miller, Westerberg, & Waldron, 1995). The Problem Oriented Screening Instrument for Teenagers (POSIT) is specifically designed to identify adolescents in need of further evaluation. The POSIT is an eight-page paper-and-pencil questionnaire containing 139 yes/no items available in both English and Spanish. It takes about 20–25 minutes to administer and covers 10 functional areas: substance use/abuse, physical health status, mental health status, family relationships, peer relations, educational status, vocational status, social skills, leisure and recreation, and aggressive behavior/delinquency (Rahdert, 1991). The Drug Use Screening Inventory (DUSI) is a closely parallel instrument with 150 items that can be used for the same purpose (Tarter, 1990). Other recommended adolescent screening measures include the Adolescent Drinking Index (ADI), which consists of 24 items representing four domains of problem drinking; the Adolescent Alcohol Involvement Scale (AAIS), a 14-item screening questionnaire; and the 40-item Personal Experience Screening Questionnaire (PESQ), which assesses problem severity, frequency and onset of use, defensiveness, and psychological functioning (Miller et al., 1995).

Diagnostic instruments, often used after a positive screen, are structured interviews based on *DSM* criteria and are used in settings where a formal diagnosis is needed (Miller et al., 1995). The Adolescent Diagnostic Interview (ADI; Winters & Henly, 1993) covers *DSM-III-R* (APA, 1987) symptoms of psychoactive substance use disorders and follows a simple structured interview format that examines the history of use and provides a diagnosis of abuse or dependence for each of the major drug classes (Rahdert, 1991). Administration of the ADI takes about 45 minutes and requires training (National Institute on

Alcohol Abuse and Alcoholism [NIAAA], 1995). While there has been an ongoing debate over the application of *DSM* substance diagnoses for adolescents, currently there is no differentiation between adults and adolescents for *DSM* substance disorder criteria. Consequently, the substance abuse sections of the Structured Clinical Interview for *DSM-IV* (SCID; First, Gibbon, Spitzer, & Williams, 1996), the Psychiatric Research Interview for Substance and Mental Disorders (PRISM; Hasin & Miele, 1997), and the Diagnostic Interview Schedule (child version) (DISC; Fisher, Wicks, Shaffer, Piancentini, & Lapkin, 1992) are also used to make *DSM* diagnoses for adolescent substance disorders (Miller et al., 1995; NIAAA, 1995).

Basic measures of substance use, simple quantity/ frequency measures, can be useful but have limited application and provide only very general information (Miller et al., 1995). A more sophisticated instrument for examining substance use is the Timeline Follow-Back (TLFB; Sobell & Sobell, 1992). The TLFB was designed for use with alcohol but can be adapted for use with other drugs as well. Participants provide retrospective estimates of their alcohol use over a specified time ranging up to 1 year. Holidays and special days such as birthdays or weddings are used as cues to aid the recall of drinking behavior for those days and the periods inbetween them. It can be administered by an interviewer, paper-and-pencil self-administered, or completed on a computer. It takes about 30 minutes to cover use during 1 year and about 10–15 minutes to cover 90 days (Sobell & Sobell, 1992). The Lifetime Drinking History (LDH; Skinner & Sheu, 1982) is another measure of alcohol use that could be adapted for use with other drugs. The LDH is used to obtain a lifetime or long-term summary of patterns of alcohol use and captures distinct phases and changes in a person's drinking style (NIAAA, 1995). In a chronological fashion, the interviewer traces the participant's use from initiation up to the present time, detailing factors associated with changes in patterns and styles of drinking. It takes about 20 minutes to complete (Skinner & Sheu, 1982).

Miller et al. (1995) pointed out that measures of alcohol consumption, although important, do not provide a full view of an individual's clinical picture. Often, adolescents brought to treatment for substance use also have a myriad of other family, school, or psychiatric problems that may be interacting with,

enhancing, or sustaining the drug use. Clinicians may be interested in a fuller range of difficulties than those covered in screening instruments, including problems that are separate from dependence symptoms and rates of use. The Rutgers Alcohol Problems Index (RAPI; White & Labouvie, 1989) is a 23-item instrument designed to assess adolescent problems associated with alcohol use that are different from *DSM* symptoms (NIAAA, 1995). In addition, the 27-item Young Adult Alcohol Problems Screening Test (YAAPST) has been developed recently for use with college students to identify those who are experiencing multiple consequences from their drinking and to evaluate the severity of those consequences (Hurlbut & Sher, 1992).

Motivation for drinking can predict treatment outcome and relapse. There are two instruments for measuring reasons for drinking designed especially for adolescents. The Alcohol Expectancy Questionnaire—Adolescent Version (AEQ-A; Brown, Christiansen, & Goldman, 1987, as cited in Miller et al., 1995), a 100 item self-report instrument, measures the effects an adolescent expects from drinking and provides scores on seven different types of expectancies. Another measure, the Alcohol Attitude Scale for Teenagers (AAST) is a 54-item paper-and-pencil questionnaire that can be used to assess three aspects of alcohol attitudes: feelings, beliefs, and intentions to act (Torabi & Veenker, 1986, as cited in Miller et al., 1995). Schafer and Brown (1991) designed a Marijuana Effects Expectancy Questionnaire (MEEQ), a self-report with 78 items, and a Cocaine Effects Expectancy Questionnaire (CEEQ), a self-report with 71 items, for adults and have recently replicated the factor structures for adolescents.

Better than selecting multiple discrete measures to evaluate separate problem areas, one can select a comprehensive assessment measure to provide a complex understanding of a case. The Personal Experience Inventory (PEI; Winters & Henly, 1989), a 45-minute paper-and-pencil questionnaire, was developed as a part of the Chemical Dependency Adolescent Assessment Package in conjunction with the PESQ and the ADI. The PEI is a multiscaled instrument for identifying the onset, nature, and degree of alcohol and other drug involvement, as well as personal risk factors that may precipitate or maintain substance abuse (Winters & Henly, 1989). The first part of the PEI is the Problem Severity Section, consisting of five basic scales (personal involvement, effects from use, social benefits of use, personal consequences, and polydrug use), five clinical scales (social-recreational use, psychological benefits use, transsituational use, preoccupation, and loss of control), three response bias scales, and two drug use history sections. The second part is the Psychosocial Section, consisting of nine personal risk factors, four environmental risk factors, six brief problem screens (need for psychiatric referral, eating disorder, sexual abuse, physical abuse, family chemical dependency history, and suicide potential), and two response bias scales (Winters & Henly, 1989). The Comprehensive Addiction Severity Index for Adolescents (CASI-A) is a 45- to 90-minute semistructured interview modeled after the Addiction Severity Index (ASI) that assesses several risk factors, symptomatology, and consequences of use within seven primary areas of functioning (Meyers, McLellan, Jaeger, & Pettinati, 1995). The Teen Addiction Severity Index (T-ASI; Kaminer, Wagner, Plummer, & Seifer, 1993), a semistructured interview with 126 questions, is another instrument modeled after the ASI but specifically designed to assess adolescents. Other recommended measures include the Adolescent Drug Abuse Diagnosis (ADAD), a structured interview of 150 items, designed by Friedman and Utada in 1989 and also modeled after the ASI, and the Adolescent Self-Assessment Profile (ASAP), a 203-item questionnaire developed by Wanberg in 1991 (both cited in Miller et al., 1995).

Treatment

Currently, there is a lack of quality research on adolescent substance abuse treatment. Existing studies are characterized by incomplete and unclear reporting, missing control groups, poor assessment measures, and inconsistent definitions of diagnoses and relapse (Bukstein, 1994; Catalano, Hawkins, Wells, Miller, & Brewer, 1991; Liddle & Dakof, 1995). In a review of the research, Catalano et al. (1991) could conclude only that some treatment is better than none and that no one treatment demonstrated superiority over any other. Relapse rates vary across studies but can be fairly high. An investigation of outcomes in an Alcoholics Anonymous/Narcotics Anonymous-based treatment program showed 2-year relapse (from abstinence) rates of 39% for females and 60% for males. However, it was also discovered that a fair percentage of relapsers had improved in other

areas, such as general behavior and school performance, providing support for the idea that some adolescents may become nonproblem users (Alford, Koehler, & Leonard, 1991).

Flaws in the research notwithstanding, there has been some success in identifying factors associated with treatment outcome. Greater pretreatment severity of drug use, early onset of use, criminal history, educational failure (Catalano et al., 1991), low perception of family independence, and high perception of family control (Friedman, Terras, & Kreisher, 1995) have been shown to predict poor treatment outcome. Factors operating during treatment that predict better outcome include motivation, perceived choice in seeking treatment, rapport with clinicians or staff, special services (education, vocational training, relaxation training, recreation, and providing and discussing methods of contraception), and parental involvement (Catalano et al., 1991). Fewer studies have examined posttreatment variables, but thoughts and feelings about drugs and cravings for drugs, less involvement in productive activities, less satisfactory leisure activities (Catalano et al., 1991), and poor skills (drug avoidance, self-control, social, and problem solving) are predictive of poorer outcomes (Jenson, Wells, Plotnick, Hawkins, & Catalano, 1993). Adolescents in treatment have special needs due to their unique developmental position: They have a dependent position in the family and in society; they are constrained by their levels of physical, social, and cognitive development; they are prone to influence from peers and popular culture; they have a strong need for educational and vocational training; they are frequently victims of comorbid psychiatric disorders; and they frequently abuse many drugs at once (Bukstein, 1994).

While the most common approach to adolescent treatment is the *Minnesota Model* based on the 12-step program of recovery designed for adults, the unique needs of adolescents suggest specific guidelines for successful treatment programs. Treatment should be of sufficient intensity and duration to achieve maximum changes in attitude as well as behavior, be comprehensive and targeted to multiple domains of the individual's life, be sensitive to individual cultural and socioeconomic realities, encourage family involvement and improvement in communication, incorporate a wide range of social services, and provide aftercare (Bukstein, 1994). Catalano et al. (1991) suggested that treatment also include academic and vocational experiences and introduce behavioral skills training as a strategy for maintaining treatment effects. Inpatient treatment is indicated for adolescents who are severely physically dependent, have failed outpatient programs, have moderate to severe psychiatric comorbidity, or need to be isolated from their environment to allow uninterrupted treatment (Kaminer & Bukstein, 1989). Several of the assessment instruments above can be used to determine whether an adolescent requires referral to inpatient treatment. Otherwise, outpatient treatment is preferable, since it is likely to be less stigmatizing to the adolescent and allows him or her to apply skills learned in treatment to real situations such as occur at home and at school.

Outpatient treatment provided by clinicians should focus on the specific needs of the adolescent. Often, adolescents brought by parents for substance use treatment may actually have more severe problems in other areas, such as family issues, learning disabilities, or problem behavior at school. A thorough assessment should be conducted in order to identify the severity of substance use problems and whether it is accompanied by problems in other areas of the adolescent's life. Treatment should concentrate on those disturbed areas. Family functioning difficulties are usually present for these adolescents, and family intervention should be a central focus of any treatment. Since some experimental use appears to be normative for adolescents, adolescents who do not yet warrant a substance abuse or dependence diagnosis may not require abstinence as a goal. Instead, treatment should be directed toward lowering the frequency and quantity of use, preventing any rapid escalation into problem use, and reducing harm from casual use (such as drunk driving, exposure to disease, or accidental overdose). Risk and protective factors should be assessed, and treatment should also aim at attempting to increase protective factors while decreasing risk factors.

With regard to inpatient treatment, there is a trend to develop alternatives to the Minnesota and 12-step models, with an emphasis on reducing the intensity and cost of treatment (Bukstein, 1994). Behavioral interventions (relapse prevention, skills training, and anger control training) appear especially promising, as do some elements of family therapy, educational and vocational rehabilitation, and medications for coexisting psychiatric disorders. Patient-treatment match-

ing to address the heterogeneity of the adolescent substance-abusing population (Kaminer & Bukstein, 1989) is another goal of program developers. The Youth Evaluation Services (YES; Babor, Del Boca, McLaney, Jacobi, Higgins-Biddle, & Hass, 1991) is an assessment and case management program designed for the early identification, referral, and monitoring of drug-abusing youth. The Adolescent Assessment/Referral System (AARS), developed by National Institute on Drug Abuse (NIDA) (Rahdert, 1991), is a similar program, where comprehensive assessment provides information for treatment referral. Both the AARS and the YES programs are still in the developmental stages but are promising approaches to the improvement of adolescent substance abuse treatment. When possible, if an adolescent requires referral to inpatient treatment, programs such as these should be sought out.

The discussion to this point has focused on one very specific, important, and as yet understudied group: adolescent substance abusers. A group at the other end of the age spectrum, elderly alcohol and drug users, is even more understudied and is of increasing significance as its numbers increase as a proportion of the population. We now turn to this group, and to the peculiar challenges its poses in terms of assessment, treatment, and understanding its peculiar patterns of use and abuse.

ELDERLY

Description

Epidemiology and Patterns of Use

The use of alcohol and other intoxicants in general declines with age, yet substance use among the elderly is a growing public health concern, one whose significance is expected to increase with the "graying" of America (Atkinson, 1990). Alcohol remains, as it is earlier in life, a commonly used drug: Researchers in the Epidemiologic Catchment Area (ECA) Study, using DSM-III (APA, 1980) criteria queried by administration of the Diagnostic Interview Schedule, found current rates of alcohol abuse and dependence among the elderly as high as 3.7% in some areas, with up to 10% of the elderly qualifying as "heavy drinkers" (Helzer, Burnham, & McEvoy, 1991). Though, also as earlier in life, rates of alcohol problems decline as Americans approach retirement age, the ECA data suggest that rates may again increase after the age of 60 and may be particularly high among males aged 75 and older (Eaton, Kramer, Anthony, Dryman, Shapiro, & Locke, 1989). In general, epidemiological data suggest that between 2% and 4% of Americans over the age of 65 have a diagnosable alcohol problem, and that 10% or so drink heavily, though there is substantial regional variability in these rates (Adams & Cox, 1995). The prevalence of alcohol problems also appears much higher in ill and service-seeking groups. Lichtenberg, Gibbons, Nanna, and Blumenthal (1993), for example, found that 17% of geriatric patients in a medical sample were alcohol abusers, with particular concentrations among the "young-old" (60–74 years old) and males. Nearly half (48%) of young-old men in this sample were diagnosed with alcohol abuse or dependence.

Drug use, especially abuse of prescription drugs, is also a problem among the elderly. The most significant problems appear to be the use of benzodiazepines and narcotic analgesics such as CoTylenol (Finlayson, 1995), to which the elderly are more likely to have been exposed, for longer times, and at larger doses, than the young. These drugs are very frequently used in combination with alcohol: A study of 216 elderly alcoholics in treatment at the Mayo Clinic found that 19% had a concurrent drug abuse or dependence diagnosis. Even illicit drug use, while presumed to be negligible among the elderly, is a cause of concern, especially in urban areas and among people of color (Rosenberg, 1995). Of the more than 7,500 drug-related deaths reported to the Drug Abuse Warning Network in 1992, 10% occurred among persons aged 55 and above. Approximately 23% of these seniors tested positive for opiates and 18% tested positive for cocaine at the time of death.

Because the aged have impaired ability to clear alcohol and other drugs, there may be no decline in hazardous use behaviors even when a decline in absolute quantities consumed is observed (Mears & Spice, 1993; Vogel-Sprott & Barrett, 1984). For this reason, it has been suggested that in the elderly, danger lies in "abuse" as much as in frank dependence (Seymour & Wattis, 1992).

One of the most important areas of research leading to the better identification of the addicted elderly is the clarification of the abuse construct, which has traditionally been neglected in the field (Langenbucher & Martin, 1996) as a "category without a content." This advice, however, is frustrated because the types of impairment which *DSM-IV* suggests for identifying abuse in clinical populations—interference with functioning in an assigned role, use in hazardous situations, legal problems, marital distress, and other social problems—are often not experienced by the elderly for ecological reasons. The most common comorbid diagnosis for alcoholism in the elderly, serious depression, is also difficult to recognize, since many cardinal vegetative and cognitive symptoms (e.g., sleep disturbance, appetite and weight loss, irritability, and inability to concentrate) are overlooked in the elderly or misattributed to age. These findings challenge the generalizability of a "cookie cutter" approach to decision rules, in which dependence in the elderly is assessed by the same set of decision rules applied to younger drinkers.

Unique Risk Factors

The elderly are susceptible to many sources of risk that distinguish them from other clinical populations, including bereavement, caring for an ill spouse, negative social stereotypes, poverty, poor physical health and encroaching dementia, and special problems faced by minority and rural elderly (Roybal, 1988). Prescription and over-the-counter (OTC) drug use becomes increasingly common with advancing age as the numbers and variety of chronic diseases increase; the elderly are the principal users of prescription drugs, taking an average of about three different compounds on a daily basis (Malcolm, 1984). Risk of iatrogenic addiction is particularly high for elders who smoke, drink, or suffer from depression (Chrischilles, Foley, Wallace, & Lemke, 1992).

Aged women may be at particular risk for alcohol and drug abuse (Rodeheaver & Datan, 1988) because of social (widowhood), economic (poverty), and psychological (loneliness) conditions associated with their age and gender. Glantz and Backenheimer (1988) suggested that elderly women, with their heavy burden of social risk factors, may be more at risk for iatrogenic addiction to sedative/hypnotic and anxiolytic preparations than any other demographic group.

Besides social factors, the aged often experience cognitive, perceptual, motor, and other psychological limitations which may promote the use of alcohol or the abuse of prescription and OTC drugs. Loss of judgment and rational capacity, along with a growing tendency to social estrangement, are characteristic of the sometimes subtle dementing processes that become increasingly prevalent as life advances into the eighth decade, affecting 50% of the elderly population in some samples. Compromised sleep regulation (Prinz, Vitiello, Raskind, & Thorpy, 1990) is another age-related condition that may tempt the use of alcohol or other soporifics. In elderly individuals, sensory deficits, particularly hearing loss, lead to social isolation and the emergence of depression, loneliness, and paranoia (Stein & Bienenfeld, 1992). In addition, because of reduced resilience and mobility and an inability to tolerate harsh weather and walking conditions, they may be much more prone to depression and isolation in the winter months (Shah, 1992). These conditions both promote the use of alcohol and other drugs and protect that use from observation by others.

Course

An important contribution to the description of elderly alcohol and drug abuse was Zimberg's (1983) model of early- versus late-onset geriatric alcoholism. The early-onset alcoholic's drinking was construed as an abusive drinking pattern that survived into old age; resulted in escalating social and psychological distress, isolation, and increasing physical disability; and was more likely to lead to liver disease, cardiac problems, neurological disorders, and a host of other emotional and physical health compromises (Schuckit, 1982). In contrast, the late-onset drinker has experienced an exacerbation of normal (or even below-normal) drinking practices because of escalating social and psychological distress, isolation, and increasing physical disability. Some suspect that late-onset alcoholism is relatively common, as is the prevalence of elderly iatrogenic drug addiction. Most agree that, in cross section, one half to two thirds of the elderly alcoholic population experienced an early onset of abusive drinking, while one third to one half experienced a late onset; however, given the covert nature of most cases of elderly alcoholism, these proportions are highly tentative and are subject to definitional constraints. A more recent adaptation of Zimberg's scheme is found in Graham et al. (1995), whose outreach and treatment work suggests that two elderly alcoholic subtypes—chronic alcohol abusers

similar to Zimberg's early-onset type and reactive problem drinkers similar to Zimberg's late-onset type—can be validated on a variety of descriptive variables.

The clinical significance of this typology may, however, be less than one would expect. Treatment response has never been shown to favor either the early-onset or the late-onset group. Rather, clinical data now suggest that over time, the treatment needs of the early- and late-onset groups converge, so that in the early-onset group, the factors that once initiated alcoholism have ceded control to factors that maintain it, and these factors—depression, frailty, losses, isolation, and so forth—are the same as those initiating and maintaining drinking in the late-onset group. Treatment needs may therefore be the same, regardless of the developmental pathway into alcoholism in the elderly.

Consequences

Changes in body composition in the elderly, including a decrease in lean tissue along with impaired liver and renal functioning, affect the pharmacokinetics of alcohol and other drugs and cause their effects to be exaggerated. Therefore, the elderly drinker and drug user is especially prone to a host of problems, including depression, restriction of functional capacity and self-care ability (Colsher & Wallace, 1990), and devastating physical injuries resulting from loss of balance (Kelsey & Hoffman, 1987). Alcohol impairs capacity to abstract (Hamblin, Hyer, Harrison, & Carson, 1984), further aggravates age-compromised sleep physiology (Prinz et al., 1990) and sensory dysfunction (Thienhaus & Hartford, 1984), and interferes with resolution of the grief process (Blankfield, 1983). Adverse drug reactions of all sorts are particularly common in the elderly (Ives, Bentz, & Gwyther, 1987). Use of benzodiazepines, barbiturates, and narcotic analgesics contributes to accidental injuries and falls (Sorock & Shimkin, 1988) and to confusional states (Larson, Kukull, Buchner, & Reifler, 1987). Cognitive impairment resulting from the use of drugs and alcohol can be a particular problem for the elderly, especially when combined with depression, since this clinical picture is often mistaken for irreversible dementia (Freund, 1984). Termed *pseudodementia* (Wells, 1979), this kind of misdiagnosis by even the best intentioned caregiver can have devastating consequences on the elderly individual's attribution of competency, even on his or her personal liberty.

Alcohol withdrawal is another particularly dangerous process for the elderly drinker, who may be at already heightened risk for hypertension, episodes of delirium, and even seizures. In addition, withdrawal signs in the elderly may be misattributed by triage staff to problems with higher base rates such as infection, pulmonary or cardiac problems, sidetracking appropriate treatment. But even when appropriate detoxification occurs, older patients generally require hospitalization and careful monitoring as well as treatment of concurrent diseases, and withdrawal may carry a higher risk of mortality (Schuckit, 1982; Thienhaus & Hartford, 1984).

The relationship between physical status, life events, and drinking in the elderly is becoming much better understood (Valanis, Yeaworth, & Mullis, 1987). In fact, the description of the elderly drinker as isolated, depressed, and at increased risk for death is one of the most robust findings in the behavioral gerontology literature (Robinson, 1989; Roca, Storer, Robbins, & Tlasek, 1990; Sunderland, Molchan, Martinez, & Vitiello, 1990). This is disturbing, since both of the symptom complexes that might focus family and professional attention, depression and alcoholism, are typically unrecognized in the elderly (Harper, Kotik-Harper, & Kirby, 1990; Rapp & Davis, 1989), in part because they may take different forms than in younger adults. Even posttraumatic stress disorder (PTSD) is underrecognized, though not uncommon, among the elderly (Rosen, Fields, Hand, & Falsettie, 1989), many of whom are survivors of extreme privation as children during the Great Depression, or of gruesome violence in the wars of this century.

We also need to better understand the interrelationships between alcohol/drug use patterns and comorbid psychopathology in the elderly. Comorbidity and subtyping studies stand at the forefront of one of the most compelling issues in health services research—patient-treatment matching—yet well-controlled studies of comorbidity among substance users (e.g., Helzer & Pryzbeck, 1988; Nace, 1990) have focused increasingly on younger rather than older subjects or have used exclusively male samples, a poor recipe for furthering knowledge of a clinical group that is both elderly and more often female than younger subject groups. In addition, though most subtyping studies focus on the dyscontrol of ego and

affect-regulatory functions that characterize youthful users, none encompass the neuropsychological impairment and the peculiarities of symptom expression that mark the older drinker. Instead, subtyping work with elderly groups is based on case study and clinical observation and lacks the rigor found elsewhere in the field.

Neurocognitive impairment must be thoroughly assessed, particularly abstraction, learning, computation, and visuospatial ability (Fein, Bachman, Fisher, & Davenport, 1990). Problems may be exacerbated by nutritional deficits, head injury, comorbid cognitive disorders including Alzheimer's and multi-infarct dementia, and other factors.

Assessment and Treatment Issues

Assessment Issues

Numerous barriers to delivering quality substance abuse treatment services to the elderly have been identified. One group of barriers undercuts systemic incentives for accurate assessment and referral, including limited access to health and mental health care (Coyne & Gjertsen, 1993), lack of trained specialists in geriatric health and mental health care, and inadequate addictions treatment benefits under prepaid health plans and Medicare/Medicaid (Roybal, 1988). Another group of barriers makes it difficult to appropriately identify older problem drinkers and get them to treatment and so can be usefully discussed here.

One barrier to services involves the typical behavior of the alcoholic elderly themselves, who, indisposed to seek health services, tend to age-in-place in an isolative fashion, undetected and untreated. For most elders with alcohol and other drug problems, interventions occur on an emergency basis and at a late stage of problem development, precluding clinically effective and cost-effective measures (Coyne & Gjertsen, 1993).

Another barrier concerns the diagnostic practices of caregivers. The symptoms typically manifested in younger alcoholics—heavy consumption by objective standards, work-related difficulties, driving arrests, marital problems—are not always apparent in elderly alcoholics (Marion & Stefanik-Campisi, 1989), whose signs and symptoms (loss of balance, confusion, depression) can be difficult to distinguish from features of the normal aging process. Diagnosticians must be thoroughly schooled in the use of a high index of suspicion but a low diagnostic threshold when evaluating drinking problems among the elderly if cases are not to be overlooked and inappropriately referred elsewhere simply because they fall below the typical diagnostic threshold for younger adults (Caracci & Miller, 1991). Even when symptoms are robust, however, research suggests that many family members and even professional caregivers conspire in the elder's denial of a problem (Beresford, Blow, Brower, & Adams, 1988) because the complications of alcoholism in the elderly are perceived as so dire, life expectancy so short, and expectations for improvement so limited. For example, Rains and Ditzler (1994), in a study of 383 elderly patients referred for outpatient geriatric assessment, found that alcohol consumption was common but rarely recognized as a factor contributing to medical deterioration. Adams, Magruder-Habib, Trued, and Broome, (1992) found that about 14% of elderly emergency department patients were current alcohol abusers but were detected as such by their physicians in only 21% of cases, a problem that may be particularly acute when patients are white, female, or educated beyond secondary school (Curtis, Geller, Stokes, & Levine, 1989). And even when elderly alcoholics are referred to treatment and treatment begins, they are less likely to be retained than younger patients (Booth, Blow, Cook, & Bunn, 1992), especially when their drinking onset was earlier in life (Schonfeld & Dupree, 1991). All of this points to a crucial need for the better understanding of symptom patterning, illness recognition, and help seeking in the alcoholic elderly, in order to implement more efficient outreach services.

Many factors combine to keep the elderly away from caregivers who might recognize their problems with alcohol or other drugs. That alcoholic elderly are far less likely to seek care than their sober peers may be due to a convergence of metabolic, health belief, and ecological factors: A flattening of the body's immune response to infection and trauma because of normal aging and heavy drinking, combined with neurocognitive impairment of the ability to recognize illness when it exists, may result in elderly alcoholics' experiencing their physical problems as diffuse and nonspecific, like fatigue and generalized malaise, rarely exceeding a threshold that will lead them in the face of ambulatory problems and transportation difficulties to the physician's office. Alcohol analgesia effects (Cutter, Maloof, Kurtz, & Jones,

1976) during mild pain crises may merely aggravate this natural tendency.

Though not enough is yet known about how to assess alcoholism in the elderly, some promising developments have been recently reported. For example, in the face of convincing evidence that one of the most popular screening devices for alcoholism, the Michigan Alcoholism Screening Test (MAST; Selzer, 1971), is highly insensitive to alcohol problems in the elderly (Blankfield & Maritz, 1990; Maisto, Connors, & Allen, 1995), Blow (1991) developed an elder-specific version, the MAST-G, with an excellent sensitivity/specificity profile. The CAGE questionnaire (Ewing, 1984), too, appears to perform well in the detection of elderly alcoholism (Buchsbaum, Buchanan, Welsh, Centor, & Schnoll, 1992; Maisto et al., 1995). DeHart and Hoffmann (1995) have offered the U-OPEN screen—probing for unplanned use, objections from family and friends, preoccupation with drinking, emotional distress drinking, and neglect of responsibilities—as a highly sensitive indicator of alcohol problems in the elderly, though its specificity is unknown. Common to all of these instruments is their disregard of alcohol tolerance, viewed by most authorities as an insensitive indicator of alcohol problems in the elderly. Instead, the useful domains for assessment appear to combine aspects of drinking for relief or relaxation, problems with family, guilt, isolative drinking, salience of drinking, and loss of control.

Treatment

Treatment needs among early- and late-onset alcoholics may be parallel because of a convergence of maintaining if not etiological factors. It is therefore possible to extract from the literature a common set of clinical targets for both early- and late-onset geriatric alcoholism. These can be used to supplement the cognitive behavioral approach to addictions treatment that is of growing interest to the field, so as to constitute an elder-specific treatment technology that may produce improved outcomes over the standard approach.

Though elder-specific addictions treatment is a relatively new idea, a few reports have already emerged. The first (Wiens, Menustik, Miller, & Schmitz, 1982–1983) tested an elder-specific program based on aversive counterconditioning to alcohol and its cues. Results were encouraging: Nearly two thirds (65.4%) of subjects were abstinent at 1-year follow-up, a success rate comparable to that obtained with younger patients. But problems with this treatment approach include medical risks of counterconditioning and its unacceptability to a majority of treatment-eligible individuals. In a more sophisticated program, the Gerontology Alcohol Project of Dupree, Broskowski, and Schonfeld (1984) piloted a partial hospital approach with an emphasis on functional analysis, self-management skills training, and reconstruction of social supports. Unfortunately, though the project generated some interesting descriptive (e.g., Schonfeld & Dupree, 1991) and case study reports (Dupree & Schonfeld, 1989), reliable outcome data have not been reported.

Two elder-specific programs developed in Veterans Administration settings have been reported. At the Portland VA, Kofoed, Tolson, Atkinson, and Toth (1987) found that elder-specific treatment was superior to mainstreaming with regard to treatment retention, compliance, recovery from relapse, and abstinence at discharge, but the VA-based sample included only two females and is not generalizable. The other study of an elder-specific program, also limited to males, was reported from the VA Medical Center in Dallas (Kashner, Rodell, Ogden, & Guggenheim, 1992). In this study, 137 older patients were randomly assigned to one of two inpatient units and followed for 1 year after discharge. One unit was a standard milieu of confrontative and 12-step-oriented treatment: the other, an elder-specific unit, offered reminiscence therapy and greater focus on developing subjective self-worth and social relationships. Patients in the elder-specific program were more than twice as likely to be abstinent at 1 year as those in the traditional treatment unit, an effect that was magnified in patients above the age of 60. Unfortunately, the study's definition of age 45 and above as "older," its restriction to males, and its use of an inpatient level of care reduce its usefulness as a guide to general program development.

The most recent report on elder-specific treatment is an evaluation of the Community Older Persons Alcohol (COPA) program in Toronto (Graham et al., 1995). In this study, the authors reviewed the demographic characteristics, typology, prognostic factors, and clinical interventions applied to a large sample of community-dwelling alcohol and drug users. Though the COPA program is ostensibly "client-centered" in orientation, the actual interventions applied—and those shown most efficacious—include a variety of cognitive behavioral (CB) techniques, including goal setting, stimulus control, and functional analysis. Of special interest is the community-based nature of the program. However, COPA's emergence in the unique Canadian health care environment, its availability to the nonelderly (COPA admits a large proportion of middle-aged and "young-old" patients), and especially its provision of services within open-ended treatment contracts make it difficult to generalize findings to the time-limited treatment of the elderly and very elderly in the U.S. system.

Though quite limited, research on elder-specific treatment reported so far, in addition to findings from the literature in behavioral gerontology, prompts a number of recommendations for future development of both treatment process and content. In terms of treatment process, while the group format is often touted as the preferred mode in addictions units, the aged alcoholic may have difficulties in forming and managing intimate bonds (Brantner, 1987). Elder-specific treatment should therefore include a reduction of group therapy in favor of additional individual therapy and should also feature more obvious components, such as the use of visually and auditorily enhanced educational materials, as well as treatment schedules that allow for impaired attentional capacity and subject fatigue. Also, alcohol and drug abuse has traditionally been treated in very-high-level-of-care and costly inpatient settings. McCrady et al. (1986), however, demonstrated the effectiveness and cost-effectiveness of the intensive outpatient or partial hospital setting, which has since become one of the most rapidly expanding clinical modes in the addictions treatment industry. The behavioral gerontology literature suggests that the partial hospital may be particularly suitable for the treatment of elders, whose anxiety, limited flexibility, and deeper roots in the community make them resistant to overnight stays away from home (as in standard inpatient care), yet whose needs for social support and network building cannot be met by very limited clinical contact (as in standard outpatient care). The intense contact with treatment staff and other patients available in the partial hospital, combined with the partial hospital's ability to offer treatment for long calendar periods while controlling costs and maintaining the elder's daily contact with home, may make it an ideal choice at the programmatic level for the treatment of addiction in the elderly.

Other suggestions for improved content of treatment have also emerged. Dupree et al. (1984) have urged that treatment of the older alcoholic, like that of his or her more youthful peers, emphasize the functional analysis of drinking behavior and the acquisition of improved self-management skills, including the ability to identify high-risk situations, to employ drink-refusal and other coping skills, and to self-monitor urges and use behaviors. They also warn, however, that most older alcohol and drug users require vastly improved social support networks, and that treatment should target the enlistment and hardening of social supports, through family, neighbor, and community involvement, and through teaching communication and social skills to the older patient. These recommendations for treatment content are very similar to those used in Graham et al.'s (1995) COPA program. In addition, treatment programmers express the need to intervene in problems which may interfere with treatment completion by the elderly (Dupree et al., 1984), since the elderly are so difficult to identify and engage and may have relatively few "chances" for success left to them. These problems include serious illnesses, cognitive impairment, and a variety of logistical barriers (e.g., lack of transportation, inability or unwillingness to venture outdoors in the winter), so that effective elder treatment programs should have ready access to medical and neuropsychological consult services, and to community agencies ready to provide the necessary logistical support. Finally, treatment of the elderly alcohol and drug user should address the very prominent role of loneliness and depressive symptomatology in the elderly (e.g., Colsher & Wallace, 1990; Warren, Grek, Conn, & Herrmann, 1989). Effective interventions include the use of CB techniques to teach the skills necessary to rebuild the elder citizen's frayed social network, but timely administration of antidepressant medication will also prove useful in many cases.

SUMMARY

The age-limited populations of adolescents and the elderly have many important epidemiological, risk, course, and comorbidity features that distinguish them, and that call for special consideration in the design of assessment and treatment measures. As we "broaden the base of treatment" for alcohol and other drug problems (Institute of Medicine, 1990), and as we move into a new century of more empirically supported and more effective treatment (McCrady & Langenbucher, 1996), it is important that we give this special consideration to adolescents and to the elderly for three reasons.

First, demography urges us: Children of the baby boomers, now entering their reproductive years, will produce, within the next decade and a half, a large group of adolescents. To this will be added a group of elderly who, by early in the next century, will be 20% of the population. Failure to adequately provide specialized services to groups as large as these would, in our view, constitute a major planning failure in public health.

Second, clinical needs urge us: Adolescence is a critical period for personal growth that must be navigated successfully if severe consequences associated with substance use are to be avoided, and if personal potential is to be expressed fully. Similarly, old age is fraught with many dangers and disabilities without the added health burden of alcohol and other drug use.

Third, science urges us: As this chapter makes clear, we now understand many features of both adolescent and geriatric substance use which were formerly obscure, and we stand poised to benefit from this progress in applied settings. The preference of adolescents for multiple drug use (Kandel et al., 1992), the diminishing gender differences in patterns of use among adolescents (Martin et al., 1993), and the role of peer selection as well as peer influence processes (Oetting & Beauvais, 1987)—all have dramatic and meaningful implications for how we assess, treat, or possibly prevent drug use among youth. Similarly, the importance of depression and cognitive impairment among older alcoholics (Sunderland et al., 1990) and the early promise of elder-specific treatment programming (Graham et al., 1995) have important bearing on clinical services for the elderly. Demographic projections, acutely growing clinical need, prospects for scientific progress—our response to them must be as creative and dedicated as has been our response to other challenges with other clinical groups.

Key References

Catalano, R. F., Hawkins, J. D., Wells, E. A., Miller, J., & Brewer, D. (1991). Evaluation of the effectiveness of adolescent drug abuse treatment, assessment of risks for relapse, and promising approaches for relapse prevention. *International Journal of Addictions*, 25(9a & 10a), 1085–1140.

Chen, K., & Kandel, D. B. (1995). The natural history of drug use from adolescence to the mid-thirties in a general population sample. *American Journal of Public Health*, 85, 41–47.

Graham, K., Saunders, S. J., Flower, M. C., Timney, C. B., White-Campbell, M., & Pietrapaolo, A. Z. (1995). *Addictions treatment for older adults: Evaluaton of an innovative client-centered approach.* Binghamton, NY: Haworth Press.

References

Adams, W. L., & Cox, N. S. (1995). Epidemiology of problem drinking among elderly people. *International Journal of the Addictions, 30,* 1693–1716.

Adams, W. L., Magruder-Habib, K., Trued, S., & Broome, H. L. (1992). Alcohol abuse in elderly emergency department patients. *Journal of the American Geriatrics Society, 40,* 1236–1240.

Adger, H., & DeAngelis, C. D. (1994). Adolescent medicine. *Journal of the American Medical Association, 271,* 1651–1653.

Alford, G. S., Koehler, R. A., & Leonard, J. (1991). Alcoholics Anonymous–Narcotics Anonymous model inpatient treatment of chemically dependent adolescents: A 2-year outcome study. *Journal of Studies on Alcohol, 52,* 118–126.

American Psychiatric Association. (1980). *Diagnostic and statistical manual of mental disorders* (3rd ed.). Washington, DC: Author.

American Psychiatric Association (1987). *Diagnostic and statistical manual of mental disorders* (3rd ed. Rev.). Washington, DC: Author.

American Psychiatric Association. (1994). *Diagnostic and statistical manual of mental disorders* (4th ed.). Washington, DC: Author.

Arria, A. M., Tarter, R. E., & Van Thiel, D. H. (1991). The effects of alcohol abuse on the health of adolescents. Special Focus: Alcohol and youth. *Alcohol Health and Research World, 15,* 52–57.

Atkinson, R. M. (1990). Aging and alcohol use disorders: Diagnostic issues in the elderly. *International Psychogeriatrics, 2,* 55–72.

Augustyn, M., & Simons-Morton, B. G. (1995). Adolescent drinking and driving: Etiology and interpretation. *Journal of Drug Education, 25,* 41–59.

Babor, T. F., Del Boca, F. K., McLaney, M. A., Jacobi, B., Higgins-Biddle, J., & Hass, W. (1991). Just say Y.E.S. matching adolescents to appropriate interventions for alcohol and other drug-related problems. *Alcohol Health and Research World, 15,* 77–86.

Bailey, S. L. (1992). Adolescents' multisubstance use patterns: The role of heavy alcohol and cigarette use. *American Journal of Public Health, 82,* 1220–1224.

Bates, M. E., & Convit, A. (in press). Neuropsychology and neuroimaging of alcohol and illicit drug abuse. In A. Calev (Ed.), *Neuropsychological functions in psychiatric disorders.* Washington, DC: American Psychiatric Press.

Beresford, T. P., Blow, F. C., Brower, K. J., & Adams, K. (1988). Alcoholism and aging in the general hospital. *Psychosomatics, 29,* 61–72.

Blanken, A. J. (1993). Measuring use of alcohol and other drugs among adolescents. *Public Health Reports, 108,* 25–30.

Blankfield, A. (1983). Grief and alcohol. *American Journal of Drug and Alcohol Abuse, 9,* 435–446.

Blankfield, A., & Maritz, J. S. (1990). Female alcoholics: 3. Some clinical associations of the Michigan Alcoholism Screening Test and diagnostic implications. *Acta Psychiatrica Scandinavica, 81,* 483–487.

Blow, F. (1991). *Michigan Alcoholism Screening Test— Geriatric Version (MAST-G).* Ann Arbor, MI: University of Michigan Alcohol Research Center.

Booth, B. M., Blow, F. C., Cook, C. A., & Bunn, J. Y. (1992). Age and ethnicity among hospitalized alcoholics: A nationwide study. *Alcoholism: Clinical and Experimental Research, 16,* 1029–1034.

Brantner, J. (1987). Intimacy, aging and chemical dependency. *Journal of Chemical Dependency Treatment, 1,* 261–268.

Bry, B. H., McKeon, P., & Pandina, R. J. (1982). Extent of drug use as a function of number of risk factors. *Journal of Abnormal Psychology, 91,* 273–279.

Buchsbaum, D. G., Buchanan, R. G., Welsh, J., Centor, R. M., & Schnoll, S. H. (1992). Screening for drinking disorders in the elderly using the CAGE questionnaire. *Journal of the American Geriatrics Society, 40,* 662–665.

Bukstein, O. G. (1994). Treatment of adolescent alcohol abuse and dependence. *Alcohol Health and Research World, 18,* 296–301.

Caracci, G., & Miller, N. S. (1991). Epidemiology and diagnosis of alcoholism in the elderly (a review). *International Journal of Geriatric Psychiatry, 6,* 511–515.

Catalano, R. F., Hawkins, J. D., Wells, E. A., Miller, J., & Brewer, D. (1991). Evaluation of the effectiveness of adolescent drug abuse treatment, assessment of risks for relapse, and promising approaches for relapse prevention. *International Journal of Addictions, 25*(9a & 10a), 1085–1140.

Chassin, L., Curran, P. J., Hussong, A. M., & Colder, C. R. (1996). The relation of parent alcoholism to adolescent substance use: A longitudinal follow-up study. *Journal of Abnormal Psychology, 105*(1), 70–80.

Chen, K., & Kandel, D. B. (1995). The natural history of drug use from adolescence to the mid-thirties in a general population sample. *American Journal of Public Health, 85,* 41–47.

Chrischilles, E. A., Foley, D. J., Wallace, R. B., & Lemke, J. H. (1992). Use of medications by persons 65 and over: Data from the established populations for epidemiologic studies of the elderly. *Journal of Gerontology, 47,* M137–M144.

Clayton, R. R. (1992). Transitions in drug use: Risk and protective factors. In M. Glantz & R. Pickens (Eds.), *Vulnerability to drug abuse* (pp. 15–51). Washington, DC: American Psychological Association.

Colsher, P. L., & Wallace, R. B. (1990). Elderly men with histories of heavy drinking: Correlates and consequences. *Journal of Studies on Alcohol, 51*, 528–535.

Conry-Cantilena, C., VanRaden, M., Gibble, J., Melpolder, J., Shakil, A. O., Viladomiu, L., Cheung, L., DiBisceglie, A., Hoofnagle, J., Shih, J. W., Kaslow, R., Ness, P., & Alter, H. (1996). Routes of infection, viremia, and liver disease in blood donors found to have hepatitis C virus infection. *New England Journal of Medicine, 334*(26), 1734–1735.

Coyne, A. C., & Gjertsen, R. (1993). Characteristics of older adults referred to a psychiatric emergency outreach service. *Journal of Mental Health Administration, 20*, 208–211.

Crumley, F. E. (1990). Substance abuse and adolescent suicidal behavior. *Journal of the American Medical Association, 263*, 3051–3056.

Curtis, J. R., Geller, G., Stokes, E. J., & Levine, D. M. (1989). Characteristics, diagnosis, and treatment of alcoholism in elderly patients. *Journal of the American Geriatrics Society, 37*, 310–316.

Cutter, H. S. G., Maloof, B., Kurtz, N. R., & Jones, W. C. (1976). Feeling no pain: Differential responses to pain by alcoholics and nonalcoholics before and after drinking. *Journal of Studies on Alcohol, 37*, 273–277.

DeHart, S. S., & Hoffmann, N. G. (1995). Screening and diagnosis of "alcohol abuse and dependence" in older adults. *International Journal of the Addictions, 30*, 1717–1747.

Donnermeyer, J. F. (1992). The use of alcohol, marijuana, and hard drugs by rural adolescents: a review of recent research. *Journal of Drugs and Society, 7*, 31–75.

Dupree, L. W., Broskowski, H., & Schonfeld, L. I. (1984). The Gerontology Alcohol Project: A behavioral treatment program for elderly alcohol abusers. *Gerontologist, 24*, 510–516.

Dupree, L. W., & Schonfeld, L. (1989). Treating late-life onset alcohol abusers: Demonstration through a case study. *Clinical Gerontologist, 9*(2), 65–68.

Eaton, W. W., Kramer, M., Anthony, J. C., Dryman, A., Shapiro, S., & Locke, B. Z. (1989). The incidence of specific DIS/DSM-III mental disorders: Data from the NIH Epidemiologic Catchment Area program. *Acta Psychiatric Scandinavica, 79*, 163–178.

Ewing, J. A. (1984). Detecting alcoholism: The CAGE questionnaire. *Journal of the American Medical Association, 252*, 1905–1907.

Fein, G., Bachman, L., Fisher, S., & Davenport, L. (1990). Cognitive impairments in abstinent alcoholics. *Western Journal of Medicine, 152*, 531–537.

Finlayson, R. E. (1995). Misuse of prescription drugs. *International Journal of the Addictions, 30*, 1871–1901.

First, M. B., Gibbon, M., Spitzer, R. L., & Williams, J. B. W. (1996). *Structured clinical interview for DSM-IV axis I disorders (SCID-I)*. New York: Biometrics Research Department, New York State Psychiatric Institute.

Fisher, P., Wicks, J., Shaffer, D., Piacentini, J., & Lapkin, J. (1992). *NIMH diagnostic interview schedule for children, version 2.3*. New York: New York State Psychiatric Institute.

Fowler, R. C., Rich, C. L., & Young, D. (1986). San Diego suicide study: 2. Substance abuse in young cases. *Archives of General Psychiatry, 43*, 962–965.

French, S. A., Perry, C. L., Leon, G. R., & Fulkerson, M. A. (1994). Weight concerns, dieting behavior, and smoking initiation among adolescents: A prospective study. *American Journal of Public Health, 84*, 1818–1820.

Freund, G. (1984). Aging and alcoholism: Neurobiological relationships between aging and alcohol abuse. In M. Galanter (Ed.), *Recent developments in alcoholism*, (Vol. 2, pp. 203–221). New York: Plenum Press.

Friedman, A. S., Terras, A., & Kreisher, C. (1995). Family and client characteristics as predictors of outpatient treatment outcome for adolescent drug abusers. *Journal of Substance Abuse, 7*, 345–356.

Gilbert, M. J., & Alcocer, A. M. (1988). Alcohol use and Hispanic youth: An overview. *Journal of Drug Issues, 18*, 33–48.

Glantz, M. D., & Backenheimer, M. S. (1988). Substance abuse among elderly women. *Clinical Gerontologist, 8*, 3–26.

Graham, K., Saunders, S. J., Flower, M. C., Timney, C. B., White-Campbell, M., & Pietrapaolo, A. Z. (1995). *Addictions treatment for older adults: Evaluation of an innovative client-centered approach*. Binghamton, NY: Haworth Press.

Hamblin, D. K., Hyer, L. A., Harrison, W. R., & Carson, M. R. (1984). Older alcoholics: Profiles of decline. *Journal of Clinical Psychology, 40*, 1510–1516.

Harper, F. D. (1988). Alcohol and black youth: An overview. *Journal of Drug Issues, 18*(1), 7–14.

Harper, R. G., Kotik-Harper, D., & Kirby, H. (1990). Psychometric assessment of depression in an elderly general medical population: Over- or underassessment? *Journal of Nervous and Mental Disease, 178*, 113–119.

Hasin, D., & Miele, G. (1997). *Psychiatric research interview for substance and mental disorders*. New York: New York State Psychiatric Institute.

Helzer, J. E., Burnham, A., & McEvoy, L. T. (1991). Alcohol abuse and dependence. In L. N. Robins & D. A. Regier (Eds.), *Psychiatric disorders in America:*

The Epidemiologic Catchment Area Study (pp. 81–115). New York: Macmillan.

Helzer, J. E., & Pryzbeck, T. R. (1988). The co-occurrence of alcoholism with other psychiatric disorders in the general population and its impact on treatment. *Journal of Studies on Alcohol, 49,* 219–224.

Hurlbut, S. C., & Sher, K. J. (1992). Assessing alcohol problems in college students. *Journal of American College Health, 41,* 49–58.

Huselid, R. F., & Cooper, M. L. (1994). Gender roles as mediators of sex differences in expressions of pathology. *Journal of Abnormal Behavior, 103,* 595–603.

Institute of Medicine. (1990). *Broadening the base of treatment for alcohol problems.* Washington, DC: National Academy of Sciences.

Ives, T. J., Bentz, E. J., & Gwyther, R. E. (1987). Drug-related admissions to a family medicine inpatient service. *Archives of Internal Medicine, 147,* 1117–1120.

Jenson, J. M., Wells, E. A., Plotnick, R. D., Hawkins, J. D., & Catalano, R. F. (1993). The effects of skills and intentions to use drugs on post-treatment drug use of adolescents. *American Journal of Drug and Alcohol Abuse, 19,* 1–17.

Jessor, R. (1987). Problem-behavior theory, psychosocial development, and adolescent problem drinking. *British Journal of Addiction, 82,* 331–342.

Johnston, L. D., O'Malley, P. M., Bachman, J. G. (1995). *National survey results on drug use from the monitoring the future study, 1975–1994: Vol. 1. Secondary school students* (NIH Publication No. 95-4026). Washington, DC: Government Printing Office.

Kaminer, Y. (1991). The magnitude of concurrent psychiatric disorders in hospitalized substance abusing adolescents. *Child Psychiatry and Human Development, 22*(2), 89–95.

Kaminer, Y., & Bukstein, O. (1989). Adolescent chemical use and dependence: Current issues in epidemiology, treatment and prevention. *Acta Psychiatrica Scandinavica, 79,* 415–424.

Kaminer, Y., Tarter, R. E., Bukstein, O. G., & Kabene, M. (1992). Comparison between treatment completers and noncompleters among dually diagnosed substance-abusing adolescents. *Journal of the American Academy of Child and Adolescent Psychiatry, 31*(6), 1046–1049.

Kaminer, Y., Wagner, E., Plummer, B., & Seifer, R. (1993). Validation of the Teen Addiction Severity Index (T-ASI). *American Journal on Addictions, 2*(3), 251–254.

Kandel, D. B., Johnson, J. G., Bird, H. R., Canino, G., Goodman, S. H., Lahey, B. B., Reiger, D. A., &

Schwab-Stone, M. (1997). Psychiatric disorders associated with substance use among children and adolescents: Findings from the Methods for the Epidemiology of Child and Adolescent Mental Disorders (MECA) Study. *Journal of Abnormal Child Psychology, 25*(2), 121–132.

Kandel, D. B., & Logan, J. A. (1984). Patterns of drug use from adolescence to young adulthood: 1. Periods of risk for initiation, continued use, and discontinuation. *American Journal of Public Health, 74,* 660–666.

Kandel, D. B., Yamaguchi, K., & Chen, K. (1992). Stages of progression in drug involvement from adolescence to adulthood: Further evidence for the gateway theory. *Journal of Studies on Alcohol, 53,* 447–457.

Kashner, T. M., Rodell, D. E., Ogden, S. R., & Guggenheim, F. G. (1992). Outcomes and costs of two VA inpatient treatment programs for older alcoholic patients. *Hospital and Community Psychiatry, 43,* 985–989.

Kelsey, J. L., & Hoffman, S. (1987). Risk factors for hip fracture. *New England Journal of Medicine, 316,* 404–406.

Kofoed, L. L., Tolson, R. L., Atkinson, R. M., & Toth, R. L. (1987). Treatment compliance of older alcoholics: An elder-specific approach is superior to mainstreaming. *Journal of Studies on Alcohol, 40,* 47–51.

Labouvie, E. (1996). Maturing out of substance use: Selection and self-correction. *Journal of Drug Issues, 26*(2), 457–476.

Labouvie, E., Bates, M. E., & Pandina, R. J. (1997). Age of first use: Its reliability and predictive utility. *Journal of Studies on Alcohol, 58,* 638–643.

Langenbucher, J. W., & Martin, C. S. (1996). Alcohol abuse: Adding content to category. *Alcoholism: Clinical and Experimental Research, 20,* 270A–275A.

Larson, E. B., Kukull, W. A., Buchner, D., & Reifler, B. V. (1987). Adverse drug reactions associated with global cognitive impairment in elderly persons. *Annals of Internal Medicine, 107,* 169–173.

Lewinsohn, P. M., Rohde, P., & Seeley, J. R. (1995). Adolescent psychopathology: III. The clinical consequences of comorbidity. *Journal of the American Academy of Child and Adolescent Psychiatry, 34*(4), 510–519.

Lichtenberg, P. A., Gibbons, T. A., Nanna, M. J., & Blumenthal, F. (1993). The effects of age and gender on the prevalence and detection of alcohol abuse in elderly medical inpatients. *Clinical Gerontologist, 13,* 17–27.

Liddle, H. A., & Dakof, G. A. (1995). Efficacy of family therapy for drug abuse: Promising but not definitive. *Journal of Marital and Family Therapy, 21,* 511–543.

Maisto, S. A., Connors, G. J., & Allen, J. P. (1995). Contrasting self-report screens for alcohol problems: A review. *Alcoholism: Clinical and Experimental Research, 19,* 1510–1516.

Malcolm, M. T. (1984). Alcohol and drug use in the elderly visited at home. *International Journal of the Addictions, 19,* 411–418.

Marion, T. R., & Stefanik-Campisi, C. (1989). The elderly alcoholic: Identification of factors that influence the giving and receiving of help. *Perspectives in Psychiatric Care, 25,* 32–35.

Martin, C. S., Arria, A. M., Mezzich, A. D., & Bukstein, O. G. (1993). Patterns of polydrug use in adolescent alcohol abusers. *American Journal of Drug and Alcohol Abuse, 19,* 511–521.

Martin, C. S., Clifford, P. R., & Clapper, R. C. (1992). Patterns and predictors of simultaneous and concurrent use of alcohol, tobacco, marijuana, and hallucinogens in first-year college students. *Journal of Substance Abuse, 4,* 319–226.

Martin, C. S., Kaczynski, N. A., Maisto, S. A., Bukstein, O. M., & Moss, H. B. (1995). Patterns of DSM-IV alcohol abuse and dependence symptoms in adolescent drinkers. *Journal of Studies on Alcohol, 56,* 672–680.

Martin, C. S., Langenbucher, J. W., Kaczynski, N. A., & Chung, T. (1996). Staging in the onset of DSM-IV alcohol symptoms in adolescents: Survival/hazard analyses. *Journal of Studies on Alcohol, 57,* 549–558.

McCrady, B. S., & Langenbucher, J. W. (1996). Alcohol treatment and health care system reform. *Archives of General Psychiatry, 53,* 737–746.

McCrady, B., Longabaugh, R., Fink, E., Stout, R., Beattie, M., & Ruggieri-Authelet, A. (1986). Cost-effectiveness of alcoholism treatment in partial hospital versus inpatient settings after brief inpatient treatment: 12-month outcomes. *Journal of Consulting and Clinical Psychology, 54,* 708–713.

Mears, H. J., & Spice, C. (1993). Screening for problem drinking in the elderly: A study in the elderly mentally ill. *International Journal of Geriatric Psychiatry, 8,* 319–326.

Meyers, K., McLellan, A. T., Jaeger, J. L., & Pettinati, H. M. (1995). The development of the Comprehensive Addiction Severity Index for Adolescents (CASI-A): An interview for assessing multiple problems of adolescents. *Journal of Substance Abuse Treatment, 12*(3), 181–193.

Miller, W. R., Westerberg, V. S., & Waldron, H. B. (1995). Evaluating alcohol problems in adults and adolescents. In R. K. Hester & W. R. Miller (Eds.), *Handbook of alcoholism treatment approaches* (pp. 61–88). Boston: Allyn & Bacon.

Nace, E. P. (1990). Substance abuse and personality disorder. *Journal of Chemical Dependency Treatment, 3,* 183–198.

National Institute on Alcohol Abuse and Alcoholism. (1995). *Assessing alcohol problems: A guide for clinicians and researchers.* (NIH Publication No. 95-3745). Washington, DC: J. P. Allen, & M. Columbus (Eds.).

Newcomb, M. D. (1987). Consequences of teenage drug use: The transition from adolescence to young adulthood. *Drugs and Society, 1,* 25–60.

Newcomb, M. D., & Felix-Ortiz, M. (1992). Multiple protective and risk factors for drug use and abuse: Cross-sectional and prospective findings. *Journal of Personality and Social Psychology, 63*(2), 280–296.

Oetting, E. R., & Beauvais, F. (1987). Peer cluster theory, socialization characteristics, and adolescent drug use: A path analysis. *Journal of Counseling Psychology, 34,* 205–213.

Pandina, R. J. (1996, September). *Risk and protective factor models in adolescent drug use: Putting them to work for prevention.* Paper presented at the National Conference on Drug Abuse Prevention Research, Washington, DC.

Prinz, P. N., Vitiello, M. V., Raskind, M. A., & Thorpy, M. J. (1990). Geriatrics: Sleep disorders and aging. *New England Journal of Medicine, 323,* 520–526.

Rahdert, E. R. (1991). *The adolescent assessment/referral system manual.* Washington, DC: Alcohol, Drug Abuse, and Mental Health Administration.

Rains, V. S., & Ditzler, T. (1994). Alcohol use disorders in cognitively impaired patients referred for geriatric assessment. *Journal of Addictive Diseases, 12,* 55–64.

Rapp, S. R., & Davis, K. M. (1989). Geriatric depression: Physicians' knowledge, perceptions, and diagnostic practices. *Gerontologist, 29,* 252–257.

Raveis, V. H., & Kandel, D. B. (1987). Changes in drug behavior from the middle to the late twenties: Initiation, persistence, and cessation of use. *American Journal of Public Health, 77,* 607–611.

Robinson, J. R. (1989). The natural history of mental disorder in old age: A long-term study. *British Journal of Psychiatry, 154,* 783–789.

Roca, R. P., Storer, D. J., Robbins, B. M., & Tlasek, M. E. (1990). Psychogeriatric assessment and treatment in urban public housing. *Hospital and Community Psychiatry, 41,* 916–920.

Rodeheaver, D., & Datan, N. (1988). The challenge of double jeopardy: Toward a mental health agenda for aging women. *American Psychologist, 43,* 648–654.

Rohde, P., Lewinsohn, P. M., & Seeley, J. R. (1996). Psychiatric comorbidity with problematic alcohol use in high school students. *Journal of the American Academy of Child and Adolescent Psychiatry, 35* (1), 101–109.

Rosen, J., Fields, R. B., Hand, A. M., & Falsettie, G. (1989). Concurrent posttraumatic stress disorder in psychogeriatric patients. *Journal of Geriatric Psychiatry and Neurology*, 2, 65–69.

Rosenberg, H. (1995). The elderly and the use of illicit drugs: Sociological and epidemiological considerations. *International Journal of the Addictions*, 30, 1925–1951.

Roybal, E. M. (1988). Mental health and aging: The need for an expanded federal response. *American Psychologist*, 43, 189–194.

Schafer, J., & Brown, S. A. (1991). Marijuana and cocaine effect expectancies and drug use patterns. *Journal of Consulting and Clinical Psychology*, 59, 558–565.

Schedler, J., & Block, J. (1990). Adolescent drug use and psychological health: A longitudinal inquiry. *American Psychologist*, 45(5), 612–630.

Scheier, L. M., Newcomb, M. D., & Skager, R. (1994). Risk, protection, and vulnerability to adolescent drug use: Latent-variable models of three age groups. *Journal of Drug Education*, 24(1), 49–82.

Schonfeld, L., & Dupree, L. W. (1991). Antecedents of drinking for early- and late-onset elderly alcohol abusers. *Journal of Studies on Alcohol*, 52, 587–592.

Schuckit, M. A. (1982). A clinical review of alcohol, alcoholism, and the elderly patient. *Journal of Clinical Psychiatry*, 43, 396–399.

Schwartz, R. H. (1995). LSD its rise, fall, and renewed popularity among high school students. *Pediatric Clinics of North America*, 42, 403–413.

Selzer, M. L. (1971). The Michigan Alcoholism Screening Test (MAST): The quest for a new diagnostic instrument. *American Journal of Psychiatry*, 127, 1653–1658.

Seymour, J., & Wattis, J. P. (1992). Alcohol abuse in the elderly. *Reviews in Clinical Gerontology*, 2, 141–150.

Shah, A. (1992). Seasonal affective disorder in an elderly woman. *International Journal of Geriatric Psychiatry*, 7, 847.

Skinner, H. A., & Sheu, W. J. (1982). Reliability of alcohol use indices: The Lifetime Drinking History and the MAST. *Journal of Studies on Alcohol*, 43, 1157–1170.

Sobell, L. C., & Sobell, M. B. (1992). Timeline followback: A technique for assessing self-reported alcohol consumption. In R. Litten & J. Allen (Eds.), *Measuring alcohol consumption* (pp. 41–72). Totowa, NJ: Humana Press.

Sorock, G. S., & Shimkin, E. E. (1988). Bezodiazepine sedatives and the risk of falling in a community-dwelling elderly cohort. *Archives of Internal Medicine*, 148, 2441–2444.

Stein, L. M., & Bienenfeld, D. (1992). Hearing impairment and its impact on elderly patients with cognitive, behavioral, or psychiatric disorders: A literature review. *Journal of Geriatric Psychiatry*, 25, 145–156.

Sunderland, T., Molchan, S. E., Martinez, R. A., & Vitiello, B. I. (1990). Treatment approaches to atypical depression in the elderly. *Psychiatric Annals*, 20, 474–478.

Tarter, R. E. (1990). Evaluation and treatment of adolescent substance abuse: A decision-tree method. *American Journal of Drug and Alcohol Abuse*, 16, 1–46.

Thienhaus, O. J., & Hartford, J. T. (1984). Alcoholism in the elderly. *Psychiatric Medicine*, 2, 27–41.

Valanis, B., Yeaworth, R. C., & Mullis, M. R. (1987). Alcohol use among bereaved and nonbereaved older persons. *Journal of Gerontological Nursing*, 13, 26–32.

Vogel-Sprott, M., & Barrett, P. (1984). Age, drinking habits and the effects of alcohol. *Journal of Studies on Alcohol*, 45, 517–521.

Warren, E., Grek, A., Conn, D., & Herrmann, N. (1989). A correlation between cognitive performance and daily functioning in elderly people. *Journal of Geriatric Psychiatry and Neurology*, 2, 96–100.

Weiss, C. J., & Millman, R. B. (1991). Hallucinogens, phencyclidine, marijuana, inhalants. In R. J. Frances & S. I. Miller (Eds.), *Clinical textbook of addictive disorders* (pp. 147–170). New York: Guilford Press.

Wells, C. E. (1979). Pseudodementia. *American Journal of Psychiatry*, 36, 895–900.

White, H. R., & Labouvie, E. W. (1989). Towards the assessment of adolescent problem drinking. *Journal of Studies on Alcohol*, 50, 30–37.

Wiens, A. N., Menustik, C. E., Miller, S. I., & Schmitz, R. E. (1982–1983). Medical-behavioral treatment of the older alcoholic patient. *American Journal of Drug and Alcohol Abuse*, 9, 461–475.

Winters, K. C., & Henly, G. A. (1989). *Personal Experience Inventory (PEI) test and manual*. Los Angeles: Western Psychological Services.

Winters, K. C., & Henly, G. A. (1993). *Adolescent Diagnostic Interview (ADI)*. Los Angeles: Western Psychological Services

Yamaguchi, K., & Kandel, D. B. (1984a). Patterns of drug use from adolescence to young adulthood: 2. Sequences of progression. *American Journal of Public Health*, 74, 668–672.

Yamaguchi, K., & Kandel, D. B. (1984b). Patterns of drug use from adolescence to young adulthood: 3. Predictors of progression. *American Journal of Public Health*, 74, 673–681.

Zimberg, S. (1983). Alcohol problems in the elderly. *Journal of Psychiatric Treatment and Evaluation*, 5, 515–520.

27

Ethnic and Cultural Minority Groups

Felipe G. Castro

Rae Jean Proescholdbell

Lynn Abeita

Domingo Rodriguez

THE MINORITY EXPERIENCE: SOME COMMON ISSUES

Life Context Regarding the Experience of Ethnicity

The experience of ethnicity and self-identification as a person of color carry a special meaning for members of the major ethnic/racial groups in the United States. These groups are African-Americans, Hispanics/Latinos, Asian-Americans, Pacific Islanders, and Native Americans/American Indians. To be a person of color is to be "different" somehow, and to feel a sense of separateness from mainstream American society (Ramirez, 1991). Some ethnic persons feel shame over this difference, while others feel pride.

In certain social environments or communities, ethnic differences (language, skin color, religious beliefs, lifestyle) prompt ridicule and discrimination. In these situations, some ethnic persons, children or adults, especially if feeling isolated, attempt to "fit in" by disavowing their ethnicity and disappearing into the mainstream culture. By contrast, other ethnic persons, especially if they can rely on an extended family or ethnic network of peers, resist these social forces that induce assimilation. The manner in which an ethnic person copes with this sense of difference and with social attitudes that discriminate against ethnicity, influences his or her preferred ethnic identification and his or her attitudes towards assimilation into the mainstream culture.

The experience of ethnicity lies at the heart of group heritage, as it offers a sense of connectedness with a community of peers who share various values, beliefs, symbols, and community norms. These shared attributes promote a sense of kinship and affiliation with the culture and forge a common identity that binds a people, particularly in the face of discrimination from others (Castro & Gutierres, 1997; Harwood, 1981).

Despite this sense of connectedness with ethnic peers, the life of a person of color is often stressful.

For ethnic minority adolescents, the usual stressors of growth through adolescence are often compounded by the pressures of responding to conflicting demands made by two distinct cultures: the Euro-American culture and the youth's own ethnic culture (Castro, Boyer, & Balcazar, in press). In relation to these demands, there are several reasons why persons of color would use illicit drugs. Among those are (a) for the pleasurable or reinforcing effect (the high) obtained from these drugs, (b) to cope with aversive emotional states (e.g., anxiety or depression), and (c) to belong to a certain peer group (Khantzian, 1985; Oetting & Beauvais, 1987; Shiffman & Wills, 1985). In addition, for some people of color, selected psychoactive drugs are used (d) as part of cultural or religious ceremonies, but not for recreational purposes. Except when used in solemn cultural ceremonies, the casual or "recreational" use of illicit drugs often extends to abuse and then to dependence (American Psychiatric Association [APA], 1994). Accordingly, the ongoing use of an illicit drug can be regarded as maladaptive coping, especially when used to cope with feelings of anger, anxiety, or depression or other forms of distress.

In looking at the relationship of ethnicity to the use of illicit drugs, the question arises: Does being an ethnic/racial minority person increase that person's chances of using illicit drugs? While the answer to this question is complex, the basic answer is no. Clearly, a child born to ethnic minority parents is not destined to use illicit drugs unless that child is exposed to drug-filled environments and is led to believe that illicit drug use offers certain rewards (economic or emotional) that are not otherwise available by other means. Thus, while being "ethnic" in and of itself does not "cause" illicit drug use, this does not mean that the experience of ethnicity is irrelevant to the risks of using illicit drugs. As noted previously, for ethnic minority youths the risk of using illicit drugs is related to the adverse life conditions in which he or she is raised. Furthermore, not all minority persons experience adverse living conditions such as living in poverty, racial discrimination, or alienation from mainstream social institutions. However, a disproportionately large number of ethnic minorities do face poverty and other adverse life conditions, and it is the composite experience of being a person of color and being raised in an adverse environment that creates the setting conditions for illicit drug use and/or dealing in illicit drugs.

"Ethnicity" and Illicit Drug Use

In survey research, *ethnicity* is a broad, superficial variable that seldom offers in-depth information about the ways in which the experience of ethnicity (i.e., ethnic identity and lifestyle) relate to drug use and abuse. This superficial property of the variable *ethnicity* has been referred to as *ethnic gloss*. (Trimble, 1995). In other words, an ethnic label does not capture the richness, complexity, and diversity of the experience of ethnicity.

For example, the superficial demographic label of ethnicity, such as *American Indian*, refers to members of that group but glosses over the diversity and differences that exist *within* that group. Here, the label *American Indian* refers to almost 2 million persons and to over 500 tribes, offering no information about the identity of a given person or group and telling us little about that person's or that group's motivations to use drugs. In practice, the label of an ethnicity must also be examined in conjunction with socioeconomic status to take into account real lifestyle differences that exist within the group as related to a person's economic and educational status and as these factors may also relate to the use of illicit drugs (Collins, 1995). More refined analyses that disaggregate broad ethnic categories such as American Indian, into more specific subcategories, such as Navajo adolescents from the Navajo reservation or urban Americans Indians from Albuquerque would specify subgroups or subcultures whose "experience of ethnicity" and its related links to drug use may be more easily identified. This strategy calls for more local/regional surveys that are designed specifically to examine drug use within a more specific region, as well as for more specific subgroups or subcultures within an ethnic category.

From a related perspective, today progress is needed to move us beyond contemporary demographically based descriptive analyses that offer limited insights into the link between ethnicity and rates of drug use and abuse. Progress is thus needed in the development of culturally competent theory that captures significant aspects of the experience of ethnicity as it relates to motivations and other factors that promote the use of illicit drugs among ethnic/racial youths and adults. In the drug field today, there exist over 40 contemporary theories on the antecedents and consequences of drug use and abuse (Lettieri, Sayers, & Pearson, 1980). However, few of these theories directly address the social process by which ethnic and cultural factors may influence various aspects of illicit drug use. Moreover, these theories focus more on initiation, continuation, and transition to heavy use, while offering little detail on factors that influence cessation, treatment efficacy, and relapse. Thus, well-developed theory on factors that affect drug use among ethnic minority persons remains limited. In summary, the field of drug abuse today offers little in the areas of empirical data and theory-driven accounts that describe or explain specific aspects of cessation, treatment, and relapse, as these occur among various ethnic and minority clients.

EPIDEMIOLOGICAL DATA ON ETHNIC/RACIAL MINORITIES AND SUBSTANCE ABUSE

Table 27.1 presents a comparison and contrast of selected demographic data for each of the major eth-

nic/racial groups in the United States. These data are abstracted from the U.S. Census and show that in 1995, the United States had a population of 263 million residents that could be partitioned by ethnicity into the following groups: 193.9 million non-Hispanic whites (73.6%), 33.5 million African-Americans (12.7%), almost 26.8 million Hispanics (10.2%), almost 9.2 million Asian-Americans and Pacific Islanders (3.4%), and 1.9 million American Indians/Native Americans (0.7%) (Campbell, 1996; U.S. Bureau of the Census, 1994). The projected U.S population for the year 2000 is 276.2 million, with relative increases in the total population percentages of Hispanics and Asian-Americans, while there will be relative reductions in the percentages of non-Hispanic whites and African-Americans (Campbell, 1996).

In 1995, when compared with a median age of 35.3 for members of the mainstream population (non-Hispanic whites), each of the ethnic/racial populations had a younger median age. Similarly, from available data for 1992, African-Americans and His-

TABLE 27.1 Demographic Characteristics of the Major U.S. Ethnic/Racial Groups

Characteristic	Total	Non-Hispanic white	African-American/ black	Hispanic/ Latino(a)	Asian-American and Pacific Islander	American Indian/ Native American
Population[a]						
1995	263.434	193.900	33.503	26.798	9.161	1.927
1995 percentage	100	73.6	12.7	10.2	3.4	0.7
2000 estimate	276.241	197.872	33.741	31.166	11.407	2.055
2000 percentage	100	71.6	12.2	11.3	4.1	0.7
1992 median age (%)	33.4	35.3	28.6	25.8	30.2	27.0
High school grad (%)	80.2	81.5	70.4	53.1	NA	NA
School dropouts (%)	12.7	12.2	16.3	33.9	NA	NA
1993 unemployed (%)	6.8	6.0	12.9	10.6	NA	NA
1993 Median family income ($)	36,812	38,909	21,161	23,901	NA	NA
1992 Families below poverty (%)	11.7	8.9	30.9	26.2	11.9	NA
Lifestyle behaviors (%) Exercise regularly	—	41.5	34.3	34.9	—	—
Two or more drinks per day	—	5.8	4.3	4.6	—	—
Current smoker	—	25.6	26.2	23.0	—	—
20% or more overweight	—	26.7	38.0	27.6	—	—

Note. From U.S. Bureau of the Census. (1994). *Statistical abstract of the United States—1994* (114th ed). Washington, DC: Government Printing Office.

[a]Population numbers are in millions.

panics had *lower* levels of education than non-Hispanic whites. Whereas 81.5% of white adults ages 25 and older had completed high school or more, only 70.4% of African-Americans, and only 53.1% of Hispanics had done so. Also, as measured by the proportion of students who had dropped out of school at any time, relative to a rate of 12.2% for non-Hispanic whites, 16.3% of African-Americans had dropped out, and 33.9% of Hispanics had done so. These data underscore the problem of educational underachievement among African-Americans and Hispanics, and especially as this relates to the risks of drug involvement among youth who drop out of school at an early age (Chavez, Edwards, & Oetting, 1989).

Economic disparities between the white and minority populations are also evident as measured by indicators of economic resources. First, in 1993, the rate of unemployment for non-Hispanic whites was 6.0%. By contrast, among African-Americans, it was 12.9%, and among Hispanics, it was 10.6%. Second, for non-Hispanic whites, the median family income was $38,909, compared with $21,161 for African-Americans and $23,901 for Hispanics (U.S. Bureau of the Census, 1994). Moreover, these data do not show that many minority persons who worked full time might still be underemployed, as they may have worked at or near minimum wage, and without having insurance benefits. As a result, many of these families could be categorized as "the working poor." And among non-Hispanic whites, 8.9% of families lived below the 1992 poverty line, compared with 30.9% of African-Americans and 26.2% of Hispanics. Thus, as measured by various indicators of socioeconomic status in 1993, African-Americans and Hispanics, as minority populations, exhibited a clear profile of disadvantage relative to non-Hispanic whites.

Among these populations, certain patterns of health-related behaviors and lifestyle behaviors are also evident. According to the U.S. Bureau of the Census (1994), in 1990, 41.2% of non-Hispanic whites indicated that they exercised or participated in sports on a regular basis, compared with 34.3% of African-Americans and 34.9% of Hispanics. By contrast, for alcohol consumption that involved consuming two or more drinks per day, non-Hispanic whites had a higher rate: 5.8% drank in this fashion, relative to 4.3% of African-Americans and 4.6% of Hispanics. Furthermore, the population percentage of current cigarette smokers was highest among the African-Americans (26.2%), relative to 25.6% for non-Hispanic whites and 23.0% for Hispanics. One remark-

able difference among ethnic/racial groups in lifestyle and health behaviors was the percentage of members of these populations who were 20% or more overweight. Here, 38.0% of African-Americans were overweight relative to 27.6% of Hispanics and 26.7% of non-Hispanic whites. In summary, these data provide an overview of comparative differences among these populations as examined by ethnic/racial status.

For these ethnic/racial groups, table 27.2 presents demographic characteristics regarding substance use and AIDS cases. Using 1993 as the population base, table 27.2 shows that the total U.S. population was 257.9 million. For this population total, the population percentages for each of the major ethnic/racial populations were non-Hispanic whites (74.4%), African-Americans (11.9%), Hispanics (9.7%), Asian-Americans (3.2%), and Native American Indians (1.8%). The Substance Abuse and Mental Health Services Administration (SAMHSA) reports that nationally in 1993, there were 11.7 million illicit drug users (4.5% of the U.S. population) (Rouse, 1995). Among these, the rates of illicit drug use covaried in close congruence with the relative percentages of each ethnic/racial group within the general U.S. population. Thus, among illicit drug users, 74% were non-Hispanic whites, while 14% were African-Americans, and 9% were Hispanics.

The SAMHSA data also report on current "heavy drinking," which was defined as "drinking five or more drinks per day on each of five or more days in the last 30 days." Among the 10.9 million Americans who were classifiable as "heavy drinkers," 81% were non-Hispanic whites, as compared with 9% who were African-Americans and 9% who were Hispanics. The SAMHSA report also indicates that about 1% of current heavy drinkers were Native American Indians, Asian-Americans, and others.

Table 27.2 also presents data from the SAMHSA report on the major drugs of abuse at the time of treatment entry for members of the major ethnic/racial groups. These data for 1993 show numbers of cases of illicit drug use and percentages by ethnicity, as reported by 6,679 treatment providers throughout most of the United States (Rouse, 1995). Here, the total number of cases (810,918), included 379,420 African-Americans; 73,552 Hispanics; 8,478 Asian-Americans; and 31,240 Native American Indians.

As minority persons enter treatment two critical questions are (a) Which is their principal problem drug? and (b) does the type of problem drug differ

TABLE 27.2 Demographic Characteristics of the Major U.S. Ethnic/Racial Groups, 1993–1995

Characteristic	Total	Non-Hispanic White	African-American/ Black	Hispanic/ Latino(a)	Asian-American and Pacific Islander	American Indian/ Native American
Population						
1993[a]	257.927	191.899	30.768	25.085	8.298	1.878
1993 percentage	100	74.4	11.9	9.7	3.2	0.7
Ilicit drug use						
Number of users[b]	11.7	8.7	1.6	1.1	—	—
Percentage users	100	74	14	9	—	—
Heavy drinking						
Number of users[b]	10.9	8.9	1.0	0.9	—	—
Percentage users	100	81	9	9	—	—
Primary substance upon treatment entry						
Total Cases	—	810,918	379,420	73,552	8,478	31,240
Alcohol (%)	—	67.8	39.0	46.2	48.8	81.6
Cocaine (%)	—	9.6	41.9	8.2	12.4	4.8
Heroin (%)	—	10.6	12.9	34.2	17.1	4.8
Other (%)	—	12.0	6.2	11.4	21.7	8.8
AIDS cases—men						
Total cases	376,889	198,822	110,958	62,934	2,667	888
Percentage IDU	30.4	16.7	46.7	46.1	8.3	30.3
AIDS cases—women						
Total cases	58,428	14,166	31,821	11,909	290	159
Percentage IDU	66.6	60.3	67.8	71.9	30.3	71.1

Note. From U.S. Bureau of the Census. (1994). *Statistical abstract of the United States—1994* (114th ed). Washington, DC: Government Printing Office; B. A. Rouse (1995). *Substance abuse and mental health statistics sourcebook.* DHHS Pub. No. (SMA) 95-3064. Washington, DC: Government Printing Office.

[a]Population numbers are in millions.

[b]Numbers of users are in millions.

by the ethnic/racial identity of the client? For each ethnic/racial group, the percentages presented within a column in table 27.2 indicate the proportion of the total treatment cases for which a given drug (alcohol, cocaine, heroin, and other) served as the principal problem drug. For all groups, the highest proportion of cases was for treatment of alcohol abuse as the principal problem substance. However, for alcohol abuse, remarkable differences appear by ethnic/racial status. For alcohol abuse, Native American Indians showed the highest proportion (81.6%) of clients presenting for treatment who suffered from alcohol abuse as their principal problem. This proportion is contrasted with the relatively lower proportions observed for non-Hispanic whites (67.8%), African-Americans (39.0%), Hispanics (46.2%), and Asian-Americans (48.8%).

By contrast, cocaine appears as the major problem drug for African-Americans, for whom 41.9% of

379,420 cases involved treatment for the abuse of cocaine as the principal problem drug. By contrast, the second highest percentage for cocaine abuse is observed for Asian-Americans, although with only 12.4% of over 8,000 cases involving a need for treatment for the abuse of cocaine as the principal problem drug. Also by contrast, heroin appears as the principal problem drug for Hispanics, with 34.2% of over 73,000 cases involving a need for treatment for heroin abuse.

Given the relationship between HIV infection and illicit drug use, table 27.2 also presents 1993 data for AIDS cases among men and women. Here, it is noteworthy that nationally, the number of AIDS cases for men was about 6 times higher than for women. Among the ethnic/racial groups, the rates of AIDS cases among men relative to women ranged from 3 times to 14 times higher. Among men, the rates of AIDS cases attributable to injection drug use

(IDU) were highest for African-Americans and for Hispanics, for whom 46% of these cases were attributable to IDU.

While the total *numbers* of AIDS cases were considerably lower for women, the *proportion* of cases among women that were attributable to IDU was remarkably high. Except for Asian-American women, the percentage of women's cases attributable to IDU exceeded 60%. Clearly, IDU was a significant risk factor for HIV infection among women, although it should be recognized that infection did not necessarily involve their own use of needles, but the sharing of needles contaminated by HIV or a sexual relationship with a partner who used contaminated needles. Moreover, these data on IDU suggest that needle cleaning had not been practiced sufficiently to protect many minority addicts from HIV infection.

In summary, the data presented in table 27.2 offer some specific features of illicit drug use related to ethnic/racial group. Thus, in 1993, for African-Americans, cocaine abuse was the major problem, where the use of injection as a route of drug administration also increased the risk of HIV infection among African-American men and women. For Hispanics, alcohol abuse and heroin use appeared as the major problem drugs. In addition, for Hispanics, injecting drugs constituted a significant risk for HIV infection, particularly among women. By contrast, Asian-Americans exhibited the lowest drug problem profiles, alcohol abuse being the most notable problem drug. However, the relatively lower rates of drug abuse problems observed among Asian-Americans should not be taken to mean that drug and alcohol abuse did not constitute significant problems for all members of Asian-American communities. And for Native American Indians, alcohol abuse appeared as the most significant drug problem. The magnitude of this problem is evident if we examine the relatively high number of cases of substance abuse problems despite the relatively small size (less than 2 million) of the Native American Indian population in the United States.

CULTURAL COMPETENCE IN DRUG ABUSE TREATMENT

Cultural competence refers to the capacity of a service provider or of an organization to understand and work effectively with the cultural beliefs and prac-

tices of persons from a given ethnic/racial group. *Cultural competence* has been defined as

a set of academic and interpersonal skills that allow individuals to increase their understanding and appreciation of cultural differences and similarities within, among, and between groups. This requires a willingness and ability to draw upon community-based values, traditions, and customs and to work with knowledgeable persons of and from the community in developing focused interventions, communications, and other supports. (Orlandi, Weston, & Epstein, 1992, p. vi)

Cultural competence is of paramount importance in the delivery of effective health and human services to members of diverse special populations, and it includes but is not limited to service delivery to members of ethnic/racial populations. By contrast, when services fail to acknowledge and appreciate the values, beliefs, and practices of persons of color, the result may be that minority clients feel misunderstood or skeptical about the helpfulness of a service and ultimately drop out of treatment (Sue, 1977). The health services literature indicates that clients are inclined to participate actively in their own treatment when they feel that the services offered to them are culturally responsive and thus helpful and worth attending (Kolden, Howard, Bankoff, Maling, & Martinovich, 1997; Sue, Fujino, Hu, Takeuchi, & Zane, 1991).

The capacity to work effectively with members of ethnic/racial populations is a matter of degree. As a conceptual framework, a continuum of increasing cultural capacity has been proposed that underscores the importance of continued learning in the ongoing process of building cultural competence (Cross, Bazron, Dennis, & Isaacs, 1989; Kim, McLeod, & Shantzis, 1992). The lowest stage of cultural capacity is *cultural destructiveness*, which involves negative attitudes that regard minority cultures as "inferior" to the dominant mainstream culture. This type of thinking prompts discriminatory and insensitive behavior toward the ethnic/racial culture and its people. This type of thinking when practiced within drug treatment programs is destructive. Here, having the dual identity of "minority person" and "drug addict" could prompt a culturally destructive service provider to justify a denial of services.

A step forward along the cultural capacity continuum is *cultural incapacity*. This stage of cultural capacity endorses the notion of "separate but equal" treatment as a viable approach to service delivery to minority clients. The concern here is that separate is rarely equal. From this perspective, segregation and discrimination would be regarded as acceptable ways to treat persons of color. Within the drug treatment setting, the attitudes consistent with cultural incapacity reflect counselor views that alternate treatments are acceptable because minority clients are seen as incapable of benefiting from the conventional treatment that is being offered. Here, it would be true that clients who speak a different language may need and could benefit from a separate form of treatment (Sue et al., 1991). However, caution is needed to avoid making a linguistically separate program a lesser program in terms of content and resources offered to these clients.

The next stage along the cultural competence continuum is *cultural blindness*. While this stage improves on the others, it also presents significant problems. The culturally blind viewpoint asserts that "all people are alike," and therefore, that all people should be treated equally. While psychologically this view appears democratic and equitable, it ignores the issue of diversity and suggests that "one size fits all." Accordingly, service providers who espouse attitudes consistent with being culturally blind also express views that one should avoid dealing with ethnic and cultural issues because these issues serve only as distracters from the real work of recovery from drug abuse, and that attention to ethnic issues divides people rather than bringing them together.

Moving forward along the cultural capacity continuum to a positive level, the next stage is *cultural sensitivity*. Cultural sensitivity is the positive entry level of cultural capacity, in which the counselor is open to working with issues of culture and diversity. The limitations of cultural sensitivity are that the provider holds only a limited repertoire of knowledge about a minority client's values, beliefs, traditions, and practices and may become perplexed when faced with complex issues and apparent contradictions based on a minority clients' complex life situation that may be difficult to interpret. At times, the culturally sensitive provider, while paying respect to cultural issues, may still think in terms of stereotypes and may think in terms of simplistic notions about the minority client's life situation. Issues of complexity and the multiplicity of problems may be particu-

larly common among drug-using minority clients who enter a drug treatment program.

The next stage in this continuum is *cultural competence*. Cultural competence is characterized by the provider's capacity to examine and understand nuances that must be appreciated with the introduction of apparent contradictions as a complex case unfolds. Thus, cultural competence may be regarded as full cultural empathy. With full cultural empathy, the provider is able to examine, consider, weigh, and interpret complex case information for a minority client. And in this complex process, the culturally competent provider is able to stand in the client's shoes and thus is able to understand the client from the client's own cultural perspective. Thus, the provider is able to conduct effective interventions that promote positive treatment outcomes.

Finally, the highest level of cultural capacity is *cultural proficiency*, which is characterized by the provider's capacity to understand in greater depth the qualities and issues involved in a minority client's complex life situation. Cultural proficiency also involves the ability to understand nuances in greater depth, and to propose and design new approaches or interventions that aid in the delivery of services to ethnic/racial clients. Cultural proficiency also involves a commitment to research and leadership in presenting new findings to others in order to increase the knowledge base on how better to treat various clients from diverse ethnic/racial populations (Castro, 1998).

MULTICULTURAL PERSPECTIVES

Common Sociocultural Features Across Ethnic/Racial Groups

As noted previously, the demographic information available from the U.S. Census shows that economic insufficiency and its related social and psychological problems introduce a common set of challenges and a lower quality of life for many people of color (Johnson et al., 1995). Indeed, low socioeconomic status, the old notion of poverty, is the most prominent common factor that creates similarity in the lives of many African-Americans, Hispanics, Asian-Americans, and Native American Indians. This is especially the case for ethnic minority clients who enter drug treatment programs.

Covarying with lower socioeconomic status are low levels of education, underemployment, lack of health insurance and thus limited access to health care, and a set of health problems that are associated with limited access to health services (American Medical Association, 1991; Ginzberg, 1991). For minority clients, these problems of poverty provide a life context, background conditions against which substance abuse problems must be examined. Epidemiological data for minority adolescents indicates that their salient health and social issues include high rates of school dropout, teenage pregnancy, self-concept and ethnic identity conflicts, violence, and death by unintentional injuries such as motor vehicle accidents (Chavez et al., 1989; U.S. Bureau of the Census, 1994). Similarly, for minority adults, salient health and social issues include addiction to cigarettes; being overweight; having high blood pressure, heart disease, diabetes, cancer, or another chronic degenerative disease; being unemployed or underemployed; and being a victim of violence, including homicide (Flack et al., 1995; U.S. Bureau of the Census, 1994). These complex and multiproblem social contexts observed frequently in the treatment of ethnic/racial minority clients add to the already difficult challenge of providing people of color with effective drug abuse treatment.

With all these mentioned, it must also be noted that the minority experience does not always involve life in lower socioeconomic status. In the past two decades, growing numbers of young adults from ethnic/racial backgrounds have advanced into the middle class, as many benefited from access to higher education, including access by way of affirmative action/equal opportunity educational advancement programs. Accordingly, these adults and their children constitute a new young cohort of middle-class minorities, some of whom have also been affected by drug abuse and the need for drug abuse treatment. Middle-class minority adults and adolescents present cases that enjoy relatively greater social resources that aid in their recovery from drug abuse. However, these middle-class minorities also experience the psychological conflicts of facing new challenges and family situations never before experienced by their parents or grandparents. For many new middle-class minority professionals and their families, these new challenges and conflicts may be just as troubling as the challenges faced by their peers who live in poverty. These middle-class challenges may be particularly stressful for those minority professionals who lack well-developed systems of social support that include knowledgeable persons who understand their professional challenges from a distinctly ethnic minority perspective (Comas-Díaz, 1997).

Unique Sociocultural Features by Ethnic/Racial Group

African-Americans

Overview African-Americans are the largest ethnic/racial minority population in the United States, with an estimated population size in 1997 of 34 million (Campbell, 1996; U.S. Bureau of the Census, 1994). Since 1980, however, the African-American population has exhibited an increase in the percentage of families that are maintained by a single parent: In 1994, only 47% of African-American families consisted of married couples (Bennett & DeBarros, 1997). From 1970 to 1993, the annual high school dropout rate for African-Americans decreased from 11% to 5%. Also, African-Americans with a higher level of education have shown considerable increases in median yearly earnings relative to African-Americans with less education. And African-American married couples with children have exhibited a higher median family income compared with married African-American couples that do not have children (Bennett & DeBarros, 1997). These demographic trends reported by the U.S. Bureau of the Census illustrate the economic advantages of African-Americans who have been successful in obtaining a higher education and who have established a stable and more conventional family system.

Historical Perspective African-Americans are just over 12% of the total U.S. population (U.S. Bureau of the Census, 1996). Over half of all African-Americans currently live in the southeastern United States (U.S. Bureau of the Census, 1995d), where many of their ancestors worked as slaves until the mid-1800s. Although slavery ended in the nineteenth century, equal rights for African-Americans were only given lip service until the 1950s. During the 1960s, the work of civil rights leaders and thousands of African-Americans came to fruition as U.S. racial policy was changed from one of "separate but equal" facilities to one of racial integration. While the last two generations have witnessed substantial changes in the treatment of and opportunities for African-Americans, the current wave of anti-affirmative-action sentiment is eroding various gains made during the civil rights era.

For African-Americans, the continued economic impact of inequality in social policy and economic opportunity (racism) is revealed by statistics. The median income for African-American families in 1994 was $24,698, 36% lower than the median income for all U.S. families (U.S. Bureau of the Census, 1996). One out of five (21%) of African-American families earns under $10,000. In 1994, of all African-American families, 27.3% lived below the poverty level, compared with only 11.6% of all U.S. families combined.

Patterns of Drug Use   Generally, substance use remains a serious problem among African-Americans, although recent national surveys indicate that drug use prevalence rates for a younger cohort of African-Americans are decreasing (Johnson, O'Malley, & Bachman, 1996; Watson, 1992). Also, the High School Seniors Survey administered from 1985 to 1989 reveals that African-Americans who stayed in school were less likely than Anglo-American students to use illicit drugs (Johnson, O'Malley, & Bachman, 1991). Specifically, only 4% of these African-American youth reported using cocaine during the past 12 months, compared with 11% of Anglo-American youth. Also, 24% of these African-Americans reported marijuana use, compared with 38% of their Anglo-American peers. These figures are promising, although prevention and treatment efforts need to be maintained to sustain this decreasing trend.

Cultural Beliefs and Practices   Drug treatment staff should know about a number of cultural beliefs and practices in order to work effectively with African-Americans. First, spirituality has long played an important role in the lives of African-Americans. The belief that a better life lies ahead has helped sustain African-Americans through the trying times of slavery and overt racism (Robinson, Perry, & Carey, 1995). The hymns and sermons of the African-American church were developed to inspire hope. For example, during their struggle for equal rights in the 1950s and 1960s, gospel songs were a source of strength

for African-Americans, and churches often served as meeting halls.

Historically, the church, with its pastor and broad network of brothers and sisters, has served as a reliable source of social support for many African-Americans. Indeed, pastors are expected to help church members during times of need by offering advice and direction (Robinson et al., 1995). Further, many churches provide needed funding to church members when a tragedy occurs, as well as serving as soup kitchens and homeless shelters for the poor of all faiths.

Another important aspect of the African-American culture is the role of women and the elderly. African-American elders are afforded a special reverence, while women are often seen as the heart of the family (Robinson et al., 1995). In certain West African tribes, from which many African-Americans are descended, women were considered the souls of society, while the men were considered the heads of society.

Today, the African-American family is strongly woman-centered, although it is not necessarily woman-dominated, as the myth of the black matriarchy suggests (Gaines, 1994). In 1994, 46% of African-American families had a female head of household without a spouse present (U.S. Bureau of the Census, 1996). By contrast, only 7% had a male head of household without a spouse present. While these figures highlight the role of women (Robinson et al., 1995), caution is needed against labeling female-headed households dysfunctional; it is often the case that children are coparented by one or more persons living in an extended-family system. In fact, many African-Americans view child rearing as a communal responsibility, much as in the African proverb: "It takes a whole village to raise a child."

This concept of *collectivism*, or the concern for the welfare of the whole group is part of the multifaceted philosophy behind Afrocentrism (White & Parham, 1990). Afrocentrism places the needs and interests of people with African ancestry at the heart of all discussions (Harris, 1992). It encourages African-Americans and others to immerse themselves in African history so that they may develop a new perspective of the world that includes placing their lives within the context of this African history. The new outlook that emerges often changes the way people view existence, meaning, reality, and time. Existence is changed from the Eurocentric view expressed by Descartes ("I think, therefore I am") to the collectivist Afrocentric perspective ("we are, therefore I exist") (Harris, 1992, p. 156).

Thus, existence is viewed not in terms of individualism, but in terms of relationships with the community and nature; reality is restructured (Harris, 1992). This restructuring allows meaning to be found not in individualistic pursuits of a better job or more money with which to buy material items, but instead in forces found within the community. From the Eurocentric point of view, these forces appear to be external to the individual and therefore constitute a communal source from which to derive meaning. However, from the Afrocentric perspective these community forces are the expression of an individual's potential. This transcendent order from where meaning is found influences the African-Americans' perception of reality. Reality from the Eurocentric perspective is defined by scientific demonstrations, but reality from the Afrocentric perspective is defined by personal experience that captures aspects that science is unable to demonstrate.

Along with changes in the concepts of existence, meaning, and reality, in Afrocentrism the concept of time also changes (Harris, 1992). Instead of viewing time as linear, time is seen as cyclical. From this cyclical perspective, progress is no longer viewed as something that is new today because it was not in place yesterday. Instead, what appears to be change may be more accurately seen as a recurrence in a repeating cycle.

The Afrocentric perspective has influenced the terms that African-American people use to describe themselves. The term *black* tends to be preferred by people who do not identify with the time period before slavery, whereas the term *African-American* is preferred by people who wish to acknowledge their African heritage and to express a feeling of closeness to Africa, "the mother continent" (Robinson et al., 1995). Within the African-American population, individuals differ in the extent to which they accept and espouse the core values of a traditional Afrocentric life orientation.

To summarize, the long history of slavery and racism experienced by African-Americans still affects them in negative ways (e.g., economically) and in positive ways (e.g., spiritually). The church is a strong source of social support for many African-Americans, and women are often viewed as the heart of the community, while they simultaneously head a large percentage of single-parent households. The Afrocentric perspective to which many African-Americans adhere employs a communal orientation which lends a different perspective to existence, meaning, reality, and time.

Latinos/Hispanics

Overview   Latinos/Hispanics constitute the second largest ethnic/racial minority population in the United States, with an estimated population size in 1997 of 29.1 million (Campbell, 1996; U.S. Bureau of the Census, 1994). Hispanics are one of the two fastest growing populations in the United States (the other is the Asian-American/Pacific Islander group): By the year 2000, Hispanics are expected to have a population of 31.1 million and, by the year 2005, are projected to grow to 35.7 million and to surpass African-Americans as the largest ethnic/racial population in the United States. Latino/Hispanics can be of any race, given that Latinos vary in skin color and appearance from light-complexioned to indigenous dark brown and include black-complexioned Latinos from the Caribbean (Cuba, the Dominican Republic, etc.).

Historical Perspective   In the United States, Latinos/Hispanics are a composite group that includes several subgroups, including Mexican-Americans, Puerto Ricans, Cubans, and persons from Central and South America. The Spanish language and certain cultural customs and traditions that are based on Catholicism and old Spanish culture bind many Hispanics with a sense of common culture: *nuestra cultura Latina* (U.S. Bureau of the Census, 1993). Nonetheless, given their diversity in cultural and racial backgrounds, various Latinos/Hispanics disagree about the term that should be used to refer to them. The terms *Latino (a)* and *Hispanic* are general terms that refer to the overall population as a composite group (Aguirre-Molina & Molina, 1994). The U.S. Census Bureau has adopted the term *Hispanic* in its surveys and publications. Some members of this population, such as those who live in northern New Mexico, prefer the term *Spanish American*, as they identify exclusively with their ancestors from Spain, and not at all with Mexico. By contrast, other Latinos/Hispanics prefer the term *Latino* for the male gender and *Latina* for female gender, noting that

Hispanic is an imposed term and refers to Spain, whereas the many Latin American nations that obtained their independence from Spain prefer to avoid an identification with their colonizers.

While choice of identifying label may seem to be a trivial issue, its importance lies in the psychology of personal and national identity, and in the social meaning that comes from who a person is, and how he or she self-identifies. As one example, persons from the United States may prefer to be known as *Americans* (or as *Notreamericanos* among Latinos) and might object to being called "English people" simply because they speak English and are from areas colonized by Great Britain.

The largest of the Hispanic groups is Mexican-Americans. Mexican-Americans constitute over 60% of the U.S. Hispanic population. Most of them are concentrated in the states of California, Arizona, Colorado, New Mexico, and Texas. However, growing enclaves of Mexican-Americans can be found in the Midwest, around the Chicago area, and in other parts of the country. A long history of conflict between the United States and Mexico, including wars and border disputes, has led to the development of a bilingual/bicultural identity among the people in the Southwest who trace their roots to Mexico, but who have been raised in the United States. Some Mexican-Americans, in recognition of their hybrid identity and as an expression of cultural pride and political activism, have chosen to call themselves *Chicanos* or *Chicanas*. Others, however, do not like to use this term.

The large influx of documented and undocumented immigrants from Mexico and other parts of Latin America have helped enrich the Mexican and other Latino influences found within U.S. Hispanic neighborhoods that are called *barrios*. The presence of Spanish-language mass media and other sources of cultural information and identity have sustained the Hispanic presence in the Southwest, in Los Angeles, in San Antonio, and in other parts of the country, most notably in Miami, New York, and Chicago. Spanglish, combined English and Spanish terms, reflects the hybrid, dual-culture identity of many Latinos/Hispanics. For example, instead of using the Spanish term *mirar* in referring to watching something, a bilingual speaker may use the term *wachar*, as in *alli te wacho* ("I'll see you around").

Puerto Ricans are U.S. citizens, many of whom have a history of migration between the mainland and the island of Puerto Rico. A major existential issue for Puerto Ricans is the issue of national and personal identity, as for over 300 years, Puerto Ricans have been colonized by Spain and then by the United States, thus not having had the comfort of a true sovereign identity for three centuries. As a group, Puerto Ricans are concentrated in the New York and New England area, although other enclaves live in various portions of the southeastern and southwestern United States.

Members of the third largest Hispanic group, Cubans and Cuban-Americans, are concentrated in Dade County in southern Florida. Historically, a first wave of Cuban immigrants came to the United States in the early 1900s after the Spanish-American war of 1890. A second large wave of immigrants from Cuba came to the United States after the political takeover of Cuba by Fidel Castro in 1959. Most of the Cuban refugees of the 1960s were middle-class Cubans, and thus, the culture and mindset of today's Cuban elders reflect this middle-class orientation. A third wave of Cuban immigrants came in the *Mariel* boatlift in 1980 (Aguirre-Molina & Molina, 1994). Thus, differing cohorts of Cubans live in the United States, although demographically the middle-class value system of the second wave of Cuban immigrants prevails as the core orientation of Cuban Americans today.

Patterns of Drug Use Mexican-Americans, Puerto Ricans, Cuban-Americans, and other Hispanics/Latinos vary in their drug use in relation to the age cohort and the region of the country that is examined. Heroin has been a main drug of use among several generations of opiate-using families in East Los Angeles, California, and in San Antonio, Texas—families that identify with gangs and with the *pachuco* or *cholo* (wild and crazy homeboy) lifestyle (Desmond & Maddox, 1984; Moore, 1990). In the late 1990s, heroin continues to be a drug that most adversely affects the lives of Mexican-Americans/Chicanos who live in certain lower-class *barrios*. As reported by SAMHSA, data from substance abuse treatment admissions for 73,552 persons of Mexican background show that the illicit drug of abuse most often has been heroin (34.2%), while the most frequently used legal substance has been alcohol (46.2%) (Rouse, 1995, p. 80). Generally, health survey data indicate that among Hispanics, the use of illicit drugs and alcohol tends to increase with greater level of acculturation (Amaro, Whittaker, Coffman, & Heeren,

1990), although gender and other factors also influence the extent of this relationship between drug use and level of acculturation.

Cultural Beliefs and Practices   Catholicism and "old Spanish culture" are potent sources of cultural influence that have strongly affected the indigenous cultural groups that were conquered by the Spaniards. Today, this influence remains strong in the form of the Spanish language, family beliefs and practices, and patterns of social interaction. And within the core Hispanic/Latino culture, there exists a set of "traditional" values (Ramirez, 1991), although it is essential to note that Hispanics vary in the extent to which they agree with and adopt as their own various traditional Hispanic values, beliefs, and practices.

Several of these values, beliefs, and practices will be reviewed here briefly. "Traditional" Hispanic culture is primarily conservative. As one example, it features strong and distinct male and female gender roles (Ramirez, 1991). Despite this traditionalism, as the result of acculturation and modernization, changes in the family structure are challenging these traditional beliefs and practices, although today some of these are still active in original or in modified form. Some of the most prominent values within the Hispanic cultures are *respeto* (respect), the importance of deference and obedience to elders and to persons of higher rank (Marin & Marin, 1991); *personalismo* (personalized relations), the importance of attentiveness to the thoughts and wishes of others; and *confianza* (trust), the importance of developing a strong interpersonal relationship, one that features mutual trust, although the highest level of trust is usually reserved for the most intimate of relationships.

Machismo is a pattern of beliefs and behaviors that has had dual meanings and that has been linked to drug and alcohol abuse (Chavez et al., 1989; Desmond & Maddox, 1984). In its original and positive sense, the responsible *macho* male was seen as a strong and able defender of the family. Accordingly, at its root, *machismo* is a positive attribute that involves serving as a courageous and strong protector of the family. However, in the negative sense, *machismo* also refers to males who are irresponsible, domineering, jealous, and violent, and who abuse alcohol. Males who are insensitive to women, who are unfaithful and promiscuous, and who may be abu-

sive are also considered to be acting as *machos* as defined in this negative sense. This "Hollywoodized," more negative version of *machismo* has been the more "colorful" and enduring version and the one that prevails as the sense in which the term *macho* is typically used today. When viewed as a *DSM-IV* character or personality disorder (APA, 1994), *machismo* can be seen as a personality disorder that features antisocial and/or narcissistic characteristics. For Hispanic drug addicts who exhibit these *macho* or antisocial/narcissistic features, recovery from drug abuse is likely to be complicated and more difficult, as is any recovery from drug abuse when codiagnosed with strong aspects of personality disorder.

In summary, Hispanics are a heterogeneous population consisting of Mexican-origin people (Mexican-Americans, Chicanos, Mexicans) as well as Puerto Ricans, Cuban-Americans, and other Hispanics/Latinos. Catholicism and old Spanish cultural values, beliefs, and traditional practices govern the behavior of most Hispanics in varying degrees, although some of these factors are changing as the result of the forces of acculturation and modernization. Extent of drug use and the type of drug used by Hispanics/Latinos varies in relation to subgroup (gender, nationality, level of acculturation), region of the country, or the community which is examined.

Asian-Americans

Overview   Asian-Americans are perhaps the most diverse of the major U.S. ethnic/racial groups. In 1994, the Asian-American and Pacific Islander population of the United States was estimated to be 8.8 million, up from 7.3 million in 1990 (U.S. Bureau of the Census, 1995a). The 1990 U.S. Census lists 10 major subgroups under the general category of Asian-Americans and Pacific Islanders. In order of their population size, these groups are Chinese, Filipino, Japanese, Asian Indian, Korean, Vietnamese, Hawaiian, Samoan, Guamanian, and other Asian or Pacific Islander. In 1990, the Asian and Pacific Islander population was 7.2 million, the largest groups being Chinese, 1.64 million; Filipino, 1.41 million; and Japanese, 847,000 (U.S. Bureau of the Census, 1995a). In terms of percentage increase, the Asian-American population is the fastest growing of all the U.S. ethnic/racial populations: in 1997, its population was 10.0 million, and in the year 2000, it is expected to increase to 11.4 million (Campbell, 1996).

Historical Perspective   The Chinese were the first Asian immigrants to enter the United States in large numbers (Kitano, 1974, 1980), as they were welcomed into the United States as a source of cheap labor. In the 1850s in California, Chinese immigrants participated in the construction of the railroad and labored in various menial jobs that Americans would not take.

The Japanese were the second Asian group to come to the United States, also in response to the demand for cheap labor. Whereas the Chinese came from a primarily agricultural nation and thus exhibited a rural and agrarian lifestyle, the Japanese came from a more industrialized nation and thus exhibited a more industrialized lifestyle (Kitano, 1974). In the past, Japanese-Americans have been considered the "model minority," as they have actively pursued upward mobility, although by exhibiting a "low social profile," in which they avoided social confrontation and conflict with mainstream Euro-American society. Accordingly, many Japanese-Americans have been successful in establishing a stable standard of living, despite many instances of racism and discrimination, including the wartime evacuation of Japanese to internment camps from 1942 to 1945. Despite being confronted with adversity, most Japanese-Americans and many Chinese-Americans have a relatively high level of education. For example, in 1994, nearly 9 out of 10 Asian-American and Pacific Islanders 25 years and older had completed at least a high school diploma, and a high proportion had attained executive or professional occupations (U.S. Bureau of the Census, 1995a).

After the Japanese, Filipinos migrated to the United States as *nationals* (similar to the case for Puerto Ricans), as the United States owned the Philippines in the early 1900s, and thus, Filipinos were able to come to the United States as a source of cheap agricultural citizen labor (Kitano, 1974). Years later, other Asian groups such as the Koreans and the Vietnamese came in waves following war in their country (Locke, 1998).

The Asian-American population of the United States is very diverse in terms of great variability in the languages spoken, their cultures, and their recency of migration. Asian-Americans reside mostly in the western United States and mostly in metropolitan areas. Other characteristics of members of this group are that relative to non-Hispanic whites, Asian-Americans have a higher level of educational attainment, cans have a higher level of educational attainment, have larger families, have a comparable level of median family income, and have more females who have a college education and work year-round (Bennett & Martin, 1997).

Patterns of Drug Use   Unfortunately, the data on patterns of drug use among Asian-Americans are limited. In the past, Asian-Americans as a group appear to have exhibited comparatively low levels of drug and alcohol abuse. Unfortunately, population-based national epidemiological data on Asian-American and Pacific Islanders (APIs) have been almost nonexistent (Yu & Whitted, 1997). Thus, the perceived low rates of drug use by APIs might reflect low levels of surveillance for that population, rather than actual low rates of drug use. Moreover, even for the available data for Asian-Americans in general, Yu and Whitted (1997) have indicated that because of "lumping diverse ethnic groups which do not even share a common history, linguistic roots, or religious belief, gross disparities in morbidity risks and mortality patterns between groups are glossed over" (p. 105).

In contrast to the "model minority" syndrome, new data for recent immigrants from Japan and for higher acculturated U.S. citizens of Chinese background have identified these subgroups of Asian-Americans as exhibiting high rates of heavy alcohol consumption (Myers, Kagawa-Singer, Kumanyika, Lex, & Markides, 1995). Moreover, rates of cigarette smoking for some of the least acculturated Asian-American immigrants are also worthy of concern. The growing social observation that many new immigrants from China and from Southeast Asia are heavy cigarette smokers has been corroborated in part: High prevalence rates for current cigarette smoking have been observed for Laotians (92.0%), Kampucheans (70.0%), and Chinese Vietnamese (54.5%) (Myers et al., 1995). Moreover, in the 1990s, with the growing wave of new immigrants from lower socioeconomic status that include Asian gang activity, drug problems that were heretofore less prevalent in Asian-American communities have now emerged among Asian-American adolescents and young adults.

Cultural Beliefs and Practices   Given the broad diversity that exists within the Asian-American population, it is difficult to make broad generalizations about specific cultural practices. However, there does exist a core set of Pan-Asian values that are based on Confucianism, Buddhism, and Taoism (Dana, 1993).

Confucianism emphasizes order, the balance of forces, and filial piety. Buddhism emphasizes avoiding worldly activities in favor of an ascetic lifestyle and the view that life involves suffering. Taoism emphasizes harmony between human beings and nature and the avoidance of confrontation.

Thus, Pan-Asian values and practices that govern the beliefs and behaviors of many Asian-Americans include the following: (a) the importance of the family as the unit of social and cultural activities, (b) the importance of observing a social hierarchy of respect and deference to elders or persons of higher social rank, (c) personal restraint and suppression of emotion, (d) using discipline and self-directedness in action, and (e) the role of shame in motivating behavior that is, actions that bring shame to the family should be strongly avoided. Based on the Asian-American person's level of cultural involvement in traditional ways, and perhaps in relation to level of acculturation, individual Asian-Americans vary in the extent to which they accept as their own and practice various Pan-Asian values, beliefs, and behaviors.

In summary, APIs are a very diverse and fast-growing ethnic population. While rates of illicit drug use appear to have been low in the past, limited health data may have failed to document accurately the extent of the problem of drug abuse among APIs. Alternately, secular trends, including acculturative effects and the drug-using behavior of new immigrants, may actually be contributing to the higher rates of drug use observed among APIs in some recent studies. New epidemiological data guided by improved sampling methodologies for special or rare populations, along with improved conceptual categories and measures would aid in generating better data on the extent of illicit drug use among Asian Americans and Pacific Islanders (Yu & Whitted, 1997).

Native American Indians

Overview   Native American Indians constitute a diverse population, with more than 554 federally recognized tribes and Alaskan native villages, each with unique customs, social organization, and ecology (U.S. Department of the Interior, 1996). Based on 1990 U.S. Census data, within a Native American Indian population of 1.93 million, the largest American Indian tribes were Cherokee (369,035); Navajo, (225,298); Sioux

(107,321); and Chippewa, (105,988) (U.S. Bureau of the Census, 1995b).

While there are commonalities that are shared by Native American Indians, striking differences in values, customs, and history exist between tribes (Snipp, 1989). These differences are partly the result of geography, which has led to grouping Native American Indians based on location: Plains, Southwest, Eastern Woodlands, Great Basin, California, Plateau, and Northwest Coast (Snipp, 1989; Stubben, 1997). While this section discusses Native American Indians broadly, it should be noted that the diversity found among Native American Indians requires a knowledge of specific tribal customs in order for a counselor or therapist to work most effectively with various individuals of American Indian heritage.

Historical Perspective   When Europeans first arrived in North America, they considered the people they encountered less than human and stripped them of basic civil rights (Clark, 1993). Over the next several centuries, people of European descent assaulted the social, religious, and governmental practices of Native American Indians (Clark, 1993). Part of this assault occurred during the 1800s and early 1900s as Euro-Americans tried to force Native American Indians to conform to their culture. For example, Native American Indian children were sent to boarding schools located far from their reservations. At these boarding schools, the children were not allowed to speak their native languages or practice their traditions. Despite such extreme attempts at forced assimilation, these policies failed to attain their goals (Olson & Wilson, 1986).

In 1953, the U.S. Bureau of Indian Affairs (USBIA; U.S. Bureau of Indian Affairs, 1991) instituted another assimilationist policy that relocated Native America Indians to urban areas. Despite the training and financial support provided by the Bureau of Indian Affairs, many Native American Indians suffered from poverty and disease and returned to their reservations (Snipp, 1989). Finally, the U.S. government ended its efforts to assimilate Native American Indians but left them with good reasons to be suspicious of future policies.

Today, Native American Indian tribes constitute sovereign nations and maintain their own governments that interface with the U.S. government (Clark, 1993). Native American Indians have dual citizenship, so they may be citizens of both their own tribal nation and the United States. As of the 1990 Census, Native American Indians composed 0.7% of the total U.S. population, making Native American Indians the smallest minority group in the United States (U.S. Bureau of the Census, 1995b). In terms of language, there are approximately 250 American Indian languages spoken in the United States today (USBIA, 1991). Of the almost 2 million Native American Indians documented by the U.S. Bureau of the Census (1995c), 90% could speak English, although 39% could not speak English very well; 23% could speak a language other than English. As of the 1980 Census, the majority (53%) of Native American Indians lived on or near Indian lands; only 23.8% lived in urban areas (Snipp, 1989).

Living in poverty is a reality for many Native American Indians. The land the U.S. government chose for Native American Indian reservations was of little economic value, thus making it difficult for Native American Indians to live prosperously (Beauvais, 1992). Historical injustices, such as relocation, continue to impact the social and psychological functioning of Native American Indians both on the reservations and in urban settings, thus contributing to their levels of poverty. On average, Native American Indian families earned $21,619 in 1990, 39% less than the average income for all American families combined (U.S. Bureau of the Census, 1995c). Over one in four Native American Indian families (27%) earn a wage that put them at or below the poverty level.

Native American Indians have valid historical reasons to resent the U.S. government and to feel hostile toward members of the majority culture. As described above, the effects of racism have been experienced by Native American Indians for centuries, and even in recent history, Native American Indian culture has been portrayed negatively by the mainstream media. While these facts have led many to hypothesize that Native American Indians may have low self-esteem and feel hostile and alienated, careful research has revealed otherwise (Trimble, 1987). A questionnaire on the psychological constructs of self-perception and alienation was developed in conjunction with 30 Native American Indian groups from eight geocultural regions of the United States. The questionnaire was then completed by 791 Native American Indians from 114 different tribes. The re-

sults indicate that Native American Indians have a moderately positive self-image and do not feel very alienated. In addition, respondents did not express feelings of powerlessness, social isolation, or normlessness. Also, the majority of respondents did not resent their current situation. Thus, working with Native American Indians requires sensitivity to their history and acknowledgment of grave injustices; nevertheless, it would be inaccurate to assume that most American Indians are resentful of their current conditions or feel bad about themselves.

Patterns of Drug Use As noted earlier, the Native American Indian population is extremely diverse. Accordingly, tribes differ in the type of substance used most and in the severity of their substance use problems. While members of some tribes are plagued by alcohol abuse, adolescents in other tribes experience problems with inhalant use (Closser & Blow, 1993). Interestingly, although Native American Indians as a group have higher rates of alcoholism than the total U.S. population, Native American Indians also have more people who abstain entirely from alcohol use. The enormous variability in deaths due to violence and alcohol abuse among some Native American Indian tribes raises questions that remain unanswered about the causes and mechanisms that mediate these differences (Yu & Whitted, 1997). This lack of answers reflects the significant knowledge gap that exists in our current understanding of the factors that affect the health and well-being of Native American Indians.

It is known that alcohol consumption among American Indians varies across time periods and from tribe to tribe. Variables that influence drinking patterns are age, geography, social norms, and local political and legal policies. Urban Indian populations have higher drinking rates than reservation populations. Unfortunately, binge drinkers (those who consume more than five to seven drinks per episode) constitute the largest proportion of those American Indians who drink alcohol (May, 1996).

Rates of tobacco use among American Indians also vary by geographic region. Smoking rates among regions between 1985 and 1988 have ranged from 18% to 48% for men and from 15% to 57% for women (Sugarman, Warren, Oge, & Helgerson, 1992, as cited in Myers et al., 1995). Smokeless tobacco (chewing tobacco and snuff) is also a problem among

American Indians, where rates of smokeless tobacco use have been reported to be between 15% and 20% among Plains Indian men, three to four times the rate among Anglo-American men.

In addition to alcohol and tobacco use, some American Indians consume high amounts of other substances. The High School Seniors Survey (HSSS) from 1990 included over 500 American Indian high school seniors (Johnson et al., 1991). The results indicate that American Indian youth had the highest prevalence rates for the use of several illicit drugs, including marijuana (43%), hallucinogens (10%), tranquilizers (8%), inhalants (7%), methaqualone (3.5%), and heroin (1%). Other prevalence rates included cocaine at 15% and stimulants at 18%.

Cultural Beliefs and Practices   There are a number of cultural aspects to consider when working with Native American Indians. One of the most important aspects to understand is the involvement of extended kin relationships in the lives of Native American Indians (Red Horse, 1982). These relationships emphasize the inclusion of community members of all ages in daily activities, discussions, and ceremonies. Even the peers of Native American Indian youth are often relatives who are close to their own age (Beauvais, 1992). Given that peer influence is a powerful determinant of individual substance use, a common mainstream approach to preventing and treating addiction problems is to help youth find abstinent friends. However, this approach may be difficult and unwise for Native American Indian adolescents whose peers are also part of their extended kin network (Beauvais, 1992).

In addition to incorporating extended kin relationships into their lives, Native American Indians maintain a strong sense of group identity (Red Horse, 1982). Sometimes, this group identity is so strong that it creates a closed system. Especially in this situation, outside helpers need to immerse themselves in the community to "join" the group in order to earn credibility before they can participate as helpers (Szapocznik & Kurtines, 1989). Within the group, Native American Indians respect the role of the individual, while group members are also mutually interdependent and will take on specific roles and responsibilities. Behavior that needs correcting is considered the individual's responsibility. However, individuals who leave the group to attend a substance abuse treatment program may experience group disapproval and imposed feelings of guilt upon their return (Colorado, 1986).

Spirituality also plays a strong role in the lives of Native American Indians. In essence, spirituality aims to achieve harmony between the mind, body, spirit, and the environment (Olson & Wilson, 1986). Thus, spiritual leadership promotes harmony with others via the Native American Indian focus on extended-family relationships and group identity (Red Horse, 1982). Spirituality and spiritual leadership may well operate as strong motivators for avoiding the abuse of drugs because many tribes believe that substance abuse results from deviating from the natural order of things (i.e., losing the balance between the mind, body, spirit, and the environment) (Colorado, 1986). As a traditional activity that promotes spirituality, Red Horse (1982) endorsed the value of engaging spiritual leaders to provide spiritual guidance during traditional ceremonies and through contemporary intertribal gatherings such as powwows.

In sum, Native American Indians constitute a diverse group which shares a history of culturally destructive policies and practices imposed by the U.S. government. Nevertheless, Native American Indians continue to draw on their strengths to maintain cultural values and customs (Olson & Wilson, 1986). Concepts which are central to the Native American Indian experience include extended kin relationships, group identity, and spirituality. These concepts should be considered and understood when working with Native American Indians.

PRACTICAL CONSIDERATIONS IN TREATMENT AND SERVICE DELIVERY

Client-Provider Relationships

In the past, minority clients have questioned the utility of seeking mental health and drug abuse treatment from a mainstream human service agency (Echeverry, 1997). The high dropout rate observed among many minority clients who have sought mental health services has been remarkable, as it has been observed to approach 50% after a single session (Sue, 1977). During the first session, if the therapist fails to engage the minority client in a manner that establishes rapport and raises positive client expectations for help in treatment, then a minority client is likely to drop out of treatment.

In the provision of drug treatment services to minority clients, the likelihood of client attrition depends on several factors: the client's level of preparedness to participate in treatment (DiClemente & Scott, 1997), whether the treatment is forced or voluntary, the presence of psychopathology (Kolden et al., 1997), whether the treatment is inpatient or outpatient in form, and even if the client pays directly or has the benefits of insurance coverage. However, as related to the client-provider relationship, the presence of cultural and/or linguistic mismatches is also a potential source of client-therapist clash that can lead to limited client participation in a program of recovery (Sue, 1988).

For increased success in treatment, clients do not necessarily need to be matched with their therapists by ethnicity (ethnic matches). However, for effective treatment, therapists do need to be knowledgeable about ethnic clients' cultural background (cultural matches) (Sue et al., 1991). This point raises the need to train therapists and counselors in a way that builds their "cultural empathic" capacities and their cultural competence, in order to meet the client more than halfway, and to create a therapeutic atmosphere that will motivate sustained client participation. In addition, efforts at matching the intervention to client characteristics, such as by severity of addiction or by cultural orientation, may also improve client motivation for treatment and treatment outcome (Miller, 1989). Research that examines cultural factors in the client-treatment matching of ethnic/racial minorities is much needed (Castro & Tafoya-Barraza, 1997).

Clearly, treatment for drug addiction won't work if the addict is not engaged and retained in treatment (Onken, Blaine, & Boren, 1997). Onken and colleagues point out that as an incentive to enter drug treatment, drug addicts may seek to escape the social, financial, criminal, and medical problems related to drug addiction. However, drug addicts also do not want to give up the pleasure associated with drug abuse. This conflicting situation creates a motivational problem for full participation in drug abuse treatment programs.

Given this context, how does one keep the drug addict involved in his or her own treatment (Onken et al., 1997)? From a different perspective, entering a medically based treatment program has typically created a stigma, especially for ethnic minority clients. Establishing more community-based programs

that are delivered within local community-based organizations (CBOs) will offer a more inviting setting for various clients, especially when these programs emphasize health promotion, lifestyle management, and relapse management as broader contexts in the task of recovery from drug abuse (Marlatt, Tucker, Donovan, & Vuchinich, 1997). Managed-care guidelines for allowable drug abuse treatment should take into account these issues (Kushner & Moss, 1996).

Assessment

One aspect of enhanced therapist/counselor cultural capacity (cultural competence) is to improve the therapist's skills at assessing and understanding the within-group variability in a given ethnic/racial group. For each group, level of within-group variability can be assessed using a core dimension that ranges from high cultural involvement and acceptance of the traditional culture's values to low or no cultural involvement. Dana (1993) referred to this key dimension as a "moderator variable," a variable that identifies levels or gradations for this dimension.

For African-Americans, this dimension is called *Afrocentricity* or *Nigrescene* (White & Parham, 1990). Measures of the Afrocentric worldview have been developed that aim to provide an indicator of an individual's level of involvement within the traditional or core African-oriented culture (Baldwin & Bell, 1985; Montgomery, Fine, & James-Meyers, 1990).

Similarly, for Hispanics and for Asian-Americans, scales that measure level of acculturation assess this within-group variability, which ranges from being strongly culture-bound (low acculturated), to being bilingual/bicultural, to being highly acculturated (culturally distant or assimilated). The ARSMA (Acculturation Rating Scale for Mexican Americans) was developed in 1980 and has been a core scale from which other scales have been derived to rate levels of acculturation among Mexican-Americans and other Hispanics (Cuellar, Harris, & Jasso, 1980). A similar scale has been developed for use with Asian-Americans (Suinn, Rickard-Figueroa, Lew, & Vigil, 1987).

In these approaches, three within-group types of individuals have been identified: (1) the low acculturated, individuals who identify strongly with the mother culture; (2) the bilingual/bicultural, those who have skills and an orientation to participate in both cultures; and (3) the highly acculturated or assimilated, those who have little connection with the

TABLE 27.3 Cultural Orientation: Six Major Ethnic Types within an Ethnic/Racial Group

	Assimilated	Acculturated	Pluralistic (Afr.-Amer.) or bilingual/bicultural (Hisp., Asian-Amer., Native Amer.)	Traditional African-American	Separatist	Marginalized
African-Americans						
Self-concept	Identifies solely with the white, dominant culture	Identifies mostly with white dominant culture; some identification with black culture and community	Identifies both with African-American and white cultures and communities; affirms African American consciousness	Identifies mostly with African-American culture; some white or other culture identification	Identifies solely with African-American culture; no identification with the white, dominant culture and community	Identifies with no specific culture; sees self solely as an individual
Attitudes toward ethnicity	Negative attitude toward race and ethnicity; avoids ethnic/racial issues; espouses white values	Positive attitude toward the dominant culture; ambivalence about issues of race and ethnicity	Positive attitude toward both the dominant and ethnic culture, and toward other ethnic cultures	Positive attitude toward own African-American culture; some interest in the dominant culture and community	Negative attitude toward the dominant culture; strong loyalty toward own African-American culture and community	Neutral attitude toward own ethnicity; no feelings of pride or of belonging to any ethnic/cultural group
Social and political involvements	Involved solely with people from the dominant culture and community	Involved mostly with people from the dominant culture and community	Involved with people from both the dominant and African American cultures and communities	Involved mostly with people from own African American culture and community	Avoids persons from the dominant culture; mostly involved in own African American culture and community	Indifference towards others from own ethnic/cultural group

Hispanics, Asian-Americans, Native American Indians						
Language	Speaks only English	Speaks mostly English	Speaks English and own ethnic language about equally well	Speaks mostly or only own ethnic language	May speak one or more languages, but prefers own ethnic language	Likely to speak English
Self-concept	Identifies solely with the white dominant culture	Identifies mostly with the white dominant culture; some identification with own ethnic culture	Identifies both with the dominant culture and with own ethnic culture	Identifies mostly with own ethnic culture; some identification with the dominant culture	Identifies solely with own ethnic culture; may dislike the dominant culture and community	Identifies with no specific culture; sees self solely as an individual
Attitudes toward ethnicity	Negative attitude toward race and ethnicity; avoids ethnic/racial issues	Positive attitude toward the dominant culture; ambivalence about issues of race and ethnicity	Positive attitude toward both the dominant and ethnic culture, and toward other ethnic cultures	Positive attitude toward own ethnic culture; some interest in the dominant culture	Antipathy toward the dominant culture; strong loyalty toward own ethnic culture	Neutral attitude toward ethnicity; no feelings of pride or of belonging to any ethnic/cultural group
Social and political involvements	Involved solely with people from the dominant culture and community	Involved mostly with people from the dominant culture and community	Involved with people from the dominant and ethnic cultures and communities	Involved mostly with people from own ethnic culture and community	Involved entirely with people from own ethnic culture and community	Indifference toward others from own ethnic/racial or cultural group

mother culture, and who seem uninterested in getting involved in the mother culture.

Within this context and as an extension, table 27.3 presents six levels or types of cultural orientations that involve language (except for African-Americans), self-concept, attitudes toward ethnicity, and social and political involvements as major aspects of cultural orientation. These groups describe six recurring types of individuals who have been observed within each of the four major ethnic/racial groups. For Hispanics, Asian-Americans, and Native Americans, these six types of persons are (a) assimilated, (b) acculturated, (c) bilingual/bicultural, (d) traditional, (e) separatist, and (f) marginalized. In parallel fashion, for African-Americans, these types are better described as (a) assimilated, (b) acculturated, (c) pluralistic, (d) traditional African-American, (e) separatist, and (f) marginalized.

As presented in table 27.3, these are prototypical profiles, and actual clients do not always exhibit all the characteristics noted. However, these typologies are intended to enhance the clinician's cultural capacity to understand, appreciate, and work with the large within-group diversity found within each of the major U.S. ethnic/racial groups. Each of these types of minority clients offers distinct challenges to recovery from drug abuse based on the type of cultural orientation. These six types are similar to the four types of adaptation to the conflicts of acculturation: assimilation, integration, rejection, and deculturation, described by Berry (1980). These six types are also similar to the typology that describes levels of involvement in American Indian culture, that is, the five categories of "Indians" described by La Fromboise, Trimble, and Mohatt (1990).

As noted, this schema provides a set of recurring types of clients as seen from the perspective of within-group differences. While presented along a general continuum, these six types of cultural orientations are not ordered by increasing degree of cultural involvement. They do, however, represent different types of orientations toward a core ethnic culture. A client who presents for treatment may be evaluated according to this schema on his or her here-and-now cultural orientation.

Moreover, from a developmental perspective, for some minority clients, a life history analysis of cultural orientation could also reveal a process of change in cultural orientation across time in which the client has shifted from one cultural orientation to another across a lifetime. For example, during adolescence, a client might assimilate toward mainstream white (Euro-American) values and behaviors in order to "fit in," as the result of education and/or in relation to efforts at upward social mobility. Subsequently, in adulthood, that same client could exert efforts to move back toward the mother culture (toward lower acculturation or toward biculturalism) when seeking to recapture lost aspects of his or her culture and identity (White & Parham, 1990). This shift back to the mother culture, to cultural roots, and toward recapturing a lost part of the self may have therapeutic value for some recovering drug users (Castro, Sharp, Barrington, Walton, & Rawson, 1991; Westermeyer, 1984). Further research is needed to determine the therapeutic effects of this process of "cultural renaissance," as this identity shift may promote effective recovery from illicit drug use and addictive dependence on illicit drugs.

Beginning with Group 1 as shown in table 27.3, assimilated minority clients (white-oriented African-American clients) exhibit a minimal identification and involvement with traditional cultural values, ethnic issues, people, and communities. Within treatment, these clients may disavow any identification or involvement with their ethnic community and are often uncomfortable and resistant when dealing with ethnic/racial issues. Usually, these clients are best treated using the conventional/standard mainstream treatment program.

Acculturated clients (Group 2), are culturally oriented more toward the mainstream/dominant culture than toward their own ethnic/racial culture. These clients can relate to ethnic issues in treatment, although with some ambivalence. The provider should assess the individual client's willingness to discuss ethnic/racial issues and the degree to which this client's lifestyle and social relations include sufficient ethnic interests to merit addressing these as part of treatment for recovery from drug abuse.

The bilingual/bicultural (pluralistic African-American client; Group 3) has a dual-culture or multicultural identity and social involvement. Accordingly, this client type has a lifestyle and social relations that embrace ethnic/racial issues as important aspects of his or her life. In the recovery of the bilingual/bicultural client, issues of ethnic identity, sources of family support, and the challenges of shuttling between two cultural environments should be examined, as these issues relate directly to the challenge of recovery from drug abuse.

Traditional (low acculturated; Group 4) clients

typically have a limited capacity to participate in drug abuse treatment that is offered in English, although this language issue does not apply to African-American clients. Thus, many of these clients need a linguistically compatible treatment program. Traditional clients who have fewer years' residence in the United States may also exhibit a lower awareness of mainstream U.S. social norms and expectations in treatment. These issues need attention in tailoring the treatment to the needs of these traditional clients, who exhibit linguistic and life values that differ from those of persons from the mainstream culture. Among African-American clients, those described here as traditional African Americans are involved primarily in the African-American community. These clients identify more closely with African-American culture and traditions and identify strongly with the African-American values of spirituality, communal relations, collaboration, extended-family relations, and experiential ways of knowing (Montgomery et al., 1990).

The separatist client (Group 5) exhibits a notable resistance to any treatment that espouses Euro-American values and expectations. A culturally relevant drug treatment program that promotes issues of ethnic cultural pride and respect for ethnic values and practices may help the separatist client relate to the treatment program. Resistance to participation in drug abuse treatment by drug-abusing clients with a separatist cultural orientation has been described by drug researchers working with Hispanic heroin addicts (Desmond & Maddox, 1984).

Finally, a marginalized client (Group 6) exhibits a notable lack of identification with both the mainstream and his or her own ethnic culture, thus "belonging" to neither culture (Stonequist, 1935). In the United States, this strongly nonconformist client, who doesn't fit in, speaks English but expresses an individualized self-concept that disavows any identification with or involvement in the conventional mainstream or ethnic cultures. Ramirez (1991) described a "mismatch syndrome," in which a socially alienated person feels alone, helpless, and misunderstood. This marginalized person expresses a lack of interest in affiliating with ethnic peers and in participating in ethnic institutions or activities. These individuals can be seen as being at the primitive "diffuse identity" stage of identity development (Phinney, 1989) in which the person does little to explore his or her own ethnic identity and has no clear understanding or appreciation of his or her own culture and ethnicity. Many drug-abusing youths, especially neglected youths

from dysfunctional families who have received little or no ethnic cultural guidance and education from their parents, would be expected to exhibit these marginalized characteristics. These marginalized youth may participate in nonconformist subcultures of their own and may belong to subcultural groups that have unique social norms and attitudes, including attitudes accepting of illicit drug use.

Treatment

Enhancing Conventional Treatment Programs

The literature on the treatment of drug-dependent ethnic/racial clients has little that provides clear guidelines. Currently, typical inpatient or residential treatment programs for recovery from illicit drugs feature several basic treatment goals: (a) eliminating substance use; (b) reducing criminal and/or maladaptive behaviors; (c) reducing comorbidity, especially among dual-diagnosis clients; (d) establishing a viable system of social supports; and (e) establishing gainful employment and/or a stable living situation.

Regarding programmatic content, the curriculum of various drug treatment programs contains a series of educational and training activities, for example, (a) emotional management, or the management of grief, anger, and stress, and self-concept enhancement; (b) personal organization, or values clarification, goal setting, and relapse prevention; and (c) improving interpersonal relations, or conflict resolution, boundary setting, resisting peer pressure, developing a support system, and effective community reentry. The addition of other culturally relevant activities would increase the cultural capacity of these drug abuse recovery programs. Such culturally relevant activities include (a) cultural identity clarification and development, (b) family systems issues affecting risks of relapse, and (c) minority community dynamics that affect the ability for reintegration into the local community.

Client-Treatment Matching

Matching clients with therapists by their shared attitudes, values, and common life experiences may lead to a more effective therapeutic alliance than simply matching client and therapist by demographic ethnic label (e.g., having a Hispanic therapist assigned to a Hispanic client) (Beutler, Zetzer, & Yost, 1997). This match by similarity of values and lifestyle is a strategy to promote better treatment outcomes, as the client may better identify with a therapist who is similar to himself or herself. In addition, this may prompt the client's perception of the therapist as a more credible individual who is capable of helping. More research is needed to identify key client factors (problem severity and coping style—internalizing versus externalizing), and to examine the potential of client cultural orientation, as depicted in table 27.3, to establish more effective matching of ethnic/minority clients to therapist and/or to treatment. For example, ethnic minority clients who are assimilated or acculturated would be expected to do well with conventional/mainstream treatment programs that include no ethnic content. By contrast, bicultural (pluralistic), traditional African-American and separatist ethnic minority clients would be expected to relate better to, and benefit more from, a drug treatment program that includes culturally relevant content. The client-treatment matching literature suggests that improving such client-treatment matches yields better treatment outcomes and is more likely to promote the client's continued participation in treatment (Onken et al., 1997).

While client-treatment matching is a promising strategy, this approach may not be viable in drug treatment agencies that focus on offering a single treatment approach. A major challenge to drug treatment programs nationally is to balance the complexity and cost of offering a diversity of programs with the importance of a specific set of program options (e.g., treatment modules) to meet the treatment needs of a diverse client population.

Along these lines, a culturally relevant approach to treatment of ethnic/racial minority clients would emphasize the potential for successful recovery and drug avoidance by helping the client change his or her identity as a "regular user" (Castro et al., 1991), with the aim of developing a new identity as a "recovering addict." This identity includes a concept of self as a nonuser and as a person with a renewed or newly constituted ethnic identity that includes a commitment to be drug-free and to participate as a contributing member to his or her family, to the local community, and to society (Castro et al., 1991).

Role of Traditional Values and Practices

In addition, a culturally relevant intervention for minority clients would encourage a pursuit of traditional ethnic values and practices, under the working assumption that certain traditional cultural values may promote protection against drug use and abuse. The core values found within traditional/agrarian societies, which promote the survival of the group, if reestablished within the modern social context might contribute to successful drug avoidance (Castro & Gutierres, 1997). Here the values of (a) collectivism and cooperation, (b) concerns for serving as a contributing member of the group or family, (c) respect for elders, and (d) spirituality that involves care and concern for the well-being of other members of the community may each serve to counter the effects of certain modernistic values that promote drug use, such as narcissism, self-centeredness, and hedonistic self-gratification. In this regard, for drug-dependent bicultural, traditional, and separatist clients, culturally relevant interventions can focus on ethnic self-concept and values clarification that include promoting (a) ethnic pride, (b) family responsibility, and (c) responsibility to contribute to one's community and culture (Castro & Gutierres, 1997). More research is needed to clarify the effects on treatment outcomes that may accrue by promoting positive antidrug attitudes, and by preventing drug relapse in clients matched by using cultural orientation and examined in progress in a culturally relevant drug treatment program.

Relapse Prevention

Relapse is a major problem among clients recovering from drug abuse, and unfortunately, its occurrence is the rule rather than the exception (Gorski & Miller, 1982; Marlatt & Gordon, 1985). Among ethnic/cultural minority clients, the strong family relations and mutual obligations that are prominent features of many ethnic/racial families can operate as sources of social support. However, conversely, family relations may also operate as sources of distraction from recovery or may prompt relapse episodes (Castro & Tafoya-Barraza, 1997).

In conveying the concepts of addiction and relapse with long-term Chicano heroin addicts, Jorques (1984) used the metaphor of the *tecato guzano* ("stomach worm"). This metaphor asserts that this worm must be "kept asleep," because to awaken it will induce the experience of cravings. This metaphor serves as a descriptive aid in reminding these addicts that addiction, its related cravings, and the potential for relapse are realities that the heroin addict must face constantly. Thus, the recovering drug addict must always keep in mind that he or she must cope with this *tecato guzano* actively and on an ongoing basis. More research is needed on the effects of similar metaphors and related culturally relevant interventions, as these may aid in helping ethnic/racial minority clients to develop culturally meaningful cognitive and behavioral strategies and skills that will aid them in avoiding drug relapse.

Identifying triggers to relapse is an important relapse prevention strategy that should be taught to minority clients within the context of their life situation. Given the importance of the family to many minority clients, identifying sources of social support (including members of the extended family) is likely to be an important strategy for relapse prevention. Conversely, some family members will themselves serve as triggers to relapse, and here, culturally competent strategies should be used to neutralize the disruptive influences of these family members, without creating undue antagonism and conflict within the client's family (Szapocznik & Kurtines, 1989).

Agency Operations

The delivery of culturally competent drug treatment services cannot be separated from the operational characteristics of the agency itself. Core agency practices that greatly affect an agency's capacity to offer culturally competent services to a diverse clientele can be examined in the areas of (a) staffing and staff training, (b) program activities, (c) organizational structure, and (d) organizational policies.

Staffing and Staff Training

For many ethnic groups, the messenger is as important as the message. Therefore, the staff member's personal style and delivery are of paramount importance. Thus, to support staff training, agencies should hire qualified consultants to offer staff development support groups in which staff can openly address and reconcile their own prejudices and/or cultural biases without fear of retribution. The goal is to have the messengers of the agency (i.e., staff counselors, therapists, and other providers) work to acknowledge and respect the individual client's cultural experiences while also encouraging these clients to participate in behavioral and attitudinal change.

Moreover, for practitioners and clinicians, cultural competence does not happen in a vacuum. Too often, an agency hires an ethnic individual who is expected serve as the sole person responsible for addressing a broad array of linguistic and cultural issues in treating a variety of minority clients. This practice can create hostility and/or divisiveness in the ranks and becomes a source of job-related stress and/or dissatisfaction for that overburdened individual. Here, one concern is that ethnicity in and of itself does not guarantee that the ethnic counselor is capable of being culturally competent. Cultural competence is a set of acquired skills and is not a preestablished capability just because the provider is a person of color. Furthermore, the organization's cultural capacity is the product of an integrated program of activities, not the product of the actions of a single "type-cast" individual.

Another challenge to staff training involves the lack of preparation observed among newly graduated college students who enter the professional social service arena. Colleges and universities have not met the challenge of preparing students to negotiate various aspects of fieldwork that involve issues of managed care and cultural competence. Ethnic leaders and communities must meet the challenge of impacting the system of higher education so that issues of color are not confined to a single course or class presentation. Issues of race/ethnicity and gender must be incorporated into course work across the curriculum. One significant activity for promoting cultural competence is to teach students skills in "cultural decentering," in which a student must reframe his or her own academic and/or Eurocentric worldview by temporarily adopting the worldview of various people of color. In addition, an activity to foster capabilities for work in the managed-care environment is to provide students with a variety of hands-on training activities within a variety of community-based health service organizations.

Here also, staff training should target all agency personnel regardless of their job classification or role within the agency. This is important because many times, receptionists, administrative assistants, cooks, and other agency staff have daily contact with clients or with individuals in the community, and these support staff members should also develop skills in cultural competence that relate to their roles within the agency.

Program Activities

Agencies should identify community resources (healers/spiritualists) to complement their conventional treatment activities if these nonconventional activities are part of the belief and/or support system of the individual client or group of clientele seen often within the agency. Agencies should also address the needs of multilingual ethnic groups (Hispanics, Asian-Americans) that need parallel and equally effective treatments delivered in their own language. This addition will also improve and expand the marketability of the drug treatment program, while also providing clients the option to receive treatment in the language in which they feel most comfortable and/or can best express themselves.

Organizational Structure

Providers/organizations of color (POCs) must redefine themselves if they are to survive in this more competitive climate of drug abuse service delivery under the rules of managed care (Kushner & Moss, 1996). This paradigm shift offers the greatest threat to the survival of small social service agencies. Organizations that do not understand managed-care idioms or principles, and/or that lack the requisite technology, clinical capacity, or service diversity, will not survive unless they reorganize in response to the new demands of managed care. However, this threat can also be seen as an opportunity to excel and diversify where POCs can serve as major players and providers of substance abuse treatments that truly serve the needs of ethnic/racial communities.

To survive and compete in the new-managed care environment, POC organizations must excel in the following three areas. First, network development is needed where smaller organizations should consider a merger with larger organizations and/or consider developing a partnership along with agreements for joining existing networks that can support and utilize their services.

Second, advocacy is another strategy in which POCs can participate actively in defining the local guidelines that govern managed care. At present, there is no universal definition of managed care. Therefore, each site will need to define and structure its own care system (eligibility, benefit plans, process, and structure). To ensure ethnic participation, to enhance and support cultural competency, and to advocate for the needs of community-based providers, POCs must develop a unified community plan. This strategy can also include advocacy so that ethnic leaders in the field can participate on the policy level

in defining and developing the characteristics of the local managed-care system.

And third, technology will also be important. Organizations must develop or enhance their capacity for automation and should develop a management information system so that clinical and financial data can be integrated and used in examining program operations. This automated information can be used to monitor and evaluate program outcomes, and to develop more potent programs based on data that monitor program progress and that identify factors associated with more positive treatment outcomes.

Organizational Policies

Treatment agencies must also be guided by governing policies, procedures, and quality assurance standards (state/federal/licensing) that address and endorse culturally appropriate programming for ethnic/racial populations. In turn, these treatment agencies must also adopt policies and standards that mandate the inclusion of a diverse representation of culturally competent community board members, managers, providers (therapists/counselors), and support staff.

SUMMARY AND CONCLUSIONS

The experience of ethnicity is unique and somewhat different for each of the more than 70 million persons of color who currently constitute over 25% of the U.S. population. This considerable diversity has been typically described according to ethnic/racial identity by referencing one of four major ethnic/racial groups: African-Americans, Hispanics/Latinos, Asian-Americans and Pacific Islanders, and Native American Indians. Within each of these four groups, however, there exist subgroups and subcultures that differ in their collective experiences of ethnicity based on variations in nationality, in the tribe or geographic region where raised, by urban-rural status, and/or by the cultural orientation of the members of a subgroup. Today, more refined analyses are needed to move beyond "ethnic gloss" in order to better describe and understand how various experiences of ethnicity may relate to the use and abuse of various illicit drugs.

In understanding this diversity, along with the cultural commonalities that bind a people and create a sense of belonging, drug abuse service providers should work diligently to develop and expand their levels of cultural competence. A commitment to cultural competence is expected to promote the delivery of more culturally relevant and more effective drug abuse prevention interventions and/or drug treatment services for people of color. In this spirit, attending to the cultural aspects of the client-provider relationship, of client assessment, of drug treatment and relapse prevention, and of agency organization, policies, and procedures is expected to contribute to improving the quality of care and treatment effectiveness as delivered to the various people of color who need these services.

Key References

La Fromoise, T. D., Trimble, J. E., & Mohatt, G. V. (1990). Counseling intervention and American Indian tradition: An integrative approach. *Counseling Psychologist, 18,* 628–654.

Trimble, J. E. (1995). Toward an understanding of ethnicity and ethnic identity, and their relationship with drug abuse research. In G. J. Botvin, S. Shinke, & M. A. Orlandi (Eds.), *Drug abuse prevention with multiethnic youth* (pp. 3–27). Thousand Oaks, CA: Sage.

Westermeyer, J. (1984). The role of ethnicity in substance use. *Advances in alcohol and substance abuse, 4,* 9–18.

References

Aguirre-Molina, M., & Molina, C. (1994). Latino populations: Who are they? In C. W. Molina & M. Aguirre-Molina (Eds.), *Latino health in the US: A growing challenge* (pp. 3–22). Washington, DC: American Public Health Association.

Amaro, H., Whittaker, R., Coffman, G., & Heeren, T. (1990). Acculturation and marijuana and cocaine use: Findings from HHANES 1982–84. *American Journal of Public Health* 80(Suppl.) 54–60.

American Medical Association. (1991). Hispanic Health in the United States. *Journal of the American Medical Association, 265,* 248–252.

American Psychiatric Association. (1994). *Diagnostic and statistical manual of mental disorders* (4th ed.—DSM-IV). Washington, DC: Author.

Baldwin, J. A., & Bell, Y. R. (1985). The African self-consciousness scale: An Africentric personality questionnaire. *Western Journal of Black Studies, 9,* 61–68.

Beauvais, F. (1992). An integrated model for prevention and treatment of drug abuse among American Indian youth. *Journal of Addictive Diseases, 11*(3), 63–80.

Bennett, C. E., & DeBarros, K. A. (1997). *The black population.* [Internet]. Internet address: www.census.gov/population/www/pop-profile/blackpop.html.

Bennett, C. E., & Martin, B. (1997). *The Asian and Pacific Islander population.* Washington, DC: Bureau of the Census.

Berry, J. W. (1980). Acculturation as varieties of adaptation. In A. M. Padilla (Ed.), *Acculturation: Theory, models and some new findings.* Boulder, CO: Westview Press.

Beutler, L. E., Zetzer, H., & Yost, E. (1997). Tailoring interventions to clients: Effects on engagement and retention. In L. S. Onken, J. D. Blaine, & J. J. Boren (Eds.), *Beyond the therapeutic alliance: Keeping the drug dependent individual in treatment* (pp. 85–109). NIDA Research Monograph No. 165. Rockville, MD: National Institute on Drug Abuse.

Campbell, P. R. (1996). *Population projections for states by age, sex, race and Hispanic origin: 1995–2025.* Washington, DC: Bureau of the Census.

Castro, F. G. (1998). Cultural competence training in clinical psychology: Assessment, clinical intervention, and research. In A. S. Bellack & M. Hersen (Eds.), *Comprehensive clinical psychology* (Vol. 10, pp. 127–140). Oxford: Pergamon.

Castro, F. G., Boyer, G., & Balcazar, H. (in press). Healthy adjustment in Mexican American and other Hispanic adolescents. In R. Montemayor (Ed.), *Advances in adolescent development: Vol. 9. Adolescent experiences: Cultural and economic diversity in adolescent development.*

Castro, F. G., & Gutierres, S. (1997). Drug and alcohol use among rural Mexican Americans. In E. B. Robertson, Z. Sloboda, G. M. Boyd, L. Beatty, & N. J. Kozel (Eds.), *Rural substance abuse: State of knowledge and issues* (pp. 498–533). NIDA Research Monograph No. 168. Rockville, MD: National Institute on Drug Abuse.

Castro, F. G., Sharp, E. V., Barrington, E. H., Walton, M., & Rawson, R. A. (1991). Drug abuse and identity in Mexican Americans: Theoretical and empirical considerations. *Hispanic Journal of Behavioral Sciences, 13,* 209–225.

Castro, F. G. & Tafoya-Barraza, H. (1997). Treatment issues with Latinos addicted to cocaine and heroin. In J. G. Garcia & M. Zea (Eds.), *Psychological interventions and research with Latino populations* (pp. 191–216). Boston: Allyn & Bacon.

Chavez, E. L., Edwards, R., & Oetting, E. R. (1989). Mexican American and white American dropouts' drug use, health status, and involvement in violence. *Public Health Reports, 104,* 592–604.

Clark, L. W. (Ed.). (1993). *Faculty and student challenges in facing cultural and linguistic diversity.* Springfield, IL: Charles C Thomas.

Closser, M. H., & Blow, F. C. (1993). Special populations: Women, ethnic minorities, and the elderly. *Psychiatric Clinics of North America, 16*(1), 199–209.

Collins, R. L. (1995). Issues of ethnicity in research on prevention of substance abuse. In G. J. Botvin, S. Schinke, & M. A. Orlandi (Eds.), *Drug abuse prevention with multiethnic youth* (pp. 28–45). Thousand Oaks, CA: Sage.

Colorado, P. (1986). *Native American alcoholism: An issue of survival* [CD-ROM]. Abstract from Silver Platter File: Dissertation Abstracts Item: AAI8722511.

Comas-Díaz, L. (1997). Mental health needs of Latinos with professional status. In J. G. García & M. C. Zea (Eds.), *Psychological interventions and research with Latino populations* (pp. 142–165). Boston: Allyn & Bacon

Cross, T. L., Bazron, B. J., Dennis, K. W., & Isaccs, M. R. (1989). *Toward a culturally competent system of care.* Washington, DC: Georgetown University Child Development Center.

Cuellar, I., Harris, L. C., & Jasso, R. (1980). An acculturation scale for Mexican American normal and clinical populations. *Hispanic Journal of Behavioral Sciences, 2,* 199–217.

Dana, R. H. (1993). *Multicultural assessment perspectives for professional psychology.* Boston: Allyn & Bacon.

Desmond, D. P., & Maddox, J. F. (1984). Mexican American heroin addicts. *American Journal of Drug and Alcohol Abuse, 10,* 317–346.

DiClemente, C. C., & Scott, C. W. (1997). Stages of change: Interactions with treatment compliance and involvement. In L. S. Onken, J. D. Blaine, & J. J. Boren (Eds.), *Beyond the therapeutic alliance: Keeping the drug dependent individual in treatment* (pp. 131–156). NIDA Research Monograph No. 165. Rockville, MD: National Institute on Drug Abuse.

Echeverry, J. J. (1997). Treatment barriers: accessing and accepting professional help. In J. G. García & M. C. Zea (Eds.), *Psychological interventions and research with Latino populations* (pp. 94–107). Boston: Allyn & Bacon.

Flack, J. M., Amaro, H., Jenkins, W., Kunitz, S., Levy, J., Mixon, M., & Yu. E. (1995). Epidemiology of minority health. *Health Psychology, 14,* 592–600.

Gaines, S. O. (1994). Generic, stereotypic, and collectivistic models of interpersonal resource exchange among African American couples. *Journal of Black Psychology, 20,* 294–304.

Ginzberg, E. (1991). Access to health care for Hispanics. *Journal of the American Medical Association, 265,* 238–241.

Gorski, T. T. & Miller, M. (1982). *Counseling for relapse prevention.* Independence, MO: Herald House.

Harris, N. (1992). Afrocentrism: Concept and method. *Western Journal of Black Studies, 16*(3), 154–159.

Harwood, A. (1981). *Ethnicity and medical care.* Cambridge: Harvard University Press.

Johnson, K. W., Anderson, N. B., Bastida, E., Kramer, B. J., Williams, D., & Wong, M. (1995). Macrosocial and environmental influences on minority health. *Health Psychology, 14,* 601–612.

Johnson, L. D., O'Malley, P. M., & Bachman, J. G. (1991). *Drug use among American high school seniors, college students, and young adults, 1975–1990.* Rockville, MD: National Institute on Drug Abuse.

Johnson, L. D., O'Malley, P. M., & Bachman, J. G. (1996). *National survey results on drug use from the Monitoring the Future Study, 1975–1994: Vol. 2. College students and young adults.* Rockville, MD: National Institute on Drug Abuse.

Jorquez, J. S. (1984). Heroin use in the barrio: Solving the problem of relapse or keeping the tecato gusano asleep. *American Journal of Drug and Alcohol Abuse, 10,* 63–75.

Khantzian, E. J. (1985). The self-medication hypothesis of addictive disorders: Focus on heroin and cocaine dependence. *American Journal of Psychiatry, 142,* 1259–1264.

Kim, S., McLeod, J. H., & Shantzis, C. (1992). Cultural competence for evaluators working with Asian American communities: Some practical considerations. In M. A. Orlandi, R. Weston, & L. G. Epstein (Eds.), *Cultural competence for evaluators* (pp. 203–260). Washington, DC: Office of Substance Abuse Prevention.

Kitano, H. H. L. (1974). *Race relations.* Englewood Cliffs, NJ: Prentice Hall.

Kitano, H. H. L. (1980). *Race relations* (2nd ed.). Englewood Cliffs, NJ: Prentice Hall.

Kolden, G. G., Howard, K. I., Bankoff, E. A., Maling, M. S., & Martinovich, Z. (1997). Factors associated with treatment continuation: Implications for the treatment of drug dependence. In L. S. Onken, J. D. Blaine, & J. J. Boren (Eds.), *Beyond the therapeutic alliance: Keeping the drug dependent individual in treatment* (pp. 110–130). NIDA Research Monograph No. 165. Rockville, MD: National Institute on Drug Abuse.

Kushner, J. N., & Moss, S. (1996). *Purchasing managed care services for alcohol and other drug treatment: Es-*

sential elements and policy issues. Rockville, MD: Center for Substance Abuse Treatment.

La Fromboise, T. D., Trimble, J. E., & Mohatt, G. V. (1990). Counseling intervention and American Indian tradition: An integrative approach. *The Counseling Psychologist, 18,* 628–654.

Lettieri, D. J., Sayers, M., & Pearson, H. W. (1980). *Theories on drug abuse: Selected contemporary perspectives.* NIDA Research Monograph No. 30. Rockville, MD: National Institute on Drug Abuse.

Locke, D. C. (1998). *Increasing multicultural understanding: A comprehensive model* (2nd ed.). Thousand Oaks, CA: Sage.

Marin, G., & Marin, B. V. (1991). *Research with Hispanic populations.* Newbury Park, CA: Sage.

Marlatt, G. A., & Gordon, J. (1985). *Relapse prevention.* New York: Guilford Press.

Marlatt, G. A., Tucker, J. A., Donovan, D. M., & Vuchinich, R. E. (1997). Help-seeking by substance abusers: The role of harm reduction and behavioral-economic approaches to facilitate treatment entry and retention. In L. S. Onken, J. D. Blaine, & J. J. Boren (Eds.), *Beyond the therapeutic alliance: Keeping the drug dependent individual in treatment* (pp. 44–84). NIDA Research Monograph No. 165. Rockville, MD: National Institute on Drug Abuse.

May, P. A. (1996). Overview of alcohol abuse epidemiology for American Indian populations. In G. D. Sandefur, R. R. Rundfuss, & B. Cohen (Eds.), *Changing numbers, changing needs: American Indian demography and public health* (pp. 235–261). Washington, DC: National Academy Press.

Miller, W. R. (1989). Matching individuals with interventions. In R. K. Hester & W. R. Miller (Eds.), *Handbook of alcoholism treatment approaches* (pp. 261–271). New York: Pergamon.

Montgomery, D. E., Fine, M. A., & James-Myers, L. (1990). The development and validation of an instrument to assess an optimal Afrocentric world view. *Journal of Black Psychology, 17,* 37–54.

Moore, J. (1990). Mexican American women addicts: The influence of family background. In R. Glick & J. Moore (Eds.), *Drugs in Hispanic communities* (pp. 127–153). New Brunswick, NJ: Rutgers University Press.

Myers, H. F., Kagawa-Singer, M., Kumanyika, S. K., Lex, B. W., & Markides, K. S. (1995). Behavioral risk factors related to chronic diseases in ethnic minorities. *Health Psychology, 14,* 613–621.

Oetting, E. R., & Beauvais, F. (1987). Peer cluster theory, socialization characteristics and adolescent drug use: A path analysis. *Journal of Counseling Psychology, 34,* 205–213.

Olson, J. S., & Wilson, R. (1986). *Native Americans in the twentieth century.* Urbana: University of Illinois Press.

Onken, L. S., Blaine, J. D., & Boren, J. J. (1997). Treatment for drug addiction: It won't work if they don't receive it. In L. S. Onken, J. D. Blaine, & J. J. Boren (Eds.), *Beyond the therapeutic alliance: Keeping the drug dependent individual in treatment* (pp. 1–2). NIDA Research Monograph No. 165. Rockville, MD: National Institute on Drug Abuse.

Orlandi, M. A., Weston, R., & Epstein, L. G. (1992). *Cultural competence for evaluators.* Rockville, MD: Office of Substance Abuse Prevention.

Phinney, J. S. (1989). Stages of ethnic identity development in minority group adolescents. *Journal of Early Adolescence, 9,* 34–49.

Ramirez, M. (1991). *Psychotherapy and counseling with minorities: A cognitive approach to individual and cultural differences.* New York: Pergamon.

Red Horse, J. (1982). Clinical strategies for American Indian families in crisis. *Urban and Social Change Review, 15,* 7–19.

Robinson, R., Perry, V., & Carey, B. (1995). African Americans. In U.S. DHHS, PHS, SAMHSA., & CSAT, *Implementing cultural competence in the treatment of racial/ethnic substance abusers* (pp. 1–21). Rockville, MD: Technical Resources.

Rouse, B. A. (1995). *Substance abuse and mental health statistics sourcebook.* DHHS Publ. No. (SMA) 95–3064. Washington, DC: Government Printing Office.

Shiffman, S. & Wills, T. A. (1985). *Coping and substance abuse.* New York: Academic Press.

Snipp, C. (1989). *American Indians: The first of this land.* New York: Russell Sage Foundation.

Stonequist, E. V. (1935). The problem of the marginal man. *American Journal of Sociology, 58,* 264–281.

Stubben, J. (1997). Culturally competent substance abuse prevention research among rural American Indian communities. In E. B. Robertson, Z. Sloboda, G. M. Boyd, L. Beatty, & N. J. Kozel (Eds.), *Rural substance abuse: State of knowledge and issues* (pp. 459–483). NIDA Research Monograph No. 168. Rockville, MD: National Institute on Drug Abuse.

Sue, S. (1977). Community mental health services to minority groups: Some optimism, some pessimism. *American Psychologist, 53,* 616–624.

Sue, S. (1988). Psychotherapeutic services for ethnic minorities: Two decades of research findings. *American Psychologist, 43,* 301–308.

Sue, S., Fujino, D. C., Hu, L., Takeuchi, T., & Zane, N. W. S. (1991). Community mental health services for ethnic minority groups: A test of the cultural responsiveness hypothesis. *Journal of Consulting and Clinical Psychology, 59,* 533–540.

Sugarman, J. R., Warren, C. W., Oge, L., & Helgerson, S. D. (1992). Using the Behavioral Risk Factor Surveillance System to monitor year 2000 objectives among American Indians. *Public Health Reports, 107*, 449–456.

Suinn, R. M., Rickard-Figueroa, K., Lew, S., & Vigil, P. (1987). The Swinn-Lew Asian self-identity scale: An initial report. *Educational and Psychological Measurement, 47*, 401–407.

Szapocznik, J., & Kurtines, W. M. (1989). *Breakthroughs in family therapy with drug-abusing and problem youth.* New York: Springer.

Trimble, J. E. (1987). Self-perception and perceived alienation among American Indians. *Journal of Community Psychology, 15*(3), 316–333.

Trimble, J. E. (1995). Toward an understanding of ethnicity and ethnic identity, and their relationship with drug abuse research. In G. J. Botvin, S. Shinke, & M. A. Orlandi (Eds.), *Drug abuse prevention with multiethnic youth* (pp. 3–27). Thousand Oaks, CA: Sage.

U.S. Bureau of the Census. (1993). *We the American . . . Hispanics.* Washington, DC: Author.

U.S. Bureau of the Census. (1994). *Statistical abstract of the United States—1994* (114th ed.). Washington, DC: Government Printing Office.

U.S. Bureau of the Census. (1995a). *Statistical briefs: The nation's Asian and Pacific Islander population—1994.* Washington, DC: Author.

U.S. Bureau of the Census. (1995b). *Top 25 American Indian tribes for the United States: 1990 and 1980* [Internet]. Table 1. Internet address: wwww.census.gov/population/socdemo/.

U.S. Bureau of the Census. (1995c). *U.S. Census Bureau: The official statistics* [Internet]. Internet address: www.census.gov/population/socdemo/race/indian.

U.S. Bureau of the Census. (1995d). *U.S. Census Bureau: The official statistics* [Internet]. Table 4. Internet address: www.census.gov/population/socdemo/race/black.

U.S. Bureau of the Census. (1996). *U.S. Census Bureau: The official statistics* [Internet]. Table 2. Internet address: www.census.gov/population/socdemo/race/black.

U.S. Bureau of Indian Affairs. (1991). *American Indians today: Answers to your U.S. questions.* Washington, DC: Department of the Interior.

Watson, D.W. (1992). Prevention, intervention, and treatment of chemical dependency in the Black community. In R. L. Braithwaite & S. E. Taylor (Eds.), *Health issues in the black community* (pp. 64–78). San Francisco: Jossey-Bass.

Westermeyer, J. (1984). The role of ethnicity in substance use. *Advances in alcohol and substance abuse, 4*, 9–18.

White, J. L., & Parham, T. A. (1990). *The psychology of blacks: An African-American perspective.* Englewood Cliffs, NJ: Prentice Hall.

Yu, E. S., & Whitted, J. (1997). Task Group I: Epidemiology of minority health. *Journal of Gender, Culture, and Health, 2*, 101–112.

28

Women

Edith S. Lisansky Gomberg

Addictive behaviors involve a wide range of substances. Omitting recently discovered addictions to work, exercise, chocolate, religion, love relationships, and the like, we will confine this discussion of female addiction to psychoactive substances. These include abuse of or dependence on nicotine, banned or illegal drugs, psychoactive medications, and alcohol. The gender ratio of male abusers to female abusers varies with the substance: Men are abusers of alcohol and illegal drugs in greater numbers than women, but women outnumber men in the frequency of misuse/abuse of prescribed psychoactive medications. In nicotine use, the gender ratio is almost even. In addition to gender, there are patterns of use and abuse that vary with age, education, marital status, employment, race and ethnicity, and the alcohol/drug usage of spouse or significant other.

In a study of age differences among problem-drinking women in treatment (Gomberg, 1989b), younger alcoholic women reported use of stimulants, sedatives, marijuana, cocaine and heroin signifi-

cantly more often than older women; the same kind of age differences existed in a comparison of younger and older alcoholic men. It is probably safe to assume that similar age differences exist in the general population.

More female drinking is associated with higher educational achievement (Celantano & McQueen, 1984), and more female drinking is associated with nonmarried status (i.e., being single, divorced, separated, or cohabiting) (Wilsnack & Wilsnack, 1991). Both social drinking and heavy drinking by a woman are associated with the drinking of her significant other (Wilsnack & Wilsnack, 1991). Epidemiological surveys have consistently found women of higher income more likely to be drinkers than women of lower income. Data on employment have shown ambiguous results (Parker & Harford, 1992; Wilsnack & Wilsnack, 1992); some studies show women at home more likely to drink, and other studies show women in the workplace more likely to drink.

If we look at the percentage of drinkers by racial/

ethnic group, the largest percentage occurs among white women, followed by Native American, Hispanic, African-American, and Asian-American women in that order; for heavy drinking, the rank order is most by white women and less by black and Hispanic women (Wilson & Williams, 1989). Abstinence is highest among black women, almost as high among Hispanic women, and quite a bit lower for white women (68%, 66%, and 46%, respectively). Interestingly enough, heavy drinking occurs most frequently among white, black, and Hispanic women in the age group 35–54. How to explain these differences and similarities is not clear: We believe that the Hispanics in the United States bring their cultural attitudes about male and female behaviors with them, and until they are assimilated, those attitudes influence drinking patterns. Differences between black and white women may relate to the history of slavery, the composition of the family, perceived sex roles, and/or the significance of religious participation. Whatever the reasons, Mexican-American women are more likely to be abstainers than Anglo women (Holck, Warren, Smith, & Rochat, 1984), and black women are more likely to be abstainers than white women (Herd, 1988).

In a National Institute on Drug Abuse (NIDA) survey (1991), women between the ages of 18 and 34 reported on their use of alcohol and/or drugs in the last month. More than half the sample reported alcohol use, but 13.4% of the 18- to 25-year-old women and 11.2% of the 26- to 34-year-old women reported use of some illicit drug during the last month. Approximately 10% of the women reported marijuana use, and 1% reported use of cocaine over the same time period. Past surveys have reported more men than women using heroin, but the popularity of heroin picked up considerably during the 1990s.

When alcoholic women studied in treatment were queried about experience with drugs other than alcohol ("Have you ever used . . . ?"), 29% reported experience with cocaine and 8% with heroin (Gomberg, 1989b). A control group of age-matched nonalcoholic women reported 16% had experienced use of cocaine and 1.5% of heroin (Gomberg, 1989b). The ages of the women surveyed were 20–50. Interestingly enough, while 53% of alcoholic women had used marijuana, 50% of the control group reported similar use. Note that use and abuse are synonymous with these drugs: They are all illegal. Typical behavior of those women using illicit substances was to

prefer one while using other substances, primarily alcohol, at the same time (Lex, 1993).

As with alcohol, it is generally noted that genetic, family-related factors and environmental influences are the base for the development of polysubstance abuse (Clayton, Voss, Robbins, & Skinner, 1986; Lex, 1993). Robbins (1989) examined gender differences in *consequences* of illicit drug use: intrapsychic problems, difficulties in social functioning and consequences of substance use episodes (e.g., blackouts, disputes with significant others). Robbins's findings were that women showed more depression and distrust, and that drug-abusing men reported more difficulties in social functioning. Of great interest was the lack of gender difference in belligerence associated with drug intake. As for *comorbidity*, comparison of male and female polydrug abusers showed a higher rate for the polydrug abusers but did not differ by gender. Patterns of comorbidity did differ, however: no gender differences for schizophrenia or affective disorders, but more female reports of bulimia, anxiety, and psychosexual disorders than male (Ross, Glaser, & Stiasny, 1988).

Nicotine has a more recent history for women than for men. Nicotine has been used since the 16th century, but women smoked little until World War I. The availability of cigarettes (rather than chewing tobacco, snuff, etc.) and the relaxed standards encouraged female use of nicotine (first advertisement featuring a woman appeared in 1919). During World War II, when there was an increase in the number of women in the workplace, there was again an increase in the number of women who smoked.

Since the annual Surgeon General's reports warning of the hazards of smoking, women's cigarette use—like men's—has dropped. The latest figures from the National Center for Health Statistics (1996) show that for all women, 18 and over, 22.7% were smokers. For the whole group, the numbers were 23.7% for white women and 19.8% for black women. Even more striking is the contrast between white and black women in the 18–24 age grouping: 26.8% of white female adolescents and young adults smoked while only 8.2% of black female adolescents and young adults were smokers.

The consequences of smoking are well known (Pomerleau, Berman, Gritz, Marks, & Goeters, 1994). Association of nicotine and cancer, coronary disease, stroke, and pulmonary disease are known, and in 1986, female deaths from lung cancer surpassed the number of deaths from breast cancer. Smokers are more likely to use other drugs: more caffeine, more alcohol, more prescription drugs. There are great differences in the proportion of alcoholic women who are currently heavy smokers and matched control women of the same age and social class (Gomberg, 1989a); interestingly enough, younger women, in their 20s, have the largest proportion of smokers compared to older alcohol women. The proportions are reversed for the control women. The concern about the relationship between alcohol and tobacco has produced a research monograph from the National Institute on Alcohol Abuse and Alcoholism (Fertig & Allen, 1995).

RISK FACTORS

Those events and experiences that put a woman at risk have been best studied in the development of alcohol abuse, but it is likely that addictive behaviors in general follow approximately the same course of risk. Although it is useful to distinguish risk factors at different stages of the life span, one must first review those risk factors that are present throughout the life span. These include positive family history; heavy alcohol/drug use by peers, by spouse, or by any significant others in the woman's life; stress, distress, and coping mechanisms; impulse control; and depression (Gomberg, 1994). The important role of genetics has been described frequently (e.g., Kendler, Neale, Heath, Kessler, & Eaves, 1994). The role of family, friends, peer groups, and the community in women's alcohol/drug use has been reported for all age groups (Gomberg, 1995b; Hesselbrock et al., 1984; Schulenberg, Dielman, & Leech, 1993), and in countries other than the United States (Hammer & Vaglum, 1989). The important role not so much of early unhappy life events, but of *response* to such events (i.e., distress), has been emphasized, and the role of coping mechanisms and their adequacy/inadequacy has also been emphasized (Gomberg, 1989a). Impulse control may be more heavily a risk factor among *younger* women, but it apparently is tied up with risk taking that remains a significant antecedent variable throughout the woman's life. And finally, the association between alcohol/drug abuse and depression among women is reported very frequently in the literature; while such depression may well be a result of the drug/alcohol abuse and its consequences, it is

noted—at least for alcohol abuse—that where depression and alcoholism occur together (in 66% of women studied), depression *precedes* drinking problems (Helzer, Burnam, & McEvoy, 1991). Perhaps, for women, alcohol/drugs are an attempt at self-medication.

Adolescents

Risk factors for adolescent girls include peer use of alcohol/drugs, behavior problems and school problems, feelings of alienation, and expectancies about the effects of alcohol and/or drugs. High-risk adolescent girls report early experience with alcohol and marijuana, positive family history and a dysfunctional early family environment, many school absences, and low educational aspiration. Frequently, there is a history of antisocial or aggressive behavior, including vandalism, shoplifting, and tantrums (Gomberg, 1994). Schulenberg and his colleagues (1993) found that peer influence plays a more significant role with girls than with boys in the misuse of alcohol. Younger adolescent females used alcohol because of a combination of individual vulnerability and exposure to alcohol through their peer group. Cigarette use dropped among female adolescents from the late 1970s, leveled off in the 1980s, and began rising again in the 1990s; this was true for 8th-, 10th-, and 12th-graders surveyed in the National High School Senior survey sponsored by the National Institute of Drug Abuse (University of Michigan News and Information Service, 1995). The problem is that in addition to alcohol, tobacco is another "gateway drug" for adolescents, its use appearing before the illicit drugs are used (Kandel & Logan, 1984).

Young Adult Women

Shifts in role behaviors occur as women get into the workplace, get married, and have children. High risk for problem drinking in the workplace is associated with nontraditional occupations, low-status jobs, part-time employment, recent layoff, or unemployment (Wilsnack & Wilsnack, 1991). Women who are single, divorced, separated, or cohabiting are more likely to be using alcohol/drugs than married women. Heavy drinking and/or drug use by a significant other is a risk factor. Those women who drink and/or use drugs are more likely to be users of nicotine, and the combination of alcohol/drugs/nicotine raises the question of health consequences that may produce, in turn, more attempt at self-medication. Some of the health consequences may be gynecological: It is not clear which comes first, but problem-drinking women show a significant relationship between their drinking (Gomberg, 1986), on the one hand, and miscarriage and hysterectomy, on the other.

Middle Age

In American culture, middle age is considered loss by most women: loss of sexual attractiveness, loss of children as they leave home. Historically, the average age at which women showed up at alcoholism treatment facilities used to be between 40 and 45 (it is now closer to the mid-30s). Risk factors in this age group consist of difficulty in adaptation to new roles, "empty-nest" status, heavy spousal drinking, depression, and heavy use of prescribed psychoactive medications (Gomberg, 1994; Moos, Finney, & Cronkite, 1990). It should be noted, however, that though women may present themselves for treatment in their 40s, one study of alcoholic women in treatment in their 40s found the mean age at onset to be 36.5 (Gomberg, 1986). For reasons that are not clear, the 30s seem to be an at-risk decade; Fillmore (1987) noted that the gender ratio of risk for heavy drinking and alcohol problems, although always larger for males, converges in the 30s.

Old Age

Among older women, it is likely that the biggest drug problem in terms of numbers is misuse/abuse of prescribed psychoactive drugs (Glantz & Backenheimer, 1988). There are relatively few older women who abuse banned substances, but it should be noted that older men and women approach parity in their use of nicotine. Although the numbers are relatively small compared to other age groups, there are older women problem drinkers. Although many are undetected and others are viewed as responding to loss and widowhood with alcohol, there is evidence that there has been heavy drinking, frequently with the spouse, before widowhood (Hubbard, Santos, & Santos, 1979). Still, a recent report of elderly alcoholic women in treatment (Gomberg, 1995b) shows significantly later onset for older women than for older

men, more frequent report of a heavy-drinking spouse by the women, more depression, and more dependence on prescribed psychoactive drugs. Research reports have been few, but it would be of interest to study risk factors for older women (e.g., widowhood, retirement, or the influence of moving to a retirement community) (Alexander & Duff, 1988).

Trauma as a Risk Factor

In 1957, a review of literature about female alcoholism described "precipitating circumstances . . . some concrete situation" as more likely to be associated with female alcoholism than with male (Lisansky, 1957). The concept of such precipitants was challenged by Allan and Cooke (1985), who argued that "heavy drinking produced an increased frequency of stressful life events rather than vice versa" (p. 147). They argued further that citing such stressful precipitants was likely to "elicit sympathy" (p. 147). In the current scene, the trauma or stressful event often cited is physical and/or sexual abuse.

There are problems with definition: Incest is almost always child or adolescent abuse, whereas rape may occur at any life stage. Violence, too, may occur early in life or later; that is, it can be parental violence, spousal violence, or assault by a stranger. Studies consistently reveal a higher rate of self-reports of a history of sexual assault among alcoholic women than among nonalcoholic comparison samples (Stewart, 1996). Younger alcoholic women who do more drinking in public are significantly more likely to report an assault than the older women alcoholics. Female drinking and intoxication are more socially disapproved than similar behavior by men (George, Gournic, & McAfee, 1988; LeMasters, 1975; Marolla & Scully, 1979).

The question remains: Is childhood sexual abuse a causal factor in the development of female alcohol problems? There is a fair amount of evidence which says yes (Wilsnack & Wilsnack, 1993); women problem drinkers cite early-life abuse more frequently than non-problem-drinking women. However, it should be noted that early sexual abuse is also associated with depression among problem drinkers and that suicidal thoughts, use of drugs other than alcohol, and violent relationships characterize the lives of both problem drinkers and non-problem-drinkers with a history of early abuse (Wilsnack & Wilsnack, 1993).

SUBSTANCE ABUSE PATTERNS, COURSE, AND CONSEQUENCES

Heroin

Interviews were conducted with 170 heroin-addicted women, 175 nonaddicted women, and 202 heroin-addicted men (Binion, 1982; Colten, 1982; Tucker, 1982). Binion (1982) compared men and women addicts in family dynamics and concluded that "drug use for women was more closely related to interpersonal affiliative issues," (p. 43). Poor self-image and unhappy family situations are likely motivaters for women's drug use, but both genders are similar in preference for mother rather than father and their "need to work through early family relationships" (p. 43).

Colten (1982) compared mothering attitudes, experiences, and self-perceptions of the addicted and nonaddicted women and found few differences; addicted women expressed more concern about their adequacy as mothers. Tucker (1982) compared male and female addicts and noted a pattern unique to the women: The absence of social support is associated with the use of "non-social, potentially dysfunctional coping strategies" (p. 17).

Kosten, Rounsaville, and Kleber (1985) interviewed 522 opiate addicts in treatment; a quarter of the subjects were women. The women reported more positive family history than the men, more comorbid depression and anxiety disorders, and more medical, family, and social consequences. A recent ethnograph of women addicts in Scotland (Taylor, 1993) indicates marked differences in drug experience (e.g., women raise drug money by shoplifting, fraud, or prostitution). Those women with children deal with the constant threat of losing the children to social services.

Cocaine

Griffin, Weiss, Mirin, and Lane (1989) compared 95 male and 34 female cocaine abusers. The women reported fewer years of cocaine use (3.9 and 5.4 years' duration), and although both genders' mean age at hospitalization was in the 20s, the women were significantly younger. Fewer women than men cocaine abusers were married, but more women lived with a drug-dependent partner than did men.

Most frequent comorbid diagnoses were depression for women and antisocial personality for men. Women reported "a significantly lower level of overall social adjustment" (p. 125) than did men. Griffin et al. noted that women reported significantly less guilt as an *effect* of cocaine than did men, and they concluded that the "guilt-reducing properties of cocaine" (p. 125) may have made the drug particularly reinforcing for women.

Marijuana

Lex (1994) reviewed gender comparisons in moderate or heavy use of marijuana and stated that "there may be distinct patterns of marijuana use for men and women, e.g., women's smoking patterns are likely to reflect social influences such as weekday vs. weekend smoking. Significant differences in alcohol use distinguished heavy from light marijuana smokers" (Lex, Griffin, Mello, & Mendelson, 1986). Heavy marijuana smokers were somewhat younger than light smokers and significantly younger at onset. Job instability was associated with marijuana use by both men and women, and interpersonal factors, such as social relationships, appeared to be more significant for female smokers (Kandel, 1984).

ALCOHOL ABUSE: PATTERNS, COURSE, CONSEQUENCES

Male/female comparisons of alcohol abusers show the following:

1. *Family history.* Women report more positive family history of alcohol abuse/dependence than do men. This is apparently true for both alcoholic (Bissell & Haberman, 1984) and general populations (Schoenborn, 1991). However, although there is apparently an association between positive family history and earlier onset among men, this association did not seem to be true for alcoholic women (Gomberg, 1991).

2. *Onset.* Women have their first drink at a later age than do men (Schuckit, Anthenelli, Bucholz, Hesselbrock, & Tipp, 1995). Problem-drinking men start abusing alcohol earlier (Lisansky, 1957; Ross, 1989). Since women show up in treatment with shorter duration and apparently telescoped development of alcoholic pathology, they seek treatment ear-

lier in the course of their alcoholism than do men (Schuckit et al., 1995).

3. *Spouse drinking.* The etiological significance of spousal heavy/problem drinking as related to female problem drinking has been reported by many investigators in the United States (Gomberg, 1994) and in other countries.

4. *Depression.* Depression is linked more with female problem drinking than with male; it is estimated that about a third of problem-drinking women experienced depression antecedent to the heavy drinking (Turnbull, 1988).

5. *Quantity and contexts.* Reports disagree. There are reports that women drink smaller quantities (Bromet & Moos, 1976; Orford & Keddie, 1985). Orford and Keddie (1985) added, "The size of the difference was such that differences in body weight would not account for the difference" (p. 275). On the other hand, York and Welte (1994) reported that the amount of alcohol consumed on drinking days, expressed "as a function of total body water" (p. 745) was very similar for men and women alcoholics. There is no ambiguity about the contexts of drinking: Women drink at home, either alone or with a companion, more than do men, who are more likely to drink in public places (Gomberg, 1986).

6. *Use of drugs other than alcohol.* Women are more likely to use prescribed psychoactive drugs, such as minor tranquilizers and sedatives, both in the general population and among alcoholic women compared to alcoholic men (Ross, 1989). Data from national surveys suggest that males are more likely to be users of illicit substances, and this difference appears to be true of alcoholic men and women as well. There are age differences in use of drugs other than alcohol for both sexes, but they are alike in being multidrug abusers. Younger problem drinkers are more likely to use "street drugs."

7. *Marital status.* There is more marital disruption among women problem drinkers than among men (Lisansky, 1957; Ross, 1989). Interestingly enough, if widowhood is considered along with the marital statuses of never-married, divorced, or separated, these spouseless categories describe women alcoholics more than male alcoholics in *all* age groups studied (Gomberg, 1995b). Marriage, however, does appear to lessen the effect of "an inherited liability for drinking" (National Institute on Alcohol Abuse and Alcoholism [NIAAA], 1990).

8. *Comorbidity patterns.* Psychiatric symptoms that indicate dual diagnoses differ for men and women. Males who become alcoholic are more likely to be diagnosed as antisocial personality; women report an association of alcoholism and depressive disorder, estimates being that a quarter to a third of women alcoholics show depression *before* the onset of alcoholism. While male alcoholics often present with depression, alcoholism seems to precede depression; among women alcoholics, depression is more frequently antecedent (Helzer & Prysbeck, 1988). In the question of gender comparison in the *prevalence* of dual diagnoses, women alcoholics have a second diagnosis significantly more frequently than males. Helzer and Pryzbeck (1988), analyzing data from the NIMH Epidemiology Catchment Area Study, found 44% of male alcoholics and 65% of female alcoholics to have secondary diagnoses.

9. *Consequences: Medical.* There is general agreement that women are "more vulnerable than men to the pathophysiological consequences of drinking (NIAAA, 1992). Schenker (1997) recently put the question: "Medical consequences of alcohol abuse: Is gender a factor?" He concluded that based on current data, women are more at risk medically when alcohol is abused than men. Women alcoholics are at greater mortality risk than men; a greater percentage of female alcoholics develop alcohol-related consequences, such as cirrhosis, hemorrhagic stroke, or brain damage (NIAAA, 1992). Hepatic disorder occurs more frequently among women and after a shorter duration of heavy drinking in spite of lesser consumption. Although lifetime intake is lower than that of men, female alcoholics are apparently as vulnerable to cardiomyopathy and myopathy as male alcoholics (Urbano-Marquez et al., 1995).

Gynecological-reproductive disorders among women alcohol abusers should be noted. Menstrual difficulties and ovarian pathology have been observed, and a comparison of 301 women alcoholics with 137 matched controls showed the alcoholic women reporting significantly more history of miscarriage and hysterectomy (Gomberg, 1986). It is not a medical consequence which impinges on the woman drinker per se, but fetal alcohol effects and the fetal alcohol syndrome may occur with women who drink heavily through their pregnancies.

Both male and female alcohol abusers are at some risk for contracting AIDS. The association of alcohol use with unsafe sexual activity has been reported by Leigh (1990) and other investigators. Although the major transmission category for the HIV virus for women in the general population is injection of drugs (Windle, Carlisle-Frank, Azizy, & Windle, 1994), women alcoholics need to be aware of the risk involved in alcohol use and unsafe sex.

10. *Consequences: Familial and social.* Women problem drinkers show a higher proportion of marital disruption than reported by male problem drinkers. Whether women's alcohol problems develop before or after marital disruption is a question: Drinking probably develops as a problem for some women as a response to marital disruption and for some as an antecedent. Wilsnack and Wilsnack (1991) found the relationship between divorce/separation and women's drinking weaker than it was a generation ago. Pressure from a spouse to enter treatment is different for the genders; one report cites 28% of male patients enter treatment at the spouse's suggestion compared with 6% of the female patients (Beckman & Amaro, 1986). The same report shows women entering treatment with a higher proportion of suggestion and pressure from a parent or from the woman's children than is true among men. At the same time, it is believed that women tend to drop out of treatment more readily because of family pressure.

An alcoholic mother's or father's relationship with children is an open question. Traditionally, it was assumed that an alcoholic mother was more destructive of children's mental health, but there is some question about that; a review of relevant studies show the evidence to be ambiguous (Williams & Klerman, 1984). Clinical observation indicate that women alcoholics are more concerned about the effect of their drinking on the children than are male alcoholics. There is some limited evidence of greater guilt on this issue among women problem drinkers (Gomberg, 1989a), and there is more risk of social service intervention in families where the mother is a heavy drinker than for families where the heavy drinker is the father.

11. *Consequences: Occupational and legal.* Since men are more likely to be in the workplace than women, there may be greater consequences of alcoholism for men in this area. Interestingly enough, Beckman and Amaro (1986) reported that twice as high a percentage of women alcoholic patients were referred to treatment by their employer as men.

Since men much more frequently drink in public places than do women, they are also more likely to encounter legal difficulties, and they are more likely to be cited for driving under the influence; although the trend is toward more drinking-and-driving consequences for women, women still manifest this consequence less than do men (Wells-Parker, Popkin, & Ashley, 1996).

12. *Eating disorders.* The relationship between eating disorders and addictive behaviors has been reviewed (e.g., Krahn, 1993; Wilson, 1993). A report of eating pathology among women with alcoholism and/or anxiety disorders (Sinha et al., 1996) shows that both alcoholic women and women with anxiety disorders have significantly higher scores on an eating disorders examination, and women with both alcoholism and anxiety disorders have higher rates of bulimia.

ALCOHOL ABUSE: ASSESSMENT, TREATMENT, PROGNOSIS

Assessment

Dissatisfaction has frequently been expressed with the most widely used screening instruments as measurements of female alcoholism; the (MAST) and the (CAGE) contain items which are far less relevant to female experience with alcohol than male. One report of an attempt to identify unique measures of women's drinking problems was summarized by Saltz and Ames (1996): First, a list of "novel" indicators was incorporated into a general population instrument, and then the instrument was tested.

> Results suggest that indicators of "high capacity for alcohol," "seeking out a 'wet' environment," and "planning opportunities to drink" are promising for both women and men, with more qualified support for less "frequent illness" for women. (Saltz & Ames, 1996, p. 1041)

A report about gender differences in the Self-Administered Alcoholism Screening Test (Davis & Morse, 1987) showed women more likely to report "loss of control," to report alcohol problems in their families (gender differences in spousal heavy drinking?), to experience emotional consequences of their drinking, and to have sought help for their problems.

A comparison of "symptom profiles" among alcoholic men and women (Turnbull, Magruder-Habib, & Landerman, 1990) produced three significant sex differences: Drinking a fifth or its equivalent in 1 day was more prevalent among men, while "inability to function without drinking" and "physical fights" were more prevalent among women. McCrady and Raytek (1993) reported that "asking detailed questions about women's alcohol intake and asking these questions by beverage type" (p. 325) is a better screening approach to identifying female problem drinkers than the frequently used MAST or CAGE. They also found laboratory tests (e.g., carbohydrate-deficient use transferin) useful in identification, although questions have been raised about their value other than using them as adjuncts to clinical interviews (Russell, Chan, & Mudar, 1997): Their value is limited because "they tend to develop after years of abuse making them relatively insensitive to early problem drinking" (Russell et al., 1997, p. 436).

Braiker (1994) discussed some of the issues and methods in assessment, which is the initial stage of treatment. Assessment usually begins with a detailed inquiry about consumption, including the contexts of drinking and the consequences. A record of consumption for outpatients (i.e., self-monitoring) is recommended. Formal assessment instruments and questionnaires may be used, but at the same time, the woman's own view of her drinking problem and the role alcohol plays for her should be queried. Such an assessment might cover more than a single session and depends a good deal on the therapist's sensitivity and rapport with the client. It is important to ask about significant others' drinking, about the woman's past attempts at treatment, and about other self-destructive behaviors.

It is useful to find out about the client's past work history and her financial status. It is absolutely necessary that there be a physical examination and that the health status of the client be dealt with if there are problems.

Russell and her colleagues (1997) reviewed the work on gender and screening, discussing the issue of "gold standards" and the development of the Diagnostic Interview Schedule for epidemiological work. After a review of the MAST, CAGE, the Alcohol Use Disorders Identification Test (AUDIT; Saunders et al., 1993), and two screening instruments designed for detection to periconceptual and pregnancy risk drinking—the (T-ACE; Sokol et al., 1989) and the

(TWEAK; Russell, 1993)—they concluded that brief questionnaires are easiest to administer, least expensive, and most effective. They also concluded that gender differences in alcoholism justify the use of different gender-relevant screening methods.

Patterns of Treatment Utilization

What of women's use of treatment resources and their availability? Data have indicated that women alcohol abusers are likely to seek help earlier than men in the course of the disorder (i.e., to come for help after a shorter duration of problem drinking) (Dawson, 1996; Moos et al., 1990; Piazza, Vrbka, & Yeager, 1989; Weisner & Schmidt, 1992). Schuckit and his colleagues (1995) examined clinical data for the sequence of alcohol-related behaviors in men and women. Dawson (1996) analyzed data from the 1992 National Longitudinal Alcohol Epidemiological Survey. Both studies report male alcohol abusers presenting for treatment later than women.

A clinical study of admissions to a variety of mental health facilities including alcoholism treatment facilities (Weisner & Schmidt, 1992) showed that women alcohol abusers were more likely than males to use "non-alcohol-specific health care settings, particularly mental health services" (p. 1872). It is relevant to note that women generally use medical services more than men do; exceptions are males and females younger than 15 and the elderly, 75 and older, when the average number of physician visits approached parity (Gomberg, 1995a).

Barriers to initiating treatment contact may come from a number of sources. Some are external, for example, pressure on the woman to fill traditional sex role expectations and take time from her responsibilities as wife and mother. Another external barrier is the stigma attached to female alcoholism. Barriers also include depression and guilt (i.e., internalized states); this is particularly true of women's feeling of responsibility for child care. Women may also perceive more negative consequences in treatment, perhaps loss of a job or disrupted family relationships. There are barriers within the treatment system: stereotypes about women problem drinkers, the belief in a poorer prognosis for women, and the like. It is useful to know that women tend to choose to enter treatment in services which include services for children and in treatment facilities which provide aftercare.

Presenting Problems

When women problem drinkers arrive in treatment, they very frequently present a clinical picture of depression. In fact, a study of alcoholic women in treatment (Gomberg, 1986) indicated that mounting, unbearable depression was the major reason most of them came for help. Low self-esteem is a major issue, and guilt and shame—particularly surrounding the maternal role—are great (Gomberg, 1988). There is also a great load of anger and resentment, often directed toward spouse, family members, and others who women feel have failed them. Because they feel guilty and angry at the same time, these ambivalent attitudes are very likely to be expressed early in treatment. It has been hypothesized by some clinicians that women arrive at treatment facilities in poorer physical shape than men.Whether this proves to be a valid observation or not, the questions of physical status and appearance need early attention.

Treatment Modalities

Detoxification and the relief of physical distress are the early steps. A treatment plan may then be evaluated with other clinic workers, and such a plan may include (a) pharmacological treatment (there is disagreement among schools of therapy as to whether drugs such as antidepressants or benzodiazepines should be used); (b) evaluation of the woman's life situation, including assets and liabilities; (c) treatment recommended (counseling, psychotherapy, cognitive behavior therapies, etc.); (d) choices and availability of group work; (e) didactics, including parental effectiveness training and training in coping skills; (f) possible referrals to self-help organizations, physical rehabilitation, or vocational training; (g) the question of family therapy and its feasibility, possible advantages, and disadvantages; and (h) relapse prevention.

The genders may vary in response to different treatment modalities. Early clinical papers suggested that women did better in individual therapy and men did better in group therapy; there is, however, little empirical support for this view (Vannicelli, 1984). Related to this distinction is the evidence that women problem drinkers are more successful in medically oriented programs and men in peer-group-oriented programs (Moos et al., 1990). In the light of available information, it is a good assumption that women will do better in programs which include child care, assessment of comorbid states and treatment, support of and work with family members, and training in coping strategies.

Do women do better in gender-specific treatment facilities? In spite of some evidence which supports such facilities, evidence is not clear enough for policy recommendation.

McCrady and Raytek (1993) discussed the heterogeneity of women alcohol abusers in terms of age, socioeconomic status, ethnic and racial diversity, sexual orientation, health status, and marital status. The authors described a clinical model for treatment which includes a range of services (e.g., inpatient and residential facilities, emergency counseling, aftercare, and community referral sources). Some authors have emphasized the primary need for child care services as part of outpatient treatment and the use of vocational and educational agencies, domestic violence centers, and self-help groups such as Alcoholics Anonymous. McCrady and Raytek (1993) raised the question of treatment goals, and they discussed the reported preference—when alternatives are offered—of male problem drinkers to choose continued but controlled drinking and of women to prefer abstinence as the goal.

There have been several comprehensive reviews of research and clinical findings about alcohol-abusing women in treatment (Annis & Liban, 1980; Braiker, 1984; McCrady & Raytek, 1993; Vannicelli, 1984). All of these reviews have emphasized the limited study of women and the extent to which past research has omitted women from subject pools; this has improved somewhat in the last decade, but there is still relatively little information about the woman problem drinker in treatment. Braiker (1984) examined the evidence relating to the view of female problem drinkers as "more psychologically disturbed" than male problem drinkers: The evidence includes more psychiatric treatment reported by women and more frequent reports of depression and anxiety. There are reports of "greater symptom severity" (Weisner & Schmidt, 1992) and of more comorbidity among women (Helzer & Przbeck, 1988). All reviews of work relating to women alcoholics stress the heterogeneity of the women: Groups of women in treatment or in surveys include all ages, ethnic groups, socioeconomic classes, marital statuses, and so on. Braiker (1984) examined the various classifications or subtypes offered; these include primary versus secondary alcoholism (Schuckit, Pitts, Reich, King, & Winokur, 1969); abuse of multiple substances versus abuse of alcohol alone; age at onset; socioeconomic class; ethnicity; and marital status.

Special Considerations in Treatment

The primary emphases which have emerged from clinical and research literature of female alcoholics in treatment are attention to comorbid and physical disease aspects of female alcoholism and the need for child care. One must also consider the fact that women in treatment situations are worse off then men financially: As heads of single-parent families and as individuals relatively untrained for good salaried jobs, this is part of the reality of female alcoholism.

Prognosis and Outcome

There are few studies of predictors of treatment outcome that include both men and women subjects. Several studies with a female sample alone report indicators of poor outcome to be marital problems, dysfunctional relationships, isolation, and multiple life problems. Cronkite and Moos (1984) found unmarried women doing better in treatment, while married men did better. Rounsaville, Dolinsky, Babor, and Meyer (1987) reported that depressed alcoholic women did better in treatment than those with no comorbid condition, while men with depression did worse than those with no comorbidity. And predictably, patients with diagnoses of antisocial personality and/or other drug abuse did relatively poorly in treatment.

Although it was stated in earlier literature about female alcoholics that they had a poorer prognosis than male alcoholics, several reviews of outcome literature do not show a strong empirical base for such a contention. Annis and Liban's (1980) review reported 5 studies with significantly greater improvement among women patients, 3 studies with significantly greater improvement for males in treatment, and 15 studies with no gender difference in outcome. The conclusion of these reviewers was that women admitted to the treatment programs reviewed did *not* show poorer response to treatment. Vannicelli's (1984) review of treatment outcome studies concluded that there was little empirical evidence to substantiate these views: (a) Women have poorer

prognosis, (b) the course and quality of recovery differs by gender, (c) women should be treated by women therapists, and (d) woman-specific treatment facilities or modalities are essential for female treatment.

ALCOHOL ABUSE: PREVENTION

Primary prevention (i.e., heading off any manifestations of problem drinking) should be directed toward high-risk groups. Among adolescents, these include children in alcoholic families and high school students who are not interested in school and who manifest early sexual precocity and marijuana use. Among adult women, these include young single women who are unemployed or part-time employed, blue-collar women in high-stress occupations, depressed divorced women with young children, and women in the military; those women whose significant other drinks heavily are also at risk. Prevention campaigns are also directed toward pregnant women and toward those who manifest early eating disorder or phobic anxiety disorder.

Secondary prevention involves early intervention with those who have early indications of alcohol abuse. Settings which are useful in identifying such abusers are (a) the employment setting, (b) the medical setting, and (c) the legal system (McCrady & Raytek, 1993). Referrals in employment settings seem to relate to supervisor education, attitudes, and training. The medical setting is apparently most useful when the patient is asked in detail about her drinking per se (e.g., amount, type of beverage, contexts), rather than when a formal screening instrument is used. There are few data about women referred through the legal system; in fact, it is primarily men who are referred, and women are more likely to come with a "personal referral" (i.e., self, family, friends, an employer, or a clergyman).

Tertiary prevention is treatment, and one of the major sources of referral is through medical services; it should be noted, however, that women are likely to present with complaints of insomnia, gastritis, depression, and the like, and that heavy drinking must be inferred.

Why special prevention approaches for women? Ferrence (1984) suggested that sex differences in physiology and in social roles are relevant. A review of prevention of alcohol/drug abuse for women (Nirenberg & Gomberg, 1993) emphasized the heterogeneity within the population of women (e.g., differences in age, health status, social class, ethnic grouping) and suggested that a single message directed to *all* women is not particularly effective. The review points to the difference between individual-oriented prevention strategies and community-oriented ones. The former includes campaigns to modify and change individual behavior; the latter involves attempts to modify the law, the availability of alcohol/drugs, and so on. (These approaches are discussed in greater detail in chapters 30 and 31 of this volume.) Nirenberg and Gomberg (1993) also emphasized the need for specific messages directed toward specific target groups (e.g., "Good friends don't let their friends drive drunk"). Nonspecific messages are those directed toward improving mental health or lowering stress level. Multiple strategies, both individual and community, are more effective than any strategy alone. Further research on the pre-substance-abusing behavior of women is needed; when more is known about the early predictor behaviors, prevention strategies will be more effective.

AFTERTHOUGHTS

It was once believed that women patients had poorer prognosis than men. Although there are signs of greater severity (e.g., more comorbidity, more medical consequences, more depression, more use of pre-scribed psychoactive drugs), women seem to do as well as and, in some settings, even better than men in treatment. This occurs in spite of difficulties in getting into treatment and pressures to get out of treatment. Men and women are constituted differently, and there are strengths in those women who do recover that need to be looked for and developed in those who do not have these strengths.

SUMMARY

In addition to gender differences, there are patterns of female use and abuse of alcohol and drugs that vary with age, marital status, education, employment status, race, and ethnicity. Risk factors may be viewed as those that remain relevant throughout the life span and those that characterize adolescence, young and middle-aged adulthood, and old age. The patterns of

use and the course and consequences of abusive use of heroin, cocaine, and marijuana were reviewed briefly; there is a paucity of information about these addictions among women. The patterns, course, and consequences of alcohol use were reviewed, many of the features probably being applicable to all female drug abuse. The consequences of abusive use of alcohol are divided into medical consequences, familial and social consequences, and occupational and legal consequences. Treatment, treatment outcome, and prognosis were examined for women alcohol abusers. There is currently general agreement that neither gender has superior prognosis in treatment. Prevention of alcohol/drug abuse was discussed, and some aspects of prevention strategies were outlined.

ACKNOWLEDGMENT   This review was supported by National Institute on Alcohol Abuse and Alcoholism Grant P50 AA 07378.

Key References

Gomberg, E. S. L. (1993b). Women and alcohol: Use and abuse. *Journal of Nervous and Mental Disease, 181*(4), 211–219.

Gomberg, E. S. L. (1994). Risk factors for drinking over a woman's life span. *Alcohol Health and Research World, 18*(3), 220–227.

Gomberg, E. L. S., & Nirenberg, T. D. (Eds.). (1993). *Women and substance abuse.* Norwood, NJ: Ablex.

References

Alexander, F., & Duff, R. W. (1988). Drinking in retirement communities. *Generations, 12,* 58–61.

Allan, C. A., & Cooke, D. J. (1985). Stressful life events and alcohol misuse in women: A critical review. *Journal of Studies on Alcohol, 46,* 147–152.

Annis, H. M., & Liban, C. B. (1980). Alcoholism in women: Treatment modalities and outcomes. In O. Kalent (Ed.), *Research advances in alcohol and drug problems: Vol. 5. Alcohol and drug problems in women* (pp. 385–422). New York: Plenum.

Beckman, L. J., & Amaro, H. (1986). Personal and social difficulties faced by women and male heroin users. *Journal of Studies on Alcohol, 47*(2), 135–145.

Binion, V. J. (1982). Sex differences in socialization and family dynamics of female and men entering alcoholism treatment. *Journal of Social Issues, 38*(2), 43–58.

Bissell, L., & Haberman, P. W. (1984). *Alcoholism in the professions.* New York: Oxford University Press.

Braiker, H. B. (1984). Therapeutic issues in the treatment of alcoholic women. In S. C. Wilsnack & L. J. Beckman (Eds.), *Alcohol problems in women* (pp. 349–368). New York: Guilford Press.

Bromet, E., & Moos, R. (1976). Sex and marital status in relation to the characteristics of alcoholics. *Journal of Studies on Alcohol, 37,* 1302–1312.

Celentano, D. D., & McQueen, D. V. (1984). Multiple substance use among women with alcohol-related problems. In S. C. Wilsnack & L. J. Beckman (Eds.), *Alcohol problems in women* (pp. 91–116). New York: Guilford Press.

Clayton, R. L., Voss, J. L., Robbins, C., & Skinner, W. P. (1986). Gender differences in drug use: An epidemiological perspective. In B. A. Ray & M. C. Braude (Eds.), *Women and drugs: A new era for research* (pp. 80–99). NIDA Research Monograph No. 65, DHHS Publication No. (ADM) 86–1447. Washington, DC: Government Printing Office.

Colten, M. E. (1982). Attitudes, experiences and self-perception of heroin addicted mothers. *Journal of Social Issues, 38*(2), 77–92.

Cronkite, R. C., & Moos, R. H. (1984). Sex and marital status in relation to the treatment and outcome of alcoholic patients. *Sex Roles, 11,* 93–112.

Davis, L. J., Jr., & Morse, R. M. (1987). Age and sex differences in the responses of alcoholics to the Self-Administered Alcoholism Screening Test. *Journal of Clinical Psychology, 43,* 423–430.

Dawson, D. A. (1996). Gender differences in the probability of alcohol treatment. *Journal of Substance Abuse, 8*(2), 211–225.

Ferrence, R. G. (1984). Sex differences in the prevalence of problem drinking. In O. Kalent (Ed.), *Research advances in alcohol and drug problems: Vol. 5. Alcohol and drug problems in women* (pp. 69–124). New York: Plenum.

Fertig, J. B., & Allen, J. P. (Eds.), (1995). *Alcohol and tobacco: From basic science to clinical practice.* Research Monograph No. 30, National Institute on Alcohol Abuse and Alcoholism, NIH Publication No. 95-3931. Washington, DC: Government Printing Office.

Fillmore, K. M. (1987). Women's drinking across the adult life course as compared to men's. *British Journal of Addiction, 82,* 801–811.

George, W. H., Gournic, S. J., & McAfee, M. P. (1988). Perception of post-drinking female sexuality: Effect of gender, beverage choice, and drink payment. *Journal of Applied Social Psychology, 19,* 1295–1317.

Glantz, M. D., & Backenheimer, M. S. (1988). Substance abuse among elderly women. *Clinical Gerontology, 8,* 3–24.

Gomberg, E. S. L. (1986). Women and alcoholism: Psychosocial issues. In *Women and alcohol: Health-related issues* (pp. 78–120). Research Monograph, No. 16. National Institute on Alcohol Abuse and Alcoholism. DHHS Publication No. (ADM) 86-1139. Washington, DC: Government Printing Office

Gomberg, E. S. L. (1988). Shame and guilt issues among women alcoholics. *Alcoholism Treatment Quarterly, 4*(2), 139–155.

Gomberg, E. S. L. (1989a). Alcoholic women in treatment: Early histories and early problem behaviors. *Advances in Alcohol and Substance Abuse, 8*(2), 133–147.

Gomberg, E. S. L. (1989b). Alcoholism in women: Use of other drugs. Abstract. *Alcoholism: Clinical and Experimental Research, 13,* 338.

Gomberg, E. S. L. (1991). Comparing alcoholic women with positive vs. negative family history. Abstract. *Alcoholism: Clinical and Experimental Research, 15*(2), 363.

Gomberg, E. S. L. (1994). Risk factors for drinking over a woman's life span. *Alcohol Health and Research World, 18*(3), 220–227.

Gomberg, E. S. L. (1995a). Health care provision for men and women. In M. V. Seeman (Ed.), *Gender and psychopathology* (pp. 359–376). Washington, DC: American Psychiatric Association Press.

Gomberg, E. S. L. (1995b). Older women and alcohol: Use and abuse. In M. Galanter (Ed.), *Recent developments in alcoholism: Vol. 12. Women and alcoholism* (pp. 61–79). New York: Plenum.

Griffin, M. L., Weiss, R. D., Mirin, S. M., & Lane, U. (1989). A comparison of male and female cocaine abusers. *Archives of General Psychiatry, 46,* 122–126.

Hammer, T., & Vaglum, P. (1989). *The increase in alcohol consumption among women: A phenomenon related to accessibility or stress?*

Helzer, J. E., Burnam, A., & McEvoy, L. T. (1991). Alcohol abuse and dependence. In L. Robins & D. A. Regier (Eds.), *Psychiatric disorders in America: The epidemiologic catchment area study* (pp. 81–115). New York: Free Press.

Helzer, J. E., & Pryzbeck, T. R. (1988). The co-occurrence of alcoholism with other psychiatric disorders is the general population and its impact on treatment. *Journal of Studies on Alcohol, 49*(3), 219–224.

Herd, D. (1988). Drinking by black and white women: Results from a national survey. *Social Problems, 35,* 493–505.

Hesselbrock, M. N., Hesselbrock, W. M., Babor, T. F., Stabenau, J. R., Meyer, R. E., & Weinman, M. A. (1984). Antisocial behavior, psychopathology and problem drinking in the natural history of alcoholism. In D. W. Goodwin, K. T. Van Dusen, & S. A.

Mednick (Eds.), *Longitudinal research in alcoholism* (pp. 197–214). Boston: Kluwer-Nijoff Academic.

Holck, S. E., Warren, C. W., Smith, J. C., & Rochat, R. W. (1984). Alcohol consumption among Mexican-American and Anglowomen: Results of a survey along the U.S. Mexico border. *Journal of Studies on Alcohol, 45,* 149–154.

Hubbard, R. W., Santos, J. F., & Santos, M. A. (1979). Alcohol and older adults: Overt and covert influences. *Social Casework, 60,* 166–170.

Kandel, D. B. (1984). Marijuana users in young adulthood. *Archives of General Psychiatry, 41,* 200–209.

Kandel, D. B., & Logan, J. A. (1984). Patterns for drug use from adolescence to young adulthood: 1. Periods of risk for initiation, continued use and discontinuation. *American Journal of Public Health, 74,* 660–666.

Kendler, K. S., Neale, M. C., Heath, A. C., Kessler, R. C., & Eaves, L. J. (1994). A twin family study of alcoholism in women. *American Journal of Psychiatry, 151,* 707–715.

Kosten, T. B., Rounsaville, B. J., & Kleber, H. D. (1985). Ethnic and gender differences among opiate addicts. *International Journal of Addictions, 20,* 1143–1162.

Krahn, D. D. (1993). The relationship of eating disorders and substance abuse. In E. S. L. Gomberg & T. D. Nirenberg (Eds.), *Women and substance abuse* (pp. 286–313). Norwood, NJ: Ablex.

Leigh, B. (1990). The relationship of substance abuse during sex to high-risk sexual behavior. *Journal of Sex Research, 27,* 199–213.

LeMasters, E. E. (1975). *Blue collar aristocrats.* Madison: University of Wisconsin Press.

Lex, B. W. (1993). Women and illicit drugs: Marijuana, heroin, and cocaine. In E. S. L. Gomberg & T. D. Nirenberg (Eds.), *Women and substance abuse* (pp. 162–190). Norwood, NJ: Ablex.

Lex, B. W. (1994). Women and substance abuse. A general review. In R. R. Watson (Ed.), *Addictive behaviors in women* (pp. 279–327). Totowa, NJ: Humana Press.

Lex, B. W., Griffin, M. L., Mello, N. K., & Mendelson, J. H. (1986). Concordant alcohol and marijuana use in women. *Alcohol, 3,* 193–200.

Lisansky, E. S. (1957). Alcoholism in women: Social and psychological concomitants. *Quarterly Journal of Studies on Alcohol, 18*(4), 588–623.

Marolla, J. A., & Scully, D. H. (1979). Rape and psychiatric vocabularies of motive. In E. S. L. Gomberg & V. Franks (Eds.), *Gender and disordered behavior* (pp. 301–318). New York: Brunner-Mazel.

McCrady, B. S., & Raytek, H. (1993). Women and substance abuse: Treatment modalities and outcomes.

In E. S. L. Gomberg & T. D. Nirenberg (Eds.), *Women and substance abuse* (pp. 314–338). Norwood, NJ: Ablex.

Moos, R. H., Finney, J. W., & Cronkite, R. C. (1990). *Alcoholism treatment, context, process and outcome.* New York: Oxford University Press.

National Center for Health Statistics (1996). *United States, 1995.* Hyattsville, MD: Public Health Service.

National Institute on Alcohol Abuse and Alcoholism. (1990, October). *Alcohol Alert (No. 10, PH290): Alcohol and Women* (4 pp.).

National Institute on Alcohol Abuse and Alcoholism. (1992). *Alcohol-induced medical consequences in women* (2 pp.).

National Institute on Drug Abuse. (1991). *National household survey on drug abuse: Population estimates, 1989.* Washington, DC: U.S. Department of Health and Human Services.

Nirenberg, T. D., & Gomberg, E. S. L. (1993). Prevention of alcohol and drug problems among women. In E. S. L. Gomberg & T. D. Nirenberg (Eds.), *Women and substance abuse* (pp. 339–359). Norwood, NJ: Ablex.

Orford, J., & Keddie, A. (1985). Gender difference in the functions and effects of moderate and excessive drinking. *British Journal of Clinical Psychology, 24,* 265–279.

Parker, D. A., & Harford, T. C. (1992). Gender-role attitudes, job competition and alcohol consumption among women and men. *Alcoholism: Clinical and Experimental Research 16*(2), 159–165.

Piazza, N. J., Vrbka, J. L., & Yeager, R. D. (1989). Telescoping of alcoholism in women alcoholics. *International Journal of the Addictions, 24,* 19–28.

Pomerleau, C. S., Berman, B. A., Gritz, E. R., Marks, J. L., & Goeters, S. (1994). Why women smoke. In R. R. Watson (Ed.), *Addictive behaviors in women* (pp. 39–70). Totowa, NJ: Human Press.

Robbins, C. (1989). Sex differences in psychosocial consequences of alcohol and drug abuse. *Journal of Health and Social Behavior, 30,* 117–130.

Ross, H. E. (1989). Alcohol and drug abuse in treated alcoholics: A comparison of men and women. *Alcoholism: Clinical and Experimental Research, 13,* 810–816.

Ross, H. E., Glaser, F. B., & Stiasny, S. (1988). Sex differences in the prevalence of psychiatric disorders in patients with alcohol and drug problems. *British Journal of Addiction, 83,* 1179–1192.

Rounsaville, B. J., Dolinsky, C. S., Babor, T. F., & Meyer, R. E. (1987). Psychopathology as a predictor of treatment outcome in alcoholics. *Archives of General Psychiatry 44,* 505–513.

Russell, M. (1993) TWEAK. In N. Burke & D. Caldwell (Eds.), Maternal substance use assessment methods reference manual. *A review of screening and clinical assessment: Alcohol, tobaco and other drugs.* Rockville, MD: CSAP National Resource Center for the Prevention of Perinatal Abuse and Alcohol and Other Drugs.

Russell, M., Chan, A. W. K., Mudar, P. (1997). Gender and screening for alcohol-related problems. In R. W. Wilsnack & S. C. Wilsnack (Eds.), *Gender and alcohol: Individual and social perspectives* (pp. 417–444). New Brunswick, NJ: Rutgers Center of Alcohol Studies.

Saltz, R., & Ames, G. (1996). Combining methods to identify new measures of women's drinking problems: 2. The survey stage. *Addiction, 91,* 1014–1051.

Saunders, J. B., Aasland, O. G., Babor, T. E., de la Fuente, J. B., Grant, M. (1993). Development of the Alcohol Use Disorders Identification Test (AUDIT): WHO collaborative project on early detection of persons with harmful alcohol consumption, Part 2. *Addictions, 88,* 791–804.

Schenker, S. (1997). Medical consequences of alcohol abuse: Is gender a factor? *Alcoholism: Clinical and Experimental Research, 21,* 179–180.

Schoenborn, C. A. (1991). *Exposure to alcoholism in the family: United States, 1988* (13 pp.). Advance Data, Vital and Health Statistics of the National Center for Health Statistics. HHS, Centers for Disease Control, Washington, DC: Government Printing Office.

Schuckit, M. A., Anthenelli, R. M., Bucholz, K. K., Hesselbrock, V. M., & Tipp, J. (1995). The time course of development of alcohol-related problems in men and women. *Journal of Studies on Alcohol, 56,* 218–225.

Schuckit, M. A., Pitts, F. N., Jr., Reich, T., King, L. J., & Winokur, G. (1969). Alcoholism: 1. Two types of alcoholism in women. *Archives of General Psychiatry 20,* 301–306.

Schulenberg, J., Dielman, T. E., & Leech, S. L. (1993, June). *Individual versus social causes of alcohol misuse during early adolescence: A three wave prospective study.* Paper presented at the Research Society on Alcoholism, San Antonio, TX.

Sinha, R., Robinson, J., Merikangas, K., Wilson, G. T., Rodin, J., & O'Malley, S. (1996). Eating pathology among women with alcoholism and/or anxiety disorders. *Alcoholism: Clinical and Experimental Research, 20,* 1184–1191.

Sokol, R. J., Martier, S. S., & Ager, J. W. (1989). The T-ACE questions: Practical prenatal detection of risk-drinking. *American Journal of Obstetrics and Gynecology, 100,* 863–870.

Stewart, S. H. (1996). Alcohol abuse in individuals exposed to trauma: A critical review. *Psychological Bulletin, 120,* 83–112.

Taylor, A. (1993). *Women drug users: An ethnography of a female injecting community.* New York: Clarenden Press.

Tucker, M. B. (1982). Social support and coping: Applications for the study of female drug abuse. *Journal of Social Issues, 38*(2), 117–138.

Turnbull, J. E. (1988). Primary and secondary alcoholic women. *Social Casework: The Journal of Contemporary Social Work* 290–297.

Turnbull, J. E., Magruder-Habib, K. M., & Landerman, R. (1990). Similarities of symptom profiles among alcoholic men and women. Presentation, Research Society on Alcoholism, Toronto. *Alcoholism: Clinical and Experimental Research,14,* 347.Abstract 501.

University of Michigan News and Information Service. (1995, July 17). *Smoking rates climb among American teenagers.*

Urbano-Marquez, A., Estruch, R., Fernandez Sola, J., Nicolas, J. M., Pare, J. C., & Rubin, E. (1995). The greater risk of alcoholic cardiomyopathy and myopathy in women compared with men. *Journal of the American Medical Association, 274*(2), 149–154.

Vannicelli, M. (1984). Treatment outcomes of alcoholic women: The state of the art in relation to sex bias and expectancy effects. In S. C. Wilsnack & L. J. Beckman (Eds.), *Alcohol problems in women* (pp. 369–412). New York: Guilford Press.

Weisner, C., & Schmidt, L. (1992). Gender disparities in treatment. *Journal of the American Medical Association, 268*(14), 1872–1876.

Wells-Parker, E., Popkin, C. L., & Ashley, M. (1996). Drinking and driving among women: Gender trends, gender differences. In J. M. Howard et al. (Eds.), *Women and alcohol: Issues for prevention research* (pp. 215–238). NIAAA Research Monograph 32. NIH Publication No. 96-3817. Washington, DC: Goverment Printing Office.

Williams, C. N., & Klerman, L. V. (1984). Female alcohol abuse: Its effect on the family. In S. C. Wilsnack & L. J. Beckman (Eds.), *Alcohol problems in women* (pp. 280–312). New York: Guilford Press.

Wilsnack, R. W., & Wilsnack, S. C. (1992). Women, work and alcohol: Failure of simple theories. *Alcoholism: Clinical and Experimental Research, 16*(2), 172–179.

Wilsnack, S. C., & Wilsnack, R. W. (1991). Epidemiology of women's drinking. *Journal of Substance Abuse, 3*(2), 133–158.

Wilsnack, S. C., & Wilsnack, R. W. (1993). Epidemiological research on women's drinking: Recent progress and directions for the 1990s. In E. S. L. Gomberg & T. D. Nirenberg (Eds.), *Women and substance abuse*, 62–99.

Wilson, G. T. (1993). Binge eating and addictions disorders. In C. C. Fairburn & G. T. Wilson (Eds.), *Binge eating: Nature, assessment and treatment* (pp. 97–122). New York: Guilford Press.

Wilson, R. W., & Williams, G. D. (1989). Alcohol use and abuse among U.S. minority groups: Results from the 1983 National Health Interview Survey. In D. Spiegler et al. (Eds.), *Alcohol use among U.S. ethnic minorities* (pp. 399–410). NIAAA Research Monograph 18, DHHS Publ. No., (ADM) 89–1435. Washington, DC: Government Printing Office.

Windle, M., Carlisle-Frank, P., Azizy, L., & Windle, R. C. (1994). Women and health-related behaviors: Interrelations among substance use, sexual behaviors, and Acquired Immunodeficiency Syndrome (AIDS). In R. R. Watson (Ed.), *Addictive behaviors in women* (pp. 415–436). Totowa, NJ: Humana Press.

York, J. L., & Welte, J. W. (1994). Gender comparisons of alcohol consumption in alcoholic and nonalcoholic populations. *Journal of Studies on Alcohol, 55,* 743–750.

29

Gay Men, Lesbians, and Bisexuals

Rodger L. Beatty

Michelle O. Geckle

James Huggins

Carolyn Kapner

Karen Lewis

Dorothy J. Sandstrom

The goal of this chapter is to assist those individuals who treat persons with substance abuse to better comprehend the unique substance abuse issues and needs within the lesbian and gay male communities. Overall, practitioners who treat gays for substance abuse will be more effective if they comprehend (a) how these communities are constituted and defined, (b) the distinctive patterns and unique risk factors of substance abuse within gay communities, and (c) treatment options and resources for lesbians and gay men.

As a whole, individuals oriented to members of the same sex are often referred to as homosexuals. However, because the term *homosexual* is often considered too clinical and focused solely on sexual behavior, the term *gay* will be used to refer to both gay men and lesbian women throughout this chapter, except where specific reference is being made to lesbian women. The term *gay* reflects more fully the social, cultural, and affective dimensions of this subculture. The term *bisexual* has not been adequately defined nor sufficiently utilized in previous or current research on substance use to distinguish specific drinking patterns; therefore, no conclusions can be made, and bisexuals will not be discussed separately in this chapter.

Lesbians and gay men are a substantial and increasingly visible minority of the American population (D'Augelli & Patterson, 1995). Gays may be "passing" as heterosexual, living as an integral part of the larger culture and wanting to remain that way, or immersed in a subculture with its own norms, mores, and activities, which differ from those of the larger culture. Each subdivision of the gay community has its own distinct culture with its own books, magazines, newspapers, music, activities, interests, and meeting places. Additionally, within each subculture, there are many smaller subdivisions. In other words, the terms *lesbian* and *gay* refer not to unified, sharply definable communities, but to loose aggregates of people who are diverse in character, values, and attitudes. Members of some of these subcultures may never intermix, while others may work together on common social and political goals and/ or may share certain social activities.

LESBIANS AND GAY IDENTITY DEVELOPMENT AND EXPRESSION

According to Cabaj (1989), three characteristics distinguish sexual minorities from everyone else: (a) having a sexual orientation that leads to the desire to have affectional, sexual, sexual fantasy, and/or social needs met more often by a same-sex partner than an opposite-sex partner; (b) needing to negotiate a process of self-identity and self-recognition as a gay man or woman who is different from the majority—a process known as *coming out*; and (c) confronting widespread, culturally sanctioned, and insidious dislike, hatred, and/or fear of gays, homosexual sexual activity, and homosexual feelings, known as *homophobia*.

To understand sexual minorities, it is important to distinguish between the terms *gender identity* and *gender role*, which are often erroneously used interchangeably, and to emphasize the difference between sexual orientation and sexual behavior. *Sexual orientation* refers to the desire for sex, love, and affection from or with another person, including sexual fantasies, whereas *sexual behavior* refers strictly to sexual activities or conduct. For any individual, sexual behavior may not always or consistently coincide with the more primary and enduring sexual orientation. For example, a man could be homosexual in orientation yet behave heterosexually. *Gender identity* is simply the sense of self as male or female. *Gender role* refers to the propensity to carry out "everyday" behaviors which are viewed as appropriately masculine or feminine by the mainstream/dominant culture.

Gay men and lesbians have been described as men or women whose primary sexual and affectional attractions are to men or women, respectively, and who have self-identified as a sexual minority. That is, they recognize through the use of language or symbolic expression that their sexual orientation places them apart from the sexual mainstream, even though they may not describe themselves as "gay" or "lesbian." Central to the definition is the view that gay men and lesbian women see their relationships with and connections to the same sex as primary, whether acted upon or not, and identify themselves as outside the sexual mainstream.

Golden (1987) described how some gay women perceive choice as an important element in their sexual orientations. Gay men, on the other hand, typically perceive their sexual orientation as a given, a central aspect of themselves, and feel that choice has little to do with it. Lesbians appear to perceive affectional orientation and relationship dynamics as central to self-definition, while gay men appear to view sexual behavior and sexual fantasy as central. It may even be that the nature of sexual orientation is different for men and women.

Substance abuse treatment issues become complicated when alcohol and/or drugs are used by gay clients to conceal inner conflict related to issues surrounding same-sex attraction, a not uncommon or necessarily conscious process. Hence, presented here is a basic, and widely utilized, model of gay identity development (Coleman, 1985) which conceives of the coming-out stages as (a) precoming out (awareness of a sense of difference which is not yet identified as same-sex attraction); (b) coming out (awareness and acceptance of same-sex attraction and disclosure of this to others); (c) exploration (experimentation with same-sex social and sexual activity); (d) first relationships (meeting needs for intimacy and a more stable, committed relationship); and (e) integration (of a gay sexual orientation into the larger self-concept with an overall positive valence). Throughout this process, denial, ambivalence, personal and interpersonal conflicts, and resulting crises of identity may occur. Individual reactions vary and may shift between acting out and internalization. Thus, aggression, suicidal ideation, and substance abuse are all major concerns in need of monitoring throughout the coming-out process.

In summary, to be identified as gay is more complex than is suggested by the typical dichotomies prevalent in American thinking. It is a complex association of sexual orientation, sexual behaviors, gender identity, and gender role, as well as possible identification with a subculture and a defined or diffuse community. Different cultural subgroups experience different alcohol and drug abuse patterns and problems.

EPIDEMIOLOGY

Earlier research (Fifield, DeCresenzo, & Latham, 1975; Lohrenz, Connely, Coyne, & Spare, 1978; Saghir & Robins, 1973) has reported rates of alcoholism and problem drinking to be about 33% of the gay population as compared to 10–12% of the general population. However, these early studies suffer from substantial methodological flaws (poor controls, poor samples, and failure to have uniform definitions of alcohol dependency and homosexuality). More recent studies (McKirnan & Peterson, 1992; Ostrow & Kessler, 1993; Stall & Wiley, 1988) have reported less dramatic contrasts between heterosexual and gay/lesbian rates of heavy drinking and of drinking-related problems, and these studies represent substantial methodological improvements in sampling lesbian/gay populations.

In a recent review, Bux (1996) drew four conclusions from comparisons of previous and recent research relative to gays' use of alcohol. First, gays appear to be less likely than heterosexuals to abstain from alcohol consumption. Second, gay men appear to exhibit little or no elevated risk for alcohol abuse or heavy drinking, using categories defined by the National Institute of Alcoholism and Alcohol Abuse as 60 or more drinks per month, relative to heterosexual men. Third, lesbians appear to be at higher risk for heavy drinking, and possibly for drinking-related problems as well, than heterosexual women. At times, lesbians have been found to match gay and heterosexual men in rates of heavy and/or problem drinking. Fourth, studies examining trends in drinking have reported recent decreases in drinking and alcohol-related problems among gay men. This may reflect the community's response to the health threat of AIDS, changes in community norms around drinking and other health-related behaviors, and declining rates of alcohol use among the general population, as reported by Midanik and Clark (1994) in their study of the demographic distributions of U.S. drinking patterns from 1984 to 1990.

The demographic, lifestyle, and mental health information on 1,925 lesbians from 50 states who participated as respondents in the National Lesbian Health Care Survey (1984–1985) is the most comprehensive study of U.S. lesbians to date (Bradford, Ryan, & Rothblum, 1994). Survey respondents indicated that 30% of them drank alcohol more than once per week, 6% drank daily, and 16% of the sample had sought counseling for substance abuse problems. The results of this survey correspond with those of McKirnan and Peterson's (1989) large-scale survey of 3,400 gays and lesbians in the Chicago area. The highest rates of alcohol use among lesbians were re-

ported by those aged 55 or older, least open about their sexual orientation, and least connected to the organized lesbian community.

In summary, more recent research on substance use indicates higher rates of alcohol-related problems among gays than among heterosexuals, but these differences do not appear to be as great as many of the earlier, but methodologically flawed, studies indicated. Rates of heavy drinking are comparable among gay and heterosexual men, but higher among lesbian than among heterosexual women.

Discrete research on use of drugs other than alcohol is limited for gays; however, on occasions where drug use was discussed, the most frequent associations were with noninjectable drugs, referred to as *recreational drugs*, such as marijuana, amyl nitrates, ecstasy, crystallized methamphetamine, and crack cocaine. Prior to 1978, gays indulged in the use of volatile nitrates more than any other group (Sigell, Kapp, Fusaro, Nelson, & Falck, 1978). Nitrates are used primarily during sexual activity because they reduce social and sexual inhibitions, heighten sexual arousal, relax the sphincter, and are thought to prolong orgasm. Nitrates have become popular drugs that are inhaled to alter consciousness, enhance meditation, stimulate dancing, and intensify sexual experience (Ortiz & Rivera, 1988).

Over half of gay/bisexual respondents, compared to 33% of the overall sample in three California communities, reported injecting methamphetamine as the primary mode of use (Frosch et al., 1996). San Francisco's Operation Concern reports that in their treatment-seeking gay and bisexual men, methamphetamine has replaced alcohol as the most common drug use mentioned. Much of methamphetamine's attraction for gays is its initial aphrodisiac effects (National Association of Lesbian and Gay Addictions Professionals [NALGAP], 1996).

Mailed surveys were returned by 1,067 self-identified gays and lesbians to the Trilogy Project, a 5-year longitudinal study of social issues relevant to gay men and lesbians living in and around Lexington and Louisville, Kentucky (Skinner & Otis, 1992). The data reveal that within this population, lesbians are more likely than gay men to experiment with different types of drugs sometime in their life but do not currently use these drugs. Lesbians are more likely to currently use marijuana than any other illicit drug. Gay men are significantly more likely than lesbians to have ever used and to currently use inhalants.

Prevalence rates for past-year and past-month use of stimulants and sedatives are also significantly higher for gay men than for lesbians. Gay men are significantly more likely to currently use alcohol while significantly less likely than lesbians to have ever used or to currently use cigarettes.

Research indicates that a problem with substance use and abuse may exist in the gay community. While the extent of that problem is uncertain and, in fact, may not be as pervasive as previous research indicates, it does exist. One needs to recognize both the differences and the similarities between gay and lesbian substance abusers and their nongay/lesbian counterparts. Given this reported rate of substance abuse problems among gays, are there particular risk factors that may be contributing to this phenomenon?

RISK FACTORS AND CONSEQUENCES

Although numerous theories have emerged to explain the etiology of problem drinking in gays, empirical support for most of these theories is lacking. Among the factors that do enjoy at least some support as possible etiological influences are: (a) the role of the gay bar as a primary socialization vehicle, (b) fewer family and societal supports, (c) socioeconomic and psychosocial conditions associated with minority status, and most significant, (d) stresses related to the developmental process of gay identity formation/coming out and (e) internalized homophobia.

Gay bars are one of the major social institutions in the gay community. Until recently, gay bars in most cities were one of the few legitimate places where gays could meet and socialize with other gays. As many gays are hidden to various degrees about their sexual orientation, the gay bar is perceived as a relatively safe place where one can openly be one's true self. Only large cities offer alternatives to gay bars, such as community centers, coffee houses, and clubs, and many of these also serve alcoholic beverages. Formal and informal communication and activity networks of the gay community continue to revolve around the gay bars and the concomitant use of alcohol. Thus, alcohol has been built into the fabric of gay and lesbian social life. Furthermore, many gays perceive the bars as the major and often the only sanctuary from an uninformed, rejecting, or hostile world (Nardi, 1982; Ziebold & Mongeon, 1982). The bars provide an "it's okay to be me" atmosphere

and may be the only place available to meet and be with other sexual minorities. Drinking for sexual minorities may also be a way of relaxing in order to "fit into" their communities, to provide the courage to approach other gays, and to deal with the fear of rejection by gay peers. Thus, drinking may be used by gays not solely or always to escape from something, but to join something: the gay community. For better or ill, the primary means of identification and connection with their own community for most gays remain the gay bars (Kus, 1988; McKirnan & Peterson, 1989).

A second risk factor for substance abuse among gays and lesbians has its basis in the fact that public attitudes and private sentiment about gays are still largely negative. Gays are openly barred or more subtly discouraged from participation in most community institutions which typically sustain heterosexuals (e.g., organized religion). While it has been proposed that the natural remission of heavy drinking and alcohol-related problems among young adults in the general population is associated with an increase in conventionality and social stability achieved through the assumption of adult social roles such as marriage and parenthood, these attenuating factors do not operate for most gays. Marriage is not an option, and gay "commitment ceremonies" are not accorded equal status, legitimacy, or rights. Parenthood, while certainly an option, can be an arduous and complicated undertaking for gays, so that only relatively few gays attain this status (Paul, Stall, & Bloomfield, 1991).

Many gays face life without the usual, full complement of benefits from family, peer, and friendship supports. It is the rare gay person who enjoys undiminished support from family, intimates, and associates following disclosure of gay sexual orientation. Some degree of ostracism is probably the norm, and complete ostracism is not uncommon. Creating and maintaining a positive sexual minority identity and larger self-concept while attempting to relate as mature adults to family and friends present daily challenges and stresses for gays that have no counterpart in the lives of heterosexuals. Young gays are particularly vulnerable in this respect. Alienation, isolation, loneliness, and excessive reliance on an intimate partner and/or a small number of select and trusted friends can all serve to increase the risk of substance abuse for gay men and lesbians (Neisen, 1993). Stress-related use of alcohol was strongly correlated with alcohol problems; a substantial number of both gay males and lesbians (23% and 13%, respectively) reported using alcohol at least half the time to cope with personal stress (Paul et al., 1991).

Finally, there are socioeconomic and psychosocial realities of belonging to a minority community that may negatively influence rates and patterns of substance abuse among gays and lesbians. McKirnan and Peterson (1992) found underemployment, residential instability, low occupational status, and religious nonaffiliation to be associated with problem drinking for gay men, although not for lesbians. However, the lesbian participants in the National Lesbian Health Care Survey reported that almost one third used tobacco on a daily basis, 30% drank alcohol more than once a week, and 6% drank daily. These lesbian participants actually constituted a more "privileged" group, or "best case scenario," among lesbians, as well as in comparison to women in the general population. The majority of survey participants were white, young, well educated, metropolitan, and employed full time in professional and managerial positions and thus were not representative of rural and isolated settings. Lesbians who were not represented in the study are more likely to be cut off from a sympathetic community and therefore to be at greater risk of distress and need for supportive help. While "privileged," these lesbians were also found to be significantly underpaid relative to educational status (all but 12% earned less than $30,000 per year, and 64% earned less than $20,000). One is left to wonder about the rates of substance abuse and related problems among poor and rural lesbians.

Additionally, a high prevalence of stressful life events and behaviors related to substance abuse and mental health problems were found among the national lesbian sample. Over one third had been physically abused, one third had been raped or sexually assaulted, and nearly one fifth had been victims of incest while growing up. Unfortunately, the rate of incest among lesbians (18.7%) is quite similar to the rate reported among the general female population (16%; Russell, 1984). Childhood sexual abuse among gay men, and its profound impact on their mental health and substance use patterns, has only very recently been acknowledged by both health care professionals and the gay community itself. Bartholow et al. (1994) focused on various health behaviors associated with a history of childhood and adolescent sexual abuse among approximately 1,000 adult gay men attending urban sexually transmitted disease clinics. Sexual abuse was found to be associated with mental health counseling and hospitalization, psychoactive substance use, depression, suicidal thoughts and actions, sexual identity development disruption, and HIV risk behavior.

Sexual minority status may entail personal confrontation with prejudicial attitudes, discriminatory behaviors, unfairness and unequal power, hatred, and verbal, emotional, or physical abuse. Minimally, gays can expect to be the object of strong antipathy. This pervasive discrimination can lead to actual or fear of loss of job and residence and rejection by family and peers, which in turn might lead to a "double" life in an attempt to keep the discrimination from occurring. The overall result of these facts of life can be immeasurable psychological stress, and many gays seek an escape with alcohol and other psychoactive substances. Mental health professionals have long experience with what the available literature suggests: Alcohol use among gays is associated with reported low self-esteem, shame, guilt, depression, anxiety, anger, frustration, isolation, problems concerning sexuality and relationships, and the patronizing of a lesbian or gay bar in social interaction. These problems are likely to be exacerbated for gays who are also members of racial/ethnic minority groups, since they are subjected to both antigay and racist attitudes and treatment. Moreover, they are stigmatized, in turn, by their own racial/ethnic and sexual minority communities, and they occupy a peripheral position in these, as well as within the dominant/mainstream culture (Icard & Traunstein, 1987).

Bux (1996) emphasized that research on the issue of gay/lesbian cultural factors that facilitate alcohol abuse has been sparse and results are inconclusive. Inconsistencies in the theoretical accounts warrant caution in accepting them uncritically, and he further asserted that there is little reason at present to conclude that a particular gay or lesbian "lifestyle" contributes to heavy or problem drinking. It will be essential in future research to separate preconceptions from reality in developing models that account for such factors in the development of drinking problems.

ASSESSMENT ISSUES

Assessment of drug or alcohol use in the gay client, as in any client, must go beyond superficial and cursory questions concerning consumption. Specifics concerning quantity and frequency of use must be obtained, along with details as to the impact of drinking or drug use on major functional areas in clients' lives. At minimum, therapists should know the impact of drug and alcohol use on physical and psychological well-being, sexual functioning, functioning in intimate relationships, and socially and within the family, and whether the client has experienced legal or financial problems as result of alcohol/drug use. It is possible that the gay client may request therapy with an initial complaint of drug or alcohol problems; however, this presentation is rare. More commonly, clients present with global reports of anxiety or depression or with specific problems in one or more life areas that are the result of drug or alcohol abuse (McCandlish, 1982). It is incumbent upon therapists to assist clients in associating their presenting problems with their drug or alcohol use, and this cannot be done if the therapist is uninformed of details of this use.

There are no specific assessment instruments that have been developed and tested relative to issues such as sexual orientation and stages of "coming out" and so on. Treatment facilities utilize standard assessments; therefore, the initial assessment needs to be comprehensive and gay-sensitive. Finnegan and McNally (1987) asserted that counselors need to take a thorough psychosocial-sexual history in a caring, relaxed manner. They also reported that gay men and lesbians who have been in treatment repeatedly reported they felt better when their counselors asked questions that gave positive signals. The importance of asking these questions is underscored by the many gay and lesbian alcoholics who report they were never asked about their sexual orientation during treatment. Substance abuse, among any population, presents a myriad of challenges for therapists. For the gay population, basic substance abuse issues are compounded by sexual orientation issues. To be effective, treating therapists need to develop a treatment plan that incorporates both issues.

The attempt to assess an individual's sexual orientation is difficult; however, it must be made, along with helping individuals address their alcohol and drug use, as sexual orientation issues might affect their ability to remain sober. An accurate assessment requires a certain level of knowledge about sexuality in general and, when dealing with gay clients, an understanding of gay sexual activities and an awareness of the coming-out process. Therapists who are relatively well versed in these matters, and comfortable discussing them, can help clients explore their

sexuality, rather than jumping to conclusions or urging actions that may not be appropriate. It is imperative that therapists be as clear as possible about issues regarding sexuality and sexual orientation, because clients, whether sexual minorities or not, are often confused and frightened about these matters. Many were confused about sexual matters before they started drinking. During their active alcoholism, many clients engage in sexual behaviors or experience emotional attractions which further confuse and frighten them. Knowledgeable therapists with nonjudgmental attitudes can help ease the turmoil somewhat and reassure their clients (Finnegan & McNally, 1987). Knowledge here allows the therapist to help distinguish whether or not the client is simply having fantasies or thoughts versus activities and actions. Someone's fantasizing about same-sex sex does not necessarily mean that she or he is gay or lesbian.

A foremost concern for therapists of gay clients is to identify which stage of the coming-out process their clients are in. This is significant, because clients' degree of comfort with their sexual orientation will directly impact the therapeutic process. Although there is variation in how far and at what rate individuals progress through the coming-out process, a common and highly stressful point is reached when clients begin to think about disclosing their sexual orientation rather than hiding it or "passing." Undoubtedly, disclosure to family members and friends of gay sexual orientation is one of the major stressful events in the lives of gay men and women. While this is so, it has also been well documented that "outness" is positively correlated with better psychological adjustment (Anderson & Adley, 1997). To facilitate and ease coming out and disclosure for gay clients, therapists may assist in such tasks as performing a cost-benefit analysis regarding disclosure, planning and rehearsing "how to," and developing effective means of coping with negative reactions from significant others. It also helps when clients realize that they are not "the only one" who has gone or is going through this process. However, the therapist must be familiar with the process to help the client recognize this.

TREATMENT ISSUES

Ratner (1988) believes that effective chemical dependency treatment, whether inpatient or outpatient, should focus on the following specific sexual minority concerns: (a) a treatment environment that affirms gay lifestyles as positive alternatives to traditional heterosexual lifestyles; (b) increased self-awareness and self-acceptance as a sexual minority; (c) appropriate ways of coping with the discrimination and rejection sexual minorities frequently encounter from society, their family of origin, and others, and with the stresses they will encounter while recovering from substance dependence; (d) a nontraditional family network; (e) integration of their sexuality into a philosophy of life based on sobriety, quality, spirituality, and self-worth; (f) medical information that is tailored to their special needs; and (g) role models who illustrate the diversity of the gay community.

In recognition of the special problems of alcohol-dependent gays, a small number of specialized residential treatment programs have become available. For example, Pride Institute in Minneapolis, established in 1986, became the first inpatient treatment center for chemically dependent lesbians and gay men in the United States. The Fellowship of Alcoholics Anonymous reports over 500 gay groups throughout the country, and many AA groups are "gay-friendly." Today, most major metropolitan communities have outpatient centers that provide chemical dependency services for gays. Other centers have added special "track" programs for these clients. Still, gay-specific inpatient treatment centers are scarce, considering the number of gay individuals with alcohol and drug abuse problems (Amico & Neisen, 1997).

On July 4, 1979, the National Association of Lesbian and Gay Addictions Professionals (NALGAP) was created by a group of 15 lesbian and gay alcoholism professionals who were attending the Rutgers Summer School of Alcohol Studies in New Jersey. NALGAP operates to create a network for support and communications among addictions professionals, to educate agencies and organizations about sexual minorities and addictions, to act as a clearinghouse for resources (the world's largest collection of unpublished literature on sexual minorities and addictions is housed at the Rutger's Center of Alcohol Studies), to raise the sexual minority community's consciousness and combat its denial of the problem of addictions, and to improve substance use treatment for sexual minorities. Therapists are encouraged to both utilize and contribute to the resources of this specialty organization.

Early recovery issues for sexual minorities include not only the cessation of the substance abuse and the teaching of relapse prevention skills but also a self-analysis and a redefining of self. If alcohol and/or drugs were used to conceal inner conflict related to issues surrounding same-sex attraction, redefining oneself and one's self-worth, then it is essential to address those issues of internalized homophobia to help alleviate feelings of guilt and shame. To effectuate behavioral change, treatment plans need to center on the underlying drives that are used as excuses for substance abuse. With the focus on issues of identity, orientation, self-esteem, self-worth, anger, denial, and the development of coping mechanisms, effective and lasting treatment will also require the identification of positive role models and community supports that will facilitate the healing process.

The excuses used to support substance abuse are infinite in any population. However, with gay clients, these excuses are often confused with and/or compounded by the negative effects of internalized homophobia, which include feelings of low self-worth, guilt, shame, and repressed anger, and the associated issues of acceptance by family, friends, and society. The construct of internalized homophobia is closely related to the coming-out process and must be understood and utilized in the treatment of gays with substance abuse problems (Finnegan & McNally, 1987). Internalized homophobia is the process wherein gays come to internalize and believe societal antigay attitudes, beliefs, and stereotypes, with resultant devaluation and negativity about the self. Education around antigay prejudice and internalized homophobia can convey to clients the origin of prejudice, the element of power, and how oppression leads to shame and guilt. Therapists can help gay clients eliminate residual self-hatred by recognizing their shame as a product of homophobia, rather than of their sexual orientation or behavior. For some individuals, homophobia may, in fact, be reinforcing a preexisting low self-esteem. Therapeutic efforts directed toward helping clients understand this internalization process should be accompanied by attempts to integrate sexual orientation with overall self-concept. Clients can then begin to develop or reconstruct a positive self-image, a process which is best begun as early as possible in treatment.

Denial and rationalization may play an adaptive role in staving off anxiety related to an antigay culture. That is, gay clients may at times employ denial to protect themselves from the stress of dealing with and living in an uninterested, uncaring, or hostile environment. Therapists must be skillful in untangling enabling excuses (such as "Everyone is doing this"; "The bar is the only place I can meet people") from adaptive defenses (such as "It is easier to cope with and talk to others"; "It is easier to accept myself and have sex"). Therapists need to confront the former and judge when and how to leave the latter intact. Enabling excuses allow the abuse/addiction to continue. Adaptive defenses help the individual cope and to live with herself or himself. If the ego is too weak and the defenses are maladaptive and removed, the person will function/adapt in a less healthy manner. The task is to concurrently support the individual's personal growth and strength, combat less effective defense mechanisms, and teach new, healthier defense mechanisms/coping skills. Therapists must also help clients understand how experiences with antipathy and discrimination can undermine a positive self-concept and efforts to value and care for oneself. All in all, it is the therapist's challenging task to discern rationalizations and excuses from real or legitimate blocks to recovery and growth.

Hall (1993) recommended that providers explore the degree to which lesbian clients associate drinking with other life experiences, such as family history and sexual abuse. They should be prepared to acknowledge and address the association of alcohol use practices with the political and social realities of lesbian life, without stereotyping individual experiences. Concerns about sexual trauma, social control, heterosexism, and male dominance should not be dismissed as avoidance or denial of the real alcohol problem in lesbian clients.

Family therapy and aftercare treatment remain vital for those in recovery. The traditional family network may not be in place for many gays. It is not unusual for gays to be completely ostracized from their family. Depending on the situation, reconciliation and/or maintenance of ties with the biological family may or may not be a focus of treatment. Identification and recognition of the nontraditional or "chosen" family support system are highly beneficial for the continuance of recovery (Paul et al., 1991).

Bittle (1982) offered two important suggestions for gays when utilizing AA: (a) The early acquisition of a sponsor who is either lesbian or gay or who is altogether comfortable with and knowledgeable about sexual minorities is of prime importance, and (b) it must be assumed that a majority of lesbians and gay men coming into AA will need more than the AA group if their continued sobriety is to be successful and reasonably secure. Many of the problems

they bring with them will not be considered in AA meetings, and it is imperative that they maintain contact with gay support groups. The concepts of "higher power" and "spirituality," central to Alcoholics Anonymous, have acted as barriers for many gays to participating in traditional 12-step programs. Many religious organizations have been extremely judgmental and condemning of gays; hence, gays associate such terms with organized religion. Therapists may need to clarify for clients AA's definition and use of these terms to help overcome client resistance. Not all lesbians in recovery prefer lesbian AA meetings. Some lesbian problem drinkers have supplemented or replaced AA involvement with an alternative mutual help group called Women for Sobriety, which according to its founder stresses empowerment and positive self-appraisal rather than powerlessness and ego deflation (Kirkpatrick, 1978). This program, however, is not as geographically accessible as AA.

Hall (1993) expounded upon the importance of considering the historical origins of alcohol use practices and sociocultural factors in the definition of alcohol problems. Rather, alcohol problems are more appropriately seen as substantially unique difficulties experienced by specific subcultural groups, such as lesbians.

The consumption of alcohol has long been associated with sexual behavior. Drinking often occurs in social settings in which sexual contacts are sought. Substance use also frequently occurs at parties and other social gatherings at which sexual encounters are commonplace. Alcohol also acts as a depressant which induces disinhibition, which in turn may be conducive to sexual behavior combined with a decline in caution (Plant, 1990). Moreover, from the earliest reports of AIDS-defining illnesses in gay men, clinical investigators have noted a high prevalence of recreational drug use by the affected patients (U.S. Department of Health and Human Services, 1981). Associations have been found between unsafe sex and use of alcohol and drugs in both cross-sectional studies (e.g., Kelly, Lawrence, & Brasfield, 1991; Leigh, 1990) and longitudinal cohort studies (e.g., McCusker et al., 1990; Stall, McKusick, Wiley, Coates, & Ostrow, 1986). Gay men who drink heavily or use other drugs appear more likely to engage in sexual risk-taking behaviors. However, within actual sexual situations, alcohol and drug use does not consistently predict HIV-risk-related sexual behaviors.

Infection with human immunodeficiency virus (HIV) is a special issues that cannot be ignored, because it affects gay men, injection drug users, bisexual as well as heterosexual people, and alcoholics (whatever their sexual orientation), who are often a high-risk group because of sexual experiences while drinking. Finnegan and McNally (1987) suggested that counselors need to understand what AIDS is and know enough to teach and reassure other staff and clients; they need to know their agencies' policies toward persons living with HIV infection and the potential affects of a fatal diagnosis on attitudes about sobriety.

SUMMARY

Effective and lasting treatment of substance abuse for sexual minorities must address the primary symptoms of substance abuse with sensitivity to societal and interpersonal concerns that make gays unique. Effective therapists are knowledgeable about, skillful in, and comfortable with certain topical areas above and beyond standard clinical substance abuse treatment. These include (a) gay culture and communities and their historical development in the United States, (b) effects of sexual minority status and contemporary societal antipathy toward gays, (c) internalized homophobia, (d) gay sexual identity formation/the coming-out process, and (e) the local gay community and how to facilitate "coming-out sober" in it.

ACKNOWLEDGMENTS This chapter was supported in part by the National Institute on Alcohol Abuse and Alcoholism, Grant AA09324. Special thanks to Christopher M. Ryan, Ph.D., for editorial guidance.

Key References

Bux, D. A. (1996). The epidemiology of problem drinking in gay men and lesbians:A critical review. *Clinical Psychology Review, 16,* 277–298.

Finnegan, D. G., & McNally, E. B. (1987). *Dual identities: Counseling chemically dependent gay men and lesbians.* Center City, MN: Hazelden Educational Materials.

Paul, J. P., Stall, R., & Bloomfield, K. A. (1991). Gay and alcoholic: Epidemiologic and clinical issues. *Alcohol Health and Research World, 15,* 151–160.

References

Amico, J. M., & Neisen, J. H. (1997). *Sharing the secret: The need for gay-specific treatment.* Presentation at the National Association of Alcoholism and Drug Abuse Counselors Annual Conference.

Anderson, C. W., & Adley, A. R. (1997). *Gay and lesbian issues: Abstracts of the psychological and behavioral literature 1985–1986.* Washington, DC: American Psychological Association.

Bartholow, B. N., Doll, L. S., Joy, D., Douglas, J. M., Jr., Bolan, G., Harrison, J. S., Moss, P. M., & McKirnan, D. (1994). Emotional, behavioral, and HIV risks associated with sexual abuse among adult homosexual and bisexual men. *Child Abuse and Neglect, 18,* 747–761.

Bittle, W. E. (1982). Alcoholics Anonymous and the gay alcoholic. In T. O. Ziebold & J. E. Mongeon (Eds.), *Alcoholism and homosexuality* (pp. 81–88). New York: Haworth Press.

Bradford, J., Ryan, C., & Rothblum, E. D. (1994). National lesbian health care survey: Implications for mental health care. *Journal of Consulting and Clinical Psychology, 62,* 228–242.

Bux, D. A. (1996). The epidemiology of problem drinking in gay men and lesbians:A critical review. *Clinical Psychology Review, 16,* 277–298.

Cabaj, R. P. (1989). AIDS and chemical dependency: Special issues and treatment barriers for gay and bisexual men. *Journal of Psychoactive Drugs, 21,* 387–393.

Coleman, E. (1985). Developmental stages of the coming-out process. In J. C. Gosiorek (Ed.). *A guide to psychotherapy with gay and lesbian clients* (pp. 31–44). New York: Harrington Park Press.

D'Augelli, A. R., & Patterson, C. J. (Eds.). (1995). *Lesbian, gay, and bisexual identities over the lifespan.* New York: Oxford University Press.

Fifield, L., DeCresenzo, T. A., & Latham, J. D. (1975). *On my way to nowhere: Alienated, isolated, drunk.* Los Angeles: Gay Community Services Center.

Finnegan, D. G., & McNally, E. B. (1987). *Dual identities: Counseling chemically dependent gay men and lesbians.* Center City, MN: Hazelden Educational Materials.

Frosch, D., Shoptaw, S., Hubber, A., Rawson, R. A., & Ling, W. (1996). Sexual HIV risk among gay and bisexual male methamphetamine abusers. *Journal of Substance Abuse Treatment, 13,* 483–486.

Golden, C. (1987). Diversity and variability in women's sexual identities. In Boston Lesbian Psychologies Collective (Eds.), *Lesbian psychologies: Explorations and challenges* (pp. 18–24). Urbana: University of Illinois.

Hall, J. M. (1993). Lesbians and alcohol: Patterns and paradoxes in medical notions and lesbians' belief. *Journal of Psychoactive Drugs, 25,* 109–119.

Icard, L., & Traunstein, D. M. (1987). Black, gay, alcoholic men: Their character and treatment. *Journal of Contemporary Social Work, 267–272.*

Kelly, J. A., Lawrence, J. S., & Brasfield, T. L. (1991). Predictors of vulnerability to AIDS risk behavior relapse. *Journal of Consulting and Clinical Psychology, 59,* 163–166.

Kirkpatrick, J. (1978). *Turnabout: Help for a new life.* New York: Doubleday.

Kus, R. J. (1988). Alcoholism and non-acceptance of gay self: The critical link. *Journal of Homosexuality, 15,* 25–41.

Leigh, B. (1990). The relationship of substance use during sex to high-risk sexual behavior. *Journal of Sex Research, 27,* 199–213.

Lohrenz, L., Connely, J., Coyne, L., & Spare, L. (1978). Alcohol problems in several midwest homosexual populations. *Journal of Studies on Alcohol, 39,* 1959–1963.

McCandlish, B. M. (1982). Therapeutic issues with lesbian couples. In *Homosexuality and psychotherapy.* New York: Haworth Press.

McCusker, J., Westnhouse, J., Stoddard, A. M., Zapkin, J. G., Zern, M. W., & Mayer, K. H. (1990). Use of drugs and alcohol by homosexually active men in relation to sexual practices. *Journal of Acquired Immune Deficiency Syndrome, 53,* 729–736.

McKirnan, D. J., & Peterson, P. L. (1989). Alcohol and drug use among homosexual men and women: Epidemiology and population characteristics. *Addictive Behaviors, 14,* 454–553.

McKirnan, D. J., & Peterson, P. L. (1992). *Gay and lesbian alcohol use: Epidemiological and psychological perspective.* Paper presented at the Research symposium on alcohol and other drug problems among lesbians and gay men, Los Angeles.

Midanik, L. R., & Clark, W. B. (1994). The demographic distribution of U.S. drinking patterns in 1990: Description and trends from 1984. *American Journal of Public Health, 84,* 1218–1222.

Nardi, P. M. (1982). Alcoholism and homosexuality: A theoretical perspective. In T. Zeibold & J. Mongeon (Eds.), *Journal of Homosexuality: Alcoholism and Drug Abuse.* New York: Haworth Press.

National Association of Lesbian and Gay Addictions Professionals. (1996, Spring). *NALGAP Reporter, 17,* 3–4

Neisen, J. H. (1993). Healing from cultural victimization: Recovery from shame due to heterosexism. *Journal of Gay and Lesbian Psychotherapy, 2,* 49–63.

Ortiz, Z. J. S., & Rivera, V. L. (1988). Altered T-cell helper/suppresser ratio in mice chronically exposed to amyl nitrate. In H. W. Haverkos & J. A. Dougherty (Eds.), *Health hazards of nitrate inhalants* (pp. 59–73). NIDA Research Monograph 83.

Ostrow, D. G., & Kessler, R. C. (1993). *Methodological issues in AIDS behavioral research.* New York: Plenum Press.

Paul, J. P., Stall, R., & Bloomfield, K. A. (1991). Gay and alcoholic: Epidemiologic and clinical issues. *Alcohol Health and Research World, 15,* 151–160.

Plant, M. A. (1990). Alcohol, sex, and drugs. *Alcohol and Alcoholism, 25,* 293–301.

Ratner, E. (1988). A model for the treatment of lesbian and gay alcohol abusers. *Alcoholism Treatment Quarterly, 5,* 25–46.

Russell, D. E. H. (1984). *Sexual exploitation: Rape, child sexual abuse, and work place harassment.* Beverly Hills, CA: Sage.

Saghir, M. T., & Robins, E. (1973). *Male and female homosexuality: A comprehensive investigation.* Baltimore: Williams & Wilkins.

Sigell, L. T., Kapp, E. T., Fusaro, G. A., Nelson, E. D., & Falck, R. S. (1978). Popping and snorting amyl nitrates: A current fad for getting high. *American Journal of Psychiatry, 135,* 1216–1218.

Skinner, W. F. (1994). The prevalence and demographic predictors of illicit and licit drug use among lesbians and gay men. *American Journal of Public Health, 89,* 1307–1310.

Stall, R., McKusick, L., Wiley, J., Coates, T. J., & Ostrow, D. G. (1986). Alcohol and drug use during sexual activity and compliance with safer sex guidelines for AIDS. *Health Education Quarterly, 13,* 359–371.

Stall, R., & Wiley, J. (1988). A comparison of alcohol and drug use patterns of homosexual and heterosexual men: The San Francisco men's health study. *Drug and Alcohol Dependence, 22,* 63–73.

U.S. Department of Health and Human Services, Centers for Disease Control and Prevention. (1981). Morbidity and mortality report. *Epidemiological Notes and Reports, 30,* 305–308.

Ziebold, T., & Mongeon, J. (Eds.). (1982). *Journal of homosexuality: Alcoholism and drug abuse.* New York: Haworth Press.

Part VII

Prevention, Policy, and Economics of Substance Use Disorders

30

Prevention Aimed at Individuals: An Integrative Transactional Perspective

Mary Ann Pentz

After a hiatus in the 1980s, drug use, including tobacco, alcohol, and marijuana use, among youth is again on the rise (Johnston, O'Malley, & Bachman, 1997). The increase, appearing since 1991, has been attributed to poor implementation of prevention programs, a decrease in perceived risk and consequences of use, high demand for use, and increases in perceived social norms and acceptance of use, with access to drugs remaining high and unchanged (Bachman, Johnston, & O'Malley, 1991; Pentz, in press). All of these factors can be addressed in prevention programs aimed at individuals.

Drug abuse prevention aimed at individuals typically means those programs and strategies that initiate from and radiate outward in impact from an individual's changing his or her own drug use behavior. These strategies are in contrast to strategies aimed at changing systems, environments, or policies that are initiated apart from individuals but are expected at some point to impact on individuals' behavior. In the field of drug abuse prevention, which includes tobacco, alcohol, marijuana, and other drugs, the dif-

ferences in these strategies can be aligned with demand or supply reduction (Pentz, Bonnie, & Shopland, 1996). Since most prevention efforts are aimed at youth, this chapter focuses on a model of prevention as it applies to children and adolescents. However, the model presented here should be applicable to prevention with other populations as well, particularly young adults.

The majority of interventions aimed at individuals are focused on changing their demand for drugs by changing attitudes, perceptions, and behaviors concerning drug use. In contrast, interventions aimed at systems, environments, or policies are focused primarily on changing supply of or access to drugs. Effective demand reduction approaches are those which train individuals to (a) counteract personal and social risk factors for drug use, sometimes referred to as social influences or resistance programs; (b) promote personal, social, and environmental protective factors; or (c) both (Hawkins, Catalano, & Miller, 1992). These approaches tend toward programmatic interventions; the more effective interventions include programmatic, process, *and* organizational intervention, such as student training that also includes school development or training that also includes community organization and policy change (Becker et al., 1989).

The most effective prevention programs aimed at individuals are those that focus on counteracting social influences to use drugs (Hansen, 1992). These programs address person-level factors of resistance skills, appraisal of drug use situations and models (P) and situation-level factors of perceived social norms and avoidance of drug-using groups and drug use opportunities (S) (Hansen, 1992; Pentz, 1986; Tobler, 1992). A few also include coping and support-seeking skills (e.g., Pentz, Pentz, & Gong, 1993) or general social skills related to coping, such as problem-solving and assertiveness skills (Botvin, Baker, Dusenbury, Botvin, & Diaz, 1995). Most P- and S-level prevention programs are implemented in schools, agencies, or familiar settings. Most are designed to affect psychosocial risk factors operating at the P and S levels. Community-based programs, on the other hand, can address individual and group-level risk factors with school and parent program components, and E-level risk factors by including mass media, community organization, and policy change strategies.

The magnitude and longevity of program effectiveness is dependent upon the extent to which intervention acknowledges and involves the interaction of intrapersonal, interpersonal, and environmental change. In personality research, these interactions have been expressed as a simultaneous series of transactions that affect the ecology or balance of an individual's personality (Magnusson, 1981).

Transactional theory posits that an individual's personality is formed or changed as a result of the interaction of intra-, inter-, and extrapersonal factors (Magnusson, 1981). Applied to the understanding of drug use development and prevention, an adolescent's drug use behavior is formed or changed as a result of the interaction of person-level (P) factors (intrapersonal history of prior drug use, skills, support seeking, and physiological reaction), situation-level (S) factors (interpersonal and group influences on drug use modeling, pressures or offers to use drugs, peer and family communication and support, and peer group transitions), and environment-level (E) factors (extrapersonal media influences, resources, community norms and policies, and demographic factors; cf. Hawkins et al., 1992; Murray & Perry, 1985; Pentz, 1986, 1994a, b, 1995).

In drug abuse prevention research, these interactions have been expressed in several different theories and models that imply longitudinal rather than simultaneous transactions. For example, problem behavior theory posits that person, situation, environment, and drug use behavior factors interact to affect subsequent drug use behavior, and that the interaction effects are accentuated during periods of adolescent transition, such as school or peer group transition (Jessor, 1982; Perry & Jessor, 1985). Peer cluster theory posits that the social influences represented by an adolescent's peer group, as well as the personal and environmental factors that contribute to the formulation of a particular peer group, predict the course of drug use onset (Oetting & Beauvais, 1986). The risk and protective factors model posits that individuals and communities can be diagnosed for drug use risk on the basis of the presence of certain personal, familial, peer, and community demographic risk factors (Hawkins et al., 1992). The theory of triadic influence posits that intrapersonal factors affect behavioral skills and self-efficacy, social situations affect bonding and social normative beliefs, and cultural-environmental factors affect knowledge, values, and attitudes toward drug use (Flay & Petraitis, 1994). Public health models interpret behavior change in terms of the interactive and causal relationships among the host of disease risk behaviors, the agent of transmission of those behaviors, and the environment that supports those behaviors; such models have been applied primarily to the understanding of alcohol use prevention (e.g., Green, Wilson, & Bauer, 1983; Holder & Wallack, 1986).

Integrative transactional theory (ITT) posits the cumulative and redounding influences of personal attitudes and behavior on social group norms and support and, consequently, on community norms, media, fiscal resources, and policy change (Pentz, 1986, 1993). The remainder of this chapter categorizes individual-aimed prevention strategies according to integrative transactional theory involving person (P), situation (S), and environment (E) interactions.

UNDERSTANDING INDIVIDUAL-AIMED INTERVENTIONS IN TERMS OF P, S, AND E LEVELS OF INFLUENCE

When first described, ITT focused on articulating P, S, and E levels of risk factors for adolescent drug use

(Pentz, 1986). The model was intended to guide the development of a comprehensive community-based drug abuse prevention intervention (Midwestern Prevention Project) that consisted of five components: a school program, a parent education and organization program, community organization and training, mass media programming, and community drug use policy change (Pentz et al., 1989). Since its original description, ITT has been expanded to include transitions, opportunity, and access as risk factors for drug use based on research showing significant relationships of these factors to drug use (Pentz, 1993). The modified $P \times S \times E$ risk factor model is shown in figure 30.1. ITT assumes (a) that risk as well as behavior change targets operate on youth simultaneously; (b) that intervention aimed at changing behavior can be focused initially on individuals' own behavior (P or intrapersonal), with a sufficient "mass" of change subsequently affecting group (S) and environment (E) aggregates of individuals' behavior (i.e., behavior change effects initially radiate outward); and (c) that the different levels are reciprocally determined over time. The factors shown in figure 30.1 are based collectively on results of epidemiological research on

drug use development (e.g., Hawkins et al., 1992; Pentz, 1993; Yamaguchi & Kandel, 1984).

Although the general ITT model is useful for describing influences on drug use development, it does not articulate specific variables that are useful as behavior change targets. Sometimes referred to as *intervention mediators*, these change targets are shown for P, S, and E levels of intervention in figures 30.2, 30.3, and 30.4, respectively.

Person-Level Risk and Prevention

Figure 30.2 differentiates the hypothesized paths of person-level (intrapersonal) risk factors for drug use and the hypothesized paths of prevention program mediators that are aimed at reversing or counteracting these risk factors. As multiple studies have shown, the single risk factor accounting for the most variance in subsequent drug use is one's own prior experimentation with drugs (Hawkins et al., 1992; Pentz, 1993; Yamaguchi & Kandel, 1984). To continue use, an individual may consciously rationalize the benefits of use (similar to the concept of reducing dissonance in cognitive dissonance theory;

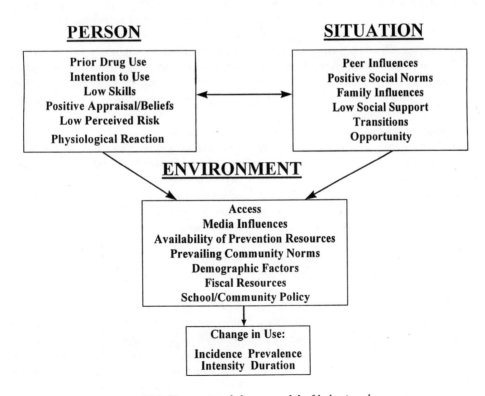

FIGURE 30.1 Transactional theory model of behavior change.

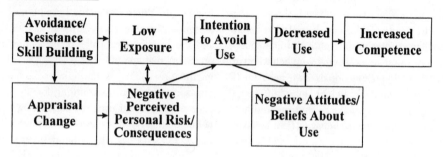

FIGURE 30.2 Interventions aimed at individuals: Effects on person (P)-level behavior.

Flay & Petraitis, 1994; Pentz, 1993), that is, develop positive beliefs about use, minimize perceived risk and consequences of use, and appraise drug use occurrences and opportunities as a positive experience (Azjen & Fishbein, 1980). Alternatively, the individual may spontaneously encounter a drug use opportunity that later appears to be positive, for example, drinking at a party, which appears to increase fellowship and camaraderie among peers. Whether positive perceptions of use are rational decisions or spontaneous outcomes of an opportunity, the perceptions are hypothesized to increase intentions to use in the near future and subsequent use. Intentions to use cigarettes, for example, are considered a major indicator of an adolescent's susceptibility (predictor) of subsequent use (Pierce, Choi, Gilpin, Farkas, & Merritt, 1996). A continued pattern of use is hypothesized to involve a repetition of positive perceptions about use, intentions to use, and positive physiological reinforcement for use. Positive physiological reinforcement includes feelings of getting high, not getting sick, a general sense of well-being, and/or temporary diversion from depression or anxiety.

Most prevention programs aimed at changing P-level risk factors have been limited to changing an individual's knowledge about drugs and consequences of use, affect or feelings about drug use, feelings about self (self-esteem building), or personal decision making and problem solving about drug use (Hansen, Johnson, Flay, Graham, & Sobel, 1988; Pentz, 1993; Tobler, 1992). None of these approaches have shown effects on either delaying or reducing drug use in youth, when restricted to the P-level context without consideration of social contexts. Most of these programs have been used in schools as part of health education; some have been used in student assistance programs (SAPs) as part of a counseling process, or in agency settings or group homes where adolescents who are already users or at high risk for use receive counseling.

It is conceivable that a P-level prevention program could achieve some effects on youth drug use if all or most of the P-level risk factors were addressed in sequence as shown at the bottom of figure 30.2. However, there is no evidence in the published literature that such a risk-inclusive program has been evaluated. In such a hypothetical program, personal drug avoidance/resistance skills would be taught first. As differentiated from resistance skills taught in S-level prevention programs (see below), personal resistance skills would focus on cognitive "self-talk" and visualization of avoiding drug use and drug use opportunities, without the context of social pressures. Sufficient cognitive practice of these skills might be expected to result in aversion to drugs (appraisal change), avoidance of drug use opportunities (low exposure), and an increase in perceived risks and negative consequences of drug use. Continued negative perceptions about drug use and avoidance of drug use opportunities would be expected to reinforce avoidance intentions and negative beliefs in the future and consequently decrease use. Based on what is known about risk and protective factors for drug use, continued avoidance of use should contribute to prosocial and academic competence (Hawkins et al., 1992).

Person-level programs have at least three major limitations. One is that they are likely to be labor-intensive and to reach fewer youth than other types of programs involving large groups or populations; cognitive practice skills, for example, may have more utility in clinical settings with individuals or small groups. Second, P-level programs rely heavily on cognitive processes. Changing perceptions have been shown to be necessary but insufficient conditions of behavior change in youth (Flay et al., 1995). Third, P-level programs do not prepare youth for the considerable social pressures they encounter to experiment with drugs.

Situation-Level Risk and Prevention

Consistently, etiological and epidemiological research has shown that the major risk factors for drug use onset are social influences, including the interpersonal social situations that an adolescent encounters and perceives around him or her. These include exposure to adult and peer modeling of drug use; peer pressure to try drugs; social situations that represent immediate access, opportunity, and availability of drugs; perceived peer norms for drug use; perceived approval or acceptability of drug use by peers and adults; and proximity and attachment to users (Donaldson, Graham, & Hansen, 1994; Hansen, 1992). Along with prior use for youth who have already tried drugs, these immediate social influences typically account for 30% or more of the variance in youth drug use (Donaldson et al., 1994). According to problem behavior theory (Jessor, 1982), these social influences escalate in importance during periods

of social transition, particularly the transition from elementary to middle school. This period represents a period of vulnerability and attempts by adolescents to emulate the behavior of older or more mature peers, including trying drugs (Jessor, 1982; Pentz, 1993).

The hypothesized sequence of S-level risk factors is shown in the top half of figure 30.3. Exposure to drug use models and social transition may contribute to attachment to users; attachment and exposure to models increases perceived (and actual) social norms for use. Together, these risk factors increase opportunities for use and seeking opportunities for use, subsequent use, and social reinforcement, by peers, for continued use.

The bottom half of figure 30.3 shows the hypothesized sequence of change in drug use via changing social situational influences. Skills training can be provided to youth that includes how to resist peer pressure and drug use offers, and how to judge and avoid situations where drugs are used. Training that also includes assertiveness and approach skills, such as life skills training (Botvin et al., 1995), should increase a youth's resistance and avoidance ability, as well as enable a youth's ability to seek social support from trusted adults when resistance skills are not sufficient to counteract peer pressure (Barrera, 1986). Resistance, avoidance, and support seeking, if consistently applied, should promote gravitation or attachment to nonusing peers as friends over time. Such friends represent and confirm among each other a negative social norm for drug use and concern about negative consequences of drug use. Attachment to nonusing friends is likely, in turn, to increase avoidance of activities and situations that involve drug use (opportunity avoidance), decrease use, and promote selection of nonuse alternative activities for the nonusing peer group.

To date, most S-level prevention programs implemented during the early adolescent years have included avoidance, peer pressure resistance, and/or assertiveness skills training, weighing positive and negative consequences of drug use, and correction of perceived social norms for use (Hansen, 1992; Tobler, 1992). A few programs implemented during the elementary school years have focused on bonding with nonusing peers (e.g., Hawkins et al., 1992). These programs are considered primary or universal prevention programs that include whole populations of school-attending youth. Only programs that are

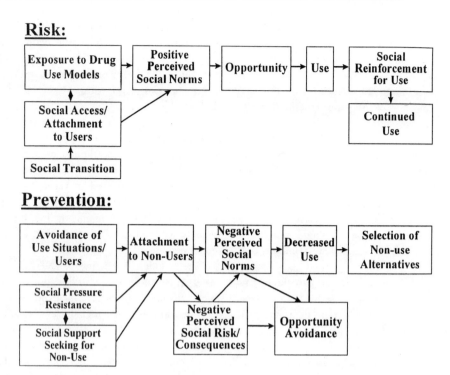

FIGURE 30.3 Interventions aimed at individuals: Effects on situation (S)-level behavior.

considered selective or indicated prevention programs (Kumpfer, 1989)—that is, programs that target youth who are already exhibiting problem behavior—have emphasized social support seeking and selection of nonuse alternatives (e.g., Eggert, Seyl, & Nicholas, 1990; Kumpfer, 1989).

Both universal and selective prevention programs that target at least two to three of the influences in figure 30.3 have demonstrated 20–40% net reductions in drug use, calculated as the difference in rates of drug use increase between program and control groups divided by the control group rate of increase (Pentz, 1994a). However, relatively little is known about the effects of either universal or selective/indicated programs on the selection of nonuse activities, or about the health or social benefits of such activities.

Most prevention programs focused on counteracting social influences have been based in schools (Hansen, 1992; Tobler, 1992); to a lesser extent, programs have focused on or have included parents or families (Aktan, Kumpfer & Turner, 1996; Dishion & Andrews, 1995). Most rely on social learning theory principles of training behavioral skills (Bandura, 1977). Referred to as *guided participant modeling*, these principles include the use of modeling, role playing, group discussion and feedback, and extended skills practice in real-life settings, usually through the use of interactive homework activities involving peers or parents. There is substantial evidence to indicate that social influence programs are effective in delaying and reducing adolescent drug use for periods of 5 years or more (Botvin et al., 1995; Hansen, 1992; Pentz, 1993; Resnicow, Cross, & Wynder, 1991; Tobler, 1992). In some cases, however, programs that have focused on counteracting social influences have shown either no effects on drug use (Ennett & Bauman, 1994), or effects dissipated shortly after the end of intervention (e.g., Ellickson, Bell, & McGuigan, 1993). With the exception of poor program implementation, reasons for program failure or weak effects have not been evaluated to the same extent as reasons for program effectiveness (tests of program mediators; Donaldson et al., 1994; Dusenbury & Falco, 1995; MacKinnon et al., 1991). Some possibilities are worth noting. One may be the type of individual(s), instructional method, or support to implement programs. For example, DARE, which is based on sound principles of social learning theory and addresses social influences of peer pressure, resistance skills, norms, and consequences of use, may show no effects on drug use because the type of implementer (police) is not considered a normative educator by youth (Ennett & Bauman, 1994). Programs with effects that dissipate after the end of intervention may encounter poor school support for prevention programs (Ellickson et al., 1993). Another possibility is that some social influence programs may not address all of the hypothesized risk factors shown in figure 30.3. For example, most S-level programs include social pressure resistance and avoidance skills, as well as changing social normative expectations and perceived risks and consequences of drug use (Hansen, 1992). Bonding (attachment to nonusers) is addressed in only a few programs (e.g., Hawkins et al., 1992), as is seeking social support for nonuse (e.g., Eggert et al., 1990). In addition, few programs include or give equal attention to selecting alternative nonuse situations.

Environment-Level Risk and Prevention

Environment-level risk factors are those that represent influences larger than a youth's immediate familial or social group environment, including school, neighborhood, and larger community. After personal use and family and peer influences, neighborhood and community influences have been shown to account for a significant proportion of the variance of adolescent drug use (White, Boorman, & Breiger, 1976).While other environmental factors such as state drunk-driving laws and national alcohol-warning labels also have an impact on use (e.g., Hingson et al., 1996; MacKinnon et al., 1991), this chapter focuses on local environmental influences that are modifiable by individuals.

Figure 30.4 shows the relationship of E-level risk factors to drug use and a hypothesized sequence of E-level prevention strategies. Five factors are shown as initial influences on adolescent drug use, although two—media beliefs and exposure—are somewhat modified from factors evaluated in previous research (e.g., Flynn et al., 1992). Glamorized images and modeling of drug use in the media have been shown to affect, at a minimum, adolescents' attitudes toward drug use. However, since such images are readily available to most youth everywhere, a more predictive factor that differentiates some environments

from others may be adolescents' positive beliefs about such images. Beliefs covary with youth exposure to a drug use environment, for example, an urban housing complex where drugs are readily used and acknowledged; exposure, in turn, is likely to be related to youth access to drugs. However, the two factors are not redundant, since several studies have shown that while over 90% of youth everywhere report easy access to drugs, relatively few youth live in environments where they are likely to be exposed to drug use on a regular basis (e.g., Johnston et al., 1997). Collectively, these factors contribute to positive perceived environmental norms for drug use, including acceptability of drug use in the community and consequent use (Pentz, 1994b). If policies are poorly enforced as well as implemented, few negative consequences such as school suspension or juvenile court appearances ensue, and use continues.

A preventive intervention sequence that mobilizes individuals to counteract environmental influences on drug use is shown in the bottom half of figure 30.4. Radio, television, and print media managers could develop mass media programs and campaigns that could focus on either direct advertising to counteract glamorized drug use images, training youth in media literacy to interpret the limitations of media, and/or providing messages that change perceived environmental norms for use. Local law enforcement officers, town government leaders, school administrators, and neighborhood volunteers could engineer attractive and safe no-use settings for adolescents to congregate in and, in the process, increase avoidance of settings (environments) where drugs are used or sold. Business leaders can organize with community leaders to raise local funds and resources to maintain prevention programs in schools, develop campaigns and services that complement school programs, provide parent prevention training, and strengthen implementation and enforcement of policy. While no study has systematically evaluated the causal relationship between resource generation and community organization for drug abuse prevention, existing models of community prevention interventions suggest that the order consists of interested leaders developing a sense of empowerment, developing an organization or partnership for prevention, and subsequently developing strategies to raise funds and change policy (e.g., Butterfoss, Goodman, & Wandersman, 1996; Goodman, Wandersman, Chinman, Imm, & Morrisey, 1996; Manger, Hawkins, Hag-

Risk:

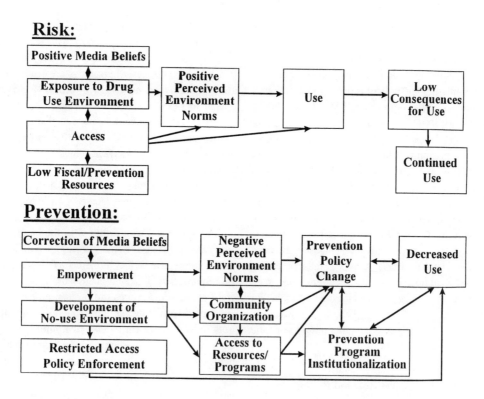

Prevention:

FIGURE 30.4 Interventions aimed at individuals: Effects on environment (E)-level behavior.

gerty, & Catalano, 1992; Mansergh, Rohrbach, Montgomery, Pentz, & Johnson, 1996). Collectively, these changes would be expected to decrease adolescent drug use. Recent research also suggests that the combination of decreased drug use and increased empowerment may contribute to subsequent efforts to refine or change policy and institutionalize prevention programs (Florin & Wandersman, 1990; Pentz & Newman, 1997).

The majority of interventions that have already addressed one or more E-level influences have consisted of either mass media programs or campaigns, policy enforcement or policy change intervention, or community coalitions or partnerships organized for drug abuse prevention. While no study has systematically compared the efficacy of each E-level approach, several studies have combined them in an attempt to reinforce each approach's prevention message and/or disseminate prevention to a larger community audience.

Mass media programs for drug abuse prevention have mostly targeted youth (e.g., Flay et al., 1995; Flynn et al., 1992). Moderate effects have been

achieved in changing attitudes toward drug use and beliefs about consequences; small effects have been noted on intentions to use drugs in the future (Donohew, Sypher, & Bukowski, 1991; Flay et al., 1995; Flynn et al., 1992). Studies of campaigns have been focused primarily on young adults rather than adolescents, particularly in the area of drunk driving (e.g., Hingson et al., 1996; Holder & Blose, 1987); these campaigns have shown changes in perceived consequences of use as well as short-term changes in drunk driving and related behaviors in young adults.

Local policy interventions for youth have concentrated on restricting youth access to tobacco and alcohol through community ordinances or school policy (Pentz et al., 1996). Collectively, results of these studies suggest that (a) prevention or support-oriented policies are associated with lower tobacco use, while punishment-oriented policies have no relationship to lower use (Pentz et al., 1989); (b) restricted access policies that involve youth in enforcement—for example, through activism or "sting" operations—have an effect on decreasing tobacco sales and purchases by youth and may decrease alcohol consumption (Forster, Hourigan, & Kelder, 1992; Jason, Li, Anes, & Birkhead, 1991; Perry & Jessor, 1985); and (c) changes toward more restrictive policy may represent a reactive effect to high rates of youth tobacco or alcohol use in a community rather than proactive support of restricted access policy. With the exception of one recent study (Forster, Wolfson, Murray, Wagenaar, & Claxton, 1997), effects of restricted access policy interventions appear to be limited to decreased sales and short-term consumption patterns rather than prevalence.

Other interventions have focused on training servers and sales people to comply with restricted-access policy by voluntarily restricting sales of tobacco and alcohol to minors in bars, restaurants, and stores (e.g., Altman, Rasenick-Douss, et al., 1991; Holder & Wallack, 1986; Mosher & Jernigan, 1988). These studies have shown significant short-term reductions of up to 40% in sales to minors, although effects tend to erode after prompts for compliance, such as sting operations and media coverage, are removed.

Community coalitions or partnerships organized for drug abuse prevention have been evaluated in a series of demonstration grants, for example, Center for Substance Abuse Prevention (CSAP) Community Partnerships, Robert Wood Johnson Foundation Fighting Back Initiative, and Kaiser Family Health Foundation Community Organization program. Collectively, these represent organization efforts in over 300 cities and communities across the United States. Most of the results obtained to date have concentrated on changes in the process of community organization, rather than drug use outcomes for youth. Results of process evaluations of these studies have shown that perceived empowerment, positive and regular interpersonal communication, and development of specific, time-limited objectives predict community leader participation, intentions to continue to participate, satisfaction with work, and completion of coalition objectives (Butterfoss et al., 1996; Carlson, 1990; Mansergh et al., 1996). For some communities, obtaining a champion or affiliating with a larger, credible organization predicted a coalition's ability to achieve objectives and maintain itself over time (Saxe et al., in press). The effects of community coalitions on changing youth drug use are less clear. For example, initial results from the CSAP Community Partnership grants indicated that while the majority of partnership communities reported smaller increases in youth drug use over time relative to comparison communities, differences were significant on only two of eight drug use variables measured (Yin & Kaftarian, 1997). It is not known whether the lack of statistically significant effects is due to insufficient power to detect the small differences between community groups, as yet unanalyzed mediational effects of coalition process on drug use outcomes, or ineffectiveness of coalitions as a strategy to reduce youth drug use. Effects of E-level interventions aimed at individuals appear to be stronger to the extent that interventions are combined. For example, large short-term reductions (40%) in youth tobacco sales were achieved in one study by combining a community ordinance with youth sting operations and mass media programming (Jason et al., 1991). In another study, relative reductions of up to 20% in youth tobacco use prevalence were achieved by combining community and youth activism to promote restricted access policy and local mass media support (Forster et al., 1997).

Person × Situation × Environment Risk and Prevention

The integration of all three levels of risk is shown in figure 30.1. Interventions aimed at individuals assume an outward direction of influence; that is, P-level interventions or intervention components affect attitudinal and belief change in a critical mass of individuals; attitudinal change builds support and willingness to participate in S- or group-level interventions; participation in S-level interventions changes perceived social norms for use and support for environmental changes such as changes in mass media, policy enforcement, and program institutionalization; and subsequent E-level changes effect reductions in use prevalence and consumption among youth. Over time, reversed and reciprocal directions of influence may operate to maintain each level of intervention. For example, policy changes that incorporate set-aside funding for prevention skills training should affect future maintenance of S- and P-level programs and program participation.

Interventions aimed at individuals have attempted to integrate P-, S-, and E-level components in comprehensive community-based programs. Examples of these types of programs include the youth-smoking-prevention program of the Minnesota Heart Health Project (Perry, Kelder, Murray, & Klepp, 1992), the youth-smoking-prevention program of the North Karelia Project (Puska et al., 1982), Project Northland for youth alcohol use prevention (Perry et al., 1992), the Community Smoking Prevention Trial (Biglan et al., in press), and the Midwestern Prevention Project for tobacco, alcohol, and drug use prevention (Pentz, in press, 1998; Pentz et al., 1989). All of these comprehensive programs have included multiple components representing P, S, and E levels of intervention, usually by combining school programs with parent, mass media, and/or community organization training. All have shown significant (20–60%) reductions in use prevalence by youth compared to control conditions; where evaluated over the long term, several have shown maintenance of effects of 8 years or more.

The capacity of comprehensive community-based prevention programs to address person, situation, and environment risk factors across the board may be more likely than school-based programs to produce a larger synergistic or interactive effect rather than a simple additive effect on reducing drug use risk and, consequently, drug use behavior. For example, avoiding drug use situations and peers is likely to produce a decrease in perceived social norms for drug use and, over time, an actual decrease in social norms for drug use in the community (Hansen, 1992). Lower social norms, in turn, should produce an intolerant attitude toward drug use, which results in a change in formalized drug policy. This sequential synergistic effect is larger than the simple effect of an individual's resistance to a drug use offer, resulting in a decrease in that individual's drug use behavior. The synergistic effect is also larger than any additive effect derived from combining person- and situation- or group-level skills. For example, an individual youth's resistance plus a parent's choice to no longer model drug use—for example, cigarette smoking, in the presence of that youth—may affect family members' drug use. However, youth resistance and parent behavioral choices may steer the family toward greater involvement in community prevention activities, which reinforce nonuse social norms in the community.

DIRECT VERSUS INDIRECT MODELS OF PREVENTION AIMED AT INDIVIDUALS

On a cursory level, within and across levels of influence, prevention efforts can be roughly categorized according to whether they directly address drug use by focusing on skills and strategies to resist drug use and avoid drug use environments or indirectly address use by either focusing on early risk factors for problem behavior or early protective factors against later drug use. The distinction may have practical significance for planning or funding purposes. For example, a school program focused specifically on drug use resistance may be funded by Safe and Drug Free Schools funding, whereas a program focused on academic and social competence as protective factors against later drug use may be funded as part of the regular school budget or as part of a special educational grant. The distinction is not important for judging effectiveness, since there is no research available that compares the relative effectiveness of direct and indirect approaches to drug use prevention.

At the P level, some of the more common direct approaches include school health education programs focusing on knowledge of tobacco or drug use (e.g., SHEE; Connell, Turner, & Mason, 1985) and individual counseling student assistance programs focusing on seeking assistance for cessation as a means of harm reduction (McGovern & Dupont, 1991; Swisher et al., 1993). Indirect approaches include peer tutoring to enhance academic competence, individual counseling focusing on stress reduction and anger management, and mentoring to build self-esteem (Tobler, 1992). Direct knowledge-based and self-esteem programs have shown no effect on drug use. Tutoring, as part of larger interventions aimed at changing the school climate for learning, has shown some effect on building academic competence, a protective factor against later drug use (Hawkins et al., 1997). However, effects of the tutoring components, independent of other effects, have not been determined.

At the S level, direct approaches include school drug use resistance training programs, parent skills training for monitoring youth and changing drug use modeling influences in the family (e.g., Kumpfer, 1989), group counseling programs focused on moving adolescents away from drug-using peers and settings as a means of harm reduction (e.g., Eggert, Thompson, Herting, Nicholas, & Dicker, 1994), and school skills-training programs aimed at secondary prevention, cessation, decision making about drug use, and motivation to achieve among youth identified as at high risk for school failure (e.g., Sussman, 1996). Indirect approaches include school programs focused on building academic and social competence among peer groups and bonding with schools, competent peers, and parents (e.g., Hawkins et al., 1992); parent programs aimed at building parenting support and parent-child communication skills to avoid the development of problem behavior (e.g., Dishion & Andrews., 1995); and job or recreational time management skills training offered through youth-serving agencies, such as Boys and Girls Clubs (e.g., Schinke, Orlandi, & Cole, 1992; St. Pierre, Kaltreider, Mark, & Aiken, 1992). Indirect approaches also include group counseling programs for secondary prevention, focused on providing support, stress management, and anger control to youth who have been identified as at high risk for school failure (Gensheimer, Ayers, & Roosa, 1993; Sussman, Dent, Burton, Stacy, & Flay, 1995). Both direct (resistance) and indirect (competence) skills programs have shown lasting effects on preventing tobacco, alcohol, and marijuana use (e.g., Botvin et al., 1995; Hansen et al., 1988).

Most longitudinal evaluations of S-level interventions have focused on school programs. Effects of school-based direct and indirect programs have been shown to last an average of 3–5 years, achieving 20–40% relative net reductions in drug use (Tobler, 1992). The similarity in effectiveness of direct and indirect programs may be due to a focus on common mediating mechanisms for behavior change. For example, both drug-use-resistance skills-training programs such as SMART and ALERT (Ellickson et al., 1993; Hansen et al., 1988) and social-skills-training programs such as Life Skills Training (Botvin et al., 1995) teach assertiveness and counteracting perceived social norms in the context of resisting peer pressure. Both of these skills have been shown to mediate behavior change in adolescents (MacKinnon et al., 1991; Pentz, 1985). SMART and AAPT (Hansen et al., 1988) teach self-efficacy to refuse drug use offers; job skills and decision-making skills-training programs teach self-efficacy to practice prosocial behaviors that involve choosing alternatives to drug use (e.g., Schinke et al., 1992). Yet no published study is available that systematically compares direct and indirect S-level interventions.

At the E level, direct approaches include the development and monitoring of drug-free zones, community policing for drug use, and campaigns aimed at developing safe communities (Becker et al., 1989). Where evaluated, these approaches have shown some changes in attitudes toward drug use, but not in drug use behavior (e.g., Ennett & Bauman, 1994). Campaigns and mass media programs focused directly on preventing drunk driving and heavy drinking, on the other hand, have shown significant short-term reductions in alcohol use (e.g., Holder & Blose, 1987; Wagenaar, Murray, Wolfson, Forster, & Finnegan, 1994). Local policy interventions aimed at restricting youth access to tobacco and alcohol have also demonstrated short-term reductions in sales to youth and use prevalence (Forster et al., 1997; Jason et al., 1991; Perry & Jessor, 1985). Indirect approaches have included neighborhood clean-ups and attempts to improve housing and public grounds (Wandersman & Giamartino, 1980) as well as interventions designed to improve school climate (Hawkins et al., 1997). These latter approaches have not yet been evaluated for their effectiveness in preventing drug use. However, there is evidence to suggest that improving and monitoring the physical environment where drugs are used helps to decrease crimes and violence associated with drug use (Sampson, Raudenbush, & Earls, 1997). As with S-level interventions, there are no studies that have systematically compared the efficacy of direct and indirect E-level interventions. However, mechanisms by which each approach might affect drug use behavior can be hypothesized according to figure 30.4. Direct approaches attempt to develop empowerment and apply community organization and resources directly to the problem of restricting access to drugs and removing drugs from the environment. Indirect approaches attempt to develop empowerment and build safe environments which are nontolerant of problem conditions and behaviors, including drug use and crime.

TARGET POPULATIONS

Youth

The majority of prevention programs have targeted youth, particularly school-attending adolescents. Most of these programs are referred to as *universal* or *primary prevention programs*, that is, programs delivered to whole populations of youth in normative settings such as classrooms, at the beginning of or just prior to drug use onset (Kumpfer, 1989). Typically, these programs target early adolescents during the transition year to middle or junior high school, considered the first risk period for drug use onset (Pentz, 1993). Evaluations of these programs suggest that intervention is effective with early adolescents regardless of sex, ethnicity, or risk background defined by peer, family, or prior self use (e.g., Chou et al., 1998; Johnson et al., 1990; Tobler, 1992). There is recent evidence to suggest that universal school-based prevention programs may be more effective with early adolescents in private/parochial compared to public schools, although differences in effectiveness have been linked with differences in program implementation (e.g., Donaldson, Graham, Piccinin, & Hansen, 1995; Pentz, 1998).

Indirect approach programs, which seek to protect against later drug use by building social and academic competence skills, are typically initiated during the upper-elementary-school years (e.g., Hawkins et al., 1992; Kellam & Rebok, 1992). Programs that are considered selective or indicated prevention programs—that is, programs delivered to subgroups of youth who have been identified as at high risk for drug use or who are already drug users—are typically targeted to older adolescents of high school age (e.g., Eggert et al., 1994; Sussman, 1996). Exceptions include recent indirect approach programs for social competence and impulse control, which target children and early adolescents who are at risk for conduct disorder or attention deficit disorder and their parents or families (e.g., Dishion & Andrews, 1995). These programs are usually delivered in small counseling groups, in schools apart from the regular classroom setting, after school, or in youth-serving agencies.

For adolescents of high school age, most prevention efforts have focused drug use identification and referral on the use of no-use campaigns or organizational efforts, such as SADD, or indicated skills, or counseling programs for high risk youth, such as SAPS (e.g., Kantor, Caudill, & Ungerleider, 1992; Pentz, 1994a; Swisher et al., 1993). Programs targeting high-risk youth of high school age tend to show the largest, most immediate reductions in drug use, although most have not followed youth for several years to determine how long effects maintain (50–60% average reductions in use and problem behaviors related to use; e.g., Eggert et al., 1994; Kumpfer, 1989; Sussman, 1996). In contrast, primary prevention programs for early adolescents have shown large sustained effects (20–60% or greater net reductions in use; Tobler, 1992).

Young Adults

Compared to prevention programs for children and adolescents, fewer prevention programs target young adults, although there is some suggestion that post-high-school may represent a second risk period for onset of drug use, particularly for tobacco use and binge drinking in college students and young adults in blue-collar occupations (Haines & Spear, 1996; Hingson et al., 1996; Holder & Wallack, 1986; Johnston et al., 1997; Wechsler, Isaac, Grodstein, & Sellers, 1994). Prevention approaches offered on college campuses include the use of campaigns aimed at correction of perceptions of use, monitoring fraternities and dorms for alcohol and drugs, counseling offered through student counseling services, and cognitive behavioral skills training to reduce acceptance of binge drinking (Fromme, Marlatt, Baer, & Kivlahan, 1994; Haines & Spear, 1996; Wechsler et al., 1994). Community approaches targeting young adults include the use of alcohol warning messages in bars, campaigns and server-training programs for limiting alcohol consumption and using designated drivers, tobacco and alcohol taxation and identification checks, and drunk-driving roadblocks and checks (e.g., Hingson et al., 1996; Holder & Wallack, 1986; Mosher & Jernigan, 1988; Wagenaar et al., 1994). In controlled trials, cognitive behavioral skills training has shown effects on reducing acceptance of drinking and binge-drinking behavior among young adult drinkers (Fromme et al., 1994). Feedback to correct college student perceptions of self-drinking and social norms for drinking, either through surveys, diaries, or campus campaigns, has also shown effects on decreasing perceived norms for drinking by 18% or more, and for binge drinking by 8% or more (Agostinelli, Brown, & Miller, 1995; Haines & Spear, 1996). However, most alcohol and drug abuse prevention programs conducted as part of college campus services are not effective (Werch, Pappas, & Castellon-Vogel, 1996). Finally, relatively little is known about the systematic use or efficacy of employee assistance or community education programs for prevention of drug use in young adults.

Women

Universal and indicated prevention programs tend to include both males and females; most focus on S- or E-level risk and prevention. These programs have typically shown no differences in program effects on drug use, with occasional exceptions of long-term program effects on smoking males versus females (cf. Schinke et al., 1992; Vartiainen, Fallonen, McAllister, & Puska, 1990).

There is some evidence to suggest that with low-income pregnant women, nurse home visits may have a long-term impact on decreasing behavioral impairment due to alcohol or other drugs (Olds et al., 1997). Home visits may have an effect by providing social support, since other studies suggest that the presence of supportive mentors or parents may contribute to reduced alcohol use (e.g., Rhodes, Gingiss, & Smith, 1994). Self-help manuals may improve alcohol quit rates, at least for light drinkers (Reynolds, Coombs, Lowe, Peterson, & Gayoso, 1995). Comprehensive health education programs for pregnant adolescents may encourage reduced alcohol and other drug use (Sarvela & Ford, 1993). However, most programs for pregnant women that have shown these effects are not randomized trials (Schorling, 1993); thus, definitive conclusions about the efficacy of these approaches are not possible. There is no clear evidence to suggest that drug prevention programs are more or less effective with females than with males. Few drug prevention programs have been designed specifically for females; most of these have included drug abuse prevention as part of a larger set of program components or skills aimed at protecting the health of pregnant adolescents and young adults, a population in which drinking has increased substantially in the 1990s ("Alcohol consumption," 1997). Results of these programs, which include P- and S-level interventions, are mixed, with some showing no effects of indirect social skills training on pregnant adolescent use behavior (Jones & Mondy, 1994; Palinkas, Atkins, Miller, & Ferreira, 1996) and some showing more declines in use from health education compared to a control condition (Sarvela & Ford, 1993).

Ethnic Groups

As with males and females, most prevention programs include whatever ethnic groups are represented in the normative settings used for intervention. Universal and indicated S-level prevention programs based in schools have shown significant program effects on different ethnic groups (e.g., Eggert et al., 1990; Johnson et al., 1990; Schinke et al., 1992; Sussman, 1996). There is little published information on the relative efficacy of P- or S-level parent-based prevention programs on different ethnic groups, since most populations studied are primarily white (Dishion & Andrew, 1995; Kumpfer, 1989). Programs that have utilized youth-serving agencies

have shown effects of prevention programs on Hispanic and African-American youth and have also reported that tailoring the situational context of prevention material to reflect culture, language, and dress of the particular group may enhance program effects on drug use and HIV risk behavior (e.g., Schinke, Gordon, & Weston, 1990; Schinke et al., 1992). E-level interventions, primarily mass media and community-based prevention programs, have focused on specific ethnic groups rather than on cross-ethnic comparisons. Thus, assessment of relative efficacy of these types of prevention programs compared to programs for white populations is difficult. However, some research suggests that mass media programs emphasizing strong family bonds and tailoring language and content to culture might be effective with both Hispanic and African-American youth and communities (e.g., Kaufman, Jason, Sawlksi, & Halpert, 1994; Romer & Kim, 1995). At least two studies suggest that community-based health promotion and organization for alcohol and drug abuse prevention may decrease rates of alcohol and marijuana use in Native American communities compared to other, mixed-ethnicity communities (Ary et al., 1990; Cheadle et al., 1995).

EFFECTIVENESS AND COST-EFFECTIVENESS

As noted earlier, S- and E-level prevention programs aimed at individuals can effect 20–40% or more average net reductions in youth drug use, with a net reduction defined as the difference between program and control group rates of increase divided by the control group rate of increase, and 2–6% actual changes in drug use prevalence (Pentz, 1994a). Costs of prevention have been estimated for school programs (approximately $6 per student per year) and community programs (approximately $24 per student and family per year) (Kim, Coletti, Crutchfield, Williams, & Hepler, 1995; Pentz, 1986; Rothman, 1995). Estimates of health care cost savings have been estimated for smoking (ranging from $4,000 to $40,000 per prevented smoker) and short-term treatment ($2,000–$20,000 per individual; Pentz, 1994a). Thus, cost-benefit can be estimated by calculating costs of program delivery and prevented users in terms of the number of individuals reached by intervention. Cost-effectiveness may be estimated by comparing the interventions discussed here with a typical school-based health education program that shows no effects on youth drug use.

SUMMARY

This chapter discusses prevention programs aimed at individuals within a theoretical framework that represents person (P), social situation (S), and environment (E) influences on drug use. In general, P-level interventions have had no effect on youth drug use. The majority of evaluated programs have focused on S-level interventions, which have shown substantial and lasting effects on reducing youth tobacco, alcohol, and other drug use. E-level interventions, including mass media, community coalition building, local policy, and multicomponent community interventions, have shown short-term effects on tobacco and alcohol use, with multicomponent interventions showing the most long-term effects. S- and E-level interventions aimed at individuals appear to be cost-effective methods to prevent health care costs associated with drug use, particularly if implemented during the early adolescent years.

Key References

Hansen, W. B. (1992). School-based substance abuse prevention: A review of the state of the art in curriculum, 1980–1990. *Health Education Research, 7*(3), 403–430.

Hawkins J. D., Catalano R. F., & Miller J. Y. (1992). Risk and protective factors for alcohol and other drug problems in adolescence and early adulthood: Implications for substance abuse prevention. *Psychological Bulletin, 11*(1), 64–105.

Pentz, M. A. (1993). Primary prevention of adolescent drug abuse. In C. B. Fisher & R. M. Lerner (Eds.), *Applied Developmental Psychology* (pp. 435–474). New York: McGraw-Hill.

References

Agostinelli, G., Brown, J. M., & Miller, W. R. (1995). Effects of normative feedback on consumption among heavy drinking college students. *Journal of Drug Education, 25*(1), 31–40.

Aktan, G. B., Kumpfer, K. L., & Turner, C. W. (1996). Effectiveness of a family skills training program for substance use prevention with inner city African-American families. *Substance Abuse and Misuse, 31*(2), 157–175.

Alcohol consumption among pregnant and childbearing-aged women—United States, 1991 and 1995. (1997). *Morbidity and Mortality Weekly Report. 46*(16), 346–350.

Altman, D. G., Rasenick-Douss, L., et al. (1991). Sustained effects of an education program to reduce sales of cigarettes to minors. *American Journal of Public Health, 81*, 891–893.

Ary, D. V., Biglan, A., Glasgow, R., Zoref, L., Black, C., Ochs, L., Severson, H., Kelly, R., Weissman, & Lichtenstein, E. (1990). The efficacy of social-influence prevention programs versus "standard care": Are new initiatives needed? *Journal of Behavioral Medicine, 1*, 281–296.

Azjen, I., & Fishbein, M. (1980). *Understanding attitudes and predicting social behavior.* Englewood Cliffs, NJ: Prentice-Hall.

Bachman, J. G., Johnston, L. D., & O'Malley, P. M. (1991). Explaining the recent decline in cocaine use among young adults: Further evidence that perceived risk and disapproval lead to reduce drug use. *Journal of Health Social Behavior, 31*(290), 173–184.

Bandura A. (1977) *Social learning theory.* Englewood Cliffs, NJ: Prentice-Hall.

Barrera, M., Jr. (1986). Distinctions between social support concepts, social support inventory: Measure and models. *American Journal of Community Psychology, 14*(4), 413–445.

Becker, S. L., Burke, J. A., Arbogast, R. A., Naughton, M. J., Bachman, I., & Spohn, E. (1989). Community programs to enhance in-school anti-tobacco efforts. *Preventive Medicine, 18*(2), 221–228.

Botvin, G. J., Baker, E., Dusenbury, L., Botvin, E. M., & Diaz, T. (1995). Long-term follow-up results of a randomized drug abuse prevention trial in a white middle-class population. *Journal of the American Medical Association, 273*(14), 1106–1112.

Butterfoss, F. D., Goodman, R. M., & Wandersman, A. (1996). Community coalitions for prevention and health promotion: Factors predicting satisfaction, participation and planning. *Health Education Quarterly, 23*(1), 65–79.

Carlson, C. E. (1990). HIPP: A comprehensive school-based substance abuse program with cooperative community involvement. Special Issue: The Virginia experience in prevention. *Journal of Primary Prevention, 10*(4), 289–302.

Cheadle, A., Pearson, D., Wagner, E., Psaty, B. M., Diehr, P., & Koepsell, T. (1995). A community-based approach to preventing alcohol use among adolescents on an American Indian reservation. *Public Health Reports, 110*(4), 439–447.

Chou, C-P., Montgomery, S. B., Pentz, M. A., Rohrbach, L. A., Johnson, C. A., Flay, B. R., & MacKinnon, D. (1998). Effects of a community-based prevention program on decreasing drug use in high risk adolescents. *American Journal of Public Health*, 88(6), 944–948.

Connell, D. B., Turner, R. R., & Mason, E. F. (1985). Summary of findings of the school health education evaluation: Health promotion effectiveness, implementation, and costs. *Journal of School Health*, 55(8), 316–321.

Dishion, T. J., & Andrews, D. W. (1995). Preventing escalation in problem behaviors with high-risk young adolescents: Immediate and 1-year outcomes. *Journal of Consulting and Clinical Psychology*, 63(4), 538–548.

Donaldson, S. I., Graham, J. W., & Hansen, W. B. (1994). Testing the generalizability of intervening mechanism theories: Understanding the effects of adolescent drug use prevention interventions. *Journal of Behavioral Medicine*, 17(2), 195–216.

Donaldson, S. I., Graham, J. W., Piccinin, A. M., & Hansen, W. B. (1994). Resistance-skills training and onset of alcohol use: Evidence for beneficial and potentially harmful effects in public schools and in private Catholic schools. *Health Psychology*, 14(4), 291–300.

Donohew, J., Sypher, H. E., & Bukowski, W. J. (1991). *Persuasive communication and drug abuse prevention*. NJ: Erlbaum.

Dusenbury, L., & Falco, M. (1995). Eleven components of effective drug abuse prevention curricula. *Journal of School Health*, 65(10), 420–425.

Eggert, L. L., Seyl, C. D., & Nicholas, L. J. (1990). Effects of a school-based prevention program for potential high school dropouts and drug abusers. *International Journal of the Addictions*, 25(7), 773–801.

Eggert, L. L., Thompson, E. A., Herting, J. R., Nicholas, L. J., & Dicker, B. G. (1994). Preventing adolescent drug abuse and high school dropout through an intensive school-based social network development program. *American Journal of Health Promotion*, 8(3), 202–215.

Ellickson, P. L., Bell, R. M., & McGuigan, K. (1993). Preventing adolescent drug use: Long-term results of a junior high program. *American Journal of Public Health*, 83(6), 856–861.

Ennett, S. T., & Bauman, K. E. (1994). The contribution of influence to adolescent peer group homogeneity: The case of adolescent cigarette smoking. *Journal of Personality and Social Psychology*, 67(4), 653–663.

Flay, B. R., Miller, T. Q., Hedeker, D., Siddequi, O., Britton, C. F., Brannon, B. R., Johnson, C. A., Hansen, W. B., Sussman, S., & Dent, C. (1995). The television, school and family smoking prevention and cessation project. *Preventive Medicine*, 24, 29–40.

Flay, B. R., & Petraitis, J. (1994). The theory of triadic influence: A new theory of health behavior with implications for preventive interventions. *Advances in Medical Sociology*, 4, 19–44.

Florin, P., & Wandersman, A. (1990). An introduction to citizen participation, voluntary organizations, and community development: Insights for empowerment through research. *American Journal of Community Psychology*, 18, 41–53.

Flynn, B. S., Worden, J. K., Secker-Walker, R. H., Badger, G. J., Geller, B. M., & Constanza, M. C. (1992). Prevention of cigarette smoking through mass media intervention and school programs. *American Journal of Public Health*, 82(6), 827–834.

Forster, J. L., Hourigan, M. E., & Kelder, S. (1992). Locking devices on cigarette vending machines: Evaluation of a city ordinance. *American Journal of Public Health*, 82, 1217–1219.

Forster, J. L., Wolfson, M., Murray, D. M., Wagenaar, A. C., & Claxton, A. J. (1997). Perceived and measured availability of tobacco to youths in 14 Minnesota communities: The TPOP Study: Tobacco Policy Options for Prevention. *American Journal of Preventive Medicine*, 13(3), 167–174.

Fromme, K., Marlatt, G. A., Baer, J. S., & Kivlahan, D. R. (1994). The Alcohol Skills Training Program: A group intervention for young adults drinkers. *Journal of Substance Abuse Treatment*, 11(2), 143–154.

Gensheimer, L. K., Ayers, T. S., & Roosa, M. W. (1993). School-based preventive interventions for at-risk populations. *Evaluations and Program Planning*, 16, 159–167.

Goodman, R. M., Wandersman, A., Chinman, M., Imm, P., & Morrisey, E. (1996). An ecological assessment of community-based interventions for prevention and health promotion: Approaches to measuring community coalitions. *American Journal of Community Psychology*, 24, 33–61.

Green, L. W., Wilson, R. W., & Bauer, K. G. (1983). Data requirements to measure progress on the objectives for the nation in health promotion and disease prevention. *American Journal of Public Health*, 73, 18–24.

Haines, M., & Spear, S. F. (1996). Changing the perception of the norm: A strategy to decrease binge drinking among college students. *Journal of American College Health*, 45(3), 134–140.

Hansen, W. B. (1992). School-based substance abuse prevention: A review of the state of the art in curriculum, 1980–1990. *Health Education Research*, 7(3), 403–430.

Hansen, W. B., Johnson, C. A., Flay, B. R., Graham, J. W., & Sobel, J. (1988). Affective and social influences to the prevention of multiple substance abuse among seventh grade students: Results from Project SMART. *Preventive Medicine, 17*, 135–154.

Hawkins, J. D., Catalano, R. F., & Miller, J. Y. (1992). Risk and protective factors for alcohol and other drug problems in adolescence and early adulthood: Implications for substance abuse prevention. *Psychological Bulletin, 112*(1), 64–105.

Hawkins, J. D., Catalano, R. F., Morrison, D. M., O'Donnell, J., Abbot, R. D., & Day, L. E. (1992). The Seattle Social Development Project: Effects of the first four years on protective factors and problem behaviors. In J. McCord & R. Tremblay (Eds.), *The prevention of antisocial behavior in children* (pp. 139–161). New York: Guilford Press.

Hawkins, J. D., Graham, J. W., Maguin, E., Abbott, R., Hill, K. G., & Catalano, R. F. (1997). Exploring the effects of age of alcohol use initiation and psychosocial risk factors on subsequent alcohol misuse. *Journal of Studies on Alcohol, 58*(3), 280–290.

Hingson, R., McGovern, T., Howland, J., Heeren, T., Winter, M., & Zakocs, R. (1996). Reducing alcohol-impaired driving in Massachusetts: The saving lives program. *American Journal of Public Health, 86*(6), 792–797.

Holder, H. D., & Blose, J. O. (1987). Reduction of community alcohol problems: Computer simulation experiments in three counties. *Journal of Studies on Alcohol, 48*,124–135.

Holder, H. D., & Wallack, L. (1986). Comtemporary perspectives for preventing alcohol problems: An empirically derived model. *Journal of Public Health Policy, 7*, 324–339.

Jason, L. A., Ji, P. Y., Anes, M. D., & Birkhead, S. H. (1991). Active enforcement of cigarette control laws in the prevention of cigarette sales to minors. *Journal of the American Medical Association, 266*(22), 3159–3161.

Jessor, R. (1982). Problem behavior and developmental transition in adolescence. *Journal of School Health, 52*(5), 295–300.

Johnson, C. A., Pentz, M. A., Weber, M. D., Dwyer, J. H., MacKinnon, D. P., Flay, B. R., Baer, N. A., & Hansen, W. B. (1990). The relative effectiveness of comprehensive community programming for drug abuse prevention with risk and low risk adolescents. *Journal of Consulting and Clinical Psychology, 58*(4), 447–456.

Johnston, L. D., O'Malley, P. M., & Bachman, J. G. (1997). *National survey results on drug use from the Monitoring the Future Study, 1975–1996: Vol. 1. Secondary school students.* Rockville, MD: U.S. Department of Health and Human Services (NIH Publication No. 94-3809).

Jones, M. E., & Mondy, L. W. (1994). Lessons for prevention and intervention in adolescent pregnancy: A five-year comparison of outcomes of two programs for school-aged pregnant adolescents. *Journal of Pediatric Health Care, 8*(4), 152–159.

Kantor, G. K., Caudill, B. D., & Ungerleider, S. (1992). Project Impact: Teaching the teachers to intervene in student substance abuse problems. *Journal of Alcohol and Drug Education, 31*(1), 11–27.

Kaufman, J. S., Jason, L. A., Sawlski, L. M., & Halpert, J. A. (1994). A comprehensive multi-media program to prevent smoking among black students. *Journal of Drug Education, 24*(2), 95–108.

Kellam, S. G., & Rebok, G. W. (1992). Building developmental and etiological theory through epidemiologically based preventive intervention trials. In J. McCord & R. E. Tremblay (Eds.), *Preventing antisocial behavior: Interventions from birth through adolescence.* New York: Guilford Press

Kim, S., Coletti, S. D., Crutchfield, C. C., Williams, C., & Hepler, N. (1995). Benefit-cost analysis of drug abuse prevention programs: a macroscopic approach. *Journal of Drug Education, 25*(2), 111–127.

Kumpfer, K. L. (1989). Prevention of alcohol and drug abuse: a critical review of risk factors and prevention strategies. In D. Shaffer, I. Philips, & N. B. Enzer (Eds.), *Prevention of mental disorders, alcohol and other drug use in children and adolescents.* Monograph 2. Rockville, MD: Office of Substance Abuse Prevention.

MacKinnon, D. P., Johnson, C. A., Pentz, M. A., Dwyer, J. H., Hansen, W. B., Flay, B. R., & Wang, E. Y. I. (1991). Mediating mechanisms in a school-based drug prevention program: First-year effects of the Midwestern Prevention Project. *Health Psychology, 10*(3), 164–172.

Magnusson, D. (Ed.). (1981). *Toward a psychology of situations: An international perspective.* Hillsdale, NJ: Erlbaum.

Manger, T. H., Hawkins, J. D., Haggerty, K. P., & Catalano, R. F. (1992). Mobilizing communities to reduce risks for drug abuse: Lessons on using research to guide prevention practice. *Journal of Primary Prevention, 13*(1), 3–22.

Mansergh, G., Rohrbach, L., Montgomery, S. B., Pentz, M. A., & Johnson, C. A. (1996). Process evaluation of community coalitions for alcohol and other drug prevention: Comparison of two models. *Journal of Community Psychology, 24*, 118–135.

McGovern, J. P., & DuPont, R. L. (1991). Student assistance programs: An important approach to drug abuse prevention. *Journal of School Health, 61*(6), 260–264.

Mosher, J. F., & Jernigan, D. H. (1988). New directions in alcohol policy. *Annual Review of Public Health*, 10, 245–279.

Murray, D. M., & Perry, C. L. (1985). The prevention of drug abuse: Implications of etiological, developmental, behavioral, and environmental models. In C. L. Jones & R. J. Battjes (Eds.), *Etiology of drug abuse: Implications for prevention*, NIDA Research Monograph 56.

Oetting, E. R., & Beauvais, F. (1986). Peer cluster theory: Drugs and the adolescent. *Journal of Counseling and Development*, 65, 17–22.

Olds, D. L., Eckenrode, J., Henderson, C. R., Kitzman, H., Powers, J., Cole, R., Sidora, K., Morris, P., Pettitt, L. M., & Luckey, D. (1997). Long-term effects of home visitation on maternal life course and child abuse and neglect: Fifteen-year follow-up of a randomized trial. *Journal of the American Medical Association*, 278(8), 637–643.

Palinkas, L. A., Atkins, C. J., Miller, C., & Ferreira, D. (1996). Social skills training for drug prevention in high-risk female adolescents. *Preventive Medicine*, 25(6), 692–701.

Pentz, M. A. (1985). Social competence and self-efficacy as determinants of substance use in adolescents. In T. A. Willis & S. Shiffman (Eds.), *Coping and substance abuse*. New York: Academic Press.

Pentz, M. A. (1986). Community organization and school liaisons: How to get programs started. *Journal of School Health*, 56, 382–388.

Pentz, M. A. (1993). Primary prevention of adolescent drug abuse. In C. B. Fisher & R. M. Lerner (Eds.), *Applied developmental psychology* (pp. 435–474). New York: McGraw-Hill.

Pentz, M. A. (1994a). Adaptive evaluation strategies for estimating effects of community-based drug abuse prevention programs. *Journal of Community Psychology*, 26–51.

Pentz, M. A. (1994b). Target populations and interventions in prevention research: What is high risk? In A. Cazares & L. A. Beatty (Eds.), *Scientific methods for prevention intervention research*, (pp. 75–94). NIDA Res Monograph. 139. NIH Publication No. 94-3631.

Pentz, M. A. (1995). The school-community interface in comprehensive school health education. In S. Stansfield (Ed.), *Institute of Medicine annual report*. Committee on Comprehensive School Health Programs, Institute of Medicine, Bethesda, MD. Washington DC: National Academy Press.

Pentz, M. A. (in press). Intervention: Prevention in the Community. In R. T. Tarter, R. T. Ammerman, & P. J. Ott (Eds.), *Sourcebook on substance abuse: Etiology, methodology and intervention*. Allyn & Bacon.

Pentz, M. A. (1998). Preventing drug abuse through the community: Multi-component programs make the difference. In Z. Sloboda & W. B. Hansen (Eds.), *NIDA Research Monograph*, 73–86. No. 98-4293.

Pentz, M. A., Bonnie, R. J., & Shopland, D. S. (1996). Integrating supply and demand reduction strategies for drug abuse prevention. *American Behavioral Scientist*, 39(7), 897–910.

Pentz, M. A., Brannon, B. R., Charlin, V. L., Barrett, E. J., MacKinnon, D. P., & Flay, B. R. (1989). The power of policy: The relationship of smoking policy to adolescent smoking. *American Journal of Public Health*, 79(7), 857–862.

Pentz, M. A., Dwyer, J. H., MacKinnon, D. P., Flay, B. R., Hansen, W. B., Wang, E. Y. I., & Johnson C. A. (1989). A multi-community trial for primary prevention of adolescent drug abuse: Effects on drug use prevalence. *Journal of the American Medical Association*, 261(22), 3259–3266.

Pentz, M. A., & Newman, T. L. (1997). Influence of community interventions on tobacco change. (Unpublished manuscript.)

Pentz, M. A., Pentz, C. A., & Gong, A. (1993). Different strokes for different folks? Effects of two adolescent smoking prevention programs on different racial/ethnic groups. *Annual Meeting of the Society of Behavioral Medicine*, San Francisco, March 10–13.

Perry, C. L., & Jessor, R. (1985). The concept of health promotion and the prevention of adolescent drug abuse. *Health Education Quarterly*, 12, 170–184.

Perry, C. L., Kelder, S. H., Murray, D. M., & Klepp, K. I. (1992). Communitywide smoking prevention: Long-term outcomes of the Midwest Heart Health Program and the Class of 1989 Study. *American Journal of Public Health*, 82(9), 1210–1216.

Pierce, J. P., Choi, W. S., Gilpin, E. A., Farkas, A. J., & Merritt, R. K. (1996). Validation of susceptibility as a predictor of which adolescents take up smoking in the United States. *Health Psychology*, 15(5), 355–361.

Puska, P., Vartiainen, E., Pallonen, U., et al. (1982). The North Karelia Youth Project: Evaluation of two years of intervention study on health behavior and CVD risk factors among 13- to 15-year-old children. *Preventive Medicine*, 11, 550–570.

Resnicow, K., Cross, D., & Wynder E. (1991). The role of comprehensive school-based interventions: The results of four "Know Your Body" studies. *Annals of the New York Academy of Sciences*, 623, 285–298.

Reynolds, K. D., Coombs, D. W., Lowe, J. B., Peterson, P. L., & Gayoso, E. (1995). Evaluation of a self-help program to reduce alcohol consumption among pregnant women. *International Journal of Addictions*, 30(4), 427–443.

Rhodes, J. E., Gingess, P. L., & Smith, P. B. (1994).

Risk and protective factors for alcohol use among pregnant African-American, Hispanic, and white adolescents: The influence of peers, sexual partners, family members, and mentors. *Addictive Behaviors, 19*(5), 555–564.

Romer, D., & Kim, S. (1995). Health interventions for African American and Latino youth: The potential role of mass media. *Health Eduction Quarterly, 22*(2), 172–189.

Rothman, M. L. (1995). The potential benefits and costs of a comprehensive school health education program. (Unpublished manuscript.)

Sampson, R. J., Raudenbush, S. W., & Earls, F. (1997). Neighborhoods and violent crime: A multilevel study of collective efficacy. *Science, 277*(5328), 918–924.

Sarvela, P. D., & Ford, T. D. (1993). An evaluation of a substance abuse education program for Mississippi Delta pregnant adolescents. *Journal of School Health, 63*(3), 147–152.

Saxe, L., Reber, E., Hallfors, D., Kadushin, C., Jones, D., Rindskopf, D., & Beveridge, A. (in press). Think global, act local: Assessing the impact of community-based substance abuse prevention. *Evaluation and Program Planning.*

Schinke, S. P., Gordon, A. N., & Weston, R. E. (1990). Self-instruction to prevent HIV infection among African-American and Hispanic-American adolescents. *Journal of Consulting and Clinical Psychology, 58*(4), 432–436.

Schinke, S. P., Orlandi, M. A., & Cole, K. C. (1992). Boys and Girls Clubs in public housing development: Prevention services for youth at risk. *Journal of Community Psychology, Special Issue*, 118–128.

Schorling, J. B. (1993). The prevention of prenatal alcohol use: A critical analysis of intervention studies. *Journal of Studies on Alcohol, 54*(3), 261–267.

St. Pierre, T. L., Kaltreider, D. L., Mark, N. N., & Aiken, K. J. (1992). Drug prevention in a community setting: A longitudinal study of the relative effectiveness of a three-year primary prevention program in Boys and Girls Clubs across the nation. *American Journal of Community Psychology, 20*(6), 673–706.

Sussman, S. (1996). Development of a school-based drug abuse prevention curriculum for high-risk youths. *Journal of Substance Abuse, 8*, 361–370.

Sussman, S., Dent, C. W., Burton, D., Stacy, A. W., & Flay, B. R. (1995). *Developing school-based tobacco use prevention and cessation programs.* Thousand Oaks, CA: Sage.

Swisher, J. D., Baker, S. B., Barnes, D., Gebler, M. K., Hadleman, D. E., & Kophazi, K. M. (1993). An evaluation of student assistance programs in Pennsylvania. *Journal of Drug and Alcohol Education, 39*(1), 1–18.

Tobler, N. S. (1992). Drug prevention programs can work: Research findings. *Journal of Addictive Diseases, 11*(3), 1–28.

Vartiainen, E., Fallonen, U., McAllister, A-L., & Puska, P. (1990). Eight year follow-up results of an adolescent smoking prevention program: The North Karelia Youth Project. *American Journal of Public Health, 60*(1), 76–79.

Wagenaar, A. C., Murray, D. M., Wolfson, M., Forster, J. L., & Finnegan, J. R. (1994). Communities mobilizing for change on alcohol: Design of a randomized community trial. *Journal of Community Psychology* (CSAP Special Issue).

Wandersman, A., & Giamartino, G. A. (1980). Community and individual difference characteristics as influences on initial participation. *American Journal of Community Psychology, 8*(2), 217–228.

Wechsler, H., Isaac, N. E., Grodstein, F., & Sellers, D. E. (1994). Continuation and initiation of alcohol use from the first to the second year of college. *Journal of Studies on Alcohol, 55*(1), 41–45.

Werch, C. E., Pappas, D. M., & Castellon-Vogel, E. A. (1996). Drug use prevention efforts at colleges and universities in the United States. *Substance Abuse and Misuse, 31*(1), 65–80.

White, H., Boorman, S. A., & Breiger, R. (1976). Social structures from multiple networks: L. Block models of roles and positions. *American Journal of Sociology, 81*, 730–780.

Yamaguchi, K., & Kandel, D. B. (1984). Patterns of drug use from adolescence to young adulthood: 3. Predictors of progression. *American Journal of Public Health, 74*, 673–681.

Yin, R. K., & Kaftarian, S. J. (1997). What the national cross-site evaluation is learning about CSAP's community partnerships. In N. R. Chavez & S. J. O'Neill (Eds.), *Secretary's youth substance abuse prevention initiative: Resource papers* (pp. 179–196). SAMHSA Prepublication Documents. Washington, DC: U.S. Department of Health and Human Services.

31

Prevention Aimed at the Environment

Harold D. Holder

Environmental strategies for the prevention of alcohol problems, smoking, and illicit drug use target the context in which those substances are used, that is, the physical, economic, social, and cultural surroundings. The environmental approach to prevention seeks to reduce risk and harm for all persons rather than for specific subgroups or high-risk groups. This chapter will first describe a systems or environmental prevention approach that is in contrast to an individual target group or catchment approach. Next, the chapter will review a variety of environmental strategies beginning with the prevention of alcohol problems (particularly acute problems), then the reduction of smoking (particularly by young people), and finally with illicit drug use (primarily interdiction of supply and severity of punishment).

CATCHMENT VERSUS SYSTEMS PERSPECTIVES

Health problem prevention has commonly focused on individuals at risk. Such a focus is based on a "catchment area" perspective, in which a "community" is viewed as a collection of target groups with adverse behaviors or associated risks. Prevention is intended to reduce or eliminate these behaviors by finding the individuals at risk and treating, educating, or otherwise responding to them in an appropriate manner to reduce their risk.

For example, cirrhosis mortality might be an identified alcohol-induced problem in a low-income, transient neighborhood. The city or a local service organization might naturally target this neighborhood and seek to reduce the drinking levels of heavy, chronic (usually dependent) drinkers by establishing a recovery center. Similarly, adolescents' use of alcohol and other drugs within a local middle school might be targeted with strategies aimed at increasing preadolescents' resistance skills against peer pressure to drink, along with developing afterschool activities and school-based and family-focused education programs. *Not* affected in this model would be community members not directly involved with the targeted at-risk populations. Retail sales of alcohol and the informal sources of alcohol and drugs to young people might also be ignored.

Prevention planners using the catchment area approach select strategies that alter individual decisions and behavior or that provides direct services to individuals. Education-based activities are favored, as are early identification and intervention. Educational efforts often include mass media announcements, focus groups, targeted communication, health promotion, health awareness, and physician education efforts. One-on-one and group treatment and counseling may be used. Many community prevention trials for heart disease and cancer have employed some form of a catchment area approach. The targets of these trials have been well-defined states or conditions with which individual residents of a community can be accurately associated. For example, if heavy smoking is the target, then heavy smokers can be identified so that education programs for smoking reduction and cessation can be directed at them. Community heart disease projects make effective use of the link between diet, exercise, smoking, and genetics to assist at-risk individuals in adjusting or moderating their behaviors.

The catchment area perspective has clear limitations in substance abuse problem prevention. Heavy users of alcohol and drugs have the greatest individual risk rates for most problems. For example, heavy drinkers are more likely to have a traffic crash when they drink and drive. However, they are not collectively the *largest* at-risk group. Their absolute numbers are often so small that they contribute only modestly to most aggregate problems. For example, infrequent and moderate users of alcohol, who are not currently nor likely ever to be dependent on alcohol, account for a greater number of alcohol-involved traumas such as auto crashes, falls, or drownings than do heavy users (see Edwards et al., 1994). Young people, in particular, account for a disproportionately large number of alcohol-related problem events, such as traffic crashes and accidental injuries. Most heavy, addicted drinkers continue their drinking pattern throughout their lives and never incur an alcohol-involved traffic crash or an encounter with the police. On the other hand, an 18-year-old with limited driving and drinking experience may cause a serious auto crash with only a small amount of alcohol in the blood system. Physical and cognitive impairment begins as soon as the body begins to metabolize ethanol. Impairment increases as more ethanol enters the blood, and the individual can become increasingly impaired over time as drinking continues. The rate of impairment is a function of such factors as alcohol experience and tolerance, body weight, amount of food consumed while drinking, and rate of alcohol intake.

A community systems approach to health problem prevention has been used less commonly than a catchment area approach, perhaps because the systems perspective is conceptually more complex. In this perspective, a "community" is viewed as a set of persons engaged in shared social, cultural, political, and economic processes. Prevention is intended to modify the *system* in an appropriate manner to reduce health problems identified in the community (see Holder, 1998).

Because substance abuse is viewed as a product of the system (not simply attributable to a few maladapted individuals), prevention strategies focused on the community at large can be more effective than those focused on specific individuals at risk. *Collective risk* will be reduced by intervening to change the processes that contribute to alcohol problems, smoking, and illicit drug use.

Environmental strategies have been employed in community public health initiatives, including some heart disease and cancer prevention trials. For example, some projects have persuaded restaurants to offer low-fat menu alternatives, to make low-salt food products available and prominently displayed in grocery stores, to get warning labels on the hazards of smoking installed at points of sale for cigarettes, and to increase the number of nonsmoking areas within public spaces and in the workplace. Some community health trials have used public policy mandates requiring the availability of low-fat food alternatives, or increasing the retail price of cigarettes, or legally restricting availability of cigarettes by banning vending machines.

The community is a dynamic system. The system changes and adapts as new people enter and others leave, as alcoholic beverage or cigarette marketing and promotion evolve, and as social and economic conditions, including employment and disposable income, change. No single prevention program, no matter how good, can sustain its impact, particularly if system-level changes are not accomplished (see Holder & Wallack, 1986; Wallack, 1981). Even if all high-risk individuals (e.g., alcoholics, drug addicts, or heavy smokers) could be identified and somehow magically "fixed," if the system structure remained unchanged then high-risk replacements naturally would be generated by the system.

ALCOHOL PROBLEM PREVENTION

Environmental strategies to prevent alcohol problems are those that affect the drinking context, including the general economic and physical availability of alcohol for consumption.

Price

Perhaps the area of research with the most consistent evidence is the study of alcohol price and consumption. Price has historically been an important part of alcohol problem prevention in many parts of the world. Alcoholic beverages appear to behave in the market like other goods: As prices decline and/or income increases, then alcohol consumption tends to increase. A number of studies have estimated this relationship (the elasticity or sensitivity of alcohol consumption to changes in price and income). See, for example, Ornstein and Levy (1983), Saffer and Grossman (1987), Levy and Sheflin (1983), and Cook and Tauchen (1982). See Österberg (1995) for a review of international research on the price elasticity of alcohol.

The price elasticity of alcohol is influenced by many other factors. It has been pointed out that the more restricted the availability of alcohol, the smaller the influence of changes in prices and incomes of consumers will be. See Malmqvist (1948) and Huitfeld and Jorner (1972) for analyses of Swedish data and Gruenewald, Ponicki, and Holder (1993) for recent analyses of U.S. data.

Since the overall consumption of distilled spirits, as well as consumption of spirits by heavy drinkers, can be demonstrated to be sensitive to price, it is reasonable to hypothesize that other alcohol-related problems will also be price-sensitive. Cook (1981) investigated the short-term effects of changes in liquor tax on the auto accident death rates and found that such fatalities declined as taxes increased (and thus, increased retail prices).

Physical Access to Alcoholic Beverages

Restrictions on physical and economic availability are intended to limit consumer access or to intervene in the drinking context. Alcohol availability received considerable attention worldwide during the early part of the 20th century with Prohibition and, in more recent years, with debates about increasing or relaxing restrictions on retail availability of alcohol.

Of course, a number of countries have monopolies on some form of retail sale, and total prohibition is practiced in many Muslim countries. The socialist countries in central and eastern Europe, as well as France, Switzerland, and the Scandinavian countries, operate some form of retail or wholesale monopoly. In North America, Canadian provinces and some U.S. states operate monopolies for distilled spirits and wine.

The opening of new types of alcohol outlets in many countries has been accompanied by increased consumption and, in many cases, associated increases in problems. Kuusi (1957) showed that opening state alcohol shops in Finnish rural communities increased consumption for males by 40% and 15–19% for females. Amundsen (1967) found that opening a wine outlet in Notodden, Norway, in 1961 increased wine consumption, while spirits and illegal alcohol declined only slightly. Nordlund (1974) concluded that opening off-license monopoly outlets in Notodden, Elverum, and Ålesund was associated with no essential changes in overall consumption. This research has been subjected to some methodological criticisms as using only self-reported survey data (Ahlström-Laasko, 1975).

The availability of distilled spirits for on-premise consumption by the individual drink (called *liquor by the drink*, or LBD) is now commonplace in most of the United States and other countries. At the end of the U.S. Prohibition, all states except nine legalized LBD. Since 1968, however, all nine states have legalized the sale of LBD, and yet studies that specifically evaluated LBD in the United States were rare and provided limited information. Bryant (1954) found no increase in alcohol problems after implementation of LBD in the state of Washington. His findings are confounded by limited time series data (a long series of observations after the intervention but only one prior), reliance entirely on measures that are particularly sensitive to enforcement (e.g., public drunkenness arrests), and other biases. Womer (1978) found a minor impact of LBD on consumption in Virginia, but he used no control group and felt his analysis was inconclusive. Hoadley, Fuchs, and Holder (1984) utilized multiple-regression analysis with cross-sectional time series data to analyze the impact of state-level regulatory measures on per capita distilled-spirits consumption during the period 1955–1980. Their results suggested that the absence of LBD was associated with higher distilled-spirits consumption.

Holder and Blose (1987) conducted an interrupted-time-series analysis of counties within the state of North Carolina and found that spirit sales rose by between 6% and 7.4% in counties implementing LBD. LBD was also associated with statistically significant increases of 16–24% in both the number of police-reported alcohol-related accidents and single-vehicle nighttime accidents among male drivers 21 years of age and older in counties implementing LBD. No change in alcohol-related accidents was found for non-LBD counties. Therefore, when distilled spirits are made available in bars and restaurants, consumption and drinking and driving increase.

Another change in alcohol availability has been the introduction of wine sales into privately licensed outlets such as grocery stores and liquor stores. Mulford and Fitzgerald (1988) concluded that the end of the state retail wine monopoly in Iowa did not increase wine consumption. Macdonald (1986) found that the introduction of wine privatization in Idaho, Maine, Virginia, and Washington produced greater wine consumption in three of the four states. Smart (1986) concluded that the introduction of wine into grocery stores in the Canadian province of Quebec produced no increase in wine sales or total per capita alcohol consumption. Wagenaar and Holder (1991a) completed interrupted-times-series (Box & Jenkins, 1976) analyses of the elimination of the state retail wine monopoly in Iowa in 1987 and West Virginia in 1981 and found statistically significant increases in both states for total absolute alcohol consumption.

Iowa was also the first state since the end of Prohibition in the United States to end its retail spirits monopoly; it did so in 1987. In a separate study, Holder and Wagenaar (1990) completed a time series analysis of wine as well as spirits and beer sales for Iowa and for total alcohol consumption for all bordering states. They concluded that there was a net increase in absolute alcohol consumption, which accounted for a 13.7% decrease in wine sales, no change in beer sales, and a 9.5% increase in spirit sales. No changes were found in spirit sales in all states bordering Iowa. Overall, the evidence supports

a conclusion that ending state monopolies on retail sale of alcohol increases alcohol consumption.

Density of Alcohol Outlets

The number and concentration of alcohol retail outlets are suggested to increase consumer convenience and possibly provide a social reinforcement of drinking behavior. Support for this observation was provided by Colon (1982), as well as for the counterobservation that outlet densities are only a response to demand for alcoholic beverages (Ornstein & Hanssens, 1985). Restricting alcohol availability by using the law has been a central part of policy efforts in Canada, the United States, and many other parts of the world (Kortteinen, 1989; Room, 1987).

The other domain of effects for public monopolies is from overall reduction in alcohol availability. Nordlund (1981) examined the effect on total consumption in two towns of a net reduction of beer outlets by concentrating beer in one or a few specialty beer stores. Nordlund found that this so-called beer monopoly produced a reduction in beer sales but that some of this reduction was replaced by sale of wine and spirits. No overall reduction in total alcohol consumption was found.

A critical subset of economic studies have been reported that included market variables in their analyses of time series (McGuinness, 1983; Walsh, 1982) and time series cross-sectional (Wilkinson, 1987) data on physical availability and consumption. The first two studies, using data from the United Kingdom, suggest that availability (measured in terms of outlet densities) may be related to consumption rates but are limited by the shortness of the series studied (at most, 25 years). A study by Wilkinson (1987) suggested a small but significant relationship between the variable number of outlets and alcohol sales.

Godfrey (1988) analyzed alcohol sales data and indicators of availability in Great Britain. Using time series data, she found evidence that outlet densities are related to use for spirits, wine, and beer but that only beer consumption is related to density of beer outlets.

A stronger design and associated analysis was reported later by Gruenewald et al. (1993), who conducted a time series cross-sectional analysis of alcohol consumption and alcohol outlets by type of beverage (beer, wine, and spirits) over the 50 U.S. states. The authors analyzed data over the period

1975–1984 for spirits and wine. Beer had an insufficient time series database to support an analysis of beer. The design and analyses used by these authors included beverage prices and income as covariates, as well as a subset of sociodemographic variables hypothesized to be related to consumption. The design includes a relatively large time series data set of 114–290 time series cross-sectional units. The results yielded elasticities of the response of retail sales of alcohol to outlet densities of from .1 to .3 for spirits and .4 for wine.

There has been increased interest in the United States in local regulation of the density of alcohol outlets (Curry, 1988; Wittman & Hilton, 1987; Wittman & Shane, 1988). For example, the state of California has limited the number of distilled spirits outlets per 100,000 population for both on-premise and off-premise sales in each county.

These studies of a variety of changes in alcohol availability support a conclusion that the number and concentration of alcohol retail outlets have been suggested to increase consumer convenience, and thereby, to increase consumer purchases and consumption.

Minimum Age of Purchase

At the end of U.S. Prohibition, each of the states established a minimum age of purchase or drinking. The states varied in terms of the established legal age: some 18, some 19, and some 21. In addition, some states established different legal ages by beverage (e.g., 18 for beer and wine and 21 for spirits). In the 1980s, all U.S. states were required to adopt a uniform 21 minimum age for all beverages.

A number of studies were undertaken to determine the effect of this uniform age (see summaries in Holder, 1987; Wagenaar, 1983). The U.S. General Accounting Office (USGAO) (1987) reviewed 32 published research studies both before and after the law changed. However, many of these studies were judged to be of insufficient scientific quality to inform policy decisions. Of the 14 studies that did meet the USGAO's methodological criteria, 4 addressed fatal crashes across several states and 5 addressed fatal crashes in individual states. The USGAO concluded that there was solid scientific evidence that increasing the minimum age for purchasing alcohol reduced the number of alcohol-involved traffic crashes for young people under 21

years old. A later study by O'Malley and Wagenaar (1991) found that the minimum age effect on traffic crashes continued well into young adulthood and did not decay after young people reached the legal drinking age.

Surveys of students in Canada reported findings similar to those in the United States. In 1971, the drinking age for Ontario was lowered from 21 to 18. Cross-sectional surveys of Toronto high school students were undertaken in 1968, 1970, 1972, and 1974. The proportion of students who had used alcohol at least once increased between the surveys immediately before and after the age change (1970–1972), but an even larger increase occurred between 1968 and 1970 (Smart & Fejer, 1975). A study of Toronto college students found an increase in frequency, but not in quantity per occasion, due to the law (Smart, Fejer, & White, 1972).

Whitehead et al. (1975) and Williams, Rich, Zador, and Robertson (1975) found an increase in the incidence of alcohol-related car crashes among the young. Schmidt and Kornaczewski (1975) found significant increases in the number of traffic accidents among Ontario drivers 16–19 years old. Whitehead (1977), following up an earlier study (Whitehead et al., 1975), found that the higher rates of alcohol-related crashes among young drivers continued over the 4 years of his study period after the age change.

A study of alcohol-related crashes for 16- to 20-year-old Saskatchewan drivers by Shattuck and Whitehead (1976) found that after the minimum drinking age was lowered in 1972, there was an increase in such crashes. Bako, MacKenzie, and Smith (1976) found over a 100% increase in the incidence of auto crash fatalities in Alberta among youthful drivers whose blood alcohol levels were 0.08% or more, related to the lower minimum drinking age. Increasing the minimum age for purchase or drinking alcohol can reduce consumption and alcohol-involved traffic accidents among youth.

Service of Alcohol

Bars and restaurants licensed to serve alcohol are increasingly viewed as locations for interventions with drinkers. Reviews of the impact of beverage server intervention can be found in Saltz (1987, 1989, 1993), Russ and Geller (1986), Gliksman et al. (1993), and McKnight (1988). More recent research studies of server training (Saltz, 1988; Saltz & Hennessy,

1990a, 1990b) have demonstrated that server training is most effective when coupled with a change in actual serving policy and practices of a bar or restaurant. A policy can reinforce the server. Such research supports a conclusion that changes in server behavior can lower the blood alcohol level (BAL) of patrons leaving licensed establishments and thus the subsequent risk of becoming involved in a traffic crash or other alcohol-involved problem (Saltz, 1989).

A study by Holder and Wagenaar (1994) found that in the one U.S. state (Oregon) that mandated server training for all persons who sell alcohol, such training produced a statistically significant reduction in alcohol-involved traffic crashes when at least 50% of servers had completed training. In general, server-training and alcohol-serving policies by bars and restaurants can reduce acute alcohol problems.

Server Liability

Server liability is civil liability faced by both commercial servers and social hosts for injuries or damage caused by their intoxicated or underage drinking patrons and guests. A study by Holder et al. (1993) found that the level of actual liability in a state appears to be linked to the level of publicity about such liability and to the awareness of such liability by owners and managers of licensed establishments and thus to differences in self-reported serving practices. This liability directly affects outlets that serve or sell alcohol. It is based upon a policy that alcohol-serving or sales establishments are legally liable for the negative consequences caused by customers who were inappropriately provided alcohol in the establishment. The prevention approach here is to encourage establishments to engage in safer alcohol-serving and sales practices. This liability has been established in many U.S. states following such situations as alcohol being served to an obviously intoxicated person who subsequently crashes his or her car and injures others, or as serving to an underage drinker who is later involved in a trauma event (Holder et al., 1993; Mosher, 1979). The potential of such liability to bring about positive changes in the serving practices of retail establishments has not been comprehensively evaluated. Wagenaar and Holder (1991b) found that a sudden change in server liability in the state of Texas produced a statistically significant 6–7% reduction in alcohol-involved traffic crashes. Unfortunately, this macrolevel study was not able to directly document changes in server behavior in response to liability, and further replication of the study in other locations is necessary. The potential for liability to affect bar and restaurant alcohol-serving practices is supported, however.

Restrictions on Time of Retail Sale

Smith (1987, 1988a, 1988b, 1988c) conducted a series of studies on a variety of changes in hours and days of sale made in various cities and states of Australia (see also Lind & Herbert, 1982), and one descriptive study has been reported on the impact of extended operating hours at Scottish public houses and hotels (Bruce, 1980). These studies present some, at least anecdotal, evidence for impacts of changes in hours and days of sale upon a number of alcohol problems.

Smith (1988c), for example, presented a study in which the introduction of Sunday alcohol sales in the city of Brisbane, Australia, was related to casualty and reported property damage traffic crashes. However, these results are not unequivocal, as these effects could be contaminated by other trend effects on Sunday sales and nonequivalent distribution of crashes over days of the week (see Gruenewald, 1991).

Olsson and Wikstrom (1982) examined the effects of an experimental Saturday closing of liquor retail stores in Sweden. They found an 8% reduction in alcohol sales and a corresponding reduction in intoxicated persons and the number of police interventions in domestic disturbances. Nordlund (1985) analyzed the effects of an experimental 1-year Saturday closing in Norway for state stores. The findings were that the Saturday closings had little effect on overall consumption and that consumers adjusted to the closing by purchasing wine and spirits on other days or by purchasing beer. He did find that effects on heavy, problematic abusers were significant. The number of police reports of drunkenness and domestic problems on Saturdays and early Sundays decreased dramatically.

Reducing the days and times of alcohol sales restricts the opportunities for alcohol purchasing and can reduce heavy consumption.

Alcohol Content

Lower-alcohol beverages have been used in recent years in many countries as a potential means to reduce levels of absolute alcohol consumed and, thus, associated levels of intoxication. These lower-alcohol beverages have often been taxed at lower levels, which produces lower prices in countries such as Sweden, Norway, and Finland, where such low-alcohol beer is sold in grocery stores rather than in state-monopoly retail stores. This lower taxation has been used in many Scandinavian countries, which have encouraged three classes of beer according to their alcohol content and at least two classes of wine. See Österberg (1991) for a summary of such policies.

The introduction of medium-strength (3.6% alcohol by weight) beer in Sweden and Finland provides additional evaluation of the results of changes in the form of alcohol availability. Noval and Nilsson (1984) found that total alcohol consumption in Sweden was substantially higher when medium-strength beer could be purchased in grocery stores (i.e., between 1965 and 1977), rather than only in state monopoly stores. The private sale of medium-strength beer in Sweden ended in 1977. In Finland, the sale of medium-strength beer began in 1969 in all food stores and most cafés. Medium-strength beer had been available for a number of years in the state monopoly stores and restaurants (Österberg, 1991). Mäkelä (1970) concluded that the number of drinking occasions on which the blood alcohol level reached 0.10% increased by as much as 25% in 1 year following the change, and there was a substantial increase in the estimated numbers of heavy drinkers (Bruun et al., 1975). Skog (1988) analyzed the effect of the introduction of light beer in Norway in March 1985 and found a substitution of lower for higher alcohol content beer, but the estimate was not statistically significant. He concluded that the data do not permit unequivocal evidence of substitution or addition.

Providing beverages with lower alcohol content provides the consumer with choices in strength of beverage that has the potential to reduce the level of alcohol impairment.

Drinking and Driving Laws

Public policy intended to reduce alcohol-involved traffic crashes and associated injuries and deaths is most often represented in each country by laws concerning drinking and driving. Most developed countries have increased the penalties for drunk driving and their enforcement of such laws. A considerable research base exists that documents the relative effec-

tiveness of per se laws, drinking and driving enforcement, and sanctions or punishment.

Per se laws specify the blood alcohol level or concentration at which a driver is considered legally impaired (i.e., the level at which a driver can be arrested and charged with drinking and driving). The per se level has been declining in Europe, Australia, New Zealand, and North America. This reduction in the legal level of driver impairment has been associated with reduced crash levels (Liben, Vingilis, & Blefgen, 1987; Ross, 1982; Zador, Lund, Fields, & Weinberg, 1989).

Drinking-and-driving enforcement has also been increased in many countries in the past decade. Ross (1982) pointed out that it might be that the threat of enforcement, or public expectation that one may be stopped and arrested, has had more influence than the actual enforcement. However, increased public expectations of arrest must be reinforced with actual increased enforcement to have sustained effect (see reviews by Hingson, Howland, & Levenson, 1988; Vingilis & Coultes, 1990; Zador et al., 1989).

The use of random roadside checks by police for alcohol-impaired drivers in such countries as Australia (Homel, 1986, 1990), Canada (Mercer, 1985), and Great Britain (Ross, 1988a, 1988b) has demonstrated the effectiveness of this type of drinking-and-driving enforcement. Sanctions or punishment of a person convicted of drinking and driving has also increased in most countries. License revocation is one type of punishment that has been shown to be effective in reducing repeated incidents of drinking and driving. The threat of loss of one's driver's license has been shown to have important effects in deterring drinking and driving by persons previously convicted of DUI (driving under the influence) (see review by Ross, 1991).

Zero-Tolerance Laws

The National Highway Systems Act in the United States provides incentives for all states to adopt "zero-tolerance laws" that set maximum blood alcohol concentration (BAC) limits for drivers under 21 to 0.02% or lower beginning October 1, 1998 (National Institute on Alcohol Abuse and Alcoholism [NIAAA], 1996). An analysis of the effect of zero-tolerance laws in the first 12 states enacting them found a 20% relative reduction in the proportion of single-vehicle nighttime (SVN) fatal crashes among drivers under

21, compared with nearby states that did not pass zero-tolerance laws (Hingson, Heeren, & Winter, 1994; Martin, Grube, Voas, Baker, & Hingson, 1996).

Administrative License Revocation Laws

Laws permitting the withdrawal of driving privileges without court action have been adopted by 38 states to prevent traffic crashes caused by unsafe driving practices, including driving with a BAC over the legal limit (Hingson et al., 1996). These laws were associated with a 5–9% decline in nighttime fatal crashes in some studies (Hingson, 1993; Zador et al., 1989).

Curfew Laws

Curfew laws establish a time when children and young people below certain ages must be home. While this policy was not initially considered an alcohol-problem prevention strategy, research has shown positive effects. In those states that established such curfews, alcohol-involved traffic crashes for young people below the curfew age have declined (Preusser, Williams, Zador, & Blomberg, 1984; Williams, Lund, & Preusser, 1984).

Restrictions on Drinking Locations

Specifying locations where drinking cannot occur is a policy that has been employed in a number of forms throughout the world but has not been systematically evaluated. The policy has been implemented with laws about public drinking and/or public intoxication, as well as those prohibiting drinking in parks or recreational locations, or at the workplace. Discussions of these types of interventions are contained in Giesbrecht and Douglas (1990) and "Communities Mobilize to Rescue the Parks" (1991).

Automobile Ignition Interlocks

These are devices that can check the blood alcohol level of the driver before he or she begins to drive. The automobile cannot be started if the level is above zero or some other preset limit. This device has been discussed as a potential means to reduce all drinking and driving but has been used in the United States primarily as a means to prevent a multiple

drinking-and-driving offender from starting his or her auto after drinking (Voas, 1988).

Self-Extinguishing Cigarettes

Such cigarettes are an example of a safety approach to reduce the likelihood of fire, for example, in bed. Research has shown that often persons are drinking and smoking and a fire is begun in bed or on a cloth-covered piece of furniture. Self-extinguishing cigarettes will not continue to burn unless regularly used by a smoker. Such cigarettes are proposed as a means to reduce the chance of fires at home or in hotels. There has been little published research on this strategy.

Health Education and Warnings

Health education is not typically an environmental strategy for prevention as education seeks to change the behavior of individuals directly. However, the use of warning messages in the environment also shapes the overall drinking context. For example, the U.S. government has required, as of November 1989, that all containers for alcoholic products contain the following warning:

> GOVERNMENT WARNING: (1) According to the Surgeon General, women should not drink alcoholic beverages during pregnancy because of the risk of birth defects. (2) Consumption of alcoholic beverages impairs your ability to drive a car or operate machinery, and may cause health problems.

There are at least three rationales for requiring a warning label on alcohol containers: (a) to acknowledge the government's recognition of health and safety risks associated with alcohol as a commercial product, (b) to inform the public that these risks exist and reduce the specific alcohol-involved problems cited on the label, and (c) to be a part of a comprehensive alcohol policy to reduce problems.

Alcohol warning labels are intended to lower risk associated with drinking while pregnant and/or while operating machinery. See Hilton (1992, 1993) for reviews of existing research on warning labels. For warning labels to be successful, people must read the warnings and thus be aware of the message. If read, the content of the warning should be familiar.

Greenfield, Graves, and Kaskutas (1992) conducted three waves of national telephone surveys during the survey years of 1989, 1990, and 1991 and found that the percentage of respondents reporting conversations about dangers associated with drinking increased from 45% in 1989 to 51% in 1991.

A lower recognition of the warning among women of childbearing age was observed by Hankin et al. (1993a) among black, inner-city pregnant women. Mazis, Morris, and Swasy (1991) found slow diffusion of the warning label in Gallup Polls from 1989 to 1991. A report by Parker, Saltz and Hennessy (1994) comparing pre- and postwarning label data found that drinker-drivers and impaired drivers (based on self-reports) were more likely to recall the warning label and its content.

For the warning to reduce risk, people must be concerned about the content of the warning and actually change their drinking. Greenfield et al. (1992) found an increase in self-reported limits on drinking among women of childbearing age in the national surveys. Hankin et al. (1993b) found little increase in the perceived risk of drinking during pregnancy among pregnant women in prenatal clinics. Hankin et al. (1993b) found a 7-month lag in the impact of the warning label on the drinking of pregnant women. Among pregnant drinkers, there was a significant reduction in alcohol consumption among light drinkers but no change among heavy drinkers. This finding is similar to the conclusion of Parker et al. (1994), who found no change in drinking-and-driving behavior among self-reported at-risk drinkers.

Greenfield et al. (1992) found in their national survey that the proportion of people who reported deciding not to drive after "having too much to drink" rose from 35% in 1989 (prelabel) to 43% in 1990 (postlabel). Young males increased from 72% to 81% in their response to this question. Andrews, Netemeyer, and Durvasula (1991) reported that college students found the drinking-and-driving warning to be believable. Overall, the U.S. alcohol container warning labels have achieved greater awareness over time, particularly among drinkers most at risk for alcohol-related problems noted in the warning. However, there is little evidence of behavioral change among those at-risk groups as a result of the warning label. But there is evidence of increased discussions among people about the dangers associated with alcohol consumption as a result of the public's exposure to warning labels. The limited change in behav-

ior is not surprising since educational efforts alone have rarely been shown to produce long-term behavioral change.

One illustration of this point comes from traffic safety. Public service information campaigns on TV have become the most frequent types of general education and are produced by the federal government, the National Association of Broadcasters, and beverage producers such as Coors and Anheuser-Busch. Public service announcements (PSAs) are intended to change drivers' behavior by raising awareness of risk.

Evaluation of the effects of PSAs on drinking and driving is quite sparse. Worden, Waller, and Riley (1975) found that a media campaign conducted in conjunction with enforcement produced significant changes in knowledge, attitudes, and related behavior. However, the authors found that the effect decayed rapidly over time. In a review of 15 years of mass communication campaigns designed to change drinking-and-driving behavior, Haskins (1985) concluded that very little had been learned.

Atkin (1988) concluded, following his review of public service information programs for the Surgeon General's Workshop on Drunk Driving, that drunk-driving educational campaigns appear to have relatively little effect on drinking and driving. And this finding is consistent with campaigns concerning safety belt promotion, substance abuse prevention, and other health practices.

Publicity alone has rarely produced lasting changes in safety behavior (Wilde, L'Hoste, Sheppard, & Wind, 1971). The best understanding of effects from media attention to DUI enforcement can be seen as an interaction between mass media information and the personal experience of drivers. Thus, Ross (1982), in his report on the British Road Safety Act of 1967, noted that the public was initially led to believe that the probability of being tested for alcohol and arrested was much higher than it actually proved to be. He stated, "It seems reasonable to me to ascribe (the subsequent reduction in effectiveness of the law) to the gradual learning by U.K. drivers that they had overestimated the certainty of punishment under the law" (p. 34).

An alternative finding was reported by Worden, Flynn, Merrill, Waller, and Haugh (1989), who conducted a public information campaign using "BAC Estimation" cards which told drivers the steps for determining their own BACs. These "Know Your

Limit" cards were widely distributed in an experimental community. Using roadside survey and community survey data, the authors found, following the campaign, that only 0.06% of drivers in the experimental community were over the legal limit, while 3.00% of drivers were over the limit in the control community.

Educational strategies such as warning labels can play at least two important roles in a comprehensive prevention program. First, warning labels seem to increase public awareness of the relationship between a specific health problem (e.g., birth defects related to drinking by a pregnant woman) and alcohol itself. This relationship, which may seem so obvious to scientists involved in the study of alcohol and to public health advocates, is simply not understood by either the general population or women of childbearing age. The research summarized above does support optimism that warning labels can increase awareness of alcohol risks among women of childbearing age and drinking drivers as well as the general public. Thus, one can infer that the alcohol warning label contributes to public awareness and that public awareness leads to support for preventive action and public policy.

SMOKING PREVENTION

Like alcohol problem prevention, smoking prevention and reduction have a history of research about the effectiveness of environmental or policy strategies for the reduction of current smoking and reducing smoking initiation by young people. However, not as many environmental prevention alternatives have been attempted for smoking as for alcohol problems.

Environmental strategies for smoking prevention described here are generally of three types: (a) price, (b) restrictions on availability, and (c) restrictions on location of smoking. Examples of prevention research conducted on these approaches are reviewed below.

Two overviews of the potential effectiveness of prevention efforts to reduce smoking were provided by Brownson, Koffman, Novotny, Hughes, and Eriksen (1995) and Reid, McNeill, and Glynn (1995). Brownson et al. (1995) concluded that environmental strategies are among the cost-effective strategies to reduce tobacco use and prevent cardiovascular disease. The authors recommended that priority be given to clean indoor air policies, restrictions on tobacco advertising and promotion, policies to limit access to tobacco by youth, comprehensive school health programs, and excise tax and other economic disincentives. Reid et al. (1995) reached similar conclusions and argued that isolated interventions targeting young people, particularly countersmoking advertising, are less likely to have long-lasting effects. They argue that schools alone cannot be expected to change historical community values that tolerate smoking. Such youth-targeted educational programs, Reid et al. (1995) also concluded, are unlikely to affect the smoking behavior of high-risk (of multiple problems) youth. They do believe that public educational efforts can affect the general attitudes and norms of the community and provide favorable support for environmental strategies. The following reviews the research support for various smoking-prevention strategies based upon an environmental approach.

Price

Price of cigarettes (and other tobacco products), like price of alcohol, is directed at creating an economic barrier against the purchase of such products. Cigarette purchases respond to price changes as do other retail products.

Economists have often studied the link between the price and consumption of cigarettes. Like alcohol, cigarettes are a commercial product subject to the same laws of supply (expressed in level of price) and demand as other products. This may be especially true for young people who are at the point of initiation and who may not have as much disposable income as adults. For example, Baltagi and Levin (1986) employed a pooled cross-sectional analysis of cigarette demand in response to changes in price from 1963 to 1980 from 46 U.S. states and found an important elasticity relationship; that is, as price increased (relative to inflation), demand declined, and when price declined, demand increased. This finding was replicated by Keeler, Hu, Barnett, and Manning (1993), who used monthly time series data from 1980 to 1990 from California. The price elasticity of cigarettes has also been confirmed in research in Canada, where it was possible to test the effects of a purposeful increase in taxes (thus affecting price) (Lewit, Coate, & Grossman, 1981), and in the United Kingdom (Godfrey & Maynard, 1988; Townsend, 1987). See discussion and review of the variety of estimates of the price elasticity of cigarettes by Zimring and Nelson (1995).

The major means available to alter the price of cigarettes are the excise taxes applied to the product by the federal and/or state governments. While producers, wholesalers, and retail outlets can make adjustments in prices to accommodate increases in excise taxes, the net effect of any increase in excise taxes is an increase in the final retail price (see Sweanor et al., 1992).

In summary, the research evidence supports a conclusion that smokers respond to cigarette prices and that excise taxes can be an effective prevention strategy.

Restrictions on Availability

These are primarily directed at young people and generally include the minimum age of purchase of cigarettes and the control of retail sources for cigarettes, especially vending machines. Establishment of a minimum age for the purchase of cigarettes is the same environmental strategy used in smoking prevention for youth as is the minimum age for purchasing alcohol (i.e., to create a legal barrier to purchase as a means to deter or reduce smoking). While many governmental units, national, state, or local, have set a minimum age of cigarette purchase, there is good evidence that the existence of such laws does not prevent purchase. A report in the state of California (University of California, San Diego, 1990) found very high rates of purchases of cigarettes by persons under 18, the legal age of purchase. DiFranza and Tye (1990) estimated that more than 3 million Americans under 18 consumed almost 1 billion packs of cigarettes and 26 million containers of smokeless tobacco, which generated approximately 3% of tobacco industry profits in 1988.

Consequently, enforcement of the minimum purchase age is an environmental strategy that has shown promise. Jason, Ji, Anes, and Birkhead (1991), in a survey of Woodbridge, Illinois, retail outlets for cigarettes, showed that between 60% and 80% of underage purchase attempts were successful. In the 3 months following initiation of increased enforcement of the sales law by local police through warning letters and actual citations using "stings," the underage sales rate fell to 35%. Within the next 6 months, the sales rate fell below 5%. The effects of increased enforcement are confirmed by Feighery, Altman, and Shaffer (1991), who found in four Northern California communities that increased community education alone had limited effect in reducing illegal tobacco sales to minors. But education did promote community support for more aggressive enforcement, and education plus enforcement decreased over-the-counter cigarette sales significantly. Vending-machine sales were unaffected. Thus, the restrictions or bans on vending machines as described below become quite relevant.

Every state has a minimum purchase age that has a variety of levels of enforcement across states and across communities within a state. The control of retail sources of cigarettes has been largely directed at restrictions or bans on cigarette-vending machines that provide an unsupervised source of cigarettes for underage persons.

DiFranza, Savageau, and Aisquith (1996) found that in communities with no requirements for lockout devices for cigarette-vending machines, illegal sales were far more likely from vending machines than from over-the-counter sources. Locks on vending machines made them equivalent to over-the-counter sources in terms of illegal sales to youths. Vendors participating in voluntary industry-sponsored programs were as likely to make illegal sales as nonparticipants.

Forster, Hourigan, and McGovern (1992) found that 12- to 15-year-old male and female confederates attempting to purchase cigarettes from all cigarette outlets in three communities achieved a success rate of 53% over the counter and 79% from vending machines. According to the researchers, these results show that minors can purchase cigarettes in all types of businesses, even those characterized as "adult" locations. Boys in this study had more difficulty than girls in purchasing cigarettes over the counter, and younger individuals had more difficulty than 15-year-olds. However, these differences were not found in vending-machine sales. Similarly, over-the-counter sales of cigarettes were significantly reduced following a statewide increase in the penalty for tobacco sales to minors, but vending-machine sales were not affected.

In a study evaluating a requirement that vending machines be fitted with electronic locking devices in St. Paul, Minnesota, Forster, Hourigan, and Kelder (1992) used a random sample of vending-machine locations selected for cigarette purchase attempts ucted before implementation of electronic lock-ᶾ and at 3 and 12 months postimplementation. ᴛhe rate of noncompliance by merchants was 34% after 3 months and 30% after 1 year. The effect of the law was to reduce the ability of a minor to purchase cigarettes from locations originally selling cigarettes through vending machines from 86% at baseline to 36% at 3 months. The purchase rate at these locations rose to 48% at 1 year. The authors concluded from these results that cigarette-vending-machine locking devices may not be as effective as vending-machine bans and require additional enforcement to ensure compliance with the law.

The impact of a local ordinance designed to prevent tobacco sales to minors was assessed (Hinds, 1992) via surveys of 10th-grade students before and after the implementation of the ordinance. Tobacco use declined from 25.3% to 19.7% overall, with a statistically significant decline from 26.4% to 11.5% among girls. There was also a statistically significant increase from 29.3% to 61.5% in the proportion of students reporting they were asked for proof of age when they attempted to purchase tobacco.

Restrictions on the availability of cigarettes have been shown to reduce access to cigarettes by young people and consequently to reduce smoking initiation and smoking levels.

Restrictions on Location of Smoking

Restrictions or bans on smoking location have assumed a considerable public presence over the past 10 years, extending from bans on smoking on domestic airliners (as well as in airports themselves), to bans on smoking in public buildings and on public ground transportation, to nonsmoking areas in restaurants or outright bans, to bans or restrictions on smoking in the workplace. There is limited research concerning the effects of these restrictions, but the evidence of controlled studies or analyses generally supports the effectiveness of such efforts.

Longo et al. (1996), in a study of workplace smoking bans, found that beginning with the smoking ban and continuing for 5 years after implementation, statistically significant differences in the postban quit ratio were observed between employees of smoke-free hospitals who were smokers and counterparts in the community. Despite preban differences in smoking intensity, the overall difference in postban quit ratios remained significant even after multivariate ad-justment for socioeconomic, demographic, and smoking-intensity variables. For those sites that were 5 years postban, the quit ratio (smokers who quit in relation to the number of total smokers) was 0.506 in smoke-free workplaces compared with 0.377 in workplaces where smoking was permitted. In all but one category, the intervention group was further along the stages-of-change continuum toward quitting smoking than the comparison group. The authors concluded that American hospitals' experiences with smoking bans, which directly affect more than 5 million workers, should be examined by other industries as a method of improving employee health.

Restrictions on location of smoking would appear to be a potentially effective strategy to encourage current smokers to quit. However, at this time, the research evidence is limited.

ILLICIT DRUG USE PREVENTION

Environmental approaches to the prevention of illicit drug use have been concentrated on restrictions in the supply of drugs, primarily interdiction of the supply at both the international and the local level. Such strategies have primarily been in the hands of law enforcement (local police, military, customs officials, and the U.S. Coast Guard). This interdiction approach to drug supply has a complementary emphasis on sanctions against those convicted of supplying drugs. As a result of the increased severity of sanctions against supplying drugs, a considerable amount of the jail and prison space in the United States is devoted to convicted drug-supplying felons.

Reducing Drug Supply

While an environmental policy for reducing drug supply has received considerable attention in public discussion and debate, there have been few controlled studies of the relative effectiveness of these strategies in reducing drug use. A report by the U.S. General Accounting Office (1993) identified the major pro and con arguments regarding drug law enforcement and the alternative approaches most often discussed. The federal government has steadily increased its annual drug control budget from $2.8 billion in 1986 to $12 billion in 1992, allocated approximately 70% to supporting drug enforcement efforts and 30% to prevention and treatment. Supporters of the enforcement emphasis claim that law enforcement activities in recent years have led to substantial drug seizures and to the arrest, prosecution, and punishment of many drug traffickers and users. Supporters are content that these seizures and arrests have reduced the availability and use of illegal drugs, both directly and through deterrence. They also claim that the connection between illegal drugs and crime is so strong that an intense law enforcement response to drugs has been necessary. Advocates of alternative strategies suggest that the federal strategy, with its emphasis on enforcement, has not made a serious dent in the nation's continuing drug problem. This report identifies a range of alternative approaches that rely less on enforcement but present no research evidence of effectiveness.

DiNardo (1993) examined the relationship between drug law enforcement and the price and use of cocaine, using data from the Drug Enforcement Administration's (DEA) System to Retrieve Information from Drug Evidence (STRIDE) and Monitoring the Future (MTF). His analysis applied a variety of grouped data estimators and related these estimators to instrumental variables, techniques, quasi-experiments, and classical experimental design. The data covered 1977–1987. Results revealed no indication that regional and time variation in DEA seizures of cocaine is helpful in explaining variation in either the demand for/or the price of cocaine.

A study undertaken by the U.S. Congress House Subcommittee on Crime (1994) investigated the effectiveness of strategies to reduce the supply of drugs in the United States and the wisdom of readjusting the proportion of funds given to supply and demand efforts to combat illegal drug use. The study noted that interdiction programs failed to prevent the rapid growth of cocaine imports in the 1980s. In the last few years, imports seem to have stabilized at historically high levels, notwithstanding a significant growth in late-1980s interdiction expenditures.

Caulkins, Crawford, and Reuter (1993) presented a computer simulation of the smuggling and interdiction of illicit drugs that specifically allows for adaptation across routes and modes (air, land, sea). The Simulation of Adaptive Response (SOAR) is used to examine several issues associated with the interdiction of cocaine shipments into the United States. The authors concluded that when one considers the existence of a "backstop" technology (smuggling small shipments over land), the low cost incurred by smugglers as a function of the fraction of all routes on which the interdiction rate is increased, and the reality that not all smuggling costs are caused by interdiction, it would appear that increasing interdiction would not have a substantial impact on U.S. cocaine consumption except under extraordinary circumstances.

Increasing Drug Prices

Like the demand for alcohol and cigarettes, drug demand is affected by retail price. However, since drugs are illegal, the only current means to increase price is to reduce the supply.

Rydell and Everingham (1994) presented a model-based policy analysis of alternative methods of controlling cocaine use in the United States. The study focused on ways to intervene in the supply and demand processes to mitigate the cocaine problem. Heavy users consumed cocaine at a rate approximately eight times that of light users, so the trend in consumption by heavy users roughly canceled the downward trend in consumption by light users. The result was that total consumption of cocaine in the United States remained at its mid-1980s peak for almost a decade. Four interventions were analyzed: source-country control, interdiction, domestic enforcement, and treatment of heavy users. This study analyzed the relative and, to a lesser extent, absolute cost-effectiveness of these programs. The first three programs focus on supply control, and the fourth is a demand control program. The cost-effectiveness of these programs was examined. The analysis concluded that money spent on supply control programs increases the cost to producers of supplying the cocaine. Further, they found that supply costs increase as producers replace seized product and assets, compensate drug traffickers for the risk of arrest and imprisonment, and devote resources to avoiding seizures and arrests. These costs get passed along to the consumer as price increases, which in turn decrease consumption.

Severity of Punishment

Cavanagh (1993) analyzed the methods that are currently available in the United States for punishing and controlling criminal behavior. Special attention was given to the capacity of the U.S. corrections system and how that capacity is currently affected by drug crime convictions. He also analyzed New York City's Tactical Narcotics Teams, an attempt to reduce drug-related crime by increasing the certainty, severity, and celerity of punishment for drug dealing and possession. He concluded that increasing the certainty, severity, and/or celerity of punishment for drug-related crimes would require large additional investments in all parts of the criminal justice system and corrections system. Even if it were possible to increase punishment levels, current research provides no clear answer as to whether this would ultimately reduce drug-related crime.

Kleiman (1989) concluded that any change in marijuana consumption that an increase in enforcement resources might produce should be weighed against the adverse societal effects caused by the illicit market enterprise. In principle, drug enforcement can create public benefits by reducing drug consumption, by controlling the "spillover" of violence and corruption from illicit markets, and by limiting the problems of perceived fairness and the damage to public morale caused by notorious criminal wealth. Since new money spent on federal marijuana enforcement efforts will have little effect on drug consumption, its justification must come from its benefits in terms of "spillover" crime and perceived fairness. It is not clear, however, that increased enforcement will ameliorate these problems rather than exacerbate them. According to Kleiman, a 13% rise in marijuana retail prices and localized marijuana shortages, although slightly ameliorating the marijuana consumption problem, will tend to concentrate the marijuana-trafficking problem.

Community Policing

Community policing has been proposed as a strategy to reduce crime and especially drug availability. Such a policy emphasizes crime prevention based upon close cooperation between police and residents in reducing both crime and fear of crime. Fleissner and Heinzelmann (1996) concluded that Crime Prevention Through Environmental Design (CPTED) and community policing can be viewed as part of a comprehensive crime prevention strategy, including reducing drug supplies. The authors explained that police, citizens, and government have a role to play in preventing crime under the CTPED/community-policing approach:

- Police involvement within neighborhoods can include both foot patrol and working with community groups to strengthen citizens' sense of security and solve neighborhood problems that contribute to crime and fear of crime and reduce the visibility of drug use and drug supplies.
- Residents can work together to improve neighborhood appearance and deter criminals.
- Government can use building codes and inspection power to increase environmental security and discourage drug use and other criminal activities.

Uchida, Forst, and Annan (1992) used Oakland, California, and Birmingham, Alabama, as test sites for the effectiveness of several different policing models for controlling the problem of street-level drug trafficking. The authors tested and assessed the models to determine their effectiveness. The findings showed that the treatments had dramatic effects on citizen perceptions of quality of life, property crime, and satisfaction with police services. Further, violent crimes reported to the police declined substantially where police-citizen contacts occurred.

Summary Thoughts on Drugs

Illicit drugs represent a special challenge for environmental (as well as any type of) prevention approaches. As a commodity, illicit drugs respond to the economic rules of price and availability just as alcohol and cigarettes do. However, since these are illegal commodities that operate outside the administrative regulation and control domains utilized for alcohol and tobacco, special problems are presented. The illicit drug market is unregulated and therefore can become (and often does) a freewheeling economic system (almost a pure system of supply and demand, unaffected by government licensing or formal restrictions). This is not to imply that restricting the supply of illicit drugs is not a potentially effective prevention strategy. There is no reason to conclude that an unlimited supply of drugs would not produce more problems. It most certainly would.

The most central barrier to current efforts to eliminate supply is that there are strong economic incentives to meet demand. Thus, the scarcer the product (when an unmet demand exists), the greater the potential profit for retail drug suppliers. In this situation, police and military interdiction of supplies can actually increase profit opportunities by making supplies scarce.

On the other hand, if interdiction strategies do reduce supply and demand is unchanged, then price will increase, thus providing economic disincentives like those achieved for alcohol and tobacco through excise taxes. High prices can provide barriers to experimental or occasional drug users. The policy dilemma for a supply strategy is that lowering the supply increases the cost for heavy (often dependent) users and stimulates other activities such as burglary or prostitution to obtain money to purchase illicit drugs. A full discussion of this conundrum is beyond the purpose of this paper, but see Levin, Roberts, and Hirsh (1975).

Therefore, it should be noted that a reduction-of-supply strategy for illicit drugs has special by-products that are more severe than those for licit (but regulated) products. This chapter is not advocating a legalization of any drugs. Such legalization could reduce price, increase supply, and increase use. Rather, this chapter points out the lack of scientific evidence that the current ongoing interdiction strategies are having the desired effect of reducing use. This does not imply, however, that an environmental strategy to reduce supply of illicit drugs cannot prevent drug use, especially experimental or nondependent use. The main issue is one of effectiveness of current approaches to reduce supply, given the demand for illicit drugs.

Interdiction to physically confiscate illicit drug supplies is not the same as establishing very high sanctions and penalties for the possession, distribution, and sale of illicit drugs. There is no solid controlled evidence that high sanctions do reduce supply. The high economic incentives and the low certainty of being caught combine to override the major deterrent effect of reducing supply. In other words, as long as there is sufficient profit, suppliers of illicit drugs are likely to find that potential gain exceeds the low risk of arrest even with severe punishment. Experience from other environmental strategies to deter use or abuse suggests that certainty of detection (not necessarily severe punishment) could be a more effective environmental approach.

SUMMARY

This chapter has provided a brief overview of some environmental changes that may reduce the inci-

dence and prevalence of alcohol misuse or alcohol-involved problems, smoking (primarily by youth), and illicit drug use. Many of the approaches described above have been evaluated through research. Other promising approaches await evaluation.

The largest number of environmental prevention strategies have been developed and tested for alcohol. For smoking reduction, environmental prevention strategies have been devised to reduce the initiation and smoking levels of young people. This is based upon the premise that most smokers begin as young people and if an environmental barrier can be created for access to cigarettes, then youth smoking incidence and prevalence can be reduced. For illicit drugs, the environmental strategies that have received a great deal of attention are efforts to reduce availability, including blocking the delivery of drugs and deterring suppliers of drugs via harsh penalties. Environmental strategies for reducing illicit drug use are largely untested. They have not received as much scientific evaluation as have strategies directed at alcohol problems and smoking.

Rationale for Environmental Strategies

Environmental strategies do not usually target a specific risk group; rather, they alter existing structures to reduce the potential risk of harm or of a social problem. For example, setting a minimum drinking age for alcohol or purchase age for cigarettes is a state policy to reduce access to alcohol or cigarettes by persons below a certain age.

There are at least three positive features of environmental prevention policies:

1. *Research evidence.* In general, policy (which usually addresses environmental strategies) has scientific evidence of effectiveness, especially for alcohol and cigarettes. This includes such policies as retail price, availability, location and type of alcohol outlets including hours and days of sale, retail and social access to alcohol or cigarettes by young people, and enforcement and sanctions against high-risk alcohol use (e.g., drinking and driving). See Edwards et al. (1994) for a review of policy research on alcohol.

2. *Lower cost.* There are few cases in which the actual cost of environmental prevention programs or policies has been documented. However, on the average, policies, as they involve changes in rules and regulations or increased emphasis for existing activities, are likely to be lower in cost than specially

funded local educational prevention programs, which require an ongoing investment in staff, materials, and other resources. For example, the cost of teacher and school administrator time, curriculum materials, and other elements of a school-based educational program is likely to exceed the cost of a local policy of reduced retail sales of alcohol or cigarettes to underage persons via increased enforcement. Raising the retail price of alcohol or cigarettes at a local level by imposing local special-purpose taxes generates increased revenue and, at the same time, is a low-cost prevention strategy.

3. *Sustainability.* Policies directed at the environment have a longer potential effective life, once implemented, than prevention programs that must be maintained and thus funded each year. A policy of requiring training for alcoholic beverage servers through an existing adult education system has a longer potential effectiveness than a mass media campaign that must be planned, funded, and implemented each year. Even when the potential effectiveness of any policy decays over time due to lower compliance or lowered regulation or enforcement, policies continue to have some sustaining effect, even without reinforcement. One example is the minimum drinking age. O'Malley and Wagenaar (1991) found that the effects on drinking and driving resulting from the increased minimum age were more sustained in states with higher drinking ages than in states with lower ages (18 to 19).

The recent advances in environmental approaches to prevention have been based upon the careful analysis of specific policies and their effect on problems. These advances were made possible by both more sophisticated causal theory and better statistical techniques to isolate effects.

Environmental strategies have at least two difficulties. First, they are often controversial and thus politically difficult to implement, especially for alcohol and tobacco, which are legal retail products. There must be political will and public support for such strategies. Second, environmental strategies, especially those conducted at the community level, often do not provide the level of immediate public satisfaction and personal reward to program staff that educational or service strategies provide. This can mean that environmental strategies may not be as attractive to community members, especially volunteers.

In general, environmental approaches to prevention of alcohol problems, smoking, and illicit drug use present alternatives to strategies that target individuals or high-risk groups. Environmental strategies are intended to alter the context in which these problems occur. Such strategies do not target specific persons at risk; rather, they reduce convenience, availability, and access to the substances of abuse. There is substantial evidence of effectiveness for the environmental strategies for alcohol problems and smoking but little evidence for illicit drugs. Such a situation suggests the need for more controlled research into the interdiction and severe punishment strategies used to reduce illicit drug use that are the major environmental strategies being used.

Key References

DiFranza, J. R., Savageau, J. A., & Aisquith, B. F. (1996). Youth access to tobacco: The effects of age, gender, vending machine locks, and "it's the law" programs. *American Journal of Public Health*, 86(2), 221–224.

Edwards, G., Anderson, P., Babor, T. F., Casswell, S., Ferrence, R., Giesbrecht, N., Godfrey, C., Holder, H. D., Lemmens, P., Mäkelä, K., Midanik, L. T., Norström, T., Österberg, E., Romelsjö, A., Room, R., Simpura, J., & Skog, O-J. (Eds). (1994). *Alcohol policy and the public good.* New York: Oxford University Press.

Keeler, T. E., Hu, T-W., Barnett, P. G., & Manning, W. G. (1993). Taxation, regulation, and addiction: A demand function for cigarettes based on time-series evidence. *Journal of Health Economics, 12,* 1–18.

References

Ahlström-Laasko, S. (1975). *Drinking habits among alcoholics* (No. 21). Helsinki: Finnish Foundation for Alcohol Studies, Forssa.

Amundsen, A. (1967). Hva skjer når et vinutsalg åpnes? [What happens when a wine outlet is opened?] *Norsk Tidsskrift om Alkoholsp rsmålet, 19*(2), 65–82.

Andrews, J. C., Netemeyer, R. G., & Durvasula, S. (1991). Effects of consumption frequency on believability and attitudes toward alcohol warning labels. *Journal of Consumer Affairs, 25*(2), 323–338.

Atkin, C. K. (1988). Mass communications effects on drinking and driving. In U.S. Department of Health and Human Services, *Surgeon General's workshop on drunk driving: Background papers* (pp. 15–34). Rockville, MD: U.S. Department of Health and Human

Services, Public Health Service, Office of the Surgeon General.

Bako, G., MacKenzie, W. C., & Smith, E. S. O. (1976). The effect of legislated lowering of the drinking age on total highway accidents among young drivers in Alberta, 1970–1972. *Canadian Journal of Public Health, 67,* 161–163.

Baltagi, B. H., & Levin, D. (1986). Estimating dynamic demand for cigarettes using panel data: The effects of bootlegging, taxation, and advertising reconsidered. *Review of Economics and Statistics, 68,* 148–155.

Box, G. E. P., & Jenkins, G. M. (1976). *Time series analysis: Forecasting and control* (Rev. ed.). San Francisco: Holden-Day.

Brownson, R. C., Koffman, D. M., Novotny, T. E., Hughes, R. G., & Eriksen, M. P. (1995). Environmental and policy interventions to control tobacco use and prevent cardiovascular disease. *Health Education Quarterly, 22*(4), 478–498.

Bruce, D. (1980). Changes in Scottish drinking habits and behaviour following the extension of permitted evening opening hours. *Health Bulletin, 38,* 133–137.

Bruun, K., Edwards, G., Lumio, M., Mäkelä, K., Pan, L., Popham, R. E., Room, R., Schmidt, W., Skog, O-J., Sulkunen, P., & Österberg, E. (1975). *Alcohol control policies in public health perspective* (No. 25). Helsinki: Finnish Foundation for Alcohol Studies. Forssa.

Bryant, C. W. (1954). Effects of sale of liquor by the drink in the state of Washington. *Quarterly Journal of Studies on Alcohol, 15,* 320–324.

Caulkins, J., Crawford, G., & Reuter, P. (1993). Simulation of adaptive response: A model of drug interdiction. *Mathematical and Computer Modelling, 17*(2), 37–52.

Cavanagh, D. P. (1993). *Relations between increases in the certainty, severity and celerity of punishment for drug crimes and reductions in the level of crime, drug crime, and the effects of drug abuse.* Cambridge, MA: BOTEC Analysis Corporation.

Colon, I. (1982). The influence of state monopoly of alcohol distribution and the frequency of package stores on single motor vehicle fatalities. *American Journal of Drug and Alcohol Abuse, 9,* 325–331.

Communities mobilize to rescue the parks. (1991, Winter). *Prevention File, 6*(1), 7–8.

Cook, P. J. (1981). The effect of liquor taxes on drinking, cirrhosis, and auto accidents. In M. H. Moore & D. R. Gerstein (Eds.), *Alcohol and public policy: Beyond the shadow of prohibition* (pp. 255–285). Washington, DC: National Academy Press.

Cook, P. J., & Tauchen, G. (1982). The effect of liquor taxes on heavy drinking. *Bell Journal of Economics, 13*(2), 379–390.

Curry, R. L. (1988). Alcohol demand and supply management in developing countries. *British Journal of Addiction, 83,* 25–30.

DiFranza, J. R., Savageau, J. A., & Aisquith, B. F. (1996). Youth access to tobacco: The effects of age, gender, vending machine locks, and "it's the law" programs. *American Journal of Public Health, 86*(2), 221–224.

DiFranza, J. R., & Tye, J. B. (1990). Who profits from tobacco sales to children? *Journal of the American Medical Association, 263,* 2784–2787.

DiNardo, J. (1993). Law enforcement, the price of cocaine and cocaine use. *Mathematical and Computer Modelling, 17*(2), 53–64.

Edwards, G., Anderson, P., Babor, T. F., Casswell, S., Ferrence, R., Giesbrecht, N., Godfrey, C., Holder, H. D., Lemmens, P., Mäkelä, K., Midanik, L. T., Norström, T., Österberg, E., Romelsjö, A., Room, R., Simpura, J., & Skog, O-J. (Eds.). (1994). *Alcohol policy and the public good.* New York: Oxford University Press.

Feighery, E., Altman, D. G., & Shaffer, G. (1991). The effects of combining education and enforcement to reduce tobacco sales to minors. *Journal of the American Medical Association, 266*(22), 3168–3171.

Fleissner, D., & Heinzelmann, F. (1996). *Crime prevention through environmental design and community policing.* Washington, DC: Bureau of Justice Assistance, Office of Justice Programs, U.S. Department of Justice.

Forster, J. L., Hourigan, M. E., & Kelder, S. (1992). Locking devices on cigarette vending machines: Evaluation of a city ordinance. *American Journal of Public Health, 82*(9), 1217–1219.

Forster, J. L., Hourigan, M., & McGovern, P. (1992). Availability of cigarettes to underage youth in three communities. *Preventive Medicine, 21*(3), 320–328.

Giesbrecht, N., & Douglas, R. R. (1990, January 11–13). *The demonstration project and comprehensive community programming: Dilemmas in preventing alcohol-related problems.* Paper presented at the International Conference on Evaluating Community Prevention Strategies: Alcohol and Other Drugs, San Diego.

Gliksman, L., McKenzie, D., Single, E., Douglas, R., Brunet, S., & Moffatt, K. (1993). The role of alcohol providers in prevention: An evaluation of a server intervention program. *Addiction, 88,* 1189–1197.

Godfrey, C. (1988). Licensing and the demand for alcohol. *Applied Economics, 20,* 1541–1558.

Godfrey, C., & Maynard, A. (1988). Economic aspects of tobacco use and taxation policy. *British Medical Journal, 297*, 339–343.

Greenfield, T. K., Graves, K. L., & Kaskutas, L. A. (1992, March 25–27). *Do alcohol warning labels work? Research findings.* Paper presented at Alcohol Policy 8, National Association for Public Health Policy, Washington, DC.

Gruenewald, P. J. (1991, October 10–11). *Alcohol problems and the control of availability: Theoretical and empirical issues.* Paper presented at the NIAAA Conference "Economic and Socioeconomic Issues in the Prevention of Alcohol Related Problems," Bethesda, MD.

Gruenewald, P. J., Ponicki, W. B., & Holder, H. D. (1993). The relationship of outlet densities to alcohol consumption: A time series cross-sectional analysis. *Alcoholism: Clinical and Experimental Research, 17*(1), 38–47.

Hankin, J. R., Sloan, J. J., Firestone, I. J., Ager, J. W., Sokol, R. J., Martier, S. S., & Townsend, J. (1993a). The alcohol beverage warning label: When did knowledge increase? *Alcoholism: Clinical and Experimental Research, 17*(2), 428–430.

Hankin, J. R., Sloan, J. J., Firestone, I. J., Ager, J. W., Sokol, R. J., Martier, S. S., & Townsend, J. (1993b). A time series analysis of the impact of the alcohol warning label on antenatal drinking. *Alcoholism: Clinical and Experimental Research, 17*(2), 284–289.

Haskins, J. B. (1985). The role of mass media in alcohol and highway safety campaigns. *Journal of Studies on Alcohol, 10*, 184–191.

Hilton, M. E. (1992, May 30–June 5). *Perspectives and prospects in warning label research.* Paper presented at the 18th Annual Alcohol Epidemiology Symposium, Toronto, Canada.

Hilton, M. E. (1993). Overview of recent findings on alcoholic beverage warning labels. *Journal of Public Policy and Marketing, 12*(1), 1–9.

Hinds, M. W. (1992). Impact of a local ordinance banning tobacco sales to minors. *Public Health Reports, 107*(3), 355–358.

Hingson, R. (1993). Prevention of alcohol-impaired driving. *Alcohol Health and Research World, 17*(1), 28–34.

Hingson, R., Heeren, T., & Winter, M. (1994). Lower legal blood alcohol limits for young drivers. *Public Health Reports, 109*(6), 738–744.

Hingson, R., McGovern, T., Howland, J., Heeren, T., Winter, M., & Zakocs, R. (1996). Reducing alcohol-impaired driving in Massachusetts: The Saving Lives Program. *American Journal of Public Health, 86*(6), 791–797.

Hingson, R. W., Howland, J., & Levenson, S. (1988). Effects of legislative reform to reduce drunken driving and alcohol-related traffic fatalities. *Public Health Reports, 103*(6), 659–667.

Hoadley, J. F., Fuchs, B. C., & Holder, H. D. (1984). The effect of alcohol beverage restrictions on consumption: A 25-year longitudinal analysis. *American Journal of Drug and Alcohol Abuse, 10*, 375–401.

Holder, H. D. (Ed.). (1987). *Control issues in alcohol abuse prevention: Strategies for states and communities.* Greenwich, CT: JAI Press.

Holder, H. D. (1998). *Alcohol and the community: A systems approach to prevention.* Cambridge: Cambridge University Press.

Holder, H. D., & Blose, J. O. (1987). Impact of changes in distilled spirits availability on apparent consumption: A time series analysis of liquor-by-the-drink. *British Journal of Addiction, 82*, 623–631.

Holder, H. D., Janes, K., Mosher, J., Saltz, R., Spurr, S., & Wagenaar, A. C. (1993). Alcohol beverage server liability and the reduction of alcohol-involved problems. *Journal of Studies on Alcohol, 54*(1), 23–36.

Holder, H. D., & Wagenaar, A. C. (1990). Effects of the elimination of a state monopoly on distilled spirits' retail sales: A time-series analysis of Iowa. *British Journal of Addiction, 85*, 1615–1625.

Holder, H. D., & Wagenaar, A. C. (1994). Mandated server training and reduced alcohol-involved traffic crashes: A time series analysis of the Oregon experience. *Accident Analysis and Prevention, 26*(1):89–97.

Holder, H. D., & Wallack, L. (1986). Contemporary perspectives for preventing alcohol problems: An empirically-derived model. *Journal of Public Health Policy, 7*, 324–339.

Homel, R. (1986). *Policing the drinking driver: Random breath testing and the process of deterrence.* Canberra: ACT, Federal Office of Road Safety.

Homel, R. (1990). Random breath testing and random stopping programs in Australia. In R. J. Wilson & R. E. Mann (Eds.), *Drinking and driving: Advances in research and prevention.* New York: Guilford Press.

Huitfeld, B., & Jorner, U. (1972). Efterfrågan på rusdrycker i Sverige: En ekonometrisk underökning av konsumtionens utveckling efter motbokens avskaffande [Demand for alcoholic beverages in Sweden: An econometric study of the development of consumption following the abolishment of the personal ration book.] *Rapport från alkoholpolitiska utredningen* (APU)(p. 91). Stockholm: Statens Offentliga Utredningar, Finansdepartementet.

Jason, L. A., Ji, P. Y., Anes, M. D., & Birkhead, S. H. (1991). Active enforcement of cigarette control laws in the prevention of cigarette sales to minors. *Journal of the American Medical Association, 266*(22), 3159–3161.

Keeler, T. E., Hu, T-W., Barnett, P. G., & Manning, W. G. (1993). Taxation, regulation, and addiction: A demand function for cigarettes based on time-series evidence. *Journal of Health Economics, 12*, 1–18.

Kleiman, M. A. R. (1989). Dynamics of marijuana supply: Enforcement effects on illicit markets. In M. A. R. Kleiman (Ed.), *From marijuana: Costs of abuse, costs of control* (pp. 107–121). Westport, CT: Greenwood Press.

Kortteinen, T. (1989). *State monopolies and alcohol prevention* (Report No. 181). Helsinki: Social Science Institute of Alcohol Studies.

Kuusi, P. (1957). *Alcohol sales experiment in rural Finland.* Helsinki: Finnish Foundation for Alcohol Studies.

Levin, G., Roberts, E., & Hirsh, G. (1975). *The persistent poppy: A computer aided search for heroin policy.* New York: Ballinger.

Levy, D., & Sheflin, N. (1983). New evidence on controlling alcohol use through price. *Journal of Studies on Alcohol, 44*, 920–937.

Lewit, E. M., Coate, D., & Grossman, M. (1981). The effects of government regulation on teenage smoking. *Journal of Law and Economics, 24*, 545–570.

Liben, C. B., Vingilis, E. R., & Blefgen, H. (1987). The Canadian drinking-driving countermeasure experience. *Accident Analysis and Prevention, 19*(3), 159–181.

Lind, B., & Herbert, D. C. (1982). *The effect of "Sunday trading" on traffic crashes* (SR 82/112). Traffic Accident Research Unit, Traffic Authority of New South Wales.

Longo, D. R., Brownson, R. C., Johnson, J. C., Hewett, J. E., Kruse, R. L., Novotny, T. E., & Logan, R. A. (1996). Hospital smoking bans and employee smoking behavior: Results of a national survey. *Journal of the American Medical Association, 275*(16), 1252–1257.

Macdonald, S. (1986). The impact of increased availability of wine in grocery stores on consumption: Four case histories. *British Journal of Addiction, 81*, 381–387.

Mäkelä, K. (1970). Dryckesgångernas frekvens enligt de konsumerade dryckerna och mängden före och efter lagreformen [Frequency of drinking occasions according to kind and amount of beverages before and after the legislative reform.] *Alkoholpolitik, 33*, 144–153.

Malmqvist, S. (1948). *A statistical analysis of demand for liquor in Sweden: A study of the demand for a rationed commodity.* Uppsala University.

Martin, S. E., Grube, J., Voas, R. V., Baker, J., & Hingson, R. (1996, November). Zero tolerance laws: Effective public policy? *Alcoholism: Clinical and Experimental Research, 20*(8, Suppl.), 147A–150A.

Mazis, M. B., Morris, L. A., and Swasy, J. L. (1991). An evaluation of the alcohol warning label: Initial survey results. *Journal of Public Policy and Marketing, 10*, 229–241.

McGuinness, T. (1983). The demand for beer, spirits and wine in the U.K., 1956–79. In M. Grant, M. Plant, & A. Williams (Eds.), *Economics and alcohol: Consumption and controls* (pp. 238–242). New York: Gardner.

McKnight, A. J. (1989). *Development and field test of a responsible alcohol service program. Volume III. Final results.* Washington, DC: NHTSA.

Mercer, G. W. (1985). The relationships among driving while impaired charges, police drinking-driving roadcheck activity, media coverage and alcohol-related casualty traffic accidents. *Accident Analysis and Prevention, 17*(6), 467–474.

Mosher, J. (1979). Dram shop liability and the prevention of alcohol-related problems. *Journal of Studies on Alcohol, 9*, 733–798.

Mulford, H. A., & Fitzgerald, J. L. (1988). Consequences of increasing off-premise wine outlets in Iowa. *British Journal of Addiction, 83*, 1271–1279.

National Institute on Alcohol Abuse and Alcoholism. (1996). *Alcohol Alert No. 31: Drinking and Driving* (PH 362). Bethesda, MD: Author.

Nordlund, S. (1974). Drikkevaner og vinmonopolutsalg [Drinking habits and state monopoly sales of alcohol]. Oslo: Universitetsforlaget.

Nordlund, S. (1981). *Effects of a drastic reduction in the number of beer outlets in two Norwegian towns.* National Institute for Alcohol Research, SIFA Mimeograph No. 42, Oslo. Paper presented at the 25th International Institute on the Prevention and Treatment of Alcoholism, Tours, France.

Nordlund, S. (1985, June 2–7). *Effects of Saturday closing of wine and spirits shops in Norway.* National Institute for Alcohol Research, SIFA Mimeograph No. 5/85, Oslo. Paper presented at the 31st International Institute on the Prevention and Treatment of Alcoholism, Rome, Italy.

Noval, S., & Nilsson, T. (1984). Mellanölets effekt på konsumtionsunivån och tillväxten hos den totala alkoholkonsumtionen [The effects of medium-strength beer on consumption levels and the rise in overall alcohol consumption]. In T. Nilsson (Ed.), *När mellenölet försvann [When middle-strength beer disappeared]*, (pp. 77–93). Linköping: Samhällsvetenskapliga institutionen, Universitetet i Linköping.

Olsson, O., & Wikstrom, P-O. H. (1982). Effects of the experimental Saturday closing of liquor retail stores in Sweden. *Contemporary Drug Problems, 11*(3), 325–353.

O'Malley, P. M., & Wagenaar, A. C. (1991). Effects of minimum drinking age laws on alcohol use, related behaviors and traffic crash involvement among American youth: 1976–1987. *Journal of Studies on Alcohol, 52,* 478–491.

Ornstein, S. I., & Hanssens, D. M. (1985). Alcohol control laws and the consumption of distilled spirits and beer. *Journal of Consumer Research, 12,* 200–213.

Ornstein, S. I., & Levy, D. (1983). Price and income elasticities and the demand for alcoholic beverages. In M. Galanter (Ed.), *Recent developments in alcoholism* (Vol. 1., pp. 303–345). New York: Plenum Press.

Österberg, E. (1991). Current approaches to limit alcohol abuse and the negative consequences of use: A comparative overview of available options and an assessment of proven effectiveness. In O. Aasland (Ed.), *The negative social consequences of alcohol use* (pp. 266–269). Oslo: Norwegian Ministry of Health and Social Affairs.

Österberg, E. (1995). Do alcohol prices affect consumption and related problems? In H. D. Holder & G. Edwards (Eds.), *Alcohol and public policy: Evidence and issues* (pp. 145–163). Oxford: Oxford University Press.

Parker, R. N., Saltz, R. F., & Hennessy, M. (1994). The impact of alcohol beverage container warning labels on alcohol-impaired drivers, drinking drivers and the general population in northern California. *Addiction, 89,* 1639–1651.

Preusser, D. F., Williams, A. R., Zador, P. L., & Blomberg, R. D. (1984). The effect of curfew laws on motor vehicle crashes. *Law and Policy, 6,* 115–128.

Reid, D. J., McNeill, A. D., & Glynn, T. J. (1995). Reducing the prevalence of smoking in youth in Western countries: An international review. *Tobacco Control, 4,* 266–277.

Room, R. (1987, January 20–22). *Alcohol monopolies in the U.S.A.: Challenges and opportunities.* Paper presented at a meeting on "The Role of Alcohol Monopolies," organized by the Swedish Systembolaget, Vaxholm.

Ross, H. L. (1982). *Deterring the drinking driver: Legal policy and social control* (2nd ed.). Lexington, MA: D. C. Heath.

Ross, H. L. (1988a). Deterrence-based policies in Britain, Canada and Australia. In M. D. Laurence, J. R. Snortum, & F. E. Zimring (Eds.), *The social control of drinking and driving* (pp. 64–78). Chicago: University of Chicago Press.

Ross, H. L. (1988b). Editorial: British drink-driving policy. *British Journal of Addiction, 83,* 863–865.

Ross, H. L. (1991, April). *Administrative license revocation for drunk drivers: Options and choices in three states.* Prepared for the AAA Foundation for Traffic Safety.

Russ, N. W., & Geller, E. S. (1986). *Evaluation of a server intervention program for preventing drunk driving* (Final Report No. DD-3). Blacksburg: Virginia Polytechnic Institute and State University, Department of Psychology.

Rydell, C. P., & Everingham, S. S. (1994). *Controlling cocaine: Supply versus demand programs.* Santa Barbara, CA: Rand Corporation.

Saffer, H., & Grossman, M. (1987). Beer taxes, the legal drinking age, and youth motor vehicle fatalities. *Journal of Legal Studies, 16,* 351–374.

Saltz, R. F. (1987). The roles of bars and restaurants in preventing alcohol-impaired driving: An evaluation of server intervention. *Evaluation and Health Professions, 10*(1), 5–27.

Saltz, R. F. (1988). Server intervention and responsible beverage service programs. In *Surgeon General's workshop on drunk driving—Background papers* (pp. 169–179). Rockville, MD: U.S. Department of Health and Human Services, Office of the Surgeon General.

Saltz, R. F. (1989). Research needs and opportunities in server intervention programs. *Health Education Quarterly, 16*(3), 429–438.

Saltz, R. F. (1993). The introduction of dram shop legislation in the United States and the advent of server training. *British Journal of Addiction, 88*(Suppl.), 95S–103S.

Saltz, R. F., & Hennessy, M. (1990a). *The efficacy of "responsible beverage service" programs in reducing intoxication* (working paper). Berkeley, CA: Prevention Research Center.

Saltz, R. F., & Hennessy, M. (1990b). *Reducing intoxication in commercial establishments: An evaluation of responsible beverage service practices* (working paper). Berkeley, CA: Prevention Research Center.

Schmidt, W., & Kornaczewski, A. (1975). The effect of lowering the legal drinking age in Ontario and on alcohol-related motor vehicle accidents." In S. Israelstam & S. Lambert (Eds.), *Alcohol, drugs, and traffic safety: Proceedings of the sixth international conference on alcohol, drugs, and traffic safety, Toronto, September 8–13, 1974* (pp. 763–770). Toronto, Canada: Addiction Research Foundation.

Shattuck, D., & Whitehead, P. C. (1976). *Lowering the drinking age in Saskatchewan: The effect on collisions among young drivers.* Saskatchewan, Canada: Department of Health.

Skog, O.-J. (1988, June 5–11). *The effect of introducing a new light beer in Norway: Substitution or addition?* Presented at Kettil Bruun Society Meeting, Berkeley, CA.

Smart, R. G. (1986). The impact on consumption of selling wine in grocery stores. *Alcohol and Alcoholism, 21,* 233–236.

Smart, R. G., & Fejer, D. (1975). Six years of cross-sectional surveys of student drug use in Toronto. *Bulletin on Narcotics, 27*(2), 11–22.

Smart, R. G., Fejer, D., & White, J. (1972). *Drug use trends among metropolitan Toronto students: A study of changes from 1968 to 1972.* Toronto, Canada.

Smith, D. I. (1987). Effect on traffic accidents of introducing Sunday hotel sales in New South Wales, Australia. *Contemporary Drug Problems, 14,* 279–295.

Smith, D. I. (1988a). Effect on casualty traffic accidents of the introduction of 10 p.m. Monday to Saturday hotel closing in Victoria. *Australian Drug and Alcohol Review, 7,* 163–166.

Smith, D. I. (1988b). Effect on traffic accidents of introducing flexible hotel trading hours in Tasmania, Australia. *British Journal of Addiction, 83,* 219–222.

Smith, D. I. (1988c). Effect on traffic accidents of introducing Sunday alcohol sales in Brisbane, Australia. *International Journal of the Addictions, 23,* 1091–1099.

Sweanor, D., Ballin, S., Corcoran, R. D., Davis, A., Deasy, K., Ferrence, R. G., Lahey, R., Lucido, S., Nethery, W. J., & Wasserman, J. (1992). Report of the tobacco policy research study group on tobacco pricing and taxation in the United States. *Tobacco Control, 1*(Suppl.), S31–S36.

Townsend, J. L. (1987). Cigarette tax, economic welfare and social class patterns of smoking. *Applied Economics, 19,* 355–365.

Uchida, C., Forst, B., & Annan, S. (1992). *Controlling street-level drug trafficking: Evidence from Oakland and Birmingham.* Washington, DC: Bureau of Justice Assistance, Office of Justice Programs, U.S. Department of Justice.

U.S. Congress House Subcommittee on Crime. (1994). *International drug supply, control, and interdiction: Hearing before the U.S. House Subcommittee on Crime and Criminal Justice of the Committee on the Judiciary, July 15, 1993.* Washington, DC: Superintendent of Documents.

U.S. General Accounting Office. (1987). *Drinking-age laws: An evaluation synthesis of their impact on highway safety* (Report to the Chairman, Subcommittee on Investigations and Oversight, Committee on Public Works and Transportation, House of Representatives). Washington, DC: Superintendent of Documents.

U.S. General Accounting Office. (1993). *Confronting the drug problem: Debate persists on enforcement and alternative approaches.* Washington, DC: Author, General Government Division.

University of California, San Diego. (1990). *Tobacco use in California, 1990.* Sacramento, CA: Department of Health Services.

Vingilis, E., & Coultes, B. (1990). Mass communications and drinking-driving: Theories, practices and results. *Alcohol, Drugs and Driving, 6*(2), 61–81.

Voas, R. B. (1988). Emerging technologies for controlling the drunk driver. In M. Laurence, J. Snortum, & F. Zimming (Eds.), *Social control of the drunk driver* (pp. 321–370). Chicago: University of Chicago Press.

Wagenaar, A. C. (1983). *Alcohol, young drivers, and traffic accidents: Effects of minimum-age laws.* Lexington, MA: Lexington Books.

Wagenaar, A. C., & Holder, H. D. (1991a). A change from public to private sale of wine: Results from natural experiments in Iowa and West Virginia. *Journal of Studies on Alcohol, 52*(2), 162–173.

Wagenaar, A. C., & Holder, H. D. (1991b). Effects of alcoholic beverage server liability on traffic crash injuries. *Alcoholism: Clinical and Experimental Research, 15*(6), 942–947.

Wallack, L. (1981). Mass media campaigns: The odds against finding behavior change. *Health Education Quarterly, 8,* 209–260.

Walsh, B. M. (1982). The demand for alcohol in the UK: A comment. *Journal of Industrial Economics, 30,* 439–446.

Whitehead, P. C. (1977). *Alcohol and young drivers: Impact and implications of lowering the drinking age.* Research Bureau Monograph Series No. 9. Ottawa, Canada: Department of National Health and Welfare, Health Protection Branch.

Whitehead, P. C., Craig, J., Langford, N., MacArthur, C., Stanton, B., & Ferrence, R. G. (1975). Collision behavior of young drivers: Impact of the change in the age of majority. *Journal of Studies on Alcohol, 36,* 1208–1223.

Wilde, G. J. S., L'Hoste, J., Sheppard, D., & Wind, G. (1971). *Road safety campaigns: Design and evaluation* (75 pp.). Paris, France: Organization for Economic Cooperation and Development.

Wilkinson, J. T. (1987). Reducing drunken driving: Which policies are most effective? *Southern Economic Journal, 54,* 322–334.

Williams, A., Lund, A., & Preusser, D. (1984). *Night driving curfews in New York and Louisiana: Results of a questionnaire survey.* Washington, DC: Insurance Institute for Highway Safety.

Williams, A. F., Rich, R. F., Zador, P. L., & Robertson, L. S. (1975). The legal minimum drinking age and fatal motor vehicle crashes. *Journal of Legal Studies, 4*, 219–239.

Wittman, F., & Hilton, M. (1987). Uses of planning and zoning ordinances to regulate alcohol outlets in California cities. In H. D. Holder (Ed.), *Control issues in alcohol abuse prevention: Strategies for states and communities* (pp. 337–366). Greenwich, CT: JAI Press.

Wittman, F. D., & Shane, P. (1988, October 31). *Summary description: A manual for community planning to prevent problems of alcohol availability.* Prepared for distribution at the conference "America Focuses on Alcohol: A National Drug Problem," The Second National Conference on Alcohol Abuse and Alcoholism, San Diego.

Womer, W. W. (1978). Drinking laws in the Commonwealth of Virginia. In J. A. Ewing & B. A. Rouse (Eds.), *Drinking* (pp. 291–305). Chicago: Nelson-Hall.

Worden, J. K., Flynn, B. S., Merrill, D. G., Waller, J. A., & Haugh, L. D. (1989). Preventing alcohol-impaired driving through community self-regulation training. *American Journal of Public Health, 79*(3), 287–290.

Worden, J. K., Waller, J. A., & Riley, T. J. (1975). *The Vermont public education campaign in alcohol and traffic safety.* Burlington, VT: Department of Mental Health.

Zador, P., Lund, A., Fields, M., & Weinberg, K. (1989). Fatal crash involvement and laws against alcohol-impaired driving. *Journal of Public Health Policy, 10*, 467–485.

Zimring, F. E., & Nelson, W. (1995). Cigarette taxes as cigarette policy. *Tobacco Control, 4*, 525–533.

32

Economic Issues and Substance Abuse

Jeffrey Merrill

The economics of substance abuse encompasses a variety of issues dealing with how substance abuse services have been financed in the past; the emerging phenomenon of managed care and its impact on how substance abuse services are now financed, organized, and delivered; and the costs, costs-benefits, cost-effectiveness, and cost offsets associated with substance abuse prevention and treatment. This chapter will address these issues both separately and from the perspective of how they interrelate.

FINANCING SUBSTANCE ABUSE SERVICES

Payment Mechanisms

In health care in general—and in substance abuse as well—financing is the critical component in determining the location, scope and duration, and nature of the services provided. The reason is the fact that "services follow the money." In other words, what the various *payment mechanisms* (Medicare, Medicaid, private insurance) cover will determine what services will be available, how much will be offered, and who will provide them. A good example of this phenomenon is nursing-home care. Until Medicaid started to cover nursing-home services in the mid-1970s, there were few nursing homes in existence for the elderly and disabled (there had been convalescent homes before that, but they were available only to those who either could pay or benefited from charity). However, once Medicaid started to cover these services, the nursing-home industry grew dramatically. Now, we cannot imagine a time when this benefit did not exist.

In addition, with the advent of managed care, financing has become more intertwined even with clinical decision making. At one time, providers made decisions about the extent and type of coverage, and the insurance followed the clinical decisions. Increasingly, however, the nature and limitations of the coverage as determined by the insurer dictate the services to be provided.

Traditionally, the financing of substance abuse services paralleled that of other health care services, albeit always on a more limited level and with more public support. The main sources of dollars to pay for substance abuse services are fourfold: private insurance, Medicaid and Medicare, the federal substance abuse block grant to states, and state and local funding. In addition, some specific federal programs fund treatment for groups that are eligible to receive their services. These include the Veterans Administration and Community Health and Mental Health Centers. Obviously, this list includes only those sources that encompass the bulk of funding. Many people with private resources pay for their own treatment, and voluntary and charitable organizations also help others to gain such services.

Private insurance, including Blue Cross/Blue Shield plans, as well as other commercial carriers (e.g., Prudential, Aetna) and HMOs, offer plans with a substance abuse treatment benefit. However, the existence of that benefit and the scope of the coverage vary from plan to plan (i.e., private insurance plans offered by the same carrier differ depending on the scope of benefits desired by an employer and the amount the employer is willing to pay for such coverage).

It should be noted that this discussion deals almost exclusively with payments for the *treatment* of alcohol and drug abuse. While tobacco use remains the most prevalent of all drugs and is the most costly to our health system, very little public or private insurance funding is used to support smoking cessation. While there are efforts both at the government level and among some private employers in the areas of both the prevention and the treatment of tobacco addiction, these contribute a relatively small amount of the total funding spent either on health care in general or, more specifically, on substance abuse treatment. In addition, prevention programs for drug and alcohol use are not funded through these mechanisms either. Most prevention funding comes from direct government support through the Center for Substance Abuse Prevention (CSAP) and the Department of Education Drug Free Schools and Communities Program.

Coverage Limitations

At one time, many of these plans offered a range of services, but it was common for them to include a 28-day hospital or residential treatment program as the typical benefit used. However, over time, given a lack of convincing evidence that 28-day residential programs—or, for that matter, any inpatient programs—were any more effective than either a shorter length of stay or an alternative outpatient program, companies began to be less generous with this benefit.[2] As a result, there are often strict limits on the number of residential days, or plans require that outpatient services be used instead. As managed care became more prevalent (see below), the limitations on these options increased, and inpatient and residential services are even less likely to be covered.

In addition to where the services may be provided, a similar financing issue has to do with the level of provider that is covered. At one time, financing for substance abuse treatment services might have covered therapy provided by psychiatrists and psychologists. Over time, however, coverage has tightened, and services offered by lower level personnel, including certified counselors, are more likely to be paid for than those of higher cost practitioners. Further, rather than covering individual sessions, payers have encouraged greater use of group therapy.

Cost Sharing

One other aspect of the nature of private financing for substance abuse treatment has to do with the cost sharing that may be required by private insurers. *Cost sharing* refers to that portion of the bill that the individual is required to pay. Various mechanisms for cost sharing exist, including deductibles, copayments, and coinsurance. A deductible is an up-front payment for services that patients must pay for their own care before the insurance plan starts to cover the services. In other words, if the deductible is $200, then the first $200 of services must be paid by the beneficiary before the insurer will pay. Copayments are a fixed amount for each unit of service that the patient must pay (after the deductible, if any, has been met). The copayment is irrespective of the actual amount of the charge. For example, a copayment of $10 per visit means that if the visit is $40, the patient pays $10 and the insurer $30, but if the visit is $60, the patient still pays $10.

On the other hand, coinsurance does vary with the cost of the service. Coinsurance is similar to co-payments in that it is an ongoing responsibility, except that it is a fixed percentage of the cost rather than a fixed amount. Therefore, 20% coinsurance on a $40 visit is $8, but if the visit costs $60, the coinsurance amount is $12.

Two other mechanisms are used by private insurers, including managed-care plans, that are related to cost sharing. One of these is a stop-loss provision, which limits the total out-of-pocket responsibility of the insured. In other words, a policy might have a provision that once a patient has paid a predetermined amount in deductibles or coinsurance, the insurer will pick up 100% of the costs. This approach is not prevalent with respect to substance abuse treatment coverage. On the other hand, a lifetime (or annual) limit on coverage is more likely to be in effect. Working the opposite way from stop-loss coverage, the insurer caps its own risk by limiting the amount it will cover either in a given year or over the life of the policy. In other words, once the insurance company has paid out this amount in benefits, the individual is no longer covered. While this provision usually applies to overall medical coverage, what is common in substance abuse coverage may be a limit on the number of treatment episodes that would be paid for. Insurers might rationalize this on the basis of the fact that a person who has not responded to multiple treatments will not be a good candidate for further treatment.

Cost sharing can be a critical factor in a patient's access to care. Since these are out-of-pocket payments, they can determine whether an individual can afford to seek treatment and limit how much care he or she receives. Additionally, particularly in the case of coinsurance, cost sharing can determine what level of personnel a patient sees, since the cost per visit for a psychiatrist or psychologist could be much higher than that of a counselor (or group sessions), making the cost of the coinsurance prohibitive. Policies may include coinsurance rates as high as 50%.

New Arrangements

More recently insurers have begun offering *preferred provider* arrangements (related to cost sharing) where,

if a patient uses a provider from a list offered by the insurer, the cost sharing may be reduced or even eliminated. The so-called preferred providers are those who have agreed to charge the payer less for services than ones not on that list. As a result, individuals who choose other providers would pay more for their care. The most typical form of this arrangement is referred to as a *point-of-service plan*, where beneficiaries pay little or no cost sharing if they use the preferred providers in the plan's network. However, they are free to choose other providers if they are willing to pay an increased portion of the bill.

Private insurance has never been a major source of payment for substance abuse treatment. One reason is that, because of their problem, many substance abusers are either unemployed or employed in marginal jobs that do not offer health insurance. In addition, insurers continue to be skeptical about the effectiveness of substance abuse treatment services. In an era of cost consciousness, payers are likely to evaluate different services in terms of their overall cost-effectiveness, and substance abuse treatment has typically not fared well in comparisons with other, more "medical" care. As is discussed below, this problem makes it more imperative that research do a better job of demonstrating the costs-benefits of substance abuse services.

Public Financing Mechanisms

Most public support for treatment comes either through Medicaid[3] or the federal substance abuse block grant. Medicaid is a state program to pay for health care for the poor, but the federal government actually reimburses the state for a portion of these funds (depending on the state, the federal matching share is anywhere from 50% to 83%).

However, the federal government matches state payments only for services covered under the federal program and for people who meet the federal eligibility guidelines. In order to be eligible for the federal Medicaid share, an individual has to be either eligible for welfare (now called Temporary Assistance to Needy Families, or TANF) or permanently and totally disabled. Those eligible by virtue of TANF are usually single, unemployed parents (mostly women) and their children. With respect to the disabled (who include male adults), until recently, having a drug or alcohol addiction could qualify an individual for both Supplemental Security Income (SSI; a federal income benefits program) and, as a result, for Medicaid. However, legislation passed in 1996 took away this eligibility category. Now, to be eligible for Medicaid as a disabled person requires a serious physical or mental disability (not including alcohol or drug addiction) that makes it impossible for that individual to be employed.

In addition, in most states, a person can qualify for Medicaid if he or she has medical bills that are sufficiently high to reduce that individual's income below a level prescribed by that state. In other words, if the state's income eligibility level is $5,000, a person who earns $15,000 would have to "spend down" at least $10,000 of her or his income in medical bills to become eligible for Medicaid.

Thus, Medicaid eligibility is limited to only the group that meets these specific categorical or spend-down requirements.[4] But even if a person is eligible for Medicaid, there is still no guarantee that he or she will be able to get substance abuse treatment paid for. There is no federal requirement that states offer substance abuse treatment as a covered service under their Medicaid program. To the extent that they do cover these services, they are usually limited to outpatient treatment or services provided in general hospitals. Medicaid excludes most residential care for both substance abuse and mental health services.

On the other hand, to the extent that a state does pay for substance abuse services, Medicaid law does prohibit any cost sharing on the part of the patient. In addition, in a growing trend, most states that offer substance abuse treatment services under Medicaid do so through managed-care arrangements.

A significant portion of substance abuse treatment is paid for through the federal Substance Abuse Block Grant (SABG). Money from this fund is allocated to the states and covers the cost of prevention and treatment services for those who cannot pay for services and who are also not eligible for Medicaid. While a large portion of the SABG funds are directed at men (since many more women would qualify for TANF and Medicaid as single parents), there are specific set-asides in the block grant for pregnant women. The funds, administered by the state substance abuse agency, pay providers to deliver these services. As with Medicaid, many states are contracting with managed-care plans both to manage and to provide these services.

The federal government also pays for substance abuse services through a number of other mechanisms as well although they are less well recognized. For example, the Department of Veterans Affairs provides a significant amount of drug and alcohol treatment for veterans. In addition, a network of both community health centers and community mental health centers supported by government funds offers substance abuse services to low-income individuals throughout the country. Some of the health centers, located in rural areas, are among the few treatment venues for residents of those communities.

MANAGED CARE AND SUBSTANCE ABUSE

Over the past decade, the world of health care has changed significantly, and these changes have been felt particularly acutely in the financing, organization, and delivery of substance abuse services. The overarching event in our health care system that has led to this dramatic change has been the emergence of managed care. While the term *managed care* is used widely, it means many different things, and its specific implication, like that of beauty, is often in the eye of the beholder.

What Is Managed Care?

Before talking about the myriad issues that encompass the economics of substance abuse and its relationship to the proliferation of managed care, it is important to agree on what we mean by the term *managed care* and how it has affected all facets of substance abuse services. Interestingly, if one were to describe managed care a decade ago, the task would have been much simpler. At one time, *managed care* was synonymous with the notion of the health maintenance organization (HMO). The traditional HMOs, like Kaiser Permanente, Group Health of Puget Sound, or the Harvard Community Health Plan, were not-for-profit organizations with whom a group or individual contracted for a fixed amount to provide all the agreed-upon health services. The provision of these services was accomplished through a group of doctors and facilities closely related to the HMO. Most of these relationships were characterized as *closed-panel* arrangements where the individual providers worked exclusively for that HMO (hospitals were either owned by the HMO or contracted with by the HMO, but the care of the HMO members was controlled by the HMO's physician panel). The closed-panel HMO was organized in either a *staff* or a *group model*. In the staff model, the providers worked directly for the HMO as employees, while in the group model, the providers formed a group that had an exclusive contract with the HMO.

Some HMOs, referred to as *independent practice associations* (IPAs) used an *open-panel* model, where the arrangements between the providers and the HMO permitted physicians to contract with the HMO for patients but also allowed them to have private practices or even contract with another HMO as well. It is out of this open panel model that the modern-day breed of managed-care plans emerged.

A Different Breed of Managed Care

At first blush, it may seem like splitting hairs to distinguish the traditional HMO from its more contemporaneous managed-care relative. Both contract with individuals and groups to provide all care, both require a fixed per capita payment (capitation) as the basis for financing services, and both use panels of physicians, other practitioners, and facilities under contract to them to provide those services. Yet the differences between managed care in its modern incarnation and its ancestors (many of which, like Kaiser, still exist) are great and affect the nature, scope, and duration of the services provided.

The most fundamental difference between the historical HMO model and today's managed care is the arrangement between the providers and the managed-care entity. Traditionally, the providers joined an HMO out of a shared philosophy with the HMO about how medicine was practiced. The notion was to have the provider manage the care of the patient, acting not only as the gatekeeper but, more important, as the coordinator of care, guiding the patient through the system, determining the nature and content of that care. Greater emphasis was placed on *health maintenance*, including prevention, early intervention, and the judicious use of specialty and inpatient care. Today, the reasons for a physician to join a managed-care plan are much more economic than philosophical. Managed-care plans create networks of providers based on the quid pro quo of help-

ing to increase—or at least maintain—the providers' patient base in return for discounts and external management of clinical decisions. Providers often do this for defensive reasons out of the fear that if they do not join a given managed care plan, they will lose patients or not get new ones.

Rather than the providers' managing the patients' care, the managed care plan now manages the physicians' decisions through a series of utilization control mechanisms that range from review of referral and admissions decisions to concurrent review of the need for—and nature of—continuing care, to retrospective review of a physician's overall utilization practices.

Thus, no longer motivated by a philosophical predilection to join a managed-care plan, the current provider is often motivated out of a fear of losing market share. In addition, rather than being granted greater clinical discretion, the provider now is often a captive of the decisions of clerks and other reviewers, who have wide discretion in permitting the practitioner to deliver a given service, make a desired placement, or continue providing the service.

Further, instead of the old model, where a provider tended to have allegiance to one HMO, a modern-day provider is forced for economic reasons to be a part of many of these plans, with little or no loyalty to any one managed-care group. In fact, what may emerge instead of loyalty is conflict between the needs of the patients, on the one hand, and, on the other, the bottom line of the managed-care plan. Ultimate success, now measured by Wall Street, may be more a function of profits and losses than of indicators of quality, which are often elusive and thus easily disregarded.

Advocates of managed care correctly assert that in a market economy, quality and consumer satisfaction remain important elements of competition. However, opponents argue that most people's health care needs are minimal in a given year, and therefore, it is easy to satisfy them. They also point out that people who are dissatisfied tend to disenroll and may not even be included in the assessment of a given plan. Further, "quality" is not easily measured, and despite efforts by groups like the National Committee on Quality Assurance (NCQA), there are no good, objective measures of quality (this is particularly the case for substance abuse treatment). Thus, despite the usual market notion of *product differentiation* based upon quality, this does not really exist with respect to health care in general and substance abuse treatment in particular.

Clearly, there remain exceptions to the problems of the current managed-care system, and good models of patient care management do continue to exist. However, much of managed care is driven by cost and profit considerations. In addition, while it is possible for providers and managed-care plans to work well in tandem, adversarial relationships characterize much of the managed health care system.

Substance Abuse and Managed Care

Managed care has had a particularly profound effect on the financing, organization, and delivery of substance abuse services. Not the least of these effects is the emergence of the notion of carving out substance abuse services from the general set of health care benefits, and merging substance abuse with mental health in a new category called *managed behavioral health care*. In other words, under a carve-out, the managed-care company responsible for treating medical problems has no responsibility either to pay for or to provide mental health or substance abuse services. While not all companies carve out behavioral health, this is currently a common practice among managed-care plans.

The reasons for this carve-out are manifold but are not necessarily justified. One reason for the carve-out is the notion that a high proportion of those with mental illness also suffer from substance abuse problems. Thus, the argument goes, by combining these services, the patient can benefit from having both problems treated concurrently and in a coordinated fashion. While this may be true, many of these patients also have serious medical problems, ranging from HIV infection, AIDS, or other infectious diseases including hepatitis or TB, to problems with pregnancy, to stroke, cancer, or enteric or liver problems. Thus, treating their substance abuse is important, but it is equally critical to address these other conditions. The carve-out may make the coordination of such services with substance treatment more—rather than less—difficult.

The rationale for carving out mental health and substance abuse is also, in part, a function of the fact that these services are not universally considered a part of the acute medical care system. Managed

care's focus is on the treatment of acute problems (i.e., those that can be treated and cured). This ranges from treating an infection to removing an appendix to delivering a baby to repairing a broken bone. Managed care does not view itself as a financing mechanism for treating chronic diseases, where treatment is not curative but is geared to alleviating a problem that is continuous or relapsing.[5] In the same way that nonacute services for Alzheimer's or other dementia patients, as well as for other chronic ailments suffered by the elderly and disabled, are usually excluded from managed-care coverage, substance abuse and mental health services are not included. The concern of managed-care plans, as well as most health insurance carriers, is that these are not only expensive patients, but ones whose problems do not end. Therefore, they must be carved out if they are to be covered at all.

Issues surrounding the notion of carving out behavioral health care are even further complicated by the population served. The fact is that the public does not necessarily view those with substance abuse and, to a lesser extent, mental health problems as having a disease. There is, at a minimum, skepticism as to whether treatment interventions can be effective and, at the other extreme, a too commonly held belief that substance abuse stems from character weakness rather than from a physical or medical etiology. Thus, despite the long-term expensive nature of these behavioral problems, the allocation of health care dollars is likely to shortchange behavioral services by a financing system that places its emphasis on treating medical problems.

Whether this current carve-out will remain a permanent change in the financing and organization of health care or will eventually disappear is still debatable. What is more certain, however, is that the carve-out already has a number of major implications for the financing and delivery of substance abuse treatment. The first—and most obvious—is that separating medical care from substance abuse care can lead to other health problems' being either addressed poorly or not addressed at all. In the same way, people being treated in the medical care system may not be identified or referred to needed substance abuse services. If different providers, in different locations, financed through different managed-care plans, are attending to the patient's medical problems than those who are treating the substance abuse problem, gaps are bound to exist. Substance abuse providers may have trouble identifying health problems or getting them treated once they are identified. On the other hand, medical providers may not identify substance problems or know where to refer the patient if they do find them. Little coordination of care is possible given this split in responsibility between two distinct entities.

But the problem is deeper than this. The focus of managed care on keeping costs down can create conflicts between the overall managed-care company and the behavioral health concern. At the most basic level, medical managed-care companies may try to attribute a health problem to substance or mental health causes to get out of paying for treatments. In the same way, a behavioral health company may attribute a problem to a physical ailment so as not to have to provide substance abuse care. An example will show how this can play out in the real world:

A patient was admitted to a hospital with a serious heart condition requiring open-heart surgery. However, the patient also had an alcohol problem, and it was deemed necessary to put the patient through detox before operating. Detox was not the responsibility of the medical managed-care plan but fell to the behavioral health plan. That plan agreed to the need for detox but did not cover inpatient detox services and would not pay for hospital-based detox. It also contended that if this was related to a medical problem, it should be paid for by the medical managed-care company. Thus, it demanded that the patient be moved from his cardiac intensive-care hospital bed (CCU) to a nonhospital setting. The hospital refused, but the managed-care company refused to pay for the detox. While the behavioral health care company eventually made an exception and paid for the inpatient detox, the delay unnecessarily put the patient's life in increased danger and actually increased the cost of care since, during the period that the two sides fought, someone had to pay for the patient's stay in the CCU.[6]

While depicting an actual case, this story may be an extreme. However, it does make the point that dividing the responsibility for financing and care responsibility between two different managed-care companies can create perverse incentives that may not benefit the patient nor even cover the total costs of care.

COSTS, COST-BENEFIT, AND COST OFFSETS

Introduction

Managed care has put the substance abuse treatment industry on the defensive. Basic questions are being raised about both the value of treatment in general and the comparative merit of one modality over another. In an era when economic concerns and judgments may take precedence over clinical decisions, knowing what substance abuse prevention and treatment programs cost and demonstrating their cost-benefit and cost-effectiveness become vital.

The Costs of Substance Abuse

The notion of the *costs of substance abuse* encompasses a variety of different concepts. We can, for example, be referring to the actual cost of a prevention or treatment program or even the costs of an individual treatment episode or visit. But the notion of costs goes well beyond this narrow definition. Substance abuse itself has costs associated with it that make the cost of treatment pale in comparison. Some of these are individual costs, some are costs to industry, and some are larger societal or public costs.

One of the most easily understood is the health care cost associated with tobacco, alcohol, and drug abuse. While we can immediately bring to mind smoking and lung cancer, or alcohol and cirrhosis, or IV drug use and HIV infection, the health effects of substance use go far beyond this. The National Center on Addiction and Substance Abuse at Columbia University found, after a search of the epidemiological literature, more than a thousand medical diagnoses where tobacco, alcohol, or drugs could be identified as the etiological or causal factor leading to that health problem. For example, diseases ranging from different types of cancer to heart disease to emphysema to adverse birth outcomes are associated with smoking. In addition, even where a health problem is not directly caused by tobacco, smoking can exacerbate a problem and increase the costs of treating it. An individual with a respiratory problem like asthma or pneumonia who smokes is more likely to have a serious or chronic case requiring hospitalization, and even for those hospitalized for other illnesses, the costs of treating a problem that is complicated by tobacco, alcohol, or drug abuse may require more services or a longer stay (Fox, Merrill, Chang, & Califano, 1995).

Alcohol and drugs also have serious health effects. For example, as much as 70% of all trauma cases among the nonelderly can be attributed to alcohol and drug use (Fox et al., 1995). This includes not only traffic accidents but also violent injuries, including gunshot or stab wounds and fractures or burns. Additionally, alcohol abuse is associated with many cancers (an individual who smokes *and* drinks heavily is 133 times more likely to get a throat cancer than one who does neither) (National Center on Addiction and Substance Abuse [NCASA], 1993). In addition, pregnant women who drink or use drugs are placing themselves at considerably greater risk of an adverse birth outcome. Further, drug use accounts for almost two thirds of all strokes among people under the age of 65 (NCASA, 1993).

The costs of these substance-use-attributable health problems are enormous. While estimates differ, more than one in seven dollars spent on health care in the United States can be attributed to tobacco, alcohol, or drug use. In a trillion-dollar health care system, this amounts to as much as $150 billion (Merrill, Fox, Pulver, & Lewis, 1996).

It is interesting that despite the concern currently expressed over rising health care costs, little mention or investment of dollars is made on treating substance problems that contribute so heavily to these other costs. As a result of the Medicare, Medicaid, Veterans Health, and a variety of other health care programs, the federal government spent more than $320 billion on paying for health care in 1995 (U.S. Office of Management & Budget, 1996). Of this, 19%, or $60 billion, was spent treating health care problems attributable to substance abuse (NCASA, 1995). Yet the amount of government spending on substance treatment was less than $5 billion (NCASA, 1995).

In the same way, while employers and managed-care plans are increasingly cost-conscious, the amount spent on paying for substance treatment is actually declining. It should also be noted that these costs do not fall only to the medical needs of the substance abuser. The toll of substance abuse is felt by the abuser's whole family and can result in increased health benefit costs to the spouses, parents, and children as well (Langenbucher, 1994).

Why does this apparent paradox exist between the high costs of substance abuse to the health care system and a lack of greater investment in treatment? A number of factors explain this, but at the heart of much of this is a continuing skepticism about the effectiveness of treatment. While, as will be discussed later in this chapter, there is a literature that demonstrates that treatment can be effective, this is not the perception held either by the public or by those who make decisions about how public and private health benefit dollars will be spent.

In part, this skepticism is due to the fact that we tend to view all substance abuse as though it were an acute rather than a chronic problem that has recurring acute episodes. As a society, we tend to hold substance abuse treatment up to a higher standard for success than we do treatment for other, similar diseases, such as diabetes or even cancer. Successful treatment is measured by complete and permanent abstinence from smoking, drinking, or drug use. If this is not attained, then either treatment is viewed as ineffective or the problem is attributed to a character weakness in the patient rather than to a disease process. We expect this treatment to function as though it were both an antibiotic with immediate curative results and a vaccine that prevents long-term relapse. Imagine if treatment for a diabetic were held to the same standard of success.

In addition, even if the notion of a chronic problem requiring more than one treatment episode is accepted, the skepticism will not disappear. Many view this not as a medical problem, but as one associated more with social or personal characteristics. Despite the evidence to the contrary, many still consider substance abuse a problem of the poor, or of those who lack moral strength. To some extent, the notion of carving out behavioral health care from the mainstream of managed care reflects this distinction.

They also see treatment, to the extent that it does work, in terms more of AA or NA than of services provided by the medical care system. Why, therefore, should the system pay for such treatment when it can be delivered for nothing through a local AA chapter?

But the concerns over the effectiveness of treatment extend beyond treatment's impact on health care costs. On the one hand, many of the largest costs to society, including criminal justice, welfare, disability, and economic productivity, are associated with substance abuse. On the other, the support for treatment, particularly in the public sector, does not reflect this link. For example, more than half of all criminal activity is closely linked with drug and alcohol abuse. Whether we are referring to crime involving people trafficking in illegal substances (distributive crimes), people committing crimes to get money to purchase drugs and/or alcohol (acquisitive crimes), or people committing crimes as a result of being under the influence of these substances (pharmacogenic crimes), substance abuse is at the heart of the crime committed. Associated costs are manifold, including the costs of law enforcement, the courts, and the corrections system. Yet those who make funding decisions at the federal, state, and local levels do not look to treatment as the best way of investing dollars to reduce crime in our society. More jail cells, longer and determinate sentences, and charging juveniles as adults—all take precedence over treatment as the desired solutions. In the same way, solutions to the welfare problem, and to reducing worker's compensation and other disability expenditures, seldom highlight substance abuse treatment. Despite a bipartisan concern at the federal level about the drug problem and its influence on crime and other social problems, in 1996 two thirds of the federal money spent in the so-called War against Drugs went to supply reduction, and only one third to demand reduction. This means that instead of investing in prevention and treatment efforts to reduce the demand for drugs, funds were more targeted on law enforcement activities here and abroad intended to reduce the supply of drugs.

Assessing the Economic Costs and Benefits of Treatment

What role does the study of the economics of substance abuse play in addressing this decoupling of the relationship between substance abuse treatment and the reduction of both the prevalence and the costs of the societal problems? Part of the answer is to increase public awareness about the costs of substance abuse to society. For example, the research of Kelman, Miller, and Dunmeyer (1990), as well as of Harwood, Napolitano, Kristiansen, and Collins (1984), points to the link between substance abuse and the its high cost to society. Rice et al. estimated that in 1990, substance abuse cost American society $166 billion. In addition, studies by Inciardi, McBride, McCoy, and Chitwood (1994), Ball, Lange,

Myers, and Friedman (1988), and Merrill (1991)[7] established the strong link between crime and the use of drugs and alcohol (although they did not put cost figures on these links). Merrill and his colleagues have also estimated that at least one in five welfare recipients is suffering from an alcohol and/or drug problem (NCASA, 1994). While this does not mean that they necessarily became welfare recipients because of substance abuse, it does mean that getting them off welfare will be difficult if this problem is not addressed. In an era of welfare reform, this should be considered an important piece of information. In a paper on the impact of substance abuse and its impact on federal entitlement programs, Merrill and his colleagues estimated that in 1995, the cost to the federal government resulting from its inability to get people off the public assistance roles because of their substance abuse problems was $3 billion (Merrill, in press; NCASA, 1995).

Making people aware of the costs of substance abuse to society is far from sufficient. As has been noted, the real concern is to convince those who make decisions about program funding (whether in the public or in the private sector) that an investment in substance abuse treatment does, in fact, yield dividends not only by reducing the chance of relapse, but also by decreasing a variety of other costs. The managed-care company must be convinced of the fact that substance abuse treatment is effective and that it can also reduce other health and mental health costs. The employer will be interested in a variety of other costs ranging from health benefits, to disability and workers' compensation, to absenteeism and productivity, to even the quality of the product or service produced. Finally, both government and society as a whole will be concerned about treatment's impact on health care, criminal justice, public assistance, and taxes. As a staff member of the White Office on National Drug Control Policy (ONDCP) put it, "The public is more concerned with whether, after treatment, the addict will rob them and hit them over the head than with whether he is drug free."[8]

The success of substance abuse treatment must therefore be measured not only in clinical terms (i.e., abstention, clean urines, and no relapse), but also in economic terms. Treatment research must demonstrate not only that a dollar spent on treatment yields savings that exceed that dollar (*cost-benefit*), but also that spending the dollar on substance abuse treatment will yield greater savings than investing that same dollar in something else *(cost-effectiveness)*. In other words, not only is a given intervention compared to no intervention, but it is also weighed against other interventions as well.

But in an era of budget constraints and managed care, cost-effectiveness comparisons go beyond simply testing one substance abuse intervention against another. A dollar spent on substance abuse prevention and treatment must also yield greater benefit than if the same dollar is spent on a medical procedure. For example, will a managed-care company derive more cost savings from putting more of its resources into substance abuse treatment than into an exercise and diet program?

Cost-Benefit

To determine the cost-benefit and cost-effectiveness of substance abuse programs, it is important to define exactly what we mean by these terms.[9] For the purposes of this discussion, we will define *cost-benefit* as a comparison of the costs of a given intervention and its benefits. The cost-benefit involves looking at the costs and benefits of a given intervention compared with doing nothing. Cost-benefit can be defined as a ratio of the benefits to the costs. In other words, if the ratio has a value greater than 1, then the benefits outweigh the costs. We can then say, for example, that a cost-benefit ratio of 4:1 means that for every $1 we spend, we yield $4 in benefit. The recent CALDATA study found that in California, for every $1 spent by the state for substance abuse services, $7 were saved through reduced health, criminal justice, and welfare expenditures (Gerstein et al., 1994). Thus, CALDATA demonstrated a 7:1 cost-benefit ratio.

However, some argue that using a cost-benefit ratio may be misleading. For example, if the benefits equal $4 and the costs equal $1, is this the same as an intervention that costs $100 but saves $400? While the ratios are the same, the potential savings are greater in the latter case (when we discus cost-effectiveness, this will become clearer). Thus, another way of looking at cost-benefit might be in terms of a *net cost offset*. Under this approach, rather than dividing benefits by costs, the costs are subtracted from the benefits. In this way, a positive result would indicate a cost-benefit, and the larger the result, the greater the net benefit.

Cost-Effectiveness

Often, cost-effectiveness is defined as the marginal improvement in some outcome given a marginal increase in the cost of the studied intervention. In other words, if we were to increase treatment from two to three sessions a week for a 50% increase in the costs of treatment, would the number of people who avoid relapse within 6 months increase by more or less than 50%? If this added cost leads to a proportionately greater increase in reduced relapses (in this case, 50%), then the added costs are deemed to be cost-effective.

However, for the purposes of this discussion, cost-effectiveness is a comparison of the cost-benefit of two or more interventions. In other words, how can we reap the biggest return on our investment? If we compare two different interventions, which will yield the most benefit?

But this might lead to somewhat misleading conclusions. For example, Intervention A costs $50 per person and yields a 5:1 cost-benefit ratio, and Intervention B costs $100 per capita and yields a cost-benefit ratio of 4:1. Thus, it would appear that Intervention A is more cost-effective. Possibly, but another way of looking at this is that by investing $100 per capita, we can save a net of $300 with Intervention B, while A saves only $200. Which is a more effective intervention? The answer is that this would depend upon a number of variables. First, it depends on whether the benefit accrues to the entity that is paying the costs. In other words, if state money is being used for the treatment, but half of the savings is reaped by the federal government (as with Medicaid), then the cost-benefit of A is reduced to 1:1, while the cost-benefit of B is 1.5:1, making B the clear winner. On the other hand, if there is a limited pot of money to treat a large population, then A may be the only option, since its lower per capita cost would permit more people to be served. Conversely, for a given population and with no limit on the available funds, spending more money—as in Alternative B—will yield greater savings. Thus, there is no simple answer, and each situation must be viewed in terms the individual conditions involved.

Costs and Benefits

What do we mean by costs and benefits? *Costs* are defined as the personnel, facilities, equipment, and supplies (including medications) that are required.[10] However, depending on the context, costs have to be further defined (i.e., costs to whom?). For example, the costs that a managed-care company is interested in are only the ones for which it is responsible. Costs being borne by the patient or a provider may not enter into its evaluation of cost-benefit. On the other hand, an overall evaluation of cost-benefit might have to define costs more broadly to include the total costs, regardless of who is responsible for them. Another issue in defining costs is to ensure that we account for all the costs. An example can be seen in much of the early work done on evaluating the cost-benefit of home care services for the elderly. If we look at the costs of the actual home care services and evaluate them in terms of the benefits accrued, we see considerable cost-benefit for the Medicare program compared to nursing-home care. However, by keeping people in their homes, we now have many other costs, including housing, food, and transportation, which may also be paid by the government (although not by Medicare). Using this definition of costs, as well as looking at the cost-benefit of home health care to the entire government (not just Medicare), we may not find that home care is more cost-effective than nursing-home services.[11]

Defining benefits is an even more complex undertaking. *Benefit* can be defined narrowly in terms of simply the cost of future treatment (e.g., relapse), or it might be viewed very broadly in terms of all the health and social cost reductions that are generated. Again, we must view this in the context of "benefits to whom?" For example, the concerns of a managed behavioral health care company would revolve exclusively around the question of whether the cost of an intervention will yield benefits in terms of reduced relapse rates and less mental health morbidity. On the other hand, a full-service managed-care plan (which includes physical, mental health, and substance abuse services) might be more interested in the benefits that result from fewer health problems overall.

An issue related to the above is the timing of when the benefits will accrue. For example, while there is no question that smoking cessation can have a tremendous impact on reducing some cancers and cardiovascular diseases, the savings will probably not be seen for years. Thus, while a managed-care plan must pay the costs of that intervention now, they may never benefit from any of the savings. On the other hand, drug and alcohol treatment may yield immediate or short-term benefits. The impact of drug and alcohol use on a variety of health problems ranging from HIV infection and other needle-related infectious diseases to adverse birth outcomes to stroke to trauma related problems is short-term.

Thus, eliminating or reducing these substance problems can yield immediate benefits. An example might be the benefits resulting from a methadone program. Just looking at HIV seroconversion rates of those receiving methadone maintenance and treatment for their heroin addiction compared to the rates of those who are not is dramatic. Given the high cost of this disease, particularly in a drug-abusing population, fairly dramatic decreases in health care costs can be realized quickly. The author's own research shows as much as a 4:1 difference in the seroconversion rates between the two groups (Merrill, 1997).

Benefits can be defined in a number of ways. Clearly, the most narrow definition of benefits would include only the costs saved in terms of having to treat the disease (in the case of prevention programs) or to prevent relapse (in the case of treatment programs). Ironically, however, this is the most problematic benefit to isolate and define. Substance abuse treatment is not like an antibiotic, where administration of the drug can actually eliminate the infection and prevent future medical costs. Instead, like diabetes, substance abuse is a chronic, recurring problem, where long-term or permanent abstinence is less likely (particularly as a result of a single treatment episode). Instead, the benefit may more likely be delaying the problem, and the savings may be both harder to quantify (than, in the case of an infection, the costs of continuing to treat the disease) and longer term. Thus, cost-benefit analysis of treatment may not provide convincing evidence where a short-term, easily understood result is required.

The benefits of substance abuse interventions can be more easily identified in terms of their *cost offsets* to other programs. In other words, offsetting the cost of, for example, treatment are savings to the medical care (including mental health), criminal justice, and welfare systems. In addition, the impact on employment can be viewed in terms of such measures as gains in productivity (e.g., reduced absenteeism) and increased tax revenues. These measures can be viewed separately or can be combined to calculate a total cost offset. If we subtract the costs of the actual intervention from this, the result can be called the *net cost offset*. This net cost offset provides us with a measure of the net savings that result from the intervention.

An example of this type of calculation is a study done in the state of Oregon which looked at the cost savings that could be attributed to publicly supported treatment programs. For those who had completed treatment, the state estimated that the savings to the Medicaid, food stamp, child welfare, and criminal justice systems amounted to more than $83.1 million. The total cost of public treatment programs was almost $14.9 million. Thus, the *net cost offset* was $68.2 million, and the cost-benefit ratio was almost 5.6 : 1 (Finigan, 1996).

As already mentioned, a cost offset can be counted only if it is relevant to the group for whom one is calculating the benefit. Obviously, to a state government, while many of these measures are important, only that portion of the costs that it pays can be counted. For example, with respect to health care costs, a state is responsible only for those costs which are paid by Medicaid or through other state funds. In addition, even for Medicaid, only those reduced costs that the state pays (the federal government pays more than half) can be considered a potential benefit. On the other hand, benefits accrue to more that just the individual being treated. As Langenbucher (1996) and Lennox, Scott-Lennox, and Holder (1992) have pointed out, treating the alcoholic improves not only his or her health status, but also that of the whole family, thus reducing health care costs even further.

It should also be noted that, for some of these measures, it would be difficult to quantify the actual cost offset in terms of dollars saved. While reducing crime is important, one cannot say that for each reduced arrest, the full savings can be counted. When we talk about health care cost savings to, for example, Medicaid, we can say that if someone did not get sick, Medicaid actually saved the money for those services. However, simply because someone is not arrested does not mean that the criminal justice system saves money. It is not as though a jail cell can be eliminated, or the number of police officers or judges will change. Significant reductions in crime have to occur before any sizable offsets can be identified. On the other hand, because crime is of such concern to society, and substance abuse and crime are so closely linked, we cannot ignore this measure.

While it may not be possible to determine whether there was any cost-benefit, the impact of prevention or treatment programs in terms of their *social* benefit still must be considered an important measure of the *efficacy* (defined as the nonmonetary benefit) of these interventions.

Another caveat about how we define benefits is that from a cost perspective, not all benefits are actually "benefits." This apparently contradictory statement stems from the fact that while a beneficial outcome is attained, it may not actually save money. For example, while health prevention programs involving exercise, better nutrition, and smoking cessation have led to healthier people who live longer, the effect of this on overall health care costs is actually to increase those costs. People dying at younger ages from strokes and heart attacks are now living much longer lives at considerably greater expense to Medicare and Medicaid. More acute services and a much greater need for long-term care contribute greatly to the costs of these programs. Thus, while we cannot argue about the benefits of a more healthy lifestyle, there may actually be no cost-benefit (i.e., the ratio is less than 1).

This problem may or may not apply to substance abuse. An example is the argument that despite the costs of smoking to the health care system, smoking cessation would actually increase overall health care costs, particularly for Medicare (Manning, Keeler, Newhouse, Sloss, & Wasserman, 1991). Opponents of current efforts at both the state and federal levels to increase tobacco taxes as a way of reducing smoking argue that these increased taxes, while raising revenues in the short term, may lead to increased longer term public expenditures. On the other hand, to date, research would refute this argument. For example, the study by Manning et al. (1991) found that the cumulative impact of excess medical care required by smokers at all ages outweighed the shorter life expectancy. In addition, a study by Hodgson (1992) showed that, in fact, payers that cover the younger groups (i.e., private insurance and Medicaid) bear a greater burden of smokers' costs than does Medicare.

Some Examples

Cost-benefit analysis has been used to examine treatment effectiveness for many years. For example, in the early 1970s, researchers like Holohan (1979),

Leslie (1971), Maidlow and Berman (1972), and Tabbush (1986) were attaching cost-benefit ratios in the range of 7.9:1 to 18.7:1 to methadone maintenance programs. The wide range may, in part, be explained by the fact that not all of these researchers defined benefits in the same way, some looking more at criminal justice, others including hospital benefits or employment and earnings.[12] But, regardless of how the benefits were specified, all of these studies essentially were designed to show how a dollar spent on treatment can lead to benefits that exceed that cost.

Many of these earlier efforts focused on the cost-benefit associated with a single program or a small set of such programs. One of the difficulties with this "micro" approach is that it may be hard to generalize from such information. For public policy purposes, using individual studies may not convince policymakers of the benefits of investing more dollars in prevention and treatment programs. One example of an effort to look more broadly at the cost-benefit associated with treatment was the Treatment Outcome Prospective Study (TOPS), which assessed the impact of 41 treatment programs. While not showing quite the high cost-benefit in some of the individual studies, TOPS nevertheless found a benefit of $1.66 for every $1 spent on treatment (Hubbard, Rachal, Craddock, & Cavanaugh, 1984).

More recently, a number of "macro" studies have been done that attempt to evaluate the cost-benefit of an entire state program. These efforts, in California (Gerstein et al., 1994), Ohio (Ohio Department of Alcohol and Drug Addiction, 1996), and Oregon (Finigan, 1996), were not focused on the cost-benefit of an individual program or modality, nor did they examine the outcomes of treatment on preventing abstention or relapse. Rather, their focus was on reductions in other state expenditures that result from treatment, and all of these studies reported sizable cost-benefits to the state resulting from substance abuse treatment expenditures. As discussed earlier, their emphasis was on savings in terms of overall Medicaid, welfare, and criminal justice expenditures. In this way, such studies have tried to demonstrate in the language of hard dollars and cents that investing in drug and alcohol treatment represents a beneficial use of public dollars. Some might argue that this is a callous approach to evaluating treatment, since it puts no emphasis on patient outcomes with respect to reducing the substance problem and rather reduces the debate to purely economic terms. On the other hand, in an era of fiscal conservatism, as well as the fact that there is little public sympathy for the problems of much of the population being treated, economic arguments will be more persuasive with respect to influencing public policy.

FINAL THOUGHTS

In every sense, economic issues surrounding substance abuse are undergoing dramatic changes. A changing financing environment, the growing influence of managed care, the carving out of behavioral health services from other medical care, and a general cost consciousness in both the private and the public sectors create an unsettling situation for all those involved in preventing and treating substance abuse.

These effects can already be seen in reduced funding for prevention and no increases—if not reductions—in spending for treatment. Not all of this is necessarily bad, however. Many argue that the system was throwing money away on ineffective and unnecessarily costly prevention and treatment programs. The era of the 28-day hospital treatment program, of inpatient detoxification, and even of some forms of lengthy outpatient care are over. Instead, new, shorter modalities, provided by lower level personnel, are the rule.

But these changes are not necessarily positive. The truth is that we currently know little about what the impact of the emerging, leaner system will be on access, quality, and outcome of services. Part of this requires clinical studies that assess these new interventions from the perspective of their outcomes. However, particularly as costs become such a critical factor in the decision-making process, cost-benefit and cost-effectiveness analyses grow in their importance. We now must prove not only that a given modality makes a difference in patient status, but also that it represents a wise investment of those treatment dollars when compared to other modalities, and that cost-effectiveness must also be demonstrated in terms of comparing the benefits of a given modality to other, non-substance-abuse services.

To many, this may appear as a bleak perspective, one that does not bode well for growth in substance abuse programs. As has already been mentioned, given the chronic, recurring nature of the disease of addiction, it may be difficult to demonstrate that a given episode of treatment is effective, particularly compared with a medical or surgical intervention for an acute disease. The future may require us to assess substance abuse programs in different ways that may put a more positive light on their impact. For example, we may find it more accurate to look at substance abuse treatment from the perspective of the cumulative effects of multiple treatment episodes rather than to assess the impact of a single episode. In addition, we must ensure that we are comparing treatment impact with that of the treatment of other chronic, recurring diseases like diabetes. To some extent, this requires correcting the prevailing public attitude about the nature of substance abuse as an acute disease.

Finally, we must start to look at the cost-benefit of prevention and treatment programs in terms of their cost offsets to other programs including health care, welfare, criminal justice, employment, and worker productivity. While society may not care as much about whether an individual addict recovers, they do care about reducing public expenditures and crime, and about increasing taxes and profits.

These may be tough times for the substance abuse treatment industry. But they also represent a challenge, one that will depend on a better understanding of all of the issues associated with the economics of substance abuse.

Notes

1. It should be noted that managed care is *not* a financing mechanism per se. Instead, as will be discussed below, managed care is a means of using financing to organize care and control the available resources. Managed care is used by all financing mechanisms, both private insurance and public funding programs.

2. It should be noted that the 28-day hospitalization was an arbitrary length of stay. In some ways, it was simply a compromise between 6-week and 2-week stays. Actually, there is a dearth of articles that would demonstrate the comparative effectiveness of inpatient substance abuse treatment. One example is McLellan, Grissom, Brill, and Durell (1993).

3. While Medicare does provide some funding in this area for individuals over the age of 65 and for working people who have become disabled, most of this is for inpatient alcohol treatment only. In addition, with respect to outpatient care, the cost sharing is very high (50%), and there is a limit on total expenditures that Medicare will cover.

4. It should be noted that, while what is described are the federal Medicaid rules, many states have their own general assistance category (mainly for men), which may also pay for services under Medicaid. However, these funds are not matched by the federal program.

5. Ironically, there is no clear dividing line, since diabetes and even some heart conditions and cancers are relapsing but are grouped with acute diseases. The reason is that as opposed to substance abuse or mental health, these are considered "mainstream" medical services (i.e., they respond to medical interventions such as drug therapy or surgery). While both mental health and substance abuse may also respond to chemotherapeutic interventions, they (particularly substance abuse treatment) are still not viewed as "mainstream."

6. This was a true story told to me by the director of the Employee Assistance Program for the company where the patient worked.

7. Unpublished analysis of data from the *Survey of inmates in state correctional facilities* (1991) conducted by the national Bureau of Justice Statistics, the U.S. Department of Justice. This survey (the data tapes are publicly available) interviews about 12,000 inmates in state prisons throughout the country and provides data on all facets of their lives including information on prior arrests and convictions as well as on substance abuse history.

8. A comment made by a senior policy official at the Office of National Drug Control Policy at a meeting in April 1997.

9. For a good discussion of these terms see Langenbucher (1996).

10. For discussion on how the costs of substance abuse treatment may be calculated, there are a number of good articles, for example, Dunlap and French (1995) and Zarkin, French, Anderson, and Bradley (1994).

11. It should be noted that this discussion is entirely about *cost*-benefit. There may be very compelling non-cost reasons for keeping people in their own homes that totally outweigh the notion of cost-effectiveness of home versus nursing-home care.

12. For a more thorough description of the cost-benefit literature related to drug treatment, a paper by Cartwright (1997) is available from the National Institute on Drug Abuse.

Key References

Finigan, M. (1996). *Societal outcomes and cost savings of drug and alcohol treatment in the State of Oregon.* Portland: Oregon State Office of Alcohol and Drug Abuse Programs.

Langenbucher, J. (1996). Socioeconomic analysis of addictions treatment. *Public Health Reports, 111*(2), 135–137.

Manning, W. G., Keeler, E. B., Newhouse, J. P., Sloss, E. M., & Wasserman, J. (1991). *The costs of poor health habits.* Cambridge: Harvard University Press.

References

Ball, J. C., Lange, W. R., Myers, C. P., & Friedman, S. R. (1988). Reducing the risk of AIDS through methadone maintenance treatment. *Journal of Health and Social Behavior, 29*(3), 214–216.

Cartwright, W. (1997). *Cost-benefit and cost-effectiveness analysis of drug treatment services.* Washington, DC: National Institute on Drug Abuse.

Dunlap, L. J., & French, M. T. (1995). *A comparison of two methods for estimating the costs of drug abuse treatment.* Chapel Hill, NC: Research Triangle Institute.

Finigan, M. (1996). *Societal outcomes and cost savings of drug and alcohol treatment in the State of Oregon.* Salem, OR: Office of Alcohol and Drug Abuse Programs.

Fox, K., Merrill, J. C., Chang, H., & Califano, J. A. (1995). Estimating the costs of substance abuse to the Medicaid Hospital Care Program. *American Journal of Public Health, 85*(1), 48–54.

Gerstein, D. R., Johnson, R. A., Harwood, H. J., Fountain, D., Suter, N., & Malloy, K. (1994). *Evaluating recovery services: The California Drug and Alcohol Treatment Assessment (CALDATA).* Sacramento: California Department of Alcohol and Drug Programs.

Harwood, H. J., Hubbard, R. L., Collins, J. J., & Rachal, J. V. (1988). The costs of crime and the benefits of drug abuse treatment: A cost-benefit analysis using TOPS data. In C. Leukfeld & F. Tims (Eds.), *Compulsory treatment of drug abuse: Research and clinical practice.* NIDA Monograph No. 86. Rockville, MD: U.S. Department of Human Services.

Harwood, H. J., Napolitano, D. M., Kristiansen, P. L., & Collins, J. J. (1984). *Economic costs to society of alcohol and drug abuse and mental illness: 1980.* Chapel Hill, NC: Research Triangle Institute.

Hodgson, T. A. (1992). Cigarette smoking and lifetime medical expenditures. *Milbank Quarterly, 79*(1), 81–125.

Holohan, J. (1979). *The economics of drug addiction and control in Washington, DC: A model for the estimation of costs and benefits of rehabilitation.* Special report to the Office of Planning and Research, Department of Corrections, District of Columbia. Washington, DC.

Hubbard, R. L., Rachal, J. V., Craddock, S. G., & Cavanaugh, E. R. (1984). *Treatment Outcome Prospective Study (TOPS) client characteristics and behaviors before, during and after treatment.* NIDA Monograph 51. Rockvillle, MD.

Inciardi, J. A., McBride, D. C., McCoy, H. V., & Chitwood, D. D. (1994). Recent research on the crack/cocaine/crime connection. In: *Studies on crime and crime prevention (vol. 3).* Washington, DC.

Langenbucher, J. (1994). Offsets are not add-ons: The place of addictions treatment in American health care reform. *Journal of Substance Abuse, 6*(1), 117–122.

Langenbucher, J. (1996). Socioeconomic analysis of addictions treatment. *Public Health Reports, 111*(2), 135–137.

Lennox, R. D., Scott-Lennox, J. A., & Holder, H. D. (1992). Substance abuse and family illness: Evidence from health care utilization and cost-offset research. *Journal of Mental Health Administration, 19*(1), 83–95.

Leslie, A. C. (1971). *A benefit/cost analysis of New York City's heroin addiction problems and programs.* New York: Health Services Program.

Maidlow, S. T., & Berman, H. (1972). The economics of heroin treatment. *American Journal of Public Health, 62*(10), 1397–1406.

Manning, W. G., Keeler, E. B., Newhouse, J. P., Sloss, E. M., & Wasserman, J. (1991). *The costs of poor health habits.* Cambridge: Harvard University Press.

McLellan, A. T., Grissom, G. R., Brill, P., & Durell, J. (1993). Private substance abuse treatments: Are some programs more effective than others? *Journal of Substance Abuse Treatment, 10*(3), 243–254.

Merrill, J. (1997, November). *The impact of methadone maintenance on HIV sero-conversion rates and related costs.* Delivered as part of the NIH Consensus Development Conference on Methadone Maintenance, Washington, DC.

Merrill, J. C. (1998). Impact of substance abuse on federal spending. In W. J. Bukoski & R. I. Evans (Eds.), *Cost-benefit/cost-effectiveness research of drug abuse prevention.* NIDA Monograph No. 176. Rockville, MD.

Merrill, J. C., Fox, Pulver, G., & Lewis, S. (1996). *The costs of substance abuse to the American health care system.* New York: National Center on Addiction and Substance Abuse (unpublished.)

National Center on Addiction and Substance Abuse. (1993). *The costs of substance abuse to the American health care system, Report 1: Medicaid hospital costs.* New York: Author.

National Center on Addiction and Substance Abuse. (1994). *Substance abuse and women on welfare.* New York: Author.

National Center on Addiction and Substance Abuse. (1995). *Substance abuse and federal entitlement programs*. New York: Author.

Ohio Department of Alcohol and Drug Addiction. (1996). *Cost-effectiveness study, the final report: Comprehensive analysis of results*. Columbus: Author.

Rice, D. P., Kelman, S., Miller, L. S., & Dunmeyer, S. (1990). *The economic costs of alcohol and drug abuse and mental illness*. Washington, DC: Government Printing Office.

Tabbush, V. C. (1986). *The effectiveness and efficiency of publicly-funded drug abuse treatment and prevention programs in California: A benefit-cost analysis*. Los Angeles: University of California Press.

U.S. Office of Management and Budget. *Budget of the United States government, Fiscal year 1996*. Washington, DC: Author.

Zarkin, G. A., French, M. T., Anderson, D. W., & Bradley, C. J. (1994). A conceptual framework for the economic evaluation of substance abuse interventions. *Evaluation and Program Planning, 17*(4), 409–418.

Index

Note: Page numbers followed by "f" indicate figures. Those followed by "t" indicate tables.